The History Of The County Palatine Of Chester

J H. Hanshall

A2

The Right Revd George Henry Law, D.D. F.R.S.

LORD BISHOP OF CHESTER.

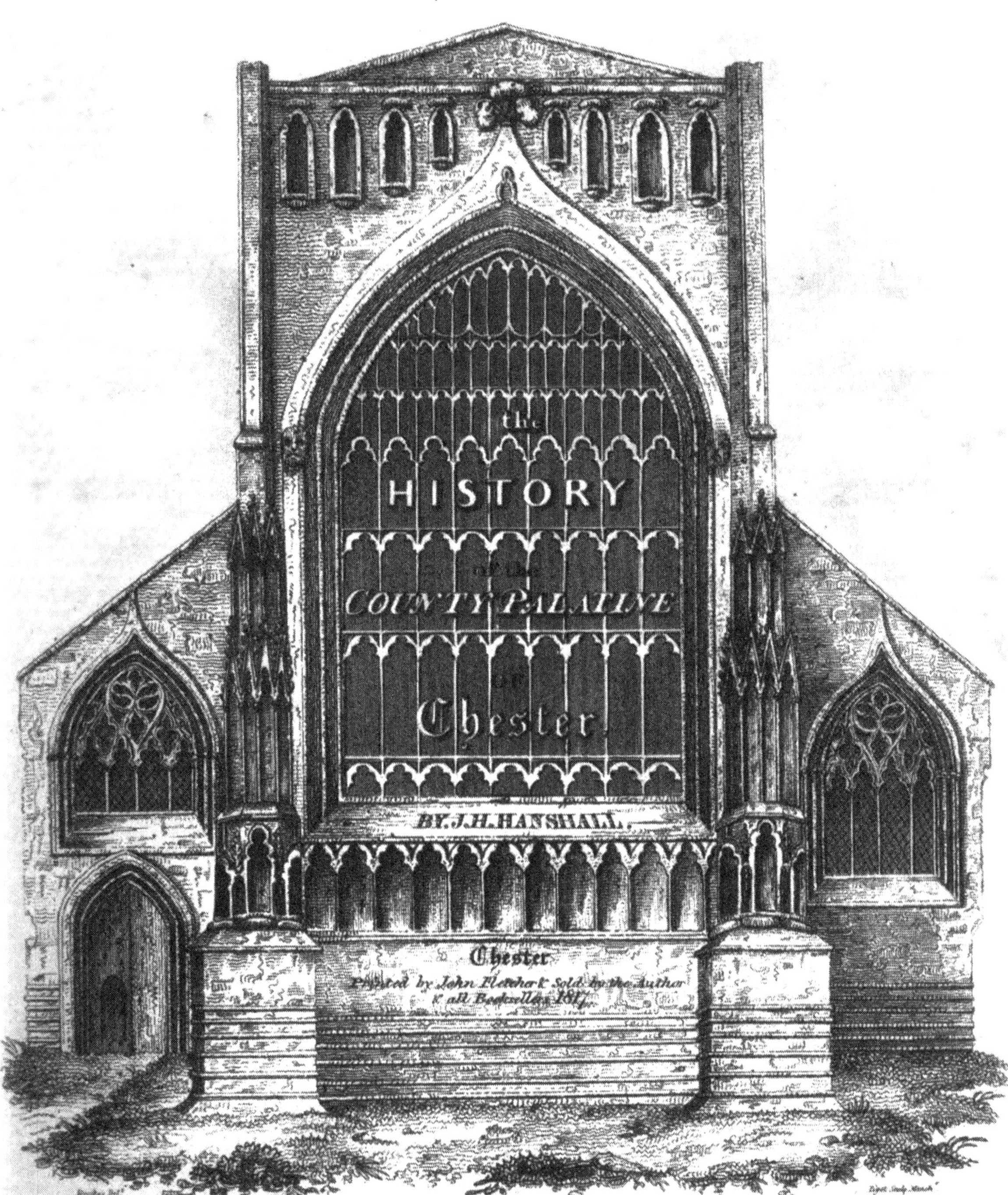
the
HISTORY
of the
COUNTY PALATINE
OF
Chester
BY. J.H. HANSHALL.
Chester
Printed by John Fletcher & Sold by the Author
& all Booksellers 1817.

South End of S^t. Oswalds Church Cathedral Chester.

BODLEIAN
-8 NOV. 1932
LIBRARY

TO THE

Right Rev. Geo. Henry Law, D. D. F. R. S.

&c. &c. &c.

LORD BISHOP OF CHESTER;

A PRELATE EMINENTLY ENDOWED WITH THOSE PRACTICAL VIRTUES WHICH
RENDER HIM AN ORNAMENT TO THE CHURCH,
AND THE BEST FRIEND TO THE INTERESTS OF TRUE RELIGION;
WHOSE LIBERALITY AND PERSONAL ACTIVITY, DURING HIS PASTORAL CARE
OF
A GREAT PORTION OF THE POPULATION OF ENGLAND,
HAVE BEEN EXERCISED IN WORKS OF CHARITY AND PUBLIC IMPROVEMENT,
AND TO WHOM HIS EXTENSIVE DIOCESE GENERALLY,
AND THE
MORAL AND PUBLIC INTERESTS
OF THE
CITY OF CHESTER IN PARTICULAR, ARE UNDER SO MANY LASTING OBLIGATIONS,

THIS WORK,

SANCTIONED BY HIS PATRONAGE, IS RESPECTFULLY DEDICATED,
BY

The Author.

Chester, Oct. 1823.

SUBSCRIBERS' NAMES.

A.

Richard Pepper Arden, Esq. Pepper Hall, Yorkshire, *large paper*,
Nicholas Ainsworth, Esq. Newton, Middlewich, *large paper*,
John Smith Adam, Esq. *large paper*,
J. Ablett, Esq. Llanbedr Hall, Denbighshire,
Mr. Ankers, Chester,
Mrs. Adeane, Palace, Chester,
Mr. J. Antrobus, Liverpool,
Mrs. Aston, Middlewich,
Mr. Wm. Acton, Nantwich,
Mr. Ansdell, Northwich.

B.

The Viscount Belgrave, M. P. Eaton House
Ald. H. Bowers, Chester, *large paper*,
Rev. Chas. Burton, B. D. Gorton Hall, Lancashire,
Rev. T. Burrowes, Dodleston,
Rev. Dr Blackburn, Warrington,
Thos. Barnes, Esq. Budworth
J. Beswick, Esq. Macclesfield,
David Browne, Esq. Macclesfield,
Samuel Brittain, Esq. Upton.
Roger Barnston, Esq. Chester,
Thos. Broster, Esq. Collector of Customs, Chester,
Thos. Bagnall, Esq. Chester,
J. Billington, Esq. Chester,
R. F. Buckley, Esq. Chester,
Mr. Bateman, Conveyancer, Chester,
Mr. Buckley, Chester,
Mrs. Brassie, Chester,
Mr. B. Brassey, Chester,
Mr. J. Bebbington, Chester,
Mr. Batenham, Artist, Chester,
Mr. Baker, Proctor, Chester,
Mr. A. Booth, Chester,
Mr. S. Brown, Herald Painter, Chester,
Mr. J. Berrington, Chester,
Mr. Benson, Chester,
Mr. Booth, Congleton,
Mr. S. Boam, Lord-street, Liverpool,
Mr. W. Barton, Litherland, Lancashire,
Mr. E. Bayley, Macclesfield,
Mr. Beckett, Malpas,
Mr. W. Betteley, Nantwich,
Mr. G. Beckett, Nantwich,
Mr. J. Burgess, Cheer Brook, Nantwich,
Mr. J. Barnes, Northwich,
Mr. Jas. Massey Bancroft, Stockport,
Mr. Birchwood, Sutton,
Mr. Bromfield, Tattenhall,
Mr. Blake, Halwood Academy, Runcorn

C.

Lord Bishop of Chester, *large paper*,
The Most Hon. the Marquis of Cholmondeley, Cholmondeley Castle,
Sir F. Cunliffe, Bart. Acton, Denbighshire,
Sir J. Cotgreave, Knt. Netherlegh-House, Chester, *large paper*,
Rev. Archdeacon Clarke, Coddington,
Rev. F. Casson, Chester,
Rev. Mr. Church, Ince,
Captain Carter, R. C. M. Chester,
Dr. Currie, Boughton, Chester,
Thos. Chorlton Clutton, Esq. Chorlton,
W. Court, Esq. Middlewich,
Miss Cortney, Chester,
Mr. Collier, Veterinary Surgeon, Chester
Mr. Crimes, Canal Agent, Chester,
Mr. Chaplow, Chester,
Mr. J. Colley, Chester,
Mr. T. Cartwright, Chester,
Mr. C. Colton, Liverpool,
Mr. Chegwin, Bookseller, Liverpool,
Mr. Ralph Cappur, Nantwich,
Mr. G. Carnes, Northwich.

D.

Davies Davenport, Esq. M.P. *large paper*
R. Darlington, Esq. Solicitor, Sandbach, *two large copies*
Thos. Crewe Dod, Esq. Edge,
Thos. Dixon, Esq. Littleton, *large paper*,
Jas. Dixon, Esq. Chester, *large paper*,
Mr. S. Davies, Chester,
Mr. Denson, Dodleston,
Mrs. C. Dutton, Chester,
Mr. R. Davies, Liverpool,
Mr. Dempsey, Liverpool,
Mr. S. Dutton, Liverpool, *large paper*,
Mr. Joseph Denson, Northwich,
Mr. R. Dewhurst, Macclesfield,
Mr. Dawson, Bookseller, Stockport,
Mr. J. Dunn, Hartford.

E.

Sir John Grey Egerton, Bart. Oulton Park, *large paper*,
Wilbraham Egerton, Esq. M. P. Tatton Park,
Rev. J. Edwards, Aldford,
Mr. Wm. Edwards, Chester,
Mr. J. Evans, Chester,
Mr. J. Eaton, Liverpool,
Mr. G. G. Elwall, Nantwich,
Mr. J. Ellson, Northwich,
Mr. James Evans, Macclesfield,
Mr. Edmundson, Trafford.

F.

John Feilden, Esq. Mollington Hall, *large paper*,
John Ford, Esq. Abbeyfield,
Alderman Francis, Chester,
J. Finchett, Esq. Chester, *large paper*,
J. Fletcher, Esq. Chester, *large paper*,
W. H. Folliott, Esq. Chester,
Mr. J. Faulkner, Solicitor, Chester,
Mr. G. Franks, Chester,
Mr. Fitzgerald, Chester,
Mr. Foden, Chester,
Mr. S. Farnworth, Holywell,
Mr. S. Franceys, Liverpool,
Mr. John Farrington, Macclesfield,
Mr. Thomas Farrall, Macclesfield,
Mr. C. J. Fox, Middlewich,
Mr. Fox, Bookseller, Nantwich, 3 copies.
Mr. Firth, Northwich.

G.

The Right Hon. the Earl Grosvenor, Eaton House, *large paper*,
Lieut. General Thos. Grosvenor, M. P. Stocking Hall, *large paper*,
The Hon. Lady Glynne, Hawarden Castle,
Rev. Wm. Garnett, Nantwich,
Matthew Gregson, Esq. Liverpool,
Thos. Grimsditch, Esq. Macclesfield,
John Glegg, Esq. Withington,
Mr. Garner, Chester, *large paper*,
Mr. S. Gibson, Chester,
Mr. Gaman, Brewer's Hall, Chester,
Mr. Ralph Green, Chester,
Mr. C. Griffiths, Chester,
Mr. C. Gaman, Chester,
Mr. Gunnery, Kelsall,
Mr. Gunnery, Solicitor, Liverpool, *large paper*,
Messrs. Gregory & Taylor, Booksellers, Liverpool, two copies,
Mr. J. Green, Prescot, Lancashire,
Mr. Golding, Maesbury, Salop,
Mr. J. Galliard, Nantwich,
Mr. Goulborne, Nantwich,
Mr. Goulborne, Cam-yr-Alyn, Denbighshire.

H.

Rev. G. Heron, Daresbury,
Rev. J. Halton, Chester, *large paper*,
Rev. J. Hill, Clotton,
Captain Hincks, R. C. M. Chester,
W. M. Henderson, Esq. Castle, Chester,
S. Humphryes, Esq. Prothonotary, Chester, *large paper*,

H.

Edw. Hawkins, Esq. Dylais, near Neath, Glamorganshire, *large paper*,
Henry Hesketh, Esq. Newton Hall,
Thomas Hilditch, Esq. Blackden
John Hill, Esq. Attorney General for Cheshire,
G. N. Hill, Esq. Chester,
G. Harrison, Esq. Chester,
Mr. W. H. Haswell, Chester,
Miss Hanshall, Chester,
Mr. Hankey, Chester,
Mr. Hudson, Castle, Chester,
Mr. Hugh Hughes, Liverpool,
Mr. Harper, Macclesfield, *large paper*,
Mr. J. Harrop, Manchester,
Mr. John Harding, Nantwich,
Mr. James Hughes, Nantwich,
Mr. Hales, Wem, Salop,
Mr. Haddock, Bookseller, Warrington, Lancashire.

I.

Rev. J. Ireland, Chester,
Jas. Ikin, Esq. Headingley, Yorkshire,
Mr. S. Ingham, Henllan, Denbighshire.

J.

David Francis Jones, Esq. Recorder of Chester, *large paper*,
Rev. Wm. Jones, Northop, Flintshire,
Rev. Lloyd Jones, Wrexham,
John Jones, Esq. Lincoln's Inn, London,
Mr. Thos. Jones, Chester,
Mr. Jones, Land Surveyor, Northop,
Mr. Jones, Plas yn Bonwm, Corwen,
Mr. Johnson, Congleton,
Mr. Johnson, Sychtyn, Flintshire,
Mr. J. Johnson, Middlewich,
Mr. Jarvis, Chester,
Mr. E. W. Jefferies, Liverpool,
Mr. C. Jackson, Manchester,
W. A. Jump, Esq. Nantwich,
Mr. Janion, Rock Savage,
Mr. Jones, Prescot, Lancashire.

K.

Right Hon. the Lord Kenyon, Gredington Hall, Flintshire, *large paper*,
Mr. Kaye, Courier Office, Liverpool,
Mr. Kelsall, Customs, Liverpool,
Mr. R. Kent, Nantwich,
Mr. Kent, Bookseller, Northwich, five small and two *large copies*.

L.

Rev. Chancellor and Prebendary Law, Lichfield,
Rev. Mr. Leigh, Middlewich,
Rev. Mr. Littler, Goostrey,
Richard Llwyd, Esq. Chester,
Thos. Leacroft, Esq. Chester, *large paper*,
Mr. Lawrence, Chester,
Mr. T. Lindop, Chester,
Mr. Thos. Lloyd, Chester,
Mr. Henry Lord, Chester, *large paper*,

L.

Mr. S. Leet, Chemist, Chester,
Chester General Public Library,
Mr. T. Low, Congleton,
Mr. J. Long, Knutsford,
Mr. James Leigh, Nantwich,
George Lowe, Esq. Nantwich,
Mr. J. Leigh, Nantwich,
Mr. Lindop, bookseller, Sandbach, four copies.
Mr. John Leech, Stockport,
Mr. Lowndes, Somerford.

M.

Sir Thos. Mostyn, Bart. M. P. Mostyn, Flintshire, *large paper*,
The Rev. Charles Mytton, Eccleston, *large paper*,
The Rev. Prebendary Maddock, Chester,
Rev. Richard Massie, Chester,
Rev. F. Master, Runcorn,
Wm. Massey, Esq. Mayor of Chester, 1822-3,
Robert Morris, Esq. Mayor of Chester, 1823-4,
S. Mostyn, Esq. Calcot, Flintshire,
Edward Mainwaring, Esq. Bromborow,
Mr. Moss, Chester,
Mr. J. Manley, Canal, Chester,
Mr. J. Meredith, Chester,
Miss Miller, Farndon,
Mr. Moulsdale, Huxley,
Mr. Major, Bookseller, Skinner-street, London, *large paper*,
Mr. Major, ditto, small paper,
Mr. George Morton, Liverpool,
Mr. M. Moss, Liverpool,
Mr. D. Mason, Liverpool,
Mr. Alex. Mosses, Artist, Liverpool,
Mr. Minshull, Gazette Office, Lancaster,
Mr. Maddock, Nantwich,
Mr. T. Mulliner, Nantwich,
Mr. Nichols, Parliament-street, London.

N.

Hon. and Rev. Geo. Neville, Rectory, Hawarden,
—. Newton, Esq. Solicitor, Stockport, two copies,
Mr. Noyes, Picture Dealer, Chester,
Alderman Wm. Newell, Chester,
Mr. Nield, Chester,
Mr. J. Norbury, Northwich,
Mr. D. T. Nickson, Nantwich,
R. Nuttall, Esq. Norley.

O.

Mr. R. Oulton, Middlewich.

P.

Rev. Henry Parry, Llanasa, Flintshire,
Capt. Pennington, Macclesfield,
David Pennant, Esq. Downing, Flintshire,
Wm. Pownall, Esq. Chester,
Stephen Palin, Esq. Chester,
Mr. T. Parry, Solicitor, Chester,

P.

Mr. Pickering, Artist, Chester,
Messrs. Poole and Harding, Chester, two copies,
Mr. Parry, Bookseller, Chester,
Miss Peers, Chester,
Mr. Phelan, Book-binder, Chester,
Mr. Pugh, Bookseller, Dolgelle, Merionethshire, two copies,
Mr. Parsonage, Aldford,
Mr. J. W. Platt, Bookseller, Liverpool, *large paper*,
Mr. W. Pott, Middlewich, *large paper*,
Mr. Pigot, Engraver, Manchester,
Mr. W. Perry, Macclesfield,
Mr. G. Pownall, Macclesfield,
Mr. Price, Bookseller, Oswestry, Salop,
Mr. Pratchitt, Nantwich,
J. Poole, Esq. Nantwich.

R.

Rev. W. Richardson, Chester,
W. Richardson, Esq. Collector of Excise, Chester,
Thomas Roberts, Esq. Mollington,
Mr. Reid, Solicitor, Llanrwst, Denbighshire,
Mr. Rowson, Solicitor, Prescot, Lancashire,
E. Roberts, Esq. Chester,
Mr. W. Roberts, Chester,
Mr. Rooke, Chester,
Mr. Ridgway, Duddon,
Mr. R. Roberts, Liverpool,
Mr. S. Ryder, Manchester,
Mr. R. Reid, Middlewich,
Mr. G. Remer, Nantwich,
J. Richardson, Esq. Nantwich,
Mr. T. Robinson, Stockport.

S.

The Right Hon. the Earl of Stamford and Warrington, Lord Lieutenant of Cheshire, Dunham Massy,
Sir Thomas Stanley Massey Stanley, Bart. Hooton,
Rev. J. Slade, Preb. of Chester, and Vicar of Bolton, Lancashire,
Alderman Wm. Seller, Vicar's Cross, Chester,
Charles Sedgwick, Esq. Hoole,
John Stanton, Esq. Hoole,
Samuel Stone, Esq. Solicitor, Macclesfield,
John Cross Starkey, Esq. Wrenbury,
Mr. J. Sothern, Canal,
Mr. Joseph Shallcross,
Miss Shallcross, Chester,
Mr. Snelson, Eccleston,
Thos. Stanton, Esq. Ellesmere,
Mr. J. Smith, Middlewich,
Mr. Saxon, Solicitor, Northwich,
Mr. Sparrow, Holyhead,
Mr. Stringer, Wheelock.

T.

Rev. Prebendary Trevor, Eastham,
Dr. Thackeray, Chester,
John Thompson, Esq. Wigan, Lancashire,

T.

Robert Taylor, Esq. Lymm Hall,
Thos. Townshend, Esq. Chester,
O. Titley, Esq. Chester,
Captain Tregent, Castle, Chester,
Thos Tolver, Esq. Chester,
Mr. Taylor, Surgeon, Middlewich,
Mr. Taylor, Chester,
Mr. Twemlow, Sandbach,
Mrs. Telford, Chester,
Mr. John Thomas, Chester,
Mr. Geo Topham, Chester,
Mr. John Tushingham, Chester, *large paper*,
Mr. John Turner, Chester.
Mr. William Topham, Nantwich,
Mr. John Turner, Nantwich,
Mr. Tomlinson, Manchester,
Mr. W. Taylor, Macclesfield.

V.

Sir R. Williames Vaughan, Bart. M. P. Nannau, Merionethshire, *large paper*,
Rev. G. Vawdrey, Nantwich,
Rev. T. Vanbrugh, Aughton, Lancashire,
Mr. Venables, Blue School, Chester,
Mr. Vaughan, Malpas,
Mr. Thomas Voce, Macclesfield.

W.

Edward Bootle Wilbraham, Esq. M. P. Lathom House, Lancashire,
Rev. J. Ward, Chester,
Rev. Mr. Watkins, Guilden Sutton,
Rev. Dr. Wynne, Bangor, Flintshire,
Lieut. Wettenhall, R. N. Chester,
Dr. Whittell, Chester,
Alexander Alaric Watts, Esq. Leeds, Yorkshire,
Richard Willett, Esq. Hawarden, Flintshire,
E. O. Wrench, Esq. Chester,
S. Woodhouse, Esq. Bronte House, Liverpool.
— Whitelegg, Esq. Solicitor, Manchester,
George Whitley, Esq. Norley,
James White, Esq. Sutton,
Mr. J. Walker, Assay Master, Chester,
Mr. Walker, Chester,
Mr. Wilbraham, Chester
Mr. Whittle, Canal, Chester,
Mr. R. Whitfield, Eccleston,
Mr. J. W. Willan, Gresford,
Mr. Watts, Waverham,
Mr. Witter, Clotton,
Mr. Whittakers, Middlewich,
Mr. Wilson, Macclesfield, three copies,
Mr. J. Walton, Macclesfield,
—. Wright, Esq. Solicitor, Macclesfield,
Mr. Joshua Worsley, Stockport,
Mr. John Worsley, Stockport.

Y.

Mr. Youde, New Burlington-street, London.

The generally expressed desire for a History of this County Palatine, combining all the main features of Chronological event with economy in price, induced the Author to undertake the present work. It is completed; and if it falls short of that interest which might have been excited in its favor, it is hoped some of the censure of his Subscribers may be ameliorated by the recollection, that it has been arranged and written during the Author's indispensable attention to the various laborious but important duties connected with the editorial management of a popular Provincial Newspaper.

All the earlier Histories of Cheshire, and of the City of Chester, have been very inadequate to the object they professed to attain: Sir Peter Leycester's is unquestionably a work of considerable magnitude and great research, but it was limitted to the description of only *one* Hundred (Bucklow) and some general details appertaining rather to a History of England generally, than to that of one of its provinces; and, in fact, till the appearance of Mr. Ormerod's splendid and costly volumes, it was the only standard work of any authority, so far as it professed to go.—King's Vale Royal, however, was in existence, and it may, perhaps, be considered by some, as a local history; but it has no system of detail,—and it is composed of such a mixed mass of materials, that, although valuable in themselves, they are lost in effect from the irregularity of their arrangement.

This Work is compiled from all the Authors, ancient and modern, who have treated on Cheshire History, particularly as connected with the History of the Country at large. Access has been had to numerous curious MSS., to rare works, and to the Records of the Corporation of Chester and of other Towns. The Author is under considerable obligations to John Finchett, Esq. Town Clerk of Chester, to Thomas Leacroft, Esq.

Stephen Palin, Esq. Matthew Gregson, Esq. of Liverpool, Edward Jones, Esq. Proctor in the Diocesan Court, W. M. Henderson, Esq. and other valued friends, for their kind assistance with information, oral or written, drawings, &c. necessary for the arrangement of a work of this description.

Whether another edition of this History may be called for or not, is a question which cannot *now* be answered—it probably remains for the decision of another generation. If, however, such a manifestation of public approval should show itself during the Author's existence, he will endeavor to render it worthy of their sanction. In the *possible* contingency of this event, he therefore respectfully solicits the communication of any omissions or other errors which appear in THIS edition, from the numerous enlightened friends who have patronised it; and in the mean time, he will not be inattentive to passing events, and to the collection of such facts and materials as may serve to illustrate another, and, under any circumstances he hopes, an improved edition.

It was first contemplated and announced, to give in this edition a Copy of the *Cheshire Domesday Book*,* to which frequent reference is had in the course of the work; its

* *Domesday Book*, one of the most ancient and memorable Records of England, is the Register from which Judgment was to be given upon the value, tenure, and services of Lands therein described; and it has been more effectually preserved by being printed with a general dissertation, index, &c. pursuant to the orders, and under the inspection, of the Royal Record Commissioners. The Commissioners' introduction is exceedingly interesting. Domesday Book appears to have been known by various other names, such as *Rotulus Wintoniæ,—Scriptura Thesauri Regis—Liber de Wintonia*, and *Liber Regis*. Sir Henry Spelman adds *Liber Judiciarius*, &c. Among Dr. Rawlinson's Manuscripts, in the Bodleian Library, at Oxford, is a fragment of a survey of all the Manors belonging to the Deanery of *St. Paul's*, taken in 1181, and called *Domisday Radulphi de Diceto*. Diceto was the Dean under whose directions it was made. A manuscript note of Bishop Kennett, also in the same Library, in a *Cowel's Law Interpreter*, quotes the *Domesday of the Nuns of Haliwell*. This last, the Record Commissioners say, it is probable was only a *Leiger Book* of the Monastery. The exact time of William the First undertaking the Survey, is differently stated by Historians. The *Red Book of the Exchequer* seems to have been erroneously quoted, as fixing the time of entrance upon it in 1080; it being merely stated in that Record (in which *the original Dialogus de Scaccario is found,*) that the work was undertaken at a time subsequent to the total reduction of the Island to William's authority. From the memorial of the com-

great length, however, and, generally speaking, want of interest, induced the Author to omit it.—For the same reason a GENERAL INDEX only is introduced, which will answer every needful purpose, and not clogg the work with a mass of useless pages.

In conclusion, the Author conceives an apology is due to his Subscribers for the delay which has taken place in the completion of the work;—certain impediments, however,

---

pletion of this Survey at the end of the second volume, it is evident that it was finished in 1086. Mathew Paris, Robert of Glocester, the *Annals of Waverley*, and the "Chronicles of Bermondsey," give the year 1083, as the date of the Record. Henry of Huntingdon places it in 1084. The Saxon Chronicle in 1085. Bromton, Simeon of Durham, &c. in 1086; and the Ypodigma, &c. in 1087. Ingulphus affirms, that the survey was made in imitation of the policy of Alfred, who, at the time he divided the Kingdom into Counties, Hundreds, and Tithings, had an "inquisition" taken, and digested into a Register, which was called from the place in which it was deposited, the "Roll of Winchester." Bishop Kennett, in his Parochial Antiquities, states, that Alfred's Register had the name of *Dome-boc*, from which the name of Domesday-book was only a corruption. This may, perhaps, serve as a clue to the explanation of the name; though the Dom-boc was in reality the code of Saxon laws. It is noticed as such in the laws of Edward the Elder, and more particularly in those of Æthelstan. The *Saxon Chronicle* furnishes a passage, under the year 1085, which enters minutely into the motives for the formation of this survey; and which, if correct, also fixes the time of its commencement to that year. By the completion of this survey, William I. acquired an exact knowledge of the possessions of the Crown. It afforded him the names of the landholders; it furnished him with the means of ascertaining the military strength of the country; and it pointed out the possibility of increasing the revenue in some cases, and of lessening the demands of the tax collectors in others. It was, moreover, a register of appeal for those whose titles in their property might be disputed. Sir W. Blackstone has observed, that from the prodigious slaughter of English Nobility at the battle of Hastings, and the fruitless insurrections of those who survived, such numerous forfeitures had accrued, that William was enabled to reward his Norman followers with very large and extensive possessions. Eadmer, Ingulph, and Henry of Huntingdon, complain heavily of the extirpation of the English from offices of honour, power, and emolument in Church and State. Yet, continue the Record Commissioners, this must have been the natural consequence of such a change as that which was occasioned by the arrival of the Normans. The soldiers and ministerial dependents of the Conqueror were to be rewarded; and we cannot wonder so see them form the larger portion of tenants *in capite*. We find the Churches and Monasteries, however, still retaining their ancient patrimony, in some cases with considerable additions from the Conqueror himself. Of the importance which William himself attached to the completion

presented themselves which it was impossible to foresee or avert, and which, more or less, tended to retard it from its commencement to its final termination.

For the accommodation of local readers, not Subscribers, a few Copies of the HISTORY OF THE CITY OF CHESTER have been printed, detached from the general County History, which may be had of the Author.

---

of the survey, we have sufficient evidence at the close of a grant which he made soon afterwards to the Abbey of Westminster. And that the value of the great survey was thoroughly perceived at a time but little subsequent to the "Conquest," we learn from Robertus Mortensis, who informs us it was imitated in Normandy by Henry II. The exact time of the removal of this record from Winchester to Westminster, if there were originally but one copy, cannot now be ascertained. It is described at a very early period in the *Dialogus de Scaccario*, as the inseparable companion of the Royal Seal. At Westminster it was kept with the King's Seal, by the side of the Tally Court in the Exchequer, under *three locks and keys*, in the charge of the Auditor, the Chamberlains, and Deputy Chamberlains of the Exchequer; till in 1696 it was deposited among the valuable records in the CHAPTER-HOUSE, *where it now remains.*

Introduction.---Ancient Roads, &c. &c.

On the subject of the Ancient British or Roman Roads which formerly intersected this County, and the particular sites of Roman stations, the ingenuity and research of the Antiquary have been long ago exhausted. That in many instances, however, his conjectures have been well-founded, will not admit of contradiction;—their situation—the materials of which they have been formed—and the existing remains of them, all conspire to support his hypothesis.

Upon these and similar inquiries, great light has been thrown by the ingenious Dr. Whittaker, in his singular but learned work, the History of Manchester. In compiling, therefore, what will be arranged under this head, the observations of the Doctor will be introduced in an indiscriminate manner; and such observations as may be necessary, drawn from the Lysons, Ormerod, and other authorities, will follow. The following remarks are contained in Vol 1. 8vo. edit. of the History of Manchester:

On the Situation of Condate.—To settle the particular position of Condate, hath long embarrassed the historical critics. Fixed originally at Congleton, because of some remaining sameness in the name, that only guide in the infancy of antiquarian learning, it has been lately placed upon better principles at or near Northwich. But it was at neither one nor the other. The site of the station is pointed out by the course of the road. And this is ascertained by the broken remains of it, which sometimes appear, by the direction of them, where they cease, and the sure signatures of the name of Street, where both fail us.

Richard's 6th Iter runs thus,		And Antonine's 2d thus,	
From MANCUNIUM		From MANCUNIUM to	
FINIBUS MAXIMÆ			
ET FLAVIÆ m. p.	18	CONDATE	18
CONDATE	18		
Deva	18;	Deva	20.

Richard's 10th goes		And Antonine's 10th	
From MANCUNIUM to		From MANCUNIUM to	
CONDATE	23	CONDATE	18
Mediolano	18;	Mediolano	18.

The road to Condate did not take the direct way from the station to Throstle-nest, but made a large curve on the south to reach it. A right line would have carried it from the south-western angle of the camp, across the channel of the Medlock, and in the line of the new canal into the road at Corn-brook. But this route was prevented by the steepness of the bank, the want of a ford there across the channel, and the prudence of retaining both in their natural state, as the principal barriers of the camp on the south.

The way to Condate and Cambodunum commenced at the same time from the eastern gate of the station, and proceeded in one line along the eastern side of the Castle field. And, parting at the extremity of the field, the former winded along the descent to the river, and, a little on this side of Corn-brook, turned on the right to gain the course in which it should originally have moved. Passing from this point along the track of the present highway, but twisted into angles by the unequal encroachments of the inclosures upon it, it proceeded through the village of Stretford to the Bridge over the Mersey. And, as no appearance of the Roman workmanship can be expected along the line of the present road, so none are discoverable, I believe, on the borders of the adjoining fields. In the unvarying level of those low meadows particularly, which extend from the village to the ford, the least elevation of a road would be immediately perceived. And, in the coat of river sand which covers them to a considerable depth, the smallest seam of gravel would as readily be distinguished. But no traces of a ridge appear to the eye above, and no remains of a foundation are discovered by the spade below.

The road, having passed the meadows and crossed the ford, continued along the present lane to the village of Cross-street, and proceeded through it to Broad Heath. There, the present way begining to wind upon the left, and to point towards the town of Altrincham, the Roman deserts it, and enters the fields that have been lately inclosed from the heath. And the line of gravel is frequently found in them by the spade, lying upon the black turf and white sand. And, at the farther end of them, the road was discovered in cutting the canal, and the traces of it appear at present in the gravelled side of the bank. It then entered the inclosures of Oldfield Hall, is invisible in the first, but very visible in the other three. These appear to have been originally a part of the neighbouring moss, which is denominated Seaman's, which once spread into a large extent on the right, and has still some narrow remains immediately on the left. And the road was constructed along them with a good elevation. Within these very few years, the gravel has been carried away to the depth of a yard in many places. And yet the seam remains very conspicuous along the third and fourth fields.

But, leaving these, the roads enter a close that was hedged in from the moss only a few years ago. This was the most boggy part of it in the time of the Romans, as even now the soil is so extremely loose and soft, that with great facility I pushed a whalebone whip a full yard into the ground. Over such a tract of land, the road was necessarily raised with gravel to a considerable height. And it still carries a lofty ridge, being popularly called the Upcast, and having a fall for ten or twelve yards on either side. And it lately carried a loftier; a great quantity of gravel having been taken off from the summit soon after the inclosing of the field, and equally dispersed along the sides.

Having crossed the moss, it leaves the low grounds to which it had hitherto been confined, and begins to ascend the Dune or hill that terminates the valley of Manchester to the south-west, and gives name to the neighbouring Dunham. Not mounting the summit, but passing along a lower shelve, it enters Dunham-park, and once communicated the name of Street-head to the height. And this is retained by the only habitation which is near it, a small house at the foot of it, and upon the margin of the present road.

Descending the slope of the hill, and leaving the park, it crossed the little valley beyond, and its rivulet the Bollen, and once more fell into the present road near New-bridge. This one significant circumstance indicates of itself: the whole length of the present road from New-bridge to Buckley-hill is denominated Street. The Roman road, therefore, stretched away from the angle immediately beyond the bridge, along the course of the present road, and left Rostherne-Mere about a bow-shot from it on the left. It thus proceeded to Bucklow-hill, being all the way popularly known by the expressive appellation of Street. From Bucklow-hill it passed to Mere-town, going in the same line and retaining the same name. And about two miles beyond the latter, passing the hollow channel of a brook, it assumes the name of Holford-street, and preserves it for half a mile together. A little beyond the conclusion of this, the present road beginning to tend too much towards Northwich, the Roman insensibly steals away to the left. But about a mile beyond the point, and in the direction of the course, we recover it again. And the new part of it is a well gravelled lane, denominated Street, and extending in a right line for four or five miles together. The appellation of it is written Kind-street by the only antiquarians that have named it, Mr. Horseley and Mr. Percival; but is invariably spoken King-street by the people. The former, however, is pretty certainly the name, and the latter merely a corruption, resulting from the natural humour among all nations, of assimilating strange to familiar names in popular pronunciation. And it formerly led to Condate, and now leads to Kinderton. At its commencement, leaving the town of Northwich about half a mile to the right, the Kind-street goes on about twelve or fourteen yards in breadth, a great public road, and wanting considerable repair. And the name of the lane is heard of no more.

Here, therefore, the termination of the road and the length of the distance invite us strongly to search for a station. The name of Condate is pretty loudly echoed in that of Kinderton. And, what is much more weighty, this is the first place convenient for a camp about the requisite distance from Manchester.

The Kind-street, pointing down the bank of the river to the Bridge of Ravenscroft, forded the channel two or three yards to the right of the bridge, and entered the field beyond it. And here it has been actually discovered. This is denominated the Harbour's field, and was plainly the site of the Roman station. The particular position of the ground betwixt the rivers Croco and Dane, is a strong argument of itself. The appellation of the close is an additional evidence, the Harbour's field signifying the area of the military station. And the site and name, the remains about it, and the tradition concerning it, are a decisive proof.

The ground is nearly a parallelogram about ten statute acres in extent, and bounded by a natural bank, lofty and steep, upon one side, and the little Croco curling at the foot of it, and by another, less lofty but more steep, on a second, and the Dane running directly under it. And the former falls into the latter at the angle of the field. Upon the third side, but several yards within the hedge, are the considerable remains of a ditch, rising up the ascent, and being once continued probably in the same line, and along the hollow of the adjoining lane. And upon the fourth the antient ditch preserves its original perfection, being a steep foss about ten yards in depth, and eight in breadth at the top; formerly converted, like a part of the other, into the course of a road, and lately made the channel of a current.

Such was the station of Condate. And a road has been discovered commencing from it, traversing a field immediately without the camp, and frequently visible in a dry summer for the whole length of the close beyond both. This is ordinarily called the Roman road, and from its direction appears to have gone to Mediolanum in Shropshire. Another went by Home-street-Hall to Chester. And a third extended by Street-forge and Red-street to Chesterton near Newcastle.

This then is Condate, the station so long lost and so vainly sought. And, that it has been sought and lost so long may justly excite our admiration. The road pointing towards Chester, because to that City one Iter of Antonine carries it; and pointing equally to the south or south-east of Chester, because another of his takes it into Shropshire; the course of it might have been easily investigated. The sure signatures of Stretford, Cross-street, Street-head, Street, Holford-street, and King-street, names all occurring in the line, all pointing out either well-known villages, conspicuous eminences, or public roads, and some retained for several miles together, trace out the course of it in the plainest colours. And the clear tradition of a Roman camp, and the appellation of Kinderton, at the conclusion of the whole, shed the fullest light upon the site of Condate.

The CORNAVII and BRIGANTES.—*The Peninsula of Wirral.*—Within this peninsula, and along the contiguous parts of the County, the Carnabii originally resided. And from them they originally sallied out, and spread their dominions over the rest of the county, over the whole of Staffordshire, and the neighbouring parts of Shropshire, Warwickshire, Leicestershire, and Flintshire. While they were confined within the precincts of West Cheshire, they seem to have had only the towns of Deva and Condate. And the latter appears from its name to have been the capital, being composed of the words Conda Te, and signifying the principal City.—Thus was Kinderton the capital of West Cheshire, and, after the acquisition of the rest of the County, Staffordshire, and the neighbouring parts of Shropshire, Warwickshire, Leicestershire, and Flintshire, the metropolis of all. But, as it had been stript of its dignity before the arrival of the Romans, so did it most probably lose it in consequence of an invasion from the Brigantes. When this active and spirited tribe, about the commencement of the Christian æra, had seized all the fortresses that guarded the passes of the Yorkshire hills, and subdued the country that lay betwixt them and the sea; they appear to have carried their victorious arms to the south and north, crossed the Mersey and Solway, and conquered the Selgovæ of Anandale and the Carnabii of Cheshire. The reduction of the former is evinced by a statue, which has been discovered in their country, and is inscribed to the Goddess Brigantia. And the conquest of the latter is equally shown by an altar, which has been found at Chester, and was addressed to the Goddess-Nymph of the Brigantes. The Carnebii and Selgovæ had received themselves, and communicated to the Romans, the worship of the peculiar or tutelar divinity of the Brigantes; and therefore, at the Roman invasion, must have been both subject to their dominion. Nothing can be a fuller proof of the reduction of one British tribe by another, than the desertion of its own national Deity, and its adoption of the other's.

ROAD NEAR STOCKPORT.—The whole range of the present road from Manchester to Stockport, is popularly denominated High-street, and thereby sufficiently bespeaks itself to be Roman. But the first half-mile of it, being remarkably direct, has obtained the significative appellation of Longsight. Thus passing along the present highway, the road crossed the Mersey at the ford, which from the steap, stop, or steep, upon either side of it, received the appellation of Stopford among the Saxons, and was about two hundred yards above the present bridge of Stockport, and about sixty below the union of the Mersey and the Tame. And it then mounted the brow of the Castle-hill to the market-place, and traversed the site of the town to Buxton.

THE CEANGI.—The Cheshire pieces of lead,* were originally designed by the Romans as a monument of triumph and the record of a victory over the Ceangi. And this design of them ascertains at once the position of that people. Being the servants of the Carnabii and the attendants upon their cattle, they lived in the northern woods of their country, that skirted the marshy grounds which still extend for many miles by Norton, Runchorne, and Frodsham along the shore of the Mersey. Here the pieces were dug up, and here was the victory obtained. And the Ceangi, over whom it was gained, were very distinct from the three bodies of herdsmen with whom they have been often confounded. In the year 76, the Ceangi of Cheshire had not yet been attacked by the Romans. In the summer of 78, when Agricola assumed the command of the troops in the island, the whole range of our north-eastern coast, including North Wales and extending to Scotland, was yet unsubdued by the Roman arms. The most southerly of these Britons, the Ordovices of North Wales, had been previously attempted by Paulinus; but all the more northerly were first attacked by Agricola. And, having totally conquered the former in the autumn of 78, Agricola equally conquered the latter in the summer of 79. This, therefore, is the highest date to which any Cheshire inscription can refer, as the county was first invaded and first conquered in that year. This is also the lowest to which an inscription concerning Vespasian can be reduced, as he died upon the twenty-fourth of June in it. And to this, therefore, the original probably referred, and was thus written, IMP. VESP. VIII. T. VESP. VII. COSS.

* See p. 11

MANCHESTER and BUXTON ROAD.—The Roman road from Manchester to Buxton runs considerably to the west of its general direction from Stockport, in order to touch at some intermediate station. It proceeds by Pepper-street fold in Bramhall, and passes over Street-fields beyond it, pointing towards Hanford Mill, on the Bollen. And Hanford appears to have had three or four roads of the Romans converging to it. One crossed the present highway to Macclesfield about half a mile to the north of Adlington Hall, a long lane on the left still bearing the appellation of Street-lane; and in two or three miles would coincide with the other about Hanford Mill. This is the continuation of the road from Manchester, as it leaves the station at Hanford, and bears directly from Buxton. And two others appear to have reached it from two opposite quarters, having bequeathed their name of Street to a lane in Alderley for three quarters of a mile, and to one in Cheadle for more than a mile together.

ROMAN STATION AT STOCKPORT.—A station was

seated equally on the course of a Roman road and the margin of the Mersey. It was settled at Stockport. And the town appears to be a common center to three or four very variously directed ways of the Romans. The High-street advances to it from Manchester, and the Pepper-street from Hanford. And in the parish of Ashton and near the foot of Staley-bridge is a third road, commonly denominated Staley-street for a mile together. A branch of this was the above-mentioned way to Stretford. And the main line lies pointing from Castleshaw to Stockport. These are sure signatures of a station here. And the general sameness in the position of this and the former fort, this being placed, like that, upon the limits of two provinces and the banks of the limitary stream, and settled, like that, in the road betwixt two considerable stations, demonstrates a sameness in the design, and requires a similarity in the nature of both. It was therefore fixed upon the plane of the Castle-hill at Stockport. This is exactly such a position as the Romans would select for the station. It is a small area, about half a statute acre in extent, projecting from the side of the Market place, and connected with it only by an isthmus. And it is a square knoll, which looks down upon a rocky bank, equally long and steep, and is guarded by the Mersey at the foot of it. This was the site of a fortress in the earliest period of the Saxons, as a port or castle originally communicated its name to the town; and was denominated Stock-port from the woods around it. And the hill is still incomparably strong in itself, and the position happily fitted for the ford. The station had a steep of a hundred yards in descent on three sides of it, and would naturally be fortified by a foss across the isthmus. And the Roman road into East Cheshire was effectually commanded by it, being obliged by the winding current of the Mersey to approach very near to the castle, and from the remaining steepness in the other parts of the bank appearing to have actually advanced up to it, and to have ascended the brow in a hollow immediately below the eastern side of it.

ROMAN LEGIONS AT CHESTER.—The Head-quarters of the 20th Legion, were in all probability fixed at Chester, by the direction of Agricola, at the termination of his war, as it certainly resided there within seventy years afterwards. We have also the positive authority of Malmesbury, perhaps the vehicle of tradition, but probably the copier of history, that one or more of the Julian legions, those commanded by Julius Agricola, were actually settled at Chester; and the better and more express attestation of Richard, that Chester was constructed by the soldiers of the twentieth. And the Frisians, who resided at Manchester, were in all probability a part of its auxiliaries; one of the eight cohorts which were annexed to the ten of the legion, and which ordinarily accompanied it upon expeditions in war, and were ordinarily disposed within the stations that lay nearest to it in peace.

But the whole of this cohort, as I have previously mentioned, was not lodged in the camp on the Medlock. Six detachments from it were constantly kept in the six fortresses of Stretford and Stockport, of Lowcaster and Raineshaw, and of Castle-hill and Hill-wood. And the first would require about nine Contubernia, or a hundred men, for a garrison; the third and fourth about a hundred and twenty. Thus about three hundred and fifty of the Mancunian Frisians were constantly detached upon duty to these six subordinate camps. Each corps would be under the same discipline as the main body. And each would be speedily recalled to the duties of the principal station, and succeeded by a new draught from the principal garrison.

NANTWICH AND CHESTER.—This road, part of one extending originally from Chester through Staffordshire, to Leicester, is now with great difficulty to be traced. Some remains, however, of it are to be seen near Bunbury, where the modern road inclines to the left, whilst the Roman road proceeds in a straight line upwards of two miles, close under the south-east side of Beeston Hill, on which it has been conjectured, from its commanding situation, there was formerly a post.

CHESTER AND SALOP.—This road is partially retained in the present one to Eccleston; it diverged, however, into the fields on the left hand, beyond Iron Bridge, and thence proceeded direct through Eaton Park to Aldford, where it remains, cut out of the solid rock; thence to Stretton, and to Shocklach, where the Church is built upon its site; and onwards to Bangor, where it branched off in the direction of the Verniew, and in the line to Wroxeter.

There was also a road from Melandra Castle, in Derbyshire, to Stockport, which although it has not been formally traced, is nevertheless pretty evident from local appearances, and from the quantity of gravel dug up in its course.

Little remains of the ancient road between Northwich and Middlewich.

The Legionary Garrisons of Cheshire and its dependencies probably amounted to about 13,000 men.

Several of the present principal roads in the County are of Roman origin; and the passes in the hills approaching towards Chester—as Barnhill, Kelsall, &c.—are undoubtedly the work of that people. All of them have been crowned with their exploratory fortresses, as may be seen at Maiden Castle, in the fields on the north side of Kelsall Hill, Eccleston Hill, and in various other situations.

A new road is now (1823) forming between Handley and Whitchurch, which, avoiding the lofty ascent of Barnhill, runs beneath Broxton, and unites with the ancient line at Hampton Post.

Mr. M'Adams's system of improving roads is becoming pretty general throughout the County; and the roads from Chester towards Delamere Forest, Parkgate, the Liverpool Ferries, Hawarden, Wrexham, and Whitchurch, have partially undergone the process.

Brown, *desig.* Mosses, *sc.*

HISTORY OF CHESHIRE.

From Camden, folio edition, translated by Holland,

1610.

DESCRIPT.

THE Fifth and last of those countries, which in old time the CORNAVII held, is the county of Chester; in the Saxon tongue Cestre-scyre, commonly called Cheshire, and the County Palatine of Chester (for that the Earls thereof had royalties and princely privileges belonging to them; and all the inhabitants owed allegiance and fealty to them, as they did to the King). As for this term Palatine that I may rehearse again, that which I have said before of this name, was in times past common to all those, who bare any office in the King's court or palace: and in that age Comes Palatinus, was a title of dignity conferred upon him who before was Palatinus, with authority to hear and determine causes in his own territory; and as well his Nobles whom they called Barons, as his Vassals were bound to repair unto the Palace of the said Court, both to give him advice and also to give their attendance, and furnish his Court with their presence.

County Palatine.

Petr. Pithœus in the description of Campaine.

This country (as WILLIAM of MALMESBURY saith) is scarce of corn, but especially of wheat, yet plentiful in cattle and fish. Howbeit RANULPH, the Monk of Chester, affirms the contrary: "Whatsoever Malmesbury

Ioh. Tillus.

CAMDEN'S DESCRIPT.

dreamed (saith he) upon the relation of others, it aboundeth with all kinds of victuals, plenteous in corn, flesh, fish, and salmons especially, of the very best: it maintaineth trade with many commodities, and maketh good return, For why, in the confines thereof it hath salt pits, mines, and metals." And this moreover will I add, the grass and fodder there, is of that goodness and virtue, that cheeses be made here in great number of a most pleasing and delicate taste, such as all England again affordeth not the like; no, though the best dairywomen otherwise and skilfulest in cheese making be had from hence. And whilst I am writing this, I cannot choose but marvel by the way at that which STRABO writeth, that in his time some Britons could not skill of making cheese: and that PLINY afterwards wondered, that barbarous nations, who lived of milk, either knew not or despised, for so many ages, the commodity of cheese, who had otherwise the feat of curding it to a pleasant tartness, and to fat butter. Whereby it may be gathered, that the device of making cheese came into Britain from the Romans. But however this region in fertility of soil cometh behind many counties in England, yet hath it always bred and reared more Gentry than the rest: For, you have not in all England again any one province beside, that in old time either brought more valourous Gentlemen in the field, or had more families in it of Knights degree. On the Southside it is hemmed in with Shropshire, on the Eastside with Staffordshire, and Derbyshire, on the North with Lancashire, and on the West with Denbigh and Flintshires. Towards the Northwest it runneth far into the sea with a long cantle * or Promontory, which being closed within two creeks receiveth the ocean on both sides entering into the land: into which two creeks, also all the rivers of this Shire do discharge themselves. Into that creek which is more western passeth the river DEE that divideth the county from Denbighshire: into that on the east-side, both WEAVER, which runneth through the midst of the shire, and MERSEY also, that parteth it from Lancashire, issue themselves. Neither see I any better way of describing this county, than if I follow the very tracts of these rivers. For all the places of greatest note, are situate by the sides of them. But before I enter into any particular description, I will first propose out of LUCIAN the Monk, thus much in commendation of Cheshire: for he is a rare author and lived a little after the Conquest. "If any man be desirous (saith he) either fully, or as near as may be, to treat of the inhabitants, according to the disposition of their manners, in respect of others that live in sundry places of the realm. They are found to be partly different from the rest of the English, partly better, and partly equal unto them. But they seem especially (the best point to be considered in a general trial of manners) in feasting friendly, at meat cheerful, in giving entertainment liberal, soon angry but not much, and as soon pacified, lavish in words, impatient of servitude, merciful to the afflicted, compassionate towards the poor, kind to their kindred, spary of their labour, void of dissimulation and doubleness of heart, nothing greedy in eating, far from dangerous practices, yet by a certain licentious liberty, bold in borrowing many times other men's goods. They abound in woods and pastures, they are rich in flesh and cattle, confining on the one side upon the Welsh Britons, and by a long intercourse and transfusion of their manners, for the most part like unto them. This also is to be considered, in what sort the Country of Chester enclosed upon one side with the limit of the wood Lime, by a certain distinct privilege from all other Englishmen is free, and by the indulgences of Kings, and excellencies of Earls, hath been wont in assemblies of the people to attend upon the Earl's sword rather than the King's crown: and within their precincts to hear, and determine the greatest matters with more liberty. Chester itself is a place of receipt for the Irish, a neighbour to the Welsh, and plentifully served with corn by the English: finely seated, with gates anciently built, approved in hard and dangerous difficulties. In regard of the river and prospect of the eye together, worthy according to the name to be called a City: guarded with a watch of holy and religious men, and, through the mercy of our Saviour, always fenced and fortified with the merciful assistance of the Almighty."

The most commendable cheeses.

** Wirrall.*

Lucian the Monk, of the praise of Cheshire.

The river* DEE, called in Latin Deva, in British Dyfr-dwy, that is, the Water of Dwy, breeding very great plenty of Salmons, ariseth out of two fountains in Wales, and thereof men think it took the name: for Dwy in their tongue signifieth Two. Yet others, observing also the signification of the word, interpret it Black

Deva.

** The river Dee.*

CAMDEN'S DESCRIPT.

Divona. Water, others again, God's Water, or Divine Water.—But although AUSONIUS noteth that a Spring hallowed to the Gods, was named Diuvona in the ancient Gaul's tongue (which was all one with the British) and in old time all rivers were reputed, Διιπετεῖς, that is Descending from Heaven, yea and our Britons yielded divine honour unto rivers, as GILDAS writeth, yet I see not why they should attribute Divinity to this river Dwy above all others. The Thessalians, as we read, gave to the river Pæneus divine honour, for the pleasantness thereof; the Scythians to Danubius for the largeness; the Germans to Rhine because it was counted a judge in the question of true and undefiled wedlock. But wherefore they should impose a divine name, upon this river, I see no reason, as I said before, unless peradventure, because now and then it changed the channel, and thereby foreshewed a sure token of victory to the inhabitants upon it, when they were in hostility one with another, according as it inclined more to this side or to that, after it had left the channel: for, thus hath GIRALDUS CAMBRENSIS recorded, who in some sort believed it; or else, because they observed that contrary to the wonted manner of other rivers, upon the fall of much rain it arose but little, and so often as the south wind beateth long upon it, it swelleth and extraordinarily overfloweth the grounds adjoining. Peradventure also the Christian Britons thought the water of this river to be holy, for it is written, that when they stood ready to join battle with the English Saxons, and had kissed the earth, they also drank very devoutly of this river, in memorial of CHRIST's most sacred and precious blood. But, Dee which seemeth to rush rather than to run out of Wales, no sooner is entered into Cheshire but he passeth more mildly with a slower stream by Bonium, in some written copies of ANTONINE, Bovium, a City that had been of great name in that age, and afterwards a famous Monastery. Of the choir or quire whereof, it was called by the Britons Bon-chor and Banchor, of the ancient English Bancornabyrigt, and Banchor, and among many good and godly men, it fostered and brought up (as some write) that most wicked Archheretick PELAGIUS, who injuriously derogating from the grace of God, troubled along time the West Church with his pestiferous doctrine. PROSPER AQUITANUS in this verse of his, termeth him the British adder, or land-snake.

Bonium.

Banchor

PESTIFERO VOMUIT COLUBER SERMONE BRITANNUS.

A British snake, with venomous tongue,
Hath vomitted his poison strong.

Neither have I made mention of him for any other reason, but because it is behovable to each one to know vices and venoms. In this Monastery, as saith BEDE, "there was such a number of Monks that being divided into seven portions, which had every of them a several head and ruler over them, yet every one of these had no fewer than three hundred men who were wont to live all of their handy labour." Of whom EDILFRED, King of the Nordan-humbers, slew twelve hundred, because they had implored in their prayers Christ's assistance for the Christian Britons against the English Saxons, then infidels. The profession of this Monastical life (that I may digress a little) began, when Pagan tyrants enraged against Christians, pursued them with bloody persecutions. For then good devout men, that they might serve God in more safety and security, withdrew themselves into the vast wilderness of Egypt, and not (as the Painims are wont with open mouth to give it out) to enwrap themselves willingly in more miseries because they would not be in misery.

Monkery.

Rutilius Claudius.

Where they scattered themselves among mountains and deserts, living in caves and little cells here and there in holy meditations, at first solitary and alone, whereupon in Greek the Monachi, that is Monks: but after they thought it better (as the sociable nature of mankind required) to meet together at certain times to serve God, and at length they began to cohabit and live together for mutual comfort, rather than like wild beasts to walk up and down in the deserts. Their profession was to pray, and by the labour of their own hands to get living for themselves, and maintainance for the poor, and withal they vowed poverty, obedience, and chastity. ATHANASIUS first brought this kind of Monks, consisting of laymen, into the West Church. Whereunto after that, Saint AUSTEN in Africk, Saint MARTIN in France, and CONGELL in Britain and Ireland, had adjoined the function of regular Clergy. It is incredible, how far and wide they spread, how many and how great Cœnobies were built for them, so called of their communion of life; as also Monasteries, for that they kept still a

CAMDEN'S DESCRIPT.

certain shew of solitary living, and in those days none were more sacred and holy than they, and accordingly they were reputed; considering how by their prayers to God, by their example, doctrine, labour, and industry, they did exceeding much good not only to themselves, but also to all mankind. But as the world grew worse and worse, so those their holy manners, as one said, REBUS CESSERE SECUNDIS, that is, GAVE BACKWARD IN TIME OF PROSPERITY. Now let me return unto my matter, craving your pardon for this short digression.

That Banchor which St. Bernard, speaketh of in the life of Malachi, was in Ireland.

After these days, this Monastery fell utterly to ruin; for in the time of WILLIAM OF MALMESBURY, who lived presently after the Normans coming in, "There remained here, (as he saith) so many tokens of Antiquity, so many walls of Churches half down, so many windings and turnings of gates, such heaps of rubbish and rammel, as hardly a man should have found elsewhere."—But now is left to be seen scarcely the face and outward show of a dead City or Monastery, and the names only remain of two gates Port Hoghan and Port Cleis, which stand a mile asunder, between which are found, very oft, pieces of the Romans' money. But, that I may tell you of one thing, this Bonium or Banchor, is not reckoned within this County but in Flintshire; a piece whereof severed (as it were) from the rest, lieth here between Cheshire and Shropshire.

Bonium, or Banchor, is of Flintshire

Dee, where he entereth first into this shire seeth above him not far from his bank, Malpas, upon a high hill, which had in it a Castle, and for the bad, narrow, and cumbrous way was termed in Latin Mala platea, that is Ill-street, and thence also took this latter name Mal-pas from the Normans, whereas in times past the Englishmen, almost in the very same sense, called it Depenbach. The Barony hereof Hugh Earl of Chester gave to ROBERT FITZ-HUGH. In the reign of Henry the Second, WILLIAM PATRICK the son of WM. PATRICK held the same, of whose line ROBERT PATRICK standing outlawed, lost it. After some few years DAVID of MALPAS by* a writ of Recognisance, got the one half of that town which was GILBERT CLERKE'S; but a great part of this Barony went afterwards hereditarily to those SUTTONS that are Barons of Dudley, and a part also thereof came to URIAN SAMPIER. And from Philip a younger son of DAVID OF MAL-PAS, is decended that worshipful family of the EGERTONS, who took this name from the place of their habitation: like as from other places, divers gentlemen of this race received the surnames of COTGRAVE, OVERTON, CODDINGTON, and GOLBORN. As touching the name of this place, give me leave, before I depart hence, in this work, to insert a pretty jest out of GIRALDUS CAMBRENSIS. "It happened, (saith he) in our days, that a certain Jew travelling towards Shrewsbury, with the Archdeacon of this place, whose surname was Peche, that is Sin, and a Dean named Devil, when he heard by chance the Archdeacon telling that his Archdeaconry began at a place called Ill-street, and reached as far as to Mal-pas towards Chester. He considering and understanding withal as well the Archdeacon's surname as the Dean's, came out with this pleasant and merry conceit: Would it not be a wonder, (saith he) and my fortune very good, if ever I get safe again out of this country, where Sin is the Archdeacon, and the Devil the Dean; where the entrance into the Archdeaconry is Ill-street, and the going forth of it, Malpas."

Out of the Roll of Doomsday of Cheshire.

Barons of Malpas.

* Per breve recognitionis.

Itinerar. lib. 2 cap. 13.

From hence, Dee runneth down amain by Shoclach, where sometime was a Castle, by Aldford, belonging in times past to the ARDENS; by Pulford, where in the reign of Henry the Third, SIR RALPH OF ORMSBY had his Castle; and by Eaton the seat of the famous family of GROS-VENOUR, that is, THE GREAT HUNTER, whose posterity now corruptly go under the name of GRAVENOR.

Shoclach.

Grosvenour.

Somewhat higher, upon the same river near unto Deemouth, which PTOLEMY calleth Seteia, for Deia, standeth the noble Citie which the said PTOLEMY named Devnana, ANTONINE the Emperor Deva, of the river, the Britons Caer-Legion, Caer-Leon Vawr, Caer-Leon ar Dyfyr Dwy, and by way of excellence Caer, like as our ancestors, the English Saxons Legea-cester, of the Legion's camp, and we more short, West Chester, of the West situation, and simply Chester, according to the verse,

Deunana. Deva.

Chester.

Cestria de castris nomen quasi Castria sumpsit.

Chester of Castra took the name,
As if that Castria were the same.

For, these British names, without all doubt were de-

CAMDEN'S

rived from the Twentieth Legion named Victrix. This legion in the year that GALBA the Emperor was the second time Consul, together with TITUS VINIUS, was transported over into Britain, which being out of awe, and therefore dreaded of the Lieutenants, as well those which had been Consuls as Prætors, had JULIUS AGRICOLA appointed Lieutenant over it by VESPASIAN the Emperor; was at length placed and seated in this City, which I suppose was not built many years before, and set as one would say at the back of the Ordovices, to restrain them, although there are some, who avouch it to be of greater antiquity, as they say, than the moon, as founded forsooth by LEON VAWR the Giant, I know not how many hundred years before. But the very name itself might give the check unto these trivial antiquaries, and withhold them from so gross an error. For, they cannot deny, but that Leon Vawr, in British, signifieth a Great Legion. Now, whether it stands more with reason and equity, that a City should take name of a Great Legion, than of Leon a Giant, let the learned judge; seeing, that in the part of Spain called Tarraconensis, there is a realm now called Leon of the seventh Legion Germanica, considering also, that the twentieth Legion, which they termed Britannica Valens Victrix, and some falsely Valeria Victrix, abode in this City, as PTOLEMY, ANTONINE, and the ancient coin of SEPTIMIUS GETA do prove; by which, it appeareth for certain, that this City also was a Colony. For, in the reverse or back side thereof standeth this inscription COL. DIVANA LEG. XX. VICTRIX. But to testify the Romans' magnificence, there are remaining indeed at this day very few tokens, beside pavements of four square chequer work; howbeit in the former ages it presented many, which, RANULPH a Monk of this city shall tell you out of his Polychronicon, in these his own words.— "There be ways here under the ground vaulted marvellously with stone-work, chambers having arched roofs over head, huge stones engraven with the names of ancient men; here also are sometimes digged up pieces of money coined by Julius Cæsar and other famous persons, and stamped with their inscriptions." Likewise ROGER OF CHESTER, in his Policraticon, "When I behold (saith he) the ground work of buildings in the streets laid with monstrous big stones, it seemeth that it hath been founded by the painful labour of Romans or Giants, rather than the sweat of Britons." The City, built in the form of a quadrant, four square, is inclosed with a wall that taketh up more than two miles in compass, and hath eleven parishes. But that of St. John's without the Northgate* was the fairest, being a stately and solemn building, as appeareth by the remains, wherein were anciently Prebendaries, and, as some write, the Bishop's See. Near unto the river standeth the Castle upon a rocky hill, built by the Earls, where the Courts Palatine, and the Assizes, as they call them, are kept twice a year.

Chester a Colony of the Romans.

DESCRIPT.

[* This is evidently an error. ED.]

The Rows

The houses are very fair built and along the chief streets are galleries or walking places, they call Rows having shops on both sides, through which a man may walk dry from one end unto the other. But it hath not continued evermore in the tenor of prosperity. First it was rased by EGFRID King of Northumberland, then by the Danes, yet re-edified again by ÆDELFLED Lady of the Mercians; and soon after it saw King EDGAR in magnificent manner triumphing over the British Princes. For, sitting himself in a barge at the fore-deck, KENNADY King of the Scots, MALCOLINE King of Cumberland, MACON King of Man, and of the Islands, with all the Princes of Wales, brought to do homage, and like watermen working at the oar, rowed him along the river Dee, in a triumphant show, to his great glory and joy of the beholders.

Marian. Scotus.

About the year 960.

Certain years after, and namely about the year of our redemption, 1094, when as in a devout and religious emulation, as one saith, "Princes strove avie, that Cathedral Churches and Minsters should be erected in a more decent and seemly form, and when as Christendom rouzed as it were herself, and casting away her old habiliments, did put on every where the bright and white robe of the churches," HUGH the first of the Norman blood, that was Earl of Chester, repaired the Church which Earl LEOFRICK had formerly founded in honour of the Virgin St. WERBURGA, and by the advice of ANSELM, whom he had procured to come out of Normandy, granted the same unto Monks. And now it is notorious, for the tomb of Henry the Fourth, Emperor of ALMAIN, who as they say gave over his empire, and lived here an Hermit's life; and for the Bishop's see therein establish-

Churches repaired.

Rodolphus Glaber.

ed. Which see immediately after the Norman conquest, Peter Bishop of Lichfield, translated from Lichfield hither: but when it was brought to Coventry, and from thence into the ancient seat again, West Chester lay a long time bereft of this Episcopal dignity, until in our fathers' days King Henry VIII. having thrust out the Monks, ordained Prebendaries, and restored a Bishop again, under whom, for his Diocese, he appointed this County, Lancashire, Richmond, &c. and appointed the same to be within the Province of the Archbishop of York. But return we now to matters of greater antiquity. When as now the said Cathedral was built, the Earls that were of the Norman line, fortified the City both with walls and castle. "For as the Bishop held of the King that which belongeth to his Bishoprick, (these are the words of Doomsday Book, made by King William the Conqueror) so the Earls with their men held of the King wholly, all the rest of the City. It paid geld or tribute, for fifty hides, and four hundred and thirty-one houses were thus geldable, and seven mint masters. When the King himself in person came thither, every carrucata yielded unto him two hundred Hesthas, and one tun full of ale, and one rusca of butter." And in the same place, "for the re-edification of the City wall and the bridge, the Provost gave warning by an edict, that out of every Hide in the County one man should come: and look whose man came not, his Lord or Master was fined in forty shillings to the King and the Earl." If I should particulate the scufflings and skirmishes hereafter between the Welsh and English in the beginning of the Norman's time, their inroads and their outroads, the often scarfires of the suburbs of Handbridge beyond the bridge, whereupon the Welsh called it Treboeth, that is The Burnt Town, as also the wall made there of the Welshmen's sculls that went a great length, I should seem to forget myself, and thrust my sickle into the historian's harvest.

But ever since the said time, hath Chester notably flourished, and King Henry the seventh made it a county by itself incorporate. Neither wanteth any thing there that may be required in a most flourishing city, but that the ocean being offended and angry (as it were) at certain mills in the very channel of the Dee, hath by little withdrawn himself back, and affordeth not unto the city the commodity of an haven, as heretofore. The longitude of this place is twenty degrees and three and twenty scruples: the latitude three and fifty degrees and eleven scruples. If you desire to know more touching this city, have here these reports out of Lucian that monk abovesaid, who lived almost five hundred years ago. "First, it is to be considered, that Chester is built as a city, the site whereof inviteth and allureth the eye, which being situate in the west parts of Britain, was in times past a place of receipt to the legions coming a far off to repose themselves, and served sufficiently to keep the keys, as I may say, of Ireland, for the Romans, to preserve the limits of their Empire. For being opposite to the north-east part of Ireland, it openeth the way for passage of ships and mariners with spread sails passing not often but continually to and fro, as also for the commodities of sundry sorts of merchandise. And whilst it casteth an eye forward into the east; it looketh toward not only the See of Rome, and the Empire thereof, but the whole world also, so that it standeth forth as a kenning place to the view of eyes, that there may be known valiant exploits, and the long train and consequence of things; as also whatsoever throughout the world hath been done by all persons, in all places, and at all times, and whatever hath been ill done may also be avoided and taken heed of. Which city having four gates from the four cardinal winds, on the east-side hath a prospect toward India, on the west toward Ireland, north-eastward the greater Norway, and southward that straight and narrow Angle, which divine severity, by reason of civil and home discords, hath left unto the Britons; which long since by their bitter variance have caused the name of Britain to be changed into the name of England.—Over and beside, Chester hath by God's gift a river to enrich and adorn it, the same fair and fishful, hard by the city walls, and on the south side a road and harbour for ships coming from Gascony, Spain, and Germany, which with the help and direction of Christ, by the labour and wisdom of merchants, repair and refresh the heart of the city with many good things, that we being comforted every way by our God's grace, may also drink wine often, more frankly and plenteously; because those countries enjoy the fruit of the vineyards abundantly. Moreover the open sea ceaseth not to visit it every day with a tide, which according as the broad shelves and bars of sands are opened or hidden by tides and ebbs incessantly, is wont more or less either to send or exchange one thing or other, and by this reciprocal flow and returns, either to bring in or to carry out somewhat."

From the city, northwestward, there shooteth out a languet of land, or promontory of the main land into the sea, enclosed on the one side with DEE-MOUTH, on the other side with the river MERSEY—we call it WIRALL; the Welsh Britons, for that it is an angle, term it KILL-GURY. In old time it was all forest and not inhabited, as the dwellers report, but King Edward the Third disforested it: yet now, beset it is with towns on every side, howbeit more beholden to the sea than to the soil, for the land beareth small plenty of corn, the water yieldeth great store of fish. At the entry into it on the south side standeth SHOTWICH, a castle of the King's, upon the salt water; upon the north standeth HOOTON, a manor, which in King Richard the Second's time, came to the STANLEY's, who fetch their pedigree from ALANE SYLVESTRE, upon whom Ranulph the first of that name, Earl of CHESTER, conferred the BAILLY-WICK of the FOREST OF WIRALL, by delivering unto him a horn. Close unto this is POOLE, from whence the Lords of the place that have a long time flourished, took their name, and hard by it STANLAW, as the monks of that place interpret it, a STONYHILL; where JOHN LACY, Constable of Chester, founded a little monastery, which was afterwards by reason of inundations, translated to WHALEY, IN LANCASHIRE.

Wirall.

Law, what it is.

1173.

In the utmost brink of this Promontory, lieth a small, hungry, barren and sandy isle, called IL-BRE, which had sometime a little cell of Monks in it. More within the county and eastward from WIRALL, you meet with a famous forest, named the Forest of DELAMERE, the foresters whereof by hereditary succession, are the DAWNS of UTKINTON, descended of a worshipful stock, from RANUPH DE KINGLEIGH, unto whom Ranulph the First, Earl of Chester, gave that Forestership, to be held by right of inheritance. In this forest ÆDELFLED, the famous Mercian Lady, built a little city called Eadesburg, that is, by interpretation, HAPPY-TOWN, which now having quite lost itself hath likewise lost that name, and is but an heap of rubbish and rammel, which they call THE CHAMBER IN THE FOREST. And about a mile or two from hence, are to be seen the ruins of FINBARROW, another town built by the same Lady Ædelfled.

Il-bre.

Finborrow.

Through the upper part of this forest, the river WEVER runneth, which ariseth out of a poole in the south side of the shire at RIDLY, the dwelling-house of the respective and ancient family of the EGERTONS, who flowered out of the Barons of MALPAS, as I have said. Near hereunto is BUNBURY contractedly so called for BONIFACE BURY, for St. Boniface was the patron Saint there, where the Egertons built a college for priests.— Over against which is BEESTON which gave surname to an ancient family, and where upon a steep rising hill, Beeston Castle towereth aloft with a turretted wall of a great circuit. This castle the last Ranulph Earl of Chester built; whereof LELAND our countryman, being rapt both with a poetical and prophetical fury, writeth thus:

Ridly.

Beeston.

Assyrio rediens victor Ranulphus ab orbe,
Hoc posuit Castrum terrorem gentibus olim
Vicinis, patriaeque suae memorabile vallum.
Nunc licet indignas patiatur fracta ruinas,
Tempus erit quando rursus caput exeret altum,
Vatibus antiquis si fas mihi credere vati.

When Ranulph from Assyria return'd with victory,
As well the neighbour Nations to curb and terrify,
As to fence his own country, this famous Fort he rais'd,
Whilom a stately thing, but now the pride thereof is raz'd.
And yet though at this present time, it be in mean estate
With cracks and breaches much defac'd & fouly ruinate;
The day will come when it again the head aloft shall heave,
If ancient prophets, I myself a prophet, may believe.

But to return to the river, WEVER first holdeth his course southward, not far from WOODHAY, where dwelt a long time that family of the WILBURHAMS, knights, in great reputation; also by BULKELEY and CHOLMONDELEY, which imparted their names to worshipful houses of knight's degree; not far off on the one hand from

Woodhay.

Bulkley.

CAMDEN'S DESCRIPT.

BADDELEY, the habitation in times past of the ancient family DE PRAERYS: of the other, from CUMBERMER, in which WILLIAM MALBEDENG founded a little religi-
1134. ous house. Where this river cometh to the south limit of this shire, it passeth through low places, wherein, as also elsewhere, the people find often times and get out
Trees under ground. of the ground, trees that have lain buried, as it is thought, there, ever since Noah's flood. But afterwards, watering fruitful fields, he taketh to him out of the east a riveret by which standeth WIBBENBURY, so called of WIBBA, king of the Mercians. Hard to it lies HATHERTON, the seat of in old time of the ORBEIES, then of the CORBETTS, but now of the SMITHES; DODINTON, the possession of the DELVES'S; BATHERTON, of the GRIPHINS; SHAVINGTON of the WODENOTHS, (who by that name may seem to have descended from the English-Saxons) beside the places of the respective families wherewith this county everywhere aboundeth. From thence runneth Wever down by NANT-WICH, not far
Saltpits. from MIDDLEWICH, and so to NORTHWICH. These are very famous SALT-WICHES, five or six miles distant asunder, where brine or salt water is drawn out of pits, which they pour not upon wood while it burneth, as the ancient Gauls and Germans were wont to do, but boil over the fire, to make salt thereof. Neither doubt I, that these were known unto the Romans, and that from hence was usually paid the Custom of Salt, called *Salarium*. For, there went a notable highway from Middlewich to Northwich, raised with gravel to such an height, that a man may easily acknowledge that it was the work of the Romans, seeing that all this country over, gravel is so scarce: and from thence at this day it is carried to private men's uses.

MATHEW PARIS writeth, that King Henry III. stopped up these SALT-PITS, when in hostile manner he wasted this shire: because the Welshmen, so tumultuous in those days, should not have any victuals or provision from thence. But when the fair beams of peace
Nantwich. began once to shine out, they were opened again. NANTWICH, which the river WEVER first visiteth, is reputed the greatest and fairest built town of all this shire after Chester, the Britons call it HELLATH WEN, that is the WHITE WICH OR SALT PIT, because the whitest salt is there boiled: and such as writ in Latin, named it VICUS MALBANUS, haply of one William named MALBEDENG and MALBANC, unto whom, at the Norman's Conquest of England, it was allotted. It hath only one Salt-pit, they call it the Brine-pit, about some fourteen feet from the river, out of which they convey salt water by troughs of wood into houses adjoining, wherein there stand little barrels pitched fast in the ground, which they fill with that water, and at the ringing of a bell, they begin to make fires under the leads; whereof they have six in every house, and therein seeth the said water: then certain women, they call them Wallers, with little wooden rakes fetch up the salt from the bottom, and put it in baskets, they call them Salt-barrows, out of which the liquor runneth, and the pure salt remaineth. The Church (and but one they have) is passing fair, and belonged, as I have heard, unto the Abbey of CUMBERMER: from hence, Wever holding on his course crooked enough, is augmented with a brook, coming out of the East, which runneth down from CREW, a place inhabited in old time by a notable family of that name. And farther yet from the west-side of the river, CALVELEY sheweth itself, which gave both habitation and name Calveley. to the worthy family of the CALVELEYS, out of which in the reign of RICHARD II. Sir HUGH CALVELEY, Knight, was for his chivalry in France so renowned, that there occurred no hardy exploit but his prowess would go through it. From whence Wever eyeth apace MINSHULL, the House of the MINSHULLS, and by VALE ROYAL, an Abbey founded by King EDWARD I. in a Vale Royal. most pleasant valley, where now dwelleth the ancient family of the HOLCROFTS, unto NORTHWICH, in British called HELLATH DU, that is THE BLACK SALT-PIT: Northwich. where also very near the brink of the river DAN, there is a most beautiful and deep Brine-pit, with stairs made about it, by which they that draw water out of it in leather buckets, ascend half naked into the troughs, and pour it thereinto, by which it is carried into the wich houses, about which there stand on every side many stakes and piles of wood. Here Wever receiveth into his channel the river Dan, whose tract and stream I will now follow.

This DAN, or more truly DAVEN, flowing out of those hills which on the East-side sever Staffordshire from Cheshire, runneth along to CONDATE, a town mentioned

CAMDEN'S by ANTONINE the Emperor, now called corruptly CONGLETON, the middle whereof the little brook HOWTY, on the East side DANING-SCHOW, and Northward DAN itself, watereth. And albeit this town for the greatness and frequency thereof, hath deserved to have a Mayor and six Aldermen, yet hath it but a Chapel and no more, and the same made of timber, unless it be the Quire and a little Tower-steeple, which acknowledgeth ASTBURY, about two miles off, her mother Church: which verily is a very fair Church, the West-porch whereof is equal in height to the very Church as high as it is, and hath a Spire-steeple adjoining thereto. In the Church-yard lie two portraitures of Knights upon sepulchres, in whose shields are two Bars. But for that they be without their colours, hardly can any man say, whether of the BRERETONS, MANWARINGS, or VENABLES, which are the most noble familes in those parts, and indeed such BARS do they bear in their coats of arms, but in divers colours.

Then cometh DAVEN to DAVENPORT, commonly *Damport,* which hath adopted into her own name, a notable family: and HOLMESCHAPEL, a town well known to wayfaring-men: where, within the remembrance of onr Grandfathers, J. NEEDHAM built a bridge. Near unto which, at RUDHEATH, there was sometime a place of refuge and sanctuary, as well for the inhabitants of this shire as strangers, who had trespassed against the laws, that there they might abide in security for a year and a day. Then runneth it under KINDERTON, the old seat of the ancient race of the VENABLES; who, ever since the first coming in of the Normans have been of name and reputation here, and commonly are called *Barons of Kinderton.* Beneath this, Southward, the little river CROCO runneth also into DAN, which flowing out of the pool called BAGMERE passeth by BRERETON: which, as it hath given name to the worshipful, ancient, and numerous family of the BRERETONS, knights: so Sir WM. BRERETON, Knt. hath of late added very much credit and honor to the place, by a magnificent and sumptuous house that he hath there built. A wonder it is that I shall tell you, and yet no other than I have heard verified upon the credit of many creditable persons, and commonly believed, that before the heir of this house of the BRERETONS dieth, there be seen in a pool adjoining, bodies of trees swimming for certain days together. Like unto that which LEONARDUS VAIRUS reporteth from the testimony of Cardinal GRANVELL, namely, that near unto the Abbey of Saint MAURICE, in BURGUNDY, there is a fishpond, in which are fishes put according to the number of the Monks of that place; and if any one of them happened to be sick, there is a fish seen also to float, and swim above the water half dead, and if the monk shall die, the said fish a few days before dieth. DESCRIPT. Lib. 2. de Fascino.

As touching these matters, if they be true, I wot not what to say, I am no Wizard to interpret such strange wonders, but these and such like things are done either by the holy tutelar Angels of men, or by the devils, who by God's permission mightily shew their power in this inferior world. For, both the sorts of them being intelligent natures, upon a deliberate purpose and to some certain end, and not for nought, work strange things. The Angels seek after, and aim at the safety and health of mankind; the devils contrarywise plot to mischief, vex, or else to delude them. But all this may seem impertinent to our purpose. Angels. Devils.

CROKE, the riveret aforesaid, being past BRERETON, within a while visiteth MIDDLEWICH, very near unto his confluence with DAN, where there be two wells of salt water, parted one from the other by a small brook: *Sheathes* they call them. The one stands not open, but at certain set times, because folk willingly steal the water thereof, as being of greater virtue and efficacy. From hence runneth DAN to BOSTOKE, in times past BOTESTOCK, the ancient seat of the family of the BOSTOKES, knights, which by the marriage with ANNE, only daughter of RALPH, son and heir to Sir ADAM BOSTOKE, Knt. passed together with a very great livelihood, unto Sir JOHN SAVAGE. Out of this ancient house of the BOSTOKS, as out of a stock, sprung a goodly number of the same name, in Cheshire, Shropshire, Berkshire, and elsewhere. Middlewich. Bostock

When as DAN, beneath NORTHWICH that I speak of, hath united his stream with WEVER, then Wever runneth forthright, and taketh in from the East, PEVER, that floweth hard by PEVER, and giveth it the name, Peven.

where, that ancient notable family of MEINILWARIN, commonly MANEWARING is seated, out of which RALPH married the daughter of HUGH KEVELIOC, Earl of Chester, as appeareth by an old Charter in the custody of Ranulph the heir now of the same house.

From thence speedeth WEVER by WININGTON, which gave both habitation and name to the ancient family of the WININGTONS; and not far from MERBURY, which being so called of a MERE under it, conferred likewise the name upon that respective ancient family of the MERBURIES. Hence the river holdeth on his course Dutton. near unto DUTTON, the inheritance of that great and worthy family of DUTTONS, who derive their descent from one HUDARD, allied to the Earls of Chester; who by an old order and custom have great authority over all the pipers, fidlers, and minstrels of this province, ever since that one of the DUTTONS, a young gentleman full of spirit and active withall, having hastily gathered a tumultuary power of those kind of people, valiently delivered RANULPH, the last Earl of Chester, Chronicles of Wales. from danger, when he was beset with Welsh enemies. Neither must I pass over in silence NETHER WHITLEY in this tract, out of which came the TUSCHETTS or TOWCHETTS, Towchet. who are now Barons of AUDLEY. By this time WEVER aforesaid, flowing between FRODSHAM, a Rock Savage. Castle of ancient note, and CLIFTON, now ROCK SAVAGE, an house of the SAVAGES, new built, who here by marriage attained to rich and fair revenues, entereth at length into MERSEY MOUTH. And this is so called of the river MERSEY, which running as a bounder between Cheshire and Lancashire, is there at length discharged into the sea, after it hath among other small towns of meaner note watered STOCKPORT, which had some time a Baron, of the Earls of Chester, and WARBURGTON, so named of S. WERBURGH, the habitation of a family thereof surnamed, but branched from the DUTTONS; hereby it entertaineth the river BOLLIN out of that spa-Macclesfield cious forest of MACCLESFIELD. Upon this BOLLIN standeth MACCLESFIELD, one of the fairest towns in this county which gave name unto that Forest, where T. SAVAGE, first, Bishop of London, and afterwads Archbishop of York, built a College, wherein some of that race of the SAVAGES lie entombed: also, DUNHAM, which from Sir HAMON of MASCY, by the FITTONS and VENABLES descended hereditarily unto the family of BOOTH. From thence MERSEY cometh to THELWALL before it be far past KNOTSFORD, that is *Canutus his ford*, which is divided into the upper and the nether; Thelwall also to LEE, from whence there is a family bearing the same surname, that is not only of gentle blood and of especial note, but also fair and fairly propagated into a number of branches. As for THELWALL, now it is an obscure village, but in times past a large town, built by KING EDWARD the ELDER, and so called, as FLORILEGUS witnesseth, of bodies of trees the boughs being cut off, firmly fastened in the ground, wherewith he walled it all round. For the Saxons, in their tongue, called the trunks and bodies of trees, Del, and a *Wall*, as we do now.

At the very mouth of the river standeth RUNCORN, founded in the same age by Lady EDELFLEDE commonly Runcorn. called ELFLED, and brought by the mutability of time Elfled or Ethelfled. to a few cottages. This Lady EDELFLEDA (to tell you at once, of whom I have oft made mention) sister to King EDWARD the ELDER, and wife to ETHELRED, a petty King of the MERCIANS, after her husband's death governed the Mercians in most dangerous and troublesome times, for eight years, with high commendation; touching whom these laudatory verses in praise of her, we read in the history of HENRY of HUNTINGDON.

O Elfleda potens, o terror virgo virorum,
Victrix naturae, nomine digna viri.
Tu, quo splendidior fieres, natura puellam,
Te probitas fecit nomen habere viri.
Te mutare decet, sed solam, nomina sexus,
Tu regina potens, Rex que trophaea parans,
Jam nec Caesarei tantum meruere triumphi,
Caesare splendidior virgo virago, Vale.

O mighty ELFLED, virgin pure, that men dost terrify,
And nature pass, right worthy you in name a man to be.
To grace thee more, dame Nature once thee shap'd a maiden brave,
But virtue thee hath caused now the name of man to have.
It thee becomes, but thee alone, the name of Sex to change:
Of great Queens and triumphant Kings thou standest in the range.

CAMDEN'S DESCRIPT.

From CÆSAR's triumphs for desert thou bear'st away the bell,
No CÆSAR ever was thy match: Thus MANLY-MAID farewell.

Beneath RUNCORN, somewhat within the country, HALTON, the town and castle, both shew themselves, which HUGH LUPUS, Earl of Chester, gave unto NIELE a NORMAN, to be by tenure and service constable of Chester, by whose posterity, through the variable change of times, it is come into the HOUSE of LANCASTER. Neither would this be over passed in silence, that WILLIAM, the said NIELE's son, founded the Abbey adjoining, at NORTON, which now appertaineth to the BROKS of ancient descent. Whether I should place in this shire, or elsewhere the CANGI, an ancient nation of Britain, that have been so much and so long sought for, I have as long and as much doubted. For continuance of time hath now so obscured them, that hitherto by no footings they could be traced and found out. And albeit, JUSTUS LIPSIUS, that flower of exquisite learning, taketh me for a Judge, herein I frankly confess, I know not what judgment to give, and rather would I commend this office of judging to any other man, than assume it to myself. Yet nevertheless, if CEANGI and CANGI were the same, as why not? it may be probable enough, that they were seated in this tract. For, whilst I perused these my labours, I understood by some of good credit, that there were here upon the very shore gotten out of the ground, twenty sows of lead, long in form, but four square. On the upper part where of in an hollow surface is to be read this inscription.

IMP. DOMIT. AVG. GER. DE CEANG.

But on the other—

In the year of Christ 78

IMP. VESP. VII. T. IMP. V. COSS.

Which monument seemeth to have been erected for a victory over the CANGI. Hereto maketh also the very scite upon the Irish sea, for thus writeth TACITUS, in the 12th book of his *Annals*: "Whilst NERO was Emperor, there was an army led by OSTORIUS, against the Cangi: the fields were wasted, booties raised every where, for that the enemies durst not come into the field, but if they attempted closely and by stealth to cut off the army as it marched, they paid for their deceitful cunning. Now were they no sooner come near unto the sea coast, towards IRELAND, but certain tumults and insurrections among the Brigantes, brought the General back." But by the inscription abovesaid, it should seem that they were not subdued before DOMITIAN's time: and then by computation of the times, when as that most warlike JULIUS AGRICOLA was Propreator in Britain. PTOLEMY likewise placed the Promontory ΚΑΓΓΑΝΩΝ, that is, *of the* CANGI, *as this shore.* Neither dare I seek elsewhere than in this tract, that Station CONGANII, where, in the declining state of the Roman Empire, a company or band, called VIGILES, that is *Watchmen*, with their Captain under the DUX BRITANNIÆ, kept watch and ward. Notwithstanding I leave to every man for me his own judgment herein, as in all things else of this nature.

Anno 51.

Earls of Chester.

Touching the Earls, that I may pass over the English-Saxons, Earls only by office, and not by inheritance.—King WILLIAM I. created HUGH, surnamed LUPUS, son to the VISCOUNT of AURANCHES, in Normandy, the first hereditary EARL of CHESTER, and COUNT PALATINE, and "gave unto him, and his heirs, all this county, to be holden as freely by his Sword, as the King himself held England by his Crown," (for these are the words of the donation) who forthwith appointed under him these Barons, viz. NIELE, Baron of Halton, whose posterity afterwards took the name of LACIES, for that the LACIES inheritance had fallen unto them, and were EARLS of LINCOLN: ROBERT, Baron of Mont-hault, Seneschall of the County of Chester, the last of whose line, having no issue, by his last will, ordained ISABEL, Queen of England, and JOHN of Eltham, Earl of Cornwall, his heirs: WILLIAM MALDEBENG, Baron of Malbanc, whose nephew's daughters, by marriage, brought the inheritance to the VERNONS and BASSETS: RICHARD

Barons to to the Earl of Chester.

CAMDEN'S

VERNON, Baron of Shipbroke, whose inheritance for default of heirs males, in the end came by the sisters unto the Wilburhams, Staffords, and Littleburies: ROBERT FITZ-HUGH, Baron of Malpas, who, as it seemeth, died, as I said before, without issue: HAMON DE MASCY, whose possessions descended to the Fittons of Bollin: GILBERT VENABLES, Baron of Kinderton, whose posterity in the right line have continued and flourished unto these our days: N. Baron of Stockport, to whom at length, the Warrens of Pointon, budded out of the honorable family of the Earls of Warren and Surry, in right of marriage succeeded. And these were all the Barons of the Earls of Chester, that ever I could hitherto find, who, as it is written in an old book, "had their free Courts of all Pleas and Suits or Complaints, except those Pleas which belong unto the Earl's sword." And their office was to assist the Earl in counsel, to yield him dutiful attendance, and oftentimes to repair unto his Court for to do him honour; and as we find in old parchment records, "Bound they were, in time of war in Wales, to find for every Knight's fee, one horse, with caparison and furniture, or else two without, within the Divisions of Cheshire. Also, that their Knights and Freeholders should have Corslets and *Haubergeons, and defend their* Fees by their own bodies.

* Hauber-gella.
* Lands & possessions.

After HUGH, the first Earl beforesaid, succeeded RICHARD, his son, who, in his tender years, perished by ship-wreck, together with WILLIAM, only son of King HENRY I. and other Noblemen, between Normandy and England, in the year 1120. After Richard, succeeded RANULPH DE MESCHINES, the third Earl, son to the sister of Earl Hugh, and left behind him his son RANULPH, named GERNONYS, the fourth Earl of Chester, a warlike man, and who at the siege of Lincoln, took King STEPHEN prisoner. HUGH, surnamed KEVELIOC, his son, was the fifth Earl, who died in the year 1181, and left his son RANULPH, named BLUNDEVILL, the sixth Earl; who after he had built the Castles of CHARTLEY and BEESTON, and the Abbey also DE of LA CRESSE, died without children, and left four sisters to be his heirs. MAUDE, wife of David, Earl of Huntingdon; MABILE, espoused to William d' Albeney, Earl of Arundel; AGNES, married to William Ferrars, Earl of Derby, and AVIS, wedded to Robert de Quincy. After Ranulph the sixth Earl, there succeeded in the Earldom JOHN, surnamed the SCOT, the son of Earl David, by the said Maud, the eldest daughter. Who, being deceased likewise without any issue, King HENRY III. casting his eye upon so fair and large an inheritance, laid it unto the Domain of the Crown, and assigned other revenues elsewhere to the heirs, not willing, as the King himself was wont to say, that so great an estate should be divided among distaves. And the Kings themselves, in person, after that this Earldom came into their hands, for to maintain the honour of the PALATINESHIP, continued here the ancient rights and Palatine privileges, and Courts, like as the Kings of France did in the county of Champagne. Afterward, this honour of Chester was deferred upon the King's eldest son, and first unto EDWARD, King Henry the Third's son; who being taken prisoner by the Barons, and kept in ward, delivered it up for his ransom, unto SIMON MONTFORD, Earl of Leicester. But when Simon was soon after slain, it returned quickly again unto the blood Royal, and King EDWARD II. summoned his eldest son, being but a child, unto the Parliament, by the titles of Earl of Chester and Flint. Afterwards King RICHARD II. by the authority of Parliament, made it of an Earldom a Principality, and to the same Principality annexed the Castle of LEON,* with the Territories of BROMFIELD and YALE, CHIRK CASTLE, with CHIRK LAND, OSWALDS-STREET CASTLE, the whole hundred, and eleven towns belonging to that castle, with the castles of ISABEL and DELALEY, and other goodly lands, which, by reason that RICHARD, Earl of Arundel, stood then proscript and outlawed, had been confiscate unto the King's Exchequer; and King RICHARD himself was stiled Prince of Chester; but within a few years after, that title vanished away. After that, King HENRY IV. had once repealed the laws of the said Parliament, and it became again a County or Earldom Palatine, and at this day retaineth the jurisdiction Palatine, and for the administration thereof, it hath a Chamberlain, who hath all jurisdiction of a Chancellor within the said County Palatine; a Justice for matters in Common Pleas, and Pleas of the Crown, to be heard and determined in the said County; two Barons of the Exchequer, Serjeants at Law, a Sheriff, an Attorney, an Escheator, &c.

DESCRIPT.

* Quere, Lions, Holt.

CHESHIRE.
EXPLANATION
City as ... CHESTER
Market & Borough Towns ... Nantwich
HUNDREDS
1 Wirral
2 Edisbury
3 Broxton
4 Bucklow
5 Macclesfield
6 Northwich
7 Nantwich
A. Kingswood
B. Edisbury
C. Delamere
D. Oakmere
Chester
Liverpool
Prescot
Warrington
Stockport
Altrincham
Knutsford
Northwich
Macclesfield
Middlewich
Congleton
Sandbach
Tarporley
Nantwich
Malpas
YORKSHIRE
LANCASHIRE
DERBYSHIRE
STAFFORDSHIRE
SHROPSHIRE
FLINTSHIRE
DENBIGH SH
FLINT SHIRE
IRISH SEA

CAMDEN'S DESCRIPT

And the inhabitants of the said County for the enjoying of their liberties, were to pay at the change of every owner of the said Earldom, a sum of money (about 3000 marks) by the name of a MIZE, as the County of FLINT, being a parcel thereof about 2000 marks, if I have not been misinformed.

This County containeth about 68 Parishes.

I shall not, I hope, be blamed, for introducing as an AVANT COURIER *to this work, a sketch of Local History, written nearly Two Hundred and Twenty Years ago.---I need not apologize for it, inasmuch as it is the production of one of our most valuable and venerable Historic Authors :---the sanction of* HIS *name is a passport to its approval ; and altho' I have in some degree modernized the orthography, I have preserved all the quaintness of stile which characterized the literature of the early part of the 17th century. It has besides, in my opinion, another recommendation : we have in it a picture of the* THEN *existing state of the county---and notices of many of its families, several of which are now extinct. It may not, therefore, form an uninteresting contrast, with the* PRESENT *state of the County Palatine of Chester. Having said thus much in the way of explanation, I shall proceed with the regular detail.*

In the ruins of the Castle of Halton, from a drawing taken 1795.

Brown, sculp. Morris, del.

Adopting the plan of others who have gone before me, I have made the ornamental parts of the work, subservient to its general purposes.—This vignette is a representation of an ancient piece of sculpture, on a rock, in a field on the west side of the Bridge, at Chester. It is noticed by Malmesbury, who wrote in 1140; by Hoveden, who wrote in 1192; by Selden, Camden, and even in Polychronicon, and the Saxon Chronicle. It is supposed to be intended for the figure of PALLAS (*Diva Armigera* of the Romans). The Goddess is depicted in her warlike dress, with her altar, spear, and quiver, on the top of which is seen her favorite bird, the Owl.—Adjoining this figure, is a considerable indentation in the rock, to which tradition has given the name of *Edgar's Cave*.—It would be difficult to account for the origin of this very ancient relic. Before the present bridge was built, however, there was a ferry from what is familiarly called the *Hole-in-the-Wall*, across the river to Edgar's Field, where the great Roman Road into *Venedotia*, or North Wales, from Chester, commenced. Is it unlikely, that the "CAVE" was made, to receive the pious offerings of passengers, for the Goddess's protection on their journey?

Ancient History---Earls of Chester.

ANCIENT HISTORY.

CHESHIRE, which owes its name to the Saxon Ceastr-Scyre, formed part of the district of the *Cornavii*, a British tribe, the whole island previous to the Roman Invasion, being apportioned into grand divisions, each taking the name of the tribe or clan which inhabitted it.—Thus, Cheshire, Staffordshire, Shropshire, Worcestershire, and Warwickshire, as now existing, were occupied by the Cornavii. Camden confesses his inability to give any etymology of the name; it continued, however, until the decline of the Roman Power, for certain regiments which served under the later Emperors, were distinguished by the addition *Cornavii*.* During the early stay of the Romans in this country, Cheshire was included in Britannia Superior, but on the subsequent division into provinces, it was a portion of Flavia Cæsariensis. We know the period in which they colonized and maintained rule in England, but it would be difficult—perhaps impossible, to ascertain the precise time† of their quitting these parts. On their final abandonment of the island, when policy rendered it necesary to draw closer their resources, the Britons again possessed themselves of this county, and its capital became that of North Wales.—They remained undisturbed for a long period; for we have no accounts of a warlike interruption till 607, when the Britons were defeated under the walls of Chester, and the city was taken by Ethelfled, King of Northumberland.—It reverted to the Britons six years afterwards; for in 613, they held a national Meeting there, and elected Cadwan their King.—The Mercian Kings possessed themselves of Chester several times, but the Welsh and Mercian dominion over the county appears to have finally terminated in 828, when King Egbert attacked Chester, and highly incensed that the Welsh had supported the Danes, in their predatory excursions, after its capture, he caused the brazen effigies of Cadwalhon, King of Britain, to be pulled down, and

* More of this may be seen in the book, *Notitia Provinciarum*.

† An old author says, that the Roman Legions were in Chester in 223, when Marcus Aurelius Alexander was Emperor, and the 20th Legion remained there till 330.—This evidence, how-

forbade them re-erection on pain of death. Under Egbert, the union of the Saxon heptarchy* took place, but Cheshire was added to the Mercian Monarchy, which then became tributary to Egbert.†—Previous to the subjugation of Cheshire by this monarch, we have no direct history of local affairs: yet a considerable hiatus may be occupied by the acts of Ethelred, and his Countess Elfleda. Sir Peter Leycester, in his Antiquities, has collected these under one head; and from his work, as they have a general reference to our domestic annals, I shall transcribe them:—

Anno Chr. 908 ETHELDRED and his Countess restored *Caerlleon*, that is, *Legecestria*, now called *Chester*, after it was destroyed by the Danes, and enclosed it with new Walls, and made it nigh such as it was before; so that the Castle that was sometime by the Water without the Walls, is now in the Town within the Walls. So TREVISA in his translation of Polychronicon, lib. 6. cap. 4. whereunto agreeth Florentius, and Matthew of Westminster. But Hoveden placeth it Anno 905. Which town of *Chester*, remained in possession of the Britons or Welshmen, till it was taken by Egbert, the Saxon Monarch of England, about the Year 824. Trevisa, lib. 5. cap. 28.

910. Also, he and his Countess translated the bones of St.
911. Oswald, King and Martyr, from *Bardeny* to *Gloucester*, where they built an Abbey in honour of St. Peter.—Polychronicon.

The Danes breaking their truce with King Edward and this Etheldred, wasted *Mercia*, and were beaten by the English at *Totenhale*, in *Staffordshire*; and afterwards at *Wodenesfield*, within a mile of *Wolverhampton* in *Staffordshire*, was a great battle fought on the 5th day of August in the same year, wherein the Danes were routed, and three of their Kings slain, Healfdene, Eywysle, and Igwar. *Stow.—Ethelwerd in Chronico suo, lib 4. cap. 4; and Trevisa, fol.* 267.

Ethelred Eximiæ vir Probitatis, Dux et Patricius,
912. *Dominus et Subregulus Merciorum, decessit, Anno* 912.

So Florentius, whose death is placed by Hoveden *sub Anno* 908. He had only one daughter, called Elfwine or Algiva; at whose birth Elflede her mother was so much astonished with the pain, that ever after she refrained the embraces of her husband for almost forty years, saith Matth. Westminst. *pag.* 359. protesting often, that it was not fit for a King's daughter to be given to a pleasure that brought so much pain with it; and thereupon grew an heroic Virago, like the ancient Amazons, as if she had changed her sex as well as her mind. Ingulphus, *pag.* 871. Malmesbury, *pag.* 46.

This Lady Elflede, is variously written by our ancient 913.
Historians, as Edelfled, Ethelfled, Egelfled, and Elflede; and from the time of her husband's death she governed all *Mercia* excellently, except *London* and *Oxford*, which King Edward her brother retained to himself.

She built a fort at *Sceargete*, and another at *Bridge* 914.
upon *Severn*, wich I conceive is now called *Bridgenorth*.

She repaired *Tamworth*, near *Lichfield*, and built a fort at *Stafford*.

She built the town of *Eadsbury*, in the forest of *Che-* 915.
shire, whereof now nothing remains, but that we now call *The Chamber of the Forest*. And the same year she built *Warwick*.

She built also *Ciricbyrig*, now called *Monks-Kirkby*, 916.
in *Warwickshire*, saith Dugdale in his *Warwickshire, pag.* 50. and another called *Weadbirig*; and a third called *Runcovan*, but now called *Runcorn*, in *Cheshire*. This was long since demolished. *Polychronicon. Florentius.*

She took *Brecannemere*, or *Brecknock*, and carried 917.
away the Queen of Wales, and 33 of her men, prisoners into *Mercia*

She took the town of *Derby* from the Danes, and the whole province thereof. In storming of which town she lost four of her chief officers, *antè Calendas Aug.*

Elflede died at *Tamworth*, the 12th day of June, *Anno* 918.
919, and was buried in St. Peter's Church, at *Gloucester*. 919.
Florentius, Westminster, Polychronicon, and Hunting-

ever, is apocryphal; it may not be irrelevant here to state, that 20,000 Britons were transported by Vespasian to Africa, and were at the sacking of Jerusalem.—But this is rather an historical fact, than an evidence of occupancy.

* We find it recorded, that an *export* Slave trade, fed by the frequent wars between the Welsh and Saxons, was carried on in Chester!

† *Fabian*, in his Chronicle, notices an Earl of Chester, during the Mercian sway, named *Edol* or *Edolfe*, who lived in the time of Vortiger, King of the Britons, A. D. 471. He was called *Earl of Caerlegion*; by some he is written *Sarsalin*, temp. King Arthur, A. D. 616. Geoffrey of Monmouth, calls him one of the Knights of the Round Table.

ton. But Hoveden placed her death *sub Anno* 915.—And so Ethelwerd, *lib.* 4. *cap.* 4. So much do writers vary for the time.

In the same year wherein she died, King Edward built a fort or town at *Thelwall*, in *Cheshire*, and garrisoned it; and also made another garrison at *Manchester*, which was then in the outmost border of the kingdom of *Northumberland* this way; and took *Mercia* from his niece, Elfwine, into his own hands. Florentius. Polychronicon.

I cannot here pass by Henry Huntington's contradiction of himself, *Lib. quinto Histor. pag.* 353, where he tells us that *Edred Dux Merciæ* died *Anno* 8 *Edwardi Regis Angliæ*, which falls *Anno Christi*, 908. And in the same page a little after he says, that *Ethered Dux Merciæ*, father of *Edelfled*, died in the 18th year of King Edward's reign, which must needs be a mistake, unless there were two Ethereds, Governors of *Mercia* successively, and two Elfledes, mother and daughter; of whom I find no mention in other authors.

The Countess Elflede was a prudent woman, and of a manly spirit. She much assisted King Edward her brother, as well by counsel as by her actions. She was beloved of her friends, and feared by her enemies.—*Thus far Leycester.*

There is a list extant, of those who bore the title of Duke and Earl of Mercia, from Alfere, who died a horrible death* in 983, to Leofric who is the first personage, in express terms, that took the title of Earl of Chester. Huntington has it "*Leofricus*† *Consul Nobilissimus Cestriæ.*"—This Leofric was witness to a Charter granted by Canute to the Abbey of Croyland, in 1032, in the following terms: "+ *Ego Leofricus Comes Concessi.*" Lib. 6. p. 366.

Leofric married the celebrated Godiva:‡ and he and his Countess built, endowed, or repaired, the Monasteries of Coventry, Wenlock, and Worcester; St. John, and St. Werburgh, Chester; and others. Leofric died at Bromley, Aug. 31, 1057, and was buried in the Monastery at Coventry. He was succeeded the same year by his son,

Algar. Leycester's Antiquities.

ALGAR.—He married, says Burton, the sister of William Mallet, and had two sons: Edwin, Earl of Mercia, and Morcar, Earl of Northumberland; and two daughters, Aldith and Lucy. Aldith married Griffith, King of Wales; and on his death, became the wife of King Harold. Lucy had three husbands: the first, Ivo Talbois, Earl of Anjou, Roger de Romara, by whom she had William de Romara, Earl of Lincoln; Randle de Meschines Viscount Bajeux, in Normandy, Lord of Cumberland, and afterwards Earl of Chester.—Algar died and was buried at Coventry, in 1059.

Edwin.

EDWIN, son of Algar, succeeded to the general title of Earl of Mercia, but not with the peculiar distinction of Earl of Chester. He and his brother Morcar fought valiantly against the Conqueror, but in the end, he lost his Earldom.—He lived to the fourth year of the Reign of William, when he was slain on his way to join Malcolm King of Scotland; but Ingulphus says, "*Comites Edwinus et Morcarius ambo à suis per insidios trucidati.*"

Gherbod 1st Earl of Chester.

After the Conquest of England, Chester, and the County were given to Gherbod, a Flemish Nobleman of considerable rank. His gallant conduct, in the border conflicts with the Welsh, gained for him the esteem of his royal patron. He obtained leave to return for a short time to his native country; where he fell a victim

* Malmesbury says, "he was eaten to death with lice."

† The word Earl was introduced into England about the period of Ethelstan's sovereignty, and was used as a synonomée to ETHELING. This last, was a title attributed to those only of Royal Blood, sons and brothers of the King, and inferred, that the bearer was Nobly Born. This, in the Saxon era, was written in Latin *Clyto*} from the Greek Κλυτος, synonimous to noble, eminent, or famous. Earl, therefore, did not then bear out its present meaning; but with the Danes, its application was nearly consonant with its modern signification. On the establishment of the Danish Power, the title of *Earl*, was borne by those whom the Saxons called *Ealdormen*, and the latter was used till about 1020, expressed in Latin by Duces, Comites, &c. Subsequent to the Conquest, Earl has almost uniformly been used as a translation of Comes. These explanatory notes, which will be introduced when necessary, may not be uninteresting to the general reader.

‡ The tradition relative to this good-natured Lady, altho' well known, may not inaptly be introduced here: On condition that she would ride through Coventry, without any covering but her hair, her spouse consented to grant the town a Charter, freeing it from all toll, except that on horses.—It is scarcely necessary to say, she performed the task!

to the existing feuds; for being taken prisoner there it seems his confinement terminated only with his life.

Another Earl, was then appointed in the person of Hugh Lupus,‡ Kinsman of William, who had previously held the Castle of Tutbury, Staffordshire, which on his appointment was given to Henry, son of Walcaline de Ferrers.—This Hugh was the son of Richard, surnamed Goz, Earl of Auranges, Viscount of Abonica, and of Margaret, daughter of Harlowine, a Nobleman of Normandy, who married Harlet, the daughter of a Burgess of Valois, who was also the mother of the Conqueror. The newly appointed Earl ‖ was not long inactive. It was the policy of William, to drive the unfortunate Welshmen to their native fastnesses, and the conquered territory was given to those who gained it.—Such an inducement exactly suited the habit of Hugh's soul; and we find that in conjunction with Robert of Rothelent, and Robert of Malpas, they made considerable conquests, and shed much Cambrian blood.§—Hugh was possessed of immense property: he had land in twenty different counties, which are thus noticed in Andrew du Chesne's Appendix to ancient Norman Writers;† Comes Hugo, Hampshire, Berkshire, Dorset, Somerset, Devon, Buckingham, Oxford, Gloster, Huntington, Northampton, Warwick, Salop, Derby, Chester, Nottingham, Rutland, York, Lincoln, Norfolk, and Suffolk.—It appears from Doomsday-Book, that with the exception of the lands held by the Bishop, and these enumerated, all the remainder of the County was held by the Earl direct from the King, *cum suis hominibus*.—The following towns in Cheshire were held by Earl Hugh, in 1086.

Waverham	Coddington
Kennardsly†	Lay
Dunham-o'-th'-hill	Rushton
Elton	Upton jux. Rushton
Trafford	Little Budworth
Manley	Oulton
Helsby	Over
Frodsham	Eastham
Alseton‡	Trafford
Alderley, inferior	Edlave‖
Done	Macclesfield
Eddisbury, in the Forest	Adlingson
Eaton, in Broxton	Gawsworth
Lea, in Broxton	Hungerweniton¶

‡ Hugh Lupus, called by the Welsh HUGH FRAS or the Fat; the 2d Earl.

‖ His surname of Lupus probably took its rise from his armorial cognizance, viz. Azure, a Wolf's head erased, arg.

§ They overran the promontory of Lleyn, Carnarvonshire, leaving it a complete desert.—Hugh was possessed of the Lordships of Tegengle, & Ryforrior, in Wales.

† Printed at Paris, 1619.

* Some account of this Robert of Rothelent may be introduced here. He is described by Ordericus as "a valiant and active soldier, eloquent, liberal, and commendable for many virtues, but of a stern countenance. He was knighted by Edward the Confessor. His piety is instanced, in giving to the Monks of Utica, in Normandy, the Church of Telliolis, and the tythe of his mills, lands, and the *Beer in his cellar*—this latter bequest was no doubt very palatable to the reverend fraternity. He also gave them of his English possessions, two carucates of land, and twenty *villates*, the Church of Cumbivel, the town, tythe, and church of West Kirby, in Wirral; the church of the *island* (perhaps the cell or chantry on Hilbree) and the Church of St. Peter, in Chester. How this Chieftain became possessed of the latter, does not appear. After the death of the Confessor, he returned to Normandy, but again visitted England with Hugh Lupus, on whose appointment to the Earldom of Chester, Robert was made Commander of his forces, and Governor of the County. The Castle of Rothelent *(Rhyddlan)* was then given to him by the Conqueror, newly built; this was a commanding situation, and he proved a dreadful enemy to the Welsh. His policy afterwards led him to rebuild the fortress--of *Dagannoth* (probably Deganwy first founded in 600). This was seated close to the sea, and for 15 years his name was a terror to his Cambrian neighbours. It was resolved to destroy him, if not by open force, at least by cunning. On the 3d of July, 1088, Griffith King of Wales, landed with a strong force from three ships under the hill called *Hormaheva*. He ravaged the adjacent country and retreated to his vessels. Robert was rendered furious by the intelligence: he saw his enemies shipping their plunder,—he could no longer restrain his rage, but ran violently down the hill towards them, attended only by one soldier. Availing themselves of his imprudence, they immediately attacked him, but at a distance, with arrows: he was soon mortally wounded; yet such a terror had he inspired, that none of his foes dared to approach him. He fell from loss of blood. Then it was that they rushed upon him, and cutting of his head, they hung it in barbarous triumph to the mast of the ship. His body was brought by his soldiers with great lamentation to Chester, and was buried in the Monastery of St. Werburgh.

† Kenardeslie, was in the ancient hundred of Roelent, Eddisbury.—‡ Alsetune, in the ancient hundred of Hamestan, Macclesfield.—‖ Edelave, in the ancient hundred of Wilaveston, Wirral.—¶ Hungerweniton, in the ancient hundred of Hamestan.

Ancient History.

Merton	Alsager
Chelford	Sandbach
Henbury	Clive
Capesthorne	Sutton, near Middlewich
Henshall	Wimboldsley
Tintwistle	Weaver
Hollingworth	Occleston
Werneth	Upton, in Wirral
Romilly	Stanney
Leighton	Antrobus.

This Hugh in his closing days, became a great benefactor to Holy Church. He founded the Monastery in St. Werburgh's Church. Malmesbury mentions this circumstance thus: "*In urbe (Cestriæ scilicet) fuit ex Antiquo Sanctimonialium Monasterium, nunc per Hugonem Cestrensem Comitem Monachis repletum.*"—The first abbot he appointed, was Richard his Chaplain, at the suggestion of Anselm, Abbot of Becci, in Normandy, who came to administer comfort to the Earl in his sickness. The Abbey of St. Werburgh had previously been filled by secular Canons, but these were easily transformed into regular Monks.

Some old authors have asserted, that the Castle and Walls of Chester were built by Hugh; but this needs not a formal contradiction: the Walls themselves bespeak their Roman origin, of which more will be said in
About 908. the proper place—and we are told that Elfleda REPAIRED the walls, and enlarged their compass, bringing the CASTLE within their circuit, which before stood without. Here we have evidence of a Castle being in existence a century and a half BEFORE Earl Hugh's time. It is likely, however, that he strengthened the Walls, and the Castle, and beautified them.—He died on the 27th July, 1101, having been Earl of Chester, thirty-one years.—The event of his demise is thus noticed by ORDERICUS VITALIS, Anno 1101. "**Interia Hugo Comes Cestriae in lectum decidit, et post diuturnum languorem Monachatum in Caenobio, quod idem Cestriae construxerat, sus cepit: atque post triduum sexti Calendas Augusti obiit.**"—The *Polichronicon* thus notices it, Anno 1102. "**Hugo Comes Cestrensis, Nepos Regis Willielmi Conquestoris ex parte Sororis, obiit.**"—It will be seen, that a year's variation occurs in the time stated of Hugh's death.—This local Monarch, it is recorded, in conjunction with Robert de Beaumont, was a principal means in the elevation of Henry I. to the crown of England. He was undoubtedly a man of great influence.

RICHARD, the only son of Hugh, succeeded his father in the year of his death, being then only seven years of age. He married Maud, daughter of Stephen Earl of Blois, but soon after their union, returning to England from Flanders, they were both drowned. The story is thus related by an old author: "The master of the ship was Thomas, the son of Stephen, who came to King Henry I. then in Normandy, and ready to take shipping for England, and offered him a mark of gold (valued at six pounds in silver) desiring, that as Stephen his father had transported the Conqueror, when he fought against Harold in England, and was his constant Mariner in all his passages between England and Normandy, he himself might have the transportation of Henry with all his attendance as it were in fee, and as he had a good ship, called *Candida Navis*, or the *White Ship*, well fitted out for the purpose. The King thanked him, but said he had already made choice of another ship, which he would abide by, yet he would recommend him to his two sons William and Richard, with others of his Nobility. The Seamen was much rejoiced at this, and requested some wine to drink. They were presented with *Tres modios Vini* (three hogsheads), and were soon intoxicated.—Three hundred persons of various degrees, embarked in this ship, and the complement of mariners was rated at "50 skilful galleymen, had they not been drunk." They were totally incapacitated from managing the vessel; it struck on a rock, sunk, and all perished, excepting a butcher of Rouen, named *Berolde*.—He was taken up the following morning, after suffering dreadfully throughout a frosty night. With great difficulty he was restored to health, and from him the melancholy fate of the passengers was obtained. He lived twenty years afterwards." This catastrophe took place on the 7th Dec. 1129, according to Ordericus; but Hoveden, Huntington, Paris, and Camden place it in 1120. Hoveden is express in his mention of it: "*Anno* 1120, *in Scopulos, dictos Chaterase, fracta est Navis 6 cal. Decembris, feriâ quintâ, noctis initio apud Barbefleet* (*Harefleet*).

Richard. He bore crusilly or, a Wolf's head erased, arg.

Ordericus.

ANCIENT

HISTORY.

Randle I. he bore Or, a lion rampant, gules. Anno reg. 20.

RANDLE DE MESCHINES, obtained the Earldom, in right of heirship, from Henry I. he being nephew to Hugh Lupus. He is noticed by the old historians, for his fidelity to Henry during a desperate insurrection in Normandy, in 1119.* By paternal descent, Randle became Lord of Cumberland and Carlisle. He had a brother, William de Meschines, who gave the Church of Dyserth to the Abbey of St. Werburgh.—Randle married the widow of Roger de Romara; she was the daughter of Algar, the Saxon Earl of Mercia, and sister to Edwin Earl of Mercia, and Morcar Earl of Northumberland, the intrepid opponents of William the Conqueror. By her, Randle had issue, Randle the second, his successor, William who became Earl of Cambridge, but of whom we know little calculated to interest the reader of a local history, Agnes, who married Robert de Grentmaisnil—and Adeliza, who became the wife of Richard, son of Gilbert de Clare, by whom he had three sons. Randle died in 1128, after enjoying his Earldom eight years. He was a liberal benefactor to the Church, in conformity to the pious custom of the day. Lucy, his wife, founded the Priory of Spalding, in Lincolnshire; and in conjunction with her two sons, instituted a Priory for Cistercian Nuns, at Stikeswold, in the same county. It does not appear she was partial to a matrimonial life, for in the Pipe Roll, temp. Stephen, we find she paid a fine of 500 marks, not to be compelled to marry within five years: a great sum in those days.

Richard was slain in a conflict with the Welsh.

His armorial coat was gules, a lion rampant, argent.

RANDLE II. surnamed Gernons, being born at Gernons or Vernons Castle, in Normandy, succeeded to all the patrimony of his father in England and Normandy. In 1139, the fury of Randle was raised against his Sovereign, in consequence of Stephen making Henry, son of David, the Scotch King, Earl of Northumberland, enriching his title with the whole of Cumberland, including Carlisle, which Randle considered as his exclusive patrimony, descending to him from his predecessors.—The civil war, which shortly afterwards broke out, at once decided the cause which the Earl would adopt.—He espoused the part of the Empress Maud; surprised, and in 1141, took the Castle of Lincoln, and conquered the whole of that County. The King was highly incensed, and immediately collected together a strong force; he marched suddenly on the insurgent Earl, and so rapid were his movements, that he possessed himself of the city and seventeen of the rebellious soldiers.—The Earl of Chester, and William de Romara, his half-brother on the mother's side, fled to the Castle with what force they could, under such circumstances, raise: and were closely besieged by the furious Monarch. Randle, however, with a few select friends, availing himself of the darkness of the night, succeeded in making his escape, and reached his Palatinate in safety. Here he succeeded in gathering together a numerous army; and in conjunction with Robert Earl of Glocester, his father-in-law, marched directly on Lincoln.—The King was advised to avoid a general battle; but rage overcoming his reason, he arranged his army in three divisions, placing in the front his Flemish and Welsh Auxiliaries, commanded by William de Ipro, and Alan de Dinau.—Opposed to these was also a body of Welsh troops, on which great reliance was placed.—Randle displayed great intrepidity, and cheered his Cheshire forces.—Addressing the Earl of Glocester, and his army, *Huntington* puts in Randle's mouth the following words:—" I humbly thank you, most invincible General, and you the rest of my fellow Soldiers, that you have so faithfully and courageously expressed your affection to me, even to the hazard of your lives. Since I have been the cause of this your danger, it is but reasonable I should lead the way, and first give the onset to the army of the perfidious King, who has broken the truce made. Out of the confidence of your valor, and the injustice of the King, I doubt not to dissipate his forces; and, with my sword, make my way through my enemies. Methinks I see them run already!" In the sequel, we find his confidence was not misplaced. *Huntington* gives here an oration by Baldwin de Clare, on the behalf of the King, in which the Earl of Chester is described as a man " having nothing in him to be feared, for whatsoever he began like a man, he ended like a woman. He was unfortunate in all his undertakings. In his encounters

* Leycester quotes an ancient roll of Knight's fees due to the Dukes of Normandy: " Comes Cestriæ Servitium Militum de S. Severio et de Bricasart; et ad suum servitium L. I milites et dimidium, et quartam partem, et octavam unius militis."

he was generally vanquished; and if by chance he obtained a victory, it was with greater loss on his part, than on that of the conquered."—Baldwin proved to be a false prophet; for soon after the commencement of the action the Flemings, and Welsh allies of the King, fled in a cowardly manner.* Stephen fought gallantly on foot, with sword and battle-axe, but was compelled to surrender himself prisoner to the Earl of Glocester, and sent to Maud, at Bristol, where he was closely confined, but in the end he was exchanged for his Conqueror, who became a prisoner to some of Stephen's party.

The battle was fought on Candlemas day, 1141.

In 1145, a reconciliation took place between the King and Randle, and the latter accompanied his Sovereign to Wallingford, with a strong force.—The unsuspecting Earl afterwards followed the Court to Northampton, but here he was thrown into prison by the King, till he surrendered up his conquests in Lincolnshire.† The Chieftains who sided with him, interceded with the King for his enlargement, and offering security for the restoration of the conquered land, he was released, on taking an oath never to take up arms against the King.—But oaths in those days, were rendered subservient to the policy of the moment—he raised a numerous army, attacked the flower of the King's troops at Lincoln—and blocked up the castle of Coventry. The King hastened to assist the garrison, and forcing his way through the Earl's army, threw in some victuals. In one of the skirmishes which took place, the King was wounded; but recovering, he fell on the Earl's forces, put them to flight, and Randle with great difficulty escaped, desperately wounded.—In 1150, Randle was present at a magnificent entertainment given by the King of Scotland, at Carlisle, to Henry, son of Maud the Empress: at this conference, an alliance took place, at which it was agreed, that Randle should have the *Honour* of Lancaster; and that his son should marry one of the Prince of Scotland's daughters.—The Earl promised to meet King David and his son Henry at Lancaster, with a large force, but failing in his performance, this hostile union against Stephen, which at one time wore a most serious aspect, was dissolved, and the King of Scotland returned to his own country.—In 1151,‡ the Earl of Chester again suffered imprisonment, but having given his nephew Gilbert de Clare, for an hostage, he was released.—He again broke out into acts of violence, and finding that the life of his hostage was in jeopardy, invited the Duke of Normandy|| into England, promising him all the aid in his power. The Duke accepted the invitation, and was soon joined by Robert Earl of Leycester, and many other Noblemen of distinction and power. Stephen saw the mischief which threatened him, and the necessity, if not by force, at least by
diplomacy, of breaking up this formidable league.—He 1152
contrived to bring Henry to terms, and Randle also.—The following year brought the troublesome life of this Potentate to a close. The event is recorded in the
CHRONICA GERVASII: "A. D. 1153, *Ranulfus ille No-* Dec. 16.
bilis et Famosus Comes Cestriæ, vir admodùm militaris, per quendam Williemum Peverellum (ut fama fuit) veneno infectus post multos agones Militaris Gloriæ, vir insuperabilis audaciæ vix solâ morte territus et devictus, vitam finivit temporalem." This Randle was a great benefactor to the Church;—offerings of conscience—as some compensation for the evils which he had brought upon it. He gave to the Cathedral of St. Werburgh, the townships of Eastham and Bromborow.
This deed is witnessed by Walter then Bishop, *et aliis.* 1152
He founded a Nunnery at Chester, the Priory of Trentham, in Staffordshire; the Priory of Mentings, in Lincolnshire. To the Abbey of Basingwerk, Flintshire, he gave one half of Lache, and £5. *per ann.* from the city of Chester; the Monks of Coventry he permitted to have two carts, to be employed daily, excepting Holydays, in gathering fuel from his woods, &c. in that neighbourhood. But all this liberality did not prevent the censures of the Church falling heavily on him: he died excommunicated by Walter Bishop of Lichfield; and for his absolution, his wife Maud, and Hugh his

* Leycester says the King was betrayed; for although his Nobles attended him in person, they directed their contingents to join the enemy.

† Polychronicon says, that the Welsh, availing themselves of the Earl's bondage, invaded Cheshire, laid a great part of it waste, but being intercepted at Nantwich, were driven back.

‡ I take here the authority of Sir Peter Leycester; although *Radulfus de Diceto, Chronica Gervasii, Brompton, Chronica Normaniæ, Matt. Paris, and Matt. Westminster*, state the date as 1145: *Hoveden* says 1146.

|| Son of the Empress Maud.

ANCIENT HISTORY.

son and successor, gave to the Bishop the town of Styshall, near Coventry.

* He bore az. 6 garbs, Or: 3, 2, 1.

HUGH, surnamed CYVEILIOC, from his having been born in the district Cyveilioc, in Powis-land, succeeded his father in 1153, of whose martial spirit he possessed no small share.—The first act of his government, was the raising an army, with which he invaded Wales, and soon possessed himself of the large extent of country, now called Bromfield and Iâl.—In 1172 he formed a coalition with the King of Scotland, and Robert Earl of Leicester, against his Sovereign Henry II. and the following year, with the assistance of Raufe de Filgiers, completed the conquest of nearly the whole of *Little Britain*, in France, then attached to the English crown.
1173. Henry summoned a strong force, marched against the insurgent Nobles, and beat them. They fled to the Castle of Dole, where they were besieged by the Brabant auxiliaries of Henry. On the 26th August they were compelled to surrender themselves prisoners.—Hugh remained in close confinement more than three years; but at a Parliament held at Northampton, in
1177. January, 1177, he obtained his liberty, and with it the restoration of all his lands. In 1181, this Earl died at Leek, in Staffordshire, and was buried at Chester. He was Earl of Chester twenty-eight years; and had issue, by Bertred, daughter of Simon Earl of Evereux, in Normandy—Randle, surnamed Blundeville, and four daughters, Maud, Mabile, Agnes, and Hawise. Sir P. Leycester, has a long argument in his *Antiquities*, in order to prove, that Amicia, who married Raufe Mainwaring, was an illegitimate daughter of the Earl Hugh, and censures very strongly "the boldness and ignorance of that herald, who gave to Mainwaring, of Peover, the quarterings of this Earl of Chester's coat armorial."—I shall not in this work, enter into a discussion on so barren a subject—it can afford but little interest in these days; and those who are fond of tracing family descents, and pedigree hunting, may have ample gratification in the work I have alluded to—and in the replication of Sir Henry Mainwaring, who refutes the unfavorable arguments of Sir Peter Leycester.—The latter certainly speaks very fairly on this curious subject; he says, "I must ever acknowledge myself to be a descendant from this Amicia by my own Mother; but you know the old saying of Aristotle, *Amicus Plato, Amicus Socrates, sed Magis amica veritas*."—It may be proper, however, to state, that, in a deed referred to by Sir Peter, this Amicia is called "*Filia Hugonis Comitis*:" but this, says the Antiquarian "it was very usual to do in those elder ages, without the addition of Bastard."* It is certain, that neither Higden, nor Knighton, in recording the issue of Hugh Cyveilioc, notice Amicia in any way.

RANDLE BLUNDEVILLE* succeeded his father in 1181. In 1188, he was Knighted by Henry II. who gave him to wife Constance, the widow of Geoffery his fourth son, daughter and heiress of Conan, Duke of *Little Britain* and Earl of Richmond †—He maintained the military name and power of his predecessors: In 1194, John, Brother to Richard I. (then a prisoner in Austria) having garrisoned Nottingham castle for himself, against the captive King,—David, Brother of the Scotch King, Earl Randle, and the Earl Ferrars, raised a powerful army, and besieged him there; but they were unsuccessful till the King returned, and assaulted it in person.—In 1216, chiefly by the great influence of Halo, the Pope's Legate, Peter Bishop of Winchester, and the Earl of Chester, Henry III. then only nine years old, Oct. 28.
was crowned at Gloucester.—In 1217, Lewis with his French troops, invited over by the discontented Barons, having been brought to battle at Lincoln, by the young King's forces, commanded by Earl Randle, they were defeated, and so many of the French troops slain, that Lewis for a sum of money then given, readily gave up his conquests, and returned home.—In 1218, Randle, having entered into a Treaty with Llewellyn, Prince of Wales, went to the Holy Land, visitted Jeru-

* He bore azure three garbs, Or, 2 and 1—this with the addition of the sword, is the present armorial coat of the City of Chester.

* William the Conqueror, in a letter to Alan, Earl of LITTLE BRITAIN, begins—"*Ego Willielmus cognomento Bastardus*," &c.

† In 1189, Chester was visitted by Archbishop Baldwin, attended by Giraldus Cambrensis, the historian. Giraldus remarked, that "Constance, Countess of Chester, kept a herd of milch hinds, made cheese of their milk, and presented three to the Archbishop: that he saw an animal there, the compound of an ox and a stag: a woman born without arms, who could sew as well with her feet as others of her sex with their fingers: and finally, that he HEARD of a litter of whelps begotten by a Monkey!"—Travellers, sometimes, see and hear A GREAT DEAL.

ANCIENT HISTORY.

salem, and is supposed to have been present at the battle of Damietta.—Randle returned in 1220, built Beeston Castle; Chartley Castle, Staffordshire; and the Abbey of De-la-Crosse, near Leek, for the Cistercian order.—The expense of building these Castles, was defrayed by a general tax throughout all his territory.—In 1224, we have the Earl, John Constable of Chester, and others, endeavoring to inflame the mind of the King against Hubert de Burgo, whom they charged with having unduly used the Royal influence against them, threatening to occupy the King's Castles unless he was discharged: but this storm, it seems, was hushed;—and in 1220, when King Henry had assembled his army at Portsmouth, and, discovering the vessels for transporting the troops insufficient for the purpose, threatened to kill Hubert de Burgo, whom he charged with being bribed by the French Queen, we find Randle protecting this Hubert, from the King's fury.—The same year, according to Matt. Paris, the Earl of Chester refused to pay tythe or impost to the Pope: thus was an example set by this high-spirited Earl, which Royalty did not follow till three centuries afterwards.—In 1230, the King having appointed him Commander-in-Chief in *Little Britain*, Randle marched thro' Anjou, and possessed himself of several strong holds.—In 1232, when the King demanded money for the discharge of the debts in which his wars had involved him, the Earl of Chester, on the behalf of the Nobility of the Kingdom, told him, that they who held of him *in capite*, attended him in person, and had exhausted all their money in his service,
1232 and therefore nothing was granted. The same year, Hubert de Burgo was again indebted to the Earl for his life, and saved by his prudence and advice from the fury of 20,000 persons, who had assembled in a tumultuous manner to destroy him.—A curious circumstance is related in some of our old local historians, relative to an extraordinary *ruse de guerre* played off by Roger de Lacy, Baron of Halton, and Constable of Chester, to accomplish the deliverance of Randle.*—I quote this account at length, from the authority of Sir Peter Leycester: Randle among the numerous border feuds in which he was engaged, was sorely distressed by the Welsh, and forced to retreat to the Castle of Rhuddlan, in Flintshire, where they besieged him: this was about the reign of King JOHN. He presently sent to his Constable of Cheshire, Roger Lacy, surnamed HELL, for his fierce spirit, that he would come with all speed, and bring what forces he could towards his relief. Roger having gathered a tumultuous rout of Fiddlers, Players, Cobblers, debauched persons, both men and women, out of the city of Chester (for it was then the Fair-time in that City), marched immediately towards the Earl.—The Welsh perceiving a great multitude coming, raised the siege and fled. The Earl coming back with his Constable to Chester, gave him power over all the Fiddlers and Shoemakers in Chester, in reward and memory of this service. The Constable retained to himself and his Heirs, the authority and donation of the Shoemakers, but conferred the authority of the Fiddlers and Players on his Steward, which then was Dutton of Dutton; whose Heirs enjoy the same power and authority over the Minstrelsy of Cheshire, even to this day;* who in memory hereof keep a yearly Court upon the Feast of St. John the Baptist, at Chester, where all the Minstrels of the County and City are to attend and play before the Lord of Dutton: And none ought to use their Minstrelsy but by order and license of that court, under the hand and seal of the Lord Dutton, or his Steward, either within Cheshire or the city of Chester. And to this day the heirs of Dutton, or their deputies, do in a solemn manner yearly, upon Midsummer-day, being Chester Fair, ride, attended through the city of Chester, with all the Minstrelsy of Cheshire playing before them on their several instruments, to the Church of St. John, and at the Court renew their licenses yearly. I cannot here pass by the gross mistake of Powel, on the Welsh history, page 296, whom Camden in his Britannia seems to follow; where Raufe de Dutton is said to have gathered this Army, and to have rescued the Earl: whereupon he had the power over the Minstrelsy granted immediately from the Earl.—For first there was never any such an heir of Dutton of Dutton, that was called *Raufe de Dutton*. But I shall, for more satisfaction, transcribe the Original Deed made to Dutton, remaining among the evidences of that family, which now by a daughter and heir, is devolved to the Lord Gerard, of Gerards Bromley, in Staffordshire.

Sciant præsentes et futuri, quòd ego Johannes Constabularius Cestriæ, dedi et concessi, et hâc præsenti Char-

* Privilege of the Duttons of Dutton.

* Not exercised since 1745.

tâ meâ confirmavi, Hugoni de Dutton, et Hæredibus suis, Magistratum omnium Leccatorum et Meretricum totius Cestershiriæ, sicut liberius illum Magistratum teneo de Comite; Salvo jure meo mihi et Heredibus meis. Hiis Testibus, Hugone de Boidele, Alano Fratre ejus, Petro de Goenet, Liulfo de Twamlow, Adu de Dutton, Gilberto de Aston, Radulfo de Kingsley, Hamone de Bordington, Alano de Waleie, Alano de Mulinton, Willielmo Filio Ricardi, Martino Angevin, Willielmo de Savill, Galfrido et Roberto Filiis meis Bletheris, Herdberd de Waleton, Galfrido de Dutton.*

* It is either thus, as I have put it; or, Galfrido and Roberto Filiis meis, Blethero Herberd de Waleton, &c. I leave it to the Reader to judge.

In which deed it is, John Constable of Cheshire, (not Earl of Chester) grants to Hugh de Dutton, (not to Raufe de Dutton) the authority over all the Letchers and Whores of all Cheshire; *Salvo jure meo.* So as the right was the Constable's, which he held of the Earl; but now transfers it over to Hugh Dutton, about the end of King John's reign. By the ancient Roll it should seem Roger Lacy rescued the Earl, and now John his son, transfers this power to Dutton: Which original grant mentions nothing of the rule of Fiddlers or of Minstrels; but ancient custom has now brought it only to the Minstrelsy. For anciently, I suppose, the Rout which the Constable brought to the rescuing of the Earl, were debauched persons, drinking with their Sweethearts in the Fair, Fiddlers, and such loose kind of Persons as he could get; which tract of time hath reduced only to the Minstrels. I find in the Records of Chester, *inter Placita* 14 *Hen.* 7. a *Quo Warranto* brought against Laurence Dutton, of Dutton, Esq. why he claimed all the Minstrels of Cheshire, and in the City of Chester, to meet before him at Chester yearly, at the Feast of St. John the Baptist, and to give unto him at the said feast, *quatuor Lagenas Vini, et unam Lanceam*; that is, four bottles of Wine, and a Lance; and also every Minstrel to pay unto him at the same Feast Four-pence Halfpenny: And why he claimed from every Whore in Cheshire, and in the City of Chester, *Officium suum exercente,* Four-pence, to be paid yearly at the feast aforesaid, &c. Whereunto he pleaded prescription. And whereas by the Statute of 39. Eliz. cap. 4. Fiddlers are declared to be Rogues; yet there is an especial Proviso in the Statute, for the exempting of those in Cheshire, licensed by the heirs of Dutton of Dutton, as belonging to his ancient Custom and Privilege, so that the Fiddlers of Cheshire, licensed by the heirs of Dutton of Dutton, are not Rogues! But enough of this.

I shall advert at greater length to this singular privilege in another part of this work; at present I shall proceed in the regular historical account of the Earls of Chester.

Randle appears to have been perpetually desirous of aggrandizing himself by the extension of his dominions: in 1230, we find him purchasing the lands of Roger de Meresey, which lay between the rivers Ribble and Mersey. This purchase is recorded in a deed in the Couchir office of the Duchy of Lancaster, and is witnessed by "*Domino Waltero Abbate Cestriæ, Domino Willielmo de Vernon Justiciario Cestriæ, Radulfo de Bray, Waltero Dayvill, Ricardo de Biron, Johanne de Lexington, Simone et Johanne Clericis.*"—This addition to the estates of the Earl, received a confirmation from Henry III. viz. of the town and wapentake of West-derby, the borough of Liverpool, the town and wapentake of Salford, the wapentake of Leyland, with all Forests, Appurtenances, &c.—After his marriage with Constance, which I have before noticed, Randle assumed the titles In 1200
of "Dux Britanniæ, et Comes Cestriæ et Richmondiæ, &c.—After his divorce, however, he relinquished his titles of Dux Britanniæ, et Comes Richmondiæ.—In 1217, on the forfeiture of Gilbert de Gant (Ghent), who had taken part with the Barons, Randle was created by Henry III. Earl of Lincoln, and from this period, till his death, he maintained the title; but it does not appear that he took the title of Earl of Leicester, although Camden informs us it was also granted to him by Henry III.

Randle died at Walingford, in 1232, and, according to Higden, was buried at Chester: *et sepultus est apud Cestriam in Capitulo Monachorum, cùm Progenitoribus suis,*"

John, surnamed the Scot, succeeded Randle, in right 1232.
of Maud, his Mother, eldest sister and co-heir to Randle, he dying without issue, leaving his whole inherit-

He bore Or, three Piles, gules.

ANCIENT  HISTORY.

ance to be shared by his four sisters —John's father, David, was own brother of William King of Scotland, and being Knighted by Henry II. was by him created Earl of Huntington: so that on his death, he became Earl of Huntington, in addition to his Earldom of Chester.

In 1236, at the marriage of King Henry, to his Queen Eleanor, John Scott carried before them the Sword of State; and here, for the first time, is the title of Earl Palatine distinctly used: "*Sub Anno* 1236. *Comite Cestriæ Gladium Sancti Edwardi, qui* CURTEIN *dicitur, antè Regem baiulante in signum quòd* COMES EST PALATII, *et Regem (si oberret) habeat de jure potestatem cohibendi: suo sibi, scilicet Cestrensi Constabulario ministrante, et Virgâ Populum (cùm se inordinate ingereret) subtrahente.*"

Matt. Paris.

John married Helen, daughter of Llewellyn, Prince of North Wales; and this union was considered as a final ratification of the Peace entered into by John's Predecessor.

John Scott, the eighth and last Earl of Chester, as an independent Potentate, died at the Abbey of Darnhall, June 7, 1237, and strong suspicions were entertained of his having been poisoned by the wicked machinations of his wife Helen.—Be was buried at Chester.

A complete Revolution now took place in the Local Sovereignty of the Earls of Chester. The crown had, no doubt, long looked with a jealous eye on the increasing power and influence of the Chiefs of the Palatinate they had control over a great extent of country, and were in possession of many strong fortresses. A favorable opportunity had now arrived for extinguishing this extraordinary jurisdiction altogether. John Scott having died without issue, Henry III. under the pretence that so great an inheritance as the Earldom of Chester should not be divided amongst distaffs (alluding to the late Earl's sisters), seized the whole domain into his own hands, and attached it to the crown, giving to Margaret, Isabelle, Maud, and Alda, the four sisters of John Scott, other lands in lieu thereof. From this seizure to the present time, the Earldom of Chester has been vested in the Crown,* and the title generally given to the Prince of Wales.—In the failure of a Prince of Wales, it is preserved in the Crown till a new creation.

* With an exception.—Henry III. and Prince Edward, being taken prisoners by Simon de Montfort, Earl of Leicester, at the Battle of Lewes, the Prince surrendered up the Earldom to Simon to obtain his release.—But the ambitious Earl enjoyed his new dignity little more than a year, for being slain at the battle of Evesham, the Earldom reverted again to the Prince.

The Barons of the Earls of Chester.

ANCIENT

HISTORY.

The assumption of the title of Barons, by these Nobles of the county, appears to have been coeval with that of the Earls. In the charter granted by Hugh Lupus to the Monastery of St. Werburgh, in Chester, the conclusion thereof runs, "*Ego Comes Hugo et mei Barones confirmarimus ista omnia coram Anselmo Archiepiscopo,*" *&c.* As the Nobility of the Palatinate Court, the Barons assisted the Earl with their advice and Counsel upon all state affairs. Leycester says, "In relation to others out of the County, I conceive them inferior to the rank of the Barons of our Realm: for these are but titularly or analogically Barons (as I may so speak) to those of the Kingdom; nay, in place beneath all Knights: but they were the greatest men in the county under the Earl for power and Estate."—Some diversity of opinion has prevailed, as to the gradations of rank observed by these Barons, inasmuch, as in some old Charters, Robert Fitz Hugh, Baron of Malpas, has taken the pre-eminence in his signature. In a Charter, however, temp. Stephen, made by Randle Gernons, the question is at once put to rest:

"*Ranulfus Comes Cestriæ,*" &c. *Proculdubio sciote me reddidisse et dedisse Eustachio Filio Johannis totum honorem qui fuit Willielmi Filii Nigelli Constabularii Cestriæ, in rebus et dignitatibus omnibus: et ipsum Eustachium constituisse hæreditariè Constabularium, et supremum Consiliarium post me super omnes Optimates et Barones totius terræ meæ.*" &c.

The order of their rank, has thus been arranged by Spelman and others:—

1 Nigel or Niel, Baron of Halton, High Constable of the Palatinate in Fee.
2 Robert, Baron of Montalto,* High Steward, of the Palatinate in Fee.
3 William, Baron de Wich Maldebeng.
4 Robert Fitz Hugh, Baron of Malpas.
5 Richard de Vernon, Baron of Shipbrook.
6 Hamon de Massey, Baron of Dunham Massey.
7 Gilbert Venables, Baron of Kinderton.
8 N. or Nicholas, Baron of Stockport.

* Or Hawarden.

The history of this little Aristocracy remains in great obscurity; and there are many doubts, whether such a personage as the Baron of Stockport ever existed.—The author of the Antiquities very properly notices, that in Doomsday Book, there is no mention whatever made of any person then holding Stockport, from which he argues, that it might then have been waste and uninhabited.—The direct succession of these Barons has long since been extinct, save that of the Barony of Kinderton, which continues now vested in the person of the Lord Vernon, a descendant from Gilbert de Venables.

The Barons of the Earl of Chester, had each of them extraordinary privileges on their own estates, even to the trial and execution of Criminals: and so late as the year 1597, we find this right exercised in the Baronial Court of Kinderton, where Hugh Stringer was tried for Murder, convicted, and executed.†

The following is a translation of the Charter of Randle Blundeville to his Barons, extracted from a Book in the Records of the Duchy Office, Gray's Inn:

† In the History of the County Palatine of Lancaster, there is no notice taken of any of these peculiar privileges and exercises of right, and therefore we may conclude, that none such existed there. In the Patent, however, of John of Gaunt, as Duke of Lancaster, we read, "that he was entitled to all other liberties relating to a County Palatine, *as freely and fully as the Earl of Chester is known to enjoy them within the County of Chester.*"

Randle Earl of CHESTER, To his Constable, Steward, Judge, Sheriff, Barons, Bailiffs, and to all his Tenants and Friends, present and to come, that shall see or hear this Charter, sendeth Greeting. KNOW YE, that I being signed with the Cross* for the love of God, and at the request of my Barons of CHESHIRE, have granted to them and their Heirs, from me and my Heirs, all the liberties in this present Charter under-written, to have and to hold for ever: to wit, that every one of them may have his own Court free from all Pleas and Plaints moved in my Court, except such Pleas as belong to my Sword†: And if any of their Tenants shall be taken for any offence within their Fee or Lordship, he shall be replevied without any ransom, so as his Lord bring him to three County Courts; and then he may carry him back again as acquit, unless ‡SAKERBORH do follow him. And if any stranger (who is faithful) shall come upon their Land, and desires to dwell there, it shall be lawful for the Baron of that Fee to have and retain him, saving to me the advowries who shall come to me on their own accord, and others who for any trespass elsewhere, shall come unto my dignity, and not to them. And every one of my Barons, when need requireth, shall in time of War, do the full service of so many Knights Fees as he holdeth: and their Knights and Freeholders shall have their Coats of Mail and Haubergeons; and may defend their own land by their bodies, although they be not Knights: and if any of them be such a one, that he cannot defend his own land by his body, he may put another person in his place: neither will I compel their villains to take arms; but I do hereby acquit their villains, which by RANDLE of DAVENHAM shall come to my protection, and other their villains, whom they can reasonably shew to be their own. And if my Sheriff, or any Officer, shall implead any of their Tenants in my Court, he may defend himself by THIRTNIC‖ for the SHERIFF's-TOOTH, which they do pay, unless fresh suit do follow him. I do also grant unto them acquittance from the Corn and oblations, which my Serjeants and Beadels were wont to require; and that if any Judger§, or Suitor of the Hundred or County-Court, shall be amerced in my Court, the Judger shall be quit from his amercement for two shillings, and the Suitors for twelve-pence. I do also grant unto them liberty of Inclosing their Lands within the boundaries of their tillage in the Forest: and if there shall be a Land or parcel of Ground within the boundary of their township, which had been formerly manured, where no wood groweth, it shall be lawful to till the same without grazing: and they may also take HOUSEBOTE and HAYBOTE in their Woods, of all manner of Wood, without the view of my Forester; and may give or sell their dead Wood, to whom they please, and their tenants shall not be impleaded for the same in the Forest Court, unless they be found in the manner or very act. And every one of my Barons may defend his own Manors and Lordships in the County or Hundred Court, by having a Steward present. I do also grant, that the wife upon the death of her husband, shall remain in her house forty days: and the heir (if he be at age) shall have his Heritage for reasonable relief, to wit, Five Pounds for a Knights Fee: nor shall the widow, nor the heir, be married, where they may be disparaged, but shall be married by the free assent of their kindred. None of them shall lose his villain by reason of his coming into the City of CHESTER, unless the same hath remained there a year and a day without claim. And in regard of the great Service which my Barons do me in CHESHIRE, none of them shall do me service beyond the LIME¶, but at their own free will, and at my cost. And if my Knights from ENGLAND shall be summoned, which ought

* Those were said to be signed with the Cross in these ages, who had undertaken a Voyage to Jerusalem, in defence of the Holy Land; and as a badge of their warfare, they wore a Cross on their right shoulder. *Spelman.*

† The Pleas of the Sword were the Pleas of the Dignity of the Earl of Chester, who held his Earldom as freely by the Sword, as the King held England by the Crown.

‡ Sakerborh, Sakber, and Sacraber, is as much as a Pledge to Sue: one that puts in surety to prosecute another. *Spelman.*

‖ Thiertnic, or Thirdnicht, is Trium Noctium hospes. *Hoveden, pag.* 606. Here it seemeth to signify three Nights Charges, for the Sheriff's Tooth. Sheriff's Tooth was a common Tax, levied for the Sheriff's Diet.

§ It is in the Deed Judex, which is sometimes taken for a Judge, sometimes for a Juryman or Freeholder; which Freeholders are by Law the Judges of a Court Baron.

¶ That is, out of the Limits of the County, as I conceive, Lima, being an old word for Limes.—*Leycester.*

to ward at CHESTER, and are come to keep their ward, and that there be no army of my enemies at present from some other place, and that there be no need, then my Barons may in the mean time return unto their own houses, and take their ease: and if an army of my enemies be ready to come into my land in CHESHIRE, or if the Castle be besieged, the aforesaid Barons upon my summons, shall immediately come with all their army, to remove the enemy according to their power: and when that army of the enemy shall retreat out of my land, the said Barons may return to their own homes and rest, while my Knights from ENGLAND keep the Guard, and that there shall be no need of my Barons, saving unto me the services which the Barons ought to do. I do also grant unto them, that in time of Peace, they may have only twelve serjeants itinerant in my land, with one horse of the master serjeant, which shall have no provend from Easter to Michaelmas, but by courtesy; and that the serjeants eat such meat as they shall find in men's houses of the Barons. And in the time of war, shall be appointed Serjeants sufficient for the keeping of my land, by my advice, and by the advice of my Judge and Barons, as need shall require. And you are to know that my Barons aforesaid have for them and their heirs, released to me and my heirs, the petitions under-written, which they desired from me, so that they can challenge nothing hereafter of them, but by my free favour and mercy:

To wit, my Steward hath released his Petition of WRBO, and of Fish cast upon his Land by the Sea, and liberty of shooting Deer in my Forest for three shoots*, and for the running of his Dogs.

Others their petition for Ley of their Swine in my Forest, and shooting at Deer for three shoots, and for running their greyhounds in the Forest going to CHESTER, upon summons, or in returning; and also the Petition of the Judgers of the WICH of thirty walms of Salt; but the amercements and laws of the WICH shall be such as they were before.

I do therefore grant, and by this present deed confirm, from me and my heirs, to all my common Knights and Gentlemen of CHESHIRE, and their Heirs, all the aforesaid Liberties, to have and to hold of my Barons, and of other their Lords, whosoever they be, as the same Barons and Knights, and other Gentlemen, hold the same of me. These being Witnesses, Hugone, Abbate Sanctæ Werburgæ Cestriæ, Philippo Orreby tunc temporis Justiciario Cestriæ, Henrico de Aldithley, Waltero Deyvell, Hugone Dispensario, Thoma Dispensario, Willielmo Pincerna, Waltero de Coventrey, Ricardo Phitton, Roberto de Cowdres, Ivone de Caletoft, Roberto de Say, Normanno le Painter, Roberto Dispensario, Roberto Deyvell, Mattheo de Vernon, Hamone de Venables, Roberto de Massy, Alano de Waley, Hugone de Columbe, Roberto de Pulford, Petro Clerico, Hugone de Pasey, Joceralino de Hellesby, Ricardo de Bresby, Ricardo de Kingsley, Phillippo de Terven, Liulfo de Twamlowe, Ricardo de Perpoint, et toto Comitatu Cestriæ.

This Charter was confirmed afterwards by Prince Edward, son of Henry III. when he was Earl of Chester.

It will appear, from the above historical account of the Earls of Chester, and their Barons, that a jurisdiction every way peculiar, was exercised by them within the county of Chester, and its dependencies.—Every act of Sovereignty emanated from the Earl himself; and he held his authority under the sanction and protection of the King of England He had his hereditary Constable, and his hereditary Steward—and summoned his own Parliaments.—In the reign of Henry VI. at the Parliament of Leicester, a Commission was issued, for rendering Cheshire liable to the subsidy in common with the other counties. This was considered a serious attack on the privileges of the County palatine. A General Meeting was held of the Abbots, Priors, and Clergy, the Barons, Knights, Esquires, and Commons of the County; and a Petition to the King was adopted, in which they state, that the Earls of Chester always held their high Courts of Parliament at will—that by the grant of the Earldom to Hugh Lupus to be held by the Sword, they had their Courts of Common Law, and as the tenor of the indictments by the Law of England, ran, "*contra coronam et dignitatem*—so in the Courts of the Palatinate it was, "*contra dignitatem gladii Cestriæ*"—that they had their Courts of Exchequer, Chan-

* The Deed runs thus, Et de Bersbare in Foresta mea ad tres Arcus, Birsare, i. e. Telo configere: a Germ. Birsen; So *Spelman*: To shoot an arrow or dart.

Ancient History.

cery, and Common Pleas, and had never sent any representatives to any Parliament holden out of the County. The petition was attended to; and they were freed from the operation of the levy.—The Baron of Halton (Neigel, or Neil) who, as I have before observed, was the first in point of precedence, was by his office bound to lead the van of the Earl's army, in his inroads into Wales, and had the entire charge of the whole armament. The whole time of the Government of the Earls did not exceed 174 years, as will appear from the following computation :—

They commenced in the reign of

1 William, whose reign was .... 21 years.
2 William Rufus 12
3 Henry I. 35
4 Stephen 18
5 Henry II. 38
6 Richard I. 9
7 John 17
8 Henry III. 56

King gives this pedigree, as "The stemme of the Earls of Chester:"—

ROBERT=ARLET=HERLWINE

WILLIAM the Conq. EMMA=RICHARD, Earl of Auranches in Constantine, in Normandy.

JOHN BOHUN, Earl of Cumberland, Lord of Carlisle =2 MARGARET

I. HUGH LUPUS=ERMENTRUDE

MAUD, daughter to STEPHEN, Earl of Blois =II. RICHARD

2. OTTWEL
4. GEVA.

3. ROBERT, Abbot of Bury.

III. RANULP I. de Meschyn.=MAUD, daughter to Aubrey de Vere, Earl of Guisnes and Oxon.

IV. RANULF de Gernon=ALICE, daughter to ROBERT Earl of Glocester.

BEATRICE, daughter of RICHARD LACY, Chief Justice of England.=V. HUGH II. KEVILIOCK

VI. RANULF III. de Blundeville. He built Beeston Castle.

MAUD=DAVID, Earl of Angus and Galloway, in Scotland, and Earl of Huntington, in England.

MABEL
AGNES
AVISA.

VII. JOHN SCOTT.

King, also states, that Hugh Lupus had full power from the Conqueror, to create Barons, to whom he granted their own free Courts of all pleas. They were bound in time of war to find for every Knight's Fee, a horse with caparison and furniture, or two horses without furniture,* in the several divisions of Cheshire†; also, that their Knights and Freeholders should have corslets and haubergeons, and defend their fees with their own bodies.—Mr. King gives us a full history of these Barons, but little dependence can be placed upon its authenticity; and names "those of the spirituality" who held seats in the Earl's Parliament, viz.

The Spiritual Barons.

* See Charter.

† The mode of summoning the Eddisbury tenantry; in those ages of feudal power, was peculiarly singular: a perforated wooden ball was carried from Village to Village, on sight of which the retainers of the Earl, his Barons, or their Knights,

1. The Bishop of Chester.
2. The Bishop of Bangor, whose Diocese comprehended a great portion of the territories of the Earl in Carnarvonshire, Denbighshire, and Anglesea.
3. The Abbot of St. Werburgh.*
4. The Abbot of Combermere.
5. The Abbot of Stanlaw.†
6. The Abbot of Norton,
7. The Abbot of Birkenhead.
8. The Abbot of Vale Royal.‡

* The day dedicated to Saint Werburgh in the Saxon Calendar is the 3d. Feb.

As far as the materials which are extant go, I have endeavored to give a brief but correct analysis, of what may not inaptly be termed, the Feudal History of Cheshire. I shall now direct my attention, to the General History of the County.

were bound to give their immediate service, according to their tenures.—It is probable the same custom prevailed over the whole of the County.—WALTER SCOTT mentions the *burning cross*, a symbol for the like purpose, in his *Lady of the Lake:* "When a Chieftain designed to summon his clan, upon any sudden emergency, he slew a goat, and making a cross of any light wood, seared its extremities in the fire, and extinguished them in the blood of the animal. This was called *The Fiery Cross*, also *Cream Tarigh*, or the *Cross of Shame*, because disobedience to what the symbol implied, inferred infamy.—It was delivered to a swift and trusty messenger, who ran full speed with it to the next hamlet, where he presented it to the principal person, with a single word implying the place of rendezvous. He who received the symbol, was compelled to send it forward, with equal dispatch, to the next village; and thus it passed with incredible celerity throughout all the district which owed allegience to the Chief, and also among his allies and neighbours, if the danger was common to them. At sight of the Fiery Cross, every man from sixteen years old to sixty, capable of bearing arms, was obliged instantly to repair, in his best arms and accoutrements, to the place of rendezvous. He who failed to appear, suffered the extremeties of fire and sword, which were emblematically denounced to the disobedient by the bloody and burnt marks upon this warlike signal. So late as the Civil War of 1745-6, the Fiery Cross made its Circuit, and on one occasion, passed thro' the whole district of Breadalbane, a tract of thirty-two miles, in 3 hours!"—Mr. SCOTT puts in the mouth of Brian, the Hermit, the following lines:—

"When flits this Cross from man to man,
"Vich-Alpine's summons to his clan,
"Burst be the ear that fails to heed!
"Palsied the foot that shuns to speed!
"May ravens tear the careless eyes,
"Wolves make the coward heart their prize!
"As sinks that blood-stream in the earth!
"So may his heart-blood drench his hearth!
"As dies in hissing gore the spark,
"Quench thou his light, Destruction dark!
"And be the grace to him denied
"Bought by this sign to all beside!"
He ceased—no echo gave agen,
The murmer of the deep—Amen!

Happily, in these peaceful days, we need neither perforated balls, nor burning crosses!

† "This Abbey," says King, "was the burial place of several of the Earls of Lincoln and Constables of Chester."—This must be an error in the Historian.

‡ The Abbey of Vale Royal was not founded till long after the annexation of the Earldom to the Crown, and the removal of the Monks of Stanlaw to Whalley.

General County History---Historical Events, &c.

CHESHIRE HISTORY.

In the reign of Henry VIII. many of the privileges of the County Palatine, if not altogether destroyed, were considerably abridged, and reduced almost to a dead letter. Some of them, however, were retained, and received a confirmation from Elizabeth, in 1568. By her patent, she guarantees the offices and powers of the Justice of Chester, and of the Chamberlain, an officer answering in a great measure to that of Chancellor. The patent also declares, that all pleas of lands, &c. and all contracts and causes, rising and growing within the said county, except in cases of error, foreign plea, or voucher, could legally be tried within the county of Chester only; and that the President and Council of the Principality had no jurisdiction within the county or city of Chester. For the enjoyment of these liberties, the county was to pay a fine of three thousand marks, called a *mize* on the accession of every new Earl.—In the 32d year of the reign of Henry VIII. the Act of Parliament was passed for doing away with the privileges of Sanctuary throughout the kingdom, except in Churches, Hospitals, and Church-yards, excluding certain offences, from its benefits.—By this enactment, Manchester, among other places, was made a sanctuary for life, for all petty offenders. But the next year, the inhabitants of that town, who, as their petition declared, then carried on a great trade in bleaching, making linen, and woollen cloths, and dressing cottons*, having suffered much loss, from the depredations of idle and dissolute persons who resorted thither under the Act—and having no Mayor, Sheriff, nor Bailiff in the town, and which had no gaol for the imprisonment of offenders,—they prayed, that the sanctuary might be removed elsewhere. The petition was attended to, and the sanctuary was removed to Chester, which, as the Act states, had no trade of merchandize, had a strong gaol for malefactors, and a Mayor and other head officers. The Act, nevertheless, reserved to the King, the power of again removing the sanctuary, if Chester should not be found a proper place for it. Its continuance at Chester, was of short duration. Soon after the passing of the Act, the Mayor, Mr. Hugh Aldersey, accompanied by Mr. Foulk Dutton, went with a petition to the King, representing that Chester was an unfit place for a sanctuary, being a port town, and situated on the borders of Wales; and that it would be attended with inconvenience to the merchants and inhabitants, &c. Upon this, the Sanctuary was ultimately fixed to be at Stafford; but by the Act, 21 James I. the ridiculous privilege was abolished altogether.—By the Act, 27th Henry VIII. it was enacted, that for the future, Justices of the Peace should be appointed in Cheshire and Wales, as in other parts of the realm.

It was not till the year 1542 that the County Palatine of Chester, sent representatives to the great Council of the nation, when the people petitioned, that they might send Knights and Burgesses to Parliament, as the other Counties, &c. of the Kingdom did; accordingly, two Knights were returned to Parliament for the County, and two Burgesses for the City.

* Manchester, at this early period, was growing into prosperity. It has continued its march of Industry without impediment, and may now be called, the first manufacturing town in Europe.

CHESHIRE

The station of the 20th Roman Legion (Victrix) so long at Chester*, and the extension of its out-posts so far as Holt, near Farndon, on the River Dee; and Caergwrle†, in the parish of Hope, about 8 miles S. W. of Chester, leave little doubt, from the many gallant attempts made by the Britons to recover their independence, but what Chester and its neighbourhood, were long the scenes of hostile contention. The Chronicon Cestrense tells us, that the names of the ancient inhabitants of Cheshire were, the *Cornavii*, the *Devanii*, and the *Cangi*. Respecting the *Cornavii*, Ptolemy says, after speaking of the Ordovices, "They lie east of those whose city is Devana, and the 20th Legion, the Conqueror, in garrison." The 20th Legion was raised by Aug. Cæsar‡, and was first placed in Gallia Belgica, but by the command of Claudius, was transported into Britain‖, and the Emperor followed them.

‡ Dion Cassius.

‖ A. D. 43.

The last of the Romans left England about 437; it is likely, therefore, that the garrison was withdrawn from Chester before that period. It is reasonable to suppose, that a detachment from the 20th Legion lay at Caerhûn, in Carnarvonshire, where bricks, 18 inches square have been found, bearing the inscription LEG. XX. V.—The *Devanii*, says the same book, have been mentioned only in modern authors, as inhabiting the borders of the river Dee, particularly by Humphrey Lloid.—With respect to the *Cangi*, we have merely a re-statement of Camden's opinion.—There is a pretty observation on the City's Antiquity: "If we should date the epocha of Chester's nativity at the vulgar year of Christ 61, it wants at this time but five years of being 1600 years old; which I think is a gallant age, especially as she breaks but little, and holds her complexion so bravely. The unhappy burning of Foregate-street, in the late *uncivil* wars, and the shallowness of the river's channel threatening the consumption of her radical moisture, have plowed her beautiful forehead with a few presaging wrinkles of mortality."

HISTORY.

1653.

On the departure of the Roman troops from this island, the Britons took possession of Cheshire, but were dispossessed of the country in 607, by Ethelfrid, King of Northumberland, who came to compel the submission of the British Monks and Bishops, to the Metropolitan Jurisdiction of the Papal Missionary, Augustine, for whom Canterbury was, for the first time, erected into a See.§—On this occasion, 1200 Monks, from the great Monastery of Bangor, who had assembled on a height near to the field of Battle, to offer up their prayers for

* It is supposed by some authors, that Chester was one of the fortresses erected by Ostorius Scapula: but this is merely supposition, yet nevertheless, by no means improbable or unlikely.

† This fact is well supported by the following extract from Camden, Art. FLINTSHIRE:—Near unto Hope, a certain Gardener, when I was first writing this work, digging somewhat deep into the ground, happened upon a very ancient piece of work, concerning which there grew many divers opinions of sundry men. But he that will with any diligence read *M. Vitruvius Pollio*, shall very well perceive, it was nothing else but a *stouph*, or hot-house, began by the Romans, who as their riotous excess grew together with their wealth, used Baths, exceeding much. In length it was five ells, in breadth four, and about half an ell deep, inclosed with walls of hard stone, the paving laid with brick, *pargetted* over likewise very smooth, having holes here and there through it, wherein were placed certain earthen pipes of potters' work, by which the heat was conveyed; and so as he saith, *Volvebant hypocausta vaporem*, that is "the *stuples* did send away a waulming hot vapour."—And who would not think this one of these kinds of work which Giraldus wondered at, especially in Isca?—"That (saith he) which a man would judge among other things notable, there may you see on every side *stouphs* made with marvellous great skill, breathing out heat closely at certain holes in the sides, and narrow tunnels."—Whose work this was the tiles did declare, being imprinted with the words LEGIO XX. that is, the *Twentieth Legion*."—On a lofty hill, above the village of Hope, in a most commanding and beautiful situation, stands the Castle of Caergwrle, a fortification, no doubt, of British origin. It was here Edward I. sought shelter from an attack by the Welsh on a division of his army—and here the Queen of that Sovereign reposed, on her way from Carnarvon to London.

§ If any thing were wanting to shew the complete independence of the British Church, of any foreign prelate, the historical fact here recited is sufficient to prove it.—It is clear, it owed spiritual obedience to its own pastors ONLY,—and their conduct in the extremity of battle proves, that they had no inclination of becoming subservient to the temporal power of the See of Rome.—Yet we find Augustine dubbed by some Catholic writers, with the title of "APOSTLE OF BRITAIN," as if he had brought about the conversion of the inhabitants!—It is probable there was more real Christianity in Britain, at this early period, than what existed in Rome itself.

their countrymen, fell victims to the bloody bigotry of Rome, which manifested itself at this early period.—This massacre excited the most determined spirit of revenge in the British Princes. They assembled a powerful army, followed Ethelfrid beyond Chester, gave him battle, and defeated him with such great slaughter, that he was obliged to retreat beyond the Humber.—After this triumph, the Britons elected Cadwan, one of the victorious Princes, their King.—In 828, King Egbert, took possession of Chester, and attached it to the Kingdom of Mercia, then tributary to him.—"Ethelwolfe," says Harding, in his Chronicle, "was crowned at Chester in a most royal manner, and reigned 19 years, and died A. D. 858."—In 892, the Danes, in great force, who had taken forced marches from Northumberland, made themselves masters of Chester. They were closely followed by King Alfred, but too late to prevent their possessing themselves of so important a post. But Alfred, by destroying all the cattle and provisions in the neighbourhood, and intercepting their supplies, drove them to great extremities; and in the end, they were glad to give up the city, and ensure a safe retreat into North Wales.—In 915, and the following year, Ethelfleda, the celebrated "Mercian Lady," and daughter of King Alfred, to whom, after the death of her husband, was entrusted the Government of Mercia, built a town at Edisbury, in the Forest of Delamere, and a fortress at Runcorn.—In 920 Edward the Elder founded the fortress of Thelwall,* on the banks of the Mersey, and placed therein a strong garrison.—King Edgar visitted Chester in 971, and received the homage of eight Sovereign Princes. by them he was rowed from his Palace to the Church of St. John, "in royal estate." This story is noticed by Webb, in the following rhymes:—

Higden.

* Not a relic of which exists.

Edgar, England's famous King, of nations great Commander,
About the Northern British coasts did pass the seas with wonder;
With navy great he did at last the City of Legions enter,
To whom eight other petty Kings their homage there did tender.
The first of them was——call'd, and King of Scots was then,
And Malcolm of Cumberland, with Macon, King of Man.
The other five were called thus——South Wales ruling.
Sfreth and Huall, both of them all North Wales then commanding:
King James, a man of great renown, did Galloway command,
And Inkil, then a famous King, did rule all Cumberland.
All these at Edgar's high command, made haste, and then did swear,
To serve him truly, sea and land, and put their foes in fear.
These all at once a barge did take, where Edgar took the helm,
And plac'd the rest at oar each one, he being then supreme,
Did guide his course, they rowing hard upon the river Dee,
Thereby he well might boast himself the English King to be.
Thus by so many under Kings which he had [illegible]
His royal state and dignity with honor was maintain'd.

There are doubts, nevertheless, of the occurrence of this aquatic excursion.—In 981, Higden tells us, nearly the whole of the county was wasted by Pirates.—In 1121, the Welsh made a desperate inroad, burnt two castles†, and committed various devastations. They were, however, compelled to make a precipitate retreat.—In 1150, the turbulent Cambrians made another inroad, and penetrated into the heart of the county: but at Nantwich, they were taken in the rear by a strong force, and suffered a dreadful slaughter.—In 1156, Henry II. encamped his army on Saltney Marsh‡, before making his unfortunate attack on the Welsh; and in 1164, this Monarch made a second visit; with a large army, threatening an invasion of the Welsh territory. He staid some time at Chester, disbanded his forces, and gave up his expedition.—King John, acted a similar part: he also marched with an overwhelming force to Chester, threatening to take ample vengeance on the Welsh, for another attack on the frontiers which they made in 1212, and in which they made an immense booty. But the King hearing of the Pope's absolving his Barons from their allegiance, and receiving information that his personal safety was in great hazard, he disbanded his army, and made the best of his way to London§.—Matt. Paris says, that in 1245, in order to prevent the Welsh from obtaining provisions in their inroads into the Palatinate, Henry III. on his way from an expedition into Wales, ordered the brine pits to be destroyed, and the frontier parts of the County to be

Caradoc's Wales, edit. 1774.

† The Lysons suppose, without giving any reason, that the Castles destroyed, were those of Shocklach and Old Castle (near Malpas).—The supposition is far from being improbable, as their situation is close upon the borders of the Principality.

‡ Called by the Welsh *Morfa-Caer-Lleon*—about a mile and a half from the City of Chester.

§ In 1237, Hugh le Despenser, Stephen de Segrave, and Henry de Audley, were invested with the military command of the Castle of Chester.

"spoiled and impoverished." A dreadful famine was the natural consequence.—An instance occurred in 1256, of the miseries resulting from impolitic and unjust Government. Sir Geoffrey de Langley was appointed by Prince Edward Lieutenant of the Principality; and ruled the unhappy Cambrians with a rod of iron. They could not bear his tyrannic oppression, and broke out into open insurrection, Cheshire was invaded, and their vengeance carried to the City gates. In 1257, under their Prince Llewellyn, they again ravaged the County, and drove back Prince Edward, who had with a strong force marched to attack them. These repeated insults at last roused the King. He summoned all who held of him by Knight's Fee to meet him on
1257 St. Magdalen's-day at Chester, in the same year. The army assembled was amply sufficient for the purpose intended; but in order, as he thought, to distress the enemy, he took the PRECAUTION of destroying all the standing corn, it being harvest season. He entered Wales, but soon felt that want of sustenance for his troops, which he had intended for the Welsh. The destruction of the harvest caused a temporary famine, and in an inglorious manner was the Monarch compelled to retreat from those foes, whom he had looked upon as already in his power.*—A contest now took place between James Lord Audley and the Welsh, in revenge for their destruction of his Castles,† when in Germany. It was carried on with extreme bitterness on both sides, for a long time, so much so, that an old
Matt. Paris. author informs us, the confines of Cheshire and Wales, exhibitted the appearance of an uninhabited wilderness. In 1258, another expedition was determined upon by the King. All who held of him by Knight's service, were ordered to attend him at Chester the Monday before St. John the Baptist's day, fully equipped to accompany him into Wales. The Welsh, however, with great policy, seeing the preparations making against them, sued for, and obtained a Peace. This expedition, therefore, was also laid aside. Llewellyn, in Nov. 1274, was summoned to Chester, to pay homage to Edward I. The Cambrian Prince, suspecting the safety of his person, should he comply, refused the interview unless a pledge was given for his safe conduct.—In 1276, King Edward placed a powerful army on the frontier, as a check upon the predatory operations of the Welsh; but Llewellyn still continued his ravages, unawed by the force which overlooked him: this state of things was not at all satisfactory to the mind of a bold and warlike Prince like Edward. Assembling an army, about the Festival of St. John, in 1277, the King marched to Chester. He immediately employed a portion of his troops in cutting a passage through the extensive woods that intervened between himself and the enemy; and soon obtained a free passage for his army, without running the risk of surprise or ambuscade. The King then entered Wales, and, it would appear, unopposed. Llewellyn hastily made his submission, and Edward returned home in triumph. The fiery disposition of Llewellyn, would allow him but a short state of quiet. In 1281, he re-commenced his depredations. Another army was sent against him; and in a skirmish in the same year with Lord Mortimer, 1281
this last of the Welsh Princes fell in the field of battle. The subjugation of the Principality followed, and an end was, for a time, put to the bloody feuds which had so long existed between the two countries.

During the wars of the Barons, in the reigns of King John, and Henry III. which, although afflicting, considered in a national point of view, were nevertheless so glorious in their results, in obtaining for the Country that grand guarantee of our Liberties, emphatically termed "THE GREAT CHARTER,"—Cheshire appears to have remained in a state of comparative quiet.—The City of Chester, it is true, was occupied by the Earl of Derby, in 1264, with the forces he had employed in the defeat of William Lord Zouch, and his confederates.‡ The following year, Luke de Taney, who had charge 1265.

* This brings to recollection the WISE precaution of Gen. Whitelock, who attacked Buenos Ayres, a strong city, without permitting his troops to load their muskets, or even to carry a flint in them. The melancholy consequences need not be recited here.

† "One of these," say the Lysons, "MUST have been Newhall Castle, in the parish of Audlem, near Nantwich, of which we have no notice, EXCEPT in a record nearly as old as these transactions."—This, I conceive, is as good an authority as could be wished, inasmuch as it is cotemporaneous.

‡ The Earl of Derby was a strong Partizan on behalf of the cause espoused by the Barons. The Lord Zouch, James

of the City for the Barons, was ineffectually besieged eight weeks in the Castle.—In 1277, Edw. I. passed through Chester, on his way to Rhuddlan, when he ordered, that all persons in the County, possessing £20. per ann. should be made Knights at their own expense. We are not told how many attended to the summons.

Another insurrection breaking out in Wales, Edward
1294. marched through the County with a strong army, forced his way into the fastnesses of the Principality, and made himself master of Anglesea.—Dugdale informs us, that an insurrection being apprehended on account of the dearness of provisions, the Black Prince, with the Earls of Stafford and Warwick, and a body of military, arrived at Chester, to protect the King's Justices, Sir Rich. Willoughby, and Richard Mareschall from the threaten-
1299. ed danger.*—The gallantry of Lord Audley and his four Esquires, Sir Robert Foulshurst, Sir John Delves, Sir John Hawkstone, and Sir Thomas Dutton, at the battle of Poictiers, in 1356, has been honorably noticed by several of our historians. Local tradition, as might be expected, has extolled their exploits wonderfully, and interwoven with them, no little of the marvellous.—Henry of Lancaster was at Chester, soon after he took arms against his Sovereign, and inspected his army under the Walls. This visit was on the invitation of Sir John Legh, Sir Robert Legh, and many others, who went to him at Shrewsbury, and assured him of their fidelity to his cause, expressing themselves as though they were deputed by both City and County. Henry signalized his stay here by putting to death Sir
†Of the Adlington family. Peers Legh,† and placing his head on the highest tower of the City.‡ At this time, the ill-fated King was at the Castle of Conway, from whence he removed to Flint Castle. At the latter fortress it was that the wily Lancaster played so well his part of hypocritical obedience to the King, which eventually placed Richard in his hands, and his crown on his head.—Lancaster brought his Royal Prisoner to Chester, lodged him in the Castle, and tradition says the place of this Monarch's confinement, was a tower that faced the north, in the outer ward——but there is nothing certain in this: it is, in a great degree, merely 'a tale of other times.' The consequences of this event are too well known to be repeated. Henry's assumption of the throne, was followed by the
rebellion of the Earl of Northumberland. The Earl's In 1403.
son, Lord Percy, surnamed from his military impetuosity Hotspur, visited the County, and it was twice proclaimed at Chester, that King Richard was still alive, and in the Castle of Chester, where he might be seen; the same proclamation was general throughout the County. Whether a representative was found for the deceased Monarch, or how the deception was carried on, does not appear. In the battle of Shrewsbury, the Men of Cheshire bore a distinguished part, and rendered memorable their valour, In this conflict, the good fortune of King Henry prevailed—the loss was tremendous on the part of the Cheshire auxiliaries of Northumberland. The Baron of Kinderton and Sir Richard Vernon fell into the hands of the King, and were beheaded. Upwards of two hundred Knights and Esquires were slain, with a great number of their retainers. On this occasion, as on others, we find the political sentiments of the County in some degree divided. In the ranks of the King, were Sir John Calveley, and Sir John Massey, of Puddington, who were killed in the battle.||

During the bloody contentions between the houses of York and Lancaster, the feelings of the County were singularly divided. At the battle of Blore Heath, in

Lord Audley, and David, brother to Llewellyn, the Prince of Wales,—supported the interests of the King, but were completely dispersed by the activity of the Earl of Derby.

* In 1300, several of the Nobility of Wales, did homage to Edward of Carnarvon, in the Castle.

‡ The remains of this faithful partizan of the King, the Harleian Manuscripts inform us, were buried in the Church of the White Friers, in Chester. In the Legh's Chapel, in Macclesfield, is a tablet to the memory of him and his father. It has the following lines:—

Here lyeth the bodie of Perkin a Legh,
That for King Richard the dethe did die,
Betrayed for righteousnesse;
And the bones of Sir Peers his sonne,
That with King Henry the Fifthe did wonne,
In Paris.

|| In 1405, on paying a fine of 500 marks, a pardon was granted to the Citizens of Chester, for the part they had taken in this insurrection; but the Mayor, John de Ewloe, was superseded.

1459; this was exemplified, in the almost equal division of the chief houses of the County under the banners of the respective "roses." Margaret, the Queen of Hen. VI. had no doubt enlisted a large portion of the gentry under her banners, by a previous visit.* Hall thus notices the battle in his CHRONICLE:—"In this battail, wer slain, xxiiij C. persons. But the greatest plague lighted on the Chesshire men, because one halfe of the shire, was on the one part, and the other on the other part, of whiche numbre wer Sir Thomas Dutton, Sir Jhon Dunne (Done) & Sir Hugh Venables. But therles§ twoo sonnes, the one called Sir Jhon Nevel, and the other Sir Thomas, wer sore wounded, whiche soberly iorneng into the Northcountrey, thinking there to repose them selves, wer in their iorney aprehended by the Queen's frendes, and conveyed to Chester; but their kepers delivered them shortly, or elles the Marche Men had destroyed the Gayles. Such favor had the commons of Wales to the Duke of Yorkes band and his affinitie, that thei could suffre no wrong to be doen, nor evil word to be spoken of hym or his frendes."—In addition to those of Knightly estate, mentioned by Hall as being left dead on the field, were Sir Richard Molineux, Sir Wm. Troutbeck, Sir John Legh of Booths, and Sir John Egerton.—Drayton in the 22d song of his "Polyolbion," beautifully notices this fatal battle—with the conception of a Poet, he represents the conflict as partaking of the form of a duel, in which one relative falls a a sacrifice to the resentment of the other.—There is so much of FIGURATIVE in the lines, that there need no apology for quoting them:—

§ Earl of Salisbury's.

There Dutton Dutton kills; a Done doth kill a Done;
A Booth a Booth; and Leigh by Leigh is overthrown:
A Venables against a Venables doth stand,
And Troutbeck fighteth with a Troutbeck hand to hand:
There Molineux doth make a Molineux to die;
And Egerton the strength of Egerton doth try.
Oh! Cheshire! wert thou mad of thine own native gore,
So much until this day thou never shedd'st before!
Above two thousand men upon the earth were thrown,
Of whom the greatest part were naturally thine own.

Cheshire furnished a large number of men, for the army of the King in his Northern broils. At the battle of Flodden Field, so fatal to the Scots, great numbers of the Men of Cheshire fell. Amongst them Sir 1513.
John Savage, Mayor of Macclesfield, and many of the Burgesses of that town.†—The son of Sir John Savage was subsequently knighted by the Earl of Hertford, after a victory over the Scots, at Leith, with nearly twenty other gentlemen of Cheshire.—From 1594, to 1598, large bodies of military passed through the County, to embark for Ireland, to quell the rebellion of Tyrone. The County appears to have enjoyed a state of quiet till the commencement of the civil wars between Charles I. and his Parliament; and of that unnatural conflict Cheshire largely partook. Civil War.

So early as the autumn of 1642, the partizans of the Parliament had occupied and strengthened Nantwich: And in July 1643, Chester was first assailed.‡—Lord Grandison possessed himself of Nantwich by a coup-de-main; but he withdrew his garrison with some precipitancy previous to the battle of Edge Hill. On the 23d Dec. 1642, a County Meeting was held at Bunbury, for the purpose of neutralizing the inhabitants in the existing war. Lord Kilmorey appears to have been

* Chester took a decided part on behalf of the unfortunate Henry VI. In 1445, his illustrious Queen visitted the City and several parts of the County, when she distributed to the King's partizans, WHITE SWANS, in silver, as cognizances of the House of Lancaster.

† "From this circumstance (says a History of Macclesfield, published in 8vo. last year) the tradition doubtless originated, that the Men of Macclesfield distinguished themselves with so much ardor at the Battle of BOSWORTH, in the cause of the Earl of Richmond (Hen. VII.) that the major part of them fell: insomuch, that the survivors were obliged to petition the victorious Prince, to grant them the continuance of their Charter, though they could not muster a sufficient number of Aldermen to constitute a Corporation."—It does not appear that Henry VII. granted any Charter to Macclesfield.

‡ On the 18th August, 1642, Sir Wm. Brereton, who afterwards acted so conspicuous a part, tried the temper of the Citizens, by beating up for recruits for the Parliament.—The inhabitants, proverbial for their loyalty, immediately rose in a body, expelled the drummer and his party, and it was with great difficulty the Mayor (Wm. Ince, Esq.) saved Sir William himself from the popular fury. The County, however, was not so remarkable for its loyalty: it is true it raised for the King a ship of 240 tons, and 96 men; but it also furnished in one year for the Parliamentary cause no less than £6944!

active in this Congress, and a treaty of LOCAL peace was signed and agreed to. But Parliament soon annulled this document, as being contrary to a former resolution of "maintaining and assisting the common cause." Sir Wm. Brereton was sent down to enforce this edict, accompanied by a regiment of Dragoons: and the King, on the behalf of his own cause, constituted Sir Nicholas Byron, to the office of Governor of Chester, and Colonel General of Cheshire and Shropshire. Sir Nicholas soon set about executing his important charge. He raised a strong force, and harrassed the Parliamentary troops, whose head-quarters were at Nantwich, by repeated skirmishes. On the 20th Feb. the Parliamentary forces sustained a defeat on Tilston Heath;* but on the following day, they possessed themselves of the important fortress of Beeston Castle. On the 22d there was a sharp contest on Tiverton Common, near Tarporley: several officers fell on both sides, and were interred at Tarporley. The arrival of the Lord Capel in the County, with a large body of horse and foot, appears for a time to have shaped military matters decidedly in favor of the King: Sir Wm. Brereton was much harrassed at Nantwich; and the garrison of Chester were enabled to extend and improve its fortifications, and provide better for its security.—March 13, Sir Wm. Brereton, who had advanced from Nantwich with his army, gave battle to the forces under the command of Sir Thomas Aston, near Middlewich, in which the latter were completely routed.†—Sir Edward Mosley, Captains Massie,‡ (of Coddington) Hurlestone, and Starkey, eight subordinate officers, and about 500 common soldiers, fell into Brereton's hands. The neighbourhood of Burleydam Chapel was the scene of a skirmish on the 11th of April; and on the 18th, a battle was fought between the Nantwich forces, and the King's garrison from Cholmondeley Hall. The latter was put to flight.—May 17th, Lord Capel failed in an attack upon Nantwich.—A party from Nantwich, on the 12th June, attacked and took the house of Mr. Leche, at Carden, carrying him off prisoner to Nantwich.—In the Month of June, Bunbury Church was burnt by the King's garrison of Cholmondeley Hall.—July 18, Sir William Brereton having concentrated his forces, made a forced march to Chester, attacked it in a spirited manner, but was, in the end, compelled to retrogade.—Another unsuccessful attack was made by the Lord Capel on Nantwich, on the 3d August.—On the 16th October, his Lordship took possession of Acton Church, and Dorfold Hall, preparatory to a third assault, but evacuated those positions on the 17th Oct.—Tarvin had been some time occupied by the Parliamentary troops; and on 12th Nov. a portion of them which had advanced to Stamford Bridge, were there totally defeated by a detachment from Chester. Such was the continued state of hostility prevalent in this County during this troublesome period.

1643.

Towards the end of November, the Royalists received a strong reinforcement from Ireland, which was placed under the orders of Lord Byron,‖ nephew to the Governor. They were soon employed in the reduction of several strong positions, particularly Beeston Castle,

‡ Ancestor of the Rev. R. Massie, of Chester.

* Sir Rt. Cholmondeley distinguished himself in this action: his services are noticed in his patent of Peerage.

† In the PARLIAMENTARY CHRONICLE, we are informed, that soon after Sir William Brereton went down into Cheshire, being then with his troops at Congleton, and hearing that Sir Thomas Aston and Sir Vincent Corbet, two active Commissioners of array, were about to take possession of Nantwich with their forces, he sent a party on or about 28th Jan. 1643, to recover that town—that Sir Thos. Aston marched to Nantwich, and attacked the town five several times, but was as often repulsed; and that he and Sir Vincent Corbet were entirely defeated by Sir Wm. Brereton, who soon afterwards came up with his troops.—At Congleton, the influence of the Parliament was predominant: In 1642, five shillings and sixpence were paid by that borough as a ley for trained soldiers at Nantwich,—in 1645, five pounds were paid by the Corporation to a Parliamentary Cornet Singleton, as a compensation for his horse, which had been stolen out of a stable in the town:—six men were summoned to do military duty at Nantwich, and paid—TWO PENCE per day each!

‖ This gallant Nobleman, (who was afterwards Governor of Chester) the Ancestor of the present Lord Byron, and equally celebrated for his poetic works, communicated regularly with the heroic garrison of Latham House, Lancashire; during the siege of which, a Dog was the means of carrying dispatches to and from the besieged. He was kept till nearly in a state of starvation, and then beat out, when he went to his Mistress, about three miles distant, by whom the dispatches were forwarded.—Eventually, the poor animal was shot by one of the Parliamentary soldiers.—STRANGER IN CHESTER, p. 26.

CHESHIRE HISTORY.

Crewe Hall, Doddington Hall, Barthomley Church, Acton Church, and Dorfold Hall—the last was taken on the 2d Jan. 1644.—Great cruelties were committed by the Royalists at Barthomley Church: and the Lysons, in a note, incorrectly say, that these outrages formed one of the articles against King Charles I. Acton Church maintained a stout resistance; but the almost impregnable Castle of Beeston,* perched on a steep hill, accessible only on one side, surrendered without resistance to Captain Sandford, who had arrived with the Irish reinforcements. This enterprising partizan, with only eight of his soldiers, availing himself of the darkness of the night, contrived to mount the steep ascent, escaladed the wall, and got possession of the upper ward before morning, and on the same day it was surrendered. The Governor, Captain Steele, was afterwards shot at Nantwich for his conduct.—Crewe Hall surrendered only for want of provisions and ammunition: it made
1643. a most heroic defence. In the month of December, the whole of Sir W. Brereton's forces were totally defeated near Middlewich by Lord Byron. The fugitives fled to Nantwich; and Northwich fell into the hands of the King's troops. On the 2d Jan. 1644, Nantwich, which had long been in part invested, was formally besieged†—the attacks of Lord Byron were almost incessant, continuing throughout nearly the whole of the month: but Sir Thomas Fairfax, and Sir Wm. Brereton, concentrating their forces, put Lord Byron's army to the rout in great disorder, and compelled them to retreat to Chester. Many of the Officers took refuge in Acton Church, and Dorfold, but were obliged to surrender.‡—The arms of the Parliamentarians, seem to have been generally triumphant: for, on the 4th January they got possession of Crewe Hall—on the 7th they occupied Doddington; and towards the end of January, they were victorious
1644. in an action at Tarvin.—A detachment from Chester made an attack on the Parliament Post at Christleton: it was a commanding situation, and the resistance was obstinate, but in the end the King's forces put their opponents to the route. The following day, the Parliament troops were more fortunate. Adlington Hall surrendered to them; and on the 25th, they occupied Withenshaw, both of them Royal garrisons.—On the 25th of May, a body of 3000 cavalry and infantry, under the command of Colonel Duckenfield, which had occupied Stockport, were attacked by Prince Rupert, and sustained a signal defeat. The loss was very great. The Prince, after the contest, immediately crossed the Bridge, and passed through that town on his way to Manchester.

In June, Sir Wm. Brereton received his appointment from the Parliament as Major-Gen. of Cheshire. Invested with the supreme command, he put all his energies into action. On the 7th July, the King's garrison at Cholmondeley Hall, after a brave resistance, surrendered to the Earl of Denbigh. August 18, fell Colonel Marrow, Deputy Governor of Chester: he was killed in an attack made on the Parliamentary garrison at Croughton Hall.—A division of Sir Wm. Brereton's army from Northwich, which had advanced on a recognizance to Tarvin, was there surprised by the King's troops, and put to flight.—Oldcastle-heath, near Malpas, was the scene of a sharp conflict on the 25th August, in which the King's troops were defeated with the loss of several distinguished officers, amongst them, Col. Vane, Col. Conyers, and others.—The Parliament troops repossessed themselves of Tarvin on the 5th Sept. placed a garrison there, and fortified it: they also garrisoned Huxley Hall.—In the same month, the horse of Prince Rupert were put to flight close to Malpas, and with difficulty escaped to Chester.—With the exception of Chester, and Beeston Castle, the whole County appears at this time to have been in the possession of the King's enemies. A concentration of their forces now took

* This fortress, it appears, was in a state of great dilapidation before the Civil Wars commenced. I find, that on the 23d Jan. 1636, a commission was granted to Lieut.-Colonel F. Conningsby, appointing him Commissary-General of and for all the Castles and fortifications of England and Wales.—It is probable, about this time, that Beeston Castle was repaired.

† It was during this siege, that a convoy, composed of a strong body of horse, with arms and ammunition, for the King's forces, was attacked and defeated by Colonel Mytton: Sir Nicholas Byron (Governor of Chester), was made prisoner, and the warlike stores fell into the hands of the Parliament troops.

‡ Amongst these prisoners was Colonel Monk, afterwards celebrated in the part he took as General Monk, in bringing about the restoration of Charles II. Monk was carried prisoner to the Tower, and remained there a greater part of the War, when he obtained his release under cover of espousing the Parliamentary cause.

place, and their sole object was confined to the reduction of these important fortresses. A line of circumvallation was drawn round Chester, which was gradually contracted. Birket House in Wirral, occupied by the King's troops, merely for the sake of maintaining a communication with Liverpool and the opposite shore, was taken. In Nov. Beeston Castle was invested by the Nantwich forces; and military posts were placed by Sir Wm. Brereton, at Tarvin, Rowton, Huntington, Eccleston, Aldford, Upton, and Trafford: subsequently he established posts at Lache, Netherlegh, and Dodleston. Christleton was strongly fortified, and there the Parliament forces fixed their head-quarters. Jan.
1645. 18, the Royalists were repulsed in a smart action with the Parliament forces from Christleton,—but the particular details of the siege of Chester, I shall reserve for the local history of the City.

March 17, the Castle of Beeston was relieved by Prince Rupert, and Prince Maurice, after a siege of more than three months. There does not appear to have been much discipline in the contending armies at this period, for we find the soldiers of Prince Rupert setting fire to Beeston Hall, and also plundering the village of Beeston. On the departure of the Prince, the siege was resumed, and mounds thrown up in order to facilitate its operations. Towards the end of March, the head-quarters of the Parliament troops were removed to Netherlegh, near the Lach-eyes, about a mile and a half south-west of Chester.—Early in May, the Parliament commanders drew off their forces from the various posts they had established on the Chester side of the County, excepting, however, from Nantwich and Tarvin. This movement, was in consequence of the intelligence of the King's advance, with a powerful army.—May 20th, Sir William Brereton retreated from his position before Chester, to Nantwich, and on the 22d, the city was relieved.—Ridley Hall, in which was a small Parliamentary garrison, was suddenly but unsuccessfully attacked on the 4th of June, by a party from Beeston Castle.—On the 27th September, an end was put to the King's power in the County, by the fatal battle of Rowton and Hoole, in which the army of Sir Marmaduke Langdale was completely routed by the forces under General Poynton and Col. Jones. In this action fell the Earl of Lichfield, a gallant nobleman, who, with the Lord Gerard, had made a vain attempt to recover the day's fortune Burghall informs us, that the King himself was in this battle, at least in that part of it of which Hoole Heath was the scene. On the 28th September, the King left Chester, with an escort of 500 horse, and was accompanied to Denbigh by Sir Francis Gamull, Alderman Cowper, and Captain Thropp. Nov. 20, after nearly a year's siege, Beeston Castle surrendered to Sir Wm. Brereton.—Early in Dec. this Commander, having been joined by Colonel Booth's troops, and a strong reinforcement from Lancashire, removed his head-quarters to Dodleston—at this time, Chester was completely invested, but, notwithstanding the extremes of privation which it underwent, held out till the 3d February following, and then surrendered by capitulation, on very honorable terms.

The conquest of Chester, put an end to the war in Cheshire: but in May, 1648, the Cheshire gentry, in the interest of the Commonwealth, possessed themselves of Chester, which they put in a strong posture of defence, and engaged to raise three regiments of foot,
and one regiment of horse if necessary. This activity 1648.
gained for them the thanks of Parliament.—A division of the retreating army of the Duke of Hamilton, after the battle of Preston, passing through the County, in August, was attacked in various places by the gentlemen of the County, and near 500 of them made prisoners.—The Scotch army under Charles II. were, in Aug. 1651, for a time quartered in Nantwich, previous to the memorable, but unfortunate battle of Worcester.—In the following month, a flying party of the King's horse, passing through Sandbach, on the market day, was assailed by the Country people, and 100 captured.—In June and July, 1655, a number of Cheshire Gentry, including Sir Richard Grosvenor, Peter Venables Baron of Kinderton, Mr. Warren, of Poynton, near Stockport, Mr. Massey of Puddington, were arrested, and lodged in Chester Castle, on suspicion of being disaffected to the Protector's Government—In August 1659, Sir G. Booth, under a commission from Charles II. appointing him Commander-in-Chief in Cheshire, Lancashire, and North Wales, assembled an army of 3000 men. Rowton Heath, rendered memorable by

CHESHIRE the defeat of Langdale and the Royalists a few years before,§ was the rendezvous of this force, and there a declaration was published, stating that the cause of their assembling in arms, was to obtain a free Parliament, and deliver the nation from the intolerable slavery under which it labored.* The Parliament soon took alarm at this hostile movement, and General Lambert being dispatched with a sufficient force, came up with Booth's troops at Winnington Bridge, near Northwich. An action took place on the 16th August; but it was not long doubtful: the new league was soon dispersed, Sir G. Booth with great difficulty escaping from the field in disguise. Being taken soon after at Newport Pagnell, he was sent prisoner to the Tower. The Parliamentarians, again triumphant, marched to Chester, then under the Government of Colonel Croxton, and they no sooner appeared before the walls, than the City surrendered.—Previous to the Revolution of 1688, the son of Sir Geo. Booth, Henry Lord Delamere, who had long been suspected of partiality to the Royal cause, and had undergone a trial before the execrable Jefferies, but was acquitted, having heard of the landing of the Prince of Orange, soon mustered a strong force in this County and Lancashire, declared his determination to support his cause, and marched to meet him. Chester in the interim was taken possession of for the King, by the Lords Molineux and Aston: but the abdication of James speedily following, the County once more was restored to a state of Peace.—About 60 years after this, the "clarion of war" again disturbed the county with its terrific sound. On the 1st December, Cheshire was invaded by the Scotch army under the command of Charles Edward Stuart, commonly called the "Young Pretender," and on the same day, this adventurer, the last military scion of an unfortunate house, entered Macclesfield at the head of his troops, by way of Jordan Gate. They remained but two days, and then marched in the direction of Leek, on their projected journey to London. The circumstances of their speedy retreat, on hearing of the advance of the Duke of Cumberland, need not be recited here:† but the alarm it created, at least in the breasts of some individuals, may not be unworthy of record. Several disposed of their property, and actually removed to distant places where they imagined greater security was to be found.—To exemplify this fact, the following deed of bargain is adduced as authentic‡—it will serve to show the value of property in those days:— HISTORY.

§ 1645.

1745-6.

Know all men by these presents, that I, John Swindells, of Raynor, in the Parish of Prestbury, and County of Chester, gent. have, in consideration of the sume of sixty-five pounds of lawful money of Great Brittaine, to me in hand paid at and before the sealing and delivery of these presents, by my Mother-in-law, Sarah Dearneley, now of, or in Raynor, in the parish and county aforesaid, widow, the receipt whereof I do fully acknowledge, and myself fully therewith satisfied, have bargained, sold, and by these presents doo bargain and sell unto the said Sarah Dearneley, six cowes, four year old calves, two mares, one cart and wheels, one plow, and all other husbandry geire implements; and all the goods, household stuff, implements of house-

* Sir Geo. Booth was supported and accompanied in this affair by the Earl of Derby, the Lords Cholmondeley and Kilmore, and a great number of other gentlemen of the county.

† The History of Macclesfield, before alluded to, says, in speaking of this irruption, "Though undiciplined and boisterous, they did not injure the persons, nor destroy the property of the inhabitants, except in the article of food, of which they took a supply. They amounted to some thousands of men, chiefly of the Highland Clans, led by their Chieftains.—They were mostly armed with the broad sword and targe, a kind of shield. A small proportion of them were musketeers, and besides their general, Prince Edward, they were commanded by several Scotch noblemen of distinction, particularly the [gentleman named Drummond, calling himself the] Duke of Perth, the Duke of Athol, the Marquis of Dundee, the Marquis of Montrose, the Earl of Cromartie, and Eleven other Scottish Noblemen, and Thirteen Knights, mostly Highland Chiefs who were knighted by the Prince, prrticularly Sir James Mackenzie, Sir Hector M'Lean, Sir Wm. Gordon, Sir David Murray, Sir Hugh Montgomery, Sir Geo. Witherington, Sir Wm. Dunbar, &c. The troops were indifferently cloathed, yet they appeared to be in high spirits. They marched under the banners of their respective Chiefs, to the music of the Highland Pipes, and the drum." On the retrograde movement made by Prince Edward, the whole of his force was compelled to cross the River Mersey at a ford, in consequence of the Bridge at Stockport being destroyed to impede his retreat.

‡ History of Macclesfield.

hold, and all other goods whatsoever, mentioned or intended to be mentioned, of what nature, kind, or property the same may be, remaining or being in the custody and possession of me the said John Swindells, or elsewhere can be found within the realme of Great Brittaine. To have and to hold, all and singular the said goods and premises, and every part and parcell of them, by these presents bargained and sould unto the said Sarah Dearneley, her executors, administrators, and assigns for ever. And I, the said John Swindells, for myselfe, my executors, and administrators, all and singular the said goods, chattels, household stuffe, and implements, unto the said Sarah Dearneley, her executors, administrators, and assignes, against me the said John Swindells, my executors, administrators, and assigns, against all and every other person and persons whatsoever, shall and will warrant and for ever defend by these presents, of which Goods, I, the said John Swindells, have put the said Sarah Dearneley in full possession, by delivering her one pewter dish, in full of all the said premises, at the sealing hereof. In witness whereof, I the said John Swindells, have hereunto put my hand and seale, this third day of March, in the twelfth year of the reigne of our Sovereigne King George, in the yeare 1745.*

JOHN SWINDELLS.

Sealed, signed, and delivered in the presence of us,
Joshua Broadhurst.
Josiah Broadhurst.

Another interval occurs of nearly 70 years, in which the county enjoyed a state of quiet.—It was interrupted, however, in 1812, by a sort of mercantile, rather than political, insurrection, the particulars of which, collected from the Chester Chronicle, are embodied in the following brief statements :—

Riots at Macclesfield and Stockport.—It is with much reluctance we announce, that the disturbances which have so long disgraced Nottinghamshire, Derbyshire, Lancashire, and some other of the Northern counties, have at last spread into Cheshire. A riot took place at Macclesfield on Monday, and it was not till the Magistrates interfered, and the Riot Act was read, that the meeting was dispersed. It does not appear that there was any specific object in view. Three of the ringleaders, John Jackson, John Tunstall, and Thomas Livesley, were apprehended, and have been lodged in our County Gaol.—Since writing the above, further distressing, and truly alarming accounts have reached the office of this paper. On Wednesday about twelve o'clock at noon, the manufacturers of Stockport and Edgley, to the number of some hundreds, met in a disorderly manner in the streets of the former place. The shops were shut; and the mob proceeded to break the windows of the houses of some of the most considerable inhabitants. The exhortations of the Magistrates availed little; they were obliged to read the Riot Act; and it was some time after the Military were called out, before order was restored. Seven of the most active in the mob were seized, and are now confined in our Castle. We have not had further information on this truly distressing subject. We are indeed apprehensive there are others of a higher class than labouring manufacturers, who are the fomenters of these unlawful proceedings, and abettors of a misleaded but patient and valuable class of the community. We trust the Magistrates will exert themselves, and pry, if possible, into the motives of the secret movers of these disorders.—They deserve the severest punishment.—Chester Chronicle, April, 17, 1812.

Owing to the exertions of the Magistracy, and the prompt, but forbearing conduct of the military, we are

* I find the following paragraph in a London paper of September, 1789:—"The Pretender, in 1745, marched to Preston, on an assurance from Sir W. W. Wynn, that a body of Welsh troops should meet him there: on the disappointment which he experienced after this promise, the Prince called for a glass of wine, and drank the health of his friends, that being the only token of attachment he had received from them. Though Sir Watkin did not raise forces for the Pretender, he did certainly raise contributions from every well-wisher to his cause; and presented the money so raised as a gift of his own!—The late Duke of Norfolk, often mentioned the circumstance, not without some acrimony, he having contributed in that subscription £100."—During the rebellion of 1745, Cappuch, the Pretender's pretending Bishop of Carlisle, was confined in the Castle of Chester.

CHESHIRE

1812.

happy to say that, at present, the towns of Macclesfield and Stockport, remain tranquil. We hail this intelligence with joy, because we think, that the misguided men engaged in the late outrages, will not again feel inclined to provoke the interference of the strong hand of the law.—The disturbances in the neighbourhood of Stockport are subsiding; and by the activity of the Magistrates and the Scotch Greys, several persons concerned in the late attacks at Mr. Goodair's and Major Parker's, have been apprehended. There are now, not less than fifteen offenders in the Gaol of this County, who have been implicated in these tumults,—amongst whom is Wm. Walker, otherwise Gen. LUDD.—Colin Linden, James Wilson, James Bennett, Foster Roach, Richard Wood, James Tomlinson, and Wm. Thomson, for a riot at Etchells and the neighbourhood, and having by numbers and intimidation, unlawfully and feloniously obtained seven shillings from John Parker, Esq. of Etchells. Richard Lowndes, James Torkington, and John Henshall, charged on the oath of Thomas Barlow, of Styall, John Millett, and Hesketh Goddard, of Pownall Fee, for a riot at Styall and Pownall Fee, on the 14th inst. in assembling mutually to assist each other against whoever should oppose them, and for feloniously demanding various sums of money from Hesketh Goddard, Thomas Barton, and Thomas Barlow. Charles Hulme, and John Field, for a riot at Cheadle Bulkeley, and for having, with divers other rioters, to the number of some hundreds, assembled about the dwelling-house of John Goodair, of Edgley, manufacturer, and wilfully, and feloniously SET FIRE to and BURNT part of the said HOUSE. The offences of Hulme and Field, are of a most serious description; and we trust it will not be our disagreeable duty to record a repetition of these disgraceful and certainly thoughtless acts.—The behaviour of the rioters at Macclesfield, was most determined; and it was not till the military advanced amongst the crowd, that the mob despersed. Mr. Higginbotham, and Mr. Grimsditch, a respectable attorney, serving in the cavalry, were both severely hurt by the rioters. The former had his arm broken. It is supposed that the number of the disaffected assembled exceeded 5,000!—CHESTER CHRONICLE, APRIL 24, 1812.

HISTORY.

1812.

THE CHESTER CHRONICLE of the 8th May, 1812, noticing the agitated state of this County and Lancashire, says, "Our accounts, to yesterday evening, state every part as enjoying perfect tranquility. The pleasure we feel in announcing this is considerably enhanced by its contradictory tendency to reports in circulation in this city, on Monday and Tuesday last—that discord and riot were spreading about the northern parts of the county, and that the mansion-house of F. D. Astley, Esq. at Duckenfield, had been burnt and destroyed by the intemperate multitude. These rumours had no foundation: Every thing has been quiet during the last sixteen days, and we trust the reign of order and peace is again restored. That there has been a regular communication between the disaffected in the different counties, appears to be evident—their proceedings were approaching to a systemized plan of opposition to the laws, and to the quiet classes of the community. The destruction of machinery, and the obtaining an advance in the average of wages, were not the only objects aimed at—there was a grand, a more dangerous attempt lying dorment, till opportunity should give scope for action—and we feel not the least hesitation in giving it as our decided opinion, that political measures were hid under the garb of misery and want, put into motion by the exertions, epistolatory and declamatory, of characters, whose elevated rank in life should have taught them better, and shewn them the folly—the extreme danger of tampering with the feelings and prejudices of the ignorant. To any one who will take the trouble of adverting to the conduct of the mob in Nottinghamshire, in Derbyshire, in Lancashire, and in Cheshire, he will find that in all these districts they were headed by a particular individual, whom they styled General Ludd, whose orders they implicitly obeyed and who ruled his adherents with the most despotic authority. Independent of what they were taught to think their duty, they were tied to one another by the most solemn and impious oaths, of one of which, we have been told, three verses of the 21st chapter of Ezekiel* formed part.—We do not, however, pledge ourselves for the correctness of our information, altho' we have received it from a respectable source. If true,

* "And thou Prince of Israel, polluted and wicked, whose day is come, when iniquity shall have an end. Thus saith the Lord God, I will take away the diadem, and take off the crown; this shall be no more the same; I will exalt the humble, and

CHESHIRE

1812. however, the FACT SPEAKS FOR ITSELF.—Two of these provincial leaders are now in custody in Chester and Lancaster Castles, and we expect disclosures on their trials which will astonish those now entertain different opinions of the motives which actuated the disaffected * * * * * * *

Among the plans proposed by the disaffected, and the conspiracies entered into, one was to have been put in execution immediately, and the signal was to have been the stopping of certain Mail Coaches—the non-arrival of which at their usual hour and place, was to be considered as the command for the general rising.—Happily all those plots were put an end to, by the spirit of the Magistrates, the courage and conduct of the Yeomanry cavalry,* and the persevering exertions of Mr. Lloyd, solicitor, of Stockport. On the 25th May, a Special Commission† was opened for the trial of the whole of the Prisoners, whose offences were connected with the lawless proceedings of the LUDDITES (as they were called)----The whole of them were convicted. —SIX were sentenced to imprisonment for different periods—EIGHT were transported for seven years—and FOURTEEN were condemned to suffer death. Five were left for execution, but two only paid the dreadful penalty of the Law, JOHN TEMPLE,‡ and WM. THOMPSON.

HISTORY.

1812.

* During the whole of these disturbances, the Earl of Chester's Yeomanry, Legion, commanded by Sir John Leicester, particularly distinguished themselves.

will abase him that is high. I will overturn, overturn, overturn it, and it shall be no more until he come, whose right it is, and I will give it him.—EZEK. xxi, 25, 26, 27.

† The Special Commissioners were, the Earl of Stamford and Warrington, Lord Lieutenant—the Hon. Robert Dallas, the Hon. F. Burton, his Majesty's Justices of Assize—Hugh Leycester, Esq. Recorder of Chester—S. Yate Benyon, Esq. Attorney General for the County—Bagot Read, Esq. Prothonotary—S. Humphryes, Esq. Chas. Potts, Esq. and Stephen Leeke, Esq.

‡ Particulars respecting this person's offence, extracted from the evidence produced by the prosecutor: who stated that about 12 o'clock the family went to bed, the doors and windows being first secured.—Was alarmed a while after by the tinkling of glass, and a violent shock at the windows, the glass flying up the room—all the windows were broken. Went to the window and a voice called out "Open the door."—He was asked, "What do you want?"—When witness was answered, "We are informed you have fire arms in the house, 2 guns and a brace of pistols. Open the door or we'll set the building on fire."—This was about one o'clock.—They said they would not stand dallying there, but demanded the door should be opened, as they had 50 more houses to call at that night. They then beat violently on the door, and as witness thought, it would presently give way, being only a pannelled door, a boy went to open it, but when he got to it, his heart failed; it was at last opened by the servant man, and a man entered with a sword in his right hand, and a stick in his left—the rest of the gang followed, presenting pistols at the family as they passed along the lobby. They said, they were *General Ludd's men*, and called themselves not by names, but by numbers. The man who came in first called the numbers; and when he was in, he said, "Gen. Ludd, walk forwards;" when presently there came from the door, a stout man, in a black coat and pantaloons, and he they called Gen. Ludd. He had a handkerchief about his mouth; and they were all disguised by handkerchiefs tied round their heads. They first searched the capboards, and took out silver spoons; they then looked in all the drawers, one of which was locked, but before the keys could be fetched, it was broken open, and searched, and they found a little silver. After these proceedings, they demanded money, but they were told there was none, the rent having been paid the Monday before. The gang then went up stairs, and after a general search, they came down, when they were asked, "Gentlemen, what do you want? If you want meat and drink you shall have plenty." Bread and cheese were then put before them, and one stood on the top of the cellar stairs, whilst others went down and drew what drink they thought proper. After eating, they insisted on all the family going into a room up stairs, whilst they were collecting all the things together, which was complied with; but the boy before mentioned, happening to be crossing the lobby, one of the robbers put a pistol to his breast, and said, if he would not keep his own room, he would blow him through!—All the drawers were stripped, and they looked whether they had left any thing behind them.—Witness said to them, "this is sad work," and was answered, "it shall be sadder!"—After collecting together a vast quantity of butter, cheese, bread, bacon, clothes, &c. they mustered their numbers, and went away the same as they came. They were called number 1, 2, 3, 4, and so on, and the persons who were the numbers, answered "here"—they were not called by him, styled General Ludd. They were altogether about an hour in the house. Witness has seen one man since before the Magistrates at Stockport, and knows him particularly well, as he took up a new pair of shoes, which were in the house. A young woman saw him eyeing them, and caught them in her hand, intending to take them away, when he immediately seized the shoes out of her hand, and threw them down. The boy to whom they belonged, said, "Don't take those shoes, I shall want them to-morrow," when he immediately pulled his own shoes off, and put those on, shuffling and dancing in them. He did not, however, walk in

CHESHIRE HISTORY. 1812.

JUNE 26.—It is with much concern we have to notice the repetition of those disorders in this county, which, we hoped, the force of the dreadful example exhibitted on Monday week,* combined with the unceasing exertions of the Magistrates, had put a complete and permanent stop to. From intelligence which we have had from that quarter, it appears, that in the beginning of the last week, a strong body of those deluded men, calling themselves LUDDITES, surrounded the house of a lady, the widow of an officer, residing at Edgeley, near Stockport, and with horrid threats demanded entrance, to search for arms. The inhabitants, under an impression of dreadful consequences resulting from a refusal, opened the door, when a number of armed men rushed into the house, and after very minutely searching all parts, took away with them eight swords, leaving the affrighted immates in a state of extreme consternation. The party consisted of from eighty to one hundred, variously armed, and they paid the strictest obedience to the commands of one who acted as their leader, and who was of a respectable appearance.—We wish we could, with that degree of justice we owe to the public's information, here close this article; but we are sorry to say, the lapse of each day discloses some new object of alarm—some new act calculated to impress upon us the most alarming sensations and apprehensions for the general peace and safety of the country. It has been told us, that assemblies nightly take place in secluded places to the number of some hundreds, that oaths are administered, and that the names of those who are parties to the abominable and seditious compact, are called over at the several places of rendezvous with all the regularity and appearance of system and discipline.

* The Execution of Temple and Thompson.

The CHESTER CHRONICLE of a date, (July 3) subsequent to the extracts before made, says, "We stated in our last, our intention of laying before the public this week, some particulars respecting the state of the county. We have been disappointed, however, in the receipt of some promised particulars from a friend, and are consequently under the necessity of postponing other remarks we had in preparation. In the mean time, we have not fallen short of a supply of—RUMOURS, most of which now in circulation, as they respect the disturbed districts, have every thing to recommend them but truth—they are either totally false or grossly exaggerated.—That occurrences of a most alarming nature have lately taken place, cannot be denied—and it is equally certain, a partial disaffection predominates in particular districts. We have heard names mentioned as the instigators of mischief, at which probability recoils, and the patriotic heart sickens. We should be fearful, were we even satisfied of the fact, of giving them to the public.—In a former paper, we adverted to the copious confession made by Thompson, lately executed here, but observed, that at a period like the present, it would not be altogether prudent to publish its contents. A short time before his sacrifice to the violated laws of the country, he acknowledged, that a regular organization of disaffected manufacturers had existed some time in Cheshire, Lancashire, the Northern Counties, and in Scotland—that there are concealed depôts of arms—and that this confederacy owes its origin to the intrigues of men of EXALTED RANK, but whose names he was unacquainted with. Those engaged in this conspiracy have taken the diabolical oath, which has before appeared in this paper†—with the tenor of which Thompson was well acquainted, having been sworn of the compact. This was not ascertained on his trial. We had nearly omitted mentioning, that the avowed object of this infernal association, is to overturn the government, and establish on its ruins a Commonwealth, 'similar to that

them to Stockport. Witness knew this man again, having seen his face when he was gathering up the shoes—knew him perfectly well, and recognised his handkerchief and waistcoat, when before the Magistrate—it was the Prisoner.

† "I, A B. of my own free will, do solemnly swear, that I will not reveal, to any person or persons, in any place or places, under the canopy of heaven, the names of the persons who composed the *Secret Committee*, either by word, deed, or sign their proceedings, meeting places, abode, dress, features, marks, complexions, or connexions, nor by any thing else that may lead to the discovery of the same, under the penalty of being put out of the world, by the first brother who shall meet me—my name and character blotted out of existence, and never to be remembered, but with contempt and abhorrence. I further swear, that I will use my best endeavours, to *punish with Death*, any traitor or traitors, should any rise up against me, he or they; *and though he should fly to the verge of nature, I will pursue him with unceasing vengeance.*—So help me God, to keep this Oath inviolate."

1812. under Oliver Cromwell!' On this disclosure, we leave the reader to his own reflections. Such is the information which has come to our knowledge on this most serious and important subject, which perfectly satisfies us, that the distresses of the times, which we have all alike to lament, have been availed of for the worst of purposes, and been made the pretext, by designing and wicked men, for consolidating treason and unnatural rebellion. It is consolatory, notwithstanding, in our being enabled to say, that a becoming vigilance is observed both by the civil and military officers; and we have every confidence in their exertions for the preservation of the public peace."

This confidence, it would appear, was well founded. At this distressing period of our County History, should be recorded the patriotic and praise-worthy conduct of the Royal Chester Local Militia.—The following paragraph is extracted from the paper before quoted :—On Wednesday morning May 6, the right wing* of that fine body of men, the Royal Chester Local Militia, consisting of the rifle company, a detachment of the artillery, with two guns, the grenadiers, and 1st, 2d, 3d, and 4th battalion companies, left this city, for Northwich, on their way to Stockport, where they arrived the next day.— The alacrity with which the men stepped forward, is an earnest of what might be expected from them at a more serious period. Many of them resided at Liverpool, Manchester, and the towns and villages in the neighbourhood of Chester; and although there were little more than three days' notice for the assembly of the detachment, few were returned absentees. The time of the meeting happened most unfortunately for the SPORTING members of the corps—the very " push and onset" of the races! This might be supposed to have damped the ARDOR of the men—but the contrary appeared the fact—they freely sacrificed the gaieties of the week, and marched off in high spirits, cheering as they passed along the streets.—The division remains at Stockport, for fourteen days' permanent duty.

* The left wing was embodied in the City during the sitting of the Special Commission; at this time, Chester exhibited the appearance of a garrison apprehensive of being seized by the *coup de main* of an enemy. The Local Militia alternately, took the Castle Guard, and every night mounted a picquet of 100 men, to each of whom were delivered six ball cartridges. The military were placed under the controul of the Mayor, and " domiciliary visits" (as our Gallic neighbours term them) were made at all the lodging houses in the city and suburbs.— In the midst of these serious events, a ludicrous occurrence would sometimes happen.—One night, about twelve o'clock, a division of the picquet was sent to the North district, to pay their unwelcome visits. Under the windows of one of the receptacles for weary travellers, the guard drew up *à la Militaire*.—" Open your door," said the officer in command. In a short time, a figure something like that of a female, appeared at the window, and inquired what was wanted?—" We are the picquet, and must search your house, for suspicious characters open the door, I say!" I'll be —— if I do, cried mine hostess, for there are no suspicious characters here.—With some difficulty, however, after a long colloquy, the door moved on its hinges,—the officer entered, and put the usual questions: " Have you any lodgers in the house, and who are they?" —" God bless your Honor (observed the Lady in reply, with a strong Hibernian accent) there's not a soul in the house, but there's a poor cratur up stairs in bed."—Where does he come from? " He told me from Stockport!"—From Stockport! exclaimed the military commander. This was enough! Up stairs went the whole guard, formed round a wretched bed, and the sleeper was awoke to the pleasing sight of some ten muskets and bayonets!—In bed with him was his daughter, about seven years old.—" You come from Stockport, eh?" *Yes, Sir*, said a voice which betrayed a thorough-bred Cambrian.—" What are you doing in Chester?" *Why you see I was go to Holywell to get work.* " At what Trade?" *I was be in Cotton works.* —" Aye, aye, you'd all have the same story: Come out of bed with you, you must be examined."—Expostulation was useless, and from beneath the dirty blankets of his straw couch, emerged one of the most spare-figured Welshmen ever beheld. Having put on his ragged clothes, accompanied by the tears and intreaties of his daughter not to leave him, the son of St. David was placed in the midst of the guard, and marched off to the guard-room in the Blossom's Inn Yard. Here sat the Mayor, attended by his officers. The Welshman trembled at the scene which presented itelf. A number of questions were put to him, and from his answers it appeared, that having been compelled by the stagnation of trade at Stockport, to quit his situation (occasioned by the riots,) he had with his daughter bent his steps towards his own country in the hope of gaining employ, to obtain a maintenance.—His story was every way satisfactory—the apprehensive Lieutenant's fears were allayed—a few shillings were collected for the suspected Luddite, and he was escorted back to his bed, to complete that tete à tete with Morpheus from which he had been so abruptly torn!

CHESHIRE HISTORY.

1817. In 1817, the County was again disturbed by a Combination, which threatened the most serious consequence, even that of the overthrow of the Constitution itself:— The County had long been deluged with seditious and blasphemous pamphlets, originally issued from the Presses of Cobbett, (a notorious renegade) Wooller, and other revolutionists in London, who under the pretence of seeking a reform in Parliament, urged on the ignorant to acts of illegality, and inflamed their passions by blank forms of petition, addressed to the Legislature, couched in the most threatening and unequivocal language. These had their effects, and excited the desperate attempts of deluded and wicked men. Lancashire proved, in this instance, the hot-bed of one of the most diabolical conspiracies on record. On March 10th, the disaffected in Manchester, assembled at what they called a Public Meeting, and itimated, in the annunciation of it, that the numbers thus collected, would, each with one of the petitions above alluded to, march to London, to present it in person to the Prince Regent, in order to 'undeceive' him. The people of Stockport were invited to join in the illegal assembly, and unfortunately too many of the cotton spinners, and characters of the worst description of that town, accepted the summons. —The Police had timely notice of their proceedings: under the active superintendance of Sir John Byng, the Commander of the District, a strong military force was mustered. The Earl of Chester's Cavalry received orders to assemble—also the Stockport troop, two troops from Macclesfield, and three from the neighbourhood of Knutsford,—the whole regiment obeyed the command with patriotic alacrity—they assembled on Sale Moor, near Manchester, ready to act in any case of emergency. A strong division of the 85th regiment of the line, by forced marches, arrived from Chester—with ample supplies of ammunition, should resistance be offered.—On the day appointed (the 10th) the mob assembled in immense numbers near St. Peter's Church, Manchester —it is said nearly 70,000 persons were present in the course of the day.—A temporary stage was erected for the accommodation of Johnson, Ogden, and the other incendiaries who acted as Orators to the Multitude. About half-past ten, in the midst of a violent inflammatory speech, a party of the 1st Regiment of Dragoon Guards, by a rapid and unexpected movement, made their 1817. appearance, galloped up to the erection, and made prisoners all who were upon it! A dispersion of the mob now began to manifest itself—numbers were provided with Blankets* and knapsacks, to shelter them in their journey to London, and this numerous proportion, moved in the direction of Stockport, on their projected expedition. At Stockport bridge, they were encountered by a body of Life Guards, and the Macclesfield troop of the Cavalry Legion, No attempt was made to force a passage—many threw themselves into the river and crossed where it was fordable. About 500 only of this immense multitude reached Macclesfield, and here they were finally dispersed.—The soldiery behaved with the greatest patience, notwithstanding the repeated insults which they received; and it must be gratifying to notice, that only two men were wounded in this affair, one of whom afterwards died in the Manchester Infirmary, from a sabre wound. Some hundreds were made prisoners, and of these twenty-one were sent to Chester Castle; by the leniency of the Crown they were afterwards discharged from Custody, on finding security, &c.†—On the 28th March, a Conspiracy was detected in Manchester, the object of which was to destroy that town by fire, on the Sunday night following.—The discovery of this horrible plot, the arrests which afterwards took place, and the suspension of the Habeas Corpus Act, happily put an end to the hellish machinations of the disaffected, and since the above period, the county has enjoyed a state of profound repose, rendered still more pleasing by the bright prospect of increased trade, and renovation of our unrivalled manufactures.

I cannot better conclude this division of the work, than by introducing the following flattering, but deserved tribute of acknowledgment, for the essential services of one of the most valuable and efficient Yeomanry Corps in the Kingdom:—

* Which singular accoutrement obtained for the mob the name of "Blanketeers."

† The mob was divided into parties of ten, every tenth man bearing a petition—and the money of his nine compatriots.

Cheshire History

1817. 1817.

EARL OF CHESTER'S LEGION.

COPY OF A LETTER FROM LORD SIDMOUTH, TO COL. SIR JOHN FLEMING LEICESTER, BART.

Whitehall, April 3d, 1817.

SIR,

It was not till this morning, that I was honored with your letter of yesterday, with an enclosure from Lieutenant Colonel Townshend.

Being fully convinced that the presence and conduct of the Regiment of Yeomanry Cavalry, of which you have the command, materially contributed to arrest the danger with which the town and neighbourhood of Manchester were recently threatened; I have to request that you will accept, and communicate to Lieut. Col. Townshend, and through him to the Officers and Privates of your distinguished corps, the assurance of the high sense entertained by his Majesty's Government, of the additional proof which they have afforded, upon this important occasion, of their zeal and loyalty, and of their constant readiness and determination when properly called upon, to afford their powerful aid to the civil power, in enforcing obedience to the Laws, and in maintaining the public tranquility.

I have the honor to be, Sir,
Your obedient and faithful Servant,
SIDMOUTH.

To Col. Sir John F. Leicester, Bart.
&c. &c. &c.

COPY OF A LETTER FROM MAJOR-GENERAL SIR JOHN BYNG, TO LIEUT.-COL. TOWNSHEND.

Head Quarters, Pontefract, April 5, 1817.

My Dear Sir,

I have this day received a Letter from Lord Sidmouth, from which I send you the following extract :—

" Altho' I have expressed to Sir John Leicester, the " Colonel of the Cheshire Regiment of Yeomanry Ca- " valry, the sense entertained by Government, of the " services of that corps upon the late occasion, I cannot " be silent upon the subject, when writing to you, who " have witnessed and rendered full justice to their pub- " lic spirited, and most exemplary conduct."

I send you this, that the Corps, as well as yourself, may know, that I have not failed in my desire, to do you full justice, for I really entertain the greatest respect for them, not only in their readiness in coming out at this, to them most important period of the year, but for assembling in such numbers; your casualties, by the return you favored me with, appear less than I should have probably found in any regular regiment.

Believe me, your obliged, and
Very faithful,
J. BYNG.

To Lieutenant-Colonel Townshend,
H. R. H. the Prince Regent's
Regiment of Yeomanry Cavalry.

The Regiment mustered at a few hours' notice, on the 10th of March, in aid of the civil power, 397, exclusive of officers; and on the 30th March, 395.

LOCAL HERALDS.

The County of Chester has had some share in heraldic, and chivalric distinctions. It has now a herald of Arms, attached to the College, in London, and the office is at present filled by G. M. Leake, Esq.—In the reign of several of our Kings, Cheshire has been distinguished by its peculiar heraldic officers. In the 6th year of Edward III. Calveley Herald brought home the intelligence from the army in Flanders. This local title certainly cannot be classed as partaking in the least degree of any national appointment. It is most likely he was attached to Sir Hugh Calveley's celebrated Crusade into Flanders and France. Froissart says, Sir Hugh Calveley was one of the most renowned Soldiers in Europe. Camden informs us, nothing was held impregnable to his valour. In 1364, this renowned hero commanded the rear-guard at the battle of Auray. In the 47th year of Edward III. he was a Banneret, Captain-General of the forces in Arragon, and Seneschal of Limoisin. Ann. 50, the same reign, he was Commander of Calais. In the 3d year of Rich. II. he was Captain of the Castle of Cherbourg, and Governor

of Guernsey, Jersey, Sark, and Alderney—thus far a portion of Sir Hugh's exploits.—CHESTER HERALD was sent into France by Hen. V. on the 24th July, 1415, to demand the surrender of that Kingdom. In the 5th year of the reign of Edward IV. CHESTER HERALD carried Lord Scales' challenge to the Bastard of Burgundy. At the Coronation of James II. CHESTER HERALD took precedence of Somerset Herald; and at the Coronation of George II. CHESTER HERALD was marshalled in the Procession, immediately before Richmond Herald. On a reference to Edmondson's Heraldry, I find, that on the 7th of June, in the 21st year of Richard II. the King created William Bruges, Chester Herald, and on the same authority it is stated that Chester had a Pursuivant at Arms.

To the general reader, this notice of the Heraldic distinctions of the County may be deemed superfluous and useless—but there may be some, nevertheless, whom it may at least gratify as a reference for curiosity.

Mosses sc.

Canal Bridge, and Water Tower, Chester---from a Drawing taken in 1802.

Geography of the County---Geological Description--- Produce, &c.

CAMDEN has well defined the Boundaries of the County in the introduction to this work. The extreme length of the County, from the Hundred of Wirral to the confines of Yorkshire is about 58 miles—its breadth from North to South about 30 miles. The collective acreage of the county may be about 676,600: of these, observes Mr. Holland, in his agricultural survey, 620,000 are cultivated; 28,000 peat bogs and mosses, and between 9000 and 10,000 acres of Sea Land. The soil of the County, generally speaking, is composed of clay and sand. At the north-west extremity of Wirral, sand is found in great abundance; in the Hundred of Broxton (immediately in the neighbourhood of Chester); in the Hundred of Nantwich; throughout nearly the whole of Eddisbury Hundred; in the southern part of Macclesfield Hundred, &c. Clay is found in great abundance in Wirral; in Broxton Hundred; in Nantwich Hundred; near Northwich; and the northern extremity of Macclesfield Hundred. There are large tracts of peat-moss, and black moor land, on the borders of Yorkshire, and Derbyshire. Coppenhall Moss,* which was remarkable for the discovery therein made of oak, beech, and fir trees, broken in various places, and bearing marks of the operation of fire,† is nearly cleared of the peat it contained. There is a Moss of some extent at Warmincham.

* Thro' this Moss passed a gravel road, no doubt of very remote antiquity. It is hazardous to conjecture its original direction.

† The fir, in particular, bore the marks of fire

HISTORY.

Cheshire was celebrated some centuries ago, for the great extent of its forests and heath lands. Its principal forests were those of Delamere (or Mara and Mondrum), Wirral, and Macclesfield, all of them abounding with timber.—The forest of Delamere must have been of extraordinary size; not less than FIFTY townships were within its boundary, viz. :—

Bridge Trafford,	Rushton,
Wimbolds Trafford,	Eaton,
Thornton,	Tarporley,
Ince,	Church Minshull,
Elton,	Aston,
Hapsford,	Worleston,
Stoney Dunham,	White Poole,
Alvanley,	Cholmondeston,
Manley,	Stoke,

Helsby,
Newton,
Kingsley,
Norley,
Crowton,
Coddington,
Onston,
Acton,
Winnington,
Castle Northwich,
Hartford,
Horton,
Wettenhall,
Oulton,
Oulton Lowe,
Little Budworth,
Rudheath,
Wardle,
Calveley,
Alpraham,
Tilston Fernall,
Tiverton,
Utkinton,
Willington,
Clotton,
Duddon,
Ashton,
Great Mouldsworth,
Little Mouldsworth,
Horton-juxta-Ashton,
Great Barrow,
Little Barrow.

Tarvin, Hockenbull, and Kelsall, although within the purlieus of this forest, were not considered as belonging to it, as they lay within the liberties of the Bishop of Lichfield and Coventry. Weverham, Merton, and Over, similarly situated, were classed within the liberties of the rich Abbey of Vale Royal,—Frodsham, Overton, Netherton, Bradley, and the Woodhouses, are described as being parcel of the demesnes of the Earls of Chester. The division of the forest called Mondrem, was the south part, extending almost to Nantwich — The township of Aston, in the parish of Acton, near Nantwich, is called Aston-in-Mondrem. In 1461, the offices of Master Forester in Fee, Surveyor, and Ranger of the Forest, were granted to Thomas Lord Stanley and his heirs, to hold the same as fully as Thomas Lord Stanley, his father, had done. By inheritance from the Dones and Kingsleys, John Arden, Esq. is Bow-bearer of this Forest,* and is also the Chief Forester.

It is highly probable, that all those parts of Delamere Forest, not clothed with timber, were at one period in a state of cultivation, altho' the soil† does not now appear to be well suited to agricultural purposes.—Within the last two centuries, it contained much more than 11,000 acres. Two thousand acres have long since been inclosed; and the cultivation of the soil is now in great progress of improvement under the sanction of an Act of Parliament, which passed the Legislature, and received the Royal Assent 9th June 1812.‡—Some of the rising grounds, in the neighbourhood of the Old and New Pales, (which have been detached from the forest

* The Bugle Horn, by which his ancestors held this office under the Norman Earls, is now preserved by Mr. Arden.

† Intermixed with gravel and white sand.—There is peat moss to be found in various places on this Forest.

‡ The following are the principal features, of the Act of Parliament:—

The Act, which is of considerable length, occupies forty pages in folio and received the Royal Assent on the 9th June, 1812. It enacts, that Robt. Harvey, and Joseph Fenna, Gents. be commissioners, saving a right in his Majesty's Commissioners of woods and forests, to appoint others in the event of their death or incapacity---and empowering John Arden, Esq. and four other proprietors to call a meeting for that purpose, of which 21 days' notice shall be given in the Chester Chronicle. Non-attendance of commissioners to be considered a refusal to act---an umpire to be appointed to determine differences which may arise---Mr. Joseph Hill, to be surveyor; and in the case of his death, or refusing to act, the commissioners to appoint another.---Proprietors are to produce surveys of their respective claims.—The commissioners to sit at least twelve days in every two months.---Parties dissatisfied with the bounries set out, may try their rights by law. All claims to be delivered to the commissioners, who are empowered to settle disputes, but not to determine titles to estates.---Quantity and value of the land to be adjudged by the Commissioners, but all ancient messuages are considered of equal value.—Encroachments made within forty years to be considered in setting out allotments, and where encroachments are taken away, compensation shall be made.—Allotments to be made for the purpose of getting stone, &c. but no stone, &c. to be carried out of the Forest.—Commissioners authorised to stop or turn the directions of roads, scour out brooks, and make ditches, &c. —Oakmere, and Eddisbury Hill Quarry, not to be considered any part of the Lands to be allotted—a similar claim extends to Hatchew Meer and Fish Pool—When the boundaries of the Forest, and the value and extent of encroachment within the last forty years, are ascertained, the Forest to be divided into Moieties, one half of which shall be allotted to the King, as nurseries for wood and timber only, and for no other use, intent, or purpose whatsoever.—A further allotment, not to exceed the annual value of 200l. made to the King, of land of the yearly value of 20s. per acre, who is to erect a church on it, which shall be adequate to the probable population of the Forest when under cultivation—together with a Parsonage House and Burial Ground.—The district to be then called Delamere Parish, and to be divided into two or more townships to be called by such names as the commissioners shall appoint.

land by Royal Grants) are now beautifully feathered by healthy thriving plantations of various timber and other Trees Thomas Cholmondeley, Esq. of Vale Royal, has some extensive plantations; and Nicholas Ashton, Esq. planted about one hundred and thirty-three acres of land, with 477,000 trees, chiefly larches and Scotch firs, for which he received the premium from the Society for the encouragement of Arts, Manufactures,

The presentation to the said church to be invested in the King for ever, and all marriages solemnized in the church to be valid. The Rectory of Delamere to be subject to the same laws as are now in force, concerning rectories, parishes, &c. The forest having always been hitherto extra-parochial, is to be exempt from the payment of tythes for ever. Any person obtaining any grant of inclosure, trees, &c. the grant to be void, and the person obtaining it to forfeit treble the value thereof. Each moiety of the forest to be divided so that each portion may have an equal quantity of bad and good land. His Majesty is empowered to grant a lease of the Old and New Pale to George James Earl of Cholmondeley, for any term of years not exceeding 61, in possession and not in reversion. A proportionable allotment to be made to Mr. Arden, for the value of the conies, fisheries, &c. he shall prove himself entitled to, as Chief Forester, and Bowbearer: The outermost fence shall be raised and made at the expense of his Majesty.—Moss pits and turbaries incapable of being drained to be left open for the use of such persons as have heretofore enjoyed them.—Any person cutting and taking away turf from the forest to pay a penalty of 5l.—Immediately after the allotments are made, rights of common are to cease.—Rights of common may be extinguished or suspended before the execution of the award.—Owners of rights of common, if desirous, may have their allotments laid together.—All allotments are to be delineated in a plan, and shewn to the proprietors.—Allotments made under this act, to be held by the same tenures, customs, &c. as heretofore.—After the final award of the commissioners, all lands, as well those inclosed as those intended to be inclosed, shall be disafforested, save and except that John Arden, his heirs and successors shall continue, if he or they think fit, to retain the title of Chief Forester, Bowbearer, and Forest Bailiff. Exchanges of allotments allowed to be made—Leases at rack-rent void as to allotments.—No sheep or lambs to be kept in any of the new inclosures during the space of seven years, unless the same be properly fenced.—Satisfaction to be made for unequal shares of boundary fences.—Expenses of the act to be paid by his Majesty and the persons interested in the premises.—Land to be sold for defraying expenses of the act, at least twenty days notice thereof being given in the Chester Chronicle—and all deficiencies to be made good by the proprietors.—Money may be raised by mortgage till the same can be raised by sale.—The final award to be left with the clerk of the peace, where it may be inspected by persons interested on paying one shilling.—The account of the commissioners to be balanced annually before two Magistrates, at a public meeting, whereof twenty-one days notice shall be given in the Chester Chronicle.—Money advanced to be repaid with interest.—Appeals must be made to the justices at the general quarter sessions within three calendar months after the cause of complaint shall have arisen. The right of his Majesty to be preserved in all mines of coal, salt, lead, &c.—Profits of stone quarries to belong to persons entitled to allotments.

The Preamble to the Act runs thus:—

Whereas the King's Most Excellent Majesty is seised to himself, his Heirs and Successors, of the Forest or Chase of MERE and MONDRUM, otherwise DELAMERE, in the County of CHESTER, containing by estimation Eight Thousand Acres of Land or thereabouts, now lying open and uninclosed; and also of Two Ancient Inclosures situate within the Boundaries of the Forest, called THE OLD PALE and THE NEW PALE, containing together by estimation Seven Hundred and Fifty Acres, or thereabouts; the said Old Pale being the exclusive property of his said Majesty, his Heirs and Successors, subject nevertheless to such Rights of Agistment and Commonage, or other Rights, as the Owners and Occupiers of any Messuages, Lands, Tenements and Hereditaments, in the several Townships, Hamlets or Places, adjoining or lying near to the said Forest, may prove themselves entitled unto, in, over, and upon the open and uninclosed parts thereof:

And whereas the whole of the said Forest and the said Inclosures therefrom, are Extra-parochial:

And whereas the Right Hon. GEORGE JAMES Earl CHOLMONDELEY, is Lessee under his Majesty, for a term of years yet to come and unexpired, of the Agistment, Herbage, Pasturage and Pannage of Hogs, Turbary, Fern, Crops and Brakes, upon the whole of the uninclosed parts of the said Forest, and also of the said Inclosures called THE OLD and NEW PALES:

And whereas JOHN ARDEN, of Harden in the county of Chester, Esq. is Chief Forester, Bowbearer, and Forest Bailiff of the said Forest, and in such right and by virtue of several Grants from the Crown, made to him and those under whom he derives his Title, claims for himself and his Underkeepers, to be entitled to certain ancient Lodges and Offices, and several Sheepwalks, in and upon the said Forest, and to divers Messuages, Cottages, Buildings, Lands, and Hereditaments belonging thereto; also to the Conies and Fishings, and the Pasturage of Conies and Sheep, in and upon the said Forest, or some part or parts thereof, and to certain Rents, and other Rights and Interests in and upon the said Forest:

And whereas THOMAS CHOLMONDELEY, of Vale Royal, in the said county of Chester, Esq. as Owner of the Scite of the dis-

CHESHIRE HISTORY.

and Commerce, and is entitled besides to the grateful thanks of his country.*

Our dates as to the Forest of Macclesfield, are not very particular. By Lucian the Monk, this dreary tract was called the Forest of Lyme† and he describes it as the boundary between Cheshire and Derbyshire. Lord Stanley was made Master Forester of this forest in 1461, with reversion to him and his heirs. Vivian de Davenport was appointed Chief-Serjeant of the forest by Randle Blundeville, with reversion also to his heirs.—Macclesfield Forest contained TWENTY-THREE townships within its limits, according to a MS. in the Harleian Collection, viz.—

North Rode	Pott Shrigley
Bozley	Adlington
Gawsworth	Poynton
Sutton	Norbury
Downes	Offerton
Hurdsfield	Torkington
Titherington	Marple
Upton	Disley
Bollington	Taxall
Prestbury	Kettleshulme
Butley	AND
Rainow	Whaley.

The lapse of a few years, it is to be hoped, will put Macclesfield Forest in the same track of improvement, as Delamere Forest, and under the same authority—an Act of the Legislature.

So early as the year 1376, the forest of Wirral was disforested, in compliance with a request from the Black Prince, on behalf of the people of Cheshire, who com- Temp. 51, Edw. III.

solved Monastery of VALE ROYAL, and of divers Messuages, Lands, Tenements, and Hereditaments, heretofore parcel of the possessions of the Abbot and Convent of Vale Royal aforesaid, claims to be entitled to a certain Mere or piece of Water, in and upon the said Forest, called OAKMERE, with a certain extent of the Turbary and Moss Ground, adjoining thereto, and a certain Stone Quarry called EDDISBURY HILL QUARRY; and also to Rights of Agistment, and other Rights in, over, and upon the uninclosed parts of the said Forest, for and in respect of the Scite of the said Monastery, and the said Messuages, Lands, Tenements, and Hereditaments:

And whereas JOHN EGERTON, of Oulton, in the County of Chester, Esq. claims to be entitled to two certain Pools of Water in and upon the said Forest, called HATCHEW MERE, and FISH POOL, with all the Fish therein, and the right of fishing of and in the said Pools, by virtue of a Demise or Grant thereof, from his Majesty to Philip Egerton, Esq. deceased, dated the 10th day of November, 1777, for the term of ninety-nine years, determinable on three lives:

And whereas an Act was passed in the Forty-first year of the reign of his present Majesty, intituled, "An Act for consolidating in one Act, certain provisions usually inserted in Acts of Inclosure, and for facilitating the mode of proving the several facts usually required on the passing of such Acts:"

And whereas from the great and increasing difficulty of procuring a supply of Timber from foreign countries, and from the Estates of private individuals in the United Kingdom, it has become necessary to adopt measures for securing a more adequate supply of Timber in this Kingdom; and if his Majesty were empowered to inclose certain parts of the said Forest, and such parts were appropriated for the growth and preservation of Wood and Timber, the same would be of great advantage to his Majesty, and the Public in general:

May it please Your Majesty, &c.

* As planting forms a very important feature in the improvements of this County, it may not, perhaps, be irrelevant, briefly to state the successful exertions of a gentleman in Chester in that branch. In the Autumn of 1804, Dr. Thackeray commenced planting in Wales; and has, since that period, covered between 500 and 600 acres of land, *incapable of tillage*, with forest trees of all kinds; and their present thriving appearance has raised its value far beyond his most sanguine expectations. Judiciously thinning and pruning *annually*, have contributed greatly to their present flourishing condition, and hold out, at no distant time, the prospect of a very profitable return. If such examples were more generally followed, all apprehensions of a future supply of timber would be removed, and we should no longer have occasion of sending to other countries, for what our own mountains would as liberally furnish. It is scarcely necessary to say, that Dr. Thackeray has also been presented with the honorary reward of the Society for the Encouragement of Arts, &c.

† It is most likely this forest is alluded to, in a passage of the Charter of Randle Blundeville to his Barons (see p. 26) which runs thus: "*Et propter grave Servitium quod in Cestershiria faciunt, nullus eorum extrâ Limam Servitium mihi faciat nisi per gratum suum et ad custum meum,*" *&c.* This quotation shows, that the services of the Barons are not to be extended beyond the forest of Macclesfield, or Lyme—and this is, I think, a much better construction than that put upon it by Leycester, in the page above noticed.

 plained to the King of having sustained many damages, grievances, and suits, by reason of the said forest. Its thickets harboured pirates, and plunderers of all descriptions, and rendered the entire district particularly obnoxious to the Citizens of Chester. The bailiwick of this forest was given by Randle Gernons, to Alan Sylvester, and passed by a succession of female descendants, to the familes of Bamville and Stanley. It has remained in the latter family ever since. The present Bailiff is Sir Thos. Stanley Massey Stanley, of Hooton, Bart. who is in possession of the ancient horn, which was granted with the office to his ancestors.—Wirral still abounds with timber, but much of it is stunted.

It has been justly observed by Mr. Holland, in his Agricultural Survey, that although there are few woods and plantations in Cheshire, of any great extent, yet the quantity of timber growing in the county, in hedge rows, coppices, &c. far exceeds the general average of the Kingdom—and it is, perhaps, worthy of note, that the great portion of this timber is Oak.

The estates of the Earl of Stamford and Warrington, Earl Grosvenor, (who has lately considerably extended his plantations) the Marquis of Cholmondeley, and some others, abound in uncommon fine timber. Alderley Park boasts some very fine beech; and it is said, nearly 100,000 oaks, and other timber trees, were planted at Dunham Massey, by the late Earl of Stamford and Warrington.

There are various parts of Cheshire which possess much picturesque beauty.—Wirral boasts many delightful marine views, frequently well filled up by a range of barren hilly land, terminating near Hoyle-lake. The prospect of the Welsh Coast from Parkgate and its neighbourhood, including the venerable ruins of Flint Castle—the town of Flint—the town of Holywell, &c. is rendered more pleasing and busy from the numerous vessels constantly employed in the Coasting and Coal trades, continually passing and repassing.—In the interior of the county, there are some fine sketches of landscape. The vicinities of Macclesfield, Astbury, Nantwich, and Sandbach, have strong claims to diversified scenery; but Nature, clothed in her magnificence, presents splendid and luxuriant prospects from Barnhill, Kelsall-hill, and from the summit of the rocks of Beeston and Halton. The view from Halton, is extensive and varied, enriched by the liquid mazes of the Mersey, and carrying the eye over a large district of Lancashire—from Beeston, the "Vale Royal" of the County is seen, in all its far-fam'd beauty, highly cultivated, and decked with numerous woods and coppices of thriving timber. In the distance are the lofty Mountains of Wales—and the estuary of the Dee forms a gratifying perspective to the picture. The situation of the Castles of Beeston and Halton, is uncommonly romantic—

——————" Wide around
Hillock and Valley, Farm and Village smile;
And ruddy roofs, and chimney tops appear,
———— up wafting to the clouds
The incense of Thanksgiving."

Generally speaking, the surface of Cheshire is flat. There is a lofty range of hills, however, bordering on Astbury, Prestbury, Mottram, &c. Bucklow Hills form prominent features in Cheshire scenery. Alderley Edge is a singular insulated hill, something similar to the Rock of Beeston. The prospect from the majestic summit of Mowcop is very extensive, as it is also from the Shuttingslow hills. The hills near Frodsham, which may be considered as the extreme boundaries of Delamere Forest, have a bold termination at Helsby. I have particularized these elevated situations in this stage of the work, merely to shew that the county is not deficient in picturesque scenery, as has been represented by some of our modern topographers. Chester, and its immediate neighbourhood, lie much lower than the other parts of the County—the traveller has a considerable descent to make in entering the city from every quarter.

PRODUCE—SALT, CHEESE, &c.

Salt, and Cheese, may be considered as the chief staple commodities of this County, both of them forming articles of exportation to a very great amount.

It does not appear from any historic facts, that the Salt Works were known during the stay of the Romans, but it is very probable they were. We know, however, that before the Conquest, the Salt Works were carried on in this County, and this is ascertained from the best authority that can now be produced—DOOMSDAY-BOOK. So early as the reign of the Confessor, they produced a considerable revenue to the Crown; but after this period they fell into decay. The works at Middlewich, and Nantwich belonging to the King and the Earl, became unproductive, and were entirely disused,* altho' they had some time before produced a rent of £16. per ann. no inconsiderable sum in those days.†—When the general Survey was taken, the WICHES, as they were termed, were farmed by the Crown at the following sums—works at Nantwich at £10. at Northwich at £1. 15s. at Middlewich, £1. 5s. Certain duties were paid for every waggon load, horse load, &c. but these duties varied, according to the custom of the Wiches. The Earl's salt pit at Nantwich,‡ was toll free, but then the produce was limitted to the purposes of his own household—if he sold any, account was to be made to the King for two thirds of the toll.—Great quantities of salt were carried into Wales, which was the principal medium of consumption.—The various works in the county, were much injured by Henry III. who in his wars with the Cambrians, directed them to be destroyed, and the pits to be stopped up.—In the reign of Hen. VI. a meterial improvement in the manufacture of salt took place, under the supervision of John de Sheidam, and sixty other persons, specially invited to England, by that Sovereign for the purpose. Nantwich was then the principal place of manufacture, and continued so till long after the Civil Wars between Charles I. and his Parliament, at which time there were 216 Wich-houses or Salt-works there; at present, however, there are only two.—Early in the eighteenth century, Mr. Lowndes received a Parliamentary Reward, for the publication of certain improvements in Salt-making; and about the same time Dr. Brownrigg suggested some advantageous alterations in the making of common salt, which were then adopted. The manufacture of White Salt, during the last century, has greatly increased—about the year 1700, it was little more than adequate to the consumption of the County.|| In 1806, a patent was obtained by Messrs. Marshall and Naylor, for making salt of a large grain, and particularly well adapted for curing fish and provisions. It is now used at most of the fisheries.—Rock Salt was first discovered by accident in 1670, near Marbury, in the parish of Budworth, whilst searching for coal. This has proved of high importance to the salt works generally. There are many pits of Rock Salt now worked near Northwich, in Marston, Wincham, and Witton. About 100 tons have been raised from some of these pits in one day! In its transit for exportation, a considerable portion of rock salt is refined at Frodsham, and other places on the Mersey. Liverpool is the great mart of export. During the last seventeen years, the average quantity of rock salt sent down the Weaver is about 52,000 tons. Above 3000 hands are employed in the salt works.—The manufacture, &c. of salt, is thus described by Mr. Holland, in his Agricultural Survey:—

"The natural form of the crystals of muriate of soda, is that of a perfect cube; and they regularly assume this figure, when the due arrangement of their particles has not been interrupted by agitation, or the application of strong heat. These cubes exhibit diagonal striæ, and frequently on each side, produce squares parallel to the external surface, gradually decreasing inwards; circumstances which shew the vestiges of their internal structure; for every cube is composed of six quadrangular hollow pyramids, joined by their apices and external surface; each of these pyramids filled up by others similar, but gradually decreasing, completes the form. By a due degree of evaporation, it is no difficult matter to obtain these pyramids separate and distinct; or six

* At this time there were eight Salt Works in the County.

† Temp. Hugh Lupus.

‡ Called by the Welsh HELLATH WEN, or the WHITE SALT PIT.

|| The principal brine pits in Cheshire are at Wheelock, Lawton, Roughwood, in Leftwich, Middlewich, Anderton, Betchton, and near Northwich and Winsford.—In the year ending May 1806, the salt manufactured at the Cheshire Brine-pits (exclusive of Nantwich and Frodsham) was 16,590 tons, 77 bushels. The annual average of White Salt sent down the Weaver, for the different fisheries, the Colonies, the Baltic, the United States of America, Newfoundland, &c. during the last seventeen years, has been about 140,000 tons. It is supposed, that within the same period, the manufacture of salt at Northwich, has been doubled.

CHESHIRE

of such, either hollow or more or less solid, joined together round a centre. If we examine the hollow pyramid* of salt farther, we shall find it composed of four triangles, and each of these formed of threads parallel to the base; which threads, upon accurate examination, are found to be nothing more than series of small cubes.† The perfect crystallization of the salt can, however, take place only under the circumstances above mentioned, a freedom from agitation, and from an evaporation of the water which holds the salt in solution: and it is principally on the presence or absence of these causes, that the variation in the appearance of the manufactured salt depends.

The manufacture is conducted in several different ways, or rather heat is applied in various degrees, to effect the evaporation of the water of solution; and according to these different degrees of heat, the product is the stoved or lump salt; common salt; the large grained flaky; and large grained or fishery salt.

In making the STOVED, OR LUMP SALT as it is called, the brine is brought to a boiling heat; which in brine fully saturated, is 226 degrees of Fahrenheit. Crystals of muriate of soda are soon formed on the surface; and almost immediately, by the agitation of the brine, subside to the bottom of the pan. If taken out, each of them appears, at first sight, to be granular or a little flaky; but if more accurately examined, it is found to approach to the form of a little quadrangular, though somewhat irregular, pyramid. The boiling heat is continued through the whole process; and, as the evaporation proceeds, similar little crystals continue to form themselves, and to fall to the bottom of the pan. At the end of twelve hours, the greatest part of the water of solution is found to be evaporated; so much only being left as is sufficient to cover the salt and the bottom of the pan. The fires are then slackened, and the salt is drawn to the sides of the pan with iron rakes. The waller then places a conical wicker basket, or barrow as it is called, within the pan; and having filled this with salt, by means of a little wooden spade, he suffers the brine to drain from it for a short time into the pan; and then carries it to one of the benches, at the side of the pan-house, where the draining is completed. It is afterwards dried in stoves, heated by a continuation of the same flues which passed under the evaporating pan, and is reckoned to lose in this about one-seventh of its weight. In making this salt, the pan is twice filled in the course of twenty-four hours.

HISTORY.

On the first application of heat, if the brine contains any carbonate of lime, the acid may be observed to quit the lime, and this being no longer held in solution, is either thrown up to the surface, as the ebullition takes place, along with the earthy or feculent contents of the brine, whence it is removed by SKIMMERS; or it subsides to the bottom of the pan, along with the salt first formed, and with some portion of the sulphate of lime; and is raked out in the early part of the process. These two operations are called CLEARING the pan; some of the brines scarcely require them at all, and others only occasionally.

The LARGE GRAINED FLAKY SALT is made with an evaporation, conducted at the heat of 130 or 140 degrees. The salt formed in this process is somewhat harder than the common salt, and approaches nearer to the natural form of the crystal of muriate of soda. The pan is filled once in 48 hours. As salt of this grain is often made by slackening the fires betwixt Saturday and Monday, and allowing the crystallization to proceed more slowly on the intermediate day, it has got the name of SUNDAY SALT.

To make the LARGE GRAINED OR FISHING SALT, the brine is brought to a heat from 100 to 110 of Fahrenheit; and at this heat, the evaporation of the water, and the crystallization of the salt, proceed. No agitation is produced by it on the brine; and the slowness of the evaporation allows the muriate of soda to form in large, nearly cubical crystals, seldom however quite perfect; with this heat it takes five or six days to evaporate the water of solution.

In the course of these several processes, various addi-

* The bases and altitudes of these little pyramids are in general equal; thus showing the salt's disposition to form a cube.

† See Burgman's Essays, vol. ii. page 12, 13.

tions are often made to the brine, with the view of promoting the separation of any earthy mixture, or the more ready crystallization of the salt. These additions have been different at different works; and many of them seem to have been made from particular, and often ill-founded prejudices; and without any exact idea as to their probable effects. The principal additions which have at various times been made, are, acids; animal jelly and gluten; vegetable mucilage; new or stale ale; wheat flour; rosin; butter; and alum."

Whilst on the relation of the natural produce, of the County of Chester, there is a strong inducement to enter rather fully into the chemical habitudes of common salt; not because they are little known, but, because some of its properties may, if judiciously attended to, contribute to the promotion of the interests of the salt trade, and to the advancement of the art of its manufacture. This salt, chemically denominated muriate of soda, has been known and in common use as a seasoner of food, from the earliest ages: sometimes it is called SAL GEM and SEA SALT, but in this country the term salt is usually applied to it without any addition. Common salt is a compound body, formed by the union of an acid, and an alkali, viz muriatic acid and soda; hence it is denominated by the new nomenclature—muriate of soda. The nature of its acid was first discovered by Glauber, and is the same with what is vulgarly called Spirit of Salts; the nature of its base has more recently been discovered by Sir H. Davy. In the year 1807, this distinguished chemist ascertained by a series of the most splendid experiments, that the base of common salt is a metallic oxide, to which, when freed of oxygen, he gave the name of SODIUM. The properties of this new metal are very singular and striking: it is as white as silver, has great lustre, and is a conductor of electricity. It enters into fusion at about 200° Fahrenheit, and rises in vapour at a strong red heat. Its specific gravity is 9.5, water being 10; thus it will be seen, that this curious metal is lighter than water.—When heated strongly in oxygen gas, it burns with great brilliancy, and after the combustion, soda is again produced. When thrown upon water it effervesces violently, but does not inflame, (as is the case with potassium, the base of potash, also discovered by Sir H. Davy) swims on the surface, gradually diminishes with great agitation, and renders the water a solution of soda.—Such are the striking properties of one of the constituents of common salt; equally remarkable are those of the other, but, as chemists themselves are not agreed concerning its real nature, I decline going into the detail of its properties. Considering the vast quantity of common salt found native in this county, and the facility and economy with which it is extracted, one feels peculiarly interested for the discovery of a process, which shall effect, at a cheap rate, its decomposition, with a view to the separation of its alkali. The more, indeed, we reflect on this subject, the more the importance of such a discovery appears. There is annually imported into this country from Spain, upon an average, 8622 tons of barilla (impure subcarbonate of soda) which is consumed principally in the manufacture of English soap: now this takes an enormous capital every year from us to enrich our less deserving neighbours; not only so, but makes us in some measure dependent on them for this essential article, for in the event of a declaration of hostilities at any time betwixt the two countries, there will be either an entire scarcity, or the price of barilla will amount to a prohibition of its use—such, indeed, has been the case. On these occasions we have recourse to substitutes, the consequence of which is the production of a worse article, though manufactured at a higher price. Here then is a strong case presented to us for the exercise of our inventive faculties, strengthened and confirmed by the fact, that common salt, a product almost peculiar to this county, contains more than half its weight of pure soda! It ought not to be concealed, that attempts have been made, though unsuccessful, for the accomplishment of this valuable desideratum; by unsuccessful attempts I mean, that the methods discovered for the separation of the soda of common salt, are not in a commercial point of view, sufficiently economical, though at the same time I must honestly declare what is my firm opinion, that hitherto the subject has not received the considera-it so imperatively demands. This indifference may probably be owing to the oppressive operation of the duty on salt, and whenever the period shall come for the removal of this excessive impost, I have no doubt means will soon be devised, by the present improved state of

chemistry, to furnish soda from common salt, at a rate infinitely below that which is now required for its importation. A principal difficulty in the way of our arriving at the most economical means of decomposing common salt, is the ignorance under which we labour of the real nature of muriatic acid, so far having resisted all our attempts at decomposition. We cannot, (by theoretical reasoning) until this is removed, suggest any means by which the combined muriatic acid may be destroyed; and until its constitution be correctly ascertained, we can only seek to discover some cheap substance that will effect the decomposition of salt by double affinity, The late Bishop Watson suggested the propriety of ascertaining, "Whether the alkaline part of rock salt may not be obtained by calcining it in conjunction with charcoal, in open fires." The experiment in consequence has been made by many, but without success, owing no doubt to the indestructibility of muriatic acid. That illustrious Swedish chemist, Scheele, did, indeed, by mere accident discover, that common salt is decomposed, and its soda separated, by being kept in contact with quicklime: and to me this appears the cheapest method hitherto devised, for the purpose under consideration, though no extensive application has yet been made of the fact. He prepared a mass, consisting of unslacked quicklime, moistened with a solution of common salt, and placed it in a moist cellar; in fourteen days afterwards, the surface was covered over with carbonate of soda, which was scraped off, and the remainder left in the cellar. In another fortnight, more alkali was formed on the surface, which was likewise removed from the mass. Water was then poured on what remained, and it was well stirred and filtered. The solution had a strong taste of lime-water, on which account it was allowed to stand a few days in the open air, by which means the lime was precipitated. To determine with more certainty, whether the lime was all precipitated, the solution was tested with muriate of mercury (corrosive sublimate) when it remained colourless. The whole was again filtered, and a solution of carbonate of soda added to it, by which a considerable quantity of carbonate of lime was thrown down. By these experiments, it is clearly demonstrated, that muriate of soda is decomposed by quicklime when thus employed, and new combinations formed, the muriatic acid leaving the soda, and attaching itself to the lime, producing muriate of lime, whilst the soda on being separated, meets with carbonic acid (which is always present in considerable quantities in cellars,) producing carbonate of soda.

CAUSES OF DELIQUESCENCE.

Besides muriate of soda, there is constantly found in rock salt, the muriates of lime and magnesia, which being deliquescent salts, are the causes of that dampness we some times perceive in common salt, when the latter has not been freed of them. Muriate of soda, in its PURE state, is not altered by exposure to the atmosphere; so that when we notice the contrary to be the case, it is owing to admixture with foreign bodies. A ready way of ascertaining whether common salt contains any earthy muriates, is to dissolve about two drams in a wine glass full of distilled or clear rain water, and add to the solution a few drops of another of carbonate of soda, when if any of the foreign salts are present, a white cloud will be visible in the mixture. It is now well known, that the purest and best salt is that made in Cheshire, as will be seen by the following table:—

GENERAL STATEMENT OF SOME OF THE RESULTS OF DR. HENRY'S EXPERIMENTS, ON VARIOUS KINDS OF COMMON SALT.

1000 Parts, by weight of each kind of Salt.	Insol. Matter.	Earthy Muriates.	Sulph. Lime.	Sulph. Magnesia.	Total Impurities.	Pure Muriate of Soda.
St. Ubes Bay Salt	9	3	23½	4½	40	960
Oleron Salt	10	2	19½	4¼	35¾	964¼
Scotch, from Sea Water	4	28	15	17½	64½	935½
Common Lymington ..	2	11	15	35	63	937
Cheshire crushed Rock	10	0¼	6½	....	16¾	983¼
Ditto for the Fisheries ..	1	1	11¼	....	13¼	986¾
Ditto Common	1	1	14½	....	16½	983½
Ditto Stoved	1	1	15¼	....	17¼	982¾

From the few observations here made, the following inference may be very justly drawn, viz. that the acquirement of chemical knowledge ought to be a most essential and paramount consideration with every individual at all concerned in the salt trade of this country—that, contemplating the many important applications resulting from the nature of common salt, whether in that state, or in the uses of its constituents, the advantage which must inevitably accrue from the discovery of a process effecting its economical decomposition, and the extreme plenty with which nature has favoured

this county in particular; I must repeat, that it ought to be an object of the first consideration with the proprietors of salt works, to make themselves perfectly acquainted with every well established principle of chemical philosophy.*

The following is the average strength of the different brines from experiments made:—

Winsford brine.—This brine contains 25.312 per cent. of pure muriate of soda; and in an ale pint of it there are 6 oz. 1 dr. of this salt. It contains 2.500 per cent. of earthy salts.

Leftwich brine.—This brine contains 21.250 per cent. of muriate of soda; and 4 oz. 15 dr. of this salt in an ale pint of it. Of earthy salts it contains only .625 per cent.

Northwich brine,—contains 25.312 per cent. of muriate of soda, and in an ale pint 6 oz. 1 dr. The earthy salts in it amount to 1.562 per cent.

Witton brine,—contains 23.125 per cent. of muriate of soda, and in an ale pint 5 oz. 7 dr.; the earthy salts in it amount to 1.562 per cent.

Anderton brine.—The brines raised in different parts of Anderton vary in strength from 25 to 26.566 per cent. and contains from 6 oz. to 6 oz. 6 dr. in an ale pint.—The earthy salts amount to 1.875 per cent. The strongest of the brines here has a greater specific gravity than a saturated solution of muriate of soda in pure water.

Lawton brine.—This brine contains 25.312 per cent. of muriate of soda; and in an ale pint of it, there are 6 oz. 1 dr. of this salt. Of earthy salts it contains 1.560 per cent.

Roughwood brine.—This brine has a greater specific gravity than a saturated solution of muriate of soda in pure water. It yields 25.625 per cent. of muriate of soda; and an ale pint of it contains 6 oz. 2 dr. of this salt. The earthy salts in it amount to 2.490 per cent.

Wheelock brine.—This contains 25 per cent. of muriate of soda, and an ale pint of it contains 6 oz. The earthy salts are .625 per cent.

Middlewich brine.—This contains 25.625 per cent. of pure muriate of soda, and an ale pint of it 6 oz. 2 dr. of this salt. The proportion of earthy salts contained in it, is only .625 per cent.

Experiments.—On examining the brines by re-agents, it was found that—

1. All the brines gave immediately a copious white precipitate on the addition of muriate of barytes.
2. On the addition of oxalic acid, there was a precipitation in each of them.
3. On the addition of a few drops of tincture of galls, a slight purple tinge was given to the Anderton, Witton, and Northwich brines; and after standing a few hours, there was a good deal of brown sediment at the bottom of the phials. A similar addition to the Winsford, Lawton, Roughwood, Wheelock, and Middlewich brines, produced no immediate change. After standing some hours, there was in each of them a very slight brown sediment.
4. All the alcalies fixed and volatile, threw down an abundant white precipitate in each of them.

The first and second experiments indicate sulphate of lime; the third shews the presence of iron in the brines. Those in the neighbourhood of Northwich contain more iron than the others; but even in these it is very inconsiderable in quantity. The precipitate thrown down on the addition of carbonated kali, was found to consist of a mixture of carbonate of lime, and carbonate of magnesia: principally the former.

It is perhaps needless to dilate on the valuable qualities of Salt as a manure. In a work of this nature, devoted to general history, particular instances of its effects even as an article of FOOD FOR CATTLE, may not be looked for: but I cannot refrain from noticing the testimonies of the first farmers this or any other country produces, in favor of this most valuable and plentiful

* I am indebted for these interesting remarks, on the Chemical habitudes of Common Salt, to Mr. S. Leet, of Chester.

product of the county of Chester. The name of CURWEN alone, is in itself sufficient to recommend the use of Salt to the Agricultural World.*

CHEESE MAKING.

The making of Cheese, forms a most important feature in the History of Cheshire, and impressed with this consideration, I shall enter at some length into the operations of the Dairy. It is supposed, that there are about 93,000 or 94,000 cows kept in Cheshire, for the purpose of the Dairy, from which, averaging the quantity of cheese made from each cow, at 250lbs. we shall have annually 9,791 tons, or 23,500,000lbs.

Mr. Fenna gives a produce of 11,500 tons from 92,000 cows, which is equal to 300lbs. per ann. per cow.

It need scarcely be premised, that much depends on the selection of the Cows, as connected with profit to the pocket of the farmer. It has been stated, that the points of a good milker are—a large thin skinned udder; large milk veins, shallow and light fore-quarters, wide loins, a thin thigh, a white horn, a long thin head, a brisk and lively eye, fine and clean about the throat; these, however, are mere points of opinion, and after all, a good milker is generally ill shaped: but it is found by experience, that those cows which possess an aptitude to fatten, are seldom if ever profitable milkers.† Mr. Holland remarks, in his Survey, "That an exact uniformity does not prevail, in every part of the process, is no wonder; for there is not any of the business which is conducted in a dairy, that tends in the least to chemical exactness. Where there is no precision, there can be no just comparison; and where no comparison can be made, there exists no foundation for an attempt at uniformity. The degree of heat at setting the milk together, is never measured; the quantity of steep is

* The Salt Duties have long been an intolerable burthen not only on the Agricultural Interests of the County, but on those of the Kingdom in general—and to their amelioration has the farmer long looked forward, with anxious expectation, but with little hope of eventual gratification. A brighter prospect now presents itself—more cheering results are anticipated;—there prevails an almost unanimous opinion, that their continuance will be prejudicial to the well being of the Country at large. On the 20th Jan. 1818, a Meeting was held at Northwich to take the subject of the pressure of the Salt Duties into consideration—it was attended by nearly EIGHT THOUSAND persons—and the result was the adoption of a Petition to the Legislature, praying for a repeal of them. A copy of it is subjoined; and it is confidently hoped, that its prayer will be attended to.—Sir T. Bernard has "done good service" in illustrating the necessity of their repeal, in several able pamphlets:—

To tha Hon. the Commons of the United Kingdom of Great Britain and Ireland, in Paliament assembled.

The humble Petition of the Nobility, Gentry, Clergy, Freeholders, and Farmers, of the County Palatine of Chester,

SHEWETH,

That your Petitioners have learnt with great satisfaction, that the consideration of the Salt Duties is to be revived in your Honorable House, in the course of the ensuing Session of Parliament. That your Petitioners humbly submit, that the excessive Duties imposed upon Salt, are very injurious to the Agriculture, Manufactures, Trade, and Fisheries of this Country; and are particularly oppressive on the Occupiers of Dairy Farms, of which this County is principally composed; and in which the greater part of the Salt used throughout the Kingdom is produced. That from experiments already made, the use of Salt for Agricultural objects, is likely to be attended with the most beneficial effects; but the allowance of Salt for those purposes granted in the last Session of Parliament, is charged with so heavy a Duty, and clogged with so many perilous restrictions, that Farmers cannot avail themselves of the liberty offered. That the burthen of the Salt Duties on the Poor is so heavy, as to take from the laborer a great proportion of his weekly earnings. That a Tax thirty times greater than the intrinsic value of the article Taxed, presents to the minds of the poor and indigent, irresistable temptations to Fraud and Theft, and occasions the prevalence of Crimes to an alarming and increasing extent. Your Petitioners therefore humbly pray, that your Honorable House will take their case into your most serious consideration, and grant such relief as to your Honorable House shall seem fit.

† The Lysons, in a note, observe, that the cows in Cheshire are now housed in the winter, although they are not in many other counties, and in some districts much celebrated for the excellency of their cheese, as the Vale of Glocester, North Wiltshire, Berkshire, &c. The richest and best cheese made in Cheshire, is said to be produced from land of an inferior nature; but the greatest quantity from the richest land. Amongst the places and districts most celebrated for making the prime cheese, may be reckoned the neighbourhood of Nantwich for a circuit of five miles; the parish of Over; the greater part of the banks of the river Weaver; and several farms near Congleton and Middlewich, among which, Croxton Hall farm has been particularly mentioned.

guessed at, and its quality not exactly known; the quantity of salt necessary is undefined; and the *sweating* or fermenting of the cheese, when made, is accidental. Under these circumstances, we cannot help expressing, by the way, a wish that a cheese farm of experiment might be established in this county, under the patronage of the Board of Agriculture, and under the management of a person well skilled in chemistry, that something like scientific principles might be discovered, on which to conduct the process." Cheese is generally made with two meal's milk, and that in dairies where two cheeses (each averaging 60lbs.) are made in a day. In the beginning and end of the season, three, four, and even five or six meal's milk are kept for the same cheese. It is difficult to say what proportion of the cream is withheld from the milk, before it is put together; the quantity may be varied, either through supposed judgment and skill in the art, or from other motives. The general custom, however, in the best dairies, is to take about a pint of cream, when two meal cheeses are made from the night's milk of twenty cows. In order to make cheese of the best quality, and in the greatest abundance, it is admitted that the cream should remain in the milk; but whether the cream that is once separated from it, can by any means be again so intimately united with it, as not to undergo a decomposition in the after process, admits of some doubt. There is, at least, no absurdity in attempting to prevent the separation of the two bodies, which it is our professed intention to unite again. If a cheese, made entirely of the night's milk, on which the cream has risen, be as rich as one made of new milk, all other circumstances being alike, it is a proof that milk and cream, after being separated, may, by heating only, become, as it were, new milk again. Experiment alone can decide this point; but the practice here is to unite the milk and cream; and the dairy-men say, that when so united, it differs not from new milk, as to the purposes of cheese making."

It would occupy too much room to go into detail on the general process of Cheese making adopted in this county: but the curious may be amply gratified on this subject, by a perusal of Mr. Wedge's Agricultural Report of the county,—or by reference to Mr. Holland's Survey.

Strabo says, the Britons were ignorant of the Art of Cheese-making, but there is little doubt, but what the historian, in this instance at least, was incorrect. Some of our old writers, borrowing the same erroneous idea, assert with similar improbability, that we are indebted to the Romans for the introduction of this highly useful art. It is likely, however, that the manufacture of Cheese, was known to the earliest inhabitants of the island. Fuller, in page 68, of his "Worthies," quaintly says, "This county (Cheshire) doth afford the best Cheese, for quantity and quality, and yet the cows are not (as in other shires) housed in the winter; so that it may appear strange that the hardiest kine should make the tenderest cheese. Some essayed in vain to make the like in other places, though from thence they fetched both their kine and dairy-maids: it seems they should have fetched their ground too (wherein is surely some occult excellency in this kind) or else so good cheese will not be made. I hear not the like commendation of the butter in this county, and perchance these two commodities are like stars of a different horizon, so that the elevation of the one, tends to the depression of the other."

POTATOES.

This invaluable vegetable is cultivated to a very great extent in this county,—formerly neglected and despised, it is now looked upon as an essential article upon every table—and certainly may be classed amongst the necessaries of life. Four times a greater extent of ground is now occupied by it, than it called for thirty years ago—and perhaps it is raised at an earlier period in Cheshire, than in any other county in England. Lancashire, also, has a great breadth of land laid down with potatoes, but the Manchester and Liverpool markets are very largely supplied with this vegetable, from the Northern parts of this county. Manchester, in particular, has an immense supply from the vicinity of Altrincham, and from Frodsham; and Liverpool from the hundred of Wirral, which possesses a soil admirably calculated for its production.—The produce varies in different parts of the county, according to situation.—The following account of the cultivation of potatoes in Wirral, was originally written by the Rev. R. Jacson, of Bebington—a gentleman to whom the county is under obligations for his example as an Agriculturist, and his activity as a Magistrate:* "From the situation, of the hundred of Wirral, between the estuaries of the Mersey and Dee, the climate of this district is mild and temperate, and particularly favorable to the cultivation of potatoes. The immediate vicinity of Liverpool, creating a large demand for this vegetable, has given rise to an improved mode of raising the early kinds, which deserves the attention of the practical agriculturist. The following is the method pursued:—The potatoes designed for the sets are got up in September or October, or even before; the sooner after they are mature, the better; and in November are laid up in a warm dry room, where they are spread rather thinly, not more than two, or at most three potatoes in thickness, and covered with wheat chaff, or dry sand. They are further protected from frost, whenever it is necessary, by a blanket or rug spread over them. By this mode of management, they are generally well sprit by the month of February or the beginning of March; if this should not be the case, the sprouting is accelerated by sprinkling them from time to time with a little water. A potatoe is said to be well sprit, when it has a shoot from two to four inches long, as thick as a small quill, and terminated by two little leaves. In this state they are planted whole: all the shoots being cut off, excepting one, as early in February as the season will allow; they are set not more than five or six inches asunder, the tops just within the ground. As long as there is any danger from an exposure to the frosts, they are carefully protected by a covering of straw or peas-haum; which is taken off in the day, unless the weather be extremely severe, and put on again at night. By this management, potatoes are now as plentiful in the Liverpool market, in the middle of May, or even sooner, as they were, before it was practised, in the middle of June. At the same time, the culture of this vegetable is productive of very considerable profit to the farmer; a second crop being in almost every instance, raised from the same land in the same year. The land is always manured for potatoes in Wirral, except a naturally rich spot, or one that has some time before been well manured, is allotted to the early crop. Under these favorable circumstances, both this crop, and that which is allowed to come to maturity, are generally much better in kind than is otherwise the case. The early kinds of patatoes, held in most estimation in this district, are the early Manleys; the Fox's seedlings; the Broughton's dwarfs; and some other sorts; all of which it must be remarked never blossom: the kinds usually grown for the winter crop, are the pink eye, the ink eye, the Scotch white, the ox-noble, &c. Besides these, there are some very good sorts ripe in August or September, and continuing fresh till Christmas: to these, various names are given, but it seems probable that they were all originally from the same stock; and that any difference now found among them, is the result of differences in the mode of their culture, or of varieties produced from the same species. The crop of those potatoes, which acquire their full growth, varies in this district, from 150 to 250 bushels of 90lb. each, on a statute acre. The pink eyes generally give the smallest, the ox-noble the largest produce. Considerable quantities of the early potatoes are sent to the Manchester and Chester markets, as well as to Liverpool. Good eating potatoes sell for 1s. 6d., 2s., and in the spring for 3s. per bushel; the ox-noble for 1s. or 1s. 6d. The early potatoes vary very much in price. When they are first brought to market, they are sometimes as high as 2s. 6d. per lb.; and, as the season advances, sink gradually down to 1d. The practice of giving potatoes to cattle, &c. in Wirral, is not so general as, of itself, to afford any inducement to their culture. Where they are given, it is generally in the raw state: sometimes, however, they are boiled by steam for this purpose."—Mr. Wedge, of Sealand, near Chester, in his Agricultural View, says—The method of raising early potatoes was first practised by one Richard Evans, of Wallasey, in Wirral. "The secret consists in nothing more than in transplanting the sets, which should be of the earliest kind, during winter; carefully guarded from the frost, in a warm place, where they may sprout at least three inches by the beginning of March. As soon after that time, as the weather happens to be favorable, they are, with the sprout on, to be carefully planted in a dry soil, in drills, with a small rib of earth between each drill, and the end of the

* The Rev. Mr. Jacson, is Chairman for the County Quarter Sessions, held in Chester.

CHESHIRE

HISTORY.

sprout just under the surface of the ground. The plants should be kept covered with straw, or rushes, every night as long as the frost continues, and uncovered every favorable day." Potatoes, thus early raised, are frequently sold in Chester Market so high as 4s. per lb. which price has gradually diminished, in the progress of the Season, to A HALFPENNY. A friend of mine has raised potatoes still earlier, by the simple process of placing the sprouts in flower-pots, in a compost of tanner's knaps (exhausted bark), old horse manure, and common soil: and then putting them in his hot-house. Many thousands of bushels are now annually exported (if I may bē allowed the term in a limitted acceptation) to the Welsh coast, from this county, and in particular from the hundred of Wirral, and from the neighbourhood of Frodsham.

Holland's Survey.

COMMON POTATOE CULTURE IN CHESHIRE.—Independently of the particular districts, which have on been mentioned, the cultivation of the potatoe is carried to a great extent in every part of Cheshire; both on the more considerable farms, and on the small spots of ground attached to the cottage of the laborer—Where potatoes are set by the cottager for the early supply of the market, a bank sloping to the east, or south east, is usually selected for this purpose; and much pains is taken to guard the crop from the spring frosts, which, in the course of a few hours, will frequently blacken, and destroy every leaf that has appeared above the surface of the ground. Probably if a southern, or south western bank, was substituted, which would be less exposed to the influence of the morning sun, the frosts would be less destructive, and the crops earlier and more abundant. It is with vegetable as with animal life; effects highly injurious are produced by sudden changes in the action of the vessels, whilst no evil is experienced when such changes are made by a more gradual operation.—The mode of potatoe culture usually pursued by the cottager varies but little.—A space is left between the beds, proportioned to their width and to the depth of the soil, that the plant may be covered as soon as it appears above the surface.—This is generally done by the cottager with a spade, and is esteemed of the most essential service to the crop: it preserves the early kinds from the frost; and by adding soil to the beds, gives encouragement to the potatoe to form near the surface, where the best are always found. For eradicating the couch grass, a fork is usually employed, being less apt than the spade to divide the creeping fibres of the couch. Where the cottager is in possession of a pig or cow (which is now much more generally the case than formerly), the manure obtained from these is put upon his potatoe ground; or, if he lives near a high road, his children are employed in collecting the dung from the passing horses; in short, every article that can be scraped up is applied to his crop of potatoes, Turf ashes, I am informed, have been used with considerable success in a moist season; but they are apt to make the potatoes scabby; pig dung is esteemed one of the best manures for this crop. The common method of keeping potatoes, during the winter, is to pile them up in heaps of considerable size, for which a foundation has been previously secured by a small excavation made in the ground. These heaps are covered with straw and mould, and sods are laid over as a superficial covering to the whole. The contracts by the cottager, for the land on which he cultivates his potatoes, are of various kinds. In some instances, he has it rent free for the year, on condition of laying on a sufficient quantity of manure: in others, the cottager furnishes the manure, which is carried, and the land prepared by the farmer; the former planting and attending to the crop while in the ground, and paying a higher or lower rent, according to the value of the land. If these agreements are properly adjusted, no better or more profitable system of husbandry can be pursued. The cottager is accommodated with land for potatoes (a circumstance which adds materially to the comforts of his situation); while the farmer has an excellent preparation for a future crop, either of wheat or barley, wishout the necessity of an unprofitable fallow.

[In my notice of the beneficial qualities of Salt, in page 57, the following letter should have been introduced as referential to the interesting and important subject. It was addressed by Mr. Curwen, to Mr. S. Brittain, of Upton, near Chester, and was read by Mr. Brittain at the Meeting at Northwich, on the 20th

January, for the purpose of petitioning Parliament to repeal the Salt Duties :—

"WORKINGTON-HALL, JAN. 10, 1818.

"SIR,

"Feeling as I do on the subject of the Salt Tax, you could not have done me a greater pleasure than to have called on me for a detailed statement of the experiments I have undertaken in giving salt to my stock. I have always viewed the Salt Tax as not less oppressive on the laboring classes, than impolitic and grievous, as it affected agriculture and our fisheries. The only persons interested in its continuance are those who enjoy the monopoly, and the tax-gatherers. If fairly proposed, the public would willingly commute the duty and give the million and a half that arises from it. The tax taken off salt, the consumption would double in the space of one year. These were my sentiments before I had an opportunity of confirming them by a trial of the effect of salt. I commenced the use of salt about six weeks ago, giving four ounces per day to my milch cows and oxen, above a hundred in number; three ounces to young cattle, and two to calves; four ounces to horses, and two to sheep. To milch cows the salt is given in steamed chaff. It makes them take with avidity two stone per day of this very inferior food. The cattle are all in high health. On the milk it has had a very powerful effect; though the cows have eight stone of turnips a-day, there is no longer any taste of the turnips; various experiments have been made, and it does not appear there is the least taste remaining of the turnip. On those horses which are fed with steamed potatoes a very striking improvement appears since the salt was given: the horses clear their own cribs so completely, that no attention to them is now required. The dung which was formerly very fetid, is now perfectly sweet. I am strongly of opinion that salt will both increase the quantity of milk, and accelerate the fattening of animals: whatever promotes digestion, must increase the appetite of the animal. The sheep crowd round the shepherd, and will take the salt from his hand. It has made all the young animals so familiar, that they come to my call, and take the salt mixed with bran out of my hand. The general health of all the stock disposes me to think most favorably; the next effect will, I apprehend, shew itself in the casting of the animals. In many cases I would express a fear that my enthusiasm might mislead my judgment; not so on the present occasion. For one and all of the people concerned with the stock witness to the benefit they conceive already received. Finally, I wish your example of petitioning for the repeal of the duty may be followed by every town in the empire. Justice and policy are on the side of the repeal, and if strenuously followed up, it must succeed. The public are greatly indebted to Sir Thomas Bernard. We ought to have carried the investigation of the business last Session; I trust we shall in the present.

"I am, SIR, &c.

"J. CURWEN."]

Grand Stand, Chester Race Course; erected by Subscription, in the year 1817.

Population Return, 1811.

Hundreds, Parish, Township, or Extra-Parochial Place.	Families Employed: Agriculture.	Families Employed: Manufactures.	Families Employed: Various employ.	Persons: Males.	Persons: Females.	Total of Persons.
BROXTON, High Div.						
Aldford, Parish: *						
Aldford† .... Township	46	8	23	204	187	391
Churton by Aldford Township	25	6	9	100	95	195
Bunbury Parish:‡						
Burwardsley ...... Township	52			125	125	250
Coddington, Parish:						
Aldersey .... Township	19	6		74	83	157
Chowley .... Township	11			31	37	68
Coddington ...... Township	7	2	7	59	74	133
Farndon, Parish:						
Barton .... Township	19	8	6	89	88	177
Churton by Farndon, Towns.	18	7		58	70	128
Clutton .... Township	12	3		38	46	84
Crewe............ Township	5	1	1	18	20	38
Farndon.......... Township	14	16	41	165	172	337
Handley, Parish:*						
Handley.......... Township	39	11	2	106	109	215
Harthill .... Parish	22	7	1	89	131	220
Kingsmarsh Extra-Parochial	6			24	16	40
Malpas, Parish:						
Agden............ Township	17		2	60	40	100
Bickerton........ Township	57	10		165	143	308
Bickley .... Township	51	15	13	204	215	419
Bradley .... Township	10			31	32	63
Broxton .... Township	49	9	2	165	166	331
Bulkeley.......... Township	29	5	1	82	83	165
Chidlow .... Township	2			5	7	12
Cholmondeley .... Township	42	3		116	135	251
Chorlton .... Township	14	2		39	55	94
Cuddington ...... Township	33	8	6	107	118	225
Duckington ...... Township	8	1	6	40	32	72
Edge .... Township	48			119	157	276
Egerton .... Township	10	5	2	52	59	111
Hampton .... Township	33			95	95	190
Larkton .... Township	11			33	31	64
Macefen.......... Township	9	1	1	25	29	54
Malpas .... Township	21	74	107	478	460	938
Newton .... Township	1		1	9	7	16
Oldcastle .... Township	16			42	52	94
Overton .... Township	16		1	49	52	101
Stockton .... Township	4	2		10	18	28
Tushingham.... with Grindley } Township	38	3		100	116	216
Wichalgh .... Township	4			16	14	30
Wigland .... Township	23	11	1	73	95	168
Shocklach, Parish:						
Caldecot.......... Township	11		1	30	26	56
Shocklach, Church Township	23	5	2	73	83	156
Shocklach, Oviatt Township	29			70	85	155
Tilston, Parish:						
Carden .... Township	27	5	6	85	98	183
Grafton .... Township	1			9	8	17
Horton .... Township	11	1	9	59	57	116
Stretton .... Township	8	1	7	44	57	101
Tilston .... Township	24	7	35	146	148	294
	975	243	293	3811	4026	7837
BROXTON, Lower Div.						
Aldford, Parish:‖						
Boughton, Great Township	86	58	13	307	353	660
Buerton .... Township	10			26	30	56
Churton Heath .. Township	1			4	3	7
Christleton, Parish:						
Christleton ...... Township	87	13	10	288	272	560
Cotton Abbots.... Township	1	1		11	11	22
Cotton Edmunds.. Township	11	1		35	40	75
Littleton .... Township	6	1		24	20	44
Rowton.......... Township	14	1	1	30	39	69
Dodleston, Parish:						
Doddleston ...... Township	36	4	2	117	112	229

* Partly in Broxton Hundred, Lower Division.---† Including Edgerley.---‡ The greater part of Bunbury Parish is in Eddisbury Hundred, First Division.---‖ Partly in Broxton Hundred, High Division.

CHESHIRE POPULATION RETURN, 1811.

Hundreds, Parish, Township, or Extra-Parochial Place.	Families Employed: Agriculture.	Manufactures.	Various Employ.	Persons: Males.	Females.	Total of Persons.
BROXTON, Lower Div. continued.						
Kinnerton Lower Township	16	1		46	49	95
Eccleston, Parish:						
Eaton .... Township	4		2	26	28	54
Eccleston ...... Township	28	6	11	137	129	266
Guilden Sutton, Parish	24	1	1	62	58	120
Handley, Parish:*						
Golborn-David .. Township	4		7	27	31	58
Mary, St. Parish:†						
Gloverstone‡ .... Township						
Marlston with Leach ...... Township	20	1	1	49	61	110
Moston .... Township	1			1	5	6
Upton .... Township	26	2	2	93	89	182
Oswald, St. Parish:†						
Bach .... Township	2			6	15	21
Huntington .... Township	16			61	63	124
Lea-Newbold .... Township	6	1		28	30	58
Newton .... Township	7	7	11	43	85	128
Saighton .... Township	9	4	36	124	123	247
Wervin .... Township	10	1		33	34	67
Plemonstall, Parish: ‖						
Caughall .... Township	2			9	9	18
Hoole .... Township	30	3	7	88	125	213
Pickton .... Township	14	1		53	47	100
Mickle-Trafford.. Township	37	14	1	123	125	248
Pulford, Parish:						
Poulton.......... Township	18	4	2	66	66	132
Pulford .... Township	12	4	21	83	88	171
Tarvin, Parish: §						
Foulk-Stapleford.. Township	31	8	11	130	113	243
Tattenhall, Parish:						
Golborn-Bellow.. Township	13	3		35	40	75
Newton.......... Township	11			33	33	66
Tattenhall ...... Township	144			331	337	668
Waverton, Parish:						
Hatton .... Township	23	1		74	73	147
Huxley .... Township	30	7		102	110	212
Waverton........ Township	44	8	1	133	130	263
	834	156	140	2,821	2,993	5,814
BUCKLOW.						
Ashton-upon-Mersey, Par.						
Ashton-upon-Mersey Towns.	95	57	14	467	451	918
Sale .... Township	92	67	7	445	456	901
Bowden, Parish:						
Agden, part of ¶ Township	10	3		52	38	90
Altrincham ...... Township	82	276	57	973	1,059	2,032
Ashley .... Township	51	7		178	172	350
Baguley .... Township	51	16	12	237	227	464
Bollington part of ¶ Towns.	25	18	4	118	115	233
Bowden.......... Township	46	18	8	195	208	403
Carrington ...... Township	27	49	8	239	241	480
Dunham-Massey.. Township	126	15	28	467	469	936
Hale .... Township	97	48	21	467	462	929
Partington ...... Township	26	44	4	203	209	412
Timperley........ Township	93	30		323	301	624

Hundred, Township, Parish, or Extra-Parochial Place.	Families Employed: Agriculture.	Manufactures.	Various Trades.	Persons: Males.	Females.	Total of Persons.
BUCKLOW—continued.						
Budworth, Great Parish:**						
Anderton .... Township	9	37		97	123	220
Antrobus......... Township	63	4	14	179	206	385
Aston............ Township	19	4	43	210	192	402
Barnton .... Township	27	62	17	241	239	480
Bartington ...... Township	13	1		39	42	81
Budworth, Great Township	36	59	16	233	271	504
Cogshall .... Township	11	[illegible]		[illegible]	[illegible]	[illegible]
Comberbach...... Township	16	16	4	88	75	163
Crowley.......... Township	2	1		68	71	139
Dutton .... Township	47	7		165	148	313
Hull and Appleton Township	105	149	4	571	602	1,173
Leigh, Little .... Township	48	10	14	158	182	340
Marbury .... Township	3	2	3	22	19	41
Marston .... Township	21	39	7	177	172	349
Peover, Little.... Township	9	9	5	50	49	99
Pickmere .... Township	27	4		85	83	168
Plumley.......... Township	63	4		191	176	367
Seven Oaks...... Township	19	7		70	77	147
Stretton.......... Township	26	16	4	123	110	233
Tabley, Inferior.. Township	16	5		68	61	129
Whitley, Lower.. Township	30	5		120	113	233
Whitley, Over .. Township	35	14	2	130	136	266
Wincham........ Township	50	22	8	229	191	420
Grappenhall, Parish:						
Grappenhall .... Township	57	8	5	182	179	361
Latchford........ Township	95	94	7	426	518	944
Knutsford, Parish;						
Bexton .... Township	8	1		27	31	58
Knutsford, Nether Township	26	276	173	993	1,121	2,114
Knutsford, Over., Township	14	37	3	103	140	243
Ollerton.......... Township	40	2	4	117	112	229
Toft .... Township	27	6	5	102	109	211
Lymm .... Parish ..	123	193	30	923	985	1,908
Mobberley .. Parish ..	180	54	2	606	546	1,152
Rosthern, Parish:						
Agden, part of..†† Township						
Bollington, part of†† Towns.						
Leigh, High .... Township	118	33	10	419	441	860
Martall with .. Warford ...... Township	42	7		130	140	270
Mere .... Township	61	21	22	288	280	568
Millington ...... Township	27	20	1	109	176	285
Peover, Superior Township	68	13	6	241	239	480
Rosthern .... Township	21	32	16	130	120	250
Tabley, Superior Township	59	10	14	221	188	409
Tatton .... Township	15		10	57	73	130
Runcorn, Parish:						
Acton Grange .. Township	15	5		73	62	135
Aston Grange .... Township	4			13	16	29
Aston juxta Sutton Township	31	4		82	85	167
Clifton, alias .. Rock Savage .. Township	2			18	18	36
Daresbury ...... Township	6	16	2	47	67	114
Halton .... Township	65	102	10	463	431	894
Hatton .... Township	49	9	5	144	127	271
Kekwick .... Township	11			29	32	61
Moore .... Township	28	4	3	91	95	186

* Partly in Broxton Hundred, High Division.—† For the greatest part of St. Mary's and St. Oswald's, see Chester City, at the end of the County.—‡ The site converted into Barracks.—‖ Partly in Eddisbury Hundred, Second Division.—§ The greatest part of Tarvin Parish is in Eddisbury Hundred, Second Division.—¶ Partly in Rosthern Parish: but the whole is entered here.—** Part of Great Budworth Parish is in Northwich Hundred, part in Eddisbury Hundred. †† Agden and Bollington are partly in Bowden Parish, and are there entered.

CHESHIRE POPULATION RETURN, 1811.

Hundreds, Parish, Township, or Extra-Parochial Place.	FAMILIES Employed.			PERSONS.		
	Agriculture.	Manufactures.	Various Employ.	Males.	Females.	Total of Persons.
BUCKLOW---continued.						
Newton by Daresbury .. Township	17			57	57	114
Norton .... Township	24	5	1	110	111	221
Preston on the Hill Township	13	53	4	196	185	381
Runcorn .... Township	34	339	27	948	1112	2060
Stockham........ Township	6			23	15	38
Sutton.......... Township	12	11	26	131	134	265
Thelwall .... Township	60	5		167	159	326
Walton, inferior . Township	35	15	7	131	154	285
Walton, superior.. Township	22	9	11	83	92	175
Weston .... Township	23	15		90	99	189
WARBURTON. .... Parish	52	33	2	235	235	470
	3034	2562	710	15933	16473	32403
EDDISBURY, First Div:						
BUDWORTH, LITTLE Parish	66	23	6	230	240	470
BUNBURY, Parish :*						
Alpraham .... Township	32	16		161	172	333
Beeston .... Township	57	8	11	195	215	410
Bunbury........ Township	78	42	1	294	280	574
Calveley .. .. Township	34	4		97	104	201
Haughton........ Township	22	3	1	69	69	138
Peckforton ...... Township	34	11	10	143	138	281
Ridley .... Township	8	2	6	67	56	123
Spurstow .... Township	65	11		180	193	373
Tilston Fearnall.. Township	26	3		75	70	145
Tiverton .... Township	62	28		249	244	493
Wardle .... Township	11	8	10	70	62	132
MIDDLEWICH, Parish :†						
Weever .... Township	22	6		67	64	131
OVER, Parish :						
Oulton, Low .... Township	6			32	30	62
Over .... Township	37	33		938	858	1796
Wettenhall...... Township	42	5	288	126	142	268
TARPORLEY, Parish :						
Eaton .... Township	76	8	4	197	172	369
Rushton .... Township	42	10	4	141	144	285
Tarporley........ Township	36	93	28	317	384	701
Utkinton ..... Township	80	16		262	235	497
WERBURGH, St. Parish :						
Iddinshall ...... Township	2			8	10	18
WHITEGATE, or NEW CHURCH Parish :						
Darnhall .... Township	18	9	3	90	85	175
Marton .... Township	111			251	265	516
	987	339	372	4,259	4,232	8,491
EDDISBURY, Second Division.						
BARROW, Parish:						
Barrow Great and Little .. Township	95	5		299	286	585
BUDWORTH GREAT, Parish:‡						
Castle-Northwich Township	2	15	73	230	192	422
Hartford .... Township	69	22	55	309	358	667
Winnington .... Township	6	31	5	89	103	192
FRODSHAM, Parish :						
Alvanley .... Township	56			142	145	287

Hundreds, Parish, Township, or Extra-Parochial Place.	FAMILIES Employed.			PERSONS.		
	Agriculture.	Manufactures.	Various Trades.	Males.	Females.	Total of Persons.
EDDISBURY 2d. Div. continued.						
Frodsham ...... Township	170	72	37	662	687	1,349
Frodsham ...... Lordship	100		37	375	381	756
Helsby.......... Township	41	2	10	144	153	297
Kingsley .... Township	121	14		318	338	656
Manley .... Township	23	5	25	139	123	262
Newton .... Township	13	3		52	48	100
Norley.......... Township	66	11	2	193	198	391
INCH........ Parish	61	23	1	203	223	426
PLEMONSTALL, Parish:‖						
Bridge Trafford.. Township	9	2	1	27	40	67
TARVIN, Parish :§						
Ashton .... Township	46	20	29	169	196	367
Bruen-Stapleford Township	34	2		100	98	198
Burton .. Township	12			37	40	77
Clotton Hoofield.. Township	52	13		145	167	312
Duddon .... Township	37	8		120	123	243
Hockenhull .... Township	3	2		21	19	40
Horton with Peele Township	3	2		18	21	39
Kelsall.......... Township	57	36	9	300	257	557
Mouldsworth .... Township	24	4		61	64	125
Tarvin.......... Township	95	6	27	461	460	921
THORNTON Parish :						
Dunham .... Township	19	10	23	143	146	289
Elton .... Township	25	3		85	80	165
Hapsford........ Township	12	3		47	45	92
Thornton in the Moors ...... Township	25			76	82	158
Wimbolds Trafford Township	20			43	60	103
WHALLEY, Parish :						
Willington ...... Township	17			52	57	109
WEAVERHAM, Parish :						
Acton .... Township	35	14		140	123	263
Crowton .... Township	66	9		186	169	355
Cuddington...... Township	32	10	3	105	112	217
Onston .... Township	9	2		35	25	60
Wallerscoat...... Township	1			3	2	5
Weaverham with Weaverham .... Township	84	70	64	559	561	1120
	1537	474	392	6,088	6,182	12270
MACCLESFIELD.						
ALDERLEY, Parish :						
Alderley, superior Township	66	8	1	204	220	424
Alderley, inferior Township	57	23	15	277	264	541
Warford, great .. Township	36	20	7	154	174	328
ASTBURY, Parish :¶						
Somerford Booths Township	49			134	133	267
CHEADLE, Parish :						
Cheadle-Bulkeley Township	36	393	52	1225	1284	2509
Cheadle-Moseley.. Township	62	179	19	578	718	1296
Hansforth, with Boxden .... Township	49	207	3	628	687	1315
GAWSWORTH.... Parish	115	5	1	377	380	757
MOTTRAM-IN-LONGDENDALE Parish :						
Godley .... Township	9	71		216	235	451
Hattersley ...... Township	11	80		229	244	473
Hollingsworth Township	8	186	4	569	520	1089

* Part of Bunbury Parish is *in* Broxton High Division.—† The greatest part of Middlewich Parish is in Northwich Hundred.—‡ Part of Great Budworth Parish is in Bucklow Hundred, part in Northwich Hundred.—‖ The greatest part of Plemonstall Parish is in Broxton Hundred.—§ Part of Tarvin Parish is in Broxton Hundred. ¶ The greatest part of Astbury Parish is in Northwich Hundred.

CHESHIRE POPULATION RETURN, 1811.

Hundreds, Township, Parish, or Extra-Parochial Place.		FAMILIES Employed. Agriculture.	Manufactures.	Various employ.	PERSONS. Males.	Females.	Total of Persons.
MACCLESFIELD CONTINUED.							
Motley	Township	5	46		152	159	311
Mottram in Longdendale	Township	2	267	3	710	736	1446
Newton Moor....	Township	13	253	4	732	713	1445
Stayley	Township	11	216	2	592	512	1104
Tintwistle	Township	25	189		662	684	1346
PRESTBURY Parish: *							
Adlington	Township	46	129	1	472	468	940
Birtles	Township	6	1	1	15	17	32
Bollington	Township	74	140	71	727	791	1518
Bosley	Township	74	21		246	236	482
Butley with Newton	Township	67	53	3	308	327	635
Capesthorne	Township	5		6	38	32	70
Chelford	Township	17	4	6	97	91	188
Eaton..........	Township	31	6		117	111	228
Fallibroom	Township	6			13	12	25
Henbury with Pexall	Township	55	10	1	189	196	385
Hurdsfield	Township	16	100	3	351	383	734
Kettleshulme	Township	73	7		188	216	404
Lime Handley ..	Township	38	6		115	132	247
Macclesfield Forest	Township	35	17		150	135	285
Macclesfield*....	Township						
Marton	Township	44	9		162	158	320
Mottram Andrew	Township	29	4	37	168	181	349
Newton..........	Township	11	10		57	51	108
Poynton	Township	16	60	10	244	253	497
Pott Shrigley	Township	8	20	39	168	162	330
Prestbury........	Township	29	35	17	203	212	415
Rainow	Township	107	164	24	753	842	1595
Rode, North	Township	37	6		122	118	240
Siddington	Township	58	15	6	237	211	448
Sutton Downs and Wicell	Township	125	302	1	930	1166	2096
Tytherington ...	Township	19	39	1	172	183	355
Upton	Township	7	2		28	39	67
Wildboar Clough	Township	48	31		197	195	392
Wincell	Township	40	35		198	230	428
Withington Lower	Township	81	14	13	297	287	584
Withington Old ..	Township	24	3		81	97	178
Woodford	Township	30	36		179	197	376
Worth	Township	11	26	9	122	132	254
ROSTHERN, Parish: †							
Snelson..........	Township	17	3	2	57	61	118
STOCKPORT, Parish:							
Bramhall	Township	34	152	6	555	579	1134
Bredbury........	Township	37	283		82	885	1706
Brinnington	Township	14	330	3	771	934	1705
Disley	Township	34	240	9	707	708	1415
Duckinfield......	Township	16	405	81	1476	1577	3053
Etchells	Township	59	125	44	651	625	1276
Hyde	Township	11	302	4	884	922	1806
Marple	Township	33	396	6	1062	1192	2254
Norbury	Township	40	62	21	233	218	451
Northenden	Township	64	60	9	275	333	608
Offerton	Township	20	65	1	235	258	493
Romily	Township	17	168	1	521	494	1015
Stockport	Township	153	3304	106	7977	9568	17545
Torkington	Township	15	22	7	113	141	254

Hundreds, Parish, Township, or Extra-Parochial Place.		FAMILIES Employed. Agricultural.	Manufactures.	Various Employ.	PERSONS. Males.	Females.	Total of Persons.
MACCLESFIELD CONTINUED.							
Wernith	Township	19	214	8	649	655	1304
TAXALL, Parish:							
Taxall	Township	34	5		86	96	182
Whaley with Yeardsley	Township	19	8	23	136	151	287
WILMSLOW, Parish:							
Bolled Fee	Township	61	265	6	851	904	1755
Chorley..........	Township	37	43		206	220	426
Fulshaw	Township	15	31	1	100	132	232
Pownal Fee	Township	84	126	7	626	671	1297
		2653	1057	703	33775	36848	70623
NANTWICH.							
ACTON, Parish:							
Acton	Township	26	14	12	147	140	286
Aston juxta Mondrum	Township	22	2	1	72	74	146
Austerson	Township	6			28	29	57
Baddington	Township	12	2	1	64	49	113
Brindley	Township	22	5		74	79	153
Burland	Township	93	27	6	230	204	434
Cholmondeston	Township	10		23	95	94	189
Cool Pilate......	Township	5			20	23	43
Eddleston	Township	15	3		39	45	84
Faddiley	Township	35	13		122	119	241
Henhall	Township	6	7		27	30	57
Hurleston........	Township	12	3	15	86	90	176
Newhall	Township	140	31	2	423	436	859
Poole	Township	28	4		84	92	176
Stoke............	Township	22	8		66	74	140
Worleston	Township	43	17		150	144	294
AUDLEM, Parish:							
Audlem	Township	192	52	2	512	528	1040
Buerton	Township	60	10	3	209	220	429
Dodcot cum Wilkesley ‡	Township	80	27	12	308	314	622
Hankelow........	Township	23	12	7	109	107	216
Sound	Township	40	4		91	116	207
Tittenley	Township	5			18	25	43
BADDI EY	Parish	42	16		147	141	288
BARTHOMLEY, Parish:							
Alsagar	Township	56	13	2	173	177	349
Barthomley	Township	71	8		231	234	465
Crewe	Township	42	6	4	140	140	280
Haslington	Township	160	21		456	466	922
COPENHALL, Parish:							
Copenhall Church	Township	44	5	2	133	133	266
Copenhall Monks	Township	20	2		57	57	114
MARBURY, Parish:							
Marbury with Quoisley	Township	49	19	6	196	195	391
Norbury	Township	61	20		190	197	387
MINSHULL Church,	Parish	59	18		120	138	258
NANTWICH Parish:							
Alvaston	Township	3		1	21	12	33
Leighton	Township	38			87	69	156
Nantwich........	Township	90	609	152	1875	2124	3999
Woolstanwood ..	Township	5		2	24	24	48
SANDBACH, Parish: ‖							
Bechton	Township	97	28	11	354	347	701

* The Town of Macclesfield is entered at the end of the County.—† The greatest part of Rosthern Parish is in Bucklow Hundred.—‡ Partly in Wrenbury.—‖ The greatest part of Sandbach Parish is in Northwich Hundred.

CHESHIRE POPULATION RETURN, 1811.

Hundreds, Parish, Township, or Extra-Parochial Place.		FAMILIES Employed. Agriculture.	Manufactures.	Various Employ.	PERSONS. Males.	Females.	Total of Persons.
NANTWICH---CONTINUED.							
SANDBACH, Par.—continued.							
Hussall	Township	30	1	1	102	103	205
WHITCHURCH, PARISH :*							
Wirswall	Township	10	1	4	53	59	112
WISTASTON	Parish :	39	11	5	144	151	295
WRENBURY, Parish :							
Bramhall..	Township	25	1		82	84	166
Chorley	Township	29	1		88	98	186
Dodcot with .. Wilkesley †..	Township						
Woodcot.........	Township	4	1		12	14	26
Wrenbury with Frith	Township	49	30	19	234	221	455
WYBUNBURY, Parish :							
Batherton	Township	2	1		15	14	29
Basford	Township	7	3		33	31	64
Blakenhall	Township	31	2		119	100	219
Bridgemere......	Township	30	10		105	103	208
Checkley, with Wrinehill ..	Township	26	2	3	66	86	152
Chorlton........	Township	15	3	2	51	39	90
Doddington	Township	5	3	2	28	34	62
Hatherton	Township	56	12		165	214	379
Hough	Township	18	20	4	117	121	238
Hunsterson	Township	35	3	1	93	107	200
Lea	Township	5	6		34	39	73
Rope	Township	13	3		48	42	90
Shavington .... with Gresty	Township	36			92	107	199
Stapeley	Township	42	7	1	117	144	261
Walgherton......	Township	27	16	2	101	105	206
Weston	Township	54	24	2	212	214	426
Willaston	Township	23	9	6	107	107	214
Wybunbury......	Township	37	32	16	174	177	351
		2384	1207	323	9568	10000	19568
NORTHWICH.							
ASTBURY, Parish :‡							
Buglawton	Township	79	35		283	301	584
Congleton........	Township	158	750	78	2023	2593	4616
Davenport	Township	14		1	41	48	89
Hulme Walfield ..	Township	13	1	1	61	57	118
Moreton Alcomlow	Township	15	5		73	67	140
Newbold Astbury	Township	77	30	9	292	304	596
Odd Rode	Township	93	73	18	494	509	1003
Radnor	Township	2			6	6	12
Smallwood	Township	60	11	16	257	239	496
Somerford	Township	1[illegible]	2	5	62	52	114
BRERETON with SMETHWICK ..	Parish	101	5		303	284	587
GREAT BUDWORTH, Parish :‖							
Allostock	Township	71	8		24[illegible]	222	462
Birches..........	Township	1			6	6	12
Holse...........	Township	6	1		21	21	42
Lach Dennis	Township	5			29	21	50
Lostock Gralam..	Township	42	15	26	226	227	453
Northwich	Township	14	181	117	650	732	1382
Peover Nether ..	Township	25	14	4	118	120	238
Witton with .. Twambrook	Township	54	313	75	983	983	1966

Hundreds, Township, Parish, or Extra-Parochial Place.		FAMILIES Employed. Agriculture.	Manufacturer.	Various Employ.	PERSONS. Males.	Females.	Total of Persons.
NORTHWICH CONTINUED.							
CHURCH LAWTON..	Parish	19	67	4	242	246	488
DAVENHAM, Parish :							
Bostock	Township	28	3	1	98	109	207
Davenham	Township	42	30	2	161	156	317
Eaton...........	Township	1			6	7	13
Leftwich	Township	77	61	67	518	461	979
Moulton	Township	18	15	2	85	102	187
Newall..........	Township	2			5	5	10
Rudheath	Township	53	4		145	158	303
Shipbrook	Township	11	1		44	40	84
Shurlach	Township	8	1	1	28	29	57
Stanthorne	Township	2	2		68	66	134
Wharton	Township	15	144	8	449	439	888
Whatcroft........	Township	8		1	33	38	71
MIDDLEWICH, Parish :							
Byley with Yate House	Township	21		1	62	73	135
Clive...........	Township	22			54	64	118
Croxton	Township	4	1		26	29	55
Kinderton with Hulme......	Township	31	21	37	212	237	449
Middlewich.. ...	Township	2	228	37	551	681	1232
Minshull Vernon..	Township	63	3		125	130	255
Mooresbarrow with Parme..	Township	3			12	15	27
Newton	Township	41	106	140	585	616	1201
Occlestone	Township	14	1		39	47	86
Ravenscroft......	Township		2		2	2	4
Sproston	Township	9	11	1	74	70	144
Stublach	Township	11			25	29	54
Sutton	Township	5			14	14	28
Wimboldsley	Township	17	3		62	67	129
SANDBACH, Parish :§							
Arclid	Township	8	3	4	40	42	82
Blackden	Township	21	2	3	73	79	152
Bradwell	Township	39	2	1	117	141	258
Church Hulme ..	Township	8	46	17	174	172	346
Cotton	Township	3	11	2	38	43	81
Cranage	Township	12	64	5	188	199	387
Goostrey with Barnshaw ..	Township	19	24	5	133	128	261
Leese	Township	7	12		63	63	126
Sandbach........	Township	117	368	36	1146	1165	2311
Twemlow	Township	16	4		78	74	152
Wheelock........	Township	25	42	1	160	169	323
SWETTENHAM, Parish :							
Kermincham	Township	25			89	84	173
Swettenham	Township	41			116	111	227
WARMINGHAM, Parish :							
Elton...........	Township	61	9		179	198	377
Moston..........	Township	19	13		83	79	162
Tetton	Township	18	14		80	77	157
Warmingham	Township	42	12	3	165	180	345
		1885	2774	730	12815	13726	26541
WIRRAL, HIGHER DIV.							
BACKFORD, Parish :							
Backford	Township	26	3	2	76	70	146
Chorlton	Township			12	26	27	53

* The greater part of Whitchurch Parish is in Salop (North Bradford Hundred).—† Partly in Audlem Parish, where the whole is entered.—‡ Part of Astbury Parish is in Macclesfield Hundred.—‖ Part of Great Budworth Parish is in Bucklow Hundred—part in Eddisbury Hundred.—§ Part of Sandbach Parish is in Nantwich Hundred.

CHESHIRE POPULATION RETURN, 1811.

Hundreds, Parish, Township, or Extra-Parochial Place.	FAMILIES Employed. Agriculture.	Manufacture.	Various Employ.	PERSONS. Males.	Females.	Total of Persons.
WIRRAL HIGHER DIVISION CONTINUED.						
Lea .... Township	11	2		51	39	90
Mollington, Great Township	21			48	65	113
BROMBOROW .... Parish *	28	7	9	114	105	219
BURTON, Parish:						
Burton .... Township	44	9	5	149	151	300
Puddington ...... Township	19	2	2	75	72	147
EASTHAM, Parish:						
Eastham .... Township	61	9	1	156	169	325
Hooton.. .... Township	16	2	2	58	51	119
Pool, Nether .... Township	1		1	15	14	29
Pool, Over, ... Township	10	3	3	37	34	71
Sutton, Great .... Township	25	2		88	78	166
Sutton, Little .... Township	36	8		103	16	219
Thornton, Childer Township	8	13	2	43	53	96
Whitby.. .... Township	30	2		38	37	75
HOLY TRINITY, Parish: †						
Blacon with Crabhall .... Township	6			30	24	54
MARY, ST. Parish: †						
Mollington, Little Township	3			13	13	26
NESTON, Parish:						
Ledsham .... Township	13	1		41	34	75
Leighton .... Township	30	15	12	104	183	287
Ness ...... Township	49	2	1	293	169	462
Neston, Great .... Township	20	200	109	609	723	1332
Neston, Little .... Township	56			117	126	243
Raby.. .... Township	22		2	83	67	150
Thornton Mayow Township	25	4	7	87	92	179
Willaston........ Township	41			89	92	181
OSWALD'S ST. Parish: †						
Croughton ...... Township	3			17	13	30
SHOTWICK, Parish:						
Cappenhurst .... Township	25	1	1	70	95	165
Saughall, Great .. Township	47	9	1	155	149	304
Saughall, Little .. Township	4	1	4	32	32	64
Shotwick .... Township	17			44	37	81
Woodbank, alias Rough Shotwick Towns.	6	3		25	18	43
SHOTWICK PARK, Extra-Par.	2			18	11	24
STANLOW HOUSE, Extra-Par.	1			7	5	12
STOKE, Parish:						
Stanney Great .... Township	3			10	6	16
Stanney Little, .. Township	20	7	11	95	134	229
Stoke .... Township	18	1	3	51	65	116
	748	306	190	3,062	3,169	6,231
WIRRAL, LOWER DIV.						
BEBBINGTON, Parish:						
Bebbington, Higher Towns.	17	11	5	93	98	181
Bebbington, Lower Towns.	24	22	12	125	154	279
Poulton with Spittle Towns.	16		1	38	45	83
Storeton .... Township	22	5	5	98	81	179
Tranmere ...... Township	29	31	34	208	266	474
BIDSTON, Parish:						
Bidston with Ford Township	30	6		101	97	198
Birkenhead...... Manor	4	7	7	52	53	105
Claughton with Grange ...... Township	12	2		43	45	88

* Partly in the Lower Division of this Hundred.—† The greatest part of the Holy Trinity, St. Mary's and St. Oswald's Parishes, is in the City of Chester.—‡ Partly in the Higher Division of this Hundred.—‖ Part of St. Mary's and St. Oswald's Parish, is in Broxton Hundred, part in Wirral Hundred.—§ Part of the Holy Trinity Parish is in Wirral Hundred.—¶ In Prestbury Parish.

Hundreds, Parish, Township, or Extra-Parochial Place.	FAMILIES Employed. Agriculture.	Manufacture.	Various Employ.	PERSONS. Males.	Females.	Total of Persons.
WIRRAL, LOWER DIVISION CONTINUED.						
Moreton .... Township	37	3		105	125	230
Saughall Massey.. Township	19		2	58	59	117
BROMBOROW, Parish: ‡						
Brimstage .... Township	21	5		68	55	123
HESWALL, Parish:						
Gayton.. .. .... Township	14	4	1	60	55	115
Heswall with Oldfield Towns.	59			166	157	323
THURSTASTON, Parish:	14		1	23	[illegible]	[illegible]
UPTON, or OVER CHURCH .... Parish	15	6	5	80	83	163
WALLAZEY, Parish:						
Liscard .... Township	40	7	7	171	118	289
Poulton with Seacomb ...... Township	15	4	23	105	109	214
Wallazay .... Township	65	16	13	174	266	440
WESTKIRBY, Parish:						
Caldey, Great.. and Little .. Township	14	1		51	47	98
Frankby .... Township	18			44	49	93
Grange.......... Township	14			47	46	93
Greasby .... Township	18	4		56	57	113
Hoose .... Township	1	16	3	52	48	100
Meolse, Great... Township	22	2	4	71	77	148
Meolse, Little .... Township	25			50	35	85
Newton with Larton Towns.	7			28	22	50
Westkirby ...... Township	28	9	1	59	82	141
WOODCHURCH, Parish:						
Arrow .. .. Township	13	1		45	37	82
Barnston........ Township	23			54	56	110
Irby .... Township	19	2		54	56	110
Landican........ Township	5	1		20	27	47
Noctorum ...... Township	2			6	8	14
Oxton .... Township	22	5		70	58	128
Pensby.......... Township	4			10	17	27
Prenton.......... Township	13		6	42	42	84
Thingwell ...... Township	12	1		36	39	75
Woodchurch .... Township	7	6		42	34	76
	720	171	130	2,610	2,738	5,348
CHESTER, CITY:						
Bridget, St. .... Parish	22	112	22	297	436	733
Cathedral Church Precinct Little St. John Extra-Par.		15	32	83	150	233
John, St. Baptist .. Parish	17	477	456	1958	2286	4244
Martin, St. .... Parish	47	108	21	269	413	682
Mary, St. upon-the-Hill ‖ .... Parish	40	382	153	1139	1330	2469
Michael, St. .... Parish		96	57	250	405	655
Olave's, St .... Parish	56	33	10	158	223	381
Oswald's, St. ‖ ...... Parish	151	587	21	1547	1869	3416
Peter, St. .... Parish	5	176	7	382	551	933
Spittle-Boughton . Extra-P.	24	13	2	71	99	170
Trinity, Holy and Undivided § .... Parish	35	297	271	853	1371	2224
	397	2296	1052	7,007	9,133	16140
MACCLESFIELD TOWN ¶	244	2458	26	5,629	6,670	12299

SUMMARY—CHESHIRE POPULATION RETURN, 1811.

HUNDREDS.	FAMILIES EMPLOYED.			PERSONS.		
	Agriculture.	Manufactures.	Various employ.	Males.	Females.	Total of Persons.
BROXTON	1,809	399	433	6,632	7,019	13,651
BUCKLOW	3,034	2,562	710	15,930	16,473	32,403
EDDISBURY	2,524	813	764	10,347	10,414	20,761
MACCLESFIELD	2,653	10,057	705	33,775	36,848	70,623
NANTWICH	2,382	1,207	323	9,568	10,000	19,568
NORTHWICH	1,885	2,774	7	12,815	13,726	26,541
WIRRAL	1,468	477	320	5,672	5,907	11,579
CITY OF CHESTER	397	2,296	1,152	7,007	9,133	16,140
MACCLESFIELD TOWN	244	2,458	26	5,629	6,670	12,299
LOCAL MILITIA*	....	....	....	3,466	....	3,466
TOTAL	16,396	23,043	5,003	110,841	116,190	227,031

* The Chester (or First Regiment of Cheshire) Local Militia, was assembled for fourteen days' service, on the 15th May, 1811, to the number of 1,332, Officers included. The Stockport Regiment was assembled on the 20th May, to the number of 1,111. The Macclesfield Regiment on the 27th May, to the number of 1,023.

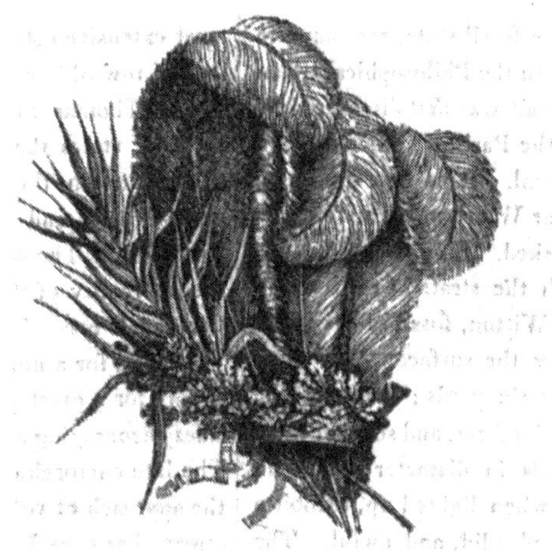

Brown, del. Mosses, sc.

Curious carved Door-post, Dean's-stall, Chester Cathedral.

Natural History, Minerals, &c.

CHESHIRE HISTORY.

BEDS of salt, and coal, in a fossil state, are found in many parts of the County. In the Philosophical transactions it is said, that rock salt was first discovered by accident, near Marbury, in the Parish of Budworth, in 1670, whilst searching for coal. It is now found in great abundance in and near Wincham, Marston, and Witton, where pits are worked. Sulphate of lime is generally found mixed with the strata of earth above the beds of rock salt. At Witton, fossil salt is found about forty-two yards below the surface. The usual depth of the salt pits is thirty-six yards; many of the mines are worked into a circular form, and some of them are near three hundred yards in diameter; those in the vicinity of Northwich, when lighted up, exhibit a scene at once interesting, splendid, and awful. The analysis of the different brines is noticed in page 57. Lysons.

Coal is found in great plenty in numerous parts of the County, and particularly on the North-east side of it, in the townships of Adlington, Bollington, Hurdsfield, Norbury, Pott-Shrigley, Poynton, Worth, &c. It is from the collieries in these places, that Macclesfield, Stockport, and Manchester, are supplied with this article so essential to manufacturing purposes. One of the most extensive collieries in the kingdom, is at Dennah, in the township of Ness, near Parkgate, the property of Sir Thomas Stanley Massey Stanley, Bart. Mr. Holland states the stratum of coal to be from five feet to six feet in thickness. It extends from high water mark a mile and three quarters under the bed of the river Dee! The coal as it is procured, is carried from the extremity of the mine in boats, the colliery having two canals beneath. These works were first opened in 1750, and for a number of years furnished a plentiful supply for a great part of the Hundred of Wirral, besides encouraging a considerable export trade to Ireland. The late encroachment of the sands, however, prevents the approach of vessels of burden; the trade in consequence has considerably decreased, and it is now carried on in flats and barges, when the tides afford facility for approach.

The Sand-pits in Cheshire (says the Author of the Survey), are frequently accompanied with a very curious phenomenon. At Mere, near the seat of Peter Brooke, Esq. I saw a sand-pit, containing the fragments of pit coal, and cinders, deposited in a stratified manner thro' a considerable extent of the bank. I have observed the 1808.

CHESHIRE

same appearances at Mobberley, near Knutsford. The above fragments of coal and cinders lay six or seven feet below the surface of the earth; and I have lately been informed by a gentleman of that neighbourhood, that such appearances are not peculiar to the sand beds of Mere and Mobberley, but that they are almost universal wherever sand-pits are dug in Cheshire. On these remarks, Sir John Thomas Stanley, Bart. in the way of NOTE, observes, "The small fragments and thin layers of coal, which are often found in beds of sand and other strata in Cheshire, have evidently been brought from a distance, and deposited by the same floods or torrents which have deposited the sand. The quantity is two insignificant to be worthy of any attention, otherwise than as the smallest quantity of any substance must prove that a portion of the same substance has had an existence in the place from which it had been originally conveyed. So many changes have taken place on the sarface of the country over which the water depositing the strata of Cheshire has flowed, that it would be now impossible to ascertain where the substances forming the strata were detached from their primary positions. The colliery at Pott Shrigley, produces coal of a superior description; and the beds at Poynton and Worth offer an almost inexhaustible supply.

Veins of Copper and Lead have been found at Alderley Edge, at a considerable altitude; and a strata of sand stone three or four yards in thickness, which is separated by those above and below by thin seams of marl, occasionally tinged with a slight colouring of copper.—In the formation of this singular hill, there are three or four divisions of the strata of sand stone They extend across from west to east, and are intermixed with masses of sulphate of barytes, running through which are many veins of lead and copper. Lead-ore has also been found, but like the copper much blended with the grit or sand stone. Cobalt has also been met with;* and the veins of all these metals have been found to ramify with increasing richness, at a depth from thirty to forty yards. The author of the Survey observes, that in all probability, they extend much further into the body of the hill. A Shropshire gentleman, named Abbadine, about a century ago, cut a tunnel a yard wide, and five feet high, through a great part of the hill, at the depth of thirty yards from the summit. On arriving at the centre, he found that the valuable part of the ore was much below the level he was working on, and he abandoned his scheme. Various attempts at the same speculation have subsequently been made. Mr. Rowe, of Macclesfield, embarked in the attempt. He was sanguine of success, and employed nearly fifty persons in the enterprise. The Pary's Mine, in Anglesea, however, was discovered about this time, and Mr. Rowe, being engaged in this also, withdrew his workmen for the new scheme, which promised more productive results. About 1806, a few veins of good ore were unexpectedly discovered at the extremity of the old works. Several Gentlemen of Stockport, soon joined in a speculation, smelting works were erected, and the mine has been long worked in a successful manner. Lead and copper ore have been found at Mottram St. Andrew, on lands belonging to L. Wright, Esq. and on the Peckforton Hills, on the estate of John Egerton, Esq. (now Sir John Grey Egerton, Bart.) At the latter place, works were commenced, at considerable cost, but the expectations which had been indulged in, failing, the attempt was given up. Sir J. T. Stanley, Bart. notices the discovery of Cobalt Ore at Alderley Edge, in 1807, in these words:—"It is found near the surface in very thin veins or filaments in rock or sand-stone, often contiguous to veins of copper and lead ore; it is of a very dark blue colour, and many specimens appear like nothing more than grains of sand adhering together; some of the veins are of a much richer quality than others: the cobalt in all of them appears intimately mixed with lead, iron, copper, and manganese; a considerable quantity of cobalt procured from the mines at Alderley Edge, has been conveyed to Ferry Bridge, in Yorkshire, where it has been manufactured into smalt; little inferior in colour to that imported from Saxony."

* 1807.

HISTORY.

There are several Quarries of excellent Free-stone in Cheshire—those at Manley and Runcorn, are the most considerable. The quarry at Great Bebington, furnished the stone which built Hooton Hall, the beautiful seat of Sir T. S. M. Stanley, Bart. From the quarry at Runcorn,—Liverpool, Manchester, and other places in the way, have plentiful supplies. The buildings at

CHESHIRE

Chester Castle, including the magnificent County Hall;* and Eaton-House, near Chester, the splendid seat of Earl Grosvenor, are entirely of stone from Manley Quarry. Near Pott-Shrigley is a firm sand stone, admitting of a good polish. A species of sand stone is met with at Kerridge, on the Hills, near Macclesfield, well adapted for flagging and whetting tools. Previous to the introduction of Welsh slates, it was used to a great extent in this part of the county, for roofing houses, and other buildings, and in this way it is still partially used. Mr. Kirwan, in his Elements of Mineralogy, describes this stone as a silicious grit, with an argillaceous cement, and states its specific gravity at 2.544.

Lime-stone is peculiar to Newbold Astbury, about three miles south of Congleton: great quantities of it are prepared upon the spot. It is much heavier than the lime-stone found near Buxton, and when burnt has more of a grey colour.

Marl is pretty generally found throughout the county, and is used as a manure. Its varieties are distinguished by the names clay-marl, stone-marl, and slate-marl.†

No extraneous fossils have hitherto been found in Cheshire, excepting the trunks of trees, and some vegetable remains, which had undergone but a slight change from their original state.—Woodward notices oak, alder, yew, birch, and fir—the cones of fir, and hazel nuts, as having been found in the mosses near Wilmslow, and in the Forest of Delamere. It is certain that great quantities of oak and fir have been raised from many of them, and used for fuel, &c.—It has been stated, that the fir, slit into thin pieces, has also been used by the indigent as a substitute for candles; but if this practice ever prevailed, it has probably long since been disused.

* The Pillars of the Portico of the County Hall, are particularly worthy of notice. They are twelve in number, each twenty-two feet high, three feet one inch and a half in diameter, and formed of a single stone.

† In the Appendix to Mr Holland's Agricultural Survey, is a very clever paper "On the nature and origin of Marl," by Sir J. T. Stanley, Bart.—Although it possesses great merit, it is too long to transcribe here. The writer observes, that Marl is seldom found as a stratum, or layer of any length; but generally a few feet below the surface, in detached masses of twenty or thirty roods in extent, and eight or ten yards in depth, covered with clay, and resting on a bed of sand or gravel. It has been spread over land in Cheshire for many centuries; and leases granted in the reigns of Edw. I. and II. contained clauses obliging the Tenants to make use of it. It may be interesting to inquire what could possibly have been the origin of Marl. As it obviously consists of an union of the crumbled remains of many of the primary and secondary strata, we shall be obliged to look back to some great deluge, which must have carried along with it, from distances more or less remote, so many different earths from their original respective beds, mixed them in its course, and then deposited them, while in a state of agitation too great for their gradual subsidence according to their distinct and respective gravities. No adequate idea can be formed of the impetuosity of such a flood, for in almost every marl-pit an immense number of stones are found, heaped together in the greatest disorder, many of them a ton weight; and all of them worn round, probably by their attrition against each other, as they were rolled along. They are of all kinds—some of granite, some sand-stone, others whin, and a few lime. From whence could these have been conveyed? No rock of granite or of whin, is now to be found in Cheshire, or in any of the adjacent hills. That such rocks have existed, their fragments prove beyond a doubt; but they have disappeared. The ground which we now contemplate, must be considered as a new creation formed from the wreck of an ancient world, different under every aspect, with hills where we now have vallies, and vallies where we now have hills. How far the devastation extended—whether this formidable revolution was partial, or common to a great portion of the globe, must be left to conjecture. It is probable that it was accompanied by Earthquakes which overthrew the existing masses of solid rock; but no subterraneous heat seems to have acted with sufficient force, to re-consolidate the materials into stone; such as must have occurred during, or subsequent to the general deluge, of which we have an account in the Scriptures. One thing remains to be considered—that if marl is an assemblage of the ruins of ancient works (and we must admit the fact as self-proved) it may have retained qualities fit for the improvement of land, which clay, sand, and lime acquired, when they first became indurated. The subjection of any substances to a violent heat, alters their nature in a great degree. It is a well known fact, that the vegetation at the base and on the side of volcanoes, is exceedingly luxuriant, whenever a sufficient time has been allowed for the thorough decomposition of the lava, and it seems by no means improbable that marl may have derived some of its qualities from a similar action on its component parts. However this may be, the inquiry is interesting in a philosophical point of view, and is gratifying to curiosity.

HISTORY.

CHESHIRE

GRASSES, FIELD PLANTS, &c.

Almost every description of grass is to be found in Cheshire, but not sown with any economical attention. The following may be noticed as generally prevalent.

Meadow Fox-tail Grass—*alopecurus pratensis.*
Meadow fescue grass—*festuca pratensis.*
Smooth stalked Meadow grass—*poa pratensis.*
Rough stalked Meadow grass—*poa trivialis.**
Sweet scented vernal grass—*authoxanthum odoratum.*†
Crested dog's-tail grass—*cynosurus cristatus.*
Field fox-tail grass—*alopecurus agrestis.*
Rough cock's-foot, or orchard grass—*dactylis glomerata.*‡
Meadow soft grass—*Holcus lanatus.*‖
Tall oat grass—*avena elatior.*
Meadow cat's tail, or Timothy grass—*phleum pratense.*
Annual Meadow or Suffolk grass—*poa annua.*
Couch grass—*triticum repens.*
Running grass, or—*fiorin.*§
Perennial clover—*trifolium medium.*
Tufted Vetch—*vicia cracca.*¶
Yellow rattle, or penny grass—*rhinanthus crista galli.*
Meadow vetchling—*lathyrus pratensis.*
Bird's-foot trefoil—*lotus corniculatus.*
Ragged robin—*lychnis flos cuculi.*
Butter flower—*ranunculus acres.*
Common sorrel—*rumex acetosa.*
Curled dock—*Rumex crispus.*
Cow weed—*chaeryphyllusor sylvestre.*
Yarrow—*Achillea millefolium.*
Ragwort—*Senecio Jacobæa.***
Way thistle—*senatula arvensis.*
Spear, or bur thistle—*carduus lanceolatus.*
Knapweed—*Centaurea nigra.*
Cockle—*agrostemma githago.*
Corn poppy—*papaver rhœas.*
Ox-eye, or great daisy—*chrysanthemum leucanthemum.*
Corn-marigold—*crysanthemum segetum.*
Corn camomile—*anthemis arvensis.*
Rape, or cole seed—*brassica napus.*
Charlock, or wild mustard—*sinapis arvensis.*
Colt's-foot—*tussilago farfara.*
Ladies' mantle—*Alchemilla vulgaris.*
Cow parsnip—*heracleum sphondylium.*
Meadow sweet—*spiræa ulmaria.*
Bistort—*polygonum bistorta.*

ARTIFICIAL GRASSES.

Red clover, or honey-suckle trefoil—*trifolium pratense.*††
White clover—*trifolium repens.*‡‡
Ray, or Rye grass—*lolium perenne.*‖‖
Hop medick, or trefoil—*medicago lupulina.*§§
Ribwort plaintain, or rib grass—*plantago lanceolata.*¶¶
Saintfoin—*hedys arum onobrychis.*
Lucerne—*medicago sativa.*
Vetches, or tares—*vicia sativa.****

* These are four of the best grasses which this country produces; horses, cows, and sheep, are particularly fond of them. The Bath Society ranks the *poa pratensis* in the highest class.

† This grass is by no means productive, and is common on sandy loams.

‡ This is coarse, but extremely productive. It should be cut early.

‖ Mr. Wilbraham had a field sown with this grass, by mistake: its produce was abundant; but his cows being fed with the hay from it, gave a much less quantity of milk.—(SURVEY.)

§ Much has been said on the valuable qualities of this grass, which some agriculturists estimate as little better than couch grass—however, many very respectable testimonials have appeared in its favor; and the farming journals for the last eight years, have abundant matter, for and against its cultivation.

¶ These are most valuable plants, and produce abundance of seed.

** This grows only on rich soils, but may be considered as worse than useless.—The farmer, notwithstanding, takes a pride in showing it, as a proof of the superiority of his land.

†† This plant is in general cultivation in Holland, and Flanders. It is usually mown for hay, or cut as green food for horses; but little of it, however, is grown in Cheshire.

‡‡ Mr. Fenna says, there is but little land that will suit the white clover; it requires a deep free soil, to bring it to any luxuriance.—(SURVEY.)

‖‖ A good deal of this is sown in Cheshire; a light soil will suit as well as a clay soil.

§§ This is often mixed with clover, to prevent the swelling of cattle.

¶¶ Cattle are not fond of this grass alone; mixed with other herbage, it forms a grateful food.

*** There are two kinds of these: winter and spring vetches. It is thought that the best time for sowing winter vetches, is

RARE PLANTS.

Marsh saxifrage—*saxifraga hirculus.*
Near Knutsford, on a low swampy soil, not 60 yards square.
Marsh cinquefoil—*comoram palustre.*
Buckbean—*Merryanthes trifoliata.*
Early orchis—*orchis mascula.*
Common tway-blade—*ophrys ovata.*
Nodding double tooth—*bidens cernua.*
Cranberry—*vaccinium oxycoccos.*
Brook lime—*veronica becabunga.*
Marsh louse-wort—*pedicularis sylvestris.*
Marsh marigold—*caltha palustris.*
The nine last mentioned plants, were found on the same piece of ground where the marsh saxifrage was discovered.
Water gladiole—*butomus umbellatus.*
In Budworth mere.
Wall cabbage—*brassica murialis.*
South side city walls, Chester, overlooking the Roodeye.
Water feather foil—*Nottonia palustris.*
In ditches near Lachford.
Navel wort—*colyledon umbilicus.*
At Rock Savage.
Frog bit—*hydrocharis morsus sanæ.*
In ponds, near Groppenhall.
Bitter Vetch—*orobus sylvaticus.*
In the woods of Vale Royal, and on the banks of the river Bollin.
Water-bennet—*geum rivale.*
At Capesthorne.
Dusky crane's-bill—*geranium phæum.*
In the meadows, at Ashley.
Herb Paris—*Paris quadrifolia.*
In the woods at Tabley Park.
Middle flea-bane—*inula dysenterica.*
In the neighbourhood of Toft.
Great bladder snout—*utricularia vulgaris.*
In ponds at Mobberley—at Churton Heath.
Fresh water soldier—*stratiotes aloides.*
In ponds at Tabley.
Broom rape—*orobanche major.*
Near Hill-cliff.

The following notices were collected by Mr. Okell, for Messrs. Lysons :

VERONICA SCUTELLATA—on the road between Wrexham and Chester; *Utricularia minor,* in the bogs in Delamere forest; *Menyanthes, nymphoides,* in the bogs in Delamere forest; *Gentiana Pneumonanthe,* on the wastes, near Parkgate; *Gentiana Campestris,* near Hoylelake and Parkgate; *Sison inundatum,* on Backford-heath; *Statice reticulata,* on Hilbree Island; *Drosera Anglica,* on the Marsh, near Holmes Chapel; *Acorus calamus,* near Holford Hall; *Narthecium ossifragum,* on Delamere Forest; *Alisma ranunculoides,* near Tarvin; *Andromeda polifolia,* Delamere Forest; *Saxifraga aizoides,* at Beeston Castle; *Stratiodes aloides,* in the Pools, about 4 miles from Holmes Chapel; *Thalictrum minus,* on the banks of the Dee, below Parkgate; *Lathrea squamaria,* on the side of the river Dane, below Congleton; *Bartsia viscosa,* near Hoylelake; *Cochlearia Danica,* at Parkgate; *Scutellaria minor,* in the bogs in Delamere Forest; *Iberis midicaulis,* Weston hill; *Geranium sanguineum,* on the banks of the Dee, near Parkgate, *Fumaria claviculata,* at Broxton, and Sandiway-head; *Lathyrus Nissolia,* at Blacon Point; *Vicia sylratica,* in the woods near Vale Royal; *Hypericum Androsæmum,* in the woods near Rock Savage; *Senecio Saracenicus,* on the Banks of the Dee, near Eaton House; *Imula Helenium,* at Eccleston; *Viola lutea,* on the hills bordering on Derbyshire; *Orchis conopsæa,* on Knutsford Heath; *Serapias palustris,* at Blacon Point; *Littorella lacustris,* on Little Budworth Common; *Empetrum nigrum,* Congleton Edge; *Pillularia globifera,* on Congleton Moss; *Dianthus deltoides,* near West Kirkby Church.

Under the general head of this division of the Work, I may introduce a brief Notice of the

in the month of September; which gives the farmer sufficient time to prepare his land properly for a crop of wheat and turnips the ensuing season.

CHESHIRE

MINERAL SPRINGS IN CHESHIRE.

The Brine Springs, for which this County is so remarkable, are found chiefly in the vallies through which run the Weaver and the Wheelock,—there are springs, however, at Dirtwich; and one of little consequence at Dunham, on the river Bollin. The author of the Survey correctly observes, that by means of the Brine Springs, an importance is given to the river Weaver, which it would not otherwise possess; and there is probably a greater bulk of carriage on this stream, than on any other river in the island, in itself so little considerable.—Brine springs have been found at Anderton, Aldersey, Austerson, Baddeley, Barnston, Baddington, Brine-pit farm, between Audlem and Nantwich,—Combermere, Dirtwich, Dunham, Hatherton, Hartford, Leftwich, Middlewich, Moulton, Newton, Waverham, Warmingham, &c.—There is a spring at Bug Lawton, containing sulphur, Epsom salts, and calcareous earth, the water of which has been found serviceable in scorbutic cases; at Shaw's-heath, near Stockport, there is a chalybeate spring of some strength.* A pamphlet was published in 1600, under the title "News out of Cheshire, concerning the New-found-Well."—The well here mentioned, was situated about a mile and a half from the Old Pale or Chamber, on the Forest of Delamere, and its medical qualities discovered by J. Greenway, of Utkinton, who being advised by his Physician, to try the effects of some pure spring water, by drinking it, and bathing in it, went to this well, and received wonderful relief. Persevering in this cheap prescription, he was restored to health, and his wonderful cure, together with that of his two sons, who were cured of fits by the use of the water, soon brought great numbers of valetudinarians to this Hygeian Bath. Two pools were filled with its waters for the purpose of bathing—immense numbers assembled from all parts to share its sanative bounties; and it is said that its daily visitors amounted to nearly TWO THOUSAND!—This influx of company induced Mr. Done, the then Chief Forester, to appoint one of his Keepers to preserve order amongst the multitude, and he was permitted to make a regular bathing-place of the spring, by providing entertainment for such as could pay for it.†

HISTORY.

I have now to notice another discovery, which promised the most satisfactory results from several analysis of the waters made by Mr. B. Whittell, of Chester, in the year 1816:‡—The first called Spurstow White Water, is an abundant Spring, on the estate of Sir T. Mostyn, Bart, not far from the village of Spurstow, about three miles from Beeston Castle, the same from Bunbury, and about five from Tarporley. It appears in a field forming part of the rising ground behind the Peckforton Hills. The stratum, out of which it comes, is a red and white clay, containing much gypsum, which has been penetrated into, to the depth of about nine feet. There was formerly a pit or hollow, at the rise of the spring for the convenience of bathing, but through neglect, it was filled up, and formed a sort of little bog, out of which the water forced its way with difficulty.—About sixty or eighty years ago, this water was in considerable repute for the cure of various disorders, and was used both internally and as a bath; and, till lately, crutches and other memoranda of its cures, were deposited in the farm house belonging to the estate. If the water be allowed to remain long in contact with the air, and with vegetable matter, it exhales the smell of sulphurated hydrogen gas, and a pellicle of sulphur is formed on its surface. The ingredients contained in a gallon of the water, are 190 grains of dried solid matter, besides carbonic acid, and perhaps other gases. Of this solid matter about 50 grains appear to be purgative salts, containing about ten grains of the muriates of lime and magnesia. The remaining 140 grains are composed of sulphate and carbonate of lime, the latter constituting about 20 grains of it.||

* Leigh speaks highly of this spring as more powerful than several others which he notices, in Lancashire and the adjoining counties.

† The nature of the water cannot be gathered from the indistinct notice which is given of it. It is supposed to have been cathartic, and is described by the pamphlet, as having "some smatch of an allum-like composition."

‡ From a paper read by Mr. Whittell, before the Chester Philosophical Society, March 8, 1816.

|| See Murray's view of the composition of mineral waters, in No. 35 of Thomson's Journal.

CHESHIRE HISTORY.

HORSELEY BATH.—From Helsby Point to Barnhill, may be traced the same formation of clay and slate, marl and red sand-stone, pushing out at a considerable angle with the horizon, and forming the whole range of hills existing between those two points, as Carden Cliff, Orton's Scar, Bolesworth, Rawhead, Dutton's Hill, Peckforton Hill, Beeston Castle, &c. From under the highest hill which overlooks, and is contiguous to Beeston Castle, the beautiful spring of Horsely rises. It comes immediately out of a red sand-stone rock, and flows into a very capacious bath, from whence it passes off along a hollow ground, forming a small brook or rivulet. Over the fountain head is the following Latin inscription:—

SANITATI SACRUM.

Obstructum referat durum tute humida siccat
Debile fortificat si tamen arte bibis.

This water is so pure and soft, that the people of the neighbouring farm-house are in the constant habit of using it to wash and brew with. A solution of soap mixes with it uniformly and without curdling; salts of silver, barytic salts, and oxalate of ammonia, are very slightly affected by it; lime water considerably so. A pint of the water during evaporation, yielded much air, and left a solid deposit, which collected as accurately as it could be, weighed only a ¼ of a grain. It dissolved with a slight effervescence, in distilled water, and a drop or two of muriatic acid, yielding the same indications with tests as the water itself, with perhaps an extremely minute trace of iron. These experiments prove it to be a most pure and excellent water, nearly equal to distilled water, and resembling the highly celebrated waters of Malvern.

The other spring hitherto unknown—rises about a mile from the last-mentioned spring, and about three and half from the former, from under one of the strata forming the base of Beeston Hill. It is not the surface spring, but pushes up through a very porous red sand-stone. There are altogether, about ten places where this water rises, in a narrow lane, at the top of which stands a farm-house, and a blacksmith's shop. When fresh, this water is clear and pellucid, sparkling with great brightness; it is devoid of smell, but has a strong and sensible chalybeate taste. Half a pint or a pint of the water, proved highly refreshing after a tedious ride, probably owing to the carbonic acid it contained, causing it in some degree, to resemble the artificial soda water. It deposits, on exposure to the air, a ferruginous sediment. It exhibits the following appearances on the addition of tests. Tincture of galls gives an immediate and intense brown or blackish tinge; prussiate of potash is precipitated of a bluish green; lime water is largely precipitated; barytic salts are precipitated: salts of silver yield a whitish precipitate, becoming, in about a minute, brown or chocolate coloured; oxalate of ammonia is considerably affected. These experiments were made on the spot, in an intense light; it is therefore difficult to ascertain and describe the exact shade of color, but the effects of all the tests, were strong and decisive; they indicate the following ingredients:—iron, lime, carbonic acid, muriatic acid, sulphuric acid; but are not adapted to ascertain the presence of a salt with base of alkali, or with base of alumine; or the presence of silicious earth, or that of any other gas than the carbonic acid.—A pint of this water during evaporation, gave out a considerable quantity of fixed air, and deposited an ochery brown powder, which, when the water was about half boiled away, was collected, and weighed about ½ a grain. The boiling being continued till the water was entirely evaporated, a further quantity of the powder of a lighter color was obtained, weighing exactly a grain. The solid contents are therefore 1½ to a pint or 12 grains to the gallon. From these few and imperfect experiments, the water is shewn to resemble the noted waters of Tunbridge, but considerably stronger, as the solid contents of a gallon of Tunbridge water, is only 5 grains.*—Mr. W. recapitulates the names of the three waters, and glances at their chemical properties:—Spurstow White Water, is saline, calcareous, and carbonic, slightly purgative, and perhaps best suited to external use.—Horseley Bath Water, is free from earthy matter, brisk and pleasant from the presence of carbonic acid, and resembles the water of Malvern.—Beeston Spa, similar to the Tunbridge water, but stronger than it, highly chalybeate and tonic, perhaps slightly purgative, and exceedingly refreshing, from the presence of fixed air.

* A solution of Epsom or Glauber's Salts, added to the Beeston Spa, forms a chalybeate resembling the Cheltenham Water.

Mosses, del. et sculp.

Portrait of Sir Piers Dutton, of Hatton (see page 23), on whom was confirmed the advowry of the Cheshire Minstrels by Henry VIII. from a rare painting in the possession of Mr. Gunnery, solicitor, of Liverpool, by whose permission it is copied.

Rivers and Canals.

CHESHIRE HISTORY.

The Chief Rivers of Cheshire, are the Dee, the Mersey, the Weaver, the Bollin, the Dane, the Wheelock, the Peover, and the Tame.

The Dee* is only partially a Cheshire river. It rises in Merionethshire, runs thro' Bala Pool, skirts the counties of Denbigh and Flint, and becomes a boundary to Cheshire near Shocklach and passes by Farndon to Aldford, where it penetrates into the county. It then runs on by Eaton and Eccleston, to Chester, where it is received into an artificial channel, the first sod of which was cut on the 20th April, 1733, and carried on along the marshes under Hawarden Castle, to the estuary, the latter spreading over an extent of sands, in some parts, seven miles in width. The Dee empties itself into the Sea near the little Island of Hilbree. In ancient times, the Dee was a river of high importance, the fleets of several of our Sovereigns have floated on its bosom; but it was ruined as a haven early in the 15th century. In 1449, a Commission of Inquiry was instituted to ascertain the state of the Navigation; and in the middle of the 16th Century,† a new Quay was erected about eight miles from the City. A collection, in the way of BRIEF, was made for the new haven at Chester, in the Churches throughout the Kingdom, in 1560; and in 1567, the City was assessed for the same purpose. The new port was, however, in the end completed, and for a long time, goods and merchandize going to and from Chester, were there taken on board or discharged. The first project for the improvement of the Dee navigation, was suggested by Andrew Yarranton, in 1677, in a work entitled "England's improvement by Sea and Land." At that period

* Called by the Welsh *Dyfrdwy*, the Dee Water.

† In the Harl. MSS. No. 3082, f. 14, is a letter from the Citizens of Chester to the Marquis of Winchester, Lord Treasurer, praying his intercession with the King for a sum of money in aid of the new haven or quay in Wirral, then building, all of stone, "in the face and belly of the sea, which would at least cost £5000. or £6000."

CHESHIRE HISTORY.

we are informed, the river was navigable only for vessels of 20 tons burthen, and those could come up only as high as Neston. He suggested, that an Act of Parliament should be obtained, for improving the navigation of the Dee, and enabling the ships to come up to Chester, by a new channel to be formed out of the river, nearly opposite Neston, passing by Flint, to Chester.—In 1693, another proposal was made by Evan Jones, to make the Dee navigable, so as to permit vessels of 100 tons to be brought to the Roodee. He offered to undertake the scheme, entirely at his own cost, provided, that all such lands as he should recover from the river, should be vested in him, on paying the usual rent to the Crown, and a fourth of the clear rents or profits to the City Companies,—and that he and his heirs should be entitled to certain duties on coal, lime, and lime-stone. He proposed that the profits of the fourth part should accumulate, for the purpose of building, fitting-out, and freighting a ship for each company, to be employed in trade for their respective advantage: the yearly profits to be paid to the Aldermen and Stewards, and distributed in equal portions. This, at the present day, may appear a curious proposal—but Mr. Jones's speculation had a methodical arrangement in it. The plan was rejected, and it seems in a great measure on account of the duties on coal, &c. which he stipulated for.—We now approximate to the completion of these projects. In 1698, a Mr. Gell, of London, submitted a proposal nearly similar to that of Mr. Jones, to the Corporation, but with some difference as to the duties on coal, &c. Not making any allotment in favor of the City companies, his scheme was, in the first instance, rejected.* He, nevertheless, did not abandon the proposition: he made a second offer, expressing his readiness to deposit £2000 in the hands of trustees for the completion of the work. This obtained the notice of the Body Corporate; and in a short time, a petition was presented to Parliament for leave to bring in a Bill to enable the Mayor and Citizens of Chester to recover and preserve the navigation of the River Dee. So successful was the application, that an Act passed the Legislature in 1700. Another Act was passed in 1732, empowering the Company (who had been subsequently incorporated) to inclose a large tract on the banks of the Dee, called the White Sands, on the condition that they made a navigable river from the Sea to Chester.† In 1735,§ the new cut was commenced and the undertaking was completed in 1737, when the water of the Old Channel entered the new one. So early as 1754, upwards of 1400 acres of land were recover-

§ Not in 1733, as stated by Messrs. Lysons.

* His plan was to make the Dee navigable for vessels drawing 12 feet water, AT ALL TIDES, from Flint Castle to the New (Water) Tower.—CORPORATION RECORDS.

† As might be expected, the cutting of the New River excited great popular attention in Chester: the inhabitants looked forward to the City becoming one of the first ports in the Kingdom—it was the theme of numerous essaical productions—and even Astrology was called in, to sanction their expectations!—In a curious pamphlet of the day, addressed "to our Trusty and Well-beloved Richard Manley, Esq. our prime friend to the Navigation," are a variety of Astrological calculations: the writer remarks, that he must "shew the state and condition of the Common People in Chester, distinct from the Magistrates." He then commences:—"In the first face of SCORPIO, ascends the Figure of two Men fighting and tearing each others hair. In the last face of Scorpio ascend two Women fighting, one striking the other on the head with a staff. Can any figure in the world represent the posture of the common people of Chester better than this doth? Now the World may see by this, that nothing is done on the face of all the earth, but the figure of it is to be seen first in the heavens; Astrology is the key that opens these secrets of nature. O Chester! How many of the evil angels of Mars have been permitted to ravage within thy walls, scattering the poison of the Scorpion amongst us, infecting us with anger, wrath, malice, and all uncharitableness; and all this under pretence of Religion and Justice, whilst honest Jupiter, the author of Peace, Honesty, Religion, Justice, and Sobriety, is got over head and ears in the Scorpion with the rest. This tells me, there are some, nay a great many of sober, peaceable, religious men among us; but alas! what could they do? Jupiter is weak and disabled for doing what he would. But that men should cover the most treacherous and wicked designs, under the pretence of religion, is the very nature of Scorpio. But come, Gentlemen, I have better tidings for you than this: I told you at Midsummer last was twelvemonth, there were in this city, and belonged to it, some learned, wise, and active men, who would lay out themselves with courage and industry to recover our navigation. And though some doubt it, yet gentlemen this scheme shews me that your governing angel Michael is strong, and hath orders to bind those angels of Mars, and cast them into the bottomless pit, and not let them deceive the nation for thirty years, and about the 20th of December next, Jupiter

CHESHIRE HISTORY.

ed from the sea; 664 acres were also recovered in 1763; and in 1769, in addition, 348 acres. A further inclosure of about 900 acres of land was also made in 1790, and other inclosures are in progress.—Immense sums were expended in cutting and embanking the new Channel, and inclosing the wastes adjacent; in consequence of which, no profits were received from the undertaking, till 1775, and then only two per cent. was divided on the principal stock. And though at the present time, the annual proceeds are very considerable,* yet if the loss of interest be taken into the account, the Representatives of the original Subscribers do not now receive more than one half per cent. on the sums embarked in the undertaking.†

† Mr. Wedge.

The provisions of the different Acts of Parliament, which are given in a note,‡ are certainly sufficiently explicit. They allow no room for quibbling on terms and conditions. Notwithstanding, however, proper attention, it is thought, has not been paid to the preservation of the Dee Navigation. Complaints have been made for some time of the imperfect state of the river, and doubts are entertained whether the depth prescribed by the Act, can by any means be maintained.—Vessels of 800 tons burthen have been launched at Chester; and some of heavy burthen, engaged in the cheese and general mercantile trade, have frequented its wharfs, fully laden: but that period is gone by. Several plans have nevertheless been devised: it has been suggested, to cleanse the bed of the river as well as existing circumtances will permit, to erect flood-gates at the mouth of the channel,§ and, during heavy freshes, to employ the operation of back floods in scouring the river from its choaking sands. This would be a work of time, and certainly of immense expense. Another plan, which perhaps is the only one that can succeed, in a commercial point of view, as connected with the prosperity of the city, is for the present River Dee Company, to obtain a new Act of Parliament, empowering them to cut an entire new channel, from near the Water Tower, or from the Sluice House, at Chester, running nearly in the line of the Canal from Chester to Whitby, where it would form a junction with the river Mersey. The channel to be deep enough for allowing vessels of 500 tons burthen to cross the Peninsula of Wirral in full sail, to and from Chester. It is supposed the expense of doing this would be about Seventy Thousand Pounds.

§ Near Connah's Quay.

will mount the fiery archer with power, to send forth his good angels, to undeceive and lose what the evil angels of Mars have bound, and to create peace, and a better understanding among the inhabitants of this city. But I must observe what company the Sun is in, and how beheld by the other planets: And I find him just separating from the conjunction of Mars and square of Saturn, and Jupiter from two signs Taurus and Scorpio, rugged company I will assure you. This posture of the Sun plainly shews me with what difficulty from seeming friends within, and powerful enemies without, he carried the Bill through both Houses of Parliament. I likewise see there are some that are not his friends, but his Sun in the regal sign Leo tells me, if a man is made a governer of a city, and his own radical ascendant is not the same as the ascendant of that city, or in Sextile or Trine to the ascendant of that city, he neither cares nor seeks the peace and prosperity of that city, neither shall his government endure. Now the Heavens have favored us with a Governor whose ascendant is the same with our city, whose significator hath majesty, power, and goodness, to be a father to his city. I shall now give you the character of a man signified by the Sun in Leo, he is very faithful, keeping promises with all punctuality, a desire to rule where he comes, prudent, and of incomparable judgment, of great majesty and stateliness, industrious to acquire honour, and large patrimony, yet as willingly departing therewith again. Now this is the character the Heavens give to the man that is designed to bring peace to this city, and all prosperity to a divided and disjointed neighbourhood, not only to encourage but command peace among us. And now I hope, every one that is a son of peace will heartily pray with me: Give peace in our time O Lord: And long life to our noble and pious Governor."—The very broad compliments in conclusion, are intended for "The noble and puissant George Earl of Cholmondeley," who we are informed "entered the city to take possession of the castle, on the 12th July, at which time twenty degrees of Leo is (are) upon the 10th house."—Mr. Hugh Williams also comes in for a large share of praise!—But enough of this.

* It was at first intended that the New Channel was to be made for ships of 200 tons burthen; but vessels of 600 tons have safely navigated in it.

‡ The Act 6th Geo. II. states, in the preamble, that "the said river (the Dee) not being navigable, is chiefly owing to the breadth of the sands, and to the shifting of the Channel from one side thereof to the other, as the winds and tides vary," and that the "vesting the said White Sands in the Undertak-

This certainly would draw closer the connexion between Liverpool and Chester, and as certainly would it render Chester a place of no small commercial importance in its trade with the southern counties of Salop, Stafford,

ers would be a considerable encouragement to the undertaking" of making the river navigable, &c. It then enacts, that Nat. Kinderley, Gent, and his assigns, are impowered to make and keep navigable the River Dee, at their own charge, "from the sea to Wilcox Point within the liberties of the City, in such manner that there shall be sixteen feet water, in EVERY part of the said river at a moderate spring tide." If vessels laden with cheese for London, drawing 14 feet water, cannot safely pass down the river, the Commissioners appointed by the said Act, on fourteen days' notice being given to them, are to inquire into the facts, and may order N. Kinderley, &c. to make a wet Dock capable of holding twenty ships AT LEAST; and if such dock be not finished by them, or is neglected in repairs, the said Commissioners may appoint others to do it, and pay them from the proceeds of the Duties, &c. vested in Kinderley, his assigns, &c. who are to deposit £10,000. in South Sea Annuities as a fund for answering any damage that may be sustained by the river overflowing, &c. The Commissioners' Meetings are to be held at the Castle of Chester, on the 1st Tuesday in August in every year. Pleasure boats are allowed to be used on the river without interruption, and the royalties and liberty of fishing are not to be prejudiced.—The undertaking to be completed between the 24th June, 1735, and the 24th June, 1742. Two ferry boats to be kept on the river when not fordable on horseback at low water.—Nothing in this Act is to be construed as affecting the rights of the City of Chester, or of Sir R. Grosvenor, or Jonathan Robinson, gent. or to prevent John Crewe, Esq. or the Lord of the Manor of Blacon, from using their marshes, &c. No alteration in the Channel is to affect the boundaries of Chester; and N. Kinderley is to set up meer stones to distinguish boundaries, &c.

By the Act 14th Geo. II. the joint Stock of the Company is to consist of £52,000.

§ Ann. Reg. Decimo Septimo, Georgii II.

The next Act § repeals the previous rates of tonnage, and fixes other rates.—It enacts, as the river in dry seasons is liable to be silted up with sand, so that at a moderate spring tide there may not be sixteen feet water, until the said sands are removed by freshes, that instead of the said depth of sixteen feet at a moderate spring tide, the said Company shall at ALL times maintain the said river from the sea to Wilcox Point, that at a moderate spring tide, as marked on the standard, there shall be fifteen feet water, &c. and in order to ascertain this the Mayor, &c. of Chester, may appoint a supervisor, and the Company another, who shall have power at any time, and from time to time, for three successive tides, when required by the said Mayor, &c. to take soundings, and if the bottom or channel of the said river shall be silted or choaked up, so that according to the standard at the TEN GATE SLUICE, there be not fifteen feet water, they shall make affidavit thereof before any Justice of the Peace for the City or County of Chester, and a Copy thereof shall be given to the Company's Collector, or any person appointed by them; and if the Company shall, for four Calendar Months following the delivery of such Copy of the Affidavit, suffer the river to continue [illegible] choaked up, &c. the payment of the tonnage duties shall be suspended, and not be payable till the depth of fifteen feet be regained: and if the Company shall allow the river to continue choaked up, for eight months after such notice, then it shall be lawful for the Commissioners, present at a Meeting to be held for the purpose, of which twenty days' notice exclusive shall be given in the London Gazette, and by notice on the Castle gate at Chester, to authorise such person or persons as they may appoint, to enter upon the White Sands, Lands, Gardens, &c. of the said Company, and take possession thereof, and receive all rents and profits, or distrain for the same till they have raised money to be expended in regaining the depth of fifteen feet in the said river. Not less than thirteen Commissioners to make such order.—The ascertaining the depth of fifteen feet to be reckoned to be level with the height of nine feet above the bottom, floor, or apron of the TEN GATE SLUICE, as the same is marked on the standard. The Supervisors, at the cost and charge of the said company, shall erect two or more piles of timber or other materials, to be fixed in such parts of the said river as they shall direct, so as the tops thereof shall be exactly level with the height of nine feet above the bottom of the TEN GATE SLUICE; and any person wilfully destroying the same, shall forfeit Two Hundred Pounds. The Supervisors appointed, to be registered within one month after the making thereof, with the Town Clerk of Chester.—The Supervisors books of soundings to be open for inspection by the Mayor and Citizens of Chester; and copies thereof lodged with the Clerk of the Peace, to be good evidence in Law.—On death or removal of Supervisors, others to be appointed within a month, and the Mayor, &c. or the said Company respectively, shall for every week they shall not have a Supervisor, forfeit the sum of Five Pounds, to be recovered by action. The Supervisor wilfully refusing or neglecting to sound the river in the manner directed, shall forfeit Ten Pounds, to be recovered by action of debt. From and after the 25th May, 1744, two ferry boats shall constantly be kept on the river at the costs and charge of the Company. Passengers to be carried over at ALL TIMES the boatmen may be required; good roads to be made to and from the said ferries, to lead to the City of Chester, and to the towns of Shotwick and Saughall, to be made and repaired by the Company, the Commissioners

CHESHIRE

and the bordering ones of the Principality.* But are there not conflicting interests in carrying into effect such a scheme? It is a duty to state these circumstances, as they have come under consideration; time alone can shew whether any of them will be carried into execution.

Tradition says—but there is nothing like a good ground work for it—that the present Channel of the Dee, from beyond where the Allen empties itself, to Chester, is the work of Roman art, and that the old bed of the river ran through the marshes below Hawarden, round by Dodleston, Pulford, &c.—where to this day, on the line marked out by such authority, marine remains are to be found. To this tradition Dr. Cowper alludes in his "IL PENSEROSO,"† when speaking of the delightful scenery that marks the mazy winding of the Dee to its bounding the beautiful peninsula of the Earl's Eye, he says,—

† Page 5.

NOT that ‡ DIVONA here, her watry course
Originally held; of yore, she deign'd
No kindly visit to our Cestrian walls,
Averse and distant: Now its pride and boast,
And source of much emolument and weal.
This affluent guest we owe to Latian bands,
Brought by much toil, their station to improve,
From a far tract, beyond where Allen swift,
From || vales Elysian, with translucent stores
Abounding, enters the Cornavian climes.

The hardy Vet'rans this atchiev'd, what time
§Paulinus, and ¶Agricola return'd,
The ** Ordovices quell'd; and Druids 'sperst
From hierarchal sway, so long possest:
And nearer ††Mona's wave-dash'd holds reduc'd.

By channels apt, and regularly form'd,
Mostly thro' living rock, by labour hewn,
(The Roman labour could all tasks perform)
To this new bed completed, nothing loth,
By guidance meet, the wond'ring waves were led.

Thro' that rich glebe they flow, where long has wonn'd
The Grosv'nor-Race, a house of high repute,
Of lineage fam'd, and qualities admir'd,
Erst NORMAN heroes, BRITISH patriots since.
To latest ages may endure the name,
That ancient name, deservedly rever'd!

HISTORY.

to assess a fine on the Company for breach of duty in this respect. The royalties, &c. of Sir John Glynne, in the manor of Hawarden are preserved. No person to fix nets or stakes across the river, to the prejudice of the said navigation.

The Act Anno vicessimo sexto Geo. II. is merely confirmatory of an agreement between the Company and Sir John Glynne, as Lord of Hawarden, &c. and several freeholders, &c

* In the event of such a scheme being undertaken, the present channel of the Dee from the Sluice House downwards, might be reduced to the common width of a canal, which would be amply sufficient for the tonnage and importance of the present trifling coasting trade with the Principality. The ground thus obtained, would no doubt materially add to the revenue of the River Dee Company. But it has been suggested, that, if this scheme were executed, the present channel must be entirely annihilated; and the Estuary itself become a marsh.—Difficulties present themselves in most undertakings; and remedies may probably be found, for those which may appear on the first view of this project.

'‡ DIVONA. One of the appellations of the river Dee; which name (as Ausonius tells us) among the Gauls, signified, *A fountain sacred to the Gods*, and, perhaps, hence it was, that Milton in a poem stiles it, "*The ancient hallow'd Dee:*" as Drayton does, "*The holy Dee:*" and the late N. Griffith, Esq. in his applauded poem, THE LEEK, calls it "*Deva's holy Tide.*"'

'|| They who are acquainted with that variety of beautiful landscapes, and delightful scenes, in, and about, the vallies just below Gresford, through which the river Allen hastens towards Cheshire, will readily allow the expression—*Vales Elysian.*'

'§ Seutonius Paulinus, one of Nero's generals, having conquered a large part of North Wales, made Chester (then Deva) a station or garrison.'

'¶ Caius Julius Agricola, an eminent commander under the emperor Vespasian, having entirely subdued the Ordovices and Mona, fixed at Chester the twentieth legion, stiled Valens and Victrix. Anno Christi, 80.'

'** ORDOVICES.----These were the inhabitants of North Wales; of all which country, Deva (Chester) was, in early ages, the capital, or metropolis.'

'†† Mona (the nearer) Anglesea, where the famous Druids had, for many ages, held their hierarchy; from which island, such of them as escaped from the Romans, fled into the further Mona (the Isle of Man) which was the Mona of Cæsar; as Anglesea was the Mona of Tacitus.'

CHESHIRE HISTORY.

From hence, along the verdant sloping banks
Of ‡‡Hunditona, glide the ductile streams,
Fast by that crystal fount, ‡‡Boestona's boast;
Where from her grot, with liberal dispense,
The Naiad issues her salubrious stores.

With soft advance, these next to Cestria bring
Bounties abundant, salutary aids,
And various blessings; then are roll'd along,
O'er Syrts * Vergivian, to the boist'rous main.

Such is the description, which the poetic imagination of the learned Doctor gives of the Dee. There are, however, extant, in the Harl. MSS. some ancient pleadings at law relative to the Dee Mills, which tend to confirm the tale which tradition has furnished. It is there inferentially stated, that the bed of the River Dee at Chester is artificial, and that it was cut by Hugh Lupus. But there are no appearances on the line of the asserted artificial channel, which corroborate it; and little credence, therefore, can be given to the story.

THE MERSEY,

Like the Dee, is also only partially a Cheshire River, forming a great boundary to the Counties of Chester, and Lancaster, from Stockport, to the Irish Channel. The Mersey is formed by the junction of two minor streams, the Etherow and the Goyt.—The latter rises in the forest of Macclesfield, and for nearly nine miles, forms a boundary between Cheshire and Derbyshire, passing by Taxall, Whaley, Disley, and Marple. The Etherow rises near Woodhead, at the point of meeting between the Counties of York, Derby, and Chester, and also forms a boundary between the two latter Counties. It enters Cheshire between Comstall and Marple bridges, and forms a conflux with the Goyt. Here the streams take the name of the Mersey, and pass by Chadwick, between Offerton and Bredbury, to Stockport; thence by Sale, Ashton, Carrington, Warburton, Warrington, and Runcorn to Liverpool. Opposite Warrington, it first meets the tide water, and there its width is about forty yards; but at Runcorn Gap, where a communication is formed with the Grand Trunk, and Duke of Bridgewater's Canal, its width is above three hundred yards, and below spreading into a fine expanse of upwards of three miles in width. Below Frodsham it receives the contributory waters of the Weaver; it then swells for many miles to considerable breadth, but opposite Liverpool, and some distance further, it does not much exceed a mile. The channel, however, is more than ten fathoms deep at low water, and safe and convenient for shipping. At the Rock Perch, it falls into the sea, by two channels, which, although much incommoded by sands, are rendered safe by various buoys—by the light-houses—and the superior system of pilotage adopted by the Merchants of Liverpool.—The whole course of the river is about forty-four miles.

The Dee and Mersey wash the narrow peninsula of Wirral on its South and North Sides: on the West it is bounded by the waters of the Irish Channel; and a valley, that runs across in an angular direction from the Mersey, via Stoke, Croughton, Chorlton, Backford, and the Mollingtons, to the river Dee, forms its limits on the East side. On this latter disposition of the country, Mr. Ormerod, in his magnificent work, builds an ingenious theory: he observes, that the raised terrace formed by Wirral, between the waters of the Estuaries of the Dee and Mersey, after being broken by the valley before-mentioned, continues its course onwards in a South-east direction towards the foot of the Broxton Hills, retaining still on its sides two deep and broad vales, each of which is a continuation of the line of the respective Estuaries. On the North-east, the vale is traversed in its whole length by the Gowy. On the South-west, the vale forms on its upper part the bed of the Dee, but which instead of proceeding down the residue of the vale to the Estuary in a straight line, is diverted to the walls of Chester by a deep channel, formed in the elevated line he before-mentions, which

'‡‡ HUNDITONA, BOESTONA. Townships, on the Dee, near to Chester, so written in Doomsday-Book, now called Huntington, and Boughton: in the latter is that noted spring, called Barrel Well, from whence much excellent water is daily fetched into the city. There is a record extant (in the first year of king Edward I.) "*De aquæductu faciendo a fonte in Boghton juxta Furcas.*"'

'* VERGIVIAN. The channel between England and Ireland, is called by Ptolemy, MARE VERGIVIUM.—(See also Milton's Lycidas.) This abounds with banks and shifting sand-beds, extremely dangerous, and often fatal, to shipping.'

CHESHIRE carries the river past Chester, in a direction nearly semicircular, till it joins the Estuary and the line of the great vale again, near Blacon Point.—That the waters, before the retiring of the sea from the Western Coast of Britain,† occupied the line of these vales, will be doubted by no one who has looked down on the general level of the county, either from the Forest Hills, or from the ridge of the great natural terrace before mentioned, between Aldford or Churton. A tide a very few yards higher than usual, would now cover them to a considerble extent. Mr. Ormerod afterwards observes, that having thus shown that vestiges exist, in the general face of the county, manifesting that the waters occupied a wider range than the present height of the tides allows, it remains to mention that a tide much lower than would suffice to cover these levels, would fill the before-mentioned smaller valley, which intervenes between Wirral and Broxton, and render the former Hundred a complete island, as the tradition of the country maintains it to have been at a (very) distant period. The variation of level is indeed so inconsiderable, that it was once proposed to take the Dee through this line into the Mersey,* instead of forming its present artificial channel by embankment.†—Assuming, then, that the estuaries of the two rivers met in the valley between the hundreds of Wirral and Broxton, this theory will raise the tide in a similar manner in a creek which parts Bromborow and Bebington, and carry it up the corner of a deep valley crossed by an ancient road below Poulton Lancelyn. The fields on each side this pass still retain the name of the MARFORDS,‡ as the other ancient points of crossing the valley, (supposed formerly to be subject to the tides) still are called Stanford, Trafford, and Backford.||—At the extremity of Wirral, next the Irish sea, is a long level plain, only protected from the ravages of the sea by a line of sand hills, and opening to the Dee by a deep rocky vale, near Thurstaston, and to the Mersey by another valley, extending, between Birkenhead and Wallesey, to Wallesey Pool. The tide which would insulate Wirral, and divert the present road by Bromborow Mill to the higher point at the Marfords, would also fill these vallies, and cover the low range, protected by the Sand-hills, on the edge of the Irish Sea, in which case the Dee and the Mersey would present only one large mouth, common to both rivers,§ from which would rise the two rocky islands, the parishes of West Kirkby, and Kirkby in Wallesey, in the ancient name of which (WALLEIA) we yet find an allusion to its insular situation.

‡ MAWR. Brit. *great*; and *ford*.

HISTORY.

As has been before observed, this is a very ingenious theory of Mr Ormerod, and it may be said a very bold one too. But it serves that learned gentleman to reconcile "difficulties of importance" in the "ancient Geography of Britain" at once—and this he does with an equal degree of ingenuity: "It will be necessary," says he,¶ "to mention that the *Seteia Portus*, and the *Morícambe* of Ptolemy, are universally acknowledged to be the mouths of the Dee and the Ken, and that the same Geographer having inserted between them only two rivers, *Segantiorum Portus*, and *Belisama Æstuarium*, it has been a subject of dispute, whether the Mersey, the Ribble, or the Lune, which now intervene, must be considered the river omitted. Mr. Whittaker has contended, that the Ribble was overlooked; and the later learned Antiquary of the same name, has abundantly proved that the Mersey, and not the Ribble, is the river undescribed, which he accounts for, by having no celebrated port on its banks, and consequently not attract-

¶ p. 188.

† What period does Mr. Ormerod fix for this removal?

* See page 79.—The plan is still in projection, although there are no immediate symptoms of its being acted upon.

† This suggestion, Mr. Ormerod says, induced Mr. Pennant to make a series of observations, which led to the connexion of the Dee and Mersey by the present canal to Whitby.

|| We are told the soil has been examined in Chorlton, Caughall, and other parts of the valley crossing that district, and at a yard below the surface, it has been uniformly found to be composed of the coarse grey sea sand, as the ground which has been recovered from the Dee by embankments. Considerable quantities of sea-shells are also found there; more particularly seen after showers of rain.

§ To establish this position, Mr. Ormerod must first rid himself of the rocky promontory of Burton, and consider the bleak range of hills behind Gayton, Heswall, &c. as never having existence.—Besides, the extreme altitude of the waters at this doubtful period, (temp. Ptolemy we will suppose) would have inundated one half of the Vale Royal, if we allow that the hundred of Wirral formed the bed of the two rivers, thus formed into one! The situation of West Kirkby and Wallesey, as forming two islands at the mouth of the rivers thus united, may easily be imagined.

ing the notice of the Mariners, from whom Ptolemy had his observations. As the mouths, and not the rivers are described, IF the theory which has been advanced, *is allowed* to have been *proved*, the difficulty will vanish. The arguments which have been stated in favor of the Ribble, being intended by the *Belisama*, will remain unshaken; and as the two rivers mingling through the channels of Thurstaston and Wallesey, would present conjointly one mouth, broken only by two inconsiderable islands, they would together form the *Seteia Portus*, and leave no impeachment in this point, on the accuracy of the informants of Ptolemy."* All this would seem to be confirmed, by a reference to any of the old Maps of Cheshire; and Mr. Ormerod remarks, that the reader may be surprised 'at the pains taken to prove an established point:' but those who projected the Maps have been misled by a brook rising near the middle of the valley, one branch of which joined the stagnant waters of the Gowy, near Thornton, the other flowed to the Dee, connecting the rivers, indeed, by a line of natural water, but not bringing them into confluence, at so recent a period. The track and appearance of the stream here alluded to, may perhaps be rendered more easy of conception by this imperfect sketch:—

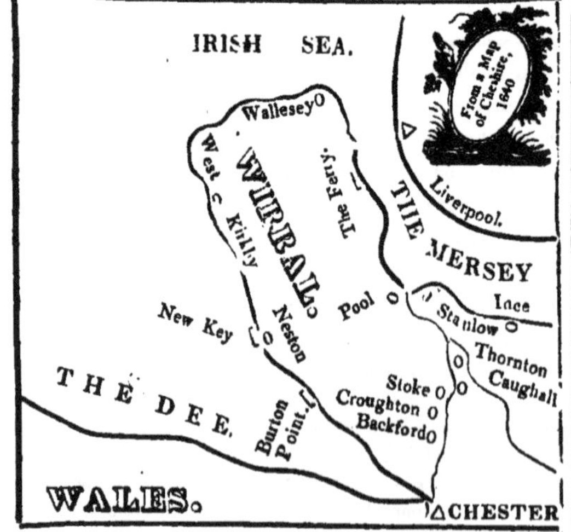

THE WEAVER,

Is justly termed *A Cheshire River*. It rises on Buckley Heath, in the parish of Malpas, and runs direct through the County to its confluence with the Mersey, at Weston, near Frodsham.—It passes through Ridley, by Cholmondeley Castle, to Wrenbury—by Audlem, Hankelow, Nantwich, Minshull, and Weaver, to Winsford Bridge; thence to Vale Royal, and Eaton, to Hartford Bridge, and Northwich, where it joins the Dane, and shortly afterwards the Peover: having formed this junction, it passes by Waverham, Acton, Dutton, Frodsham, and Rock Savage, to Weston, where it joins the Mersey. The Weaver, in its original state, was navigable only at high tides; but in 1720, the Hon. Langham Booth, Sir Geo. Warburton, Bart, Philip Egerton, Esq. John Egerton, Esq. Henry Legh, Esq. Randle Dod, Esq. J. Amson, Esq. H. Mainwaring, Esq. T. Vernon, Esq. J. Williams, Esq. Peter Warburton, Esq. and J. Mainwaring, Esq. formed a Subscription, the object of which was, the obtaining an Act of Parliament, for making the Weaver navigable, from Frodsham Bridge to Winsford Bridge—a distance of nearly 20 miles. It was agreed by them, and provided by the Act which they subsequently obtained, that after payment of the subscriptions, (receiving 5 per cent. interest, and 1 per cent. profit, per ann. for their risk) the entire income arising from tonnage, &c. should be applicable to all the purposes of the County Rate.†—In 1778, all incumbrances were paid off: and since that period upwards of £120,000. have been received by the Treasurers of the County Rate.—For the last 18 years, the tonnage has greatly increased, averaging £17,000 per annum, which is expended in the execution of the trust, and in maintaining and improving the navigation of the river. A great portion of the expense attending the erection of that magnificent pile, the County Gaol, Assize Hall, and other necessary buildings in Chester Castle, was defrayed solely from the receipts of the income arising from the Weaver. About ten years ago, in consequence of the great increase in the salt trade,

* Ptolemy wrote about the year 140.

† It is seldom such an instance of genuine public spirit occurs—the speculation gave the promise, almost the certainty, of an immense return (as has been since experienced), and yet we see these real patriots sacrificing it for the general advantage of the County. Such men are truly worthy of 'immortal remembrance.'

CHESHIRE HISTORY.

the then existing accommodations of the river were found inadequate to the multiplicity of business carried on; a Canal was accordingly cut from near the Weir, at Frodsham, to Weston Point, in order to prevent delays arising from the shallowness of the river at low tides. This, and the improvements which have since taken place, have cost nearly £45,000.—The entire course of the Weaver, is about 33 miles; it is narrow and deep, with a slow stream.

THE DANE

Has its rise in the Forest of Macclesfield, close to the Three Shire Meer. It forms a boundary between Cheshire and Staffordshire for a considerable distance, and then enters Cheshire about two miles from Congleton.—It passes from thence by Radnor Bridge, Davenport, the Hermitage, to Cranage and Byley Bridges; then by Middlewich, Croxton, Shipbrook, and Davenham, to Northwich, where it forms a junction with the Weaver. The Dane runs about 22 miles; is broad, swift in its course, but shallow.

THE PEOVER

Also falls into the Weaver near Northwich. It is formed of the waters of two streams, one rising near Macclesfield, the other near Gawsworth: these join at Chelford, and then pass to Over Peover, Nether Peover, Holford, and Wincham Bridge. The length is about 15 miles.

THE BOLLIN,

Like the Dane, rises in Macclesfield Forest, from several heads, the two principal of which, issue from the foot of Thutlingslow-hill, near Ridge, and united pass by Sutton, Macclesfield, Bollington, Prestbury, Newton, Wilmslow, Pownall, Ringey, Ashley, Dunham, and Warburton, to Rixton, and there fall into the Mersey, after a course of near 20 miles.

THE WHEELOCK

Composed of three streams, rises near Lawton, Rode, and Moreton Hall, and joins near Sandbach, whence it passes by Wheelock, Elton, and Warmingham, falling into the Dane at Croxton. It has a run of about 12 miles.

THE TAME

Originates in the county of York; during almost the whole of its course, (about 10 miles) it becomes a boundary to Cheshire and Lancashire: on the Cheshire side it passes by Staley, Duckinfield, Hyde-hall, and Harden Hall, between which and Stockport, it becomes tributary to the Mersey.

THE GOWY

Is a small stream, rising near Bunbury;—from thence it passes by the Castle of Beeston, Tiverton, and Huxley, to Stapleford, Barrow, Plemstall, Bridge Trafford*, Picton, Stoke, and Stanney, and near Stanlow House it is received into the Mersey;—during the whole of its course, it forms a boundary between the hundreds of Eddisbury and Broxton.

* Here it is called Trafford Brook.

THE BETLEY

Rises at Apedale, in Staffordshire, and running by Doddington, Wybunbury, and Bartherton, empties itself afterwards into the Weaver.

THE ASHBROOK

First shows itself in the Forest of Delamere, and then passes by Over, and Little Budworth, to the neighbourhood of Darnhall, forming Darnhall Pool. It empties itself into the Weaver, near Weaver Hall.

THE BIDDLE

Comes from Staffordshire, and is a very inconsiderable stream: it falls into the Dane, near Congleton.

THE BIRKIN

Springs near Chelford, and passing Mobberley, falls afterwards into the Bollin.

THE CROCO

Runs from Bagmere; it then passes by Brereton hall, Kinderton Park, and through Middlewich; and falls into the Dane at Croxton.

THE WALWERN

Is first traced near Barthomley, passes by Crewe Hall and Coppenhall, and forms a Junction with the LEA

CHESHIRE

which comes from Lea and Wistaston: they afterwards fall into the Mersey.

THE GRIMSDITCH

Comes from Grimsditch: it passes by Preston, Daresbury, and Kekwick, falling into the Mersey, at Norton Marsh.

THE MAR

Runs out of Mere Pool, and after a short course, joins the River Bollin.

THE FLOOKERSBROOK

Is a small stream, rising close to Chester; it runs to the Bach, near which it joins a rivulet (now nearly merged in the line of the Canal to Whitby) which in its way by Caughall, Moston, and Mollington, divides the hundred of Wirral. Conjointly they fall into the Dee below Chester.

There is a stream which rises at Harthill (receiving many local names) and taking its course by Tattenhall, Golborne Bellow, and Lea Hall, is joined near the latter place by a brook coming from Grafton, by Cuddington, Aldersey, and Bechin; it is received by the Dee, at Aldford.*

HISTORY.

LAKES AND MERES

ARE numerous in Cheshire. COMBERMERE is a noble piece of water, considerably more than a mile in length. It gave name to Combermere Abbey, now the romantic seat of the gallant Lord Combermere.—CHAPEL-MERE, and MOSS-MERE, are two beautiful sheets of water in front of Cholmondeley Castle. BAR-MERE is a large pool of water in Malpas Parish. The other Meres are Quoisley Mere, Rosthern-mere, Bagmere, Pick-mere, Oak-mere, Mere Pool, &c. Ridley Pool, noticed by Leland† as being one of the largest in the County, has long since been drained and in tillage.

CANALS.

THE principal Canals of the County, are the Duke of Bridgewater's—the Trent and Mersey, or Grand Trunk—the Ellesmere and Chester‡—and the Peak Forest Canal.

DUKE OF BRIDGEWATER'S CANAL.

This cut first gave celebrity to Mr. Brindley;|| who designed and executed it. It was commenced in 1761;

* The Rivers and Meres of Cheshire, abound with various sorts of fish. The salmon of the Dee is noted throughout the Country, and particularly in the Metropolis. At one time it was so plentiful at Chester, that Masters were prohibited by their Apprentices' indentures, giving them that delicate food more than twice in each week! At present there are no apprehensions of Masters committing themselves in this respect: the Salmon Fishery has been declining some years. In 1813, however, a "Society for the Preservation of the Salmon Fishery in the Dee," was instituted at Chester, Meetings were held, Advertisements published, Rules issued, and strong symptoms of perseverance, manifested. But this bustle was of short duration; it soon went to sleep, and has not since been heard

§.1818. of! The fishermen attribute the present§ scarcity of Salmon to the Steam Boat, employed between Chester and Bagillt: they say that it has frightened the fish out of the river! The Mersey abounds with plaice, flounders, smelts, &c. but, like the Dee, it has experienced a great falling off in the Salmon Fishery.

† Noticed, also, it may be said, by Nixon, of prophetic fame. His prophecy relative to it was, says Oldmixon, in his life of Nixon,—

"Thro' Weaver Hall shall be a lone,§ § lane.
"Ridley Pool shall be sown and mown,
"And Darnhall Park shall be hacked and hewn."

"The two wings of Weaver Hall are now standing, and between them is a cart road; Ridley Pool is filled up, and made good meadow land; and in Darnhall Park the trees are cut down, and it is made into Pasture Ground."—So much for the renowned Prophet, and his Biographer!—And yet to disbelieve the seer's prescience, in many parts of the county, would be deemed, at least, irreligious!.

‡ These Canals were united in 1813, under one Proprietary.

|| This extraordinary man was born in 1716, at Tunsted, in the Parish of Wormhill, Derbyshire; his father dissipated a small property by keeping company above his rank; and at 17 years of age, James Brindley bound himself apprentice to one Bennet, a Mill-wright, near Macclesfield. Here he made a wonderful progress in mechanical knowledge, that gave the confident promise of his ultimate fame. In 1752, he erected a very extraordinary water engine at Clifton, in Lancashire, for the purpose of draining some coal-mines, which before were worked at an enormous expense. The water for the use of this engine was brought out of the river Irwell, by a subter-

and in 1772, the communication between Manchester and Liverpool was opened. In 1776, the whole of the

raneous tunnel, nearly six hundred yards in length, carried through a rock; and the wheel was fixed thirty feet below the surface of the ground. In the year 1766, Mr. Brindley undertook to erect a steam engine, near Newcastle-under-Line, on a new plan. The boiler of it was made with brick and stone, instead of iron plates; and the water was heated by fire-flues of a peculiar construction; by which contrivances the consumption of fuel, necessary for working a steam-engine, was reduced one half. He introduced, likewise, in this engine, cylinders of wood, made in the manner of cooper's ware, instead of iron ones; the former being not only cheaper, but more easily managed in the shafts; and he substituted wood for iron in the chains which worked at the end of the beam. The period that stamped his exalted genius, was now at hand—and his biographer thus notices it:—"His Grace the Duke of Bridgewater had, at Worsley, about seven miles from Manchester, a large estate, rich with mines of coal, which had hitherto lain useless in the bowels of the earth, because the expense of carriage by land was too great to find a market for consumption. The Duke, wishing to work these mines, perceived the necessity of a canal from Worsley to Manchester; upon which occasion, Mr. Brindley, who was now become famous in the country, was consulted. Having surveyed the ground, he declared the scheme to be practicable. In consequence of this, an act was obtained in 1758 and 1759, for enabling his Grace to cut a Canal from Worsley to Salford, near Manchester, and to carry the same to or near Hollin Ferry, in the county of Lancaster. It being, however, afterwards discovered, that the navigation would be more beneficial, both to the Duke of Bridgewater, and the public, if carried over the river Irwall, near Barton-bridge, to Manchester, his Grace applied again to Parliament, and procured an Act, which enabled him to vary the course of his canal agreeably to this new plan, and likewise to extend a side branch to Longford-bridge in Stretford. Mr. Brindley, in the mean time, had begun these great undertakings, being the first of the kind ever attempted in England, with subterraneous tunnels, and elevated aqueducts. When the canal was completed as far as Barton, where the Irwell is navigable for large vessels, Mr. Brindley proposed to carry it over that river, by an aqueduct of thirty-nine feet above the surface of the water. This, however, being generally considered as a wild and extraordinary project, he desired, in order to justify his conduct towards his noble employer, that the opinion of another engineer might be taken; believing that he could easily convince an intelligent person of the practicability of his design. A gentleman of eminence was accordingly called in; who being conducted to the place where it was intended that the aqueduct should be made, ridiculed the attempt; and when the height and dimensions were communicated to him, he exclaimed, "I have often heard of castles in the air, but never before was shown where any of them were to be erected." This unfortunate verdict did not deter the Duke of Bridgewater from following the opinion of his own engineer. The aqueduct was immediately begun; and it was carried on with such rapidity and success, as astonished all those who but a little before condemned it as a chimerical scheme. This work commenced in September, 1760, and the first boat sailed over it on the 17th of July, 1761. From that time, it was not uncommon to see a boat loaded with forty tons drawn over the aqueduct, with great ease, by one or two mules; while below, against the stream of the Irwall, persons had the pain of beholding ten or twelve men tugging at an equal draught: a striking instance of the superiority of a canal navigation over that of a river not in the tideway. The works were then extended to Manchester, at which place the curious machine for landing coals upon the top of the hill, gives a pleasing idea of Mr. Brindley's address in diminishing labour by mechanical contrivance. The Duke of Bridgewater obtained, in 1762, an Act of Parliament for branching his canal to the tideway in the Mersey. This part of the canal is carried over the rivers Mersey and Bollin, and over many wide and deep vallies. Over the vallies it is conducted without the assistance of a single lock; the level of the water being preserved by raising a mound of earth, and forming therein a mould, as it may be called, for the water. Across the valley at Stretford, through which the Mersey runs, this kind of work extends nearly a mile. A person might naturally have been led to conclude, that the conveyance of such a mass of earth must have employed all the horses and carriages in the country, and that the completion of it would be the business of an age. But our excellent mechanic made his canal subservient to this part of the design, and brought the soil in boats of a peculiar construction, which were conducted into caissoons or cisterns. On opening the bottoms of the boats, the earth was deposited where it was wanted; and thus in the easiest and simplest manner, the valley was elevated to a proper level for continuing the canal. The ground across the Bollin was raised by temporary locks, which were formed of the timber used in the caissoons just mentioned.—In 1766, the canal, called by the proprietors, "The Canal from the Trent to the Mersey," but more emphatically, by the engineer, the "Grand Trunk Navigation," on account of the numerous branches which, he justly supposed, would be extended every way from it, was begun; and under his direction, it was conducted with great spirit and success, as long as he lived. Mr. Brindley's life not being continued to the completion of this important and arduous undertaking, he left it to be finished by his brother-in-law, Mr. Henshall, who put the last hand to it in May 1777, being somewhat less than eleven years after its commencement. It need not be said, that the final execution of

CHESHIRE

projected works were finished.—This canal commenced at the Duke of Bridgewater's estate at Worsley, Lancashire, and enters Cheshire near Ashton on the Mersey: it then passes near Altrincham, Dunham Massey, Bollington, Lymm, Groppenhall, Higher Walton, Preston-on-the-Hill, and Moor, through Sir Richard Brooke's estate at Norton, and thence to Runcorn, where it joins the Mersey. At Runcorn it has a rise of nearly ninety-five feet, by means of ten locks; and this is the only variation from the general level of the Canal. At the Vales of Mersey and Bollin, there are embankments made for its preservation.

TRENT AND MERSEY CANAL.

The Act for making this branch of our inland navigation, sometimes called the Grand Trunk Canal, was passed in 1766. At Preston-brook, it communicates with the Duke of Bridgewater's, and thence passes by Dutton, Barnton, Little Legh, Northwich, Shipbrooke, and Middlewich; runs near Sandbach to Lawton, a short distance beyond which it enters the county of Stafford. There are not less than four tunnels, in the course of this Canal, viz. at Preston-on-the-Hill, in length 1241 yards; at Barnton in Great Budworth, 572 yards long; at Satersfield, in Great Budworth, 572 yards long; and another at the Hermitage, in length 130 yards.

THE ELLESMERE CANAL,

From the Tower Wharf, Chester, to Ellesmere Port, in the Township of Whitby, has a course of about nine miles. It was cut under the superintendance of Mr. Telford, engineer, of Salop; and passes the east-end of the Hundred of Wirral, and the south-east part of Broxton Hundred, running thro' Whitby, Great Stanney, Stoke, Croughton, Chorlton, Caughall, Moston, to Chester, where it joins the river Dee by several locks, on a lower level.—There is a branch of this Canal from Whitchurch, which enters this county at Grindley-brook in Wirswall, and then passes by Quoisley, Marbury, Norbury, Wrenbury, Baddeley, and Hurleston. In Hurleston township it joins the Chester and Nantwich Canal. The Act, which was passed in 1793, authorised the proprietors to cut the line from the Dee, by the Lach-eyes, Rough-hill, Pulford, through Denbighshire, to join the Severn near Shrewsbury; this, however, has been abandoned, the line of communication being along the Chester Canal, the Whitchurch Branch, to all its different ramifications.

HISTORY.

THE CHESTER AND NANTWICH CANAL,

Now united with the Ellesmere Canal, and the Proprietors incorporated as "The Ellesmere and Chester Canal Company," was completed in 1776. The Act authorising the scheme was passed in 1772. It passes from Chester, via Great Boughton, Christleton, Waverton, Hargrave, Huxley, Beeston, Tiverton, Tilston Fernall, Wardle, Barbridge, Stoke, Hurleston, and Acton, a little beyond which, near Nantwich, it terminates. On the project for this Canal being announced, shares in the speculation were greedily purchased, and the most sanguine anticipations were entertained of very profitable results. It turned out, notwithstanding, an unprofitable undertaking; and shares in it were sold, within the last twenty years, at less

the Grand Trunk Navigation gave the highest satisfaction to the proprietors, and excited a general joy in a populous country, the inhabitants of which already receive every advantage they could wish from so truly noble an enterprise. This canal is ninety-three miles in length; and besides a great number of bridges over it, has seventy-six locks and five tunnels. The most remarkable of the tunnels is the subterraneous passage of Harecastle, being 2880 yards in length, and more than 70 yards below the surface of the earth. The scheme of this inland navigation had employed the thoughts of the ingenious part of the kingdom for upwards of twenty years before, and some surveys had been made. But Harecastle hill, through which the tunnel is constructed, could neither be avoided nor overcome by any expedient the ablest engineers could devise. It was Mr. Brindley alone who surmounted this and other difficulties, arising from the variety of measures, strata, and quick-sands, which none but himself would have attempted.—Mr. Brindley conquered all obstacles by his foresight and skill, and lived to complete a great number of other stupendous undertakings. He died at Turnhurst, in Staffordshire, Sept. 30, 1772, in the 56th year of his age, and was buried at New Chapel, in that county. The interest of the subject, may perhaps apologize for the length of this biographical digression."

CHESHIRE HISTORY.

than ONE per cent. on their original value! After the junction of this canal with that to Whitby, and with the Whitchurch branch at Hurleston, shares were enhanced in value, and ROSE to £30. for the £100.—It was intended, that a branch of this canal should be cut, from Wardle Heath to Middlewich, but this project has not yet been commenced, nor is it likely now to take place.

THE PEAK FOREST CANAL

Was completed under the authority of an Act of Parliament, passed in 1794. This Canal crosses Cheshire from Lancashire, and enters Derbyshire near Whaley-bridge. It enters Cheshire crossing the Tame at Duckinfield, and runs through the townships of Hyde, Wernith, Bredbury, Romiley, Marple, Disley, and thence to Whaley. At Marple, it is carried over the Mersey by a stupendous aqueduct, second only in magnitude to that at Pontcysyllte,* near Llangollen, Denbighshire. It has three arches, each 60 feet in span, and 78 feet high: the whole being about 100 feet in height.

* The following are the dimensions of this magnificent structure:—

	F.	IN.
Length of the Iron Work	1007	0
Height from the surface of the rock, on the south side of the river, to the top of the side plates	126	8
Breadth of the water way, within the iron work	11	10
Number of stone pillars besides abutments	—18—	
Distance of ditto, from each other at the top	45	0
Depth of the iron plates for canal part	5	3
Length of earthern embankment, south side the river	1500	0
Height of ditto, at the south abutment	75	0

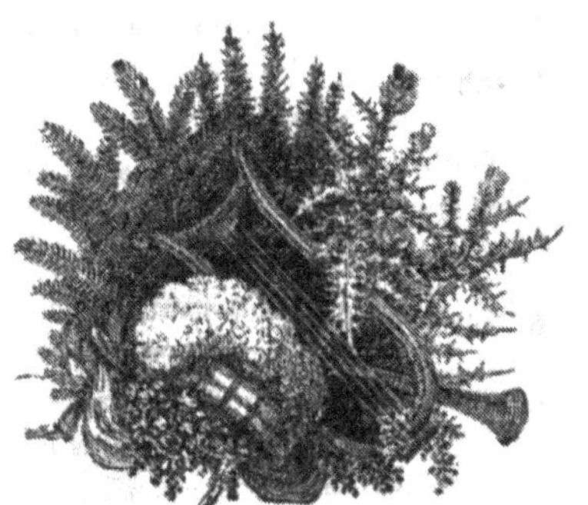

Cheshire---Ancient and Modern.

Cheshire

It appears that when the county was originally divided, it contained TWELVE hundreds, of this we have ample proof by reference to that valuable record, Domesday-book. They are there thus named—

Old Hundreds.	Present Hundreds.
1 Wilaveston	Wirral
2 Dudestan, and 3 Centre	Broxton
4 Riseton, and 5 Roelau	Edisbury
6 Mildestvic	Northwich
7 Warmondestrou	Nantwich
8 Hamstan	Macclesfield
9 Bochelau, and 10 Tunendune	Bucklow
11 Atiscros	———
12 Exestan	———

The Towns in the two last Hundreds have long been detached from Cheshire,* and incorporated with the counties of Flint and Denbigh, with the exception of Dodleston, Marlston, (near Eccleston) Claverton, and Lache; now attached to the hundred of Broxton. The modern division of the county into hundreds, is not much older than Edw. III, At the great Survey of Domesday, there were not so many towns in the county, as may now be enumerated. The population has wonderfully increased, and villages and houses have increased in the same proportion.—No account is here taken of the lands between the Ribble and Mersey, now forming part of Lancashire, and which were divided into six hundreds, viz.

History.

Derbie Hundret	Neweton Hundret
Walintune Hundret	Blacheburne Hundret
Salford Hundret	Lailand Hundret.

These were deemed part of Cheshire.—It is probable that the Survey of Domesday was not made upon any regular system, but given in merely by general estimation; and this appears pretty evident from the mode in which towns are entered following each other, when they are, perhaps, at extreme points of the county.—It may also be inferred from ancient records, that Wirral lost its name *Wilaveston*, soon after the Norman Conquest, and acquired that of Caldey.

The hundreds are held by Lords or Bailiffs, by lease from the Crown; thus—

Wirral.. is held by ..	J. B. Glegg, Esq.
Broxton	Sir J. G. Egerton, Bart.
Edisbury *Nantwich*	Marquis Cholmondeley.
Northwich	The Duke of Leeds.
Macclesfield	The Earl of Derby.
Bucklow	Wilbraham Egerton, Esq.

The following table gives the former and present names of the townships, with the hundreds in which they were and are now situated. It will be seen, that several townships, formerly in *Dudestan* hundred, are now in the hundred of Edisbury.

* See Stat. 33 Henry VIII. c. 13.

CHESHIRE—ANCIENT AND MODERN.

Former Name.	Present Name.	Ancient Hundred.	Present Hundred.
Acatone and Actune	Acton	Warmondestrou	Nantwich
Aculvestune	Occleston	Mildestvic	Northwich
Alburgham	Alpraham	Dudestan	Edisbury
Aldelime	Audlem	Warmondestrou	Nantwich
Aldredelie	Over & Nether Alderley	Bochelau and Hamestan	Macclesfield
Aldretune	Ollerton	Ditto	Bucklow
Alretune		Hamestan	Macclesfield
Altetone	Oulton	Dudestan	Edisbury
Ascefie	Ashley	Bochelau	Bucklow
Bagelie	Baguley	Ditto	Ditto
Bedelei	Baddiley	Warmondestrou	Nantwich
Berchesford	Barksford	Ditto	Ditto
Berdeltune	Bertherton	Ditto	Ditto
Bernestone	Barnston	Wilaveston	Wirral
Bero	Barrow	Riseton	Edisbury
Bertemeleu	Barthomley	Warmondestrou	Nantwich
Bertintone	Bartinton	Tunendune	Bucklow
Bertintune	Barnton	Ditto	Ditto
Bevelei	Byley	Mildestvic	Northwich
Bichelei	Bickley	Dudestan	Broxton
Bicretone	Bickerton	Ditto	Ditto
Blacheholl	Blacon-hall	Wilaveston	Wirral
Blachenhale	Blakenhall	Warmondestrou	Nantwich
Bocitone	Boughton	Dudestan	Broxton
Bodevrde	Little Budworth	Ditto	Edisbury
Bogedone	Bowdon	Bochelau	Bucklow
Boliberie	Bunbury	Riseton	Edisbury
Boselega	Bosley	Hamestan	Macclesfield
Botestoche	Bostock	Mildestvic	Northwich
Bramall	Bramhall	Hamestan	Macclesfield
Bretburie	Bredbury	Ditto	Ditto
Bretone	Brereton	Mildestvic	Northwich
Brochetone		Atiscros	
Brossee	Broxton	Dudestan	Broxton
Bruge	Handbridge	Cestre	
Brumhala	Bromhall	Warmondestrou	Nantwich
Budeverde	Great Budworth	Tunendune	Bucklow
Buistane	Beeston	Riseton	Edisbury
Burtone	Burton	Ditto	Ditto
Bartune	Barton	Warmondestrou	Nantwich
Burwardeslei	Burwardsley	Dudestan	Broxton
Burwardestone		Ditto	
Butelege	Butley	Hamestan	Macclesfield
Caldecote	Caldecot	Dudestan	Broxton
Calders	Caldey	Wilaveston	Wirral
Calmundelei	Cholmondeley	Dudestan	Broxton
Calvintone	Shavington	Warmondestrou	Nantwich
Cedde		Hamestan	
Celeford	Chelford	Ditto	Macclesfield
Celelea	Chowley	Dudestan	Broxton
Cepmundwicke	(Over Peover)	Bochelau	Bucklow
Cerdingham	Caringham or Kermincham	Mildestvic	Northwich
Cerlere		Warmondestrou	
Cerletune	Chorlton	Ditto	Nantwich
Chelmondestone	Cholmeston	Ditto	Ditto
Chenoterie	Knoctorum	Wilaveston	Wirral
Chingeslie	Kingsley	Roelau	Edisbury
Christetone	Christleton	Dudestan	Broxton
Cimbretune	Kinderton	Mildestvic	Northwich
Claventone	Claverton	Atiscros	
Cliftune	Clifton	Tunendune	Bucklow
Clive	Clive	Mildestvic	Northwich
Clotone	Clotton	Riseton	Edisbury
Clutune	Clutton	Dudestan	Broxton
Cocheshalle	Cogshall	Tunendune	Bucklow
Cocle		Riseton	
Cogeltone	Congleton	Mildestvic	Northwich
Colburne	Golbourn Bellow, and Golbourn David	Dudestan	Broxton
Copehall	Coppenhall	Warmondestrou	Nantwich
Copestor	Capesthorne	Hamestan	Macclesfield
Cotintone	Coddington	Dudestan	Broxton
Creu	Crewe	Warmondestrou	Nantwich
Creuhall	Crewe by Farndon	Dudestan	Broxton
Croeneche		Hamestan	
Crostone	Croughton	Wilaveston	Wirral
Crostune	Croxton	Mildestvic	Northwich
Cunetesford	Knutsford	Bochelau	Bucklow
Cuntitone	Cuddington	Dudestan	Broxton
Deneport	Davenport	Mildestvic	Northwich
Depenbech	Malpas	Dudestan	Broxton
Deveneham	Davenham	Mildestvic	Northwich
Dochintone	Duckington	Dudestan	Broxton
Dodestune	Dodleston	Atiscros	Broxton
Done			
Doneham	Dunham Massey Dunham on the Hill	Bochelau Roelau	Bucklow Edisbury
Duntune	Dutton	Tunendune	Bucklow
Ecclestone	Eccleston	Dudestan	Broxton
Edelaue		Wilaveston	
Edisberie	Edisbury		
Edulvintune	Adlington	Hamestan	Macclesfield
Eghe	Edge	Dudestan	Broxton
Eleacier		Mildestvic	
Eltone	Elton	Tunendune	Edisbury
Elveldelie	Alvanley	Roelau	Edisbury
Enelelei	Enley in Norton	Tunendune	Bucklow
Entrebus	Antrobus	Tunendune	Bucklow
Epletune	Appleton	Tunendune	Bucklow
Estham	Eastham	Wilaveston	Wirral
Estone, Estune, and Ressetune	Aston, Aston-Grange, Aston-Mondrum, &c.	Riseton, Tunendune, and Warmondestrou	Bucklow and Nantwich
Eswelle	Heswall	Wilaveston	Wirral
Eteshalle		Mildestvic	
Etingehalle	Iddenshaw	Riseton	Edisbury
Etone	Eaton	Dudestan	Broxton
Ferentone	Farndon	Dudestan	Broxton
Frotesham	Frodsham	Roelau	Edisbury
Gaitone	Gayton	Wilaveston	Wirral
Gostrel	Goostrey	Mildestvic	Northwich
Govesurde	Gawsworth	Hamestan	Macclesfield
Gravesberie	Graisby	Wilaveston	Wirral
Gropenhale	Gropenhall	Tunendune	Bucklow
Hale	Hale	Bochelau	Bucklow
Hamiteberie	Henbury	Hamestan	Macclesfield
Hanlei	Handley	Dudestan	Broxton
Hantone	Hampton	Dudestan	Broxton
Haregrave	Hargrave	Wilaveston	Edisbury
Haretone	Hatherton	Warmondestrou	Nantwich
Hefingel		Hamestan	
Helesbie	Helsby	Roelau	Edisbury
Heletune	Halton	Tunendune	Bucklow

FORMER NAME.	PRESENT NAME.	ANCIENT HUNDRED.	PRESENT HUNDRED.
Herford	Hartford	Roelau	Edisbury
Hofinchel		Hamestan	
Hoiloch	Wheelock	Mildestvic	Northwich
Holisurde	Hollingworth	Hamestan	Macclesfield
Hotone	Hooton	Wilaveston	Wirral
Hunditone	Huntington	Dudestan	Broxton
Hungrewenitune		Hamestan	
Inise	Ince	Roelau	Edisbury
Kenardeslie		Roelau	
Lai	Lea	Dudestan	Broxton
Laitone		Hamestan	
Landechen	Landican	Wilaveston	Wirral
Lautune	Lawton	Mildestivic	Northwich
Lavorchedone	Larkdon, or Larton	Dudestan	Broxton
Lece	Lees	Mildestvic	Northwich
Leche	Lache	Atiscros	Broxton
Lege	High Legh	Bochelau	Bucklow
Legh	Little Leigh	Tunendune	Bucklow
Lestone	Leighton	Wilaveston	Wirral
Levetesham	Ledsham	Wilaveston	Wirral
Lime	Lymm	Bochelau	Bucklow
Maclesfield	Macclesfield	Hamestan	Macclesfield
Maneshale and Manesselie	Church Minshull Minshull Vernon	Meldistvic	Northwich
Melas	Meoles	Wilaveston	Wirral
Menlie	Manley	Roelau	Edisbury
Mera	Mere	Bochelau	Bucklow
Merburie	Marbury	Warmondestrou	Nantwich
Meretone and Merutune	Marton	Hamestan	Macclesfield
Merlestone	Marleston	Atiscros	Broxton
Midestune	Mid-Aston, or Middleton Grange	Tunendune	Bucklow
Moletune	Moulton	Mildestvic	Northwich
Molintone	Mollington	Wilaveston	Wirral
Motburlege	Mobberley	Bochelau	Bucklow
Motre	Mottram	Hamestan	Macclesfield
Mulintune	Millington	Bochelau	Bucklow
Nesse	Nesse	Wilaveston	Wirral
Nestone	Neston	Wilaveston	Wirral
Newbold	Newbold Astbury	Mildestvic	Northwich
Newentone	Newton	Centre	Broxton
Newtone	Newton	Mildestvic	Northwich
Nordberie	Norbury	Hamestan	Macclesfield
Nortune	Norton	Tunendune	Bucklow
Norwordine	Norden, or Northenden	Bochelau	Bucklow
Oltetone	Oulton	Riseton	Edisbury
Olretune	Ollerton	Bochelau	Bucklow
Optone	Upton	Dudestan and Wilaveston	Broxton and Wirral
Ovre	Over	Dudestan	Edisbury
Ovreton	Overton	Dudestan	Broxton
Pevre	Peover	Bochelau	Bucklow
Pevreton	Peckforton	Riseton	Edisbury
Pictetone	Picton	Wilaveston	Broxton
Pol	Poole	Warmondestrou and Wilaveston	Nantwich and Wirral
Pontone		Warmondestrou	
Pontone	Poolton	Wilaveston	Wirral
Potitone	Podington	Wilaveston	Wirral
Prestune	Prenton	Wilaveston	Wirral
Pulford	Pulford	Dudestan	Broxton
Rabie	Raby	Wilaveston	Wirral
Redeclive	Radcliffe	Centre	

FORMER NAME.	PRESENT NAME.	ANCIENT HUNDRED.	PRESENT HUNDRED.
Rode	Odd-Rode	Mildestvic	Northwich
Rodesthorne	Rosthorne	Bochelau	Bucklow
Rodo	North-Rode	Hamestan	Macclesfield
Rumelie	Romily	Hamestan	Macclesfield
Rusitone	Rushton	Dudestan	Edisbury
Salhale, or Salhare	Saughall	Wilaveston	Wirral
Saltone	Saighton	Dudestan	Broxton
Sanbec	Sandbach	Mildestvic	Northwich
Santune		Warmondestrou	
Senelescune	Snelson	Bochelau	Macclesfield
Cibroc	Shipbrook	Mildestvic	Northwich
Socheliche	Shocklach	Dudestan	Broxton
Sotowiche	Shotwick	Wilavestan	Wirral
Sprostune	Sproston	Mildestvic	Northwich
Spurestone	Spurstow	Riseton	Edisbury
Stabelei, or Stablei	Tabley-Over and Nether	Bochelau	Bucklow
Stanei	Stanney	Wilaveston	Wirral
Stanlei *		Warmondestrou	
Stapleford	Stapleford	Dudestan	Broxton and Edisbury
Storeton	Stourton	Wilaveston	Wirral
Sudendune	Sidington	Hamestan	Macclesfield
Sudtone, or Sutone	Sutton	Meldestvic and Wilavestan	Northwich and Wirral
Sumreford	Somerford	Mildestvic and Wilaveston	Northwich and Wirral
Sundreland	Sunderland in Dunham Massey	Bochelau	Bucklow
Surveleg	Shurlach	Mildestvic	Northwich
Tadetune	Tetton	Mildestvic	Northwich
Tatenale	Tattenhall	Dudestan	Broxton
Tatune	Tatton	Bochelau	Bucklow
Tengestivisie	Tintwistle	Hamestan	Macclesfield
Tereth		Warmondestrou	
Terve	Tarvin	Riseton	Edisbury
Tevretone	Teverton	Riseton	Edisbury
Tidulstane	Tilston-Fernall	Riseton	Edisbury
Tellestone	Tilston	Dudestan	Broxton
Titesle		Hamestan	
Torintone	Thornton	Wilaveston	Wirral
Torintune	Thornton in the Moors	Dudestan	Edisbury
Torpelei	Tarporley	Riseton	Edisbury
Traford	Trafford	Wilaveston	Broxton
Trafford, Troford, or Trosford	Bridge Trafford Wimbold's Trafford	Roelau	Edisbury
Tuigwelle	Thingwell	Wilaveston	Wirral
Turastaneton	Thurstaston	Wilaveston	Wirral
Tusigeham	Tushingham	Dudestan	Broxton
Ulvre		Riseton	
Walcretune	Walgherton	Warmondestrou	Nantwich
Walea	Wallasey	Wilaveston	Wirral
Wareburgetune	Warburton	Bochelau	Bucklow
Wareford	Warford	Bochelau	Macclesfield
Wareneberie	Wrenbury	Warmondestrou	Nantwich
Warehelle	Wardle	Riseton	Edisbury
Warnet	Werneth	Hamestan	Macclesfield
Watenhale	Wettenhall	Riseton	Edisbury
Warretone	Waverton or Warton	Dudestan	Broxton
Wenitone	Winnington	Roelau	Edisbury
Werblestune	Worleston	Warmondestrou	Nantwich
Westanestune, or Wistetestune	Wistaston	Warmondestrou	Nantwich

* This had been formerly classed as part of the manor of Weston in Wybunbury.

FORMER NAME.	PRESENT NAME.	ANCIENT HUNDRED.	PRESENT HUNDRED.	FORMER NAME.	PRESENT NAME.	ANCIENT HUNDRED.	PRESENT HUNDRED.
Westone	Weston	Tunendume and Warmondestrou	Bucklow and Nantwich	Wireswelle	Wirswal	Warmondestrou	Nantwich
				Wisdelea		Wilaveston	
Wevre	Weaver	Mildestvic	Edisbury	Witelai	Whitley	Tunendune	Bucklow
Wibaldelai	Wimbaldesley	Mildestvic	Northwich	Witune	Witton	Mildestvic	Northwich
Wilavestune	Willaston	Warmondestrou	Nantwich	Wiveleade		Warmondestrou	
Wimeberie	Wybunbury	Warmondestrou	Nantwich	Wivevrene	Wervin	Wilaveston	Broxton
Wimundesham	Wincham	Bochelau	Bucklow	Wivreham	Weverham	Roelau	Edisbury
Wisfletone		Riseton					

It is very remarkable, that the parishes of Aldford, Astbury, Backford, Bebbington, Bidston, Brereton, Bromborow', Burton, Cheadle, Eastham, Harthill, West-Kirkby, Plemstall, Prestbury, Runcorn, Stoke, Stockport, Swettenham, Tattenhall, and Woodchurch, are not noticed in the Survey of Domesday, by name; notwithstanding this apparent omission, it contains several of their component Townships.—But there are many townships altogether omitted in the above, and several other parishes.

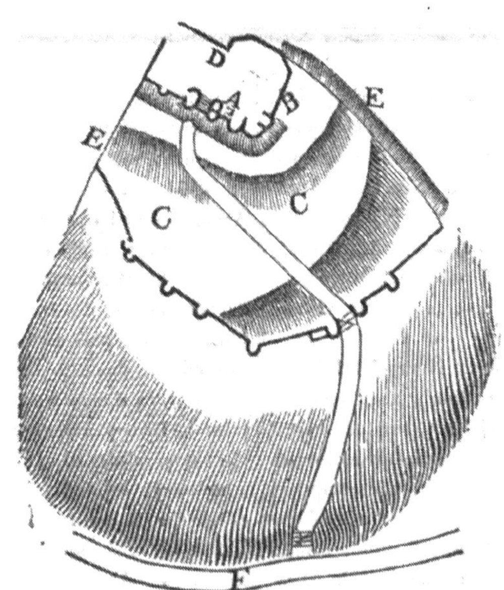

PLAN OF BEESTON CASTLE.

A—The Draw-well. B—The Ditch. C C—Outer Ward. D—Inner Ward, or Keep. E E—Precipice sides of the Rook. F—Cross-road to Tarporley, &c.

Episcopal Jurisdiction, &c.

Cheshire

The Bishops of Mercia had, at a very early period, occasionally their seats at Chester.—After the Conquest, Peter, then Bishop, removed the see to Chester, and some of our old Historians inform us he made choice of the Church of St. John for his Cathedral.—For nearly three centuries his successors were called Bishops of Chester, although Robert de Lindsey, who succeeded Peter, removed the episcopal seat to Coventry, and

† Ann. 1541 built there a splendid palace.*

Chester was made a Bishopric by Henry VIII.† and the diocese attached to it is certainly the largest in England. It includes the Archdeaconries of Chester and Richmond (which were detached from the dioceses of Lichfield and Coventry, and York)—and comprises the whole of Cheshire and Lancashire; part of the counties of York, Cumberland, and Westmoreland; four parishes in Flintshire, and a Chapelry in Den-

‡ Iscoyd. bighshire.‡ It is within the province of York, being transferred from that of Canterbury,|| by Act of Parliament of the 33d of Henry VIII. Originally the Bishops of Chester were invested with extensive temporalities. They had the manor of Weston, in the county of Derby, the manor house of which was erected for a country seat for the Bishops, and by the same Act,§ it was ordained to be within the Diocese of Chester, although it was a part previously of the Bishopric of Lichfield and Coventry;—also, the Manor of Cotton Abbots, in the Parish of Christleton—and other lands and impropriate rectories belonging to the dissolved Monastery of St. Werburgh,—and the revenues of the two Archdeaconries of Chester and Richmond. Dr. Wm. Knight, being possessed of BOTH these Archdeaconries, surrendered them to the King, who directed that the Archdeacons should each receive fifty pounds per ann. from the Bishop, in lieu of their former estates.—Among the temporalities of the Archdeacon of Chester,¶ was a messuage adjoining St. John's Church-yard; it was called the *Archdeacon's House*, and was his residence. This was in the same reign subsequently leased to the Breretons. About forty years ago it was rebuilt in a handsome manner, and Edw. Vernon, Esq. the Lessee, resided in it. It is now occupied by Mr. R. Williams, one of the Aldermen of the Body Corporate. Another house was built in the adjoining orchard, by Bishop Peploe, and is the residence of Wm. Wynne, Esq. the Lessee.**—Certain valuable mortuaries were attached to

History.

§ 33 Hen.

¶ Lysons.

* Matt. Paris says, in his days the Bishop had three seats, viz. at Chester, Lichfield, and Coventry.

|| By the Charter of Creation by Hen. VIII. the new Bishopric was placed in the province of the Archbishop of York.

** Both of these houses are delightfully situated, and have obtained the name of Dee Bank.

the Archdeaconry of Chester, viz. on the death of every Rector and Vicar within its jurisdiction, were claimed the best horse or mare with the bridle and saddle, boots and spurs; the best hat, the best book, the best upper garment, cloak, gown, or coat; cassock, doublet, and breeches; girdle, shoes, and stockings; best tippet, garters, shirt, band, and cuffs; gloves, seal, ring, purse, and all the money in it at the time of his death.—An Act of Parliament, however, was passed in the 23d year of Henry VIII. for relieving poor persons and others from payment of excessive mortuaries,—which in future were regulated in proportion to the value of the personal property of the deceased; but this act, nevertheless, acknowledged and confirmed the rights of the Archdeacon, although more burthensome, perhaps, than any other existing. The Act passed in 1755, relieved the Clergy of the Archdeaconry from these extraordinary claims; the mortuaries were finally abolished, and the Rectory of Waverton annexed to the see in lieu thereof.

The Archdeaconry of Chester is one of the largest in England: it includes the whole of Cheshire; all that part of Lancashire south of the Ribble; the four parishes in Flintshire, and the Chapelry in Denbighshire. The division of the Archdeaconry immediately within the county of Chester, is sub-divided into seven Deaneries, viz. Chester, Frodsham, Macclesfield, Nantwich, Malpas, Middlewich, and Wirral.

Bishop Bird, in 1547, surrendered to the King, the Manor of Weston, and all the temporalities of the see, receiving in exchange a few impropriate rectories, and rents in several counties, which* still are included in the revenues of the Bishop.

The Diocese at present, contains 87 parishes,† of which 9 are in the City of Chester. Of these 46 are rectories, 22 vicarages, and 18 donatives or Curacies.‡ Before the dissolution, the tythes of about 20 Parishes were appointed to the support of the different monasteries and religious houses. Most of these are in lay hands, but some three or four still belong to the See.||

† Camden says 68.

* Excepting the Rectory of Workington, in exchange for which Queen Mary, in 1557, gave a fee-farm rent of £148. 16s. 2½d. in St. Bees, the rectories of Cartmel, and Childwall, Lancashire, and the patronage of all the Prebends in Chester Cathedral.

‡ From the following extracts from the charge to the Clergy of this Diocese (in 1814) by that exemplary and truly apostolic Prelate, Dr. Law, now Bishop of Chester, some interesting facts may be gathered, as to the state of the Church immediately under his pastoral care:—

"We have to lament, that in consequence of these bills, (alluding to the Acts lately passed, with respect to the residence of the Clergy) a very general but erroneous opinion has gone abroad, with respect to the residence of the Clergy. From the late parochial returns it appears, that though there are some who had sinned against the letter of the law, there were comparatively very few, who were real and virtual offenders—few who could be charged with wilful dereliction or neglect. In this Diocese, of so great an extent, and of such an immense population, there are not many incumbents who do not at least serve one of their Churches. The total number of benefices is five hundred and ninety-two.---Upon these there are three hundred and ninety who do their own duty; five only are absent without license, or exemption. The proportion also of those who have licenses is much diminished.—Some absentees of necessity there always must be, from age, from indisposition, and various other causes of just and legal exemption. But, upon the whole, I am satisfied, there are not many, of whom, in this particular, there is just ground of complaint. The quantity also of duty which is performed, is not a little creditable to the Clergy of this Diocese. In most of the Churches or Chapels, both morning and evening service, are administered each Sunday, with two sermons; and this duty is performed upon very many livings, the value of which does not amount to £100. per ann. Let not then the services of the Parochial Clergy be lightly esteemed or underrated. With relation to the stipends of the Curates, upon which so much has of late been observed, I have no cause of complaint. The average of their salaries throughout the Diocese is £71. per annum, exclusive of the Parsonage Houses. Now when the smallness of some of the benefices themselves is taken into account, together with the expenses to which themselves or families may be subjected, this sum must be allowed to be as large, as could with propriety be demanded or wished for."

|| "Wee find no mention of a Bishop of Chester, before the Norman Conquest, onely wee find yt Divina a Scotsman, was made Bishop of Mercia, by King Osway anno, 648—whereof Cheshire was a small parcell, and that he had his Seat at Lichfield anno. 656.—From wch there remained a Succession of Bishops in the See, untill by Doome of Canon Law, all Bishops were to remove to the greater Cities in their Dioceses.—Therefore Peter Bishop of Lichfield removed his Seat from Lichfield to Chester, and was then commonly stiled Bishop

In 1740, Knutsford was made a parish by Act of Parliament. The parishes of the county, generally, are of very great extent, comprising numerous townships, and more than one chapelry.* There are many chapels of ease within the county.

Sir Peter Leycester calls those *Chapels*† *of Ease*, which have been originally built for the accommodation of one or more " townships, not having liberty of Baptism or Burial."—*Domestic Chapels* he classes as " Oratories erected in the houses of Great Persons, for the use of a private family."—*Parochial Chapels* he terms such, as being " built by a more numerous multitude of the neighbourhood, consisting of one or more villages, have got a liberty for Baptism and Burial with Consecration thereof by the Bishop, and sometimes an allowance in Money or Tythes from the Mother Church: these are, indeed, lesser parishes created within the greater for the benefit of the neighbourhood."

The following is a list, corrected by the late Wm. Nicholls, Esq. of Chester, for Messrs. Lysons, of the Parochial and Domestic Chapels in the county. To those erected within the last century, the date of Consecration is added:—

CHAPELS.	IN THE PARISH OF
D. Adlington..................	Prestbury
P. Alsager (consecrated 1789)....	Barthomley
P. Altrincham (consecrated 1799)	Bowden
* Alvanley (not now used)	Frodsham
*P. Aston	Runcorn
*Birkenhead..................	Extra Parochial
*Bosley.....................	Prestbury
P. Bruera, on Church-on-Heath	St. Oswald's, Chester
*Burleydam	Acton
*Burwardsley (consecrated 1735)	Bunbury
*Capesthorne	Prestbury
*Carrington (consecrated 1759) ..	Bowden
Chad	Malpas
*Chadkirk....................	Stockport
*Chelford	Prestbury
D. Cholmondeley..............	Malpas
Christ Church, or Chapel, Macclesfield, consecrated 1799	Prestbury
*P. Congleton	Astbury
*P. Daresbury	Runcorn
*P. Disley....................	Stockport
D. Duckenfield (not now used) ..	Stockport
*Forest Chapel...............	Prestbury
*P. Goosetrey	Sandbach
*Haslington	Barthomley
*P. Halton	Runcorn
P. Hargrave	Tarvin
P. Holmes Chapel	Sandbach
*Little St. John's, Chester, (Blue School)	Chester
*Latchford (consecrated 1781) ..	Groppenhall

of Chester.—But Robert de Lindsey the next Successor after Peter, leaving Chester, fixed his Seat at Coventry anno 1095, wch was brought back to Lichfield by Roger Clinton in the Reign of Hen. I. but so as his title was Bishop of Lichfield and Coventry.—From wch time downward, the Bishops were sometimes stiled Bishops of Coventry, from the place where they fixed their residence, having then three Sees, one at Coventry, another at Lichfield, and a third at Chester, yet all of them, one and the same Bishoprick.—At last King Hen. 8 made Chester an entire Episcopal dignity, Anno Regni sui 33. Turning the monastery of Werburg in Chester into a Bishop's Pallace, unto wch jurisdiction was allotted Chesshire, Lancashire, Richmondshire, and part of Cumberland, and was appointed to be within the Province of York.—One Thos. Clark, who had been the last Abbot of Chester, was made the first Dean of Chester, after the Erection of the new Bprick."---*From a MS. in the possession of Mr. S. Palin. Chester.*

* As this sheet is passing thro' the press, an Act is passing the Legislature, for the appropriation of 1,000,000l. towards the building of New Churches, and the enlargment of others, already in existence.—It is to be hoped, in the quota of the grant to be assigned to the portion of the Diocese within this county, that the extensive and populous parishes of Malpas, Prestbury, Budworth, &c. will not be forgotten.

† Sir Peter has the following curious definition of the word Chapel: he says the word Capella, *quasi* Capsella, is a diminutive from Capsa, which signifies a Chest or Coffer, because the relics of Saints or Holy Persons were kept in such a Chest; and the place where such Chest was kept, was so called also; *undè nomen* Capella, Capellanus, &c. *Beatus Rhenanus*, and *Durand*, do derive the word Capella, from Capa or Cappa. St. Martin's hood being so called barbarously, and carried about for good luck by Lewis the French King, in all his wars. But others derive it à *Pellibus Caprarum*, wherewith such portable tents for God's Service, as were to be removed in their Warlike Expeditions, were covered.

CHESHIRE

CHAPELS.	IN THE PARISH OF
*D. High Legh	Rostherne
*P. Little Leigh	Great Budworth
P. Macclesfield	Prestbury
P. Marbury	Whitchurch, Salop
*P. Marple	Stockport
*P. Marton	Prestbury
* Norbury	Stockport
P. Over Peover	Rostherne
D. Nether Peover	Great Budworth
*P. Pott Sbrigley	Prestbury
*P. Poynton	Prestbury
* Rainow	Prestbury
* Ringey	Bowden.
* Sattersford, or Jenkin Chapel (consecrated 1794)	Prestbury
*P. Siddington	Prestbury
* Stockport, St. Peter (consecrated 1768)	
D. Nether Tabley	Great Budworth
* Thelwall	Runcorn
P. Warburton	Annexed to a mediety of the Rectory of Lymm.
* Wettenhall	Over
D. Nether Whitley	Great Budworth
* Wincle	Prestbury
*P. Witton	Great Budworth
* Woodhead	Mottram
D. Woodhey	Acton
*P. Wrenbury	Acton.

In this list, those marked with an asterisk (*) have had an increase from Queen Anne's Bounty.—Burleydam Chapel is at the extreme angle of the Chapelry of Wrenbury, in the parish of Acton, but within the township of Dodcots-cum-Wilksley.—At Chad Chapel, Malpas, there are no christenings, although some burials have within these few years occurred there.—Chelford Chapel was pulled down, and another built on its site and consecrated in 1776.—Christenings are permitted in Christ's Church, Macclesfield, but the burials there are registered at the Old Chapel.—There are baptisms at Norbury, but no burials.—Poynton Chapel was built and consecrated in 1789.—Sattersfield Chapel was erected in 1739, but was not consecrated till 1794; divine service nevertheless, was performed in it in the interim. Wrenbury, though it differs in no respect from other parochial chapelries, is called a parish by Webb in his Itinerary.—The domestic Chapels mentioned here, are those only which are detached from the mansion.*—There were chapels formerly at Spittle Boughton, at Congleton-bridge, at Moreton (Wirral) Newton, Poosey, Stretton, Over Tabley, Wervin, and Poulton, near Eaton, but they have long since been destroyed or in ruins †

HISTORY.

Sir Peter Leycester observes, that "Brereton Church was formerly a Chappel within Astberie parish, built about the Reign of Richard the First, and dedicated to St. Oswald, whose wakes or feast of Dedication, is on the 5th of August yearly; and was made a Parish Church, and endowed with the tythes of Brereton-cum-Smethwick, about the reign of Henry VIII."

Following is given a list of the Bishops of Chester, and other dignitaries of the Church, from the foundation of the See by Henry VIII.‡

* At Hooton, and Puddington, in Wirral Hundred, the seats of Sir Thomas Stanley Massey Stanley, Bart. are two beautiful Chapels, where the service of the Church of Rome is performed.

† Leycester in his own copy of the Antiquities, in a marginal note, mentions two other domestic Chapels in these words:—also "at the Hall of Rock Savage.—Since the printing of this booke, a neate Chappell built by Sr. Peter Leycester, at his house at Tabley."

‡ The endowment of the Bishopric by Hen. 8th, was as follows:—The Archdeaconries of Chester and Richmond, with all their appurtenances, rights, &c. the manors of Abbots Cotton, county of Chester, Lands in the parishes of St. Mary, St. Martin, St. Michael, St. Werburgh, and Trinity, in Chester; City Lands in Mancot, Hawarden, Christleton, Nantwich, Northwich, Middlewich, Over, Wollaston, Neston, Heswell, Bidston, Sandhough, i. e. Sandbach, Thornton, Eccleston, Rosthern, and Davenham; Parcel of St. Werburgh's late Monastery; the advowson of Over rectory, pensions issuing out of Handley rectory, Budworth Chapel, and Bidston rectory; parcel of Birkenhead Abbey; advowsons of Tattenhall and Waverton; rectories of Clapham, Easingwold, Thornton, Stuart, Bolton-in-Lonsdale, Bolton-le-Moor, and prebend of Bolton-le-Moor, in Lichfield Cathedral; the manor of Weston, Derbyshire; habend. to the Bishop and his successors. The impropriations

Bishops.

JOHN BIRD, S. T. P. consecrated Bishop of Chester, August 5th, 1541. He suffered deprivation in 1554, for breaking his vow of celibacy. He died aged 81.

GEORGE COTES, S. T. P. consecrated to the see, 1st April, 1554. He died at Chester, January, 1555.

CUTHBERT SCOT, S. T. P. He was deprived of his Bishopric by Queen Elizabeth, and retired to Louvain, where he died.

WILLIAM DOWNHAM, A. M. consecrated May 4th, 1561. Died December 3d, 1577.

WILLIAM CHADERTON, S. T. P. consecrated Nov. 9, 1579. He was translated to the see of Lincoln, in 1595, and died at Southoe, April 11th, 1608.

HUGH BELLET, S. T. P. was prefered from the see of Bangor to Chester, June 25th, 1595. He died at Berse, near Wrexham, June 13th, 1596.

RICHARD VAUGHAN, S. T. P. translated from Bangor, May 16th, 1597. He caused the bells to be new cast, and hung in the great tower, and considerably promoted the reparation of the Cathedral of Chester. He was translated to London, Dec. 1604, and died March 30, 1607.

GEORGE LLOYD, S. T. P. He died at Thornton, and was buried in the Cathedral, August 1614.

GERARD MASSIE, S. T. P. nominated by King James to this see, but died whilst settling matters for his consecration, at London, January 16th, 1615.

THOMAS MORETON, S. T. P. consecrated July 7th, 1616. He was translated to Lichfield in 1618, and afterwards to Durham.

JOHN BRIDGMAN, S. T. P. elected Bishop March 15, 1618, and died at Little Moreton, about the year 1657.

BRIAN WALTON, S. T. P. consecrated December 2d, 1660. He died November 29th, 1661.

HENRY FERNE, S. T. P. consecrated on 7th of Feb. and died 16th March, 1662.

GEORGE HALL, S. T. P. consecrated May 11th, 1662, and died August 23d, 1668, in consequence of a wound from a knife in his pocket, on falling down a mount in his garden at Wigan, Lancashire.

JOHN WILKINS, S. T. P. brother-in-law to Oliver Cromwell. He was consecrated November 15th, 1668. Died 19th November, 1672.

JOHN PEARSON, S. T. P. consecrated February 9th, 1672. This learned Bishop after publishing a valuable Exposition of the Creed, died July 16th, 1686. He bequeathed twenty pounds to the poor of St. Oswald's.

THOMAS CARTWRIGHT, S. T. P. consecrated to this see, Oct. 17th, 1686. He was afterwards nominated to the see of Sarum, by James II. Died in Dublin, 15th April, 1689.

NICHOLAS STRATFORD, S. T. P. consecrated Sept. 15, 1689. He was particularly zealous in repairing the Cathedral, and constantly resided in his diocese. Died 12th Feb. 1706-7.

SIR WILLIAM DAWES, Baronet, S. T. P. consecrated 8th Feb. 1707. Translated to York, Feb. 26th, 1713.

and advowsons which Bishop Bird was compelled to receive by the crafty Henry in lieu of the above, were the vicarages of Cottingham, Yorkshire, Kirby, Ravensworth, Patrick Brompton, Wirklington, Ribchester, Chipping Mottrum, Bradley, Staffordshire; Castleton, Derbyshire; Wallasey, Weverham, Backford, Boden, yielding and paying as a chief rent £15. 19s. 9d. The Bishop of Chester was patron of his six Prebends and two Archdeaconries; with about thirty livings, all in his own diocese, except the following:---Llangathen, V. Carmarthenshire; Llanbeblic, V. Carnarvonshire; Castleton, V. Derbyshire; Essingwold, V. Yorkshire; in York diocese, and Bradley-le-Moor, Staffordshire; but this last the Bishop has not presented for several years.

FRANCIS GASTREL, S. T. P. consecrated to this see, 19th April, 1714.

SAMUEL PEPLOE, S. T. P. installed 19th April, 1716. He erected the galleries on the south and north sides of the Choir, in 1745, and 1749. Died 1752.

EDMUND KEENE, S. T. P. installed by proxy, April 2d, 1752. Soon after his promotion, he re-built, out of his own private property, the Episcopal Palace, at the expense of £2,200. He was translated to Ely in 1771, and died there in 1781.

WILLIAM MARKHAM, L. L. D. installed Bishop of Chester, Feb. 23d, 1771, and appointed tutor to the Prince of Wales the same year. He was translated to the Archbishopric of York, in 1777,

BEILBY PORTEUS, S. T. P. installed February 14th, 1777, and translated to the see of London, 1787.

WILLIAM CLEAVER, S. T. P. installed Feb. 12th, 1788, and translated to Bangor 1799, and afterwards to St. Asaph, where he died 1815.

HENRY WILLIAM MAJENDIE, S. T. P. installed on the 27th, 1800, and translated to the see of Bangor, in 1810, which he still holds.

EDMUND BOWYER SPARKE, S. T. P. installed Feb. 7th, 1810. Translated to Ely in 1810.

GEORGE HENRY LAW, LL. D. & F. R. S. installed July 28th, 1812.

When King Henry VIII. dissolved the Monastery of St. Werburgh, and erected it into a Cathedral, he founded a Deanery, two Archdeaconries, six Prebends, &c. granting valuable property and patronage to the Dean and Chapter.*

---

* The grants by Patent to the Dean of Chester, were the Manors of Huntington, and Sutton, the last in Wirral H. Upton, Bromborough, Ireby, Ince, Saighton, Barnshaw, Fernell-*cum-Pertinentiis*; Lands in Backford, Huntington, Cheveley, Sutton, Bromborough, Upton, Boughton, Newton, Wervin, Croughton, Stamford, Christleton, Chorlton, Lee, Morton, Salghall, Shotwick; right of the Fishery in the Dee, as customary appertaining to several of these places; rectories of Shotwick, Bromborough, Upton, West Kirkby, Prestbury, great and little Neston, Willaston, and Ince; parcel of Chester late Monastery; tythes in St. Oswald's parish, in Chester; rectory and advowson of Bampden, Gloucestershire; pension of forty pounds issuing out of Rufford manor, Lancashire; pensions out of Christleton, and the churches of St. Mary, and St. Peter, in Chester, Bebington, Eastham, West Kirkby, Thurstaston, Dodleston, Coddington, Handley, Astbury, and Northenden; advowsons of Christleton, and St. Mary's and St. Peter's, in Chester, Bebington, Thurstaston, West Kirkby, Dodleston, Coddington, Handley, Astbury, and Northenden; advowsons of the vicarages of Neston, Prestbury, St. Oswald's in Chester, and Eastham, with all lands belonging to those places which were ever parcel of Chester late Abbey: *habend.* to them and their successors *in puram et perpetuam elymosynam.* August 5. The value of the above, on founding, was as follows:—

	£.	s.	D.
Impropriations of Huntington and Cheveley manors	49	9	4
Sutton manor	11	12	2
Upton	21	11	4
In Boughton, Newton, Wervin, Croughton, Backford, Chorlton, Stamford, Christleton	104	18	2
In Moston, Salghall, Civ. Cest. cum Vico. Malbano	67	18	11
Bromborough manor	34	15	7
Bebington-cum-Eastham	21	18	6
Ireby manor	27	17	7
Ince-cum-Membris	223	2	1
	563	3	8
SPIRITUALIA.			
St. Oswald's, Chester, Prestbury, Ince, Campden, Shotwick, Upton, Neston, cum pensionibus ecclesiarum	358	10	2
	921	13	10

Out of the revenue, the Chapter had to pay according to the foundation, per annum:—

To the Dean	100	0	0
Six Prebends, twenty pounds each	120	0	0
Six Minor Canons, ten pounds each	60	0	0
The Gospel and Epistle reader at the altar, 6l. 13s. 4d. each	13	6	8
Four students at Oxford, 6l. 13s. 4d. each	26	13	4
Master of the Choristers	10	0	0
Eight Choristers, . s. 8d. each	26	13	4

CHESHIRE

HISTORY.

The Deans.

The following have been Deans of this Cathedral, from its foundation to the present time :—

THOMAS CLERK, B. D. the last Abbot, was made first Dean, August, 1541. He died or resigned in less than half a year.

HENRY MANN, S. T. P. possessed the deanery March 28th, 1542. He was installed Bishop of the Isle of Man, 1546.

WILLIAM CLIFF, L. L. D. presented May 30th, 1547. Died in London, about Dec. 7th, 1558.*

RICHARD WALKER, A. M. who died in the neighbourhood of Lichfield, 1567.

JOHN PEERS, S. T. P. presented Oct. 4th, 1567. He resigned towards the close of 1571.

RICHARD LANGWORTH, S. T. P. Died about the 19th of April, 1579.

ROBERT DORSET, S. T. P. presented August 17th, 1579. He died May 29th, 1580.

THOMAS MODESLEY, B. D. presented August 12th, 1580. Died in the beginning of June, 1589.

JOHN NUTTER, B. D. presented July 4th, 1589.—Died March 30th, 1602.

WILLIAM BARLOW, S. T. P. installed June 12th, 1602. He resigned on being consecrated Bishop of Rochester, 1605.

HENRY PARRY, S. T. P. installed August 1st, 1605, He was consecrated Bishop of Gloucester, 1607.

THOMAS MALLORY, B. D. installed July 25th, 1607. Died April 3d, 1644.

WILLIAM NICHOLLS, S. T. P. installed April 12th, 1644. He died Dec. 16th, 1657.

HENRY BRIDGMAN, S. T. P. presented July 13th, 1660. He died May 15th, 1682.

JAMES ARDERNE, S. T. P. installed July, 1682. He died August 18th, 1691. As an example to the Clergy, he bequeathed the bulk of his estate to the Cathedral, not willing to sweep all away from the Church and Charity, amongst their lay kindred, who are not needy.

	£.	s.	D.
Master of the Grammar School	16	13	4
Under Master	8	0	0
Twenty-four Scholars, 3l. 6s. 8d. each	80	0	0
Six Almsmen, 6l. 13s. 4d. each	40	0	0
In Alms	20	0	0
To be expended in repairs	20	0	0
For first fruits (and afterwards a tenth ann.)	106	16	5
	648	3	1

The Dean and Chapter, at this time, present to no livings but those in Chester.

* It was in this Dean's time, that the great loss in the Chapter Revenues took place. On the 20th Nov. 1550, the manor of Idenshaw was surrendered by the Dean, and on the 14th of May, 1553, he had a license granted to alienate the manor of Huntington and Cheveley, to Sir R. Cotton, Comptroller of the Household to Edw. VI. Sir Robert, it is stated, having procured the imprisonment of the Dean and two Prebendaries, compelled them by intimidation to make over the Church estates to him. Subsequently, the Chapter having discovered that the grant of Henry VIII. was null, by the omission of the word CESTRIE, made known the fact to Queen Elizabeth, praying she would re-grant to them the estates illegally obtained by Sir R. Cotton. The petition was attended to, and twice argued in the Court of Exchequer. The fee-farmers in possession of the estates (Sir Robert having sold them to Cheshire gentlemen at very low prices) apprehensive that they might lose them, bribed the Earl of Leicester, on their behalf, with six year's rent of the land. This powerful stimulus speedily prompted the Earl to put a stop to further proceedings, and he obtained a Commission for hearing the matter BEFORE HIMSELF and other Lords of the Privy Council; the result, as might be expected, was, that in 1580, the Old Charter of the Chapter was recalled by the Queen, and the estates were confirmed to the fee farmers, on the payment of certain rents, with which, and a few impropriations, she re-endowed the Chapter, preserving, however, the old rate for first fruits and annual tenths:

LAWRENCE FOGG, S. T. P. installed November 2d, 1691. He died Februray 27th, 1718.

WALTER OFFLEY, A. M. installed March 27th, 1718. Died August 18th, 1721.

THOMAS ALLEN, LL. D. installed Dec. 6th, 1721. Died in the year 1733.

THOMAS BROOKE, LL. D. installed July 18th, 1733. He died in 1758.

WILLIAM SMITH, D. D. installed July 28th, 1758. In the course of an active life, he published many very valuable works. He died January 12th, 1787.

GEORGE COTTON, LL. D. installed February 10th, 1787. Died at Bath, in 1806.

HUGH CHOLMONDELEY, B. D. installed 28th March, 1806. This valuable man set on foot the reparation of the Cathedral, opened the different avenues in the cloisters, and other parts long before blocked up, and erected the iron palisadoes in front of the Cathedral. He was beloved for his unostentatious charities, and admired for his exertions in promoting objects of real utility. He died 25th Nov. 1815.

ROBERT HODGSON, D. D. installed December, 1815.

Archdeacons.

The Rev. UNWIN CLARKE, M. A. Archdeacon of Chester.

The Rev. JOHN OWEN, B. A. Archdeacon of Richmond.

Prebends.

Rev. T. WARD, A. M. Rev. T. T. TREVOR, D. D. Rev. U. CLARKE, A. M. Rev. T. MADDOCK, A. M. Rev. J. SLADE, A. M. Rev. J. T. LAW, A. M.

Minor Canons.

Rev. T. MAWDESLEY, A. M. Rev. J. EATON, A. M. (Precentor) Rev. J. IRELAND, A. M. Rev. T. ARMITSTEAD, B. D. Rev. T. MOLINEUX, A. M. Rev. M. TAYLOR, A. M.

Ecclesiastical Courts, &c.

A list of Ecclesiastical Courts and Peculiars, within the Diocese of Chester:

CONSISTORY COURT OF CHESTER, having jurisdiction throughout the Diocese of Chester.

CHANCELLOR—Rev. T. Parkinson, D. D.

RURAL DEAN—Rev. Unwin Clarke, M. A.

REGISTRAR—B. Keene, Esq. Deputy, Wm. Ward, Esq.

Mr. Edw. Pate,
S. Baker,
E. Jones,
W. Ward, jun. } PROCTORS

RURAL DEAN'S COURT, having a limited jurisdiction within the Archdeaconry of Chester. Registrar, Wm. Ward, Esq.

HAWARDEN, in the county of Flint. A Peculiar, under the jurisdiction of the Rector thereof; has cognizance of Ecclesiastical Causes, proves Wills, grants Letters of Administration, and Marriage Licenses. Registrar, Francis E. Barker, Esq. Chester.

CONSISTORY COURT OF RICHMOND, in the county of York, having limitted jurisdiction within the Archdeaconry of Richmond. Registrar, Benjamin Keene, Esq. Deputy, Octavius Leefe, Esq.

NOTE.—There was a Consistory Court at Lancaster, within the Archdeaconry of Richmond, in which Courts were formerly held, but which have been for several years discontinued, and the parties cited to Richmond.

There is still a Registry at Lancaster, for Probate of Wills, granting Letters of Administration, Marriage Licences, &c. within the Deaneries of Amounderness, Lonsdale, Kendal, Furness, and Copeland. Registrar, Benjamin Keene, Esq. Deputy, John Dowbiggin.

Cheshire History.

HALTON, in the county of Lancaster.—The Lord of the Manor, WILLIAM BRADSHAW BRADSHAW, Esq. claims Probate of Wills, and Letters of Administration within the same; his Steward acts as Actuary or Registrar.

MARSHAM, otherwise MASHAM CUM KIRKBY MALZERD, in the county of York, a Peculiar, claimed by Thomas Hutchinson, of Hipwell Lodge, county of York, Esq.

MIDDLEHAM Deanery, in the county of York, a Royal Peculiar. Registrar of Richmond

KIRKBY IRELITH, in the county of Lancaster; and ALDBOROUGH, BURTON LEONARD, DUNSFORTH, HORNBY, } In the county of York, Peculiars claimed by the Dean and Chapter of York. Registrar, Wm. Mills, of York.

USBORNE PARVA, a Peculiar in the county of York, claimed by the Præcentor of the Cathedral Church of York.

HUNSINGSORE, in the county of York, assumes exemption from the Bishop of Chester's jurisdiction, except in Institution by him.

THE DIOCESE OF CHESTER.

Contains two Archdeaconries, in which are 599 Churches and Chapels.
1 The Archdeaconry of Chester has 12 Deaneries, containing 320 Churches and Chapels;
2 The Archdeaconry of Richmond has 8 Deaneries, containing 279 Churches and Chapels.

EXPLANATION.—Names in Small Capitals are Rectoral or Vicarial Churches; those in Small Letters are dependent Churches or Chapels, many of which are Parochial. Those in Black Letter are Borough Towns. R. Rectory.—V. Vicarage.—CI. Curacy to an Impropriation.—Dis. signifies a Living discharged from the Payment of First Fruits.

ARCHDEACONRY OF CHESTER.

Chester Deanery.

Having 28 Churches & Chapels.
In Chester City.

ST. BRIDGET'S .... R
ST. JOHN BAPTIST V
St. John Little
ST. MARY'S .... R
St Michael's
St. Olave's
ST. OSWALD'S dis. V
Bruera, or Church on Heath
ST. PETER'S, dis. .... R
TRINITY, dis. .... R
CATHEDRAL CHURCH OF CHRIST AND THE BLESSED V. M.

In Cheshire and Wales.

BARROW .... R
CHRISTLETON .... R
DODLESTON .... R
ECCLESTON .... R
FARNDON CI
GUILDEN SUTTON CI
HAWARDEN .... R
HOLT CI
Iscoyd
INCE CI
PLEMONSTALL CI
PULFORD .... R
TARPORLEY .... R
TARVIN V
Hargrave
THORNTON .... R
WAVERTON .... R

Wirral Deanery.

Having 16 Churches and Chapels.

BACKFORD, dis V
BEBINGTON .... R
BIDSTON CUM FORD CI
Birkenhead
BROMBOROW CI
BURTON CI
EASTHAM, dis. V
HESWALL .... R
NESTON V
OVERCHURCH CI
SHOTWICK CI
STOKE CI
THURSTASTON, dis. .... R
WALLASEY MED. dis. .... R
WEST KIRKBY .... R
WOODCHURCH .... R

Bangor Deanery.

Having 4 Churches and Chapels.

BANGOR .... R
Overton
HANMER V
WORTHENBURY .... R

Malpas Deanery.

Having 11 Churches and Chapels.

ALDFORD .... R
CODDINGTON, dis. .... R
HANDLEY, dis. .... R
HARTHILL CI
MALPAS .... RR
St. Chad
Whitwell
SHOCKLACH .... R
TATTENHALL .... R
TILSTON .... R
Threapwood, Consecrt. 1817.

Nantwich Deanery.

Having 16 Churches and Chapels.

Acton V
Burleydam
Wrenbury
AUDLEM V
BADDELEY, dis. .... R
BARTHOMLEY .... R
Haslington
Alsager
BUNBURY CI
Burwardsley
COPPENHALL .... R
MINSHULL CI
NANTWICH .... R
WYBUNBURY V
WISTASTON, dis .... R
Marbury in the Parish of Whitchurch

Middlewich Deanery.

Having 15 Churches and Chapels.

ASTBURY .... R
Congleton
BRERETON .... R
BUDWORTH PARVA CI
DAVENHAM .... R
LAWTON, dis. V
MIDDLEWICH, dis. V
OVER dis. V
Wettenhall
SANDBACH V
Goostrey
Holmes Chapel
SWETTENHAM .... R
WARMINGHAM .... R
WHITEGATE, dis. V

Macclesfield Deanery.

Having 32 Churches and Chapels.

ALDERLEY .... R
CHEADLE .... R
GAWSWORTH .... R
MOBBERLEY .... R
MOTTRAM V
Woodhead
NORTHENDEN .... R
PRESTBURY V
Adlington
Bosley
Capesthorne
Chelford
Forest Chapel
Macclesfield
Christ Church, Macclesfield
Pott
Marton
Newton
Poynton
Rainow
Saltersford
Siddington
Wincle
STOCKPORT .... R
St. Peter's, Stockport
Chadkirk

Disley
Duckenfield
Marple
Norbury
TAXALL, dis. .... R
WILMSLOW .... R

Frodsham Deanry.

Having 26 Churches & Chapels.

ASHTON ON MERSEY .... R
BOWDEN V
Carrington
Altrincham
Ringey
BUDWORTH MAGNA V
Little Leigh
Nether Peover
Witton
FRODSHAM V
Alvanley
GROPPENHALL .... R
Latchford
KNUTSFORD V
LYMM .... RR
Warburton
ROSTHERN V
High Leigh
Over Peover
RUNCORN V
Aston
Daresbury
Thelwall
Halton
WAVERTON V
DELAMERE .... R

Manchester Deanry.

Having 70 Churches & Chapels.

ASHTON-UNDER-LINE .. R
Lees
Mosley
Stayley Bridge
BOLTON-IN-THE-MOOR, dis V
Little Bolton
Blackrod
Bradshaw
St. George
Rivington
Turton
Walmsley
Lever
BURY .... R
St. John's
Etonfield
Heywood
Holcomb
DEAN, dis. V
Horwich
Peel
Westhoughton
ECCLES, dis .... V.
Ellenbrook
Swinton
Pendleton
FLIXTON CI
MANCHESTER COLLEGE
St. Ann's, Manchester R
St. John ditto .... R
St. Mary ditto .... R
St. Paul ditto .... R
St. Peter's Church
Ardwick
St. James's Chapel.
Birch
St. Michael's
Blakeley
Chorlton.
Cheetham
Denton
Didsbury
Gorton
Heaton Norsis
Newton
Salford
St. Stephen's
Stretford
MIDDLETON........ R
Ashworth
Cockey
PRESTWICH .... R
Royton
Oldham
St. Peter's ditto
Hollinwood
Ringley
Unsworth Church
Shaw
ROCHDALE .... V,
Hundersfield in Roch Town
Littlebrough
Milnrow
Saddleworth
Friarmere
Dobcross
Todmordin
Whitworth
Lydiate
RATCLIFF .... R

Warrington Deanry

Having 59 Churches & Chapels.

ALTCAR........ CI
AUGHTON........ R
CHILDWALL V
Hale
Wavertree
Garston
HALSALL .... R
Maghull
Melling
HUYTON, dis. V
LEIGH, dis. V
Astley
Atherton or Chowbent
Liverpool, Old Ch. R
Trinity
St. Stephen's
St. Matthew's
Christ Church
St. Peter
St. George
St. James
St. John
St. Paul
St. Thomas
St. Ann Rich.
St. Mark's
St. Andrew's
NORTHMEOLS .... R
ORMSKIRK, dis. V
Shelmersdale
PRESCOT V
St. Helen's
Farnworth
Rainford
Sankey
SEPHTON .... R
Crosby magna
Seaforth
WALTON .... RV
Formby
Kirkby
West Derby
Edge Hill
Everton
Toxteth
WARRINGTON........ R
Burtonwood
Hollinfare
Trinity
Wigan .... R
St. George
Billing
Hindley
Holland
WINWICK .... R
Ashton
Lowton
New Church
Newton

Blackburn Deanry,

Having 27 Churches & Chapels.

BLACKBURN V
St. John's
Balderston
Darwen
Harwood
Lango
Law Church, or Walton
Samlesbury
Salesbury
Tockholes
WHALLEY V
Altham
Acrington
Bacup
Burnley
Holme
Clithero
Church Kirk
Colne
Marsden
Downham
Goodshaw
Haslingden
New Church, in Pendle
New Church in Rossendale
Padiam
Whitewell

Leland Deanry.

Having 16 Churches & Chapels.

BRINDLE, dis. .... R
CROSTON .... R
Beconstall
Chorley
Rufforth
Tarleton
ECCLESTON .... R
Douglas
HOOLE, dis. .... R
LEYLAND V
Euston
Heapy
PENWORTHAM CI
Longton
STANDISH .... R
Coppul

ARCHDEACONRY OF RICHMOND.

Amounderness DEANRY.

Having 39 Churches & Chapels.

BISHAM CI
Chipping V
COCKERHAM, dis. V
Ellell
Shireshead
GARSTANG V
Garstang
Pilling
KIRKHAM V
Goosnargh
White Chapel
Hambleton
Lund
Rigby, or Ribby
Singleton
Warton
Lancaster .... V.
St. John
St. Anne
Admarsh
Littledale
Overton

Poulton
Stalmin
Wyresdale
Lytham CI
St. Michael's, dis V
Cop, or Eccleston
Woodplumpton
Poolton, dis. V
Preston V
Marton
St. George
Broughton
Grimsargh
St. Lawrence
Ribchester V
Longridge
Stidd

Lonsdale Deanry.

Having 28 Churches & Chapels.

Bentham .... R
Ingleton
Ingleton Fell, or Chapel in the Dale
Clapham, dis. V
Claughton, dis. .... R
Kirby Lonsdale, dis. ... V
Barbon
Firbank
Hutton Roof
Killington
Mansergh
Middleton
Melling, dis. V
Archolm
Hornby
Sedberg, dis. V
Dent
Garsdale
Howgill
Tatham .... R
Tathamfel
Thornton V
Burton
Tunstall, dis. V
Leck
Whittington .... R
Caton and Cressingham, in Lancaster Parish

Kendal Deanry.

Having 36 Churches & Chapels.

Betthom, dis. V
Witherslack
Bolton-in-the-Sands dis. V
Overkellet
Burton, dis. V
Preston Patrick
Grassmere .... R
Ambleside, part in Windermere Parish
Langdale
Halton .... R
Aughton
Heversham V
Crossthwaite
Crosscrake
Heysham .... R
Kendal V
St. George
Burnside
Crook
Grayrigg
Helsington
Hugil, or Ings
Kentmire
Natland
Long Sledal
New Hutton
Old Hutton
Selside
Stavely
Underbarrow
Winster
Warton V
Borwick
Silverdale
Windermere .... R
Troutbeck

Furness Deanry.

Having 29 Churches & Chapels.

Adlington .... R
Dendron
Cartmel CI
Cartmelfel
Fieldbroughton
Flookborough
Lindale
Stavely
Coulton CI
Finsthwaite
Russland
Dalton, dis. V
Kirby Irelith
Ramside
Walney
Hawkshead CI
Satterthwaite
Kirby, dis. V
Broughton
Seathwaite
Woodland
Pennington CI
Ulverston V
Egton
Blawith
Coniston
Lowick
Torver
Urswick, dis. V

Copeland Deanry.

Having 44 Churches & Chapels.

Arlecden CI
Bootle .... R
St. Bridget's CI
Brigoham, dis.
Cockermouth
Seemurthy
Embleton
Lorton
Mosser
Buttermere
Wythrop
St. Bees CI
Ennerdale
Eskdale
Hensingham
Lousewater
Nether Wasdal
Wasdal Head
Trin. Chapel, St. Nicholas, St. James } Whitehaven
Cleater CI
Corney, dis. .... R
Dean .... R
Distington .... R
D[illegible] CI
Egremont, dis. .... R
Gosforth, dis. .... R
Harrington, dis. .... R
Hayle CI
St. John's CI
Irton CI
Lamplugh .... R
Millam, dis. V
Thwaites
Ulpha
Moresby, dis. .... R
Muncaster CI
Ponsonby CI
Waberthwaite, dis. .... R
Whitbeck CI
Whicham, dis. .... R
Workington .... R
Clifton

Richmond Deanry.

Having 38 Churches & Chapels.

Ainderby Steeple, dis. V
Arkengarthdale CI
Barningham .... R
Bowes CI
Brignall V
Cleasby CI
Croft .... R
Danbywiske .... R
Yeaforth
Easby V
East-Cowton, dis. ...... F
Gilling V
Barton St. Mary's
Eryholm
Forcet
Hutton Magna
South Cowton
Grinton, dis. V
Muker
Kirkbywisk .... R
Kirkby Ravensworth .. CI
Langton-on-Swale, dis. R
Manfield V
Marrick CI
Marsk .... R
Melsonby .... R
Middleton Tyas V
Richmond .... R
Trinity
Romaldkirk .... R
Laithkirk
Rookby, dis. V
Sneaton .... R
Stanwick V
Barton Cuthberts
Startforth, dis. V
Wycliff .... R
Bolton on Swale, in Catterick Parish

Catterick Deanry.

Having 40 Churches & Chapels.

Aisgarth, dis. V
Askrigg
Hardrow
Hawes
Lunds
Stalinbusk
Bedale .... R
Burneston V
Leeming
Catterick V
Bolton on Swale
Hipswell
Hudswell
Coverham CI
Horsehouse
Downholm CI
Eastwitton V
Finghall .... R
Hawkswell .... R
Hornby, Pec. dis. V
Kirkby Fletham, dis. .. V
Kirklington .... R
Marsham ...., Kirkby Malzerd .. } V
Middleham, Decanus, Pec.
Patrick Brompton CI
Hunton
Pickhall, dis. V
Spenithorn .... R
Bellerby
Scruton .... R
Tanfield .... R
Thornton Steward, dis. V
Thornton Watlas .... R
Wath .... R
Well, dis. V
Wensley .... R
Bolton
Redmire
West Witton CI

Boroughbridge D.

Having 25 Churches & Chapels.

Aldborough dis V
Boroughbridge
Dunsforth
Allerton Malleverer CI
Burton Leonard, dis. Pec. .... } V
Copgrave, dis. .... R
Cundal V
Farnham V
Goldsborough .... R
Hunsingore, Pec V
Kirkby-sup.-Moram dis. V
Marton-on-the-Moor
Kirkhamerton CI

CHESHIRE					HISTORY.
	Knaresborough .. V Harrowgate Arkendale	MARTON CUM GRAFTON dis V NIDD, dis. .... V NUNMONKTON CI	OUSEBURN MAGNA, dis. .. V OUSEBURN PARVA, Pec. . CI RIPLEY.................. R	STAINLEY .... CI STAVELEY.............. R WHIXLEY.............. CI	

Population of the Diocese, according to the Returns to Parliament, in 1801.

CHESHIRE	191,751
LANCASHIRE	672,731
YORKSHIRE (NORTH RIDING)	51,103
WEST DITTO	20,343
CUMBERLAND	37,833
WESTMORELAND	24,230
WALES	9,255
TOTAL	1,007,246

The greatest length of the diocese is .... 120 miles.
The greatest width 90
The length of the boundary line 570

Other particulars relative to the Diocese will appear under the Head CATHEDRAL OF CHESTER, in that portion of the work appropriated to the HISTORY OF CHESTER.

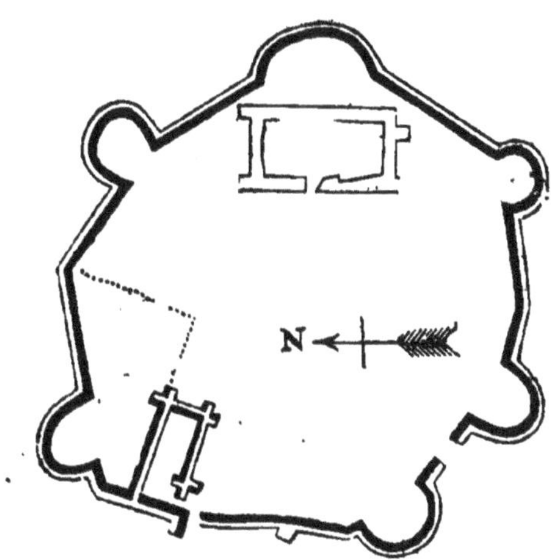

PLAN OF SHOTWICK CASTLE.

Market Towns in Cheshire.

History.

There are but fourteen Market Towns in this County, viz. Chester, Altrincham, Congleton, Frodsham, Knutsford, Macclesfield, Malpas, Middlewich, Nantwich, Neston, Northwich, Sandbach, Stockport, and Tarporley. At Winsford-bridge, between Middlewich and Over, there is a weekly provision market. The principal corn-markets, are held at Chester, Nantwich, Sandbach, Congleton, Middlewich, Macclesfield, and Stockport: but most business is transacted at the Four-lane-ends, near Tarporley. In addition to the customary market, there is a cattle market held at Nantwich, from the first Saturday in February, to the last Saturday in May; this is called the New Market. Neither Neston nor Tarporley are mentioned by King as being Market Towns; but from its being clearly ascertained that Markets were held there long before the time of that writer, it has been conjectured they were then discontinued—they are now, however, revived.—Aldford, Alderley, Audlem, Brereton, Coddington, and Upton, had Charters for Markets, but they have long since been discontinued, with the exception of Audlem, the market of which was revived in the year 1817, by Mascie Taylor, Esq. Lord of the Manor, under the authority of the Charter, granted by Edw I. to Thoma de Aldelym. A market, by prescription, was formerly held at Halton, but it has long been decayed: Sir Piers Dutton, however, temp. Hen. VIII. intended to have procured a Charter for it, but death prevented him. The fairs at Northwich, are chiefly for the sale of Yorkshire goods; but those at Chester and Macclesfield, are for general sales, as Cattle, Wool, Cloth, Linen, Cotton, Hardware, &c.—These will be properly noticed under the respective heads of the towns.

ITINERARY

OF

THE HUNDREDS OF CHESHIRE;

THE

Parishes inserted in Alphabetical Order.

COMMENCING

WITH

THE HUNDRED OF BROXTON.

The notices of Principal Land Owners—of Noble and Knightly Families, &c. with their seats—Families Extinct and Existing—Ancient and Modern Roads—Customs, &c. &c. &c. will be introduced after the Itinerary of the different Hundreds, together with the copy of Domesday-book, so far as it relates to Cheshire, and other curious and interesting matter.—The History of Chester, which will probably commence in Part V. will be more copious than any hitherto published.

The Oratory, in the Refectory of St. Werburgh's Monastery, Chester.

Hundred of Broxton.

PARISHES.

ALDFORD	ECCLESTON	MARY, ST.	SHOCKLACH
BUNBURY	FARNDON	MALPAS	TARVIN, PART OF
CHRISTLETON	GUILDEN SUTTON	OSWALD, ST.	TILSTON
CODDINGTON	HANDLEY	PLEMONSTALL	TATTENHALL
DODLESTON	HARTHILL.	PULFORD	WAVERTON

HINDMARSH (Malpas) Extra-parochial.

PARISH OF ALDFORD,

CONTAINS FOUR TOWNSHIPS,

ALDFORD, BUERTON, CHURTON, PART OF EDGERLEY.

CHESHIRE HISTORY.

Aldford is 5 miles S. E. of Chester, pleasantly situated on the banks of the Dee, over which it has a good bridge. In former times, it had a Market on Tuesday, granted to Walkelin de Arderne, about 1253, and a fair for three days, at the Festival of the Holy Cross. It is somewhat remarkable, that Aldford is altogether unnoticed in the Survey. It no doubt, however, formed part of the extensive estates of Bigot at the Conquest; and took its present name about the time of Randle Blundeville. In the reign of Henry II. Robert de Aldford, took to wife Mary daughter of Richard Fitz Eustace, baron of Halton;* and it is probable about this time the Castle which it once possessed, was erected. Aldford afterwards became the head of a great fee, held in capite by military service from the Earls.—Richard de Aldford was the Lord in the time of King John.—Between the 10th of King John, and the 13th Hen. III. Sir John Arderne† succeeded to the fee of Aldford, and occupied the Castle. By the Charter of Confirmation granted to him, he is entitled to the privilege of free duel in his Court, and ordeal by fire and water, "*Et libertate duelli habendi in curiâ suâ, et cum juisio ignis et aquæ*, et cum omnibus libertatibus et aisiamentis intra villam et extra villam, et cum advocatione ecclesiarum et capellarum, et cum omnibus prædicto feodo de Aldeford pertinentibus." The witnesses to the charter,

* Ormerod.

† This Sir John Arderne is supposed to be the Son-in-law of Richard de Aldford.

CHESHIRE

are "Philippo de Orreby tunc justiciario meo, Rogero de Montealto seneschallo meo, Henrico de Audelegh, Warino de Vernon, Willielmo de Venables, Hamone de Massy, Rogero de Meingarin, Roberto Patricio, Waltero de Leynet,* Petro clerico meo Hugone, Thoma, Henrico, et Gilberto Dispensatoribus."

This fee descended lineally to the Ardernes of Aldford and Alvanley, till the reign of Edward III. Sir John Arderne then dying without any legitimate heirs, settled Aldford and some of its dependencies on Thomas, his son by Ellen his wife, but born previous to marriage. From this Thomas, the descent is clear to the present time. In the 3d. of Edward IV. Thomas Stanley, of Elford, Esq. died; he married Maud, daughter and heiress of Sir John Arderne, Knt. who was seized of the manors of Aldford, Alderley, and Etchells, after the death of Maud with remainder to their son, Sir John Stanley, Knt.—It continued in this branch of the Stanley (or *Standley)* family, till the reign of Henry VIII. when by the death of Christopher Savage, son and heir of Anne, daughter and coheiress of the before-mentioned John, Aldford and its dependencies became vested in Sir William Stanley, of Holt; and after his attainder and execution, was purchased from the Crown by Sir William Brereton, seventh son of Sir Randle Brereton, of Shocklach; but in 1546, he also was attainted and executed.—Another grant from the Crown was then made to Edw. Peckham, the King's Cofferer, for 30 years, on payment of an annual rent of 100l. with reversion to Margery Monitor, subject to a rent of 60l. per Annum. The grantees dying, in the 3d and 4th of Philip and Mary, the Manor of Aldford, and its dependencies, were sold to Sir E. Fitton, and Robert Tatton, Esq.—From the Fittons it passed to Charles Gerard,† Lord Brandon, who became Earl of Macclesfield, whose niece Lady Mohun, jointly with her third husband, Charles Mordaunt, Esq. sold it in 1729, to Sir Richard Grosvenor.—It is now the property of the Right Hon. Robert Earl Grosvenor.

The ford, from which the town derives its name, is situated a short distance below the town; and a little above it are thrown up some earthworks, intended for the defence of this important point of communication between the northern and southern Watling-streets.

HISTORY.

The foundations of the Castle, moated half round, are still visible. The Keep is on an eminence, now called the Blobb Hill. The outer Court forms an unequal triangle, the sides of which are about 130, 120, and 55 yards in length, the whole encircled by a foss nearly 20 yards wide. The keep is perfectly circular, and is surrounded by a Moat 40 yards wide.

At present there is a Court Leet and Baron held here; and the freeholders of Thornton and Elton attend it, but have distinct juries. Formerly the fee of Aldford had jurisdiction over Mobberley, Ollerton, Sutton, Occleston, Wimboldsley, Baguley, Thornton, half of Farndon, and Weaver, Nether Alderley, Siddington, *Yeaton*, Norbury, Offerton, Torkington, and Sharlston.

A handsome school was a short time ago erected here by Earl Grosvenor, but it is supported by the inhabitants.

Aldford Church nearly adjoins the old Castle Moat. It consists of nave, chancel, and short spire steeple, having a ring of four bells.—The advowson of the Rectory is attached to the Manor; and the Rector has tythe of all the townships, excepting a modus for hay. Buerton pays hay-tythes of agistment.—The present Rector is the Rev. R. Massie, A. M. instituted Jan. 28, 1811.

There are no remarkable funeral mementoes in the Church: in the Church-yard, is the recumbent figure of a female, in red stone.

BUERTON

Was held by the Pulfords of Pulford, under the Ardernes, in the reign of Hen. III. and by an Inquisition temp. Edw. I. we find it was held by service of repairing the fortifications of Aldford Castle, or assisting in its defence. This Manor passed by female heirs to the Grosvenors, of Hulme; but in the reign of

* Probably the father of Walter Lynnett, first Mayor of Chester, on record.

† Nephew of the last Sir Edward Fitton.

Edw. IV. Agnes, daughter and co-heiress of Robert Grosvenor, brought Buerton as her portion to Sir Wm. Stanley, of Hooton, in which family it has since continued, and passed, with Hooton, to Sir Thomas Stanley Massey Stanley, Bart. the present proprietor. On the Church-on-Heath side of the Township, is the site of an old moated mansion.

CHURTON.

All the northern part of this Township, is in the parish of Aldford. Roger Barnston, Esq. is the proprietor.

EDGERLEY,

Although not noticed in Doomsday, no doubt formed part of the greater dependency of Coddington, which was formed of three Saxon manors. It belonged originally to the Montalts—then to the Botilers of Wem, and was purchased from them by William Massie.§ The estates of this family were partitioned in the reign of Edward IV. when Edgerley was given to Morgan Massie, and he it was who founded the Massies of *Edgerley*, in whom the manor was vested till about the end of the 17th century, when a Mr. Smallwood purchased it.—His descendant, Mr. Thomas Smallwood, possessed it in 1759, when it was purchased by the Rev. Thomas Ince. Townshend Ince, Esq. of Christleton, is the present proprietor.

§ 18 Henry VI.

THE PARISH OF BUNBURY,

CONTAINS TWELVE TOWNSHIPS:

ALPRAHAM	BURWARDESLEY	PECKFORTON	TIVERTON
BUNBURY	CALVELEY	RIDLEY	TILSTON FERNALL
BEESTON	HAUGHTON	SPURSTOW	WARDLE.

ALPRAHAM is situated about three miles and a half from Tarporley.—About 1380, the manor was divided amongst the seven daughters of Matthew de Alpraham, in whose family it had long been vested. About the 4th Richard II. Thomas Bulkeley, having married one of the co-heiresses, was possessed of a share of the manor: this portion descended by a succession of female heirs to the Ardernes and Stanleys.—The estate was divided between the Crewes, Leghs (of High Legh), Mostyns, and Wilbrahams, in 1701; but in 1662, the manor was the property of Sir Thomas Wilbraham, although in the reign of Elizabeth, it belonged to Sir Thomas Egerton. The Earl of Dysert, as representative of the Wilbrahams, is the present owner. The Crewes possessed three shares out of seven of the manor, by inheritance from the Dones.

BUNBURY,

At the period of the Conquest, was granted to the Baron of Malpas, Robert Fitz-Hugh; and on a subsequent division of the Barony, Bunbury fell to the lot of Patrick, who married Letitia, eldest daughter and coheir of Robert Fitz-Hugh. In their descendants, the paramount Lordship was vested.

About the reign of King John, Humphrey de Bunbury dying without male issue, the manor was divided between his two daughters, Almeria and Joan. The moiety of Almeria descended to the Patricks, from whom it passed to the St. Pierres. The daughter and heiress of Urian de St. Pierre, Isabella, brought it in marriage to Sir Walter Cokesey, early in the 14th century; and it continued in this family and its representatives, the Gryvell's, nearly two hundred years. In an Inquisition, 22d Henry VII. the heir to the estate was found to be John Younge, then Somerset Herald.—This moiety eventually passed to the Wilbrahams, by purchase from Lord Keeper Egerton, in 1598; and it appears from the Harl. MSS. that in 1671, Sir Thomas Wilbraham ranked as Lord of the Manor of Bunbury.* All the

* It is probable the manerial rights were divided, as we find that in 1662, Thomas Bunbury, Esq. of Stanney, is de-

manerial rights are now vested in the Earls of Dysert, Grace Wilbraham, daughter and co-heiress of Sir Thos. Wilbraham, having married Lionel Tolmache, then Earl of Dysert.

The other moiety passed by descent from Alex. de Bunbury to David de Bunbury, and he settled the advowson of the Church of Bunbury, and the manor of Stanney, by fine, on his son, William de Bunbury.

The joint rights of manor remained in the family till the time of the late Sir William Bunbury: disputes then arose; and the matter being sent to reference, it was decided that the Earl of Dysert had the sole manerial right.

A Court Leet and Court Baron for the manor, is now held by the Earl of Dysert, in conjunction with his Court for Tilston Fernall, which is an adjoining township.

In the 14th century, the Bunbury family removed to Stanney; but Sir Thomas Charles Bunbury, Bart. has still an estate in the parish; so also has Sir Thomas Mostyn, Bart. and Samuel Aldersey, Esq. of Aldersey.

Bunbury is situated about thirteen miles from Chester, and about two miles from the right hand of the great road from Chester to Nantwich. It is divided by the Gowy, which runs between the upper and lower towns.—Bunbury has long been celebrated for its wake, which like the generality of these Cheshire saintly carnivals, is held on the Sunday before the day of Saint Boniface.* The Estate of PRESTLAND GREEN, adjoining Bunbury Green, was at a very early period, the property of the Bulkeleys, (Bulkileh) of Bulkeley. It was sold in 1603, to Thomas Wilbraham, Esq.† for £500. and from him it has become the property of the Earl of Dysert.

The Church is a very handsome structure, and although the present exterior is not of very ancient date, there is no doubt of a church being in existence here so early as the period of the Survey. The presentation to the church was alternately exercised by the Bunbury and St. Pierre families; but subsequently to 1389, Sir Hugh Calveley purchased the right from them, which was vested solely in him.

Ann. Reg. 10, Richard II. Sir Hugh obtained license‡ to found a college or chantry here for a master and six chaplains, to celebrate mass for the souls of the King, of Sir Hugh Calveley, and their ancestors—to endow the same with the rectory advowson, and two acres of land; which the master and chaplains were to appropriate for their own benefit, and that of their successors. Thomas de Thornetone was collated first warden, in 1389, on the presentation of Sir Hugh, as "Magister vel custos cantariæ collegii Sancti Bonifacii, ecclesiæ de Boneberie."—John Woodward was the warden at the Dissolution, when the establishment of the college was a warden, six chaplains, and two choristers.

scribed as Lord *of the Township*, and Sir Thomas Wilbraham, as Lord *of the Court*.

* It is not improbable, but what the following lines, which are so often heard in our nurseries, originated from some grotesque exhibition, formerly characteristic of the Wake:—

> "Ride a-cock horse, to Bunbury cross,
> To see the old woman jump on the white horse;
> A ring on her finger, a bell to her toes,
> That she may have music wherever she goes."

† He purchased it from William Prestland, Esq. successor to the Bulkeleys.

‡ It runs thus:—"Licentia Regia Hugeni de Calveley Chv'r concessa pro fundatione Cantariæ collegii de Bonebirie.—Rex omnibus ad quos, &c. salutem.—Sciatis quod cum dilectus et fidelis noster Hugo de Calveley, chevalier quandam cantariam et collegium, septem capellanorum, viz. unius magistri et aliorum sex capellanorum in ecclesià de Bunbury, in comitatu Cest. ad exorandum et divina celebrandum pro salubri statu nostro, et ipsius Hugonis dum vixerimus, et animabus nostris cum ab hac luce migraverimus, ac animabus progenitorum nostrorum, et antecessorum prædicti Hugoni, ac omnium fidelium de functorum, mediante licentià nostra facere intendit et fundare; nos sanam intentionem, se piam devotionem præfati Hugonis in hàc parte merito commendantes; capientesq. hujusmodi laudibile propositum quatenus ad nos attinet (prout reputamus multum fore Deo gratum), ex regia benignitate fœliciter promovere; de gratià nostra speciali, et pro quadraginta libris quas idem Hugo nobis solvit, concessimus et licentiam dedimus," &c.

The chantry of Sir Ralph Egerton, had two priests.—The whole lived on pensions, with the exception of two of the Chaplains. The clear value of the college was returned by the commissioners at £49. 10s. 8d.; of the chantry £12. 2s.

In the Church is still remaining the Monument of Sir Hugh Calveley. His tomb is an elegant piece of workmanship, in alabaster, ornamented with Gothic niches, between each of which is a shield, with the arms of Calveley, and Browe and Knolles thereon, alternately placed. The effigies of Sir Hugh is 7 feet 10 inches long, in plate armour, richly ornamented down the seams, with gorget, and skirt of mail: at the feet is a lion; on the surcoat are the arms of Calveley, viz. *Arg. a fesse gules, between three calves passant, sable*: and under the head the family crest, a calf's head issuing from a ducal coronet. The helmet is pointed, and ornamented with jewels: the hands are joined, in the attitude of prayer.

Sir Hugh's character ranks too high in the chivalry of some of our proudest days, to be passed over here in silence.* He was the younger son of Kenrick de Calveley, of Calveley Hall, in Bunbury, and highly distinguished himself in the French wars. His valour previous to the Treaty at Bretagny in 1360, first introduced him as "one of the celebrated in arms," and after that truce, he became the leader of an independent army of disbanded veterans. They called themselves "The Companions," and committed dreadful ravages in many of the French provinces, holding themselves in readiness to join any warlike expedition, that might be projected. They assisted John de Montford in enforcing his claim to Britanny; and at the battle of Auray, in 1364, under the command of Sir John Chandos, the tide of victory was turned in favor of John de Montford, mainly by the exalted bravery of Sir Hugh Calveley, who commanded the rear-guard.† "The Companions" afterwards assisted in driving Peter, surnamed "The Cruel," from the Spanish throne: but the Black Prince espousing the cause of Peter, they re-assembled under the command of their immortal Prince, and won the great triumph of Najara. In this victory Sir Hugh covered himself with laurels.—In 1375, Sir Hugh was appointed by his Sovereign, Edw. III. to the important Government of Calais; and in 1377, he destroyed a great part of the town of Boulogne, and burnt twenty-six ships in the harbour—re-took the Castle of Marke, the day on which it had been lost through negligence—and plundered Estaples.—In 1378, he and Sir Thomas Percy were made Admirals of England; and in 1379, he succeeded in conveying the Duke of Britanny to St. Maloes, driving off several French gallies intended to oppose the enterprise.‡ Sir Hugh engaged in a variety of other military expeditions: his last, it is conjectured, was with Sir Henry Spencer, the Martial Bishop, in Flanders. In this he was accompanied by Sir Thomas Fogg, of Chester. On his return, the Bishop was blamed for misconduct; and on a suspicion of treachery, several of his companions in arms were sent to the Tower. Sir Hugh, however, met with the protection of the Duke of Lancaster, and it does not appear that he was molested, for he retained the Government of Guernsey till his death, in 1394.

It has been asserted, that Sir Hugh Calveley married a Queen of Arragon; but this assertion is, no doubt, a fiction. It has not the slightest historic corroboration. Fuller, indeed, states, that the arms of this Queen, who in some pedigrees is called Margaret, were quartered with his on his tomb; but Randle Holme, who was cotemporary with Fuller, and one of the best heralds of the day, expressly particularizes the arms on the tomb, as those of Calveley—and gules, on a chevron argent, three roses of the field, placed alternately round it.

Another pedigree describes Sir Hugh, as having sub-

* Sir Hugh Calveley's history is so connected with that of the Church of Bunbury, that it has been thought not improper to introduce a notice of it here.—A biographical sketch of the celebrated natives of this county, will be collected, and introduced in the conclusion of the work.

† It was during these wars, that Sir Hugh, Sir Robert Knolles, and twenty-eight other companions in arms, engaged in the romantic combat with thirty Bretons, whom they completely defeated.

‡ Shortly after this, he narrowly escaped shipwreck in a storm, in which Sir John Arundel, several officers, and more than a thousand seamen perished.

CHESHIRE

sequently married the heiress of Mottram.* This is as well founded as the other; and the probability is, he was never married.

† Lysons.

† "Sir Robert Knolles, who has been mentioned with Sir Hugh, was a native of Cheshire, but the place of his birth is unknown; he attained at least equal celebrity with Sir H Calveley; and in 1358, he distinguished himself by taking the city of Auxerre, and the town of Chatelon sûr Soigne, for the King of Navarre: he had the command of a battalion at the siege of Auray, and shared in the glories of the victory of Najara. In 1369, the Black Prince made him Commander in Chief of his forces in Gascony. The next year, Sir Robt. Knolles, having in the mean time paid a visit to his native country, was sent with the chief command of an army into France, where he burnt several towns, and laid waste the country to the gates of Paris. Lambard, in his Perambulation of Kent, says, that the sharp points and gable ends of the buildings then laid in ruins, were many years afterwards called Knolles' Mitres! The last public act of Sir Robert Knolles' life was, the service be rendered in suppressing the rebellion of Wat Tyler, in 1381. It has been already mentioned that the place of Sir Robert Knolles' birth is not known, nor has any thing been handed down to posterity relating to his family or connexions;‡ but he is said to have been of humble origin. It is a singular circumstance, that Sir Hugh Calveley should have had a nephew named Robert Knolles, the son of his sister Eve, who married Richard Knolles, on which Robert, the manor of Lea, in case of the failure of issue male from Sir Hugh Calveley, and his brother David, was entailed, by a deed of the 10th April, 1354: and it is further remarkable, that the arms which were borne by the family of Knolles, are placed alternately with those of Sir Hugh Calveley, on Sir Hugh's tomb. Did not the circumstance of their being evidently so near of an age render it improbable, there would be strong reasons for supposing that the two celebrated Cheshire warriors were uncle and nephew. They certainly both went to the Continent about the same time; but the name of Sir Robert Knolles is first mentioned by our Historians, as one of the officers who accompanied the Black Prince to France, in 1356. Sir Hugh Calveley, who is called by Hollinshead, an "Auncient Captain," in 1383, died at an advanced age, in 1394: Sir R. Knolles died in 1407, at which time Fuller conjectures that he must have been nearly 90 years of age. Sir Hugh Calveley, Sir Robert Knolles, and Sir John Hawkwood, were joint founders of an English Hospital at Rome, in 1380.

HISTORY.

Besides the monument of Sir Hugh Calveley, there was formerly in the Church the monument of his son, also Sir Hugh Calveley, who died in 1415, and of Christian his wife. There is a memorial for Dame Mary, the widow of the last Sir Hugh Calveley, of the senior branch of that family, who died without issue male in 1648: his widow Mary died in 1705, after surviving her husband 57 years.

Their coheiresses were married to Cotton, of Combermere, and Legh, of Lyme: Stapleton, Baron Combermere, of Combermere, is the sole representative of the elder branch of the ancient family of Calveley.

The Chancel, which was founded 11 Richard II. remains in its primitive state; and the tracery work in the east window is truly magnificent. The nave is in the architecture of the 15th century, the windows large and handsome, with obtuse arches. There are eight large windows on each side; and it is separated from the aisles by five elegant clustered pillars. The parapet is enriched with beautiful gothic tracery. In the East window of the Church, was a very curious painting of the root of Jesse, with this inscription underneath:—"*Sanctus Bonifacius intercedat Deum pro David de Bonebury rector' ejusdem * * * * * * qui in ejus honorem hanc feuestram composuit in vita Ano*

* From inquisitions among the county records, it appears, it was Sir Hugh's brother, David, who married this heiress of Mottram.—The Lysons observe, that "The only Queen of Arragon, who could have married Sir Hugh Calveley, was Eleanor, Dowager of Alphonso IV. who became a widow nearly twenty years before Sir Hugh went on the Continent; and we have no evidence that she was then living."

‡ This is an extraordinary omission of the historians of the age.

Dni. M°.CCC°.XLV°." On the north side of the Chancel is a rich gothic shrine of stone, ornamented in the lower part with grotesque figures, flowers, &c. painted in chiaro scuro; above sculptured foliage, and shields of arms, and on a frieze, "This chapel was made at the coste and charge of Syr Rauffe Eggerton Knyght, in the year of owre Lord God M.CCCCC.XXVII." Two of the arches in the south side are filled with skreens, in light gothic open work, the lower part ornamented with scriptural paintings, and inscriptions, in black letter, viz. "Salutatio Sancte Marie per Gabrielem Archangelum,"—"Sancta Juliana," &c. —In the Church are also three stone stalls, unequal in height, having plain ogee arches, with semi-quatrefoils inclosed.

There are monuments, &c. in the Church for the Beeston family.

In the Spurstow Chapel, for George Spurstow, Esq. of Spurstow, who died 1669.

For Sir George Beeston, who died in 1601, aged 102 years, one of the illustrious commanders in the victory over the Spanish Armada. He is represented in armour, and from the inscription it appears he was 89 old when he was knighted for his valor in that memorable engagement.*—On this monument is also a commemoration of his Lady, Alice Davenport, of Henbury, who died in 1591, after having been wedded to him sixty-six years!—also of Sir Hugh Beeston,† his son, who died 1627, and of Sir George his grandson, who died in 1611.—There are several other monuments, and funereal emblems in the Church and Church-yard, which are not of sufficient interest to obtain notice in this work: they are mentioned, however, generally, in Mr. Ormerod's description of the Church.

The Parish registers are kept in good condition, but there is a chasm from 1706 to 1725.—They notice some curious squabbles between the Ministers and the Lessees of the Rectory, as to their respective rights: An article with the signature "John Swanne, 1630," abuses in a violent manner Earl Cholmondeley and Mr. Aldersey, for dividing the hearse of Lady Calveley with the Parish Clerk: the Minister asserts his right, quoting the authority of Mr. Holme, herald of the Diocese of Chester. Mr. Aldersey, it would seem, possessed himself of the church key, on a Sunday afternoon, and on the following day divided the plunder with the Clerk, Mr. Swanne exclaiming against the partition in the Church-yard! In 1649, the hearse of Sir Hugh Calveley was seized in the same way, by Mr. Aldersey: Mr. Swanne again protests against this invasion of his rights, and says, that Mr. Aldersey is merely "farmer of the tythes." This assertion is repelled, in the following laconic epistle: "Mr. Swanne is mistaken; he is neither preceptor, vicar, nor curate, but a stipendiary, and all he can claim is his £20. THOS. ALDERSEY."

On the 20th June, 1643, the Church was set on fire by a party from Cholmondeley-house, then garrisoned for the King; and received considerable injury.

The site of the College of Bunbury, the ruins of which remained so late as 1622, belongs to the Earl of Dysert. In 1575, Thomas Aldersey, Citizen and Haberdasher, of London, purchased the Rectory and Advowson of Bunbury from the Queen; the rectory was leased for a term of years, at the rent of £27. 18s. from which £20. per ann. were to be appropriated for maintaining two Ministers. On the expiration of this lease, about 1592, Mr. Aldersey granted a long lease to his own family, of all the Rectory, (excepting the tythes of Ridley, which he similarly leased to the Egerton family, for £8. per ann.) at the rent of £122. providing that 100 marks per ann. the best house, and land of

* "Hic situs est Georgius Beeston, eques auratus, virtutis et veritatis cultor, a juventute bellicis artibus emeritus; ab invictissimo Rege Henrico III. cum obsideret Boloniam in cohortem pensionarior. co-optatus; meruit sub Edwardo VI. in prælio contrà Scotos Musselborow; postea sub eodem rege, Marià et Elizabethâ, bellis navalibus, vel ut classis præfectus. A quâ post profligatam potentissimam illam classem Hispanicam 1588, equestri dignitate ornatus est, jamque gravescente ætate, cùm fidem principibus, fortitudinem hostibus agregiè probasset, Deo gratus, bonisque charus, Christum diu expectans, in Christo, anno 1601, ætatis suæ 102, obdormivit ut in ipso lætus resurgat."

† He is described as "receptoris generalis omnium reventuum coronæ tam in comitatu palatino Cestriæ, quam in comitatibus North Walliæ," &c.

CHESHIRE

about the value of 20 marks, (now about 24 acres) per ann. should be given to the preacher; £20. per ann. to an assistant, or curate; £20. per ann. a small portion of land (about an acre and a half), and a house for the school-master; £10. per ann. with a house and garden, to an usher, to be appointed by the Haberdasher's Company of London, in which, after the expiration of the lease, the fee was vested. For the foundation of the School, letters patent were granted to him by the Queen, on the 2d Jan. ann. reg. 36. He had permission to frame rules for the regulation of the Charities, and he orders, that any of the persons enjoying his benefaction, may be displaced by the Haberdashers for unfitness; for accepting any additional charge; for absence without their approval; or for being detected in, accused, or strongly suspected of incontinency! The school to be visitted by the Preacher, who must have taken the degree of A. M. in an English University.—The amount of the stipends, from the original endowment in money, instead of land, to the present day remains unaltered, and is, of course, inadequate to the founder's benevolent intentions.—In noticing these endowments, the Lysons observe, in a note, "We could not learn for certain, the extent of the term for which the lease was granted (it is said to have been
1810. for 500 years, of which about 235 have expired)*, nor in what manner the profits of the estate are eventually to be disposed of. The deed of gift does not appear to have been enrolled either in Chancery, or in the Exchequer at Chester; and we were unsuccessful in our endeavours to procure information from any other quarter." To this statement, nothing further can be added here.

About the year 1750, Mr. Thomas Gardener, late of Chester, gave the interest of Two Hundred Pounds to the Minister and Church Wardens of the Parish, in trust, for the purpose of establishing a school for all the poor children in the parish, not of the township of Bunbury. Sixty pounds, part of this money were laid out in the purchase of a moiety of a tenement, in Foulk Stapleford, for three lives, on the 11th October, 1751. On the 26th Dec. 1808, the lease became void, by the death of Samuel Lea, the last surviving life.

BEESTON,

Adjoins Bunbury, on the north-west side; and at the Conquest formed part of the extensive possessions of Robert Fitz-Hugh, Baron of Malpas. It was held from his successors, by the Beestons.

In the reign of King Stephen, the Bunburies settled in the township of Bunbury, and were the ancestors of the Beestons and Bunburies. In the 33d Henry III. Henry, the son of Alexander de Bunbury, and his wife Margery, the daughter of William de Beston, granted their lands in Beeston, to Richard the son of William de Bonebury. In an inquisition temp. Henry VI. William, the son of Thomas de Beeston, held the manor of Beeston in demesne from John, the son of John Sutton, then Baron of Malpas, at the annual valuation of 20 marks; also a seventh of a fourth-part of the Thornton share of the fee of Kingsley, in Picton, Stoke, Cuddington, Onston, Norley, Acton, Elton, Poulton Lancelyn, Newton, Arrowe, and Chester: with half of the manor of Helsby; and lands in Tiverton, Huxley, Burwardesley, Alpraham, and Bradley,—Thomas Beeston being son and heir.—The estates regularly descended to Sir Hugh Beeston, son of Sir George, whose achievements have been noticed under the head "Bunbury;" and from his daughter and heiress Margaret, it passed by marriage to the Whitmores, of Leighton, a younger branch of the Whitmores, of Thurstaston.—From the Whitmores it passed to the Savages, by the re-marriage of Margaret Beeston, the widow of Sir Edward Somerset, K. B. with Thomas, the second son of Thomas, the first Viscount Savage. The issue of this marriage was Darcie Savage, whose daughter and heiress Bridget, brought the estates of the Beestons and Whitmores, by marriage, to Sir Thomas Mostyn, of Mostyn, in the county of Flint, Bart. The manerial lordship of Beeston is now vested in Sir Thomas Mostyn, Bart. M. P. for the county of Flint.

Beeston Hall has long been the residence of respectable farmers; but of the ancient mansion, the seat of the Beestons, little now remains. It was moated, and during the civil wars was almost destroyed, being fired

CHESHIRE by the soldiers of Prince Rupert, on the 19th March, 1645; on which day, tradition says, the Prince "dined with the Lady of the house; after dinner he told her he was sorry to make so bad a return to her hospitality, advised her to secure her valuables, for he must order the house to be burnt that night, that it might not be garrisoned by the enemy!"*

* Pennant p. 9.

The village of Beeston encircles the hill, but is built chiefly of mean cottages, of an ancient date. Their situation, however, is truly picturesque. It is stated,† that in the year 1745, this estate, with the manor of Peckforton, were offered for sale for 9000*l.* and in 1756 for 11,000*l.* but there were no purchasers; in 1801, however, the timber alone on the estates was valued at 30,000*l.* and the chief part of it grew on the eminences occupied and fortified during the siege of the Castle!‡

† Ormerod.

In this township, on a rocky insulated hill, at an elevation of about 366 feet, stands the castle of Beeston. The hill rises in a regular and steep slope, and terminates in a precipice. The building is in the Saracenic style of architecture, introduced from the Holy Land by the Crusaders, of irregular form, with a wall and eight round towers,‖ thrown across from side to side. The upper ward, or inner bullium, occupies something less than an acre of land; and the access to it is over a narrow ruinous platform, up a steep flight of steps, over which the draw-bridge fell. On each side is a massy round tower, with a pointed arch forming the gateway. The two sides of the inner ballium flanking the ascent, are protected by a moat, cut out of the solid rock, which must have been a work of immense labor; the outer walls are beautifully covered with ivy, and a variety of plants and shrubs. On the right hand, after entering the inner Court, is the well mentioned by Webb: it is now nearly filled up: but in his time, it was 275 feet in depth, and was originally sunk to a level with Beeston-brook.§ The two sides of the Keep, not defended by the moat and towers, are partly open to a frightful precipice, giving to the curious spectator an association of ideas with those of our immortal Bard on the Cliffs of Dover— HISTORY.

* * * * How fearful
And dizzy 'tis, to cast one's eyes so low!
The crows and choughs,¶ that wing the midway air,
Shew scarce as gross as beetles. Half way down
Hangs one that gathers samphire; dreadful trade!
Methinks he seems no bigger than his head.
* * * * I'll look no more,
Lest my brain turn, and the deficient sight
Topple down headlong.

¶ a kind of Sea Bird.

The view from the summit is most magnificent and extensive. A tolerable conception of the fortifications and appearance of the hill, may be formed by a reference to the plan in page 93.

The Castle was built by Randle Blundeville, the sixth Earl, "after he was come from the Holie Land,"** and towards the erection of Beeston and "Chartlei, he took toll throughout all his Lordships, of all such persons as passed by the same, with any cattel, chaffre, or merchandize."†† John Scot, the last of the local Earls dying in 1237, Henry III. previous to possessing himself of the Earldom, seized on the Castles of Chester and Beeston, and Hugh Despenser, Stephen de Segrave, and Henry de Aldeley, were appointed Commissioners for the purpose.—In 1256, Prince Edward paid a visit to his Palatinate, and inspected the fortresses; and Fulco de Orreby, Justice of Chester, was placed in charge of the "castles of Chester, Beeston, Dissard, Schotewyke, and Vaenor."‡‡ In 1264, the partizans of Simon de Montford, possessed themselves of Beeston Castle; but the news of the escape of Prince Edward from Hereford the following year, stimulated his Cheshire friends; and James de Audley, and Urian de St. Pierre, made themselves masters of this almost impregnable fortress. About June, the Prince, accompanied by Humphrey de Bohun, Henry de Hastings, and Guy

** Higden.

†† Ibid.

‡‡ Dugdale.

‡ This fact affords a practical illustration of the advantages of planting, in a pecuniary point of view: there is no necessity of expatiating upon its value as a national desideratum.

‖ The accompanying plate conveys an accurate representation of the entrance to the Keep, or Inner Ballium.

§ Those fond of the marvellous in the adjacent villages, have a tradition, in which they put implicit faith, that at the BOTTOM of this well is great store of gold and silver: but no discovery has, as yet, been made, to corroborate it!

GATE OF BEESTON CASTLE.

Engraved for Hanshalls History of Cheshire.

CHESHIRE

de Montfort, his prisoners at the Victory of Eversham. In the 5th year of Edward II. Robert de Holland was appointed Governor of the Castle; and in the 32d of Henry III. Prince Edward, Earl of Chester, nominated Robert de Houghton to the Constableship of Beeston, and to receive the produce of the lands and tenements of John de St. Pierre, *durante placito*, at the salary of 4*l.* per ann.

In 1399, Beeston Castle received a garrison of 100 men at arms, and was well victualled by order of Richard II. who made it the depôt of his treasures, to the value
Stow. of 200,000 marks, which were subsequently carried to Chester. The name of "the haughty Bolingbroke" operating here as in other places, the fortress was abandoned.—During the short peace between Henry VI.
1406. and his successor, the Castle was given to the Duke of York, who being declared heir to the throne, it was enumerated in the list of Manors and Castles appurtenant to the Earldom.

Eighty years after this, Leland describes the fortress as being in a state of ruin; but during the desolating wars between Charles I. and his Parliament, a party of 300 of the "Roundheads" got possession of it in the night of Feb. 21, 1642, and put it in a state of defence
* Burghall's Diary. On the 13th Dec. 1643,* a little before day, Captain Sandford, a devoted royalist, who came out of Ireland with eight of his firelocks, crept up the steep hill of the Castle, and got into the Upper-ward, of which he took possession, although it was deemed "most impregnable." Captain Steel, who then commanded in it for the Parliament, was tried for cowardice, and suffered death for it on Monday, Jan. 28, 1644, but it was supposed unjustly, inasmuch as some of his men betrayed symptoms of fear, and he himself did not feel safe in trusting to them. "What made much against Steele, (says Burghall) he took Sandford down into his chamber, where they dined together, and much beer was sent up to Sandford's men;† and the Castle after a short parley, was delivered up: Steele and his men having leave to march, with their arms and colours, to Nantwich; but as soon as he was come into that town, the Soldiers were so enraged against him, that they would have pulled him to pieces, had he not been immediately clapped in prison. There were much wealth and goods in the Castle, belonging to gentlemen and neighbours, who had brought it thither for safety, besides ammunition, and provisions for half a year at least; all which the enemy got."

HISTORY.

On the 20th Oct. 1644, the Parliament's "Council of War" at Nantwich, hearing that the enemy at Beeston were in want of fuel and other necessaries, laid close siege to it; but on the 17th March following, it was relieved by Prince Rupert and Prince Maurice, at the head of a strong force: they plundered nearly the whole of Bunbury Parish, and burnt Beeston Hall.—In the following month it was again besieged: a mound‡ was raised, moated round, and fortifications erected upon it: but the King approaching from Shropshire, the works were abandoned, and the Parliamentary army marched towards Nantwich.—On the 4th of June, the garrison sallied out, and assaulting Ridley Hall, were driven back with loss.

After the battle of Rowton, the Parliament troops again sat down before the Castle in the latter end of September; and after undergoing a siege of about seven weeks, it was surrendered on the 16th November. Burghall thus notices it:—"Nov. 16, Beeston Castle, that had been besieged almost a year (at different periods) was delivered up by Capt. Valet, the Governor, to Sir William Brereton: there were in it 56 soldiers, who by agreement had liberty to depart with their arms, colours flying, and drums beating, with two cart loads of goods, and to be conveyed to Denbigh; but 20 of the soldiers laid down their arms, and craved liberty to go to their own homes, which was granted. There was neither meat nor drink found in the Castle, but only a piece of a turkey pie, and a live peacock and peahen."

Soon after the taking of Chester, in 1646, Beeston Castle was dismantled, and has since been sinking into the beautiful ruin which it now presents.

† This was "Mars surrendering to Bacchus" with a vengeance.

‡ Still in existence on the North East side of the hill.

The site of the Castle being alienated from the Earldom by Elizabeth, was granted to Sir Christopher Hatton, from whom, it is supposed, the Beestons purchased it ; it has descended with the manor to the present proprietor, Sir Thomas Mostyn, Bart. who takes considerable care in preserving the remains of this once formidable fortress from further dilapidation.

In the outer court of the Castle, is a considerable stone quarry. Sir Thomas Mostyn possesses the whole of the township, excepting about 150 acres ; and holds a Court Leet and Court Baron.

The mineral spring discovered in the township, has been before noticed in page 75.

Leland, in his "*Genethliacon, Eaduerdi Principis,*" has the following lines, allusive to Beeston Castle ; and he inferentially mentions the Sixth Edward as the person who was to restore it to its former consequence.—His predictions, nevertheless, proved him to be like many modern prophets—no conjurer :—

Explicuit dehinc Fama suas perniciter alas,
* * * * * * ocellis.
Sidereos figens Bisduni in mœnia Castri
Qui locus excelso consurgit vertice rupis,
Unde licet, velut et speculà, quoscunque jacenteis
Circum monticulos, vallesque videre feraces.
Huc se præcipitem celeri dedit illa volatu,
Atque tenens arcis fastigia summa superbæ
Concussit pennas alacri fervore strepenteis,
Oraque deinde sono tali facunda resolvit ;
"Assyrio rediens Victor Ranulphus ab orbe
Hoc posuit castrum, terrorem gentibus olim
Vicinis, patriæque suæ memorabile vallum.
Nunc licet indignas patiatur fracta ruinas,
Tempus erit quando rursus caput exseret altum,
Vatibus antiquis si fas sit mihi credere vati
Forsan et Edverdus precium feret omne laboris."

BURWARDSLEY,

Is about five miles S. S. W. from Tarporley. This manor at a very early period was given by the Abbot of St. Werburgh, at Chester, to Roger de Combre, or Fitz Alured, on condition that he should become Champion for the Monastery ; from his daughter and coheir a great part of this estate descended to the Touchetts. In 1662, Robert Lord Cholmondeley was described as Lord of the Manor ; but latterly, the Lordship has been considered as subordinate to the manor of Tattenhall, which was the property of the Touchetts. In 1804, Burwardsley was sold by John Crewe, Esq. (since ennobled) to Thomas Tarleton, Esq. of Bolesworth Castle, and he is the present proprietor. In 1735, a chapel of ease was consecrated in this township. It is built on the common, by subscription, chiefly raised by a Mr. Kyffin. A small quantity of land, as an endowment, was given by Mr. Hodgkis, and it has been augmented by Queen Anne's bounty. The Trustees of the endowment appoint the Minister.

CALVELEY

Is not mentioned in Domesday-book, although it is pretty clear it was then parcel of the great Barony of Shipbrook ;—and this is confirmed by a grant made by Richard de Vernon, in the early part of the 13th Century, to Hugh Calveley, (ancestor of the celebrated Sir Hugh Calveley) of Lea Hall, in Bruera Chapelry.—About the reign of Edward III. the elder branch became extinct by the death of Sir Hugh's uncle, Robert, and his daughter brought Calveley in marriage, to a younger branch of the Davenports, of Davenport, which family became extinct in 1771, by the death of Richard Davenport, Esq. John Bromley, Esq. marrying the elder daughter and coheiress of Mr. Davenport, the manor became vested in him ; but dying without issue, the reversion is vested in Davies Davenport, Esq. of Capesthorne, M. P. for the County, whose father married the younger daughter of the before-mentioned Richard Davenport.

The entire township is now the sole property of Mr. Davenport, excepting about 250 acres, and is in the jurisdiction of the manerial court of Alpraham, held by Earl Dysart.

About thirty years ago, the old hall of Calveley was pulled down. The rooms were large and lofty, and the house surrounded by a brick wall, loop-holed, enclosing about two acres. The present house is an old timber building, cased with brick, and is the residence of Edw. D. Davenport, Esq. Adjacent to the house is a park of about 60 acres of land, in which are some deer.—Calveley is 14 miles from Chester.

HAUGHTON,

Or Halghton, was possessed by a family of that name at a very early period, and was held under the Barony of Malpas. It is likely it was included in the grant of lands made at the Conquest to Fitz-Hugh.—The first of the family named, is Robert de Halton, the father of John, surnamed Molendinarius de Halghton, and William, by whom in the 4th Edw. II. lands were confirmed to Richard the son of Robert de Brundelegh, &c.

It continued in regular descent in this family till about 1740, when it was purchased from the coheiresses of the last male heir, —— Haughton, Gent. by the family of Comberbach; —— Comberbach, Esq. re-sold it in 1790, to Thomas Garnet, Esq. of Nantwich, who is Lord of the Manor, and holds a Court Baron.

The Bulkeleys, of Haughton, a family long settled here, were the descendants of William de Halghton, a younger brother of the manerial Lords, and were, 39th Edw. III. seized of lands in Halghton and Tarporley. It appears from an inquisition, 19th Henry VII. on the body of Urian Bulkeley, of Halghton, lately slain, the jurors presented, that he assaulted Thomas Halghton, of Halghton, who fled till he was stopped by the fosse of Wister Long, and then in his own defence, he slew the said Urian. The Bulkeleys have long since quitted the township, and the house they lived in was taken down by Mr. Comberbach, with the materials of which he repaired Haughton Hall.

* Ormerod. The following is given* as the acreage of the Township: Mr. Garnett 200 acres, Earl Dysart 200, Mr. J. Billington 100, Mr. C. Salmon 100, Trustees of Mottram School 60, Mr. R. Owen 55, Mr. John Broster, of Chester 40, Mr. Court 70, Mr. R. Crewe 37, Mr. Wickstead 30, &c.

PECKFORTON

Lies about 5 miles S. S. W. from Tarporley; and was included in the grant of lands to Robert Fitz Hugh, the Norman Baron of Malpas; and according to Domesday Survey, "*Valebat octo solidos modo XX solidos reddit.*" The foundation Charter of the Monastery of St. Werburgh, at Chester, recites that "*Billeheld, uxor Baldrici, dedit Pecfortunam; teste Normanno de Arretio, multisque aliis.*" This grant the Monks afterwards exchanged with Humphrey, the Kinsman of William Patrick, for Stanney Mill, Alrithesholme, and all that belonged to them in marsh or meadow, on the sides of Stanney and the Mersey, with the water, &c.

Urian de St. Pierre was afterwards enfeoffed with the manor; and with his daughter Isabella, it passed with the other family estates to Sir Walter de Cokesey, Knt. in whose family it remained till the reign of Henry VII. when by an Inquisition Ann. Reg. 16, Roger Horton was found next heir to Thos. Cokesay; and another Inquisition of 22d of the same King, also found John Younge, Somerset Herald, heir: this contention of title brought on a sale, when a share of the barony was purchased, with other manors, by Edmund Dudley, Esq. and were passed by fine† by Sir John Dudley, Knt. † 28 Henry VIII. and Jane his wife, to Rowland Hill, merchant. From the Hills, by marriage settlement, and fine, Peckforton was settled on Peter Corbett, by Alice Hill, who married Sir Reginald Corbett, Knt. Justice of the Common Pleas. The manor was subsequently sold to the Beestons, and Sir Hugh Beeston, Knt. was Lord in 1626. From him, through the Whitmores, and Savages, Peckforton descended to the Mostyns, and is now the property of Sir Thomas Mostyn, Bart. M. P. who holds a Court Leet and Baron for the same.—The estate of Peckforton Hall, which belonged to a family bearing the local name of Peckforton, and was sold by one of them to Sir J. Crewe, of Utkinton, Knt. before the year 1662, is now occupied as a farm. Part of the highway, each side Peckforton Hall, is within two gates; and from the intervening space being called Calveley's-lane, it has been conjectured, that this house was the seat of the Calveleys, of Peckforton.

In this township is the manor or reputed manor of HORSLEY, which passed with Peckforton to the Mostyns. Horsley Bath is also situated here, and will be found noticed at length in page 76.

RIDLEY,

Or Ridgeley, is about 6 miles W. N. W. of Tarporley, and is situated in a singularly romantic spot. It probably formed part of the estates of the great Barony of Malpas, but it is not mentioned in Domesday Survey. This manor was held in the reign of Edward III. by a family which took the name of Rydlegh, or Rodelegh, from the Knights of St. John of Jerusalem, and the St. Pierres. From the Ridleys it passed by female heir to the Danyels, and subsequently from Robt.
* 32 Henry VI. Danyel, to Sir Wm. Stanley,* and it would seem in rather a mysterious manner, from what Leland says on the subject :—" Ridle longid to Danyel, that was servant to Syr W. Standle, and few men know what became of this D*****." Sir Wm. Stanley, says Leland, made " Ridle Hawle, of a poore old place, the the fairest gentleman's howse of al Chestreshire." In another place he says, " Ridle Hawle is a right goodly house of stone and tymbre, buildid by Sir William of Standeley, that much favorid King Henry the VII. parte at Bosworth-feelde."†

It was afterwards given by Henry VIII. to his standard bearer, Sir Ralph Egerton,‡ whose descendants, in the reign of Charles II. sold it to Sir Orlando Bridgeman, Lord Keeper of the Great Seal. It passed, in 1720, by the foreclosure of a mortgage, to the Pepys family, and is now the property of Sir William Pepys, Bart.|| A Court Leet and Court Baron are held every four or five years for this manor, and its jurisdiction extends over the townships of Ridley, Haughton, Peckforton, Bickerton, and Broxton.

The hall of Ridley, which stands under the romantic hills of Peckforton, is of a quadrangular form, with a massy gateway. During the local wars, the royalists sallied out from Beeston Castle, and attacked the Hall, but were defeated by the garrison, consisting of only sixteen soldiers, leaving five men killed on the spot.—Within the gateway, is an old building called the Star§ Chamber, which was anciently the Court-house.

Ridley Pool, which has long been in tillage, is mentioned by Nixon, in what is called his *Prophecy*.

SPURSTOW¶

Is about four miles S. by E. from Tarporley, and was also parcel of the Barony of Malpas, descending from them to the St. Pierres and Cokeseys. From an Inquisition of the 35th Edw. III. it appears that Spurstow was held by a descendant of William Spurstow, who was Sheriff of Cheshire, in the 9th and 10th Edw. I. it continued in the Spurstow family till 1685, when by

† He was the second son of the first Lord Stanley, and brother of the first Earl of Derby.

‡ This distinguished warrior was made joint escheator of Cheshire, with Roger Mainwaring; and Ranger of Delamere Forest, by Henry VIII. In 1513, he received the honor of Knighthood for his bravery at the battle of Spurs, and the sieges of Terouenne and Tourney. In Jan. 1514, he was appointed Standard Bearer of England, during life, with a salary of One Hundred Pounds per ann. He served under the Earl of Derby, at Flodden, and it is probable the high office of standard bearer was granted to him, for his valour in that decisive conflict. Indeed, this is somewhat confirmed by Weber's reprint of " Flodden Field:"—

Lancashire and Cheeshire, said the Messenger
They have done the deede with their hande:
Had not the Earl of Derby been to the true,
In great adventure had been all England.

Then bespake our Prynce with a high worde,
Sir Rauphe Egerton, my marshall I make thee!

The last public act of this distinguished character, was his accompanying his Royal Master to Canterbury, to meet the Emperor Maximilian. He died on the 9th March, 1527, and was interred at Bunbury.

|| Created June 23d, 1801.

§ From a number of lozenges in the upper part of the building, carved in a form somewhat resembling stars.

¶ A finger-post, pointing to Spurstow, and Bunbury, was some time ago set up at a junction of roads, in this parish;—it bore the following whimsical inscriptions :—

☞ If you are troubled with sore or flaw,
This is the way to Spurstow Spa:

☞ If all your sores you've left in the lurch,
This is the way to Bunbury Church!

CHESHIRE HISTORY.

the death of Charles Spurstow, Esq. the estate became the property of Sir John Crewe, of Utkinton, by purchase, and is now vested in his descendant, the Right Hon. John Lord Crewe.

The Estate of Lower Spurstow Hall, is subject to the Manerial Court of Spurstow, but no sittings have been held for some years. This estate passed by a female heir from John Stalker, Esq. to the Aldersey family, in the reign of Henry VI. Samuel Aldersey, Esq. of Aldersey, and Spurstow, is the present proprietor.

The hall stands under the elevated ground between Bunbury and Ridley. About 60 years ago, one of the wings was pulled down. It is now occupied as a farm: it was of considerable size, with a large entrance hall.

An analysis of the mineral spring in this township, formerly in no mean celebrity, will be found in page 75.

TIVERTON,

Sometimes called Teverton, is about two miles S. from Tarporley: it was included in the great possessions of the Baron of Malpas. No subsequent heirs occurring to that immense fief, it is supposed the Earls of Chester resumed the grant of this township, and bestowed it on the Barons of Shipbrook, whose descendants, the Vernons and Audleys, have always been recognized as the Chief Lords.

The mesne manor was vested in a branch of this house, which took the name of Verdun. About the time of King John, or Hen. III. Henry de Verdun granted an estate in Tiverton with his daughter, in marriage, to Matthew, son of Matthew de Hulgrave.—From the Hulgraves, the manor descended by female heirs, to the Beestons and Actons. In 1662, it belonged to Sir Thomas Wilbraham; and is now the property of Earl Dysart, his lineal representative.

At Bressie Green, was the seat of a younger branch of the Bressies, of Willcott's Heath, in Wistaston, settled here before the reign of Henry IV.—The daughter of the last of the Bressies, married Mr. Garnett, and resided here in 1804.

Burghall, in his Diary, records, that on the night of the 21st Feb. 1642-3, " three hundred of the Parliament men had taken Beeston Castle, who coming down to assist the military, were met by the horse of the array, on Tiverton Town Field, when one of Col. Mainwaring's officers was slain on the Parliament side, and a few others of the King's, who were buried at Tarporley."—With the exception of a small piece of marshy ground, the scene of this conflict is now inclosed.

The Earl of Dysart holds a Court Baron, for the Manor of Tiverton.

TILSTON FEARNALL,

Fernall, or Fernhall, is about three miles S. E. from Tarporley, and formed part of the Barony of Malpas. —Shortly after the conquest, it was vested in the Monastery of St. Werburgh, and the grant confirmed by Pope Clement. In the Harl. MSS. we find that William de Burmyncham gave all his lands in Tidulstan, to sustain a Chaplain in the monastery of St. Werburgh, to pray for his soul, that of Margery his wife, and all the faithful.

At the Dissolution, this manor was given to the Dean and Chapter of Chester, but shared in the common fall of their lands into the hands of Sir Richard Cotton.* * See Note, page 100. Before the accession of Eliz. the Wilbrahams held lands here under the Cottons; and subsequently the manor became united to their estate. It is now in the possession of the Earl of Dysart.—There are no remains of the former residence of the Wilbrahams,† excepting a few of the out-buildings which have been converted into a farm-house.

† During the Civil Wars, there was a considerable skirmish on Tilston-heath; and in the Patent of Robert Viscount Cholmondeley, his services, in this affair, are particularly noticed.

History.

WARDLE,

Or Wardhull, is about 5 miles N. W. from Nantwich. At the Conquest it was given to Hugo de Mara, probably one of the King's Norman followers. The local name was early assumed by the family in possession; and it appears from an old deed, that Catherine de Wrenbury, gave all her lands in Wrenbury to Philip, son of David de Egerton, which lands are described as Wordel Park, and le Breres. By Inquisitions, temp. Hen. VI. Rich. III. and Hen. VII. these lands were found to be held from the Grosvenors, of Holme.—The Breretons afterwards held them from the Egertons, with the moiety of Malpas Barony. Wardle, afterwards, was possessed by the Prestlands; and in the 44th Eliz. William Prestland sold the manor of *Wordhull*, to Thomas Wilbraham, of Woodhey, Esq. from which family it has descended to the Earl of Dysart, with their other estates.

THE PARISH OF CHRISTLETON,

CONTAINS THE TOWNSHIPS OF

CHURCH CHRISTLETON,
COTTON ABBOTS,
COTTON EDMUNDS,
LITTLETON,
AND
ROWTON.

Christleton—lies about 2½ miles from Chester, and formed part of the Barony of Malpas. At that time, it was of considerable extent, and more populous than Malpas itself. Soon after the Conquest, Robert Fitz Hugh, gave to the Abbey of St. Werburgh "Capellam de Christleton, et tenam cujusdam rustiçe, et ipsum rusticum."—His daughter Letitia de Malpas, afterwards granted the entirety of Christleton to the Abbey, together with Bechin, but it is probable there was a resumption of this grant, Philip Burnel, and his wife Isabel, subsequently confirming to the Monks of St. Werburgh, in right of their manor of Christleton, a fountain, from which water was conveyed in pipes to the Cloisters of the Abbey. A branch of the Cholmondeley family, had a portion of the Malpas estate here; and assumed the local name.

Before the reign of Edw. I. the Birminghams had possession of this manor. In the reign of Edward II. William de Birmingham gave the manor to his son William, as an endowment for Isabel, daughter of Sir Thomas de Estley. It passed to the Browes, and the Pens; the former was attainted by Henry IV. and *"the King gave all his lands in Cheshire to John Mainwaring, who gave them to Sir T. Grosvenour, who feoffed divers Chaplains therewith, who feoffed therewith John de Kingsley, Esq. who enfeoffed Randle, son of Wm. Mainwaring, and others to the use, I suppose of his d. or st. Catharine, who brought these lands, &c. to ——— de Macclesfield; and John Macclesfield, son of Catherine de Kingsley, passed over this manor, &c. 10th Henry V. and Ralph, his son, sold it 21st Henry VI. to Humphrey Earl of Buckingham."

* Dr. Williamson.

Ultimately the manor became vested in the Staffords; and Sir Wm. Sneyd, in the 1st and 2d of Philip and Mary, obtained from Lord Stafford and his wife Ursula, several messuages and lands, for him and his heirs.—From the Sneyds, it passed by purchase, in 1617, to Sir John Harpur. In 1771, Sir Henry Harpur, Bart. sold the manor to Thos. Brock, Esq. uncle of John Brock Wood, Esq. only son of his eldest sister, who is the present proprietor.

During the Civil Wars, Christleton was fortified by the partizans of the Parliament, and for a length of time, was the head-quarters of Sir William Brereton; on the siege of Chester being raised, in Feb. 1645,

CHESHIRE Christleton was nearly destroyed by fire, in a sally by the Citizens.*

* Holme.

In Birch-lane, was an ancient seat of the Bavands, who lived here many generations; the last of them, Robert Bavand, M. D. dying without issue in 1741, it passed with the other estates here to John Nicholls, Surgeon-General to the forces in Ireland, and Edward Nicholls, Esq. Mayor of Chester, in 1747, sons of the sister of the said Robert Bavand.—From their heir it passed by will to William Richards, Esq. late Town Clerk of Chester.

An ancient mansion, formerly the seat of a younger branch of the Egertons, is now the property of Bell Ince, Esq.—Christleton Hall, is a modern built house, delightfully situated, and is the seat of Townshend Ince, Esq. It was erected by Robert Townshend, Esq. Recorder of Chester, whose family had long lived here.

The Church, no doubt, existed at the Conquest, when in the grant to the Monks of Saint Werburgh, it was described as "*Capella de Christleton.*"—This grant was made before 1093. It was vested in the Abbey of St Werburgh, till the Dissolution; after which the advowson fell to the Cottons. It was the property of the Mostyns, of Mostyn, in the county of Flint, before 1598, and they are the present patrons.

The Church has a nave, chancel, and side aisles, rebuilt of brick; the tower is of stone, was built about 1530, and contains a tolerable peal of six bells. There are no remarkable monuments in the Church—the registers begin in 1697. The parochial bequests do not exceed £46. the interest of which is given to the Poor.

The present Rector of Christleton is the Rev. Griffith Lloyd, A. M. instituted May 6, 1809.

† "Isdem Robertus tenet Christletone. Edwinus comes tenuit. Ibi VII hidæ geldabiles. Terra est XIV. carucarum. In dominio sunt una caruca, et II ancillæ, *et XII villani*, et V bordarii, et II præpositi cum VIII. carucis. Ibi molinum de XII solidis, et II radmans ibi,"—&c.

In 1800, a school house was built here, chiefly at the expense of John Hignett, Esq. who bequeathed £100 for that purpose; the ground being given by Mr. John Seller, who also gave a croft of nearly three acres of land, called *Lower Withway croft*, the income of which to be employed in the education of the poor children of Christleton and Littleton. HISTORY.

CHURCH CHRISTLETON.

This township was inclosed under the provisions of an Act of Parliament, passed in 1791, but the lands were not exonerated from the tythe.

COTTON ABBOTS,

Or Abbot's Cotton, anciently called Cotes, and Ordrick's Cotes, is about four miles E. from Chester. It formed a part of the original vill of Christleton.

About the year 1093, this manor was given by the Baron of Malpas to the Abbey of St. Werburgh, at which time one Ordrick resided here. It is probable he was one of the twelve *villans*, mentioned in the Survey.†

At the dissolution, the temporal estates of the Abbey here, were valued at £12. 16s. 8d.; some short time‡ previous to which event, the Abbot had leased the Conventual lands to Foulk Dutton, afterwards Mayor of Chester, for 89 years, and this lease was confirmed by the Dean and Chapter. Catharine the daughter and heiress to this branch of the Duttons, in 1558, brought those lands in marriage to Thomas Daniel, Gent. of Over Tabley; they afterwards fell into the possession of Sir Thomas Smith, of Hatherton, and by him were sold to Mr. John Anderson, of Chester, who again sold them to Colonel Whitley.|| One of the Coheiresses of Col. Whitley brought this manor to the Mainwarings,

‡ 26th Hen. VIII.

|| It appears, that in 1695, the Colonel leased the estate for three lives to Joshua Horton, who being attainted, in 1700, of high treason, for keeping a press and implements for coining, his interest became forfeited to the Crown, and was granted in the 5th of Anne, to Sir Salathiel Lovel, one of the Barons of the Exchequer, &c.

by whom it was sold under the will of Lady Mainwaring to Ralph Leycester, Esq. of Toft, and in 1780, his son, George Leycester, Esq. conveyed it to the late Thomas Brock, Esq. by whose settlements, and the will of his brother Richard, then Rector of Davenham, the manor has passed to the eldest son of his eldest niece, Thomas Clutton, Esq. of Kinnersley Castle, in Herefordshire, who took the name of Brock, and is now proprietor.

The township is pleasantly situated on the banks of the Gowy; and included in the Court Leet with Cotton Edmunds. The ancient hall is occupied as a farm house.

COTTON EDMUNDS.

This township no doubt took its name from Edmund de Cotton, whose family had possessed it as early as the reign of Henry III. and held the whole of it from the Earl, with the exception of Cotton Wood. It continued in this family till the reign of Henry VII. when Eleanor, daughter of Richard de Cotton,* the last male heir of the elder branch, brought the township in marriage to William Venables, Baron of Kinderton. The late Lord Vernon sold the manor to Thomas Brock, Esq. and it has descended with his other estates.

The hall, now called Cotton Hook, is an ordinary farm house.

ROWTON AND LITTLETON,

(Or Row Christleton, and Little Christleton) are within the manor of Christleton,—Rowton being about three miles and a half S. E. from Chester, and Littleton about two miles and a half E.

At Rowton, is the seat of the late John Hignett, Esq. which has passed to his nephew, John Litherland, Esq who has assumed the name of Hignett. In 1787, a small estate was incorporated with this, which had been the property of the Brosters, of Rowton, and was sold by the uncle of Mr. John Broster, of Chester, to the late Mr. Hignett.

It was in this township, and its immediate vicinity, that the battle took place, which terminated so fatally to the cause of the unfortunate Charles I. of which more will be said in another place. On Rowton Heath was the rendezvous of the Cheshire gentry, who assembled to declare for a free Parliament, at the time of the premature attempt of Sir Geo. Booth, to restore Charles II. in 1659. A great portion of the Heath was inclosed in 1690.

At Littleton is the beautiful seat of Thomas Dixon, Esq.; and on the opposite side of the road from Chester to Tarporley, a handsome mansion was erected in 1810, by Wm. Seller, Esq.

* The Cottons, of Connington, in Huntingdonshire, and of Connington, in Cambridgeshire, both extinct, descended from a younger branch of this family.—LYSONS.

PARISH OF CODDINGTON,

CONTAINS THE TOWNSHIPS OF

CODDINGTON-CUM-BECHIN,	ALDERSEY, AND CHOWLEY.

CODDINGTON is about nine miles S. S. E. from Chester. Previous to the Conquest, Coddington comprised three manors, held by distinct proprietors, but who were all driven from their patrimony, by the triumph of the Normans.—These were given to the Earl.

Subsequently, the manor became the property of a branch of the Malpas Barony, which assumed the local name; but the Barons of Montalt were the paramount Lords and Grantees. Indeed, so early as 1093, Hugh Fitz Norman had presented the Church of Coddington to the Abbey of St. Werburgh, at Chester.—The Botilers succeeded the Coddingtons, for we find that in the 6th Edw. I. Sir Ralph Botiler held a Knight's fee in Coddington; and in the 14th Edw. II. Sir Ralph Botiler was presented for making a mill pool in Coddington. Hawise le Botiler, 34th Edw. III. held in fee the vill of Coddington, from William le Botiler, of Wem, as half a Knight's fee, the said William holding the same from Wm. de Montacute, Earl of Sarum, as of his Castle of Hawarden, and the said William holds the Castle of Hawarden from the Earl of Chester, in capite, by military service. Hawise le Botiler also held a place called Bechin, part of the said vill, but not in fee. In an Inquisition 14th Hen. VI. Philip, the son of Ralph le Botiler, held as of fee the manor of Hawarden, from the then late King Henry, by Knight's service; and also the manor of Bechin, from Hugh de Calveley, as of his manor of Lee.

In the 18th Hen. VI. Sir Philip Botiler sold the manors of Coddington, Bechin, Edgerley, &c. to Wm. Massie, subject to a rent of 25 marks per ann. but by a subsequent deed*, the rent was fixed at 40 marks.—This Wm. Massie was the third son of Hugh Massie, who having intermarried with the Bolds, of Coddington, had been some time settled here. Some doubts exist as to the line of his parentage, and nothing has yet been advanced to settle the disputed point satisfactorily.

* 6th Hen. VIII.

Mr. Ormerod says, "his father's parentage has long been a matter of dispute, some of the pedigrees making him a younger son of Sir John Massey, of Tatton, who died 8th Hen. V. and others of Sir John Massey, of Puddington, who fell at the Battle of Shrewsbury, in 1403. The probabilities are in favor of the Tatton branch, as far as can be argued from correspondence of dates; and no stress can be laid on a subsequent settlement made by John Massie† in the 16th Century, whereby he settled Coddington, in remainder, on the Puddington family, in the event of his issue failing, as this settlement overlooked acknowledged nearer relations, the Massies, of Broxton, and the Massies, of Edgerley."

The Lysons, *per contra*, say "The Massies, of Coddington, are descended from a younger branch of the Massies of Puddington, who derive their descent from a younger branch of the Masseys, Barons of Dunham Massey, being perhaps the only remnant in the direct male line, of the Cheshire Barons."

† Edward Massie, the Parliamentary General, was third son of John Massie, Esq. of Coddington, who married a daughter of Richard Grosvenor, Esq. of Eaton: his elder brother was Captain in the King's army. What an illustration have we here, of the effects of political difference in one family!—Mrs. Massey, of St. John's Church-yard, Chester, has a valuable portrait of Edward Massie, the General.—Among the tracts in the British Museum, relative to this Massie, are—Proceedings of G. M. touching the King of Scots—An Invitation to Soldiers to serve under Colonel M.—An order for paying Colonel M. 20,000—Copy of his letter respecting the fight between Colonel M. and Prince Rupert, at Ledbury—Declaration of Colonel M. and Colonel-General Poyntz—G. M. Bartholemew Fairings—An outcry against the speedy

CHESHIRE

It is evident the line of descent cannot very well, at this distant period, be traced. All the facts known, are here given, and the reader may draw from them his own conclusions.

§ Called Pipard-st.

William Massie, with Coddington and Bechin, also purchased lands in Edgerley, Church-on-Heath, Aldersey, Crewe, Handley, Coddington, Chorlton, Churton, Barton, Clutton, Carden, and had all Pepper§-street, in Chester, and these he divided in the 3d of Edw. IV. between his eldest son, Morgan Massie, of Edgerley, and his second son John Massie, of Coddington.

It appears from an Inq. 2d Edw. VI. that Roger Massey, of Coddington, held the manor of Coddington, and lands in Bechin, from Lord Dacres, as of his Manor of Wem, by fealty, and the presentation of a rose yearly. He also held lands in Barton, Clutton, Farndon, Churton, Cuddington, Burwardsley, Edge, Aldersey, and Milton. John Massye was found son and heir; and he settled these large estates on his sons, John and William, with remainder in default of male issue to Geo. Massey, of Puddington; in default, &c. to his brother, John Massey, of Coghall; and in default, &c. to William Massey, of Chester.—It was from this John Massie, that the Manor of Coddington descended to the present proprietor, the Rev. Richard Massie, A. M. of Stanley-Place, Chester.

Coddington-hall no longer exists. It was an ancient timber building, and stood a short distance N. E. from the Church. In the field opposite, is a tumulus of red sand, about 10 yards in perpendicular height, and about 90 yards in circumference at the foot; altho' a considerable portion of it has been taken away, its centre has not been penetrated; and the object of its formation remains a secret. Its summit commands a very fine prospect.

HISTORY.

Coddington Church is an old structure, and is dedicated to St. Mary. It is probable it was founded between the period of the Survey, and 1093; and it appears from the Foundation Charter of Chester Abbey,* that it was granted to the Abbot by Hugh Fitz Norman, and the grant afterwards confirmed.

Coddington, was one of the few possessions of the Abbey, which remained to the Dean and Chapter; the advowson of which was confirmed to them by the second charter, Ann. Reg. Eliz. 22.

The Church consists of a nave, chancel, and side aisles, which are separated from the body by cylindrical pillars. In the north aisle, is the chancel belonging to the Massies, of Coddington. The church is surmounted by a mean wooden bell-loft. The Registers commence in 1724.

The Rectory-house is prettily situated on the side of a brook, and possesses a pleasant look-out towards Carden Cliff, the hills of Broxton, &c. The Rev. Unwin Clarke, A. M. Prebendary, and Archdeacon of Chester, is the present Rector, on the cession of the Rev. Thomas Maddock, A. M. Prebendary of Chester Cathedral.

The rector of Coddington, has all the tythes of Coddington, with the exception of part of the hamlet of Bechin, which pays composition to Malpas. He has also those of Aldersey, and half of those of Chowley.

The Reverend John Stones, A. M. who was instituted to the Rectory in 1710, made considerable

hue and cry after G. M. and Colonel Poyntz—Virtue and Valor vindicated, or the late Hue and Cry after G. M. and Poyntz retorted—Arraignment of G. M. and others—A Message sent from Scotland, to G. M.—Declaration to the City and Kingdom, from G. M. and others—Declarations of the grounds and reasons, moving G. M. and others to take up arms—Declaration and Speech of Colonel Massey, concerning enthroning the King of Scots—Declaration on his Death-bed—The Reformado righted (an answer to G. M.'s "Bartholemew Fairings.")—Corbet's Historical relation of the Military Government of Glocester (under Massie) —True relation of the Manner of taking Evesham—Verses on the siege of Glocester and Colonel Massie—Nine tracts relating to the Siege of Glocester—Impeachment of Major-General Massie and others—&c. &c.—[General Massie was living in 1670, and was buried at Abbey Leix, in Ireland.]

* "Hugo filius Normanni, et Radulphus frater ejus dederunt partem suam de Lostoke, et ecclesiam de Contintuna, et terram ecclesiæ, et decimam illius villæ, et de Lai similiter. Teste Willielmo Malbedeng, et aliis."

CHESHIRE

collections towards a local history. He left to his successors, Rectors of Coddington, a large folio volume, with a charge, which thus concludes: "If these collections shall chance to fall into any other hand, I charge the person to restore them to the right owner, the Rector of Coddington for the time being, as he or she expects justice in this world, or hopes for mercy in another, J. S." This book, however, is, in a great measure, mere blank paper.

The HAMLET of BECHIN adjoins the township of Coddington, and formed part of the Saxon vill of Coddington. It descended from the Botilers to the Massies; and subsequently by purchase became the property of the Wilbrahams, and Colonel Roger Whitby; from the Whitbys it descended by marriage, to the Mainwarings of Peover; Lady Mainwaring dying, bequeathed her estates, after payment of debts, &c. to James Mainwaring, Esq. Baron of the Exchequer at Chester, who sold the estates in Bechin, on the 20th June, 1747, to the Rev. Thomas Ince, A. M. Rector of Handley, and grandfather of Townshend Ince, Esq. of Christleton, the present proprietor.

ALDERSEY.

This township, also, was a part of the great Barony of Malpas.—A family which were proprietors of the Manor, assumed the local name at a very early period; and about the reign of Edward III. it was divided into two branches: William, eldest son of Hugh de Aldersey, had one half, which afterwards passed to the Hattons, of Hatton: The second son, Adam de Aldersey, had the other half, which has descended in a direct line to the present proprietor S. Aldersey, Esq.

The Hatton portion, passed by marriage to the Duttons, of Hatton; and so late as the reign of James I. Rowland Dutton, held the *manor* of Great Aldersey, Middle Aldersey, and Crooke Aldersey, from William Brereton, as of his manor of Malpas, by service which is not stated. This moiety was subsequently purchased by the Alderseys, from the Duttons.*—The manor is now called Crook,† and Great Aldersey, and a Court is held by Mr. Aldersey, but the tenants owe suit and service, to Handley.

HISTORY.

† Qy. Kirk

Mr. Aldersey is almost the exclusive land-owner, and is impropriator for a third of the tythes.

Leland, in his Itinerary, notices the existence of Salt Works in this township. There is, indeed, at the present time, a brine spring of considerable strength here; but from the great distance of coals and other necessaries and conveniences, a number of years have elapsed, since Salt was made here.

The hall of Aldersey, is a modern building, of white stone, re-erected about the year 1811, and altho' in a low situation, commands a delightful prospect of the Broxton Hills.—Thomas Aldersey, the benefactor to the Church of Bunbury, and who corrected by his researches, the list of Mayors of Chester, &c. was of this family.

CHOWLEY,

Formed part of the territorial possessions of the Barons of Malpas.—At a very early period, the Pulfords of Pulford, had possessions here; and Hugh de Pulford, in the 18th Edw. I. died, seized of an eighth of this manor, held from the Barons of Malpas, as the eighth of a Knight's fee. The heiress of this family, Joan, afterwards brought this estate in marriage to the Grosvenors, of Holme; and in an Inquisition 8th Henry VII. it is stated, that Thomas le Grosvenor held in demesne, a fourth part of the manor of *Cholley*, from Sir John Sutton, Knight, in socage, but by what service is not known.

The direct male line of this family becoming extinct, their share of Chowley passed in marriage, with Eliz. Grosvenor to Peter Dutton, of Hatton, who previously had considerable estates in Chowley, through the Vernons, from the Hattons, of Hatton. In an Inquisition 3d

* Speaking of the Hatton portion, the Lysons observe, "the latter (i. e. the Duttons) possessed it so late as the year 1582; it afterwards belonged to the Calveleys, from whom it descended to the late T. P. Legh, Esq. of Lyme; but no manerial rights are exercised for this moiety."

James I. Rowland Dutton, of Hatton, is stated as holding the manor of Chowley from Sir William Brereton, Knt. as of his manor of Malpas, by unknown service. Peter Dutton, of Hatton, Esq. temp. Charles II. sold Chowley manor to Thomas Knevet, of London, who settled it on Peter Calf, of Tottenham, Middlesex, in marriage with his daughter. Their son devised it to Edw. Donne, of Shrewsbury; and it afterwards passed in marriage from the Donnes, to Thomas Gardiner, Esq. of Shrewsbury; his family sold it in 1786, to John Crewe, Esq. of Bolesworth, and it passed with Bolesworth to the Moseleys. In 1805 it was bought, under a Decree of Chancery, by Thomas Tarleton, Esq. of Bolesworth, who is proprietor of the manor; but the greater portions of this 1114
estate, being separated from the manor, were the property of Stephen Leeke, Esq. of Chester, who recently re-sold a part thereof to the late Wm. Leche, Esq. of Carden, in whose representatives, and Mr. Tarleton, the estates, including a moiety of the tythe of the entire estates, are now vested.

The tenants attend at Mr. Tarleton's Court, at Tattenhall; Chowley being long since disused as a distinct manor.

Brown, del. Mosses, sc.

Saxon Arch, Chester Cathedral, from the East Cloister, entering into the Broad Aisle.

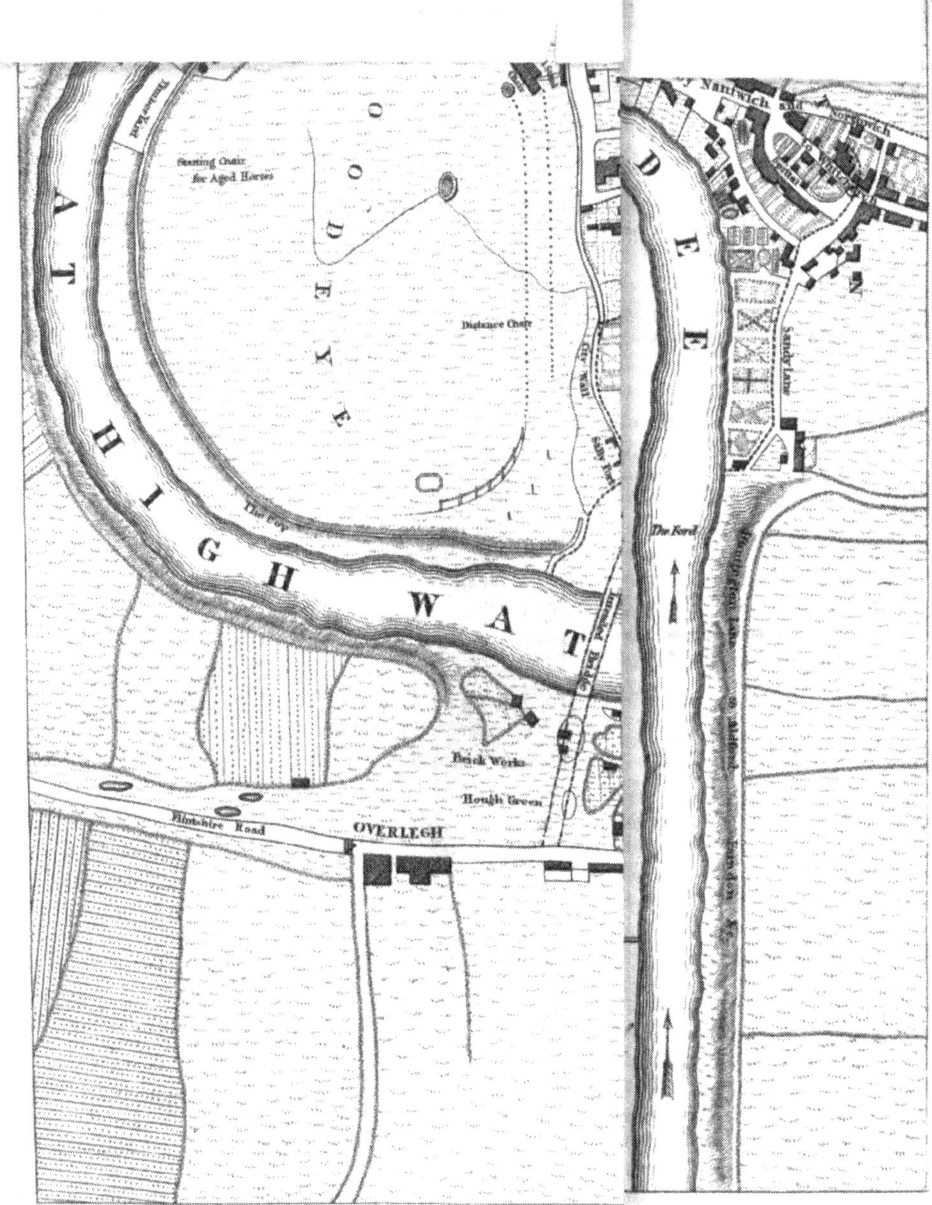

O O D E Y E
Starting Chair for Aged Horses
Distance Chair
AT HIGH WAT
D E E
The Ford
Sandy Lane
Brick Works
Hough Green
Flintshire Road
OVERLEGH
Nantwich and Northwich

COAT ARMORIAL OF THE CITY OF CHESTER.

Copy of the Grant—temp. Eliz. extracted from the exemplification itself, in the records of Chester; now first published.

Omnibus et singulis tam regibus ad arma sive Heraldis, quam nobilibus cæterisq. hoc scriptum visuris vel audituris Willms Flower, armiger, aliter dictus Norroy, rex armorum, et principalis Heraldus partiu regni Angliæ boreaīlu, Salutem in Domino sempiternam. Quum venerabiles viri Maior et cives civitatis Cestriæ', sicut et eorum prædecessores, multis, et egregiis privilegiis à regibus Angliæ' Comitibusq. Cestriæ palatinis, &c.—Virtute cujus quidem incorporationis Civitas prædicta, sicut et aliæ regni Angliæ civitates Armorum sive insigniorum longo usu ac demonstratione', clarior et spectabilior multo efficitur.—Quoniam verò, relictis Armis sive insigniis prædictæ civitatis antiquis, et feré penitus è memoria deletis, alia nova insignia prætensa sibi assumpserat eisdemq. per multos annos elapsos usi sunt, &c.—Inciaco ego prædictus Norroy rex Armorum, non solum quod est officii mei in reformatione' delictorum priorum temporum exequutus, Arma sive insignia antiqua coloribus rubeo, et asorio sive ceruleo per longu' distincta, quorum pars prior (quæ et regia appellari merito potest) dimidiatos tres leones gradientes et respicientes aureos, quam speciosissime' ostentat, altera verò pars ab ipsis Comitibus olim Palatinis mutuata, spicarum fascem unum integrum, et dimidiatu aliu aureu præ' se' fert, dictæ civitati plenarie,' et in integru restitui per præsentes. Ac Insuper, &c. civitati et societati tam præclaræ', deq. principe' et patria nra tam bené meritæ gratificarer: pro maiori et ampliori ornamento Civitatis prædictæ', pro Crista supra galeam, regalitatis et justiciæ' symbolu gladium vaginatum, erectum, cinguloq. cinctum, totu deauratum, assignavi, situatum super torquem aureis, rubeis, asoriisq. coloribus distinctu, simul cum manteltis sive' appendicibus, partim rubeis, partim asoriis intrinsecus argento duplicatis. Et ulterius in clypei sive' scuti sustentationem, leonem aureum, corona argentea circa collum redimitum à dextro, et lupum argenteum, aurea similiter corona circa collum cinctum, à sinistro latere, destinavi: quemadmodum in margine' præsentiu pro pleniori notitia magis ad vivum suis metallis atq. coloribus illuminanda, delineanda, depingendaq. curavi, &c. Habenda, utenda, et ostendenda honoris gratia quibuscunq. loco et tempore pro eorum arbitrio, aliquo impedimento, contradictione', aut probibitione', id ut ne' fieri possit, non obstantibus. In Quorum, &c. ego Norroy rex Armoru prædcus his præsentibus nomen meum manu mea propria subscripsi, et appensione' sigilli officii mei præsens meum diploma corroboravi.—Datum Cestriæ' tertio die' Septembris, anno Christi Salvatoris M.D. LXXX. regni veró Serenissmæ' reginæ Elizabethæ', vicessimo atq. secundo.

Motto: "Antiqui colant Antiquum Dierum,"

Per moi Wyllam Flower, Esquyer, alias Norroy Roy D'Armes.
Confirmed by me Richard St. George, Norroy King of Armes,
in my visitation, 1613.

TRANSLATION.

To all and singular, as well Kings of Arms, as Nobles, and others, to whom these presents shall come (to sight or ear): I, William Flower, Esq. alias Norroy, Principal Herald, and King of Arms, of the north parts of England, sendeth greeting, in our Lord everlasting. Forasmuch as the venerable (Worshipful) Men, the Mayor and Citizens of the city of Chester, also as their predecessors, by many and distinguished privileges from the Kings of England, and the Earls Palatine of Chester, &c. By virtue of which Incorporation, the said city, in like manner as other cities of the kingdom of England, is rendered much more distinguished and respectable by its ancient use and display of the Coats of Arms. But forasmuch as the said city had relinquished its ancient arms, so that their very memory had become nearly obliterated, and in their place took up and has used new arms for these many past years, &c. In consideration whereof, I, the said Norroy King of Arms, &c. having executed the duty pertaining to my office touching the amendment of former delinquency, have by these presents fully, and in their pristine state, restored to the aforesaid city, the Armorial Coat or Ancient Insignia, marked with gules and azure; the first side (which may be likewise justly called the regal side) exhibiting three demy-lions passant regardant, or, accurately depicted; and the second side presenting a whole wheat sheaf, and a half of another, or. And moreover, &c. to do pleasure to a city and society so distinguished, and of such great deservings from our Prince and country, have allowed, for the greater and ampler ornament of the said city, for the crest upon the helm, the symbol of royalty and justice, a sword sheathed, erect, girt with a belt, thorough gilt, situated above the torce, distinguished with gold, red, and azure below; moreover, with mantlings (or appendants) part red, part azure, doubled argent. And moreover, for the support of the shield, I have designed, on the right side a lion, or, ducally collared, argent; and on the left side, a wolf, argent, alike ducally collared, argent. For the fuller information of which, and more to the life, I have ordered the above to be illuminated, delineated, and depicted in the margin of these presents, with the respective metals and colors, &c. To use, bear, enjoy, and shew forth as token of honour at any time and place, at liberty and pleasure; any impediments, contradiction, and prohibition to the contrary notwithstanding. In witness whereof, &c. I, the Norroy King of Arms, have signed these presents with my hand; and by the appendant of my seal of office, have confirmed this my diploma. Given at Chester, the 3d day of September, in the year of our Saviour, M.D.LXXX, and in the 22d year of the reign of Her Most Serene Highness Queen Elizabeth.

THE CITY OF CHESTER.

(FROM WEBB.)

HISTORY.

That there hath been so much wrestling and striving to find out the ancient names, and the first original of the City of Chester, is to me one argument of the ancientness thereof; for as there is no certainty known, how can it be but beyond the reach of all intelligence; that the laborious writers of all ages have endeavoured after: Whereupon I hold it for a conclusion, that many monuments in this kingdom, whereof there can be found no memory of their foundation, are more antient than those which have their foundations either certainly known, or probably conjectured.

And to come briefly to our purpose in hand: altho' for my part, I see not any but very weak grounds for their conjectures, who would bring our city of Chester's foundation from beyond all possibility of records; yet I will not prejudicate any in their surmises, nor defraud them of the praises that any shall think good to bestow upon those who have labored in collections of that kind.

The first name that I find this city to have been supposed to have borne, was Neomagus; and this they derive from Magus, the son of Samothes, who was the first planter of inhabitants in this isle, after Noah's Flood, which now containeth England, Scotland, and Wales; and of him was called Samothea; and this Samothes was son to Japhet, the third son of Noah; and of this Magus, who first built a city even in this place, or near unto it, as it is supposed, the same was called Neomagus. This conjecture I find observed by the learned Knight Sir Thomas Elliott, who saith directly, that Neomagus stood where Chester now standeth, in vol. 1. *Chronic. de Descript. Britan. pag.* 2.

Whether it carried that name for any long time of continuance, or when it lost the same, I find no certainty.

Ranulphus, a monk of Chester, and author of the old Polychronicon, hath another foundation from a giant, forsooth, called Leon Gawer: which Gawer Marius calls the vanquisher of the Picts, who laid the first foundation of this city, as it were, in a kind of rude and disorderly fashion; which afterwards by Leir, King of Britain, was brought to a more pleasant fashion of building, which is best expressed in the verses of Henry Bradshaw, another monk of Chester, who writ the life of St. Werburg, and therein these verses:

> The founder of this city, saith Polychronicon,
> Was Leon Gawer, a mighty strong giant;
> Which builded caves and dungeons many a one,
> No goodly buildings, ne proper, ne pleasant.
>
> But King Leir, a Briton fine and valiant,
> Was founder of Chester by pleasant building,
> And was named Caer Leir by the King.

Touching which foundation, supposed by this Leon Gawer, I do, by so much less, give approbation, by how much methinks that opinion of Mr Camden's seems most probable, drawn from the antient British language, of whom it hath been called Caerlegion, Caerleon vaur, Caerleon ar Dufyr dwy, as the Britons calls it. Which names are derived from that legion of the Romans, called Vicessima Victrix, which were first placed here in the second consulship of Galba, with Titus Vinius; and afterwards established under the government of Julius Agricola, appointed by this city; being, as he thinks, not long before that time, built in this very place, and intended for a oak to the, &c. And, saith he, the very name may serve to confute such plebeian antiquaries, as would derive it from Leon Vaur, a giant, seeing Leon Vaur, in the British language, signifieth nothing else but The Great Legion.

By whom, or howsoever, the city had her first foundation, it is manifest enough that it is exceeding antient; and even the doubtfulness of the first foundation makes it, as before I touched, of undoubted antiquity.

The names thereof, indeed, have been variable and

diverse; but those which the Britons, upon the plantation of the Roman Legions, have fastened upon it, I hold most authentic, as those names before mentioned of *Caer, par excellentiam*, amongst the ancient writers; and those which the Saxons afterwards took from the addition of *Castra*, which might signify either castles, or camps of soldiers, and thereupon, it is likely, they made the name—many other cities or towns yet retaining that part of the name; namely, Caster, or Cester, or Chester; with some difference added either to the beginning or end thereof. But this our city, being the first city, made famous by that renowned Legion aforementioned, called Victrix, was more properly or primarily called Cester, or Chester, being indeed an abbreviation of *Legecestria*, which name it obtained by the entertaining of those Legions in the winter-time, which first Julius Cæsar the Emperor sent, when he proposed the winning of Ireland; and after which Claudius Cæsar placed here, when he intended the surprising of the Orcades. And hence it is, that we may well affirm that old verse to be as antient as the name itself:

Cestria de Castris nomen quasi Castria sumpsit.

Which verse I find in an old author, thus prettily turned into an English Hexameter:

Chester, Castle Town, as it were, name took of a Castle.

And that this my conjecture of the name of this city, is not without authority, I suppose that the mention of one other city of legions, together with this, which the fore-cited author gives in the life of St. Werburg, lib. 2, cap. 3. will give some satisfaction.

Two cities of legions in chronicles we find,
One in South-Wales, in the time of Claudius,
Called Carrusk, by Britons had in mind;
Or else Caer Leon, built by king Belinus:
Where sometimes was a legion of knights chivalrous.
This city of legions was whilom the bishop's see,
To all South-Wales nominate [illegible].

Another city of legions we find also
In the west part of England, by the water of Dee,
Called Caer Leon of Britons long ago,
After named Chester, by great authority.
Julius the Emperor sent to this said city
A legion of knights to subdue Ireland;
Likewise did Claudius, as we understand.
This city of legions, so called by Romans,
Now is nominate, in Latin, of his property,
Cestria quasi Castra, of honour and pleasure,
Proved by building of old antiquity,
In cellars, and low vaults, and halls realty;
Like a comely castle, mighty strong and sure,
Each house like a castle, sometimes of great pleasure.

As well the authorities of Ptolemy, and Antoninus, who placed here that legion, which was called *Vicessima*, and *Victrix*; as also some old pieces of money here found stamped by *Septimius Geta*, do prove it; upon the reverse or back-side whereof, is this inscription, *Col. Divana leg.* xx. *Victrix.*

But for other tokens, or monuments, to testify the Romans' magnificence, time, the devourer of all things, hath eaten up almost all, of which there remain only in these late ages, some pavements of four square chequer-work stones, but in former times were many more, as we may learn from the words of the fore-named monk Ranulphus Cestrensis. There be here, saith he, ways under ground, vaulted marvellously with stoneworks, chambers, having arched roofs over head, huge stones engraven with the names of ancient famous persons. Here are also sometimes pieces of money digged up, coined by Julius Cæsar, and other Emperors, or men of fame, and stamped with their inscriptions.—And to this may be added, the report of another author, called Roger of Chester, in his Polychronicon: When I behold, saith he, the ground work of buildings in the streets, laid with main strong huge stones, it seemeth, that it has been founded by the painful labour of Romans, or Giants, rather than by the industry of Britons.*

* There are who have written, that Chester has been a city for many centuries of years before the entrance of the Romans into Britain; that a certain very ancient British king, called Lisle, when he first built the city Carlisle, repaired and made

The situation of the city is not the least matter for the commendations thereof, which made Lucian, a monk, who lived near the time of the Norman Conquest, to write thus: Chester is built as a city, the sight whereof inviteth and allureth the eye; which being situate in the west part of Britain, was, in times past, a place of receipt for the Legions, sent from afar to repose themselves, and served sufficiently to keep the keys, as I may say, of Ireland, for the Romans to preserve the limits of their empire. For being opposite to the north-east part of Ireland, it opens a way for the passage of ships and mariners to spread their sails, passing not often only, but continually, to and fro; as also for the commodities of sundry sorts of merchandize. Which description I find comprised in Camden.

Chester itself, is a place of resort to the Irish, a neighbour to the Welsh, and plentifully served with corn by the English; finely seated, with gates anciently built, approved in hard and dangerous difficulties; in regard of the river, and prospect of the eye, worthy, according to the eye, to be called, a city guarded with a watch of holy and religious men; and, through the mercy of our Saviour, always fenced and fortified with the merciful assistance of the Almighty.

I have purposely here omitted what divers writers have delivered touching other names, which they say this city has been called by, some of them being like, originally, to those afore-mentioned; and some of them either merely barbarous and insignificant, or fantastical and frivolous, being conscious to myself, that I herein intended no historical narration, but a plain topographical description of this noble city and shire; wherein notwithstanding in such passages as serve best for the illustration of the foundation and worthy esteem of the same, where the historical narrations of my authors will best express the truth thereof, I hope to find pardon in such recitals; and in that hope will crave patience for some little further stay upon the state of this city in former times, before we come to the present survey.

We find that the same city hath had many variable changes, sometimes in a flourishing, and other times in a depressed condition; yet at no time

good the decays and ruins of the city of Chester, worn out with age, about 900 years before Christ. A book, the title of which is Flores Historiarum, seriously ascertains (nor is it a modern author) that the same king Lisle reigned here in Britain at the same time king Solomon reigned in Jerusalem; which, according to history, was about the year of the world 3049: And though all historians commonly differ from one another concerning the year of the world when our Lord Christ was born, as is to be seen in Selden; however, the most reverend archbishop Usher, of Armagh, in his Annals, has set forth that Christ was born in the year of the world 4004; but the before described book also sets forth, that Ebrancus, a certain British prince, built York at the same time that David reigned in Israel; and that Rudibrass, son and survivor of the before-mentioned Lisle, built the cities Canterbury and Winchester, so that Chester is of so great as well as remarkable antiquity, that in the days of Solomon, and when York, Canterbury, and Winchester, although cities very ancient, were first built, then Chester, thro' decay and extreme antiquity, wanted repairing and making good its defects.

Rome, the foundation thereof laid by Romulus, round about Mount Palatine, on the 21st of April, 750 years before Christ, so that to the year 1700, it is 2450 years since that; and from the above statement it is plain it is 2655 years since Chester was repaired by king Lisle as above, and 205 years before the laying of the foundation of Rome by Romulus as aforesaid, to the said year 1700. It is 2808 years since the foundation of London, and 1755 years from Julius Cæsar's invasion of England, being 110 days before Christmas-day, which was September the 5th.

This account of the very remote antiquity of Chester corresponds with those given by Geoffry of Monmouth, Higden, and Henry Bradshaw, writers who were, unquestionably, either often deceived through an excess of credulity, or intended to recommend themselves to an ignorant age, which is always delighted with whatever carries an air of the wonderful, by promulgating as truths the exaggerated tales of tradition. Leland and Selden, names to which an infinitely greater degree of respect is due, suppose this city to have been founded by the Romans. Yet there are not wanting some, and those of a respectable class, who, from its advantageous situation, and other corroborating circumstances, maintain, with great appearance of probability, that Chester, was a place of some consideration before the invasion of Britain by that people by whom, however, they allow it to have been considerably improved and enlarged.

brought so low, but, by God's goodness and mercy, it hath again recovered all losses and impeachments; which plainly appears, as well in those times of the Roman government spoken of before, as more especially in the times of those variable jurisdictions of Saxons, Danes, and Normans, and also of later times.

The truth whereof will be manifested in the next part for our description, which shall be of the walls; for, albeit, much may be found in ancient relations, beyond the mention of the walling of this, or any other city in this kingdom, except the walls of turf, or earth, before the invention of stone-walls; which Mr. Stowe ascribeth to one Bennet, a monk of Wirral, *anno* 680, in his Survey of London, fol. 9. Yet, that which our writers tells us of our city's walling, both first and last, shall be all that I will offer to my readers in this kind, and that in their own words.

The walls of this city were first built by Marius, king of Britain, who reigned about the year of our Lord 73. But Ethelfleda, that noble Mercian Lady, about the year 908, greatly repaired and enlarged this city, making the walls thereof anew, and compassing in the castle, which, as it seemeth before that time stood without the walls; all which the fore-mentioned monk, Henry Bradshaw, thus expresseth:

King Marius, a Briton, reigning in prosperity,
In the west part of this noble region,
Amplified and walled strongly Chester city,
And mightily fortified the said foundation.
Thus each author holdeth a several opinion,
This Marius slew Readerick, king of Picts land,
Calling the place of his name Westmorland.
The year of our Lord nine hundred and eight,
This Elfleda, Duchess, with mickle royalty
Re-edified Chester, and fortified it full right:
Church-house, and Wall, decayed piteously,
Thus brought into ruin was Chester city.
First by Ethelfred, king of Northumberland,
And by Danes, North Wales vexing all England.
Also, she enlarged this old city
With new mighty walls strong all about;
Almost by promotion, double in quantity,
To the further building brought without doubt,
She compassed in castle, enemy to hold out.
Within the said walls, to defend the town,
Against Dane and Welshmen, to drive them all down.

Of which famous lady I will say somewhat further, though it be with some iteration; and imitate my author, in prosecuting her praises, and will relate that story which seems most pertinent to our purpose.

This Ethelfleda (saith he), after the death of her husband Ethelred, governed the kingdom of the Mercians. She was a virtuous and valiant queen, and inclined herself to do good in the common-wealth: She repaired Stafford, Warwick, Tamworth, Shirsbury, or Shrewsbury, and built up new Runcorn and Eddesbury. She translated the body of St. Oswald, king and martyr, from Bradney to Gloucester, where she built a monastery, in the honour of St. Peter, over St. Oswald's body; and she was there buried, anno Dom. 919.

My author proceedeth further; and Mr. Stowe, it seems, followed him in these words, in his Summary, fol. 16. :—Leil the son of Brutus Greenshield, that destroyed the giant out of his land, being a lover of peace, in his time built Caerleil, that is now called Chester; the first founder whereof, saith Randal Higden, was Leon Gaur, of Neptune's progeny, a mighty strong giant, who built the same city, with caves and walls under the earth. But this king Leil, of whom we have spoken before, was founder thereof, with pleasant buildings, and fair houses, and named it Caerleil: Since that time, by the Romans this city was re-edified, when a legion of Roman knights and soldiers were sent thither, and by them named, the city of Legions, which is now called Cestria, of the ancient buildings with vaults and towers, each house like a castle, which were sometimes of great pleasure. And in the same, fol. 26. he saith, that in the seventy-third year of Christ, that Marius, the son of Arviragus, repaired, walled, and fortified the city of Caerleon, now called Chester.

And fol. 37. in the year 918, Elfleda, wife to the

duke of Mercia, repaired Chester, with other cities and towns; and that she built a town and castle in the north-end of Wales, upon the river Mersey, that is called Runcorn; and she built a bridge over Severn, called Brimsbury bridge: She was, as before said, a great repairer of Chester; with many others, whom ancient Chronicles do speak of, as Arviragus, Marius, and others.

To this, let me now add that which was cited out of the Domesday book, made by Mr. Camden: "The "earls of the Norman line fortified the city of Chester "both with walls and castle; for as the bishop held of "the king that which belonged to the bishopric, so the "earls, with their men, held of the king, wholly, all "the rest of the city. It paid gild or tribute for fifty "hides; and 431 houses were gildable, and seven mint "masters."*

Afterwards, when the king himself in person came thither, every caracata yielded unto him 200 liestas, and one ton of ale, and one rusco of butter; and for the re-edification of the wall, and the bridge, the provost gave warning by an edict, that out of every hide in the county, one man should come, and whose man came not, his lord and master was fined in forty shillings to the King and the Earl.

The afore-mentioned Marius, saith Grafton in his Abridgement, did so much esteem the city of Chester, that he repaired, walled, fortified, and greatly enlarged the same; and when he had reigned there fifty-three years, he was there buried.

And Fabian, in his Chron. page 5, cap. 15, saith, This city was of no small respect, when king Vortiger, being deposed from his kingdom, and his son Vortiger placed in his stead, was, during the life of his said son, kept under the rule of certain tutors, to him assigned in Caerlegion, now called Chester; and all that time so demeaned himself towards his son, both in counsel, and otherwise, that thereby he got the love of the Britons; and after the death of his son Vortiger, was restored again to the kingdom.

In Holinshead's Chronicle of the history of Ireland, it is said, that the Irishmen made their appearance, and

* The ancient Revenues of the Earldom of Chester; as appears by the Survey made in the 50th year of King Edward III. Collected out of the Records of the Tower of London, and divers ancient Authors. By Sir J. Dodderidge, Knt.

COUNTY OF CHESTER.

	£	s.	d.
The fee-farm of the city of Chester	1000	0	0
Other profits out of the city	4	0	0
Farm of the town of Medwick	64	0	0
Farm of the mills upon the River Dee	240	0	0
Manor of Drakelow in yearly rent	49	1	10
Farm of the manor of Dunmarsh	15	0	0
The forest of Mara, the issues and profits thereof	51	7	0
Rents and profits of Northwich	66	0	0
Rent of Shotwick manor	30	14	1
Rent of Frodsham manor	36	13	4
Profits of the Sheriffs of the county	124	4	7
Perquisites of courts holden by the Justice of Chester	100	0	0
Profits of the Escheator's-office	100	0	0
Total of the revenue of the earldom of Chester	1001	3	7

THE COUNTY OF FLINT,

	£.	s.	d.
Profits of the manor of Hope and Hopedale	63	0	0
Profits of the manor of Ellow, and of the coal-mines there	6	0	0
Profits of the constable of Rothlem, whereof he was accountable	8	14	0
Rent of the town of Flint	56	0	0
Rent of the town of Colshul	4	7	10
Rent of the town of Carouse	59	6	8
Rent of the town of Bagherge	14	3	4½
Town of Voyvol, yearly	13	16	8
Town of Rothlem, and rent thereof	72	9	2
Town of Mosten, and rent thereof	15	6	8
Profits of the office of Escheator of Englefield	56	0	0
The Bloglot of the county of Flint, which consists of the profits of 100 courts in the county	72	11	9½
Perquisites of the sessions in Flint	30	0	0
Profits of Escheator in the said county	8	0	0
Sum total of the revenues of the earldom of Chester, arising from the county of Flint	442	6	2

	£.	s.	d.
Rents of Macclesfield borough	31	0	0
Profits of Macclesfield hundred	61	14	0
Profits of Macclesfield forest	98	0	0

did homage unto King Arthur at Caerlegion, now called Chester. And Mr. Fox, in the Acts and Monuments,

	£	s.	d.
Profits of Macclesfield store	13	6	8
Herbage and agistments of the park of Macclesfield	6	0	0
Sum total of Macclesfield lordship	164	0	8
Sum total of all the revenue of the said earldom, in the counties of Chester and Flint, and lordship of Macclesfield	1694	9	8
Out of which total sum there were deducted these sums following, viz.			
Alms of the said earldom	61	6	8
To Sir Rich. Stafford 129l. as due of a rent out of the said earldom	129	0	0
Fees of the Justices yearly	100	0	0
Which being deducted, the whole revenue of of the said earldom remaining, not allowing any other fees to officers, amounted to	1304	15	5

The Revenues of the Earldom of Chester, as they stand charged to the Crown, are as follows:

THE COUNTY OF CHESTER.

	£	s.	d.
Fee-farm of the city of Chester	20	2	4½
Escheated lands within the said city	0	7	0
Rents of the manor of Drakelow and Rudheath	26	2	6
Farm of the town of Medwick	21	6	0
Profits of Mara and Mondrem	34	0	9
Profits of Shotwick manor and park	23	19	0
Fulling-mills upon the River Dee	11	0	0
Annual profits on Frodsham manor	48	0	0
Profits of Macclesfield hundred	6	1	8
Farm of Macclesfield borough	16	1	3
Profits of the forest of Macclesfield	85	12	11¼
Profits of Escheator of Chester	24	19	0
Profits of the Sheriff of the said county	43	12	3
Profits of the Chamberlain of the county of Chester	55	14	0
Sum total of the revenue of the earldom, in the county of Chester	418	1	2¼

COUNTY OF FLINT.

	£	s.	d.
Yearly value of Ellow	20	8	0
Farm of the town of Flint	33	19	4
Farm of Carouse	7	2	4
Castle of Rothlem	5	12	10
Rents and profits of Mosten	7	0	0
Rents and profits of Colshul	54	16	0
Rents of Rothlem town	44	17	6
Lands in Englefield, yearly value	23	10	0
Profits of Veyvol	5	9	0
Profits of the office of Escheator	6	11	9
The mines of coal and wood within the manor of Mosten	0	10	0
The office of the Sheriff in rents and casualties	120	0	0
The mines and profits of the fairs of Northop	8	9	2
The total sum of the said revenue in yearly rent	244	5	4
In casualties were lastly	37	0	8
	281	6	0

The Fees of the Officers of the said Earldom.

THE COUNTY OF CHESTER.

	£	s.	d.
The fee of the office of the Eschestor	10	10	0
The fee of the justices of assize in the counties of Chester and Flint	100	0	0
Fee of the attorney-general	3	6	8
Fee of four serjeants at law	14	6	8
Chamberlain of Chester, his fee	20	0	0
Sheriff of Chester, his fee	20	0	0
Constable of Chester Castle, his fee	18	5	0
Constable of Flint Castle, his fee	10	0	0
Ranger's fee of Mara forest	4	11	3
Fee of the porter of the Castle of Flint	6	1	8
Fee of the porter of the said Castle, and of the bailiff itinerant there	9	2	6
Fee of the governor of the forest of Macclesfield	12	0	0
Fee of the two clerks of the exchequer of Chester, for every of them 4l. 11s. 3d.	9	2	6
Fee of the surveyors of the works within the said county palatine	6	1	8
Fee of the keeper of the gardens of the Castle of Chester	4	11	3
Fee of the cryer of the exchequer at Chester	3	15	0
The yearly fee of the master carpenter	9	12	6
Fee of the comptroller of the counties of Chester and Flint	12	3	4
The yearly fee of the pregnatory	3	6	8
The fee of the master cementer	8	12	6
Fee of the chaplain of the Castle of Chester	2	0	0
Fee paid unto the dean and chapter of Chester	19	10	0
To the master of the hospital for his fee	4	11	0
The sum of this charge in Chester, amounteth unto	310	9	9
Which sum of 310l. 9s. 9d. being deducted out of the former total sum of 699l. 7s. 2¼d. there doth remain 388l. 17s. 5¼d. which is the clear remain of the earldom of Chester and Flint	388	17	5¼

CHESTER HISTORY.

saith, that about the same time, this city was a place of great account; and that both grammar and philosophy, with the tongues, were there taught.

The city of Chester is built in form of a parallelogram, the longest sides running north and south, inclosed with a fair stone wall, high and strong built, with fair battlements on all the four sides; and with the four gates opening to the four winds: besides some posterns and many seemly towers, in and upon the said walls. The four gates are, the East-gate, the North-gate, the Water-gate, and the Bridge-gate: Without the two first of these gates, namely the East and North-gates, the city extends itself in its suburbs, with very fair streets, and the same adorned with goodly buildings, both of gentlemen's houses, and fair inns for entertainment of all resorts.

And the Bridge-gate opening into an ancient part of the city, beyond the water over the bridge; or rather that part which some suppose was once the city itself, now called Handbridge; and the water-gate only leading forth to the river Dee; which river, even there, falls into the mouth of the sea, having first as it were, purposely turned itself aside, to leave a fine spacious piece of ground of great pleasure and delight, called the Rood-Eye; for the citizens both profit and repast, a very delightful meadow place, used for a cow-pasture in the summer time; and all the year for a wholesome and pleasant walk by the side of the Dee, and for recreations of shooting, bowling, and such other exercises as are performed at certain times by men; and by running horses in presence of the mayor of the city, and his brethren; with such other lords, knights, ladies, and gentlemen, as please, at those times, to accompany them with that view.

That which we may call the chiefest passage into the city, giving entrance to all comers from the most part of the county of Chester, and the great roads from other shires, is the East-gate, a goodly large gate, of an ancient fair building, with a tower upon it, containing many fair rooms within it.* At which we begin the circuit of the wall, which from that gate, northward, extendeth to a tower upon the said wall.

These towers, whereof there are divers upon the said walls, were, as I suppose, made to be watch-towers in the day, and lodging places in the night, and in the time of storms, for the watchmen that kept watch upon the walls, in those times of danger, when they were so often besieged by armies of enemies, and in such surprizes; though now some of them be converted to other uses.

The North-gate of the city is a reasonable strong, fair building, and used for the prison of the city, in the charge and keeping of the sheriffs successively from year to year; where are imprisoned, as well all malefactors for capital offences, taken within the liberties and county of the city; and there receiving their trials before the mayor and his brethren, by due course of the common law of England; as also, all other for trespasses, misdemeanors, and other causes whatsoever, to the same prison, by the magistrates of the city, lawfully committed; which prison hath always one sufficient well reputed keeper, or gaoler, to take charge of all prisoners thither brought; and for due performance of his office therein, standeth always bound to the sheriffs of the city, for the time being, at the appointment of the said Sheriffs.

From the Northgate, still westward, the wall extendeth to another tower; and from thence to the turning of the wall southward, at which corner standeth another fine turret, called the New Tower, and was pitched within the channel of Dee water; which new tower was built, as it is reported, in or near to the place in the river, which was the quay whereunto vessels of great burden, as well of merchandize as others, came close up to; which may the rather seem probable, as well by a deeper foundation of stone work, yet appearing from the foot of that tower, reaching a good distance in the channel; as also by great rings of iron, here and there fastened in the sides of the said tower, which if they served not for the fastening of such vessels, as then used to

* This gate and tower were taken down, and a handsome elliptic arch erected in their stead, in the year 1769.

approach to the same quay, I cannot learn what other use they should be for.

From this corner of the New-tower, the wall goeth south to the Water-gate; which gate is less than any of the other three, serving only for the passage to the Roodeye, formerly mentioned, and to the bank of the river, where are brought into the city all such commodities as coal, fish, corn, and other things; which barks and other small vessels, bring up the river Dee.*

And still south from the same Water-gate, reacheth the wall in a straight line, before it hath gotten beyond the castle, and then turns itself towards the east.

From that turning is the Bridge-gate situate at the north-end of a very fair and strong stone-bridge, with another fair gate at the south-end of it.

The river Dee doth here incline to enlarge itself, having gotten so near the sea, but that it is soundly girt in on either side with huge rocks of hard stone, which restrain the pride of its force.

This Bridge-gate, being a fair strong building of itself, hath of late been greatly beautified by a seemly water-work of stone, built steeple-wise, by the ingenious industry and charge of a late worthy member of the city, John Terer, gent and hath served ever since, to great use, for the conveying of the river water from the cistern, in the top of that work, to the citizens houses, in almost all the parts of the city, in pipes of lead and wood, to their no small contentment and commodity.

The wall thence continueth along the river side eastward, to another remainder of a turret, and then turneth itself northward; and certain paces from thence is a postern, of old called Woolfield-gate; but of later times named Newgate, which in the year 1609 was augmented and adorned with a fair building, and made as a passage both for horses and carts, serving to great use; and for a more compendious way to all passengers, horse, foot, carts, or coaches, which either desire not to behold the beauty of the middle streets of the city, or delight not to be seen of many eyes, but make more speed than some do: and from this gate, our wall having another turret now unto it, called Wall-tower, stretcheth itself still along, till it meeteth with the East-gate, at which it began.

This wall is so fairly built with battlements on the outward part, as was said before, and with a foot-pace, or floor, a yard or four feet under the notch of the battlement, that you may go round about the walls, being a very delectable walk, feeding the eye, on one side, with the sweet gardens and fine buildings of the city; and on the other side, with a prospect of many miles into the county of Chester, into Wales, and into the sea. And this wall, although it serveth not so much in these days for defence and safety against the invasions of enemies and dangers of siege, as in ancient times it did, yet have the citizens here, by continual care and no small charge, maintained the same in sound and good reparations, for the ornament, credit, and estimation of the city: the special care whereof belongeth to certain officers yearly, either new elected, or confirmed, called the murengers, being usually of the most ancient aldermen of the said city, who have the receipt of the customs and tolls for the most part of the city, especially in shipping and sea-matters; out of which is defrayed the charge of the reparation of the wall; and that toil hath been allotted to this very purpose.

I find this record in the year 14 Edward II. the custom of Murage was granted to this city for two years, to the reparation and amendment of the walls of the city, and for the paving of the streets: In which grant, there are set down some particulars, which are to be paid for thus, viz.: For every cranock of all kind of corn, a halfpenny; and of all meat and malt, a farthing. And for what was not in the said grant expressed, there should be paid for the value of every two shillings a farthing, which was two-pence halfpenny a pound.—

* Since the time of King, the river Dee has been made navigable, by virtue of two Acts of Parliament, passed in the years 1733, and 1744, at the expense of above £80,000. so that vessels of 200 and 300 tons burden can navigate up to the city.

But of these customs and tolls, it may be we shall have more occasion to say somewhat hereafter.

Upon the south-side of the city, near unto the said river Dee, and upon a high bank, or rock of stone, is mounted a strong and stately castle,* round in form; the base-court likewise enclosed with a circular wall, which, to this day, retaineth one testimony of the Romans' magnificence, having therein a fair and ancient square tower; which, by testimony of all the writers I have hitherto met with, beareth the name of Julius Cæsar's tower: Besides which there remain yet many goodly pieces of building; whereof one of them containeth all fit and commodious rooms for the lodging and use of the honorable justices of assize, twice a year. Another part is a goodly hall, where the court of common-pleas, and gaol-delivery; and also the sheriff of the county's court; with other business for the county of Chester, are constantly kept and holden: And is a place, for that purpose, of such state and comeliness, that I think it is hardly equalled by any shire-hall, in any of the shires in England.

The city is also adorned with many fine and decent churches, there being within the walls eight parishes, and parish-churches, St. Oswald's or Werburgh, St, Peter's, Trinity Church, St. Martin's, St. Mary's, St. Olave's St. Michael's, and St. Bridget's. And in the suburbs without the walls, St. John the Baptist; besides little St. John, without the Northgate; all which churches, or the most of them, as they are of a very ancient, so they are of a very comely building, and have their situations so in open view of the streets wherein they stand, and are so well maintained, both for their fit and decent reparations, without, and their clean and handsome keeping within, that they are so many beautiful ornaments to the city. But here I thus pass by them, until by coming particularly to them in their places, and order, I shall have more occasion to describe them. &c. &c. &c.

* From Grose's Antiquities of England and Wales.

This Castle, it is said, was either built, or greatly repaired by Hugh Lupus, earl of Chester; nephew to William the Conqueror: this castle is built of a soft reddish stone, which does not endure the weather, and is at present much out of repair, several large pieces of the walls having lately fallen into the ditch. Indeed, its trifling consequence, as a fortress, would hardly justify the expense of a thorough repair. It is, however, commanded by a governor and lieutenant-governor, and is commonly garrisoned by two companies of invalids. In Peck's Desiderata Curiosa, Chester Castle stands in the list of queen Elizabeth's garrisons, with the following officers, and salaries:

CHESTER.

	£	S.	D.
Constable of the Castle; fee	6	13	4
Porter; fee	4	11	3
Keeper of the gardens; fee	6	1	8
Surveyor of the works within Cheshire and Flint; fee	6	1	8
Master mason; fee	8	12	4
Master carpenter; fee	9	2	6

It still continues to be a royal garrison, and has a governor and lieutenant-governor, each at ten shillings per diem; and two independant companies of invalids are stationed here. During the civil war under Charles the First, Chester was besieged, and at length, Feb. 3, 1645, taken by the parliamentary forces, commanded by Sir William Brereton; but the Castle neither made any particular defence or separate capitulation. The church, seen near the Castle, is dedicated to the Virgin Mary, and called St. Mary's of the Castle. In and near the angles under the great window, appears the rock on which the Castle is founded.

These are accurate representations of the Seal of the "Mayor and Citizens" of Chester—and of the Hospital of St. John, Chester.—It is very probable, that the former was the ANCIENT Coat Armorial of the City.

THE CITY OF CHESTER.

CHESTER

HISTORY.

IT would be very difficult, if not impossible, to fix any data, for the building of this city. It is, however, extremely probable, that long before the arrival of the Romans, it enjoyed some distinction amongst its neighbours from being the metropolis of one of the great tribes into which Britain was then divided. It has been before observed, that Chester was included in the district occupied by the *Cornavii*;* and we have nothing to disprove an assertion, that this city was the chief seat of their Government. It is true, that few BRITISH relics have been found upon its present site, whilst the discovery of ROMAN antiquities has taken place, almost yearly: but its advantageous situation only, divested of all other considerations, induces a belief that it was a place of note at that early period.

The extract from *Webb's Itinerary*, which introduces this portion of the work, is sufficient to prove the fallacy of any attempt to ascertain the origin of this ancient city.—Whilst we may argue for its *British* origin, we have ample proofs of its being a *Roman* station.—The 20th Legion,† distinguished by the proud title of "THE VICTORIOUS," established itself in Chester, in the time of Galba; but there is no doubt that, anterior to this, it had been a Roman garrison. The importance of its situation, rendered it necessary that the

* Speaking of this tribe, Camden observes, (edit. 1610), "The derivation or etymology of the name, let others sift out. As for myself, I would draw the force and signification of that word to this and that diversly; but seeing none of them doth aptly answer to the nature of the place, or disposition of the people, I chuse rather to reject them, than here to propound them. According therefore to my purpose, I will severally run over those provinces which after Ptolemy's description the *Cornavii* seemed to have possessed; that is to say, *Warwickshire*, *Worcestershire*, *Staffordshire*, *Shropshire*, and *Cheshire*. In which there remaineth no footing at this day of the name of *Cornavii*, although this name continued even until the decline of the Roman Empire; for certain companies and regiments of the Cornavii, served in war under the latter Emperors, as we may see in the Book, *Notitia Provinciarum*."

† This Legion, it appears, was removed from Chester to Bath.

CHESTER

strength of its garrison should correspond with it; and we find that the out-posts of the Legion extended, on the Dee, as far as Aldford; and to Caergwrle,* in the parish of Hope, Flintshire. The relics of Roman works in and near Chester,† are very numerous; and the city walls yet remain perfect, a standing monument of their military magnificence. It has been conjectured, that Chester (speaking of it as a *fortress*) was one of the garrisons erected by Ostorius Scapula, after the defeat of Caractacus; and Mr Pennant instances the direction of *Vitruvius*,—that the walls of all Roman cities should be only of a breadth to admit two armed men to pass abreast—as a proof of their foundation by the Legions. It is pretty certain, however, that Chester was a walled town previous to the year 908, for the Saxon Chronicle informs us, that Ethelred, the Mercian Duke, and his illustrious wife, Ethelfleda,‡ in that year REPAIRED the walls, which had been much injured by the Danes, and enlarged them to double their former extent.

* See note, p. 31.

A brief notice of particular events from the earliest period may be introduced here. In 607 the City was taken from the Britons, by Ethelfrid King of Northumberland, who had previously defeated their army under the walls. But in 618, the Britons recovered possession of it; and at a solemn assembly in that year held here, they elected Cadwan to be their King. It is noticed by Hardyng, in his Chronicle, that Cadwall the son and successor of Cadwan, was also crowned King of the Britons in Chester. About A. D. 830, the victorious Egbert, having united the Heptarchy under his authority, finally drove the Britons from Chester, and annexed it to his dominions; and it is said by Hardyng, that his successor "Athelwolfe, was crowned kyng at his cittee of West Chester, in all royal estate." In 894, Chester fell into the hands of the Danes, and they underwent a siege, during which they were compelled to feed on horse flesh. Matthew of Westminster, however, maintains,‖ that this occured at Buttingden; and that the Danes who escaped from thence, joined a garrison of their own countrymen at Chester, where Alfred followed and besieged them, but finding them too strongly posted to hope for success, he wasted the adjacent country, to prevent them obtaining supplies of provisions.—The city however, reverted to the Mercian Government, for in 907, it was repaired and beautified by Ethelfred, and his wife Ethelfleda.

HISTORY.

‖ In his work, page 179.

The Welsh afterwards regained possession of the

† At a very early period this city bore the name of Chester, but the old Monkish historians have bestowed upon it a variety of other names. In Fletcher's M.S. 1640, (a book in the possession of Thomas Dicas, Esq. of Chester, it is thus noticed: "*Neomagus*, because Magus, sonne to Simothes, sonne to Japet, the third sonne of Noah, first built it, and called it so. *Civitas Legionum*, or the cittie of Legions, so named of the Romans, because Julius Cæsar sent his Legions of Souldiers and Knights unto this cittie to winne Ireland; and there is a tower in the Castle of Chester, knowne by the name of Julius Cæsar's tower. *Deva*, *Devania*, because it was situate upon the River of Dee. *Caerleon Arddeur dwy*, in the Brittish or Wailch speech; in English the City of Legions on the river of Dee. *Ostelirm*, so called of writers, signifieing the qualllity of the place, viz.: a stong hold, rocke, or island. *Legecester*, or *Legecestria*, so called of the Lattins. *Caerlegion*, a common name of the Brittaines and of diverse writers, also alluding to the name the Romans gave it. *Leogrica*, or *Locrinus lande*, because it fell into the part of Locrine his inheritance, when Brute divided this land unto his three sonnes, Locrine, Albanet, and Camber. *Westchester*, currently it is called in the furthest parts of Englande, and to difference it from the other Chesters, and because they think it so standeth. *Chester*, the only and proper name now of this citty, allthoughe there be many Chesters, townes and citties called by this name, as Manchester, Dorchester, Winchester, and others. But this city is called Chester without all manner of addittion, as though it were the only Chester, or principall Chester of all others in the Kingdome. This name Chester, in the Saxon speeche, signifies a castle, or strong hould in English, or else, quasi *Castra*, for lodging of the souldiers. It is builded upon a rocke; many cellars are in it, digged under the ground, as it may seeme to hide souldiers; and many rare workes are found under ground; which shew great antiquitie."

‡ She was the daughter of King Alfred. On the birth of her first child it is said she parted from her husband, being deterred by the pangs and danger of parturition, from hazarding their recurrence, observing, "That it was beneath the daughter of a King to pursue any pleasure attended with so much inconvenience." She afterwards devoted herself to acts of piety, and deeds of heroism, building and refounding cities, and erecting no less than nine castles. She was dignified with the titles of *Lord* and *King* those of Lady and Queen being thought unworthy of her greatness.—*See page 10.*

CHESTER

city, but they were expelled by King Edward in 923;* and we are told, the heads of Gruffydh, Prince of Wales, and Leofrid, a Danish auxiliary, were cut off, and set upon the gates by the Conquerors. About the year 971, King Edgar, with his army, and the whole of his naval forces, came to Chester. It was at this time "he was rowed from his Palace on the south side of the Bridge, to the Monastery of St. John, by eight petty Sovereigns,† who had previously paid their homage to him." This Legend, unfortunately for its veracity, has for its chief authority, merely the traditions of the *Saxon Chronicle*;‡ but it is pretty certain, nevertheless,

HISTORY.

† See p. 32.

* William of Malmsbury says 924.

‡ The following account is extracted from Campbell's lives of the Admirals, vol. 1, p. 46.:---

EDGAR, very justly styled the Great, succeeded his brother Edwy; and, from his first ascending the throne, demonstrated himself worthy of being the heir of Alfred and Ethelstan. He thoroughly understood, and successfully pursued their maxims; for he applied himself, from the beginning of his reign, to the raising a mighty maritime force, and the keeping in due subjection, all the petty princes. In one thing only he was blameable; that he gave too much into foreign customs, and indulged the Danes in living promiscuously with his own people; which gave them an opportunity of knowing thoroughly the state of all parts of the nation, of which they made a very bad use in succeeding times. In all probability, he was led into this error by his love to peace, which indeed he enjoyed, much more than any of his ancestors had done. But he enjoyed it, as a king of this island ought to enjoy it; not in a lazy fruition of pleasure, unworthy of a prince; but by assiduously applying himself to affairs of state, and by an activity of which few other kings are capable, even in times of the greatest danger. But it is necessary to enter into particulars, since we are come to that king who most clearly vindicated his right to the dominion of the sea, and who valued himself on his having justly acquired the truly glorious title of Protector of Commerce. All writers agree, that his fleet was far superior to that of any of his predecessors, as well as much more powerful than those of all the other European princes put together; but they are by no means of the same mind, as to the number of ships of which it was composed. Some fix it at three thousand six hundred; others at four thousand; and there wants not authority to carry it so high as four thousand eight hundred. However, the first seems to be the most probable number; and, therefore, to it we shall keep.—These ships he divided into three fleets, each of twelve hundred sail, and them he constantly stationed; one on the east, another on the west, and the third on the north coast of the kingdom; neither was he satisfied with barely making such a provision; he would likewise see that it answered the ends for which he intended it. In order to this, every year, after Easter, he went on board the fleet stationed on the eastern coast; and, sailing west, he scoured all the channels, looked into every creek and bay, from the Thames mouth to the Land's end in Cornwall: then, quitting these ships, he went on board the western fleet, with which, steering his course to the northward, he did the like, not only on the English and Scots coasts, but also on those of Ireland and the Hebrides, which lie between them and Britain: then, meeting the northern fleet, he sailed in it to the Thames mouth. Thus surrounding the island every summer, he rendered any invasion impracticable, kept his sailors in continual exercise, and effectually asserted his sovereignty over the sea. As a farther proof of this, he once held his court at Chester; where, when all his feudatory princes had assembled, in order to do him homage, he caused them to enter a barge; and sitting four on one side, and four on the other, they rowed, while he steered the helm; passing thus in triumph, on the river Dee, from his palace, to the monastery of St. John, where he landed, and received their oaths to be his faithful vassals, and to defend his rights by land and by sea; and then, having made a speech to them, he returned to his barge, and passed in the same manner back to his palace. The names of these princes were Kenneth, king of Scotland; Malcolm, king of Cumberland; Maccusius, king of Man, and of the isles, and five petty kings of the Britons. When the ceremony was over, the king was pleased to say, that his successors might justly glory in the title of kings of the English; since, by this solemn act, he had set their prerogative above dispute. In the winter, he travelled by land through all parts of his dominions, to see that justice was duly administered, to prevent his nobles from becoming oppressors, and to protect the meanest people from suffering wrong.—These were the arts by which he secured tranquillity to himself; while he kept foreigners in awe, and his subjects in quiet. By being always ready for war, he avoided it; so that, in his whole reign, there happened but one disturbance, and that through the intemperate fury of the Britons, who, while he was in the north, committed great disorders in the west.—On his return, he entered their country with a great army; and, that they might feel the effects of plundering, suffered his soldiers to take whatever they could find: but when he saw the people reduced to extreme misery, he rewarded his army out of his own coffers, and obliged them to restore the spoils; by which he left those, whom he found rebels, the most affectionate of all his subjects. Well, therefore, might our ancient historians boast, as they did, of this prince; and say, that he was comparable to any of the heroes of antiquity. In truth, he far surpassed them; for whereas many of them became famous by acts of rapine and robbery, he established his reputation on a nobler foundation—that of reigning sixteen years without a thief found in his dominions on land, or a pirate

CHESTER  HISTORY.

that the Kings of Mercia had a regal palace here. The first field, after crossing the Bridge into Handbridge, on the right hand side, still retains the name of "*Edgar's Field*;" and Dr. Cowper, in a note on his "IL PENSEROSO," says, "The foundations of his (Edgar's) princely mansion, are *now** *apparent* just below Chester Bridge, southwards." There is not a relic in existence at the present time.†

* About 1747.

There is a considerable hiatus in our local annals, from the year 971, till the Conquest; and then we are enlivened with a tale told by *Giraldus Cambrensis*,‡ who says, that after the wound received by Harold at the Battle of Hastings, he fled to Chester, and spent the remainder of his days there as an hermit.—This is not worth contradiction. We have too many proofs in our national annals, to render this tale at all probable.‖—But let us hear all that has been *hazarded* on this topic. Bromton tells us, that his tomb was shewn in the middle of the area behind the Cross§ at St. John's Church: he also says, that many asserted he was alive when Hen. I. returned to Chester from his Cambrian expedition, and that the monarch had an interview with him here.¶ It is well ascertained, nevertheless, that Harold fell at the battle of Hastings, and was interred at Waltham. Giraldus has another marvellous story respecting Henry IV. Emperor of Germany, who after giving up his crown, passed over seas into England; and lived the life of a hermit, near Chester, on his death bed only confessing his high rank. The historian styles him, "*Imperatorem Romanum Henricum*;" and Camden supposes he alludes to Henry IV. The Lysons say, that the circumstances mentioned by Giraldus, apply to Hen. V. but he died *at Utrecht*, May 22, 1125.** The traditional story related of this imperial incognito is, that he led a recluse life here, under the name of Godescallus, or Godstallus; and in the Red Book of Chester Abbey, the following entry occurs: "*Anno* 1110, *Rex Henricus dedit filiam suam Godescallo, Imperatori Alemannæ, qui nunc Cestriæ jacet.*" Voltaire says, that in the letter which Henry IV. sent to his son, he entreats him to allow the Bishop of Leige to grant him an asylum:—"Allow me (says Henry) to continue at Liege, if not an Emperor, at least a refugee. Let it not be said to my shame, or rather to your's, that I am forced to beg lodgings in Easter time. If you grant me what I ask, I shall be greatly obliged to you; if you refuse me, I will go and rather live as a poor Cottager, *in a foreign land*, than wander thus from one disgrace to another, in an empire which was once my own."††—This may be considered by some as an allusion to his voluntary exile; the circumstance, also, of a lane called Godstall-lane,‡‡

heard of at sea. One thing more I must mention, as being much to my purpose, though slighted by many of our modern writers. It is the preamble of a decree of his, made in the fourteenth year of his reign; wherein his style runs thus:---"*Ego Edgarus, totius Albionis Basileus necnon maritimorum seu insulanorum regum circumhabitantium*," &c. That is, I Edgar, monarch of all Albion, and sovereign over all the princes of the adjacent isles, &c. Which plainly asserts his naval dominion. As he lived, so he died, in peace, and full of glory."

† Early in the reign of Elizabeth, an engraved plan of Chester was executed in the usual style of the day: in which the site of this field has the reference: "*Ruinoso domus Comitis Cestriensis.*" In this field is the very ancient Roman relic of Minerva and her bird.—See vignette, page 14.

‡ Bromton also notices this.

‖ See Barnard's History of England, page 57:---Harold II. was killed by the random shot of an arrow, which entering at the ball of his eye penetrated into his brain. His two brothers were also numbered among the slain. The courage or rather hopes of the English fell with these undaunted leaders. They immediately gave way in several places, and fled from the field of battle, leaving their standard and victory with the Norman conqueror. In this decisive battle of Hastings, William had three horses killed under him, and lost near fifteen thousand men; but the loss of the English was still more considerable: it continued from sun rising to sun set. The body of king Harold was found besmeared with blood, which William restored to his mother, who buried it in Waltham Abbey."

§ The situation of which was in the present ruin.

¶ Might not this tale have arisen from the circumstance, of Algitha, the Queen of Harold, who immediately after the Conquest was removed to Chester, by the Earls Edgar and Morcar, her brothers?

** See Voltaire's Annals, 12mo. edition.

†† Annals of the German Empire, vol. 15, p. 195, 12mo. edit. 1762.

‡‡ This lane is described in a survey of the streets, "in the dais of King Henrie the third," in those terms:—"On the south side of the said streete is a lane that goeth out of the said streete, by the house side of William Tanner, and so into the Church-yarde of St. Oswalde's, called Lean-Lane; and

adjoining the Cathedral Church, might be brought in to support the tradition, as taking its name from that which the deposed Emperor assumed: but, considered wholly, there does not appear to be the slightest foundation for it.

We learn from the Harl. MSS. that after the imprisonment of Gherbod, the first Earl,* William I. invest-
* Sep. 16. ed Hugh Lupus with the Palatine dignity: he accompanied him on his way to his new possession, and at Malpas, Hugh was solemnly presented with the Earldom. The Conqueror returned to his Metropolis; and the Earl advanced to Chester, which, after being thrice defeated, he took, and subjected to his sway.—Shortly after this, the King being determined on humbling the power of the Welsh Princes, arrived at Chester with a powerful army: it was at this time he rebuilt the Castle, and to this period we may attribute the erection of such ancient parts of it as still remain. In 1156, Henry II. visitted Chester on his way to Wales, encamping his army on Saltney Marsh; and in 1157, he received here the homage of Malcolm the Scots King.†—In 1212 King John spent several days here: It was here he received the intelligence of the defection of a great portion of his subjects, which put an end to his projected Welsh expedition.‡ In 1237,‖ Chester Castle was seized by the King's Commissioners Hugh le Despencer, Stephen de Segrave, and Henry de Aldithley. This took place on the death of John Scott, the last Earl, when the King seized the Palatinate into his own hands. In 1256, Prince Edward, who had recently been created Earl of Chester, arrived here on the festival of St. Kenelm. On the road he was met by the Clergy and Citizens, in solemn procession; he remained three days, receiving the homage of the Nobles of Cheshire and Wales—and after making a military survey of his garrisons in the Earldom and Principality, returned through Chester, and according to the Chronicle of Chester Abbey, proceeded to Darnhall. The following year, the King summoned his Barons to meet him with their vassals at Chester, preparatory to an inroad into Wales, which it does not appear took place.—In 1264, William le Zouch, Justice of Chester, apprehensive that the City might be besieged either by the rebellious Barons, or the Welsh, considerably improved its fortifications, and dug a deep ditch on the north side. Considerable damage was in consequence done to the property of the Abbot in Bagge-lane (Wall's-lane), near the Northgate, and for which an equivalent was promised.§ Notwithstanding these preparations of defence, the City and Castle were taken by the Earl of Derby on the behalf of the Barons. The King and his son, soon after falling into the hands of Simon de Montfort, were compelled to sue for peace; and the Earldom was given to him.—His son Henry, was subsequently sent here, and in his father's name, received the homage of the Citizens of Chester, and of the Nobles and Freeholders of the County, before his departure,¶ appointing Luke de Taney Justice. The next year brought about a change of fortune: James de Aldithley, and Urian de St Pierre, with the concurrence of the people of Chester, laid siege to the Justice and his adherents in the

beneath it upon the *same side nearer the Eastgate*, is a lane called St. Goddellstall, and so goeth out of the said streete, into the said Church-yard: this Goddellstall lieth buried within the Abbey Church, in Chester, and he was an Emperour, and a virtuouse disposed man in his liveing; and this lane lieth betweene the house sometime of Robert Chamberlaine, and the house late in the houlding of William Humphrey. And upon the same side, *nearer the Eastgate*, there is a lane called St. Warburge's-lane, and goeth into the aforesaid Church yard," &c.---It is probable, therefore, that Godstal-lane was upon the site of the passage leading from Eastgate-street to the Cathedral, now called the *London Baker's entry*.

† In a book printed towards the close of the 17th century, entitled, "A dispute concerning Homage," this is strenuously denied.

‡ Matt. Paris thus notices it: "Cumque adhuc spretis his communicationibus, ad Cestriam venisset, iterum venerunt ad eum nuncii et literæ, quod videlicet rex, si bellum aggrederetur inceptum, aut a suis magnatibus perimeretur, aut hostibus ad perdendum traderetur."

‖ About this period, some peculiar customs prevailed in Chester; among them, whenever the King came, he claimed from all ploughland 200 HESTHAS, or capons; one CUNA or vat of ale; and one RUSCA of butter—and whoever made bad ale was either to pay forty shillings, or sit in a tumbril, or dung cart.

§ On the patent roll 51 Hen. III. there is an order for inquiring into the extent of the damage, and making compensation.

¶ He staid here about ten days.

CHESTER

Castle, for nearly ten weeks; which being in a good state of defence, held out stoutly. But the news of the result of the battle of Evesham arriving, and of the advance of Prince Edward to the Castle of Beeston, with many prisoners of distinction, operated strongly on de Taney, and surrendering the Castle, he threw himself upon the mercy of the King, who soon after gave him his liberty.—In 1276* and the following year, the city was honored, with the presence of Edw. I.—In 1282,† the King remained here from the 6th June till the 4th July, and granted protection to great numbers in Cheshire, that their corn, &c. should not be taken to his use; to others also he gave safe convoy to facilitate the victualling of his army. In 1283, he gave public thanks in the Cathedral Church, on the day of St. Augustine, when he heard Mass, and presented to the Convent an altar cloth of great value.

In 1284, Queen Eleanor staid here a few days, in her way to Carnarvon.‡ The King was also here four days in the beginning of September.—On the feast of St. Nicholas, in 1294, the King passed through Chester, to repel the rebellion of Madoc in North Wales.—In 1300, the Welsh were completely subjected to the rule of England, and did homage at Chester to their new Prince, Edward of Carnarvon.|| Edward II. in 1312, arrived here to meet his favorite Piers Gaveston, coming from Ireland.

‡ Cowp. MSS.

HISTORY.

In 1353, Edward the Black Prince, the Earls of Warwick and Stafford, and a strong armed force came to Chester, for the protection of the Justices Itinerant (Sir Richard Willoughby, and Sir Richard Snareshull) from the popular fury.§—Cowper's MSS. notice a remarkable occurrence on the Friday before St. James's Day, in 1393. Sir Baldwin de Rudyngston, John Hert, Griffith Reynolds, Roger Wall, and others, excited a riot within the precincts of the Abbey of Chester, but were finally driven out of the City, after a serious disturbance, in which the Mayor was ill treated, one of the Sheriffs made Prisoner, and the other much hurt.—This Baldwin escaped into Lancashire, but returned in a few days with 300 horse, raised for him by Sir John Stanley, of Latham, and attempted to surprize the City, but failed in the attempt, and many of his followers were taken prisoners.—In 1394, Richard II. attended by the Duke of Gloucester, the Earls of March, Salisbury, Arundel, Nottingham, Rutland, and others of high distinction, came to Chester, on their way to Ireland. Richard had always a remarkable partiality for the men of Cheshire, and it is noticed by our historians, that at the period when he was forsaken by his former friends, he appointed a corps of 2000 Cheshire archers 1397.
for his body guard. It was in 1398, that he exhibitted a further manifestation of the Royal favor to this County, having ordained, at the Parliament held at Shrewsbury, that from thenceforth it should be called and known by the name of the PRINCIPALITY of CHESHIRE,

* 1276.—The King went towards Chester, that thither Llewellyn Prince of Wales might have more free access to him; but he denying to do him homage, the King gathered an host of men, with the view of expelling the Prince out of his inheritance.—He built the Castle of Flint, strengthened the Castle of Rhyddlan, and others against the Welshmen.—*Howes' Chronicle.*

† "David, Lord of Denbigh, being reconciled to his brother Prince Llewellyn, against whom he had been a traitor, upon condition y^t^ he should never after serve the Kyng of England, but become his utter enemy,—laid siege to the Castle of Hawarden, and took therein Sir Roger Clifford, a noble Knight, slaying all y^t^ resisted, and after spoiling all the country."—*Alders. MSS.*—"In 1278, the King came to Chester, and after some time to Shotwick, and so over into Wales, having ordered that all the gentry in Cheshire that could expend £20. per annum, should come and be made Knights."—*Cowp. MSS.* "In 1280, the King compelled the Citizens of Chester to rebuild Dee Bridge at their own charge, contrary to the privileges which had been granted to them."—*Red Book of St. Werburgh.*

|| Powell in his history of Wales, enumerates the following who did homage: Henry Earl of Lancaster, for Monmouth; Reginald Grey, for Ruthin; and Foulk Fitz Warren, for his lands. These, also, for their lands: Lord William Martyn, Roger Mortimer, Henry Lacy Earl of Lincoln, Robert Lord Montalt, Gryffydh, Lord Poole, Tudor ap Grous, Madoc ap Tudor, Einion ap Howell, Tudor ap Griffydh, Llewellyn ap Ednyfed, Gruffydh Fychan, son of Gruffydh ap Torwerth, Madoc Fychau d' Englefield, Llewellyn Bishop of St. Asaph, and Richard de Puleston.

§ The cause of this insurrection is not known, but it probably arose from the scarcity of provisions. Knighton says, that the people of Chester, conscious of the enormity of their offences, (but which he does not particularize) purchased an exemption from the Eyre of the Justices, by a promise of paying the Prince v thousand LX marks in four years.

CHESTER " for the love he bare to the Gentlemen and Commons of the Shire of Chester." From this time he assumed the title of PRINCE of CHESTER in his public acts.*—
† 1398. The same year,† the King was present at the Installation of John Brughill, Bishop of Lichfield and Coventry, in the Church of St. John, then a Cathedral of that Bishopric, after which he entertained many of the Prime
‡ Cowp. MSS. Nobility.‡ In 1399, Henry of Lancaster, having announced himself against the King, several gentlemen of Cheshire, amongst them Sir Robert Legh, and Sir John Legh, went to Shrewsbury, to render to the haughty Duke their submission. They accompanied him back to Chester, and during his stay, the Duke made a muster of his troops under the City Walls; and Sir Piers Legh, of Lyme, the trusty adherent of King Richard, was put to death, and his head fixed on the highest tower of the
‖ See note p. 55. Castle.‖ Hollinshead says, that the Duke of Surry, having been sent on a message by the King to the Duke of Lancaster, was by the latter imprisoned in the Castle.—On the 19th August, the Duke marched to Flint, when he drew up his army under the Castle, on the shore of the Dee. The occurrences that there took place, ending with the capture of the King, need not be noticed here at length:§ the conference ended in the unfortunate King being brought to Chester on the following day, and the place of his imprisonment was a tower over the great outer gateway of the Castle,¶ pulled down about 30 years since. HISTORY. ¶ Cowp. MSS.

In 1400, an order was received by the Mayor, to apprehend and imprison John and Adam Heskseth, because they and their confederates had assaulted the Castle, had taken away the keys of the Eastgate, had beheaded Thomas Molineux, and made various proclamations in Chester against the Duke, and in behalf of Richard II. Cowper's MSS. say, that in 1409, the Mayor (John Ewloe) was removed from his Mayoralty, and Sir Wm. Brereton, Knt. was made Lieutenant or

* The Act, creating the County into a Principality, was repealed the following reign.

§ The following account of the behaviour of Bolingbroke to the King, at Flint, does not need an apology for its appearance:—" Richard was met by Earl Percy, at Conwy, who there delivered the purport of his diplomacy. On the king's, who had been too much addicted to reliance on *espionage*, mistrusting the sincerity of the message, and the professed intentions of the Earl; the latter, to quiet, or if possible allay the royal apprehension, accompanied him to the Temple of Deity; attended high mass; and at the altar took the oath of allegiance and fidelity. The snare was effectually laid, but when they had proceeded to a defile, in the mountainous recesses, near Penmaen Rhos, the king perceived his error, in having placed confidence in a sacramental oath, by the appearance of a numerous military band, bearing upon their standards the Northumberland arms. He would have escaped from the decoy; but Percy, springing forward, caught the bridle of his horse, directed his course towards Flint; and the poor deluded prince had only time to reproach the miscreant with his perjury; by observing, that the God he had sworn before that morning, would do him justice, and amply retaliate the blasphemous transaction, at the day of judgment. After halting with his royal prisoner at Rhuddlan, for the purpose of refreshment, he conveyed him with that promptitude, which is proverbial, because essentially requisite, for the completion of treacherous designs, to the castle of Flint. The next day he was received with that mock appearance of respect, which can only be necessary, when the last act of wicked conception is to be perpetrated. The next day after dinner the duke of Lancaster entered the castle all-armed, his basenet excepted King Richard came down from the Keep to meet him, when Bolingbroke falling on his knees, with his cap in his hand, immediately as he saw the king, assumed, by repeating the same ceremony, a dutiful and respectful appearance. On seeing this apparent act of rational submission, the king then took off his hood and spoke first. 'Fair cousin of Lancaster, you are right welcome.' The Duke bowing still more courteously replied, 'My liege lord, I am come before you sent for me, the reason why I will shewe you. The common fame among your people is such, that ye have for the space of twenty, or two and twenty years, ruled them rigorously; but if it please you my lord, I will helpe you to govern them better.' Then the king answered, 'Fair cousin of Lancaster, sith it pleaseth you, it pleaseth me well.' The intrigue then had its denouement: the contriver of the plot quickly threw off the mask, and adding insolence to infamy, 'with a high sharpe voyce, the duke badde, bring forth the king's horses; and then two little nagges, not worth forty franks, were brought forth; the king was set on the one, and the earl of Salisbury on the other, and thus the duke brought the king from Flint to Chester, where he was delivered to the duke of Gloucester's sonne, and to the earle of Arundel's sonne, that loved him but a little, for he had put their fathers to death, who led him strait to the castle.' And thus in this '*dolloreus castelle*,' as Halle styles it, was deposed the unfortunate, because inefficient monarch, king Richard II."—*Beauties of England and Wales, vol.* 17, *page* 654.

Governor of the City; John Preston was appointed his Deputy. It is supposed this took place in consequence of some dissatisfaction still prevailing, from the Citizens having taken part with Henry Percy at the battle of Shrewsbury.—Percy was well known here, having been appointed Constable of the Castle in 1399. When he passed through Chester on his way to Shrewsbury, a great number of Cheshire men joined his standard under the persuasion that Richard was then living; but after the battle, an amnesty was published by the Commissioners of Prince Henry, in favor of the adherents of the late King in this county.—Eleanor, Duchess of Gloucester, who was condemned to perpetual imprisonment in 1447, for practising the King's death, was confined some time in the Castle.*—In 1453, the city was gratified with the presence of Margaret of Anjou, the Queen of Henry VI. She came "upon progresse with manye greate lordes and ladyes with her, and was graciously received by the Mayor and Citizens."—In the year preceding the battle of Blore Heath, the Queen again visited Chester; and won the hearts of the Citizens by her Royal Courtesy, and hospitality.† After the battle the two sons of the Earl of Salisbury, taken in the fight, and sent to be imprisoned in the Castle here, were released by an order from the King to Sir John Mainwaring—who delivered them to the Lord Stanley as his prisoners, together with Sir Thos. Harrington, James Harrington, Raufe Rokesby, Thomas Ashton, Robert Evereux, and others. In 1465, a remarkable occurrence took place: "there happened a bloody fray, between Reginald ap Griffith ap Bleddyn. (ancestor of the Wynne's, of Tower) at the head of a great number of the Welsh; and many Citizens of Chester. There was a dreadful slaughter on both sides; and Reginald having taken prisoner, Robert Brynn (Brown), who had been Mayor of Chester three years before, carried him away to his fortress near Mold, and then hanged him, in the large ground room within the Tower. There are now (1756) in the hands of the owner of Rainallt's Tower, several copies of verses composed by the Welsh Bards, congratulating Rainallt on his several triumphs over the English, and particularly for one single victory, when he pursued his adversaries to the gates of Chester, and plundered and burnt all Handbridge. This Reynallt bravely defended Harlech Castle, in Merionethshire, for Henry VI. which was the last fortress that held out for the unhappy Prince. On this account Reynallt was attainted by Edw. IV."‡

† Harl. MSS.

From an Inquisition taken in the 28th year of Henry VI. the City of Chester is there described as being so decayed and depopulated, by reason of the choaking of its harbour, by sands, and the consequences of Glyndwr's Rebellion in Wales, that the Citizens were unable to pay their rent to the Crown.

In 1470, the King was at Chester, and granted to William Stanley, of Hooton, the Sheriffalty of Cheshire. In 1475, Edward Prince of Wales, son to Henry VI. came to Chester before Christmas, "and was immediately conveyed to the Castle in great triumph:" so says, the Aldersey MSS. but as Mr. Ormerod justly observes, "this is palpably incorrect," this Prince being, murdered after the battle of Tewksbury in 1471. Prince Edward son of Edw. IV. must be the Prince intended. July 18, 1494, Henry the VII. his Queen, and Mother, arrived in Chester with a great retinue, and proceeded to Hawarden, the Earl of Derby attending, with a number of "Chester Gallants." In 1499,|| Chester was honored with the presence of Prince Arthur, and he was

|| Aug. 4.

* It is said that one Robert Needham, a Chester gentleman, supposed to be concerned with the Duke of Glocester in planning her deliverance, was with others hung at Tyburn, taken down alive, and pardoned, *after having been stripped by the Executioner to be quartered!*

‡ Llwyd, in his "Translations from the British," thus tells the story:—"This Reynallt ap Gryffydd ap Bleddyn, was one of the brave defenders of Harlech Castle: he afterwards dwelt at the Tower, near Mold, but was always at variance with the Citizens of Chester. A great number of them being at Mold fair, in 1465, a scuffle ensued, and much slaughter, in which Reynallt succeeded in taking Robt. Byrne, Mayor of Chester, in 1461, and hung him on the staple still remaining in the hall of his house, at Tower: 200 "tall men" afterwards sallied from Chester to besiege Reynallt's house, upon which, retiring to a wood, he permitted them, in part to enter it, when rushing from his covert, he degraded himself, and sullied his former triumphs by burning them in it, and pursued the remainder into the Dee, in which they perished.—Lewis Glyn Cothi, a cotemporary of Reynallt, celebrates his exploits, and uncharitably describes Chester "as the habitation of the seven deadly sins."

HISTORY.

gratified with the performance of "The Assumption of our Lady," at the Abbey Gates This Prince left Chester on the 9th Sept.* In 1515, "There was a fray at St. Werburgh's-lane-end, between the Citizens and the Welshmen; but there was little hurt done, as the Welshmen fled.† In 1522, the city raised sixty men well armed to serve under the Earl of Surrey in Scotland.‡

The year 1554, was rendered memorable by the Execution of George Marsh, who fell a sacrifice to the sanguinary spirit of Popery, and the cruel intolerance of a bigotted Queen. He was burnt at Spital Boughton, "and did endure his martyrdom with such patience as was wonderful"|| Dr. Cowper asserts, that after the exhibition of a conditional pardon by Vawdrey, the Vice Chamberlain, and Marsh's heroic refusal of it, the people, headed by Sheriff Cowper, pressed forward to accomplish his rescue: but the other Sheriff, however, prevented the rescue, and Mr. Cowper was obliged to fly the City, effecting his escape by way of Farndon and Holt, into Wales. He was soon after outlawed, and his estates were seized by Government. He remained privately in Carnarvonshire, till the death of the Queen.

In the year 1558, occurred the very extraordinary interruption to Dr. Cole's commission for the persecution of the Irish Protestants. §The Doctor came to Chester, on his way to Ireland, with a commission, from the Queen for prosecuting (or rather persecuting) the Protestants in that kingdom. The commissioner lay at an inn, then called the Blue Posts, in Bridge-street, (the house now occupied by Mr. Brittain, woollen draper) where he was visited by the mayor, to whom, in the course of conversation, Dr. Cole communicated his errand, by taking a leather box out of his cloak-bag, and saying, in a tone of exultation, "Here is what will lash the heretics of Ireland!" This declaration accidentally struck the ear of the mistress of the house, who had a brother in Dublin; and, whilst the commissioner was complimenting his worship down stairs, the good woman, prompted by an affectionate fear for the safety of her brother, opened the box, took out the commission, and placed in lieu of it a pack of cards, with the knave of clubs uppermost. This the Doctor carefully packed up, unobserved and unsuspecting; nor was the deception discovered till his arrival in the presence of the Lord Deputy and Privy Council at the Castle of Dublin. The surprise of the whole assembly, at the sight of their *warrant officer*, the KNAVE, may be more easily imagined than told! The Doctor, in short, was immediately sent back for a second commission, but before he could return to Ireland, the Queen providentially died. Elizabeth, her successor, rewarded the woman (whose name was Elizabeth Edmunds) with a pension of forty pounds a year during her life."

§ Stranger at Chester.

In 1573, a controversy broke out between the City and the Vice Chamberlain. ¶"For Mr. Wm. Aldersey, and Mr. John Aldersey, his son, were disfranchised, and put from their Aldermen's rooms. On the 22d Feb. the Mayor was served by a pursuivant with the council's letters, to appear before them with all speed; where, at his coming, there were twenty-three articles of information laid against him by Mr. Glaziour, vice-

¶ Cowper's MSS.

* Henry VIII. by his mandate, granted an exemption to the Inhabitants of Chester, "from being pressed in the wars, by the Royal placards, it being meet that they should remain at home for the defence of the City."—HARL. MSS.

† For many centuries, there was a sort of warfare existing between the people of Wales, and the Citizens of Chester; and even at the present day there are proverbial sayings among the Cambrians, allusive to those feuds, and to the commercial importance of the City.—Mr. Llwyd, the author of "BEAUMARIS BAY," has noticed the following:—

Mwy nag un bwa y'w Ynghaer
More than one yew bow in Chester.
Allusive to its means of Defence.

Codi cin cwn Caer. Up before the dogs at Chester. Expressive of the Citizen's Vigilance.

A favorite lullaby in North Wales is an allusion to its former commercial importance.

Gurru, gurru, gurru i' Gaer,
I briodi merch y Maer.
Trotting, trotting, trotting to Chester,
To marry the Mayor's daughter.

‡ In 1519, there was an order made by the Mayor, that none go to Priests' offerings, first mass, gospel ales, or Welsh weddings, within this city, under a penalty of ten shillings.

|| The ashes of the sufferer were carefully collected, and privately interred in the burial ground of the Spital Chapel.

CHESTER HISTORY.

chamberlain, which the mayor did answer. After long debating of the matter, it was agreed, that the exchequer should be the chancery court, as well for the city as the whole county palatine, and articles set down how far the said exchequer should deal with the mayor and citizens, and wherein they should obey that court.—Also, that if William Glaziour, William Aldersey, and John Aldersey, did come and desire to be restored to their former liberties, that then the Mayor should restore them. Divers other things were accorded, too long here to rehearse; as the confirmation of the charter, and the taking out of this word, Pretorial, by which the citizens were exempt from the exchequer. The 19th of April, Mr. Mayor came from London, and the 26th day of the same month being Monday, in the common hall, at a portmote, in the presence of the whole citizens, and the bishop, who was also appointed by the council for the same purpose; all the orders were openly read between the city and the exchequer. Wherein, amongst other things, the mayor is not now to appear in the exchequer for every light matter, except for some great cause: Also, one freeman of the city not to sue another there, except it be for want of justice before the mayor, &c. with divers others, as appeareth in record in the city. The same day Mr. William and John Aldersey, came to the common-hall, before the mayor and all the citizens, and desired to have their former liberties; upon whose request they were restored, the first to his aldermanship, and his son a merchant as he was before. Also, Mr. Glaziour, vice-chamberlain, at his coming from London, was restored at his request, according to the council's order."

In 1578, "many soldiers being in Chester, two of the Captains did strive which should bring their company first from the Rood-eye, which had like to have bred much hurt between them; but the Mayor did commit them both to the Northgate, until he had heard from the Privy Council, and then both the Captains were discharged, and others put in their place, and martial law was used in the city."

June 3, 1583, Robert Earl of Leicester, Chamberlain of the County Palatine, came to Chester, accompanied by the Earls of Derby and Essex, and the Lord North, and also met and attended by most of the gentlemen of the shire, with their whole train, in the whole about 1500 horse. At the High Cross, they were received by the Mayor and his Brethren, and the whole Council of the City. They were lodged at the Bishop's Palace; and on the 4th June, dined with the Mayor, who presented the Earl of Leicester, with a gilt cup, containing 40 angels. This civic fete, it appears, occasioned a general meeting of the Corporation, in Assembly, on the 13th May preceding, in order "to settle how the Earl of Leicester should be entertained: it was proposed that there should be a banquet, and that for the present supply of money, all Members of the Corporation should lend from 20s. to 6s. 8d. according to their degree.". But this intention was given up; and it was determined "that 40 angels of gold should be presented in a cup value £18.—From this time till 1602, the City was thronged with soldiers, passing through to the wars in Ireland, the general place of embarkation, being Hoyle-lake, in Wirral.

In 1594, the Mayor was under the necessity of erecting a Gibbet, *in terrorem*, at the High Cross, "whereon three soldiers had like to have been hanged." In 1598, "the Earl of Essex, Lieut.-General for the wars in Ireland, arrived here, and with him three other Earls, besides many other Lords, Knights, and Gentlemen, who were honorably received by the Mayor and his brethren, and after a banquet prepared for them in the Pentice there was given unto the Earl of Essex, a fair standing cup, with a cover doubly gilt, and in the same 40 angels of gold,"

Feb. 14, 1599, arrived the Lord Mountjoy, Deputy of Ireland, and with him a great train, who dined with the Mayor on the 17th; and on the 19th Feb. went towards Wales, to take shipping for Ireland.—In 1603, the celebrated Earl of Tyrone, having surrendered to the Lord Mountjoy, was brought through Chester, and lodged in the house of Hugh Glaziour.*

* In 1606, "A stranger and his wife arrived, who both danced on a rope tied overthwart the street at the High Cross, and showed strange feats of activity."

CHESTER HISTORY.

On the 23d Aug. 1617, King James, the "Solomon of the North," came to Chester, "attended by many honorable Earls, reverend Bishops, and worthy knights and courtiers, besides all the gentry of the shire, and rode in state through the City, being met by the Sheriffs' Peers, and Common Council, every one with his foot cloth, well mounted on horseback. All the train soldiers standing in order without the Eastgate, and every company with its ensigns in seeming sort, did keep their several stations on both sides of the Eastgate street. The Mayor and all the Aldermen took their places on a Scaffold, railed and hung about with green; and there in most graceful and seemly manner, they attended the coming of his Majesty. At which time, after a learned speech from the Recorder, the Mayor presented to the King, a fair standing cup, with a cover double gilt, and therein an hundred Jacobins of Gold, and likewise the Mayor delivered the City's sword to the King, who gave it to the Mayor again. And the same was borne before the King, by the Mayor, being on horseback. And the sword of Estate, was borne by the Right Hon. William Earl of Derby, Chief Chamberlain of the County Palatine of Chester. The King rode first to the Minster, where he alighted from his horse, and in the West aisle, he heard an oration delivered in Latin, by a scholar* of the Free-school.—After the oration, he went into the Choir, and there, in a seat made for the King, at the higher end of the Choir, he heard an Anthem sung: And after certain prayers, the King went from thence to the Pentice, where a sumptuous banquet was prepared at the City's cost, which being ended, the King departed to the Vale Royal: and at his departure, the order of Knighthood was offered to the Mayor, (Mr. Edw. Button) but he refused the same."—It appears from the "Annals" of Chester, among the Harl. MSS. that "on the 18th Sept. 1630, came to Chester, being Saturday, the Duchess of Tremoyle, in France, and Mother-in-law to the Lord Strange, and many other great estates, and all the gentry of Cheshire, Flintshire, and Denbighshire, waited to meet her at Hoole Heath, with the Earl of Derby, and at least 600 horse; all the Gentlemen of the Artillery-yard lately erected in Chester, met her in Cow-lane, in very stately manner, all with great white and blue fethers, and went before her chariot in a march to the Bishop's Pallas, and making a lane, let her through the midest, and there gave her three volleys of shot, and so returned to their yard: also the Mayor and Aldermen in their best gownes and aparel, were on a stage in the Eastgate-street, to entertayn her, and the next day she came to the Pentice, after the Sermons in the afternoone, to a banquet, being invited by the Maior; and the next day went to Whitchurch, but it was reported that so many Knights, Esquires, and Gentlemen never were in Chester together—no, not to meet the King James, when he came to Chester."—In 1636,† the celebrated Puritan, "Maister Prynne," caused no small stir in the City; and the Bishop, in a pastoral letter, dated Aug. 28, 1637, after stating Prynne had been entertained here by some "scismaticall persons of the City of Chester," says, "that they have thereby manifested their owne inclination to the like faction and scism, for which it is likely that they shall receive condign punishment: but in the mean time, by reason thereof this citty, which hitherto (God be praised!) hath continued free from any inconformity and scismaticall practices, is thereby much defamed," &c. the Bishop "doth hereby order that every lecturer in any Parish Church of the City, before every his lecture or sermone, shall henceforth in his surplisse, read prayers distinctly, &c. as is prescribed in the Book of Common Prayer, &c. And that such lecturers, vicars, &c. shall in their next lecture, after notice had of this order, make public expressions of their heartie detestation of the offences for which the said offenders were censured."‡ These "censures" were rather rigorously enforced: some were fined £500, some 300, and others £250.—Mr. Peter Ince, a stationer, and one of the offenders, made a public recantation before the Bishop, in the Cathedral; as did Calvin Bruen, of Stapleford, in the

* It would be gratifying now to hear, that the scholars were qualified for the same task.

† This year a collection of £53, was made for Preston, and other places afflicted with the plague.

‡ It would seem that the Diocesan was fully obeyed, some of the Rev. Preachers calling Prynne and his friends, in their sermons, "symatiques, rebels, traytors, factious and seditious persons, worse than Priests or Jesuits, Rogues, Rascals, Witches:" and comparing them to "Corah, Dathan, and Abiram."

Town Hall.* Two others, Mr. Peter Lee, and Mr. Richard Golbourne, suffered their bonds to be estreated in the Exchequer, refusing to make the acknowledgement. At this time there were a great number of Portraits of Prynne, in Chester; and the Archbishop therefore issued an order, for spoiling and defacing the pictures; *after which*, they were to be delivered to Thomas Pulford, of Chester, limner, (who drew them!)—A subsequent order was issued for burning the obnoxious portraits, which was accordingly done at the High Cross, on the 12th Dec. 1637, with all the formality of an '*Auto da Fè*,' "the Mayor, Aldermen, Citizens, and persons to the number of 1000, attending, the people exclaiming, and crying, *Burn them, Burn them!*"

On the 27th June, in the same year,† the Mayor, the Earls of Derby, and Rivers, were appointed by the King, Commissioners of Array, for the County of the City.—That important period of our local History, the Siege of Chester, now steps closely on our Chronological notice of remarkable events; and the greater portion of the following detail, is arranged from the best authorities that could be obtained, and more particularly from the account given in Mr. Ormerod's recent work.

† 1637.

* Before the Mayor, Dec. 12, 1637. Several other prosecutions were intended; but the offenders bought their peace of the Archbishop (Laud) "for TWO BUTTS OF SACK!"—It appears that Bruin had been summoned before the High Commissioners at York, and there confessed his intimacy with Prynne.

Blue Coat Hospital, Chester.

SIEGE OF CHESTER.

CHESTER HISTORY.

It was on Monday the 8th Aug. 1642, that the first symptom of "civil dudgeon" broke out at Chester. By the direction of Sir Wm. Brereton, a drum was beat publicly in the streets for the parliament, and on the interposition of the constables, a tumult ensued, which was quelled by the personal exertions of the Mayor, Thomas Cowper. Sir William Brereton was brought to the Pentice, but afterwards discharged, having been saved with difficulty from the fury of the populace. It appears from the law documents in the Harl. collection, that there were personal animosities between Sir William and the city, arising from the assessment of his estate (the nunnery lands, supposed to be rate free) for the contribution of ship-money. His subsequent severities are stated to have proceeded from his resentment on this occasion, and the Chester annalists bitterly lament, that the activity of the Mayor had on this occasion preserved the life of the author of their succeeding calamities.

The King having set up his standard at Nottingham, on the 25th of August marched towards Shrewsbury, in order to proceed to Chester, and dispatched, on Sept 18, a letter under the royal signet, to the mayor, to notify his intended visit. Accordingly on Friday, the 23d of the same month, his Majesty, with a numerous train of nobility and gentry, came to Chester, and passing through the Foregate-street, which was lined with the trained bands, and was received with the same honors his father had been received with, twenty-five years before. His Majesty with his train was lodged in the episcopal palace, and the next day was entertained by the corporation at the Pentice, when two hundred pounds was presented in their name, by the Mayor, to the King, and one hundred was ordered as a present to the prince. During his stay at Chester, his Majesty issued a commission to search for concealed arms, dated "at our Court at Chester, this 26th September, in the 18th year of our reign;" and his Majesty's declaration to all his loving subjects upon the occasion of his late messages to both houses of Parliament, and their refusal to treat with him for the peace of the kingdom. "Given under our royal signet at our Court of Chester, this 27th of Sept. &c."

At two o'clock on the following day, the King proceeded to Wrexham, and was escorted by the Corporation to the city boundary. On the following day he was waited on at Wrexham by the Mayor, who had declined the honor of knighthood, and was here presented by Garter, agreeably to his Majesty's orders, with a grant of arms, the bearings of which were coats assigned to the two first Norman Earls of the palatinate.

His Majesty, before his departure, had directed the city to be put into a state of defence, and the preparations had been previously commenced. At a common-council held on the 6th of September, 1642, an assessment of 100l. had been ordered for repairing the gates and fortifying the city.

The outworks and entrenchments were carried on*

* By the advice of Colonel Ellis, Major Sydney, and other skilful engineers, a trench was cut, and mud walls made from Dee side, without the Bars, to Dee side at the New Tower. The walls repaired and lined with earth; the Newgate, and New Tower gate, mured up; divers pieces of cannon placed both for offence and defence; draw Bridges at the Northgate, Eastgate, Bridge, and Castle: and turnpikes at all the outworks, at the Bars, Cow-lane-end, without the Northgate, and at the Mount at Dee-lane-end, near Little St. John's; besides several Mounts, pitfalls, and other devices, to protect the outworks, and annoy the enemy's approach to the city.—A proof of the decided part taken by the County in this contest, may be gathered from the fact, that it raised for the Parliament, in ONE year, 6944l. and for the King, a ship of 240 tons burthen, with 96 men."—In cutting the Chester Canal, in 1772, a great quantity of human bones were found in the Garden, near the

CHESTER HISTORY.

with great vigour. In the beginning of the next summer, the mud walls, mount, bastions, &c. were all thoroughly completed.

The out-works began about the middle of that part of the city-walls which lies between the New Tower looking towards Hawarden and the Northgate, and proceeded towards the Stone-bridge leading to Blacon; inclined then to the north-east, and took in the utmost limits of the further Northgate-street; then turning eastward near to Flookers-brook, encompassed Hornlane, the Justing Croft, and all that part of the town to Boughton: from whence the works were carried on down to the brink of the river.

Upon Friday, July 18th, 1643, Sir William Brereton came with his forces before Chester, and on Thursday morning following made a violent assault upon the works, which were so resolutely defended, that he was beat off, and forced to retire. Many of his men were killed and carried away in carts; the besieged sustained no loss, except that one person was killed who was fool-hardy enough to stand upright upon the highest part of the mud wall, in defiance of the enemy; another was wounded by exposing himself in the like manner. Sir W. Brereton being so smartly repulsed, thought proper to draw off his men, and attempt nothing further against the city at that time. Some time after, Spital-Boughton Chapel was pulled down, and all the houses thereabouts; many other houses and barns in that neighbourhood were likewise destroyed, and the great wind-mill without the Northgate was taken down to prevent the enemy making lodgments in these buildings to the annoyance of the city.

Upon Saturday, November 11th, 1743, Sir William Brereton, accompanied by Alderman William Edwards, who had been Mayor of Chester, in 1636, came with a party to Hawarden Castle (six miles from Chester); Thomas Ravenscroft, of Bretton, Esq. and Mr. John Aldersey, being then in that garrison, opened the castle gates, and received Sir William and his party very joyfully. They being in possession of that strong fortress, and likewise of the town of Hawarden, prevented all that neighbourhood from bringing coals, corn, or provisions of any kind to Chester, which proved a great inconvenience to the city.

Upon the afternoon of the same day that Sir William Brereton entered Hawarden, Mr. Ravenscroft, pretending to be of the King's party, ventured into Chester, and applied to the Governor for a barrel of gun-powder and a quantity of match, which, as he was unsuspected, were delivered to him by the store-keeper of the garrison. On the Thursday following, Sir William Brereton wrote a summons from Hawarden to Sir Abraham Shipman, then governor of Chester, expressly requiring him to surrender that city, adding some severe threatenings in case of refusal. The Governor sent him for answer, That he was not to be terrified by words, but bade him come and win it, and have it; however, upon this warning, the governor thought proper to order all the Handbridge suburbs to be burnt down. Mr. Matthew Ellis also covenanted that Overlegh Hall, with all the outhousings, should be demolished, to prevent the enemy at Hawarden from sheltering themselves there if they come to attack the city.

The day following, Mr. Whitby's Mansion, Beachhall, and Flookersbrook-hall, Sir Thomas Smith's, were burnt down, lest they might afford lodgments to enemies from another quarter. A party of the King's forces, which had been employed against the rebels in Ireland, landed about that time at Mostyn in Flintshire, and advanced to Hawarden Castle, to which they sent a verbal summons by a trumpet, to which they in the garrison returned a long paper in the puritanical style of those times, concluding thus:—"We fear the loss of our religion more than the loss of our dearest blood, and being resolved to make good our trust, we put our lives into the hands of that God, who can, and we hope will, secure them more than our walls and weapons."

Northgate. They lay in masses, and as the rock is very near the surface, at the time of interment, the bodies must have been very thinly covered indeed. The sculls were nearly perfect, and the teeth quite firm.—At the same time, several cannon shot of large size were found.

Colonel Marrow, who had summoned them by the trumpet, immediately sent the following reply :—

" Gentlemen,

" It is not to hear you preach that I am sent hither, but it is, in his Majesty's name, to demand the Castle for his Majesty's use ; as your allegiance binds you to be true to him, and not to inveigle those innocent souls that are within with you ; so I desire your resolution, if you will deliver the Castle or no ?

" Nov. 21st, 1643.

A rejoinder was soon sent from the Castle, in much the same style with their former answer, intimating, that they were satisfied with Colonel Marrow's disaffection to preaching; that God would require blood from those who shed it ; that they relied upon the Lord of Hosts, &c.

On the 22d November, more forces, being arrived from Ireland, 'came up : and another summons was sent in, from Sir Michael Ernley, and Major-General Gibson, but they received such answer as the former. They had a letter likewise from one Captain Sandford, newly come from the service in Ireland, which, as it is somewhat singular, shall be here inserted :

" Gentlemen,

" I presume you very well know, or have heard, of my condition and disposition, and that I neither give or take quarter ; I am now with my firelocks, who never yet neglected opportunity to correct rebels ; ready to use you as I have done the Irish, but loth I am to spill my countryman's blood ; wherefore, by these, I advise you to your fealty and obedience towards his Majesty, and shew yourselves faithful subjects, by delivering the Castle into my hands for his Majesty's use ; in so doing you shall be received into mercy, &c. Otherwise, if you put me to the least trouble, or loss of blood, to force you, expect no quarter for man, woman, or child. I hear you have some of our late Irish army in your company ; they very well know me, and that my fire-locks used not parley.—Be not unadvised, but think of liberty, for I vow all hopes of relief are taken from you, and our intents are not to starve you, but to batter and storm you, and then hang you all, and follow the rest of that rebel crew. I am no bread and cheese rogue, but was ever a loyalist, and will ever be, whilst I can write or name

" Thos. Sandford,
" Captain of Firelocks.

" Nov. 28th, 1643.

" I expect your speedy answer this Tuesday night, at Broad-lane hall, where I now am your near neighbour.

" To the officer Commanding in Chief at Hawarden Castle, and his Consorts there."

However, the garrison not surrendering, the besiegers thought proper to apply to Chester, to obtain a reinforcement ; whereupon Sir Abraham Shipman, the Governor, called a Council of the Commissioners, to consider of this matter, who, after some debate, resolved as follows :

" At a Council holden at the Council-chamber within his Majesty's Castle of Chester, this first day of December, 1643, we, whose names are hereunto subscribed, having duly weighed and considered the application and request of Sir Michael Ernley, Knight, and Major-General Richard Gibson, to us made, for aid and assistance, whereby to enable them to reduce the rebel garrison at Hawarden ; it is hereby ordered, that on the morrow, by break of day, 300 of the citizens and train bands, with their proper officers, together with the companies of Captain Thropp and Captain Morgell, do march to the assistance of the King's forces now at Hawarden, and that this detachment shall be commanded by Lieutenant-Colonel John Robinson.

(Signed) " Abrah. Shipman,

" Robt. Cholmondeley,	" Francis Gamull,
" Wm Manwaring,	" R. Grosvenor,
" Rob. Brerewood,	" Tho. Thropp,
" Tho. Cowper,	" Cha. Walley."

December 2d, 1643. Accordingly, this reinforcement came to Hawarden the next day, and a brisk attack

HISTORY.

being made upon the castle the day following, the besieged hung out a white flag, and December 4th, 1643, capitulated; and early next morning, the castle was surrendered to Sir Michael Ernley, on condition to march out with half arms, and two pair of colours, one flying, and the other furled, and to be safely convoyed either to Wem or Nantwich.

After this success, the party from Chester marched back to that city, without the loss of one man But the royalists, being further reinforced by some regiments from Ireland, marched into Cheshire, under the command of Sir John, lately created Lord Byron, and took Beeston-castle; for which the Parliament Governor there was soon after executed for cowardice.

Next they engaged Sir William Brereton and Colonel Ashton at Middlewich, and cut off near two hundred of their men, which occasioned Northwich to be quitted to them; and likewise Crewe-house, after a stout resistance, was forced to surrender; as also Doddington-house, and Acton-church, without much opposition.

On the 18th of January, Lord Byron made a sudden and violent storm upon Nantwich, but was beaten off with great loss, and among the slain was the famous firelock captain (Sandford) before-mentioned.

January 25th, that town was relieved, and Lord Byron routed by General Fairfax.

Upon Saturday, February 13th, a detachment of the garrison of Chester sallied forth to attack a party of the Parliament Soldiers who had made a lodgment at Christleton. The fight began near to Great Boughton, but after a very bloody engagement, the Parliament forces retired. There were slain of the King's Party, officers and soldiers, near 140, most of them Chester men. Upon the Wednesday following, Great Boughton was burned down by the garrison of Chester, to prevent the Parliamentarians from harbouring there.

Upon Monday, June 19th, 1644, a party of the King's forces, consisting of six companies of foot, and three troops of horse, marched out of Chester to reconnoitre the enemy in the neighbouring quarters, and took Captain Glegg, and his whole troop, prisoners.

August 18th, 1644. Colonel Marrow, Governor of Chester, fell upon a party of Sir William Brereton's forces, near Crowton-house, where they kept a garrison, and took fourteen of them prisoners; but the Governor himself there received a shot, of which he died soon after at Chester.

August 21st, 1644. Sir William Brereton sending out a party from Northwich, they advanced as far as Tarvin, and there engaged a party of the King's forces; but the alarm being given to Chester, they sallied out of that garrison, and routed the parliamentarians, who fled over Delamere forest, with great precipitation.

Prince Maurice coming to Chester during the siege in 1644, thought proper to issue out a precept to the commissioners there, to tender a protestation, or test, to the inhabitants of that city; the precept and test are as follow:

"To the Mayor of the City of Chester, Sir Francis Gamull, Sir William Mainwaring, Lieut.-Col. Robinson, Ald. Thos. Cowper, Lieut.-Col. Grosvenor, Col. Mostyn, Capt. Thos. Thropp, Capt. Morgell, or to any two of them."

"These are to will, authorise, and require you, or any two of you, to administer the protestation hereunto annexed, lately made for the security of this city, to all the nobility, gentry, divines, citizens, and all other the inhabitants of this city; and to all and every the officers, soldiers, and others, that shall come into, or have any commerce within the said City; and in case any person or persons refuse, deny, and will not take the same, you are hereby required to give in a list of the names of all and every person so refusing unto me. Herein you are not to fail. Given at Chester under my hand and seal at arms, this 4th day of March, 1644.

MAURICE."

THE PROTESTATION.

"I, A. B. do vow and protest, in the presence of

Almighty God, that I believe in my heart, that the Earl of Essex, Sir William Brereton, Sir Thomas Middleton, and Mr. Thomas Mytton, and all their party and adherents, are in actual rebellion against the King, and that I will with my life, and fortune, and to the utmost of my power, maintain and defend his Majesty's cause against the said rebels, and all others who are now in arms without his Majesty's express consent and command; and that I will not give, nor by any privity and consent suffer to be given, any aid, assistance, or intelligence to the aforesaid rebels, or any of their parties, in prejudice of the safety of this City of Chester, to the betraying of it, or any forces, castles, garrisons, or forts under his Majesty's express command and government, in any of his dominions, into the said rebels hands and power. And I do likewise from my soul abhor the taking of the damnable and late invented Covenant, commonly called the National Covenant, pressed by the rebels upon many of his Majesty's subjects: and to all that I have protested, I call God to witness, believing that I cannot be absolved by any power, mental reservation, or equivocation, from this my vow and protestation. So help me God, and by the contents of this book."

Friday, Sept. 19th, 1645. Colonel Jones, who commanded the horse, and adjutant-general Louthian, who commanded the foot, which were then besieging Beeston castle, drew off 1300 horse and foot from that place, about eight of the clock in the evening, and in a very private manner marched all night to Chester; and next morning before day break, they divided their forces into four squadrons, and stormed the out-works in so many different places, and got upon the works in some parts even before the guards discovered them, and so with little loss made themselves masters not only of Boughton, but likewise of St. John's Church, with the adjoining lanes, the Foregate-street, and all the eastward suburbs. They possessed themselves of the Mayor's house, with the sword and mace, &c. and made a brisk attempt upon the city itself, to the no little terror and consternation of all within.

The King having been at Hereford, left that city the very day that this attack was made upon Chester, intending to pass through Lancashire and Cumberland into Scotland: and taking his route through Wales, came to Chirk castle. As he advanced near Chester, he received intelligence of Col. Jones's late success, but his Majesty's coming, greatly encouraged the garrison, as it equally dismayed the besiegers, whom the King's troops looked upon as already in their power.

Sir Marmaduke Langdale, detached with most of the horse over Holt-bridge, that he might be on the Cheshire side of the river Dee, whilst the King with his guards, and the Lord Gerard, with the rest of the horse, marched directly that night into Chester. His Majesty lodged at Sir Francis Gamull's house, Wednesday, Sept. 24, 1645, near the bridge. Next morning Alderman Cowper went to pay his duty to the King, and was most graciously received, and had the honor to kiss his Majesty's hand; the King was pleased in a very kind manner to express his approbation of his service, and ordered him to attend him that day.

Sir Marmaduke Langdale, having passed the river at Holt, was drawn up upon Rowton-heath, three miles east of Chester, that very evening, when he intercepted a letter from Major-General Poyntz, who was advanced as far as Whitchurch, to the Parliament Commander before Chester, telling him that he was come to his rescue, and desiring him to have some foot sent to him to assist him against the King's horse. The next morning Poyntz being advanced towards Chester, Sir Marmaduke Langdale charged him with such resolution, that he forced him to retire: however, he drew up his men again, but kept at a distance, expecting the forces from before Chester, to whom he had dispatched a second courier. In the mean time they in the city, not considering, till it was too late, in what posture Sir Marmaduke Langdale was, and there being no good intelligence between him and the Lord Gerard, sent him orders to march towards Chester, where some foot, drawn up under the command of Lord Astley and Sir John Glenham, should be ready to support him: but Sir Marmaduke could not possibly obey these orders, because, had he proceeded towards Chester, Poyntz would have fallen upon his rear. About noon, Colonel Jones, and Adjutant-General Louthian, having drawn

CHESTER HISTORY.

500 horse, 300 foot, from before Chester, began a hasty march, which caused those in the city to imagine that they were upon their flight; whereupon a great part of the forces in the town were ordered out by the North-gate, and so by Flookersbrook, for the direct way was blocked up by the enemy, to pursue the besiegers, but it seems their supposed flight was only an eager haste to get up to General Poyntz; who now perceiving Col. Jones's men coming towards him, and having rallied his troops, immediately advanced upon Sir Marmaduke Langdale, and then there began a most furious fresh encounter. But General Langdale having to deal with Poyntz in the front, and Jones's reinforcements having fallen upon his rear, after having fought bravely, was at length overpowered, and routed, and forced to retire towards Chester. Poyntz pursued his victory, and followed close till he came to Hool-heath, where the Lord Gerard and the Earl of Lindsey were drawn out with their troops, who charged and repulsed him; but those disordered horse, which first fled, had so crowded up all the little passes and narrow lanes between that heath and the city, (a ground quite unfit for horse to fight upon) that when a fresh body of the enemy's musqueteers charged briskly upon them, they forced the King's horse to turn, and rout one another, and to overbear their own officers, who would have restrained them. In this fatal crisis fell many gentlemen of high rank, and officers of distinction. And amongst the slain, covered over with wounds, was Bernard Stuart, the young gallant Earl of Lichfield. A noble historian tells us, that he was the third brother of that illustrious family that sacrificed their lives in this cause; a very faultless young man, of a most gentle, courteous, and affable nature, and of a spirit and courage invincible; whose loss all men exceedingly lamented, and the King bore with extraordinary grief.

By computation not less than 600 were killed on both sides, and many persons of quality, on the King's party, were taken prisoners; amongst whom was Sir Philip Musgrave, of the North. His Majesty, attended by the Mayor, Sir Francis Gamull, and Alderman Cowper, stood upon the leads of the Phœnix-tower, and was all the while a sad spectator of most of this tragedy.* The King's routed horse were scattered about the country: several made for Holt bridge, others ventured to cross the river at Boughton-ford, for Poyntz having had enough that day, pursued them no further. His Majesty staid that night and the next morning in Chester, and at his departure, gave orders to the Lord Byron, then Governor, and to his Commissioners, "If after eight days they saw no possibility of farther assistance, to treat for their own preservation." Believing that the city must of necessity have been surrendered even before he could have well secured his own person, though the place held out against a close and severe siege twenty weeks afterwards; and had those whom his Majesty employed to relieve it, done their parts, or had not the intended assistance from Ireland been stopped, the City had not then fallen into the enemy's hands, but might possibly have been the basis of a new fortune to his Majesty.

On Thursday, Sept. 25, 1645, the King marched over Dee-bridge with 500 horse, and not without some danger passed into Wales; Sir Francis Gamull, Captain Thropp, and Alderman Cowper, attended his Majesty to Denbigh†-castle, where he arrived that night. They staid with the King till Saturday, when those loyal citizens took a sad and final leave of their Sovereign, and returned to Chester, which, if possible, they found more distressed than when they left it the Thursday before; for that very morning, about four of the clock, the enemy had again forced the works at Boughton, and re-possessed themselves of all that part of the town without the Eastgate; the citizens, tho' now confined within the narrow circuit of their own walls, earnestly applied themselves to the defence of the city.

On the Monday following, the besiegers made a breach in the walls, near to the Newgate, by the battery of 150 cannon shot, and at midnight made a sharp assault upon the breach. They likewise attempted to mount the walls with scaling ladders, but some officers

* Randle Holme says, that the King also went on the Tower of the Cathedral, where a shot from some of the assailants' works, killed an officer, with whom he was conversing, by his side.—This is not very likely.

† The Tower in which the King lodged, still retains the name of *Siamber y brenhin*—or the King's chamber.

Chester History.

and several soldiers were hauled in over the walls, some of the ladders too were dragged over, and many of the assistants thrown down and killed, and the rest forced to give over the attack.

Wednesday, October 1st, the enemy removed their battery, and planted thirteen pieces of cannon against the Eastgate, and played them furiously all that day, but with little or no damage to the city. Early next morning, the citizens made a brisk sally, dismounted most of those cannon, killed seven or eight men, and brought in a lieutenant and an engineer prisoners.

On the Saturday following, October the 4th, the besiegers removed their great ordnance and planted four large pieces against the walls between the Northgate and the New-Tower, where the besieged had some cannon planted upon Morgan's-mount. All Sunday the enemy played their artillery so violently, that they beat down some of the battlements, and forced the King's soldiers to retire from the walls; they likewise, by a shot, shattered the carriage of one of the largest cannon, which in the fall had two feet of the muzzle broken off. That night the besieged repaired the damages, and made entrenchments in the Lady Borough Hey, which they found to be very serviceable in the defence of that part of the city.

On the Monday, October the 6th, the enemy removed their ordnance about six roods downwards nearer to the New-Tower, but they had no great effect: the day following, they raised a battery upon Brewer's-hall-hill, endeavouring with those cannon to clear the line within the city.

On the Wednesday next, October 8th, there was a parley between the city and the besiegers, and an answer was to be returned the next morning; but terms could not be agreed upon, so the siege was continued with all possible rigour, and the same day they placed two pieces of cannon upon an eminence in St. John's-lane, and played them with much violence against the walls. The next day* the besiegers discharged 352 large shot against the walls; two breaches were made, but they were effectually repaired. That afternoon the enemy's horse drew up round about the town, and about five o'clock a violent assault was made in several places; the battlements were resolutely attacked, and as bravely defended; the assailants having with great difficulty gained the top of the wall, were beat off, thrown down, and killed. The King's party got a good number of arms, and dragged up several of the scaling-ladders over the walls into the city. After this day's action, the besiegers did not think fit to make any further attempt to storm the city, but changed the siege into a close blockade, in order to subdue those by famine, whom they could not overcome by force.

The Parliament forces having made a floating bridge over the river, just above Chester, the besieged finding themselves much annoyed by it, had recourse to this contrivance to burn it; upon a certain day, when there was a spring tide, they filled two boats with combustible materials, and so turned them adrift to be carried up the river by the tide; the boats floated up accordingly, and the trains took fire when they came to the enemy's bridge, but by the diligence of the guards, no great damage was done. The same day 500 horse and 200 foot made a brisk sally out of the city, and fell upon the besiegers, but being overpowered, it was thought adviseable to retire back to Chester, and but few were killed on either side.

About ten days afterwards, November 27th, Sir William Brereton sent some proposals to the besieged, but the Lord Byron, and the Commissioners, insisted upon such terms as would not by any means be complied with, so that that treaty was soon over.

In about a fortnight after, December 10th, Colonel Booth, with the Lancashire forces, who had just before reduced Latham-house, received orders to march to Chester, and reinforce Sir William Brereton; they ar-

* This day fell Sir Wm. Mainwaring, in an assault made by the besiegers on the Walls, near the Water Tower. A monument, in commemoration of his loyalty and valor, is in the Cathedral.

rived accordingly, and such dispositions were made, that the city was quite encompassed, nor was any place more straightly beleagured.

This soon occasioned a scarcity of provisions, and the poor citizens kept a Lenten Christmas. In the beginning of January, hunger and want began to occasion discontents, and murmurings encreased almost to a mutiny. The disaffected insinuated to the people, that notwithstanding their misery, the governor and commissioners lived well themselves. The Lord Byron and some of the commissioners took opportunity, severally, to invite the chief of the malcontents to dine with them, and entertained them with boiled wheat, and gave them spring-water, to wash it down, solemnly assuring them, that this, and such like, had been their only fare for some time past. When this was made known to the citizens, they all seemed inspired with the same resolution to hold it out to the very last extremity.

January 1st, 1645-6, Sir William Brereton sent a sort of threatening summons to the commanders, to which they returned no answer in five days. Upon which Sir William sent another letter to them, peremptorily requiring them to answer it that very day, which they accordingly did, and offered to come to a treaty if the King did not relieve them in twelve days, and desired a pass to send an express to his Majesty. But this was not complied with.

The governor and the commissioners had, by their judicious management, kept this town and garrison, contented to feed on horses, dogs, and cats, whilst there was the least probability of relief. They refused nine several summonses, and did not answer the tenth till they had received undoubted assurance that there were no hopes of any succours; then, and not till then, they consented to a treaty, previous to which the following letters passed between the commanders:

" My Lord,

" I cannot send you such propositions as have formerly been rejected, every day producing loss of blood and expense of treasure; neither will I trouble myself with answering the particulars of your unparalled demands, to which if I should suit mine, I should require no less than yourself and all the officers and commanders to be my prisoners, and the rest to submit to mercy. Yet to witness my desires of the preservation of the city, I have, upon serious consideration and debate, thought fit to tender these inclosed conditions, for the perfecting whereof, I am content commissioners meet concerning them, and such further particulars as may be conceived conducible to the welfare of the cities and countries adjacent; and have given commission to these gentlemen to receive your answer in writing to these propositions of mine herewith sent, touching which, I shall not be so scrupulous as to demand their return, not valuing to what view they may be exposed; therefore they are left with you if you please; and I remain,

" Your servant,

" WM. BRERETON."

" Chester Suburbs, Jan. 26, 1645-6."

To this my Lord that day returned, that he could not at present give a full answer, in regard that he must consult the gentlemen joined in commission with him: however, the next day he sent his answer, thus:

" Sir,

" Those demands of mine, which you term unparalleled, have been heretofore granted by far greater commanders than yourself, no disparagement to you, to places in a far worse condition than, God be thanked, this is yet. Witness the Bosse, Breda, Maestricht, and as many other towns as have been beleaguered either by the Spaniard or the Hollander; or, to come home, York and Carlisle, and nearest of all, Beeston-castle; and therefore you must excuse me, if, upon the authority of so many examples, I have not only propounded, but think fit to insist upon them, as the sense of all manner of people in the city. As for your conceit in demanding of myself, and the rest of the commanders and officers, to be your prisoners, I would have you know, that we esteem our honours so far above our lives, that no extremity whatever can put so mean thoughts into the meanest of us all. That to submit to your mercy is by us reckoned amongst those things that we intend never to make use of. I am nevertheless still content that the commissioners, whose names I formerly tendered unto you, meet with such as you shall appoint, in any indifferent place, to treat upon honorable conditions; and desire you to assure yourself, that no other will be assented unto, by

"Your servant,

"JOHN BYRON."

Chester, Jan. 27, 1645-6.

To which Sir William Brereton sent the reply as under:

"My Lord,

"I cannot believe that you conceive the war betwixt the Hollander and the Spaniard is to be made a precedent for us; neither can I believe that such conditions as you demanded were granted to the Bosse, Breda, or Maestricht. Sure I am, none such were given to York, Carlisle, or Beeston, though some of them were maintained by as great commanders as yourself, and no disparagement to you. I shall therefore offer to your consideration the example of Liverpool, Basing, and Latham, who by their refusal of honourable terms when they were propounded, were not long after subjected to captivity and the sword. You may, therefore, do right to all those many innocents under your command, to render their safety and the preservation of the city; for which end I have sent you fair and honorable conditions, such as are the sense of all the officers and soldiers with me; which being rejected, you may expect worse from

"Your servant,

"WM. BRERETON."

Chester-Suburbs, Jan. 27, 1645-6.

It now being thought advisable to come to a treaty, the Lord Byron fixed upon eighteen commissioners, and a greater number were appointed on behalf of the besiegers, which is taken notice of by Sir William Brereton in a letter to the Parliament, wherein he says, "I was the more desirous to have a number of commissioners, that the soldiers might be better satisfied with that which was agreed unto by their own officers; and the officers would be more careful to keep the soldiers to an observance of those conditions, which they themselves had signed and ratified."

The treaty continued six days, during which there were frequent debates among the city commissioners, when they withdrew from the others to consider of certain points. At length, conditions, consisting of eighteen articles, were agreed to, and subscribed by twelve of the city-commissioners; but as some of those articles were dissented to by others, the treaty was refused to be signed by the commissioners following: Francis Gamull, Thomas Cowper, Sir Robert Brerewood, Charles Walley, Richard Morgell, and Robert Harvey; but a great majority of the commissioners agreeing to, and subscribing, the terms subjoined, they were likewise confirmed by Lord Byron.*

* THE ARTICLES OF SURRENDER.

"ARTICLE I. That the Lord Byron, and all noblemen, commanders, officers, gentlemen, and soldiers, and all other persons whatever, now residing in the city of Chester, and the castle and fort thereof, shall have liberty to march out of the said city, castle, and fort, with all their apparel whatsoever, and no other, or more goods, horses, or arms, than are hereafter-mentioned, viz.—The Lord Byron with his horse and arms, and ten men with their horses and arms to attend him; also his lady and servants, two coaches, and four horses in either of them, for the accommodating of them and such other ladies and gentlemen as the said Lord Byron shall think meet; with eighty of the said Lord's books, and all his deeds and evidences, manuscripts, and writings in his possession. And the said lord, his lady, nor any of their attendants, carrying amongst them all above forty pounds in money, and twenty pounds in plate. The rest of the noblemen, with their ladies and servants, to march with their horses, each of the said lords attended with four men, their horses and arms; every such nobleman carrying with him not above thirty pounds in money. Every knight and colonel to march with four men, their horses and arms; no such knight or colonel to carry with him about ten pounds in money. Every lieutenant-colonel, major, and captain of horse, with one man, their horses and arms; and such lieutenant-colonel, major, and captain, not to carry with him above five pounds in money. Every captain of foot, esquire, graduate, preaching minister, gentleman of quality, the advocate and secretary to the army, every of them with his own horse and sword, the ministers without swords; none of them carrying with them above fifty

Pursuant to this, the brave and loyal city of Chester, which had held out twenty weeks beyond expectation,

shillings; and the ministers to have all their own manuscripts, notes and evidences. Lieutenants, cornets, ensigns, and other inferior officers in commission, on foot, with every man his own sword, and not above twenty shillings in money. All troopers, soldiers, gun-powder-makers, canneniers, and all others not before-mentioned, to march without horse and arms; and that none of the said persons before-mentioned shall, in their march, after they are out of the city and liberties thereof, be plundered, searched, or molested.

II. "That all women of what degree soever, that please to march out of the city, shall have all their apparel with them; and such officers' wives whose husbands are prisoners, or absent, may carry such sums of money with them, as are allowed by these articles to commanders, officers, and gentlemen, of their husbands' qualities, and no more.

III. "That none of the commanders, officers, or soldiers, or any other, at or before their marching out of the city, castle, or fort, do injure or plunder the goods of any; nor carry any thing away out of the said city, castle, or fort, but what is their own, and hereby allowed.

IV. "That all citizens and others now residing within the city, shall be saved and secured in their persons, and their goods and estates within the city and liberties be preserved and kept from the plunder and violence of the soldiers; and have the like freedom of trade as other cities and towns under the parliamentary protection have, and such immunities as they of right ought to have. And that every merchant and tradesman of Chester as shall desire to go into North-Wales to look after his goods, shall have a pass to go thither and return back again, he first giving security that during his absence he will do no act to the prejudice of the parliament; and that no such person shall at any time, without licence, carry more monies with him than sufficient to defray the charges of his journey. And that all citizens, and other inhabitants, who shall now or hereafter desire to march forth of the city of Chester, and not to act any thing against the parliament, their wives and families to have the benefit and privileges of inhabitants.

V. "That such officers or soldiers as shall be left sick or wounded within the city of Chester, or the Castle, or forts thereof, shall have liberty to stay until their recovery, and then have passes to Conway, or any of the king's garrisons not blocked up, in the mean time to be provided for.

VI. "That the said Lord Byron, noblemen, commanders, gentlemen, officers, and soldiers, and all others that shall march out of the town, shall have liberty to march to Conway, and five days are allowed them to march thither, with a convoy of two hundred horse; the Welsh officers and soldiers, to have liberty to go to their own homes, all of them to have free quarter on their march, and twelve carriages if they shall have occasion to use so many, which carriages are to be returned on the sixth day, and that passes be given them for their safe return to Chester, and that they be secured until they return thither.

VII. "That no soldier in his march shall be inveigled or enticed from his colours or command, with any promise or inducement whatsoever.

VIII. "That all such persons, citizens, or others, who have families in Chester, and are now in places remote, shall have the like benefit of these articles, as those who are now resident in the city.

IX. "That the friends of the Earl of Derby and Lichfield, or any of those whose dead bodies are not yet interred in Chester, shall have two months time to fetch them from thence, whither they please, provided that none of them come attended with above twenty horses.

X. "That no church within the city, or evidences, or writings, belonging to the same, shall be defaced.

XI. "That such Irish as were born of Irish parents, and have taken part with the rebels in Ireland, now in the city, shall be prisoners.

XII. "That all those horses and arms belonging to those that march out, and not by these articles allowed to be taken and carried out of the city, except such horses as are the proper goods of the citizens and inhabitants that shall remain in the city before the delivery of the same, be brought, the horses into the Castle-court, and the arms into the Shire-hall, where officers shall be appointed to receive them.

XIII. "That in consideration hereof, the said City and Castle, without any slighting or defacing thereof, with all the ordnance, arms, ammunition, and all other furniture and provision of war therein whatsoever, except what is allowed to be carried away, and all the records in the castle, without diminution, embezzling, or defacing, be delivered to the said Sir William Brereton, or such as he shall appoint, for the use of the King and parliament, upon Tuesday next, being the 3d of this inst. February, 1645-6, by ten of the clock in the forenoon.

XIV. "That the fort, with all ordnance, arms, ammunition,

CHESTER HISTORY.

being now subdued by famine only, was upon the third day of February, 1645-6, surrendered up to the parliament forces, who immediately took possession of it; and soon after, two thousand arms, and five hundred and twenty head pieces were brought into the castle, agreeably to the 14th article of the treaty.

The description of the siege by Randle Holme, is extremely curious. "By this time (says he, alluding to the assault made on the 29th Sept.) our women are all on fire, striving through a gallant emulation, to out-do our men, and will make good our yielding walls, or lose their lives to shew they dare attempt it. The work goes forwards, and they, like so many valiant Amazons, do outface death, and dare danger, though it lurke in every basket; seven are shot and three slain; yet they scorn to leave their matchless undertaking, and thus they continued for ten days' space, possessing the beholders that they are immaculate! Our ladies, likewise, like so many exemplary goddesses, created a matchless forwardness in the meaner sorts, by their daily undertakings, that he who saw them would have thought a hundred suns eclipsed, at least ways clouded, with our loyal dust, had he been in that place, which they wipe off with such a pleasant smile, that they seem rather silent solicitors of a new deformity, than willing partners with that purchased honor." In another place, speaking of the bursting of some grenadoes on the 10th of December, he says, "Two houses in the Watergate-street, skip joint from joint, and create an earthquake, the main posts jostle each other, while the frighted casements fly for fear: in a word the whole fabrick is a perfect chaos, lively set forth in this metamorphosis; the grand-mother, mother, and three children, are struck stocke dead and buried in the ruins of their humble edifice. About midnight they shoot seven more, one of them lights in an old man's bed chamber, almost dead with age, and sends him some days sooner to his grave, than perhaps was given him. The next day (Dec. 11) six more breake in upon us, one of which persuades an old woman to bear the old man company to heaven, because the times were evil."

Sir William Brereton's forces were not particular as to the observance of the treaty; for although the sword and mace were restored to the city, the blind bigotry of his soldiers led them to acts of violence. They pulled down the High Cross,* defaced the Cathedral Choir, much injured the Organ, broke nearly all the Painted Glass in the Church Windows, and demolished the Font.

The state of the City after the siege, is thus described in a MSS. narrative by Randle Holme:—"Thus of the moste anchante and famous cittie of Chester, in times past; but now beholde and make the ruines of it in these present times, within these few years, viz. within these three years 1643, 1644, and 1645; the particu-

and provisions therein, of what sort whatsoever, not formerly granted or allowed of, upon the signing these articles, be delivered to Sir William Brereton, or such as he shall appoint.

XV. "That upon signing these articles, all prisoners in the city, castle, or fort, that have been in arms for the parliament, or imprisoned for adhering thereunto, shall immediately be set at liberty.

XVI. "That the convoy shall not receive any injury in their going or coming back, and shall have three days allowed for their return.

XVII. "That if any persons concerned in any of these articles, shall violate any part of them, such persons shall lose the benefit of all the said articles.

XVIII. "That upon signing of these articles, sufficient hostages (such as shall be approved of) be given for the performance of the said articles.

"Signed by us the commissioners appointed on the behalf of the right honorable the lord Byron,

"EDMUND VERNEY.	"CHRISTOPHER BLEASE,
"JOHN ROBINSON.	"WILLIAM INCE.
"THO. CHOLMONDELY.	"JNO. WERDEN.
"PETER GRIFFITH.	"JOHN JOHNSON.
"HENRY LEIGH.	"EDMUND MORETON.
"THOMAS THROPP.	"THOMAS BRIDGE.

"What is done by the commissioners is confirmed by

"JOHN BYRON."

* The great CAP, (if the expression may be allowed) of the Cross, is now fixed up in the garden of Netherleigh-house, the beautiful seat of Sir John Cotgreave, Knt.

lar demolitions of it, now moste grievous to the spectators, and more woefull to the inhabitants thereof :—

" *Imprimis*, without the Barrs, the chappelle of Spittle, with all the houses, and gerdens, and edifices there.

" 2. *Item*, all the houses, barns, and buildings, near to the Barrs, with Great Boughton, and Christleton.

" 3. *Item*, In the Foregate-street, Cow-lane, St. John's-lane, with some other houses in the same street, all burned to the ground.

" 4. *Item*, without the Foregate, from the said gate to the last house, Jollye's Hall, all burned and consumed to the ground, with all lanes in the same, with the Chappelle of Little St. John, not to be found.

" 5. *Item*, from Dee Bridge over the Water, all that long street, called Handbridge, with all the lanes, barnes, and buildings, all about it, ruinated to the ground.

" 6. *Item*, all the Glover's houses under the walles of the Cittie, all pulled downe to the ground.

" 7. *Item*, all the buildings and houses att the Watergate, upon the Roodee, pulled downe to the ground.

" 8. *Item*, Besides the famous houses of gentlemen in the same cittie, and neer unto adjoining the Bachhall, Mr. Whitbies.

" 9. Mr. W. Jollye's Hall, at the Norgate-street end.

" 10. Blacon-hall, Sir Randall Crue's, with cottages belonging.

" 11. The Nunnes'-hall, Sir Wm. Brereton's.*

" 12. Mr. Ellis's hall, on the Hough-greene.

" 13. Flookersbrook-hall, Sir Thomas Smith.

" 14. Mr. Walker's, or Shermen's mills.

" 15. The Hall of Hole, Mr. Bunburie's.

" 16. The Water Tower, at Dee Bridge.

" 17. Bretton-hall, Mr. Ravenscrofte's.†

" 18. The Lord Cholmondeleye's Hall, in St. John's Church-yard, with the ruins of the said Church.‡

" 19. Mr. William Gamull's house att Newgate, with Mr. John Werden's house neare unto it.

" 20. The destruction of divers other houses in the cittie, with granadoes, too tedious to recite.

" 21. The ruines of stalls, pentices, doores, trees, and barnes, in divers lanes and places in the cittie.

" 22. The destroying of the Bishop's Palace, with stables in the barne-yard, and the ruine of the great churche.

" 23. The charge of mudd walles, sodding, carrying, and building them, with centrye houses both without the walles, and within the walles.

" 24. The drawing dry of the cittie's stockes, plate, rentes, and collections, not knowne, all which losses, charges, and demolishments, in opinion of most, will amount to two hundred thousand pounds, att the least; soe fare hath the God of Heaven humbled this famous cittie; and note, here, that if Jerusalem, the particular beloved cittie of God, of which it is said in Sacred Writ, mark well her bulwarkes, and count her towers, in man's judgement invincible; yet her sinne provoked God soe, that he leaved not a stone upon another; this may be an advertisement to us, that God's mercy is yett to be found, since he hath left us soe many streets, lanes, and churches, yet unmolested. God grant us faith, patience, and true repentance, and amendment, that a worse danger befall us not. Amen."

February 6th, 1645-6. Three days afterwards, orders came down from the parliament, to regulate the garrison, and to appoint alderman William Edwards, to be colonel of the regiment of the city.

October 1st, 1646. The parliament displaced the persons hereafter named from being justices, of the peace, aldermen, sheriffs-peers, and common-council men, by a public ordinance, which recited that these delinquents had been in arms, or had otherwise been violent fomenters of these unnatural wars against the parliament, viz. :—

Charles Walley, mayor, Nicholas Ince, Randle Holme, Francis Gamull, Sir Robert Brerewood, Thomas

* As this stood within the City, it is probable it was destroyed in RETURN for Sir William's ravages without the walls.

† This gentleman, it will be recollected, played off a successful RUSE DE GUERRE from Hawarden Castle. See p. 152.

‡ The Church was for some time garrisoned by the Parliamentarians. In Jan. 1814, a six-pound cannon shot, was found by the Sexton, in digging a grave at the west end of the north aisle of the Church. It is now in the possession of the Rev. Wm. Richardson, and probably formed part of the "warlike munition" of the garrison, or was discharged from the city batteries.

Cowper, Thomas Thropp, Sir Thomas Smith, Richard Dutton, Robert Sproston; aldermen and justices of the peace.

James earl of Derby, John earl Rivers, Thomas Savage, Richard Broster; aldermen.

Humphrey Phillips, Edward Hulton, Thomas Weston, Richard Wright, Humphrey Lloyd, Richard Taylor, and Arthur Walley; sheriffs-peers, and common-councilmen.

The parliament likewise, by an ordinance of the same date, appointed alderman Wm. Edwards to be the mayor of the city of Chester, until the time of electing a new mayor, which should be in the year 1647, and the sword and mace were restored again to the city; and this year the High-Cross was pulled down, and the founts taken away out of the parish-churches in Chester.

1648. In this year were superadded to the evils which had been endured by the city, the horrors of pestilence, caused probably by the habitual neglect of public cleanliness, and the increased annoyances which would be occasioned by the numbers cooped within the city walls during the preceding siege. Between the 22d of June in this year, and the 20th of April following, 2099 persons died of the plague in the several parishes of Chester. Grass grew at the High Cross, and in the most frequented parts of the city, and an ordinance was issued by the houses of parliament for nominating city officers, as the assembly of citizens could not be held without danger. Cabins for the infected were built under the Water-tower, and in the adjoining salt-marsh. *Cowper's MSS.*

HISTORY.

A design was discovered in August to seize the castle and garrison for the use of the King. Baker, Mouldsworth, and others concerned, who were prisoners of war, were referred to the General; but Capt. Oldham, and Lieut. Ashton, were shot in the corn-market, suffering with truly Christian resolution, and exhorting the by-standers to loyalty and fidelity towards the King and royal family. *Cowper's MSS.*

1649. King Charles II. was proclaimed a traitor at the High Cross, and other places of the city. The King's Arms were removed from the Shire-hall, and those of the Earls from the Exchequer, by order of the judges, Humphrey Mackworth (deputy to Bradshaw), and Thomas Fell. *Cowper's MSS.*

1650. The Bishop's palace, with all the furniture, was sold, Dec. 13, to Robert Maller and Wm. Richardson for £1059. *Cowper's MSS.*

1652. A court-martial was established at Chester, where the prisoners from Newport were brought for trial. Ten of these were condemned on the act against holding a correspondence with the King, and five were executed, including a Captain Simkins, who had carried the king's letter of invitation to Sir T. Middleton.

Shortly afterwards, the Earl of Derby*, Sir Timothy

* Proceedings against JAMES STANLEY Earl of DERBY, Sir TIMOTHY FETHERSTONHAUGH, and Captain JOHN BENBOW, before a Court Martial, for High Treason, 3 CHARLES II. A. D. 1651. SOMMERS' TRACTS.

On Wednesday being the 1st of this instant month, the Earl of Derby was brought to his Trial, before the Court Martial holden at Chester, in the year of our Lord God, 1651.—By virtue of a Commission from his Excellency the Lord Gen. Cromwell, grounded upon an Act of Parliament of the 12th of August last, intituled "An act prohibiting correspondence with Charles Stuart, or his party, directed to Major-General Mitton, &c." The said Court being assembled together, after silence proclaimed, the names of the Officers were called over, where were present as followeth:—

A List of the Names of the Officers at a Court Martial holden at Chester, on the 1st of October, for Trial of the Earl of Derby, Sir Timothy Fetherstonhaugh, and Captain Benbow.

Colonel Humphry Mackleworth, President.

Major-Gen. Mitton.	Samuel Smith.
Colonel R. Duckenfield.	John Downes.
Colonel H. Bradshaw.	Vincent Corbet.
Colonel T. Croxton.	John Delves.
Colonel G Twistleton.	John Griffith.
Lieut.-Col. H. Birkenhead.	Thomas Portington.
Lieut.-Col. Simon Finch.	Edward Alcock.
Lieut.-Colonel Newton.	Ralph Pownall.
CAPTAINS.	Richard Grantham.
James Stepford.	Edward Stelfax.

Featherstonhaugh, and Col. Benbow, were condemned by the same tribunal. The two first to be beheaded severally at Bolton and Chester; and the third to be shot at Shrewsbury.

After the Court was proclaimed, the President gave order for the Prisoner to be brought to the bar; and accordingly he was guarded from the Castle to the said Court, where Judge Mackworth read the Act of Parliament, prohibiting correspondence with Charles Stuart, or his party. And when his Lordship came to the latter clause of the said Act, viz. "That whosoever shall offend against this act and declaration, shall or may be proceeded against by a Council of War, who are hereby authorised to hear and determine all and every the said offences; and such as shall by the said Council be condemned to suffer death, shall also forfeit all his and their lands, goods, and other estates, as in case of High Treason." Upon which words, the Earl of Derby said, 'I am no Traitor, neither.'—'Sir,' replied the President, 'your words are contemptible: You must be silent during the reading of the Act, and your Charge.' After his Lordship had read the said Charge of High Treason, &c. the Earl pleaded, that he had quarter given him for his life by one Captain Edge, which (said he) he conceived a good bar to avoid trial for life by a Council of War, unless he had committed some new fact since quarter given, that might bring him within the cognizance of a Court Martial. Hereupon the Commissioners took the matter into consideration, and after a long and serious debate, they agreed to overrule him in his Plea, and finding him Guilty of Treason, passed Sentence upon him in these words:—

The SENTENCE against JAMES Earl of DERBY.

1. Resolved, by the Court, upon the question, "That James Earl of Derby, is guilty of the breach of the said Act of the 12th of August, last past, entitled, 'An Act prohibitting correspondence with Charles Stuart, or his party,' and so of High Treason against the Commonwealth of England, and therefore is worthy of death."

2. Resolved, &c. "That the said James, Earl of Derby, is a Traitor to the Commonwealth of England, and an abettor, encourager, and assister of the declared traitors and enemies thereof, and shall be put to death, by severing his head from his body, at the Market-place, in the town of Bolton, in Lancashire, upon Wednesday, the 15th of this instant Oct. about the hour of one o'clock of the same day."

The Honorable Court having proceeded to Sentence against the Earl of Derby; in order to the further executing of justice, began with Sir Timothy Fetherstonhaugh, and Captain Benbow, and being brought to the bar, the President likewise caused the Act of Parliament to be read; as also their Charge, consisting of High Treason: and after a short speech by them made, touching the grounds and reasons of their Engagement, the Court proceeded to Sentence, and accordingly resolved as followeth:—

The SENTENCE of the Court against Sir TIMOTHY FETHERSTONHAUGH.

1. Resolved upon the question, "That Sir Timothy Fetherstonhaugh, is likewise guilty of the breach of the said Act of Parliament, of the 12th of August last past, and so of High Treason against the Commonwealth of England, and is therefore worthy of death."

2. Resolved, &c. "That the said Sir Timothy Fetherstonhaugh, as a Traitor to the Commonwealth of England, and an abettor, encourager, and assister, of the declared traitor and enemy thereof, shall be put to death, by severing his head from his body, at some remarkable and convenient place in the city of Chester, upon Wednesday the 22d of this instant October."

The SENTENCE of the Court against Capt. JOHN BENBOW.

1. Resolved by the Court upon the question, "That Capt. John Benbow, is also guilty of the breach of the said Act of the 12th of August last, and so of High Treason against the Commonwealth of England, and is therefore worthy of death.

2. Resolved, &c. "That the said Captain Benbow, as a traitor to the Commonwealth of England, shall be shot to death at some convenient place in the town of Shrewsbury, upon Wednesday, the 15th of this instant October, about one of the clock the same day."

FROM WHITLOCKE'S MEMORIALS, p. 486.

Oct. 6, 1651. Letters, That the Earl of Derby was tried at a Court Martial at Chester, at which were twenty Officers, Captains, and above that degree, five Colonels, Major-Gen. Mitton, and Col. Mackworth the President. That the Earl confessed the plot for a general rising of the Presbyterians in Lancashire, to join with the King: but it was disappointed by the apprehending of Mr. Birkenhead. That Sir Thos. Tiddesly, Major Ashurst, and Major-General Massey, were principal actors in that Conspiracy. He confessed the matters of Treason charged against him, and submitted to the mercy of Parliament. And for plea, 1. He alledged 'he had quarter given him, and therefore was not to be tried by a Court Martial for life;' but this was over-ruled by the Court. 2. He pleaded 'ignorance of the acts of treason set forth by the Parliament;' which plea was also over-ruled; and the Court sentenced him to be beheaded for his treasons at Bolton, where he had killed a man in cold blood. The Earl seemed very desirous of life, and petitioned the Lord General upon the point of his having quarter, but had no relief from him. The Court sentenced Sir Timothy Fetherstonhaugh to be beheaded for the same treasons; and Captain Benbow to be shot to death.

Oct. 8. Letters, That Captain Young, who commanded the President frigate, coming to the Isle of Man, summoned it for the Parliament; but the Countess of Derby being there, re-

CHESTER HISTORY.

Sept. 9, 1683.—The Duke of Monmouth, with a train of 100 horse, arrived in Chester. The Citizens went out of the city to welcome him, saluting him with loud acclamations of "God Save the Protestant Duke!" On entering the city, he alighted at the Mayor's house,* where he was received by his Worship, and the Recorder, Mr. W. Williams the late Speaker, of the House of Commons. At night, his Grace supped at the Feathers Inn; the streets were illminated with flambeaux and bonfires, and the bells of the different churches loudly proclaimed his welcome! Next day (Sunday) the Mayor and Corporation went with him to Church, the Mayor and Sword-bearer walking immediately before him. The sermon was preached by the Rev. Dr. Fogge, which much galled the Duke's enemies, the Papists, Non-jurors, &c. so much so, that they reputed he did not pray for the Queen. He was attended to the Feathers by the Mayor, &c. who in the evening again conducted him to the Cathedral. He then went to the Mayor's house, attended by so great a crowd as almost to render the streets impassible. The Mayoress having been lately brought to bed, the child was that evening christened Henrietta, his Grace being the Godfather. On the Monday, followed by a numerous suite of gentry, the Duke went to Wallasey Races (Wirral), where he was received with every testimony of joy. He there rode his own horse, won the plate, and presented it to his God-daughter, the same evening.† The city presented a vast field of joy, alloyed only by the peurile attempts of the disaffected to the Church Establishment, who beat the boys in the street, and put out the bonfires. They were, however, soon obliged to desist.—Next day, his Grace went to Rock Savage; on the 14th to Dunham Massey; from thence to Trentham, Newcastle; and so on to Stafford, where he was taken into custody by a special warrant from the King.

* Mr. Peter Edwards.

† Is this plate in existence.

1745. Towards the latter end of this year, the rebel army from Scotland, marching into this kingdom, and entering Lancashire, the Earl of Cholmondeley, Lord Lieutenant of the County, and Governor of Chester, began dispositions for the defence of this city, in which was one veteran regiment and three new-raised ones. The Watergate, Northgate, and Sally-ports were walled up, and the several buildings adjoining to the walls pulled down. The main guard was kept in the Bridge Street, at the end of Common Hall Lane; subalterns had the charge of the gates, through which no one was al-

turned answer, 'That she was to keep it by her Lord's command, and without his order she would not deliver it up, being in duty bound to obey her Lord's commands.'

Oct. 13. Letters, That the Earl of Derby attempted to escape, and was let down by a rope from the leads of his Chamber, but some hearing a noise, made after him; and he was re-taken upon Dee Bank. He wrote a handsome passionate Letter to his Lady to comfort her, and advised her, as then matters stood, to surender the Isle of Man upon good conditions.

Oct. 20. Letters of the particulars of the Earl of Derby's death on the 15th at Bolton; who carried himself with stoutness and Christian-like temper.

Nov. 1. Letters, That Sir Timothy Fetherston was executed in the market-place, Chester, according to the sentence of the Court Martial, and used only a few prayers out of the Common Prayer Book.

After the Earl's sentence, he was visitted in the Castle by a Lieutenant Smith, who informed him that he was required to go to Bolton, on the following morning, and said, "Doth your Lordship know any friend or servant that would do that thing which your Lordship knows of; it would do well if you had a friend." Lord Derby replied, "What do you mean; would you have me to fix upon one to cut off my own head?" Smith said, "My Lord, IF you could get a friend." To which the gallant Earl answered, "Nay, Sir; if those men that will have my head, will not find one to cut it off, let it stand where it is: I thank my God my life has not been so bad that I should be instrumental to deprive myself of it; though he hath been so merciful to me as to be well resolved against the worst terrors death can put upon me--and for me and my servants, our ways have been to prosecute a just war by honorable and just means, and not those barbarous ways of blood which to you is a trade."

"What reward his son had for this famous Earl's loyalty, will appear by the following Inscription, fixed by the late Earl of Derby on a building erected at Knowsley, his seat in Lancashire:—

'JAMES EARL OF DERBY, LORD OF MAN AND THE ISLES, GRANDSON OF JAMES EARL OF DERBY, AND OF CHARLOTTE, DAUGHTER OF CLAUDE DUKE DE LA TREMOUILLE, WHOSE HUSBAND JAMES WAS BEHEADED AT BOLTON, XV. OCTR. MDCLII. [so in the book] FOR STRENUOUSLY ADHERING TO CHARLES THE SECOND, WHO REFUSED A BILL PASSED UNANIMOUSLY BY BOTH HOUSES OF PARLIAMENT FOR RESTORING TO HIS FAMILY THE ESTATE LOST BY HIS LOYALTY TO HIM. MDCCXXXII.'" [So in the book.]

Tindal's Rapin, fol. ed. 1743, vol. 2. p. 586, note (*e*.)

CHESTER HISTORY.

lowed to pass, but by day-light; advanced parties were placed at proper places in the suburbs, and picquet guards patrolled on the walls, all night long. On the 19th of November, orders were given that all householders should lay in a stock of provisions for a fortnight. The fortifications of the castle were repaired, and some new works added: ammunition and necessary stores were provided. On Sunday, Nov 24, the church-yard walls of St. Mary's on the Hill were taken down, and the materials removed into the Castle. It was intended to form the Church-yard into a bastion, which would have the full command of the Bridge. Several adjoining buildings were likewise taken down, and their foundations levelled, and the citadel and town were made as tenable as the time would permit. However the rebels did not approach the city, but marched through a part of the county into Staffordshire.

Dr. Cowper adds, that all trade and business ceased for some weeks, the principle inhabitants having removed all their valuables. The four regiments* quartered in the city were chiefly accommodated in private houses. Shortly after the surrender of Carlisle, a number of the rebels were brought prisoners in sixteen carts to Chester, and lodged in the castle, which they completely filled. In consequence of this, the Spring Assize was held at Flookersbrook; but no sort of business was brought before the Grand Jury.

* Two of them said to be Dutch.

Since this period, there occurred no event of sufficient importance to require notice in the account of the local History of the City of Chester, until

Aug. 15, 1814.—This day was rendered remarkable, by the splendid reception given by the City to Lords Combermere† and Hill,‡ on their return from the Peninsular and French wars. At an early hour in the morning, the bells of the different churches struck up merry peals, and about 9 o'clock the great bells of the Cathedral commenced ringing and firing.—Flags were hoisted on Mr. Mellor's, and Messrs. Walkers, Maltby & Co.'s shot towers, and on the steeples of St. John's and St. Mary's. The houses in Handbridge, Bridge-street, Northgate-street, Eastgate-street, &c. &c. were decorated with laurel and shrubs, and the Bridge-gate was ornamented in the form of a triumphal arch, the sides and the centre of the arch bound round with laurel and flowers, and on the upper compartment, on the south side, was the inscription, in large letters, "*Brave Warriors welcome,*" and on the sides in small devices, "*Almarez,*" "*Salamanca.*" On the north side of the Gate in large letters, "*Europe liberated,*"—"*Salamanca,*"—"*Almarez.*" Festoons of laurel, &c. also ornamented the Grand Gateway of the Castle; above was the inscription, "BRITAIN TRIUMPHANT." At eleven o'clock, the different trade-companies, clubs, &c. began to muster at their respective houses, and at twelve marched up to the Abbey Square, where they were marshalled; and about one o'clock the whole moved in the following

ORDER OF PROCESSION.

Four Trumpeters on horseback;
The trumpets decorated with the arms of the heroes.
Two emblematical blue banners, with the inscription—
"Cheshire's pride"—"The pride of Shropshire,"
carried by men on grey horses.
Naval flags and pendants, carried by Ship Carpenters.
Shipwrights, two and two, in blue jackets and trowsers.
The Beneficial Clubs four abreast, in the following order:—
Colours.
Friendly Society,
With a banner, on which was "Combermere and Hill."—"Peace and Plenty."
Colours.
The Original Brotherly Society.
Colours.
The True Blue Society.
Colours.
The Union Band Society.
Preceded by a large banner, bearing the inscription,
"The Reward of Victory,"
surmounted by Fame; on the reverse, "Combermere and Hill."

† Sir Stapleton Cotton, and ‡ Sir Rowland Hill, severally ennobled for their heroism, in Spain, Portugal, and France.

The members decorated with rosettes.
Colours.
The Independent Society.
Colours.
The Independent Band Society.
Colours.
The British Brotherly Society.
Colours.
The Amicable Society.
Flag.
The Building Society.
Band of Music.
Banners.

The Military. The Military.

The Innkeeper's Company, on horseback, the members decorated with rosettes.
The respective Trade-companies, preceded by their banners, four abreast.
Subscribers and gentlemen of the city.
The Committee.
THE CORPORATION,
In scarlet, and blue gowns, preceded by the Sword and Mace.

The Military. The Military.

Banners.
Inscribed, "Through Noble Deeds to Noble Honors," &c. &c. &c.

THE CAR:

An open carriage, drawn by six beautiful greys, decorated with crimson and white ribbons.

It was lined with crimson cloth, and on each side, on banners, were the armorial bearings of the Lords Combermere and Hill, tastefully painted; on the pannels, a large Baronial coronet. In front, rising from wreaths of laurel, the plume of the Earl of Chester. At the four corners, inverted Eagles in burnished gold. The whole had a very good effect. The horses rode by post boys in red liveries.

The London Royal Mail,

Drawn by six dark bay horses. The body of the coach ornamented with flags, bearing the Imperial Arms, and the words "Combermere and Hill," in letters of gold.

Another Coach drawn by four horses.
Gentlemen on horseback.
&c. &c. &c.

The procession proceeded down Northgate-street, Bridge-street, to Overlegh-hall, where it awaited the arrival of the illustrious visitors. About two o'clock Lord Hill passed through the concourse of people assembled, in a close carriage, without being recognised, and alighted at Overlegh Gates. On his arrival being generally known, the *mobility* became very anxious for the arrival of Lord Combermere. Owing, however, to the inhabitants of Holywell and Halkin taking his Lordship's horses from his carriage, and drawing him through those towns, his Lordship was unable to make his appearance till nearly half past three o'clock, in a carriage ornamented with the family arms. He was escorted by the Hawarden troop of artillery, which was placed under the command of Lieutenant Boydell. He wore the splendid dress of a British General of Cavalry, and was decorated with several military orders. Lord Hill was in the full costume of a General of Infantry. In the area fronting Overlegh House, they were complimented on their arrival by Colonel Barnston, in the name of the Committee of Management, in a most able speech. Suitable replies were made, and the Heroes mounted the Car amidst the shouts of the spectators. The procession, in return, was formed in an order similar to what is described, so far as "THE CORPORATION," which, we should have noticed, went to the Deputy Mayor's house, near the Bridge, where the Body awaited the entrance of the noble visitors. During their stay there, Mr. Ald. Newell entertained the Corporation with a splendid cold collation, of which nearly 100 gentlemen of the city and neighbourhood partook.

After the companies, &c. the remainder of the cavalcade was formed in the order following:—

The Committee, two and two.
Trumpeter of the Hawarden Cavalry.
An honorary advanced guard, of four of the Hawarden Cavalry, bearing the Standard.
LORDS
COMBERMERE & HILL,
IN THE CAR.
Hawarden Cavalry.
Gentlemen on Horseback.
Coaches.
&c. &c. &c.

Cavalry. Cavalry.

CHESTER HISTORY.

On their Lordships appearing in view of the advanced part of the procession, the Bands of Music struck up—"See the Conquering Hero Comes!" and the multitude, amounting at least to 10,000, rent the air with huzzas, and shouts of "Combermere for ever!"—"Hill for ever!"—On approaching the bridge, the scene that presented itself beggars description: The procession was literally wedged in by the crowd, and formed one solid mass. Their progress, of course, was very slow: and on entering the city, each side of the street was lined by a strong detachment of the 22d foot. As the procession passed the bridge, the guns of the castle fired a salute; and when the car approached the Bridge Gate, the military presented arms. On the north side of the Gate, the procession stopped, and the Deputy Mayor addressed their Lordships in the following appropriate speech:—

"MY LORDS,

In the absence of our highly respected Chief Magistrate, Sir Watkin Williams Wynn, Bart. the pleasing duty has devolved upon me, as his representative here, in his name, on behalf of the Corporation, and of the Inhabitants in general, to bid you welcome within our walls, and to invite you to do us the honor of accepting the freedom of this ancient and loyal city, which has been unanimously voted to you by the Corporation in Council assembled, as a tribute of their esteem for the very eminent services you have rendered to your King and Country. With your permission, I will conduct you to the Town Hall, in order that the usual ceremonies may be performed."

Their Lordships shortly replied, expressing themselves, that they accepted the invitation with pleasure.

This ceremony being over, the Corporation fell into their place in the procession, which proceeded up Bridge-street and Northgate-street, amidst the acclamations of more than 15,000 spectators. The rows and windows of the houses, were occupied by all the beauty and fashion of Chester, and an influx of elegantly dressed females from Wales, and the adjoining counties, waving their handkerchiefs, spontaneously with the greetings of the gratified inhabitants in the streets. On the arrival of the procession at the Exchange, their Lordships descended from the Car, and entered the Town Hall, which was beautifully fitted up for the occasion, with festoons of laurel, intermingled with flowers; and the floor was covered with green baize. Lord Combermere was seated on the right hand of the Mayor, and the Hero of Shropshire on the left. Mr. Finchett, (Deputy Town Clerk) then administered to their Lordships, the Oaths of Allegiance, and Supremacy, and Fealty to the Earl of Chester and the Mayor; when the Freedom of the City was presented to their Lordships, and Chester has the pride of numbering amongst its Citizens, two of the immortal heroes who have so essentially contributed to the Independence of Europe. Happy day! may it long live in her records! The shouts of a crowded Hall, evinced the pleasure of all present; and Lord COMBERMERE spoke to this effect:—

"MR. MAYOR, and GENTLEMEN of the CORPORATION,

I cannot express the gratification I feel, for the very distinguished manner in which you have been pleased to evince your opinion of my services—next to the honors which have been bestowed upon me by my Prince and my Country, I shall cordially estimate them. The pleasure I feel is also much enhanced by the reflection, that my splendid reception has been from the ancient and loyal City of Chester, the Metropolis of my native county!"—(Loud cheering.)

Lord Hill's Reply.

"MR. MAYOR, GENTLEMEN of the CORPORATE BODY,

I need not observe, that I want words to express to you the sensations of gratitude which I feel, for the high, distinguished, and I may add, unmeritted honors, which I have this day received in so flattering a manner, at your hands—I can only beg you will, in return, accept of my best thanks.—To-day, Gentlemen, brings with it the association of many pleasing ideas—it brings to my recollection, the many, many happy days, I spent in my youth within the walls of this ancient and respectable city. Be assured, Gentlemen, I shall ever feel a lively sense of the honor you have conferred upon me."—(Loud shouts of approbation.)

Preceded by the Deputy Mayor, Corporate Officers, and the sword and mace, the Heroes left the room, and re-entered the Car, the procession moving down Northgate-street, Eastgate-street, to the Hotel, where they alighted, and afterwards appeared at the window, from which they addressed the immense multitude below, and were answered by tumults of applause. Lord Combermere was attended by his beautiful bride; and Lady Corbet stood at the left hand of Lord Hill. The pillars in the front of the Royal Hotel, were ornamented with national colours, hung in draperies, surmounted by festoons of laurel and flowers.

The dinner table was laid out in the Assembly Room, perhaps one of the most handsome rooms of its size in the kingdom:—At the upper end was a beautiful canopy, tastefully hung in crimson and yellow drapery, *à la Grecq*, in a style which has seldom been equalled. The drapery was edged with a rich gold fringe, and at the extremities of the cornice was a representation of the French Eagle disgraced (inverted) in burnished gold. In the centre of the canopy were two sabres, sheathed, indicative of the termination of War, surmounted by the figure of a dove, in dead gold, holding in its beak the olive of Peace. At the sides of the canopy were the colours of the Royal Chester Local Militia. In the centre of the recess was the Chair of the Deputy Mayor, behind which were the arms of the City. On the right hand of the Mayor sat Lord Combermere—on the left Lord Hill, behind each of whose chairs were their respective coats armorial. The chairs of the Vice-presidents and Stewards, were occupied by Colonel Wrench, Mr. Leeke, Mr. H. Potts, Mr. Dixon, and Captain Henderson.—The table at which their Lordships sat, was elevated about eight inches above the level of the room. The room had been newly painted for the auspicious occasion, and had a truly magnificent appearance—the orchestra was ornamented with flowers, formed in festoons, wreaths, &c. The table was superbly laid out, and the ornamental part was of very superior taste. Beautiful temples in gold, military trophies and pacific emblems, were amongst its leading features.—A fine fat buck was sent for the dinner by Earl Grosvenor (who also liberally offered the produce of his gardens) as was also another from Oulton, by J. Egerton, Esq. M. P.* and amongst other epicurean desideratas, was an immense turtle. About 180 gentlemen dined on the occasion.

*Now Sir J. G. Egerton, Bart.

COATS ARMORIAL—EARLS OF CHESTER.

HUGH LUPUS.

RICHARD.

RANDAL I. AND II.

Civic Government of the City of Chester.

"* THE worthy Alderman, Mr. W. Aldersey, though he ever gave due respect, and reverenced the collections of other judicious men, that had laboured in the antiquities of the city, yet he found, that the most common received account of the beginning of the Mayoralty, ascribed to the 53d year of King Henry III. when Sir John Arnway, Kt. is supposed to be the first Mayor, is untrue; and that in the 26th year of the same King, the first Mayor was Walter Lynnett, concerning whom he thus delivers his opinions :—

* From Mr. Palin's MS.

" This *Walter Lynnett*, whom (I believe) also to be called *Walter Coventry*, I suppose was of Coventry, and came thence, who, as I have been informed by some skilful heralds, was a Knight, and by all conjecture, had the Government here, until Richard Clarke came to be Mayor, wch was about the 34th or 35th year of King Henry III. And I take him the sd *Walter* to be ye first yt carried the name of Maior. What name they called ye Chief Governor by, in the time of ye Earls, I cannot certainly learn; but I take it yt the Constable of Chester, who was no doubt a great man, had ye Chief Government of the Citty, under the Earls, and had Bayliffes under him.

" It plainly appears, yt the Maioralty of Chester is very auncient, and grew to a venerable and absolute authority, as long time as can be sd well near of any other citty in the Kingdom; for however the beginning of the Maioralty of London be reckoned from the 1st of Richard I. which falls to fifty-one or fifty-two years before the beginning of this Maioralty, at least by the name of a Maior; yet were that Henry Fitz Alwyn, whom they call the first Mayor of London, continued himself alive in that name and office to the 15th year of King John, which was about 24 years, and yt after him the next successors were some of them 6 yeares, some 3 yeares, some 2 yeares, some 8 yeares, some more or less, and not also without some interruption in the Government, even till it grew towards the latter end of the reign of King Henry III. which was but a very few years before the Mayor of Chester was grown to be a settled officer, and a successor now chosen every succeeding year.

" The like may be said of our SHERIFFS of the Citty of Chester, who no doubt were in this citty, as in the citty of London, formerly called *Bayliffes*, which as Mr. Stowe well deriveth from *Ballive*, which was the precinct allotted to such governments as had been under *Portgreeves*, *Aldermen*, *Shire-reeves*, *Vicounts*, or howsoever they had been called, and came at length to that one special denomination of *Sheriffs*, of wch name, two have been usually ordained to be the next immediate officers to the Mayor of each city, as one was to the Earle, of several counties, wch one Sheriff for every county, began to be titles of honor, and not of office, hath been the chief *Custos*, or rather *Quæstor* of the several shires to which he is appointed.*

"The first certainty of a Mayor's Government in the citty, by the name of Mayor, is the 26th Henry III. A. D. 1242.†"

The following is a correct list of Mayors and Sheriffs, from 1257 to 1818—a period of 561 years :‡—

Mayors.	Sheriffs.
1257, Sir Walter Lynnet	Robert Fitz James. Adam Venator.
1258, The Same	The Same.
1259, The Same	Stephen Sarazin. Robert Mercer.
1260, The Same	Richard Clark. Gilbert Marshall.
1261, Richard Clark.	Richard Apothecary. Robert Mercer.
1262, The Same	The Same.
1263, The Same	The Same.
1264, The Same	Stephen Sarazin. Robert Mercer.
1265, The Same	Oliver de Trafford. Robert de Tervin.
1266, The Same	Oliver de Cotton. Robert de Tervin.
1267, The Same	William de Hawarden. Oliver de Trafford.

Mayors.	Sheriffs.
1268, Sir John Arnway	The Same.
1269, The Same	Matthew de Daresbury. Richard le Espizer.
1270, The Same	The Same.
1271, The Same	The Same.
1272, The Same	The Same.
1273, The Same	Robert Mercer. Richard Apothecary.
1274, The Same	Adam Godwiche. Richard le Espizer.
1275, The Same	Randal Daresbury. Christopher Clark.
1276, The Same	Adam Godwiche. Richard Apothecary.
1277, Randal Daresbury	Hugh Moles. Robert Tervin.
1278, The Same	Nathaniel de Deresbury. Randal Dobley.

* The City of Chester is noted of all writers for a place of great antiquity, honor, and reputation; was first built by Lyal King of the Britons, anno ante Christo 917, at which time Jehosaphat and Ahab governed Israel and Judah. It was afterwards repaired by Julius Cæsar, at which time the houses were built in form of Castles, and were garrisoned by Roman Legions.—Concerning the government of the City of Chester, it was long before the Conquest, under the government of the King and Duke of Mercia; and according as they pleased, they appointed Governors for the County, unto whom the City was subject, and the particular government of the city was most by Consulls, who observed their matters, and were also their Captains in war. But since the Conquest, and the time of the Earls of Chester, this city was subject to the Earls, as their Chief Governors. And those Earls gave charge both to city and county round about. And for determining their matters in Law, they had a special officer, whom the Earl did appoint, and was stiled as the Earl pleased, of whom were found sometimes by the name of Lord Chief Justices of Chester—the Knights of Chester— the Stewards, Seneschall; and other officers were there called, by the name of Keepers of the Gild Mercatory, who made freemen, looked after and decided differences. But besides these Governors under the Earls, there was the Constable of Chester, which was a place of great honor as being an office belonging to the persons who had the care of the Earl, for they had the ordering of all both men and arms that belonged to the Earl; and sending and conducting of his army, both in his presence, and in his absence.

Before the City had any Charters, they used divers liberties by prescription, and enjoyed a Gild Mercatory, i. e. a Brotherhood of Merchants; and whosoever was not admitted of the Society, he could not use any trade, or traffic within the city, nor be a tradesmen there. The tenor of this Gild Mercatory did ever run in these words:—"*According as heretofore ever have used*,"—and was afterwards confirmed under the Earl's Seal. The same name of those officers remain to this day in the *Leavelookers*, who then were head and chief of the citizens, before a Mayor was ordained; and they still are reputed the head and chief of the Forty, or Common Council of the City.—*Alders. MSS.*

† The list of Mayors and Sheriffs attached, is corrected from the Corporation Records.

‡ In a MS. which I have seen, is this Memorandum :—"It would appear from an Order of Assembly, made Dec. 26th, 1573, (4th Eliz.) when Richard Dutton was Mayor, that one John Hope was Mayor of Chester, in the reign of Henry I. and that during his Mayoralty a bye law was enacted, and made, that no Citizen should make any foreign suit, or nonfreeman exercise any trade in this city," &c.—The fact is, there is no certainty of the antiquity of the office of Mayor in this city-- it is highly probable it might have been long before 1242,---at least there is nothing extant to show that a Mayor did not exist a century before that period.

Year	Mayor	Sheriffs
1279,	The Same	Hugh Moles. Robert Tervin.
1280,	Robert le Mercer	Hugh Moles. Robert Ernes.
1281,	The Same	Alexander Hurell. Robert Ernes.
1282,	Alexander Hurell	Hugh de Moles. Robert de Hole.
1283,	Robert le Mercer	Alexander Hurell. David de Molineux.
1284,	The Same	Alexander Hurell. Robert Ithell.
1285,	Robert de Tervin	The Same.
1286,	The Same	Nicholas Payne. Robert Ernes.
1287,	The Same	The Same.
1288,	Hugh de Moles	Hugh de Birchill. Nicholas Payne.
1289,	Robert de Tervin	
1290,	Rober Mercer	
1291,	The Same	Robert Earnes. Robert Caudry.
1292,	Hugh de Birchill	Nicholas Payne. Roger Dunfould.
1293,	Robert Mercer	John de Molindiners. Roger Dunfould.
1294,	Hugh de Birchill	Alexander Hurell. Robert Ithell.
1295,	The Same	Edward Molineux. Roger Dunfould.
1296	The Same	John de Warwick. Robert de Macclesfied.
1297,	Alexander Hurell	Andrew Stanlow. Robert Ithell.
1298,	The Same	Richard Candelan. Robert de Macclesfield.
1299,	The Same	Andrew Stanlow. Robert Ithell.
1300,	Hugh de Birchill	Richard Candelan. Robert Ithell.
1301,	Alexander Hurell	Richard Candelan. Mag. John de Tervin.
1302,	Hugh de Birchill	Robert Macclesfield. Roger Dunfould.
1303,	The Same	Henry de Blackbrode. William, Son of Peter de Birchill.
1304,	Richard Lew-Genour or Regenator	Benedict Stanton. John Warwick.
1305,	Hugh de Birchill	Richard Candelan. William Son of Peter de Birchill.
1306,	The Same	Gilbert Dunfould. Roger le Sparks. Hugh de Wheatley.
1307,	The Same	William, Son of Peter de Birchill. Roger de Macclesfield.
1308,	Benedict Stanton	Henry Blackmore. Richard de Hugh Moles.
1309,	Hugh Birchill	Gilbert de Dunfield. Richard de Wheatley.
1310,	The Same	John de Blund. Richard de Wheatley.
1311,	The Same	Robert Macclesfield. William Fitz Peter de Birchill.
1312,	The Same	William de Doncaster, jun. Richard Russell.
1313,	Benedict Stanton	Gilbert Dunfould. William le Peak.
1314,	John Blund	Richard le Wood. Richard de Wheatley.
1315,	The Same	Richard Russell. Richard de Wheatley.
1316,	William Doncaster	Richard le Wood. Wiliam le Blund.
1317,	John Blund, *Died* Wm. Doncaster, *Succeeded.*	William Clark. William Mulvecon.
1318,	William Doncaster	Richard de Wheatley. Richard le Bruin.
1319,	The Same	Gilbert de Dunfould. Robert de Strangeways.
1320,	William, Son of Peter de Birchill	John Daresbury. Roger le Blund.
1321,	John Birchill	Gilbert Dunfould. Richard Wheatley.
1322,	The Same	Richard Russell. Richard Wheatley.
1323,	William Clark	Rog. le Quite, or White. John de Daresbury.
1324,	William, Son of Peter de Birchill *Died.* Rd. Russell, *Succeeded.*	William Basingwerk. Richard le Bruin, *Died.* Rich. Wheatley, *Succeed.*
1325,	Richard le Bruin	Richard Ernes. Roger Norleigh.
1326,	The Same	Richard Ernes. Roger Spark.
1327,	Richard Ernes	Richard Wheatley. Thomas de Strangewayes.
1328,	The Same	Roger Macclesfield. Maddock de Capenhurst.
1329,	William de Birchill	Henry Hurrell. Maddock de Capenhurst.
1330,	The Same	Roder de Broughton. Henry Wade.
1331,	Roger le Blond, or Blund	William Basinwark. Roger le Harpur.
1332,	The Same	Roger de Norlegh. Maddock Capenhurst.
1333,	Richard de Wheatley	John Barnes. Maddock Capenhurst.
1334,	Roger le Blond	Daniel Russell Robert Ledsham.
1335,	John Blond	Henry Torrand. William Kellsall.
1336,	Roger le Blond	Daniel Russell. Roger Capenhurst.
1337,	John Blond	Henry Hurrell. Maddock Capenhurst.
1338,	The Same	John De Hawarden. Edmund de Waterfall.
1339,	The Same	The Same.
1340,	Robert de Ledsham	John de Hawarden. John de Stoke.
1341,	Richard Capenhurst.	Maddock Capenhurst. Thomas de Hargrave.
1342,	The Same	Maddock Capenhurst. Richard de Wenefleet.
1343,	John Blond	William de Doncaster. Richard Bruin.
1344,	Richard Capenhurst.	Maddock Capenhurst. Bartholomew Norworthey
1345,	The Same	John Barnes. William Hadlegh.

Chester History.

Year, Mayor	Sheriffs
1346, Henry Torrard	Hugh de Mulveston. Richard de Ridleoh.
1347, John Blond	William de Capenhurst. Richard de Ditton.
1348, The Same	Adam de Wheatley. William Darnaldshaw.
1349 Bertram Northen, or Norworthen, *was slain*. Rich. Bruin, *Succeeded*.	The Same.
1350, John Blond	William de Huxley. Stephen de Kelsall.
1351, The Same	Robert de Castle. John, Son of Adam le Quite, or White.
1352, The Same	Thomas Wyse. Adam del Hope.
1353, Richard Bruin	William Brassie, Adam Ingram.
1354, The Same	William Brassie. Roger Ledsham.
1355, John Blond	Benedict de Ridlegh. Hamon de Didsbury.
1356, The Same	Alexander Belleter. John Collie.
1357, The Same	William de Beaumaris. Thomas de Appleton.
1358, The Same	John Collie. William de Mucklestom.
1359, Alan de Wheatley	John de Garnold. Henry Walsh.
1360, The Same	Henry Done, Hugh de Stretton.
1361, The Same	William de Huxley. Thomas Peacock.
1362, The Same	Richard Manley. Jeffrey Flint.
1363, Roger Ledsham	John Collie. William Brerecroft.
1364, The Same	David de Eulow. John de Cotton.
1365, John Dalby	Robert Fox. Henry Stapie.
1366, The Same	John Chamberlain. William del Hope.
1367, Richard Bruin	Nicholas de Troughford. Richard de Hawarden.
1368, The Same	John le Armerer. William Danson, *Skinner*.
1369, John Whitmore, jun.	Thomas Doun, or Dawn. John le Armerer.
1370, The Same	Thos. de Ferse or Frere. Richard Dunfould.
1371, The Same	Ralph Thropp. Robert Collie.
1372, The Same	Robert del Broughton. Richard de Birkenhead.
1373, Alexander Belleter	Robert le Marshall. Hugh de Dutton.
1374, Richard Bruin, jun	William Bradburn. William Savage.
1375, Richard Dunfould	Robert Collie. Hugh Dutton.
1376, The Same	John Barber. John Bebindon.
1377, Thomas de Bradford	Thomas de Apulton. John le Amerer.
1378, The Same	Roger Potter. Stephen Carley.
1379, John le Chamberlain	Roger Potter. Ralph Hatton.
1380, The Same	John Hatton. Gilbert de Billiter.
1381, David de Eulowe	John Collie. William de Barton.
1382, The Same	Roger de Ditton. Richard le Hewster.
1383, The Same	Robert de Ditton. Robert Lancelin.
1384, John Chamberlain	Thomas Wood. John Preston.
1385, The Same, *Died*.	John Delwych. Richard Strangeways.
1386, John Armerer	John de Modesley. Wm. Blackrode.
1387, The Same	Henry Yeate. Jno. del Hall.
1388, The Same	Thomas Hurrell. John de Arrow.
1389, Ralph Marshall	Ralph de Polton. Jno. de Madeley.
1390, Jno. Armerer	Ralph de Hatton. Jno. de Bebington.
1391, Gilbert Trussell	Robt. Davers. Roger le Potter.
1392, The Same	Robt. Lancelin. Jno. de Preston.
1393, Jno. Armerer	Rd. le Hewston. Thomas Pigott.
1394, The Same	Hugh de Ditton. Roger de Ditton.
1395, Jno. Capenhurst	Roger Ditton. Wm. Preston.
1396, The Same	Jno. Madeley. Wm. Heath.
1397, The Same	Richard Srangeways. Jno. Hawarden.
1398, The Same	J. Fitz David de Hawarden. Richard Stalmon.
1399, The Same	John Hardyn, or Hawarden. Robt. Bradley.
1400, John Bebington	Wm. Heath. Richard Stalmon.
1401, The Same, *Died*. John Marshall, *Succeeded*.	Jno. Harden. Thos. Acton, *Died* Jno. Arrow, *Succeeded*.
1402, Roger Porter	Innocent Chesterfield. Wm. Kempe.
1403, Ralph Hatton	Jno. Hall. Jno. Arrow.
1404, Jno. Preston	Wm. Ratchdale. Thos. Allen.
1405, John Ewlowe	Robert le Chamberlain. John Hatton.
1406, The Same	Jno. Hatton. Thomas Cottingham.
1407, The Same	Jno. Walsh. Ellis Trevor.
1408, The Same	Jno. Walsh. Hugh Mutton.
1409, The Same *removed* Sir Wm. Brereton, *made Governor of the City*.	Jno. Tarpurleigh, Hugh Mutton.
1410, Roger Potter	Jno. Brown. Ellis Trevor.

Chester History.

Year	Mayor	Sheriffs
1411	Jno. Walsh	Wm. del Hope. Richard de Hatton.
1412	Jno. Whitmore	Jno. del Hope. Hugh de Mutton.
1413	The Same	John del Hope. Richard le Spicer.
1414	The Same	John del Hope. Jno Overton.
1415	Jno. Walsh	Jno. de Hatton. Robert del Hope.
1416	Jno. de Hawarden	Jno. de Hatton. Richard le Spicer.
1417	J. Overton, or Oulton	Robert Hall. Thomas Cliffe.
1418	Wm. Hawarden	Alexander Henbury. Jno. Bradeley.
1419	Jno. Hope	Robert Hall. Stephen Belleter.
1420	The Same	Wm. Malpas. Nicholas Wirvin.
1421	The Same	Richard Massey. Wm. Malpas.
1422	Jno. Walsh	Robt. Hewster. Nicholas Russell, or Trussell.
1423	Jno. Hatton	Hugh Woodcock. Richard Weston.
1424	Jno. Hope	Richard Massey. Adam de Wotton.
1425	The Same	Richard Massey. Wm. Stanneer.
1426	The Same	Roger de Walshall. Thomas de Wotton.
1427	Thos. Madeley	Thomas Madeley. John Flint.
1428	Jno. de Bradley	Thos. Bradford. Wm. Holme.
1429	Jno. Walsh	Edw. Skinner. Hugh Green, or Greys.
1430	Robt. Hope	Jno. Freeman. Richard Hankey.
1431	Rich. Massey	Jno. Pilkinton. Richard Vinkers.
1432	The Same	Thos. Walley. David Skinner.
1433	Thos. Wotton	Wm. Rogerson, *Barker*. Hugh Hickling, *Mercer*.
1434	Adam Wotton	Barthol. Byalton. Thos. Hamon.
1435	Jno. Walsh	Jno. Cottingham, *Mercer*. Robt. Eaton.
1436	Wm. Stanneer	Jno. Minor. Jno. Layett.
1437	Rich. Massey	Jno. Flint. Thos. Wood.
1438	Richard Wester, or Weston.	John Copeland, *Merchant*. Thomas Clark.
1439	Nicholas Daniel	Robert Gill, *Mercer*. Peter Savage.
1440	Jno. Pilkington	Wm. Williamson, *Barber*. Wm. Massey de Coddington.
1441	Hugh Woodcock	Thos. Lillie. Hugh Neile.
1442	John Flint	Philip Hewster. Robt. Walley.
1443	Nicholas Daniel	Jenkin Lowther. John Rochley.
1444	The Same	The Same.
1445	The Same	Richard Barrow, *Barber*. William Barker.
1446	Edw. Skinner	Rowland Hunt, *Mercer*. Richard Eccles.
1447	The Same, *Died*. Wm. Rogers, *Succeeded*.	Jenkin Williamson. Rodger Ledsham.
1448	William Rogerson, or Rogers	Jno. Yardley. Robert Bruin.
1449	Wm. Massey	Jno. Southworth. Henry Hernes.
1450	Wm. Whitmore	Rich. Hawarden. James Hurleston.
1451	Jno. Dutton de Hatton	Rich. Massey, *Merchant*. Rich. Raynford, *Walker*.
1452	Wm. Stanner, *Vinter*.	Robt. Rogerson, *Vinter*. Tho. Garrat, or Gerrard.
1453	Nicholas Daniel, Esq.	Rawlin Marshall. Jenkin Trafford.
1454	The Same	John Barrow. John Grosvenor.
1455	Jenkin Cottingham	Thomas Kent, *Mercer*. William Hankey, *Skinner*.
1456	The Same	Jenkin Ronkhorn, *Butcher* Richard Bower.
1457	Nicholas Daniel	Rich. Buckley. William Trickett.
1458	The Same	Thos. Macclesfield. Robt. Acton.
1459	Jno. Southworth	Wm. Lilley, *Mercer*. Nicholas Macclesfield.
1460	The Same	Roger Warminshaw. Henry Day.
1461	David Ferrer	Thomas Cottingham, *Mercer*. J. Chamberlain, *Vintner*.
1462	Robt. Brown, *Draper*	Jno. Goldsmith, *Butcher*. Hugh Frere, *Died*. Wm. Gough, *Succeeded*.
1463	Robt. Rogerson	Jno. Spencer, *Draper*. Alexander Stanney.
1464	Rog. Ledsham, *Draper*.	Rich. Green. Wm. Runcorn.
1465	Rich. Rainford	James Norris, *Glover*. Jno. Fenton, *Butcher*.
1466	Wm. Lilley, *Mercer*	Wm. Rawson. Wm. Thomason.
1467	John Southworth, Esq.	Wm. Sharman. Rich. Sharp.
1468	Jno. Dedwood, Gent.	Rich. Gerard. Robt. Notterville.
1469	Thos. Kent	Jno. Smith, *Mercer*. Henry Ball, *Draper*.
1470	Thos. Cottingham	Thos. Fernes. Wm. Richmond.
1471	Robt. Rogerson	Henry Port, *Mercer*. Rich. Harpur, *Butcher*.
1472	Jno. Spencer, *Draper*.	Jno. Evans, *Glover*. Nicholas Hopkinson.
1473	Jno. Whitmore, Esq.	Jno. Barrow, *Ironmonger*. Wm. Sneyd, *Draper*.
1474	Jno. Southworth, Esq.	Roger Hurleston, *Mercer*. Robert Walley, *Butcher*.
1475	The Same	Richard Smith, *Saddler*. Thos. Eccles, *Huckster*.

ITINERARY OF THE COUNTY, &c.

Year	Mayor	Sheriffs
1476,	Hugh Massey	Henry Warmingham. Roger Lightfoot.
1477,	J. Southworth, Esq.	Geo. Bulkley. Thos. Hurleston.
1478,	Robt Notterville	Robt. Elswick, *Fletcher.* Jno. Mansfield, *Apothecary.*
1479,	Wm. Sneyd, *Draper*	Robt. Walker, *Fisher.* Matthew Johnson, *Hewster.*
1480,	Jno. Southworth	Ralph Davenport. William Heywood, *Cook.*
1481,	Roger Hurleston, *Mercer*	Jno. Dedwood, *Goldsmith.* Henry Francis, *Butcher.*
1482,	The Same	Roger Taylour, *Founder.* Roger Burgess.
1483,	Jno. Dedwood	Peter Smith, *Mercer.* Jno. Runcorn, *Butcher.*
1484,	Sir Jno. Savage	Jno. Norris. Hugh Hurleston.
1485,	The Same	Thomas Barrow, *Mercer.* Rich. Gardner.
1486,	Henry Port	Randal Sparrow. Hen. Harpur, *Died.* Rich. Spencer, *Succeeded.*
1487,	Hugh Hurleston	Randal Sparrow. Nicholas Lowker.
1488,	Geo. Bulkley	Thos. Bunbury. Robert Barrow.
1489,	Ralph Davenport	Jno. Cliffe, *Mercer.* Thos. Manning.
1490,	Jno. Barrow	Rich. Wright. Rich. Wirrall.
1491,	Randal Sparrow	Edm. Farrington. Rich. Hockenhall.
1492,	Roger Hurleston	Rich. Goodman, *Merchant.* Rich. Barker.
1493,	Ralph Davenport	Ralph Manley. Rich. Grosvenor.
1494,	Geo. Bulkley	Hen. Bellfront. Jno. Walley.
1495,	Rich. Wirrall	Nicholas Newhouse, *Glover.* Randal Smith, *Sherman.*
1496,	Tho. Barlow, *Mercer.*	Thos Smith, *Mercer.* Tudor ap Thomas, *Mercer.*
1497,	Thos. Farrar	Jno Grimsditch. Rowlin Eaton.
1498,	Rich. Goodman	Richard Fletcher. Thos. Thornton.
1499,	Jno. Cliffe	Roger Smith. Jno. Walley.
1500,	Thos. Farrar	James Manley. Rich. Walton.
1501,	Ralph Davenport	Wm. Rogerson. Rich. Lowe, *Pewterer.*
1502,	Rich. Wright	Wm. Ball, *Draper.* Thos. Gill, *Butcher.*
1503,	Rich. Goodman, Esq.	Jno. Tatton. Jno. Rathborn.
1504,	Thos. Smith. sen.	Thos. Harden. Wm. Sneyd.
1505,	Thos. Thornton	Hamnet Goodman, *Sherman.* Jno. Bradfield *Baker.*
1506,	Tho. Barrow, *Mercer*	Robt. Barrow., *Mercer.* Hamnet Johnson, *Draper.*
1507,	Rd. Wirrall, *Glover.*	John Harpur, *Mercer.* Robert Goulburn.
1508,	Thomas Hawarden	Edm. Smith. Wm. Davison.
1509,	Rd. Wright, *Draper.*	Thos. Crook, *Merchant.* Rd. Brewster, *Barker.*
1510,	Wm. Rogerson	Thos. Houghton, *Bowyer.* Hen. Bradford, *Barker.*
1511,	Thos. Smith	Hugh Clark. Cha. Eaton.
1512,	Pierce Dutton	Thos. Middleton. David Middleton.
1513,	Sir. P. Dutton.	Jno. Brickdale. Robt. Aldersey.
1514,	The Same, *declared unduly elected, and superseded by* Jno. Rathbone	Wm. Hurdleston. Jno. Looker, *both superseded by* Wm. Goodman, *and* Rich. Grimsditch.
1515,	Sir Tho. Smith, Sen.	Thos. Smith, *Ironmonger.* Robt. Wright, *Draper.*
1516,	Wm. Sneyd, *Draper*	Hugh Aldersey, *Draper.* Randal Done, *Skinner.*
1517,	Wm. Davison	Wm. Offley. Nicholas Johnson.
1518,	Thos. Barrow	Pierce Smith. Robt. Middleton.
1519,	Jno. Rathbone	Jno. ap Griffith. Rich. Anyon, *Barker.*
1520,	Thos. Smith, sen.	Thos. Goulborn. Christopher Warminsham.
1521,	The Same	Ralph Rogerson. Thos. Bamvill.
1522,	Wm. Davison	Roger Barlow. Jno. Woodward, *Hewster.*
1523,	David Middleton	Roger Pike. Stephen Cross.
1524,	R. Goulbourn, *Draper*	Rich. Evans. Jno. Dimmock.
1525,	R. Aldersey, *Draper*	Jno. Walley. Henry Eaton.
1526,	Robt. Barrow, Gent.	Hugh Davenport. Foulk Dutton.
1527,	Thos. Smith, sen.	Thos. Hall. Henry Gee, *Draper.*
1528,	H. Aldersey, *Draper*	Edw. Davenport. Robt. Barton.
1529,	H. Bradford, *Tanner*	Thos. Rogerson, or Rogers, *Merchant.* Ralph Goodman, *Skinner.*
1530,	Thos. Smith, sen.	Lawrence Dutton, *Mercer.* Wm. Massey, *Draper.*
1531,	Wm. Sneyd, *Draper.*	Robt. Brerewood, *Glover.* Thos. Barrow, *Glover.*
1532,	Wm. Goodman	Wm. Beswick, *Goldsmith.* Rd. Hunter, *Tailor.*
1533,	Hen. Gee, *Merchant*	Randal Mainwaring. Hugh Hanckey.
1534,	Ralph Rogerson *Ironmonger*	John Thompson. Thos. Martin.
1535,	Sir Thos. Smith	Robt. Walley. Rd. Wrench.
1536,	Wm. Goodman, *Merchant*	Geo. Leeche, *Ironmonger.* Geo. Lightfoot, *Butcher.*
1537,	Flk. Dutton, *Draper*	Wm. Glasbour. Roger Whitehead.
1538,	David Middleton	Thos. Aldersey, *Draper.* Rd. Dixon, *Fishmonger.*
1539,	Hen. Gee, *Draper.*	Wm. Aldersey, *Merchant.* Wm. Whitelег, *Ironmonger*
1540,	Law. Smith, *Esq.*	John Smith, *Draper.* Thos. Langley, *Merchant.*
1541,	Hugh Aldersey, *Merchant*	Rich. Sneyd, *Draper.* R. Aldersey, *Merchant, Died.* Rand. Bammville, *Succeeded.*
1542,	Wm. Beswick, *Goldsmith*	Adam Goodman, *Merchant.* Edmund Gee, *Merchant.*
1543,	Wm. Sneyd, Esq.	Ralph Radford. Jno. Rosengreave.

Mayor	Sheriffs
1544, Robt. Barton, *Merch.*	William Leech, *Draper.* John Offley, *Merchant.*
1545, Wm. Holcroft, Esq. *Died* J. Walley, *Succeed.*	Richard Pool, *Merchant.* Rich. Grimsditch, *Merchant.*
1546, Hugh Aldersey, *Died* Jno. Smith, *Succeeded*	William Bird, *Tanner.* Thomas Smith, *Draper.*
1547, Ralph Goodman	Rd. Rathbone, *Draper.* Thos. Bavand, *Ironmonger.*
1548, Foulk Dutton	John Webster, *Mercer.* Robt. Jones, *Ironmonger.*
1549, Thos. Aldersey	Rd. Massey, *Upholsterer.* Morrice Williams, *Merchant.*
1550, Edmund Gee, *Died* .. William Goodman, *Succeeded*...............	Ralph Goodman, *Merchant.* Peers Street, *Butcher.*
1551, Wm. Glasеour	Ralph Rogers. Thos. Green, *Candlemaker.*
1552, Thos. Smith, *Draper.*	Thos. Saunders, *Ironmonger.* Wm. Brounkshank, *Glover.*
1553, John Offley, *Mercht.*	Hen. Hardware, *Merchant.* William Ball, *Glover.*
1554, Foulk Dutton	Robt. Amary, *Merchant.* John Cooper, *Ironmonger.*
1555, John Smith, *Draper* ..	Thos. Woodwall, *Ironmonger* John Reece, *Mercer.*
1556, Jno. Webster, *Mercer*	John Hankey, *Innkeeper.* Thomas Bellin, *Mercer.*
1557, Wm. Bird, *Tanner*..	John Newell, Gent. *Clerk of the Pentice.* Thos. Burgess, *Beer Brewer.*
1558, Sir Lawrence Smith.	John Yarworth, Gent. William Jewett, *Merchant.*
1559, Hen. Hardware, *Merchant*	Chris. Morvill, *Merchant.* Simon Mountford, *Pewterer.*
1560, William Aldersey, *Merchant.*	Robert Dryhurst, *Merchant.* Richard Boydill, *Joiner.*
1561, John Cowper, *Ironmonger*........	Richard Dutton, Gent. Thomas Pillen, *Shoemaker.*
1562, Rand. Bamvile, *Draper*	William Hamnet, *Draper.* John Harvey, *Glover.*
1563, Sir Lawrence Smith.	Hugh Rogerson, *Draper.* Gilbert Knowles, *Pewterer.*
1564, Rich. Pool, *Merchant*	Henry Leech, *Draper.* Evan de Neston, *Howster.*
1565, Thos. Green, *Tallowchandler*	Rd. Thompson, *Draper.* William Dod, *Shareman.*
1566, Sir William Sneyd ..	Wm. Bird, *Tanner.* Robert Brerewood, *Glover.*
1567, Rd. Dutton.	Edward Martin, *Draper.* Oliver Smith, *Draper.*
1568, Wm. Ball, *Glover*, ..	Edward Hanner, *Draper.* Roger Lea, *Ironmonger.*
1569, Sir John Savage	Rd. Massey, Gent. Peter Litherland, *Tanner.*
1570, Sir Lawrence Smith.	John Middleton, *Merchant.* William Styles, *Mercer.*
1571, Jno. Hankey, *Innkeep.*	Rd. Bavand, *Ironmonger.* William Ball, *Same.*
1572, Rog. Lea, *Ironmonger.*	Rd. Wright, *Draper.* Robt. Hill, *Tailor.*
1573, Rd. Dutton.	Wm. Massey, *Merchant.* Paul Chantrell, *Mercer.*
1574, Sir John Savage.	John Allen, *Draper.* Wm. Goodman, *Merchant.*
1575, Hen. Hardware, *Merchant*	William Goulbourn, Gent. David Dimmock, *Tanner.*
1576, John Hervey, *Skinner*	Thos. Lineall, *Hat-maker.* John Barnes, *Tanner.*
1577, Thos Bellin, *Mercer.*	Valentine Broughton, *Mercer* John Tilston, *Mercer.*

Mayor	Sheriffs
1578, Wm. Jewet, *Merchant*	David Montford, *Pewterer.* Randal Leech, *Merchant.*
1579, Wm. Goodman, *Merchant, Died* .. ... H. Rogerson, *Draper Succeeded.*	Robert Brooke, Gent. David Lloyd, *Draper.*
1580, Wm. Bird, *Tanner* ..	Richrad Bird, *Tanner.* Wm. Cotgreave, *Innholder.*
1581, Richd. Bavand, *Ironmonger*	Robert Wall, *Ironmonger.* John Fitton, *Same.*
1582, Wm. Stiles, *Mercer* ..	Thomas Cooper, *Draper.* Rich. Rathbone, *Merchant.*
1583, R. Brerewood, *Glover*	Thomas Fletcher, *Draper.* W Mutton, *Goldsmith, Died.* Richard Massey, *Draper, Succeeded.*
1584, Valentine Broughton, *Mercer*	William Aldersey, *Merchant.* Henry Anion, *Tanner.*
1585, Edm. Gamul, *Vintner*	Thos. Tatlow, *Merchant.* Thos. Lynaker, *Cooper.*
1586, Wm. Wall, *Ironmong.*	Rob. Amery, *Ironmonger.* Rd. Knee, *Merchant.*
1587, Robert Brerewood, *Glover*	Thos. Harbottle, *Mercer.* Jno. Williams, *Same.*
1588, Robt. Brooke, *Gent. Died.* .... Wm. Hamnet, *Draper, Succeeded*	Richard Spencer, *Gent.* William Maio, *Tanner.*
1589, William Cotgreave, *Innholder.*	Thurstan Hollinshead, *Gent.* Godfrey Wynne, *Butcher.*
1590, Wm. Massey, *Mercht.*	Jo. Ratcliff, *Beer Brewer.* John Warden, *Same.*
1591, Thos. Lyneall, *Hatter*	Ralph Allen, *Shoemaker* Richard Broster, *Tanner.*
1592, Jno. Fitton, *Ironmonger*	Peter Newell, *Merchant.* John Sise, *alias* Taylor, *Innholder.*
1593, David Lloyd, *Draper*	John Littler, *Draper.* John Francis, *Tanner.*
1594, Foulk Aldersey, *Merchant*	William Knight, Gent. *Clerk of the Pentice.* Henry Hamnet, *Draper.*
1595, Wm. Aldersey, *Merc.*	Philip Philips, *Hatter.* William Leicester, *Mercer.*
1596, Thomas Smith, Esq.	John Aldersey, *Merchant.* Rowland Barnes, *Same.*
1597, Sir John Savage, *Died* Thos. Fletcher, *Suc.*	William Throp, *Furrier.* Robert Fletcher, *Hatter.*
1598, Rich Rathbone, *Merchant.*	John Brerewood, *Glover.* Lewis Roberts, *Ironmonger.*
1599, Hen. Hardware, Esq.	John Owen, *Mercer.* John Moyle, *Draper.*
1600, Robert Brerewood, *Glover, Died* .... . Rd. Bavand, *Ironmonger, Succeeded.*	Edward Button, *Innholder.* Ed Bennett, *Shoemaker, died.* Thomas Wright, *Hatter, Succeeded.*
1601, J. Ratcliffe, *Brewer.*	Jno. Ratcliffe, jun. *Brewer.* Owen Harris, *Ironmonger.*
1602, Hugh Glaseour, Esq.	William Gamul, *Merchant.* William Johnson, *Same.*
1603, John Aldersey, *Merchant*	William Aldersey, *Same.* Wildiam Manning, *Innholder.*
1604, Edward Dutton, Esq.	Thos. Rivington, *Brewer.* Kenrick ap Evans, *Innholder.*
1605, Jno. Littler, *Draper*	Robert Blease, *Apothecary.* Thomas Harvey, *Merchant.*
1606, Phil. Phillips, *Hatter*	Thomas Throp, *Vintner.* Richard Fletcher, *Glover.*
1607, Sir John Savage	Robert Whitby, Gent. George Brooke, Gent.
1608, Wm. Gamul, *Merchant*	Edward Kitchene, *Merchant.* Robert Amery, *Ironmonger.*

Chester — History.

Year	Mayor	Sheriffs
1609,	William Leycester, *Merchant*	Charles Fitton, *Merchant.* George Harpur, *Ironmonger.*
1610,	Thos Harvey, *Merchant*	Hugh Williamson, *Mercer.* John Throp, *Tailor.*
1611,	J. Radcliffe, *Brewer*	Nicholas Ince, *Maltster.* Robert Fletcher, *Hatter.*
1612,	Robt. Whitby, Gent.	Thomas Whitby, *son of the Mayor.* Peter Drinkwater, *Ironmonger.*
1613,	Wm. Aldersey, Jun. *Merchant*	Edward Bathoe, *Clothier.* Thomas Percival, *Saddler.*
1614,	Wm. Aldersey, Sen. *Merchant*	Richd. Aldersey, *Merchant.* Robt. Bennett, *Draper.*
1615,	Thos. Throp, *Vintner.*	Randal Holme, *Painter.* Thomas Weston, *Glover.*
1616,	Ed. Button, *Innholder*	Tho. Sutton, *Innholder, Died.* Tho. Bird, *Tanner, Succeeded.* John Cooke, *Glover.*
1617,	Chas. Fitton, *Merchant.*	Foulk Salisbury, *Ironmonger.* Gilbert Eaton, *Brewer.*
1618,	Sir Randal Manwaring	John Brereton, *Innholder.* Robert Berry, *Merchant.*
1619,	Hu. Williamson, *Mercer.*	Charles Walley, *Innholder.* Thomas Ince, *Shoemaker.*
1620,	William Gamul, *Merchant*	Humphrey Lloyd, *Merchant.* William Spark, *Ironmonger.*
1621,	Robert Whitehead, Gent	William Allen, *Draper.* Richard Bridge, *Dyer.*
1622,	Sir Thomas Smith	John Williams, *Innholder.* Hugh Wicksted, *Glover.*
1623,	John Brereton, *Innkeeper*	Christopher Blease, *Merch.* William Fisher, *Innholder.*
1624,	Peter Drinkwater, *Ironmonger*	Tho. Knowles, *Ironmonger.* William Glegg, *Merchant.*
1625,	Sir Randal Manwaring	Robt. Sproston, *Haberdasher.* Robt. Harvey, *Merchant.*
1626,	Nich. Ince, *Maltster.*	Richard Bennett, *Draper.* Thos. Humphreys, *Maltster.*
1627,	Richd. Dutton, Esq.	William Edwards, *Merchant.* Thomas Aldersey, *Same.*
1628,	J. Ratcliffe, *Brewer*	Richard Leicester, *Mercer.* James Leech, *Same.*
1629,	Christ. Blease, *Merchant*	John Aldersey, *Ironmonger.* Wm. Higginson, *Innkeeper, Died.* Rob. Ince, *Draper, Succeeded.*
1630,	Chas. Walley, *Innkeeper*	Thomas Throp, *Merchant.* Thos. Cooper, *Ironmonger.*
1631,	Wm. Allen, *Draper, Died* Tho. Bird, *Succeeded.*	Richard Broster, *Tanner.* William Jones, *Linen-draper.*
1632,	Will. Spark, *Ironmonger*	William Parnell, *Merchant.* Robert Wright, *Baker.*
1633,	Rand. Holme, *Painter*	Randal Holme, *Painter, Son of the Mayor.* Richard Bird, *Merchant.*
1634,	Fran. Gamul, Gent.	William Ince, *Merchant.* Tho. Eaton, *Brewer, Died.* Edw. Evans, *Mercer, Succeed.*
1635,	Thos. Knowles, *Ironmonger,*	Thomas Crosse, *Ironmonger.* Calvin Bruin, *Same.*
1636,	Wm. Edwards, *Merchant*	Edw. Bradshaw, *Mercer.* Owen Hughes, *Merchant.*
1637,	Thos. Throp	Thomas Weston. William Wilcock.
1638,	Robert Sproston	Philip Sproson. William Drinkwater.
1639,	Robert Harvey,	Richard Bradshaw. Ralph Hulton.
1640,	Thomas Aldersey	John Whittle. Edward Hulton.
1641,	Thomas Cooper	Thomas Mottershead. Hugh Leigh.
1642,	William Ince	John Johnson. William Crompton.
1643,	Randal Holme, Jun.	William Whittell. William Bennett.
1644,	Charles Walley	Humphrey Philips. Ralph Davis, *Died.* Ran. Richardson, *Succeeded.*
1645,	The Same	*No Sheriffs this year.*
1646,	William Edwards	John Wynne. Richard Sproson.
1647,	Robt. Wright, *Died.* Edward Bradshaw, *served out the year.*	William Wright. Richard Minshull.
1648,	Richard Bradshaw,	Jonathan Ridge, Gerrard Jones.
1649,	William Crompton	Thomas Parnell. Robert Capper.
1650,	Richard Leicester	John Anderson. Thomas Heath.
1651,	Owen Hughes, *Died,* John Johnson, *served out*	Thomas Harris. Hugh Mason.
1652,	William Bennett	William Wilson. Richard Townshend.
1653,	Edward Bradshaw	Daniel Greetback. Charles Farrington.
1654,	Richard Bird,	Arthur Walley. John Griffith.
1655,	William Wright	John Witter. John Pool.
1656,	Peter Leigh,	Thomas Robinson. Ralph Burroughs.
1657,	Richard Minshull	William Street. William Bristowe.
1658,	Thomas Hand, *Died* Gerrard Jones, *Succeeded*	William Heywood. Randal Oulton.
1659,	John Johnson	Thomas Wilcock. John Knowles.
1660,	Arthur Walley	Richard Taylor. Randal Bennett.
1661,	Thomas Throp	Richard Harrison. John Hulton.
1662,	Richard Broster	John Maddocks. William King.
1663,	John Pool	Charles Leinsly. Edward Kingsey.
1664,	Richard Taylor	Robert Murray. Richard Key.
1665,	Randal Oulton	Gawen Hudson. Richard Annion.
1666,	William Street	Henry Lloyd. William Warrington.
1667,	Richard Harrison	William Harvey. Robert Caddock.
1668,	Cha. Earl of Derby	Richard Wright. John Young.
1669,	Robert Murray	Thomas Simpson. Owen Ellis.
1670,	Thomas Wilcock	William Wilme. Thomas Billington.
1671,	William Wilson	Robert Townshend, *Died.* William Wilson, *Succeeded.* Thomas Ashton.
1672,	Gawen Hudson,	George Manwaring. Benjamin Critchley.

1673, Thomas Simpson .... { William Ince, Peter Edwards.
1674, Richard Wright .... { Edward Oulton. Isaac Swift.
1675, Henry Lloyd ...... { Nathaniel Williamson. Thomas Wright.
1676, Jno. Young, *Died* ... John Maddock, *Succeeded* .... { Thomas Baker. Robert Shone.
1677, William Ince ...... { Thomas Hand. John Mottershead.
1678, William Harvey .... { Hugh Starkey. Robert Fletcher.
1679, William Wilme .... { Ralph Burrows. Francis Skellerne.
1680, John Anderson .... { John Tailor. William Starkey.
1681, Geo. Manwaring ... { Wm. Allen. Henry Bennett.
1682, Peter Edwards .... { Robt. Hewitt. William Bennett.
1683, Wm. Street, *2d time*. { John Wilme. Robt. Murray.
1684, Sir Tho. Grosvenor { Richard Harrison. John Johnson.
1685, Wm. Wilson .... { Randal Turner. Richard Oulton.
1686, Edw. Oulton .... { Puleston Partington. Nathaniel Anderton.
1687, Hugh Starkey ...... { Edw. Starkey. Jonathan Whitby.
1688, Wm. Street, *3d time*. { Robert Murray. John Coulborn.
1689, Francis Skellerne. { Edward Partington, Randal Bathoe.
1690, Nathan. Williamson. { John Warrington. Robert Dentith.
1691, Henry, Earl of Warrington .... { Thomas Maddocks. Michael Johnson.
1692, Col. Roger Whitley { Joseph Maddocks. John Burrows.
1693, The Same .... { Thomas Hand. John Kinaston.
1694, The Same .... { Arthur Bolland. Thomas Bolland.
1695, The Same .... { Timothy Dean. John Holland.
1696, Peter Bennett .... { James Mainwaring. Owen Ellis.
1697, Wm. Allen .... { Peter Edwards. William Francis.
1698, Henry Bennett .... { Thomas Parnel. Thomas Wright.
1699, William Bennett .. { Edw. Puleston. John Bradshaw.
1700, Richd. Oulton, *Died*. Hugh Starkey, *Suc.* { Humphrey Page. Thomas Bowker.
1701, Thomas Hand ...... { Wm. Allen. Wm. Coker.
1702, Wm. Earl of Derby, *Died Nov 5th*, ... Mich. Johnson, *Suc.* { John Minshull. Thomas Partington.
1703, Nat. Anderton. .... { George Bennion. John Thomason.
1704, Edw. Partington. .. { Daniel Peck. Thomas Houghton.
1705, Edw. Puleston ...... { John Stringer. Randal Holme.
1706, Puleston Partington { Thomas Davis. Francis Sayer.
1707, Humphrey Page.... { Thomas Williams. Joseph Hodgson.
1708, James Mainwaring.. { James Comberbach. Alexander Denton.
1709, Wm. Allen .... { Henry Bennett. Randal Bingley.
1710, Thomas Partington. { Hugh Colley. Edward Burroughs.
1711, Jno. Minshull .... { Thomas Edwards. Thomas Wilson.
1712, John Thomason. .... { Robert Crosby. Lawrence Gother.
1713, John Stringer. .... { John Parker. Thomas Bolland.
1714, Francis Sayer. .... { John Parker. Peter Leadbeater.
1715 Sir Rich. Grosvenor. { Wm Hughes. Thomas Brooke.
1716, Henry Bennett .... { John Pemberton. James Johnson.
1717, Joseph Hodson. .... { Trafford Massie. Geo. Johnson.
1718, Alexander Denton. { Thomas Williams. Peter Ellames.
1719, Randal Bingley .... { Wm. Johnson, *Chandler, Died*; Thomas Chalton, *Succeeded*. Thomas Bridge, *Hatter*
1720, Thomas Edwards. .. { Roger Massey, *Linen-draper*. John Cotgreave, *Same*.
1721, Thomas Wilson . .. { Nathaniel Wright, *Grocer*, John Hiccock, *Tanner*.
1722, Lawrence Gother .. { John Marsden, *Sugar Baker*. Thomas Duke, *Wet Glover*.
1723, Robert Pigot ...... { Peter Parry, *Hatter*. Chas Bingley, *Upholsterer*.
1724, John Parker, *Apothecary* .... { Edward Twambrook Sam. Jarvis, *Ribbon Weaver*.
1725, Thomas Bolland .... { Edmund Parker, *Mercer*. Arthur Mercer.
1726, John Parker, *Mercer* { James Burroughs Thomas Davis, *Clothier*.
1727, James Comberbach. { Thomas Maddock, *Goldsmith*. Thomas Gother, *Linen-draper*.
1728, William Hughes .... { Joseph Parker. Randal Bingley, *Chandler*.
1729, Thomas Brooke .... { John Francis Thos. Ravenscroft, *Tanner*.
1730, John Pemberton .... { Andrew Duke, *Wet Glover*. George Fernall.
1731, Trafford Massie .. { Henry Ridley, *Mercer*. Edw. Yearsley, *Same*.
1732, George Johnson .... { Edw. Nichols, *Apothecary*. William Edwards.
1733, Peter Ellames. .... { Ch Mytton, *Wine Merchant*. Robert Holland.
1734, Roger Massey ...... { Edw. Griffith, *Grocer*. Francis Bassano.
1735, John Cotgreave .... { William Speed, *Grocer*. Peter Potter, *Stationer*.
1736, Sir Watk. Williams Wynn .... { Thomas Bingley, *Grocer*. John Hallwood, *Same*.
1737, Sir Robert Grosvenor .... { Ralph Probert, *Hatter*. Thomas Broster, *Cutler*.
1738, Nathaniel Wright .. { John Dicas, *Chandler*. John Snow, *Weaver*.
1739, John Marsden ...... { Henry Pemberton, *Roper*. William Vizer, *Maltster*.
1740, Thomas Duke ...... { Wm. Smith, *Innholder*. Edmund Bolland, *Mercer*.

Year	Mayor	Sheriffs
1741	Charles Bingley	Edw. Partington, *Attorney.* Benjamin Peryn, *Gent.*
1742	Samuel Jarvis	R Cawley, *Watchmaker, Died.* William Cowple, *Succeeded.* John Page, *Stationer.*
1743	Thomas Davis	Benjamin Maddock, *Maltster.* John Egerton, *Brewer.*
1744	Thos. Maddock	Peter Dewsbury, *Tailor.* Rd. Richardson, *Silversmith.*
1745	Henry Ridley	George Griffiths, *Plumber.* Thos Massey, *Linen-draper.*
1746	Edw. Yearsley, *Died* Edw. Nicholls, *Suc.*	Rob. Maddock, *Linen draper.* Thos Bridge, *Hatter.*
1747	Wm. Edwards	Thomas Cotgreave, *Linen-draper.* Edw. Walley, *Hatter.*
1748	Edw. Griffith.	John Lawton, *Innholder.* Peter Ellames, *Druggist.*
1749	Thomas Bingley	Charles Parry, *Hatter.* Hen. Hesketh, *Wine Merch.*
1750	John Hallwood	John Dicas, *Barber.* Holmes Burrows, *Cutler.*
1751	Ralph Probert	John Hickcock, *Tanner.* James Briscoe, *Died.* John Bridge, *Succeeded.*
1752	Thomas Broster	Edward Burrows, *Hatter.* Thomas Hart, *Innholder.*
1753	Edm. Bolland	Rich. Ollerhead, *Apothecary.* Richard Ledsham, *Same.*
1754	Dr. Wm. Cowper	Thomas Astle, *Cabinet maker* John Kelsall, *Attorney.*
1755	John Page, Esq.	Charles Boswell, *Brewer.* Joseph Wilkinson, *Baker.*
1756	Peter Dewsbury.	John Johnson, *Plumber.* Geo. French, *Toy Man.*
1757	Richard Richardson	Tho. Craven, *Grocer.* Robt. Lloyd.
1758	Thomas Cotgreave	Thomas Randles, *Grocer.* John Lawton, *Stationer.*
1759	Sir Rd. Grosvenor	Thomas Slaughter, Esq. Peter Morgan, Esq.
1760	Th. Grosvenor, Esq.	Thos. Marsden, *Sugar-baker.* Samuel Dob, Gent.
1761	Tho. Cholmondeley, Esq.	Joseph Dyson, *Wine Merch.* Joseph Crewe, *Apothecary.*
1762	Henry Hesketh	William Dicas, *Barber.* John Drake, *Mercer.*
1763	Holmes Burrows,	Thomas Griffith, *Grocer.* Jno. Thomas, *Brazier.*
1764	Ed. Burrows, *Hatter.*	James Broadhurst, *Apothecary.* Francis Walley, *Hatter.*
1765	Richard Ollerhead.	Daniel Smith, *Innholder.* John Hart, *Same*
1766	Thomas Astle	Thomas Bowers, *Linen-drap.* William Seller, *Brewer.*
1767	Thomas Kelsall	Robt. Williams, *Skinner.* Gabr. Smith, *Watch-maker.*
1768	Charles Boswell	Joseph Snow, *Wine Merchant.* Pattison Ellames, *Druggist.*
1769	Geo. French.	Thomas Powell, *Upholsterer.* Thos. Amery, *Linen-draper.*
1770	John Lawton.	Henry Hegg, *Druggist.* John Bennett, *Wine Merch.*
1771	Henry Vigars	John Dimmock Griffiths. Thos. Edwards, *Grocer.*
1772	Joseph Crewe	John Hallwood, *Grocer.* Thomas Lea, *Tobacconist.*
1773	Sir Watk. Williams Wynn	Edw. Orme, *Organist.* Wm. Turner, *Tanner, Died.* T. Roberts, *Grocer, Succeed.*
1774	Joseph Dyson	Richard Ledsham, *Carpenter.* William Corles, *Skinner.*
1775	Thomas Griffith	Thomas Patton, *Merchant.* John Chamberlain, *Same.*
1776	James Broadhurst.	John Monk, *Printer.* Peter Broster, *Stationer.*
1777	John Hart.	John Wright, *Tanner.* George Johnson, *Apothecary.*
1778	William Seller	Thomas Richards. Charles Francis, *Clothier.*
1779	Gabriel Smith	William Birch, *Clothier.* George Binglay, *Glazier.*
1780	Joseph Snow	William Harrison, *Grocer.* Thomas Barnes, *Plumber.*
1781	Pattison Ellames	Rowland Jones, *Saddler.* John Bramwell, Gent.
1782	Thomas Patton	Joseph Turner, *Architect.* Samuel Bromfield, *Cutler.*
1783	Thomas Amery	Cotton Probert, *Hatter.* Daniel Smith, *Merchant.*
1784	Henry Hegg.	John Meacock, *Linen-draper.* Rd. Richardson, *Silversmith.*
1785	John Bennett	Jno. Larden, *Woollen-draper.* Thomas Jones, *Grocer.*
1786	Thomas Edwards	Charles Panton, *Banker.* Edmund Bushell, *Mercer.*
1787	John Hallwood	Nath. Dewsbury, *Hatter.* William Edwards, *Grocer.*
1788	John Leigh, Esq	Andr. Davison, *Wine Merch.* Thomas Bennion, *Chandler.*
1789	R. H. Vaughan, Esq.	Robert Whittell, *Roper.* Joseph Wright, *Died.* John Troughton, *Succeeded.*
1790	Thomas Powell	T. Rathbone, *Timber Merch.* John Hassall, *Wine Merch.*
1791	Peter Broster.	Roger Dutton, *Grocer.* Thomas Jenkins, *Tanner.*
1792	John Wright	Jno. Johnson, *Cabinet-maker.* Pet. Wilkinson, *Apothecary.*
1793	Thomas Richards	Wm. Seller, *Brewer.* John Thomas, *Chandler.*
1794	George Bingley	Samuel Barnes, *Plumber.* William Newell, *Brewer.*
1795	William Harrison	Thomas Evans, *Druggist.* Robert Brittain, *Clothier.*
1796	Thos. Barnes	Fr. Woods, *Tin-plate-Worker.* John Bakewell, *Druggist.*
1797	Rowland Jones,	Thomas Griffith, *Mercer.* John Webster, *Grocer.*
1798	John Bramwell	Robert Bowers, *Silversmith.* Sam. Bennett, *Wine Merch.*
1799	Daniel Smith	John Bedward, *Carpenter.* John Harrison, *Grocer.*
1800	John Meacock	John Cotgreave, Esq. Robert Williams, *Grocer.*
1801	John Larden.	Joseph Bage, *Paper-maker.* Thomas Francis, *Clothier.*
1802	Robt Hodgson, Esq.	Henry Bowers, *Druggist.* Tho. Bradford, *Linen draper.*
1803	Edmund Bushell	John Tomlinson, *Apothecary.* Thomas Richards, *Tanner.*
1804	Wm. Edwards	John Powell, *Upholsterer.* John Williamson, *Carpenter.*
1805	Tho. Bennion	Thomas Poole, *Bookseller.* Jno. Swar. Rogers, *Skinner.*
1806	Thos. Rathbone	Timothy Whitby, Gent. James Bennett, *Druggist.*
1807	Robert Earl Grosvenor	Joseph Johnson, *Wine Merch.* Jo. Stewart Hughes, *Merch.*
1808	William Newel	Joseph Hornby, *Linen-draper.* Wm. Cortney, *Ship-builder.*

Mayor	Sheriffs
1809, THOS. EVANS	WM. MASSEY, *Druggist.* JOSEPH GRACE, *Grocer.*
1810, GEN. THOMAS GROSVENOR	WM MOSS, *Merchant.* ROBT. MORRIS, *Painter.*
1811, ROBERT BOWERS	GEORGE HARRISON, *Ironfounder.* JAMES SNAPE, *Brewer.*
1812, SAMUEL BENNETT	JOSIAH THOMAS, *Druggist.* SAML. NEVETT BENNETT, *Surgeon.*
1813, SIR WATK. WILLIAMS WYNN	JOHN FLETCHER, *Printer.* GEO. HASTINGS, *Brazier.*
1814, JOHN BEDWARD	THOS. DIXON, *Banker.* TITUS CHALONER, *Currier.*
1815, JOHN COTGREAVE*	RD. BUCKLEY, *Wine Merchant.* GEO. HARRISON, *Surgeon.*
1816, THOS. FRANCIS	THOS. BAGNALL, *Surgeon.* WM. GAMAN, *Brewer.*
1817, H. BOWERS, *Druggist.*	JOHN MELLOR, *Plumber.* THOMAS WHITTELL, *Roper.*

THE CORPORATION OF CHESTER

Consists of twenty-four Aldermen, and forty Common Councilmen, from whom the Mayor, the Recorder, two Coroners, Treasurers, Murenger,† Leave Lookers, and two Sheriffs, are chosen.

It was formerly the duty of the MURENGER to receive the duties granted on imports, which were appropriated to the repair of the Walls, and to superintend their repair. This office, however, is likely to become a perfect sinecure, as the money received for that purpose, as Murage duty, is trifling indeed. The failure of this particular branch of the local revenue, may be attributed to the almost entire extinction of the Irish linen trade, and the falling off in the two great fairs in July and October.

The LEAVE-LOOKERS is a very ancient office, and is supposed to have succeeded to the first civic office known to have existed in Chester, which was called the "*Keeper of the Guild Mercatorial.*" Their duty is to prevent infringements on the rights of the Citizens, by strangers exercising any trades within the liberties—to examine the markets;‡ and receive all customs, &c. due to the Corporation.

The MAYOR has as ample a Civic *Staff* as any similar officer in the kingdom. He has Courts of CROWN MOTE and PORT MOTE,‖ which give him the privilege of trying all criminals excepting traitors—and of determining civil actions. The Courts are held "before the Mayor and Recorder;" the former presides, but the latter passes sentence of death, and may respite at pleasure. In the Port Mote Court, recoveries for landed assurance, are suffered by plaint, without writ.—The jurisdiction of these Courts extends throughout the liberties of the City, and on the River Dee from Arnold's eye, opposite the Castle of Chester, to the Red Stones, near Hoylake, so far as high water mark.§

There is another Court, called the PENTICE COURT, which is held before the Sheriffs, and although the date of its first roll is 1282, five years subsequent to the roll of the Crown Mote and Port Mote Courts, it is considered to be of greater antiquity than either of them. This Court, by custom, has cognizance by plaint of all personal actions to any amount. Suits of this Court may be removed to the Port-mote Court by order of the Mayor, or petition of suitors, but it has no jurisdiction on the River Dee. All causes brought to issue in this Court, may be tried in the PASSAGE COURT, the origin of which at this period it would be difficult, if not impossible, to trace. It is certain, however, that trials for petty assaults and misdemeanors, were heard in it. The City Sessions are held four times in each year; these sittings took place so early as the year 1347.

Attached to the office of Sheriff, is a very disagreeable duty:—that of executing all criminals, as well those tried in the County Court, as in the City Court. On the day appointed for an Execution, the Sheriffs, ac-

* Knighted during his Mayoralty, on presenting an Address to the Prince Regent, on the Marriage of the lamented Princess Charlotte to the Prince Leopold of Saxe Cobourg.

† Formerly the senior Alderman.

‡ The Mayor, in the strict execution o his office, is Clerk of the Markets.

‖ The first roll of these Courts, bears the date 1277, and they are at THAT early period noticed as having been held from time immemorial.

§ The jurisdiction of the City Coroner is precisely the same.

CHESTER. companied by their Bailiffs, and the Town Clerk, on horseback, and the Constables, proceed through the City to the verge of the Castle wall, called Glover's-stone.* Here the cavalcade halt, and one of the Bailiffs goes forward to the Constable of the Castle, to demand the body of the convict. The Constable then brings out his prisoner, under a military guard;† and at Glover's-stone, he is delivered to the Sheriffs.—Being placed in a cart, the horse led by the Executioner, the procession returns to the City Gaol—on a drop, at the back part of which, the Execution takes place ‡

The present mode of electing the Members of the Body Corporate, is nearly the same as that prescribed by the Charter of Henry VII. with the exception of the nomination of the first Sheriff by the Mayor, the filling up Corporate vacancies by the Aldermen and Common Council, instead of by popular election, annually, by the Citizens—and the general election of the whole body annually, also by the Citizens. In addition to these exceptions, the Recorder and Town Clerk are now chosen by the Mayor, Aldermen, and Common Council, as are the subordinate officers of the Body Corporate. This variation from the provisions of the Charter of Hen. VII.‖ has at different periods given rise to much litigation.—So early as 1572, the Citizens attempted to establish HISTORY.

* There was formerly a stone of immense size here; and tradition says, it was used by the Glovers, to dress their leather: and hence the name "*Glover's-stone.*"

† First employed, we believe, in 1812, at the Execution of Temple and Thompson, for rioting (See p. 43). Since that period, a sergeant's guard, has usually attended. There certainly is no necessity for a military guard in the city, and the propriety of their attendance on such an occasion may be questioned.

‡ The bodies of executed criminals are generally interred in the Castle-ditch, beneath the wall of St. Mary's Church-yard, at the south-west corner.—For centuries, previous to 1801, Boughton was the place of execution, and in the old maps of Chester, the south-side of the road is marked as the site of the Gallows. The later executions, however, took place on the north-side of the road. The last convicts executed here were Thompson, Morgan, and Clare, on the 9th May, 1801. On this occasion, when the cart had arrived at the hill, on a line with a drain that carried the water from that part of the town into the river, Clare made a sudden spring from it, and rolling down the hill, with his irons on, precipitated himself into the river. It did not appear that he had any wish to escape, as he immediately threw himself over head, and was speedily drowned. He had previously declared he was not born to be hung: however, the execution of Thompson and Morgan was postponed till the body was found, and they were all hung up together! After this, on the 3d of October following, Gee and Gibson, for burglary, were executed at the south front of the Northgate (since taken down) on a machine which obtained the name of THE DRAG. Its construction was clumsy, and no respect had for decency in carrying the awful sentence of the law into effect; for on the signal being given by the unfortunate men, they were propelled from the aperture of a large window, forty feet from the level of the street; the rope having a run of about twenty inches, and their bodies beating against the walls and the windows below, in a truly frightful manner. On the drop being first erected in its present situation behind the City Gaol, it was customary to encircle the scaffold with black curtains, which were closed till the convict were tied to the fatal beam. Of course the executioner could not be seen. An order of the Judges afterwards prevented the use of the curtains, and the execution is now public.

‖ In a document amongst the Corporation records, which appears to have been a Return to a Quo Warranto against the Citizens under the statute of 6th Edw. I. A. D. 1278,—the Constitution of the City is thus stated:—"The Maior and Citizens of the Citty of Chester clayme to have liberties under written, that is to say, that the citty of Chester be a free Citty; and that the Citizens may chuse to them a Maior of themselves from year to year, the Friday next after the Feast of St. Denyse, which shall make his oath to keep the laws of our Sovereign Lord the Prince, and the liberties and laws of the citty aforesaid. And also that they may chuse to them two Sheriffs of themselves, the day aforesaid, which in manner aforesaid the execution and commandments of the said Earl of Chester, and of the Maior and Citizens of Chester, truly shall do by their oaths, and to have *Gildam Mercalem* in the citty aforesaid, and to have free Court of Port-mote in the citty aforesaid, of all quarrels growing within the citty aforesaid to be tried, (that is to say) to have pleas of lands and tenements, and of repleven growing by plaint, in the Port-mote, or writ and pleas of dower in a writ of right, which in the aforesaid Port-mote by writ original ought to be served. And all other pleas to be holden in the Pentice of the citty aforesaid afore the Sheriff there; and to have two fairs by the year, one by a whole week next before the feast of the Nativity of St. John Baptist, and on the day of the same Feast; and one week next following: and another fair by one week next afore St. Michael, and on one week next following And two markets every week, that is to say the Wednesday and the Saturday. And whatsoever to any fair or market belongeth."—The whole of these franchises are, in effect, now enjoyed.

CHESTER HISTORY.

the Charter of Henry, the old mode of election then being in use, sanctioned by a bye-law of the Body Corporate, made in 1518: but they did not succeed. In 1693, Roger Whitley being then Mayor, he consented to the election by the popular voice, and it would appear it was acted upon till 1698, when the old mode was again introduced, and confirmed by a General Assembly; the votes being Yeas 36, Noes 3.

In the year 1733, a *Quo Warranto* was brought, to try the question as to the mode of election. The trial took place in the County Court of Cheshire, on the 28th March, in the same year, before the Hon. Mr. Verney, Chief Justice, and a Special Jury. The hearing was very long, and the following issues were found: 1st that on the 20th day of April, the 10th Henry VIII. at the city of Chester, at an Assembly of the Mayor Sheriffs, Aldermen, and Common Council, and the rest of the Citizens of the said City, then and there had in the Common Hall of the said City, being then and there assembled and met together, they did make and constitute an ordinance or bye law, whereby it was ordained and directed, that as often it should happen, one or more of the Aldermen of the said City, should die, or be amoved from his or their office or offices, or places of Aldermen of the said City, that then and so often the Mayor, and the residue of the Aldermen and the Common Council of the said City, or the major part of them, immediately after the death or amoval of such Alderman or Aldermen, *should* and *might*, without any hindrance or contradiction, assemble and meet together, in the same Common Hall, and that they so assembled, or the major part of them, *should* and *might* elect and prefer one or more, as the case should require, of their Fellow Citizens of the said City, to be Alderman or Aldermen, in the place or places of him or them, so dead or amoved, as the said George Johnstone* and others, the Defendants, have by their plea, alleged. 2d issue,—That the Ordinance or Bye Law within mentioned to be made, doth remain in force, as the said George Johnstone and others, the Defendants, have by their plea alleged. 3d issue,—That the within-mentioned Mayor and Citizens of the said City of Chester, did not accept and agree to the Letters Patent of the late King Charles II. as by the same Information is alleged. 4th issue,—That the within-mentioned Mayor and Citizens of the said City of Chester, have not conformed themselves to the said Letters Patent, &c. as by the said Information is alleged.—5th issue,—That the said Robt. Pigott, and others, as Aldermen of the said City, and Nathaniel Wright, and seventeen others, as Common Council of the said City, after the determination of the Mayoralty of the said George Johnstone, did not use and exercise the liberty and privilege of franchise, of nominating, electing, and choosing Aldermen of the City, exclusive of the Freemen, of the said Information, as is also alleged by the said Information." With this Verdict the Citizens acquiesced.

In 1747, however, at the Election for Representatives, circumstances occured, which interrupted the previous quiescent state of the City. At this Election, Sir Robt. Grosvenor, Bart. James Mainwaring, and Philip Henry Warburton, Esqrs. were candidates, and Sir Robert and Mr. Warburton were returned; but on the Meeting of the New Parliament, a Petition was presented to the House, signed by several hundreds of the Citizens, in the interest of Mr. Mainwaring, stating, "That the said James Mainwaring had an undoubted majority of legal votes of the said Mr. Hen. Warburton, and ought to have been returned accordingly, but that by the indirect and illegal practices of the said Mr. Warburton, his friends, and agents, and by the partial and unjust proceedings of the returning officers, the said Mr. Hen. Warburton, and not the said Mr. Mainwaring, was with the said Sir Robert Grosvenor, returned, in prejudice to the rights of the Petitioners, and others the Electors of the said City, and to the manifest wrong of the said Mr. Mainwaring." In consequence of this petition, the Speaker issued his warrant for the production of such of

* In the Michaelmas Term of 1732, an Information was moved for in the Court of King's Bench, against Geo. Johnstone, then Mayor, Robert Pigott, and nine other Aldermen, and Nathaniel Wright, and seventeen other of the Common Council, being the whole of the Select Body, to know by what warrant they claimed to use and exercise the right of electing the Aldermen, and Common Council, in exclusion of the Citizens. This is the case as tried before Mr. Justice Verney, and now under notice.

CHESTER

the City Records as should be wanted, in the investigation of Mr. Mainwaring's case.* A slight sketch of the proceedings shall be here introduced: The Petition was heard before the whole House, and the Petitioners' Counsel argued, that the right of election lay in such Citizens only as are inhabitants within the City or liberties,† and that had been admitted to their freedom by birth or servitude, not receiving parochial relief, &c.—This position was denied by the Counsel for Mr. Warburton, who insisted that the right of Election was in the freemen at large. The Charter of Henry VII. was then produced, to prove, that the commorant Citizens only were the Electors, as were also the subsequent Charters and Letters Patent confirmatory thereof. The House then divided on the motion, that Wm. Wall, who was a non-resident freeman, should be examined.—Ayes 160, Noes 103.—Adjourned for a week.—On the next sitting, Wall and several other witnesses were examined on the part of the Petitioners, as to the right of election by commorant citizens only; when the Counsel for the sitting member proposed to prove, and the Petitioners' Counsel admitted, that many of the persons who had polled at preceding elections, were not commorant, and also, that several honorary members, and non-resident freemen, had been elected into the offices of Mayor and Sheriffs, and had voted in elections of Mayor and Sheriffs. These and other admissions of minor import being made by the Petitioners, Counsel, the House resolved, on a division, Ayes 141, Noes 92, "That the right of election of Citizens to serve in parliament, for the City of Chester, is in the Mayor, Aldermen, and Common Council of the said City, and in such of the Freemen of the said City not receiving alms, as shall have been commorant within the said City, or the liberties thereof, for the space of one whole year next before the election of Citizens to serve in Parliament for the said City."—It is worthy of notice, that on this decision, the Petitioners' Counsel acquainted the House, "That the House having come to the said Resolution, they were instructed to say, that the Petitioners would give the House no further trouble."—Mr. Warburton was of course declared to be duly elected.‡

HISTORY.

In 1784, the Corporation had another successful trial at Shrewsbury, where they grounded their right on the Charter of Charles II. but the House of Lords afterwards determined, that this Charter, from its having been disused soon after it was granted, and only partially acted upon subsequently, could not be considered as accepted. But the Corporation, nevertheless, relying on

* This warrant produced the following Order of Assembly, of the 7th December, 1747, in which, after reciting the Speaker's Warrant, it proceeds, "It was Ordered, that the said Charters, should be produced under the care and inspection of the Mayor, the Recorder, and Aldermen Parker and Brock; and should be sent up and brought to London, &c. under the care of Thomas Lloyd, Town Clerk, or his Deputy, and such other Members of the House as the Mayor, Recorder, Aldermen, &c. should depute, &c."

† At this Election 834 non-residents polled:—for Mr. Mainwaring 183; Mr. Warburton 318; Sir Robert Grosvenor 333.

‡ The Election of Members of Parliament has ever since been governed by this Order of the House.—By an Act of the 26th Geo. II. 1753, it is recited, that within the City of Chester the usual and accustomed time of the Annual Meeting and Assembly of the Citizens of the said City, for the Election of the Mayor, Sheriffs, Treasurers, Coroners and Leavelookers, hath been on Friday next after the Feast of St. Denis yearly; and taking notice that by the Act for altering the style, the Annual Fair of Chester, commonly called Michaelmas Fair, would hereafter begin to be holden and kept on the 10th day of October yearly, which is the day next after the Feast of St. Denis, by which means the Friday next after the said Feast will always hereafter happen during the time of holding and keeping the said Fair, and therefore it would be very inconvenient to the Citizens of the said City of Chester, if the Annual Meeting and Assembly of the said Citizens, for the Election of Mayor, and the aforesaid other Annual Officers of the said City, should continue to be holden on the Friday after the Feast of St Denis: For preventing which, it is enacted, that the Annual Meeting and Assembly of the said Citizens for the Election of Mayor and other Officers, shall not at any time hereafter be holden on the Friday next after the said Feast of St. Denis, but the same and all Annual Meetings and Assemblies for that purpose, shall at all times hereafter be holden in the usual and accustomed manner, on the Friday next after the 20th day of October, in every year, and not before, any thing in the said recited Act of Parliament, or any Law, Statute, Charter, Custom, or Usage to the contrary notwithstanding.—Several instances have occurred, in which the Election for Mayor has taken place by popular poll, in direct opposition to the Charter of Charles II. which authorises such Election to be by the Mayor, Aldermen, and Common Council.

the validity of their bye-laws, and ancient custom, confirmed in 1735, continued to elect their own Members till 1813; when the Mayor, S. Bennett, Esq. in compliance with a requisition, numerously signed, called a Meeting of the Citizens at large, and proceeded to elect Members of the Corporation under the provisions of the Charter of Henry VII. The Recorder and most of the Aldermen, also, proceeded to the Election of Civic Officers in the usual way, at the same time and place, by which Chester exhibitted the singular spectacle of two Corporate Bodies, *each* claiming to be the Corporation of Chester!* The New Corporation, however, did not act in its Civic and Judicial capacity, although its Mayor, Wm. Seller, Esq. walked the Markets on the next Market Day. This state of things could not be expected to last, and the question of Election was again sent to Shrewsbury for discussion. The trial came on, on Saturday the 26th of March, 1814, when the election of an Alderman† of the New Corporation,‡ was declared null, not on the general question of the Charter, but on account of insufficiency of notice of the election, and other less material irregularities.—Other trials, were in preparation, particularly that of the legality of Sir W. W. Wynn's election; but a very heavy expense attended this first essay, and this, and other considerations, induced the parties to compromise. It was accordingly agreed, that each party should pay their own costs; and that the Old Corporation should enjoy full authority—the old mode of election in which is still followed.

The modes of Election of the Body Corporate, have been various, as before noticed.

The tenure of the City of Chester, previous to the grant by Henry VII. of the Charter, called the *Great Charter*, may be thus stated in the abstract:—The Mayor, Sheriffs, Citizens, and Commonalty of the City, had anciently holden the said City from the King and his predecessors, Earls of Chester, at and under the fee-farm rent of £100. annually payable; but in consequence of the decayed state of the haven, the King|| for services rendered by the Citizens, &c. did for himself, his heirs, and successors, Kings of England or Earls of

HISTORY

|| Hen. VII.

---

* It is worthy of remark, that both the Old and New Corporations proceeded to the Cathedral Church, in procession, on the Sunday after their election, where a sermon was preached before them by the Bishop (Dr. Law). As this was a trial of party, the friends of both Corporations attended, accompanied by an immense multitude.

† Edw. Mainwaring, Esq.

‡ It may not be improper here to introduce the names of those composing the New Corporation. Those marked (*), were Members of the Old Corporation:—

THE NEW CORPORATION,

Elected by S. Bennett, Esq. Mayor, Oct. 1813.

THE RIGHT WORSHIPFUL WM. SELLER, ESQ. MAYOR.

HUGH LEYCESTER, ESQ. Recorder.

JOHN LOWE, and THOS. WHITTLE, Coroners and Treasurers.

EDW. ROBERTS and JOHN HASSALL, Sheriffs.

RICHD. WARRE LLOYD, and WM. GORST, Leave-lookers.

Aldermen.

Hugh Leycester*	Thomas Rathbone*
Joseph Dyson*	William Newell*
John Hallwood*	Thomas Evans*
Andrew Davison*	Samuel Bennett*
Peter Broster*	Robert Brittain*
John Wright*	James Bennett*
Earl Grosvenor*	Wm. Seller*
Robert Hodgson*	Edw. Omm. Wrench
John Larden*	Edw. Mainwaring
R. E. D. Grosvenor*	William Massey.
Daniel Smith*.	Thomas Hodson.

Common Council Men.

Richard Richardson*	Edw. Titley
John Chamberlaine*	John Moulson
Thomas Poole*	John Broster*
Josiah Thomas*	John Powell*
John S. Rogers*	John Griffith
Thomas Moulson	W. O. Roberts
John Edwards	Thomas Whittle
Robert Whittle	J. Williamson, builder*
John Troughton*	John S. Hughes*
Robert Brittain*	Thomas Whittakers
William Bage	John Walker
William Coker	John Bradford*
Thomas Francis*	William Cortney*
J. Williamson, distiller	William Moss*
Henry Bowers*	Joseph Grace*
Thos. Cholmondeley*	William Massey*
John Dodd	Thomas Bradford*
William Cole	Thos. Barnes.

CHESTER

Chester, release the then Mayor, Sheriffs, Citizens, and Commonalty (or by whatsoever name they were known) £80. annually for ever from the said fee-farm of £100. so that the said Mayor, &c. and their successors, should from henceforth for ever, have and hold the said city from his said Majesty, his heirs, &c Earls of Chester, rendering to his said Majesty, &c. £20. only per ann. at the Feast of Easter, and St. Michael, by equal payments. And his said Majesty did, of his especial grace, ratify and confirm to the said then Mayor, &c. and their successors, the said city, with all liberties, franchises, advantages, and customs whatsoever, which they ever fairly and peaceably held or used in the time of any of his predecessors, Kings of England or Earls of Chester, or granted or confirmed to the said Citizens or their predecessors by his said Majesty, &c.—But the same King, Hen. VII. in the 21st year of his reign, granted another Charter—the *Great Charter,*—by which the City, severed from the shire, was made a county of itself: and the Mayor and Citizens had full power to elect annually a Mayor, who by virtue of his office was also Escheator and Clerk of the Market; 24 Aldermen, including the Mayor as one; and 40 Common Councilmen, of which number the Select Body continues to the present day. Also, two Sheriffs, two Coroners, two Murengers, or Supervisors of the Walls, two Treasurers, and two Leavelookers. This Charter was acted upon, no doubt, for it appears from an ancient Book of the
* 1517. 7th Henry VIII.* containing a list of the officers of that year, that the Aldermen were annually elected.†

HISTORY.

‡ 20th April 10th Henry VIII.

The bye-law‡ authorising the election by the Members of the Select Body, is thus noticed in the Corporation books:—"The said Mayor, Sheriffs, Aldermen, Common Council, and the rest of the Citizens of the said City, being then and there so assembled and met together for the better government and order of the said City, and for the avoiding of popular disorder and confusion, did make and constitute a certain ordinance, or bye-law, in writing, for the common benefit and utility of the Citizens of the said city, whereby it was ordained and directed, that as often as it should happen, one or more of the Aldermen should die, or be amoved from his or their office, &c. that then and so often the Mayor, the residue of the Aldermen, and the Common Council, or the major part of them, immediately after the death or amoval of such Alderman, should and might, without any hindrance or contradiction, assemble and meet together in the said Common Hall, and that they so assembled, or the major part of them, should and might elect and prefer, one or more (as the case should require) of the Fellow Citizens of the said City, to be Alderman or Aldermen, in the place or places of him or them so dead or amoved."

It is believed that the documents copied in the note, are the bye-laws, on which the Select Body acted, in taking upon themselves the Election of Aldermen and Common Councilmen: the oddity of the style in which they are composed, render them curiosities not unworthy of introduction.||

† The entry runs thus:—"Nomina viginti quatuor Aldermannos infra Civitatem Cestriæ tempore Thoma Smyth, sen. Majoris Civitatis illius: Thoma Smyth, jun. mercatoris; et Roberto Wright, vicecomitum ejusdem Civitatis die Venoris prox post festum Sancte Dionisq. anno regni Regis Henrici viij. post Conquestum Anglice Septimo usq. idem festum, tunc proximo sequentem, viz. unum annum integrum."—Here follow the names of nineteen Aldermen, including the Mayor. On the other side of the leaf in the same book, are the names of the Members of the Common Council. In the next page is this entry:—"Eastgate-street, nomina v civium de comũni consilio civitat. Cest."—After this are inserted eight names; and eight also under the head Bridge-street.

|| Amongst the Corporation Records are the two following bye-laws, entered amongst the Orders of Assembly:—"And whereas there should always be forty Common Counsellors of this City, and that when any of them fortune to die, there should be other of the saddest and most substantial Commons of the City, newly chosen in their place, which many times heretofore have been appointed and sworn by the Mayor only, without consent of his Brethren, whereby the sad and discreet Councel of the City, hath been sore decayed and greatly minished, by reason that the Mayor oftentimes hath for favor and affection, taken in such persons as have lacked convenient qualities for the same; be it therefore enacted, for the establishment and obtaining a sad and substantial Councel, to be had and continued, that from henceforth, all such persons as shall want of the said number of forty, shall be always chosen by the *Mayor, Aldermen, and the residue of the Common Council, within their Council-house at the Pentice*, of such wise, discreet and able Commons as by them shall be thought most convenient to supply the rooms that were void for the wealth and sad ordering of the City," &c.

"Whereas, the charges and expenses sustained by such as of

CHESTER

*37th Hen. VIII.

The Charter of Henry VII. was by no means perfect in its provisions; for we find, that in May, 1546,* William Howcroft, the then Mayor dying, and there being no provision by the Charter, for electing a successor, until the return of the ensuing Charter-day,† application was made to the King in Counsel, to help the City out of the dilemma: accordingly, a Royal order was made, "That on the 11th June two Citizens, discreet and honourable personages, of the twenty-four Aldermen, neither of which hath been Mayor or Sheriffs, by the space of three years before the said Election, shall be chosen, to be Mayor, by the greater part of the said Aldermen and Sheriffs; and, if there be an equality of votes in such election, then the voice of the eldest Alderman present shall be taken for two voices, and be shall administer to the Mayor then elected, the oath and charge—such Mayor to continue in office until a New Mayor be elected at the time specified in the letters patent, &c."‡

HISTORY.

‖ 5th Eliz.

In 1563,‖ a Quo Warranto was exhibited in the Court of Exchequer, by the Queen's Serjeant there, against the Mayor and Select Body, to shew by what Warrant they claimed to elect the Aldermen by the Mayor and Common Council, without the commonalty, contrary to the Charter. But the Earl of Leicester, then Chamberlain, declining to make any order therein, and referring the parties to decide the question by course of law, it does not appear any further proceedings were then had on the subject. Four years

---

late years have been called, and be called to bear the office of Mayor, within this City, is in all respects grown to be more by three or four parts than was accustomable used to be spent in that office, forty years past, so that as small charge that hath been at that time to have borne the charge of that office three or four times, as now once. And whereas, partly by the unableness and decay of such as be chosen to the rooms of Aldermen, there is such want of able persons to supply that place, as the Commons have at their yearly election purposed by their advices to have placed in such as personally have officiated in the office of Mayoraltie, which if that had so happened, had not been unlike, but to have brought him so chosen to great decay, lessening of his trade, and diminishing of his countenance. And whereas also, it hath been doubtful whether one chosen to be Alderman, might freely give another his room, or for just and lawful cause by the Mayor and Common Councel be displaced, in that the words of the Charter be, that *he the same may bear the name of Alderman for ever.* And whereas also, many being well able, have threatened that at the time of the election, if he should be so chosen, he would refuse the office, which if done at that time, might as well procure trouble as also doubtfulness of a new election: Therefore, and, in the providing of condign remedy, for all the premises, it is at this Assembly, holden the day and year above written,§—Ordered and decreed *by the Mayor, Aldermen, Sheriffs, and Common Councel* of the said City, in manner and form following: First, for the better preservation and saving of the countenance of the estate of such as have carried the office of Mayor, and to reduce the order and manner of calling to that office, to the like order as is used in London, and other good Cities, that is, not to call any that have borne the office to his double charges, oftentimes to bear the same, so long as there shall remain any of the Aldermen that have not been Mayors. It is ordered, that every year upon the Election-day, the Mayor, or Recorder, before they proceed to any new Election, shall rehearse and declare to the whole Commons the names of all the Aldermen that are of ability to be Mayors, and will then proceed out of these to the naming of two, *in as much as the words of the Charter cannot otherwise well be understood, purporting that they shall name two of the most sufficient, discreet, and honourable persons of the number of the twenty-four Aldermen:* that such are to be reputed of those that before had not borne that office oftentimes when amongst them; the most able to all respects is chosen, until one better able shall happen, he shall be continually chosen.

§ May 30, 1567.

"And that it is further ordered, that all such as be chosen, or shall be chosen Aldermen of this City, shall *be reputed and taken for Aldermen for and during their lives,* except they, or any of them shall of worthy cause, by the Mayor and Common Councel of this City, in open Assembly, be discharged, or that they, or any of them, shall for their inability, or that they be determined during their lives to dwell out of this City, make request to the Mayor, and Common Councel of this City, to give over their room and name of Alderman, and request that one more may be chosen. And if upon any such request, the Mayor and Common Councel, in open Assembly, shall consent and think meet, the person so worthy of displacement, for any of the respects aforesaid, that then it is *Ordered, that the Mayor, Sheriffs, and Common Councel, shall and may not only take order for his and their displacement, so requesting the same, but also proceed to Election for another to be chosen in his place and stead, so resigning or displaced.* And he so newly chosen, to be reputed and taken as one of the Company of the twenty-four Aldermen.

† Friday next after the Feast of St. Denis.

‡ This Decree, by an application from the Citizens, was exemplified under the Great Seal, on the 4th June, 1547, and is now amongst the Records.

CHESTER. • 19th Eliz. 1567.

afterwards, however, in the Mayoralty of Sir William Sneyd,* William Ball was elected Alderman by the commonalty at large, convened for that purpose by Order of Assembly.

In 1573, in the Mayoralty of Roger Lea, another information was exhibited in the Exchequer, founded on the infraction of the Charter, by the Election, by the Select Body, instead of by the Citizens at large. The proceedings in this case, cannot now be obtained; but it is probable, as the Body expressed their determination to defend themselves by Law, that the inquiry was hushed up.

Queen Elizabeth (ann. reg. 16.) granted a Confirmatory Charter, in which, the additional power of electing Mayor and Sheriffs, in case of death, was introduced and established; and to cover the expense incurred, in obtaining this Charter, a rate was levied on the Citizens.

In Feb. 1662, a Commission, under the Great Seal was issued to Charles Earl of Derby, and 19 other Commissioners, in pursuance of the Act of the 13th Charles II. "For the well governing and regulating of Corporations, empowering them to execute the powers therein contained, as to the City of Chester."—The Commissioners met on the 26th August, and discharged such of the Members of the Body Corporate as refused to take the Oath of Allegiance and Supremacy, placing others in their room, without the assent or concurrence of the Body, pursuant to the provisions of the Act.

In 1664, the King granted a Charter to the Mayor and Citizens of Chester, corresponding with the Charter of Henry VII. but comprising the further powers of the confirmatory Charter of Elizabeth.

In Trinity Term, 35th Charles II. the Attorney General exhibited an information (Quo Warranto) against the Mayor and Citizens of Chester, to shew by what authority they claimed to be a Body Corporate: but by an Order of Assembly, under their Common Seal,† the Mayor & Citizens refused to appear, conceiving, probably, that without such an appearance, their franchises could not be affected by any judgment that might be obtained against them: but in Hilary Term following, judgment was obtained by the Crown against the Citizens, and it was ordered, "That the liberties, privileges, and franchises, in the Information specified, should be seized into the hands of the said Lord the King, until there should be further order." A writ of seizure was accordingly issued on this judgment, directed to the Chamberlain of the County Palatine, commanding him to seize into his Majesty's hands, the liberties, privileges, and franchises of the City, and to return the precept.‡—This act of a despotic Monarch, completely extinguished the functions of the Mayor, as Judicial President of the Ancient Port-mote; as it did also those of the Sheriffs in the Pentice and County Courts; but to prevent the confusion that would necessarily arise from want of a due administration of Justice, the King, by Letters Patent, dated March 26, 1684, appointed William Wilme, Esq. "to be the Steward or Judge of this Court, called the Portmote Court, with all the profits and advantages thereto appertaining, to hold and exercise the same during his Majesty's pleasure, in as ample manner and form, as any Judge or Justice of the said Portmote Court, ever held or exercised the same"—By virtue of this Commission, Mr. Wilme actually sat as Judge of the Portmote Court until the granting of the Charter on the 4th Feb. following,‖ by which the Citizens and Inhabitants were newly incorporated§ excepting Roger Whitley, Esq. Thomas Whitley, his son, John Mainwaring, Esq. William Williams, Esq.¶ George Booth, Esq. William Street, George Mainwaring, and Michael Johnson.**—It is worthy of remark, that this celebrated Charter, which has at so many different periods created no small stir in

HISTORY. ¶ Then Recorder.

† Dated 28th Feb. 1683.

‡ Altho' this writ cannot be found, a copy of it is existing among the Corporation Records.

‖ This Charter was never enrolled.

§ No inhabitant ever claimed the rights or franchises of a Citizen, to serve upon Juries, or be exempted from toll.

** This Charter also granted an additional fair for Cattle, and Horses, in Feb. together with a Court of PIE POUDRE—also the reversion to the Corporation, of the office of Master and Keeper of the Hospital of St. John (for a fac simile of the seal of which see page 139) with all lands, tythes, &c. belonging thereto, after the death of Roger Whitley, to whom the same had been granted by letters patent of the 12th of the same King.

CHESTER.

HISTORY.

the city, is dated on Wednesday, Feb. 4, 1684, and imports to be not only under the Great Seal of England, but also under the Seal of the County Palatine, which, however, it never received in the life-time of the King, as appears by the Seal Keeper's Books. Indeed, it is scarcely possible it could have received the Seal, for the King was taken ill on Sunday the 1st Feb. of an apoplexy, and seldom spoke afterwards. He died on Friday the 6th, two days after the date of the Charter. It appears this Charter was immediately acted upon, in the Election of Mayor, Sheriffs, Murengers, Treasurers, and Coroners, in *Common Council*, in Oct. 1685; and again in 1686, but there are no data as to the mode of Election of H. Starkey, Esq. in 1687. Notwithstanding the provisions of this Charter, the mode of Election, as laid down in that of Henry VII. has ever since been adopted.

For reasons which need not be explained, James II. by order of his Privy Council, removed and displaced Hugh Starkey, Esq. (then Mayor) and also all the Aldermen and Common Councilmen acting as such: but the King granted a new Charter—in fact, a copy of that of Charles II.

In 1692, Roger Whitley, Esq. who had been disfranchised by Charles II. but restored by James II. in 1698, was Elected Mayor, and held that office successively, in 1693, 1694, and 1695.—In 1693, an Address was presented by Sir J. Mainwaring, Bart. and Geo. Booth, Esq. signed by themselves and 400 other Citizens, "praying to be admitted to the benefit of their Charters, in choosing their Common Council, according to the privilege thereby granted them." This address was read in open Court, and seconded, as was also a Protest, by Alderman Wilcocke, in the name of himself and 77 other Citizens. The address was, however, acceded to; and on the 15th June, the Mayor proceeded to an Election of the Common Council by the Citizens and Commonalty, in the Common Hall, at which forty Members were chosen, in lieu of the old Common Council, and two Aldermen, in the place of two others, then Dead, and they were sworn into Office, the same day.* —The Members of the Body, by this election ejected from office, in July following petitioned the Queen in Council, stating, that "Forasmuch as these tumultuary proceedings are not only injurious to your petitioners in discharging them from serving your Majesty in their respective stations, but do tend to the subversion of the ancient Government of your Majesty's said city, in violation of the Charters of many of your Majesty's predecessors: it is humbly prayed, that your petitioners may have such redress, and the Corporation be so settled, as to your Majesty in your wisdom shall seem fit."—To this petition was annexed a Certificate of its correctness, subscribed by Sir Thomas Grosvenor, ten other Aldermen, and twenty Common Council Men.

An answer to this petition, and certificate from the Mayor, was forwarded to the Privy Council, and read on the 5th October. It was couched in warm language; and sets out by stating, that "It is no small trouble to him to find so much disingenuity and rashness in any Members of the City, as to presume to offer to her Majesty so many gross mistakes, not to give them a worse character," as were contained in the petition and certificate: it maintains the regularity of the proceedings of the popular Election, sanctioned as it was by Charter. With respect to the certificate annexed, it said, "Nor is the certificate annexed to the Petition (to give it credit) less to be wondered at, there being several of the certifiers (and of the best quality amongst them) that were not present at the Election, but at London, or other remote places, yet presume to assert the truth of it (the petition) to your Majesty, of which they could have no cognizance, but by the misinformation of the Petitioners, or some of their mistaking adherents."—Upon reading this answer, the Privy Council dismissed the Petition, and ordered that the whole matter should be left to the determination of the law. The business was then brought into Court, by mandamus, and at the determination it was observed by the Chief Justice, Holt, that the Petitioners could not be restored on the Writ.

In Oct, 1697, after the death of Whitley, the follow-

* Twenty-six of the Old Assembly, and Common Council, protested against the proceedings, in these words: "We, whose names are underwritten, do protest against the address and irregular proceedings in the Election, June 15, 1693."

CHESTER

ing important bye-law, which has subsequently put to rest generally the question of popular elections, was agreed to :—

" At an Assembly of the Mayor, Aldermen, and Common Council,* the following Order or Bye-law, was made, touching the Election of Aldermen, and Common Council. At which Assembly—whereas the manner of Election of the Aldermen of this city, lately practised, by a poll of all the freemen, is found to be very tumultuous and inconvenient, and contrary to the ancient usage of the said city; and whereas at an Assembly holden in the said city, on the 15th day of October last past, by Roger Whitley, Esq. then Mayor, and the Aldermen and Common Council of the said city, certain proposals for the better governing and regulating the Election of the Aldermen and Common Council of this city, were presented by the said late Mayor, and approved, established, and confirmed, at the same assembly, as by the acts or orders of the same assembly may appear; and whereas it is manifested to this house, that the same proposals and manner of elections thereby directed, are contrary to the ancient way and manner of Elections of long time used, established, and approved within the said city, and may be of dangerous consequence to the peace and quiet of the said city . it is therefore Ordered, by this house, that the said proposal and order, made on the 15th day of October, for the better governing and regulating the Election of the Aldermen and Common Council of this city, shall be, and hereby it is utterly abrogated, and repealed, to all intents and purposes.—And IT IS FURTHER ORDERED, that the Mayor, Aldermen, and Common Council of the said City, do and shall immediately proceed to supply all the vacant places of Aldermen of this city, by Election of other fit persons into the same places, in such manner as was used and practised in the said city before the Mayoralty of the said Roger Whitley, Esq. (Mr. Deputy Recorder and Alderman Lloyd, only dissenting and protesting against the Election of Aldermen by this Common Council.) And then the said Mr. Recorder and Alderman Lloyd, departed from the Assembly : whereupon Sir Thomas Grosvenor, Bart. one of the Aldermen of this city, being called in before this house, declared that he had neglected to subscribe the Association, according to the direction of a late Act of Parliament, entitled ' An Act for the better security of his Majesty's Royal Person and Government,' but that he is willing to subscribe the same Association, and to qualify himself accordingly, if this house shall please to elect him a-new, to be one of the Aldermen of this city, in his said former station, which is yet vacant: and then the said Sir Thomas Grosvenor, being withdrawn,—It it Ordered, by this Assembly, that he the said Sir Thomas Grosvenor, shall be, and hereby is newly elected and chosen; and the said Sir Thomas Grosvenor being called in again, took the Oaths appointed by a late Act of Parliament, entitled ' An Act for abrogating the Oaths of Allegiance and Supremacy, and appointing other Oaths,' and likewise the Oath of an Alderman, and thereupon is established and confirmed in his said office."

* Oct. 12th 1697.

HISTORY.

A Petition against this bye-law was presented to the King and Council, but no proceedings were had in consequence of it.

Having gone pretty much at length into the History of the local Government of Chester, it will close with the following extract from an Act of Assembly, October 14, 1698 :—

" Whereas the Ancient Common Hall of Pleas of this city, is now in great decay, and unfit for the service of this city, and a new Hall† is lately built in the Northgate-street of this city, over against the Bishop's Palace, which is conceived by this House to be much more useful and commodious for the public business of this Incorporation. It is therefore Ordered by this House, that the said New Hall, from henceforth, be the Common Hall of Pleas of this city, and as such shall be accepted, used, and employed to all intents and purposes. And that the Election of a New Mayor, and other Officers of this year next ensuing, and all future Elections of Mayor and other officers, and the Courts of Crown-mote, Port-mote General Quarter Sessions of the Peace, Pentice Courts, and County Courts, and all other Courts, Meetings, and Business whatsoever, which usually have been, or by the law or custom of this city should or ought to be holden, kept, transacted, or done in the Common Hall of the said city, shall for the time

† The present Exchange.

CHESTER HISTORY.

to come, be holden, kept, transacted, and done in the said New Common Hall. And it is further Ordered, that this Order shall be immediately read and proclaimed in the said Old Hall, to the end, that all the Citizens there attending, for the Electing of their Mayor, may forthwith repair to the said New Common Hall, for that purpose.

OATHS OF OFFICE.

MAYOR.

I shall be hold and true* to the King of Great Britain, and the Earl of Chester, and unto the City and Franchises of Chester, and duly and truly execute the office of a Mayor within the City aforesaid, for this year; and do right to the poor as to the rich, and rich as to the poor; and be counselled by the twenty and four Aldermen of the said City; and the victual within the said City, oversee; and no person receive into the Franchises, contrary to the Ordinances thereupon made: So help me God.

* In 1640, the Oath began, 'I shall hold and be true,' &c.

RECORDER.

I shall be a true liege man unto the King's Grace, and to the Earldom of Chester, and true to the Franchises of Chester, and the same truly maintain with all my might and power, and truly obey my Mayor for the time being, in all things lawful; and truly occupy the office of Recorder of the City of Chester, and all that to the same appertaineth: So help me God.

SHERIFFS.

We shall truly occupy the office of Sheriffs of the City of Chester as for this year to come, and do right as well to the poor as to the rich, in our office; doing, and truly execution do, of all that is recovered in our Courts, and suffer no manner of person to retail within the franchise, contrary to the ordinance thereupon made: So help me God.

ALDERMEN AND COMMON COUNCIL.

I shall be ready as one of the twenty-four of this city, and come upon due warning to me made, to the Mayor of the City for the time being, and give him my true advice and counsel of any thing that I am required of, touching the Franchise, Weal, Governance, and good Rule of this City, as oftentimes as the case requires; and shall be assistant, and attendance give to the Mayor and Sheriffs for the time being, for the observance of the peace, as far as the franchise of the city of Chester stretches, afore all other persons, and to keep their counsel; and all lawful ordinances made by the said Mayor, and the twenty-four, and forty, or by the most part of them, shall truly keep or perform, and be ready to make such sureties as can be thought reasonable to perform these points: So help me God.

THE FOUR SERJEANTS.

I shall be hold and true† to the King of England, and to the Mayor of Chester, and their counsel keep, and to bear and draw with the City, and not to be retained with any man as long as I shall be serjeant to the said City, but unto the Mayor of Chester for the time being, and truly take, and present, and execute, all things that belong thereunto: So help me God.

† See note to Mayor's Oath.

OATH FORMERLY TAKEN BY THE MURENGERS.

We shall truly execute and occupy the office of Murengers within this City, for this year next to come, and of all customs of merchandise that come to our hands during the said year, give and yield thereof a true account to the Mayor, and his Brethren, for the time being; and all other things do that pertaineth to our said office: So help me God.

THE FREEMEN.

I shall be obedient, profitable, and true to the King of Great Britain, and to the Earldom of Chester, and to the Mayor, and to the Commonalty of the said City, and truly the franchise of Chester maintain, with all my might and power; give and yield with my Mayor and my neighbours, after my having; worship my elders, and their counsel keep, and be not assenting nor abetting to any confederacy or conspiracy against the City, nor my neighbours; nor any foreign goods conceal, in merchandise, in custom, nor other ways, and not to be retained to any other man, but only to the Mayor for the time being: So help me God.

GOD SAVE THE KING.

The following is a statement of the different Polls that have taken place for Civic Officer, from 1590, to 1817.

ELECTION FOR ALDERMEN, 1590.

For William Massey	204
Sir J. Savage	181
Thomas Lynyal	17*
John Ratcliffe	19
William Tilston	18
Thomas Smith	15
Thomas Garratt	9
William Bavand	2
Thomas Green	2
Total	627

In 1691, for the office of MAYOR, when the greater number of votes was for

The Earl of Warrington	408
1694, for the office of SHERIFF:	
Mr. Thomas Bolland	164
1695, for the same office:	
Mr. John Holland	148
1696, for the office of MAYOR:	
Mr. Alderman Allen	421
The same year for SHERIFF:	
Mr. Ellis	244

1696, for the office of MAYOR:

Mr. Henry Bennett - - - 484

For SHERIFF the same year:

Mr. Thomas Wright - - - 233

1701, for the office of MAYOR, vice Richard Oulton, who died in his Mayoralty:

Hugh Starkey - - - 11

1702, for MAYOR, vice the Earl of Derby, who also died in his Mayoralty:

Mr. Michael Johnson - - - 354

1704, for MAYOR:

Mr. Edward Partington - - 20

The same year for SHERIFF:

Mr. Hoghton - - - - 269

1705, for MAYOR:

Mr. Edward Puleston - - 412

Same year for SHERIFF:

Mr. Randle Holme - - - 288

1707, for MAYOR:

Mr. Humphrey Page - - 389

1710, for MAYOR:

Mr. Thomas Partington - - 376

For SHERIFFS the same year:

Mr. Edward Burrowes - - 317

1711, for Mayor:

Mr. John Minshull - - - 292

The same year, for SHERIFF:

Mr. Thomas Wilson - - 310

1713, for MAYOR:

Mr. John Stringer - - - 300

For SHERIFF the same year:

Mr. Thomas Bolland - - 280

1714, for MAYOR:

Mr. T. Sayer - - - - 399

The same year for SHERIFF:

Mr. P. Leadbeater - - - 320

1720, for the office of MAYOR:

Mr. Thomas Edwards - - - 480

1721, for Mayor:

Mr. Thomas Wilson - - - 923

Same year for SHERIFF:

Mr. Thomas Hiccocke - - - 802

1728, for MAYOR:

Mr. William Hughes - - 373

1732, for MAYOR:

Mr. Alderman Johnson - - 1097

——— Ellames - - 1095

——— Mainwaring - - 858

——— Bennett - - 858

1733, for the office of MAYOR:

Mr. Peter Ellames - - - 371

1734, for MAYOR:

Mr. Roger Massey - - - 70

1744, for MAYOR:

Mr. Thomas Maddock - - - 137

1771, for SHERIFF:

Mr. Rider jun. - - - 365

Mr. Thomas Edwards - - - 465

1809, for SHERIFF:

Mr. Grace - - - - 278

Mr. Brittain - - - - 216

1817, for MAYOR:

Mr. Henry Bowers - - - 268

Mr. Wm. Seller - - - 271

Mr. Thomas Bradford - - - 58

Mr. Alderman Seller, and Mr. Alderman H. Bowers, were then returned to the Court of Aldermen, by the Citizens. The election of the Court fell on Mr. Ald. H. Bowers, and he was declared duly elected.

List of Recorders.

1506, Raufe Birkenhead was appointed first Recorder by Henry VII. by Charter.

1516, Richard Sneyde.	1662, Richard Levinge.	
1540, Raufe Wryne.	1667, William Williams.*	* The persons marked thus(*) were Representatives.
1548, John Birkenhead.	1684, Sir Edward Lutwyche.	
1551, Richard Sneyde.	1686, Richard Levinge.*	
1556, William Gerrard*	1687, Sir William Williams.	
1575, Richard Birkenhead.*	1700, C. Comberbach.	
1601, Thomas Lawton*	1719, Thomas Mather.	
1606, Thomas Gamull.*	1745, William Falconer.	
1613, Edward Whitby.*	1754, Robert Townshend.	
1639, Robert Brerewood.	1787, Thomas Cowper.	
1646, John Radcliffe.*	1788, Foster Bower.	
1651, Richard Howard.	1795, Hugh Leycester.	
1656, John Radcliffe.	1814, D. F. Jones.	

So late as the beginning of the 18th Century, a Counsel was always employed by the Corporation, in the County Court, to watch over the privileges of the City, and prevent any infringements on its liberties and franchises.

Town Clerks.

1404, William de Hawarden.	1609, Thomas Whitby.
1510, John Farrar.	1619, Robert Brerewood.
1540, Raufe Wryne.	1627, Richard Littler.
1543, William Newhall.	1639, David Lloyd.
1551, Thomas Glaseour.	1648, John Jones.
—— John Yearworth.	1649, Rich. Goulbourn.
—— Anthony Harper.	1651, Ralph Davenport.
1590, William Knight.	1653, Daniel Bavand.
1600, Ellis Williams.	1655, George Bulkeley.
1602, Robert Whitby.	1688, Roger Comberbach.

1700, Richard Adams.
1712, Thomas Lloyd, and Roger Comberbach, jointly.
1756, Thomas Brock.
1786, William Hall.
1795, George Whitley.
1799, William Richards.
1817, John Finchett.

During the greater part of the last Century, those gentlemen who held the office of Town Clerk, had previously acted as Deputies to their predecessors. John Finchett, Esq. the present Town Clerk, succeeded Wm. Richards, Esq. May 2, 1817.

Representatives.

7 Edward VI.	Richard Sneyd, gent.	Ralph Mainwaring, ald.
1 Mary.	Richard Sneyd, gent.	Thomas Massey gent.
1, 2, Phil. & Mary.	Rich. Sneyd, recorder.	Thomas Massey, esq.
2, 3, Phil. & Mary.	The Same.	
4, 5, Phil. & Mary.	Thomas Gerard, esq.	Sir Law. Smith, knt.
1 Elizabeth.	Sir T. Venables, knt.	William Alsecher.
5 Elizabeth.	William Gerard, esq.	John Yearworth, esq.
13 Elizabeth.	William Gerard, esq.	William Glazeour, esq.
14 Elizabeth.	The Same.	
27 Elizabeth.	Rd. Birkenhead, esq.	Rich. Bavand, ald.
28 Elizabeth.	Rd. Birkenhead, esq.	Peter Warburton, esq.
31 Elizabeth.	The Same.	
35 Elizabeth.	Rich. Birkenhead, esq.	Gilbert Gerard, esq.
39 Elizabeth.	Peter Warburton, esq.	William Brook, esq.
43 Elizabeth.	Hugh Glaseour, esq.	Thomas Gamul, esq.
1 James I.	Tho. Lowton, recorder.	Hugh Glaseour, esq.
	Hugh Glaseour died, Kenrick ap Evan returned.	
12 James I.	Edw. Whitby, recorder.	Jno. Bingley, merchant.
18 James I.	Edw. Whitby, recorder	Jno. Radcliffe, ald.
21 James I.	Edw. Whitby, recorder.	John Savage.
1 Charles I.	The Same.	
1 Charles I.	Edw. Whitby, recorder.	William Samuel, esq.
3 Charles I.	Edw. Whitby, recorder.	Jno. Radclyffe, ald.
15 Charles I.	Sir Thos. Smith, knt.	R. Brerewood, kt. & ald.
16 Charles I.	Sir Thos. Smith, knt.	Francis Gamul, Esq.
	William Edwards.	John Radclyffe.
5 Charles II.	No Burgesses.*	
6 Charles II.	No Burgesses.*	
8 Charles II.	Edward Bradshaw, esq.*	
11 Charles II.	Jonathan Ridge, ald.	John Griffiths, ald.*
12 Charles II.	Jno. Radcliffe, recorder	William Ince, esq.
13 Charles II.	Sir T. Smith, knt.	Jno. Radclyffe, esq. but
	dying in their places,	
	Wm. Willams, esq. and	Col. Werden, were ret.
31 Charles II.	William Williams, esq.	Sir T. Grosvenor, bt.
31 Charles II.	The Same.	
32 Charles II.	William Williams, esq.	Roger Whitley, esq.
1 James II.	Sir T. Grosvenor, bart.	Robt. Werden, esq.
4 James II.	Roger Whitley, esq.	Geo. Mainwaring, esq.
1 Wm. & Mary.	Sir T. Grosvenor, bt.	Rich. Levinge, esq.
7 William III.	Sir T. Grosvenor, bt.	Roger Whitley, esq. on
	whose death was substituted Tho. Cowper, esq.	
10 William III.	Sir T. Grosvenor, bt.	Peter Shackerley, esq.
12 William III.	Henry Bunbury, bart.	Peter Shackerley, esq.
13 William III.	The Same.	
1 Anne.	Sir H. Bunbury, bart.	Peter Shackerley, esq.
4 Anne.	The Same.	
7 Anne.	The Same.	
9 Anne.	The Same.	
12 Anne.	The Same.	
1 George I.	Sir H. Bunbury, bart.	Sir Rd. Grosvenor, bart.
8 George I.	The Same.	
1 George II.	Sir Rd. Grosvenor, bt.	Tho. Grosvenor, esq. on
	whose deaths July, 1732, and Jan. 1733,	
	Rt. Grosvenor, and Sir C. Bunbury, bt. were ret.	
8 George II.	Sir Rt. Grosvenor, bt.	Sir Charles Bunbury, bt.
15 George II.	The Same. On the death of Sir C. Bunbury, bt. April, 1742,	
	Henry Warburton, esq. was substituted.	
21 George II.	Sir Rt. Grosvenor, bt.	Rich. Grosvenor, esq.
27 George II.	Sir Rt. Grosvenor, bt.	Rich. Grosvenor, esq.
	Sir Robert Grosvenor died, August, 1775, and	
	Thomas Grosvenor, esq. was substituted.	
1 George III.	Thos. Grosvenor, esq.	Rd. Wilbraham Bootle.
8 George III.	The Same.	
15 George III.	The Same.	
21 George III.	The Same.	
24 George III.	The Same.	
30 George III.	Thomas Grosvenor, esq.	Robt. Vis. Belgrave.
	On the death of Thomas Grosvenor, esq. 1795,	
	Thos Grosvenor, esq. (his son) was substituted.	
36 George III.	Robt. Vis. Belgrave.	Thomas Grosvenor, esq.
42 George III.	The Same. On Lord Belgrave's succession to the	
	Earldom of Grosvenor, in 1802,	
	R. E. D. Grosvenor, was substituted.	
47 George III.	Thos. Grosvenor, esq.	R. E. D. Grosvenor, esq.
47 George III.	Thos. Grosvenor, esq.	John Egerton, esq.
53 George III.	Thos. Grosvenor, esq.	John Egerton, esq.
59 George III.	Thos. Grosvenor, esq.	Rd. Viscount Belgrave.

* Six years' Usurpation.

The following are the Contests for the Representation of the City, from 1568.

1568,	For Mr. Warburton - - - -	198
	The Recorder - - - - -	50
	Mr. Glaziour - - - - -	40
	Mr. Bunnell - - - - -	19
	Mr. Bavand - - - - -	10
	Mr. Lynyal - - - - -	1
		318

CHESTER

HISTORY.

1727, For Sir R. Grosvenor - - -		1032
1732, For Sir R. Grosvenor - - -		1109
1747, For Sir R. Grosvenor -	1049	- 333*
Mr. Warburton - -	928	- 318*
Mr. Mainwaring -	758	- 183*
Total - - -	2735	834*
1784, For Mr. Thomas Grosvenor - -		713
Mr. R. W. Bootle - - -		626
Mr. J. Crewe - - -		480
Mr. Barnston - - - -		38
Total polled - - -		1095
1812, For General Grosvenor - - -		627
Mr. Egerton - - - - -		602
Sir Richard Brooke - - - -		575
Mr. Townshend - - - - -		537
Total number polled - - -		1188
1818, For Lord Belgrave - - -		813
General Grosvenor - - -		741
Sir John Grey Egerton - -		607
Mr. Williams - - - -		522
Total polled (exclusive of 44 rejected)		1346

* Non-residents.

The Records

Of the City, which were arranged in 1806, under the superintendance of the late Town Clerk, Wm. Richards, Esq. are preserved in excellent condition.—Few, if any, cities in the Kingdom, can boast of a more ancient, or more numerous collection of Records. The CHARTERS, (with their dates) will form a separate article: the following is the arrangement of the general Records of the City, in alphabetical order: the dates those of the year in which they commence.

	A. D.		A. D.
Assembly Orders, and Files	1409	Haven Money, papers of...	1574
Assembly Books............	1539	Inquisitions....................	1432
Amerciments, Fines, &c....	1477	Licenses	1592
Admiralty Warrants, May 4	1529	Mayor's Court Books......	1393
CHARTERS---Ran. I. temp.	1190	Mayor's Files..............	1532
Declarations................	1558	Murage Accounts	1446
Depositions.................	1553	Merchants' Statutes	1621
Election papers	1571	Outlawries	1626
Exchequer papers	1341	Pentice Court Rolls.........	1282
Examinations, temp. Eliz.	1568	Pannels	1536
Fines	1565	Precepts	1563

	A. D.		A. D.
Proclamations	1668	Sacrament Certificates......	1673
Petitions and Letters	1567	Soldiers' Notes, &c.........	1550
Prize wine accounts.........	1653	Sessions' Files..............	1347
Primage Papers	1567	Sessions' Presentiments ...	1624
Portmote and Crownmote Rolls......................	1277	Treasurers' Accounts	1464
		Tonnage and Poundage ...	1570
Passage Court Rolls.........	1377	Tolls on Horses, &c. at Fairs, temp. Eliz.......	1558
Recoveries	1547		
Records of Mayors, Sheriffs, &c.	1518	Tax Papers..................	1576
		Writ Files, temp. Edw. I...	1272
Sheriffs' Court Books......	1436	&c. &c. &c.	
Sheriffs' Files	1527		

The Charters, Grants, &c.

To the City, are preserved in regular succession among the City Archives, as before noticed:--

The first Charter is from Randle I. by which he grants to the City the ancient* privileges, liberties, and GILD MERCATORY,--sicut hactenus usi fuerint—under his seal. There are also two other Charters by the Earls of this name, but without date, confirming the preceding.

King John confirmed all Charters granted to the City, and particularly those of Henry II. (not now in existence) concerning certain privileges and liberties in the trade between Ireland and Chester, with freedom of Custom.

John Earl of Chester, granted that no Merchant shall buy or sell any merchandise brought to the said City, either by sea or land, but his Citizens of Chester, and their heirs, or by their agreement (saving at Midsummer and Michaelmas); shall make any bargain before witness, and if the sale thereof happen to come, he who made the sale shall be free from the Earl to lose or to yield, &c.; and by the same doth grant Gild Mercatory, freely as in the time of his Uncle Randulph.

King Henry III. granted three Charters under the great seal as King, by whom the Mayor was created, for he took the Earldom of Chester into his own hands in the 22d year of his reign; one of the said Charters granted by the said King Henry III. recites that he had seen the former Charters of Randulph, Earl of Chester and Lincoln, and doth grant and confirm, that none shall buy and sell merchandise in the City but Citizens, except in the fairs before in the Charters of Earl Randulph mentioned; and willeth that the said Citizens shall have the said freedoms, to them and their heirs for ever. Anno. 32. Hen. III.

Edward I. King of England, appointeth the Mayor and Citizens of

* Although there are no grants in existence from Lupus, and his son Richard, it may reasonably be inferred, from the Charter of Randle I. which is merely confirmatory, that they endowed the City with certain privileges and liberties, of considerable importance. The *Gild Mercatory*, no doubt existed soon after, if not before, the Conquest.

CHESTER

Chester, to furnish two ships, to serve in his wars in Scotland. Anno 4. Edward I.

The same King Edward I. confirmeth the former Charters of his father Henry III. and also the Charters of Ranulph Earl of Chester, for the said liberties and customs, acquittance and releasing of recognizance, and proportaments for testaments, buying and selling; and further, the same King, by the same Charter, giveth the City of Chester, with the appurtenances, liberties, and freedoms, to the Citizens of Chester, and their heirs, to be holden of him and his heirs for ever, paying yearly a hundred pounds; he granteth also the election of Coroners, the office of Coroners, and Pleas of the Crown, and that the Citizens should have Sock, Sack, Toll, Team, Infang Theif, Outfang Theif, and to be *free throughout all his lands and dominions of Toll, Passage, &c.* This Charter was dated at York, and importeth great authority. Anno 28, Edw. I.

Edward III. King of England, reciting the said Charter of the said King Edward I. his grandfather, doth confirm as well the former Charters of the said Earls, as also the said Charter of the said King Edward I. This Charter was dated at Worcester, Anno 1, Edw III.

The same King Edward III. confirmed the former Charters, and further granteth to the Citizens the vacant grounds within the City, with liberty to build upon the same, as doth appear in the Charter, dated Anno 1, Edward III.

The same King Edward III. by another Charter, confirmed the former Charters, and herein he is somewhat larger in words than in his other Charters. Anno 25th, Edward III.

Edward Prince of Wales, son of Edward III. by his Charter directed to the Mayor and Citizens, doth show that he hath granted the Fee-farm of Chester, being a hundred pounds by the year to the Earl of Arundel, for the term of his life.

The same Edward Prince of Wales, doth confirm former liberties and Charters, and setting forth the special names and boundaries of the City of Chester, beginning at Ironbridge, and so on to Saltney, the Portpool, Flookersbrook, and Boughton.* Anno 28 Edward III.

HISTORY.

Richard II. King of England, by his Letters Patent, sheweth the ruinous state of this City, and of the haven, and therefore doth release to the Citizens, seventy three pounds, ten shillings and eight-pence, parcel of the hundred pounds, for the fee-farm reserved by the Charter of Edward I. which the city was in arrearages. Anno 1, Richard II.

The same King Richard confirmeth all the former Charters, Rights, and Privileges. Anno 3d.

The same King Richard, giveth to the City, the profits of the passage, to the building and repairing of the Bridge of the Dee. Anno 11, Richard II.

The same King Richard granted to the Citizens the Murage for four years. Anno 18.

The same King Richard granteth to the Citizens the profits and prizes of the Murage, towards the reparation of the Walls of the City for five years. Anno 21, Richard II.

The same King Richard II. by the name of King of England and France, Lord of Ireland, Prince of Wales, and Earl of Chester, confirmeth the former Charters and Liberties, with larger words. This Charter is under the Seal of the County Palatine of Chester. Anno 22, Richard II.

The same King Richard, using his style next before recited, for the remedy of such demunities, as had then happened to the City, and for furtherance of Justice, in the same City to be executed, did grant to his subjects, the Mayor, Sheriffs, and Commonalty of the said City, to hold Courts, and limitteth what process they may award in Actions, Personal Felonies, Appeals, Process of Utlegary, as at the Common Law. This Charter carrieth great authority, and is granted under the

* CITY BOUNDARIES.---Edw. Prince of Wales, and Earl of Chester, son of Edw. III. granted the first Charter describing the boundaries of the City, as running thus:---" From Claverton *lone*, from opposite the Iron Bridge, and so on through a certain lane to Greene Ditch, otherwise called the Meredith, following that ditch to a certain road that leads towards the West, between the lands of Robert de Bradford, and the land of Michael Scott, as far as the top of that ditch, and so along the land of the said Robert de Bradford, as far as the land of the Priory and Monastery of Chester, which was formerly the land of Thomas Deniers; and so along a certain lane as far as a road which leads from Chester towards Kynnaston (Kidnerton); and beyond that road as far as the village of Lache, and through the middle of that village on the North as far as Lande Pull,* in Saltney, otherwise called Blake Pull, and so along that Pull, as far as the Water of the Dee; and afterwards along that water to as far as a certain ferry on the other side of the same river, at the Pull Bridge, and so along that ferry as far as Stannen Bridge, and from thence to Bache pull, and so along a stream of water to a place called Flookersbrook; and from thence as far as Bisfe-diche, and so along towards the East, and afterwards along the ditch towards the South West as far as the road leading to Stamford Bridge, towards Chester, and along that road as far as a certain ditch on the East side of the Chapel of Boughton; and so along the road which leads from Chester towards Tarporley, along that road leaving Granges le Prossey on the East, so far as the Hollow-way which leads toward Pother Bache, under the hill by the water of the Dee; and so along the bank of that water as far as Huntingdon Wood, and from thence to the Iron Bridge aforesaid."

* Pool.

CHESTER

Seal of the PRINCIPALITY OF CHESTER, 4th Aug. Anno 22, Rd. II.

Henry Prince of Wales and Earl of Chester, the elder son of Henry IV. confirmeth all the former Charters, and granteth to the Mayor and Citizens, that they shall hold and enjoy their former liberties.

The same Prince Henry granteth to the Mayor and Citizens, the profits of the Murage, and Tower of the Bridge, during pleasure, and a reservation of the Tithe of the Rood-eye, that the Rector of Trinity Church should not have it.

Henry VI. King of England confirmed the former Charters, Anno 4.

The same King Hen. VI. by his Charters, reciting what great concourse in times past, as well of strangers as others, had been used with merchandise to come to the City, by reason of the goodness of the Port of Chester, and also what great resort was out of Wales with victuals, and other things, to the great profit of the City, until the time of the rebellion, (which should seem to be that of Owen Glyndwr,) and then shewing how the said port was lamentably decayed, by reason of the abundance of the sands which had choaked the creek, he therefore releaseth to the City, fifty pounds of the fee-farm, reserved by Edw. I. Also, he released the parcel of the fee-farm for which the Sheriffs of the City were found in arrears before the Auditor. Anno 25.

Edward IV. King of England released fifty pounds of the said fee-farm, which must be either the former, or else some arrears. Anno 1, Edward IV.

Henry VII. King of England, reciting how the Mayor and Citizens of ancient time did hold the City of Chester of his progenitors, Earls of Chester, paying yearly a hundred pounds, and shewing the great resort in times past, as well of strangers as others, with ships and merchandise unto the Watergate, and other places thereabouts did come, whereby the charge for maintainance of the walls, and payments of the fee-farm were had and paid, until such time as the river, by quarring and bursting out of the water, became sandy, and merchandise was detained; in consideration thereof, remitteth seventy pounds of the yearly fee-farm.

The same King Henry the VII. granteth that the City of Chester, and the Suburbs, Towns, and Hamlets thereof (the Castle excepted), should be a County of itself, by the name of the County of the City of Chester, with divers other grants, in the same Charter contained. Anno 21, Henry VII.* (This is the celebrated Charter.)

Henry VIII. King of England, directed his letters in parchment under his privy seal to the Mayor of the City of Chester, charging that the inhabitants of the said City, should remain within the said City for defence thereof; and not to suffer any person, by virtue of his letters placards, to take any person within the City, except the same placard did especially touch the revocation of the said letters, so directed to the said Mayor. Anno 14, Henry VIII.

HISTORY.

The same King Henry VIII. by his letters patent, doth discharge the City of Chester from being a Sanctuary, Anno 34; and in his time a decree was made in the Star Chamber, concerning the election of the Mayor of the City of Chester.

Elizabeth, Queen of England, &c. by her Charter, hath confirmed the former Charters, and granteth pardon to none misusing the said liberties, and that the Charters shall be construed, most beneficially, for the City; with provision for orphans' goods, and liberty to purchase lands to a certain value, &c. Anno 16, Elizabeth.

A grant by Flower, Norroy, to the Mayor and Citizens of Chester, of a Coat Armorial, to be by them used for the said City. Anno 22, Elizabeth.† †See p. 129.

James I. King of England, &c. by a Charter under the great seal of England, hath as King, confirmed all former Charters, and most amply and fully established the liberties and privileges of the said City. Anno 1604.

James I. by letters patent Dec. 14, Anno Reg. 34, grants the reversion of Primage and Custom of Wines, to the Mayor and Citizens.

Jan. 10, 16 Charles I. a Commission under the great seal, to the Mayor, &c. for administering the oaths of supremacy, &c. to the Soldiers passing through the City to Ireland.

June 23, 1658, a patent from Oliver, Lord Protector of the Commonwealth, granting the reversion of the Mastership of the Hospital of St. John of Jerusalem, to the Mayor, Aldermen, and Citizens.

June 6, 16 Charles II. Charter to the Mayor and Citizens, confirming the provisons of the Charter of Hen. VII. as to the City being a County of itself; but vesting the Election of the Aldermen, &c. in the Select Body.

Feb. 4, 37th Charles II.—A Grant, empowering the Mayor and Recorder to appoint a Deputy; and confirming the Mastership of St. John's Hospital in the Mayor, &c.

Sept. 15, 4 James II. confirmatory of the preceding grants.

Oct. 26, 4 James II. merely a repetition of the former grants.

March 15, 12 William III. a Commission of Gaol Delivery issued to the City of Chester.

Dec. 7, 44 George III. Empowering the Mayor to appoint a Deputy, &c.

These Charters are all in a state of high preservation; the Seals of the greater part of the most ancient of them, being perfect.

RANDAL III.

JOHN SCOT.

Gilds, or Incorporated Companies.

Many years antecedent to the establishment of the office of Mayor, there existed in Chester a Gild Mercatorial, composed of various Trade Companies, severally incorporated by Charters. Of the origin of their formation, no trace now exists, neither in record nor tradition—and this is itself a sufficient proof of their extreme antiquity. By their constitution, they do homage to the Mayor, as the Chief Officer of the City, for their privileges, by attending him in all processions when required. Formerly the Members composing each Company, attended the Mayor in person; but this custom has sunk into disuse; and at present upon Festivals and public occasions, they are represented by their respective Banners, which are carried before the Mayor. The fixed days of these solemnities, are the Sunday next after the Election of City Officers, and the 29th of May,* when the banners precede the Corporation to and from the Cathedral.

Till within the last few years, the Companies were twenty-five in number; two of them, however, (the Fishmongers and the Dyers) no longer exist as distinct companies. At present they are thus classed:

1 Tanners.
2 Merchants, Drapers, and Hosiers.
3 Brewers.
4 Barbers Chirurgeons, & Tallow Chandlers.
5 Cappers, Pinners, Wire-drawers, and Linen-drapers.†
6 Bricklayers.‡
7 Wrights, and Slaters.
8 Joiners, Carvers, and Turners.
9 Painters, Glaziers, and Plumbers, Embroiderers, and Stationers.‖
10 Goldsmiths and Clockmakers.
11 Smiths, Cutlers, Pewterers, Cardmakers.
12 Butchers.
13 Glovers.
14 Cordwainers.§

* Previous to the Restoration, on Midsummer-day.

† These Companies receive together the Legacy called "Owen Jones's Charity," of which more hereafter.

‡ In 1691, the Masons petitioned for a Charter, but for some reason not specified they were refused.

‖ In 1629, this Company prosecuted Mr. Prebendary William Case, a freeman, for "cursing them, and wishing the Devil to take them all!" and for scandal against the Magistrates, "by giving out, that whatever the Recorder said the Mayor would swear, be it true or false!" Maister Prebendary was accordingly ordered to appear at the next Assembly, and then submitted himself. The cause of this dispute we are not acquainted with.

§ It would appear from the following entry in the Assembly Book, that somewhat had taken place not of the most harmonious description, in this and other Companies, during the Mayoralty of Sir Randle Mainwaring, in 1625:—"The Aldermen and Stewards of the So-

15 Bakers.*
16 Fletchers,† Bowyers,† Coopers, and Stringers.†
17 Mercers, Grocers, Ironmongers, and Apothecaries.
18 Innholders, Cooks, and Victuallers.
19 Feltmakers and Skinners.‡
20 Saddlers and Curriers.‖
21 Tailors.§
22 Fishmongers (no longer existing).
23 Cloth-workers, Walkers, and Masons.
24 Dyers (no longer a Company.)
25 Weavers.

Like many other old Institutions, these Companies are fast falling into decay—and although within the last year or two, endeavors have been made to re-establish them, it is to be feared, that the symptoms of dissolution are too strongly manifested in the system, to allow a hope of their restitution.¶ There were several festivities, &c. formerly celebrated by these companies, with great show and pageantry. The watches and show, on Midsummer Eve, first instituted in 1497 or 1498, were composed of processions of the different Companies, attended by various devices.

Among the Harl. MSS. is a contract between Sir Lawrence Smith, Mayor, in 1558, 1563, and 1570, and two contracts, "for the annual painting of the City's four gyants; one musician, one dromedarye, one luce, one camel, one asse, one dragon, six hobby horses, and sixteen naked boys."—But one of his successors, Henry Hardware, having a little more respect for decency, "caused the gyants in the show not to goe; the Devil in his feathers not to ride for the butchers, but a boy as the others, and the cupps and canns, and dragon, and

ciety or Company of Cordwainers, within the Citty of Chester, come forthe, give, and deliver you ye GLEAVES to the Master, and Wardens of the Company of Drapers, within the said Citty, to bee by them immediately presented to the Maior, and afterwards disposed of at the discretion of the said Maior, and Drapers, according to ancient order, upon payne of tenn pounds. And it is further ordered, that the Aldermen and Stewards, both of the Company of Shoemakers and Sadlers, and every Member of the said Companies, shall accordingly upon every Shrove Tuesday, for ever, doe these said homages unto the Maior for the time beeinge, in givinge their attendance upon him orderly and decently, in their gownes, from the Pentice to the Roodee, and then back againe to the Common Hall; and likewise upon the two days following, shall give their attendance upon Mr. Maior for the time beinge, decently in their gownes, from the Pentice to the Common Hall, and then back again to the said Pentice, upon payne of tenn shillings, to be paid to the Treasurers, for the use of the Citty, by any person absenting himself, except good cause bee shewed to Mr. Maior for his excuse. And that if any person so absenting himself, shall refuse, or delay the payment of the said forfeiture, then the said to be levied by distresse, at the appointment of Mr. Maior for the time beeinge. And, moreover, the said Aldermen and Stewardes of the Company of Shoemakers, shall give, and deliver up unto the Drapers, in the presence of Mr. Maior, upon Shrove Tuesday next, and yearly for ever, six silver gleaves of the same fashion, and more value than heretofore, at any time within the space of tenn days now last past, have accustomed to be by them immediately presented unto the said Maior, &c. afterwards disposed of at the discretion of the said Maior, &c. as in and by the said proclamation, and auncient orders made to that purpose, is expressed. And likewise upon Shrove Tuesday next and soe yearly, upon the same day for ever, the Aldermen and Stewards of the Company of Saddlers, shall showe and presente their horse, in a decent and comely manner, as commonly they have done, and shall also give and deliver up unto the Master and Wardens of the Drapers, one silver bell of the same value, and at any time for the space of tenn days now last past, they have done, upon payne of tenn pounds. [Here there is an order "that the Drapers shall mayntayn the rotation of drinkinge to Mr. Maior for the three days as of ould," &c.] Lastly, it is ordered, that if any person free of or admitted into any of the said several Companies of Drapers, Shoemakers, and Sadlers, shall at any time hereafter give out, publish, or divulge, any outbrauving, scandalous, or disgraceful termes, either against the other two companies or either of them, &c. concerninge their professions, liberties, and customes, and especially touching the presentiment of gleaves and bell, which is by this howse finally enacted, determined, and ordered, or to doe or offer any violence, which may any way occasion any tumult, grudge, or distraction amongst the said Companies, that then the partie offendinge in this kind, upon proofe thereof made before Mr. Maior or some of his brethren, by two or more sufficient witnesses, shall forfeit and pay unto the companie wronged and offended, the summe of tenn pounds. [This order originated, says the preamble, from some difference heretofore existing for many years, between the Company of Drapers, Saddlers, and Shoemakers, concerninge the yearly presentinge of certain gleaves, horse, and bell, upon Shrove Tuesday.]

* The Bakers had a renewal of their Charter so far back as 1462.

† These branches of "Armourie," flourished exceedingly in Chester previous to the 17th Century.

‡ So late as the last Century, the leading staple trades of Chester.

‖ United in one Company in 1639.

§ Incorporated in 1427.

¶ At the Salop Summer Assize, 1818, an action was brought by the Bakers' Company of that Town, against an individual, for practising his business, not being free of that Company. A verdict, however, was given for the Defendant, but the Company expressed their determination of having a new trial in the King's Beach.

CHESTER — naked boys, to be put away; but caused a man in complete armour to goe before the showe in their stead."— All the pageants, however, were restored by the next Mayor, and continued till the show was finally abolished. Amongst the items for the show in 1621, are

"To four men that carried the 2 beasts............ 4s. 8d.
"To the five men that held the boys that ridd...... 2s. 6d.
"For painting the beasts and hobby horses.........43s. 0d."

The puritans again put a stop to these exhibitions; and the giants, hobby horses, camels, and dragons, had a long period of rest.

In 1657, in the Mayoralty of Richard Minshull, they were again revived, as "auncient and laudable customs, by the late obstructive times much injured." The following is the estimate of the expense attending their restoration:

For new making the Citty Mount, called the Mayor's Mount, as auenciently it was; and for hyring of bayes for the same, and men to carry it ....£	03 06 08
For making a-new the Marchant's Mount, as auenciently it was, with a shipp to turn, hyring of bayes, and five men to carry it...	04 00 00
For finding all the materials, with the workmanship of the four great gyants,* all to be made new as neer as may be, like as they were before, at £5. a gyant, the least that can be; in all	20 00 00
For four men to carry them................................	00 20 00
For making a-new the elephant and castle, and cupitt to look out of it, and two men to carry it	02 16 08
For making a-new the four beasts for the leavelookers, called the unicorn, the antelop, the flower de luce, and the camell, at 33s, 4d. a-piece	06 13 04
For eight men to carry them	00 16 00
For four hobby horses, at 6s. 8d. a-piece, and four boys to carry them	01 06 08
For the two lance-staves† for the boys that ride for the Sheriffs..........	00 06 08
For six garlands‡ for Mr. Maior's halberts, 23s. 4d. a-piece, and for Mr. Sheriffs' at 20d, a-piece........	
For balls, for the Maior and Sheriffs' burches‡	00 10 08
For the making new the dragon, 5s. and for six naked boys to beat at it	00 06 00
For the Morris-dancers,‖ and tabrett and pipe........	00 20 00

HISTORY. — The whole of the expense for this pageant, amounted to £45. 9s. 8d which was paid in portions by the Mayor, Sheriffs, and Leave-lookers.

An order was made in 1666, that the Members of the Common Council should accompany the Leave-lookers from the Bars, during the Show, according to ancient custom, upon pain of forfeiting ten shillings a piece; and the Members of the Companies were also ordered to attend, on pain of forfeiting five shillings In 1670 it was ordered, that the show held at Midsummer should be observed on Whit Tuesday, being more convenient, and all those failing in attendance, without a reasonable excuse to be allowed by the Mayor, should pay five shillings; and the Company failing to "put forth" their boy and horse, to pay five pounds to the City.— This ancient custom was, in 1678, finally abolished by an order of the Corporation.

In the possession of Mrs. Nicholls, of Nicholas-street, in Chester, is a curious MS. giving a full account of the ancient plays and pastimes of our Ancestors, and from it is extracted the following detail:—It is entitled "Certayne collections of aunchiante times concerninge the anchiaunte and famous Citty of Chester, collected by that Reverend Man of God, Mr. Robert Rogers, Batchelor of Divinitie, Arch-deacon of Chester, Parsone of Gooseworthe, and Preband in the Cathedral of Chester; being but in scattered notes, and by his sonne reduced into these chapters following."

* In an estimate at the Restoration of Charles II. relative to the "shows," one curious item is, "For arsenick to put into the paste to save the gyantts from being eaten by the rats, one shilling and fourpence."

† Hand, or lance staves.---‡ Garlands.

‖ Till the present year the city was annually visitted on Whitsun Monday, by about twenty or thirty grown-up children, calling themselves Morres Dancers, bedizened with ribbons, rags, and garlands of flowers, some of them dressed in a most indecent manner, and the whole party followed by crowds of idle women and children. Opposite the principal houses, they exhibitted their performances, consisting of grotesque dancing; a non-descript character, called Meg, armed with a besom and wooden ladle, acting as clown to the party. The Mayor, however, put an end to their visit; and it is to be hoped his successors will follow his example.

CHESTER

HISTORY.

"Of the laudable Exercises yearly used within the Cittie of Chester."

Mem. "That whereas the companye and corporation of Shoemakers within the Cittie of Chester, did yearely, time out of memory of man, upon Tewsday, commonly called Shrove Tewsday, or otherwise *Goteddesse* day at afternoon, at the cross upon the Roode-Dee, before the Mayor of the said Cittie, offer unto the Company of Drapers of the same Cittie, a ball of leather, called a foote-ball, of the value of 3s and 4d. or thereabout: and by reason of greate strife which did arise among the younge persons of the same Cittie, (while diverse parties were taken with force and stronge handes to bringe the said ball to one of these three houses, that is to say to the Mayor's house, or any one of the two Sheriffs' houses of the time being); much harme was done, some in the great thronge fallinge into a trance, some having their bodies brused and crushed; some their arms, heades, or legges broken, and some otherwise maimed, or in perill of life; to avoyd the said inconveniences, and also to torne and converte the saide homage to a better use; it was thought good by the Mayor of the saide Cittie, and the rest of the Common-council, to exchange of the said foote-ball as followeth: that in place thereof, there be offered by the Shoemakers to the Drapers, six gleaves* of silver, the which gleaves they appoynted to be rewards unto such men as would come, and the same day and place, passe and overrunne on foote all others: and the said gleaves were presently delivered according to the runninge of every one; and this exchange was made in the time when Henry Gee was Mayor of Chester, A. D. 1539, and in the thirty-firste yeare of Kinge Henry the Eighth.

* Gleave is an ancient word for a Javelin, or hand dart.

"Alsoe, whereas the companye and occupation of the Saddlers, within the Cittie of Chester, did yearely by custome, time out of memorie of man, the same day, hour, and place, before the Mayor, offer upon a truncheon, staffe, or speare, a certain homage to the Drapers of the Cittie of Chester, called the Saddler's ball, profitable for few uses or purposes, as it was, beinge a ball of silke of the bigness of a bowle, it was torned into a silver bell, weighing about two ounces, as is supposed, of silver: the which saide silver bell was ordayned to be the reward for that horse, which with speedy runninge, then should rune before all others, and there presently should be given the daye and place. This alteration was made the same time, and by the same Mayor, like as the Shoemakers' foote-ball was before exchanged into sixe silver gleaves.† Also, whereas of an anchant custom whereof man's memorie nowe livinge cannot remember the original and beginninge, the same daye, hower, and place, before the Mayor, for the time beinge, every person which is married within the liberties of the saide Cittie, dwelling wheresoever without, and all those that dwelle within the saide Cittie, for one year before, and marye elsewhere, did offer likewise a homage to the saide companye of Drapers before the Mayor, a ball of silke, of the like bigness of a bowle: the same Mayor torned the same balls into silver arrowes, the which arrowes they tooke order should be given to those which did shoote the longest shoote, with divers kinds of arrowes: this exchange was made as before is mentioned of the Shoemakers' foote-ball; and the Saddlers' ball. In which exchanges there appeared wisdom, in anchant and sage senators, whoe had greate studye and regarde to torne the foresaide thinges unto soe profitable uses and exercises; so that three of the most commendable exercises and practices of war-like feates be, as runninge of men on foote, runninge of horses, and shootinge of the broade arrowe, the flighte, and the butt-shafte, in Cities of England, soe farr as I understand."

† See note p. 197.

As referential to the above, is the following copy of an order, by Henry Gee, Mayor, dated 10th January, 3 Henry VIII.:—

"Ordered by the Mayor, Aldermen, and Common-council, with the consent of the whole occupation of Drapers, Saddlers, and Shoemakers, that the said occupation of Shoemakers, (which always have, time out of mind, given and delivered yearly, on Shrove Tuesday, in the afternoon, unto the Drapers, before the Mayor, at the cross on the Roodee, one ball of leather, called a foot-ball, of the value of 3s. 4d., or above, to play at from thence to the Common-hall of the said City, and further at the pleasure of the evil-disposed persons; whereof hath arisen great inconveniences), shall give and deliver yearly to the said Drapers, before the Mayor at the said time and place, six silver gleaves, each of the

value of 27d. or above to be disposed of at the pleasure of the said Mayor and Drapers, to him that shall win a foot-race befor them, on that or any other day; and that the Sadlers, (who have out of mind given and delivered yearly, at the same time and place, every master of them, unto the Drapers, before the Mayor, one painted ball of wood, with flowers and arms, upon the point of a spear, being goodly arrayed upon horseback accordingly), shall henceforth give and deliver to the said Drapers, before the Mayor, at the same time and place upon horseback, a bell of silver, to the value of 3s. 4d. to be disposed of at the discretion of the Mayor and Drapers, to him that shall get the horse-race on that day; and that every man that hath been married* in the said City, since Shrove Tuesday, then last past, shall then and there also deliver to the said Drapers before the Mayor, an arrow of silver, to the value of 5s. or above, instead of such ball of silk and velvet, which such married men ought then to have given and delivered by the ancient custom of the said City (used time out of mind), which silver arrow shall be disposed of by the Mayor and Drapers, for the preferment of the said feat and exercise of shooting in a long bow, for avoiding the said inconveniences, any use or prescription to the contrary notwithstanding: and also, the said Drapers, and their successors, shall keep yearly their recreation and drinking, as they have used to do, time out of mind.—And that the Shoemakers and Sadlers, and persons hereafter to be married, shall observe this order, upon pain of 10*l.* for every offence, *toties quoties*, to be forfeited to the Drapers according to ancient custom."

"Of the Sheriffes Breakfaste."

"There is an anchant custome in this Cittie of Chester, the memory of man now livinge not knowinge the original, that upon Monday in Easter-weeke, yearely, commonly called Black Mondaye, the two Sheriffes of the Cittie doe shoote for a breakfaste of calves-heades and bacon, commonly called the Sheriffes' breakfaste†, the manner being thus: the daye before the drum sowndeth through the Cittie with a proclamation for all gentlemen, yeomen, and good fellowes, that will come with their bowes and arrowes to take parte with one Sherife or the other, and upon Monday-morning, on the Rode-dee, the Mayor, Shreeves, Aldermen, and any other Gentelmen, that wol be there, the one Sherife chosing one, and the other Sherife chosing another, and soe of the archers; the one Sherife shoteth, and the other Sherife he shoteth to *shode* him, beinge at length some twelve score; soe all the archers on one side to shote till it be *shode*, and soe till three shutes be wonne, and then all the winners' side goe up together, firste with arrowes in their handes, and all the loosers with bowes in their hands together, to the common hall of the Cittie, where the Mayor, Aldermen, and Gentlemen, and the reste take parte together of the saide breakfaste in loveing manner; this is yearly done, it beinge a comendable exercise, a good recreation, and a loving assemblye."

"Of St. George's Race, of late time inbented, and when alter'd."

"In A. D. 1609, Mr. William Lester, mercer, beinge Mayor of Chester, (A. D. 1608) he, with the assent of the Mayor and Cittie, at his own coste chiefly, as I conceive, caused three silver cupps of good value to be made, the whiche saide silver cuppes were, upon St. George's daye, for ever to be thus disposed: all gentlemen that woulde bringe their horses to the Rood-dee that daye, and there runne, that horse which with spede did over-runne the rest, shoulde have the best cuppe there presently delivered, and that horse which came seconde, nexte the firste, before the rest, had the second cuppe there also delivered: and for the third cuppe it was to be rune for at the ringe‡, by any gentleman, that woulde rune for the same, upon the said Roode-dee,

* Were this custom now restored, a cup of no small value might be obtained for our races!

† In the year 1640, the Sheriffs gave a piece of plate to be run for, instead of the calves-head breakfast. In 1674, a resolution was entered in the Corporation Journals, that the calves head feast was held by ancient custom and usage, and was not to be at the pleasure of the Sheriffs and Leave-lookers. In the month of March 1676-7, the Sheriffs and Leave-lookers were fined ten pounds, for not keeping the calves-head feast. The Sheriffs of late years have given an annual DINNER, but not on any fixed day.

‡ Probably the QUINTEN—a sport long since disused, and which succeeded the ancient tournaments.

and upon St. George's daye; being thus decreed, that every horse putt in soe much money as made the value of the cupps or bells, and had the money, which horses did winne the same, and the use of the cupps, till that daye twelve month, being in bond to deliver in the cupps that daye;* soe alsoe for the cuppe for the ringe, which was yearely continued accordingly, untill the yeare of our Lord 1623; John Brereton, inn-holder, being Mayor of Chester, he altered the same after this manner, and caused the three cupps to be sould, and caused more money to be gathered and added, soe that the intereste thereof woulde make one faire silver cuppe, of the value of 8*l.* as I suppose, it may be worth, and the race to be altered, viz. from beyonde the New-Tower a great distance, and soe to rune five times from that place rownd about the Rood-dee, and he that overcame all the rest the last course, to have the cuppe freely for ever,† then and there delivered, which is continued to this daye. But here I must not omitt the charge, and the solemnitie made, the firste St. George's-daye; he had a poet, one Mr. Davies, whoe made speeches and poeticale verses, which were delivered at the high-crosse, before the Mayor and Aldermen, with showes of his invention, which booke was imprinted and presented to that famous Prince Henry, eldest sonne to the blessed King James, of famous memorie. Alsoe, he caused a man to goe upon the spire of St. Peter's steeple in Chester, and by the fane, at the same time time he sownded a drum, and displayed a banner upon the top of the same spire. And this was the original of St. George's race, with the change thereof, as it is now used. Also Mr. Robert Amorye caused the jacks, or boyes, which strike quarterly at St. Peter's at High-crosse, to be made and erected in A. D. 1612."

The solemnity on St. George's Day, alluded to in the above extract, is thus described in a paper in the Harl. Coll. The prizes were two bells and one cup, and not three cups:

"The manner of the showe, that is, if God spare life aud health, shall be seene by all the behoulders upon St. George's-day next, being the 23d of April, 1610, and the same with more addytions to continue, being for the Kyng's crowne and dignitie, and the homage to the Kyng and Prynce, with that noble victor St. George, to be continued for ever.—God save the Kyng."

"Item. Two men in greene liveries, set with worke upon their other habit, with blacke heare, and blacke beards, very ougly to behoulde, and garlands upon their heads, with fir woods to scatter abroad, to maintaine way for the rest of the showe.

Item. One on horsebacke, with the buckler and head piece of St. George, and three men to guide him, with a drum before him, for the honor of Englande.

Item. One on horsebacke, call'd Fame, with a trumpet in his hand, and three men to guide him, and he to make an oration, with his habit in pompe.

Item. One called Mercury, to desend from above in a cloude; his wings, and all other matters, in pompe, and heavenly musicke, with him; and after his oration spoken, to ryde on horsebacke, with his musicke before him.

Item. One call'd Chester, with an oration, and drums before him, his habit in pompe.

Item. One on horsebacke, with the Kynge's armes upon a shield, in pompe.

Item. One on horsebacke, conteening the Kinge's crowne and dignity, with an oration, in pompe.

Item. One on horsebacke, with a *bell*, dedicated to the Kynge, being double gilt, with the Kynge's armes upon it, carried upon a sceptre, in pompe, and before him a noise of trumpets, in pompe.

* This was a strange "bond," and in our day probably the winner would not be particular as to the fulfilment of the obligation.—Among the records of the Corporation, are some articles, relative to a race for two bells, and for a cup to be run for at the ring. The bell was the prize given for the winning horse, and from this arose the proverb to "bear the bell."—It is certain there were horse races annually at Chester so early as 1582, and probably long before that period: so that this City may claim, perhaps, a priority over all other places in England, not excepting York, as to the establishment of Races.

† Considering the Roodee as having formerly included the Tower Field, the site of the two Crane-streets, and Paradise-row, this run must be considered as an extraordinary trial of STRENGTH as well as speed. In 1629, the Companies contributed to St. George's Race; and in 1640, the Sheriffs gave a piece of plate value £13. 6s. 8d. to be run for on Easter Tuesday, in lieu of the Sheriffs' Breakfast.

Item. One on horsebacke, with an oration for the Prynce, in pompe.

Item. One on horsebacke, with the bell, dedicated to the Prynce, his armes upon it, in pompe, and to be carried on a septer, and before the bell, a noise of trumpets.

Item. One on horsebacke, with the cup of St. George, carried upon a septer, in pompe.

Item. One on horsebacke, with an oration for St. George, in pompe.

Item. St. George himselfe on horsebacke, in complete armor, with his flag and buckler, in pompe, and before him a noise of drums.

Item. One on horsebacke call'd Peace, with an oration, in pompe.

Item. One on horsebacke, call'd Plentye, with an oration, in pompe.

Item. One on horsebacke, call'd Envy, with an oration, whom Love will comfort, in pompe.

Item. One on horsebacke, call'd Love, with an oration to maintaine all, in pompe."

"Item. The Maior, and his brethren, at the Pentes of this Citye, with their best apparell, and in scarlet; and all the orations to be made before him, and seene at the high-crosse, as they passe to the Roodye, wher by Gentlemen, shall be runne for by thirr horses, for the two bells on a double staffe, and the cup to be runne for at the rynge, in the same place by the Gent. and with a greater mater of the showe by armes, and shott, and with more than I can recyte, with a banket after in the Pentis to make welcome the Gent.; and when all is done, then judge what you have seene, and so speake on your mynd, as you fynd—the

Actor for the presente,"

"ROBERT AMORYE."

"Amor is love, and Amorye is his name,
That did begin this pompe and princelye game;
The charge is great to him that all begun,
Who now is satisfied to see all so well done."

Having thus traced the great antiquity of "St. George's Races," which have continued, from a period at least as early as 1512, to the present day, a recapitulation of the plates and stakes, as they were entered in 1818, may not be improper:—

MONDAY, May 4, a Produce Stakes of 25gs. each for colts, 8st. 4lb.; fillies, 8st.---Two miles.

A Maiden Stakes of 15gs. each, for horses that never won Match, Plate, or Sweepstakes, before the 1st May, 1818. Two miles.

A Maiden Plate, value 50l. the best of heats, twice round the course to a heat, to start at the Coming-in Chair.

A Match for 100gs. p. p. between J. Phibbs, Esq.'s ch. f. and J. Bailey, Esq.'s ch. c. both three years old. Two miles.

A Match for 100gs. p. p. between Sir W. Wynne's gr. h. and J. Brady, Esq.'s ch. h. both five years old. Two miles.

TUESDAY, May 5th.---The Dee Stakes of 50gs. each, h. ft. for colts and fillies, then 3 yrs. old; once round and a distance, to start at the Distance Chair.---The owner of the second horse to receive back his stake.

The Earl of Chester's Plate, of 100gs. for all ages; winners of one Plate, Match, or Sweepstakes, to carry 5lb.; of two 7lb.; of three or more 10lb. extra; one heat, three times round the course.

Sixty Guineas, (clear) the gift of T. Grosvenor, Esq. and Sir J. G. Egerton, Bart. for three year olds; the best of three two-mile heats.

WEDNESDAY, May 6th, The Stand Gold Cup, value 100gs. added to a Sweepstakes of 10gs. for all ages. Twice round the course and a distance, to start at the Distance Chair.

The Annual City Plate, of 60gs. (clear) given by the Corporation, the best of heats, three times round the course to a heat, to start at the Coming-inChair.

THURSDAY, May 7, a Sweepstakes of 20gs. each, p. p. for three year olds; once round the course and a distance, to start at the distance chair. The horses to be bona fide the property of the subscribers.

A Cup value 70l. the gift of the Right Hon. Earl Grosvenor; the best of heats, three times round the course to a heat, to start at the Coming-in Chair.

FRIDAY, May 8, A Sweepstakes of 20gs. p. p. Two miles. The horses to be bona fide the property of the subscribers. Three subscribers or no race.

A Handicap Stakes of 10gs. each, p. p. with 20gs. added by the Stewards. Two miles. The horses to be bona fide the property of the subscribers. Three subscribers or no race.

The Ladies' Purse, value 50l. the best of heats, twice round the course to a heat; to start at the Coming-in Chair. A winner of one fifty to carry 2lb. extra; of two 5lb.; and of three or more, 8lb.; Matches and Sweepstakes excepted. The second best horse to be allowed Ten Pounds.

In 1816, a Grand Stand was erected on the Roodee by subscription, from a design by Mr. Harrison, the County Architect. The sum raised was £2,500. in shares of £50. each. An engraving of the Stand will be found in page 63; and the vignette below, is a representation of the 100gs. Subscription Cup (the first year) run for in 1817. It is the production of native talent, being from the manufactory of Mr. Walker, Assay Master, of Chester, and was won by Sir T. S. M. Stanley's brown colt Hooton. These "baubles" may perhaps pass away as the "glayves" and "bells" of our ancestors have done; and our successors may then feel a gratification in viewing the taste of those who preceded them, which temporary considerations render comparatively uninteresting. Not a relic exists of the "bells," &c. formerly run for.

The Whitsun Playes.

"" These playes were the worke of one Randall Higden, a Monke in Chester Abbeye, whoe in a good devotion translated the Bible into several partes and playes, soe as the common people might learne the same by their playinge; and also by action in their sighte, and the first time they were acted, or played, was in the time of Sir John Arnewaye, about the first year of his Maioralty, aboute A. D. 1328; we must judge this Monke had no evil intention, but secret devotion therein, soe alsoe the citizens, that did acte and practise the same, to their great coste. Here I must showe the manner of the performinge of these anchent playes, (which was) all those companies and occupations, which were joyned together to acte, or performe their several partes, had pagents, which was a building of a great height, with a lower and higher rowme, beinge all open, and set upon fower wheels, and drawne from place to place, where they played. The first place where they begane, was at the Abbeye Gates, where the Monks and Churche mighte have the first sighte; and then it was drawne to the high crosse before the Mayor and Aldermen, and soe from streete to streete, and when one pagent was ended another came in the place thereof, till all that were appoynted for the daye were ended; thus of the maner of the playes, all beinge at the Citizens' charge, yet profitable for them; for all, both far and near, came to see them."

"Now follow what occupations bring forth at their charges the playes of Chester, and on what dayes they are played yearly. These playes were sett forth, when they were played upon Mondaye, Tuesdaye, and Wednesdaye in the Whitsun weke."

1. "The Barkers and Tanners bringe forth The falling of Lucifer.
2. Drapers† and Hosiers, The Creation of the World.
3. Drawers of Dee, and Water-leaders --Noe and his Shippe.
4. Barbers, Wax-chandlers, and Leeches---Abraham and Isacke.
5. Cappers, Wire-drawers, and Pinners---King Balak, and Balam, with Moses.
6. Wrights, Slaters, Tylers, Daubers, and Thatchers---The Nativity of our Lord.
7. Paynters, Brotherers, and Glaziers---The Sheppard's Offering.
8. Vintners and Merchants---King Herod and the Mounte Victorial.
9. Mercers and Spisers---The three Kings of Coline.

These nine Pagents above written, be played on the firste daye."

1. "Gouldsmiths and Masons---The slayinge of the Children by Herod.
2. Smithes, Forbers, and Pewterers---Purification of our Ladye.

† Previous to 1600, the Drapers enacted this "Play," and determined to suit the DRESS to the period, Adam and Eve appeared literally naked, and were not ashamed!---After the fall they proposed to make themselves "SUBLIGACULA A FOLIIS, QUIBUS TEGAMUS PUDENDA."---an apron of fig leaves, &c.

CHESTER.

3. Bouchers---The Pinackle with the Woman of Canaan.
4. Glovers, and Parchment-makers---The arisinge of Lazarus from Death to Life.
5. Corvesers and Shoemakers---The coming of Christe to Jerusalem.
6. Bakers and Millners---Christe's Maundye, with his Disciples.
7. Boyers, Fletchers, Stringers, Cowpers, and Torners----The Scourginge of Christe.
8. Ironmongers and Ropers---The Crucifieinge of Christe.
9. Cookes, Tapsters, Hosiers, and Innkeepers---The Harrowinge of Hell.

These nine Pagents above written, be played upon the Second Daye, being Tuesdaye in Whitson Weke."

1. "Skynners,* Cardmakers, Hatters, Poynters, and Girdlers---The Resurrection.
2. Sadlers and Fusters---The Castell of Emmaus, and the Apostles.
3. The Taylors---Ascension of Christe.
4. Fishmongers---Whitsunday---the making of the Crede.
5. Shermen---Profetts afore the Day of Dome.
6. Hewsters, and Bell-founders---Antechriste.
7. Weavers and Walkers---Domesday.

These seven Pagents above-written, were played upon the Thirde Daye, beinge Wensedaye in Whitson Weke."

"These Whitsun playes were played in A. D. 1574. Sir John Savage, Knight, beinge Mayor of Chester, which was the laste time they were played, and we may praise God, and praye that we see not the like profanation of Holy Scripture; but O the mercy of God for the time of our ignorance: God, he regardes it not, as well in every man's particular as also in general causes."

In the British Museum, is a MS. copy of the Whitsun Plays, writen by George Bellin, with a Prologue, or "Banes, reade before the beginninges of the Playes of Chester, June 14, 1600." The date 1600 appears at the end of nearly all the Plays, in this form: "Finis Deo gratias, perme George Bellin, 1600." This Bellin was merely the transcriber. The following is a copy of the prologue:—

HISTORY.

"The Banes which are reade before the beginninge of the Playes of Chester.

"Reverende lordes and ladyes all
That at this time here assembled bee,
By this messauge understand you shall
That sometymes there was mayor of this citie
Sir John Arnwaye knighte, who most worthilye
Contented hymselfe to sett out in playe
The devise of one Done Rondall moonke of Chester Abbey.
This moonke, moonke-like, in scriptures well seene
In storyes travilled with the best sorte,
In pagentes set fourth apparently to all eyne
The old and new testament with lively comforth,
Intermynglinge therewith only to make sporte,
Som things not warranted by any writt;
Which to glad the hearers he woulde men to take yt.
This matter he abbrevited into playes twenty-foure,
And every playe of the matter gave but a taste;
Leaving for better learninge the circumstance to accomplishe,
For all his proceedinges maye appeare to be in haste.
Yet altogether unprofitable, his labours he did not waste;
For at this daye and ever he deserveth the fame
Which all moonkes deserves professinge that name.
These storyes yf the testamente at this time you knowe,
In a comon Englishe tongue never read nor harde;
Yet thereof in thes pagentes to make open shewe,
This moonke and moonke was nothing afreayde,
With feare of banginge, brenninge, or cutting off heade,
To set out that all maye disserne and see,
And parte good be lefte beleeve you mee.
As in this citie divers yeares the have bene sete out,
Soe at this tyme of Penticoste, called Whitsontyde,
Allthough to all the citie follow labour and coste,
Yet God givinge leave, that tyme shall you in playe,
For three dayes together, begynnyng on Mondaye,
See these pagentes played to the best of theire skill;

† Peculiar to the Skinners' company, at the present day, is a "local" incorporation, called the Corporation of Juan. It has existed from time immemorial, and no data exist by which to trace its origin. Mr. Dodd, a very respectable member of this company, in 1817, informed me, he had been told by those who had preceded him, that the name had its origin, from Spain—from skins being brought from the plains of Juan, in that country, to be dressed at Chester, from which circumstance the Skinners eventually were called the Company or Corporation of Juan. Is it not more probable, however, that the name Juan, is a corruption of the ancient name Devana?—An election takes place for the office of Mayor of Juan, annually,—the senior apprentice is generally the person made choice of. It was customary a few years ago, for the newly elected Mayor of Juan, attended by his officers, preceded by a fiddler, and drum and fife, to proceed to the Exchange to pay his compliments to the Mayor of the City, where his Worship of Juan, and Brethren, were generally treated with half-a-pint of wine each. This formality still exists.

Where to supplye all wantes, shall be noe wante of good will
As all that shall see them shall moste welcome be,
Soe all that here them we most humblie praye
Not to compare this matter or storie
With the age or tyme wherein we presentlie stay;
But in the tyme of ignorance wherein we did straye;
Then doe I compare that this lande throughout,
Non had the like, nor the like dose sett oute.
If the same belikeinge to the commons all,
Then our desier is to satisfie, for that is all our gaine;
Yf noe matter or shewe thereof speciall
Doe not please, but mislike the moste of the trayne;
Goe backe I saye to the firste tyme againe;
Then shall you fynde the fyne witt at this day aboundinge,
At that day and that age had verye small beinge.
Condemne not our matter where grosse wordes you here,
Which ymporte at this daye small sence or understandynge,
As some tyme POSTIE LEWTES, in good manner or in feare,
With such like will be uttered in their speeches speakinge,
At this tyme those speeches carried good likinge,
Tho at this tyme, you take them spoken at that tyme,
As well matter as wordes, then all is well and fyne.
This worthy knighte Arnwaye then maior of this cittie,
This order toke, as declare to you I shall,
That by twenty-fower occupations, artes, craftes or misteries,
These pagentes should be played after briefe rehearsall;
For every pagente a carriage to be provided withall:
In which sorte we purpose this Whitsontyde,
Our pageants into three partes to devyde.
Now you worshipful Tanners, that of custome old,
The fall of Lucifer did set out, &c. &c.
——————— therefore be boulde
Lustely to play the same to all the rowtte;
And yf any thereof stande in any doubte,
Your author his author hath your showe let be,
Good speech, fyne players, with apparell comelye," &c.

The following short Extracts will serve as Specimens.

Noe and his Shippe.

"Then Noe shall goe into the arke with all his familye his wife except, the arke must be borded rounde aboute with bordes, all the beastes and fowles hereafter rehearsed must be painted, that there wordes may agree with the pictures."

NOE.

"Wife come in, why standes thou there
Thou arte ever frowarde I dare well sweare.

HISTORY.

NOE'S WIFFE.

Yea sir, set up your sayle
And row forth with evill haile,
For withouten faile I will not out
Out of this towne;
But I have my gossippes every eich one,
On foote further I will not gone;
They shall not drowne by St. John,*
And I maye save there life;
But thou wylt let them into that cheist,
Else rowe forth Noe where thou list,
And get thee a new wife.

THE GOOD GOSSIPPS.

The flood comes flitting in full fast,
One every syde that spreadeth full farr;
For fear of drowning I ame agaste;
Goode gossippes let us drawe neere;
And let us drinke or we departe,
For oft-tymes we have done soe,
For at a draught thou drinkes a quarte,
And soe will I doe or I goe;
Here is a pottell full of Malmeseye gode and stronge,
Yt will rejoice both hart and tongue;
Though Noe thinke us never so longe,
Yet we will drinke alike.

JAPHAT.

Mother we pray you all together,
For we are here your owne children;
Come into the shipp for feare of the weather.

NOE'S WIFFE.

That will I not for all your call,
But I have my gossippes all.

SEM.

In faith mother yet thou shalt
Whether thou wilt or not.

NOE.

Welcome wife into this boat.

WIFFE.

Have thou that for thy note

(ET DAT ALAPAM.)†

NOE.

Ha! ha! marye, this is hott,
It is good for to be still;
A! children methinkes my boate removes,
Our tarryinge here highly me greeves;

* Noah's wife swearing by St. John, is a strange anachronism.

† She gives him a box on the ear.

Over the lande the water spreades,
God doe as he will."

King Balack and Balaam, with the Prologue.

" Cappers and Lynnendrapers, see that you fourth bring
In well decked order, that worthy storee
Of Balaam and his asse, and of Balacke the kinge;
Make the asse to speake and set yt out livelye."

ASINA.

" Master thou doest evill sikerly,
Soe good an asse as me to nye;
Nowe thou haste beaten ma here thrye,
That bare thee thus aboute.

BALAAM.

Burnell, why begylest thou me.
When I have most nede of thee.

ASINA.

That sighte that before me I see,
Maketh me downe to lowte:
Am not I, master, thyne own asse
To bear thee whether thou wilte passe,
And many winters ready was,
To smyte me it is shame.
Thou wottest well, master, pardye
Thou hadest never non lyke to me.
Ney never yet soe served I thee,
Now ame not I to blame.

The Creation of the World.

" Then God taketh Adam by the hand, and causeth him to lye downe and taketh a rybb out of his side and sayth,--" &c. &c.

" Then God doth make the woman of the rybb of Adam; then Adam wakinge speaketh unto God as followeth."

ADAM.

" I see well Lorde through thy grace,
Bone of my bone thou here mase,
And fleshe of my fleshe hase;
And my shape through thy sawe,
Wherefore she shall be called, I wysse,
VIRAGO, nothing amisse,
For out of man taken she is,
And to man shall she drawe."

" Then Adam and Eve shall stande naked and shall not be ashamed;* then the serpent shall come up out of a hole and the devill walking shall say--

" That of woman is forbidden to doo,
For any thinge they will there too;
Therefore that tree she shall come to,
And assaye what yt is:
A manner of an edder is in this place,
That winges like a bird she hase,
Fete as an edder, a mayden's face,
Her kinde I will take:
And of the tree of paradice
She shall eate through my contyse;
For women they be full licorise,
That will not she forsake."

After the Reformation, these plays were seldom acted; in 1560, 1566, 1567, and 1571, they were re-produced, and an inhibition from the Archbishop of York, for preventing them came too late. During the Mayoralty of Sir John Savage,† the Plays were again performed, † 1574.
by order of the Mayor and Corporation. The records of the Body, however, freely allow, that these strange performances, were " to the great dislike of many, because the plague was then in the city:" but it appears they were amended and corrected.—The Archbishop, nevertheless, was not conciliated, and prosecuted the matter against Sir John Savage, Mr. Hankey, (Mayor in 1571) and such of the Citizens as performed in them. It is not now known how the affair terminated; but it appears from Mr. Rogers's MSS. they were never after repeated.‡

The Whitsun Plays were not the only specimens of

* In one of the copies the minstrels are afterwards directed to play whilst Adam and Eve are adjusting their fig-leaves!

‡ In Nov. 1588, the Bishop wrote the following letter to the Mayor, at the period of the destruction of the Spanish Armada. It is introduced here as a curious document, being, perhaps, the first order for a General Thanksgiving ever issued by a Bishop in England:—

" SAL. IN PR. FOR.—I have receyved specill dyrection from her Ma'tie to appoynte generall prayers and thankes gevynge to be made in every Churche throughout my Dyocese upon Friday wch. shall be the sixthe of this instant November (a day to be celebrated through-

CHESTER

early dramatic taste, exhibitted before the good Citizens of Chester: in 1488, "The Assumption of our Lady," was played before the Lord Strange, at the High Cross; in 1498,* it was played before Prince Arthur,† eldest son of Henry VII. at the Abbey Gate.

* August 8.

In 1515, "The Assumption," and the "Shepherd's Play," were enacted in St. John's Church-yard. In 1529, the play of Rt. Cecill was performed at the High Cross. On the Sunday after Midsummer-day, 1564,‡ the "History of Æneas and Queen Dido," was played on the Roodeye, as "sette out by W. Crofton, gentleman, and one Mr. Man, Master of Arts." at which triumph there were made two forts and shipping on thewater, besides many horsemen, well armed and appointed||.

‡ Lysons.

In 1577, the "Shepherd's Play" was performed before the Earl of Derby, at the High Cross, and the Roodeye was the scene of several "triumphs." A Play, called "King Ebranke with all his Sonnes," was performed at the High Cross, in 1589. This Ebranke is one of our ancient British Kings, in whose history is interwoven so much of the marvellous. Holinshead informs us, he had twenty-one wives, fifty-nine children, of whom twenty were sons. Ebranke is said to have built York, and his sons to have invaded and subdued Germany. But enough of this.

We find no mention of the plays since 1589, and it is probable, immediately after that period, they sunk into complete disuse.

HISTORY.

Curious Orders of the Mayors, &c.—Customs peculiar to the City.

Several of the local enactments for the Government of the City, are extremely curious. The following are mentioned so early as the record of Doomsday:—

The fine for bloodshed on certain holydays, specified	20s.
On other days	10s.
For murder in a house, the forfeiture of lands and goods, and the party to be deemed an outlaw.	
For manslaughter on specified days	80s.
On other days	40s.
Unchastity in a widow	20s.
In an unmarried woman	10s.
For a rape, if commited in a house—for robbery or insurrection	40s.
The making false measures	4s.
Making bad ale, the punishment of sitting one hour in a tumbrel, on market day, or a fine of	4s.
In case of fire, the person in whose house it broke out, was subject to a fine, not declared; besides paying to his next door neighbour	2s.

Under the rule of the Earls, a custom prevailed, that if a Debtor should come into the Exchequer Court, and swear that he would discharge his debts as soon as he was able, a writ of protection was granted to him, by virtue of which he was at full liberty, and could not be molested by his creditors. But this, perhaps, prevailed more particularly in the County: In the City itself, a custom prevailed from time immemorial, that any freeman, having been imprisoned for a debt, and unable

---

out the whole realme), for our delyverance from the Spanyards and the wonderfull overthrowe of that Power which they had prepared against us; whereof I thoughte goode to advertyse you, and the rest of yr Brethren, to the ende that you myghte be all at home and in readines to celebrate that day accordingeley, not onely in your harte, but with yr. bodyly presence at the said Prayers, in yr. most comeley and decent manner, after the order off yr. Cytye; wyshynge that you wolde also have yr. self and pr. cure yor. Brethren and other of the well affected cytizens to communicate (for there will be a generall communication) and further that you wolde cause all Shoppes, Taverns, and Typlynge houses to be shutte up all that daye (as they were and will be in London) lest throughe any worldly occasion those who are not fully grounded in good zeal myght withdraw themselves from that most godly actyon. And not doubtynge but you will have a dutyfull regarde of the premises, with my hartye commendations, I trust you to God. Manchester this xi of November, 1588.

Yor. verey lovynge friende,

Mr. Maior of Chester." W: Cestren:

† Much has been said by different writers, as to the precise place of rank and dignity which an Esquire should fill. It would seem that it was formerly a dignity by creation; for we find that on the 25th August, 1498, Prince Arthur "made the Maior, Richard Goodman, an Esquire!"

|| In 1567, the Mayor (Richard Dutton) is said "to have kepte a very worthye howse for all comers duringe all the tyme of Christmas, with a lorde of Misrule, and other pastymes"—these pastimes consisted of mummery of every description. These "pastymes," &c. appear to be in the teeth of an order of Assembly, 3d and 4th Philip and Mary, "that all mummerys and disguises be left off at Christmas tyme."

CHESTER.

to pay it; he was allowed to go before the Mayor and Sheriffs, and on swearing that the debt should be paid as soon as possible, reserving himself "mean sustentation" only, he was allowed his discharge. This is stated in a record among the orders and acts of Assembly of the Corporation,* temp Hen. VII. Fifty years after this, the practice varied; for then it appears, that any freeman petitioning the Mayor and Aldermen, and declaring himself unable to pay his debts, was permitted to reside in what was called the "Free-house," to walk at large within its liberties,† and to attend service at (Little) St. John's Church without the Northgate; but he was restricted from entering into any dwelling-house. The boundaries of these liberties were "along the walls (from the Northgate) on the west-side to the New (Water) Tower; on the east side to Newton (Phœnix) Tower, and towards the Corn Market as far as the New-houses of St. Anne's, which had been there lately built in the Bell Yard."

* Lib. A. fol. 76.

In 1459, an Order of Assembly was made, that no person in the four principal streets of the City, should willingly receive into their houses, chambers, or cellars, nor set the same, to any woman that openly misuseth herself with any wedded man, or any other man of ORDER, upon every of the twenty-four ALDERMEN paying ten shillings, and every other six shillings and eight-pence, to be levied by the Sheriffs, &c.

1508.—Ordered by the Mayor and Sheriffs, that all Innkeepers, &c, hang out lautherns, from All Saints to Candlemas, or forfeit one shilling for each neglect; and that all taverns be shut up at nine o'clock, or forfeit six shillings and eightpence.

‡ 21st Nov. 3d Henry VIII.

1512.‡—An order for avoiding of Idleness: all children of six years old or upwards, shall on week days be set to school, or some virtuous labour, whereby they may hereafter get an honest living; and on Sundays and Holidays, they shall resort to their Parish Churches, and there abide during the time of service; and in the afternoon all the said small children shall be exercised in shooting with bows and arrows for pins and points only, and that their parents furnish them with bows and arrows, pins and points for that purpose, according to the statute lately made for maintenance of shooting in long bows and artillery, being the ancient defence of the kingdom.

† This custom is closely analogous to having "the rules of the Bench," in London.

HISTORY.

|| 12th May 32d Henry VIII.

1540.||—Order of Assembly.—Whereas ALL the Taverns and Alehouses of this City, be used to be KEPT BY YOUNG WOMAN, otherwise than is used in any other place of this realme, whereat all strangers greatly marvel and think it inconvenient, whereby great slander and dishonest report of this city hath and doth run abroad; in avoiding whereof, as also to eschew such great occasions of wantonness, brawls, frays, and other inconveniences as thereby doth and may arise among youth and light disposed persons, as also damages to their masters, owners of the Taverns and Alehouses: Ordered, that after the 9th of June next, there shall be no Tavern or Alehouse kept in the said City by any Woman between fourteen and forty years of age, under pain of forty pounds forfeiture for him or her that keepeth any such servant.

Another order of the same date.—Whereas great expense and superfluous charge hath been and doth grow, by reason of costly dish meals and drinks, *brought unto women lying in childbed*, and by them likewise recompensed at their churchings; whereby such as are of mean substance strain themselves to more charge than they can well sustain; Ordered, that henceforth no such dish-meals nor wines be brought to women in childbed, or at churchings; and that no women (except the midwife, mother, sister, and sisters-in-law, of the woman churched) shall go into the house of her that is churched, but bring her to the door and so depart, on pain of six shillings and eightpence, upon the owner of the house; and three shillings and fourpence upon every person offending, *toties quoties*.§

Same year.—Ordered—That to distinguish the head-dresses of married women from unmarried women, no unmarried woman to wear any hat, unless when she rides or goes abroad into the country (except sick

§ This is a strange stretch of civic authority!

CHESTER.

or aged persons) on pain of three shillings and fourpence.

* 23d Eliz. October 26. 1581.*—Ordered, that no wife, widow, or maid, shall keep any tavern, ale or beer cellar, in Chester.

1590.—Ordered, that none should be made free, except he came in armour, or other furniture, as his ability was, and to depose it to be his own, and not borrowed.

3d and 4th Philip and Mary.—" The breakfasts used on Christmas Day, to be laid aside, that men may apply themselves to religious duties."

Same date.—Ale to be no more than a penny a quart, and that *to be full.* " All mummings and disguises to be left off at Christmas time."

† 26th Oct. 13th James. 1616.†—Ordered, that no Players be allowed to Act in the Common Hall;‡ and further that for avoiding several inconveniences, ordered, that they shall not Act in any place within the liberties of the City, after six in the evening.

|| Nov. 16. 1651 ||—An order that all of the Common Council should wear their tippets, as formerly, " to the ende they may bee knowne to bee off the Common Councell of the said Cittie."

1657.—Ordered that all Common Councilmen who had not paid their *haunch feasts;* be forthwith ordered to pay, or be disfranchised.

1657.—Ordered, that the Sheriffs, Aldermen, Sheriffs' Peers, and Leavelookers, shall attend the Maior every Monday, Wednesday, and Saturday, at ten of the clock in the Morning, to assist in the Administration of Publique Justice—and that they also attend the Maior in the Pentice, on every Sabbath or Lord's Day, in the afternoon, before Sermonne, under the penalty of four shillings, for every Justice of the Peace, and one shilling for every other person.

It was customary to hang out a Glove, to announce the coming fair, previous to 1658, for we then find an Order of Assembly, " that by unanimous consent a Glove shall be hung out to give notice of the ensuing fair as heretofore.

1663 (July 11.)—Ordered, that letters be sent unto Richard Dutton, Alderman, Richard Savage, Alderman, and Valentine Short, of the Common Council, to admonish them either to come and inhabit within the City, between and Michaelmas next, or to surrender their offices; otherwise to be degraded at the Assembly following.

Same year, (Dec. 12.)—Being put to the question, whether the Calves-head Feast be a feast to be maintained by auncient custome and usage, or at the will and pleasure of the Sheriffs and Leavelookers; it was resolved in the former question, and that it is not to bee upon the pleasure of the Sheriffs and Leavelookers.

Same year.—Ordered, that fifty pounds be granted to the children of the late John Ratcliffe, Esq. *the Member,* " he beinge in his lyfe tyme a usefull and profitable servant to this cittie, and in the service thereof had spent a great part of his tyme and estate, and by reason thereof was enforced to contract several considerable debts."

1666.§—George Watts petitioned on the behalf of himself and his company the cittie wayts, desiring to have the citties liverye to be bestowed upon them,—ordered that Geo. Watts and two others of the auncient wayts shall have clothe to be given them, to make them livery gowns, to be worn in the citie, and not elsewhere. § Dec. 14.

1671.—Ordered, that all butchers within this cittie, shall henceforth cause their swine to be killed without the walls of the Cittie, upon pain of twelve pence for every swine.

The Eastgate, it appears, was sometime the Gaol for

‡ The present Theatre; and previous to its being the Common Hall, the Chapel of St. Nicholas! The lower part is occupied as a Carrier's Warehouse.

CHESTER HISTORY.

the Prisoners; there is an Order of Assembly, in 1671, that "the Prisoners in the Northgate, by reason of the insufficiency and untenableness thereof, be removed to the Eastgate, and that it be and continue the Cittie Gaol till further orders."

1672. The City Waits ordered to have new liveries every three years, and ten shillings a year at Christmas.

1673.—All show-boards in the rows ordered to be made with hinges, to prevent people injuring themselves in walking against them at night.

1674*.—A letter from the Bishop (John) being read—and it being put to the vote, whether the parishes in this Cittie should be reduced to a lesser number (to wit) those Churches which have no endowment belonging to them, to be added to others that have, as had been done in Exeter; it was resolved in the negative.

1678.†—Ordered, that the Christmas Watch shall not bee observed at Christmas next, in regard of a late dangerous conspiracy against the peerson and life of his Sacred Majesty, and the great danger this Kingdome is conceeved to bee in of an Insurrection of the Roman Catholiques.

1679.—The Midsummer Show being disused,—Ordered, that Mr. Randle Holme be recompenced in £20. for the gyantts he had made for the same.

Same year.—The Christmas Watch again dispensed with, "in consequence of the horrid Popish Plots."

Same year.—Ordered, that the *Linen-drapers* and the *Bricklayers* should be separated as a Company, the latter being troublesome and unserviceable to the former.

1680.—The Calves Head Feast ordered to be observed.

1683.‡—Ordered, that the Treasurers shall pay for the King's picture, and for the other pictures of Justice and Prudence, sett up in the Common Hall, the summe of £7. 5s. 0d.

1689.||—Ordered, that Mr. Maior, have his kitchen fee of 20 nobles, and 40 shillings, for a Venison Feast, due to him in 1683.

1690 §—Ordered, that a deputation (there named) be appointed to wait on their Majesties at Poole, and learn whether his Majesty will be pleased to take this City in his way, &c. and in case his Majesty shall be pleased to honor this City with his presence, the Maior, &c. shall meet his Majesty on horseback, in their formalities, at the Black Lyon, in Boughton, with all possible demonstrations of duty, and loyalty; and that his Majesty be entertained at the Pentice in such manner as the Aldermen shall think fit—[The deputation went, but the King did not visit the City]

Same year.—The Corporation of Drapers fined £10. for not attending the Mayor on Shrove Tuesday, and not continuing their usual *potations*.

1693.¶—The estimate for building the New Hall (the present Exchange) amounted to £1,000.**

Same date.—Ordered, that the Mayor and Sheriffs of the City, to whom the conservation of the Dee belongeth, do inquire into the complaints alledged against the Wirrall Fishermen, for *setting stake nets, &c.* and they to be prosecuted at the charge of the City.

Same year.††—Alderman Wilcocke, the Treasurer, having refused to give up the key of the box in which the Common Seal of the City was kept, the same is ordered to be broken open.

Same year.—Ordered, that no horses are to run for St. George's race, unless they come in eight days before the races, and continue in the city.

1696.‡‡—Ordered, that the table over the Inner Pentice door, whereon is an account of the procuring

* March 4.

† Nov. 22.

‡ April 15.

|| Oct. 10.

§ June 6.

¶ April 13.

†† June 2.

‡‡ June 30.

** Sam. Farrington being chosen sword-bearer, paid £100. for the same, which was presented by the Mayor, Col. Roger Whitley, to the City, towards the building of a new Common Hall.

CHESTER HISTORY.

and bringing down of the new Charter, be taken down, and removed by the Yeoman of the Pentice, and delivered to the Treasurers to be disposed of for the benefit of the City, it containing matter both scandalous and false, and particularly that the New Charter was to the satisfaction of all good men, &c.

* Feb. 18. 1697.*—Ordered, that the Treasurers do pay unto Randle Holme, herald painter, and his son, the sum of three pounds, for their attendance and assistance in proclaiming the Peace, lately concluded between his Majesty and his Allies, and the French King.

CITY WAITS.—In the Corporation Records, I find that the Mayor of Chester, had on his civic establishmemt four *Waits*, or Musicians, to play before him on public occasions. They had annual salaries and liveries, with liberty to solicit a Christmas Box, for which they played to the *Watch*, or *Customers*, about the time of Christmas. The livery and salary have long since been discontinued, and musicians hired to attend the Mayor in processions, &c.—The *Customers* were the grantees of the four Gates, by virtue of which they were bound to watch the City by night, during the predatory incursions of the Welsh. Each of these Customers had a Musician in attendance, and hence probably arose the appellation of City Waits. The love of music, also, might have induced others of the Citizens to attend at the Gates, and thus render the watch more respectable. At the present day, half-a-dozen fiddlers perambulate the City, at midnight, for a fortnight preceding Christmas, and after striking up a lively air, bid the tenants of the different houses, a "Good-morrow:" but for this act of courtesy, they afterwards call for a return, in the shape of a Christmas Box. Some years ago, the Bellman, imagining, probably, that his bell was at least as loud as a fiddle, visitted the different streets, and tuning his melodious official instrument, bade the Citizens a "good-morrow" also. This addition to the midnight serenades has, possibly for want of taste, been dispensed with.

The Execution of the County Prisoners by the City, has given rise to much conjecture, and sagacious reasoning.—It admits, however, of easy explanation:—In an Inquisition taken in 1321, for the purpose of ascertaining the tolls payable at the City Gates, it is stated, that the Mayor and Citizens, as keepers of the Northgate, had a right to certain tolls, for which they were bound to watch the said Gate, and the prisoners in the prison of the Earl there imprisoned; to keep the key of the felon's gallows; to HANG UP THE CONDEMNED CRIMINALS; to execute the sentence of pillory; proclaim the bann of the Earl within the city,‡ &c. In another record, entitled, "The claymes of the Cittizens of Chester," after reciting their existing privileges and immunities, it states, that there were certain *Customary tenants* of the City, sixteen in number, who by their tenure were bound to watch the City three nights in the year, which are specified; and also to watch and bring up felons and thieves condemned, as well in the Court of Justiciary of Chester, IN THE COUNTY THERE, as *before the* Mayor of Chester in full Crown Mote, as far as the gallows, for their safe conduct and charge, under the penalty which attaches thereto; for which services the said customary tenants had certain privileges and exemptions. This record is without date; but from the names of Sir Hugh Hulse, and some others, to whom the houses to which their services were attached, belonged, it appears to have been about the year 1400.—Of these "*Customers*," there were five in *Eastgate-street*, viz. Hugh Hulse, Chiliver Johnson, Robert de Lancelyn, Mary Dew with John de Wigan, and Nicholas Give: in *Bridge-street*, five; John de Whitmore, Roger de Dutton, Robert le Chamberlayne, John le Tanner, and Robert de Strangeways for the Tenement in the Fields: in *Watergate-street*, four; Henry the Abbot of Chester, Corbin, Lawrence de Worcaster, and Elizabeth, who was wife of John Hawarden: in *Northgate-street*, two; Hen. de Birtheli, and John de Whitmore. This "custom" is still continued the following houses now pay the Gabel, or Execution Rent:—

In BRIDGE-STREET.—The Harp-and-Crown, public-

‡ Before the appointment of a particular local Magistracy, it is highly probable the same judicature existed throughout the county at large, including the city. The Barons of the Earl, however, held their separate Courts of Justice, within their Baronies, which were vested with as ample powers as any of our existing Criminal Courts.—See page 52.

CHESTER

house, on the south-side of Common-hall-street; the house of Mr. Brittain, woollen-draper,* on the east-side of Bridge-street; Mrs. Huntington's house, adjoining the road to the stables of the Feathers Inn; the house above the shop of Mr. Vernon, grocer, nearly opposite the Feathers; Mrs. Shone's house, east-side of Lower Bridge-street.—EASTGATE-STREET—Mr. Finchett's house, east-side of the Honey-steps; the house occupied by Mr. Alderman Bowers; Mr. Jackson's house, east-side of Newgate-street, adjoining the Royal Hotel; Mrs. Gardner's house, adjoining the Old Talbot, near the Eastgate.—NORTHGATE-STREET—The Fleece Inn; the house rented by Messrs. Leeke and Potts's, and adjoining the house of Stephen Leeke, Esq. on the south-side; Mr. John Chamberlaine's house, near the Shambles.—WATERGATE-STREET—The house occupied by Miss Williams, east-side of Goss-street; the house of Mr. Bulkeley, adjoining the last; the Castle and Falcon Tavern; the Moon Tavern; the house lately occupied by Mr. Barlow, glazier, opposite Crooke's-lane. It appears, therefore, there is one house LESS in Eastgate-street,† than is mentioned in the preceding record; one MORE in Watergate-street, and one MORE in Northgate-street: there are still five in Bridge-street.

THE CHESHIRE MINSTRELS.—In page 23, is noticed the ancient custom vested in the Dutton family, of licensing the Minstrels of Cheshire.—The particulars below will not be uninteresting:—This right‡ was exercised by the Duttons, and their representatives the Gerards and Fleetwoods, as long as they continued in possession of the Dutton Estate; and though not originally attached to the estate, but vested in the heirs of Dutton, it appears, nevertheless, to have been alienated with it. The Minstrels' Courts were, to the middle of the last century, held annually at Chester, on St John Baptist's day, by the heir or Lord of Dutton, or his steward. A banner emblazoned with the Dutton arms, was hung out of the window of the Inn where the Court was held, and a drummer proclaimed in the streets the important sitting, summoning all persons concerned to appear in the Court. At eleven o'clock, a procession was formed, and moved from the Inn as follows:—

‡ Lysons p. 524.

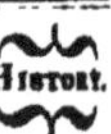

HISTORY.

A BAND OF MUSIC.

Two Trumpeters.

Licensed Musicians with white napkins across their shoulders.

The Banner.—borne by one of the Principal musicians.

The Steward,

On horseback with a white wand in his hand.

A Tabarder, his tabard emblazoned with the arms of Dutton.

The Lord or Heir of Dutton,

(if present)

Attended by the Gentry of the County and City, on horseback.

In the middle of Eastgate-street, this proclamation was made:

"Oyez, oyez, oyez! This is to give notice to all musicians and minstrels, that the Court of the Honorable Charles Gerard Fleetwood, Esq. (descendant heir of Eleanor, sole daughter and heiress of Thomas Dutton, of Dutton, in the County of Chester, Esq. by Sir Gilbert Gerard, son and heir of Thomas Lord Gerard, of Gerard's Bromley, in the County of Stafford) is this day held at the house of Robert Cluff, of the Eagle and Child, Northgate-street, Chester, where all such Musicians and Minstrels as do intend to play upon any instrument of music for gain, within the County of Chester, or within the County of the City of Chester, are required to appear and take license for the year ensuing, otherwise they will be adjudged, and taken up as rogues and vagabonds, and punished accordingly. God Save the King, and the Lord of the Court."||

* Remarkable for being the scene of the change of the warrant of Persecution against the Irish Protestants, for a pack of cards; and then a Tavern, called the "Blue Posts."—See page 147.

† It is probable that two houses might have formerly stood on the site of thatnow occupied by Mrs. Gar dner.

|| The following is found in Cowper's MSS. and copied by Mr. Ormerod in his History, from which it is now extracted:—"In this Mayoralty§ Matthew Ellis of Overleigh, and Thomas Browne of Netherlegh, within the precincts of the City of Chester, having each married a daughter of Sir Piers Dutton, of Dutton, the two weddings were kept at the same time and with much festivity at Dutton Hall, from whence the gentlemen brought their brides, on Tuesday the 24th of June, which being the feast of St. John the Baptist, and the day upon which the minstrelsy of the city and county are annually licensed at Chester by the lord of Dutton, the company before-mentioned were met on their return from Dutton Hall, by Flookersbrook-bridge, by the steward of Dutton, attended by the pursuivant and standard-bearer of that family, each properly habited, and having the insignia used at

§ Mayoralty of Hen. Gee 1539.

The procession then moved on to St. John's Church. On entering the chancel, the Musicians, by notice from the steward, played several pieces of sacred music *upon their knees;* after which Divine Service was performed, and the heir or Lord of Dutton, especially prayed for. The following proclamation was made after service :—" God save the King, the Queen, the Prince, and all the Royal Family; and the Honorable Charles Gerard Fleetwood, Esq. (heir descendant of that ancient, worthy family of the Duttons, of Dutton, in Cheshire, and of the Right Honorable Family of the Gerards, of Gerard's Bromley, in the County of Stafford), long may he live, and support the honor of the Minstrel's Court."

The procession then returned to the Inn, in the same order that it came, and entertainments were given to the Lord's friends and to the Musicians. In the afternoon a Jury was impannelled from among the licensed Minstrels, to whom the Steward delivered a charge; and directed them to inquire of any treason against the King or the Earl of Chester; likewise whether any man of their profession had exercised his instrument without license from the Lord of the Court, and what misdemeanors they had been guilty of; and whether they had heard any language amongst their fellows, tending to the dishonor of their lord and patron, the heir of Dutton.

A verdict according to circumstances, was then given by the Jury; the oath was administered to the musicians; and licenses granted to all who were adjudged worthy, empowering them to play for one year.*

The last court was held in 1756, R. Lant, Esq. being then Lord of Dutton, and possessing the advowry of the minstrels by purchase; previous to which they were not held annually as had been the custom, but every two or three years. The fee for a license was 2s. 6d. but it does not appear, that much attention was paid to the mandates of the Lord of Dutton; for in 1754, only twenty-one licenses were granted. In the charge of the steward of Mr. Lant, in the before-mentioned year, he observes—" Gentlemen of the Jury, the oath which you have just now taken, seems to make it proper to say something by way of charge; otherwise your own knowldege and experience would have rendered it quite unnecessary; but as the duty of the office of Steward of this honorable Court, and your oath require that a charge should be given to you, I shall beg leave to take up a little of your time, and say something to you concerning this honorable Court—the duty and privileges of Musicians in this City and County of Chester—and your duty as Jurors. The Records relating to this honorable Court, which are still preserved, shew it to have been of great antiquity; and the readiness and zeal

that Midsummer solemnity, preceded by all the licensed musicians with white scarves across their shoulders, ranked in pairs, and playing on their several instruments. This procession marched before the gentlemen and their guests quite through the city, to their respective mansions, where plentiful entertainment was provided on the occasion."

*Under the royall grace of the king's most excellent ma'tie and his most ho'ble counsell, the right ho'ble lord viscount Kilmurrey, lord, leader, conducter, (and under his highness) protecter of all and every music'ons and minstrells whosoever, either resident or resorting within or to ye county pallatine of Chester, and w'thin or to the citty of Chester, by virtue and authoritie of the auntiente use, custom, prebeminence, and speciall royalltie of the predecessors of the manor of Dutton, straightly chargeth and commandeth all and every the said music'ons and minstrells and other whatsoever acknowledgeinge, useinge, and p'fessinge the noble art, worthy science, and high misterie of musique and minstrellzie w'thin the said countyes, or either of them, to approach this pub'c place and attend this pub'c proclamac'on, and pub'cly here to drawe forthe their sundry instruments of musique and minstrellzie, and to play here before ye said Robert viscount Kilmurrey, or his deputy' here publ'y unto the accustomed place in dutiful manner and order customablie used by his predecessors before tyme, soe longe that the memory of man can not witnes to the contrary, which royalltie hath beene alwayes annexed and resigned to the said auncient predecessors of the manor of Dutton, and now come unto the said Robert viscount Kilmurrey, in the right of dame Elinour now wife of the said Robert viscount Kilmurrey, and sole daughter and heire of Thomas Dutton, late of Dutton aforesaid, esq. deceased, and her heirs, as p'cell and porc'on of her inheritance, and in like good dutifull order to retorne from the said place, playinge upon their said severall instruments unto the court-house, and there to make their severall appearances; alsoe to doe all other such homages, duties, and services, as by virtue thereof belongeth to the aforesaid court of ye said Robert viscount Kilmurrey: and from thence in like order, playinge upon their said severall instruments, to his lodginge, and not to dep'te without license. This omitt you nott, as you will at yo'r p'ills aboyde the displeasure of the aforenamed Robert viscount Killmurrey, the rebuke of the Court, forfeiture of your instruments, and imprisonment of your bodyes. God save the king's ma'ty, his most ho'ble counsell, and the lord of Dutton, and send us peace. Amen.—Tabley MSS.

CHESTER HISTORY.

which the Musicians heretofore shewed in redeeming their Prince, when he was surrounded by enemies, have been a means of perpetuating their service, and establishing this honorable Court, which Mr. Lant, the present Lord of the Manor of Dutton claims, and the privileges thereto belonging, from Roger Lacy, Constable of the Castle of Chester, who raised the siege at Rhuddlan Castle, and brought the Prince in great triumph to Chester; some of which privileges are, that all Musicians shall appear and do their suit and service at this Court; and no Musician shall play upon any instrument for gain, without having a license from the Lord of Dutton, or his Steward of this Court. And if any person does presume to play for gain without such license, he is not only liable to be prosecuted by a due course of law, but also to be prosecuted as a rogue, vagrant, and vagabond. These privileges have been confirmed and allowed by several Acts of Parliament;* and Mr. Lant, is determined that the power and authority of this Court shall be preserved, and that none shall exercise the employment of a Musician for gain, without a license from him or his Steward; and therefore, Gentlemen, he expects, and the oath you have just taken requires, that you should inquire of all such persons, playing upon any instrument of music, for gain, either in the County of Chester, or the County of the City of Chester; and if you know, or are particularly informed of any such, you are to present them to this Court, that they may be proceeded against, and punished according to law; which the Lord and Steward thereof are determined to do, with the utmost severity.

* 14 Eliz. c. 5.—39 Eliz. c. 4.—43 Eliz. c. 9.—1 Jac. 1, c. 25. 17 Geo. 1, c. 5.

Mosses, sc.

OLD TABLEY HALL, *the Seat of Sir J. F. Leicester, Bart.*

Mosses, sc.
Interior of St. John's Church, *Chester.*

Churches, Religious Houses, &c.

THE CATHEDRAL.

Occupies the site of the ancient religious house of
TER St. Peter and St. Paul, and the Abbey of St. Werburgh.
It has been said, that Wulphere, King of Mercia, found-
.675. ed the nunnery,* in honor of his daughter Werburgha, afterwards canonized: but this rests on vague authority; it is, however, pretty clear, that two centuries subsequent to the reign of Wulphere, there was a monastery here, dedicated to St. Peter and St. Paul; for Henry Bradshaw gives us a long account of the removal of the relics of St. Werburgha to the monastery, to prevent their being polluted by the Danes, in the invasion of 875—he also tells us of their miraculous effects, and of the army of Griffin, the Welsh King, being stricken with blindness by the interposition of St. Werburgha, whilst besieging the city. During the reign of Athelstan, the convent or monastery, was rebuilt by Ethelfleda, Countess of Mercia, who took away the *patronage* from St. Peter and St. Paul, and bestowed it on the virgin Saint, and St. Oswald, placing in it at the same time secular
Canons. Leofric, the Mercian Earl, was also a great HISTORY.
benefactor to the monastery, and put its decayed buildings in a state of complete repair. The secular canons, were expelled in 1093, by Hugh Lupus, who founded an Abbey of Monks of the Benedictine order, which was regulated by the celebrated Anselm, Archbishop of Canterbury. Henry Bradshaw says, that

> "The founder alsoe buylded within the Monasterie,
> Many sightly places convenient for Religion,
> Compassed with stronge walles on the west partie,
> And on the other syde with walls of the town,
> Closed at every ende with a sure postern,
> In south parte the cymiterie environed rounde aboute,
> For a sure defence enemies to hold out."

It is stated, that in 1101, Lupus, who had been pro-

CHESTER. fessed a monk in his sickness, died in this Abbey. He had endowed it in a magnificent manner,—and it was subsequently further enriched by donations of numerous benefactors, actuated by the religious superstition which then pervaded the Country.—It continued to flourish from the period of its foundation, to the General Dissolution of Religious Houses, by Henry VIII. when it also fell in the indiscriminate wreck. At that time its annual clear revenue was stated at £1003. 5*s*. 11*d*.—an immense sum in those days. A few years subsequent to the Dissolution, the Abbey was converted into a Cathedral Church, dedicated to Christ and the Blessed Virgin, a Dean and six Prebendaries being placed in it,—the last Abbot, Thomas Clerk, was appointed the Dean. At the same time Chester was erected into a Bishop's See, John Bird, formerly Provincial of the Carmelites, and then Bishop of Bangor, being translated to the new Diocese.* The revenue then granted to the See and Chapter was immense, and in a preceding portion of the work, there is a notice of the occasion of its alienation and loss. An Abstract of the Patent, 22d Eliz. granting the Dean and Chapter lands to the Fee Farmers, is here introduced:—

Elizabeth, Dei Gratia, &c. grants† by letters patent to Sir Geo. Calveley, Knt. George Cotton, Hugh Cholmely, Thos. Leighe, Henry Maynwaringe, Jno. Nuthall, and Richard Hurlestone, Esquires, the Manors of Huntington, Sutton in Wirral, Upton, Bromborow, Irby, Ince, Salghton, Barnshawe, and Fernell, in com. Cest. cum pert. late part, the of possessions of the dissolved monastery of St. Werburgh, and also grants to the same, all royalties and privileges in the said Manors; and further grants to the same all lands, royalties, and other privileges of the said Abbey in Backford, Huntington, Cheveley, Sutton, Bromborow, Upton, Boughton, Newton, Wervin, Croughton, Christeltone, Chorleton, Moston, Salghall, Shotwick, Crue, Bebington, Plymyard, Irreby, Greaseby, Frankby, West Kirkby, Knoctorum, Woodchurch, Walesey, Kirkby Walley, Ince, Elton, Thornton, Manley, Cattenhall, Idencote, Hellesby, Frodsham, Bridge Trafford, Plemstow, Saughton, Huxley, Coddington, Barnshawe, Goosetry, Lees, Crannage, Sandbache, Asthull, Chelford, Prestbury, Northwich, Hulse, Winnington, Nether Tabley, Plumley, Budworth, Northenden, Ferneball, Bunbury, Idenshawe, Tarvin, Great Sutton, Little Sutton, Hutton, and Thornton, in said County. Also to the same all rents in the City of Chester, which Richard Hurleston claimed by virtue of a grant from William Clyffe,‡ late Dean of Chester, and all tythes and oblations possessed by the said Monastery, in the parishes or hamlets of Brombrorowe, Upton, Eastham, Plymyard, Ince, Elton, Barneshawe, Prestbury, Idenshawe, Great and Little Sutton, Hulton, Thornton, Whitby, and Overpoole.—Also, to the same, the Rectories, and Churches of Sutton, Brombrorowe, Upton, Prestbury, Great and Little Sutton, Neston, and Willaston, and the Rectory and Church of Ince, late possessed by the said Monastery.—Also, to the same, all Granges, Glebe, &c. in Sutton in Wirral, Brombrorowe, Barnstone, Eastham, Plymyard, Childer Thornton, Hulton, Over Poole, Nether Poole, Great and Little Sutton, Prestbury, Great and Little Neston, Willaston, and Ince. Also, to the same, the Patronage of the Churches of Christletone, Bebington, and Astbury, in co. Cest. and of St. Mary's civ. Cest. late possessed by the said Monastery. All which are granted in as full and entire possession, as they were ever held by the last Abbot, or any of his predecessors, or came by virtue of surrender by the Abbot and Convent into the hands of King Henry VIII.

Saving to the Queen and her Successors, the Manor of Abbot's Cotton, late parcel of the Bishopric of Chester; all lands and messuages from which rents are due to the Crown; the Rectories of Shotwick, and St. Oswald's, in the County and City of Chester (with the exception of the Burland Tythes of Upton, near Chester, parcell of the said rectory); all Tythe Barns, Tythes, and oblations, in Shotwick, Great and Little Saughall, Crabwall, Capenhurst, Huntington, Cheveley, Saighton, Church on Heath, Boughton, Newton, Wervin, Croughton, or Bache, or in any other part of Cheshire, except as before excepted, and farther excepting certain tythe Barns specified, in Boughton, Wervin, Saughall, and Ledsham; and all Tythes of Huntington, Cheveley, HISTORY.

† Ormerod, page 240.

‡ See page 100.

* An accurate list of Bishops, and of the Endowments of the See, is given in pages 97, 98, and 99, of this work.

CHESTER

Saighton, Church on Heath. Boughton, Newton, Wervin, Croughton, Bache, Shotwick, Great and Little Saughall, Ledsham, and Capenhurst; and the Burland Tythes of the parishes of West Kirkby, and Woodchurch: in West Kirkby, Woodchurch, Thurstaston, Upton in Wirral, Irreby, Knoctorum, Greaseby, and Frankby; and the same tythes in Wybunbury, Worleston, Wigsterston, Weston, and Over Figden; also the advowry of West Kirkby, Thurstaston, Dodleston, Hanley, Coddington, Northenden, Kirkby Walley, Neston, Eastham, and St. Oswald's: excepting Cellerer's Meadow, Carter's Hey, the Pool of Bache Mill, and a fishery therein, within Upton; a Wich House in Wich Malbank, and the Isle of Hilbree, with a fishery therein: excepting also a pension of £19. 10s. called Castle Rent, and all pensions issuing from the Churches of Astbury, Christleton, St. Mary's in Chester, Eastham, Kirkby, Tattenhall, Dodleston, Weston, Handley, and Coddington: excepting also all liberties or grants of deer or other beasts, either granted to the Abbots of St. Werburgh, or the Dean and Chapter of Chester, in the forests of Mara and Mondrem, alias Delamere; excepting also the manors of Lee or Ley, near Backford, Whitby, and Overpoole, with messuages in Upton, Great and Little Sutton, Saughall, Shotwick, and Chorleton. The aforesaid manors, &c. with these exceptions, to be held from the Crown as of the manor of East Greenwich, in Kent, by the aforesaid Sir George Calveley, George Cotton, &c. and their assigns for ever, subject to certain specified reserved rents, payable to the Crown at Lady Day, and Michaelmas, at the West Gate of the before-mentioned dissolved Monastery, the said rent to be levied by duties, and if left unpaid for thirty days a forfeiture of one fourth of the value of the grant to be incurred. The said Sir George Calveley, &c. to hold the said rectories, with all ancient privileges except as befor excepted, and to be discharged from all further rents, &c. payable to the Crown, for which these letters patent shall be sufficient warrant to the Treasurers, Chancellor, and Barons of the Exchequer: the said letters patent to be enrolled, and received as evidence in all Courts of Law, and passed without fine, or fee, under the Great Seal of England.

Test. me ipsa apud Westm. xix° Decembris, a°r'i n'ri xxii, per ipsam Reginam, &c.

HISTORY.

The following is the abstract of the Charter, confirmatory of the Grants to the Fee Farmers.*

* Pat. 22 Eliz. [Orm.

Elizabeth, D. G. Ang. Franciæ, et Hib. &c. Here is introduced a recital of the preceding grant, with the exceptions, &c. reserved to the Queen,—and a recital of another grant by letter patent, dated Nov. last past, by which the Queen grants to Wm. and John Glasiour, Gents. the manor of Ley, alias Lee, by Backford, and the vills of Ley, Whitby, and Over Poole, with tenements in Moston, Upton, and Boughton, with Court Leet, and all other profits and privileges appertaining to the said manor of Ley, Whitby, &c. as possessed by Chester Abbey, saving to the Queen and her heirs, all tythes, oblations, &c. in Whitby, and Over Poole, to be held from the Crown in socage, and not in capite, as of the manor in East Greenwich, subject to a certain reserved rent to be gathered by duties, &c. Then follows a recital of Henry VIII. having by letters patent dated at Walden, Aug. 5, a°. reg. 33, founded within the site of the Abbey of St. Werburgh, a New Episcopal See, and a Cathedral Church for one Bishop, one Dean, and six Prebends, to be called the Dean and Chapter of the Cathedral Church of Christ and the Blessed Virgin Mary of Chester, the which foundation is confirmed by the Queen, who wishing that the same " may be honorably endowed for the praise and honor of Almighty God, and that He may be worshipped daily, according to her father's original intention, that the Holy Gospel of Christ may be preached constantly, that for the increase of Christian faith and piety, the youth of the kingdom may be constantly instructed there in good learning, that hospitality may be exercised by the Dean and Prebendaries aforesaid, and the poor there continually relieved," of her special grace, &c. grants to the said Dean and Chapter as follows:—

£71. 3s. 9d. annual rent, issuing from the manors of Huntington, Cheveley, the rectories of Great and Little Newton, and Willaston, and lands in Crue.—£168. 19s. 10d. issuing from the manors of Sutton and Ince, and the rectories of Sutton, Bromborow, and lands granted out in Elton, Cattenhall, Manley, Edencot, Hellesby, Bridge Trafford, and Plimstow. £31

CHESTER HISTORY.

13s. 4d. issuing from the manor of Irreby, and lands in Irreby, Greaseby, Knoctorum, Woodchurch, Frankby, and Wallasey. £51 12s. 6d. issuing from the manor of Saighton, with lands in Saighton, Church-on-Heath, Coddington, and Huxley. £54. 10s. issuing from the manor of Barnshaw, and lands in Barnshaw, Asthull, Chelford, Goostre, Lees, Cranage, Northwich, Hulse, Wynington, Nether Tabley, and Plumbley.—£5. 13s. 4d. issuing from the manor of Tilston Fernhall, and lands therein. £113. 11s. 4d. issuing from the manor and rectory of Prestbury; and premises belonging to that manor. £24. issuing from the manor of Eastham, and the appurtenances thereof. £33. 3s issuing from the Ferry, the Ferry-house, and the Wood of Eastham. £5. 5s. 11d. from lands, &c. in Plimyard. 4s. 5d. from the long meadow in Backford parish.—*In Upton*, £12. 9s. 10d. fee farm rent issuing from the Burland tythes, held by Elizabeth Browne, widow: £13. 13s. 1d. from the lands held by Robert Brock: £1. 9s. 9d. from William Smith's lands. £1. 9s. 0d. from the lands of William Heley: and 7s. 7d. from the lands of Richard Spencer. *In Boughton*, £2. 6s. 3d. from the lands of Ralph Payne; £2 9s. 3d. Thomas Foxe; £3d. 6s. 8d. Ralph Davenport; £2. Robert Hanley; 1l. 14s. 7d. Thomas Ball; 1l. 14s. 6d. Christopher Taylor; 3l. 7s. 4d. Thos Richardson; 2l. 11s. 5d. William Cooke; 3l. 8s. 2d. Thomas Browne; 1l. 2s. 8d. Hamlet Moores; 2l. 6s. 6d. Roger Whatton; 2l. 4s. 4d. John Hammond; 2l. 8s. 4d. John Ley; 3l. 12s. 8d. Thomas Dodd; 4l. 3s. 10d. Richard Ball; 7s. 10d. Richard Cotton; 9s. John Carter. 2l. 12s. 10d. issuing from Boughton windmill, paid by John Handley. 52l. 8s. 2d. arising from lands in Idinshawe, Newton, Wervin, and Croughton. 5l. 13s. 8d. issuing from Stamford mill, and lands there, in the holding of Thomas Venables.—*In Chorlton*, the following sums issuing from lands therein: Robert Cooke 7s.; Richard Ashton 2l. 12s. 8d.; Margaret Forshea 1l. 18s. 10d.; Thomas Trafford 1l. 12s. 2d.; John Kinge, 1l. 18s. 10d.; Thomas Whitefield 1s. 14s. 8d. for the windmill and lands thereto attached.—10l. 4s. 4d. issuing from the messuage, mill, and lands, &c. in Brombrow, held by Henry Hardware.—32l 13s. 3d. issuing from lands in Childer Thornton, Brombrow, and Bebington, in the holding of Richard Bavand, and William Baxter, alias Mayo.—4l. 10s. 10d. issuing from lands in Moston, in the holding of Ralph Rogerson.—4l. 10. 0d. issuing from lands ibidem, in the holding of John Ashton. 8l. 9s. 3d. issuing from lands in Salghall and Shotwick. 1l. 2s. 9d. issuing from lands in Northenden.—16s. 8d. issuing from lands in Christleton, in the holding of Wm. Cotgreave.—10l. 11s. 4d. issuing from the manor of Lee, held by William and John Glasiour.—35l. 15s. 4d. issuing from the vills of Whitby, and Overpoole, held by the same.—1l. issuing from the long Meadow in Backford, held by the same.—2l. 8s. 6d. issuing from lands in Boughton, held by the same.—2l. 6s. 10d. issuing from lands in Upton, held by the same.—Together with all rents, services, and lands, parcel of the dissolved Abbey estates, which in the previous grants to the fee farmers, the Queen had reserved to herself and her successor; given in free and perpetual alms.

The Queen further grants to the aforesaid Dean and Chapter.—The Rectories of St. Oswald and of Shotwick.—All tythes of Huntington, Cheveley, Saighton, Church on Heath, Boughton, Newton, Wervin, Croughton, Bache, Shotwicke, Great Saughall, and Little Saughall.—The tythes of Ledsham, and Capenhurst.—The tythes of Crabwall, Poole House, and Heath House, growing in the parish of St. Oswald.—The Burland tythes of West Kirkby and Woodchurch, growing in West Kirkby, Woodchurch, Upton in Wirral, Irby, Greaseby, Knoctorum, Thurstaston, Frankby, and Wallesey.—The Burland tythes of Nantwich, Wybunbury, Worleston, Wighterston, Neston, Over, Wirleston, Willaston, Eccleston, and Figden, or other places in the county aforesaid, being parcel of the dissolved Monastery.—Also, a rent of 19l. 10s. 0d. issuing from the Earldom of Chester, and previously paid to the Abbey of St. Werburgh.—Also all profits or privileges possessed in any part of England by the rectors or by the Churches of St. Oswald's, or Shotwick.—Also the advowsons of the Rectories of West Kirkby, Thurstaston, Dodleston, Hanley, Coddington, and Northenden, and of the vicarages of St. Oswald's, Eastham, and Neston, to be held in pure and perpetual alms, by paying yearly to the Queen at the Treasury, the sum of 106l. 16s. 6¾d. in lieu of tenths and first fruits.—Also all privileges within the rectories of St. Oswald's, Shotwick, West

CHESTER

Kirkby, &c.—And the Forest of Delamere, which was at any time enjoyed by the before-mentioned Abbey of St. Werburgh, and came into the hands of the Crown by the surrender thereof.—Also a license to the said Dean and Chapter, to appropriate and convert to their uses the Churches of St. Oswald's, Shotwick, or West Kirkby, or their appurtenances, which were in any manner appropriated by the Abbot and Convent of St. Werburgh, without the said Dean and Chapter appointing an incumbent thereto.

The aforesaid grants to be exonerated from pensions and payments whatever, on the condition of the Dean and Chapter paying annually the sums following:—106l. 16s. 5¾d. to the Queen, and her heirs.—4l. 6s. 8d. to the Minister of a Priest at Chelford, in Prestbury Parish.—4l. to the Minister of St. Bridget's, in Chester. 4l. 6s. 8d. to the Minister at Ince.—5l. 6s. 8d. to the Minister of Shotwick.—3l. 6s. 8d. to the Minister at Wervin.—6s. 8d. to an Assistant Minister at St. Oswald's, in Lent and Easter.—4l. 6s. 8d. to the Minister of Brombrow.—1l. 13s. 8d. to the Vicar of St. Oswald's. 3l. 5s. 4d. to the Archdeacon of Chester, in lieu of synodals, annually issuing from the following Churches: Ince 8s. 2d.—Norton 16s. 4d.—St. Oswald's 8s. 2d.—Brombrow and Eastham 16s. 4d.—Neston 16s. 4d.—All which sums the Dean and Chapter covenant to pay for themselves and their successors.

HISTORY.

Here follows a pardon of the Dean and Chapter for intrusions and trespasses on the Crown property which they might have committed to the date of the Charter, and a stipulation that in all Courts the Charter shall be interpreted as advantageously as possible for the Dean and Chapter, and as strictly as possible with respect to the interests of the Crown; no advantage to be taken of any *omissions** or contradictions therein, and the same shall be sealed with the Great Seal of England, without any fee or fine whatsoever.

* This was certainly a necessary proviso.

Teste me ipsa apud Wstmin. 22º die Decr. a.º r'i xxii.

THE CATHEDRAL is a lage irregular pile, and a considerable portion of it of great antiquity.—Messrs. Lysons, in noticing the small Circular Arches, in the exterior of the north wall of the nave, conjecture that they are as ancient as the time of Leofric, the Mercian Earl, who repaired and beautified the Church in the eleventh Century.—They certainly are of Saxon architecture, and peculiar in their ornaments—they are in the form represented in the Wood Cut:—

There is a Cellar in the Palace of the Bishop, which adjoins the west-end of the north aisle of the Nave, well worth notice: it is about nineteen feet and a half by nearly seventeen feet, with a semicircular arch on south side, the piers ornamented with the Saxon mouldings. In the west cloister is a building, formerly the cellar of the Abbey; it is ninety feet long and thirty feet wide, a line of short cylindrical pillars running down the middle, with round arches, and diagonal vaultings, springing from them. This, with the small cellar of the palace before noticed, is also probably of the time of the eleventh century. The Chapter

CHESTER. House, in the east angle of the Cloisters, is a noble room,* with lancet shaped windows, between which run slender detached shafts, with neat foliated capitals. The room has a narrow stone gallery on the east, south, and north sides, below which is an extensive library, consisting chiefly of old Divinity, with very few modern additions.

In one of the Presses on the south-side adjoining the fire-place, is the head part of a stone coffin, found here in 1723, by Mr. Henchman, a shoolmaster: the coffin inclosed a body completely enwrapped in leather, the skull and bones of which, it is said,† were quite fresh, and the strings which fastened together the ankles, were entire. This coffin is said to have contained the remains of the celebrated Palatinate Earl, Hugh Lupus, second Earl of Chester, "whose bones were transferred from the burial ground of the Monastery, to the Chapter House, in the reign of Henry I." Many, and very just doubts exist, as to the authenticity of this conclusion: it is true, the upper part of the coffin bears on it the Wolf's head erased, which was the cognizance of the Earl, but it also bears in a cypher, the letters R. S. and certainly does not possess the appearance of antiquity ascribed to it. In elucidation, it has been with great propriety observed, in the work before adverted to, that "armorial devices do not appear to have been introduced on works of art before Richard I. nor on sepulchral monuments till the thirteenth century."‡—and it further suggests, that the initials are those of Rd. Seynesbury, who was abbot in 1349, and what is now conjectured to be part of a coffin, is in fact the relic of some monument executed in his time previous to his death in 1363, and burial in Normandy.||—But the very discovery of this relic, although so recent, remains in great doubt; and the original purport of it will serve to titillate the sagacity of future historians, as it has done those who have already expressed their opinions on the subject. In the same press, in a Roman remain, cut on a red grit stone, about 24 inches by 8 inches. It was found *on the site of the Deanry*, and removed to its present situation by Dean Cholmondeley: it bears the following inscription:— HISTORY.

† Lysons, page 448.

|| p. 449.

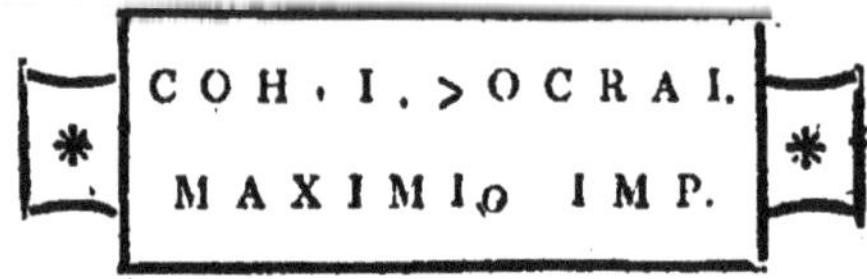

The elegant vestibule to the Chapter House, is an object of general admiration; it is singularly constructed. The roof is beautifully groined, supported by clustered pillars which unite without any capitals. The work of the whole of this building, although probably of the twelfth century, is as fresh as if it had recently come from under the chissel.§—The walk or aisle, adjoining the Chapter House, leading to the Abbey Court, affords some beautiful architectural specimens. A sketch of the south arch, of the east cloister, opening to the nave of the Church, is given at the foot of page 128.

The *Refectory* of the Monastery, formerly near 90 feet in length, and 34 wide, is a noble room, although it is now divided. On the establishment of the See, by Hen. VIII. it was converted into a School-room, for the free grammar establishment which he founded. In the south wall, on the east side, is a stone stair-case, with open arches trefoiled, leading to an Oratory.¶—In the east window are several lancet shaped parti-

¶ See p. 108.

* It has been stated, that the "SPIRAL Gothic windows" of the Chapter House, "previous to the Reformation," were "decorated with the Portraits of the Earls of Chester,"—which portraits were in April, 1818, offered for sale in Liverpool. It would be gratifying to know on what authority the assertion was made, that the Chapter House Windows were ornamented with these said ANCIENT specimens of the art. It is much doubted whether there is any record extant sanctioning it. Some portions of the "PAINTED, glass," it is well known, were the production of a LIVING artist.

‡ The Lysons here introduce a note, in which they observe, that "though the wolf's head erased is given by Brooke and others as the armorial bearing of Hugh Lupus, and his Nephew, yet there is no reason for supposing it to have been coëval with them: in later times, indeed, it was considered by the convent of St. Werburgh, as the arms of their founder," &c. This is extremely plausible: the wolf's head erased, ornamenting several parts of the Church, particularly the north Cloister, where it appear in the centre of the groins, with the arms of Wolsey, the Stanleys, &c.

§ The Chapter House is the burial place of several of the Earls of Chester.

The Interior of the Choir of Chester Cathedral

THE BISHOPS THRONE, CHESTER CATHEDRAL.

GREAT WESTERN DOORWAY, CHESTER CATHEDRAL.

Engraved for Hanshall's History of Cheshire

CHESTER.

tions, having slender pillars between, ornamented with *fasciæ* on the shafts.—There are no data to ascertain the period of the erection of this building, but it is probably as old as the 13th century, and had Randle Blundeville for its founder.

The length of the Cathedral from east to west, including the Chapel of the Virgin, is 349 feet—the width, including the side aisles, 75 feet. The nave is divided from the choir by a handsome Gothic screen of the workmanship of the 14th Century, above which is the Organ.*—The pillars of the nave and choir are beautifully clustered; the capitals of the latter are plainly rounded, but those of the nave are elegantly foliated.—The arches are pointed; but the architecture varies. The greater part of the nave is no doubt the workmanship of the 14th century, but it has subsequently undergone extensive repairs; and a great portion of the west-end appears to have been rebuilt towards the latter part of the 15th century. Indeed, the commencement of the work may be distinguished above the first arch from the cross, on the south side of the nave, where there are the remains of a gallery, the balustrades of which are tastefully formed in quatrefoils. These repairs were carried on under the directon of the Abbots Ripley and Birkenshaw. The western front,† the upper parts of the choir, and nave, and part of the north transept, and the cloisters are all of this date.‡ It would seem it was the intention of the Abbots to have vaulted the nave and choir, but the design was not completed, although the commencement of the vaultings appear in many places.

‡ Lysons.

The Choir of the Cathedral is deservedly the theme of the Traveller's admiration.—The end and sides from the Organ loft to the Bishop's throne, are ornamented with spiral tabernacle work, highly enriched, and probably not equalled in the Empire, underneath which are the stalls of the dignitaries of the Church, the Vicar's Choral, &c. The desks for the singing boys, are arranged on the sides of the Choir, projecting from the stalls of the Vicars Choral, and are evidently of a modern construction. The following rude sketch (that of the Dean's seat), may furnish an idea of the formation of the stalls generally. They appear to be of the work of the 14th century, and have *miserecords*, (seats turning up) ornamented with curious and ludicrous figures :—

Midway between the throne and the pulpit, is the Reading Desk, supported on the back of a large gilded eagle.—The Throne is on the south side of the Choir, and is one of the most splendid specimens of early Gothic architecture in the kingdom.|| It formerly stood in the Chapel of the Virgin at the east-end of the Choir, and was the pedestal on which rested the shrine of the virgin patroness of the Abbey, St. Werburgha. Soon after the Reformation, it was removed to its present situation, and converted into the Throne of the Bishop. The architecture is that of the earliest part of the 14th century: its ground plan is an oblong, 8 feet 9 inches in height, in length 7 feet 6 inches, in breadth 4 feet 6 inches. It is ornamented with six Gothic arches 6 feet 4 inches high, two on the north front, two on the south front, one at the east end, and one at the west—above these is a smaller arch, in the same style of architecture. Buttresses occupy the space between the windows, and the spandrils of the arches are filled up with quatrefoils. The foliage of the crockets is singular. There is a range of small images in the up-

|| See plate.

* Supposed to have been built by the celebrated Smith: it is certainly a very old instrument, and generally much in want of repair.

† A view of the highly-enriched door way of which is given in the plate.

per part, intended to represent Kings and Saints of the Mercian line: they hold scrolls in their hands, on which were inscribed their names, in old English letters, but in Latin. These inscriptions are now no longer in existence. Dr. Cowper thus gives the arrangement of them, commencing with the figure at the south west angle, fronting the west, and then proceeding along the north front, and thence round the east end, towards the stairs up to the throne:—

1	Rex Crieda	16	Rex ——— dus
2	Rex Penda	17	Sta ——— rga
3	Rex Wolpherus	18	——— us
4	Rex Ceolredus	19	———
5	———	20	Baldredus
6	Rex Offa	21	Merwaldus
7	Rex Egbertus	22	Rex Wiglaff
8	———	23	Rex Bertwulph
9	Stus. Kenelmus	24	Rex Burghredus
10	Sta. Milburga	25	———
11	Rex Beorna	26	Sta. ——— eda
12	Rex Colwulphus	27	———
13	———	28	———
14	Sta ——— lda	29	Rex Ethelbertus
15	——— us	30	Sta. Mildrida

Four images have been entirely cut away, two at the west end, and two at the east end. Dr. Cooper was of opinion, that all these figures represented relatives or ancestors of St. Werburgha, and thus describes them:

1. Crieda, said to be tenth in descent from Woden, founder of the kingdom of Mercia, about 584.
2. Penda, grandson of Crieda, a Pagan King of Mercia.
3. Wulphere, second son of Penda, and father of St. Werburgha, second Christian King of Mercia.
4. Coelred, nephew of Wulphere, and son of Etheldred, husband of St. Werburgha, King of Mercia.
5. * * * * * *
6. Offa, the Great King of Mercia.
7. Egbertus, son of Offa, and King of Mercia.
8. * * * * * *
9. St. Kenelm, son of Kenulff, and King of Mercia.
10. St. Milburga, daughter of Merwaldus, fourth son of King Penda.
11. Beorna, King of the East Angles, in the time of St. Werburgha.
12. Colwulphus, uncle of St Kenelm, and King of Mercia.
13. * * * * * *
14. St. [Ermini]lda, mother of St. Werburgha, daughter of Ercombert, King of Mercia.
15. Rex ——— us
16. Rex [Ethelred]us, paternal uncle of St. Werburgha, and King of Mercia.
17. St. [Keneba]rgo, paternal aunt of St. Werburgha, wife of Adelwal, Prince of Northumbria.
18. [Kenred]us, a pastoral staff in the hand, supposed to be Kenred, brother of St. Werburgha, who resigned the Crown to Ceolred, and accepted of an Abbacy, but died in the Monastery of St. Peter, at Rome.
19. * * * * * *
20. Baldredus, governor of the Kingdom of Kent, under Kenulf, King of Mercia.
21. Merwaldus, fourth son of Penda, and uncle of St. Werburgha.
22. Wiglaff, King of Mercia, tributary to Egbert.
23. Bertwulph, brother of Wiglaff, and tributary King of Mercia.
24. Burghredus, tributary King of Mercia.
25. * * * * * *
26. St. [Ethelr]eda, the aunt of St. Werburgha, under whom she was veiled at Ely.
27. * * * * * *
28. * * * * * *
29. Rex Ethelbertus, supposed to be Ethelbert, first Christian King of Kent, and great grandfather of St. Werburgha.
30. St. Mildrida, daughter of Merwaldus, and cousin of St. Werburgha.

These figures, tradition says, were of gold, but at the Reformation were replaced by wooden ones, with golden heads. The rapacity of the Puritans, soon decapitated them, and wooden heads were placed on their shoulders. The artist, it would seem, was not remarkable for skill or taste, for several of the masculine heads are placed on feminine bodies, and vice versa. The sounding boards to the Throne and Pulpit are much admired for their workmanship.

CHESTER HISTORY.

The Chancel, is divided from St. Mary's Chapel by a partition, recently erected. On each side, are stalls* intended for the officiating Monks. The Altar Piece is of tapestry; the subject from the celebrated Cartoons—"Elymas the Sorcerer stricken blind." Two galleries were erected on the south and north sides of the Choir next to the Chancel, in 1745, and 1749, by Bishop Peploe.

In the intermediate space between the arches, is introduced a grotesque figure,—and figures of this description—the propriety of which we need not here discuss, abound throughout the whole building, and particularly in the Cloisters,† where one is shown with an immense drinking cup in his hands—another playing on the bagpipes—and others in situations, the description of which will be much "better honor'd in the breach than in the observance." Between the first and second arches, on the north side after entering the Choir, are two curious figures embracing each other: a sketch of which is given here:—

The side aisles of the Choir are vaulted. In the south aisle of the Choir, under an arch indented in the wall, is a stone, ornamented with a cross-fleury, probably covering the relics of an Abbot, or some dignitary of the ancient monastery. Opposite to which is an altar tomb, which *tradition* appropriates to Henry IV. See p. 142. Emperor of Germany.‡ The sides are neatly ornamented with Gothic niches, having trefoil heads, alternate quatrefoils, and the quatrefoils alternately filled with leopards' heads, and roses. The head-stone of the lid slides, and discovers the coffin, which is of remarkably small dimensions. This tomb is not of an earlier style than the 15th century; and the mouldings of the lid nearly correspond with the screen which separates the aisle from the Choir. Mr. Ormerod, with great propriety, attributes the tomb to one of the later Abbots. On the north side of this aisle, entering the door of St. Mary's Chapel, is an elegant niche, in this form—

opposite to which is an indenture in the wall, the front ornamented in the Gothic style, which was probably appropriated to the reception of Holy Water. In the Chapel of St. Mary, formerly called the Chapel of the Virgin,|| was the High Altar, which before it was cut off from the body of the Choir, must have afforded a fine sight from the body of the Church. There are Prayers in this Chapel every morning at six o'clock throughout the winter and summer; and in the Choir daily at half-past ten in the morning, and at three o'clock in the evening.§

Mr. Stone, quoting the ledger book of the Abbey,

* Behind these are to be seen indentions, where were affixed the names or arms, probably, of the Abbots.

† In 1812, under the superintendance of the late Dean Cholmondeley, the site of the southern angle of the Cloisters, was cleared, and it was then that the Saxon arches, depicted in the preceding wood cut, were discovered.

|| Erected probably towards the 13th century—the windows, however, have much the style of the 14th century.

§ Formerly at four o'clock in the evening. This alteration in the time took place in the autumn of 1817.

CHESTER

states, that the Choir and centre Tower were finished in 1210; but it is the generally received opinion, that the Tower, the Choir, the upper part of the Nave, and the West Front, also the greater part of the Cloisters, and the greater part of the Vestibule of the Chapter-House,* were built, as is before noticed, in the Abbacies of Simon Ripley, and John Birkenshaw, between 1485, and 1535.—The elegant screen which separates the Nave from the Choir, and which consists of a series of arches, was ornamented with paintings of the Kings of England, from the Conquest to the commencement of the Tudor line. The upper pannels of the gallery, are now filled up with paintings of the arms of the Earls of Chester, from Lupus, to the continuation in the Crown. The roof of the north transept is finished in wood, the ribs supported by figures of Angels, bearing the spear, the pincers, and other emblems of the Crucifixion. The entire of the Cathedral was much injured by the Parliamentary soldiers, during the civil wars.

In part IV. of Mr. Ormerod's History of this County, are given several of the ancient deeds relative to the dissolved Monastery of St. Werburgh, amongst them—"Tituli et ordo Munimentorum Monasterii Sanctæ Werburgæ," which that gentleman describes as being transcribed from a beautiful MS. on vellum, in the Harl. Coll. 1965, drawn up by the Monks themselves. The size small 4to. After each title is a short abstract of the deed itself, which was obviously prepared, to avoid the trouble of reference to the original deeds, on common occasions. There is another copy of the same on vellum also, in large folio, in the same collection, of which a copy exists in the hand-writing of one of the Randle Holmes. Both of the vellum copies are imperfect. There is a chasm in the middle of the large one; the small one is injured by the damp at the end. The Charters of the Earls, and others of importance, precede the Charters of particular manors, and are given at large in both MSS. The Charter of Earl Randle to his Barons is amongst them, marked "Carta Communis Cestresiriæ."

The following are the most remarkable Monuments in the Cathedral:

IN THE NAVE.

HISTORY.

Near the entrance to the Parish Church, is a memorial to—

"WILLIAM NICHOLLS, of Chorlton, Esq. F. S. A. and Deputy Registrar, died Aug. 19, 1809, aged 49."

In the centre aisle, a Pyramidal Monument, by Nollekins: In the upper part a female figure leaning on a rock, against which is a broken anchor. Above, two shields, the first, sable, a lion rampant argent, between three cross-crosslets of the second. The second, azure, two bars argent, over which a bend gules; the whole elegantly executed—the inscription is

"Anna Helena Matthews, daughter of Peter Legh, Esq. of Booths, in this county, and Anne his wife, died Nov. VIII. MDCCXCIII. In Memory of her amiable disposition, her liberality of mind, and conjugal affection, her husband, John Matthews, Captain in the Royal Navy, has erected this Monument."

On the first pillar, east-end of the nave, on the north side, is a Monument in white marble, by Banks, on which is a female figure weeping, at the side of an urn. On the left three volumes, irregularly placed, lettered "Longinvs,"—"Thvcydides,"—"Xenophon,"—above which is an academic cap, inverted. The urn is inscribed, "Blessed are they that Movrn." The inscription is—

"Sacred to the Memory of William Smith, D. D. Dean of this Cathedral, and Rector of West Kirkby and Handley, in this county, who died the 12th of January, 1787, in the 76th year of his age. As a scholar, his repvtation is perpetvated by his valvable pvblications, particularly his correct and elegant translations of Longinvs, Thvcydides, and Xenophon. As a preacher, he was admired, and esteemed by his respective avditories; and as a man, his memory remains inscribed on the hearts of his friends. This monvment was erected by his affectionate widow."

On the west-side of the same pillar, a Medallion of Archdeacon Travis, and on a tablet the inscription—

"Sacred to the Memory of the Rev. George Travis, A. M. late Archdeacon of Chester, and Vicar of Eastham, in this County, who departed this life Feb. xxiv, MDCCXCVII. He was a man, whose extensive learning, active mind, and generous heart, were assiduously exerted in the service of religion, his country, and his neighbour. His loss will be long regretted, and his virtue revered. Reader! this eulogy is no flattery, but the sincere testimony of a surviving friend."

* The presses, which so much disfigure the Chapter-House, were placed there in 1727, in conformity with the will of Dean Arderne.

On the next pillar but one on the same side, the Monument of Mrs. Barbara Dod, on which is her bust, and underneath, quarterly, the arms of Dod and Morgill. The inscription is—

" To the Memory of Mrs. Barbara Dod, who divised her estate in Boughton, and Childer Thornton, in the county of Chester, to the Minor Canons of this Cathedral. She was the daughter of Randal Dod, of Edge, in the same county, Esq. by Barbara his wife, daughter and heir of William Morgill, of Gray's Inn, Esq. She died in London, July the 15th, A. D. 1703, and was interred the 26th, at Saint Martin's-in-the-Fields: and for the perpetuation of the memory of such a benefactrix, the present Minor Canons. I. D.---R. S.---T. L. I. S. have with gratitude, in honor to her name, erected this Monument, Anno Dom. MDCCXXIII.

In the aisle behind the north range of pillars, a mural Monument, decorated with military trophies, the most prominent of which is a Grecian helmet, of a size totally disproportioned to the other emblems. Beneath which is inscribed—

" Sacred to the Memory of Captain John Phillip Buchanan, of the 16th or Queen's Regiment of Light Dragoons, who, in the glorious and decisive Battle of Waterloo, on the 18th day of June, 1815, was killed by a musket shot, in the Hour of Victory, in the 27th year of his age. Accomplished in all the qualities which distinguish the Soldier, or adorn the Gentleman; his Courage, his Zeal, and Devotion to his Profession, whilst actively and unceasingly engaged in the memorable Campaigns in Portugal, in Spain, and in France, acquired him the Friendship, the Confidence, and just Admiration of his Brother Officers. In the more retired scenes of private life, he was no less exemplary. Superior to every mean and selfish Consideration, he was uniformly Liberal, Affectionate, and Unassuming. And whilst his ingenuous Disposition and unaffected Manners secured the Kindness and Esteem of ALL, the Loss which his Family and Friends have sustained by his glorious, but untimely Death, can never be contemplated without Emotions of deep and sincere Regret.---His afflicted Mother and only surviving Parent, has caused this Monument to be erected to the Memory and Virtues of a beloved and lamented Son."

On the left of the first flight of steps, leading to the great western door, above the font, is inscribed on a black tablet—

" Lateritium hic olim invenit baptisterium infans Guhelmus Moreton: marmoreum idem instituit Episcopus Kildarensis—Anno Dom. 1687."

Beyond this, against the west wall, a barbarous piece of sculpture—a medallion, encircled with foliage, and supported by two infants—

" Johanni Wainwright, avo } LL. D.
Thomæ Wainwright, patri }
Ille a Waltono
Huic a Pearsono,
Cancellariis hujusce diœceseos constitutis,
In eodem sepulchro compositis:
Quos tranquillum iter, et privatæ semita vitæ.
Detulit ad tumulum, charos æquis que bonisque:
Si non floruerint opibus, laribusque superbis,
Justitiam, morèsque, fidemque, et jura colebant.
Dives eris, patriæque decus, quicunque, nepotum
Tales laude, pari, tales virtutibus, æquas.
Johannes Wainwright, unus Baronum de scaccario in regno Hiberniæ.
P.

On the north-side of the west door, a Monument to the Memory of Sir Wm. Mainwaring. It is ornamented with wreathed pillars, figures weeping, and enriched with foliage, badly sculptured

" To the perpetual Memory of the eminently Loyal Sir William Mainwaring, Kt. eldest son of Edmund Mainwaring, Esq. Chancellor of the County Palatine of Chester; of the ancient family of the Mainwarings of Peover in the said County. He died in the service of his Prince and Country, in the defence of the City of Chester, wherein he meritted singular honour for his Fidelity, Courage, and Conduct. He left by Hester his Lady (daughter and heiress unto Christopher Wase, in the county of Bucks, Esq.) four sons and two daughters. His eldest daughter Judith, married unto Sir John Busby, of Addington, in the county of Bucks, Kt. His youngest daughter Hester unto Sir Thos. Grobham How, of Kempley, in the county of Gloucester, Kt. He died honourably, but immaturely, in the Twenty-ninth year of his age, October the 9th, 1644. His Lady Relict erected this Monument of her everlasting love, and his never dying honour, Oct. 25th, 1671.

In the Nave are also Memorials of Frederick Phillips, an American Loyalist, died 1715. The Rev. J. Winfield, died 1807. The Rev. William Russel, died 1792; and his widow Elizabeth, daughter of Sir John Byrne, died 1805. Elizabeth wife of Wm. Nicholls, Esq. of Stockport, died 1708. Dr. Peploe, Chancellor of the Diocese, died 1731. John Hamilton, Secretary at War, in Ireland, died 1781 Jane, wife of S. Vernon, Esq. died 1775; Ralph, their son, died 1799; John Vernon, died 1797; Anne, his wife died 1812. George Ogden, died 1788; Elizabeth his wife died 1781. To the memory of Richard, son of Bishop Cleaver, died 1798. Bishop Hall, died 1668. John Ford, M. D. died 1807. Lucy Joddrell, died 1786.

IN THE NORTH TRANSEPT.

Near the east wall, two large flat stone Memorials, on each a cross-floree, and shields in the form of a heart. On one of them is "Ran. de Gallitorta;" on the shield a fess, with two mullets pierced in chief.—The other cannot be decyphered.

Peter Stringer, Clerk, Precentor, and Organist, died 1670.

IN THE CHOIR.

To Bishop Stratford, who died 1706-7.

Bishop Peploe, died 1752.

To the Memory of Dean Arderne, a plain white stone, with this inscription—

"Near this place lies the body of Doctor James Arderne, of this County, a while Dean of this Church: who, though he bore more than a common affection to his private relations, yet gave the substance of his bequeathable estate to this Cathedral; which gift, his will was, should be mentioned, that Clergymen may consider whether it be not a sort of sacrilege to sweep all away from the Church and Charity into the possession of their Lay Kindred, who are not needy. Dat. Octr. 27, 1688. This plain Monument, with the above Inscription, upon this cheap Stone, is according to the express words of Dean Arderne's will.

Archdeacon Entwistle, died 1707.

IN THE NORTH AISLE OF THE CHOIR.

A plain flag stone, a Memorial of the Cheshire Antiquary—

"Here lie the remains of the Rev. John Stones, A. M. who was one of the Minor Canons, and Sacrist of this Cathedral, and Rector of Coddington: he died the 23d Feb. 1735."

The Family of the Rev. Robert Vanbrugh, A. M.

Thomas Entwistle, eldest son of the Archdeacon, died 1774; Henry the second son, died 1784.

The Rev. J. Prince, Minor Canon, died 1795.

IN THE SOUTH AISLE OF THE CHOIR.

The Rev. Thomas Ince, A. M. died 1766; Susan, his relict, died 1767.

Rev. C. Henchman, died 1780; Elizabeth Henchman, died 1804; Elizabeth, wife of the Rev. C. H. 1776; C. D. Henchman, 1803; Anne Henchman, 1810.

IN ST. MARY'S CHAPEL.

On large flag stones, two of them inlaid with marble:

"Underneath are deposited the remains of Edw. Peregrine Gastrell, Esq. who resigned this life the 24th February, 1772, aged 64. Is this his death-bed! No! it is his shrine. Behold him rising to an Angel; entering the harbour like a gallant, stately vessel, he hoists his flag of hope, through the merits of our blessed Redeemer, riding before a stately gale of atonement, till he makes, with all the sail of an assured faith, the happy port of a joyful resurrection. He lived in the fear and love of God, and died in Christ. Believe, and look with triumph on his tomb."

"Underneath are deposited the remains of Edw. Gastrell, Esq. who resigned this life May 3d, 1798, aged 58.

"Thirsting after the Bread of Heaven and Water of Life, he took up the Cross at an early period, following the steps of his Blessed Master, which enabled him to fight manfully under the banner of Affliction. He possessed a good heart, had a great mind, and supported the gentleman through the whole of his deportment. He never resented an injury; every trial he bore with exemplary patience. After finishing his warfare, he resigned his soul into the hands of his Maker, to conduct safe, and place in the bosom of Jesus. He fought the fight to win the Crown; Let us so run, that we may obtain it."

Between the two last, on a flag stone:

"The Jew and the Heathen derided, the Papist abused, but be not thou ashamed of the Cross of Christ."

Beneath, a Cross in an oblique line, on the pole of which is—

"It is not for me to glory, save in the Cross of our Lord."

And on the transverse piece—

"By this we overcome."

Afterwards—

"Eliz. Gastrell, enlisted at baptism under the Captain of our Salvation, was called early to the Standard of the Cross, which she bore manfully, through a long series of sharp conflicts, and by faith and patience overcame. Worn out in this service, her soul was exalted, August the 19th, 1747, from the militant to the triumphant estate, following the steps of her Divine Leader, who endured the Cross, despised the shame, and then sat down at the right hand of God; her body in dust here sleeps, in hopes of a joyful resurrection to life immortal. The Lord killeth, he bringeth down to the Grave, his will be done. He bringeth up, he maketh alive again—hallowed be his name."

"The body of Peregrine Gastrell, Esq. late Chancellor of the Diocese of Chester, (who July the 23d, 1748, departed this life in the same faith and hope) lies with her.

I. H. S.

Jesus, our Saviour, Glory be to the blessed Trinity, one God."

In the same Chapel are also memorials to Lawrence Fogg, who died Feb. 27, 1711. Mary his wife, Jan. 3, aged 88.—William Fynmore, Archdeacon and Prebend, April, 1686, aged 63.—Wm. Case, Subdeacon, Oct. 6, 1634.—Wm. Bishham, Jan. 6, 1685, aged 88.—Rev. E. Mainwaring, A. M. Prebend, July 30, 1780, aged 71.—Rev. Abel Ward, A. M. Archdeacon, Oct. 1, 1785, aged 68.—Anne Ward, wife of the Rev. T. Ward, Sept. 7, 1793.—Sarah, daughter of Peploe Ward, Sept. 7, 1793, aged 15.—James Falconer, Esq. Nov. 8. 1738. Mary Falconer, his wife, Jan. 12. 1754.—John Leche, Alderman, Dec. 27, 1639.—Sarah Johanna, wife of Edward Holt, Esq. July 11, 1796, aged 40.—Edw. Roberts, Deputy Registrar, July 7, 1754, aged 73; Elizabeth his wife, July 18, 1773, aged 88; Rebecca their daughter, wife of Samuel Peploe, L. L. D. Oct. 29, 1779, aged 59; Susannah, another daughter, Dec. 11, 1784, aged 60; Dorothy, another daughter, wife of the Rev. Thomas Tonman, A. M. April 18, 1785, aged 64: Rev. Thomas Tonman, A. M. March 8, 1783, aged 64; John Tonman, Esq. Sept. 2. 1786. aged 21; Charlotte, his wife, daughter of John Clarke, Esq. of Hough, April 9, 1787, aged 22.—Catharine Talbot Malpas, April 1, 1805, aged 30.—Lieut.-Gen. Henry Whitley, Colonel of the 9th regiment, and Maria his wife, Jan. 14, and Feb. 12, 1771.—Peter Hughes, A. M. Rector of Caerwys, Flintshire, June 29, 1778.—Mary, daughter of Wm. Lloyd, Esq. of Halghton, Flintshire, April, 1722; Beatrice, third daughter of Wm. Lloyd, Esq. Feb. 26, 1726.—William Williams, Vicar of Godmanchester, May 6, 1782, aged 67.—Anne, daughter of Sir Humphrey Briggs, of Houghton, county of Salop, Bt. March 29, 1740; Magdalen his daughter, April 23, 1759.—Thomas Hughes, Esq. Voynal, county of Cardigan, July 30. 1807, aged 66.—Rev. C. Henchman, A. M. Feb. 6th, 1741; Margaret, his wife, April 30th, 1752; Charles Henchman, Esq. Aug. 20, 1810, aged 72.—Frances, wife of Geo. Salusbury Townshend, Esq. March 18, 1775, aged 37.—Geo. Salusbury Townshend, Esq. Sept. 29, 1801.—Maria Georgina, daughter of Admiral Bowen, June 16th, 1810, aged 18 years, &c.

The Registers of the Cathedral commence in 1687.

Morses, sc.

BRERETON HALL.

THE GENEALOGY

Of the Kings of Mercia, which included Cheshire, with that of St. Werburgha, or Wereburg.

From Speed, 3d Edition, 1632, see fol. 210, 248, 254, &c. and other Authorities.

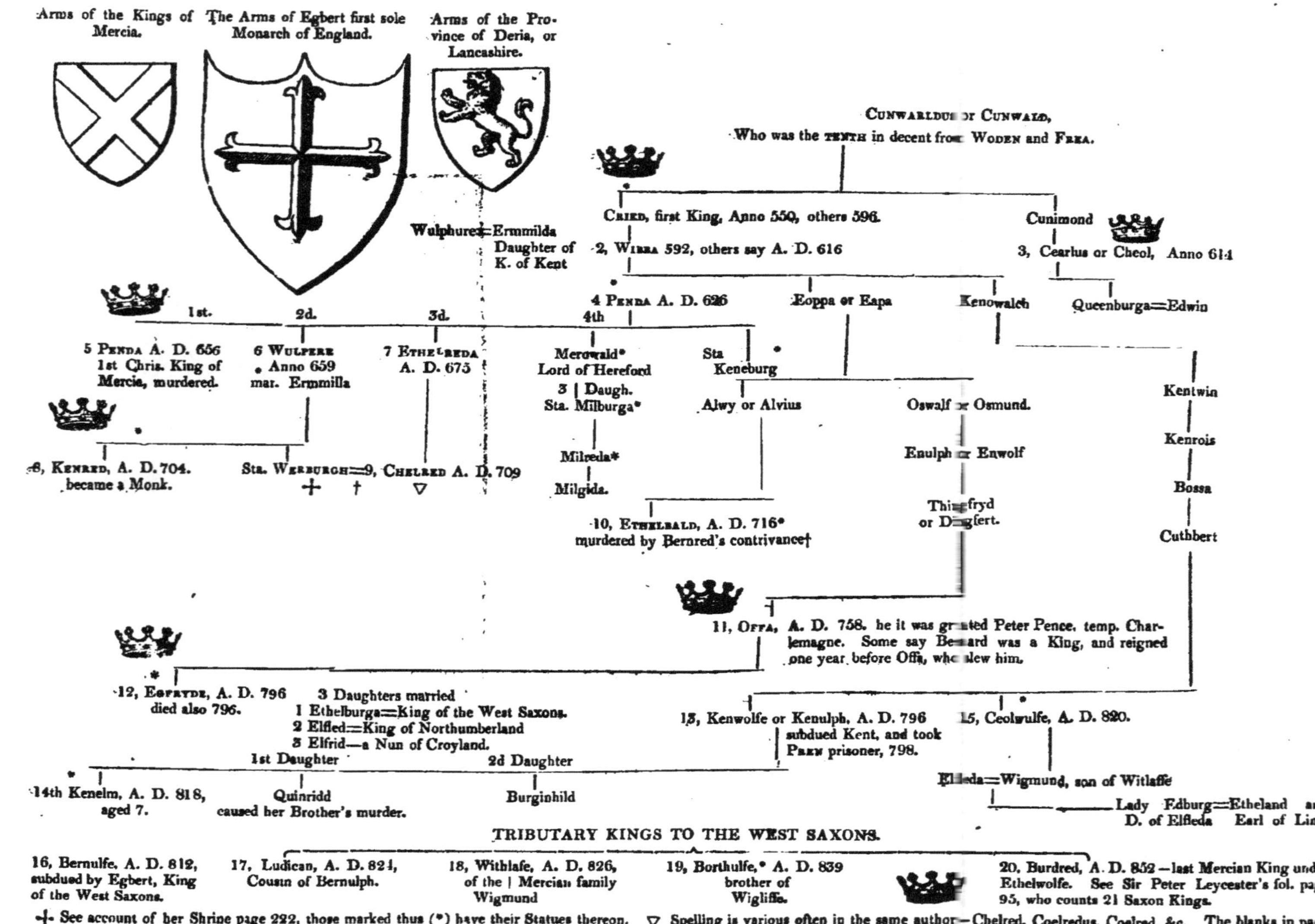

✝ See account of her Shrine page 222, those marked thus (*) have their Statues thereon. ▽ Spelling is various often in the same author—Chelred, Coelredus, Coelred, &c. The blanks in page 222, might be properly filled up by the remaining Relatives of St. Werburga, above noticed in the Genealogy. The Mercian kingdom was established A. D. 582, continued Two Hundred and Two Years, sometime in the possession of the Danes, and became part of the West Angles. † In the Genealogy of the Mercian Kings, by a Citizen of Chester, printed 1748, Bernard, or Bernred, is called the 10th Mercian King, and Penda the 5th Mercian King, is wholly omitted in that pedigree. By a Series of Medals lately discovered of Saxon Kings, another is found to exist, as laid [illegible] the British Museum.

List of the Abbots of the Monastery of St. Werburgh.

RICHARD, chaplain to Anselm, Archbishop of Canterbury, was instituted in 1093; died April 26, 1117.—Buried in the East Angle of the Cloister, near the entrance into the Church.

WILLIAM; who died Oct. 5, 1140; buried at the head of his predecessor.

RALPH; died Nov. 16, 1157: buried on the left side of the last Abbot.

ROBERT FITZ NIGEL;* died Jan. 31, 1174; buried in the East Cloister, on the right hand of the entrance to the Chapter House.

ROBERT II. died August 27, 1184. The King on his death seized the Abbacy; after keeping it two years, he bestowed it on

ROBERT DE HASTINGS,† July 13, 1186, who was deposed in 1194, and twenty-nine marks allowed him for his subsistence. He was buried at the head of William the second Abbot, in the South Cloister. The site was marked by three marbles, ornamented with images, and crosiers, on the right hand side.

GEOFFRY; died May 7, 1208; buried in the Chapter House, on the left side from the door.

HUGH GRYLLE; died April 21, 1226; buried on the left side of the Chapter House, under the second arch from the door, at the feet of the last Abbot.

WILLIAM MARMION; died August 27, 1228; buried on the left hand of the Abbot Grylle.

WALTER PYNCHBECK; died June 22, 1240; buried in the Chapter House, at the head of Abbot Grylle.

HISTORY.

ROGER FRIEND; died Sept. 23, 1249; buried in the vestibule of the Chapter House, on the right side from the door, under the second arch.

THOMAS CAPENHURST; died March 28, 1265; buried at the head of the last Abbot.

SIMON DE ALBO MONASTERIO;‡ died April 24, 1289; buried on the south side the Chapter House, under a marble stone, in an arch, supported by six marble pillars. The Abbacy again seized into the King's hands; and in 1291, given to

‡ Alias Whitchurch.

THOMAS BIRCHELSEY, alias LYTHELES, the King's chaplain; he died in 1324, and was buried on the south side of the Choir, where was a grave stone, which had a brazen effigy of him.

WILLIAM DE BEBINGTON,|| or BURINGTON, prior of the Abbey; died 1349: buried in the south aisle of the Choir, on the right hand of the last Abbot.

RICHARD SYNESBURY; deprived by the Pope in 1362, for mal-administration.

THOMAS NEWPORT, succeeded in 1363; died at Sutton, June 1, 1385; buried in the Chapter House, within the inner door.

WILLIAM DE MERSHTON; died Jan. 13, 1386; buried in the south aisle, at the right hand of Wiliam de Bebington.

HENRY DE SUTTON; died May 10, between the years 1411, and 1417; buried near the entrance to the Choir, on the north side of the first great pillar on the south, opposite to the painting on the second pillar called the "Piety of the Virgin," of which all traces have long since been lost.

THOMAS YERDELEY, was Abbot in 1418; died 1434, buried on the north side of the Choir, beyond the Throne.

* No doubt of the family of the Barons of Halton.

† 1190—About this period the Abbots of Chester received an annuity of £10. from the Irelands, of Hutt, in the county of Lancaster, for arranging a marriage between Sir J. Ireland, and Maude, daughter and heiress of John Ireland. This must have been a match of consequence, for the gratuity was immense.—Gregson's Frag. Lanc. p. 219

|| This Abbot obtained the Mitre in 1345, and the following year had an exemption from the Bishop of Lichfield's Visitation.

CHESTER HISTORY.

JOHN SALGHALL, died in 1452; buried behind the Altar, between the pillars, where his grave stone is still to be seen, and on which was his effigy in brass.

RICHARD OLDHAM; died Oct. 13, 1485.*

SIMON RIPLEY;† died at Warwick, Aug. 30, 1492; buried in the College Church there.

JOHN BIRCHENSHAW, appointed by the Pope, Oct. 4, 1493. He was Abbot in 1512; but in about twelve years afterwards, he was displaced by a faction.‡

THOMAS HYPHILE, or HYPHILD, Abbot about 1524; he was set aside in 1529, and succeeded by

THOMAS MARSHALL; who was in his turn compelled to abdicate to Hyphile, who was restored.

JOHN BIRCHENSHAW, reinstated in his dignity, at the close of 1519, or beginning of 1520; died 1535.

THOMAS CLARKE, Abbot about 1537, and maintained his place till the Dissolution in 1540, when he was appointed the first Dean of the New Diocese.

* He was a Bishop of Man.

† This Abbot beautified and rebuilt a great portion of the Church.

‡ The Editor of the 8vo. edit. of the History of Chester (Dr. Pigot) says—"I presume he (this Abbot) was a native of Wales, and from near Conway, for on the great bell of that Church, is a Latin inscription with his name."—The name, however, is by no means national.

PARISH CHURCH OF ST. OSWALD.

THIS is the most extensive parish* in the City, extending a considerable distance into the County Palatine, and containing within its limits the townships of Bach, Great Boughton, Croughton, Huntington, Idenshaw, Newton, Wervin, the island of Hilbree, at the mouths of the Dee and Mersey, the Chapelry of Bruera, or Church on Heath, which includes the townships of Lea-cum-Newbold, Huntington, and Saighton.

The Church occupies the south transept of the Choir of the Cathedral. The Dean and Chapter are the patrons; and the present Incumbent is the Rev. T. Mawdesley, A. M. instituted June 4, 1803.

It is said, this Church was formerly dedicated to St. Peter and St. Paul, and subsequently to St. Oswald, King and Martyr. On the introduction of regular Monks into the Monastery of St. Werburgh, that part of the conventual Church now dedicated to St. Werburgh, was set apart for the use of the Parishioners. A considerable time afterwards, however, the Abbot wishing to attach it entirely to the Monastic Establishment, built a Chapel a short distance south-west from it, and dedicated it to St. Nicholas.† The parishioners wishing to return to the Old Church, a composition was entered into between them and the Abbot in 1488, by which they were permitted to take possession of the present Church, which they have ever since retained — About 1665, Bishop Bridgman wished to have the Sermon preached in the broad aisle of the Cathedral, but it does not appear that he persevered, as the Citizens refused to attend.

The Church is divided by a slight wooden screen from the aisle of the Cathedral, from which it differs little in architecture, with the exception of the windows on the east side, and the small windows at the south end, which are more elegantly finished.‡ Previous to 1525,

‡ See plate for title.

* The Townships, &c. included in the different parishes of Chester, will be found under their proper heads in the Itinerary of the Hundred.

† The present Theatre is built upon its ruins; the arches, however, remain on the north and south side, and also at the east end; the Dressing Rooms are erected over the spot, where formerly stood the High Altar! After being disused by the Parishioners, and being in a dilapidated state, it was sold to the Corporation in 1545, who converted it into a Common Hall. On the Hall in Common-hall-street being built, it became a Mart for the sale of Wool; and the lower part is now a Carrier's Warehouse!—Such are the strange revolu-

there were no seats in this Church, excepting those appropriated to the Mayor and Corporation; and about 1622, the Body attended Divine Service here every morning on Sundays and Festivals. In the license for appropriation granted by William Cornhull, Bishop of Lichfield and Coventry, it is called the *Parish Church of St Werburgh*, as it is also in another document, in which the Abbot agrees to pay to the Rector of Stoke a premium, in consideration of receiving in right of *his Parish Church of St. Werburgh*, and his Chapel of Wervin, the tythes and Church dues of Stoke, and retaining the right of burying within the cemetry of St. Werburgh, the bodies of the dead in Croughton, Stoke, Stanney, Holme, and half of Whitby.*

* Lysons.

The following is an abstract of the license of appropriation, and the ordination of the Vicarage :—

"Charta Will'i Ep'i de appropriatione Vicariæ S'c'i Oswaldi et Capellar de Brucrâ et Wyrvin.

"Will'mus Covent. ep'us totum alteragium p'ochialis eccl'ie s'c'e Werburge cum ejus pertinen. et capellis de Bruera et Wirvin et earum pertinen. integre et plenarie in proprios usus monach. Cest. confirmavit; salvo quidem jure mag. Hugo de s'c'o Oswaldo, quod in illo alteragio habuit, quamdiu vixerit: ita quidem quod p't ejus decessum d'c'i monachi per aliquem ab confratribus suis parochianis d'c'e eccl'ie divina administrent."

The Vicar has the tythes of Church-on-Heath, a part of the tythes of Saighton, and the Hamlet of Newbold, with a composition of £5. from Lea. Huntington is tythe free, as is also a portion of Saighton. The value of the Vicarage is £27.

Monuments, &c.

Against the screen which divides the Church from the Choir, a plain marble tablet, above which, the arms of Howard and Booth are impaled—

"S. jacet Catherina, Georgii Booth, arm. filia, ex Warringtonia nobili domu: nupsit Jacobo Howard arm" comitis Berkeriensis nepoti, ex Norfolciæ ducum prosapia illustrium. Inter Aulicos diu vixit illa mente dotibus eximiis ornata. Erga maritum præ amore nimio, gladio infelici pectus lævum præbuit semel per viscere eheu! tenera languida penetranti. Plus autem doloris infortunium lugubre Gulielmo (luxit enim Rex Britannus) quam ipsi attulit, Deus namque sanitatem cito dedit. Omnipotentis erat semper cultrix, pauperibus munifica, omnibusq. amicis cara. Ob. Feb. d. 8 A. D. 1765, æt. 93. Nobiles æque ac ignobiles mors conculcat. Pietatem cole, mundoq. pereunte vives immortalis. F. F. Catherina Elizabetha uxor N. C. Proby arm. et Martha Maria uxor C. Hervey S. T. P. filii honorab. dom honoratiss. Johannis illust. comitis Bristoliensis, P. P."

On a plate of brass, nearly adjoining this,—

"Emma Currie, died 25th April, 1816, aged near eight months, the infant daughter of Lieutenant-Colonel Currie, who lost his life in the Battle of Waterloo, 18th June, 1815."

In the north-east angle, on a blue flag stone,—

"Thomas Booth, eldest sonne of Will'm Booth, esq. and Vere, his wife, daughter of Thomas Venables, Baron of Kinderton, deceased ye third day of January, 1662, at the house of his Grandfather Sir George Booth, Knight and Baronet, in this cittie of Chester.—Ætatis suæ 2 annis et 6 Mensi's. Subter hoc jacet. Resurgam."

On an adjoining stone, ornamented with the arms of Booth—

"Hic jacet cupus Johannis Booth, equitis, aurati, filii natu minimi Georgii Booth, de Dunham Massie, in agro Cestrensi, equites aurati et baronetti. Obiit nono die Maii, anno salutis M.DC.LXXXVIII. Duxit in uxorem primam, Dorotheam filiam Anthonii St. John de Bletso, comitis de Bullingbrok, et reliquit tres filios et unam filiam.—Duxit in uxorem secundam, Annam viduam Thomæ Leigh de Adlington in comitatu Cestrensi armigeri, per quam nullam habuit prolem. Stant rata nonulli fila tenenda da manu."—

At the feet of the last, on a mural monument, with the arms of the families of Booth and Hawtry, impaled—

"Underneath lyeth the body of Martha, the wife of George Booth, of the house of Dunham Massey, Esq. youngest daughter of Mr. Ralph Hawtry, of Purley, in the county of Surrey, who died the 6th of May, 1718, by whom she had four sons and three daughters.—George, the eldest son, was buried in St. Peter's Church, of this city;

tions which St. Nicholas' Chapel has undergone.—According to Leycester, it was sometimes called St. Oswald's Church.

HISTORY. CHESTER.

George, a third son, in the Round Church of Dublin, in Ireland,—Mary the eldest daughter, and Robert the youngest son, and Thomasin, his wife, youngest daughter of William Hanmer, of Bettesfield, in the county of Flint, Esq. lye here interred. John, Catherine, and Elizabeth, are surviving; Catherine married to James Howard, Esq. Elizabeth married to Thomas Tyndal, Esq. The above mentioned George Booth, Esq. who was eminent for his piety and learning, endowed with all the virtues that adorn a Christian, dyed the 12th of November, 1719, aged 84.

Adjoining this, a monument to

"Elizabeth Booth, died September 11th, 1734, aged 96.

Monuments and other memorials to

"Catharine, daughter of Thomas Glynne, of Glynnelivon, county of Carnarvon, died 19th April, 1696, aged 58.

"Sarah, relict of Samuel Jervis, died July 17, 1748, aged 37."

&c. &c. &c.

PARISH OF ST. OLAVE.

The Church of St. Olave is situated on the east-side of Lower Bridge-street, opposite to Castle-street, and is a perpetual Curacy, in the gift of the Bishop. In 1726 it was augmented by the Royal Bounty, and afterwards thirteen acres of land were purchased, and added to it, together with the parochial contributions.* In 1809, its value was returned at £42. 1s. certified value £1. The present incumbent is the Rev. T. Crane. The registers commence in 1611.

The Church is built of the common red sand-stone of the City, and is of great antiquity. In the 11th century this Church was possessed by the Botelars; and in the time of Earl Richard, was given by Richard Pincerna, of that family, to Chester Abbey—the gift was confirmed by Charter in 1119.—Mr. Ormerod notices the following Charter, as referential to the Church, which he conceives to have been written between 1230 and 1234.†

Sciant, &c. quod ego Rog'us Herri dedi Agneti filie mee ad se maritandam unam mansuram terre q'm Hug. Ulf et Nich. Ulf filius ej's tenuerunt, illam scill. que est jux'a eccl'iam s'c'i Olavi, quam quidem habui de decano s'c'i Joh'is Baptiste, et de ej'dem loci canonicis. Habend. &c. Reddendo inde annuatim duodecim denar. ad festum s'c'i Martini ad communam s'c'i Joh'is Baptiste Cestr, p. om'i servicio et exac'o'e. H. aut. f'c'm fuit coram toto portmoto Cestr. Testibus, Will'o de Vernon justic', Steph'o Fredvell t'c vic. Will'o Cl'ico, Germano Dobelday, Joh'e fil. Ulfkell, Will'o, Saraceno, Hamon. Herre, et multis aliis." The seal is of green wax, and much defaced; on it is a whole length figure, inscribed "✠ SIGILL. R.... ERI HERRE."

After the Siege of Chester, the Church fell into disuse, and Bishop Gastrell, who noticed it in 1722, observes:—"Here is no provision at all for a Minister, and although the Church be in some tolerable repair, it is not fit for any public service, nor is any performed, besides baptism and burial. The Minister of St. Michael takes care of the Parish at present, and has done so for twenty years past."

Many of the Charitable bequests *to the poor*, were sunk in the erection of a gallery, but the parish pays the interest of money.

Alderman Robert Hervey erected six Alms Houses in this parish, for six poor persons, which he endowed with a fourth and an eighth of the Water Tower at the Bridge, which being purchased by Messrs. Hawkins & Headley, the Engineers to the Water Works, in 1692, for £100, that sum was vested in the works, and now

* In 1771 it was augmented by £200. the interest of which was paid to the Rev. Henry Dockesey, who died 1778, since then the payment has been withheld.

† It is in the possession of W. Hamper, Esq.

produces £6 per ann. received by those occupying the houses. By the will of Elizabeth Booth, dated Feb. 7, 1732, she left £10. per annum to the Minister of St. Olave's for ever. This was charged on the Park-house, lately the residence of Mrs. Dale,* on the east-side of Lower Bridge-street. The Rev. B. Culm, left in 1764, £100. the interest to be applied in putting out apprentices, children of indigent people, not receiving alms. This sum, with accumulated interest, and £20. left by Mrs. Aubrey, has been vested in the purchase of One Hundred and Sixty-three Pounds, Thirteen Shillings, and Three Pence, Navy 5 per cents.

The Registers commence in the year 1611.

* Purchased in the year 1818, by a Company of Gentlemen, for the purpose of being converted into an Inn, Bowling-green, &c. This house, although in a central part of the City, has attached to it a small park of nearly two statute acres, ornamented with a grove of lime trees, which, it is supposed, will be cut down, to admit of the projected improvements.

PARISH OF ST. MICHAEL.

THE present Minister of the Parish is the Rev. Joseph Eaton, A. M. F. S. A. who is perpetual Curate. The certified value is £15. but it has been augmented by Queen Anne's Bounty. It is in the gift of the Bishop.

The Church stands on the east side of Bridge-street, opposite to that of St. Bridget, and has an embattled tower,* about 76 feet high, resting on four Gothic arches, containing six tunable bells, cast in 1726.† The interior consists of a Nave, Chancel, and North Aisle, which is divided from the body of the Church by three pointed arches, springing from octagonal columns, the capitals ornamented with quatrefoils. The roof of the Chancel formerly rested on brackets, which have been taken away; it is ornamented with rosettes carved in wood The Chancel was built in 1496 ‡ The roof of the Nave is nearly flat.

This Church is supposed to have been connected with the Monastery of St. Michael, which, together with a house in the City, was given to the Priory of Norton, by Roger de Lacy.

The Monuments, &c.

Are very few, and unimportant. On the second pillar near the west end, a Tablet, arms effaced,—

"Hic jacet corpus Thomæ Chaloner, nuper de hàc urbe Civis quem pater patratus a Trenta in boream, sibi ad diem obitus 14m Maii, anno 1598, surrogarat quo magno sui desiderio expiravit."

In the Chancel—

"Here lyeth interred the body of Elizabeth, one of the daughters of Sir Richard Wilbraham, Kt. and Baronet, and late wife of Sir Humphrey Brigges, Kt. and Baronet, by whome she had issue two sons and two daughters, the eldest a son only surviving her. She departed this life, the 24th June, 1659, and in the 37th yeare of her age."

On the south side of the Altar, a Tablet,—Arms Venables and Leycester—

"Near this place lyeth the body of Dame Mary Delves, relict of Sir Henry Delves, of Doddington, Bart. and daughter of Randle Leicester, of the City of Chester, Gent. She died February 1, 1690, aged 68."

In the North Aisle, a mural monument—

"Near this place rest the remains of Roger Comberbach, Esq. late Prothonotary of the Counties of Cheshire and Flint. His virtues were exemplified in the husband, the father, and the friend. He died March 27, 1771, aged 51. Also the remains of Helen Comberbach, widow of the said Roger Comberbach, Esq. who died 8th Oct. 1814, aged 74 years."

Memorials of the Ledshams, also of Adams, Lowe, Dennell, Barnston, Falconer,|| Williams, Dicas, &c.

* Although built only One Hundred and Eight Years since, it is in a very ruinous state.

† The weight of them is stated to be 30½ cwt.

‡ See King's Vale Royal.

|| The remains of Thos. Falconer, Esq. A. M. the editor of Strabo, are interred in this Church.

In 1556, the following pensions were paid to the officiating Priests who served the Church previous to the Reformation :—

" Penc. Joh'is Thompsonne presbiter', nup. celebran, in eccl'ia s'c'i Mich'is Cest. p. ann. iiij*li*."

" Georgii Hardie, unius presbiter. nup. celebran. in eccl'ia p' och. p'd. in civitat. p'd'ta, p. ann. xls. vi*d*.

The value of the living, including every source of income, was returned by the Bishop in 1809, as amounting to £44. 10s.

The following is extracted from a MS. which appears to have been a book for the account of receipt and expenditure of the Church revenue.*

" Hereafter folowith the accomptes of us George Leghe and Adam Goodman to our Parisons, of the Landes longinge to the use of Sante Mighelli, both of the same landes and peade to ye Priestes wages, with other matters and costes of reparasions and deade rites of ye aforesayd landis, given the laste day of July in the furste yeare of Kinge Edowarde the Sixte, of the Churche of Englande and Hirelande, Supreme heade—for vj yeare and one quarter before this forsayd date to this presente day above mentionedde—

	The rentes of the landis.	The Cheaf rentes of ye same landis.
Brige strete	Roger Leigh's house ...... xxxs.	To Mr. Warburton ... . xvs.
	Limme's house ....xvs.	To Mr. Bothe .... xijs.
Foreast strete.	Goode Geste's house, widow...xs.	To Mr. Witmore .... iijs.
	John Burket's house ....vijs.	To the Shearives of Chester xijs.
Fleshemongers lane.	John Lingley's house.. ......xvs.	
	Thos. Winchester's house ...xvs.	
	The late wife of Thos. Wilcocke's house . ...vijs.	
	Richard Witbey's house......viijs.	
	Also one house in the Barne lane .... ijs.	
	Som of these rents is......... vl. ixs.	

The Priestes wagis for vi years and a quarter after iiijl. to ye yeare comes to............................. .... xxvl.

Rebated of this wagis for wante of a Prieste at two times, &c................ .... vjs."

Here follows a long bill of disbursements, for repairs done to several houses in " Brige-strete, Foreaste strete, and Fleshemongers lane."

" Som of all thes wastes and reparasions is .... ixl. iiijs.

Also there remayneth unpayd for the time of our service, to Goode Geste, widow, and her son's rente .... xxjs.

The som of our accountes besides the Prieste's wagis is viijl. xixs. id.

The som of wastes and reparasions of ye landis is ....ixl. iiijs.

So these remaineth due to us George Leghe and Addam Goodman of this forsayd rente, &c. .... iiijs. xid."

*In the possession of Mr. Dicas, Solicitor.

The Charitable bequests to this parish from the year 1596, are thus stated :—

" Small legacies amounting to £100. have at different times been received, for which the parish pays interest according to the direction of the donors.

" Philip Phillips, Alderman of the City, by will dated July 5th, 1611, left a shop in Eastgate-street, which then let for forty shillings a year. This it seems has from neglect of the parishioners dwindled to, and is now only claimed as a rent charge; no more than the above sum is paid at this day.

" Henry Smith, of London, included this parish among various others, to receive the profits of his charitable gift. The share received by the church wardens of St. Michael for the year 1815, was 10l. 2s. 4d.

" Jonathan Goldson, by will of March 10th. 1679, left 15l. once in three years, to put forth a freeman's son of this parish apprentice. This bequest is chargeable, and now paid upon four houses on the south side of Pepper-street, belonging to Earl Grosvenor.

" George Bulkley, left Sept. 25, 1688, the sum of 100l. vested in trustees, who are to pay the interest to the minister, but in case of a vacancy, the interest then arising to be given to the poor of St. Michael and St. Bridget, by the church wardens of those parishes.

" Joseph Bassnet left, June 4th, 1694, 2l. every three years, towards putting a freeman's son apprentice, after the same manner as Goldson's bequest, to which it was intended as an augmentation.—Charged on his estate in the parish, and now paid by the present landlord Mr. Owen Foulkes.

" Doctor Robt. Oldfield, by will of April 24th 1695, devised two-thirds of Dunham Hall, and other Lands, and Messuages at Dunham-on-the-Hill, together with Lands at Boughton, for the purpose of paying 20l. a year to the Minister of St. Michael's, provided he held no other preferment, and of binding poor boys apprentices born in the parish, and of maintaining one or more poor boys, who should be apt to learn, at the University. Proper objects do not every year present themselves, the revenues therefore have accumulated, and together with the bequeathed property, produce an annual sum of above 200l. The present Trustees are—

ROGER BARNSTON, } ESQUIRES. { HENRY HESKETH
JOHN DRAKE, } { ROBERT BAXTER.

" William Proby, left April 3d, 1716, twelve shillings a year, charged on a Field in Handbridge, called Cook's Croft, now the property of Robert Evans, of Saltney-side.

Lettice Whitley, left a house on the east side of Bridge-street, to

CHESTER HISTORY.

the Minister and his successors, for ever, and charged the cellar under the same with 10s. a year for the clerk, and 5s. for the sexton for ever. By her will, in 1706, this house is left to a Mr. Brereton, paying 4l. a year to the Minister; but in a codicil, dated July 3d, 1708, the Minister is to have the house, and the cellar only is reserved to Mr. Brereton, paying the clerk and sexton, which by the will lay on the premises at large.

" Peter Cotton, left in 1716, thirteen large prayer books to poor widows, of the nine parishes of the city, in rotation. Paid by the Mayor of Chester for the time being, and received by this parish in the year 1811.

" Timothy Dean, left March 20th, 1726, 50l. in aid of Goldson's legacy. This was in the hands of Mr. Philip Prestbury, who died insolvent about five years since, and the legacy entirely lost.

" Rev. Thomas Leftwich, left May 10th, 1746, 10l. the interest to be laid out by the Minister and Church-wardens, in a bible, value 4s. 6d. prayer-book 2s. duty of man, 2s. 6d. preparation for the sacrament 1s. and given every year to one poor house-keeper of the parish.—Also,

Hannah Leftwich bequeathed 40l. the interest to be given to eight old maids yearly.

" Elizabeth Potter, left Jan. 9th, 1782, 40l. the interest to be paid yearly to ten poor persons in the alms-houses. These three last legacies were in the year 1789 called in, and vested in the purchase of a shop in the street, under the house belonging to this parish, on the north side of the church.

" John Matthews, Esq. (Capt. R. N.) who died in 1798, left 350l. of 3 per cent. Cons. the interest to put apprentice a poor child born in this parish, now vested in the names of the Rev. J. Eaton, and Mr. T. Dicas."

SAINT BRIDGET'S PARISH.

THE Church dedicated to St. Bridget, is situated on the west side of Bridge-street, opposite to St. Michael's Church. There is no fixed date for its foundation, but it was probably amongst the Churches founded during the reign of Offa, about 795.—The patronage of the Church was formerly vested in the Lords of Aldford, one of whom, we are told* quitclaimed the same, together with the advowson of Sandbach, to Randle Blundeville, shortly after the suit between the Earl and Sir Richard de Sandbach, in 1224. A record of the pleadings in this case, heard in the King's Bench, brought into that court by Writ of Certiorari, 38th Henry III. till exists amongst the Harl. MSS. A connexion afterwards existed between the Church of St. Bridget and a Chapel, (which belonged in the 13th century to the Arneways). This Chapel, together with Messuages in 'Brugge Streete,' was granted by Bertram, son of Wm. de Arneway, to the Abbot of St. Werburgh, and this, together with other donations, induced Simon the Abbot of Chester,† to bind himself to maintain two Chaplains to celebrate Mass for the soul of John Arneway, before the Altar of St. Leonard, in the Conventual Church, and also before the Altar of the Virgin, in St. Bridget's Church.—At the Dissolution, £4. wages were given to "Richard Lowther, Pryeste att the Churche of Saynte Bryggytt's."—The Church is now considered a Rectory; the present incumbent is the Rev. Rich Massie. The certified value £18. 14s.; the value as returned by the Bishop in 1809, including the various sources of income £68. 3s. 2d. The Rectory is in the gift of the Bishop.

* Ormerod.

† 1265-89.

The Church was formerly surrounded by a wall, which encroached several feet on the present line of the street; but in 1785, the Parishioners purchased a piece of ground on the south side of the building, into which the bodies were removed from the old Church-yard, and the public causeway considerably widened on the north and east sides.‡ The Church was at the same time repaired, the walls re-cased with stone, and a new door made at the east end of the north side. The expense of these improvements, was very great, and paid

‡ Formerly, there was a Gateway between these two Churches, erected probably as an additional means of defence, during the incursions of the Welsh.

chiefly by money sunk in annuities after the rate of 10 per cent. The steeple has been several times repaired within the last dozen years: it contains four indifferent bells. It is said a fifth bell was seized by a Churchwarden for a debt due from the parish, and sold to the parish of Waverton: there certainly is a defect in the peal between the third and fourth bells.

The Monumental Memorials in the Church, are also few and unimportant:

A Tablet to the memory of Mary Nelson; to the Rev. Wm. Nelson, who died Sept. 21, 1810.

On a marble Monument, to the memory of Henrietta, wife of William Wingfield, daughter of Sir Rich. Astley, of Pateshull, Staffordshire, died 21st February, 1720.

Randle Holme notices Memorials to the families of Wright, Jones, Savage, Simpson, Clayton, Goodman, Williams, Hulton, and Proby, as having existed in 1580; also in the Chancel, a large Tablet to the memory of Stephen Smith, Esq. Customer of the Port of Chester, Comptroller of the Port of Dublin, and Escheator of the Province of Munster, he died September 4th, 1665, aged 69.

Charitable Bequests.

This Parish has a share of an Estate at Willaston, left by Mr. Wilcox, in April 1634: It now lets for £100. but originally for £20. when it was thus apportioned:—

	£	s.	d.
To St. John's	£14	9	8
To Neston	2	16	2
To St. Bridget's	2	14	2

At the present time it is thus divided:—

	£	s.	d.	
St. John's	£0	14	5	In the Pound.
Neston	0	2	10	
St. Bridget's	0	2	9	

Belonging to this Parish is a piece of Land, in Hoole-lane, called the Croft, now let for about £5. per ann. This was purchased with legacies left by Mrs Salmon. Mrs. Booth, Mrs. Bailey, and Mrs. Swarsbrick.—An estate at Trafford, purchased for £300. from the proceed of the sale of certain houses left by Mr. Richard Harrison, brewer; the income of which is now distributed among ten poor parishioners, who receive £1. 4s. 6d. each, half yearly.—£50. left to the Churchwardens, in Nov. 1786, the interest to be appropriated to the purchase of bread for the Poor, to be distributed every Christmas. In 1798, £100. stock, in the 3 per cent. Cons. was purchased in the names of Wm. Thomas, and Wm. Massey, Esqrs. but owing to NEGLECT, in renewing the Trustees, *the money has been lost to the Parish!*—£2. charged on a house the property of Bell Ince, Esq. left by the late Recorder Townshend.—In addition to these, there are several other trifling sums distributed to the Poor.

PARISH OF ST. PETER.

THE Church is situated close to the ancient site of the High Cross. It was formerly a Rectory, but is now a Perpetual Curacy, augmented by Queen Anne's Bounty. The present Incumbent, is the Rev. John Halton.—Val. Eccl. £6. 18s. 4d; certified value, £12. 18s. 4; according to the returns made by the Bishop, in 1809, £92. 18s. 4d. including the different sources of income.

Tradition says, that this Church owes its building to Ethelfleda, who dedicated it to St. Peter and St. Paul; and this Bradshaw the Monk notices in these uncouth rhymes—

And the Old Church of St. Peter and Paul,
By a general consent of the spiritualty
With the help of the Duke most principall,
Was translated into the midst of the said city.

It is certain, however, at the survey of Domesday, it was known by its present name—

"Terra in qua est templum Sancti Petri, quam Robertus de Rodeland, clamabat at Teinland (sicut diracionavit comitatus) nunquam pertinuit ad manerium extra civitatem, sed ad burgum pertinet, et semper fuit in consuetudine regis et comitis, sicut aliorum burgensium."

CHESTER HISTORY.

This Robert de Rodeland, gave this Church, with other donations, to the Monks of St Ebrulf, at Utica, in Normandy, who ultimately quit-claimed the Rectory to the Abbot of St Werburgh. At the Dissolution, the patronage was vested by Charter, in the Dean and Chapter; about 1670, the Crown possessed it. It is now exclusively in the gift of the Bishop.

The interior of the Church consists of a Nave, and side aisles. The tower is at the south angle on the west side. It had formerly a spire, which was taken down about the year 1780, having been much injured by lightning. In 1787 the south side of the Church was re-cased with stone. In 1813, the steeple was rebuilt, and a new clock placed in it. The entire body of the church was new pewed in 1814-15. In the steeple are eight bells, of which six are a peal, cast in 1709. On the treble is "when you ring, I'll sing." The "Pentice bell" was cast so early as 1589, and was originally used for the purpose of summoning the Magistrates; it is now rung on Corporate Court days. In the beginning of the year 1818, Sunday Evening Lectures were established in this Church, under the patronage of the excellent Bishop of the Diocese, and the Lectureship was bestowed on the Rev. R. Pearson.* On Sunday evening October 18, the Church was lighted with Gas. The Registers commence in 1559.

The Monuments, &c.

Are but few, but there are a number of Tablets in the Church—the following are those chiefly worth notice—

"Neare unto this place lieth the body of Edward Bradshaw, Esq. who by his first wife Susannah, daughter and heir of Christopher Blease, of this City Alderman, had 12 children, and by his second wife Mary, the relickt of Mr. Christopher Love, had seven children: he was exemplary for his piety and charity when living, and departed this life the 31st of October, 1671, in the 67th year of his age, leaving five of his children yet alive, to continue whose memory, his son and heir, Sir James Bradshaw of Risby in the east riding of y[e] county of York, has erect this monument."

On the pillar in the middle of the Church—

"On the south-west side of this pillar, lies the body of Mrs. Ursula Bradshaw, youngest daughter of Sir James Bradshaw, Kt. and of his Lady, who was sole daughter and heir of Edward Ellerker, of Risby, in the county of York. Esq. She died at Chester, 18th Sept. 1731, ætat 43, and desiring to be buried near her grandfather, her affectionate brother, Ellerker Bradshaw, Esq. in memory of her many virtues erected this monument."

A Memorial of—

"Mary, daughter and Co-heiress of Randle Leech, merchant, and Sheriff of Chester, and late wife of Robert Ince, draper, who died July 27, 1613, leaving 5 sons and one daughter."

"Thomas Tylston, M. D. died Jan. 9, 1746; and John Tylston, M. D. his son, died June 22, 1760."

On a Mural Monument against the north wall in the gallery—

"This marble, conjugal affection, and filial piety, have erected to the memory of Henry Bennett, Esq. A Citizen who did honour to this City, a Merchant who improved and extended its commerce, a Magistrate who ruled with dignity and justice; a lover of his country, a friend of mankind, and of his God a servant zealous with knowledge: his life was such continued happiness to those whom God and nature taught him most to love, that his death, which happened on the 26th of Nov. 1747, in the 56th year of his age, became their greatest and most lasting misfortune."

On the south side of the Altar, against the wall—

"Præter fuit anno verbi incarnati MDLXXXVIII. Gulielmo Wall, honestis penatibus, Helsbeii, Frodshamiæ, nato, hujus urbis olim prætori, ordinisq. senatorii. viro gravi, et moribus suavissimis, optimorum comiti, et omnibus corni: in se potius quam sui parco; in publicum liberali. in pauperes prodigo, virtutum ejus memor memoriæq. cuttor posuit."

Behind the Pulpit, on a tablet—

"Quisquis hæc legis, scias ··· esse Thomam Cowper ··· civem Cestrensem, qui dum vixit, vixit bonus civis, paterfamilias frugi, amicis utilis, cognatis benignus, simul temperans, justus, religiosus, misericors, quodque scire, etiam te volo, duobus quos reliquit filiis et vivus et moriens, optime prospexit, e quibus natu major, hoc quod vides marmor, pietatis ergo, extrui curavit. Obiit 27° die Novembris, Anno M.DC.XCV. ætatis suæ 71°."

Beneath this inscription, the following—

"Thomæ cineribus miscentur Elizabethæ, conjugis charissimæ, viduæ mœstissimæ Joannis Baskerville de Withington arm. filiæ, et Britonum et Normannorum principibus oriundæ. Pia benefica vixit, bonis flebilis occidit, x Dec. an. Christi 1716, ætat. 72."—W. C. nepos, arm. hoc posuit."

* The expense attending the Establishment, is defrayed by public Annual Subscription.

HISTORY.

On a wooden tablet—

"Here lyethe the bodyes of Thomas Cowper of y^e citty esquier, Alderman and Justice of Peace, Maior 1641, he dyed 19th July, 1671, aged 76 yeares; and alsoe of Catherine his wife, daughter of Thomas Throppe, of the saide citty of Chester, Alderman and Justice of the Peace. She died 29th of May, 1672, aged 72 yeeres.—They had yssue five son'es and two daughters, of which three sons and one daughter survived them,"

"Humphrey Page, gent. Alderman, died April 17, 1711, aged 54, leaving issue two sons and five daughters."

&c. &c. &c.

Charitable Bequests.

William Crompton, of Kinnerton, Flintshire, left by will in 1709, one half of his lands and messuages at Higher Kinnerton, to the Poor of St. Peter's Parish, to be distributed under the direction of the Mayor and Aldermen. In 1810, the land was valued at £18. and was leased for that sum to W. Richards, Esq. of Kinnerton. A survey of this estate, made in 1775, is preserved in the Church.

Alderman H. Bennett, left by will 17th Feb. 1708, £25. the interest to be paid to 12 poor old widows, each Christmas. This was charged on his real estate, at Whitby, and was never paid to the parish. It seems, instead of the bequest of 2s. 1d. to each widow, his family gave 2s 6d. to each of the 12 widows. At the present time, £1. 12s. are paid to the Church-wardens every Christmas by Earl Grosvenor, the now owner of the Whitby property.

Twenty shillings yearly left by Mr. Witter, of Frodsham, charged on a house and shop on the west side of Upper Bridge-street.—52s. yearly, left by Mr. Cooper, to be given to the poor in bread, and 8d. to the Clerk and Sexton, for delivering the same. This Legacy is charged on the Old Talbot Inn, at the Eastgate.—Mr. Hugh Offley, on the 14th May, [illegible], left a penny loaf, and [illegible] to 12 poor people, to be given on the 1st Sunday in each month, to the eight parishes of the City, in succession, St. Olave's being omitted, it being, probably, at the date of the will, scarcely considered as a separate and independent parish; 6½d. each to the Clerk and Sexton for distributing the same. This is paid by the Treasurer of the City.—10s. left to the poor by Mr. Brereton, to be paid every St. George's Day, by the City Treasurer.

The figures which supported the old clock, originally placed there to strike the chimes, and which represented two Roman Soldiers, were removed in the month of August, 1810: one of them is still in existence.

PARISH OF THE HOLY TRINITY.

THIS Church adjoins the Custom House, on the east side, and is situated on the north side of Watergate-street, nearly opposite to Nicholas-street. It is a Rectory; the present Incumbent, the Rev. T. Maddock, A. M. Rector of Northenden, and one of the Prebendaries of the Cathedral. The advowson of the rectory was formerly vested in the Barons of Montalt, and with that Barony passed to the Crown, the Earls of Salisbury, and the Stanleys of Lathom, and is now the property of the present noble representative of that family, the Earl of Derby *

The chief part of the present Church, is built of the common red sand stone of the City, but the north wall of the north aisle, is cased with brick. The interior consists of a Nave, Chancel, and side Aisles, which are divided from the nave on the south by three pointed arches. The arches on the north side have been removed, and iron pillars introduced in their place. The Tower, is at the south angle of the west end, and in 1811 possessed a remarkable fine spire; apprehensions, however, being then entertained of its safety, and the dreadful accident by the fall of the spire at St. Nicholas Church, in Liverpool, about this time occurring, it was taken down without the least accident. Its structure was remarkably light,† and the extreme altitude 159 feet; it had frequently been injured by storms, particularly in the years 1769 and 1770; about which periods the upper part had been built not less than three times in eight years. The stones which formed the ex-

† See Butcher's Tour from Sidmouth to Chester.

* The earliest notice of this Church supposed to be in existence, is in a charter relative to the Church of Rosthern, previous to 1188, which is witnesse damong others, by William de Montalt, and Waltero, Ecclesiæ Sanctæ Trinitatis Presbytero.—ORM.

treme point, were obtained by Dr. Thackeray, and fixed as a pedestal for a basaltic column from the Giant's Causeway, in the Infirmary Garden. The east and south sides of this Church, were, in 1679, rebuilt from the foundation, being then in an extremely dilapidated condition. In 1771 the Church-yard was enlarged from land given by the Rector to the Parish, he and his successsors receiving in lieu thereof £4. a year for ever. The Church was materially enlarged from the Chancel, in 1774, 50 feet in length from Saint Patrick's aisle, and 28 feet in width from south to north, at an expense exceeding £500. In 1736, the present peal of six bells was placed in the steeple, cast by Rudhall, of Gloucester. In 1809, part of the field, in which the City Gaol is built, was purchased by the Parish at an expense of nearly £1000. and on Sept. 22, 1810, it was consecrated as a Burial ground, together with a small Chapel built thereon. Certified value of the living £33. 11s. 10; Val. Eccl. £8. 15s 6d. R. D.

The Monuments, &c.

Webb notices a number of monuments in this Church, not now in existence. The following are those most worthy of notice :—

At the Altar, a Tablet—

" Here lyeth the bodyes of Martha, 4th daughter of Philip Chetwood, of Oakley, by Esther, his wife, daughter to William Tuchett, of Whitley, who died 17th May, 1681 aged 41 years, and Eleanor, 2d daughter of the said Philip Chetwood. She died 16th March, 1682, aged 12 years."

Above this—

" Here lieth interred the remains of Martha Meredith, spinster, sister of Sir Wm. Meredith, of Henbury, in this county, Bart. who died in this city, on the 8th day of October, 1788, aged 64 years."

On the north side of the Altar, a Memorial of

" Sir Herbert Whalley, Knt. who was born at Ringmore, in Sussex, and died of a fever at Chester, May 6, 1689."

Near to this, on a marble Tablet—

" P. M. S. Thomæ Ravenscroft, nuper de Pickhill, in agro Denbighensi, armigeri. ex antiqua Ravenscroft de Bretton, in com. Flint, prosapiâ orti · Margaretæ uxoris ejus fidelissimæ, d'ni Thomæ Williams, nuper de Vaynall, in comitatu Carnarvan, ba'rti, filiæ: qui cum quadraginta annos sum'a cum felicitate amantissimi consixerunt, et ad 84 ætatis annum respective provecti pientissimi obierunt, ille 18mo. die mensis Februarii, 1681, illa 23° Octobris, 1683: in quorum piam memoriam eorum filia mœstissima et executrix Dorothea Ravenscroft, pie hoc monumentum posuit."

Near the last, on a plain Tablet—

" Near this place resteth in hope of a joyful resurrection to eternal life, the body of the Rev. James Stones, A. M. late Rector of this Parish. He died the 23d day of May, in the year of our Lord 1786, aged 68."

At the end of the south aisle, the memorials of Henry and Edmund Gee; on a black slab—

" Henry Gee, who was Maior of the City in 1539."

" Heere under lieth buried the body of Edmunde Gee, once Maior of this citty of Chester, and in the same yeare he departed, the XIII day of June, anno Domini, M.V.LI whose soul hopeth for Mercey."

" Dame Elizabeth heare interred is,
That ladie was of late
To Calverley, Kt. but first espoused
To Genry Gee her mate;
Who ruled heare a patern rare,
As cittie well can shewe;
Thus she in worship run her race,
And still in virtue grewe."

A large Marble Monument to—

" John Mainwaring, of Wrenbury, of the Baddiley family, and Steward to Lord Weymouth. Obiit March 2, 1729, aged 84."

A brass plate to the memory of—

" Peter Drinkwater, Alderman, obiit July 18, 1631; and Sarah his wife, obiit Jan. 5, 1646."

A large Monument, with a very long inflated inscription, to the memory of—

" William Allen Merchant, and Alderman of Chester, Mayor 1697, died July 1708, aged 67.

Beneath the last, was a recumbent figure in complete armour,* his shield vert, fretty Or; and around the edge of the tablet—

* It is now buried beneath the last seat at the east end of the south aisle. occupied by Dr. Thackeray. Why it was removed, has not been explained—it is certainly to be regretted that it should thus remain in obscurity.

CHESTER.

"Hic Jacet Joannes de Whitmore, obiit 3 Kal. Octob. A D. 1374."

Near this was a Tablet in a shield form, inscribed—

"Here lies John Whitmore, Esq. He was Mayor of this city four years successively. King Edward the Third then reigning."*

On a Brass Plate, within the Altar rails—

"Mutilatatis exuvias hic juxta deposuit Katharina Henry, filia unica Samuelis Hardware, armigeri Conjux admodum dilecta Matthæi Henry, S. S. Evangelii ministri, quæ primo partu (filiolâ superstite) variolis extincta ad patriam migravit 14º die Februarii, 1688-9, anno æt. 25. Posuit in lachrymis viduatus conjux.—Idem Matthæus Henry, pietatis et ministerii officiis strenue perfunctus, per labores, S. S. literis scrutandis et explicandis impensos confectum corpus huic dormitorio commixit 22ndo die Junii, 1714, anno ætat. 52; susceptis ex Mariâ Warburton, armigeri, filiâ, mœrente jam vidua, unico filio et quinque filiabus superstitibus."

A Memorial on the south side of the Altar—

"At ye foot of this pillar on ye chancell side is interred ye body of William Ince, late Alderman and Justice of the Peace of ye citey, was maior anº 1662, he was one of the burjezes in Parliament for this citey: he died ye 27th of January, aº. 1678: had issue only by his second wife, Anne daughter of Thomas Thropp Alderman and Justice of the Peace. She was interred in ye same anº. 1644. Two sons survived their father, William the eldest, and Robert the fourth. William Ince, Alderman and Justice of Peace of this citey, was maior anº. 1677."

Memorials of

Thomas Partington, Alderman, obiit February, 24, 1716.—John Stringer, Mayor, 1714, died May 30, 1715, aged 52.—Robt. Hincks, died March 12, 1779.—Margaret Hincks, died June 24, 1809, aged 58.—John Hincks, Nov. 25, 1812, aged 43.—Elizabeth Hincks, born Oct. 20, 1752, died Dec. 20, 1812.—William Wright, merchant, died Sept. 16, 1662; and Sarah his widow, daughter of Richard Bird, Alderman, May 20, 1689, aged 60.—John Buckley, Esq. died Aug. 6. 1805, aged 45, John Bennett, Alderman, died Sept. 6, 1810, aged 81; Eleanor his wife, died August 27, 1793, aged 55; Edward, Daniel, and Thomas, their sons.—Elizabeth Hinde, daughter of Henry and Alice Hesketh, died Jan. 20, 1811, aged 60.—Henry Hesketh, Esq. died Feb. 22, 1788, aged 73; Alice his wife, died Feb. 16, 1784, aged 66.—Jane, daughter of Roger Steele, registrar of Bangor, wife of John Poole, Sheriff of Chester, died June 6, 1644: Anne, 2d wife of the same, daughter of Rowland Griffiths, of the county of Merioneth, died Sept. 15, 1660.—Francis Skellern, Mayor of Chester, 1689, obiit Oct. 14, 1708, aged 78.

HISTORY.

Parnell, the Poet, (Archdeacon of Clogher) was interred in this Church, October 24th, 1718."

&c. &c. &c.

There are some fine remains of stained glass in the window on the north side of the Altar.

Charitable Bequests.

The following are still applied, subject to the directions of the Donors:—

Thomas Kenyon, carpenter, in 1711, left all his real and personal estate in trust, for the use of 12 poor widows of this parish, to be distributed on the 10th of June annually. He charged his property with his debts, and a few legacies, which were paid off with some parish bequests, and the estate was much improved. The property consisted of two houses and a stable, and yard, on the west side of Lower-lane; a barn, stable, and garden, on the east side thereof. The whole comprising 9 tenements, now let for about £59. per ann.

Alderman H. Bennett, left £25. to this parish, subject to the same regulations as his bequest to St. Peter's. In 1715, this legacy was, by order of Vestry, ordered to be paid in, to discharge a debt upon Kenyon's houses; but it does not appear that the order was attended to. The interest of the £25. chargeable on the real estate, is now paid by Earl Grosvenor

John Grosvenor, Esq. in May, 1699, left £3. a-year, to 10 decayed housekeepers, charged upon his house, garden, and premises on the south side of Watergate-street, late the property of Wm. Currie, M. D.

Peter Ince, stationer, left 20th Charles I. 52s. yearly, to be given to the poor attending the Church, in bread, charged upon the cellar of the house in which he lived.

Robert Fletcher, of Cork, son of Wm. Fletcher, of Chester, draper, in 1674, left two new houses, with £4. a-year, for four poor widows, and 4 shillings a year to repair the houses, for ever;† charged on a front, is this inscription:—"The gift of Robert Fletcher, of Corke, in Ireland, gent. ye fourth son of William Fletcher, of this citty of Chester, to 4 poor widdows of sixty years old, of ye parish of Trinitie, and 20 shillings to be paid each of them yearly by the quarter, and 4 shillings yearly to repair these houses for ever, Anno Domini 1674."

* This tablet also, was buried beneath the seat before mentioned, but was at the close of the year 1817, taken up, and affixed to the wall. The effigy was that of John Whitmore, of Thurstaston, Mayor from 1369, to 1372.

† The houses are situated at the bottom of King's Buildings. In

CHESTER HISTORY.

house on the west side of Lower Bridge-street, lately inhabited by Mrs. Hunt.*

The Parish Officers have the appointment of pensioners.

The Mainwaring family founded alms houses in Trinity-lane, for three poor widows, with an allowance each of 20s per ann. They are appointed by James Mainwaring, Esq. of Bromborow Hall, grandson of the founder.

* Purchased in the year 1818, with the Park-House, by the Proprietors of the projected New Hotel, Bowling-green, &c. and converted into a Reading-room, Billiard-room, &c. &c.---See note, page 233.

PARISH OF ST. MARTIN.

The Church is situated on the south side of the west end of Whitefriars-street, and the area in front of it is called "*St Martin's Ash*;" indeed the Church itself was formerly called *St. Martin's of the Ash*. It is a rectory in the gift of the Bishop. In 1744, it was augmented by lands purchased with £400.* £200. of which were from Queen Anne's bounty. The certified value £1. 16s. In 1809 the annual value of the living, arising from the various sources of income, was £76. 18s.

The building is of brick, erected, as appears from the tablet on the west side of the steeple, in 1721—

> This Church being ruinated, was new Erected from the Foundation, in the year 1721.
> CHARLES BINGLEY, } C. W.
> WILLIAM TERRY, }

The interior is small, but very neat, without chancel or side aisles. The origin of the foundation remains in obscurity, but it appears pretty certain to have been anterior to 1250.—Indeed, there is a deed in the possession of the Earl of Shrewsbury, by which Bernard, Lord of Tranmulle, releases to Philip le Clerk, son of Galfridus Muniter, 12d. rent arising from premises *near the Church of St. Martin*, in Chester, Adam le Zouch being then Justice of Chester.† In July, 1637, the Bishop of Chester presented William Clerke to the Rectory; but in 1699, the inhabitants elected a Minister. After this period, according to Gastrell's *Notitia*, the Rector of St. Bride's generally supplied the Church, preaching there once a month, and administering the Sacrament every quarter. There are two small bells in the steeple.

† Ormerod.

The present Rector, is the Rev. John Willan, presented in October, 1806.

The Monuments.

On the south side of the Altar, is a Mural Monument to

"Abigail, relict of Thomas Jones, of Churton, Esq. daughter of Sir John Chetwode, of Oakley, county of Stafford, Bart. She died June 11, 1776, aged 73."

Charitable Bequests.

The Charitable Bequests are but few—

Robert Shone, tallow chandler, formerly Sheriff of Chester, left 20s. to be distributed to the Poor every Good Friday: he left also 20s. to the Church-wardens, towards repairing the Church. The Clerk had a legacy from him of 10s. annually. These are charged on the Middle Rake Hey, in the parish of Hawarden.

Twenty shillings to the Poor, and ten shillings to the Minister, left by Mr. Terry, to be paid every Easter Monday, charged on a House near Glover's-stone.

The interest of £10. to be given to the Poor every Christmas-Day, left by Mr. John Langdale.

* £100. were given by a Lady unknown, and the Parishioners subscribed another £100.

PARISH OF ST. MARY,

Anciently called St. Mary de Castro—St. Mary super Montem, and now St. Mary on the Hill. This Church was given to the Abbey of St. Werburgh, by Randle Gernons, Earl of Chester. It is just within the liberties of the City, being divided from the County merely by the Castle-ditch.

Subsequent to the Dissolution, the Dean and Chapter had a grant of the Rectory; but it was lost to them in the disputes at that period;* and vested in and confirmed to the Fee Farmers, by Patent of the 22d of Elizabeth. A short time previous to the final settlement, Richard Hurleston purchased the interest of George Cotton, Esq. in it, for £100. on the behalf of John Brereton, Esq. of Wettenhall, who had presented to the Church in 1554. From the Breretons, the Rectory passed with half of Wettenhall, by sale, to the Wilbrahams, of Dorfold, and from thence by marriage, to the Hills, of Hough, in Wybunbury, who are the patrons. The parish runs considerably into the County. Upton, Little Mollington, Moston, Claverton, Marleston cum Lache, and Gloverstone, being within its limits, as is also the suburb of Handbridge.

*See p. 100.

The Church consists of a Nave, Chancel, and side Aisles, and a Tower, containing six heavy bells.† The tower is only about 50 feet high; it was repaired in 1715, and a further increase to its altitude was objected to by the Governor, because it would command a view of the Castle-yard.‡ The side aisles are separated from the nave by three arches, and the chancels are also divided from the aisles by a pointed arch, excepting the principal Chancel, which has an obtuse one.—The windows still contain a few fragments of stained glass, amongst which appears the arms of Brereton, Ipstons, &c.

† Three of them werecast by Rudhall, of Glocester; the remaining three were cast at Wigan, so early as 1557.

‡ So says the 8vo. History of Chester; but no authority is cited for the assertion.

There is a handsome octagonal font in the south chancel, but it is not used. The Troutbeck‖ Chapel formerly occupied the south aisle, and there were many curious monuments of the family here about 1660—at that period, however, they were destroyed by the falling in of the Chapel. The chapel was given up to the parish in 1690, by the Earl of Shrewsbury, the representative of the Troutbecks, and on its site was built the present aisle. The north aisle was called the chapel of St. Catharine.

In August, 1793, a neat organ was put up in the West Gallery, by Mr. Chalinor, at the expense of £175.

In the Registers of this parish, ann. 1636, occurs the following entry, which in these days it is melancholy to peruse:—"Three witchis hangid at Michelmass Assizes buryed in the corner by the Castel ditch, in Churche yarde, Oct. ye 8th.

The Monuments, &c.

The Monumental Memorials are still numerous, but many noticed by Webb, no longer remain.

In the Chancel, memorials to Emma Jane Barbara; Emma Jane Barbara; Elizabeth Anne; Robert Wilbraham, daughters and son of John and Elizabeth Hill. Capt. Peter Wilbraham, died Feb. 27, 1765, aged 40; Mary his wife, Jan. 10, 1766, aged 37.

On a brass, adjoining the Altar rails, on the north side—to

"Elizabeth, daughter of Richard Wright, S. T. B. rector of St. Mary's, and Mary his wife, daughter of John Wainwright, L. L. D. Chancellor of Chester."

On a Mural Marble Monument—

‖ Troutbecks of Dunham.---There is notice of a Chapelry here in the Eccl. Survey, 26 Henry VIII.—"Cantaria infra eccl'iam Beate Marie Cestrie Johannes Dutton, capellanus. Valet in redd' provenien' de certis terris et tenementis in civitate Cestrie annuatim per cantaristam ib'm recept' ad annuum valorem cvj^s. x^ma inde x^s. viij^d."

"Underneath lie the remains of the Rev. Middleton Jones, L. L. B. late of Cribarth, in the county of Brecon, formerly Rector of this parish, who died the 9th of November, 1755, aged 47."

A Mural Monument to the memory of

Peter Cotton, of the family of the Cottons, of Cotton, who died Feb. 16, 1715-16, leaving charitable legacies to the amount of £500. to the charities and poor of Chester, Northwich, and Witton.

A Memorial to several of the Eyton family, of Pentre Madoc.

Near the last—

"In this Chancel lieth the body of Roger Wilbraham, late of Dorfold, in the county of Chester, Esq. who departed this life on the 24th day of January, 1768, in the 52d year of his age."

At the end of the North Aisle, the Monument of Edmund Gamul—

"The bodies of the just are buried in peace, but their names live for ever." ECCLUS. 44.

"Here lieth the body of Edmund Gamul, sometime maior of this citie, who had 2 wives, Elizabeth, the daughter of Thomas Case, by whom he had issue 3 sons and 3 daughters. And Elizabeth, the widdow of William Goodman, sometime maior of this city, who died without issue; who departed this life in the yeare of his age... of..."

A curious Tomb of Thomas Gamul, late Recorder of Chester, with statues of alabaster of himself, and his wife on the right hand, his only son kneeling at his feet upon his knee, his prayer-book lying open upon his other knee; his three other children in their order pourtrayed in the arched side of the tomb, holding skeletons in their hands, being all deceased in their infancy, and the tomb compassed with a strong piked grate of iron,—at the lower end of the tomb, thus inscribed:

"Ossibus et Memoriæ

"Thomæ Gamuelis, ornatissimi armigeri, et juris consulti clarissimi, in quo eximia quædam ingenii suavitas cum summa morum gravitate ancipiti palmâ contendebat: quiq; (proh dolor!) in ipso ætatis dignitatisq; suæ flore, ardentissimâ febre correptus, et præreptus; immaturo funere tristissimum toti Cestriæ (cui per aliquot annos præfuerat) à memoriâ multiplicis suæ scientiæ, admirabilis prudentiæ, singularis fidei, spectatissimæ probitatis, et pietatis minimè vulgaris, desid. reliquit:

Alicia. uxor quondam beatissima, nunc mœstissima vidua, parvum hoc non-parvi amoris monumentum, multis cum lacrimis precibusq; profusis. ponit simul consecratq. In quo ipsa posthac sua quoq; ossa recondi et permisceri cineribus tam chari capitis nimis miserè cupit: ut ab eo jam mortuo nunquam sejungatur qui cum vivo olim conjunctissime et jucundissime vixerat. Vixit autem ille annos XLII. obiit decimo die Augusti, anno à partu Virginis MDCXIII. Ubi nunc quatuor liberorum lætus parens factus fuerat; quorum tamen hodi unus tantum superstes est, isq; minimus natu, nomine Franciscus, puerulus optimæ spei: cui ego quidem omnia bona in hoc uno voto exopto: Sit Patri simillimus.

Hunc tumulum tibi composui, charissime conjux:
Quo mea mista tuis molliter ossa cubent.
Delixi vivum, volo defunctum comitari:
Nam quos junxit amor, dissociare nefas.

A Monument to Ralph Worsley—

"Hic subtùs humatur corpus Radulphi Worsley, armig. qui fuit filius tertius Gulielmi Worsley, de Worsley Meyne, in comitatu Lancastriæ, arm. ac quondam serviens, scilicet, pagettus garderobæ robarum, ac unus dapiferorum cameræ invictiss. principis Henrici octavi, Dei gratiâ Angliæ, Franc. et Hiber. nuper regis. Cui idem rex ob bonam et fideli servitium circum regiam suam personam impensum, ex regiâ sua magnificentiâ ad terminum vitæ donaverat officia satellitis coronæ, custodiam leonum, leonarum, et leopardorum intra Turrim Londinensem; portatoris magnæ garderobæ, contra rotulator, in com. Cestr. et Flint, clerici coronæ Lanc. et esceator. com. palat. Lancast. aliasq; remunerationes. Hiis accesserunt præstontes animi dotes cœlitus ei tributæ, quibus insigniter erat imbutus, nempe singularis in Deum pietas, multifaria in pauperes beneficentia, et mira in cunctos charitas. Annos 80 natus et ultra, 27 die Decem. anno Dom. 1573, expiravit, relictâ sobole Alicia conjuge Tho. Powel, arm. qui hos sumptos fecit; Katharinâ nupta Thomæ Tutchet, arm. et Avisia Thomæ Vawdrey, gen. de Joanna filia Johannis Pike, armig. uxore sua progenitis.

——— Nulli cœlum reparabile Gazâ.

There is a figure of Philip Oldfield, dressed in the costume of the age, with a ruff round the neck, in the left hand a roll, and leaning on the right side. Below, on the side is a painted skeleton, and the slab is supported by kneeling figures of his four sons, with their right hands applied to the hilt of their swords; on the left hand are shields, with the arms of Oldfield, Wettenhall, Somerford, Mainwaring of Croxton, and Leftwich. Figures of two daughters are placed at the head, supporting shields, with the arms of Shackerley, Wettenhall, and Oldfield.

"Philippo Oldfeld, ar. ob navata' in construendis viis pontibusque operam, in erundis antiquissimis familia' stem'etibus, benè de com. hoc merito: qui in pri'um matrimonium Helenæ Guliel' Berington de Brad: hered. copulavit, ex qª Tho' et Eliz. Joh' Wettenhalle nuptam, genuit: ad secunda vota convolans, Helen Griffith, vid', fil. Guliel. Hanmer, ar., duxit; p. qua' tres filios, una' filia' p'creavit. Quoru' p'ogenit. Phi. Mariæ unicæ filiæ et hered. Joh'n. Somerford de Som', ar'. Mich' Elianoræ hered. Jacobi Mainwaringe de Croxto'. ar.—Guliel' Eliz' hered. Rob'i Leftwich de Left[h] ar'. Marga' filia' Petro Shakerley p'ogenito nepoti ex hered. Galfrid' Shakerley de Hulme, ar', in matrim' fœlicissimè elocavit, jure consulto municipali clarissimo marito suo chariss. Helena uxor relicta sepulchr. hoc monumentum consecravit. Obiit 15 Dec. 1616. ætat. suæ 75."

Beneath on a Tablet—

"In June 1788, this tombe and monument was repaired and cleaned, by order of the Rev. Doctor Richard Jackson, Prebendary of Chester, whose mother was wife of Richard Jackson, Esq. of Betchton House, near Sandbach, in this County, and who was the only daughter of Wm. Oldfield, Esq. and Lætitia his wife, and great great grandson of Philip Oldfield, Esq. and Ellen his wife, of Bradwall, in this County."

Adjoining the last, a board with arms of Holme, inscribed

"Here beneath lyeth the bodyes of Randle Holme, of ye cittie of Chester, Ald', and Justice of Peace. and was Maior thereof 1633; died ye 16th of Jany. 1655, æt. 84; also of Elizabeth his wife, daughter to Thomas Alcock, and widow to Thomas Chaloner, gent. she dyed 24th of May, 1635; and had yssue two sonnes, W[m]. Holme, y[t] dyed 1623, without yssue livinge, and Randle Holme, now livinge, who was also Maior of this citty 1643."

On the same pillar, a stone Monument, with the arms of Holme and Tenny—

"Here lyes the body of Randle Holme, gent. sewer in extraordinary to King Charles y[e] 2d, and deputy to y[e] Kings at Arms, who died 12th March, 1699; and Randle Holme his son, deputy to Norroy King at Arms, who died 30th day of August, 1707. He married Margaret, daughter of Griffith Lloyd, of Llanarmon, in the County of Denbigh, gent. by w[m]. he has issue Sara, Eliz. Kat. Randle, and Kat. who died before their father, and lye here interred."

Close to the last, on a large wooden Monument, this inscription—

"Hoc monumentum in memoria' possit' Ran'i Holme, aliquando ald'man. & Justic. pacis, huj' civitatis Cestr' majoris ejusd. anno M. DI. XLIII. Q. q'dem Ran'us fil' et h'es fuit Ran'i Holme, alderm.' et justic' pacis, et majoris anno M. DC. XXXIII. ejusd'. civitatis Cestr p'dict. (q'etiam fuit servus d'ni n'ri Henrici principis, filii pri'ogenti Jacobi R. pie memorie, ac etiam deputatus fuit p', officio armorum in comitatib' palatini Cestr' et Lancastr' et VI comitatuum Nord Walliæ) per Elizabeth uxorem ej' fil. Tho. Alcock, de civitate Cestr', et relict' Tho. Chaloner, de eadem civitate q'ando Ulster rex armorum p' Hibernie regno. Ille fuit filius et h'es Tho' Holme, de Cestr' civitate p'dic. p. Elizabeth uxore ej' fil' Joh'is Devenett de Kindton, in com. Flynt, gen. Fil', fuit ille Gulielmi' Holme, d'ni mediet' ville de Tranmor' p' Marg'ettæ' uxorem ej' fil. Ricardi Caldy, de civitate Cestr. p'dic'; fil' et he's Rob'ti H. de Tranmor' al's, Tranmol p'd'ca, p' Janam fil' Tho. Poole, de arm; fil' et h' Guliel' Holme, que obiit ano 1 Hen. VIII.; fil. et he's Robti H. qui obiit 14 Edw. IV.; fil' et h'es Tho' H. qui, vixit 24 Hen. VI; fil' et h'es Joh'is H. d'ni med' vill' de Tranmoll qui ob' 4 Hen. V; fil et h'es Rob'ti Holme, d'ni mediet. vill' de Tranmoll jure uxor' ej' Matild' fil' et unius cohe'dum Ric'i de Tranmoll, d'ni Tranmoll, fil' et h'edes Gulielmi de Tranmoll, p' Matild' fil' et un. cohe'dum Petri de Lymme, fil' Gilberti, d'ni de Lymme, qui vixit te'p'e E. I.—Ipse Ran' sup'dict' te'p'e vite ej' duxit i' uxore' Catherina' fil' Math' Ellis de Ov'legh in com'. civitat Cest' gen', p' quam h'uit 3 filios et 5 filias; p' cuj' mortem duxit in uxorem Elizabeth, fil' et h' Tho. Dod, de civitat' Cestr' reli't. Samuel Martyn, mercatoris; ille i' an'o 63, ætat. suæ obiit, die dominica, 4 Sep. XI[o] Caroli 2, annoq' D'ni CIↃ. DC. LIX."

"Underneath neere to this place lyeth interred the bodyes of Sarai, eldest dau'r of Henry Soley, Minister of the Gospell at Forton, in ye county of Salop, and late wife to Randle Holme, sworne serv[t]. and gentleman ———— ma'ties chamber in extraordinary to Kinge Charles the 2nd one ——cill of the City of Chester, and Deputy to Garter Principall Kinge of Arms; she had yssue by him Randle, Elizab. Kath. Rachell, and Sarai, y[t] dyed an infant; she dyed y[e] 5th of April, anno 1665, aged 36 years: and Katherine, sister of the said Randle, and late wife to Benj. Harpur, of London, gent. she dyed the vii of July, an'o 1664, aged 34 yeares; and alsoe, William Holme, brother to the s[d] Randle, and 2nd son of Randle Holme, alderman, dyed ye xxvi day of April anno D'ni 1666, & y[e] 35 yeare of his age: and Rafe, y[e] yongest sonne of Randle Holme, alderman, dyed y[e] — day of ——, anno 1641, aged 4 yeares."

On a brass plate in the same aisle—

"Here lyeth the body of William Brock, of Upton, in the county of Chester, esquire, who by Anne his wife, daughter and co-heir to Robert Mohune, of Baynton, in the county of Dorcet, Esq. had yssue 4 sonnes and 7 daughters. He died on the 4th day of April, 1640; and here also liethe the body of Edward Brock, his unkell, who died on the 2d day of October, 1639."

Susannah, daughter of Joseph Hockenhull, of Shotwick, Esq. wife of Wm. Brock.

William Brock, Esq. died 10th Jan. 1715, aged 73 · William Brock, of Upton, Esq. his eldest son, died Aug. 10, 1734 aged 58.

A neat Marble Monument—

"To the Memory of Mrs. Susannah Brock, who died March 20,

1766, She was daughter of Wm. Brock, Esq. of Upton, in this county, and the last of that ancient family. This monument was erected by her nephew, and nieces, the son and daughters of John Egerton, Esq. of Broxton, in this county."

In the north aisle, Memorials of—

Philippa, wife of Thomas Browne, of Netherlegh, daughter of Tho. Berrington, of Chester, by whom he had 10 sons and 5 daughters; she died aged 42, May 6, 1664.—The said Tho. Berrington, died 1669, aged 42, having married to his second wife Jane, daughter of Richard Leycester, of Great Budworth, relict of Charles Levesby, of Chester, who survived him.—Ales, daughter of Matthew Browne, of Netherlegh, and wife of Thos. Parnel, of Chester, obiit 5 Sept. 1639. Matthew Browne, gent. obiit 24 Nov. 1634. Richard Browne, of Upton, co. Cest. son & heir of Tho. Browne, by Elizabeth his wife, daughter to Henry Birkenhead, Esq. Clerk to the Green Cloth to Q. Eliz. son and heir of Rich. Browne, son and heir of Tho. Browne, of Upton. This Richard Browne died Jan. 4, 1624, having had two wives; first Frances, daughter of Sir Geo. Beverley, of Huntington, Knt. who died s. p.; and 2d Mary, daughter of Sir Thomas Ashton, of Ashton, Knt. by whom he had Thos. Browne, of Upton, and Richard, of London. She afterwards married Jaques Arnodie, gent, and died 17th Feb. 1668, aged 87 years.---Thomas Browne, son and heir, died at Munster, in Ireland, having married Grisel, daughter to —— Dobb, of Ireland, by whom he had Thomas, Robert, Francis, Richard, Mary, Judith, Grisel, and Dorothy. She died in Childbed, 19th June 1641. Thomas Browne, son and heir, married Cicily, daughter to Wm. Glegg, of Gayton, Esq. who died in Childbed of her daughter Cicily, March 16, 1661.---Thomas Birkenhead, gent. and Ales his wife; he died 12th November, 1644; she died Jan. 1, 1691.

William Holme, eldest son of Randle Holme, died 10th July 1623.

Other Memorials to—

Anne Prescott, died Feb. 3, 1772.---Gregory, their son, Oct. 4, 1725.---Anne, wife of George Prescott, died Sept. 22, 1740, aged 59---George Prescott, merchant, March 10, 1747, aged 67.---Thos. Prescott, of Eardshaw, county of Cest. esq. died Oct. 29, 1768, aged 63.---John Glegg, of Irby Hall, Esq. died Feb. 6, 1804, aged 72.--- Betty Baskervyle Glegg, his wife, died July 9, 1810, aged 77.

On a Tablet—

"Here lies interred Matthew Ellis, of Overleigh, in the county of the city of Chester, one of the gentlemen of the body guard to King Hen. 8, son of Ellis ap Dio ap Gryffyth, successor to Kenrick Sais, a British Nobleman, and lineally descended from Tudor Trevor, Earl of Hereford. He died April 20, 1574. Alice his wife, died 1547. His son, Matthew Ellis, of Overleigh, gent. died 1575, whose wife Eliz. daughter of Thos. Browne, of Netherlegh, gent. died 1570, having issue Julian, who was married to Thos. Cowper, of Chester, Esq. Margery, and Matthew Ellis, of Overlegh, gent. He died July 13, 1613. His wife, daughter to Richard Birkenhead, of Maule, Esq. died July 6, 1640, having issue Katherine, wife to Randle Holme, of Chester, gent. & Matthew Ellis, of Overlegh, gent. who died Nov. 2, 1663; his wife Elizabeth, daughter to Wm. Halton, of Baddiley, gent. married Anne, daughter to John Birkenhead, of Backford, Esq. He died Feb. 17, 1685; she died Aug. 4, 1689.

"Beati sunt mortui qui in Domino moriunter."

Beneath this, under the Arms of Cowper—

"Wm. Cowper, of Overlegh, in respect to these his ancestors and relatives, caused this decayed memorial to be restored, anno Domini 1739. He died 12th of October, 1767, aged 66.

In the Middle Aisle—

Adam Birkened, and Alice his wife, daughter and co-heiress to John Huxley, died 1516, 7th Hen. VIII.

Memorials of the

Brownes of Netherlegh; Parker of Audley.—Alexander and Edward Wynne, of Brithic, in the co. Flint, by Eliz. daughter of Walter Horton, of Catton, Esq. Edw. died 27 Sept. 1681, and Alexander Oct. 2d following.

Katherine, youngest daughter of Matthew Ellis, of Overlegh, gent. wife of Randle Holme, Sheriff of Chester, 1633, died March 15, 1640.

Hugh Whickstead, Coroner of Cheshire, died 1646; and Alice, his wife 1656; and Hugh their 2d son.

Mr. Ormerod quotes the following from the Harl. MSS. as existing in the windows in 1578—

"In the Chancel Window, over the Communion Table, the Royal Arms, with those of Hugh Lupus, Venables, Troutbeck, Dedwood, Davenport, and Leche, with the following inscriptions:—

Orate pro anima Johannis Davenport, hujus eccl'ię rectoris, qui hanc fenestram fieri fecit 1534.

Orate pro a'i'a Joh'is Willaston, quondam rectoris hujus eccl'ie, et pro a'i'abus ...... parentum ejus ...... 1400.

In St. Catharine's Chapel, a petition to pray for the souls of Randle Brereton, of Chester, and his two wives, Cecilia and Johanna, 1523.

In the window next to St. Catherine's Chapel, two kneeling figures, with the arms of Eaton, and underneath—

" Orate pro bono statu Ricardi Grosvenor, et Sibeliæ uxoris ejus, qui hoc opus fecit 1524."

In another north window, a figure of Matthew Ellis, in a surcoat, and helmet, and sons after him, and his wife in a veil, and daughters after her; and in a high window in the middle aisle—

" Of your charity pray for the soul of Matthew Ellis, and Elizabeth, his wife."

&c. &c. &c.

Charitable Bequests.

A number of small sums, originally bequeathed to the Poor by various charitable persons, were employed in the erection of Galleries; and the poor now receive the profits arising from the pews. The bequests are particularised on tablets—

Six shillings paid to the poor on St. George's day, by the Treasurers of the City; this is called Brereton's legacy.---The parish has landed property at Llai, in the parish of Gresford, which now produces £22. per ann. A portion of Henry Smith's* gift, which amounts annually to £4. 10s. or £4. 11s.

The present Rector of the Parish is the Rev. Rowland Hill, A. M. Rector of Delamere.

* Henry Smith, was formerly a silversmith in London, and having acquired a considerable fortune, formed the strange resolution of spending the remainder of his days as a common beggar with a dog. He was known by the appellation of DOG SMITH, but having given offence to an inhabitant of Mitcham, in Surry, he was, by a Justice of the Peace, ordered to be publicly whipped. This he resented so much, that he left £50. a year, or £1000. in money, to every market town in that county—Mitcham excepted. The parishes of St. Michael and St. John, also partake of Smith's bounty---being those in which, during his mendicant life, he was the best treated, in this city. His deed of Charitable uses, is dated January 26, 9th Chas. II. and 26 parishes, in different parts of the Kingdom, participate in it.

ST. JOHN THE BAPTIST'S PARISH.

THE Church stands without the City Walls, about 150 yards south-east of the Newgate.—It is a venerable pile, and affords a remarkable fine specimen of the later Saxon Architecture. It is delightfully situated, within a few yards of a red rock, jutting out above the north bank of the river Dee; and the Church-yard commands extensive views of the beautiful meadow land of the Dee, and of the Forest, Broxton, Peckforton, and Shropshire Hills. Beeston Castle, forms a prominent object in the perspective scenery, as it does in most of the county views. The Church is of high antiquity; and it is recorded, that—

" King Ethelred minding to build a Church, was told, that where he should see a white hind, there he should build a Church; which white hind he saw in the place where St. John's Church standeth, and in remembrance whereof, his picture was placed in the wall of the said Church, which yet standeth on the side of the steeple towards the west, having a white hind in his hand.*

On a large painted board in the body of the Church, on the north side, we are told, that " This churches antiquitie, the yeare of grace six hundred fourscore and nine, as sayth mine authour, a Britaine, Giraldus [*Cambrensis*] King Etheldred, minding most the blisse of Heaven, edified a Colledge Churche, notable and famous, in the suburbs of Chester, pleasant and beauteous, to the Honor of God, and the Baptiste St. John, with

* The figure, which now occupies a niche on the west side, was probably preserved from the ruins of the old steeple, and placed in that now standing, which was rebuilt about the middle of the 17th century. The statue has been finely carved, and the animal is represented as fawning upon it on the left side. It is now in a state of rapid decay.

Engraved by J. Pigot Manch.r from a Drawing by Miss.s Nicholsons Liverpool.

RUINS OF S.T JOHN'S CHESTER.

Engraved for Hanshalls. History of Cheshire.

the help of Bishop Wulfrice."—The Chronicle of St. Werburgh, has a similar notice; but Tanner is of opinion that it was founded by Ethelred Earl of Mercia, early in the 10th century. Be this as it may, it is pretty clear that it was *repaired* so early as 1057,* by Leofric the Mercian Earl, by whom it was bountifully endowed. The Domesday Survey has the following account of it—"*Ecclesia Sancti Johannis in civitate, habet viij domos quietas ab omni consuetudine: una ex his est matricularii ecclesiæ, aliæ sunt canonicorum.*"† The
1075. Diocesan see was about this time‡ fixed in the Church of St. John, by Peter, who was the then Bishop; Roger de Linesey, his successor, however, removed it to Coventry. The Church then returned to its first establishment, as Collegiate; but was subsequently denominated ONE of the THREE Cathedrals of the Diocese. Near to it the Bishop had a Palace, and there was a residence also for the Archdeacon of Chester. At the Dissolution, it possessed a Dean and seven Prebends—a number, which, a cotemporary historian observes, corresponds with that of the houses attached to the Church at the time of the Great Survey—"viij domos," &c.: in addition, there were four Vicars, a Clerk, and a Sexton. The Dean retired on a pension of £14. 5s. and was afterward, appointed Dean of Chester Cathedral. In the Ecclesiastical Taxation of 1291, the value is stated at £23. 13s. 4d.; according to the Bishop's returns 1809, £47. 7s. 4d.

In 1572, the greater part of the central steeple fell; and two years afterwards, one half of the steeple fell upon the west end of the Church, and destroyed a large portion of it. In 1581, the Parishioners having obtained a grant of the Church from the Queen, commenced the repairs of it, cutting off all the Chapels above the Choir. In 1585 (Oct. 4), Queen Elizabeth, by letters patent, granted the impropriate Rectory, and the advowson of the Church of St. John the Baptist, to Sir Christopher Hatton, Knt. her Vice Chamberlain, afterwards Lord Chancellor of England; who afterwards conveyed the same to Alexander King, Gent.|| and he || Oct. 5, 1585.
on the 16th Dec. 1587, conveyed it to Alexander Cotes, Gent.—Anne Cotes, his daughter and heiress, (one of the Maids of Honor to Queen Elizabeth) brought the same by marriage, Oct. 4, 1597, to John Sparke, Esq. who died Dec 29, 1639, and was succeeded by William Sparke, his son, Alderman and Justice of the Peace, who died Jan. 12, 1658; and he was succeeded by John Sparke, Esq. his grandson, who died July 11, 1709; and was succeeded by Thomas Sparke, Esq. his son, who died March 22, 1716. He was succeeded by Mary, his sister, relict of Lawrence Wood, vicar; she died Nov. 20, 1739; and was succeeded by Thomas Adams, Esq. her grandson, who died Jan 24, 1786; to him succeeded John Adams, gent. his nephew, who sold the same to Earl Grosvenor, in 1810. Thus the impropriation continued in one family for 223 years.§

* Chron. of St. Werburgh,—William Malmesbury, &c. See vignette, page 215.

† Redcliffe is thus noticed in Domesday—after stating that it beonged to the Bishop, it adds, "prius ad ecclesiam Sancti Johannis pertinebat."

§ Information of the Rev. W. Richardson.—In a cause before the Rev. Samuel Peploe, in the Consistory Court, the original grant of the Church is thus noticed:—"First, that the Lady Elizabeth of happy memory, heretofore Queen of England, by her Letters Patent, bearing date at Hinchingbrooke, or at about the fourth day of October, in the twenty-eighth year of her reign, did of her special Grace and Favour, for herself, her heirs, and successors, among other things give and grant to Sir Christopher Hatton, Knight, by the name of her beloved Councellor, Christopher Hatton, Knight, her Vicechamberlain, all that her Rectory, and Church of Saint John Baptist, in the City of Chester, with all and Singular the Right, Members, and Appurtenances, in her County of Chester, and all that her Tithe Barn, situate near the Bars, without the City of Chester, and all and Singular her Tithes of Corn, Hay, Herbage, Flax, Hemp, and other her Tithes whatsoever, yearly, and from time to time arising, increasing, and renewing, within the Parish of Saint John aforesaid, to have, hold, and enjoy, all and singular the premises, to the said Sir Christopher Hatton, Knight, his heirs, and assigns, for the sole and proper use of him the said Sir Christopher, his heirs, and assigns, for ever; to hold the said Rectory, and all and singular other the premises granted by the said Letters Patent, with every of their appurtenances, of the said Queen, her heirs, and successors, as of her Manor of East-grenewich, in her County of Kent, by Fealty only, in free and common Socage, and not in capite, nor by Knight Service, for all Rents, Services, Exactions, and Demands, whatsoever, therefore to the said Lady Queen Elizabeth, or her Successors, in any manner to be render'd, pay'd, or done; as by the said Letters Patents, remaining on Record in the Rolls of the Chancery of the said Queen, and the things therein contain'd, granted and expressed, more fully and clearly appears. And the party propounding, propounds every thing, jointly and severally," &c. &c. &c.

CHESTER HISTORY.

The present appearance of the Church is extremely picturesque. *At the time of the Dissolution, the remains of the Collegiate Church were included within an oblong inclosure, at the north west angle of which was the gate-house; lower down on the west side was the Dean's house, and below this was a Palace, which the Bishops of Lichfield still retained near their ancient Cathedral. On the north side were houses for the Petty Canons. The south side was formed by the cliff :† on two projections were small buildings called *Anchorite's Cells*;‡ and between these and the south door of the nave of the Church, was the Chapel of St. James.||

* Ormerod.

† Redcliff.

The Church originally consisted of a Nave and Choir, with side Aisles, Transepts, and a central Tower.—Eight arches, resting on massy cylindrical pillars separate the nave and side aisles; each of the pillars are 5 feet 6 inches in diameter. Above the arches are two rows of galleries, with lancet shaped arches, springing from light shafts. The exterior, on the south side of the Church, has the appearance of the same line of galleries. The four massy pillars, which supported the great tower, still remain at the east end of the nave.—"§East of the tower was the Choir, divided from its side aisles by three arches on each side, with galleries over. The first couple of these arches are remaining. They were of the horse-shoe form, resting on cylindrical columns with capitals. The first row of galleries consisted of a series of low semicircular arches of the same span with the arches below, resting on low semicircular shafts. The upper row of galleries is here perfectly destroyed. At the east end of the Choir, was a fine semicircular arch, with ornamented capitals, yet remaining, but in the last stage of decay, under which was the entrance to a small chancel, consisting of five sides of an octagon."¶ The present external appearance of the Church is delineated in the accompanying plate. The ancient chapels no longer exist. The house on the east side, THE PRIORY, was called "The Chambers of the Churches Priests." The present tower, is about 150 feet high, and contains a beautiful peal of eight bells, placed there, six in 1710, and two in 1734. The approach to it is through the remains of the north aisle. It is detached from the body of the church.—The sides of the tower are decorated with a rich screen, and ornamented with figures placed in niches of exquisite workmanship. The porch of the Church is much admired. The nave formerly extended considerably beyond its present site westward.

§ Ormerod.

The Church of St. John contained within its precincts, the Chapel of St. Anne, the Chapel of St. James, and the Thorneton Chantry. Bishop Tanner remarks, in his "Notitia," that "By the Lincoln Taxation of temporalities of the Clergy, made in 1291, it should seem as if there had been a Collegiate Church of the

‡ The Cliff is now called the ANCHORITE's HILL.

|| The foundations of which still remain beneath the surface.

Copy, from a Record of the Dissolved Colleges of St. John, and fraternity of St. Anne:—

"**Be yt had ever in mynde**, yt the Deane and Chanons of this Colledge Churche, have granted by their CHAPTER SEALE,* to the P'ishioners of the same for Ever, that they for such costes as ye have bene att, in the buyldinge of the Steple, shall have the belles ronge freely at all Diriges and anniversries for the inhabitants of the same without payinge any thinge to the Sextone, or any other, so yt the Clarke, yf he fynde ryngers, shall have for fyve bells viijd. iij or iiij vjd, for ijs iiijd. and yf the p'ishioners fynd ryngers of their owene costes, then the Clarke to have ijd. Alsoe, the p'ishioners bynd themselves that the belles shall not be ronge to dysturbe the Devyne service; also, p'ishioners bynd themselves to amend all faultes and charges of belles and steple within one quarter of a yeare's warninge, except the stone worke, and belles to be caste, wch must be done by the Deane and Chanons, and the p'ishioners indifferently as doth more playneley appeare in the composicion, wth doth remayne in the treasure house of this cittie."

There are no remains of the "TABLE," alluded to in the following record:—

"This is a true copye of a table of brasse, whiche was fyxed in the walle of the old steple of this Colledge Church of St. Johne's in Chester, lately fallen downe---and the same table of brasse fixed upon stone was founde the xth daie of Maye, 1583, and now remaineth in the sayd p.ish Churche, in the custodie of the Churchwardens."—It probably contained the original inscription relative to the foundation of the Church, and which is now copied on a board on the north side of the pulpit.---See preceding page.

¶ See the view of the interior of the Ruins.

* A fac-simile of the old Seal of the Chapter is given in Mr. Ormerod's history; it was of a lozenge form, representing a figure in a robe, holding what appears to be a book. All that remained of the inscription was "*Johannis, Dec.*"

Engraved by [illegible] from a Drawing by [illegible] 1818.

NORTH EAST PROSPECT, S^T. JOHN'S CHURCH, CHESTER.

Engraved for Hanshall's History of Cheshire.

name of the *Holy Cross*,* because under *Archidiaconatus Cestriæ*, and immediately before *Abbas Cestriæ*, is this memorandum,—" Portionarii ecclesiæ prebendalis S. Crucis Cestriæ, non habent temporalia, sed omnia quæ habent taxantur cum spiritualibus prout firmiter asserebant."—It appears certain from the Ecclesiastical Survey, made by the Commissioners of Hen. VIII, that there were three stalls in this Church, for the *Prebends of the Holy Cross*—" et unit. tribus stallis prebend. sancte Crucis," &c.

In 1813, the Chancel underwent a thorough repair; a completely new window was introduced, and the north and south transepts rebuilt and beautified, at the sole expense of the Earl Grosvenor, in whom, as has been before observed, the advowson of the Church is vested.†

List of Deans of St. John's College.

R. de VERDUN, about 1187, a younger branch of the Vernon family.

BERTRAM, Dec. Cestr. temp. Richard I. or John.

SIMON, temp. Henry III.

WILLIAM DE BRICHULL, temp. Edward I.

RICHARD ALCROFT.

1309.—RANDLE TORALD.

1311.—WILLIAM WISH, rural Dean of Chester.‡

1324.—THOMAS DE CLEPTON—NICHOLAS DE NORTHBURGH.

1329.—" PETRUS RUSSEL, pr'b'r post res. Nicholai de Northburgh."|| || Ormerod.

1334.—WILLIAM DE APPELLERE.

1338.—JOHN DE MARISCO.

1353.—RICHARD DE BAUNHAM.

1354.—HUGO DE THYRLINGHAM.

1356.—RICHARD DE BIRMINGHAM.

1380.—WILLIAM DE BLUMEHULL.

1386.—RICHARD SCROOP.

1389.—(temp.) JOHN DE WOODHOUSE.

1395.—JOHN LEYCOTT. [He was rector of Malpas.]

1430.—RICHARD PLEYMUNDSTOW—JOHN PATTEN, al. Waynfleet§—ROGER ASSER, rector of St. Mary's.

1485.—THOMAS WILLEY.

1490.—JOHN BIRKENHEAD, Archdeacon of Chester—CHRISTOPHER TALBOT.

1492.—HUGH OLDHAM.¶

1494.—THOMAS MAWDYSLEY, S. T. P.

1500.—ROBERT LAWRENCE, D. D.

1535.—GEOFFRY BLYTHE.

1546.—RICHARD WALKER, he surrendered the College in 1547, and was afterwards appointed Dean of Chester

---

* Dr. Cowper in his IL PENSEROSO, says,---" In this Church was an ancient rood or image of wood, of such veneration, that in a deed dated dated March 27, 1311, confirmed by Walter Langton, the Church was called *The Church of the Holy Cross, and St John*.—Richard Hawarden, of Winwick, Lancashire, by will dated March 28, A. D. 1503, left " vis. viiid. to whatever Priest would go for him to the Holy Rood, at St. John's, Chester "

† It often occurs, that repairs are attended with partial destruction to what is in existence; and it occurred so in this instance. Several curious monuments were broken and otherwise injured; and amongst them, an old tomb which stood in the Chancel,---Sacred to the Memory of Alexander Coates, the former proprietor of the advowson. It bore this inscription.---" Alexander Cotes, ætatis sexaginta duorum annorum filius natu minimus Hugonis Cotes unici filii Ricardi Cotes, unius filiorum Humfridi Cotes, armigeri, Domini de Cotes, in comitatu Staff. qui quidem Alexander modo est Feodifirmarius hujus Ecclesiæ, Deputatus Baro Scaccarii hujus Comitatûs Palatini Cestriæ, per quadraginta annos ultimos elapsos et amplius, et fuit Contrarotulator Cust: et Subsidii Dominæ Reginæ in Portu Cestriæ, per triginta annos præteritos, hunc Tumulum condidit in charam memoriam Ursulæ nuper dilectæ uxoris suæ, filiæ natu minimæ Thomæ Powell, armigeri, et Catherinæ uxoris ejus unicæ filiæ et hæredis Lancelotti Lother, armigeri, quæ quidem Ursula obiit quarto die Decembris, anno Domi 1598, ætatis suæ sexaginta et octo annorum.

Idemq. Alexander obiit sexto die Martii Anno Dom. 1609, relictâ prole Annâ, unicâ filiâ et hærede apparente prædicti Alexandri Cotes generosi et Ursulæ uxoris ejus, nupta Johanni Sparke, generoso modo Contrarotulator Cust.: et Subsidii Serenissimæ Dominæ Elizabethæ Reginæ Angliæ in Portu Cestriæ, &c. ac Secretario Inclytissimi Willi modo Comitis Derbiæ, prænobiis ordinis Garterii militi.

Idemq. Johannes Sparke, generosus, et Anna uxor ejus has suas effigies fieri fecerunt in obsequium præfatorum Alexandri et Ursulæ. Qui quidem Johannes obiit undetrigesimo die Decembris Ann. Domi. 1639; et prædicta Ann. obiit sexto die Decembris Ann. Domi 1639."

‡ Arrested for extortion, together with the Archdeacon of Chester, and others. Harl. MSS. 2072. 81.

§ A relation of the Founder of Magdalen College.---ORMEROD.

¶ " Afterwards Bishop of Exeter, the founder of Manchester School, and a benefactor to Brasenose and Corpus Colleges."—IDEM.

Prebendaries.

THOMAS DE S'C'O NICHOLAO, Archdeacon of Chester, temp. Dean Simon.
JOHN DE LONGFORD.
1310.—RADULPHUS DE HASLASTON.
1316.—RICARDUS DE LEESTRISHULL.
1318.—(about) JOHN MARCELL.
D'NUS NICHOLAUS DE SWYNERTON.
1350.—MAGISTER WALTERUS CHILTERNE.
1392.—WILLIAM HEBDEN.
1490 (about) JOHN GOODFELLOW, Rector of Waverton, and Vicar of St. Oswald's.
1493 —THOMAS HARSNAPE.

One of these Prebends, (the Petty Canonry,) was in the gift of the Breretons, of Brereton.

CERTIFICATE

Of the College of St. John, Chester, (in the Augmentation Office.)

The Certificate of Hughe Cholmeley, Will'm Brereton, Knt. John Arscotte, James Starkey, George Browne, Thom's Ffletewoode, and Will'm Laton, gent. com'yssyon's of o' sov'aing Lorde the Kinge ma.^{tie} appointed for the survey of all Colledges, &c. w^{t}in the sayd shyre, mayed in the month of Marche anno r. r.^{s} Edwardi Sexti primo, by vertew of the Kinges maiesty comyssyon to them in that behalf dyrected, bering date .... day of ...., in the second yere of the reign of o^{r} sou'ainge Lorde Edwarde the Sext, by the Grace of God of England, Ffraunce, and Ireland, Kinge, Defender of the Ffaythe, and in the Earthe of the Churche of Englande and also of Irelande the Supreme hede :

The Answer of the sayde Commissioners to the articl's hereafter following as well upon the saing of thincumbent of the same p'rnoc'ons by ther seu'all othes, and churche-wardens by ther othes, of ev'y towne and p'ysshe where the same p'rnoc'ons ar founded or appointed, as upon the righte of dyvers and sundrye ther fundac'ons and other wrytinges showed and exhibyted to the seyd com'yssyon's :

The Colledge of Saint John's within ye sayd cyte, and it beinge a paryshe Churche of itself, having MCC hoslying people wthin the same.

Rycharde Walker, of the age of xlvj yeres, Deane, hathe for his stypend in the colledge, over and besydes one cth poundes in other places xxxj*li.* xiij*s.* ij*d.*

Davi Pole, prebendary, of the age of L yeares, hath for his stypend, ou' and besides one cth poundes in other places, viij*l.*

Robert Ffowler, prebendary, of the age of xviij yeres, hathe yerely for his stypende, having no other lyvinge, viij*l.*

Thom's Snede, prebendary, of thage of lx yeres, hathe for his stypende over and besydes L*li.* in other place —

Peter Manwaring, of the age of lxvj yeres, over and besydes one cth marks in other places, hathe for his stypende —

Rycharde Smythe, of thage of lxx yeres, hathe for his stypende, over and besydes xxx*li.* in other places —

John Whyteby, of thage of L yeres, hathe for his stypende having no other lyving—

Thomas Wetton, of thage of lx yeres, hathe for his stypende, over and besides xxx m'ks in other places —

Prebendaries in the same colledge, every one of them havynge lxvj*s.* viij*d.* wch amounteth in the hole to xvj*l.* xiij*s.* iiij*d.*

Robert Bowyer, of thage of xl yeres, Thom's Latus, of thage of lj yeres, Richarde Crosse, of thage of xxvj yeres, and Roger Houghton, of the age of xli yeres, Vicars in the same colledge, hathe no other livinge, but eche of them xj*l.* yerly for the salarye.

Thom's Ratclyf, clerc of ye sayd p'ysshe churche, havinge no other lyvinge, hathe yerely xxxiij*s.* iiij*d.*

CHESTER

Phylip ap Gryffyth, sexton of the sayde Churche, of thage of xl yeres, hathe for his livinge ther xxvjs. viijd.

The yerely valewe of the same colledge cxlvil. vs. inde ——

Rep'ris thereof p'p'tuall xiiijl. xvjd.

Annuytes, ffees, and penc'ons for terme of lyves xijl. vjs. viijd.

The clere remaine cxixl. xvijs.

Plate and jewells ij.c xxxij onz. di.

In gilte clxxiij oz.

In white lix oz.

Goodes and ornaments xll. xixs. ixd.

Leade remaininge in and upon the Churche of the sayde colledge, beinge a p'yshe churche iiij^xx ffother.

Md. the bodye of the same churche thowghte suffi'ent to s've the sayd p'isioners w^t the charge of xxl. so that the hole ch'unsell, wth the twoo aisles, may be well reserved for the Kinge's ma^tie having upon them lead to the quantatye of xxxviij ffothers.*

Bells belonginge to the seyde colledge, and as yete hanginge in the churche of ye sayd colledge, ffyve.

Whereof it is thoughte sufficient to contynew—*one* !*

And ye resydew may be taken for the Kinge, and by estymacion MMMV^c lb.

Memor'd. it is requysyte to have a Vycar and one assistant to be appointed to sarve the Cure there, and Rob't. Bower and Thom's Latwys, twoo of the late Vycars of the sayd Colledge are appointed for the same accordingly.

Names of the Vicars of St. John's.†

Rev. John Dowglas	1578
Thomas Symond	1597
John Cony	1636
George Burches	1643
John Pemberton	1650
Peter Leigh	1658
Alexander Fetherston	1662
Thomas Bridge	1665
Robert Bridge	1674
Lawrence Wood, A. M.	1689
Charles Oulton	1710
Lawrence Adams, A. M.	1742
John Price	1777
William Richardson	1785

HISTORY.

Mr. Ormerod has given an incorrect list of the succession.—After George Burches, he has introduced the name of Philip Wilson, which is not to be found in the Church Books: there is, however, a Philip Wilson, *dyer*, from which, owing to the obscurity of the writing, the mistake of *Vicar*, for "dyer," might probably have arisen.

POSSESSIONS OF THE COLLEGE,

AT ITS DISSOLUTION.

	£.	s.	d.
Scite of the late Colledge aforesaid	1	9	0
Over and above £2. 4s. 8d. for rents and farms granted by King Edwd VI. in the third year of his reign, to Rich. Roberts, his heirs, and assigns for ever.			
Rents of Lands, called the Prebends lands	12	18	6
Rents, called obit rents, within the said city, parcel of the said college	12	4	8
Rents, called the repartition lands belonging to the said colledge	1	19	8
The Rectory of Guylden Sutton	11	0	0
The Rectory of Stoke	19	0	0
The Rectory of Plemstall	18	10	0
The Rectory of Farmedon	16	0	0
The Church of Shocklache, with the Chapel of St. Edith	6	0	0
The Rectory of Upton	6	0	0
Certain glebe lands, and a Messuage in Stoke	1	3	6
A capital Messuage there	0	1	0
A barn, and the tithes of grain, &c. within the parish of St. John, Chester	5	0	0
Other tythes of St. John, in the said city	5	12	4
The Rectory of St. Martin	2	13	4
The Rectory of St. Bridget	5	0	0
&c. &c. &c.			
Sum	£196.		

* What an instance of cruel rapacity !

† Information of Rev. W. Richardson.

The Monuments, &c.

In the south aisle of the Chancel a mural monument—

"Near this place are interred the remains of Wm. Falconer, Esq. Barrister at Law, and for some years Recorder of this City, who, by his abilities and integrity in that station, and by his virtues in private life, acquired the respect and gratitude of his fellow Citizens, and the esteem and affection of his friends. He departed this life June 2, 1764, aged 65 years.—In the same grave are deposited the remains of Elizabeth his wife, daughter of Randle Wilbraham, of Townsend, in this county, Esq. who resembling her husband in the practice of every Christian and social duty, deservedly gained the regard of all who knew her. She died June 27, 1782, aged 79 years.—Here also repose the bodies of five of their children: Elizabeth, born April 4, 1732, died Dec. 8, 1733; Francis, born Feb. 13, 17 , died Jan. 14, 1743; William, born August 25, 1738, died Oct. 25, 1738; Alexander, born Feb. 12, 1739, died Feb. 21, 1740; Elizabeth born May 8, 1746, aged 18 years."

Near this a Tablet to the memory of the son of Recorder Falconer, the Editor of Strabo:

"M. S. Thomæ Falconer, armigeri, filii natu maximi Gulielmi Falconer, arm. qui per plures annos officium propraetoris hujus urbis gerebat, et Elizæ, filiæ Ranulphi Wilbraham, de Townsend, in comitatu Cestriæ, armigeri, conjugis ejus. Vir fuit literarum elegantiis et morum comitate egregie ornatus, memoria præditus vix credibili, et industria quæ nec labori nec ægritudini diuturnæ succubuit: maxima autem laus est quod benevolentiâ, vitæ integritate, et erga Deum pietate, nemini fuit impar. Obiit 4to die Septembris, A. D. 1792, ætatis suæ LVI.—Vale vir summe pietatis pariter ac liberarum exemplar, Vale! Frater tui amantissimas hocce exiguum quamois cenotaphium virtutibus tuis sacrum posuit."

A Tablet to the memory of

"Robert Barker, M. D. Fellow of the College of Physicians, and Physician to the Infirmary of Chester, died 19th July, 1808, aged 30, Buried at St. Asaph."

There is a figure in the North Chancel, of a Knight, in a coat of mail and surcoat, cross-legged; it was found in the Church-yard, and near to it a slab, on which is carved a cross, with a sword on the right hand. On the left side is inscribed, "Hic jacet Johannes le Sériaun."—It is supposed to be a memorial to a Crusader.

Cornelius Hignett, of Ashton, gent. and Margaret his wife, daughter of William Hyde, of Frodsham, gent.: she died 28th of August, 1735, aged 68; and he died 26th Feb. 1785-6, leaving issue Mary wife of Thomas Aldersey, M. D. Catharine, and Margaret.

"The Rev. Lawrence Wood, M. A. Rector of St. Bridget's, and Minister of St. John's, died July 13, 1710, aged 63.

Robert Bulkeley, son of Sir Richard Bulkeley, of Beaumaris, in Anglesea, Knt. who married Priscilla, daughter of Sir Hen. Bunbury, of Stanney, Co. Cest. Knt.; he died 27th Oct. 1679, aged 69 years; she died May 26, 1682, aged 67.

On a Brass Plate—

"Hic jacet, fratrum Edmundi Borlase, Med. Doctor, et Gulielmi Borlase, filiorum Johannis Borlase, Esq. arnati et Hibernia justiciarii, reliquiæ, quirum hic XXV Nov. M.DC.LXV. obiit, ille V Januar, M.DC.LXXXII."

Monuments of—

Edward Harbert, Gent. died March 27, 1688.—Capt. Giles Peacock, 21st April, 1720.—Benjn Perryn, Esq. and Jane his wife; he died Dec. 12, 1761; she died Jan. 19, 1781.—Katharine, 5th daughter of Robt. Wynne, of Voylas, co. Denbigh, by Jane his wife, dau. of Edw. Thelwall, of Plas Edward, died 11th Sept. 1685.—Hannah, daughter and heiress of Chas. Davies, of Montgomeryshire, wife of Caldecot Aldersey, of Aldersey, Cheshire, Gent. Feb. 5, 1718, aged 24, Sidney, daughter of John Lee, of Darnhall, Esq. died Jan. 16, 1788, aged 61.

In the Warburton's Chapel, on the south side the Chancel, a Mural Tablet, with a Bust—

"In hoc sacello juxta cineres optimæ matris (cujus memoriam vivens moriensq. summo honore prosecutus est) suos etiam requiescere voluit Cecilius Warburton, arm. Georgii Warburton de Arley, in com. Cestrensi baronetti, et Dianæ uxoris ejus, natu minimus Egregias illi dotes natura concessit, quas commendavit simul et ostendit eximia vultûs elegantia et decor. Erat ille vita sincerus, moribus comis, et quanquam fracta et pœne deplorata valetudine annos plus viginti conflicatus est, constans, facilis, placidus: quibuscunque innotuit, prœcipue amicis, quos omnibus vitæ officiis sibi devinxerat, charus vixit desideratus obiit 2ndo die Maii, anno Domini 1728-9, ætat. 63."

Near this, an Altar Tomb; above it the figure of a skeleton under the arms of Warburton, holding a scroll—

"M. S. of Diana Warburton, wife and relict of Sir George Warburton, of Arley, in Cheshire, Bart. who survived her husband 17 years, in an unmarried state, with true mourning, fasting, and prayers. She was daughter of Sir Edwd. Bishop, of Parham, in Sussex, Knt. and Bart. and in her minoritie had had a virtuous and severe eduation, so as she became a great exemplar of all Christian graces and virtues, and adorned every relation she stood in. She was a loving and loyal consort, a tender and indulgent parent, a compassionate mistris to her servants, a most accomplished friend, cheerful in her family,

CHESTER HISTORY.

obliging to strangers, a daily almoner to the poor; fervent and composed in her devotion, both in public and in private; a patron to the Clergy, and a generous benefactor to the Church, and all places of her abode. She was of a quicke and piercing understanding, of a deep apprehension and discerning judgment, of great evenesse of mind, and calmness of spirit in all events; aspiring after things only solid, improving, and rational; just in her actions, candid in all her censures; ready to forgive injuries, and never prone to doe any; delighted to see good in others, commended and encouraged it in all; her religion was not a base shew or empty noise, but solid, substantial, even, and uniform; humble and patient in her sickness, and in the midst of pain, without murmuring and despondency, she submitted herself to God, and with great constancy of mind, and cheerfulness of spirit, resigned her life to Him in one continued act of devout prayers and praises, of heavenly meditations and discoursings, suitable to the entertainment of a departing soul, on the 15th March, Ann. Dom. 1693."

Memorials of

Christiana, 4th daughter, March 31, 1689; Elizabeth, 3d daughter, April 26, 1689; Frances, 2d daughter, January 29, 1694—daughters of Sir George Warburton.

Walter Warburton, Esq. May 17, 1753, aged 54.

Near the Altar, Memorials of

Elizabeth daughter of Sir John Bellot, Bart. of Moreton. Oct. 2, 1731. Eliz. Wilbram, daughter of Sir Thos. Bellot, Bart. March 6, 1737, aged 57. Mary Bellot, daughter of the before-named, Dec. 5, 1747, aged 60. John and Richard, sons of Dr. Pennington, 1687: Doctor Allen Pennington, Nov. 12, 1696: Anne, his wife, Dec. 21, 1728: Anne Maria, daughter of Capt. Thomas Pennington, March 7, 1715: Ruth Pennington, wife of Capt. Thos. Pennington, March 7, 1715. Elizabeth, wife of John Philpot, gent. Nov. 4, 1752: John Philpot, Esq. Dec. 6, 1764: Mary, wife of Nicholas Ashton, of Woolton, Esq. and daughter of J. Philpot, Esq. March 13, 1777, aged 37. Rev. Lawrence Adams, Vicar of St. John's, April 30, 1777. Rev. C. Oulton, Vicar of St. John's, Dec. 22, 1741, aged 58.—Hon. John Grey, July 12, 1802, aged 59.—Anna Christiana Farrel, Feb. 16, 1764, aged 63.—Wm. Farrel, of Broxton, Esq. Jan. 29, 1775, aged 86.—Frances, third daughter, and wife of Col. Bonner, of Chester, Aug. 18, 1813, aged 71.—Jane, daughter of Thos. Wilcock, wife of Richd. Broster, Alderman, June 30, 1660.—Humphrey Phillips, of Chester, Alderman, 27th Jan, 1662.—Thos. Gamul, son and heir of Wm. Gamul, Mayor, 18th June, 1637.—John Maddock, Mayor, 1676, Sept. 25, 1680.—John, son of Humphrey Phillips, Alderman, Oct. 3, 1665 aged 39.—Thos. Davenport, barber surgeon, younger son of Ralph Davenport, gent. of Low Cross, Cheshire, and Katherine his wife, daughter of Hugh Moulson, Alderman.—R. Whitehead, Mayor, 1621, March 31, 1624.—Wm. Wilson, Mayor 1671, Feb. 3, 1679, aged 71.—Rand. Oulton, Mayor 1665, Jan. 20, 1682, aged 68 years.—Thomas Byrd, Mayor 1631, May 13, 1644.—Dutton Bunbury, 7th son of Sir H. Bunbury, of Stanny, Knt. married Mary, daughter of John Brescy, of Ireland, gent. died 21st March, 1652, aged 42.—Near the South door, John Tilston, sculptor, of this city, 27th Sept. 1723, aged 52.*

&c. &c. &c.

Charitable Bequests.

One Pound per ann. left by will by Mr. Brereton, April 8, 1631, to be paid to the poor by the City Treasurer.†—The greater part of a small estate at Willaston, left by Mr. Wilcox, in 1634.—1l. to the Poor, 10s. to the Vicar for a Sermon on the Epiphany, left by Mr Edw. Bather, Nov. 14, 1628, charged on a house in Foregate-street; this becomes due Jan. 6.‡ He also left 1l. per ann. to be distributed on the 1st Sunday of each month; this is charged on his Estate in Huntington, called the Lower, or Meadow Farm: 10s. a year, to the Poor, charged on his estate in Huntington, called Owler Hall.—These become due at Lady Day.—A share of Henry Smith's bequest amounting to about 12l. 3s. annually.‖—11s. per annum left to the Poor, by Will, by Mr. J. Stockton, and his wife Eleanor, in 1698, and 1710, charged on a Garden, the property of Mrs. Kenrick, in the Groves. This becomes due on the 18th Oct.

Several small sums were employed in the Erection of a Gallery, the receipts of which amount to about £9. 10s. per ann.

There are four Alms Houses, for old parishioners, built by Mrs. Dighton Salmon, in 1738, but they have no endowment. In the front of them is this inscription:

> These Alms Houses were rebuilt and enlarged at the sole expense of Mrs. Dighton Salmon, of this Parish. Ann. Dom. 1738.

* This was an artist of much talent. It is said, he carved the figure of Queen Anne, and the armorial shields which adorn the front of the Exchange. It is probable, he executed also, the beautiful work in front of Pemberton's parlour, on the City Walls.—See Stranger in Chester, p. 94.

† Paid on the 4th May, annually.

‡ This same Edw. Bather also left 10s. to the Mayor, to be expended in a "BANQUET," annually, to his Worship and the Body.

‖ See note, p. 246.

ADDITIONS.

The Chapel of St. James, before noticed, existed in 1662; but it was in a ruinated state, and occupied as a stable.

The tradition relative to the wooden image of the Virgin, so roughly treated by the "*Hawarden Jews*," has been repeatedly noticed—the following is at least a *different* reading:—After its fall on the head of the Lord of the Castle's wife, (which occasioned her death) it was thrown into the Dee; the tide carried it to Chester, and left it on the Roodee. The pious Cestrians from thence carried it in grand procession to St. John's Church, where it was re-erected. After the Reformation it was used by the Master of the Grammar School, as a block, to whip his scholars on! it was subsequently burnt.

In 1770, in repairing the Anchorite's Cell, on the south side of the Church, two skeletons were found in cavities hollowed out of the rock. This building was formerly used as a Meeting Hall for some of the City Companies; it is now converted into a Dwelling-house.

Mosses, sc.

PERSPECTIVE VIEW OF BEESTON CASTLE.

Mosses sc.

LAMB ROW, CHESTER.

Hospitals, Decayed Places of Worship, &c.

CHURCH OF ST. CHAD.

History.

There is no doubt but what this Church stood at the bottom of Princess-street, on the north side, opposite to the road leading to the City Gaol—but there are now no remains of it in existence. It was standing, however, so late as the reign of Henry VII. for in a document of the 16th of that King, in the possession of Mr. Dicas, solicitor, of Chester, a certain " crofte and closet" is described as lying " nigh the Churche of St. Chadde of Chester."—In a record of the 21st of the same King, a fine was levied on account of *St. Stephen's Cross**—" *Qd. fregit et obstupuit viam quæ ducit ad Ecclesiam Stæ. Ceddæ, ad magnum nocumentum civium civitat. prædict.*"—and the following document, observes the 8vo. History of Chester, " nearly confirms the above conjecture: Robert de Stretton, constituted his brothers William and David Bellot, his attornies, to give possession to Robert Hare, Citizen of Chester, and William Troutbeck, Esq. of two Messuages, and two Gardens,—' jacent in p'. dict. civitat. Cest. super le Crofts, juxta Ecclesiam Stæ. Ceddæ existent. inter messuagia Rich^l. Coly, ex parte australi et messuag Bastrami Lyalton ex parte boreali et gardinam monach. Cest. exparte orientali, et alta strata de la crofts exparte occidentali," &c. This is completely descriptive of the situation before noticed, " above the Crofts," which Crofts now form the site of the Infirmary, City Gaol, &c.—We find a Chapel and Well, in *Little Parsons Lane*, were given by Richard Fitton, to Chester Abbey, in the reign of Henry III. which Chapel was no doubt that of St. Chad.

It would appear, from the following extract from the will of Wm. Danyess, of Daresbury, dated in 1306, this Church had a monastic establishment attached to it:

" †Item (lego) *ffratribus* Sancti Chad, vj denarios." † Ormerod

We have not the least account of the period of its destruction. The old stone wall, on the north side of the lower end of Princess-street, is probably a relic of the Old Church.

* This Cross stood at the bottom of Parson's-lane.

† The above and the preceding vignette were from drawings in the possession of M. Gregson, Esq.

THE GREY FRIARS.—The Franciscans were settled in Chester at least as early as the reign of Hen. III. This house was near the Watergate, on the north side; probably its site is occupied by the Irish Linen Hall and Stanley Place. Pennant was of opinion it stood in the *Yacht Field*, on which the Linen Hall is built.

In 1329, Sir Lawrence Dutton made a bequest to the three Friaries at Chester, and the Friary at Warrington—" *Item lego quatuor ordinibus fratrum religiosorum Cestriæ et Werington, singulis vero conventibus eorundem xx solidos.*" In 1579, Peter Warburton, Esq. of Arley, and Thomas Wilbraham, Esq. had a grant from Elizabeth, of premises in Chester, consisting of the site of the Grey Friars, then possessed by Peter Warburton, Esq. of Chester.* The buildings were entire till about 1640, at which time they were occupied by the celebrated Sir William Brereton. According to a plan in the Harl. Collect. the buildings were of an oblong form, the Church in the centre, the cloisters at the north-west angle, and the entrance on the east side.

* Ormerod.

THE BLACK FRIARS—were situated on the west side of the north-end of Nicholas-street. The precise site of the building is not known; it is likely, however, that it was near the old house, on the west side of Nicholas-street, adjoining Watergate-street, which bears the date 1591, and which was subsequently the town residence of the Stanleys of Alderley, to whom it passed from the Warburtons of Grafton. The Black Friars had a large piece of ground attached to their Convent, extending from Nicholas-street to the Watergate, and in a southerly direction to Smith's Walk, now improperly called GREY FRIARS. Large traces of the boundary wall are to be seen on the south side of Watergate-street, on the left side of the road from the Watergate to Smiths Walk, on the premises of Colonel Wrench, and in the wall of the garden, on the south side of the house occupied by S. Humphryes, Esq. in Nicholas-street. The fraternity were settled here at a very early period, and had, temp. Edw. I. a license to bring water " a fonte prope furcas," and were exempted in the 19th of Richard II. from Toll at Dee Mills.

WHITE FRIARS.—*Carmelites.*—Their Monastary was in the parish of St Martin, on the north side of Whitefriars-street. They were established in 1279, by Thomas Stadham.—In 1496, the steeple of their Church was built; after the Dissolution, Sir Thomas Egerton, erected a handsome mansion on the site of the conventual buildings; in July, 1597, the steeple was taken down; and a writer of the day, pathetically remarks, it was a " great pitie that the steeple was put away, being a great ornament to the citie. This curious spire steeple might still have stood for grace to the citie, had not private benefit, the devourer of antiquitie, pulled it down with the Church, and erected a house for more commoditie, which since hath been of little use, so that the citie lost so goodly an ornament that tymes herehereafter may more talk of it, being the only sea-mark for direction over the bar of Chester."† In 1316, there occurs a referential notice signed by Rich. de Donnes, —" prior fratrum Carmelitarum domus be'e Marie Cestr'," to a dispensation of marriage to Sir William Brereton, and Anilla Venables.—In 1772, the remains of the Mansion built by Sir Thomas Egerton, were destroyed by a dreadful explosion.‡

† 2125, Harl. MSS.

" ‡ On the 5th November, 1792, a few minutes before nine o'clock in the evening, the inhabitants of this city, were greatly alarmed by a loud unusual noise, attended with a shaking of the ground, which every one imagined to proceed from an earthquake. But the news soon arrived, that a large number of people, assembled at a Puppet Show, had been blown up by gunpowder, placed in a Grocer's warehouse, which was under the room. Amidst the universal consternation and confusion, occasioned by this dreadful calamity, it happened most fortunately, that some Gentlemen repaired to the melancholy scene a few minutes after the accident, who gave particular directions that every person who shewed the least signs of life, should be immediately carried to the Infirmary, where the Physicians and Surgeons would be ready to administer every possible means of relief.—The number admitted that night was 33, and 20 since, in all 53.

" A clean bed was provided for every patient, before the unfortunate sufferer could be stripped, which, in general, was by cutting off the clothes, to prevent the agony of pulling those limbs which were broken, burned, or bruised. In this tremendous scene of horror and confusion, that no possible means of relief might be omitted, which their humanity and skill could suggest, the Faculty assigned different offices to different persons; some were employed entirely in bleeding all who required such an evacuation; others washed several times over all the burns and bruises with Goulard's cooling water, which seemed uni-

CHESTER

ST THOMAS THE MARTYR—*Thomas à Becket.* The remains of this Chapel still exist on the west-side of the road leading to Beach Pool, near to the garden attached to the house of J. Fletcher, Esq. Its dedication may give a date to the period of its foundation; but it is clear it existed so early as 1190.* At this Chapel were held the Courts of the Dean and Chapter, which are now held in the Cathedral, under the name of *St Thomas's Court*, with jurisdiction over all residents in the City, beyond the Northgate, and the inhabitants of eight dependent Townships.† After the Reformation, it was converted into a dwelling-house; and at the

HISTORY.

* Orm. p. 278.

sally to have an excellent effect; the rest were engaged in setting fractured bones, reducing dislocations, &c. In these, and other offices, the Faculty were most assiduously engaged from nine o'clock (when the accident happened) till four in the morning. Not one that was admitted, has escaped without marks of violent contusions, or large and deep burns, on the face, hands, &c.; and generally both. The women are remarkably worse burnt than the men, especially on their arms and thighs; this circumstance may be accounted for by the particular mode of their dress. Of another peculiarity it may be more difficult to guess the cause: a greater number of broken bones, as arms, thighs, legs, &c. have happened amongst the men; yet, only one limb of a female has been fractured, which, most unfortunately, is the arm of a poor girl, who had lost the other by a former disease. It is very astonishing, that among so large a number as 53, who have been admitted into the Infirmary, with such a variety of dreadful injuries, all yet remain alive, except one, who expired in about an hour after his admission, before any means of relief could possibly be administered. However, it must be apprehended, that many patients will still die; for out of the number in the House, their burns, contusions, &c. have excited such a fever in all, that only one patient had yesterday (three days after the accident) an appetite for animal food. The chief danger now to be dreaded from so great a number of large ulcers, compound fractures, &c. in the same apartment, is, lest a putrid fever should be excited.

To guard against this dreadful calamity with all possible care, four windows in each ward are constantly kept open all the day, and not close shut at night; each patient is daily supplied with clean sheets, and a shift or shirt; the wards are daily washed with hot vinegar; all the dressings, when taken from the sores, are immediately thrown into a vessel of cold vinegar; every species of dirt is taken away with the most scrupulous care; laxative medicines are frequently administered; and all the patients are very plentifully supplied with great variety of acid, and acescent drinks.

" It happened that no person, man, woman, or child, but of inferior rank, were sufferers in this dreadful calamity; most of those at home, could not have been supplied with the necessaries of life in a state of such distress. But had they been persons of the most affluent fortunes, and carried to their own houses, none could have possibly received such immediate and effectual medical assistance as was administered to all, who were admitted into the Infirmary. Besides 23 dead, and 53 Hospital Patients, upon particular inquiry, there appears to be about 30 more in the town who have received some degree of injury, but the greater part of this number have only suffered slight contusions or burns; in all about 106.

" To prevent a like misfortune, it may be useful to relate some facts which may be learned from this melancholy accident. The inside dimensions of the building were 40 feet by 20; none of the stories were divided into separate apartments; it was composed of a cellar 12 feet high, a warehouse 7 feet high, on the ground floor, where about 800lbs. of gunpowder were lodged. The Puppet Show-room over it 11 feet high; a dwelling above this room, 7 feet, and a garret still higher.—The walls of the warehouse and show-room were of stone, 3½ feet thick. It appears clearly, that the chief force of the explosion had been exerted UPWARDS, for it was sufficient to throw off all the floors, &c. of three stories above the warehouse; yet the walls of the building continued standing on three sides, as high as the top of the room on which the powder was lodged. Even a part of the wood floor, at the opposite end of the room, on which the powder was placed, still remains standing. A house, which rested on one corner of the building, is tumbled down, but another old house, six yards distant from the warehouse, was only injured by one side falling OUTWARDS. Not a chimney is blown down, though the spot is surrounded with a great number of old houses. A great many windows have been broken all round the place, even to a considerable distance; but one circumstance deserves very particular attention; nearly all the glass fell OUTWARDS with some of the window-frames. This fact apparently proves that these windows were not broken by the explosive power of the gunpowder, but by the pressure of the air contained in the surrounding apartments, which rushed into the vacuum caused by the explosion.—However, where the force of the gunpowder was confined by narrow passages, its influence or centrifugal force took place: for two boys, walking along the rows (or passages), in Watergate-street, opposite to a passage leading to this building, were blown, one into the street, and the other against the rails; and opposite another passage into Commonhall-lane, one side of a slated room, was entirely blown off.

" Do not these facts evidently prove, that even the smallest quantity of gunpowder should be always kept in garrets? And do they not suggest a doubt, whether the distance from towns prescribed by law, for keeping larger quantities, is not greater than necessary, if the magazine be entirely separate from other buildings?"—*From Adams's Weekly Courant, Nov.* 9, 1772. [In the preceding page, it is print- 1792, instead of 1772.]

Soon after this terrific accident, a Charitable Assembly was held, when £350. were collected, for the relief of the sufferers.

† Specified in the plea to a QUO WARRANTO, 31 Edw. III. It is called the Manor of St. Thomas; and Great Boughton, and Bridge

period of the siege it was demolished ;* it was called Jolly's Hall.

* 1645.

ST. THOMAS THE APOSTLE,—The Chapel dedicated to this Saint, occupied the site of the present Deanery. It was dependent upon the Abbey.

THE HOSPITAL OF ST. GILES.—The Chapel and Hospital, which were destroyed during the siege, were situated in the extra-parochial district, called The Spital, in Boughton, just within the liberties of the City. The Hospital was founded by Randle Blundeville, Earl of Chester, who gave to the Abbey of St. Werburgh, a rent charge of xs from lands held from him by Geoffrey de Sibesey, "de quibus dicti monachi solvent leprosis de Boughton xx denarios, et de residuo pascent c pauperis, in die nativitatis patris sui infræ abbatiam Cestriæ" Several other grants were made to the Hospital, and its privileges were confirmed by Hugh Cyveilloc, and King Edward III. when it claimed "Certain toll from every thing carried to sale at Chester market: One handful from every sack of wheat, vetches, or barley, and two handsfull from every sack of oats or malt, carried either on horse or cart, or in any other way ; and of wheat, vetches, barley, oats, salt fish, produce of any other kind, and particularly salt, one handful from a sack, and two from a cart ; one cheese from every horse load or cart load of cheese ; one salmon from every horse or cart load ; and in other fish, such as sparlings, flukes, eels, &c. five from every horse's pannier, and one from every man's load. From fruits of trees, one double handful from each horse load, and three double handsfull from each cart load. From the fruits of the earth, whether horse loads or cart loads, one handful. From all packages of earthenware, one piece of the same†; to have one horse from the horse fair ; and from all carts drawn by oxen or horses carrying wood or brick, one piece of the same. To have also one boat with a fisherman above or below Dee Bridge, with stallnette, flotnette, dragenette, or any other kind of nette, night and day, and three stalls in Dee, called single lyne stalles, and not to be amenable to the justice, sheriff, or other officer of the Prince, except in the Court of the Hospital aforesaid."

Two Charters of Randle Blundeville are recited in this document.—The following are all the names of the Masters that are extant :—

Rogerus	26th Edw. I.
Radulphus de Hole	30th Edw. I.
Radulphus de Bebington	32d Edw. I.
Mathæus de Hole	2d Edw. II.
Robertus Vickars	22d Hen. VI.
David Barrs	31st Hen. VI.

During the Civil Wars,‡ as has been before observed, the Hospital and Chapel were entirely destroyed. The Burial Ground, however, still exists, and is used as a Church-yard dependent upon St. John's Parish, to the present day ; in it are mingled all the remains that could be collected of George Marsh, who was burnt here for his adherence to the reformed religion, in 1555.

‡ 1645.

The Houses on the east side of the Spital Burial Ground, occupy the site of the Hospital and Chapel.

ST. MARY'S CHANTRY.—This was situated in the great Tower, on the left hand of the entrance to the Higher Ward of the Castle of Chester. It has been by some supposed to be the same with the Church of St. Mary supra Montem ; but this is an error, inasmuch as we find by the Tax Book of Hen. VIII. that this Chantry "infra castrum Cestriæ," paid 10s. whilst the Church of St. Mary supra Montem, or de Castello, paid £5. 4s.

It was in this Chapel, that the senseless bigot, James II. received mass, during his stay in Chester. Its dimensions are about 19 feet by 16 feet, and the altitude is also about 16 feet. It has a vaulted roof, with groins, springing from slender pillars with ornamented capitals.

Trafford, still pay suit and service here, the Constables of which township, are elected by the Court.—A short time previous to the Dissolution, the Abbey claimed a Leet of all residents—"from the Northgate unto the Church of St. Thomas, once by the year to be holden, with all manner of things and articles which to a Leet do appertain."

† A similar toll is now levied, vi et armis, by the Coal Carriers on the carts of those who bring that necessary article to the City from the pits.

CHESTER

The style of the workmanship is that of the 12th century, and some writers have attributed it to the period of the completion of the Chapter House of the Cathedral. It is pretty certain, that the large square Tower, of which it forms the middle apartment, was rebuilt at a much earlier date, probably so early as the Government of the Saxon Earls of Mercia.* Tradition, which is seldom to be depended upon, attributes it to Julius Cæsar, by whose name it is still known. The walls are of immense thickness. At the Reformation, the following name occurs as the officiating Priest :—

" Petri Trafforde, cantariste Cantar. infra Castru' Cestr. p. ann. cs.

Within the last few years, the walls were ornamented with a very ancient fresco painting,† a sketch of which, made at the request of W. M. Henderson, Esq. Store Keeper, by — Musgrave, together with a view of the interior of the Chapel, is given in the accompanying plate.

The Chapel is now used as a store-house; and is nearly filled with wheel-barrows, axes, shovels, and other appendages to the pioneer department of an army. It is well worth the inspection of the curious.

BENEDICTINE NUNNERY OF ST. MARY.—There appears to have been considerable doubt, as to the precise situation of this Nunnery, but there is no doubt, but what a religious house, with this dedication, occupied the lawn, in front of the Castle Gateway, and of which a pointed arch still remains to mark the precise situation.‡ A Monastery dedicated to St. Mary, is thus noticed in the Domesday Survey :—

" In monasteria sanctæ Mariæ, quod est juxta ecclesiam sancti Johannis, jacent duæ bovatæ terræ quæ wastæ erant et modo sunt wastæ."

HISTORY.

This Monastery eventually became a Nunnery, to which Randal II. or Gernons, granted lands, by a Charter, of which the following is a copy, to erect a House and Church upon :

" **Ra'nus Comes Cestr.** ep'is, archdecanis, abbatibus, constab' &c. SALUTEM. Sciatis me dedisse et in perpetuam eleemosynam concessisse Deo, et S. Mariæ, et Monialibus Cestr. n'ris in Xto. sororibus, illas croftas quas Hugo filius Oliveri de d'nio meo tenuit, concessione et bonâ voluntate ipsius Hugonis ita quod illas clamavit quietas, coram me et comitissâ, et plurimis baronum meorum, liberas et immunes ab omnibus secularibus servitiis, et omnimoda subjectione, ad edificandam ibi ecclesiam in honore' Dei et s'tæ Mariæ, in remissionem peccatorum meorum, et ad fundationem sui edificii. Volo igitur et præcipio quod ecclesia ita in eleemosynâ mea fundata, de tolnato et omni seculari exuctione libera sit et quieta, et curiam suam et dignitatem ac liberatem, in omnibus et peromnia, prout libera exigit eleemosyna, habeat; quam vobis mando ac diligenter et in D'no obsecro, quatenus p'd'tam ecclesiam, et moniales ibidem Deo et s'tæ Mariæ jugiter servientes, cum omnibus ad illos pertinentibus, pro Deo et communi salute meæ vizt. animæ et proavorum, manuteneatis et protegatis, et n'e patiamini quod eleemosyna mea deprivetur, neque moniales in ea manentes ab aliquibus vexentur.—TEST. Joh'e et Rogero capellanis, Matilda comitissa, Hogone filio comitis, Fulcone de Brichsard, Rad'o Mansell, Ric'o Pinc'. Apud Cestriam."

This document, however, does not fix the situation of the convent, and much therefore must be left to conjec-

* This tower was newly cased with red stone, in 1817-18.

† It would be difficult to form even a conjecture of the SUBJECT of the artist. To my mind, it appears to be a representation of Moses receiving the tables of the Commandments from the Mount, whilst the Devil, in a non-descript form, is making a formidable attempt to seize them. The anachronism in the design is, however, glaring; and I must leave it to those better versed in abstract studies of the graphic art, to explain how the Pope and his companions were introduced on the occasion!—H.

‡ This Arch was the western entrance of the Church of the Benedictines, the corresponding Arch on the east side of the same, now forms the entrance to the ruins of the Old Chancel of St. John's Church, where it was removed about forty years ago.—In the Harl. MSS. 2073, a plan of the building is given, which the Messrs. Lysons have introduced in their MAGNA BRITANNIA.

In Buck's print of the Castle of Chester, there is also a view of the ruins.

‖ Harl. MSS. 2101, f. 182.

ture. But this much is certain: it shows that the grant was for lands for the erection of a NEW Church; and we may therefore infer, that the situation formerly occupied by the Convent near St. John's Church, was exchanged for a more eligible one near the Castle, where, at the Reformation, the Benedictines had a Nunnery.

Hugh Cyveilioc afterwards confirmed the Charter of Randle, which received subsequent confirmation from Edward Earl of Chester, in the 27th year of Edw. III. who exempted the tenants of the possessions of the Nunnery *(Not Freemen of the City*)* from juries, assizes, inquisitions, recognizances, or appearances before any officers of the City, or County of Chester; and from murage, stallage, passage, toll, watch, customs, postage, mizes, and exactions of Tolcest'r, assize of bread and beer, &c. and from all suits of shires, courts, pendices, hundreds, portmotes, and works of any kind: and that no officers of the Earl, or others shall enter on the premises; and that they shall have all amercements levied on any of their tenants in the Earl's Courts; and that any sheriff or Officer of the City or County, interfering with the said liberties, shall be liable to a fine of £10. of silver; provided that the said Nuns and their successors shall not bring upon their estates tenants of any other description than those which they now have, or exercise any trade injurious to the merchandize of the City." This grant, which bears date at Chester, 14th Dec. 32d Edw. III. was confirmed by Richard II. Nov. 8, ann. reg. 7.

After the Dissolution, the Breretons had a grant of the Nunnery, between which family and the Corporation, there were continually disputes. The severities exercised by Sir William Brereton, after the surrender of Chester, are attributed to this state of disagreement.

In making the improvements in the neighbourhood of the Castle, quantities of human bones were found in the area of what was once the cemetry of the Convent, the Gardens of which remained perfect till the year 1814, when they were destroyed, and the draw-wells covered up. History.

The Church is described† as being 66 feet long, 45 broad, and supported by a line of pillars in the middle. The Chapel was 27 feet by about 13 feet. The cloisters 90 feet by 63 feet. † Pennant.

The last Prioress, at the time of the Dissolution,‡ was Eliz. Grosvenor, who retired on a pension of £20. ‡ 1537.

The following were the landed and other possessions of the Nuns:—

	£.	s.	d.
Demesne Lands	15	15	4
Rents of Assize	2	6	10
Free Rent from Whalley Abbey	0	13	4
Lands, tenements, and Cottages, in various Towns	45	15	10
Lands, Tenements, &c in Handbridge‖	7	1	0
A Wychehouse in Nantwich	1	10	4
A Salthouse in Middlewich	1	6	8
A Tenement in Davenham	2	13	4
The Rectory of Llangothan, & Llanyerion, South Wales	17	6	8
Rectory of Bykkyk, and Chapel of Carnarvon, North Wales	3	0	0
Rectory of Over	8	13	4
Pension from the Rector of Handley	0	13	4
——— Chapel of Budworth	0	10	0
Money from the King's Exchequer, of old time paid	26	12	2

ST. JAMES'S CHAPEL, in St. John's Church-yard.—See page 248.

ST. JAMES'S CHAPEL, Handbridge.—The site of it is now entirely unknown; it was a very ancient establishment.

* It would appear from this, that at the period we have mentioned. non-freemen were competent to fulfil and hold the offices now filled by Freemen only.

‖ The Nuns had also a Chapel in Kettle's Croft, opposite the Castle, in Handbridge, called Little St Mary's. It was close to the river's side, and was probably on the site of the Cottage which now stands near the Quarry. It is stated, that a long time after the Dissolution, when the boundary wall had been washed down by a flood, two chapel bells were found in the rubbish.

A Chapel belonging to the Hall, at Overlegh, was destroyed during the Civil Wars.

THE CHAPEL OF ST. ANNE—stood on the north-east side of St. John's Church. It has been called the Monastery of St. Anne, and in the Patent of the 16th Richard II. "de fraternitate S. Mariæ et S. Annæ fundanda in capella S. Annæ, infra collegium S. Joannis." It was endowed with thirty houses, &c. in Chester; and the entire rental was £17. 8s. 4d.

THE CHAPEL OF ST. URSULA—was situated in Common Hall-lane, and the site of it is now occupied by six Alms Houses. After the Dissolution, it was used as the Common Hall of the City, in the windows of which, so late as the year 1663, were some remains of stained glass.

THE MONASTERY OF ST. MICHAEL—of the existence of which as a distinct Monastic Establishment, there are considerable doubts, is said to have been situated in Rock's Court, in Lower Bridge-street, some 80 yards below the Church dedicated to St. Michael. Speaking of this Court, Dr. Williamson observes, "before it was converted into Dwelling-houses, one might have beheld fair Church-like windows, and other demonstrations of its being part of a religious house."—The Annals of the City, as collected by the Holmes', and others, inform us, that in 1118, the Monastery was burnt in the great fire which happened on Midlent Sunday, at eight in the morning, all being in Church, by which a great part of the City was destroyed. It is certain, no remains of such a Monastery now exist; and, indeed, the only mention of it is in a Charter granted to the Prior of Norton, "Monasterium S'c'i Michaelis," which phraze was adopted by the later writers. It is highly probable, that the "Monastery of St. Michael," means nothing further than the present Church dedicated to that Saint.

HOSPITAL OF ST. JOHN.—The present Chapel is situated in the south wing of the Blue Coat Hospital, near the Northgate. The Curacy, which is in the gift of the Corporation, is perpetual; and is now occupied by the Rev. William Fish. In the 15th Edward III. the lands and rents of the Hospital of St. John the Baptist,* were seized by the Justices of Chester; when an Inquisition was held, formed of twelve Citizens of Chester, which found, that it was erected by Randle Blundeville, Duke of Britanny, and Earl of Chester and Richmond, in honor of God, the Virgin, and St. John the Baptist, for the sustentation of poor and silly persons, and granted in pure and perpetual alms. The Charter and grant of Randle, were confirmed by Henry III. and Edw. I. who gave the Keeping of the Hospital to the Monks of Birkenhead.—The revenues were then—

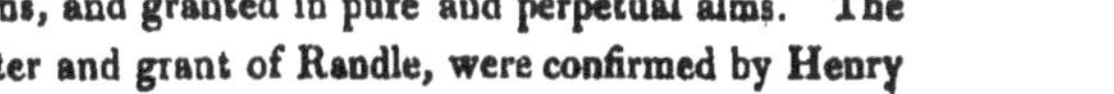

	£.	s.	d.
Given by Randle Earl of Chester, payable out of the Exchequer, yearly	4	10	0
Houses in the City of Chester	8	13	10
A Grange, at the Holme Houses, held in exchange from the Prior of Birkenhead, by the Abbot of Chester	2	0	0
A Grange at le Moss, Lancashire	2	0	0
A Dry-rent in Pensby	0	13	4
A House in Handbridge, and half an Oxgang in the Clays	2	0	0
A Wich-house in Wich Malbank	0	13	4
Other rents belonging to the Hospital	6	13	4
Total of the lands belonging to the Hospital	27	3	10

The last Prior or Keeper, was "George Hope de Dodleston, Magister sive custos, 9 Car. I."

According to the above Inquisition, it appears that there ought to have been three Chaplains to the said Hospital to say Mass daily, two in the Church, and one in the Chapel, before the poor and feeble therein maintained; also a lamp for mass, to burn every night throughout the year; thirteen competent beds, for thirteen poor men of the City, each of whom shall have daily, a loaf of bread, a dish of pottage, half a gallon of competent ale, and a piece of flesh or fish, as the day shall require, &c.

* For the Seal of which, still used by the Corporation, in the granting of leases, &c. of tenements belonging to the Hospital, see page 139. It represents St. John in a dress of Camel skin.

CHESTER

In the reign of Edward III. only one Chaplain and six poor widows were maintained in the Hospital; and in the reign of Hen. VIII. the Corporation remonstrated with the Prior of Birkenhead, for not maintaining the Hospital according to the terms of the foundation, whose answer was, that the revenues was not sufficient. William de Bache, who was Master in the 9th Edw. II. was sued by the Vicar of Eastham, for 7 white loaves, and 7 bottles of beer, such as the Master fed upon weekly, or in lieu thereof half a mark. It does not appear on what ground this claim was made.

During the siege, the Hospital and Chapel were destroyed, and Cromwell afterwards granted the site and lands to the City,* by which the Mayors, for the time being, were appointed Masters or Keepers. The Chapel and Hospital were rebuilt by Col. Roger Whitley, who obtained from Charles II. a grant of the Hospital Estate for his life, and twenty years afterwards.—On the renewal of the City Charter, in February 1685, the Mayor and Citizens obtained the reversion of this property. Whitley dying in 1697, the Corporation obtained possession in 1703.

The value of the living, which is in the gift of the Mayor, and augmented by Queen Anne's Bounty, was returned at only £18. per ann. but a considerable further sum is made up by gratuities.

In the Yard, behind the Chapel, are six Alms Houses, for Poor Widows, who were called "The Sisters."—The Corporation appoint them, and each of them receive a pension of £1. 6s. 8d. exclusive of a few perquisites.—Thirty pounds, were bequeathed to them in 1801, by Alderman Joseph Crewe, to be divided in equal portions.

Mr. Ormerod is of opinion, that the following entry, in the Ecclesiastical Taxation of P. Nicholas, relates to this Hospital:—

HISTORY.

Taxatio bonor' temporal' mag'ri Hospi' Cestr' 1291:

Magist' Hospitalis Cestr' h'et in Dec' Cestr'	£.	s.	d.
ij caruc. terr' et val' caruc' p' ann.......	0	10	0
Et h'et ib'm de redd' assis' p' ann	3	6	8
Et h'et ib'm de p'fic' staur' p' ann..........	0	13	4
S'ma..............	£5	0	0
Inde Dec'ma	0	10	0

As several new Churches are about to be built in the extensive Diocese of Chester, it may not be uninteresting to give the following comparative statement the population of parishes containing upwards of 1000, in eight English Dioceses,—the calculation made in 1811.

Diocese of	Number of Parishes.	Population	Number of Churches and Chapels.	Number of Persons they will contain.	No. of Dissenting Places of Worship.
Canterbury	67	175,625	83	67,705	113
Chester........	257	568,826	351	220,542	439
Durham	75	298,755	113	63,239	173
Exeter	159	362,551	176	152,019	234
Lichfield	129	430,231	189	122,756	294
London	132	661,394	186	162,962	265
Winchester	120	371,206	193	115,711	165
York..........	108	591,972	220	149,277	392
Total	1047	3,460,560	1511	1,054,231	2075

It appears, therefore, that with the single exception of Winchester Diocese, the Dissenting Meeting Houses have a vast majority over the Places of Worship belonging to the Established Church.

* This Grant, elegantly written, is preserved in the Archives of the Corporation; it bears the Seal of the Commonwealth.

CHESTER CASTLE in 1760.

M. Gregson, Esq. *del.* Mosses, *sc.*

WALLASEY CHURCH, WIRRAL.

Public Buildings---Charities, &c.

THE CASTLE

Is situated a short distance west of the Bridge Gate, and the building of it is ascribed to William the Conqueror.* The ground on which it stands, is exempted from the jurisdiction of the City by the Charter of Hen. VII. The destruction of the old Castle commenced in 1789, under the authority of an Act of Parliament; and in 1807, another Act was obtained, for enlarging the Castle precincts, and improving the entrance to it, under which Act, the site of the Nun's Gardens, and Nun's Lane, were purchased, and added to the County property. The Higher Ward stands on an elevated piece of ground, and is the only part of the old Castle now remaining. It is precipitous on the south and west sides; and the north side is defended by a large mound, apparently artificial. On the south side is a great Tower, described in page 258, beneath which is a Magazine for gunpowder. Further on, apartments for the Officers of the Garrison, opening on a narrow terrace, which commands a magnificent prospect. Adjoining these are the lodgings for the Judges of the Circuit †

* Ordericus.

† The present Lord Colchester, when Mr. Abbott, attended this circuit, professionally as a Barrister; and it is said received his first brief here, from the hands of Mr. Humphryes, now Prothonotary of the Court.—In recollection of this occurrence of early life, the Noble Lord has presented a Law Library, for the use of the Judges, which is fitted up in their apartments. It is somewhat remarkable, that the Chief Justice, when in Chester, assumes a Military Command. From the moment he enters the Castle, all orders emanate from him, and he gives the watch-word, &c. A guard of honor attends his Lordship, and salutes, on entering and quitting his carriage. During the stay of the Judges, their table is supplied, and their apartments are also furnished, at the EXPENSE OF THE CITY. Many conjectures might be hazarded on the origin of this custom, but nothing certain is known. It is, however, of very high antiquity; and the appointment of the Day of Assize, is immediately followed by a Writ from the Exchequer Court, of which a copy‡ is subjoined. In addition to the express stipulations of which, the body Corporate, give the Judges the loan of the City Plate, and present them with a certain quantity of Wine:—

"George the Third, by the Grace of God, of the United Kingdom of Great Britain and Ireland, King, Defender of the Faith. To the Sheriff of the said City, Greeting. Forasmuch as we are given to understand that our Justices of Chester, on the thirty-first day of August instant, are to come to our Castle of Chester, there to dispatch our and our subjects' business, and that the beds, and other necessaries are wanting for their stay, in our service, as we have heard; we command you, that as well in Woollen as in Linen, you cause to be provided for our said Justices, Six Good Beds, and other necessaries, fit for such their stay, so that we may have them within our said Castle of Chester, on the Twenty-ninth day of August next coming,

‡ Summer Circuit, 1818.

CHESTER

The west side is formed by a battery, for twelve cannon, but only four are mounted, two of which are brass six-pound field pieces, purchased for the Chester Volunteers, by subscription. Below this, in the Castle Ditch, is another Powder Magazine; such a situation
* See plate. is considered by military men as an anomaly.*—On the west side is the Old Armory,† and the Store Keeper's‡ House. The lofty battlements on this side, afford a delightful view over the Vale of Cheshire—of the Broxton and Peckforton Hills—and a large and romantic district of the Principality. A fine Walnut-tree, which occupied the centre of the square, was cut down in 1814, and another planted. The entrance to the Higher ward, is protected by strong Wooden Gates, placed there in 1817, previous to which it lay open to the Lower Yard, from the time when the two high round towers
‖ About 1807. were taken down‖—fronting which was a drawbridge and portcullice. Pennant describes the general appearance of the Old Castle, in a very accurate manner:—"It is composed of two parts, an Upper and a Lower, each with a strong gate, defended by a round *bastion* on each side, with a ditch, and formerly with drawbridges. Within the precincts of the Upper Balium, are to be seen some towers of Norman architecture, square, with square projections at each corner slightly salient. The handsomest is that called *Julius Cæsar's*. Its entrance is through a large Gothic door, probably of later workmanship. The lowest room has a vaulted roof, strengthened with ordinary square couples. The upper has been a Chapel, as appears by the Holy Waterpot, and some figures almost obsolete, painted on the walls. The arsenal, some batteries, and certain habitable buildings occupy the remaining part. On the side of the lower Court, stands the noble room called *Hugh Lupus's Hall*,§ in which the Courts of Justice for the County are held: the length is very near 99 feet, the breadth 45, the height very awful, and worthy the state apartment of a Great Baron. The roof supported by wood-work in a bold style, carved, and placed on the sides, resting on stout brackets. Adjoining to the end of this great hall, is the Court of Exchequer, or the Chancery of the County Palatine of Chester. This very building is said to have been the Parliament House of the little Kings of the Palatinate. It savors of antiquity in the Architecture, and within are a number of seats described by Gothic arches, and neat pillars. At the upper end are two, one for the Earl, the other for the Abbot. The eight others were allotted to his eight Barons, and occupy one side of the room."—In the room over the gateway of the lower ward, it is said the unfortunate Monarch, Richard II. was confined by the imperious Bolingbroke, on his way to London from Flint. Howard, the Philanthropist, gives the following account of the Old Gaol:—"The day confinement of the Prisoners, is in a little yard, surrounded on all sides by lofty buildings, impervious to the air excepting from above, and ever unvisitted by the purifying rays of the Sun. Their nocturnal apartments are in Cells, 7½ feet by 3½ feet, ranged on one side of a subterraneous dungeon, in each of which are often lodged three or four persons. The whole is rendered more (wholesomely) horrible by being pitched over three or four times in the year. The scanty air of their strait prison yard is to travel through three passages to arrive at them through the window of an adjoining room, through a grate in the floor of the said room into the dungeon, and finally through the dungeon, through a little grate above the door of each of their kennels."¶

HISTORY. 

At present the Lower Yard is thus occupied:—*The Grand Entrance* extending 100 feet in length, is the admiration of every stranger. It is in the Grecian Doric style of Architecture, consisting of three temples or pavilions, connected by short covered passages. **—The centre is a peristyle, formed of ten fluted columns, 18 feet high, and nearly 3 feet in diameter, with their anti or pilasters, the carriage entrance being through the middle intercolumniation, and on each side another for foot passengers. The entablature is crowned with a low attic, formed into pannels and over the centre of

and this, under pain that shall fall thereon, in no wise omit. Witness ourself, at Chester, the Third day of August, in the Fifty-eighth year of our Reign. BLOUNT."

† Built in the reign of William III.

‡ W. M. Henderson, Esq. holds this office.

§ This Hall was nearly rebuilt in the time of Queen Elizabeth.

¶ Written in 1784.—The annexed plate affords a pretty correct view of the external appearance of the Old Castle, the point of sight taken from the south-west angle of the City Walls.

** Octavo History of Chester.

Engraved by J. Pigot. from a Drawing by G. Barrenham.

THE CHAPEL, IN THE OLD TOWER CHESTER CASTLE.

Engraved for Hanshalls History of Cheshire.

Engraved by J. Pye Manch.r from a Drawing by Miss.s Nicholsons Liverpool.

CHESTER CASTLE.

From the City Walls.

Engraved for Hanshalls History of Cheshire.

the fronts, large tablets are placed*. The wings are temple-formed, having porticos of four columns in front, and the roofs terminate in a pediment. The ceilings are entirely of stone, divided into compartments by immense stone beams, having caissons with simple mouldings, formed after the plan of the temple of Theseus, at Athens—the whole forming a beautiful imitation of the pure Grecian architecture. There are 84 columns used in the different buildings of the Castle, each of which is formed of a single stone.† It has been observed,‡ that the Propylæa, at Athens, furnished the idea of the Architect's design, as it did also for the Brandenburgh Gate, at Berlin. The Grand Entrance is in the centre of the semi-cicrular fosse which surrounds the Castle-yard in front; the fosse is 13 feet deep; the wall 390 feet in extent, surmounted by handsome stone pedestals, and a neat but strong cast-iron railing, in the Chinese style.

On the north-east side of the Castle Yard, are the BARRACKS, containing very excellent accommodation for about 130 men. Behind them, is the PROVOST, for Deserters; the area between these buildings form an exercise ground for the prisoners. The south-west side is occupied by an extensive ARMOURY, for 35,000 stand of arms, which are kept in admirable order, and beautifully arranged; above which are rooms for military accoutrements, shot, &c. &c. The fronts of these wings, the expense of which was defrayed jointly by the Crown, and the County, are ornamented each with 10 Iönic columns 23ft. 6in. high, supporting a neat entablature, and a screen, which conceals the roofs. At the end of the Barracks, next St. Mary's Church, is the COURT OF QUARTER SESSION, a fine room, the roof of which is indented nearly similar to the roof of the entrance to the Shire Hall. The south-east side of the Court is occupied by the Entrance to the Gaol, the Shire Hall, Grand Jury Room, Record Rooms, and Prothonotary's Offices, presenting a fine front of 310 feet, the centre of which is formed by the Magnificent County Hall. It has a fine portico in front, supported by twelve immense pillars (emblematical of a British Jury) each formed of a single stone, 22 feet high, and 3 feet 1 inch in diameter. The interior of the Hall is semi-circular, the diameter eighty feet, by 44 feet high; the width, including the recess for the Judges, 50 feet. Round the semi-circle, is a colonade of twelve beautiful Iönic pillars, also formed of a single stone, 22 feet in height, supporting a semi-dome divided into square compartments, in each of which an ornamental rose is inserted, the whole gradually reducing to the centre The semi-circle, immediately above the seats of the Judges, is richly ornamented, and also divided into compartments described by a Grecian border.—The Prisoner's Box, is in the lowest part of the Court,‖ from which there is a regular elevation by broad steps, to the base of the colonade before mentioned.—The *tout ensemble* is grand and imposing, and admirably calculated to give a majectic appearance to a Judicial Court. Behind the Hall is the Constable's House,§ a Terrace, in front of which commands a view of the Felons' Yards below, five in number. Beneath the Terrace is a neat Chapel, the gallery of which is appropriated to the Debtors, whilst the divisions below, which correspond with opposite yards, are occupied by the Felons. On this level is a Hot Bath, a Cold Bath, and every convenience suitable for a prison. The Debtors' Yards form quadrangles, on the right and on the left of the Constable's House, on a level with the Castle Yard.

The whole of this magnificent pile is built from designs furnished by Mr. Harrison, the Architect of the County; who entirely superintended the erection of the whole, and to whose genius and taste it does infinite credit.¶

* After the Battle of Waterloo, "BRITAIN TRIUMPHANT!" was painted on the centre tablet, but it was afterwards obliterated.

† The stone was cut from the quarry at Manley; it is durable and finely colored: but symptoms of vegetation have already appeared in many parts of the building.

‡ Octavo History of Chester.

‖ There is a subterraneous communication between the Dock and the Gaol.

§ The Constableship of the Castle is held by Patent---the office is occupied by Mr. J. E. Hudson.

¶ It would seem, that there was formerly another Shire Hall, without the Castle Walls, at Gloverstone. The Harl. MSS. record a letter from the Magistrates of the City to Lord Burleigh, dated Feb. 4, 1587, describing it as "uncovered and in ruyn," and begging

CHESTER HISTORY.

THE BRIDGE—is one of the most ancient, as it is one of the most inconvenient structures in the Kingdom. It is probably the only stone bridge that ever existed on the present site. A wooden bridge was erected at a very early period over the Dee by the celebrated "Mercian Lady," Ethelfleda, but the precise period of the erection of the one now existing cannot be ascertained.—The notices in the "Chronicle of Chester Abbey, stating that in 1227, "Pons Cestriæ totus cecidit," and "1279, Mare excrevit, pontem Cestriæ confregit et asportavit," relate, no doubt, to the wooden bridge; and it is highly probable the stone bridge succeeded this last demolition. Indeed, we find, that in 1280, the King compelled the Citizens to rebuild the Bridge at their own charge; and in 1500 the south side of it was rebuilt, together with the tower that defended the entrance to it, which was taken down in 1782. It appears from the ledger-book of the Abbey of Vale Royal, that Chester Bridge was the rendezvous for the Earl's vassals, in his Welsh inroads. They were led by the Seneschal of the respective manors from which they held lands, and the names of defaulters were presented by him.

It has long been in contemplation to erect a New Bridge over the Dee, in a line stretching across from below the Higher-ward Battery of the Castle; and on 28th Sept, 1818, a Public Meeting was held in the Exchange to take the subject into consideration, at which the following resolutions were adopted:—

"1st.—That the present Bridge over the Dee at Chester, and the avenues thereto, which are the principal communication between the great manufacturing counties of Lancaster and York, and the whole of the North of England, with the West of England, and with Wales and Ireland, are not only highly inconvenient, but absolutely dangerous to passengers in carriages, on horseback, and on foot.

"2dly.—That the Erection of another Bridge, in addition to the present one, would be highly beneficial to the public at large—to the County and City of Chester in particular; and as a National undertaking, most important to the intercourse between England, Wales, and Ireland.

"3dly.—That it is expedient to apply to Parliament for leave to bring in a Bill for the Erection of such additional Bridge.

"4thly.—That a Committee be appointed (which consisted of 44 in number) any nine of whom be competent to act, and to receive and consider such Plans, Surveys, and Estimates; and the most expedient mode of providing Funds for carrying the foregoing Resolutions into effect; and that they do report thereon, at a subsequent Meeting, of which due notice will be given. And that this Committee have power to add to it such other Gentlemen as they may think proper.

"5thly.—That Notice be immediately given, in order that application may be made to Parliament, at the ensuing Sessions, by Mr. Finchett, and that the business relating thereto be transacted by him, as Solicitor to the undertaking," &c.

In compliance with the 5th resolution, a notice actually appeared on the Exchange Door, notifying the intention of the Committee to apply for an Act of Parliament, to enable them to commence the undertaking. It is to be apprehended, however, from the operation of party differences, and the intervention of other obstacles, (amongst which is, the depreciation in the value of property in the neighbourhood of the Bridge) that no immediate progress will be made to accomplish the desired work. It is certain that, independent of these considerations, a considerable difference of opinion prevails as to the actual expediency of a New Bridge. It has been argued, (and a plan has been prepared by the celebrated Mr. Telford) that the Old Bridge might be rendered perfectly commodious, by extending the cause-

they might have it for shambles; with the addition, that though they could not gratify his Lordship as they ought, yet they presumed to send him half a dozen Cheshire Cheeses! Mr. Glaziour, and Mr. Bostock had obtained a promise of it, but the Citizens succeeded in their suit, at the expense of £40. It was moved into Northgate-street, and placed opposite the Abbey Gate, when the lower part was converted into shambles, and the upper part into a store house for victualling the garrisons in Ireland.

Engraved by T. [illegible] from a Drawing by J. Brown, from a Picture in the Collection of [illegible] Esq. Chester by [illegible] Marine Painter to his Majesty

DEE BRIDGE 1798.

Engraved for Hanshall's History of Cheshire.

CHESTER

way to the width of the piers, by throwing over an iron railing, on the suspension principle. This would at once double the width of the Bridge, and the entire expense, it is supposed, would not exceed £3000. including a considerable improvement to the approaches of the Bridge. When the importauce of the subject, as connected with the great intercourse between the North of England, Cheshire, and the Principality, is taken into consideration, the absolute necessity of some alteration is rendered obvious, and it is to be hoped that measures will be adopted to carry the desideratum into immediate effect.

THE EXCHANGE—is a large pile, situated in Northgate-street, on the west side of the Cathedral:—It is a brick building, with stone facings, resting on pillars, with a thoroughfare on the ground floor,* forming a communication between the Fish and Green Markets, and the Butchers' Shambles. The east side forms an open piazza, but there were shops erected on the west side, in 1756, for the purpose, it is said, of strengthening the support of the building. It was begun in 1698 † In the centre of the south front, is a well executed statue of Queen Anne, in her coronation costume, but the sceptre and ball, which formerly occupied the hands, were complerely destroyed by the election mobs in 1784, and 1812. The figure was formerly handsomely gilt. On the west side is a tablet containing the Royal Arms previous to the introduction of the Hanoverian quarterings: on the east side is another tablet, and thereon, on a circular shield in the centre, the arms of the Earldom; above them, first, those of the Principality of Wales, the Earl's leading title; secondly, the coat of his Duchy of Cornwall, each having their proper coronets over them; beneath, are two dragons, as

supporters, (though not placed in the usual position as such,) each holding in his paw an ostrich feather, alluding to the plume borne as a crest by the King of Bohemia,‡ and taken by Edw. Prince of Wales, at the battle of Crecy, in 1346; the dragons evidently refer to those of ancient Briton, the cognizance of her Kings; the arrangement in this tablet, bears evident marks of science and intelligence, and was probably done by Randle Holme, the fourth and last of a name, that is, and ought to be, dear to the men of Cheshire; he was deputy to Norroy, King at Arms, and died in 1707. The arms of the Earldom were those of Randle Blundeville, the Earl, thus emblazoned:|| Azure, three garbs, or wheat sheafs, proper; but why the coat of this Earl was adopted, and not that of Hugh Lupus, the great and second Earl, continued, I do not find ascertained.§ William the Norman, gave the Earldom to his nephew, Hugh Lupus, to be held as freely by his sword, as he held by his crown; in consequence of this grant, the Earls were hereditary sword bearers of England, and the sword was borne on their official symbol; and the omission of it on this tablet, is its only defect.—The room fronting the south, is elegantly fitted up as the Assembly Room of the Corporation; it is 39 feet long, by 26½ wide, with an Orchestra in the centre on the north side.—Within the last year or two, the principal trades-people of the City, joined here monthly in the festive dance during the winter season; but the baneful influence of party spirit has banished those happy and harmless meetings. Over the fire-place on the west side, are the Armorial bearings of the City; and on the east side the Arms of Grosvenor. The centre of the building is occupied by the Common Hall of the City, a fine room, with oak wainscoating. Here the Court of Quarter Session¶ sits before the Mayor and Recorder,

Mr. § Llwyd.

* During contested Elections for Representatives, the Court of Hustings is erected here.

† See page 210.

‡ Mavor, noticing the Battle of Crecy, says—The King of Bohemia, wore in his cap three Ostrich feathers, with the motto ICH DIEN. The King, though blind by age, in order to stimulate his troops to acts of bravery, resolved to hazard his person. He accordingly ordered the reins of his horse to be tied on each side to the horses of two gentlemen of his train. He was, however, with his attendants found slain, with their horses standing near them, by Edward, who afterwards wore the plume, and the motto. The motto is [erroneously] considered by some as allusive to the King of Bohemia, being little better than a vassal under the French yoke; and by others, as allusive to the Prince, from the following passage:—"The Heir, as long as he is a Child, differeth nothing from a Servant, though he be Lord of all; but under Tutors and Governors, until the time appointed of the Father."—Gal. iv. ch. 1, 2, v.

|| The present Armorial Bearings are, Azure, a sword in pale between three garbs, or.---See exemplification, page 129.

¶ The Mayor of Chester has the peculiar privilege of respiting executions without previous application to the Crown: and the powers of the Court are as ample as those of any other judicial tribunal.

and here the Annual election of Civic Officers take place. This room has also been occupied as a banquetting room; and on more than one occasion, upwards of 400 persons have sat down in it to partake of the good things of the season. It contains on the east side portraits of Recorders Comberbach, and Leycester; on the north east angle Recorder Sir William Williams, and adjoining the last, those of Sir Henry Bunbury, M. P. for the City, and John Egerton, Esq. of Oulton: At the north west angle the portrait of Recorder Levinge; on the west side, portraits of Recorder Townshend, and Thomas Cholmondeley, Esq. Mayor, 1761. On the right and left of the Mayor's seat, are diminutive ornaments, composed of the Roman fasces, spears, &c. intended as supporters for the City Sword, and Mace.—These were introduced in 1817, in lieu of two large figures of a Lion and Wolf, tastefully allusive to the supporters of the City Arms.* In this instance the substitution has been no improvement: propriety and taste protest against it. The seats for the Barristers, Juries, &c. are very commodious. Communicating with the Common Hall is the Council Room, where the Mayor and Magistrates sit to hear and determine complaints, and other petty matters, every Monday, Wednesday, and Saturday.—Over the Mayor's seat, is a fine full length portrait of his Majesty George III. in his coronation robes, in a superb frame, the likeness by Gainsborough the drapery by Sir J. Reynolds, presented to the City by Earl Grosvenor, in 1808.—There are also full length portraits of Robert (present) Earl Grosvenor; Richard, the first Earl Grosvenor; and Thomas Grosvenor, Esq. M. P. for the City; the two last, painted by West in 1771, are in their robes as Mayors of Chester. The portrait of Robert Earl Grosvenor, in his Parliamentary robes, as a Peer of the Realm, is by Jackson: it is a strong likeness. On the south side of the room are the following Portraits of Benefactors to the poor Freemen of Chester:—

WM. OFFLEY, Sheriff in 1517.---By two wives he had 26 children. Robert Offley, the eldest son of the second wife, gave £500. to charitable uses in the city, with an exhibition yearly of 5l. towards the maintenance of a Scholar in the University, being the son of a Freeman; and 5l. towards the charge of taking the degree of M. A.---Hugh Offley, a younger son, Alderman of London, gave 200l. and an yearly rent of 5l. to charitable uses in the City. William Offley, another son, had 15 children by Anne, his wife, and left 300l. to charitable uses in the city.

SIR THOMAS WHITE, Lord Mayor of London, in 1554, left 100l. to be paid every 24 years to the City, to be lent 10 years gratis to poor freemen, particularly clothiers. The first 100l. was paid in 1585.

RICHARD HARRISON, brewer, late Sheriff, left his house, called the Star, &c. to be sold by his executors, and the produce to be given to maintain almsmen. Interest of the remainder of the money being paid quarterly to poor men till a convenient purchaser be found: 1606.

OWEN JONES, butcher, died in 1658. He left his lands and mortgages in Cheshire and Denbighshire, amounting to 46l. per ann. to the poor of the different companies, the Tanners being first; excepting 5l. to the Mayor and Sheriffs for the time being.

JOHN VERNON, a native of Chester, residing in London, left 800l. to purchase lands to be thus appropriated:—4l. each to 10 decayed freemen, 60 years old, and a gown every three years; for an annual sermon, 10s.; to the prisoners in the Northgate and Castle, 6s. 8d. each; for a banquet in the Pentice, 20s. and his will then to be read; the residue for pious and good uses. He also left 200l. to be employed in wool to set the poor at work; and he gave the city several pieces of plate, weighing 156 ounces.

JOHN LANCASTER, ironmonger, devised his lands in Shordley, Hope Owen, &c. after 14 years subsequent to his death, to the Mayor and Citizens, to pay unto 6 decayed Freemen yearly, 36l. at Michaelmas and Lady Day. -He died in 1676.

RICHARD BIRD, merchant, died at Seville, in Spain, 1681. He left 60l. to the City, for charitable uses, which was appropriated to the relief of six poor aged Citizens.

RICHARD SNEYD, cooper, by his will bearing date 1773, left 120l. the interest to be applied to the relief of an aged Citizen.

JOSPH CREWE, Alderman, by his will dated 19th April, 1799, left 120l to be applied to the relief of an aged Citizen; and by a Codicil dated 18th July, 1800, 600l. were left to the Mayor. &c. in trust, to pay 30l. per year amongst the six Chapel-yard Widows.

WILLIAM LEWIS, of Lyon House, Stamford Hill, Middlesex, on 1st February 1808, transferred to the Mayor, &c. 200l. 3 per cent. cons. to pay the dividends thereof on the 10th of February, annually, to the widow of a Freeman, having three Children under 12 years of age, and never having received parochial relief; but if such a widow cannot be found, then to be paid to any deserving widow of a Freeman, 66 years old or upwards, in straitened circumstances, and never having received relief, &c.

* Now in the possession of Sir John Cotgreave, Knt, of Netherlegh House—who has had them elegantly painted and gilt.

CHESTER

Adjoining the Council Room, on the east side, is the Town Clerk's Office, beneath which are offices for his Clerks. On the west side of the north end of the Exchange, on the street level, is the Record Room; the valuable documents contained in which are noticed in p. 193.

THE CITY GAOL AND HOUSE OF CORRECTION—nearly adjoin the Infirmary, on the south side.—The Northgate and the Eastgate, were formerly the City Prisons; but the latter, long since destroyed, had not been used as such for more than a century antecedent. The present gaol was built in 1808-9, and in that year, the Prisoners from the Northgate were removed here.—The Common Gaol fronts the west, the entrance to which is of white stone, of Doric architecture, supported by four columns. The House of Correction fronts the east; over the door-way of which, on a temporary platform erected for the purpose, execution is done on felons convicted in the county, as well as in the City.* An extensive brick boundary wall, coped with stone, surrounds both prisons. There are four yards to each prison, adjoining which are the cells and day rooms. In the centre of the building is a neat Chapel; and here the condemned receive their last religious solace, previous to mounting the Scaffold, a narrow passage from the Chapel, communicating directly with the Drop. The Gaols are under the immediate superintendance of the City Magistrates, by whom the respective Keepers are appointed. Neither of these Gaols are considered as particularly secure.

THE IRISH LINEN HALL—adjoins the City Gaol on the South. It is a large quadrangular building of brick, including a spacious area, and contains 36 double, and 24 single shops.—This Hall was built in 1778, by the Irish Merchants frequenting the Fairs, previous to which the chief Mart for Irish Linens, was in Northgate-street, in the building on the west side of the Cathedral, still called "The Old Linen Hall," but now occupied by various mechanics, and as dwelling-houses. Scarcely one-third of the Shops in the Irish Hall are now occupied, the Linen Trade having declined still more rapidly than it rose. Its commencement may be dated about 1736, when 449,654 yards were imported.† Mr. Pennant says the importation regularly increased till the last year of the then war, from which, till about 1778, it continued at par. The annual importation was about 1300 boxes and packs, including 300 boxes and packs imported into Liverpool, and sent from thence to Chester. The annual importation calculated in yards, was then at least a million each fair. In 1786, the trade had greatly increased; in that year 1684 packs, and 788 boxes were imported, exclusive of the linens imported at Liverpool, making a total of 5,500,000 yards!—Since then the trade has gradually declined: in 1796, 582 packs, and 808 boxes were imported; in 1806, only 327 packs, and 936 boxes. At present the number is very small indeed, considered as an exclusive trade.

HISTORY.

† Pennant.

THE INFIRMARY.—This excellent Institution, is pleasantly situated on the north-side of the City Gaol. It is a peculiarly neat building, of brick, remarkable for the good order and cleanliness of its interior. It is of a quadrangular form, erected in 1761, and is calculated to contain upwards of 100 beds, exclusive of every convenience for House Surgeon, Matron, and the necessary apartments for the Physicians and Surgeons; the Board Room, &c. There are cold, warm, and vapour baths, used not only by the patients, but by others, at a fixed rate of payment.‡ It is to be lamented, that owing to the inadequacy of the income of the Charity, the house never contains so great a number of patients as it is calculated to accommodate. In 1818, the annual subscriptions were £1229 19 0. The total amount of Stock £15,282 18 2, 3 per cent. Cons. is entered in the names of R. Barnston, Esq. Thos. Townshend, Esq. and W. M. Thackeray, M. D.; also, £1798 19 7. 3 per Cent. Cons.; and a further sum of £1279 18 0. 3 per cent. Reduced in the name of Roger Barnston, Esq. John Feilden, Esq. W. M. Thackeray, M. D. and J. S. Townshend, Esq. There was formerly an annuity of 10gs. a year arising from the proceeds of the Musical Fund of 1783; but this has ceased, and the principal divided amongst the different Charities.—£210. were appropriated to the Infirmary, which was

* See origin of this, page 211.

‡ The author is indebted to that benevolent character, Dr. Thackeray, for some interesting particulars, relative to this admirable establishment.

CHESTER

laid out in the 3 per cents. Reduced. There is also an additional sum of £6. per ann. for rent from the Blue Girls' School. These sums, with £60. per ann. paid by the County for Medical attendance on the Prisoners in the Castle; and £36. for the like purpose from the House of Industry, form the entire permanent income of the Infirmary. Other additions to the receipts, arise from casual donations, subscriptions of fever patients, charitable sermons, assemblies, apprentice fees, &c.

The following are the Physicians and Surgeons of the Hospital, with the dates of their appointment:—

PHYSICIANS.

1798.—Wm Makepeace Thackeray, M. D. Cambridge.
1807.—J. M. B. Pigot, M. D. Edinburgh.
1814.—Llewellyn Jones, M. D. Glasgow.
1814.—Charles Whittell, M. D. Glasgow.

SURGEONS.

1784.—Griffith Rowlands.
1801.—Samuel Nevitt Bennett.
1806.—Thomas Bagnall.
1809.—Owen Titley—Members of the Royal College of Surgeons, London.

MATRON.—Mrs Kennerley .... 1816.
HOUSE APOTHECARY.—Mr. Weaver .. 1818.

Subscribers of two guineas yearly, are Governors for the time being, having the privilege of recommending two in-patients, and an indefinite number of out-patients; a benefactor of twenty guineas has the same privilege for life; and larger sums entitle the donors to recommend a proportionate number of patients.

Statement of patients admitted during the year ending Lady Day, 1818:—

In-patients..................	650
Out-patients	1634
TOTAL	2284

In which period, the total expense of the establishment was £2338 12 10.

This Hospital was the first that introduced the establishment of distinct wards for fever cases,* which example has been followed by all the well-regulated Hospitals in the Kingdom. The northern attic story is exclusively appropriated to this purpose. This ward is open to all persons, without the necessity of applying for a recommendation, on a respectable person undertaking to pay one shilling per diem during their stay.—The House during the last year,† has had upwards of 90 patients weekly, and at present‡ contains 95. There are 101 beds for patients, 3 or 4 of which are always kept vacant for those who may meet with accidents.—It is with great propriety observed, by the humane gentleman we have before alluded to,‖ that "No place in England has been more exemplary than Chester, in the number and variety of its Charitable Institutions, and the zeal by which they have been supported—a zeal in which all ranks and parties have united."

HISTORY.

† 1818.

‡ Jan. 23, 1819.

‖ Dr. Thackeray.

An Infirmary was established here as early as April, 1755, and a part of the Charity School of the Blue Coat Hospital, was fitted up for the reception of Patients. From 1783 to 1784, the number of patients admitted was 1809—the next year, they were increased to 1521, making a difference in the two years of 712: out of these, the In-patients were 713, and many of this last class were very expensive from the nature of their complaint (typhus) and the slowness of their recovery. Experience has amply proved, that the preventive regulations, drawn up by Dr. Haygarth, were sufficient to preserve patients in the other wards, from contagion. The concerns of the Infirmary, are managed by a president, Vice President, Treasurer, and Auditors, with Committees of Subscribers. The Infirmary is certainly one of the best regulated of the many Charitable Institutions which do honor to the City.

THE BLUE COAT HOSPITAL§ is separated by the Canal from the Northgate, on the west side of the street. It was founded in 1700, at the suggestion of Dr. Stratford, then Bishop of Chester; but the greater part of the present building was completed in 1717, at the expense of the Corporation and the Benefactors.—In page 261, the ancient Hospital of St. John is noticed, on the site of which stands the present Building, which has a handsome appearance, with two projecting wings—

* At the suggestion of Dr. Haygarth, now of Bath.

§ See Vignette, page 150.

CHESTER.

the south wing forms the Chapel of St. John;* the north, the Room for the Consolidated Sunday and Working School, conducted by Mrs. Ann Richards; beneath which is the Board Room, and other offices.—The funds of this admirable Institution, at present support twenty-five boys, who remain two years, from twelve to fourteen years of age. They are dressed in blue, with caps and bands. There are also sixty-five day scholars, called the Green Caps, from their formerly wearing that distinctive colour.† They are instructed in the useful branches of learning applicable to trade and mercantile life, on a system combining the leading features of Bell and Lancaster, by Mr. S. Venables, the present active and intelligent Master. The funds arise from a variety of sources,‡ particularized in the Annual Report. The expenses of the Hospital in 1818, including the Master's Salary, &c. &c. were £643 1 1.

THE BLUE GIRLS' SCHOOL.—This Institution was established in Aug. 1718, at the Bishop's Palace, by Subscription, "For teaching Poor Girls to read and write, repeat and understand the Church Catechism, and to sew, knit, and spin;" at which time twenty poor girls were clothed and taught, but not fed. The following year, an addition of six was made to the School; but in Feb. 1778, a judicious order was made, "that the number of girls be reduced to fifteen, six of whom are to be taken into the House, at bed and board; the other nine to be day-scholars as before." In 1810, benefactions, forming a considerable fund, were raised, with which the present building was erected, in St. Martin's-in-the-Fields, at the east end of the Infirmary garden, on ground granted by the Trustees of the Infirmary, for ninety years, at £6. per ann. The day-scholars were then struck off, and twelve boarders were admitted, since increased to fourteen. In Feb. 1815, five girls were admitted as day-scholars, from whom the selection is made to fill up vacancies caused by those on the permanent establishment going out—they must be eleven years of age. On leaving school, each girl is presented with two guineas, and if she remains in her first service one year, an additional guinea is given to her.‖ The expenses of the Institution for the year, were—£254 2 6. Miss Elizabeth Parry is the present Mistress.

HISTORY.

THE KING'S, OR FREE GRAMMAR SCHOOL, was founded by King Henry VIII. for twenty-four boys, to be apointed by the Dean and Chapter. It occupies the fine room formerly the Refectory of the Monastery of Chester, above the north side of the Cloisters of the Cathedral. No boys are admitted under 9 years of age. They continue four years, generally, although occasionally, a year of grace has been obtained from the Dean. Previous to 1814, an Under Master was allowed, in conformity with the statutes of the Royal Founder; in that year, however, a regulation was made, by which, with an increase of salary, the head-master undertook the sole management and instruction of the scholars; but the number of extra, or private, pupils, was limitted to six. The Rev. James Ireland, A. M. Rector of Thurstaston, and Minor Canon of the Cathedral, is the present Master. The boys belonging to this establishment, receive each, annually, £3 4 0.§—The acquirements of the scholars now, are very different to what they were. The school once obtained a distinction of considerable classical merit. Plays were occasionally performed by the boys, which were arranged under the superintendance of Mr. Falconer, the learned Editor of Strabo. A Collection of Greek, Latin, and English exercises, was printed in Chester, under the title of *Prolusiones Poeticæ*, which were written by the Scholars, and by the Rev. Thomas Bancroft, A. M. the then Master. But age, it is pretty clear, does not improve these well-intentioned establishments.

* The Bridge which formerly opened a communication between this Chapel and the Old Northgate Gaol, taken down in 1809, is still in existence. Across this bridge the prisoners passed to attend Divine Service.

† Some years ago, they formed a distinct school, but are now taught in the Blue School, and considered probationers for that Establishment.

‡ Amongst them, a rent charge of 25l. per ann. on the Roodeye, from the Corporation, commencing May 1, 1767, in consideration of 500l. then paid. The Corporation also allows 21l. per annum towards the repairs of the Building.

‖ The Girls are wholly instructed in reading, writing, sewing, knitting, and other domestic affairs, requisite to make them notable and frugal wives, and mothers.

§ An additional sum of £2 6s. is given to the singing boys.

Chester History.

THE BENEVOLENT INSTITUTION—suggested by Mr. Rowlands, surgeon, in 1798, and aided by the Donations of the Ladies of Chester and its neighbourhood, is for the Delivery of Poor Married Lying-in Women at their own Habitations. At present all the Surgeons in the City give their gratuitous attendance, but previous to 1812, Mr. Rowlands was the sole superintending accoucheur.—Annual subscribers of half-a-guinea have the privilege of recommending a poor woman to the benefit of the Charity: and during the Patient's confinement, she is supported with all the necessary linen, sheets, &c. with two pounds of sugar, a quarter of a pound of tea, and a pound of soap. In cases of extreme poverty, baby linen is also found.—Children are expected to be vaccinated within a month after their birth. The number of poor women delivered in the year 1818, was 268, and the total annual expense of the Institution for 1817, was 163*l.* 11*s.* 2*d.*

THE DIOCESAN SCHOOL—originated in Jan. 1812, under the immediate patronage of the Bishop of Chester, Dr. Law.----These institutions are general throughout England; and the main object of them is, the education of youth in the pure principles of our venerable Church, according to Dr. Bell's, or the Madras, system. All these schools are in unison with the Central National School, in London, and in them, Masters are instructed and perfected in the mode of Education.—In 1816, the School-room, in George's-street, on the south-side immediately adjoining Upper Northgate-street, was opened for the reception of the Scholars.—It is eighty feet long, by thirty-three wide; and has convenient accommodations for 400 children. A house is built for the Master,* adjoining the School.—This institution is the great central one for the Diocese, over the entire extent of which sub-committees and corresponding members have been appointed; the whole is under the direction and superintendance of the Bishop, and the Committee at Chester. The Secretary of the Institution is the Rev. T. Armitstead.

* Mr. Richards.

EARL GROSVENOR'S FREE SCHOOL.—This excellent Foundation, so creditable to the benevolence of the Noble Earl, is situated on the north side of the Church of St. John. It is a handsome building of brick, the front ornamented with tablets of stone, and the cost of it exceeded £3000. It is calculated for the reception of 400 boys, who are instructed in writing and arithmetic, without particular limitation as to the period of enjoying the benefits of the Institution: they are gratuitously furnished also with paper, pens, ink, and every other necessary et cetera. The Master is Mr. F. Hamilton; and the system of education, is in a great measure, that recommended by Dr. Bell. The number of boys on the books, in Jan. 1819, was 260; the number educated since the establishment of the School is nearly 1000. The children admitted to this school are recommended by the Committee, which has the sole management of it:—

COUNTESS GROSVENOR'S SCHOOL—occupies the upper room of this foundation; and is calculated likewise for the accommodation of 400 girls, who are instructed in all the useful branches of learning, and domestic acquirements. The Mistress is Miss Holford; and the number of girls on the books in Jan. 1819, was 150. "Thus (observes the STRANGER IN CHESTER) by the munificence of two individuals, are nearly 500 children instructed in the necessary branches of education, and trained up in that religion, which the wisdom of our ancestors thought fit to incorporate with the constitutional economy of the country. It is perhaps superfluous here to offer the tribute of our praise; and in the name of HUNDREDS who may eventually become ornaments to their country, give the thanks, which gratitude demands."

The children in each school are treated with an excellent dinner, annually, in the school-rooms; the girls are dressed uniformly, in new frocks, presented to them for the occasion.

THE DEE MILLS—Although the property of an individual, nevertheless partake in some degree of public interest, and are therefore introduced under this head. The exact period of the first erection of Mills in this situation, closely adjoining the Bridge-gate, remains in obscurity; but there is no doubt they were built at a very early period. John Scott, the last Palatine Earl, of the original stock, granted the Mill to the Abbey of

CHESTER

St. Werburgh, from the receipts of which many public works were carried on appertaining immediately to the dignity of the Earldom. After the Battle of Poictiers, they were given to Sir Howell-y-Fwyall, in reward for the signal bravery he displayed in that glorious combat. When this grant was made, the inhabitants were restrained from grinding corn at any other place. In the 6th of Edw. VI. Sir Richard Cotton, obtained a grant of the Mills from the Crown, in fee, by Knight's service; this was in exchange for the manors of Bourne and Moreton, in Lincolnshire.—George Cotton, son of Sir Richard, granted the Mills in fee-farm to Edmund Gamul, at the rent of £100, who, it is said expended
* Ormerod. qy. 400l ? £4000,* in repairing the Causeway. In the 17th century, there was much discussion as to the utility of the causeway; it was said to be injurious to the lands above, and to the river below, by preventing the floods from scouring the bed, and thereby permitting the accumulation of sand.—In 1646, the Parliament ordered, that the Mills and Causeway should be destroyed, being a great annoyance and obstruction to trade—the work to be completed within three months from the date of the order. It was also ordered, that within a year, new courses should be erected on the Roodeye, or some other Corporation land; but nothing was done. In 1652, it was again proposed to pull down the Mills and Causeway, in order to make an harbour.† On the alienation of the Gamul property, a considerable share of the Mills became the property of Mr. Edw. Wrench, and the whole is now possessed by E. O. Wrench, Esq.
‡ 2084.157. In some pleadings in the Harl. MSS.‡ relative to the Causeway, it is said, that "The River of Dee was drawne unto the said cittie with great charge by the Earle (Lupus) or some of his predecessors before the Conqueste, from the aunciente course which it held before, a mile or two distant from the cittie, and a passage for it cutt out of a rocke under the walles of the
‖ See p. 81. saide cittie.‖ The saide Earle allso built the Corne Mills of Chester, and erected the causey, and granted threescore fisheries above the said weir to several of his dependents, commonly called *stalls in Dee*, reserving to himself the *Earle's Poole*, next to the Causey; and granted to the Abbot the tythes of the saide Mills and fishings, which the Deane and Chapter have since enjoyed. Henry III. resuming the Earldom, the Mills were retained in the Crowne to 6th Edward VI. A steward of the Mills had vj*d*. a day.—The Justice of Chester held Courts yearly, for their better regulation."

HISTORY.

THE THEATRE—is noticed in page 230. It was built upon the ruins of the Chapel of St. Nicholas, and the Town Hall, in 1772-3. A patent was obtained for it on the 16th May, 1777, then held by J. Townshend, Esq. but now by his son, J. S. Townshend, Esq. It is, on the whole, a miserable structure.

THE ENGINE HOUSE.—This is a neat building, opposite the east side of the Exchange. It was erected about the year 1680, by the Duke of Ormond, when Lord Lieutenant of Ireland, but why this mark of respect to the City was manifested, remains a secret.—It is built of brick with stone facings, ornamented with fluted Corinthian pilasters. An iron railing was placed round it in 1812, and the brick work coated with Roman cement.—The Fire Engines are kept here; and the City weights, measures, &c.

THE COMMERCIAL BUILDING.—This is a neat pile, of the Iönic order, after a design by Mr. Harrison, the County Architect. It is situated on the west side of Northgate-street, next to St. Peter's Church. On a line with the street, are two excellent shops, above which, is the News Room, 45 feet long, and 26 feet wide. At each end of the room is a fire place. Here are taken, different London and Provincial Journals, Reviews, Magazines, &c. There are one hundred proprietary shares in this Institution, and annual subscribers are admitted. The rules are certainly dictated in a spirit of genuine liberality: The Earl Grosvenor, and the Mayor, are Honorary Members, and are privileged to introduce as many strangers as they please. The Representatives for City and County, the General Officer of the District, and his Staff, have also the liberty of the Room. On the same floor, are the Committee Room, the Keeper's apartments, and the Room for the reception of the files of the newspapers.—The room above, is occupied by the City Library.

† 1248, the Mills were leased by the King for 12 years at the great rent of 200l. per ann. equal to 5000l. of our present money.

UNION HALL—was built in 1809, for the convenience of Manchester, Birmingham, Sheffield, and other Manufacturers, attending the two great Fairs.—It is situated on the south side of Foregate-street, on the site of the public house, called the Eagle & Child, and other old buildings, pulled down for the purpose.* It contains sixty single, and ten double shops, exclusive of the Upper Story, occupied chiefly by Yorkshire Clothiers. The Hall is galleried completely round.

THE COMMERCIAL HALL—was first opened at the July Fair of 1815. It is situated nearly opposite the Union Hall, in Foregate street, having an entrance for Carts, &c. from Frodsham-street. It contains 56 single, and 20 double shops, and the model of the Union Hall has been adopted in the erection of this. This hall had an entirely speculative origin—which has proved profitable—and was reared from its foundation in five weeks.

THE GRAND STAND.—The Race Course was ornamented with this very neat building in 1816, built by subscription, in shares of £50. each. It is admirably calculated for the purpose; although there is less necessity for such a building on Chester Race Ground, than on any other in the Kingdom, the City Walls commanding a view of the entire circuit.—A view of it is given in the Vignette, page 63.†

THE CUSTOM HOUSE—is a mean brick building, adjoining the Church of the Holy Trinity, on the west side.—It is extremely probable, it was not originally built for this purpose; it is large enough, however, for the trifling trade of the port. In front of the edifice, is a sun-dial, with the inscription—"Cito pede præterit Ætas." Over the principal entrance, is the Coat of Earl Randle III. without the sword. The annexed table will afford a comparative view of the trade of Chester for the last forty-three years:—

PORT OF CHESTER.—DUTIES FROM 1776, TO 1817.

TRADE OF CHESTER.	1776	1786	1796	1806	1817
Coasting Vessels entered inwards	208	241	206	149	316
Ditto ditto outwards	619	454	402	350	512
Inland inwards	146	48	82	195	180
Ditto outwards	104	103	61	329	364
America inwards	2	......	......	......	3
—— outwards	5	2	......	......	1
Isle of Man, & other Foreign parts, outwards	3	13	1	9	14
Ditto inwards	4	28	15	1	15
EXPORTED TO FOREIGN PARTS:					
Chaldrons of Coals	2877	2716	272	16519	14,039
Tons of Lead	1184	1410	16	11	Nil.
—— Ore	168	245	......	......	Nil
—— Bark	18	370	695	16	30
EXPORTED COASTWAYS:					
Tons of Lead	2813	1058	1163	2200	3167
—— Ore	431	309	376	490	313
Number of Ships in Foreign trade	22	8	6	13	17
—— Coasting trade	13	26	17	14	29
Total Amount Murage Duties	£159 9 8	293 0 0	122 0 13	61 4 0	‡ 0 13 6

* Views of these curious specimens of ancient domestic architecture, are preserved in Cuitt's Etchings. Panoramic sketches of the different streets, as now existing, are publishing in Parts, by Mr. Batenham.

† The roof was put on in December, 1816. On laying the first stone, a Masonic Procession was projected; but on due consideration of the subject, the attendance of the "Craft," did not take place.—The white stone used in the building, was cut from the quarry belonging to Mr. Gunnery, at Kelsall.

‡ In 40 years, it will be seen, that the Murage Duties, appropriated to the purpose of repairing the City Walls, have experienced a reduction of £158 16 2!

CHESTER

THE MANCHESTER HALL—is situated opposite to the Royal Hotel, in Eastgate-street, but not one half of it is now occupied, altho' within the last twelve years every shop had its regular tenant. As its name implies, it was chiefly intended for the reception of Manchester Manufactures.

THE CITY LIBRARY—is placed, as before noticed, in the Upper Room of the Commercial Building. It was first suggested by the late Mr. Peter Broster, when Mayor in 1791.—The collection is extensive and valuable; but the limitation of its rules, operated almost as an entire exclusion to tradesmen. A similar institution was commenced, on more liberal principles, in March, 1817, and is called—

THE CHESTER GENERAL PUBLIC LIBRARY.—It may not be deemed irrelevant to give a few particulars relative to the origin of this establishment.—It was first suggested by a respectable Schoolmaster,* to the Editor of this work, who immediately acted on the hint. He obtained, in the first instance, about twenty respectable names, when Mr. Fletcher, the Proprietor of the Chester Chronicle,—whose promptitude and liberality in promoting every object calculated for public utility, is well known—requested his name to be added to the list, accompanying it with a handsome donation of Twenty Guineas—and many valuable sets of books, including the *Edinburgh Encyclopædia:* Ten Guineas were also given by Mr. Feilden, of Mollington Hall. The example was quickly followed by Capt. Henderson, Dr. Whittell, and several other gentlemen, and in a few days, the subscription list received upwards of One Hundred signatures. The Library was opened for the circulation of Books† on the 21st of April, 1817, in the Philosophical Society's Room, Bolland's Court; but the patronage of Mr. Fletcher did not terminate here: An elegant room was built by him purposely for the reception of the Library, in Bridge-street, and on the 13th of September, in the same year, the books were issued from it.‡ The Library is governed by a Committee of fourteen Subscribers, and a Chairman (Mr. Fletcher); and all the subscribers have the privilege of introducing a friend, by a temporary transfer of their Tickets.||

*Mr. Venables.

HISTORY.

HOUSE OF INDUSTRY—was built by the Corporation, in 1757, on a dry bank, close to the River, on the North West side of the Roodeye.—The establishment is under the direction of the Mayor, Recorder, Aldermen, (Justices of the Peace) and 74 Guardians, who are elected by the nine Parishes of the City, in conformity to the Act passed in 1762.§—The sick are attended by the Medical Gentlemen of the Infirmary.—The expense of maintaining the in and out-poor of the nine Parishes within the liberties of the city, (exclusive of those of the Cathedral Precincts, and the extra-parochial limits of Little St. John, and the Spital) for the year terminating 27th April, 1818, was £9,615 19 0¼.

OWEN JONES'S CHARITY.—This bequest is noticed in page 268.—A lead mine was discovered on the estate in 1756, the produce of which in 21 years amounted to 12,606*l.* the greater portion of which was laid out at interest, so that the annual income is now above 400l.—Some difficulty occurring to the Trustees (the Mayor and the Sheriffs) in the appropriation of the funds, in consequence of their great increase, application was made to the Lord Chancellor, for his opinion. An order was therefore made by his Lordship, directing the mode of dividing the arrears among the Poor of the different Companies, and ordering that the future "annual income of the Charity Funds, after allowing to the Trustees the legacies given by the will, and reasonable expenses of management of trusts,—and allowing such sum or sums of money, not exceed-

† Confined to the City of Chester, and a circle of nine miles beyond it.

‡ An order appears in the Book of the Institution, to this effect:—"Dec. 22d, 1817.- Ordered, That it be proposed at the next General Meeting to open a Subscription for the purpose of procuring a Portrait of Mr. John Fletcher." This must have been forgotten by those who proposed it, or it would surely ere this have been carried into effect.--Mr. Telford, the celebrated Engineer, is amongst the Donors to this Library.

|| The Motto on the Subscriber's Ticket (the plate presented by Capt. Henderson) is---"STUDIA ET MORES."

§ This Act vests the Poor House in the Guardians for 99 years, from the 1st May 1762, at £90. per ann. allowing them, however, the privilege of terminating the engagement after the first 7 years, on giving eight months' notice.

ing in any one year 20l. which the Trustees may think proper to advance, for and towards enabling Poor Brothers to bear and draw with their respective companies, shall be distributed among the Poor Brothers of the several Companies, in rotation, pointed out by the Testator's will, and in such sums and proportions as the Trustees shall think proper, according to their several necessities, and *having regard to the circumstances of each poor brother and his family*; but that no Poor Brother shall receive more than 40l. in any one year. And when there is not in the Company first in rotation, any Poor Brother, to exhaust the said annual income, when distributed according to the regulations above specified, that then the Poor Brothers in the Company succeeding next in rotation, one after another, shall be relieved in the like manner, so as to exhaust the said income; and that the income of the following year shall begin where it ended in the year preceding; and when the distribution has gone thro' all the Companies, it shall begin again with the first company," &c. &c. The Decree then orders, "that an account of the application and distribution of the said Charity Funds, shall be kept in a book at the Town Office, where any Member of any of the Companies shall, for one month after notice in one of the Chester papers, have the inspection of the said book; and that within one month after the distribution of the Charity, an advertisement shall be inserted in one, or both of the Chester Newspapers, that the Charity had been distributed, and specify the account of the monies distributed, and number, but not the names, of objects thereby relieved."—The clear income distributed in 1818, among eleven poor brothers, Tailors, and seven poor brothers, Masons, was £400.

Alms Houses.

There are four in Little St. John-street, built by Mrs. D. Salmon, in 1738, but they have no endowment.*

* See p.253.

On the south side of Common Hall-street,† in the parish of St. Bridget, there are Alms Houses for six freemen's widows, to whom the Corporation pay annually £1. 6s. 8d.—These houses form an ancient building, formerly called the Hospital of St. Ursula, founded in 1532, by the Executors of Roger Smith, for six poor decayed persons, who had been Aldermen and Common Council Men, or their Widows, and in default of any such, for other poor persons.—The Guild of St. Ursula, in 1540, gave 30d. a year to the Hospital.

The Alms Houses in St. Martin's-in-the-Fields are noticed in page 240.

In Pepper-street are Alms Houses, founded by Wm. Jones, Esq. of the Middle Temple, London.‡ He left by will, dated July 13, 1658, lands, &c. in the parish of St. Michael, and a Croft in Claverton, to which some lands in Holt, were afterwards added, "for four poor men, and six poor women, above 55 years of age, unmarried, decayed, and impotent persons, such as frequent the public worship of the Lord's Day, and Holy Days, and are not guilty of any gross sin."—In cases of vacancy, the Poor of St. Michael's parish are always to be preferred, unless there should be two of that parish already occupants.—The Revenue now is about

† This has generally been known as Common Hall Lane; but in 1818, all the houses in the City were numbered; and all LANES, were then called STREETS—thus we have Sty-street, Skinner's-street, &c.

‡ Repaired and newly fronted in 1817.

Dissenting Places of Worship.

THE ROMAN CATHOLICS—have an elegant little Chapel on the West side of Queen-street, nearly adjoining Union-walk.—It is built of brick, with an entrance under a Doric portico; the front ornamented with tablets in stone.—This Chapel was opened in the year 1799, with the solemn services customary on such an interesting occasion.—The interior is neatly painted, and elegant pillars, colored to imitate marble, support the springs of the windows.—The altar is beautifully decorated, and over the Cross, in the recess, is an admirable painting of the Crucifixion,—The Congregation at present is not large, but it is respectable, and has considerably increased.—Previous to the erection of this Chapel, the followers of the Roman ritual, assembled for divine worship in a house in a passage in Foregate-street, about 60 yards East of Queen-street, the site of which is now occupied as a Coach Manufactory. The first Priest of the new Chapel, was the Rev. T. Penswick, since appointed Minister of the New Chapel in Seel-street, Liverpool. He was succeeded by the Rev. John Ashhurst; and the Rev. Mr. Briggs, is the present Priest.

THE WESLEYAN METHODISTS—are a very numerous and respectable body; within the last few years, they have had a great increase to the connexion. —So early as 1750, their religious labors commenced in this city, when Mr. J. Bennett, of Bolton, was, on the invitation of a Mr. G. Shaw, induced to become the pastor of the few Methodists then settled here.—Mr. G. Cotton, of Huntington Hall, it would seem, became their patron, and permitted them to preach in his house, where, in a short time, a larger congregation assembled than the House could contain; in consequence of which, they were obliged to preach in the open fields, on the River Bank. The Connexion, about this time, established itself in the house of one Robert Jones, a Pipe-maker, in Love-lane; and in the next year (1751) a barn at Martin's Ash was fitted up as a Chapel. The prejudice—not to give it a harsher term—of the day, soon manifested itself in an unequivocal manner: the Chapel was violently broken open, and nearly destroyed; and it was with great labour and exertion, that the Congregation succeeded in repairing the damage sustained. But the freedom of Divine Worship had not then the protection of legislative enactments. In the last-mentioned year, the Rev. John Wesley, the great founder of Methodism, first preached in this city. —In 1763, Chester became, for the first time, the head of a District, and regular Preachers were sent down by Conference.—The following year, a piece of land was purchased on the north side of Foregate-street, near the Bars, and here the first Chapel, properly so called, was built,—denominated *The Octagon*. It was calculated to accommodate 600 or 700 persons; and the following were the Trustees of the Building: Thomas Bennett, George Lowe, Richard Bruce, (of Acton, Northwich) Joseph Brown, (of Tarporley) Joseph Woolrich, (of Duckington) John Gardner, (of Tattenhall-lanes) and Richard Barker, (of Acton Bridge.)—A room in Common Hall-lane was also occasionally used as a Chapel at this period.—In 1782, the Methodist Sunday School was established.—In 1810, the congregation had so much increased, that the Octagon Chapel could not accommodate it; and this, coupled with the ruinous state of the building, first suggested the propriety of building a new Chapel, in a more convenient situation. Accordingly, the matter was taken into consideration at a meeting of the Principals of the Connexion, and subsequently the present Chapel, situated on the West side of St. John's-street, was built, at the cost of nearly 5,000l. 1500l. of which were raised by the Connexion in Chester, and other well wishers—and a great portion was raised on the income of the seat revenue. It was vested in Trustees, viz. Messrs. Geo. Lowe, Henry Bowers, George Walker, Thomas Shone, Robert Shearing, Joseph Betteley, Thomas Jones, Samuel Williams, Samuel Beckett, Robert Parry, John Jones, John Reece, John Hitchens, and James Hall.—The Chapel is a large handsome building, with a circular front, and three entrances, one in front, and two behind, communicating with which is a flight of steps from the City Walls. In a recess behind the pulpit is a gallery for the singers, and there are galleries

on the East, North, and South sides.—The body of the Chapel is free.*

THE KILHAMITE METHODISTS, a branch of the parent stock, have a Chapel in Trinity-street, erected in 1794, the dimensions within the walls being 36 feet by 57 feet. It is a neat structure, but much inferior to the before-mentioned Chapel, both in size and dimensions. The founders of this Chapel, originally frequented the Octagon, and were in fact, part of the Methodist Connexion there. The separation originated in some disputes concerning discipline, and in 1793, they quitted the Old Connexion, and held their meetings in Common Hall-lane Chapel, till their own was built. Their Constitution is entirely independent of the Methodists of the Old Connexion, they have their own code of Rules, their own Preachers, and their own Conference.—The present Trustees of the Chapel are Messrs. Orme, Lowe, Perry, Garner, Shone, Davies, Ingram, Allcock, Owens, Dakin, Dunning, and Bradford.

THE CALVINISTS—are a respectable, and rather numerous sect, in Chester.—Their principal Chapel is on the West side of Queen-street, beyond the Chapel of the Roman Catholics; a house for the Minister adjoins it.—The frequenters of this Chapel, are called THE INDEPENDENTS, and they are what the Presbyterians were. The Chapel was erected in 1777; it is a handsome brick building, has two entrances, an iron palisading, in front, and a burial ground attached to it. The interior is neatly fitted up, with a large commodious gallery, on the east, north, and south sides.—There was formerly a small organ in this Chapel, but it was removed on the erection of the gallery, in 1811-12. The founders of this Chapel, originally belonged to the congregation of the present Unitarian Chapel, in Crook's-lane, under the excellent Matthew Henry, from which they separated, and assembled for some time in a Court, on the south side of Common Hall-street, and afterwards in the Room on the opposite side of the street, now occupied by Mr. Wilcoxon's society.

THE BAPTISTS, in 1806, erected a small, but neat Chapel, in a yard, on the east side of Crook's-street.† The Congregation is but small. Previous to the erection of this Chapel, they occupied the room in Common Hall-street, noticed under the head Calvinists. The Rev. Mr. Inglis, is the present Minister. A dispute arising in 1810, a few of the Society separated, and now assemble with their Minister, Mr. Sim, in a large Room, in the OLD BOARDING SCHOOL YARD, Lower Bridge-street.

THE OCTAGON CHAPEL, is now the property of the sect patronized by the late pious Countess of Huntington, and closely in connexion with the followers of the late Rev. P. Oliver, a Clergyman of the Establishment. Mr. Oliver became a pious convert to the peculiar opinions of Mr. Whitfield, and appropriated some outbuildings, near his house, in Great Boughton, into a Chapel.‡ It was soon crowded with a congregation, led either by novelty or inclination, and speedily became totally inadequate to the accommodation of its frequenters. Mr. Oliver's services to his congregation were entirely gratuitous; and he possessed the leading qualifications of a good preacher: his language was nervous and persuasive; and he practically illustrated his principles by a life void of offence.—On his death, which occured July 10, 1800, aged 37,‖ he bequeathed the Chapel, with his house and garden, adjoining, to his Congregation for a term of years; but when the Wesleyan Methodists entered on their new Chapel in St. John-street, they sold their interest in it,§ and pur-

* The opening of this Chapel was graced by the nervous eloquence of Messrs. Bradburn, and Gaultier, (natives of Chester)—two men, whose oratorical powers, and mental endowments, ranked them high among the followers of the venerable Wesley. Mr. Bradburn died at London, in 1816.

† There is now a thoroughfare thro' this yard, communicating with Watergate-street, and Northgate-street, which has proved a great public accommodation.

‡ On Sunday Nov. 10, 1793, Mr. Oliver preached his first sermon in Boughton Chapel—"Unless the Lord build the house, they labour in vain who build it."—PSALM CXXVII. 1.

‖ Mr. Oliver preached his last sermon on Sunday, May 25, 1800. "Let thy hand be upon the Man of thy right hand, upon the Son of Man, whom thou madest strong for thyself."—PSALM LXXX, 17.—His remains were interred in St. John's Church-yard, followed by an immense number of people.

§ It has since been used as a Sunday School, by the Independents and Sermons are occasionally preached in it.

CHESTER — HISTORY.

chased the OCTAGON, which they newly roofed, and beautified.---The Rev. Mr. Bridgeman, and the Rev. Mr. Williams, are the present Ministers.---A small Calvinistic Society meets in the before-mentioned ROOM, in COMMON-HALL-STREET, of which Mr. Jonathan Wilcoxon, chandler, is the Minister.*

THE WELSH CALVINISTIC METHODISTS' place of Meeting, was in a room in Shoemaker's-row, Northgate-street. The situation being extremely unpleasant, they built a new Chapel in 1804, in Trinity-street, immediately adjoining to the Methodist Chapel there, on the north side. The congregation is not very large. Mr. John Parry and other Ministers from the Principality occasionally preach in it. It is scarcely necessary to observe, that the services are performed in the ancient language of Britain.

THE SOCIETY OF FRIENDS—have a Meeting House, on the east side of Frodsham-street, with a burial ground in front, planted round with poplars — It is a plain brick building, erected in 1702. The actual Members of the Society, in Chester, scarcely exceed a dozen.

THE UNITARIANS.—Their Chapel is situated between Crook's-street, and Trinity-street. It was originally built in 1700, by a large Society, formed here in 1687, by the celebrated Matthew Henry. It is of brick, with three gables in front, and has a burial ground attached. About eighteen years previous to its erection, there were three Dissenting Congregations in Chester, formed by Mr. Cook,† Mr. Hall, and Mr. Harvey--Ministers who were expelled the Established Church for non-conformity.—On their death, Mr. Henry succeeded in collecting together their congregations, and opened a Meeting-house in Whitefriers-lane. It was by them the Chapel in Crook's-street was built, which was the only Dissenting Place of Worship in Chester. Mr. Henry removed from Chester to Hackney, in 1713, and the following year died of an apoplexy at Nantwich, on a visit to his friends, in the 52d year of his age.‡—Mr. Henry was succeeded by Mr. John Gardner, and he was the first Minister that manifested a variation from the religious principles of Mr. Henry. Mr. J. Chidlaw succeeded Mr. Gardner, in 1765—he professed himself an Unitarian; and it appears the greater part of the Congregation adopted the sentiments of their pastor, for their avowed faith is that held by Dr. Priestly, Mr. Belsham, &c. &c. Mr. Chidlaw was followed in the Ministry by Mr. Thomas, Mr. James Lyon, Mr. J. Parry, Mr. Theo. Brown, and Mr. J. Bakewell, who is still the officiating Minister. The congregation is very respectable. Attached to the Chapel, are eight Alms Houses, liberally endowed for poor widows.—There are funds also for the education of Young Men for the Ministry,—for the instruction of poor children, and other charities.

* Mr. Wilcoxon, was in connexion with, and originally officiated as Minister to, the Congregation of Mr. Oliver's Chapel; but a schism breaking out amongst them, a rupture took place, and "those who loved him followed him" to Common-hall-street.

† Mr. Cooke, was ejected from St. Michael's Chester; Mr. Hall, from Mere, in Staffordshire.—During the reign of intolerance, Mr. Cooke retired to Puddington; and Mr. Hall, was imprisoned six months in Chester Jail, under the Five Mile Act. They both died the same year—1684. Mr. Harvey had been ejected from Wallasey, in Wirral, and had a congregation in a room in Bridge-street; he died in Nov. 1699, and was buried in the Cathedral.---*From Register Book of the Chapel.*

‡ He was buried in the Church of the Holy Trinity,---see p. 240. In the Register Book of the Chapel, there is the following curious notice of the arbitary policy of the bigotted James II. as connected with the City Charter:—"The Charter (says Mr. Henry) had been surrendered about 1684, and a new Charter granted, by which a power was reserved to the Crown, to put out Magistrates and put in at pleasure. This precarious Charter was joyfully accepted by those that were for surrendering the old one, that Alderman Mainwaring and some other Aldermen of the same honest principles, might be turned out, and none but those of their own kidney taken in. By this Charter, Sir Thomas Grosvenor was the first Mayor, Alderman Wilson, the second, Alderman Oulton, the third, and Alderman Starkey, the fourth. In the latter end of his time, about 1688, one Mr. Trinder came to Chester, for the new modelling of the Corporation, according to the power reserved to the Crown by the new Charter. He applied himself to me, told me the King thought the GOVERNMENT OF THE CITY NEEDED REFORMATION, and if I would say who should be put out, and who put in their places, it should be done. I told him, I begged his pardon, that was none of my business, nor would I in the least intermeddle in any thing of that nature. However, he got instructions from others, the new charter was cancelled, and another sent, of the same import, only altering the persons, and by it, all the dissenters of note in the city were brought into the government; the seniors to be Aldermen, and the juniors to be Common Council-men, and Sir Thos.

THE HORN
Of the Foresters of Wirral, in the possession of Sir Thomas Stanley Massey Stanley, Bart. of Hooton.

City Walls, and Gates.

THE City of Chester is peculiar in its fortifications, being still surrounded by a perfect wall of one mile, three quarters, and one hundred and twenty-one yards in extent,* forming a delightful promenade, and commanding the most interesting and luxuriant views.—Of their Roman origin there can be no doubt; indeed, specimens of their architecture still remain in their present site, viz. the Shipgate, about eighty yards west from the Bridge Gate, and an arch within the Walls, about fifty yards north of the Eastgate, on premises belonging to Mr. Charles Dutton, this latter, probably, formed a kind of postern to the Old Eastgate, as the style of building is precisely that shown in the different drawings of it.—The *Shipgate*, or *Hole in the Wall*, was, it is said, the only mode of egress from the city by the ferry to the opposite field.†

The Walls are entirely built of the red sand-stone of the City, and are at present very much out of repair.—It is to be apprehended they will soon fall into a state of ruin, unless something be done to preserve them.—The *Murage Duties*,‡ which were formerly sufficient for their repairs, have totally failed, and there is scarcely a single shilling of revenue, that can be appropriated to their service. It has been suggested—and it is the only method likely to preserve this delightful promenade from total dilapidation—that a New Local Act should be obtained, in which a clause might be intro-

Stanley, Mayor. This Charter was brought down, and the persons called together to have notice of it, and to have the time fixed for their being sworn, but they, like true Englishmen, unanimously refused it, and desired that the ancient charter might be restored, though they knew that none of them would come into power by that, but that many that were their bitter enemies would be restored by it. This I take to be a memorable instance both of the modesty of the Dissenters, and a proof how far they are from an affectation of power; the top of their ambition being to live quiet and peaceable lives, in the exercise of their religion according to their consciences; as also of their inviolable fidelity to the rights and liberties of their country."

* So say the Tablets on the Walls, the accuracy of which there is good reason to doubt.

† See vignette, and description, page 14.

‡ An account of the comparative state of the Trade of Chester, and the produce of the Murage Duties, will be found in page 274.

CHESTER

duced, imposing a slight levy for their use: a levy to which, we are persuaded, every Citizen of Chester, would gladly contribute his quota.

The height and width of the Walls, materially vary: the general average of the width is five feet, protected on the outside by a parapet from three to four feet high, and on the inside by a wood railing.—The height of the rampart varies from 12 feet to 40 feet.—Numerous encroachments have been made upon the walls at different periods, and on the north, east, and south sides, houses have been built closely adjoining them.

As the general ascent to the Walls is from the Eastgate, we will commence the description from that part.

THE EASTGATE—forms the principal entrance to the City on the English side.—The original gate was no doubt of Roman origin;* for in taking down the old gate, in 1767, the peculiar architecture of that people was discovered in two wide circular arches, formed of very large stones, inclosed within its workmanship. The late gate, it would seem from the four shields of arms, ornamenting its front, was erected temp. Edw. 3d. It was occasionally the city prison,† and was a handsome gate. The present gate is formed of a wide arch, with posterns; the passage over it protected by a slight iron railing. It was built at the sole expense of Rich. Lord Grosvenor, whose arms, and those of the city, occupy the centre of it. The inscription on the west side is—

Begun A. D. M.DCC.LXVIII. *John Kelsal, Esq. Mayor.*
Finished A. D. M. DCC. LXIX. *Charles Boswell, Esq. Mayor.*

On the east side—

Erected at the expense of Richard Lord Grosvenor,
M.DCC.LXIX.

The serjeantcy of this and the other gates, was considered a very honorable office. About 1270, the Serjeantcy of the Eastgate was given by Royal Mandate, to "Hervicus‡" de Bradford, and Robert his son, together with Brewer's Hall,|| as a compensation for the Manor of Bradford, ceded by the Abbey of Vale Royal. The Trussells afterwards had possession; and it appears from an inquisition post mortem, of the 2d of Richard II. that Wm. Trussell, of Cubleston, had the Custody of the Gate. In a subsequent inquisition,§ he is said to die seized of the bailiwick, &c. of this gate, together with its appurtenances, and the houses and buildings above and below the same.—In the time of Hen. IV. the keeper was called Bailiff of the Eastgate, and held it with the Manor of Bruardeshalghe, from the Earl, by the render of a penny. In the 3d Edw. IV. William Trussel held the custody of the gate, *with its buildings*, viz. five messuages, and two shops below it, together with Brewardeshalghe, and lands in Chester: The value x*l*. The serjeantcy afterwards passed with the other estates to the Veres, Earls of Oxford, from whom Sir Randulph Crewe purchased it, covenanting to release the tolls to the City, but it was not then¶ executed.—In 1662, John Crewe, Esq. released the right of toll to the Corporation, in consideration of a rent charge of 2*l*. 13*s*. 4*d*. on the Roodeye, reserving, however, to himself and heirs, the custody of the gate, and freedom from toll.—The keeper was bound to find a crannock and a bushel for measuring salt; and at the present day, the Serjeant of the Eastgate, has the inspection of the City Weights and Measures. Lord Crewe has still the appointment of the Serjeant.

HISTORY.

‡ Qy. Henricus. ORM.

|| Brueres Halgh.

§ 3d & 7th Richard II.

¶ 1630.

Proceeding from the Eastgate due North, there is a fine view of the CATHEDRAL; beyond which is a postern called the CALE-YARDS-GATE, formerly the road from the Monastery of St. Werburgh, to the Gardens beneath the Walls; but now a general thoroughfare

* It cannot for a moment be supposed, but what the present walls occupy the original site of the old Roman fortifications: And if the SHIPGATE be of Roman architecture, which no one disputes, the matter is at once put to rest. The walls, it is pretty clear, (with the exception of the slight inroad upon them by the boundary wall of the Castle,) occupy the same site they did 1700 years ago.

† In 1671, the Prisoners in the Northgate were removed to the Eastgate, by reason of its insufficiency. It would seem that this step had been some time in contemplation, for in the preceding year, an order was made, "That the Eastgate should be repaired, the Mason to have £30. and 2s. 6d. for every 'HOWELL STOY' he shall put into the Tower of the said Gate." In the same year, there is also an order of Assembly, "That the Murengers shall be allowed to get stone for the Cittie's use, between the Goblin's (Phœnix) Tower and Northgate."—CORPORATION RECORDS.

into Frodsham-street. The projecting site beyond this, was occupied by a Tower, called SADDLER'S TOWER, taken down about 1779. At the north east angle of the Walls, is the PHŒNIX TOWER,* so called from a large sculptured Phœnix, which ornaments the front. This was the place of Meeting of several of the City Companies. The view within the walls from this part, is particularly pleasant, the lofty tower of the Cathedral giving a magnificent finish to it.—The walls proceed due west to

THE NORTHGATE.—This Gate was, within the last few years, the Common Gaol of the City,† till the erection of the New Gaol near the Infirmary, in 1808;‡ but this is, in public documents, also called the Northgate Gaol.—The old Northgate was an inconvenient, dangerous structure; by no means secure in the object of its appropriation as a Prison. In 1808, the Prisoners were removed to the New Gaol, and the Gate was demolished;|| on its site was erected the present handsome Gate, the Mayor, Earl Grosvenor, and the Corporation attending at the laying of the foundation stone. It is an eliptic arch, of white stone, of the Doric order, divided on each side from smaller arches or posterns, by two handsome pillars. The design was furnished by Mr. Harrison, and the whole was built at the expense of that munificent Nobleman, Earl Grosvenor. On the south side is inscribed, in capital letters—.

‡ See p. 269.

"INCHOATA GULIELMO NEWELL, ARM. MAJ. M.DCCC.VIII. PERFECTA THOMA GROSVENOR, ARM. MAJ. M.DCCC.X.—THOMA HARRISON, ARCHITECTO."

On the north side—

"PORTAM SEPTENTRIONALEM SUBSTRUCTAM A ROMANIS VETUSTATE JAM DILAPSAM IMPENSIS SUIS AB INTEGRO RESTITUENDAM CURAVIT ROBERTUS COMES GROSVENOR. A. R. GEORGII TERTII LI."

The Northgate is situated on the highest ground within the City Walls, and commands a delightful prospect

* Formerly called NEWTON TOWER. It was from the summit of this Tower, that the unfortunate Charles I. beheld the discomfiture of his army, under Langdale, by Fairfax.—The present appearance of the Tower, and of the south angle of the City Walls, is accurately described in the accompanying plate. It is to be lamented that some efficient means are not adopted for the preservation of this and the other remains of the old fortifications of the City. The grant of it as a dwelling-house has often been suggested, but an unaccountable prejudice prevented it.

† See some particulars relative to it in page 211. With respect to the custom of executing Criminals, as there noticed, it appears it was not peculiar to this place. Mr. Ormerod cites an inquisition p. m. of John Croxton, gent. 41 Eliz. in which it is stated he held, *inter alia*, "un p'cell' terr'cu' p'tin' in Kinderton, jacent' inter terr' quond' Joh'is Licester ar', et Henry Ravenscroft, continen' p' estimac'o'nem una' acr' terr' vulgariter voc' *Hangemans Butts* de Tho. Venables, de Kinderton, ar' ut de man'io suo de Kinderton, etc. p' redd' xij*d*. solvend' an'tim et sect. cur' leete sue de Kinderton, et *inveniend, &c, p'd' Tho. et hered,' suis unu' carnificem* (Ang. a Hangman) *ad suspendend' murdratores et felones* d'c'e d'ne regine' hered' et successor' suor', quandocu'q' opus fuerit infra d'c'a baronia' sive feod' suu' de Kinderton," &c. It is to be remarked, that during the period when Chester fair was one of the privileges of the Abbey of St. Werburgh, all executions within the limitation of the Fair, were done by the Abbots' officers. It is further observed,* "that capital jurisdiction without appeal, and the power of instantaneous decapitation, were vested in the Barons of Malpas, as Serjeants of the Peace of all Cheshire, excepting the Hundred of Macclesfield; also in the Davenports, as Serjeants of that Hundred, and Foresters of the Forest of Macclesfield; in the Serjeants of the Barons of Halton, for "Haltonshire," or the Fee of Halton; in the Kingsleys, their successors the Dones, for the Forests of Mara and Mondrem; in the Storetons, and their successors the Stanleys, for the Forest of Wirral; and in all these cases, the head was presented by the Serjeant, or his Deputy, at the Castle, of Chester. The last case of execution in which this tenure did not operate, related to the jurisdiction of the Baronies; when a tenant of a Cheshire Baron appealing to the Earl's Court, was found guilty of a capital offence, or a similar verdict was passed against one who had committed a capital offence against the Baron or his tenants, the execution did not take place in Chester; but the Culprit was delivered to the Baron's Seneschal and his attendants, was guarded by them to the head of the Barony, and there suspended on the gallows." [Thus, if an offence was committed near Malpas, the sentence would be executed there.]

* Ormerod page 281.

|| It consisted of a mean round arch; with a postern. The entrance to the Gaol was under the Gate. The slide for the portcullice was complete at the period of its demolition. Immediately under the Gateway, at the depth of some thirty feet from the level of the street, was a horrible dungeon, the only access of air to which, was thro' pipes, which communicated with the street. In this frightful hole, prisoners under sentence of death, were confined—"itself a living death."

Engraved by T. Hunt from a Drawing by S. Brown.

PHOENIX TOWER.

and Part of the City Walls.

Engrav'd for Hanshalls History of Cheshire

WATER TOWER CHESTER 1750.

CHESTER HISTORY.

east, north, and west,—the view into Wales is extensive and bold;* and tracing the Dee to its estuary, Flint Castle may be distinctly seen on a clear day.—The Walls descend to the Water Tower, midway to which, are THE MOUNT, and PEMBERTON'S PARLOUR. The Mount was formerly called MORGAN'S MOUNT, and it was formed into a battery of four cannon during the siege. Further on is Pemberton's Parlour, sometimes called THE GOBLIN'S TOWER, and DILL'S TOWER. It was repaired, and converted into an alcove, for public convenience, during the Mayoralty of the Earl of Derby, who died in office, in 1702.† The Field adjoining the Walls here, on the inside, was called THE BARROW FIELD, and in some documents OUR LADY'S FIELD.—Entrenchments were thrown up in this field at the time of the siege, which are still visible at the north-west angle,‡ at which stands, on the Walls, BONWALDESTHORNE'S TOWER, forming a thoroughfare to the WATER, or as it was formerly called NEW, TOWER.‖ These towers are connected by a species of covered way, about thirty yards in length, and two yards in width, beneath which, is an arched way, through which was the general road, from the Watergate to the Sands, and the Old Haven. At the angle of the Walls, is a postern,§ leading to the Canal Wharf,¶ the Sluice-house, &c. The fine Field below the Walls on the west side, is the property of the Body Corporate, and no doubt formed part of the Roodeye.** From hence the Wall proceeds, passing by the Infirmary, the City Gaol, and Stanley Place, to—

THE WATERGATE.—The Corporation purchased the Custody of this Gate, which had long been vested in the Earls of Derby,†† about 1778.—All the Mayor's processes on the Dee, are executed by the Serjeant of this Gate. On taking down the Old Gate, which was a plain arch without towers, the present handsome Gate was erected from the proceeds of the Murage Duties, in 1788; it is wide and lofty, the passage protected by stone balustrades.—On the west side is inscribed—

IN THE XXIX YEAR OF THE REIGN OF GEORGE III. IN THE MAYORALTY OF JOHN HALLWOOD, AND JOHN LEIGH, ESQRS. THIS GATE WAS ERECTED.

THOMAS COTGREAVE } ESQRS. MURENGERS.
EDWARD BURROWES }

The Walls extend in a straight line to the CASTLE,‡‡ passing by the ROODEYE,‖‖ on the right hand, and the

* The pyramidal mountain called MOEL FAMMA, with the Jubilee Column on its apex, and the other hills of the Clwydian range, form an interesting boundary to the western view. The Church, and Castle of Hawarden may also be seen, embosomed in a thickly wooded district.

† The front is ornamented with the remains of some fine sculpture, which remained perfect before the year 1813, when it was mischievously destroyed. On the west side are the City Arms; on the east, the Royal Arms; in the centre is this inscription:—" * * * year of the glorious Reign of Queen Anne, diverse large breaches in these Walls were rebuilt, and other decays therein, were repaired, two Thousand yards of the pace were new Flagged or Paved, and the whole Improved, Regulated, and Adorned, at the expense of One Thousand Pounds and upwards. Thomas Hand, Esq. Mayor, 1701. The Rt. Honble. William Earl of Derby, Mayor, 1702, who dyed in his Mayoralty.

1702 Michael Johnson	Esquires, Mayors.	Roger Comberbach, Esq. Recorder.	
1703 Matthew Anderson		William Wilson, Aldm.	
1704 Edw. Partington		Peter Bennet, Aldm	Murengers.
1705 Edward Puleston		and (upon the death of	
1706 Pulest. Partington		the said Wm Wilson)	
1707 Humphrey Page		Edw. Partington, Aldm	
1708 James Mainwaring		Justice of the Peace.	

‡ During the Plague, vast numbers of the Inhabitants were buried in this field; it is the property of the Dean and Chapter.

‖ It was erected by John Helpstone, in 1322, who contracted to build it twenty-four yards high, and ten and a half yards in diameter; the entire expense £100. It has embrazures, and ships were formerly moored to its wall, the iron rings for that purpose remaining till within the last fifty years.

§ A few yards west of the postern, in the wall, is an arch, filled up, which was probably the original postern to the water side.

¶ A convenient Packet to Liverpool, proceeds daily to Whitby, where a handsome and commodious masted Packet conveys passengers across the Mersey.

** See further account of this in page 201.

†† It is supposed it passed to this family, with the Barony of Montalt, and the Rectory of Trinity, and was an appendage to the seneschalship of the Earldom.—ORM.

‡‡ A view of the Higher Ward, and Prison, from the south-west angle, is given in the accompanying plate.

‖‖ A few centuries ago, the river overflowed the Roodeye, and the land on which now stands Crane-street: the former, it would seem, was nearly covered, for "the Cross seemed to stand in the water."—The Roodeye, it is scarcely necessary to say, was the Champ de Mars of our Ancestors; and here they enjoyed their athletic sports.—

CHESTER — HISTORY.

NUNS' GARDENS on the left hand; from thence in a line nearly due east, passing by the boundary wall of the COUNTY GAOL, the SKINNERS'-HOUSES, and the HOLE-IN-THE-WALL,*

THE BRIDGE GATE—is crossed, opposite which are the DEE MILLS, and WATER WORKS.—It appears from Documents in the possession of the Earl of Shrewsbury, that Randle Earl of Chester, confirmed a gift of his Countess to Poyns, her servant, of premises near the Castle, *habere suo servicio*. This confirmation was witnessed by Fulco de Bricasart, Benedict, brother of the Earl, William Pincerna, Philip the Chamberlain, and others; and is supposed to allude to the Custody of the Bridge Gate.—Another deed, however, preserved among the same documents, speaks more decidedly of the locus in quo: it appears from it,† that the ancestors of Richard Bagot had long held the Custody of this Gate, but being unable by misfortune, to discharge its duties, and especially in time of war,‡ he released it at a Portmote Court, to Philip the Clerk, a Citizen of Chester, and his heirs. This was about the year 1269 or 1270. Avicia, the daughter of this Philip, married Roger Grymbald, but the Keeping of the Gate reverted to Robert de Raby, who was the next heir. It passed from the Rabys, to the Norris's, of Speke, (Lanc.) and the Troutbecks. The Corporation purchased the Norris moiety in 1624, and the other moiety they purchased from the Earl of Shrewsbury, the representative of the Troutbecks,‖ in 1660, the Earl reserving for himself and heirs, a suit of rooms in a house near the Gate, now the property of Sir John Cotgreave, Knt. The Old Gate was defended by two strong round towers; and on the west side, an octagonal lofty tower, was built for Tyrer's Water Works.§ It was taken down in 1781, and the present gate erected, composed of a large centre arch, and two smaller ones for foot passengers.—On a tablet over the western postern arch, is inscribed—

"THIS GATE WAS BEGUN APRIL M.DCC.LXXXII PATTISON ELLAMES, ESQ MAYOR, AND FINISHED DECEMBER THE SAME YEAR, THOS. PATTON, ESQ. MAYOR.

THOS. COTGREAVE, ESQ. } MURENGERS.
HENRY HESKETH, ESQ. }

JOSEPH TURNER, ARCHITECT."

On a Tablet on the eastern side—

"THIS GATE HAVING BEEN LONG INCONVENIENT, WAS TAKEN DOWN, A. D. M.DCC.LXXXI.

JOSEPH SNOW, ESQ. MAYOR.

THOS. AMERY, } TREASURERS."
HENRY HEGG, }

Much form was observed in laying the foundation of this Gate. The first stone was placed in its situation by the Mayor, and the Lodges of Freemasons attended on the occasion. A brass plate, sunk in the stone, bore this inscription:—

"*Pattison Ellames, Esq. Mayor of this City, Chester, laid this stone in the year of the Christian æra, 1782; as D. Provincial Grand Master of Free and Accepted Masons. A numerous procession of Brethren attended. A. L.* 5782.

A descent to the Roodeye, opposite the Nun's Gardens, is called the SALLY-PORT STEPS.

* For an account of this, see page 280.

† "Sciant, &c. quod ego Ricardus Bagoth de Cestr dedi, &c. et omnino quietam clamavi Philippo clerico, civi Cestr,' totum jus meum, &c. in PORTA PONTIS Cestr' cum omnibus pertinencijs suis. Habend', &c. &c. * * * * * * Et quia servicium dicte porte propter paupertatem et inpotenciam debito modo et maxime in guerra sustinere non potui, predictum jus meum," &c.—ORM.

‡ This gate was a most important situation during the predatory inroads of the Welsh.

‖ In an Inq. of 20th James I. Sir Wm. Troutbeck, is said to have held the Serjeantcy of this Gate, and the Custody of the Castle Garden, by reason of his possessing the Manors of Little Neston and Hargreave, but it does not appear at what time these tenures were connected. Philip de Raby, temp. Edw. III. had, together with the custody of the Gate, that of the Earl's Garden, at the Castle, for which service he was entitled to the fruit of a certain tree, called "A RESTYNGE-TRE," and to the fruit of the other trees after the first shaking; but he was to furnish the Earl's household with colewort from Michaelmas to Lent, and with leeks during Lent. From an Inq. 1321, it appears that the Keeper of the Gate, was bound to find locks and keys for the Bridge Gate, and the neighbouring postern—SHIPGATE' OR HOLE-IN-THE-WALL; and a man to watch, and open and shut the gates.

§ Taken down 1780, and 1781.

THOS. COTGREAVE, AND } Esquires, Aldermen,
HENRY HESKETH, } and Murengers.
JOSEPH TURNER, Architect.

"*At this time, France, Spain and the States of Holland, leagued with the British American Colonies (now in open and ungrateful rebellion !) are endeavoring the destruction of the Empire of Britain ! her Freedom ! her Religion ! her Laws ! and her Honor ! In support of which blessings, her armies and navies, are bravely contending in every quarter of the Globe,*—May the God of armies go forth with them !"

On the occasion of the arrival of the news of Admiral Rodney's naval triumph, there was indorsed on the Plate—

"*The great and joyful news was announced this day, of the British fleet under the command of Admirals Rodney, Hood, and Drake, having defeated the French fleet, in the West Indies, taking the French Admiral De Grasse, and five ships of the line, and sunk one.—The battle continued close and bloody for eleven hours.*"

The view of the Dee from the Bridge Gate, is truly delightful, and the Walk from thence to the flight of steps, called THE WISHING STEPS, was a favorite promenade of the late venerable Bishop Porteus.* On the top of the Wishing Steps, is a WATCH TOWER, which affords a delightful view of the Forest, and Broxton Hills, Beeston Castle, Bolesworth Castle, &c. About 130 yards further on in a northerly direction is NEWGATE. It was built in 1608, when the postern called WOLF'S, or WOLFADES GATE, and sometimes PEPPER-GATE† was removed. A few yards beyond the Newgate, is the remains of THIMBLEBY'S TOWER: and the wall passes by the Methodist Chapel to the Eastgate—which completes the Circuit.

* On the King's Birth-day, annually, there are boat and coracle races, on the river below this part of the Walls, which attract great numbers of people. The land beneath the Walls is called THE GROVES, from a regular line of fine trees which formerly ornamented the River side, from the BRIDGE to BARREL WELL, but most of them are now cut down, and the road itself is stopped up. The steps which lead from the Walls to the Groves, are called THE RECORDER'S STEPS, and were erected at the expense of the Corporation, about 1700, for the convenience of Recorder Comberbach, who resided in Duke-street.

† Fuller says, in support of an old tradition—that "The Mayor of the City had his daughter, as she was playing at ball with other maidens in Pepper-street, stolen away by a Young Man through the same gate, whereupon he caused it to be shut up"—from which circumstance arose the saying—"When the daughter is stolen, shut Pepper Gate."

Brown, delin. Mosses, sc.

South East View of the EXCHANGE, Chester.

The Rows, Ancient Houses, Streets, Antiquities, &c.

CHESTER HISTORY.

THE ROWS—afford an interesting walk in the most inclement weather—and are deservedly an object of attraction to the curious.—That they were originally erected for purposes of defence, is pretty obvious. Bridge-street Row and Eastgate-street Row, from the Two Churches to the Hotel, form a fashionable promenade. In hot weather, a continued stream of cold air passes along the Rows from the numerous entries or avenues which branch from them. In wet weather, they afford ample protection from the descent of the " drizzly storm."—Bridge-street, Northgate-street, Eastgate-street, and Watergate-street, have these galleries on each side, and there is little doubt the streets without the wall at one time possessed these conveniences. Even within our early recollection, several rows have been destroyed. Where the Green Dragon Inn, in Eastgate-street stands, were formerly a row and shops—there was a thoroughfare within these few years in the Lower Row on the West side of Bridge-street, the steps of which are now taken down, and the way block-up—the passage of the row (called *Broken-shin Row*) on the East side of Northgate-street, near the Theatre, is stopped.—We cannot but lament that these innovations have taken place, because we are persuaded that the Rows are at once ornamental, and highly useful to the citizens; and it is still more to be regretted, that not one protecting voice was then raised on their behalf, to save them from destruction, amongst those gentlemen who had the municiple authority. It is to hoped, however, that an order will be entered in the Corporation Books, by the enforcement of which, all further attempts to do away with so valuable a feature of the old city, will be prevented. The Rows, if we may judge from the most ancient* specimens now in exis-

* On a post at the foot of a flight of steps leading from Watergate-row, the property of Sir J. Cotgreave, Knt. is the date 1539.

tence, were formerly very low, not exceeding six feet, and generally not more than 5 feet 10 inches high; the width about 10 feet. To the front of the street was a clumsy wooden railing, and immense pillars of oak, supporting transverse beams, over which were built the houses, chiefly of wood, which hung over the street, and in some places nearly met in the centre. A little above the top of the row, run heavy slated sheds, called *Pentices*. These are removed, and within the last twenty years, the streets have assumed a new and more pleasing appearance. Many houses have been taken down, which, on being rebuilt, were to the street, decorated with a neat iron railing. These improvements are become pretty general in Bridge-street and Eastgate-street; but the *wooden antiquity* of Northgate-street and Watergate-street, remains unaltered, and is likely to continue so for some time.

* See vig. p. 265.

There is a old building called the *Lamb Row*,* still standing, which, as it is a curious specimen of the domestic architecture of the early part of the 16th cent. we cannot forbear noticing. It is situated immediately below the church of St. Bridget, on the west side of Bridge-street. It is built almost entirely of wood, and twigs of hazel, covered with clay and mortar. It projects considerably over the street, and many entertain fears (we believe unfounded ones) of its security. The inner part of the house, which has been of great size, is pannelled with oak. It was formerly, as we are informed by a friend, the residence of one of the celebrated Randle Holme's, the Chester Antiquaries—and was within the last 50 years, a public house, bearing the outward and visible sign of the Lamb; it is now, however, remarkable only for its ruins. It is divided into several dwellings.

In noticing the Rows, a friend has observed, "they are what in Covent Garden would be called PIAZZAS, or at Tunbridge THE PANTILES. The foot passengers walk the front of the first floors of the houses under colonnades, with shops on the one hand, and pleasant balconies on the other. Nothing can be more pleasant, commodious, sociable, and picturesque; at present, they are unique. The origin of this irregular style of architecture, goes back, no doubt, to the times when the neighbouring Welsh made inroads on the city, when the Inhabitants defended themselves, and beat back their assailants, from these galleries."†

† Mr. Boswell, in a letter to Dr. Johnson, dated Oct. 22, 1779, says, "Chester pleases me more than any town I ever saw.—I told a very pleasing young lady, niece to one of the Prebendaries (Miss Letitia Barnston) at whose house I saw her, 'I have come to Chester, Madam, I cannot tell how; and far less can I tell how I am to get away from it.' Dr. Johnson, in his reply says, "In the place where you now are, there is much to be observed, and you will easily procure yourself skilful directors." In another letter, dated Nov. 7, 1779, Boswell remarks, "I was quite enchanted at Chester, so that I could with difficulty quit it."—In 1769, S. Derrick, Esq. Master of the Ceremonies at Bath, published a small 12mo. vol. dedicated to the Duke of Northumberland, and he thus notices Chester, and its festivities. It must be confessed, that Boswell and he had different views of things:—"Your Lordship is so well acquainted with the City of Chester, that it would be ridiculous in me to give you any account: yet in this ancient city there is an article, my Lord, which you will permit me to mention, as it may probably have escaped your notice, it is a charity schoool, absolutely APPROPRIATED TO THE EDUCATION OF JOCKIES!—The TRUTH of the matter is this: there is a charity school without the Northgate, well endowed, having a large fund, intended by the donor to be laid out in putting the Children here educated, at a certain age, to trades. Some years ago, it was usual to bind them out to the tradesmen and artificers of Chester, and consequently when out of their time, they were admitted freemen, and had a right to vote in the election of Members to represent the town in Parliament: but it having OFTEN HAPPENED that many of them were either too honest, or too obstinate, to receive DIRECTIONS in that material point from any superior but their own conscience, the practice of making them saucy rebellious tradesmen, has been discontinued, and they are put out to horse hirers, and JOCKEYS, not free of the city!—This account I had from an old ill-natured fellow, who HATES all mankind, and fattens upon scandal, sarcasm, and ridicule!—We were invited a few days since to dine at the Town-hall with Sir Richard Grosvenor, who is NOW Mayor of the city, and deservedly the darling of the people. The Company consisted of near 400 persons. There was great plenty of every thing in season. The wines were good and of all kinds: but the most remarkable part of the Entertainment was, that there were at once served up 42 HAUNCHES OF VENISON.—Sir Richard was supported at table by the Ecclesiastic and Military powers, for he sat between the Lord Bishop of Chester, and Colonel Viner, of the Lincolnshire Militia. As I know the Clergy live well, I took up my quarters between two of the Prebends, and by this, secured myself some rational conversation, as well as a comfortable dinner: an advantage not always to be found in so large an assembly.—Stukeley, in his Itinerary 1724, describes Chester in the following words: "We passed thro' Delamere Forest upon the

CHESTER

Streets, Antiquities, &c.

There are four principle streets in Chester,* commencing at the Cross, from which the others branch. The following are the present, and former names of the streets, commencing with Eastgate-street:—

EAST.

PRESENT NAME.	FORMER NAME.
Eastgate-street	Eastgate-street.
Foregate-street	Forest-street.
Newgate-street	Fleshmonger's-lane.
Werburgh's-street	Church-lane. Werburgh's-lane.
London Baker's Yard	Godestall-lane.
St. John's-street	John's-lane.
Little St. John-street	Vicar's-lane.
Dee-lane	Fowler's-lane Sowter's-lane.
Frodsham-street†	Coole's-lane. Cow-lane
Gorst-stacks	Gorst-stacks.
Brook-street	Flookersbrook-road.
Queen-street	Queen-street.
Union-walk	
York-street	York-street.
Bold-square	
Claremont-walk	
Love-street	Love lane
Union-street	Barker's-lane.
The Headlands	
Mill-street	Star lane. Chester-lane. Horn-lane.

† So named in 1818.

HISTORY.

PRESENT NAME.	FORMER NAME.
Dee-lane	Peene's-lane.

BEYOND THE BARS.

PRESENT NAME.	FORMER NAME.
Boughton	Gallows'-street.

WEST.

PRESENT NAME.	FORMER NAME.
Watergate-street	Watergate-street.
Goss-street	Goss-lane
Crook-street	Gerard's-lane.
Trinity-street	Trinity-lane.
Bunce-street	Bunnes-lane. Bise-lane.
Nicholas-street	Nicholas-street.
Linen-hall-street	Berward-street. Lower-lane.‡
Stanley-place	
Crane-street	
Back Crane-street	
Paradise. Row	

NORTH.

PRESENT NAME.	FORMER NAME.
Northgate-street	Northgate-street.
Prince's-street	Parson's-lane
Abbey-square	Abbey-court.
Abbey-street	Abbey-street.
King-street	Barn-lane.
St. Martin's in the Fields	The Crofts. Ox-lane.
Wall's-lane	Bagge-lane.
George-street	Henwalde Lowe. Sandy-way.

Road in our way to Chester. They say here was formerly an old City, now called the Chamber on the Forest. I suppose some fort or camp to secure the road. From hence you have a fine prospect to the Welsh Mountains; such a noble scene of nature as I never beheld before. Beeston Castle is upon our left, built upon a rocky precipice. Chester is a fine old City and Colony of the Romans, the residence some time of Legio vicesscima victrix. A Hypocaust was lately found, lined with bricks, made by that Legion. I need not repeat what other authors say of the antiquities at this place. The Rows, or piazzas, are singular, through the whole town, giving shelter to foot-people. I fancied it a remain of the Roman Porticoes; four Churches besides the Cathedral, which is a pile venerable indeed for age, and almost ruin. There are shadows of many pictures upon the walls, Madonnas, Saints, Bishops, &c. but defaced. At the west end are some images of the Earls Palatine of Chester in niches: the adjoining Abbey is quite ruined. The Walls round the City are kept in good repair, at the charge of the Corporation, and serve for a pleasant, airy, walk The Exchange is a neat building, supported by columns, 13 feet high, of one stone each, over it is the City Hall, a well-contrived Court of Judicature. The Castle was formerly the Palace, and where the Earls assembled their Parliament, and enacted laws independent of the King of England; and determined all judicial trials themselves. Abundance of Roman and British Antiquities are found hereabouts." [It need scarcely be added, that little of this account is correct. H.]

* Viz. Eastgate-street, Northgate-street, Bridge-street, and Watergate street.

‡ Sometime called Chadd's-lane, from it leading to the old Church of St. Chad.

Chester

History.

PRESENT NAME.	FORMER NAME.
Canal-street	The Poole Way. Dee-lane.
Cottage-street	Stone Bridge-lane.
Further Northgate-street	
Wind Mill-street	Bessome-lane.

SOUTH.

PRESENT NAME.	FORMER NAME.
Bridge-street, (upper)	Mercer's-row.
Lower Bridge-street	Bridge-street.*
Common-hall-street	Norman's-lane. Common-hall-lane.
Dirty-lane†	Perpoyntes-lane
White-Friers'-street	Foster-lane. Custard-lane
Pepper-street	Pepur-street.
Cuppin-street	Cuppins-lane.
Weaver's-street	St. Alban's-lane. Weaver's-lane.
Martin's Ash	
Wall's-lane, ...	Arderne-lane.
Nun's-lane‡	
Castle-street	
Glover's-stone‡	
Holme-street‡	
Olave's-street	Tooler's-lane.
Duke-street	Clayton-lane.
Shipgate	Ship or Shappe-lane.

THE CROSS—is situated at the intersection of the four principal streets; the Cross which stood here, was broken down by the Parliamentary forces in 1646. The only remains of it in existence, are deposited in the garden of Sir John Cotgreave, of Netherlegh House. —The High Cross was the scene of the Civic entertainments of our Ancestors, and here the old plays were enacted.—It was also the site of occasional civic disturbances, a notice of one of which we quote from the MSS. of the first Randle Holme:—"According to the usual custom for the Mayor's farewell out of office, it chanced a contention fell out betwixt the butchers and the bakers of the cittye about their dogges then fyghtynge: they fell to blows, and in the tumult manye people woulde not be pacefyed, so that the Maior, seeing there was great abuse, being Cityzens, could not forbeare, but he in PERSON HIMSELF went out amongst them to have the peace kept: but they in their rage, lyke rude and unbroken fellowes, did lytill regarde hymm. In the ende they parted, and the begynners of the sayde brawle being found out and examined, were commytted to the Northgate—THE MAYOR SMOTE FREELY amongst them, and he BROKE HIS WHITE STAFF; and the Cryer, Thomas Knowstley, brake his mase, and the brawl ended. This took place on the 2d Oct. 1619."

Antiquities.

EASTGATE-STREET—is one of the great thoroughfares of the City.—Many of the houses yet remaining, are of considerable antiquity; and the cellars in the street, under those of the south side, worthy the inspection of the curious.—The Rows, on each side the street have several massy gothic arches, of stone, of great age.||—Numerous Roman Antiquities have been found in this street;—amongst them, an altar, now in the possession of the Rev. C. Prescot, of Stockport, was found in 1693. It is supposed to have been dedicated to the Emperors Dioclesian and Maximian. On one side of it, is a vase with two handles, issuing from which are leaves of the acanthus, on which is a basket with fruit: on the other side, a Genius, with an altar in one hand, and a cornucopiæ in the other. The back represents a curtain, festooned, with a globe above it, surrounded with a palm. Within the THURIBULUM on the top of the altar, is a human face. It was found amongst a heap of ashes, horns, and bones of animals, resting on

* A Gateway at the Two Churches, formerly completely divided the streets. It intersected the street, from St. Michael's Church to St. Bridget's Church.

† This is the vulgar appellation for what is now merely a passage to warehouses and stabling; but formerly it was a principal way to the Common-hall.

‡ Completely destroyed.

|| A view of the appearance of this street, from the Cross, is given in Mr. Ormerod's History.

CHESTER

its face. The inscription is thus given by Mr. Ormerod:

PRO· SAL· DOMIN
(ORV) ·M· NN· INVI
CTISSIMORUM
AVGG· GENIO· LOCI
FLAVIUS· LONG (VS)
TRIB· MIL· LEG· XX· (VV)
LONGINVS· FIL
(E) IVS· DOMO
SAMOSATA
V· S·

Near it were found two medals, one of which was supposed to be of Constantius Clorus, son in law of Maximian, the other of Vespasian.

In 1653, an altar was dug up in FOREGATE-STREET, which is preserved among the Arundelian marbles at Oxford. The back of it is plain; on one side a PRÆFERICULUM, on the other a sort of PATERA; within the thuribulum had been placed a piece of iron. When perfect, the inscription was

I · O · M · TANARO
T · ELVPIVS · GALER
PRAESENS · GVNTA
PRI · LEG · XX · V · V
COMMODO · ET · LATERANO
COS
V · S · L · M·

* Horsley. It is supposed* that the person named as Commodus, is not the emperor, but Ælius Verus Cæsar, whom Hadrian adopted, and who is described by Spartian, as "CEJONIUS COMMODUS QUI ET ÆLIUS VERUS APPELLATUS EST."†

HISTORY.

The line of Foregate-street extends to the BARS, where stood an old gate, with a postern, which intersected the street, and which was taken down about 40 years ago.—Beyond the Bars, is called BOUGHTON, vulgarly GALLOWS-STREET.‡—In Boughton is the Spital Burial ground, formerly belonging to the Hospital of St. Giles.§ §See p. 258. So early as the reign of Edw. I. the Black Friers had made an Aqueduct for the conveyance of water to the city; but before 1537, the works had gone to decay. In 1583, a Conduit was built for conveying water to the High Cross,|| and an agreement was entered into the following year, for making a stone house at the Cross for the Cistern.¶

QUEEN-STREET—now occupies part of the site of the JUSTING CROFT, where the tilts and tournaments of ages long gone by, were celebrated.—In a field at the bottom of DEE LANE,** is a beautifully clear spring, called BILLY HOBBY'S WELL,—how this name was applied, remains to be traced.

BRIDGE-STREET—is the great thoroughfare from the Principality into the City. It is divided into *Upper* and *Lower*, the division is marked by the two churches of St. Michael and St. Bridget. These streets have recently been much improved in appearance.††—In a cellar beneath the Feathers' Inn, occupied as a Smith's Shop, are the remains of a ROMAN HYPOCAUST and SUDATORY. The way to the Hypocaust is through a dark passage, six feet high, grooved round the outside, probably for the reception of an iron door or grating.—

† Verus Cæsar, and Sextilius Lateranus, were Consuls A. D. 154.

‡ Execution was done here on criminals for both city and county, till 1801. The site of the Gallows is now occupied by a handsome house, and the opposite side the road, the original place of execution, is converted into a Garden.—Mr. R. Morris has a lease of the ground from the Corporation for a term of years.

|| In 1573, the Mayor, Richard Dutton, made an agreement with Peter Morris for making a Conduit from St. Giles's Well, Boughton, to the Cross, at St. Bridget's Church, in Bridge-street.—There are two fine wells in Boughton, one in Sandy-lane, and the other nearer the City, called BARREL WELL; the latter is still much frequented by the Valetudinarian, but the former was called St. Giles's Well. The following is a comparative analysis of Barrel Well Bath with other waters; made Sept. 8, 1789—

Barrel Well	53°
Bowling Green Bath	53°
Dee Water	59°
Heat of the Air	59°

The Bowling Green Bath is now covered in, and no longer used. It is situated in the Groves, near the flight of steps at the east end of St. John's Church-yard leading from the river.

¶ The present Water works at the Bridge, were first constructed in 1698, and consist of six forcing pumps; the greatest lift of water about 64 feet. They are divided into six proprietary shares, worth about £1,700 each.

** The Company of Tanners lay claim to a right of washing their skins, &c. from the bank here.

†† The account of the singular occurrence at the Blue Posts, in this street, is given in page 147.

The breadth of the entrance is two feet nine inches; the length of the Hypocaust, in the inside is fifteen feet; the depth six feet seven inches. It contains thirty-three square pillars, arranged in rows, as represented in the cut:—

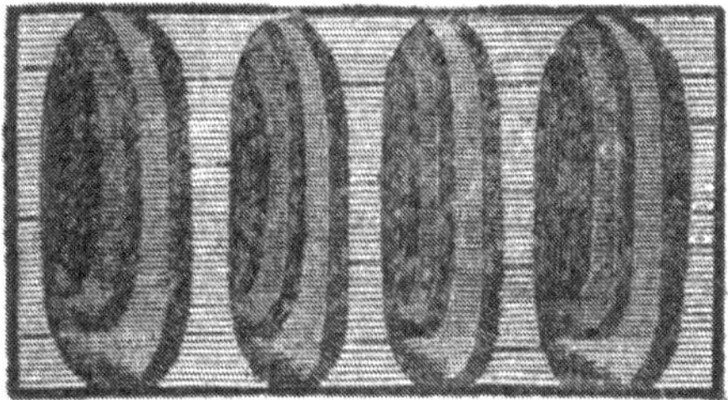

Each of the pillars is about two feet eight inches in height, and nearly a foot in diameter at top and bottom; they are distant from each other 12 and 16 inches.— They support large square perforated tiles, fixed in cement, and the surface on which they stand is covered with thick brick tiles, also laid in cement The upper part has many vents, or *spiracula*, to convey the heat upwards, and at the sides, into the tubes of iron or copper, for the use of the hot and warm baths, and the different *Sudatoria*, or sweating-rooms. The Hypocaust is surrounded by a stone wall, two feet thick.— There are now no remains of the *Bath*; it is either totally destroyed, or covered by the adjoining buildings, probably the latter. Some years ago, a Machine was erected for weighing coals, &c. a few yards south of the cellar, when part of the angle of a Roman building was pulled up, supposed to have been one end of the Bath; from thence to the Hypocaust is 35 feet, and according to the rules of architecture, laid down by Vitruvius, 35 feet more for the building must be allowed on the other side of the Hypocaust, which was uniformly placed in the centre of the building. The depth of the building must have been nearly 70 feet.*

HISTORY.

Many of the cellars behind the street shops, are well worthy of notice, as are several of the houses in the row on the west side of the street, called the SCOTCH ROW. Tradition says, there are subterraneous passages from the cellars of several of the shops, communicating with St. John's Church, the Cathedral, &c. but these are idle stories, originating in superstitious ignorance Of the existence of such passages, however, at a former time, there can be no doubt, for all the old writers mention the fact—there are not any known to be in existence at the present day. Nearly adjoining St. Bridget's Church on the south side, is the LAMB ROW.†

Immediately below Castle-street, on the west-side of the street, is the BOARDING SCHOOL YARD. The house fronting the street, was the residence of the Gamul Family, and it was here the unfortunate Charles I. was entertained by Sir F. Gamul, during the siege of Chester. The house is now divided into several dwellings, and the whole is the property of E. O. Wrench, Esq. The chimney-piece of one of the rooms, is painted in a superior manner, with the Gamul arms in the centre; probably the work of the first Randle Holme. The house on the opposite side of the street, now the brewery of Messrs. Newell & Gaman, is an antique structure, certainly as early as the beginning of the 16th century, the row adjoining which, bears evident marks of early domestic architecture.

In 1813, in sinking the foundation of the cellar of Netherlegh‡ House, the property of Sir J. Cotgreave,

* Information of Dr. Thackeray.

† It would seem that encroachments were made on the rows at a very early period. It appears from the Records of the Corporation, that on the 2d. of Sept. 1697, an Order of Assembly was obtained by Francis Skellorn, "to enclose, stop, and block up, the row on the west side of Bridge-street, adjoining White Friers-lane." A thoroughfare was afterwards made in this row, but within the last few years, it has again been completely blocked up. There are no precise data extant, to fix the period of the building of the LAMB ROW—but the probability is, that it was erected towards the middle of the 17th century. On referring to the Records of the City, I find, that in 1670, the Assembly ordered, that "the nuisance erected by Randle Holme, in his New Building in Bridge-street (near to the Two Churches), be taken down, as it annoys his neighbours, and hinders their prospect from their houses." The following year, "Mr. Holme, painter, was fined £3. 6s. 8d. for contempt to the Mayor, in proceeding in his building, in Bridge-street." In short, it does not appear that the "building" was taken down; and a letter in the possession of Mr. R. Llwyd, is addressed "To Mr. Randle Holme, at his house near the Two Churches."

‡ Netherlegh House stands on the right hand side of the road leading to Eaton, a short distance from Handbridge. Netherlegh belong-

CHESTER

a variety of Roman antiquities were found, which are thus described in the Stranger in Chester:—"A number of vases formed of red clay, similar to what flower-pots are composed of, were discovered a little below the surface of the earth, arranged in regular order, in vaults, each containing four or six vases. Some of them contained the ashes, perhaps, of illustrious warriors, now in undistinguishable obscurity. In others were lamps, of a hard white clay. One of the vases was got up, perfectly whole, and presented by Mr. Cotgreave to Earl Grosvenor; but the remainder, owing to the carelessness of the workmen, were destroyed. One of the lamps was in the possession of the Editor of this work.* About the same time, a demi-figure, somewhat resembling a Priest, was dug up. Several other memorials, such as traces of walls, and rudely sculptured stones, were destroyed. Sufficient, however, was seen, to give strength to the supposition, that this spot had been a CALVARIA, or burial place, of the Romans; and the idea is strengthened, by the vestiges in question being found in a situation adjoining the highway,—the Romans' usual place of burial."—The entrenchments of Sir Wm. Brereton, thrown up during the Siege, are visible on Hough Green, near Overlegh.†

WATERGATE-STREET.—An altar is now in the possession of Sir John Egerton, Bart. of Oulton Park, found near the Watergate, in 1779. The sides are ornamented with a cornucopiæ, urn, knife, and other sacrificial instruments. The inscription is thus decyphered—

HISTORY.

FORTVNAE · REDVCI
ESCVLAP · ET · SALVTI · EIVS
LIBERT · ET · FAMILIA
(CAII) PONTII · T · F · CAL · MAMILIANI
RVFI · (A) NTISTIANI · FVNINSVLANI
VTTO (NIA) NI · LEG · AVG
D · D

A slate was found in digging in a cellar in this street, in 1729: the inscription is imperfect—

NVMINI · AVG
ALMAE · CEr.T
NVS · ACTCR
EX · VOTO · FACI

In 1779, a Hypocaust, &c. similar to that in Bridge-street, was found in this street, the Pillars, &c. belonging to which, were removed to Oulton Park.

In 1814, in making the improvements near the Castle Gateway, a tesselated pavement was found, a great portion of which was destroyed, and the residue was covered up again.—There are several curious houses in this street: opposite Crook-street is a house built by Bishop Lloyd, with a variety of curious carved work in front, a view of which is preserved in Cuitt's Etchings.‡

ed to the Barons of Halton, and was granted in trust to Herbert de Orreby, by Geoffry de Dutton, about 1270, when he went with the Crusaders. It was afterwards held under the Warburtons by the Orrebys of Gawsworth, and passed by marriage with an heiress to the Fittons. A part was subsequently in the Stanleys of Alderley, and from thence it passed by sale in 1735, to John Cotgreave, Esq. Mayor, of Chester, from whom it descended to his collateral heir, the present proprietor. Another portion of Netherlegh is vested in the heirs of John Bennet, Esq. of Chester. It passed from the Brownes, of Upton, to Wm. Symson, D. D. of Brasenose College, Oxford.§—See account of St. Mary's, Chester.

§ Ormerod.

* Presented to the Bishop of Chester, 1818.

† OVERLEGH, adjoins Handbridge, just within the liberties of the City, and nearly opposite the Castle. The situation affords an interesting view of the City. This, as also Netherlegh, was included under the general name of "Lee," in Domesday. It was held by the Barons of Montalt, and was given by their representatives, about 1230, to the Abbey of Basingwerk, the Monks of which built a Chapel here. In 1462, the Abbot devised to Ellis ap Dio ap Gryffyd, A PLACE CALLED THE OVERLYTHE, for one hundred years, Ellis contracting to pay four marks yearly, and keep the Chapel in repair.—From thence it passed by marriage to Thos. Cowper, Esq. of Chester. The estate is now the property of C. Cholmondeley, Esq of Knutsford, to whom it passed by will of his maternal uncle Thos. Cowper, Esq. The Old Mansion was destroyed during the Siege; the present is of brick, and occupied as an academy by Mr. Smedley.

‡ Dr. Geo. Lloyd, Bishop of Man, in 1604, succeeded Dr. Vaughan, of Nyffryn, in Carnarvonshire, who was translated to London as Bishop of Chester. He appears by the arms on the front of his house in Watergate-street, to have built it. He died in 1615, and was buried at St. Werburgh's. "He was Rector of Bangor, and Thornton. He was of a most amiable and lovely countenance---of a mild and righteous nature. The King (James I.) called him the Beauty of Holiness." He was liberal to his friends, merciful to the poor; and died in the prime of life, being much lamented by all. He was Bishop of Chester about eleven years. Dr. Lloyd was the fourth son of the house of Cinmel, near St. Asaph; his brother David Lloyd, second son, in 1593 was Mayor of Chester; and Morgan Lloyd, third son, was Mayor of Beaumaris.

LLWYD

CHESTER

A little higher up the street, on the same side, on a post at the foot of a flight of steps to the Row, is carved the date 1539. About 80 yards from the Cross, on the south side of the street, on the front of an old house is the inscription—"GOD'S PROVIDENCE IS MINE INHERITANCE." Numerous have been the conjectures as to the origin of it. Some suppose it to have been built by the Earl of Orrery, who being raised from a humble to an elevated station in life, adopted these words, as a gratitudinal motto.* But it is not known that the noble Earl, or any of his family, ever possessed any property in this City. On the other hand, tradition has given a variety of meaning to it: A dreadful fire destroyed nearly the whole of Watergate-street, and the flames ceased at this house;—All the houses in the street, with the single exception of this, were infected with plague, &c. The probability, however, is, that the house was built during the prevalence of Puritanic hypocrisy, and that the saint who occupied it, adopted the words, as an outward and visible sign of the inward and spiritual grace. But at last, we are in the dark about it.

The chimney pieces of several of the houses in this street, Bridge-street, Eastgate-street, and Northgate-street, are curiously decorated with antique carved work of heraldic bearings, &c.

NORTHGATE-STREET.—In pulling down the Northgate, in 1809, the remains of the Roman architecture of the original gate, were distinctly visible. A copper coin of Claudius Gothicus, of the Lower Empire, was found by one of the workmen, near the Exchange, in laying down the Gas Pipes, in Oct. 1818; it was obtained by the Editor of this work, and presented to M. Gregson, Esq. of Liverpool. Henry Potts, Esq. has in his possession the fragment of a slate-stone, found in 1738, in digging in the market place. On it was cut in bas relief the figure of a Retiarius, with trident and net, and part of the shield of Secutor.†

Many Roman and other antiquities have been found in this city. Horsley has an engraving of a stone statue, found near the Dee bank, supposed to be Atys or Mithras; a Phrygian bonnet was on the head, on the body a short vest, with a mantle over the shoulders; in the hands, a declining torch. Leigh, in his *Lancashire*, &c. has a plate of various Roman Coins found in Chester.

‡ W. M. Henderson, Esq.

* A Gentleman,‡ whose veracity may be depended upon, informed me, that there is an old house, in Bishopsgate-street, London, bearing a similar inscription.

† There is an error in noticing the stone in the Chapter House of the Cathedral, which it may be as well to correct here: it should be—

COH · I · C · OCRATI
MAXIMINI · M · P.

In alluding to this, Mr. Ormerod observes, that this inscription is of the kind usually termed centurial, and may be read, "Cohortis Primæ Centuriæ Ocratii Maximini Mille Passus," intimating that this Century had performed so much of some public work. The name of Ocratius occurs twice in Muratoris Novus Thesaurus Inscriptionam. For the C in Centuria, an imperfect Σ is introduced, and an Ω for the N in Maximinus. If the inscription may be supposed to relate to the erection of the City Walls, the relic is of considerable interest.

Memoranda, &c.

CHESTER — THE OLD PLAYS—are noticed in page 203; but the following addition may not be unacceptable. It is in the Play of "*The Nativitye of our Lorde.*" The lines are spoken by "EXPOSITOR," whilst SIBELLA a midwife is travelling to OCTAVYAN,* with the news of Christ's birth. The other midwife (SALOME) had been previously punished for an insult to the Virgin, by the withering of her arm, which the Holy Infant miraculously restored:—

* Augustus Cæsar.

THE WRIGHTES' PLAY.

Loe lordinges all of this mirackle here,
Fryer Bartholemew in good mennere
Beareth witnesse withouten were,
  As played is you before;
Another mirackle if I maye,
I shall rehearse or I go awaye,
That befell that same daye
  That Jesus Christ was borne.

We read in Chronackles expresse,
Some tyme in Rome a temple was,
Made of such great riches,
  That wonder was witterly
For all things in it, 'leeve you me,
Was silver, goulde, and rich arraye,
Thirde parte the worlde, as reade wee,
  The Temple was worthy.

Of each provynce that boke mynde mase
There Godes Image there sett was,
And eiche one aboute his necke hase
  A silver bell hanginge,
And one his breaste written alsoe,
The landes name, and Gods bouthe too,
And set allsoe in midest of thoe
  God of Rome, righte as a Kinge.

Aboute the house alsoe, meaning there,
A man on horse stoode men to steere,
And in his hand he beare a speare
  All pure dispitiously.

That horse and man was made of brasse,
Torninge about that Image was,
Save certayne Prestes there mighte none passe,
  For Devills fantasye.

HISTORY.

But when any lande with battele
Was readye Rome to assayle,
The Godes image withouten fayle,
  Of that lande range his bell.
And torn his face dispiteouslye
To God of Rome, as reade I,
In tokeninge that they were readye,
  To feightinge fresh and fell.

The Image alsoe above standinge,
When the bell beneathe began to ringe,
Torned him al sharpley, shewinge
  Towards that lande his speare,
And when the see this tokeninge
Rome ordeyned without taryinge,
An host to keep ther cominge
  Longe or the came there.

And in this manner sothely,
By act of negromancye,
All the worlde witherlye
  To Rome were made lowte.
And that Temple† ther doubtless,
Was called therefore the Temple of Peace,
That through this sleight batayle can cease,
  Throughout the worlde about.

† The temple of Janus?

But he so cuningly this worke cast,
Asked the Devill, as he past,
How longe that temple there should last,
  That he ther can build.
The Devill answered suttely,
And sayde it shoulde last seckerlye,
Untill a mayden womanly,
  Had conceived a childe.

The harde, and beleeved therefore,
It shoulde indewer ever more;
But that tyme that Christ was bore
  It fell down soone in hie.

CHESTER

Of which howse is seen this daye,
Somewhat standinge in good faye,
But no man dare goe that waye
For feendes fantasye.

That daye was seene veramente,
Three sunnes in the firmamente,
And wonderlye together wente,
And torned into one.
The oxe, the asse these were the lente,
Honoured Christe in ther intente,
And no mirackles, as I have mente,
To play righte here anone.

Customs.

Chester must have been greatly reduced at the period of the Conquest; it then contained only 431 houses, rateable, exclusive of 56 belonging to the Bishop.—About the same time a curious custom prevailed both in city and county; whenever the King came he claimed from every ploughland 200 hesthas or capons, one cuna, or vat of ale; and one rusca of butter; and those who made bad ale, were either to pay 4s. or sit in a tumbril or dung cart for an hour.

The Bridge Gate—is mentioned in page 266. It appears from an Inq. p. m. 23d Edw. III. that Robert de Raby held in demesne, one messuage, and the custody of the Castle Garden, with other liveries, for CIS. IIId. Also, the custody of the Bridge Gate, by finding one man to make proper ward thereof, and the *Horse-gate*, and the *Shap-gate*, and to receive the profits value 20s. per ann. and one Stall on the Dee by the render of 4*d.* value viiid. and one messuage from the Prioress of Chester, &c. and a messuage from the Abbot of Basingwerk, and iiis. rent out of the Walls of Chester, one carucate in Claverton and Newbold, and vii stalls in the Dee, with a boat on the same, &c.

At the Conquest, the Provost of Chester had orders to summon one man from every hide of land in the county, to rebuild *Dee Bridge*; if he did not appear, the lord forfeited XLs. When the *Mills* were granted to Sir Howell y Fwyall, the inhabitants were restricted from grinding corn any where else: this must have been a very valuable grant.

HISTORY.

The Roodeye.—On the 9th May, 27 Eliz. the Roodeye, being then greatly impaired and neglected, was let to Thomas Lyniell, merchant, for a lease of 21 years, at £20. together with as much land as he can get from the River Dee, provided he builds a sufficient quay *near the Watergate*, for boats, &c. to come to, from which he shall have 2*d.* for every one laden. About the same year, the Mayor (Wm. Wall) was petitioned by the *comynaltie* of the City, respecting the Roodeye, which was accustomed to be let to the Poor at low rates, and which they had heard *was to be utterly taken from them.* The *silver ball* was run for in the 31st Henry VIII. in which year it was first changed for *a silver bell,* value 3*s.* 6*d.*—"In 1665,* the Sheriffes would have no calves'-head feast, but put the charge of it into a piece of plate, to be run for on Shrove Tuesday; and the High Sheriff borrowed a Barbary horse of Sir T. Middleton, which won him the plate; and being master of the Race, he would not suffer the horses of Maister Massey, of Podington, and of Sir Philip Egerton, of Oulton, to runne, because they came the day after the time prefixed for the horses to be *brought and kept in the citye*; which thinge caused all the gentry to relinquish the races ever since."

* Randle Holme, the second.

†"It had been the custom, time out of mind, for the Shoemakers yearly at the Shrove Tuesday, to deliver to the Drapers in the presence of the Mayor of Chester, at the Cross on the Roodeye, one ball of leather,‡ called a foote ball, of the value of 3*s.* 4*d.* or above, to play at from thence to the Common Hall of the said citie; which practice was productive of much inconvenience, and therefore this year, 1540, by consent of the parties concerned, the ball was changed into six glayves of silver, of the like value, as a reward for the best runner that day upon the aforesaid Roodee."

† Randle Holme the last.

‡ See p. 199.

Pressing to Death.—The punishment of pressing to death, or the *peine forte et dure,* is said‖ to have originated within the walls of the old Castle of Chester.—The statute was made in the 4th Edw. II. when Adam, son of John de Woodhouses, was charged with destroy-

‖ Pennant.

CHESTER

ing his own house by fire, and carrying away his goods. He stood mute when put upon his trial; and a Jury having decided that he could speak if he thought proper, he was imprisoned *ad dietam*. This ironical term expressed the sustenance he was to receive, which was three morsels of the worst bread on the first day; on the second, three draughts of water out of the next puddle; and so on alternately till he died. The death of this offender being notified to the Crown, the statute for *pressing to death* was enacted, as more *humane* than starving to death!

On the 19th July, 1634, the Earl of Arundel, Earl Marshal, came to Chester, and not finding the Deputy Herald then Mayor (Rand. Holme) in attendance, sent for him by warrant. The Mayor attended with all the insignia of office, when the Earl said, "Mr. Mayor, I sent for you to tell you your offence you have committed in not giving your attendance as you ought, and now do you come with your authority." He then plucked the rod from the Mayor's hand, and put it in the window, saying, "I will teach you to know yourself and attend Peers of the realm. Though I care not for your observances, yet because you want manners, I shall teach you some, and you shall further hear from me. I would have you to know, I have power to commit you, to teach you to know yourself and me, and give better attendance." The Mayor, it appears, made some excuses for this insolence, paid the Earl's fees, and was dismissed!

In the 27th Hen. VIII. the following petition was presented to Parliament from the City and County.—Burke, in his speech, for a Conciliation with the Colonies,* thus introduces it —"In the 35th of that reign, (Hen. VIII.) a complete and not ill-proportioned representation of counties and boroughs was bestowed upon Wales, by act of parliament. From that moment, as by a charm, the tumults subsided; obedience was restored; peace, order, and civilization followed in the train of liberty.—When the day-star of the English constitution had arisen in their hearts, all was harmony within and without—

* 8vo. edit. page 407.

Simul alba nautis
Stella refulsit,
Defluit saxis agitatus humor:
Concidunt venti, fugiuntque nubes:
Et minax (quod sic voluere) ponto
Unda recumbit.

HISTORY.

"The very same year the county palatine of Chester received the same relief from its oppressions, and the same remedy to its disorders. Before this time, Chester was little less distempered than Wales. The inhabitants, without rights themselves, were the fittest to destroy the right of others; and from thence Richard II. drew the standing army of archers, with which for a time he oppressed England. The people of Chester applied to parliament in a petition penned as I shall read to you:—

"**To the King our Sovereign Lord**, in most humble wise shewn unto your excellent majesty, the inhabitants of your grace's county palatine of Chester; that whereas the said county palatine of Chester is and hath been always hitherto exempt, excluded and separated out and from your high court of parliament, to have any knights and burgesses within the said court; by reason whereof the said inhabitants have hitherto sustained manifold disherisons, losses, and damages, as well in their lands, goods, and bodies, as in the good, civil and polite governance and maintainance of the commonwealth of their said country: And for as much as the said inhabitants have always hitherto been bound by the acts and statutes made and ordained by your said highness, and your most noble progenitors, by authority of the said court, as far forth as other counties, cities, and boroughs have been, that have had their knights and burgesses within your said court of parliament, and yet have had neither knight nor burgess there for the said county palatine; the said inhabitants, for lack thereof, have been oftentimes touched and grieved with acts and statutes made within the said court, as well derogatory unto the antient jurisdictions, liberties, and privileges of your said county palatine, as prejudicial unto the common wealth, quietness, rest, and peace of your grace's most bounden subjects inhabiting within the same."

"What did parliament with this audacious address?

reject it as a libel? Treat it as an affront to government? Spurn it as a derogation from the rights of legislature? Did they toss it over the table? Did they burn it by the hand of the common hangman?—They took the petition of grievance, all rugged as it was, without softening or temperament, unpurged of the original bitterness and indignation of complaint; they made it the very preamble to their act of redress; and consecrated its principle to all ages in the sanctuary of legislation."

Ancient City Games.

The Proclamation and the Maner used to this daye here followe:

Oyes! thrise—The R^t worshipfull the Mayor of the cittie of Chester willeth and requireth, and in the Queene's Majesties name straitly chargeth and commandeth all and every person and persons, of what degree or calling soever he or they be, here this day assembled, or shall assemble themselves to see the auntient games, heretofore accustomed to be played, at or upon this day, for the comfort and recreation of her Majesties subjects then present, that they and every of them doe observe and keepe her Majesties highnes peace, and be of good behaviour during the time the games be in playeinge, upon paine and peril that shall fall thereon.

FOR THE SHOEMAKERS.

Oyes—The aldermen and stuards of the societie of the shooemakers within the cittie of Chester, come forth and doe your homage in deliveringe up your gleaves and presentmentes, upon paine of ten powndes.

FOR THE SADLERS.

The aldermen and stuards of the societie and companye of sadlers, within the cittie of Chester, come forthe, doe your homage with your horse and bell, upon paine of ten powndes.

The Waches of the Mayor and the Sherifes at Christmasse yerelyé used,

Of which noe man's memorie cannot remember the origenal, yett the collections of writers doe shew the cause thereof, the time of the beginninge to be in the dayes of William the Conqueror, who driving the oulde Brittons, or as is veryly thoughte the Walshemen, who did here inhabitt, mixed with the ould Saxons, seeing the Normans to have gotten the possession, and had procured some rest, settled themselves in this cittie in peace, by force of conquest, at a season in the Christmas, when all men give themselves to securitie, the Walshmen, were neighbours, grudgeinge at their securitie and possession of their lande (as late example we had of the Irishe in Londondery in Ireland, and of later time, about 1620, of the plantation of the English in Virginia), the Walshmen came in the nighte time, and made a sudden invasion, and spoyled and burned some part of this cittie, whereupon the Conqueror gave landes with the consente of Hugh Lupe, his sister's son, and Earle of Chester, to divers who should watche and warde, and be ready to defend the city by any service at all time, the which lands are come to the possesion of divers honorable and worshipful persons and others, which now is called the gable rents, at which time of Christmasse always after they used to sett the said tenants, with all theire forces, accordinglye to watche at that season, to prevent the like danger of the Walshmen. The which service is required, and the houlders of those landes doe their homage before the mayor and sherifes, at their watchcourtes at Christmasse yerelye, to this daye, with other services proper to that tenure, only when they are required or commanded. This was the originall, the cause and continuance of this custome.

The use now of the Watches.

The use now that is made thereof is, to performe the service of the anchante tenure, and cause there appearance before them, to watche 3 nightes togeather, with most stronge and well appointed armore, not fearinge now the invasion of forraigne or civile enemye, by reson of the perfecte and long blessed peace we have enjoyed from God and our gratious princes and kinges precedente; but now we use the same, as to kepe the cittie from danger of fire, theeves, dronknes, and unmeete meetings, and drinkeinges in the nightes, which might be causes of perturbation of peace, and sin againste God, which to these times are most incidente. This is the cause of the continuance thereof now. And after the courte of theire appearance of the tennantes aforesaid, and the watche there ordered or given by the mayor or sheriffes, the 3 first nightes in Christmasse, the mayor, aldermen, and sheriffes, doe all goe togeather to the howses of the mayor and sheriffes, as their nighte is in course, and doe there banquet togeather in joy, as the time requires, not only for the birth of our blessed Redeemer, but also for rememberance of God's greate mercie, in granting us peace and plentie, but also these gracious meanes to preserve our peace and quiet, both of our soules, howses, and persons, which is in my opinion a most meet, honeste, and comendable thinge, whereat if any repine, because there may be sin, I say he or they mighte goe up to Heaven for perfection, for upon this earthe it is not to be found.

St. George's Race on the Roode Dee of late begone.

In anno Dom. 1609, Mr. William Lester, mercer, being mayor of Chester, Mr. Robert Ambrye, irnemonger, being sometimes sheriffe of this cittie, upon his own coste did cause 3 silver bells to be made of good value, which bells he appoynted to be ranne for with horses upon St. George's day, upon the Roode Dee, from the New Tower to the netes, there torning to run up to the Watergate, that horse which came firste there, to have the beste bell, the second to have the seconde bell for that year, putting in money, and for to .... and shuerties to deliver in the bells that day twelvemonth, and the winers had the money put in by those horses that runne, and the use of the bells. The other bell was appointed to be run for the same day, at the ringe, upon the like conditions. This was the first beginninge of St. George's race, to which charges, it is said, Mr. Ambrye had some allowance from the cittie.

St. George's Race, altered 1623, by John Brereton, the Mayor of Chester.

This continued until the year 1623, in which yeare Mr. John Brereton, a worthie famous citizen of Chester, altered the said race, to run from beyond the New Tower, and so round the Roode Dee, and the bell to be of greater value, and a free bell, to have it freely for ever, which shall winne the same ; to the which he gave liberally, and caused the oulde bells, with more money, to be put out in use, the which use should make the free bell yearly for ever, there to be runne for on St. George's day for ever. This I leave to the new alteration, the which, if by reporte I erre, I crave pardon, and desire it may be truly corrected.

Now of the Playes of Chester, called the Whitsun Playes.

THE AUTHOR OF THEM.

The maker and firste inventer of them was one Randoll, a monke in the Abbaye of Chester, who did transelate the same into Englishe, and made them into partes and pagiantes, as they were then played.

THE MATTER OF THEM.

The matter of them was the Historye of the Bible, mixed with some other matter.

THE FIRST TIME PLAYED.

The time they weare firste set forthe, and played was in anno 1339, sir John Arneway being mayor of Chester.

THE PLAYERS AND CHARGES THEREOF.

The actors and players weare the occupacions and companies of this cittie ; the charges and costes thereof, which was greate, was theires also. The time of the yeare they weare played, was on Monday, Tuesday, Wenesday in Whitson weeke.

THE MANER OF THEM.

The maner of these playes weare, every company had his pagiante, or parte, which pagiantes weare a high scafolde with two rowmes, a higher and a lower upon 4 wheeles. In the lower they apparelled themselves, in the higher rowme they played, being all open on the tope, that all behoulders might heare and see them.

THE PLACES AND WHERE THEY PLAYED THEM.

The places where they played them was in every streete. They begane firste at the Abay Gates, and when the pagiante was played, it was wheeled to the High Crosse before the mayor, and so to every streete, and so every streete had a pagiante playinge before them till all the pagiantes of the daye appointed were played, and when one pagiante was neere ended worde was broughte from streete to streete, that soe the mighte come in place thereof, exceedinge orderlye, and all the streetes had their pagiante afore them, all at one time, playing togeather, to see which playes was greate resorte, and alsoe scafoldes, and stages made in the streetes, in those places wheere they determined to playe theire pagiantes

Police Act.—An Act passed in the 43d year of Geo. III. enlarging the powers of an Act, passed in the 2d year of the same reign; the provision contained in it, relating to the election of Commissioners, the nightly watch, lighting, and cleansing the streets, &c. and preventing nuisances and encroachments within the same, and the making and collecting the rates, having been found inadequate to the purposes of the Act.—Any seven of the Commissioners enumerated may act, unless a larger number is specified as necessary. The Mayor, Recorder, and Justices of the Peace, also the Dean and Prebendaries for the time being, are qualified to act as Commissioners; and no other person shall be qualified to act as Commissioner, unless at the time of his acting he be seized or possessed, either in fee or for life, or for a term of not less than fourteen years, and be in actual possesion of buildings, premises, &c. rated and assessed under this act, at the yearly value of £60. or upwards, unless such person shall be the actual occupier of some house, shop, &c. within the city or liberties, rated and assessed under this act at the yearly value of £20. or upwards. Any person acting as Commissioner not qualified as above, shall for every such offence forfeit and pay the sum of £50. to any person who shall inform or sue for the same. Commissioners to take an oath to act with impartiality. Not to act in any case in which they are personally interested. A general meeting of Commissioners to be held the second Tuesday in April, in each year, which shall be called the General Annual Meeting of the Commissioners; when an account of all monies received or paid by virtue of this act shall be produced, examined, and settled, being verified by oath, which any Commissioner is qualified to administer. Commissioners may order a rate or assessment to be made, by surveyors as often as they think requisite, which shall be signed by seven or more of the said Commissioners, and shall not be deemed valid, unless so signed. Premises occupied by several persons any one or more of them may be deemed liable to pay rates. John Fletcher and John Bedward, appointed Surveyors, with such salaries as the Commissioners shall at some general meeting order and direct; if in any case such surveyors differ in opinion, then Thomas Penson, of Wrexham, Architect, is appointed to settle the difference between the said Surveyors, who are to take an oath to act impartially. Houses under the yearly value of £3. not to be rated, and no messuage, &c. to be rated higher than £70. except the Dee Mills, which shall not be rated at any greater value than 100*l.* No empty and unoccupied house, shop, &c. to be rated. Persons quitting premises before the assessments be paid, shall be liable. Agreements between any landlord and tenant concerning payment of rates not to be affected by this act. The Commissioners may cause the names of streets, &c. to be painted in any conspicuous place, and if any person shall wilfully obliterate or deface the same, he shall on conviction, by the oath of one witness, forfeit any sum not exceeding 40*s.* nor less than 10*s.* The owners and occupiers of houses and other buildings within the liberties of the city, shall at their own costs and charges, within such time and in such manner as the said Commissioners at their general annual meeting shall from time to time by notice in writing, signed by their clerk, to be delivered to such owner or occupiers, or left at their respective dwelling-houses, direct and appoint, cause all steps, stairs, posts, pillars, and pilasters, pallisadoes, pales, and rails, poles, projecting windows, porches, stalls, shew-boards, cellar windows, doors, and grates, spouts, steps into cellars and vaults, and all other encroachments and annoyances, whatsoever, belonging to their respective houses, buildings, or premises, and extending over or upon the streets, squares, lanes, alleys, passages, and public places, or any part thereof, to be removed, altered, or reformed, and also to cause the water to be conveyed from the roofs, cornices, and penthouses of their respective houses, or other buildings, by proper and sufficient pipes or trunks, to be affixed to the sides of their respective houses or other buildings; and in case any such owner or occupier shall neglect or refuse so to do, it shall be lawful for the said Commissioners to cause the same to be done at the costs and charges of any such owner or occupier; and the costs and charges attending the removal, alteration, or reformation of the same, to be ascertained and settled by the said Commissioners, shall, in case the same be not paid on demand made by any person authorised by the said Commissioners in that behalf, be levied by distress and sale of the goods and chattels of such owner or occupier, by warrant under the hands and seals of the said Commissioners, or any two, or more Justices of the Peace of the said city of Chester, (which warrant such Commissioners or Justices are hereby authorized to grant) rendering the overplus (if any) upon demand, to the person or persons whose goods and chattels shall have been so distrained and sold; and if the tenant or occupier of any such house or other building shall remove, alter, or reform, any such encroachment, obstruction, or annoyance, as aforesaid, to the satisfaction of the said Commissioners, it shall be lawful for him or her to deduct and retain the reasonable charge and expense thereof, and also any money which shall or may have been levied upon his or her goods and chattels as aforesaid, out of his or her next payment of rent; and the owner, proprietor, or landlord of every such house or other building, is hereby required to allow the same accordingly as a payment or part of payment of rent, as the case may be, and the same shall be good as such payment to all purposes whatever. Commissioners may raise money on mortgage of the rates, but it shall not exceed in the whole the sum of one thousand pounds. They may with consent of the Mayor and citizens, make, repair, or cause to be opened in all or any of the streets, such drains, soughs, common sewers, and reservoirs as they shall think proper. If any person shall trail or draw, or cause to be trailed and drawn upon, or along any of the said squares, streets, lanes, or public roads, within the said city, or the liberties thereof, any tree or piece of timber, or any stone, otherwise than upon wheel carriages, or shall suffer any tree, &c. which shall be conveyed upon such wheel carriages to drag upon any part of the said squares, streets, lanes, or public roads within the said city; or shall bring any stoned horse or stallion into any of the squares, streets, lanes, roads, or public passages aforesaid, or in the market-place, or places of the same city, otherwise than for the purpose of passing through or along the same, or shall exhibit the same in any of the places aforesaid; or shall suffer any butcher's blocks, huxter's standings, coach, chaise, waggon, cart, or other carriage, wheelbarrow, truck, timber, bricks, lime, stones, slates, hay, straw, wood, faggots, coal, tubs, casks, crates, hampers, goods, wares, or merchandise, or any other materials or things whatsoever, to be laid or placed, and left to remain in any of the said squares, streets, lanes, roads, rows, public passages, or places, for any longer time than shall be necessary for removing or housing the same, or for taking up or setting down passengers, or persons going into or coming out of any stage coach, or for the loading or unloading of any waggon, cart, or other carriage; or shall cast or throw, or cause to be cast or thrown any broken glass or earthenware, ashes, rubbish, dust, dirt, dung, filth, soap-lees, or any other nuisance, annoyance, or obstruction whatsoever, into, or laid in any of the said squares, streets, rows, lanes, roads, public passages or places, or shall leave any cellar-doors open therein, or shall drive, draw, carry, or place in any of the rows, or on any of the footways of any of the said squares, streets, city walls, lanes, ways, public passages, or places, any cart, wheel-barrow, hand-barrow, wheel-sledge, truck, or carriage, or wilfully ride, lead, or drive, any horse or other beast or cattle therein or thereon; or shall cause any bull, bear, badger, or other beast, to be baited or worried in any of the streets, rows, or squares, within the said city, every person so offending shall for every such offence forfeit and pay any sum not exceeding five pounds, nor less than five shillings, to be recovered as after mentioned; and it shall also be lawful for any person or persons to seize and detain any such cart, carriage, wheelbarrow, or other matters, and also to impound any such horse, mare, mule, ass, swine, beast, or other cattle, in the common pound of the said city, or in such other place as shall be appointed by the said Commissioners, and the same to detain in the said pound or places, until the penalty and the expenses of impounding, seizing, and detaining the same, shall be fully paid and satisfied; and in case such penalty, and all expenses attending the levying thereof, shall not be paid within four days next after such seizure, or after such, horse, mule, ass, swine, beast, or other cattle, shall be so impounded, it shall be lawful for the person or persons, who shall be appointed by the said Commissioners for that purpose, to sell, or cause to be sold, such horse, mare, mule, ass, swine, beast, cattle, or other things so distrained or seized, returning the overplus (if any be), to the owner thereof, after such penalty, and the reasonable charges occasioned by such impounding, seizure, and distress, shall be deducted and paid. No person to be subject to any penalty on account of any building materials, &c. so that there be

CHESTER

HISTORY.

convenient room for carriages to pass and repass, and the owner or occupier shall effectually inclose the same with posts and rails, and set up, and maintain a light during the night time, to prevent accidents, or mischief happening to passengers or cattle. Commissioners to appoint a time for the removal of night soil, &c. Persons summoned to give evidence before the Commissioners, liable to a penalty for refusal. Inhabitants declared competent witnesses and jurors, in all actions concerning the execution of this Act. Penalties to be recovered with costs of conviction by distress and sale of the offenders' goods, and in case of deficiency the party may be committed to the common jail without bail, for any time not exceeding six calendar months, or until such penalty, together with the costs, shall have been fully paid. Of penalties recovered, one moiety to go to the informer or informers, in such shares as the Justices shall direct, and the other to the Treasurer of the Commissioners for the uses and purposes in this Act mentioned. Charges of prosecution to be reimbursed. Any person thinking himself aggrieved may appeal to the Justices of the Peace, at the General Quarter Session for the City, within the space of seven calendar months next, after such cause of appeal shall have arisen. Proceedings not removable, nor to be quashed for want of form. Commissioners and their officers allowed to plead the general issue, and give this Act in evidence. No process to issue against them unless previous notice shall have been given to such Commissioners, Clerk, &c. Tender of sufficient amends may be pleaded in bar to such action. Plaintiffs not to recover without proof of notice. Commissioners neglecting to give notice to be at liberty to pay money into court. No evidence to be given but what is mentioned in the notice. Nothing in this Act to affect the powers of the General Turnpike Act, &c. Powers of the former Act to extend to this. Declared to be a Public Act. The royal assent was given to this Act on the 27th of May, 1803.

The same King George III. did in the 44th year of his reign, grant his letters patent, dated at Westminster, on the 7th day of November, to the Mayor and Citizens of Chester, in consequence of their petition, shewing that by the constitution of the Magistracy of the said city "the Mayor and Recorder only being Justices of the Quorum, great delays and inconveniences have arisen, and it is apprehended may hereafter arise, in the administration of justice, and particularly in the execution of the laws relating to the revenue and the poor, from the Mayor and Recorder of the said city for the time being, or either of them, being prevented by absence from the said city on account of illness, or any other reasonable cause, or by sickness, infirmity, or interest in any matter in question, from attending on or acting in the execution of the said offices of Mayor and Justices of the Peace: and that it would be of great public utility to the said city, if the Mayor for the time being were authorized to appoint a deputy, with power to execute the office of Mayor in all things in the absence of the said Mayor, for such cause as aforesaid; and that such deputy should be during his continuance in that office a Justice of the Peace of the Quorum, in like manner as the Mayor and Recorder now are." He the same King George III. did give and grant to the Mayor and Citizens of Chester, and their successors for the time being, "that it shall and may be lawful to and for the Mayor of the said city for the time being, to nominate and appoint from time to time, by any instrument or writing under his hand and seal, executed by him in the presence of, and attested by two or more credible witnesses, with the consent and approbation of any three of the Aldermen of the said city, for the time being, testified by their signing the same, one of the Aldermen of the said city, who shall have served the office of Mayor, to be deputy of him the said Mayor, and to execute and act in the said office of Mayor in the place and stead of the said Mayor for the time being, and also in any other office or offices which is, or are to be executed by the Mayor for the time being, in the place and stead of such Mayor in and over the said city of Chester, and county of the same city, at such times only as the said Mayor for the time being shall be absent from the said city, on account of sickness or other reasonable cause, or be prevented by sickness, infirmity, interest, or other legal cause from attending on and executing the same office, which said person so to be nominated and appointed, shall have and exercise by himself and together with any other or others, as the case may require, all and every the powers and authorities, jurisdictions, offices, and functions, which by the

CHESTER

Constitution of the said Corporation are vested in, or ought to be exercised by the said Mayor for the time being, by himself or together with any other or others, or as are vested in, or ought to be exercised by such Mayor as exercising any other office within the said city, and county of the same. Provided always that such instrument of appointment shall be registered amongst the proceedings of the Crownmote and Portmote Courts of the said city, within fourteen days after the execution of the same. And that it shall not be lawful for any such deputy to act under such appointment until such registration as aforesaid, and until he shall have taken an oath duly and impartially to execute the same according to the best of his skill and knowledge, which oath shall and may be administered by the Mayor or two of the Aldermen of the said city for the time being. And all acts, matters, and things, done and executed by the person so to be nominated and appointed as aforesaid, by himself or together with any other or others as the case may require, shall be as valid and effectual in the law to all intents and purposes whatsoever, as if the same had been done and executed by the Mayor of the said city for the time being, named, chosen, and appointed as heretofore accustomed. And that every such deputy so to be nominated and appointed as aforesaid, shall during his continuance of the said office of deputy, be, and be held, deemed, and taken to be a Justice of the Peace of us, our heirs and successors, of the Quorum, within the said city and county of the same, with such and the like powers, jurisdictions, and authorities, in all respects and of what nature soever, and whether the same are to be executed together with any other person or persons or otherwise, as are vested in the said Mayor and Recorder, as Justices of the Peaçe of the Quorum, and which they or either of them can or may exercise by themselves or himself, or together with any other person or persons by virtue thereof. And our will and pleasure is, that every such appointment shall continue in force during such time as the person who shall have made and executed the same as aforesaid, shall continue in the said office of Mayor, or until the same shall be revoked by instrument in writing as herein after mentioned. Provided always, and our will and pleasure is, that these our letters patent shall extend and be construed to extend to authorize and empower such person so to be nominated and appointed by the Mayor of the said city for the time being as aforesaid, to exercise or execute all or any of the said offices, powers, authorities, jurisdictions, and functions hereby granted to, or vested in him, or which he is hereby authorized and empowered to exercise and execute either in the place and stead of the said Mayor for the time being, or as a Justice of the Peace of us, our heirs and successors, of the Quorum, within the said city, and county of the same, in such cases and at such times only as the said Mayor for the time being, shall be absent from the said city, on account of sickness or other reasonable cause, or be prevented by sickness, infirmity, interest, or other legal cause, from attending on and executing the same. Provided also, that it shall and may be lawful for the said Mayor, for the time being, to revoke any such appointment by instrument or writing, under his hand and seal, executed by him in the presence of, and attested by two çredible witnesses as he shall see occasion, such instrument of revocation being registered amongst the proceedings of the Crownmote and Portmote Courts of the said city, within fourteen days after the execution thereof."

HISTORY.

The Stanley family held the forestership of Wirral, by the delivery of a horn* (to their ancestor, Allen Sylvester) with a proviso by the Earl of Chester, Ranulph, that he should blow, or cause to be blown, that horn, at Gloverstone, Chester, on every fair day, in token that the tolls or duties payable for goods bought or sold in that place during the time of the fair, belonged to him, and all his tenants there.—*History of the House of Stanley.*

*See p. 280.

The Manufactures of Chester are comparatively inconsiderable. They consist chiefly of tobacco, snuff, patent shot, white lead, iron, tobacco-pipes, and leather; a good deal of business is still done in the skinning trade. Formerly glove making was carried on here to a great extent, but it has almost entirely ceased. The Lysons say, that "there are not now (1810) more than two or three hundred persons, mostly women, employed in it:" The fact is, there are not FORTY glovemakers in the city.—Chester has long been famed for the superiority of its ship-building.

CHESTER

There are still existing the remains of two Fords over the Dee, within the city's liberties. One, called Boughton Ford, which led in a direct line to the great Watling-street, through Eaton Park, now called Eccleston-lane. The other near the bottom of Dee-lane, in Foregate-street (formerly called *Peene's-lane*), leading to the road from Boughton Ford. That there was a regular way across the stream of the Dee at THESE places, cannot be doubted; but the passage must have existed before the erection of the causeway across the river at the Bridge, which forms a breast work, and rises the water of the river above it, several feet. Tradition says, that there was formerly a ford, from the *Shipgate, or Hole-in-the-Wall*, to the opposite (Edgar's) field: but of this there is no remain.

The present Oath taken by every Freeman of the City of Chester:—I shall be obedient, profitable, and true to the King of the United Kingdom of Great Britain and Ireland, and to the Earldom of Chester, and to the Commonalty of the said City, and truly the franchises of Chester maintain, with all my might and power, give and yield with my Mayor and my Neighbour, after my having; worship my Elders, and their Council keep, and be not assenting, nor abetting, to any Confederacy, nor Conspiracy against the City nor my Neighbours, nor any Foreign Goods conceal, in Merchandize, in Custom, nor in any otherwise, and not to be retained to any other man, but only to the Mayor for the time being; and these Articles well and truly keep.

The full return of the Royal Chester Volunteers, in February, 1808, was—

Officers	69	7th	92
Grenadiers	97	8th	93
1st Company	95	9th	90
2d do	86	10th	91
3d	120	Light Company	108
4th	83	Artillery	101
5th	87		——
6th	109	TOTAL	1321

In November, 1818, there were 145 Inns, and Public Houses, in Chester; the principal Inns, are, the Royal Hotel, and Green Dragon, Eastgate-street; the White Lion, Coach-and-Horses, and Pied Bull, Northgate-street; and the Feathers, and Red Lion, Bridge-street, &c.

HISTORY.

The building of Chester appears to have been predicted at a remote period; for Tudor Aled, in his ode to the Castle of Crogen (Chirk), says—

"Mae breuddwyd am Beryddon,
"Yr ai Gaer hir ar gwr hon."

It was said of old that there would be a city, or fortress, on the shore of the Peraidd, the sweet, or delicious river, now the Dee. LLWYD.

SHERIFF'S ELECTION.*—On the 23d, 24th, and 26th days of October, 1818, a poll took place for the office of Sheriff of Chester; the Candidates were Mr. John Dodd, and Mr. G. Wildig.—The state of the poll was as follows:—

*See p. 191.

FRIDAY—Dodd 276
Wildig............ 132
——137 Majority.

SATURDAY—Dodd 586
Wildig.......... 501
—— 85 Majority.

MONDAY—Dodd 652
Wildig 571
—— 81 Majority.

Mr. Dodd was chaired by his friends through the principal streets.

ELECTION, 1818.—In Feb. 1819, a Petition was presented against the return of General Grosvenor and Lord Belgrave, elected Representatives for the City of Chester, in June, 1818; when the Committee appointed by the House of Commons, by the mouth of their Chairman, Mr. Wharton, on the 5th day of March, resolved—

That it is the opinion of the Committee, that Lord Belgrave is duly elected to serve as a Burgess in Parliament for the City of Chester.

That Lieutenant-General Thomas Grosvenor is also duly elected a Representative for the same city.

That the Petition of Sir John Egerton, Bart. and John Williams, Esq. is not frivolous and vexatious.

CHESTER

That the Defence of Lord Belgrave and Lieut.-Gen. Grosvenor, is not frivolous and vexatious.

DESTRUCTION OF THE DEE MILLS BY FIRE.—On Saturday night, March 6, 1819, a little before twelve o'clock, a fire broke out in the upper story of that extensive building, the Dee Mills, in Chester. The progress of the flames was extremely rapid—the night mild and calm; and in half an hour, the entire fabric presented one vast volume of fire. There was a great quantity of corn, both barley and wheat, on the premises, and the flames ascending to an immense height, illuminated the country throughout a circuit of several miles,—presenting a magnificent but terrific spectacle. The fire engines were soon on the spot, and also the ordnance engine from the Castle, but worked with no avail as to the immediate object--that of saving the mills. It became, then, a matter of the highest importance, to prevent the spread of the devouring element, to the property adjoining, for at one time, the Water Works, and the Paper Mill of Messrs. E. and W. Roberts, were in imminent peril. All the engines were directed to this purpose, and by great exertion those buildings were fortunately secured, and the whole line of warehouses in Skinner-street probably rescued from destruction. In the mean time, every endeavour was used to save the property in the mill; but about 100 bags of corn only, with the books, were got out, with much danger and appalling risk. Amidst this general ruin, a man far advanced in years, named Davies, fell a victim to his intrepidity—he was burnt literally to a cinder; and when found, about eleven o'clock on the Sunday morning, merely the body, shoulders, and thighs remained, parched into an undistinguishable mass, not three feet in length! The unfortunate man left a widow and eight children to lament his melancholy fate, for whom a subscription was set on foot by several gentlemen of Chester, the amount of which in a few days was upwards of one hundred pounds. About 2 o'clock on Sunday morning, the roof fell in; and by six o'clock, a portion only of the outside walls remained. One of the engines was employed nearly the whole of Sunday and Monday playing on the ruins, which continued blazing throughout the week. The premises and stock were insured to a large amount: the total loss, it is supposed, will exceed £40,000. The late building existed nearly 30 years, erected on the site of the Old Mills, destroyed under similar circumstances, about 12 o'clock, on Saturday night, Sept. 26, 1789.*

HISTORY.

* Chester Chronicle.

The Advowson of the Rectory of St Mary, in Chester, has, since the publication of the 8th part of this work, been purchased from the Hills, of Hough, by the Earl Grosvenor.

In noticing the Benevolent Institution, (see p. 272) we were in error in stating that it was suggested by Mr. Rowlands; it owes its establishment to Dr. Haygarth; and at its commencement, Mr. Geo. Harrison, surgeon, undertook the arduous and difficult office of accoucheur, in conjunction with Mr. Rowlands. This explanation we consider as but a bare acknowledgment of Mr. Harrison's Benevolence.

Page 276.—At the foot of the page, after "The revenue now is about," should have been added "£90." In 1782, Mrs. Eliz. Potter, left the interest of £40. to the occupiers of three houses; which was further increased by £100. left by C. Goodwin, Esq. in 1815.

THE PARISH OF DODLESTON,

CONTAINS THE TOWNSHIPS OF

DODLESTON	AND
HIGHER KINNERTON	LOWER KINNERTON.

Higher Kinnerton is in the County of Flint; and Dodleston Moor was perambulated as part of the Parish of Gresford, till 1642.

DODLESTON,

Together with Claverton, was included in the boundaries of a Forest, laid out by the Earl, and noticed in the Domesday Survey; it extended to Bretton, Hawarden, and probably in the direction of Northop. The founder of the Boydell family, Osborn Fitz-Tezzon, had the first grant of Dodleston. Helto, was probably the first of the family that assumed the name of Boydel, about the year 1100 or 1110. About the reign of Henry V. this family as connected with Dodleston, became extinct; and it appears, that in the 5th of Hen. V. Hugh Radiche and Margaret his wife (sister and co-heiress of Robert, son of Thomas de Boydell) obtained from John Aldburgham, and Isabella his wife, (sister of the said Robert) lands in Dodleston, Kinnerton, Gropenhall, Hale, Warrington,* &c. This Hugh, after the death of Margaret his wife, held the Manor of Dodleston and Kinnerton from the King as Earl of Chester, in capite. In the 4th Eliz. Thomas Reddishe, Esq. held the Manor, valued at £13. 13s. 4d. and lands in Dodleston, Kinnerton, &c. Maud his daughter and heiress married William Merbury, of Merbury, and in the 11th Eliz. they obtained by fine from George and Peter Redish, deforciants, the manors of Dodleston, and Gropenhall. Soon after this the Grosvenors of Eaton purchased an estate from the Merburies, which was subsequently conveyed by Richard Grosvenor, Esq. to Thomas Egerton, Esq. afterwards Lord Chancellor. About 1627, the Merbury estates were purchased by the Ravenscrofts, of Bretton, in the county of Flint; and in 1756, Thomas Powis, Esq. of Lilford, in the county of Northampton, whose father had married a co-heiress of the Ravenscroft family, sold it to Sir Robert Grosvenor, Bart. Grandfather of the present proprietor.

The site of the ancient Castle of Dodleston, formerly the seat of the Boydells, still remains. It lies immediately west of the Church, and the earthworks inclose nearly a Cheshire acre. The keep, at the north-west angle, was defended by a fosse, and circular mound—

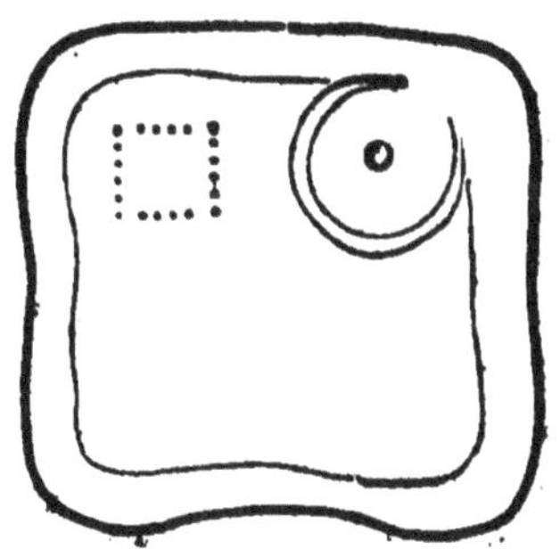

The Old Hall, which for several generations was the property of the Manleys, of Lache, stood within this site. It was, during the Civil Wars, the head-quarters of Sir W. Brereton, when he had the command against Chester. It passed by sale from the Manleys, to Sir Robert Lawley, Bart.† from whom it was purchased by Earl Grosvenor, in 1807. The old hall no longer exists, and the ground it stood upon is occupied by a farm-house. The other Hall, sold by the Grosvenors to the Lord Chancellor Egerton, was purchased from his son the Earl of Bridgewater, by R. Kelsall, Esq. of Trafford. It is now, with an adjoining estate, the property

† Lysons.

* Thomas de Boydell, 20th Ric. II. held lands in Handlegh, &c. the tolls of Warrington Bridge (cum passagio pontis de Warrington.)

of John Glegg, Esq. of Withington, to whom it came by marriage with Bridget, daughter of John Kelsall, Esq.

The Church was given by Alan de Boydell to the Abbot and Convent of St. Werburgh, at Chester, temp. King John. William, the brother of Alan, confirmed the donation; and it appears from an ancient document,* that the Monks had license to appropriate it, on the condition of endowing a vicarage, from Galfred, Bishop of Lichfield and Coventry from 1198 to 1208; the license, however, was not acted upon.—At the Dissolution the patronage was given to the Dean and Chapter, and in the 22d of Eliz. it was confirmed to them by Patent.

The present Rector is Unwin Clarke, A. M. Prebendary, and Archdeacon of Chester, instituted Jan. 16, 1806. All the tythes of the Parish are vested in the Rector.

The Church closely adjoins the moated site before described, on the east side. It has a good tower; the body consits of nave, chancel, and side ailes; and the Glegg chancel.

The grave of the Chancellor is marked by this short inscription on a white lozenge, inlaid on a stone of black marble:—

"Anchora animæ, fides et spes in Christo—Orimur,—Morimur, sequentur qui non præcesserint."

On a Monument, on the south wall of the Chancel—

"Sacred to the memory of John Kelsal, Esq. and Mary his wife. She was daughter of William Farrington, Esq. of Eardshaw, co. Cest. He died Sept. 21, 1783, aged 77. She died April 6, 1791, aged 70. His public virtues were conspicuous in the several situations he filled; his gentle and amiable disposition endeared him to his family and friends, which made their loss severe. Bridget, only child of the above-named John and Mary Kelsal, married John Glegg, Esq. of Old Withington, co. Cest. She died June 27, 1786, aged 35 years and left issue one son and daughter.

Nearly adjoining the memorial of the Chancellor, on a flat stone—

Thomas Egerton, miles filius primogenitus Thomæ Egerton, mil. Baronis de Ellesmere, Cancellarii Angliæ; in Anglia natus; in insulis Asor: dignitate militari insignitus; in Hibernia, morte immatura præreptus—occubuit in Christo, 23 die Aug. aº. 1599, æt. suæ 25; victurus cum mortua mors fuerit. Hic corpus requiescit, in cœlo anima lætatur.

On a white marble Monument, the arms of Egerton, impaling Ravenscroft of Bretton, a memorial of one of the Chancellor's wives—

Fallax gratia, vana pulchritudo,
Mulier timens d'num ipsa laudabitur.
Elizabetha condita est hic Egertona,
Pie familiam rexit, instituit natos.
Vitæ virili mente sustinuit curas,
Plusquam virili mente sustinuit morem,
Juvit jacentes pauperes manu, voce.
Desideratam sponsus et sui lugent,
Quos ipsa liquit, sed dedit suis sese.
Matri illa partem reddidit, patri partem,
Terræ illa corpus reddidit, Deo mentem,
Sic tota salva est, sic et occidit tota.
Vis plura? ocellos, flentum lege ocellos,
In his notantur plura—plura scribuntur.
Non obiit, sed abiit,
Anno d'ni 1586.

The Registers, which are very imperfect, begin in 1570.—In 1642, occurs the following entry: "This yeare the Curate of Gresford, with some of the Parishioners, having come for divers yeares to the Moor Well,† some of them over the Moor, and some of them through Pulford parish in procession, saying that they were sent thither to claim that well to be in their parish, and now this yeare, when they were in the Moor, they saw some souldiers standing by the well, which wanted to see their fashions; on which they said the Curate and his company went back again, and never came again to the well."—Several soldiers were shot in the village during the Rebellion in 1645, and were buried in the Church-yard.

The Charitable Contributions are not very numerous. There are £84, the interest arising from which, and a rent charge of 5s. together with the proceeds of land

* Chartulary of St. Werburgh.—Harl. MSS.

† The boundary of Gresford parish, on the Dodleston side, is marked by several wells, at particular distances; and it is said that a well on the Moor at Dodleston, was one of these useful boundaries.

Cheshire History.

let at £6. 7s. 6d. per ann. is distributed to the poor yearly, but 15s. of this belong exclusively to the poor of the two Kinnertons. The school which this village possesses, is supported by subscription.

LOWER KINNERTON,

Is about 4 miles S. W. by W. from Chester. It is not noticed in Domesday Book, but has uniformly passed with the Manor of Dodleston. In the 23d Edw. III. Wm. Boydell held lands in Kynarton. From the Boydells it descended to the Redishes; and in the 7th Eliz. it passed by fine to Thomas Grosvenor, and it is now vested in Earl Grosvenor. Kinnerton Hall is tenanted as a Farm House. It is a brick building, closely adjoining a small brook, which divides Cheshire and Flintshire—England and Wales. The hall is in Cheshire, but the offices, &c. are in the county of Flint.

PARISH OF ECCLESTON,

CONTAINS THE TOWNSHIPS OF

ECCLESTON, AND EATON CUM BELGRAVE.

At the period of the Survey, Eccleston belonged to the Barony of Kinderton. From an Inq. post mortem, 20 Ric. II. it appears Gilbert de Venables held (inter alia) the advowson of the Church of Eccleston, from the King, as Earl of Chester. It was then valued at xx marks. The Manor continued vested in the Venables family till after the reign of Henry. VI. In the 19th Hen. VIII. Richard Coton, who was cousin and co-heir of Sir Hugh Venables, held the Manor and advowson of Eccleston, from the King as before; value xxiii*l.** In 32d Hen. VIII. Sir Wm. Venables, Knt. held inter alia, the advowson of Eccleston, and lands, from the King, as before. In the 23d Eliz. Sir Thos. Venables, Knt. held inter alia from the Queen, as parcel of his Barony of Kinderton, the Manor and advowson of Eccleston, together with the Hamlet of Belgrave, valued at £11. 17s. 6d. On the Death of Peter Venables, the last male heir, it passed by marriage to Montague Bertie,† Lord Norris, and afterwards to the Vernons. (Lysons.) In 1758, George Venables Vernon sold the manor and advowson to Sir Richard Grosvenor, Bart. and it is now the property of Earl Grosvenor, who holds a Court Leet and Baron here, for Eccleston, Eaton, and Poulton.

A bastard branch of the Breretons, possessed an estate in this township several generations.

The situation of Eccleston is extremely picturesque, and a walk thither from Chester is a favorite exercise with the Citizens.—The Parsonage commands a fine view of the river Dee, and to the line of Broxton Hills, and the high lands of the Forest of Delamere. Below the Church, in the grounds attached to the Rectory, is a tumulis of considerable size, adjoining which is a bath.

Eccleston Hill is considerably higher than the neighbouring country, and the view from it into Wales, may vie with most in the County. There is little doubt but what the summit of the Hill was the site of a British or Roman fortification.‡ The line of the Watling-street through Eaton Park to Aldford, directly crossed it. The hill is covered with a thick plantation, and it forms a prominent object from the adjacent country, and is seen by mariners on entering the Dee from the Irish channel.

All the Houses in Eccleston are built, or painted in the Gothic style of architecture, and have a clean and handsome appearance.

Eccleston is a place of great resort from Chester, from which it is distant little more than two miles, and is much frequented by strangers, on account of the vi-

* William Venables, heir of Sir Hugh, married Eleanor, sister and co-heiress of Thomas Coton, son of Richard Coton.

‡ Several Roman coins have at different periods been found on it, and in the fields adjoining.

cinity of Eaton House, the magnificent seat of Earl Grosvenor.

FIGDALE, a hamlet of Eaton, was situated immediately beyond the Keeper's Lodge, in the present Park. It now no longer exists as a separate *vill*; the houses in it were chiefly on the bank of the Dee, and the site of them is now occupied by the Farm-house of the Bailiff, the Groom's stables, &c.

EATON BOAT, affording a convenient passage across the Dee, from Holt, Farndon, Aldford, Saighton, &c. is now in the township of Eccleston and Cheveley, having been removed from below the Old Hall at Eaton, about the period of the commencement of the present House. The right of this Ferry is vested solely in Earl Grosvenor—and the scenery in the immediate neighbourhood of it, is delightfully romantic. Perhaps the best view of this part of the Dee, and the neighbouring country, is afforded from the Bank, in front of the Keeper's Lodge, at the lower entrance to the Park from Eccleston.

THE CHURCH.—The old Church was taken down in April, 1807; it was a low structure, but of very early English architecture; with a square tower, containing 4 bells.* The body of the Church consisted of nave and side aisles. It possessed several ancient monuments of the Grosvenors, and other families. It is to be lamented, that in the zeal for rebuilding, the destruction was so indiscriminate; for ALL the old Monuments were destroyed, and the mutilated fragments of them strewed over the Church-yard.

Of the Monuments in the Old Church, as they existed in
† 2151,63. Sept, 15, 1572, the Harl, MSS.† give the following account:

" In Eaton Chappell, in the west window of the same, are these coates and subscriptions:—

" A large shield containing Eaton and Grosvenor quarterly (Eaton 1 and 4) impaling a Shield composed of the arms of Rudware, Waltheof, Falconer, and Venables, with Coton on a shield of pretence.—Crest, a falcon with wings displayed gules, beaked and belled Or.—Underneath,

' Of your charitie pray for the good state of Richard Grosvenor de Eaton, armig. and Katherine his wife, the whiche did make this windowe, A. D. 1538.'

" On either side the armes above-said are these figures in the Glasse. On the right hand, a male figure habited in a tabard, emblazoned with the arms of Eaton, with 5 male figures kneeling behind him; over his head—

' S'cus Georgius Ora pro Nobis.'

On the left hand a female figure in a hood and dress, emblazoned with the arms of Rudware, and twelve female figures kneeling behind her. Two were in the habit of nunnes. The one had a crosier staffe in her armes, for she was Lady of the Nunnes in Chester, and the other was of the same house with her. In another place of the same Chappell window, the same coate quarterly, with this writing under it—

' Orate pro anima Ricardi Grosvenor de Eaton, armigeri, qui obiit, 27° die mensis Julii, A. D. 1542.'

In another place Legh of Adlington with four quarters, impaling an unknown shield. This coat for Legh, quarterly 1st and 4th, azure three ducal coronets Or, in the centre point a bezant; 2d azure, two bars gules, over all a bend componè Or and gules, Legh; 3d argent, a cross potence sable, Legh, ancient. Underneath

' Of your charitie pray for the soul of Thomas Leigh, of Adlington, Esq. which died the 17th day of May, 1548.'

" In the north window is the figure of a Bishoppe, in his habite and crosier staffe, and on the rochette is this coat, arg. a chevron sable, between three crosses patee fitchèe sable, and on the welt,—

' S'cus Chadda Lichfeld: Ep'us.'

In another window, on the south side of Eaton Chappell, are two kneeling figure, with eight sonnes and four daughters; no arms—subscribed—

' Of your charitie pray for the souls of Raff Rogers, Maior of the Citty of Chester, and Lucey his wife, Anno 1534.'

In a window on the south south side of the Churche, two figures

* One of the bells is placed in the clock tower, in the stable yard, at Eaton Hall; another was sent to Aldford to increase the ring to four bells; and the remaining two to Farndon, making the peal there six bells.

ECCLESTON CHURCH, 1800.

Eng.[d] for Hanshalls History of Cheshire.

CHESHIRE

kneeling before desks, the tabard of the Man emblazoned with the arms of Danyell---no inscription ---On a grave-stone by the Altar, the recumbent figure of a man in plate armour, inscription mutilated---

'* * who dyed the 17th day of August, A. D. 1548.'

On the screen that parts Eaton chappell from the churche, these arms cut in wood, very aunciente: Stanley quartering Latham and Mann.

In the Chancel on grave stones—

"Here lyeth interred the body of Maud, the wife of Richard Brereton, Esq. who died the 17th day of March, anno 1616, haveing had between them 8 sonnes and 8 dau'rs, being dau. to Richard Hurleston, of Picton, Esq.

Here lyeth the body of ye s^d Richd Brereton, who dyed the --- day of ---."

On a large mural Monument, decorated with the arms and quarterings of the Grosvenors—this inscription:—

"D. O. M. To the pious memoriall of his deare parents, Richard Grosvenor, esq. with Christian, dau' to Richard Brooke, Esq. and Jane, dau' to Sir Thomas Vernon, Kt. his virtuous wives; as alsoe to the like memoriall of Lettice, dau' to Sir Hugh Cholmondeley, Kt. Elizabeth, dau' to Thomas Wilbraham, esq. and Elizabeth, yet living, daughter and heire to Sir Peter Warberton, Kt. one of the Judges of Common Pleas, wives to Sir Richard Grosvenor, Kt. and Bart. the saide Sir Richard, their thrice affectionate sonne and husbande, dedicates this monument, anno domini 1624."

The sides of this tomb were decorated with 4 niches, filled with kneeling figures, inscribed above—

"One sonne and 2 dou'rs of Sir Richard and Lettice; 14 dau'rs of Richard and Christian; 3 sonnes of Richard and Christian."

On the slab were recumbent figures of Sir Richard (in plate armour and spurs) and one of his wives, with their heads on cushions, and their hands clasped.*

There were many other Monuments in the Old Church, noticed by the Rev. T. Crane, in his account of the Parish;—among them, those of—

"Mrs. Rogers, wife of Archdeacon Rogers, the Chester Antiquary; she died the 11th Dec. 1617. John Okes, A. M. died Nov. 1710, aged 65. Henry Wigley, S. T. B. died April 27, 1701, aged 39. Elizabeth Oldfeld, wife of the Rev. Thos. Aubrey, died Nov. 19, 1738, aged 48. Rev. Thos. Aubrey, A. M. died 2d June, 1758, aged 81.--&c. &c. &c.

HISTORY.

THE PRESENT CHURCH stands on the site of the former church. It is a Rectory, the advowson of which is vested in the Earl Grosvenor. The Rev. C. Mytton, A. M. is the present Incumbent, Instituted Oct 2, 1801, on the death of his father, the Rev C. Mytton. The Rector has the tithes of the entire parish, with the exception of a modus for hay, on a farm at Belgrave, some lands in the Park, and a few meadows in Eaton.

The Church is one of the most splendid buildings, of its size, in the Kingdom. It is built, after designs by Mr. Pordon, of the red stone of Eccleston Quarry.—It has a neat Tower, 90 feet high, (containing six new bells) with buttresses, battlements, and pinnacles;—a nave, and chancel. The sides of the Church have three pointed Gothic windows; and over the communion table, is a painting of the Nativity, by Polidoro Caravaggio, presented to the Church by the present Earl Grosvenor. The interior of the fabric is beautifully decorated in the richest style of Gothic ornament. The south transept is occupied by the vestry, above which is the seat of Earl Grosvenor, lined with crimson velvet, and gold fringe. In the opposite transept is the burial place of the Grosvenor family; and a large marble slab records the names of those interred here—

"In the vault underneath are deposited the remains of Richard Earl Grosvenor, created Baron Grosvenor of Eaton, April 1761, and Earl Grosvenor Viscount Belgrave, 1784: he died August 1802, aged 71. Also the remains of Sir Richard Grosvenor, of Eaton, in the County of Chester, Knt, and Bart.: he died Sept. 14, 1645, aged 61.---Roger Grosvenor, Esq. grandson of the above Sir Richard, died Aug. 22, 1661, aged 33.---Sir Richard Grosvenor, Knt. and 2d Bart. son of the above Sir Richard, buried Jan. 31, 1664, aged 60. Hugh Grosvenor, fourth son of Sir Richard, buried Feb. 17, 1698, aged 61. Sir Thomas Grosvenor, 3d Bart. son of Roger Grosvenor, buried July 2, 1700, aged 44. Catherine, daughter of Sir Richard Grosvenor, 4th Bart. buried June 12, 1718. Jane, first wife of Sir Rich. Grosvenor, buried Feb. 6, 1719. Mary, relict of Sir Thomas Grovenor, buried Jan. 15, 1729, aged 65. Diana, second wife of Sir Richard Grosvenor, buried Feb. 28, 1729, aged 27.---Sir Richard Grosvenor son of Sir Thomas, and 4th Bart. died July 12, 1732, aged 44. Sir Thomas Grosvenor, 5th Bart. brother to Sir Richard, died at Naples, buried May 28, 1773, aged 40. Dorothy, wife of Thomas Warre, Esq. buried Aug. 30, 1736. Thomas Warre, Esq. buried August 7,

* This monument was destroyed when the Church was re-built: it was on the south side of the Chancel; but had been much defaced during the Civil Wars.

1745, aged 72. Sir Robt. Grosvenor, 6th Bart. brother to Sir Thos. buried Aug. 12, 1755, aged 60. Deborah, wife of Thos. Grosvenor, Esq. buried April 22, 1771, aged 33. Mary, daughter of Sir Robert Grosvenor, buried Feb. 14, 1774, aged 38. Jane, relict of Sir Robt. Grosvenor, and daughter of Thomas and Dorothy Warre, buried May 25, 1791, aged 86; and of Thomas Grosvenor, Esq. second son of Robt. and brother of Richard Earl Grosvenor, buried Feb. 26, 1795, aged 62. And Elizabeth Grosvenor, his sister, buried December 20, 1805, aged 67.

N. B. The two first Baronets represented the County, and the third Baronet, and all his male descendants, the City of Chester, in Parliament."

The window above this inscription is ornamented with the arms of Grosvenor, and those of other houses with which the House of Eaton have formed alliances, viz.—Mobberley, Downes, Pulford, Phesaunt, Eaton, Stockton, Coton, Rudware, Waltheof, Basing, Falconer, Thurcaston, Venables, Vernon, Davies, Warre: at the bottom are the original coats of the Grosvenors, Azure, a bend, Or; and the same with the bordure awarded in the celebrated Scroop's case,—a bordure Argent.

The roof of the Church is vaulted. An Organ has lately been erected at the west end. This Church was first opened for the celebration of Divine Service on the 10th March, 1809.

In the Church-yard, are the following Monumental Memorials:—

"Here lie the remains of Priscilla, late wife of Mr. John Banks, Manager of the Theatre Royal, Chester. She died 27th Dec. 1793, aged 43. She was a loving dutiful wife, a tender mother, a sincere friend, and a good Christian; in short "take HER for all in all, we shall not look upon her like again."

Sacred to the Memory of Thomas Cowper, Esq of Overlegh, one of his Majesty's Counsel at Law, and Recorder of the city of Chester, who died the 25th day of July, 1788, in the 47th year of his age. He was the last surviving branch of a very ancient and respectable family.

Sacred to the Memory of Harriet, widow of Thomas Cowper, late of Overlegh Hall, Esq. She died on the 3d of March, 1811, aged 59.

Sacred to the Memory of Henrietta Mytton, who died on the 12th of December, 1812, in the 38th year of her age.

Sacred to the Memory of Colonel Martin Tucker, who died the 14th of May, 1792, in the 62d year of his age.

William Lowe, who departed this life, January 21, 1809, aged 92 years.

Underneath this stone rest the remains of the mortal part of John Huxley,* late of Eaton, who departed this life, the 12th day of Sept. 1798, in the 68th year of his age—

Poor Jack; he lies beneath this rood,
And sure he must be blest,
For if he could do nothing good,
He meant to do his best.
Think of your souls, ye guilty throng,
Who knowing what is right—do wrong.

Previous to the destruction of the Weir, the Rector had for his tythe every twentieth salmon. At one period this nutritious fish must have been extremely plentiful in the Dee; so much so, that the Masters in Chester were restrained by the Indenture, from giving it to their apprentices above twice a week.

The Charitable benefactions, chiefly arose from donations from the Grosvenor family, and amounted to £222. forty-two pounds of which were sunk in the repairs of the Old Church, for which the Parishioners now pay interest. The remainder, with a further gift of £50. from Mrs. Elizabeth Grosvenor, is vested in Earl Grosvenor, and the interest is distributed to the Poor on St. Stephen's Day, annually.

The Registers, are early, but imperfect. The following are a few extracts from them:—

		£.	s.	D.
1634	To George Beeston for hanging the mad dog	0	2	6
1638	To a Preaching Minister	0	3	4
	For burying the Cobler of Holt	0	1	6
	For ringing the Coverfeu	0	3	4
1641	Given to a Minister	0	2	0
	A Bottle of Wine and Bread for the Sacrament	0	1	1
1648	Paid for killing Fox Cubs	0	0	6
	For a Fox's head	0	1	0
1654	Meat for the Bell-founder, his Son, and Man, 36 meals, at 4d per meal	0	12	0
	Grass for their two Horses, from 28th Sept. to 7th October	0	9	0

* The deceased was a well-known inoffensive ideot, who almost daily paid his visits to Chester.

CHESHIRE

		£.	s.	d.
1658	The Bell-hanger and Man, eight meals	0	2	8
1662	To writing the Creed and the Lord's Prayer	0	10	6
1666	Drink for Ringers, when we beat the Dutch	0	0	6
1670	To 6¼ days work the Slater and his Man	0	13	0
	Morning draughts for them	0	1	0
1672	To half a pound of Candles	0	0	2
	For a She Fox's Head	0	2	6
	Five Pints of Wine for the Sacrament	0	2	6
1693	April 16, Paid then at the Clerk's, being spent on the Parson which preached on that day, being a stranger	0	1	0
	To Thomas Tilston, for a Vane, 72lb. at 5d.	1	10	0
1709	Postage of a Letter from Manchester	0	0	2
	Paid the Bell-hanger for Casting two Bells	12	0	0
1713	Paid Thomas Booth, for ringing nine of the Clock	0	8	0
1714	Gave the Ringers when King George landed	0	4	0
1718	Gave to a RIGHTING Master y^t had lost ye TEUCE of his Right Thumb.	0	0	6
1738	Bottle of Wine	0	1	4½
1746	Paid the Ringers at the taking of the Rebels	0	2	6
1747	Bottle of Wine	0	1	6
1748	Ditto	0	1	8
1750	Ditto	0	1	4½
	Dinner and drink when we walked the bounds	0	17	6
1757	A Bottle of Wine for Mr. Ruddal, Bell-founder	0	2	0
	Mr. Ruddal's bill for re-casting the first Bell	7	16	0
	Ringing for the King of Prussia	0	1	0
1775	Bottle of Wine	0	1	6
1791	Ditto	0	1	7½
1796	Ditto	0	2	6
1799	Ditto	0	3	0
1804	Ditto	0	3	6
1806	Ditto	0	4	0

EATON.

Formerly called Eaton Boat.—This Township is situated about three miles and a half S. of Chester. The manor was originally given by Leofric, the Mercian Earl, to the Monks of Coventry, temp. Edward Confessor. Immediately previous to the Conquest, it formed two manors, the Saxon proprietors of which were dispossessed to make way for Ilbert, a Norman, who also had grants of Waverton and Clotton. Eaton afterwards passed through the families of Rullos and Pichot, to the Pulfords; and in the reign of Hen. III. Hamon de Pulford was the Lord; this Hamon settling one half of it on Richard his son, and Cecily his wife, daughter of Robert de Huxley, they assumed the local name of Eaton.—Their descendants were afterwards possessed of the whole manor; which in the reign of Henry V. passed by marriage with Joan, daughter and heiress of John Eaton, to Ralph, second son of Sir Thomas Grosvenor,* of Holme, who was the founder of the Grosvenors of Eaton.

HISTORY.

By an Inq. p. m. 22 Eliz. it appears Thomas Grosvenor, Esq. held the manor of Eaton, with certain messuages, a free ferry, and the Serjeantcy of Dee, by services not then known, from the Queen, of her Earldom of Chester, value £3. 6*s*. 8*d*; and also the manors of Tushingham, Belgreave, and Thurcaston, half of Dodleston, lands in Stockton, Droytwiche, Wigland, Shochlach, Hampton, Edge, Horton, Kyddington, Ouldcastle, Hargreve, Burwardsley, Greenwall,† Pulton, Pulford, Gorstilow, Rowton, Oscroft, Kynaston, Bromfield, Gresford, and Barton, right of Common in Burton, Denbighshire, and Coal Mines in Wrexham. Richard Grosvenor who was found heir by this Inquisition was Knighted in the 17th James I. who created him a Baronet. He served the offices of High Sheriff of the counties of Flint and Chester, and represented Cheshire in Parliament. The second Baronet, Sir Richard Grosvenor, was a zealous supporter of the Royal Cause, during the Civil Wars, his attachment to which, ended in his ejection from Eaton; his estate was sequestrated, and the house of a neighbour afforded him shelter till the Restoration. Roger Grosvenor, his eldest son, shared in his sufferings; and both of them saw the re-

† Parish of Dodleston?

Edw. III. * Robert de Eton,* pleading to a quo warranto, claimed by prescription—the Serjeantcy of Dee from Eaton Weir to Arnoldsheyre (opposite the Castle of Chester) by the service of clearing the river from all nets improperly placed there, and to have half of all forfeited nets, and of the fish therein, so far as stall nets were placed, (from Dee Bridge to Blacon, and from thence to Arnoldsheyre) to have one out of all the nets taken, with all the fish therein; and to have a Ferry Boat at Eaton, over the Water, for which his neighbours shall pay him according to their pleasure; but from a stranger he shall receive, if he has a horse, and is a merchant, one halfpenny; but if not a merchant, the payment to be optional. And to have toll from every FLOTE at Eton passing through his weir (de prima Knycke unum denarium qui vocatur hachepeny, et de qualibet Knycke sequente, unum quadrantem) and to have waifs and wrecks on his manor of Eton, with two stall nets, and two free boats on Dee.---Harl. MS. 2022, p. 88.

Cheshire

storation of Charles II. Roger Grosvenor's name was amongst those of the Cheshire Gentlemen who was entered on the list of the projected new Knightly Order of the Royal Oak.—Sir Thomas Grosvenor, the third Baronet, was Mayor of Chester in 1684, and Sheriff of the County in 1688; he also represented the City from the 31st Car. II. to the 1st James II.; and again in the 1st, 7th, and 10th William and Mary. It was this Baronet, by marriage with Mary, sole heiress of Alexander Davis, of Ebury, Esq. who attached to the family possessions the extensive property in the Metropolis. In 1685, he had the command of a troop, in the Earl of Shrewsbury's regiment of horse; and when the Bill was brought into the House for repealing the Penal Laws, and the Test Acts, he was closetted by the King, and offered the regiment, together with a Peerage, for his assent, which he manfully refused, prefering the religion and liberties of his country, to all honours and power. He then threw up his commission, and taking his place in the House, gave his negative to the Bill. Notwithstanding this patriotic demeanor, it was at first supposed that he was a decided supporter to the bigotted measures of the King; and this opinion receives some sanction, when it is recollected, that he was appointed by Jefferies, of execrable memory, as the Foreman of that Jury, which presented the necessity of having sureties of the Peace, from such of the Cheshire Nobility and Gentry, as entertained the Duke of Monmouth in his progress through the County.* He died in 1704, aged 44.

Sir Richard Grosvenor, the fourth Baronet, and eldest surviving son of the last, was Member for Chester, in the first Parliament of George I. as also in the 8th George I. and 1st George II.† He was Mayor of Chester in 1715.—At the Coronation of George II. he acted as Grand Cup Bearer of England, in right of his manor of Wymondelegh, in co. Herts, by presenting the first cup of wine to his Majesty after he was crowned, and receiving the cup for his fee. He was married twice; first, to Jane, daughter of Sir Edward Wyndham, of Orchard Wyndham, county of Somerset; second to Diana, only daughter of Sir Geo. Warburton, of Arley. He died in July, 1732.—Sir Thomas, the fifth Baronet, his brother, succeeded to the title and estates.—He died of a consumption at Naples, in 1733, aged 40 years.—He was an Alderman of Chester, and one of its Representatives in Parliament. Sir Robert Grosvenor, the sixth Baronet, also represented the city, in four Parliaments, and was Mayor in 1737. He married, in May, 1730, Jane, sole heiress of Thomas Warre, of Swell Court, and Shepton-Beauchamp, county of Somerset. He died in May, 1755. Sir Richard, son of the deceased, and the seventh Baronet, also officiated as Grand Cupbearer of England on the marriage of his present Majesty George III. On the 8th April, 1761, he was created Baron Grosvenor of Eaton; and on the 5th July, 1784, was dignified with the titles of Viscount Belgrave and Earl Grosvenor. In 1759, he was Mayor of Chester; and was some time Representative in Parliament for Chester.—He died in 1802. Robert the second Earl Grosvenor, was born in London, the 22d March, 1767. He represented the City of Chester in Parliament from 1790, till the death of his father. In 1789, his Lordship was appointed one of the Lords of the Admiralty, and contiuued so till 1791—he is Lord Lieutenant of the county of Flint. His Lordship married Eleanor, daughter and sole heiress of Thomas Earl of Wilton, by whom he has issue Rich. Viscount Belgrave, born Jan. 27, 1795, elected Rrepresentative for Chester in June, 1818; Thomas Grosvenor, Earl of Wilton,‡ born December 30, 1799; Robt. Grosvenor, born April 24, 1801; Amelia‖ Grosvenor, born July 19, 1802, died March 27, 1814—buried at Prestwich, near Manchester. The present Earl was Mayor of Chester, in 1807, and is the twenty-first in paternal descent from Gilbert le Grosvenor, who came to England in 1066, with his uncle Hugh Lupus, Earl of Avranches, and subsequently Earl Palatine of Chester.

The manerial rights of Eaton are co-extensive with the township; the Manor of Belgrave is unknown;

* For this presentment, an action of Libel was afterwards brought against Sir Thomas, by the Earl of Macclesfield.

† In the last Parliament he was associated with his younger brother, Thomas Grosvenor, Esq.

‡ By the limitations of a Patent, the Earldom of Wilton is entailed on the second son of Earl Grosvenor.

‖ The late Princess Amelia was her Godmother.

EAST VIEW OF EATON HOUSE.

The seat of Earl Grosvenor. from the large plate by Mr. J. Halton.

Engraved for Hanshalls History of Cheshire.

CHESHIRE

HISTORY.

nor can it be traced at what period it merged in that of Eaton. So late as the reign of Edward III. it was possessed by a family that bore the local name; it was then the property of Thomas, son of John de Belgrave, whose widow Joan de Pulford, subsequently married Sir Robt. Grosvenor of Holme—it appears, therefore, that it was connected by relative ties with the Grosvenor family, some time previous to Eaton becoming their property.

Eaton Hall.—The Old Hall has been pulled down about fifteen years. It was built by Sir Thomas Grosvenor, during the reign of William III. and was a large, plain, brick mansion, with a flat heavy roof, and immense lanthorn; a fine court yard in front, with a fountain in the centre, surrounded by iron railing, the entrance gates curiously ornamented.*—The grounds were laid out in the genuine old style of English gardening, which although superseded, has not been surpassed.—The trees were cut in long alleys, intersected by walks, and plantations of orange, the centres of the square thus formed being ornamented by some very fine statues in lead.† In the grounds was a beautiful little Theatre, which was the occasional scene of much rational entertainment: but all these no longer exist; they were destroyed without mercy by the innovating hand of what is termed modern improvement; and the delightful and romantic vistas are succeeded by a flower garden and gravel walk. A view of the Old Hall, by Kip, is preserved in the *Nouveau Theatre de la Grande Bretagne.*

The present magnificent mansion is erected on the site of the Old Hall, some parts of which have been preserved in the basement story. It is built of the white stone from Manley Quarry. The best general idea of the external appearance of the building may be formed from an inspection of the accompanying plates, being views of the east and west fronts of it. The octagonal turrets, buttresses, and richly carved pinnacles, give a splendid finish to the whole. The entrance on the east side is by an extremely wide flight of steps to an extensive terrace 350 feet long, from which the house is approached by another flight of steps, under three light but highly ornamented pointed arches, forming the centre of a fine vaulted cloister, which connects the wings of the building. Passing through folding doors of costly painted glass, the saloon is entered, which commands a most delightful prospect, (the fore-ground of which has been heightened, by the introduction of an artificial river) towards the Forest Hills, Beeston Castle, the Peckforton Hills, &c. The entrance to the west front, is under a lofty portico, vaulted, and profusely enriched with carved work. The great hall is vaulted, and is approached by a flight of steps; it is large and lofty, and nearly square. The intersection of the arches is ornamented with the various armorial devices of the family, as are also the windows. Descending from the centre is an enriched shaft, from which is suspended an immense lamp, in brass work. On the east side is a gallery, connecting the bed-rooms of the house, with a pierced screen in front, supported by five arches. Under the gallery are archways—on the right hand to the grand staircase, the library, &c. and on the left hand to the state bed room, &c. The pavement of the hall is of variagated marble; over the chimney piece on the south side is a painting of the landing of Chas. II. over that on the north side the Dissolution of the Long Parliament; both the early production of Mr. West's pencil. On each side the chimney pieces, are niches, with pedestals and canopies. Opposite the entrance, is the door of the saloon. This room has three finely painted windows, opening to the cloister front, representing William I. Odo, Bishop of Bayeuse, Gilbert le Grosvenor, and his wife, Sir Robt. Grosvenor,‡ and Johanna de Eaton.—The rooms on the right and left are finished

* They are now placed at the end of the vista on the Poulton side of the Park.

† Some few of which still remain in the wood on the south side of the Hall.

‡ Sir Robert had a famous plea with Sir Richard le Scrope, about a coat of arms, before the High Constable, the Earl Marshall of England, and others commissioned expressly for the purpose. The sentence of the Court was, that Sir Richard le Scrope should bear the said arms, with a bordure argent, for distinction. Sir Robert appealed to the King against the sentence, and his Majesty ordained, that Sir Richard Scrope should continue the same arms, and that Sir Robert le Grosvenor should either use them with a bordure, or else, instead of a bend, or, a garb, or, from the arms of the ancient Earls of Chester, to whom he fully proved his consanguinity at the trial. Sir Robert, therefore, adopted the garb in preference to the bend; and it still continues the family coat.

Cheshire

in a style of the most sumptuous magnificence; and the ceilings of the dining and drawing-rooms, which form the extremities of the suite, are richly decorated with the most exquisite fan-tracy, the effect much heightened by their being covered with burnished and dead gold.—There are some valuable paintings in these rooms; among which may be noticed, Christ on the Mount of Olaves, by Claude Lorraine, and the largest painting ever executed by him; a sea piece in the Mediterranean, by Vernet; Rubens and his wife, by himself; the Judgment of Paris, after Rubens, by Peters; full length portraits of the present Earl and Countess Grosvenor, by Barker, &c. The Library is on the south side, and the book-cases are of English Oak, carved in Gothic. It possesses numerous scarce and valuable documents, and abounds with many of the political and polemic tracts, which the civil wars gave birth to.* It has also a copy of the Chronicles of Hen. Huntington, in which is a curious drawing of the entry of King Stephen into Lincoln; a MS. on vellum, richly illuminated, containing the proceedings in the chivalric case of Scrope and Grosvenor; and an imperfect copy of the Vision of Piers Plowman. A volume of Local Collections, marked XXI. 5, in which is a transcript of a large portion of the celebrated, but lost record, the Cheshire Domesday.† The contents, however, differ materially from those of Domesday, consisting of acquittances of claims, final concords, grants to monasteries and individuals, with confirmations, &c. The dates are singular, referring to particular periods, as when Earl Hugh II. was knighted; and the Return of Randle III. from the Holy Land.—The deeds appear to be entered at the time of their execution. The extracts occupy more than twenty folio pages, after page 96, on which is written "Ex Rotulo Cartar. Antiq. vocat. Domesday." At the end of the 7th extract, p, 97, is written: "In initio præfati rotuli scribitur sic—Inceptor finem det gratia trina labori."

* Ormerod.

History.

"Hic referens rotulus multorum facta virorum
Non sinit a pacto quem resilire suo.
Fallere temptanti justos obstacula ponit,
Ne quis sic faciat, pagina sancta monet."

The entries in the original roll were esteemed of high authority.‡ In an Assize of Darrein presentment, in Cheshire, 38 Hen. III. between Roger de Sandbach and the Abbot of Deulacresse, as to the Church of Sandbach, and removed by Certiorari into the King's Bench, the Court, among other reasons assigned for judgment, observed—"Et quia convictum est p'er Domesday Cestr'. quod perpetuam habet firmitatem, et omnia quæ in eo continentur in perpetuum sunt stabilia, in quo continentur quod, &c. consideratum est."

The stables form a large quadrangle on the north side of the house, cut off by a small shrubbery, but, viewed from the south-east side, give a fine effect to the perspective. In the centre of the east angle is a large clock tower, in the Norman style. Indeed, altho' the architecture of the time of Edward III. may be deemed the ground work of the whole, it has generally been departed from, when a better effect could be produced.

The higher parts of the Park, afford some fine bursts of romantic scenery, as well on the Welsh as on the Cheshire side. There are lodges, in the castellated form, with wings and turrets, entering to the Park, below Eccleston Hill, and at Belgrave, on the Wrexham road.

The expense of the erection and furnishing of the Hall, the building of the out-offices, and the alterations in the grounds, must have been immense.

† Sir Peter Leycester mentions several deeds stolen out of the Exchequer at Chester, in his time. In the Chartulary of the Abbey of Chester,* are numerous abstracts of deeds, with brief notices—"inotulata est concordia in magno rotulo Cest. qui vocatur Domesday," but no regular transcript has yet been found.

* Harl. MSS. 1965.

‡ Mr. Illingworth; "Reports of Commissioners of Public Records."

Reduced & Eng[d] by J. Fyot Manch[r] from a Drawing by M[r] J. Halton of Chester.

WEST VIEW OF EATON HOUSE.

Eng[d] for Hanshalls History of Cheshire.

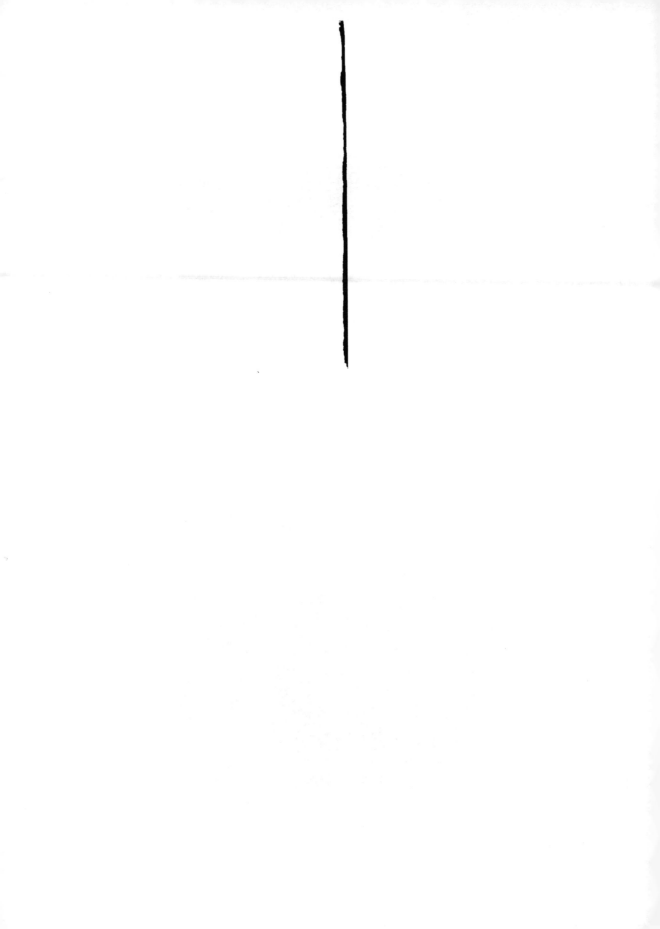

CHESHIRE

HISTORY.

THE PARISH OF FARNDON,

CONTAINS THE TOWNSHIPS OF

FARNDON
BARTON
CLUTTON
CREWE
AND
CHURTON (a MOIETY.)
HINDMARSH—EXTRA-PAROCHIAL.

FARNDON,

Is pleasantly situated on the declivity of a Hill, overlooking the Dee, about eight miles S. of Chester. The Bishop of CHESTER (Lichfield), is noticed in Domesday Book as holding one part of the Township, previous to, and after the Conquest. It appears from an Inq. temp. Hen. VII. that William Bishop of Lichfield and Coventry held the Manor from the Prince, Earl of Chester, in right of the See, valued at £10. 9s. 8*d*. per ann. The Manor is now leased from the See of Lichfield by Roger Barnston, Esq. and he holds for it a Court Leet and Baron. There is a narrow old Bridge here over the Dee, connecting Farndon with Holt, and also the counties of Chester and Denbigh, of which there is a fine, but considerably heightened view, in Mr. Ormerod's History of the County.*—There is much travelling through Farndon, it being situated on the cross-roads from Wrexham to Barnhill, Whitchurch, &c.—The view from the north side of the Bridge is delightfully picturesque.—John Speed the author of the Theatre of Great Britain, &c. was born here in 1552; he was buried at St. Giles's, Cripplegate, London, in 1629, where there is a monumental inscription to his memory, in Latin, in which he is described:—"Civis Londinensis, mercatorum scissorum fratris, servi fidelissimi regiarum majestatum Elizabethæ, Jacobi, et Caroli, tunc superstitis."

A School was built at Farndon in 1629; the Master's salary is about £14. per annum, with a small croft, and garden.

Earl Grosvenor is the impropriator of the Church, and he appoints the Curate: the gross annual value of the living in 1810,† was £72. 1*s*. 10*d*. The great tithes of Farndon, with a moiety of Churton and Clutton are attached to the impropriation; the great tithes of Barton, however, are the property of Lord Kenyon, by purchase from the Grosvenors; those of Crewe were purchased from the present Sir John Grey Egerton, Bart. (who bought them together with the royalty of the Township from Lord Crewe) by Mr. Rich. Browne. There was a Church at Farndon before the Conquest; and the unappropriated rectory was the property of the Collegiate Church of St. John, in Chester. The Church with all perquisites were afterwards leased by the Dean and Chapter of St. John's, to John Dutton, Esq. of Hatton, in 1449, for nine years, at 15 marks per ann. The valuation, 4th Edw. VI. was £16. The present

† Parl. Returns.

* There is a tragical tradition relative to this Bridge:—"Edw. I. on the death of Madoc lord of Dinas Brân, appointed the guardians to his two sons:. Of the one, who was to have had for his share the lordship of Bromfield and Yale, the castle of Dinas Brân, and the reversion of Maelor Saesneg, after the death of his mother Emma, daughter of James Lord Audley, to John Earl Warren; and of the other, who was to have possessed the lordships of Chirk and Nanheudwy, to Roger Mortimer, son of Lord Mortimer, of Wigmore.—These lords soon conspired to free themselves from their charge, and possess themselves of their estates: and accordingly caused the poor children to be drowned under Holt Bridge. This I discovered in a manuscript, communicated to me by the Rev. John Price, keeper of the Bodleian library. Before that, the manner of their deaths was current in the country, under the fable of two young fairies, who had been destroyed in that manner, and in the same place; but the foundation of the tale was, till very lately, totally lost."---PENNANT'S TOURS IN WALES.

CHESHIRE

Church stands on a red sand-stone rock, and is described in Webb's *Itinerary*, written in 1622, as a fair new building. During the Civil Wars, it was made a garrison; and at the time Holt Castle was besieged,* it was greatly injured. In 1658 it was repaired, and the window of the Barnston Chancel was ornamented with the stained glass which still remains nearly perfect. It is altogether a military memorial, the centre part representing a field of war, bordered with portraits of Sir Francis Gamul, Sir William Mainwaring, Roger Grosvenor, Esq. Capt. Barnston; pikemen, musqueteers, &c. in the costume of the day. The arms of Sir F. Gamul, have the badge of baronetcy, and it is therefore conjectured he was raised to that dignity by his ill-fated Sovereign.† The architecture of the Church is much varied, altho' the pointed Gothic is most prevalent. Five pointed arches, rising from cylindrical columns, separate the body of the Church from the side aisles. There are chancels at the end of each aisle, that on the south side is the property of the Barnstons, as is also the other, formerly possessed by the Massies of Coddington. In the Massie Chancel, is a marble monument, inscribed—

* 1645.

In hope of a blessed and joyful resurrection, are laid underneath this, ye bodies of John Puleston, of Pickhill, Esq. and Anne his wife, the second daughter of Richard Alport, of Overton, Esq.; she dyed the 14th Aug. 1715; and he dyed the 14th Jan. 1721. They were interred here by the leave of their son-in-law, John Massie, of Coddington, Esq. Here also lies by the leave of her nephew Richard Massie, Esq. the body of Hester Janns, ye younger daughter of the aforesaid John Puleston, Esq. and relict to the Rev. Mr. Thomas Janns, late Rector of Hordley, in Shropshire; she dyed the 12th Oct. 1732.—With earnest desire that their bones may remain unmoved to ye last day, this monument is erected by Mrs. Anne Maddockes, in memory of her dear and very valuable father, mother, and sister.

On the east wall of the Church, a painted wooden tablet, with the inscription—

William Barnston, of Churton, Esq. had to wife Elizabeth, eldest daughter of Roger Massy, of Coddington, Esq. Obiit (ille) 21 July, 1620: obiit (illa) 13 Jan. 1606.

On a similar tablet underneath—

Near this lie the remains of John, son and heir of William Barnston, of Churton, Esq. who died May 8, 1661: he married Alice, sole heiress of Thos. Trafford, of Bridge Trafford, Esq. by whom he had one son, Trafford Barnston; she married to her second husband the Hon. Richard Savage, by whom she had one son, who became Earl Rivers. She died Oct. 23, 1666, and was buried at Plemonstall, near Chester.

HISTORY.

Below this a third tablet—

Here lie the remains of William Barnston of Churton, Esq. He married Dorothy Brooke, daughter of Thomas Brooke, of Little Sankye, Esq. ancestor to Sir Richard Brooke, of Norton, Esq. He was a person of great worth and integrity, ventured his life and fortune with King Charles the First; was sent Prisoner from Oxford to London, where he continued till he paid his composition for his estate. He died March 8, 1664.

There are four achievements hung round the Chancel; the first for Roger Barnston, Esq.; the second for the wife of Prebendary Barnston; the third for Prebendary Barnston; the 4th the arms and crest of Robt. Barnston, Esq.

In this Church were, about the middle of the 17th century, the tombs of Sir Patrick de Barton, and two other Knights, with their effigies in mail armour, with large lozenge shields, round the edges of which were inscribed their names in Lombardic capitals. The 1st was inscribed—"Hic jacet Patricius de Barton. D'p'to'—another had—"Hic jacet Madocus...Daur...or...pro eo." The 3d was cut on a flat stone; the arms a lion rampant.—A few years ago, whilst the building was undergoing some repairs, these three figures were discovered at the east end of the Church: they were of white stone, and two of them were immediately converted into sand by the Vandals of the neighbourhood.—That of Patrick de Barton was rescued from them, and is placed under the tower. It is of considerable antiquity, representing a Knight in mail armour, recumbent, his head reclining on a cushion, his feet on a dog. The helmet is conical, and the shield bears a bend cotised.

The arms of Leche of Carden, Hurleston, and Bostock of Churton, which formerly ornamented the windows, no longer exist. The Church register, which is in a very dilapidated state, commences in 1603.

† It was repaired at the expense of the late H. Cholmondeley, Dean of Chester, whose autograph appears on the glass.

The Charities consist of £20. from Sir Rich. Grosvenor to the Poor of Farndon; and other benefactions, amounting in the whole to £110. exclusive of £18. for communion plate. A portion of this is vested in land; the rest is on security, the interest being distributed to the Poor at Christmas.

In the Church-yard, about thirty yards north of the chancel, on an old door-post, is the following inscription:—

+ 1 ❀ 5 ❀ W + B ❀ 7 ❀ 6 +
Octor. + ❀ + vi.

The stained glass window in the Gamul Chancel, is about 22 by 24 inches, cracked in two of the lower compartments. In an upper blank compartment, written on the Glass, is a memorial, that Hugh Cholmondeley, Dean of Chester, had it repaired in 1812.

CHURTON.

This Township is divided between the Manors of Aldford and Farndon. It localized the name of a family which granted lands to the Abbey of Poulton.—Churton Hall, is the seat of Roger Barnston, Esq. but it is now occupied as a farm-house. The Barnstons settled here as early as the reign of Ric. II. and were originally of Barnston, in the Hundred of Wirral, where we find Hugh de Bernston Lord of a Moiety of Barnston, temp. Edw. I. they were also the paramount Lords of Capenhurst.

The Hall of Churton is an ancient mansion of wood, surrounded by fine trees. The village is formed by a long straggling street of decayed cottages, many of them, however, bearing marks of considerable antiquity: the remain of an ancient cross marks the boundaries of the manors of Farndon and Aldford.—The family of Hankey were seated here for several generations; the elder branch became extinct temp. Eliz. but a younger branch remained as late as 1630.—Churton is about 7 miles S. E. from Chester, and the neighbourhood abounds with rich and diversified scenery

BARTON,

Is about nine miles from Chester, and was held under the Barony of Malpas, by the Bartons,* the first of whom was Patrick de Barton, who married Sybilla, daughter of David de Goulborne; they had issue David de Barton, and Patrick. The family became extinct at a very early period, and to the reign of Elizabeth, Burton is merely noticed as a portion of the Malpas Barony. In an Inq. p. m. 39 Eliz. 2 messuages, 2 cottages, and 136 acres of land, appear to belong to Sir Hugh Cholmondeley, and his son of the same name, held of the before-named Barony.—The manor afterwards was vested in the Cholmondeleys; but in 1777, George James Earl of Cholmondeley, sold it to Wm. Leche, Esq of Carden, since deceased, in the representatives of whose heir, Hurleston Leche, Esq. it still remains. Barton is considerably elevated above the Dee. A Court is held for the Manor.

CLUTTON,

Is about 10 miles S. S. E. from Chester. It is noticed in the Survey as being held by Wm. Fitz Nigell, Baron of Halton, and under him it was held by the Montalts. About the time of Henry VI. the manor became vested in the Cluttons who were settled here as early as the 21st Edw. I. It appears from an Inq. p. m. 7th Hen. VI. that William de Clutton held an estate in Aldersey, another called the *Acres*, and one in Clutton, as of the manor of Shaw †—It passed from the Cluttons to the Massies, for, temp. Elizabeth, Thomas Massie held Clutton from the Queen, in right of the Barony of Halton. The Bromleys were the next possessors, and continued so till the commencement of the 17th century, when the manor was purchased by Richard Williamson, Esq. whose descendants sold it about 1723, to John Leche, Esq. of Carden, in whose family it still continues.—Dr. Williamson, the antiquary, was born in this township. His collections commence 29th Hen. III and end 7th Car. I. and form a truly valuable historic record. A Court is held for the Manor.

* See account of the Church at Farndon.

† This Dr. Williamson takes to be Shawe Green, in Higher Clutton.

CREWE

Is situated about 9 miles S. E of Chester. Little is known of the first possessors of this manor. The Crewes, the ancient Lords, are stated* to be the descendants of the Crewes, of Crewe, in Nantwich Hundred, and they became extinct temp. Hen. IV. when Margaret and Alice, the coheirs of Jenkin Crewe, married Walter Dod, of Broxton, and Thomas Bird; the grandson of this Thomas, John Bird, had two daughters, and they again divided the estates between the Stringers, and Catherals.†—After the Dissolution, the Royalty of the township, which had belonged to the Abbey of Chester, was vested in the Crewes, of Holt, a younger branch of the Crewes, of Crewe Hall.‡—Mr Thomas Crewe, of Holt, was the proprietor of the manor in the beginning of the last century; and he sold it to Sir J. Crewe, of Utkinton, from whom it passed to the Crewes, of Crewe, in Nantwich Hundred. The present Lord Crewe, sold it and the tithes to Sir J G. Egerton, Bart by whom it has subsequently been sold, the manor to Ambrose Dutton, Esq. and the tithes to Mr. Richard Brown.

* In a paper signed by Sir J. Crewe, of Utkinton.

KING'S MARSH,

Sometimes called Over, is an extra-parochial township, between Farndon and Shocklach, and nearly opposite the ruins of Holt Castle. The manor is the property of T. S. Moulson, Esq. whose mother was the daughter and coheiress of Geo. Spurstow, Esq. a younger branch of the Spurstows, of Spurstow. It was formerly called Over Marsh, and was one of the three sanctuaries of the ancient Earldom, set apart for the reception of fugitive strangers, who, in time of war, should come under the protection of the Earl. They were allowed to live there in booths, or tents, for a year.

In an Inq 7 Edw. II. it is stated, that a certain large piece of waste, called *Overmarsh*, was in ancient times ordained for strangers of what country soever, and assigned to such as came to the support of the Earl of Chester, or to his aid, resorting there to form dwellings, but without building any fixed houses, by the means of nails or pins, save only booths and tents to live in. Over Marsh was given by Richard III. to Sir William Stanley.

† Vill. Cest. ‡ Lysons.

PLAN OF HOLT CASTLE, 1620,

Sometime called the Castle of Lyons.—The Castrum Legionis of the Romans, and an outpost to Deva.

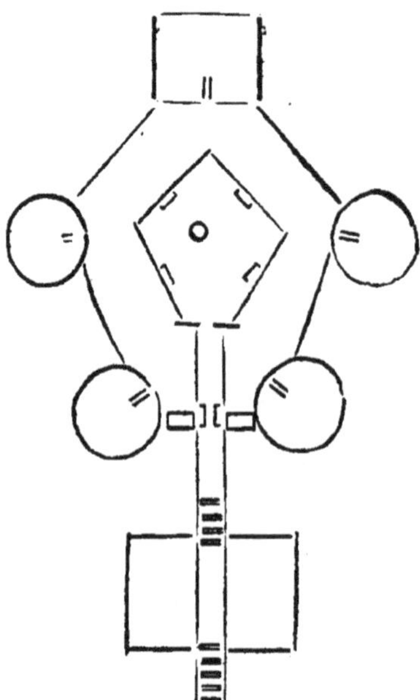

PARISH OF GUILDEN SUTTON,

CONTAINS only one Township, and not more than 900 statute acres of land.—It has sometimes been called Golden Sutton, and Guilders Sutton; and was originally given by John Lacy, the Constable, to Adam de Dutton, whose son Geoffrey, granted it to the Abbot and Convent of St. Werburgh. Soon after the Reformation,* the reputed Manor was vested in a branch of the Booths, of Dunham Massey, and they exercised a manerial right. In 1699, Elizabeth, daughter of Geo. Booth, Esq. of Woodford Hall, Over, being married to Geo. Tindale, Esq. of Bathford, Somersetshire, it passed to the Tyndales, and in 1773, James Croxton, Esq.† purchased it from them. Emma, daughter and heiress of Mr. Croxton, brought the estates in Guilden Sutton, by marriage, to the Rev. Rowland Egerton,‡ of Norley, seventh son of the late John Egerton, Esq. of Oulton Park; and Mr. Egerton is the present proprietor, and Lord of the Manor.

|| Lysons. The Grandfather|| of the late Mr. Croxton, purchased in 1725, a house and lands in this Parish, belonging first to the Breretons, and afterwards, to the Wrights: and in 1747, he purchased a Mansion, and demesne, of Launcelot Machell, Esq. of Crakenthorpe Hall, co. Westmorland. The house, which had long been the family seat of the Machells, is taken down; and that which belonged to the Wrights, is now occupied as a farm-house.—It appears from a Survey of the Cheshire Manors, among the Harl. MSS that at one period Guilden Sutton consisted exclusively of Freeholders.

* It is suspected it was amongst the estates of the Dean and Chapter, obtained by Sir R. Cotton, and by him sold to the Booths.---See Lysons, p. 767.

The Church was part of the endowment of the College of St. John the Baptist at Chester, and temp. Edw. IV. was valued at £11. After the Dissolution it fell into lay hands, and became the property of the Hardwares, of Bromborow. In the 42d Eliz. Henry Hardware, Esq. sold for £100, the Rectory, and all tithes, &c. arising within the Parish, to Peter Warburton, Esq. Serjeant at Law; from whom it passed by marriage of the daughter and heiress, to Sir T. Stanley, of Alderley, Bart. The present Sir J. T. Stanley, in 1810, sold the same, with a farm in the Parish, to the Rev. Rowland Egerton Warburton, retaining, however, the nomination of the Curate.

On the 21st Jan. 1802, the Chancel of the Church was so much injured by a storm, that it was considered necessary to rebuild it. The present is a plain brick pile, with body and chancel, and no side aisles. The Registers commence in 1595.

There are no monuments worthy of particular notice.

† Sheriff of Cheshire in 1750.

‡ Who assumed the name of Warburton, on the death of Sir Peter Warburton, of Arley, Bart.

PARISH OF HANDLEY,

CONTAINS THE TOWNSHIPS OF

HANDLEY. | GOLBORNE-DAVID.

HANDLEY is about 7 miles south-east of Chester, the turnpike road to Whitchurch passing through the village. At the Conquest it was the property of Osborne Fitz Tezzon, ancestor of the Boydells, of Dodleston, in whose family it continued till the time of Henry VI. when the male line failing, it passed by marriage with Margaret, an heiress, to Hugh Reddish. It was afterwards alienated, and a portion became the property of the Calveleys, of Lea, in 1585. By an Inq. p. m. 27 Elizabeth, it appears Sir Geo. Calveley, Knt. held, inter

CHESHIRE

alia, the manor of Handley, a Messuage called Clayley, and lands in Handley, and Milton, valued at £13. 7*s*. 3*d*. Dame Mary, relict of Sir Hugh Calveley, Knt. the last male heir of this family, died in 1707, having survived her husband 57 years. On the partition of the estates of the Calveleys, Handley was allotted to Peter Legh, Esq. of Lyme, as one of the co-heirs of the Calveleys. It is now vested in Thomas Legh, of Lyme, Esq. and M. P. natural son of the late Thomas Legh, Esq.

The Hall of the Calveleys is situated on Milton Green, in this township, and was occasionally the residence of the Leghs. It is a curious old mansion, and had a large apartment handsomely wainscotted; from the arms of the last Lady Calveley appearing over the chimney-piece, it is supposed to have been fitted up by her. The ceiling is decorated with flowers, &c. hanging in festoons. Some fine tapestry, which ornamented another room, was removed to Lyme Park, a few years ago. It formerly possessed a domestic Chapel, erected by Dame Mary Calveley, in 1690. The mansion is now occupied as a farm house by Mr. Woolrich.

The Court Leet of Handley, has authority over Golborne David, and Aldersey.

The Church is dedicated to ALL SAINTS, and was given by Alan de Boydell to the Monastery of St. Werburgh. After the Dissolution, the Advowson of the Rectory was confirmed to the Dean and Chapter of Chester. The Church has a nave and chancel, but no side aisles; and a strong tower, on the south side of which is inscribed,—

"Hoc ca'panite f'c'm e' a' d'ni M.CCCCC.XII[c] tp'e R'c'i Raulinso Rectoris ac pro o'ibus b'n'facto ribus ejusdem orate."

Over the Altar, on a Brass Plate, is this Inscription,

Memorandu' that Mr. Thomas Venables, first sonne of Thomas Venables, esquier, of Kinderton within the countie of Chester, begotton onne the bodie of Elizabeath daughtare of Sir William Breerton, Knight, within the saide countie, dyed in his minoritie, in the life time of his saide father, and was buried here in Haundley churche, in the saide countie of Chester, the xiiith daye of October, 1572.

HISTORY.

There are no other funeral monuments worth recording.

The present incumbent is the Rev. Thomas Ward, A. M. instituted April 5, 1797.

The Charities amount to about £80. the interest of which is distributed annually to the Poor. The Registers commence 1570.

The Rector has the whole of the tythes; Golborne Hall, and Golborne Bridge Estates, however, pay a modus for hay.

GOLBORNE DAVID.

Formed part of the estates of Osborne Fitz Tezzon, and was subsequently vested in the Boydells, in right of their Manor of Dodleston, but it is now included in the Court Leet of Handley. The mesne manor becoming the property of David de Malpas, he assumed the local name; and the township obtained its present addition. In the reign of Edw. III. William Golborne held jointly with his wife Margaret, this manor, from Howell ap Owain Foel, by military service, as part of his Manor of Dodleston, value 100*s*.—The manor afterwards* became the property of the Barons of Kinderton, in right of Hugh Venables, son and heir of Elizabeth, daughter of William de Golborne.

* 10 Hen. V.

The lands of the township are reputed to be the property of Freeholders, owing suit and service to the Court at Handley.

PARISH OF HARTHILL,

CONTAINS ONLY ONE TOWNSHIP.

HARTHILL,

Is situated about 11 miles S. E. of Chester. It is not noticed in the Survey, although there is little doubt of its having formed a parcel of the Barony of Malpas, and that it was vested in the St. Pierres, under whom it was held by a family which assumed the local name. From them it passed by an heiress to Thomas (or Tomlyn) Tattenhall. The following extract is quoted* from the Harl MSS. taken from "an olde writinge of Mr. Hugh Calveley, of the Lea:—"11th Jan. 16th Henry VII. Wm. Tattenal, of Harthill, hereafter declareth his pedigree of his inheritance in Harthill, and other places in the county of Chester. Imp. the said William sheweth that one Edwin Harthill, was inheritor and Lord of Harthill, and had a son and heir called David, who married one Sara, sister to one Thomas Trechett, Lord of Tattenhall, and the said Thomas gave to the said David and Sara all the lands and tenements of the said William, lying in Siddenhall; which David and Sara had issue Richard Harthull; and the said Richard had a son called Thomas, and the said Thomas had a son called Richard, and the said Richard had a son called Wilcocke Harthull; and the said Wilcocke had a daughter and heiress called Cecily, which married to Tomlyn Tattenhall, and they had an heire called Wilcocke Tattenhall, which Wilcocke was married to Maud, daughter to Wilcocke Bulkeley, and the heyre of his inheritance, which Wilcocke and Maud had issue a son and heyre, called Thomas Tattenhall, which Thomas was married unto Magaret, daughter and heyre unto Jenkin Heyre, sumtyme of Barrets Poole, which Thomas and Margaret had a son and heyre called William Tattenhall above named, which William married one Emma, daughter and one of the heyres of Randle Cotgreave, and had issue by her Thomas and Rafe, which Thomas is heyre apparent, and married unto one Margaret, daughter to Hugh Bulkeley, of Woore."—The estate eventually became vested in Eleanor, daughter of the last-named Thomas Tattenhall, and wife of Sir Hugh Calveley, of Lea, in whose family it was settled, till the division of the estates of the Calveleys, when Harthill passed to the Cottons, of Combermere, who afterwards sold it to Oswald Moseley, Esq. of Bolesworth Castle, from whom it was purchased in 1813, by Thomas Tarleton, Esq. under the authority of an Act of Parliament. The tenants of Harthill attend the Court Leet at Tattenhall.

*Ormerod.

The Church, which is dedicated to All Saints, is an augmented Curacy, in the gift of T. T. Drake, Esq. in right of his portion of the Malpas barony.

The Chapel of Herthull is mentioned in an order of Archbishop Peckham, in 1280.*—The advowson of the donative was originally in the St. Pierres, from whom it passed by marriage to the Cokeseys and Grevilles.—In an Inq. p. m. 7th Hen. IV. it is stated that the advowson was held by Sir Walter Cokesay, in capite, from the Prince, in right of his barony.

*See Dugd. Mon. 227.

The Church is beautifully situated. It is a low stone building, with large bay windows, but has no aisles.—A wooden screen separates the Chancel, on which is painted, "This Church was builded upon the Devoc'on of the Cuntrye, by the labor and travell of Ed. Tarrat, Jo. Dod, Thos. Bulkeley, Gra. Weston, P. a°. 1609." The ceiling is supported by brackets of wood, on which are the arms of Egerton, Dod, Herthull, Bulkeley, Page, and the crests of Dod and Calveley. The Church was considerably ornamented by the last Incumbent, the Rev. H. Cholmondeley, A. M.—The present Incumbent is the Rev. W. W. Drake, A. M. licensed May 7, 1816.

On a Monument, the only one in the Church, affixed to the south wall, is this inscription:—

Hic mortales in ultimum diem reposuit exuvias Georgius Bird, de Broxton, in com. Cest. arm. Non uno nomine desideratus, quippe qui vixerat amicis admodum jucundus hospes, non inhonestus artifex, summaque in pauperes misericordia, in universos charitate, in ecclesiam reverentiâ, in regem constantiâ spectabilis. Annam antiqua Whitmoreorum de Barr Hill, com. Stafford. familià oriundam, pari pietatis ingenio felicem, non indignam tali viro uxorem, in æterna cœlestum gaudia secutus, nullàque ditatus prole, fratrem Carolem heredem reliquit, solo natu minorem, jam suis accumulatum.

Hic	obiit	Jan. 5	A. D.	1724	Ætat.	54
Ille		Sept. 7		1725		63
Illa		July 6		1718		59

Gul. Glegg, gen. mœrens nepos,
M. S. P.

The Charities are described on a painted board, and were restored to the parish mainly by the exertions of the late Dean Cholmondeley. They consist of £10. from Dame Mary Calvely; and £10. from Richard Stockton, the interest to be given annually to the poor attending Church.—£6. 16s. 4d. for the Poor on St. Andrew's Day, being a rent charge from Richard Whitfield, in 1711.; £1. 13s. to be given annually to the Poor on St. Thomas's Day, being a rent charge from Thomas Bebington, of Harthill, 1733.

The value of the living, according to the Parliamentary Return, 1810, including every source of income, is estimated at £122. 10s. The registers commence so late as 1730.

PARISH OF ST. MARY, CHESTER,

(IN THE COUNTY), CONTAINS THE TOWNSHIPS OF

CLAVERTON,
GLOVERSTONE,
MARLSTON cum LACHE,
MOSTON,
AND
UPTON.

OVERLEGH, and NETHERLEGH, in this parish, are described in pages 291 and 292.

CLAVERTON,

Is within the boundary of the City of Chester, adjoining Handbridge, and is included within that manor, its Constable being sworn at the Handbridge Leet.—It was originally among the possessions of Hugh Fitz Osborne,* the predecessor of the Pulfords, when it was a free vill. It is noticed in an Inq. p. m. temp. Edw. III. as part of the estates of John de Pulford. Joan his sole heiress afterwards married Thomas de Belgrave; and he dying, she became the wife of Sir Robert Grosvenor, of Holme, and they suffered a joint recovery for this manor, 12 Ric. II. It continued in the Grosvenor family till the partition of the estates, when Claverton passed by marriage with Elizabeth Grosvenor, to Peter Dutton, of Hatton, Esq. grandfather of Sir Piers Dutton; on whose decease disputes arising, it was awarded to John Dutton, of Dutton, Esq. From the Duttons, Claverton passed to the Gerards; the greater part of the township is now, however, the property of Earl Grosvenor.

* Survey.

GLOVERSTONE,

Will be found noticed in page 181.

MARLSTON cum LACHE,

Is about two miles S. W. from Chester. At the Conquest this township formed two distinct manors, Leche, and Marlston; the former was among the possessions of the secular Canons of St. Werburgh, and the latter was the property of the Barons of Nantwich. After the conquest, Marlston was seized by the Earl, and was subsequently granted by Randle Gernons to Basingwerk Abbey. A family named Blunt, afterwards got possession of Marlston, and Lache, and held them under the Earls, certainly so late as the reign of Edw. III. The manor was then vested in the Benedictine Nuns of St. Mary; but after the dissolution, the Breretons had a grant of it. In 1654, Sir Wm. Brereton conveyed the manor, and lands in Handbridge, to Thos. Minshull, apothecary, for a certain long term; eventually it became vested in Roger Whitley, whose daughter and heiress Elizabeth brought the estate in marriage to Sir John Mainwaring, Bart of Peover. In 1725, Sir Thomas Mainwaring, Bart. of Baddeley, gave his interest in the manor to his widow Martha, who married Edw. Mainwaring, Esq. of Whitmore; and again becoming a widow, she devised all her lands, in trust, to Jas. Mainwaring, Esq. and Rowland Cotton, Esq. to be put to sale, in discharge of her debts, the residue to become the property of the said J. Mainwaring —The manor is now the property of James Mainwaring, Esq. of Bromborow, but the manerial privileges extend merely to the appointment of a Game Keeper. The entire estate is tythe free.

The hall of Lache was garrisoned by Sir W. Brereton, during the siege of Chester; by whose family it was sold to the Manleys, of Monksfield; and by them to John Snow, Esq. one of the Aldermen of Chester. Mr. Snow died in 1807, and left his estate to trustees for the benefit of his natural children.*

A large tract of waste land, called the Lache-eyes, extends from this township, to that of Dodleston. The soil is of excellent quality, and the parishioners of St. Mary's, Chester, and of Dodleston, claim the privilege of pasturing cattle, &c. on it.

MOSTON,

Is situated about two miles N. from Chester, and contains only two houses. About the year 1125, Rich. Crue granted the manor to the Monks of St. Werburgh, and a family which took the local name, held lands under them here, at a very early period.

In a plea to a Quo Warranto, 31 Edw. I. the Monks claimed the privilege of Infangtheof, wayf, stray, and chattels of natives and fugitives, and view of frank pledge for this manor at their Court of Upton.—After the Reformation, the grant to the Dean and Chapter, was confirmed to Ralph Rogerson, and John Ashton, in fee-farm, and towards the conclusion of the reign of Elizabeth, both their shares were purchased by John Morgell, Esq. Registrar of the Diocese of Chester, in whose family it continued till 1718, when Elizabeth, sister and heiress of Wm. Morgell, sold it to Methusalem Jones, Esq of Underdale, Shropshire; by whom, in 1722, it was conveyed to Hen. Bennett, Esq. Mayor of Chester in 1716, and Sheriff of the county in 1734. In 1789, the manor was purchased from his representatives, by Wm Massey, Esq. of Chester, Attorney; and Richard Massey, Esq. his natural son, is the present proprietor.

The Old Hall of Moston was taken down about five years ago. It was built of brick, four stories in height, with five gables in front. It was called by Webb, a "delicate house of brick," and was erected by Mr. John Morgell. A small house has lately been built on its site by the present proprietor.

Moston Ley for Cattle is well known; and it occupies at least two thirds of the township.

UPTON,

Lies something less than two miles N. of Chester. It was amongst the possessions of the Earl at the Conquest, and was the head of several dependant estates. Earl Hugh gave the tithes of the township to the Abbey of Chester, in 1093; and in the time of Randle Meschines, when the body of Hugh Lupus was removed to the Chapter House, a grant of the manor was made to the Abbey also.—The Grant of the first Randle runs thus: "Notum sit omnibus me Ran. Comit. Cestræ concessisse quando feci transferri corpus Hugonis Comitis anunculi mei a cemiterio in Capitulum," &c. i. e. "Be it known unto all men, that I Randle Earl of Chester, have granted at such time as I caused the body of Hugh the Earl, my uncle, to be translated from the Church Yard into the Chapter House; that on the day of my death, I should give together with my body to the Church of St. Werburgh, *Upton*, in pure alms, free from every thing, for the soul of the aforesaid Hugh, and the health of my soul, and the souls of all my kinsfolk. And whereas Hugh the Earl, before had granted to the Church of St. Werburgh, at the feast of the translation of the same, the privilege of a fair; I also do grant and confirm the same. Moreover, William Meschines my brother, hath given the Church of Dysart;

* The Trussels had an ancient estate here, which passed for a considerable length of time with the Serjeantcy of the Eastgate, and the Manor of Blacon.

Matthew of Roelent hath given the Church of Thurstaston," &c. &c.

The Abbot had view of frank-pledge at his Court here of all residents in Upton, Moston, Croughton, Wervin, Lea, Newton, and Boughton.

After the Reformation, Upton was involved in the disputes between the Dean and Chapter, and Sir Rich. Cotton; and afterwards it was granted to several fee-farmers, the principal of which were the Brocks, and the Brownes, the former of whom had the manerial right. It passed from them in 1734, by marriage of Elizabeth, eldest sister and heiress of William Brock, Esq. with John Egerton, Esq. of Oulton Park, and is now part of the jointure of her daughter in law, the widow of the late Philip Egerton, Esq. of Oulton Park.

Sir Thomas Browne, author of the celebrated *Vulgar Errors*, was of the family of the Brownes of this township.* Upton Hall, which was garrisoned during the siege of Chester, by Sir Wm. Brereton, is now occupied as a farm-house. It is of brick, with large stone bay windows.

The Abbots of St. Werburgh formerly had a Park here; and old Henry Bradshaw relates a marvellous tale, relative to the horses of some invaders, which being turned loose in Upton Park, were, by the interposition of St. Werburgh, miraculously prevented from destroying the corn, then in sheaf.

* See account of St. Mary's Church, page 245.

PARISH OF MALPAS,

CONTAINS THE TOWNSHIPS OF

MALPAS,
AGDEN,
BICKERTON,
BICKLEY,
BRADLEY,
BROXTON,
BULKELEY,
CHIDLOWE,
CHOLMONDELEY,
CHORLTON JUXTA MALPAS,
CUDDINGTON,
DUCKINGTON,
EDGE,
EGERTON,
HAMPTON,
LARTON,
MACEFEN,
NEWTON,
OLDCASTLE,
OVERTON,
STOCKTON,
TUSHINGHAM CUM GRINDLEY,
WICHALGH,
WIGLAND,
AND
ISCOYD (CO. FLINT.).

This Parish is about seven miles and a half in length, (from Whitchurch boundary to Broxton); in breadth five miles and a half (from Manley to Shocklach).

MALPAS

Was known at the Conquest by the name of Depenbeche, somewhat similar in signification to its present name, both being allusive to the difficulty of the pass where it is situated.* The site of the township as a military position is most commanding; and it was therefore selected for one of the line of fortresses which bound this side of the county, and given by Hugh Lupus to Robert Fitz Hugh, supposed to be a

* See p. 4.

natural son of his. To support the dignity of the Barony, the following estates were conferred on him,—Malpas, Bickley, Bickerton, Broxton, Cuddington, Cholmondeley, Duckington, Edge, Hampton, Larton, Overton, Tushingham, the parish of Shocklach, Bunbury, Beeston, Burwardsley, Peckforton, Spurstow, Tiverton, Tilston Fernall, Chowley, Row Christleton, Little Christleton, Tilston, Sutton in Eastham parish, and Butley; Worthenbury, and Bettiafield in Wales—and Burwardestone, and Crœneche, places not known. The chief portion of these townships formed part of the estates of Edwin, the great Saxon Earl.

Robert Fitz-Hugh died without issue male, leaving as co-heiresses, Letitia, and Mabilia, his daughters.—The latter married William Belward, and was the ancestor of the Egertons, now of Oulton. In the time of Rich. I. the Barony was divided in moieties between Robert Patric (descendant of Richard Patric, who married Letitia, daughter of Robt. Fitz Hugh) and David le Clerc. The daughter and sole heiress of the last of the Patrics, brought a moiety into the Sutton family; and on the death of William de Malpas, he left his brother Philip Gogh, surnamed de Egerton, his heir. David le Clerc, however, bastard son of William, by Beatrix de Montalt, got possession of the Barony, and bequeathed it to his daughters, Beatrix, wife of Roderic ap Gryffyn, and Idonea, wife of Urian de St. Pierre, between whom a partition was made temp. Hen. III. The portion of Beatrix passed to her daughter Isabella by her first husband Richard de Sutton, who was Lord of a moiety of Malpas; and thus the Suttons became possessed of three fourths of the Barony—the other fourth passing after some time from the St. Pierres, to the Cokesays, by marriage of Isabella, daughter of a subsequent Sir Urian de St. Pierre, to Sir Walter de Cokesay. In 1363, a suit was commenced by Isabella, one of the coheirs of David Egerton, as heir of Philip Goch, against John de Brunham, trustee of the Cokesays, and she recovered a half of another 4th from John de Sutton.—Sir Wm. Brereton, of Brereton, however, completely failed in an attempt at the same time to recover his moieties of the two fourths from John de Sutton, and from Sir Walter Cokesay, in 1379, although he was the husband of the sister of Isabella Delves—and this formed the foundation of the extensive possessions afterwards acquired by the Breretons in Malpas. Sir Wm. Brereton's share consisted of a fourth part of the half thereof, the advowson of a 4th part of the term of a moiety of Malpas Church, a second term of Tilston, and the advowson of a prebend called "Pety Chanonrye," in the Collegiate Church of St. John, at Chester.*—The other half of the fourth part of the Barony, which the Breretons failed in seizing from the Cokesays, consisted of an eighth part of the Manor of Malpas, the advowson of a fourth part of a moiety of Malpas Church, and Harthill Chapel, the Manors of Bickley and Peckforton, with the lands.† To this portion, Roger Horton was found next heir; but by another Inq. John Younge, Somerset Herald, had permission to enter on this estate, having proved a nearer degree of consanguinity.—The disputes between these heirs, terminated in the sale of the greater part of the property, which was purchased by Edmund Dudley, in the Inq. after whose attainder‡ they are mentioned. In 1527, John Sutton Lord Dudley, conveyed the manor and Castle of Malpas, and three fourths of the Barony, to George Robinson, and others; and it appears that these possessions took with them the Baronial distinctions, the Suttons being called Barons of Malpas, in an Inq. 7th Hen. V The same Lord Dudley, nine years afterwards, alienated another portion of the Barony, to Sir Rowland Hill,‖ who, in 1560, settled a 4th part of the Barony, and large estates in the parish, on his niece, Alice Greetwood, who married Reginald Corbet, one of the Judges of the Common pleas; and on his death, Richard, his son and heir, afterwards Sir Richard Corbet, of Stoke-upon-Trent, sold the share to Sir Randulph Brereton, of Shocklach, who settled it on his daughter Mary, wife of Sir Rich. Egerton, of Ridley, and Shocklach.§—In the 11th Car. I. Rich. Egerton, of Shocklach, with his brothers, John and Thomas, sold it to Richard King, Esq. of the Inner Temple, for £7,500. who conveyed it on the 30th March following, to the Right Hon. Robt. Vis. Cholmondeley, and Lady Catherine his wife. It is now vested in the Most Noble the Marquis of Cholmondeley. The other portions of the Barony, and estates, became, by purchase and descent, the property of

* Inq. 2 Ric. III. † Inq. p. m. 16 Hen. VII. ‡ 1 Hen. VIII. ‖ Then described as Rowland Hill, citizen, and mercer of London. § 37 Jac. I.

CHESHIRE

HISTORY.

the Breretons, of Brereton, from whom temp. Car. II. they were purchased by Sir Wm. Drake, the ancestor of Thomas Tyrwhitt Drake, the present proprietor.

The *Suttons* were ennobled; and John, Lord Dudley, 6th in descent from Richard and Isabella, was Lieutenant of Ireland for two years, and in the 26th Hen. VI. had an annuity of £100. from the Customs of the Port of London. He was afterwards a Knight of the Garter. The *St. Pierres* are supposed to have been a junior branch of the French Counts de St. Pierre. Urian de St. Pierre, who so heartily espoused the cause of Prince Edward, after his escape from Simon de Montfort, and who took possession of Beeston Castle for that Prince in 1265, was of this family.—The *Cokesays*, the successors of the St. Pierres, were possesors of the Manor of Cokesay, in Worcestershire; and in Kidderminster Church, is a fine altar tomb with the figures, recumbent, of Matilda, wife of Sir Walter Cokesay, between her two husbands.—*John Younge*, heir to Thomas Cokesay, was Somerset Herald. He was sent by Henry VII. to Scotland with the Princess Margaret, the betrothed wife of James IV. *Edmund Dudley*, was the Judge, who became so notorious in the time of Hen. VII. by his exactions, *Sir R. Hill*, Lord Mayor of London, rendered himself conspicuous by his many private and public virtues; he was an ancestor of the present illustrious Lord Hill, of Hawkstone.—The *Drakes* are from the Drakes, of Ash, in Devonshire.

The town of Malpas is by no means unpleasantly situated. It consists of four streets, forming a cross; the houses miserably built in general, with nothing like neatness or cleanliness to recommend them.—Not a relic remains of the Castle, once the proud seat of the ancient Barons. The Old Hall of Malpas, the residence of the Breretons,* of Shocklach, was completely destroyed by fire in 1760—Malpas is about 16 miles S. S. E. from Chester, and in 1281, had granted to it the privilege of a three days' fair, at the festival of St. Oswald. There are now three fairs, viz. April 5, July 26, and Dec. 8, but they are scarcely worthy of the name,—and the great former feature of them, was the sale of quantities of home-made linen. The market is on the Wednesday in each week. It appears from Dug. Monast. that temp. Edw. III. there was a small chantry here, belonging to the alien priory of Montacute, in Somersetshire; its establishment at that period consisted of only two Monks.

The Barons of Malpas possessed peculiar privileges: they had power of inflicting Capital Punishment in their Courts, and criminals convicted of felony, were beheaded;—and this punishment is spoken of in a record temp. Edw. II. as being the custom of the county—the heads of all felons thus executed, being presented at the Castle of Chester. In the 6th Edw. II. David Bulkeley, Serjeant of the Peace to Rich. Sutton, presented the heads of two felons, executed for burglary; and Hugh Cholmondeley, Serjeant of the Peace to John de St. Pierre, presented the head of Thomas Barnes, executed for a theft, for which he had the *radynge* fee.—In the 15th Hen. VII Sir Edward Sutton, Lord of Dudley, claimed to have view of frank pledge, with amercements, &c. in the manor of Malpas, and in its appurtenances Shocklach, Shocklach Ovyatt, Grafton, Stretton, Barton, Chollay, L. Aldersey, Broxton, Bickerton, Carden, Edge, Agden, Wigland, Chidlowe, Newton by Oldcastle, Horton by Tilston, Higher Fulwich, Tushingham, Macefen, and Bradeley. He also claimed infangtheof, outfangtheof, and pelf, and gallows, pillory, tumbrell, and thew. Also to have the Manor and Castle of Shocklach, fortified, ditched, and enkernelled, and to have a toll there for himself and Wm. Brereton. He likewise claimed in right of his frank pledge, the regulation of bread and beer, amerciaments for effusion of blood, hue raised, obstruction of ways, dilapidation of bridges, sale of corrupted flesh, fish, or other victuals, and all offences on the King's highway, by land, or water: that breaches of the peace, and hamsoken, should be presented by his bedell; and punishment of bakers, brewers, and scolds, by amerciaments for the two first offences, but for the third to punish bakers by the pillory, brewers by the tumbrel, and scolds by

* There is a curious entry in the Parish Registers, relative to the burial of a person considered at the period most essential to the conviviality and character of a Gentleman's house.—He was no doubt one of the Breretons servants:—"1572: Jan. 7, Tho. Bosewell, beynge the foole of the Hall."

the thew, i. e. by placing them in a certain seat called a *dokyn stole*. In addition, he claimed jointly with Wm. Brereton, to have a fair and market at Malpas; and to have view of frank pledge in Church Christleton, Row Christleton, and Little Christleton, with the same privileges as at Malpas.

In an Inq. p. m. 2d Rich. III. Sir Wm. Brereton, Knt. is stated to hold, inter alia, one fourth of one half, and half of another fourth, of the manor of Malpas, with the advowsons of the fourth presentation of Malpas, the alternate presentation of Tilston, and the *petty chanonrye* in the College of St. John at Chester, &c.

A *Grammar School* was founded at Malpas towards the latter end of the 17th century, by subscription, to which Hugh, the first Earl Cholmondeley, contributed £200. and the total sum raised was £536. 11s. This was charged on an estate called the Old Hall, with an annual salary of £25. for the Master, for whose use the Earl gave a house and school-room, and tenement adjoining. The present Marquis Cholmondeley, inherits the right of appointing the Master, but it will eventually lapse to the Trustees. The school is free only to the children of the representatives of the original subscribers. The School-room was rebuilt in 1795.

A *School* for twelve boys and girls was founded here by Richard Alport, Esq. of Overton, who left £500. by will dated Dec. 17, 1709, for that purpose.—As the National System of Education is introduced here, the school is become of high importance to the religious and moral improvement of the Children of the Parish.

A *Hospital* for the reception of the Indigent, was founded here by Sir Randle Brereton, of Shocklach, temp. Hen. VIII. and it was further endowed by Sir Thomas Brereton, Knt. in the reign of Car. I. charged on an estate in Newton. In 1721, Lord Cholmondeley rebuilt the Hospital, accommodating it for six poor women, five of whom receive 10*d*. per week. Each of the occupiers have a house and garden, and they are nominated by Marquis Cholmondeley.*

During the frightful operation of the plague, in the beginning of the 17th century, Malpas suffered heavily. The Parish Registers, have many melancholy notices of it. The following occurs in 1625.—"Richard Dawson, of Bradley, being sicke of the plague, and p'ceyvinge he must die at ye time, *arose out of his bed, and made his grave, and caused his nefew John Dawson, to caste strawe into the grave, wh'che was not farre from the howse, and went and layd him down in the sayde grave, and caused clothes to be layd uppon him, and so dep'ted out of this world;* this he did because he was a strong man, and heavier than his sayd nefew and another wench were able to bury. He died about the xxivth of August. Thus much was I credibly tould he did, 1625."

"John sonne of the above-mentioned Thomas, came unto his father, when his father sent for him, being sicke, and *haveing layd downe in a dich*, died in it the xxixth daye of August, 1625, in the night."—This dreadful pestilence continued more than three months.†

The Church of Malpas is dedicated to St. Oswald. From time immemorial, the Rectory has been divided into medieties; the Marquis Cholmondeley, and Mr. Drake present to the Higher Mediety alternately.—The Lower Mediety is vested solely in Mr. Drake.—An excellent parsonage house, and a glebe, is attached to each.‡—The Church is a fine specimen of the en-

* Mrs. Elizabeth Taylor, who died in Jan. 1748-9, left £500. for clothing poor men and women of the townships of Malpas and Edge. With this £771. stock, Old South Sea Annuities was purchased. For a considerable time the expenditure of the dividends was interrupted; but the dividends accumulating by the delay, were also invested in the same stock, and the whole produces about £27. per ann. The Rectors of Malpas are the Trustees. Mrs. Taylor was sister to the late Thomas Dod, Esq. of Edge. Dr. Townson, Archdeacon of Richmond, and Rector of the Lower Moiety of Malpas, left £500. in the same stock, April, 1792, for educating and clothing poor children.—These dividends, similarly accumulated, but the appropriation of them depends on certain annuitants, one of whom yet survives, on whose death £7. 10s. per ann. will fall to the Charity: at present £9. 4s. are expended on the Children; and the Rectors are trustees.—Orm. Other smaller charities are mentioned in the Parliamentary Returns.

† In the Registers, is the following record of longevity: "Burials, 1797: May 26, Catherine Richardson, widow, of Malpas, aged 107, according to her friends' account."

‡ Value: 1st portion, with St. Chad's Chapel, £48. 8s. 4d.—2d portion, with Whitewell Chapel £44. 19s. 2d.

riched Gothic which prevailed towards the conclusion of the reign of Henry VII.—It has a low tower,* with chancel, nave, and side aisles, terminating in two chancels built by the Cholmondeleys and Breretons.—The beams of the roof, which is of carved wood, are intersected by beams, decorated with foliage, and the centre compartments filled with a quartrefoil. Under a gallery, erected by Sir Robert Cholmondeley, in 1612, is a handsome grey marble font, presented by the late Philip Egerton, Esq. of Oulton. Six fine lofty arches, resting on heavy clustered columns, divide the nave and side aisles.

The *Brereton's*, now called the *Egerton's Chancel*, is separated from the other part of the Church, by an oak screen, tastefully carved; on the upper part of which is written—

"PRAY GOOD PEOPLE FOR THE PROSPEROUS ESTATE OF SIR RONDOLPH BRERETON, OF THYS WERKE EDIFICATOUR, WYTH HIS WYFE DAME HELENOUR, AND AFTER THYS LYFE TRANSYTORIE TO OBTEYNE ETERNAL FELICITIE. AMEN. AMEN."

Round the edges of the slab of an altar tomb,—

Hic jacent Randulfus Brereton, Miles Baronit' ac Camerar' Cestr', et D'na Elynora uxor ejus, qui quidem Randulfus et Elynora du". i' humanis vixerunt, hanc tumbam fieri fecerunt, scilicet in festo Sc'i Michaelis Archangeli, Anno d'ni millesimo, quingentesimo, vicesimo secundo, quorum a'i'abus p'pitietur Deus. Amen.

On the outer side of the tomb, are seven figures in niches, under fine Gothic canopies: on the slab are recumbent figures of Sir Randle, and Lady Eleanor Brereton, founders of the Oratory, executed in a very superior manner.

In the south wall of the Chancel, are some large niches, and two piscinas.

The *Cholmondeley Chancel*, adjoins the north aisle, from which it is divided, by a screen of carved oak, similar to that of the Brereton Chancel. The following sentence is inscribed on the upper part :—

"ORATE PRO BONO STATU RICHARDI CHOLMUNDELEIGH, ET ELIZABETH UXORIS EJUS, HUJUS SACELLI FACTORES, ANNO DOMINI MILLESIMO QUINGENTESIMO QUARTO DECIMO."

The monument of Sir Hugh Colmondeley, and his son Sir Hugh, is in this Chancel; it is an alabaster altar tomb, inscribed—

"Hugo Cholmundeley de Cholmondeley senior, miles, Walliæ de Marg' vice p'ses, sextus vice comes, mortem obiit, a° ætatis suæ 83, a°. d'ni 1596, et hac humo sepelitur: filiusq' heres ejus Hugo Cholmondeley miles, annum agens 50, diem clausit ultimum, a° domini 1601, et hic jacet; uxorque ejus do'i'a Maria, quæ post viri obitum propter charum illius in se amorem hoc erigi fecit monumentum a°. do'i 1605."

The figure of Sir Hugh is represented in complete plate armour, his head resting on an helmet, allusive to the family arms. His Lady is at his side, in the full costume of the day. The sides of the tomb are richly ornamented with niches, in which are figures of children—at the west end a shield of 10 quarterings, containing the armorial devices of Cholmondeley, (1) Cholmondeley (2) Cheney, Capenhurst, Dutton, Thornton, Kingsley, Hellesby, Hatton, Minshull, Holford, Toft, and Bulkeley. On a mural monument above the tomb, this inscription :—

"To the memory of the Right Hon. Mary Viscountess Malpas, wife of the Right Hon. Lord Viscount Malpas, daughter of the Right Hon. Sir Robt. Walpole, Knt. of the Garter. She died at Aix, in France, Decbr 21, 1731, in the 26th year of her age."

There are twelve ancient oak stalls in the Chancel, and two niches for the officiating Priests. The altar piece is a fine painting, by Hayman, of *Peter's denial of Christ*, given by Assheton, afterwards Lord Curzon, in 1778.

In the south aisle, a mural monument, inscribed on a convex shield—

"In hopes of a blessed resurrection, near to this place lyeth interred the body of John Stockton, of Kiddington, in this county, Esq. who changed this life for a better, on the 18th of Oct. in the year of

* There are six bells in the tower, which were re-cast in 1808.—There were formerly only five bells in the steeple, four of which bore inscriptions:—On the 2d bell, GLORIA DEO IN EXCELSIS; on the 3d, AVE MARIA, GRACIA PLENA, TECUM DOMINUS, with a cross-potence before it; on the 4th, OMNIA PROPTER SEIPSUM CREAVIT DOMINUS 1624; on the tenor bell SIR RANDLE BRERETON, KNT. CHAMBERLIN OF CHESTER, GAVE THIS BELL IN 1508. Mr. Ormerod supposes this latter date to be that of the rebuilding of the Church.

our Lord God 1700, and in ye 56th year of his age. To his lamented loss for time to come his mournfull widow consecrates this tomb."

On a brass plate—

Memoriæ sacrum.

Stocktonus pacis sumper placidissimus autor,
Sub duro situs hic marmore pace fruor.
Æstas illæsa vidui tricesima famâ,
Florentem sobolem patre cadente videt
Discede's lachrymas, quot pax si abitura reliqui.
Cœlo pacificis præmia pacto fero.
Eugenio patri posuit Eugenius filius.
Obiit 2 die Decembris, Anno Domini 1610.

On another brass plate adjoining—

Here lyes buryed Owen Stockton, Gent. who deceased the second day of December, 1610, and John Stockton his eldest sonn, who deceased the 18th day of June, 1643.

On a brass plate, a short distance from the Egerton Chapel, in capitals—

HERE LYETH INTERRED THE BODYE OF THAT VERTUOUS LADIE DAME ALICE BRERETON, LATE WIFE TO SIR THOS. BRERETON, KNIGHT, WHO DEPARTED THIS LIFE THE XII DAY OF SEPTEMBER, 1622.

On three scrolls, fixed to an escutcheon on the further pillar in the north aisle—

Heere vnder lyeth the bodyes of Robert Alport, of Overton, in ye county of Chester, Esq. who married Anne, one of ye daughters of Sr Tho. Mainwaringe, of Peever, B^t. by whom she had issue Mary y^t ob^it yonge; Richard, Anne, and Jane, s'vived y^m. She died 30th December and was buried 4th of January, 1686, aged 32. He died 27th January, and was buried ye 1st of Feb. an'o 1686. Aged 28. Virtus vivet.

On a brass plate, adjoining the pew, and ornamented with the arms of T. C. Dod, Esq.

Ranulphus Dod, Armiger, de Edge, in com. Cest. Dominus suis aliisq. exoptatissimus mortales exuvias (quas Saxo hoc texit Vidua mœstissima) deposuit Junii 16, An'o Dom. 1679, ætatis suæ 46.

Over the pew, painted on a framed board,—

M. S.

Joannis Dod, de Broxton, Armig. pacis publicæ apparatissimi custodis, privatæ gravis et fœlicis arbitri: cui fortuna pares et gloria alios habemus: virtutibus forsan neminem. Erat enim rerum et virorum prudens; et secundis temporibus dubiisq. rectus: quo nemo cultior nemo melior, nemo dignior immortalitate: sic integer ille. Amicorum, liberorum, annorum, et famæ satur obiit September xiii, M.DC.XC. et mortuus adhuc loquitur. Paucis post annis charissima conjux F. D. fatis etiam cessit et vicino in sepulchro mariti jam claudit latus: Arcta nimis tabula, et demortua virtutibus impar: non dat cæteris locum: Brevi, et vixit bene, et obiit Jan. 31°, M.DCC.IV.

In the aisle, on a brass plate—

Here lyeth Frank Shallerden, relict of John Shallerden, of the county of Kent, Esq. whose sole daughter and heiress, John Dod of Broxton, Esq. married; she dyed March 1st, 1680.

Here lyeth interred the body of Thoma Clutton, Esq. late of Clotton, who departed this life, Decemb. the 20th Anno Dom. 1729, in the 63^d year of his age.

Near the Desk, are a variety of Memorials to the Bulkeleys, of Bulkeley and Bickerton, the inscriptions much defaced.—In the Cholmondeley Chancel, on a flat white stone, ornamented with the effigy of a Clergyman, nearly obliterated,—

Hic jacet corpus Uriani Davenport, quondam Rectoris de Malpas et vicarii de Acton, qui quidem Vicarius obiit vicesimo octavo die mensis Julii anno D'ni mill'mo ccclxxxv.^to Cujus a'i'e propitietur D's. Amen.

Adjoining the last, on a brass plate, in a blue marble slab,—

Phelipp de Egerton sez fe'mez et cez enfauntez gisount icy Dieu de lo' almes eit mercy.

On a flat stone adjoining the south wall of the Chancel,—

Hea.. —ethe the bodie of Roger Brereton, of Hoton, squiar, buried the 25 of Maye, 1590.

Against the south wall of the Chancel,—

The Reverend Thomas Townson, D. D. Archdeacon of Richmond, whose remains are interred, as he directed, near the north wall of the Church Yard, was sometime Fellow of St. Mary Magdalen College, Oxford, and more than forty-one years Rector of the Lower Mediety of this Parish; whose constant attention to the temporal wants and spiritual welfare of every rank, joined with benignity of mind, and courtesy of manners, gained him universal esteem and cordial affection. He was learned, humble, pious; his writings were distinguished by classical elegance, sound argument, evangelical purity; his devotion was fervent without enthusiasm; his liberality inexhaustible, yet studiously concealed; his cheerfulness invariable, and his countenance heavenly. His life and death were alike edifying—the one was piety, the other peace. He expired full of hope in Jesus Christ, on Sunday evening, April 15, 1792, aged 77 years.

In the Chancel, on a flat stone—

Here lyeth the body of Judeth Dod, wife of Thomas Dod, of Shocklach, Gentleman, who deceased the —— day of January 1651.

Above the Communion Table, on a white marble—

M. S.

Bridgettæ Kinaston quondam uxoris Joh'is Kinaston de Morton, in com. Salop. arm. quæ obiit 8 die April. anno 1664, et hic jacet sepulta. Et Dominæ Judithæ Bridgman, eorum filiæ et cohæredis, quæ obiit 12 Julii eodem anno et sepulta Jacet Oxonii Joh'es Bridgman, Armiger, hoc pietatis et officii sui erga charissimos parentes monumentum posuit.

On a flat stone below—

Bridgetta Kinaston de Morton, vidua venerabilis et pia, obdormivit in D'no 8 April. 1641. Resurgam.

On the pavement of the Chancel—

Heare liethe the bodie of Robart Leeche Doctor of Lawe, and Chancelor to the Bushope of Chester, who died the th'rde daye of November, Anno Domini 1587.

Sarah Leech, died 28 J—— 165—

The Rectors of Malpas have the tithes of part of Bechin, in Coddington parish; and also an yearly pension of twenty shillings from the Grafton Hall estate in Tilston parish. The corn tithes of the parish are subject to an annual valuation, and there is a trifling modus for hay.—The Marquis Cholmondeley claims the impropriation of tithes in Cholmondely and some other townships, as do also Sir John Grey Egerton, Bart. in Egerton, and T. C. Dod, Esq. in Edge and Duckington.

There are TWO CHAPELS in the parish of Malpas, viz. CHAD CHAPEL, in Tushingham, about three miles from Malpas; and WHITEWELL CHAPEL, in Iscoed, distant 5 miles.

In *Whitewell Chapel* is a monument to the memory of the Rev. Rich. Congreve, who was the first person buried there—

Near this place lie the remains of the Rev. Richard Congreve, A. M. son of John, and grandson of Richard Congreve, Esquires, of Stretton and Congreve, in Staffordshire, who departed this life, in hope of a blessed resurrection, through the mercies of God in his Redeemer Jesus Christ, July 27, 1782, aged 68 years: esteemed and regretted by all who knew him for his benevolence, liberality, and diffusive charity. Martha his wife, daughter of Mr. Jones, of Fynnant, by whom he left three children, William, Richard, and Marianne, hath placed this small token of her tender regard for the memory of a kind and affectionate husband.

Chad Chapel was conveyed with the estate, and was therefore claimed by Susanna, daughter of Thomas Churton, Esq. who was possessed of the manor in 1716; but soon afterwards it was given up to the Rectors, who now have possession.

Both of these Chapels are paltry buildings, and they have no endowments. They are served by the Rectors and Curates, alternately, Divine Service being performed in one of them every Sunday, excepting when the Holy Sacrament is administered at the Mother Church. They are used as places of burial.

The present Rector of the *Higher Mediety* of Malpas, is the Rev. Philip Egerton, A. M.; of the *Lower Mediety* William Wickham Drake, A. B.—the former instituted May 3, 1804; the latter July 29, 1802.

AGDEN,

Not being mentioned in the Survey, little is known of its early history. It is situated about 17 miles from Chester, and 3 from Whitchurch, and adjoins Tushingham. There is no doubt it originally formed parcel of the Malpas Barony, falling to the portion of the Suttons. It was afterwards alienated to the Breretons and Drakes, and is now the property of Thomas T. Drake, Esq. whose ancestor gained it by purchase in the reign of Chas. II.

BICKERTON,

In the time of Edward the Confessor was held by three Saxon thanes, Dot, Edwin, and Ernuin, who were

CHESHIRE

ejected by the Conqueror, and the manor given to the Norman Baron. In the beginning of the reign of Edw. II. Wm. de Hampton, was sued by Hugh de Bickerton, and Ellen his wife, the widow of William de Bickerton, for a portion of 400 acres of land in Bickerton. The manor passing to the family of Malpas of Hampton, descended to the Egertons, and it is now the property of Sir John Grey Egerton, Bart.

The highest part of the Broxton Hills, is in this township, particularly the bold front of *Raw Head*, and *Maiden Castle*. The latter is an old British fortification, defending the pass between Bickerton Hill and Rawhead, on the summit of the former of which it is situated—commanding a most extensive and magnificent prospect. A precipice protects the south-west side. The earthworks are on the other side, forming a perfect semicircle, being about 140 yards from end to end. The ditch is 15 yards wide. The only entrance to the works is on the north side, and the entire site is nearly covered by heath and other mountain plants.—The following is a rough plan of the Castle :—

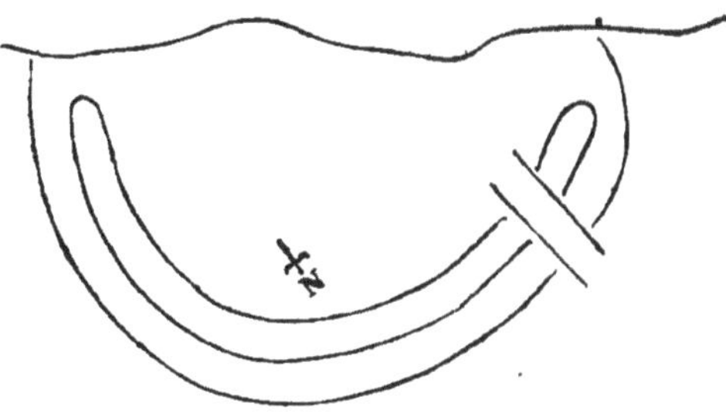

BICKLEY.

The situation of this township is truly delightful, and its population is second only to Malpas. It fell to the share of the Belwards, on the first division of the Barony ; and afterwards into the hands of David de Malpas, passing from him to the St. Pierres, Cokesays, Grevilles, and Dudleys, from the latter it became by fine the property of Sir Rowland Hill, Knight. The manor, severed from the manerial jurisdiction, was given in marriage by Sir Rowland Hill, with his niece Anne, daughter of George Dorman, Gent. of Malpas, to Sir Hugh Cholmondeley, from whom it has lineally descended to the present proprietor, the Marquis of Cholmondeley.

HISTORY.

On the Barrel Farm, in Bickley, is a chasm called the *Barrel Fall*, the ground declining on both sides to the extent of nearly a quarter of an acre. This was the scene of a remarkable phenomenon, which occurred on the 8th of July, 1657, and is described in a cotemporaneous pamphlet :—

" On Wednesday July the 8th, about three of the clock in the afternoon, there happened a very rare and memorable thing at Bulkeley [ERROR, BICKLEY] some nine miles off from Chester: a parcel of land belonging to the Lord of Cholmley, did sinke into the earth.—It was a little rise of land higher than the rest; there were goodly oaks upon it, which were ten yards high on the body (so the letters do expressly mention) before you come unto the branch; these with some other trees did sinke down with the earth into a water prepared to receive them underneath : the fall they made was hideous, representing thunder, or the roaring of a well laden cannon. It is certifyed that although these trees were of a great height, yet the waters they fell into are so extremely deep, that there is not so much as a branch, or a sprigge of any of them to be seen. At first the country people were afraid to come near the place, but one taking encouragement from the other, some at last were persuaded to go to the brink and mouth of the hollow, and one or two were let down with ropes to see what they could discover: they were neither of them let downe farre, but they importunately called to be plucked up again : they discovered as they said a great flood of water, and they heard a noise agreeable thereunto, but not any thing of the trees, either root, branch, or top, is to be seen."

The chasm formed by this singular phenomenon, is still to be seen on the Barrel Farm, in this township, occupying an extent of about an acre, perfectly dry, and nearly covered over with brush-wood, &c.—In 1812, in the process of turning over a field, on the Barrel Farm, two tablets of copper, containing a decree of the Emperor Trajan, were found. The inscription is thus decyphered by the Lysons :*—

" Imp. Cæsar divi Nervæ f. Nerva Trajanus Augustus, Germanicus Dacicus Pontifex Maximus, Tribunic. Potestat. VII. Imp. IIII. Cos. V. P. P. Equitibus et Peditibus qui militant in alis quatuor, et cohortibus decem et unâ, quæ appellatur I Thracum, et I Pannoniorum Tampiana, et I I Gallorum Sebosiana, et Hispaniorum, Vettonum C. R. et I Hispanorum, et I Valcionum Milliaria, et I Alpinorum, et I Morinorum, et I Cugernorum, et I Baetasiorum, et I Tungrorum Milliaria, et I I Thracum, et I I I Bracar. Augustanorum et I I I I Lingonum, et I I I I Dalmatarum, et sunt in Britanniâ, sub I Neratio Marcello qui quina et vicena plurave sti-

* Reliq. Brit. Romanæ.

pendia meruerunt quorum nomina subscripta sunt, ipsis liberis posterisque eorum civitatem dedit, et conubium cum uxoribus quas tunc habuissent cum est civitas iis data, aut si qui cœlibes essent, cum iis quas postea duxissent, dumtaxat singuli singulas.

A. d. xiv K. Febr.

M. Laberio Maximo II. } Co.
Q. Glitio Atilio Agricola II. }

Alœ I Pannoniorum Tampianæ, cui præest C. Valerius Celsus Decurioni Reburro Severi f. Hispan. Descriptum et recognitum extabula Anea quæ fixa est Romæ in Muro post Templum [Divi Aug]us[ti] ad Minervam.

Q. Pompei Homeri.	C. Vettieni Modesti.
C. Papi Eusbetis.	P. Atini Hedonio.
T. Flavi Secundi.	Ti. Claudi Menandri.*
P. Cauli Vitalis.	

BRADLEY

Originally belonged to the Suttons, from whom it passed by sale in 1527, to Rowland Hill, and from him to George Robinson, in 1528. It was purchased by Sir Wm. Brereton, in 1531, and his descendants sold it in the reign of Car. II. to Sir Wm. Drake, ancestor of the present proprietor.

BROXTON

Is beautifully situated about 11 miles S. E. by S. of Chester. It was given by the Conqueror to Roger Pigot, from whom it passed to the Pulfords,† and afterwards in portions, to the Leycesters, Grosvenors,‡ and the Duttons of Hatton, from whom it passed by marriage to the Massies of Coddington; and Thomas Massie sold it (reserving all minerals), to the late Philip Egerton, Esq. of Oulton, whose son Sir J. G. Egerton, Bart. is the present possessor.

Broxton Higher Hall, is delightfully situated on the top of the Hill, commanding most extensive prospects into the Principality, and to the estuaries of the Dee and Mersey, on the north side. It is built of timber and plaister, but has been repaired, and in some degree modernized, at different periods. The estate on which this house is situated was formerly possessed by the Broxtons, from whom it passed by the marriage of the daughters of Thos. de Broxton, to the Dods and Birds, the former a branch of the Edge family. In the early part of the 17th century, on the death of Thomas Dod, the estate passed by marriage of his daughter, to Edw. Tannat, of Aber Tannat, Shropshire, whose grandson sold it to Sir Philip Egerton, Knt.; it is now vested in Sir J. G. Egerton, Bart.

A stone house, a short distance north of the Higher Hall, was the seat of the Birds of Broxton, who were settled here so early as 1338; and it continued in their family till 1724, when it passed to Wm. Glegg, nephew of Charles Bird, whose nephew Edw. Glegg, sold it to James Tomkinson, Esq. of Nantwich, and he disposed of it to the Egertons, of Oulton, who are the present proprietors.

Broxton Lower Hall is a picturesque house, in a most romantic situation below the Broxton Hills. It is composed of timber and plaister, with gables and bay windows. The Massies‖, a branch of the Coddington family, were the proprietors, temp. Henry VIII. and continued so till about 1700, when Hugh Massie, Esq. sold it to John Dod, Esq. John Herbert Dod, Esq. dying without issue in 1719, the estate became vested in his sister, Anna Christiana, wife of William Farrel, Esq. of Chester, on whose death his three daughters§ sold it to the Egertons, of Oulton, who are the proprietors.

BOLESWORTH is a hamlet of this township, and was possessed by the Duttons so late as the reign of Car. I. from whom it passed to the Brownes, before 1662.—In the middle of the last century, James Tilston, Esq. purchased a considerable estate here, and built thereon a handsome pointed Gothic mansion, which he called *Bolesworth Castle*. Being appointed Consul at Cadiz, Mr. Tilston sold the estate in 1763, to John Crewe,

* These Tablets are preserved in the British Museum; and it has been observed, that "they serve to throw considerable light on the military establishment in Britain during the reign of Trajan, of which no mention is made by any Roman Historian."

† An eighth. ‡ An eighth.

‖ It appears from an Inq. p. m. temp. Eliz. that this branch of the Coddington family, possessed no less than eleven townships in Cheshire, and two manors (Haulghton and Isl) in Denbighshire.

§ Wives of Colonel Bonner, Major Henchman, and Mr. Cotgreave, of Chester.

Esq son of Joseph Crewe. Esq. Rector of Astbury and Muccleston, who again sold it about twenty-five years afterwards to Oswald Moseley, Esq. son of Sir John Moseley, Bart. of Rolleston. In 1805, Thomas Tarleton, Esq. purchased it from Mr. Moseley's representatives; he is the present proprietor, and has extended the domain by several large purchases in the neighbourhood.

The Oaks in Bolesworth, gave name to a family resident here in the reign of Henry III. from whom it passed to a branch of the Dods, and successively by female heirs to the Claytons, Stocktons, and Thicknesses. In 1739, Ralph Thickness, Esq. by will left it for sale, and it was purchased by Ald. S. Jervis, of Chester.—It subsequently became the property of the Dobbs's, and in 1785 was purchased by Mr. Thomas Cotgreave.

The romantic eminence of *Barnhill* is in this hamlet; forming the half way between Chester and Whitchurch.

BULKELEY

Is a completely secluded township, about 12 miles S. E. of Chester. Altho' it is not noticed in the Survey, there is no doubt of its having formed a portion of the Malpas barony. It gave name to a family settled here at a very early period; and we find, that in 1233, the four daughters of Robert de Bulkileh quit-claimed lands in Prestland to their brother William. The elder branch of the Bulkeleys became extinct in the 14th century, subsequent to which two estates here each bore the title of the manor of Bulkeley. One of them passed to Thomas Holford, an Esquire of the Body to Richard II. whose descendant Mary Holford, marrying Sir Hugh Cholmondeley, of Cholmondeley, about 1580, it has passed to the present proprietor, the Marquis of Cholmondeley. The other estate passed by marriage from the Bulkeleys to the Calveleys; in 1659 Lord Cholmondeley purchased it from Lord and Lady Byron; having been conveyed by Sir Hugh Calveley to Lady Byron, then Mrs. Elizabeth Booth, Dec. 30, 1646. It Is now the property of the Marquis of Cholmondeley.* The Bulkeley tenants attend the Cholmondeley Court Leet.

CHIDLOW.

This manor was at a very early period vested in the Stranges, of Blackmore, under whom it was held by the Pulfords. It was afterwards possessed by the Warrens, a bastard branch of the Plantagenets Earl of Warren; John de Warren, sixth in descent from whom, having two daughters coheiresses, the eldest, Margaret, brought Chidlow in marriage to the Mainwarings, of Ightfield. With the other Cheshire property of the family, Chidlow descended to the Egertons of Oulton; and John Egerton, Esq. in 1800, sold the reputed manor to Chas. Goodwin, Esq of Farndon. It is now the property of Hugh Maxwell Goodwin, Esq. in right of his wife, daughter and heiress of Walter Thomas, Esq. (late distributor of stamps in Chester), and niece of the said Mr. Goodwin. Chidlow is within the leet of Egerton.

CHOLMONDELEY

Is about fifteen miles from Chester, and adjoins the township of Egerton. It was included in the share of the great Barony which fell to the lot of Robert Fitz Hugh, from whom it passed to the Belwards. Robert, youngest son of Wm. Belward, took the local name, and was father of Hugh de Cholmondelegh, who married Felice, a natural daughter of Randle Blundeville, Earl of Chester, by whom he had a daughter of the same name. This Hugh had also two sons, Robert and Richard, the former of whom confirmed lands in Christleton to Chester Abbey, together with his body there to be buried. He married it is said,† first Beatrix,

* In a MS. of the date 1662, Lord Cholmondeley, Thos. Bulkeley, and Edward Bressey, or Brassey, are described as joint Lords of the Manor of Bulkeley. The Brasseys possessed an estate here by marriage with the heiress of Hadleigh, in the early part of the 15th century; and the 'fair new house" of the Brasseys, spoken of by Webb, still belongs to their descendant, Mr. Rd. Brassey, of Cotton Abbots. Thomas Bulkeley, the last male heir of that family, died in the house still called Bulkeley Hall, in 1802, at the age of 98 years, bequeathing his property here to Mr. Thomas Orton, the present proprietor. Old Bulkeley Hall is the property of the Marquis of Cholmondeley.

† MS. History of the Cholmondeley family.

CHESHIRE

daughter of Urian de Saint Pierre, by whom he had Richard; and second, Weverilla, daughter of David de Malpas, by whom he had Agnes, ancestress of the Broxtons: but the dates of both these marriages, are liable to considerable objection. Hugh son of the last-named Richard, by marriage with Margery daughter and coheiress of Richard de Kingsley, Forester of Delamere, obtained from the Rectors of Malpas, a license for a Chapel at Cholmondeley, in the 13th Edward I.* and holding the office of Deputy Serjeant of the Peace under the Baron of Malpas, he presented at Chester Castle the head of David le Cooper, decapitated for burglaries in Burwardsley and Cholmondeley. It appears from an Inq. p. m. 30 Hen. VIII. that Richard Cholmondeley, Esq. 8th in descent from the last-named Hugh, held the manor of Cholmondeley from Rowland Hill, Esq. by fealty, 12*d* rent, value per ann. £27. Also lands in Capenhurst, Upton, Chorley, Malpas, Edge, Rowton, Werswall, Bradley, Tushingham, Macefen, Norbury, Wordhull, Haughton, Northwich, Ebnall, Tattenhall, Kinnerton, Hawarden, Church Minshull, Aston, Hellesby, Weverham, Chester, and Egerton; total value £93. 13*s*. 4*d*. Hugh, brother and heir of this Richard, was on the Scotch expedition under Seymour Earl of Hertford, together with seventeen other Chester Gentlemen; and with them at Leith, in 1554, received the honour of Knighthood. Thirteen years afterwards, he raised one hundred men at his own cost, and with them joined the army of the Earl of Derby, intended to relieve Berwick from a threatened siege. In an Inq. p. m. 39 Eliz. it is stated, that he held in demense, as of fee, the manor of Cholmondeley, with its appurtenances, from the Malpas Barony, by military service, or the sixth part of a Knight's fee; also the manor or barony of Wich Malbank, the manors of Bickley, Norbury cum Althurst, Aston juxta Mondrem, half of Church Minshull, two parts of Capenhurst, the manors of Barkesford, Newbold, Edlaston, and Little Mouldsworth, and lands in Henhull, Barton, Larkton, Bickerton, Edge, Ebnall, Hampton, Malpas, Tushingham, Macefen, Stockton, Cuddington, Tilston, Horton, Duckington, Carden, Stretton, Haughton, Rowton, Worswall, Bradley, Spittle Boughton, Fadiley, Wolstanwood, Haslington, Badington, Chowley, Great Aldersey, Plumley, Northwich, Worleston, Wrenbury, Audlem, Swanbach, Egerton, Burwardsley, Golborne-Bellow, Church Shocklach, Oviatt, Sounde, Church and Monke Copnall, Woodbank, Little Christleton, Spittle in Wirral, Hoole, Backford, Newhall, Aston juxta Wrenbury, Cholmeley House in Chester, with numerous Messuages, the Manor of Hinton, and Mudford (Som.), Hinton (Salop), and Worthenbury (Flintshire). His son Hugh Cholmondeley, was knighted in the year the Spanish invasion was threatened, and was a firm friend to the Protestant interest. At the age of 20 years he commanded 130 men, raised for the suppression of the rebellion in the north under the Earls of Westmoreland and Northumberland, for the Restoration of Popery. He was Sheriff of the Palatinate, and twice Escheator. In the 42d Eliz. he, together with the Lord Chancellor Egerton, and Lord Treasurer Buckhurst, were joined in a Commission for the Suppression of Schism. He died the 23d July, 43d Eliz. Robert Cholmondeley, aged 17 years, his son and heir. On the 29th of June, 1611, Robert was made a Baronet; and in 1628, he was created a Peer, by the title of Viscount Cholmondeley, of Kellis, in the Kingdom of Ireland. He made himself particularly conspicuous during the civil wars, by his perseverance and courage in the Royal Cause; he distinguished himself in the affair of Tilston-heath, and raised several companies of foot. In 1645, he was created Baron of Wiche Malbank, and afterwards Earl of Leinster. On the final discomfiture of the Royalists, he compounded for his estates at the price of £7,742, and retiring to Bickley Hall, spent there a great portion of the residue

HISTORY.

* 1285.—This grant was in the possession of the late Hugh Cholmondeley, B. D. Dean of Chester; the appendant seals of the Rectors were in green wax.—It run thus:—

"**Omnibus** C'r'i fidelibus ad quos praesens scriptum p'rvenerit Will's de Audelym et Leodegarus de Notingh'm, rectores Ecclesie de Malo passu, salt'm in D'no. Nov'itis nos concessise Hugoni de Chelmundeleg' q'd possit h'ere cap'llm idoneu' celebrantem Divina in capella sua de Chelmundeleg' salva indempnitate matric: Ecclesia n're de Malo passu. Ita q'd cap'll's si quis ibid'm fuerit Divina celebr'na non se intromittat de aliquibus matrici Ecclesie n're spectantibus. In cujus rei testimonium huic presesenti scripto sigilla n'ra apposuimus Salt. Dat' apud Malum passum die lune in crastino S'ci Martini anno Gr'e milesimo ducentesimo octogesimo quinto."

CHESHIRE

of his life. He died without issue; and owing to some disputes, relative to the payment of his funeral expenses, his body was left uninterred for a year, when it was buried in the family vault at Malpas, Oct. 8, 1660.

Robert Cholmondeley, son of the third brother of the last Robert, succeeded to the estate, and was called to the Peerage as Lord Cholmondeley of Kellis; Hugh Viscount Cholmondeley, his son, succeeded him. He was Lord Lieutenant and Custos Rotulorem of the County and City of Chester, and also Lord Lieutenant of North Wales, previous to which by patent of Dec. 27, 1706, he was created Viscount Malpas and Earl of Cholmondeley. From these offices he was displaced in 1713, but restored on the accession of Geo. I.—Dying in 1724, he was succeeded by George second Earl of Cholmondeley. He was one of the Grooms of the Bedchamber to William III. and commanded the Horse Grenadier Guards at the celebrated battle of the Boyne, where his bravery gained him particular notice. He was wounded at the Battle of Steenkirk, in 1692. On the 15th of March, 1714-15, he was created Baron of Newburgh, Ireland; and July 2, 1716, was advanced to the English peerage as Baron Newburgh, in Anglesea. He died in 1733, and was succeeded by George the third Earl. After having previously held the offices of Master of the Robes, Commissioner of the Admiralty, and Governor of Chester, and been appointed a Knight of the Bath, in May 1735, he was made a Commissioner of the Treasury, and a Privy Councillor. He afterwards held the offices of Keeper of the Privy Seal, Vice Treasurer, Receiver General, and Paymaster of Ireland. In the Rebellion of 1745, he raised a regiment of foot for his Majesty, which was commanded by Lord Malpas his son. Soon after the accession of the present King, he retained the offices of Lord Lieutenant, Custos Rotulorem, and Vice Admiral of Cheshire, Governor of Chester Castle, Steward of the Royal Manor of Sheene, and a Privy Councillor. George James, now Marquis of Cholmondeley, was born on the 30th April, 1749, and succeeded to the title of Earl of Cholmondeley, on the death of his grandfather in 1770.—He was for some years Lord Lieutenant and Custos Rotulorem of the County, and Governor of the Castle of Chester. In June, 1782, his Lordship was appointed Envoy Extraordinary and Plenipotentiary to the Prussian Court. In April, in the following year, he was presented with the Captaincy of the Yeoman of the Guard, and admitted a Privy Councillor.* Sept. 13, 1815, he was elevated to a Marquisate, by the titles of Marquis of Cholmondeley, and Earl of Rock Savage. His Lordship is now Chamberlain, and Vice Admiral of the Palatinate, Lord Steward of the Royal Household, and Judge of the Marshalsea and Palace Courts.

HISTORY.

Cholmondeley Hall, a great portion of which is now pulled down, was re-built in the reign of Queen Elizabeth, by Sir Hugh Cholmondeley the younger. It was a timber mansion chiefly, projecting from each story. Over the great entrance door, was the armorial coat of the family, curiously carved, above which was inscribed,

"THE HOUSE WAS THEN BUILT BY WILLIAM FAWKONER, MASTER OF THE CARPENTRY AND JOYNERY WORKE, 1571."

During the Civil Wars, it was a garrison for 400 of the Royalists. In April, 1643, there was an action between the garrison and the Parliamentary forces from Nantwich, in which the latter were driven back, with considerable loss, stated so high as 50 men killed, and 600 horses, which were carried off to Nantwich.† Previous to November, 1643, the troops of the Parliament got possession, and sent off a detachment to assist their party at Tarvin. It again exchanged masters; but on the 30th of June, 1644, ‡" the Earl of Denbigh went before break of day towards Cholmondeley House, with 3 or 4 pieces of ordnance and two cases of drakes, where two Nantwich companies, volunteers, guarding the great piece of ordnance, met them; and before the break of day, they planted all their great pieces within pistol shot of the house, and about three or four in the morning, after they had summoned them, they played upon it, and shot through it many times, and they in the house shot lustily at them with their muskets. The besiegers playing still on them with their ordnance and small shot, beat them at last out of the house into their works, when they continued their valor to the utmost,

‡ Burghall's Diary.

* On the death of Horace Walpole, Earl of Orford, his Lordship succeeded to the ancient estates of that family.

† Many of the soldiers slain in this conflict, were buried at Malpas on the 22d of April.

themselves being few, killing four or five more of them, and Major Pinckney, a brave commander: but being too weak to hold out any longer, about one in the afternoon they called for quarter, which was allowed, and Mr. R. Horton, Captain of the House, let down the drawbridge, and opened the gates, when the Earl of Denbigh, Colonel Booth, and the rest entered, and took the Captain and all the rest prisoners, about 66, with all their arms and provisions." After this, the Parliamentary forces maintained entire possession of the Hall. The gardens adjoining the house are noticed by Mackay in his "Tour,"* as being remarkably fine.—At the commencement of the last century, the very serious injury which it appeared the Hall had sustained during the siege, rendered it necessary to be rebuilt; it was accordingly taken down on the south side, and the east and west sides were lengthened, and the whole cased with stone, under the superintendance of the celebrated Sir John Vanbrugh.

* 1724.

The building of *Cholmondeley Castle*, the present seat of this illustrious family, was commenced in 1801, the first stone being laid by Mr. Stephens; and the then intended work was completed in 1804. It is situated a considerable distance from the Old Hall, on a gentle elevation, commanding delightful views of a most luxuriant country. The style is the Norman castellated, with pointed windows, and its irregularity much enhances its picturesque appearance. In the front perspective is a noble Lake. In 1817, an addition was made on the north side of the Castle; and in 1819, a new wing was projected, on the south side, from a tasteful design by the Noble Marquis.† The windows of the Hall, the Library, and the Saloon, all fine apartments, are enriched with ancient painted glass, purchased by the Marquis in France. The convenience and comfort of the house is much increased, by all the principal apartments being on the ground floor.—Arranged in racks in the great hall, are the pikes of the Volunteer Corps raised by his Lordship during the late war; and the Hall and drawing room are decorated with ancient military trophies. Among a variety of other paintings in the Castle, are the following:—A portrait of Earl Hugh; of Sir Robert Walpole, and his Lady, (the former in full costume as a Knight of the Garter) after a painting at Houghton; Prince Rupert, by Lely; Lady Cholmondeley, daughter of Sir Robert Walpole, from the original at Houghton; the present Marquis, by Hoppner; the Earl of Rocksavage, by Finlater; the Hon. Wm. Henry Cholmondeley, second son of the Marquis; the late Lord Malpas, painted at Geneva; George third Earl of Cholmondeley; Holy Family by Rubens' Master; Death of Germanicus; Christ on the Mount, by Paul Veronese; St. Andrew; Italian Ruins, by Le Brun; Her Royal Highness Caroline Louisa, Princess of Wales; the Marquis, and Mr. Stephens his Steward, by Finlater; Venus attended by the Graces, copy by Romanelli from Guido, &c. &c.

The *Chapel* of Cholmondeley, noticed in page 334, is stated to have been sumptuously repaired by Robert Earl of Leinster, in 1652; and it is now conveniently fitted up for Divine Service by the Marquis.

The Court Leet and Baron of Cholmondeley, is now held at a newly erected and convenient Inn, adjoining the Castle;‡ its jurisdiction extends over the townships of Bickley, Cholmondeley, Norbury, Bulkeley, Chorley, and Wrenbury.||

† The whole exterior is of stone, procured from an excellent quarry, in the neighbouring township of Bulkeley.—The view which accompanies this, is after a painting by Breary, June 4, 1819.

‡ In 1818, in digging in a peat bog near the Castle, an ancient boat was discovered several feet beneath the surface. It is composed of the trunk of an oak tree; about twelve feet long, by nearly three feet wide--the ends have gone to decay. It has much the appearance of a canoe of the natives of the Polar regions, and has been buried many centuries. There is little doubt but what the bog was, at one time, an extensive mere.

|| In Collins's Peerage, notice is made of an ancient hospital at Cholmondeley, originally released by Rt. Fitz Nigel, Baron of Halton, to Rt. de Cholmondeley, first of the name; but it seems to rest on no authority, and to be wholly erroneous.--There was no Rt. Fitz Nigel, Baron of Halton, unless, as some suppose, the first Baron, who lived in the reign of the Conqueror, bore that name. His grandson, who assumed the name of Lacy, continued by his posterity, died about the middle of the 12th century; Robert de Cholmondeley must have lived in or about the reign of King John.---LYSONS.

From a Drawing by Drury — Engd. by J. Pigot Manchester.

CHOLMONDELEY CASTLE,

The Seat of the Most Noble George James Marquis of Cholmondeley.

Cassis Tutissima Virtus

Eng^d for Hanshalls History of Cheshire.

CHORLTON,

Was vested in Urian de St. Pierre, in right of his wife Margaret, in the 16th Edw. I. under whom it was afterwards held by the Birds and Claytons, or Cluttons. Owen Clutton was Lord of the Manor in 1671; and Thomas Chorlton Clotton, Esq. his descendant, is the present proprietor.

Chorlton Hall is moated; the house is in a state of great dilapidation. It is a timber mansion, ending in gables, situated in the least agreeable part of the township. Near the hall, is a dwelling, formerly the seat of the Mainwarings, over the door of which is written, " In the life time of George Mainwaringe, 1660."—It is now the property of the occupier, Mr. Benyon.

CUDDINGTON.

This township was the property of Robt. Fitz Hugh, Lord of Malpas, from whom it passed to the Suttons and Breretons. It was alienated by the latter family to the Drakes, and is now the property of T. T. Drake, Esq.

DUCKINGTON,

Was among the very few estates which remained to the Saxon proprietor Edwin. Before the reign of Edward II. it was possessed by the Suttons, for we find that John, son of Richard de Sutton, 17th Edward II. gave to David de Egerton, and his wife Isabella, all right to his land here. It passed from Isabella Delves, coheiress of the elder line of the Egertons, to William Brereton her nephew, in whose family it continued till 1662, shortly after which it was purchased by the Drakes, and is now the property of T. T. Drake, Esq. There are very few houses in the township.

EDGE.

It appears from the Survey, that this township formed part of the great possessions of Edwin, the Saxon Thane; and he was permitted to retain it. He was the sole proprietor of no less than eight manors, and Lord of a moiety of four, and a third of another, &c. &c. but the vicissitudes of Conquest, left him at last merely the subtenant of Rt. Fitz Hugh in the manors of Duckington, Hampton, Larton, Cholmondeley, and great and little Edge. There are no manerial rights exercised here; but an estate, called in some documents the Lordship of Edge, was possessed by the Dods, the present proprietors, so early as the reign of Hen. II. and it is pretty clear it was held by their Saxon ancestors. Mr. Ormerod gives some interesting particulars relative to this ancient, and truly *English* family, which need no apology for being introduced here :—

Hova, son of Cadwgan Dot, founder of the family in its present name, in the reign of Hen. II. then settled in Edge, and married the daughter and heiress of the Lord of Edge, and with her he had a fourth of the manor. It is conjectured, that this Lord was the son of Edwin, the original proprietor, and assuming this fact, the following particulars are inferred :—Dot was the Saxon Lord of sixteen manors, or at least of a great portion of them; he was also joint Lord of Cholmondeley, Hampton, Groppenhall, and two thirds of Bickerton, *with this very Edwin*. Dot was ejected from all his manors; and the circumstance of the heiress of the residue of Edwin's lands, uniting herself with a man who bore the name of one so closely connected with her apparent ancestor (prefixing thereto the addition of a name derived from the land* to which that friend of her ancestor would be most likely to fly for shelter) seems to make this marriage the result of old family friendship and alliance,—and to lead to a deduction of Cadwgan Dot, from the Dot of Domesday. To these very sensible observations are added, that " a descent in the male line from a Saxon, noticed in that record, would be unique in this county,"—and this descent is certainly pretty nearly proved.†

* Cambria.

† The following translation from the Survey, will illustrate the great possessions of Edwin, and Dot: and also what they held under Lupus the second Earl, and his son Robert, by military tenure, &c.:

FROM DOMESDAY BOOK.

Ispe tenet Coddington. Ernui, and Ansgot, and Dot, held it as three manors. Two hides were taxed. The land four carucates. In demesne one carucate, with two cowherds, and five villains, and one bordar, and one Frenchman born, with two carucates. There are a mill and twelve acres of meadow, &c. &c.

CHESHIRE

HISTORY.

In the Visitation of 1613, four descents were furnished by Sir Edward Dod, Baron of the Exchequer of the Palatinate, all of them subsequent to Cadwgan.—The alteration of the family surname from *Dot* to DOD, took place as early as the reign of Henry II. The Pedigree re-commences with Hova, and continues clear and defined even to the present time.* The actions of several of the family, have shed a lustre on the genealogy. Sir Anthony Dod, the 6th named after Hova, was one of the Heroes of Agincourt, and was Knighted on the field by Hen. V. His son, David, was among the gentry of the county, who addressed the Sixth Henry, relative to the liberties of Cheshire.—It appears from an Inq. p. m. 23d Eliz. that Urian Dod held lands in Edge value £3. 9s. also lands in Barton, and Little Edge,—the manor of Willaston, co. Salop, under the Earl of Shrewsbury by fealty. He died July 11, 22d Eliz. leaving Anne, Katherine, Margaret, Alice, and Elizabeth, sisters and heiresses. The senior line thus ending in female heirs, the Edge estate passed to Sir Edw. Dod, Knt. nephew of Urian, and from him it has descended uninterruptedly to the present esteemed proprietor, Thomas Crewe Dod, Esq.

The old Mansion of the family is supposed to have been situated in a place called the Hall Heyes, where still exist the outlines of the site, which was square, and of the moat which surrounded it.—The present House is in a most romantic spot, sheltered on all sides from the weather, but the immediate vicinity commanding the varied and magnificent scenery of the neighbourhood, extending over the fine Vale of Chester, and bounded only by the Welsh hills.

EGERTON,

Is not mentioned in the Survey; but there is a great probability that it was among the Baronial estates of

1 Isdem Robertus holds Cholmondeley; Edwin and Dot held it as two manors. Two hides are taxed—the land, four carucates.—Edwin and Drogo hold it of Robert, &c.

2 Isdem Robertus hold Eghe (Edge), Edwin formerly held it, and now holds it of Robert, &c.

3 Isdem Robertus holds Hampton; Edwin and Drogo hold it of him. Edwin himself formerly held it as two manors, &c.

4 Isdem Robertus holds Larton; Edwin and Drogo holds it of him. Edwin himself formerly held it as his own property, &c.

5 Isdem Robertus holds Duckington; Edwin holds it of him. Edwin himself formerly held it in domain, &c.

6 Isdem Robertus holds Eghe (Edge), Edwin holds it of him; he formerly held it in his own right, &c. [N. B. There are two Edges: Higher and Lower.]

7 Isdem Robertus holds Shocklegde, and Drogo holds it of him.—Dot formerly held it, &c.

8 Isdem Robertus holds Bickerton, Drogo holds it of him. Dot, and Edwin, and Ernuin, three Saxon Thanes, formerly held it as three manors, &c.

9 Richard the Cupbearer, holds Pontone of the Earl. Edwin formerly held it, &c.

10 Isdem Ricardus holds Calvingtone; Dot formerly held it, &c.

11 Isdem Willelm holds Estune; Dot formerly held it, &c.

12 Isdem Willelm holds Santune; Godwin and Dot formerly held it, &c.

13 Isdem Willelm holds Winelserde; Dot and Godwin formerly held it as two manors, &c.

14 Isdem Willelm holds Steple; Eluric and Dot formerly held it as two manors, &c.

15 Isdem Willelm holds Mollington; Dot formerly held it.

16 Isdem Bigot holds Mobberley; Dot formerly held it, &c.

17 Gilbertus de Venables holds Ecclestone of Earl Hugh; Edwin formerly held it in domain, &c.

18 Isdem Gilbertus holds Lege (High Leigh); Ulviet and Dot formerly held it as two manors.

19 Isdem Gilbertus holds Wincham; Dot formerly held it in demesne, &c.

20 Isdem Gilbertus holds Peover; Dot formerly held it, &c.

21 Isdem Gilbertus holds Hope, in Exeston Hundred; Edwin formerly held it, &c.

22 Gilbert the Hunter, holds Witune; Dot formerly held it, &c.

23 Osbern the son of Jesson, holds of Earl Hugh, Golbourne; Edwin formerly held it in demesne, &c.

24 Isdem Osbern holds Epletune; Dot formerly held it, &c.

25 Isdem Osbern holds Groppenhale; and Edwin holds of him. He and Dot formerly held it in domain as two manors, &c.

26 Hamo holds Estone; Edwin and Toret held it as two manors, &c.

27 Isdem Hamo holds Carlestone; and Osmond holds of him—Edwin formerly held it, &c. &c.

* It is asserted, that "the names of two undoubted descents, living now, are unnoticed altogether. These are, Thomas son of Stephen Dod, trustee of the Manor of Utkinton, 3d Edward III. and William, son of the same Stephen Dod, who grants 29th same reign, lands in Edge, to Philip de Egerton, which are most probably the lands now possessed there by the Egertons."—ORM.

Robert Fitz Hugh, whose daughter Mabilia brought a portion of it to Wm. Belward in marriage. On the death of his descendant, William de Malpas, David his natural son, obtained possession of the Barony, to the exclusion of Philip Goch, his uncle. The estate reverted to, and has continued vested in, the Egerton family, to the present time, being now the property of Sir J. G. Egerton, Bart.—In the early part of the 17th Century, Sir Rowland Egerton, bequeathed this and other estates to his second son Sir Philip Egerton, Knt.

From an Inq. p. m. 6th Eliz. it appears Sir Philip Egerton, Knt. held the manor of Egerton, and lands in Wichalch, Bickerton, and Malpas, from the Queen, of her Earldom of Chester, in capite, by military service, at the fourth part of a Knight's fee, value per annum, £34. 13*s*. 1½*d*. He also held the manor of Olton, and lands in Hampton, Egerton, Bradley, Chidlowe, Nantwich, Flaxyards, Poole, Calveley, Agden, Dirtwich, Netherwich, Tilston Heath, Newton, and Oldcastle.

On the 15th of April, 1617, Rowland Egerton was created a Baronet. By his wife Bridget, daughter and co-heiress of Arthur Lord Grey of Wilton, he had issue Sir John Egerton, of Farthingoe, Bart. (immediate ancestor of the late Earl of Wilton), and Sir Philip Egerton, Knt. a second son, who became possessed of the Churton estates.

Several of this most respectable family have distinguished themselves in the field. Urian de Egerton, temp. Richard II. had the lion rampant added to his arms, in testimony of his services in the Scotch Wars. Sir John Egerton, his grandson, was a strong partizan of the Lancasterians, and lost his life at Blore Heath. Sir Ralph Egerton, of Ridley, was by King Hen. VIII. created Chief Ranger of the Forest of Delamere, and Standard-bearer of England. The High Office of Serjeant of the Peace for Cheshire was held by the Egertons, in fee.

Egerton is situated on the banks of one of the small rivulets which empty themselves into the Weaver, near its source, and was for ages the seat of the family; in the 16th century, they removed to Oulton, and the *Old Hall* of Egerton, soon went to decay. It was moated; the inclosed area about an acre: the whole site is now in tillage. The *Chapel* stood within the moat, and part of it still remains, particularly the eastern window, which is in the pointed Gothic style. It is now occupied as a barn.

HAMPTON.

This township was originally in moieties, one of which remained to Edwin the Saxon proprietor. On the division of the barony of Malpas, it passed to the Belwards; a branch of which family assumed the local name.—Sometime after 1318, Hampton was vested in a family which bore the name of Malpas,* the male line of which became extinct temp. Henry V. Ellen and Catherine, sisters and coheiressess of the last heir, dying, the estate was divided among their four aunts, and a fourth of Hampton, was the share of Matilda, wife of Philip Egerton, of Egerton, from whom it descended to Sir John Grey Egerton, Bart. who sold it to Ambrose Brookes, Esq. and it is now vested in his sisters, Sarah the widow of Robert Brassey, Gent. and Martha Peers, of Broxton.

The *Bromleys*, who were settled in this township so early as the reign of Richard III. obtained the Hampton Hall estate in marriage with the daughter of a younger branch of the Egertons. Their descendant dying without issue, the estate was inherited by Randle Hopley, a sister's son, who in 1744, assumed the name of Dod. Soon after that period, Wm. Hanmer, Esq. of Hanmer, bought the property; which is now the property of Lord Curzon, by marriage with Esther, only daughter of Wm. Hanmer.

LARKTON, OR LARTON,

Was at the Conquest held by Edwin and Drogo.—Temp. King John, it gave name to a family residing here; it afterwards passed to the Cholmondeleys, and the Marquis of Cholmondeley is the present proprietor. The tenants of this manor owe suit and service to the

* Descended from Roger, bastard son of William Belward.

CHESHIRE

Court Leet of Cholmondeley, and they attend the Court of Egerton also.

It consists generally of miserable hovels, on the S. E. side of the Bickerton Hills, about eight miles and a half N. W. from Whitchurch.

MACEFEN.

This manor formed part of the great Barony of Malpas; it is now a very inconsiderably place, adjoining the township of Tushingham. Its early history remains in total obscurity; but it is highly probable that it passed to the Stocktons, with Tushingham, and from them descended to the Eatons, and the Grosvenors.—In the early part of the 17th century, it was included in the estates of Sir Rich. Grosvenor, who alienated the manor to the father of the present Lord Kenyon, about 1787, and his Lordship is the present proprietor.

STOCKTON.

Neither Stockton, nor Macefen, are noticed in the Survey; but it is pretty clear Stockton formed a dependency of the Malpas Barony. Long before the reign of Edward II. it became the property of a family which assumed the local name. It appears from an Inq. p. m. 17th Henry VII. that Robert Grosvenor held in demesne, as of fee, a messuage and lands in Stockton, from the heirs of Sir Thomas Cokesay, by the render of 6*d*.

Stockton passed to the Kenyons in the manner described in the notice of Macefen.

NEWTON.

This manor consists of only one farm, and adjoins the township of Cuddington, bordering on the county of Flint. It is among the possessions of T. T. Drake, Esq. having passed by purchase from the Breretons to Sir William Drake.

OLDCASTLE

Lies about 5 miles N. N. W. from Whitchurch, and was included in that portion of the Malpas Barony which fell to the St. Pierres, from whom it passed to the Cokesays, and they held it in capite from the King. By an Inq. p. m. 16th Henry VII. Roger Horton is found heir, and the same year it was transferred with the other Cokesay estates, to the celebrated Edmund Dudley, after whose attainder, in the 36th Hen. VIII. it passed by fine to Sir Rowland Hill. On the division of the Hill estates, it became the property of the Alports of Overton. It is now possessed by John W. Dod, Esq. of Clevely, co. Salop, a younger branch of the Edge family.

This township is divided from the Principality by a small brook; the ground about which is beautifully broken up. The Castle, which evidently gave name to it, was situated on a gentle eminence, some small remains of the site of which still exist. It is extremely probable that this fortress owed its erection to the Romans. It is stated in King's Vale Royal, that so early as the year 1585, not a vestige remained of its walls.

*Aug. 26th, 1644.

During the great Rebellion,* Oldcastle Heath, was the scene of a sharp conflict between 2,500 Royalist Cavalry, who had been driven out of Lancashire, and about 900 of the Parliament troops. The former were defeated; and Colonel Vane, and Colonel Conyers, together with 60 private soldies, were left dead on the field; 25 prisoners, including 2 Majors, 3 Captains, and a Lieutenant, fell into the hands of the Parliamentary troops, of whom only Lieut.-Col. Jones was wounded!†

OVERTON

Was included among the estates of Robt. Fitz Hugh; afterwards a great portion of it was vested in David de Golborne, half brother to Philip Goch, in whose descendants it continued till the beginning of the 16th century, when it passed to the Alports,‡ who were settled here some time; the paramount royalty, however, was held by the Lords of Malpas.

† So says Mr. Burghall; but the story is as marvellous as some of the Bonapartean Bulletins of the present day.

‡ Richard Alport was Lord of the manor of Overton, in 1641.—He was grandfather of Robert, who married into the Mainwaring family in 1680. He had messuages, lands, and tenements, near Fleet-street, London; also in Dorset Court, otherwise Salisbury Court, Hanging Sword Court, and Hanging Sword Alley, co. Middlesex.—Information of M. Gregson, Esq. of Liverpool.

Engraved by J. Pigot Manch.r from a Drawing in the Possession of M. Gregson Esq.r of Liverpool.

OVERTON HALL & WREXHAM VALE.

Engraved for Hanshalls History of Cheshire.

CHESHIRE

HISTORY.

-Rich. Alport, by will dated in 1718, bequeathed his lands amongst his three nieces, and left numerous legacies : among them, a rent charge of 40s. per ann. to the Curates of Malpas, for a daily service in their Church the week before Sacrament Sunday; £50. to the Blue School at Chester;* and £500. for the establishment of a School at Malpas, On his death Colonel H. Lawrence, purchased the estate, whose son Charles, in 1739, sold it to Wm. Chesshyre, Esq. of Hallwood, son and heir of the Rev. Robt. Chesshyre, M. A. Vicar of Runcorn. The manor was sold by his Executors to Mr. Thomas Prescott, merchant, of Chester, who in 1756 served the office of High Sheriff. In 1766,† he bequeathed the property to his brother Geo. Prescott, for his life, then to revert to Sir Geo. Wm. Prescott, his nephew; whose son, afterwards Sir Geo. Beeston Prescott, married Catharine Critchton Mills, upon whom he settled Overton.

†Obt. 1769.

In 1802, he obtained an Act of Parliament, to sell Overton, and to secure his wife's annuity on estates in Wales. He became possessed of Theobalds—the favorite seat of the revels of Charles II. by purchase from the Duke of Portland. Sir George Prescott, of Theobald's Park, co. Herts, died April 20, 1790; and Sir George William Prescott, his son, about the year 1801. The act above alluded to,‡ recites the object to be for exchanging the settled estate of Sir Geo. Beeston Prescott, Bart. in co. Chester, for another of greater value, in the county of Flint, to be settled in lieu thereof.—Under the provisions of this act, in Sept. 1802, the manor of Overton was purchased by Matthew Gregson, Esq. of Liverpool.‖ This gentleman has a large family; he married first, Jane, only sister of Mr. Foster, architect, af Liverpool, by whom he has a son and two daughters; secondly, Ann, eldest daughter of John Rimmer, merchant, of Warrington, by Catharine Leigh, daughter of George Leigh, Esq. of Oughtrington, by whom he has a son and three daughters living.§

‡42 George III.

§...ne, 1819

The *Hall* of Overton is situated in a very romantic dell; a great portion of the moat, including an area of about a statute acre, is filled up. —The entrance gate over the moat still exists; it is of considerable antiquity, & the arch is pointed. Very little of the old house remains; what there is, is cross-timbered, similar to many of the ancient houses in Chester, with a projecting story. A good farm-house is built here.

Overton Scar was long celebrated as the haunt of gypsies; it is an immense projecting rock, rising to a considerable altitude, beneath which was the Cavern where the wanderers sheltered. They assembled here, sometimes in a band of sixty persons; and on one occasion they were actually relieved by the parish, during the inclemency of a severe winter. This humanity of the parishioners did not, however, meet with a suitable reward; and the vagrants being detected in some nefarious practices, they were prosecuted. The gang soon after decamped; and the scene of their jollity is now covered with a plantation of thriving trees.

The *Golbornes of Overton*, a branch of the Golbornes, of Golborne,¶ were settled here long before the Visitation of 1566, and were a highly respectable family.—John Golborne, of Overton, living in 1590, married Katharine, daughter and coheiress of Randle Dod, Esq. of Edge.

* He was born in Chester.

‖ To this gentleman the author is much indebted for a variety of local information, which he takes leave here particularly to acknowledge.—Mr. Gregson, notices the similarity of the names of the principal families in Cheshire and Leicestershire,* viz. Bickerton, Cotton, Broughton, Bowden, Brooke, Corbet, Malory, &c. and reasonably attributes it to the Earls of Chester having commands in both counties, and the consequent probable interchanges of their leading chieftains, &c.

*...h. Hist.

¶ From Sir David Golborne, of Golborne.—Information of M. Gregson, Esq.

, Arms: Quarterly, Gregson, Hulgrave, Yates, Gregson; impaling Foster, and Rimmer.

CHESHIRE

TUSHINGHAM CUM GRINDLEY,

Is about two miles N. W. N. of Whitchurch. Its lofty situation affords delightful views of the surrounding country, particularly on the side of Shropshire. It was originally among the possessions of Robert Fitz Hugh; from whose descendants it passed before the reign of Edward II. to the Stocktons, who held it of the Malpas Barony. It afterwards passed by marriage of Isabella, daughter and heiress of Wm. de Stockton, to Robert de Eaton, and, with the estates of that family, became the property of the Grosvenors. In 1636, Sir Richard Grosvenor sold the manor, together with "all that Chapel of Tushingham, commonly called Chad Chapel, with a yard thereunto belonging," to Thomas Nevett, goldsmith of London, for £600.

In 1715, Edward Halsey, Esq. purchased the manor from the heirs of John Nevett, for £1100. and the following year conveyed it to Thomas Churton, gent. of Whitchurch, whose descendants sold it to Josiah Boydell, Esq. of Kilhendre, near Oswestry, who subsequently sold it to Daniel Vawdry, Esq. the present proprietor, occasionally resident at Tushingham — Tushingham gave name to a Family, which occupied lands here, in the reign of Edw. II. A Court has been held for the Manor, but the tenants now attend the Court of Egerton.

GRINDLEY, a hamlet of this township, is included in the manor.

WICHALGH.

This township is about five miles N. W. from Whitchurch. It is not noticed in the Survey, but it formed that portion of the Malpas barony which was possessed by the Belwards. It was afterwards the property of Philip de Egerton,* and continued in that family till 1800, when it was conveyed by John Egerton, Esq. to the trustees of James Broadhurst, Esq. It is now the property of Thomas Jenks, Esq. who has assumed the name of Broadhurst; and it is within the Leet of Egerton.

HISTORY.

* 20th Edw. III.

WIGLAND.

Is about four miles N. W. N. of Whitchurch. It originally formed part of the great Barony, although it is not noticed in Domesday. In the 35th Edward III.† David de Wigland, descended from Hova de Hampton, second son of Philip Goch, died possessed of Oldcastle Mill, two parts of a Salt Work, in Fulwich, and half the Manor of Wigland, excepting thirty acres held from Philip de Egerton. It then passed to the Golbornes, of Golborne, the Catheralls, of Horton, the Lawtons, of Wigland, and the Bostocks, of Bostock, and reverted to the Breretons, of Shocklach, from whom it was probably purchased by the Fletchers, of Lichfield. On the death of John Fletcher, Esq. it was vested in his nephew Thomas Wickstead, Esq. of Nantwich; on whose decease in 1814, the manor, &c. passed by will to his grand nephew Charles Tollet, Esq. of Betley, who has assumed the name and arms of Wickstead.

† Par. Inq. p. m.

DIRTWICH, sometime called Fulwich, is in this township; salt was made here in the reign of Edw. III. and probably long before that period;‡ and its manufacture still continues.—Maister Burgall says, in his Diary, "Aug. 28, 1643, Captain Croxton, and Capt. Venables, with their companies and others went to Durtwich, and cut in pieces all their pans, pumps, *salt pits*, and works, and carried some of their pans off; so their salt making was spoiled, which served Shrewsbury, and many other places in the Kingdom. The provocation of this was, that Lord Capel had issued a Proclamation, that none under his command should fetch any salt from Nantwich."

‡ Leland, in his Itinerary, says, "The Dyrte wiche a new pitte besyde the olde decayede."—"There be a II or III, but verie litle salt springs at Dertwiche, in a low botom, wher sometimes salt is made."

Cliffe, del. (See page 118.) Mosses, sc.

CALVELEY HALL, THE SEAT OF E. D. DAVENPORT, ESQ.

PARISH OF ST. OSWALD, CHESTER,

IN THE COUNTY.

CONTAINS THE TOWNSHIPS OF

CHURCH-EN-HEATH.
LEA cum NEWBOLD.
SAIGHTON.
HUNTINTON.
BOUGHTON.
BACHE.
NEWTON, AND
WERVIN.

[The three former Townships are within the Chapelry of Bruera.]

CHURCH-EN-HEATH,

Generally called *Churton Heath*, is about four miles rom Chester; it contains only one farm, which is occpied by the owner, Mr. Colley.—Wm. del Heath, 31st Edw. I. gave this manor to Robt. Bulkeley; it afterwards passed to the Malpas family, and David, son of John de Malpas, held lands here under the Suttons.—In the 15th Henry VII. the Massies of Edgerley obtained possession by purchase, and continued proprietors till the reign of Charles II. when Mr. Colley, a non-conformist Minister (ancestor of the present proprietor) purchased it from them. The entire township contains only 120 statute acres. Of late it has been esteemed a manor, but it pays suit and service to Saighton Court.

LEA cum NEWBOLD,

Is about 6 miles S. S. E. from Chester. At the period of the Survey it was divided; one moiety belonging to the Earl, the other to Bigot, being a portion of the fee of Aldford, which afterwards descended to the Aldfords and Ardernes. The tithes of Lea were given by Hugh Fitz Norman to Chester Abbey.

From Hugh Fitz Norman it passed to the Montalts. Robert de Morley, heir of Robert de Montalt, dying in 1277, conveyed Lea to Queen Isabella, with remainder to John de Eltham and K, Edward III, On that Monarch obtaining possession of it, he granted it to Wm. Earl of Salisbury, about 1337, from whom it was purchased by Sir John Wingfield, who in 1354, settled it

on Maud, the wife of Kenrick de Calveley, and her youngest son, the celebrated Sir Hugh Calveley. It continued in the Calveleys till 1648. In Sir Hugh Calveley the male line of the family terminated, and the property was afterwards divided between the families of his sisters, Elizabeth, wife of Thomas Cotton, Esq. of of Combermere, and Lettice, wife of Thomas Legh, of Lyme: the former had all lands north of the brook; the latter those on the south side.—The Cottons sold their share in [illegible] to Joseph White, Esq.; the other still continues in the Leghs, of Lyme.

SAIGHTON, or SALGHTON,

Sometimes called Saughton, Saltone, and Salktone, is about 4½ mile S. E. S. of Chester. It was amongst the gifts of Hugh Lupus to the Abbey of Chester; but his successor, Richard, wishing to regain possession of it, was refused by the Abbot,—who was threatened with the dissolution of the Monastery on the Earl's return from his Norman dominions.* The Abbot maintained his right till the Patricks, Barons of Malpas, gained possession, and did not quit till they had obtained from the Monastery £200. as an accommodation. At the Dissolution this township was involved in the disputes which took place between the Dean and Chapter and the Fee Farmers, and was obtained by Sir Rich. Cotton. In the subsequent division of the Abbey Lands, Saighton, was purchased by Sir Geo. Beverley, Knt. of Huntinton, from whom it passed to the Harpurs;—Anne, daughter of Peter Harpur, had two daughters, one of whom was married to Edward Spencer, of London, and the estate passed from him to John Spencer, whose widow brought the estate in marriage to the Rev. Rd. Williams, Rector of Hawarden peculiar, who sold it to Thomas Brock, Esq. of Chester, under whose will it passed to the present proprietor, John Brock Wood, Esq.

In the 28th Henry III. the Abbot of St. Werburgh, had a grant of free warren in Saighton, Huntinton, and Cheveley; and 22d Richard II. obtained a license to fortify the manor house of Saighton. In the 6th Hen. VIII. Abbot John had permission to make a Park of one thousand acres in the before-mentioned three townships, but this was never carried into effect.—After the Reformation, and the disputes relative to the lands of the Dean and Chapter, the manor was possessed for a great number of years by the Calveleys, and during the Protectorate it was sold under the sequestration, to Charles Walley, innkeeper, of Chester, whose great-grandson John dying without issue, his widow sold it in 1755, to Foster Cunliffe, Esq. grandfather of Sir Foster Cunliffe, Bart. of Acton, the present possessor.

A considerable portion of the Manor House, now called *Saighton Grange*, still exists, and the *great entrance*, which is of red stone, is nearly perfect.† It was built about 1489, by Abbot Ripley, and is castellated; the outer arch pointed. On the west side, is a tall square turret, with a staircase; adjoining which is a projecting window, and underneath a wolf's head erased. Above it, is a figure of the Virgin and Child, under a beautiful canopy. The House is now occupied by a farmer, and the room over the gateway is used as a granary. The appearance of the house is extremely interesting, the situation delightful, and the view from the summit of the tower extensive and magnificent.‡

HUNTINTON cum CHEVELEY,

Is about three miles S. S. E. from Chester, pleasantly situated on the right bank of the Dee; it was included with the Fee of Saighton. In 1093, Huntinton was confirmed to the Monastery of St. Werburgh. Its descent is given in that of Saighton.

The Cowpers had long an estate here, which passed by marriage with the heiress of Thomas Cowper,‖ to John Hincks, Esq. of Chester, whose descendant, Thos. Cowper Hincks, Esq. is the present proprietor.

* Old Henry Bradshaw attributes to this declaration, the subsequent shipwreck of the Earl, and the heir apparent to the Crown.

† The slide for the portcullice still remains.

‡ Mr. Ormerod notices a tract in the British Museum, under the following title:—"Letter of a sad Tragedy by Prince Griffin, at Seyton, neere Chester, and his several attempts against the Lady Caufley, and the bloody Murther for which he is fled into Scotland. London, printed for A. C. and A. W. 1648."—What this sad Tragedy was remains to be discovered—probably a republication of some popular legend of the time.

‖ Son of Thomas Cowper, Esq. M. P. for Chester, temp. William the Third.

BOUGHTON

Adjoins the east suburb of Chester, and originally formed part of the possessions of the secular Canons of St. Werburgh, being held by them with Saighton Fee. It partook of all the vicissitudes of the Cottonian litigation, and was eventually confirmed by patent of 22d Elizabeth, to eighteen fee farmers.

The largest mansion and property here, was for many generations vested in the Davenports of Henbury, from whom it passed by marriage in the first instance to Thomas Hand, merchant, of Chester; second, by marriage with Mary, daughter and co-heiress of Thomas Hand, to Hugh Foulkes, Esq. of Llechred, from whose eldest daughter and coheiress Mary, by marriage, it has become the property of the present very respectable possessor, Wm. Currie, M. D. who resides at Boughton Hall, which he has recently in part rebuilt, and greatly improved the adjoining property.

It would seem there was formerly a Chapel of Ease here; for it is mentioned in the Chartulary of St. Werburgh,* that the Vicar of St. Oswald's was to maintain a Chaplain, who should perform divine service "*in Capella de Boughton*," three days in each week, and the remaining four days with the Vicar at the Church of St. Oswald.—The Chapel of Spittle Boughton is certainly not meant here, that having an indepeudent foundation, and besides being within the precincts of the Parish of St. John.

Harl.MSS.

Boughton possesses no manerial rights; and the township is divided amongst a number of landholders.

BACHE

Is not mentioned in the Survey; but it is ascertained, that Richard the second Earl, granted the Mill here, (in addition to the manor, which he before possessed) to the Abbot of St. Werburgh, in whom the manor continued vested till the Dissolution, when it passed to the Dean and Chapter, who were dispossessed by Sir R. Cotton, under whom, and Chester Abbey, it was held by the Chauntrells, who were settled here for many generations, and resided at the Hall of Bache. It appears by an Inq. p. m. temp. Hen. VI. that William Chauntrell, held lands in Bache, Newton, and Upton, from the Abbot of Chester; together with lands in Hale, Altrincham, Dunham Massey, Stockeport, Offerton, Newton, Ashton, Bradley, Tranmore, Kelsall, Kirkby in Walley, Bebington, an eighth of the *vill* of Pulton Secum, a fourth of Liscard in Wallesey, and Newton in Wirral. The manor passed by purchase from Wm. Chauntrell, who died in the 26th Elizabeth, to Robert Whitley, Gent. whose daughter married Alderman Wm. Crompton, in whom it became vested, partly in right of his wife, and partly by purchase. Robert, grandson of this Wm. dying without issue male, it became the property of Edw. Morgan, Esq. of Golden Grove, Flintshire, who married his daughter and heiress. Bache was purchased from the Morgans by James Broadhurst, Esq. on whose death it became the property of Thomas Jenks, Esq. who has taken the name of Broadhurst.

A stream, which passes thro' the Bache Pool, gives a romantic feature to the immediate scenery. The *Mill* adjoining, now occupied by Mr. Dodd, skinner, was given to the Monastery of Chester, as before mentioned, by Richard, the second local Earl; and passed with the Abbey lands to the Dean and Chapter; from whom it was purchased by Mr. Broadhurst.†

NEWTON,

Sometimes described as *Newton juxta Sutton*, is about two miles N. from Chester. It formed part of the possessions of Chester Abbey, to which it was granted by William Fitz Nigel, the Constable, and the Abbot claimed infangtheof, outfangtheof, wayf, stray, chattels of natives, fugitives, &c. After the Dissolution it was transferred to the Dean and Chapter, from whom it passed with other property to the Hurlestons, and from them by Anne, coheiress, in marriage, to her second husband, Henry John Needham, afterwards created Viscount Kilmorey, in whose family it is now vested.

† The Dean and Chapter had a grant of the pool, and the fishery therein, in addition to the Mill.

Newton Hall, the seat of the Hurlestons, and now of the Viscount Kilmorey, is tenanted by the family of the late George Parker, Esq. It is of brick, with a high roof, and scarcely any feature to recommend it in point of situation.

Henry Hesketh, Esq. is the proprietor of a handsome mansion in this township.

FLOOKERSBROOK is a Hamlet of Newton, forming partially a suburb of Chester, and was at an early period in the family of the Masseys, of Kelsall. In the 37th Henry VI. John Massey sold it to the Bruens; and temp. Hen. VII. Richard Bruen, of Tarvin, sold it to Thos. Barrow, of Chester, from whom it passed, by marriage of a daughter, to the Sneyds. The Smiths, of Hough, afterwards bought it, and Sir Thomas Smith conveyed it to John Anderson, Esq.* of Chester.—Since the commencement of the last century, it has been divided into several small estates.

The Hall was destroyed during the siege of Chester, by the Garrison.

The situation of Flookersbrook is extremely picturesque; it was within the jurisdiction of the Court of Upton.

WERVIN.

At the time of the Survey, this manor was held by William, Baron of Wich Malbank, and the Canons of Chester Abbey.—The entirety was subsequently confirmed to the secular canons by Hugh Lupus, by consent of the said William, who was witness to the grant.—It continued among the possessions of the Abbey till the Dissolution, and then fell into the hands of Sir Rd. Cotton. Passing to the Hurlestons, it continued in that family till the death of Charles Hurleston, Esq. last male heir, when it descended to his niece and coheiress Elizabeth, wife of Trafford Barnston, Esq. on whose death it passed to her niece Mary, daughter of John Leche, Esq. of Carden, who married Mr. Thomas Roberts, and he is the present possessor.

Some remains of the ancient *Chapel of Wervin*, confirmed to Chester Abbey by a Bull of Pope Honorius, still exist. Roger, the Abbot, some time between 1240 and 1259, appropriated its revenues for the augmentation of the kitchen stores, when the number of Monks was increased to forty. The officiating Priest was provided by the Abbey, and not by the Vicar of St. Oswald's. Previous to the Great Rebellion, there was a font in the Chapel, and Randle Holme† describes it as a Parochial Chapel. It has been in ruins a great number of years, and is now used as a cattle shed, or cart house. On the north side there is a fine quatrefoil window; and the walls are nearly covered with ivy.

Wervin is beautifully situated, about four miles and a half from Chester, close to the Canal from that City to the Mersey.

* Brook House, is a pleasant residence, built in the octagonal style, by Mr. Anderson, and was for many years designated "ANDERSON'S FOLLY." It afterwards became the residence of P. Ellames, Esq. who made considerable improvements in the gardens, &c. and erected a wooden railing, which has long since been destroyed, extending from the house, considerably within the City Liberties. The House is at present tenanted by — Barnes, Esq.

† Harl. MSS, 2071, f. 204.

PARISH OF PLEMONDSTALL,*

CONTAINS THE TOWNSHIPS OF

BRIDGE TRAFFORD,	HOOLE, AND
MICKLE TRAFFORD,	PICTON.

[Bridge Trafford is in the Hundred of Edisbury.]

THE CHURCH, which is dedicated to St. Peter, is at a considerable distance from the village of Mickle Trafford, and was originally a rectory in the gift of the Monastery of St. Peter and St. Paul, at Shrewsbury, from which it passed to the College of St. John, Chester. Richard, Bishop of Lichfield and Coventry, in 1393, licensed the Dean of the College to appropriate the Rectory; and in 1403, it was endowed with 40 marks per ann.—At the Dissolution, the Marburies got possession, from whom it was purchased by Bishop Bridgeman,† and from him it descended to the Earl of Bradford, the present proprietor.

† Gastrell.

The present Rector is the Rev. Mr. Bridgeman; he has corn tythes of the entire parish. Picton and Bridge Trafford pay a modus in lieu of hay; Hoole and Mickle Trafford pay 16*d.* as a modus.

The Church is pleasantly situated on an eminence, some distance S. E. of the road from Chester to Warrington—in "a place where solitude herself might dwell." The architecture is that of the middle part of the 15th century. It consists of a nave and chancel (the latter separated from the body of the Church by a wooden screen) with an aisle, on the north side, which is also divided from the body of the building in the same way. The roof is of timber, arched, and springing from heavy brackets. The belfry is of wood. There is little doubt but all the windows were originally enriched with stained glass, some fine specimens of which still exist. At the East end of the Church is the Trafford Chapel, in the window of which is the date 1500. In the window adjoining the pulpit, are the figures of "Thomas Smyth and Marget hys wife," with their seven sons and four daughters, kneeling behind them, the whole brilliantly coloured.

On the north side of the communion table, is a white marble monument, thus inscribed:—

Underneath lie interred John Hurleston, of Picton, Esq. and Anne his wife, daughter of Thomas Wilbraham, of Woodhey, in this county, Esq.—Here also lie John Hurleston, their son and heir, and Mary his wife, daughter of Thomas Leigh, of Adlington, in this county, Esq.—Here also lie Charles Hurleston, Esq. their son and heir, and Anne his wife, daughter of Sir Geoffry Shakerley, of Hulme, in this county, Knt.—Underneath also lie John Hurleston, of Newton in Chester, Esq. son and heir of the above mentioned Charles and Anne, who died 12th Aug. 1720. He left issue by Mary his relict, eldest daughter of Sir John Williams, of Pengethly, in the county of Hereford, Knight and Baronet, four daughters, Anne, Mary, Penelope, and Elizabeth.

In the Trafford Chapel,—

Here lyes the remains of Alice Trafford, sole heiress to Thomas Trafford, of Bridge Trafford, Esq. who first married John Barnston, of Churton, Esq. by whom she had one only son Trafford Barnston; and after married the Hon. John Savage, of Rock Savage; by him she left one son, John Earl Rivers. She departed this life the 23d. of October, 1666.

In the yard, under the east window, on a tomb raised on a platform—

In this vault lies the body of Elizabeth, wife of Charles Hurleston, of Newton, Esq. youngest daughter and coheir of Thomas Lander, of Newhall, in the county of Lancaster, Esq. by Elizabeth, daughter of Edward Downes, of Shrigley, in the county of Chester, Esq.—She was beautiful in her person, discreet in her behaviour, a dutiful daughter, an observant wife, and had she lived a few weeks longer, might have been a happy mother.—She died 19th November, 1727, aged 32.‡

* It is worthy of remark, that no such township as Plemondstall exists: the Church is in the township of Mickle Trafford.

‡ In the Holme Coll. is the following remarkable memorial, now no longer existing:—"Neere unto this place lyeth interred the bo-

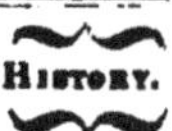

There are few charitable bequests, and they are recorded on two tablets in the Church. There is a *School* here for the education of four poor children; the Church Wardens appoint the Master.—The Registers commence in 1558.

MICKLE TRAFFORD.

This Township is noticed under the head of Wirral Hundred in the Survey, and passed from the Earls to the Fitzalans, and from them, in the reign of Hen. VI. to the Troutbecks. Margaret heiress of the Troutbecks, marrying Sir J. Talbot, Knt. it has descended to the Earls of Shrewsbury, who are the present proprietors.

HOOLE

Is vested in the Earls of Shrewsbury, in the same line of descent as the preceding township.

Hoole Heath was one of the sanctuaries for Criminals appointed by the Earls within the Palatinate.—From an Inq. 13th Edw. III. its privileges are thus noticed: Six citizens of Chester, and six men selected from the inhabitants of the county, state, that they had ridden the boundaries of *Hole Heath*, and they find it to have been holden of the Earl of Chester, and his predecessors time out of mind; and that in time of war in Wales, all lawful men of the Earl of Chester, and all other men living in peace of our Sovereign Lord the King of England, and the said Earl of Chester, were wont to have refuge, and receipt on *Hole Heath* "wt they' goods, necessaryes, and beasts, by an yer and one daye; and that the comynaltie of the cittee of Cest.' of right and of tyme out of mynde, ought to have comyn pastur upon *Hole Heath*, to they'r beasts in all tyme of the yeare; and saye also that the meares and bondes of *Hole Hethe* do begyn from the yate called Chest'r yate, nygh Flokershroke, and so folloyng Flokersbroke unto Wysnaysich, and so folloyng Wysnaysich nere a cet'cyne place wher a grange of the p'sons of the Church of Plemondestow sometime beyng; and so folloyng neare ——— that Robt. of Whitmore sometyme dyd breke, and so folloyng neare Houghshey a'ynst Pykton Dale unto Saltesway, whych is the Kyng's Highway ner Chest'r, to lede the hooste of our sovreyn Lord the Kyng in tyme of warre unto Shotwyk Ford; and so folloyng beyond Saltesway unto Sasse Diche, and so unto the town of Newton, and unto the yate of Robert the sonne of Cislie Newton, whyche sometyme was called the Shepe Yate, for whyche yate the said Robert gave money to the Kep'r of the Towne of Hole for the tyme beynge, and so folloyinge from the sd yate, by the Old Heyes of Newton unto Flokersbroke." This Inquisition complains, that the Abbot of Chester, the Whitmores, Bruchulls, &c. had made inclosures on "Hole Heath, to the gret hurt and gret exheredition of the easement of the hole citie of Chest'r."

Hoole is pleasantly situated on a gentle elevation. The Bunburys of Stanney had an estate here before the reign of Henry VI. and the seat of their descendants, *Hoole Hall*, was destroyed during the siege of Chester. In 1757, this property was purchased by the Rev. J. Baldwin, who assumed the name of Rigby, In 1800 it was sold to the Rev. Dr. Peploe Ward, whose son is the present proprietor.

There is a handsome brick house, with stone facings, built by the Rev. J. Baldwin, which was sold, together with the land immediately surrounding it, to Mrs. Fairfax, from whom it was purchased by John Oliver, Esq. It has recently become the property of Charles Sedgwick, Esq.

Hoole House, built in 1760, is the property of the Rev. James Ward, (who has assumed the name of Hamilton, in compliance with the will of his uncle, Chas. Hamilton, Esq.)—It is now tenanted by the Lady of Lieut.-Gen. Sir John Delves Broughton, Bart. sister of Sir John Grey Egerton, Bart. of Oulton Park.

Hoole Lodge,* is held by lease from the Earl of Shrewsbury, by the proprietor of the last mentioned estate.

dyes of John Hurleston, of Picton, Esq. who died the 29th day of October, 1669, aged 79 yeares; together with his loving wife Anne, the daughter of Thomas Wilbraham, of Woodhay, Esq. who died the 12th Oct. 1669, aged 79 yeares; they lived together husband and wife 60 years, and had still-born and christened 19 children, of which John his son and heir, Peter, Stephen, Francis, and Grace, only survived him.

* This is supposed to be the ancient manor house of Hoole.—Orm.

There are several other pleasant houses in the township.

PICTON.

Is about four miles and a half N. N. E. from Chester. At the Survey it was held by the Barons of Shipbrooke, and their successors the Vernons, held it till long after the reign of Hen. VI. Richard de Vernon gave the tythes of the township to Chester Abbey, before the year 1093, and Warin Vernon gave to the same Abbey, 4s. yearly, issuing from Picton Mill. Richard de Vernon who was beheaded after the battle of Shrewsbury, was possessed of the entire manor, which he held from the King in capite.

* Then of Hurleston Hall, in the county of Lancaster.

From the Vernons, Picton descended to the Savages; and towards the conclusion of the reign of Elizabeth, passed to the Hurlestons,* in which family it continued till the death of Charles Hurleston, Esq. in 1734. His estates being divided among his four nieces, Picton fell to the share of Mary, wife of John Leche, Esq. of Carden, in whose descendant it is now vested.

*** Mr. Ormerod with great propriety says, in his description of this township, that "in roads, appearance, and inhabitants," it "may be safely said to present a complete picture of barbarism."

THE PARISH OF PULFORD,

CONTAINS THE TOWNSHIPS OF

PULFORD. | POULTON.

PULFORD is about five miles S. W. from Chester, separated from the Welsh frontier by a small brook, which empties itself into the Dee. It appears from the Survey, that it was divided between the Secular Canons of Chester Abbey, and Hugh Osberne, who possessed himself of the share which belonged to the original proprietor.

Some time afterwards the manor was held by the Ormsbies and the Pulfords; the latter family had assumed the local name, and were probably descendants from the Fitz Osbernes. In 1239, Ralph de Ormesbie* granted his Castle, and lands in Pulford, to Robt. de Pulford.

From the Pulfords, the manor passed to Sir Robert Grosvenor, of Holme, Knt, in marriage with Joan, sole heiress of Thomas de Belgrave, in whom Pulford was vested. On the death of Robert Grosvenor, in 1464, Pulford passed with his daughter Catherine, to the Winningtons, of Winnington; and from Elizabeth, sister and heiress of Richard Wynyngton, by marriage, to Sir Peter Warburton,† of Arley, Knt. Pulford continued in the Warburton family for many generations, and was purchased by the late Robert Townshend, Esq. of Christleton, from Sir Peter Warburton, Bart. The latter possessor devised it by will to Trustees, for the purpose of sale, after a certain period; on the expira-

† 31 Henry VIII.

* The Lysons, are of opinion, that this name was written erroneously for the Orrebies, for it is said ‡ that Robert Pulford "held under Sir Peter Arderne, temp. Edw. I. and it was well known that the heiress of Orreby married Arderne. The Orrebies had a Castle at Aldford, but it is possible they might have had another at Pulford, as both places were so near the borders of what was in ancient time an enemy's country. Pulford Castle is said to have been built for the purpose of checking the inroads of the Welsh."

‡ Vill. Cest.

[Whilst this portion of the work is passing through the press, an account of the death of Samuel Lysons, Esq. F. R. S. & F. A. S Keeper of the Records in the Tower of London, &c. has appeared.--- A loss truly severe to all the admirers of the Antiquities of Great-Britain.---July 1, 1819.]

CHESHIRE

tion of which it was purchased in 1813, by the present Earl Grosvenor, who has once more united the manor to the paternal estates of the family.

Between the Church, and the Brook, before mentioned, is the site of the *Castle of Pulford*—in form semicircular, occupying in the whole nearly a statute acre. An idea of the ancient works may be formed from the plan:—

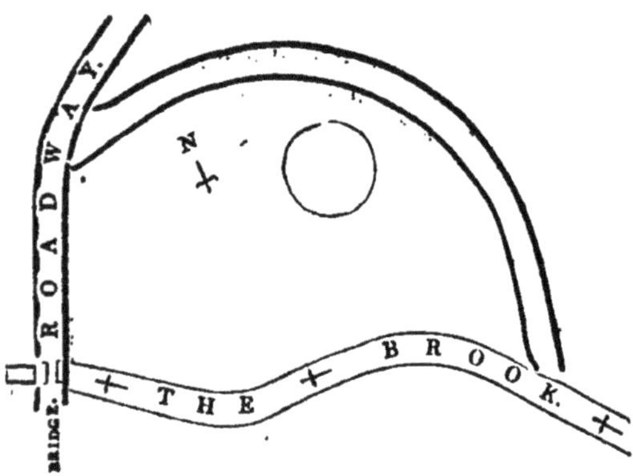

A Court Leet and Baron is held for the Manor.

The Burganeys, a respectable family, have been settled some time in this township. The last male heir of the family, John Burganey, Esq. was a Captain in the Ancient British Fencibles, commanded by Sir W. W. Wynn, Bart. and was killed during the Irish rebellion, at the Battle of Newton Barry, June 1, 1798.

The *Church* is of considerable antiquity, and adjoins the turnpike road. It is built of red stone, with a strong tower (of the style of Hen. VII.) nave, and chancel. On a wooden tablet against the south wall of the Church, is this inscription—

In the Church Yard, under a faire stone lyeth the bodies of William Burgayney, son of Anthony and of Katherine his wife. William Burganey, of Pulford, Gent. his son, student of Corpus Christi in Oxford, died 26th of August, 1689. Elizabeth his wife, daughter and coheiress of David Lloyd, of Ugh-y-monidd,* in Hope, died 25th July, 1670. William his son, Gent. married Rachael, daughter to Randle Holme, of the city of Chester, Gent. and had issue William and Rachel; she died 30th May, 1695, and was buried at St. Mary's, Chester.

* Uch y mynydd.

† 1153 says the Monasticon.

HISTORY.

The advowson of the Rectory descends with the Manor; the present Rector is the Rev. Townsend Forrester, A. M. instituted 20th June, 1809.

Among the Charities, which are trifling, are two benefactions of £10. each, by Sir Rich. Grosvenor, and Anne Club, the interest to be given to the poor not receiving parochial relief.

POULTON,

Which is about five miles S. W. from Chester, is not mentioned in the Survey; but it is ascertained that Robt. Pincerna, gave half of this township to the Monks of Combermere, to found a Convent of Cistercians, for the safety and health of the Earl his Master, Randle Gernons, then a prisoner with King Stephen—of the Earl's predecessors, his own wife Ivetta, his son and heir Richard, and the souls of his ancestors. Hugh Cyveilioc confirmed this Charter; and the Earl himself, together with the Arderncs, Boydells, Aldfords, and others, contributed to the pious undertaking. The Abbey was founded in 1158,† but the contiguity of it to the Welsh frontier, rendering the situation peculiarly irksome to the Monks, Randle Blundeville, translated the Holy Brotherhood to Dieulacres, in Staffordshire, where he built and endowed a Monastery for them about 1220. This translation, the Monasticon legend attributes to a dream with which the Earl was visitted, in which the spirit of his grandfather Randle, conjured him to go to Cholpesdale, near Leek, and there found an Abbey, to which he was to remove the monks in the 7th year of a Papal Interdiction, which he foretold! This dream the Earl told to his Countess, who exclaiming "*Deux encres!*" the Earl accordingly gave it the name of Dieulacres. But take the words of the Legend, as given in Mon. Aug.—

"**Idem Ranulfus** cum quadem nocte in strato suo quiescit, apparuit ei per visum, Ranulfus comes avus suus, dicens Vade ad Cholpesdale, quod est in territorio de Leeke, et in illo loco quo quædam capella in honore B. M. V. olim fnit constructa, fundabis Abbatiam albi ordinis monachorum, et eam edificiis instaurabis, et possessionibus ampliabis, et erit tibi gaudia et multis aliis, qui per locum illum salvabuntur. Ibidem enim erigenda est scala, per quam descendent et ascendent Angelorum preces, et vota hominum Deo offerentur, et referent gratiam, eritque nomen Domini invocatum super locum illum de precatione assidua. Et hoc tempore horum nuncio, signum erit eeclesiæ, D. papa Christianitatem, in Angliâ interdicet, sed tu interim ibis ad monachos de Pulton, quorum Abbatiam Robertus Pincerna in honore meo fundavit, et particip's ibi Sacramento Domini, habent enim privilegia hæc suis fundatoribus ministris. Et in septimo anno interdictionis transferes eosdem monachus ad locum quem prædixi. Qui cum Ranulfo Comiti et (ille) Clementiæ Comitissæ retulisset, et in dicto loco se velle construere monasterium indicasset, illa in Gallicis verbis sic respondit, *Deux encres!* et Comes congratulans ad dictum ejus, *hoc*, inquit, *crit nomen illius loci, Deulacres.*

" Ranulfus Comes Cestriæ fundavit Abbatiam de Deulacres, et cum posserit primum lapidem fundamenti ejusdem Ecclesiæ, dixit in Gallicis verbis, *Deux encres,* et alii circumstantes responderunt Amen! et Comes, hoc, inquit, monasterium vocatur Deulacres, ut nomen Domini super illud invocetur."

Another tradition respecting Earl Randle, equally credible, is quoted from the Chronicle of Dieulacres, viz. :—

That as he lay on his death bed, a great number of figures, in appearance human, with a Chieftain at their head, passed the cell of a hermit near Wallingford: he demanded their errand; when he was answered,—We are demons, and hasten to the death of Earl Randle, to bear testimony to his sins. The Hermit desired the Chieftain to return in thirty days, and acquaint him with the result of the mission. At the expiration of that period the polite demon did return, and told the Anchorite, that the Earl had received sentence of condemnation, but that the Mastiffs of Dieulacres, and the other Monasteries, had yelled so loudly when his sentence was executed, that the deepest pits of hell had been distured by the noise, *and their Prince* (Lucifer !) *had been compelled to release him !* The Demon-chief added that no greater enemy than the Earl had ever entered the Devil's dominions, inasmuch as the prayers which had been offered up for him, had released from torments the souls of thousands who had been associated with him in those orisons.*

The Abbots of Dieulacres retained temporal possession of Pulford till the Reformation. At the Dissolution, a branch of the Manleys, of Manley, which had resided at Poulton from the beginning of the reign of Hen. VII. on lands leased from the Convent, obtained possession; and continued here till the reign of Elizabeth, when Henry Manley sold the manor to Rich. Grosvenor, Esq. of Eaton, in whose descendant, the Right Hon. Earl Grosvenor, it is now vested.

Not a vestige of the Monastery exists; but some remains of the Grange-hall Chapel, probably a relic of it, is recorded to have been in a state of extreme decay in 1672. A Court Leet and Baron, is held for this Manor at Eccleston.†

* In the confirmation of the Earl, he granted the Monks of Poulton a fishery in the Dee; and exempted them from paying toll for grinding their corn at his (Dee) mills, in Chester.

† Copies of the foundation Charter, and of Earl Hugh's Charter, &c. are given by Mr. Ormerod in his History; they are too long for the limits of this work.

CHESHIRE

HISTORY.

THE PARISH OF SHOCKLACH,

CONTAINS THE TOWNSHIPS OF

CHURCH SHOCKLACH,
SHOCKLACH OVIATT,

AND
CALDECOTE.

Church Shocklach and Oviatt Shocklach, are included in one manor in the Survey, and were the property of Rt. Fitz Hugh, from whom they passed to the Suttons and St. Pierres in right of their Barony of Malpas. Sir John Dudley then obtained possession, and the manor was passed by fine to Sir Rowland Hill, from whom it devolved to Sir Richard Corbet, of Stoke, who sold it in the 14th Eliz. to Sir Randolph Brereton, Knt. The descent of the Brereton property to the Egertons of Ridley, is before noticed; but amid the general wreck of their property, they retained Shocklach, for a considerable period; when it was sold by them to the Pulestons, of Emral. It is now the property of Sir Richard Puleston, Bart. of Emral, Flintshire.

The Breretons of Shocklach, became extinct by the death of Randle Brereton, in May, 1611. *Shocklach Hall*, the "fair and goodly seat" of the Breretons, (afterwards of Sir Richard Egerton, of Ridley) was a very ancient mansion, within a moat; but it no longer exists. A farm-house occupies its site.

The *Shocklaches*, a family which assumed the local name, were resident here some time, but became extinct at an early period.

The *Dods of Shocklach*, a respectable branch of the Edge family, were settled here about 1480. Of this family was Thomas Dod, Archdeacon of Richmond, and Rector of Malpas and Astbury; also John Dod, the *Decalogist*, born here in 1547. He was a celebrated non-conformist, and was twice silenced. Afterwards he obtained the living of Fawsley, in Northamptonshire, and died there in 1645. Dr. Wilkins, Bishop of Chester, was his grandson.

The Lord of the Manor pays suit and service at Malpas; but the Court of Shocklach extends over Chorlton, Cuddington, Horton, and Wigland.

The *Church* of Shocklach, is dedicated to St Edith. The living is an augmented Curacy. The presentation passes with the manor, but it was originally vested in the Dean and Canons of Saint John's, Chester. The Church has a nave and chancel, and at the west end is a small baptistery with an ancient font. The south door has a semicircular arch considerably beautified with Saxon mouldings. The value of the Curacy is stated* to be £100. 15s.

* Par. Ret.

The Charities are trifling: a rent Charge of £10. left by Mr. Val. Broughton, 1633: £14. interest from money vested in the hands of Mrs. Anne Bennion; £3. from Joan Roden; £1. per annum for the poor of Caldecote, from Mr. Larden, &c. The Registers commence in 1538.

The *Castle of Shocklach*, of which not a vestige remains, occupied a moated site, near Castleton Bridge, on the Farndon road, adjoining a small stream. It is probable it was in a state of repair so late as the reign of Elizabeth.

CHESHIRE HISTORY.

The only idea of its extent is now to be formed from the appearance of the ground on which it stood—

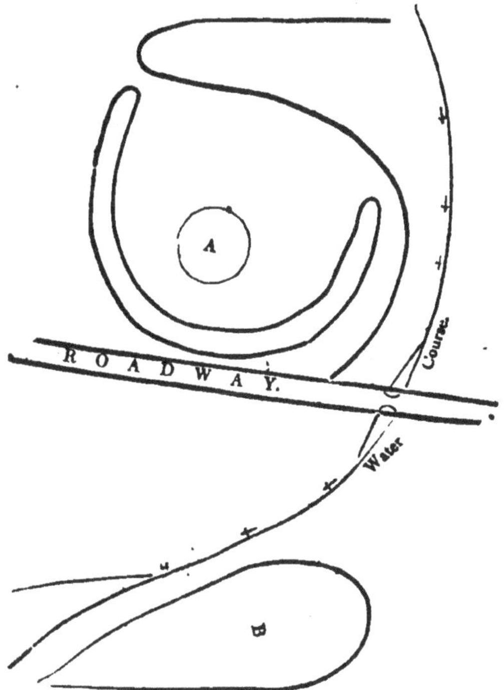

∴ A. The site of the Keep; about 22 feet in perpendicular height. B. an exterior mound; about 45 feet in width at the base.

SHOCKLACH OVIATT

Is included in the manor of Shocklach, as before noticed; it is about nine miles and a half N. W. W. from Whitchurch.

CALDECOTE

Is about eleven miles S. E. from Chester; and is noticed in the Survey as being the property of Hugh Fitz Osberne—from whom it passed as parcel of the Malpas Barony, to the Breretons, and Drakes, who are the present lords.

A branch of the *Egertons* of Egerton, were settled here so early as the reign of Edw. II. and held considerable property, which has passed to the Pulestons of Emral.

A family which assumed the local name, were also settled here temp. Edw. IV. which became extinct in the person of Randolph Caldecote, D. D. who died towards the conclusion of the 17th century, leaving behind him a certificate, stating his belief that Thomas Caldecott, of Calthorpe, co. Leicester, was descended from his family—this certificate is dated Sept. 14, 1642.

The *Yardleys* of Yeardesley, in the Hundred of Macclesfield, had estates in Caldecote, temp. Hen. VI. a branch from which settled at Farndon.

TARVIN PARISH,

(PART OF.)

FOULKE STAPLEFORD,

Is about six miles E. from Chester. The description in Domesday, "*Radulfus Venator tenet de Hugone comite Stapleford,*" probably included *Bruen Stapleford.* It is supposed the descendants of this Radulfus, assumed the local name; for it appears, temp. Richard I. William de Stapleford alienated the manor to Philip de Orreby, who was Justice of Chester in the reign of John. The Township received its prefixture from his descendant Fulco de Orreby, who was Justice of Chester temp. Henry III. This Fulco had a son, Sir John Orreby; who dying without male issue, the manor passed to Richard Corbett, Esq. of Leighton, great grandson of Alicia, sister of Sir John Orreby, and wife of Peter Corbet. From the Corbets, Foulke Stapleford passed to the Breretons, who exchanged with John Bruyn, of Stapleford; and it continued in the Bruins, till the middle of the last century, when it was sold under a decree of Chancery to Randle Wilbraham,

CHESHIRE

Esq. of Rode, in whose grandson, Randle Wilbraham, Esq. it is now vested.

An estate here called BRERETON PARK, parcel of the original estate, was purchased by the Walls, in the 17th century; and in 1702, they sold it to Sir John Werden, Bart. of Chester, with whose estates it has passed thro' the Beauclerk family to George Harley Drummond, Esq. who is the present proprietor.

HARGREAVE STUBBS—is a hamlet of Stapleford.—There is a *Chapel* here, founded in 1627, by Sir Thos. Moulson, Knt. Lord Mayor of London. He originally endowed it with £40. per ann.* The Chapel is situated on the Common; it is built of red stone, and adjoining to it is a *School House*, endowed originally with £20. per ann. *for the Government, education, and instruction of youth in grammar and virtue.*

* The Clerk to have 40s. per ann.

HISTORY.

Since the bequest was made, so great has been the alteration in the value of landed property, that the lands have been let for £252. per ann. An order of Chancery has been obtained for the appropriation of the property, under which, the Bishop, and Dean of Chester, (for the time being) the Right Hon. Earl Grosvenor, Rand. Wilbraham, Esq. the Rev. J. Oldershaw, (Vicar of Tarvin) and the Rev. Richard Massie, (then Rector of Coddington), were appointed Trustees. They are empowered to raise the Minister's salary to any sum not exceeding £150, per ann. the Schoolmaster's not exceeding £60, the Clerk's not exceeding £10, and the residue to be applied to such Charitable purposes, as the Trustees shall think proper.

The Registers of the Chapel commence four years after the foundation.

THE PARISH OF TILSTON,

CONTAINS THE TOWNSHIPS OF

TILSTON,	HORTON,
CARDEN,	AND
GRAFTON,	STRETTON.

TILSTON

Is about twelve miles south from Chester, situated in a sequestered district, and consists generally of Farmhouses and Cottages. It formed part of the great Barony of Malpas, and as such is noticed in the Survey.—It afterwards passed to the Belwards, and to David the Bastard; from whom it descended to the St. Pierres and Cokesays. A portion of Tilston was recovered by Isabella Delves, from the Cokesays; and the whole of the Sutton share* eventually passed through the Hill, Brereton, (of Shocklach), and the King families, to the Cholmondeleys; when it was sold by the present Marquis Cholmondeley, about 1788, to John Leche, of Carden, Esq.—The recovered share, viz. that of Isabella Delves, passed to the Breretons of Brereton, who afterwards alienated it, together with the advowson of the living of Tilston, to the Drakes of Shardeloes, who are the present proprietors: this share is considered as 11-12ths of the entire manor, which is within the jurisdiction of the Court of Malpas.

* As Barons of Malpas.

A family which bore the local name, was settled here at an early period. William de Malpas released to Einion, the son of Richard de Tilston, for his homage, the lands in Tilston, which he had given to him by Einion ap Cadwgan.† The lands of the Tilstons passed by purchase to the Coddingtons, who with them held a sixth part of Tilston Mill.

† Ormerod.

The *Church* is dedicated to St. Mary, and the Drakes and Cholmondeleys,* notwithstanding the inferiority of the share of the latter, alternately present to the Rectory. The present incumbent is the Rev. William Garnett, A. M. instituted Feb. 1. 1798.

Some portions of the Church have the appearance of considerable antiquity; it has a nave, chancel, and tower, with a small division on the north side, called the *Stretton Chancel.* There are no monumental memorials of much interest: they are chiefly to the Leche family.

The Rector has the entire tythes of the Parish; the Registers commence 1558.

The Charities are few: A rent charge of £1. 14s. 8d. left in 1679, by Mr. Wright, the produce to be given in bread to the poor of Tilston and Malpas.—A similar charge of £5. per ann. for the instruction of poor children, left by Mr. Bradshaw.—A rent charge of £5. left by Mr. Fitton, for the relief of the Poor.—And £156. left by persons unknown, the interest of which is given to the poor.

Tilston Heath Hall belonged to the family of Gardner, in 1662.†

CARDEN.‡

It is very probable this manor was originally included within that of Tilston, for no mention is made of it in the Survey. Before the reign of Hen. III. a family which assumed the local name, was settled here; and after the time of Hen. IV. Carden was divided into *Lower*, and *Over Carden*, the former possessed by the Leches,|| the other by the Fittons. Towards the conclusion of the 17th century, Over Carden was sold by the Fittons to the Bradshaws, of Pennington, co. Lanc. and afterwards to Joseph Worrel, Attorney, who disposed of it in several lots, the whole of which are now included in the manor of Lower Carden.

Lower Carden, continued altogether in the Leches, and is now vested in John Hurleston Leche, Esq. a minor, fifth in descent from John Leche, last mentioned in Dugdale's Visitation. Of this family, were the Leches of Nantwich and Mollington.

The *Hall* of Carden is a curious timber mansion of the early part of the 16th century, situated on a small eminence, commanding extensive and splendid views into Wales, the Vale of Chester, and to the estuaries of the Dee and Mersey. It is backed by abundance of large timber, behind which rises the higher range of the Broxton Hills. The Park has long been celebrated for its fine deer.

Carden is within the jurisdiction of Malpas Leet, but the Leches hold a Court for it.

GRAFTON

Is not noticed in Domesday, but it nevertheless was portion of the Malpas Barony. It gave name to a family settled here in the reign of Edward III. from whom it passed with an heiress to David de Crue, of Sonde, before the time of Henry VI. It afterwards became the property of the Wards and Massies, in the latter of whom it was finally vested. In the reign of Elizabeth, Gerard Massie, B. D. Rector of Wigan, alienated it; it was subsequently purchased by Sir Peter Warburton, Knt. one of the Judges of the King's Bench, who left Elizabeth, wife of Sir Thomas Stanley, of Alderley, Bart. sole heiress.—It has continued in the Stanleys of Alderley and Winnington to the present time.

Grafton Hall, erected by Sir Peter Warburton about 1613, is still standing, and in good repair; it is occupied as a farm house. It is of brick, with stone facings, gables, and bay windows; the chimnies are lofty and turretted. A handsome gateway leads to the garden in front of the house.

HORTON.

This Township also is not noticed in the Survey; but it was claimed as portion of the Malpas Barony.§ It was possessed by the Corlets, and Breretons, and passed from them to the Pulestons; Sir Richard Puleston, Bart. being the present proprietor.

This township gave name to a family possessed of considerable property here, which passed to the Aldersey and Catherals, about the reign of the first Edward. The Catherals were a younger branch of the Cathe-

* This share is now in the Leches.

† Harleian Manuscripts.

‡ Sometimes called Cawarden, Caerddyn, Caurthin, &c.

|| From John Leche; stated in the pedigree as a younger brother of the Leches, of Chatsworth, Derbyshire.

§ By Lord Sutton, in plea to Quo Warranto, 15th Henry VII.

rals of Catheral, co. Lanc. and were settled at Horton for *fifteen* generations; when about the year 1700, Dutton Catheral sold the estate to a Mr. Dodd, linen-draper, of London.

Horton Hall, formerly the seat of the Catherals, is in a state of ruin, but it bears the appearance of having been at one time a respectable mansion. It is built of timber and plaister, the roof finished with gables; and a stone gateway in front.

STRETTON

Is about ten miles S. S. E. from Chester, and probably took its name from the ancient Roman road, which passed through the town, or its immediate vicinity.—It was at an early date held by the Stranges of Blackmere, under the Malpas Barony; in the reign of Hen. V. it passed to the Warrens, and from them by marriage of Margaret, an heiress, to William, second son of Randle Mainwaring, of Peover. In the 38th Hen. VIII. it was bought from the Mainwarings by Rich. Wright, Arthur Starkey, and Thos. Barnston, Esqs. for £2000. and on the purchase being divided, the Manor became the property of the Leches, of Carden, excepting the Stretton Hall Estate, which was retained by Richard Wright, Esq. and continued in his family for five generations, when on the death of Edw. Wright, Esq. last heir male, in 1752, it became vested in his brother-in-law, John Leche, Esq. who dying without issue in 1785, the estate passed to his cousin J. Leche, Esq. a Major in the Army; he also died issueless, in 1814, when it passed to his elder brother Wm. Leche, Esq. of Carden. It is now the property of John Hurleston Leche, Esq. a minor.

The *Hall* is a good house, delightfully situated on the cross-road from Wrexham to Barnhill.

PARISH OF TATTENHALL,

CONTAINS THE TOWNSHIPS OF

TATTENHALL,
GOLBORNE BELLEW, AND
NEWTON.

TATTENHALL

Lies about eight miles S. E. from Chester, and formed a portion of the possessions of the Barons of Wich Malbank. It was afterwards given by Randle Gernons to Henry Touchet and the Lords Audley; on the attainder of James Touchet, Lord Audley, 12 Hen. VII. the Manor was forfeited to the Crown. About 1600, it was purchased from the Cottons by Ralph Egerton, Esq. for £1000. and afterwards passed to the Crewes, of Utkinton, and the Crewes of Crewe, whose descendant, John Crewe, Esq. sold it to Thos. Tarleton, Esq. of Bolesworth Castle, the present proprietor.

The Court Leet of Tattenhall, which extends over the entire Parish, has jurisdiction also over the manors of Burwardsley, Harthill, Chowley, and Huxley.

The *Hall* of Tattenhall belonged to the Bostocks, of Bostock, who sold it to the Bradshaws; in 1666 it was the property of Sir J. Bradshaw, of Chester. It is of brick, with gables and bay windows; and forms parcel of the manor.

The *Tattenhalls*, of Tattenhall, had estates here, which they inherited from the Herthulls, long since extinct. John Larden, Esq of Chester, (Mayor in 1801), has a handsome property here.

The *Church*, which is dedicated to St. Alban, has a nave, chancel, and side aisles, with a square tower, and five bells. Some remains of rich painted glass still exist; and in the east window is a figure of St. Alban, patron of the Church. The rest is elegantly traced tabernacle work,—the arms of the Touchetts, &c.—The Church and Tythes were given by William Malbedeng to the Abbey of Chester; and after the Dissolution,

CHESHIRE HISTORY.

the advowson was attached to the Bishopric of Chester. The tythes are the property of the Rector; a modus is paid for hay.

The Monumental remains are few. There is an inscription near the altar to the Rev. Sam[l]. Davie, A. M. Rector of the parish 41 years, who died Oct. 19, 1742, aged 72. Another monument to John Davie, A. M. Rector of St. Mary's, White Chapel, London, who died August 9, 1756, aged 46.

Memorials of the Rev. Wm. Southcoat, many years Curate of Tattenhall, died May 21, 1760, aged 46. George Bird, of Broxton, Gent. died Dec. 31, 1702, aged 79, &c.

The present incumbent is the Rev. James Thomas Law, A. M. instituted Feb. 5, 1816.

There are several Charitable Benefactions to this Parish: An Annuity of 8*s.* from Hugh Dod, 1652.—The sum of 9*l.* 10*s.* in the hands of John Larden, Esq. given by Dr. Peploe, for the clothing of one poor person alternately in Newton and Golborne Bellow.—200*l.* 3 per cent. consols, producing 10*l.* 0*s.* 10*d.* per ann. to be distributed to the Poor attending Church, and not receiving alms.—60*l.* in the hands of J. Larden, Esq. given by the Rev. S. Davie, in 1742, for apprenticing poor boys to farmers.—13*l.* in the hands of Mr. Geo. Peck, for the relief of the poor of Newton, given by Mr. John Handley, in 1724.—13*l.* 6*s.* 4*d.* annually, from lands bequeathed by Robert Farral, and Richard Whitfield, for the relief of the poor.—Twenty-seven Benefactions sunk in the purchase of an estate value 300*l.* vested in trustees, and the interest of 45*l.* the gross interest of the whole of which is expended in educating and clothing poor children.

GOLBORNE BELLOW,

Or *Bellew*, or as it was anciently written *Belleau*, is about six miles and a half S. E. E. from Chester. It was the property of William Baron of Nantwich, and was under him held by the family of Bella-Aqua, Belleau, or Bellew, from which it passed successively to the Golbornes, Hattons, Vernons, and Duttons. This was a mesne manor, but it is not now considered one, being annexed to Mr. Tarleton's manor of Tattenhall; its officers are sworn in at Handley Court.

In this *vill* is Rushill, Rushee, or Rushall Hall, formerly a seat of the Duttons, of Hatton,* and afterwards of Sir Peter Pindar. It is the property of Miss Giffard, of Nerquis, and is occupied as a farm-house, the site of it moated.

A place called the *Cleys*, was situated near Newton,† the seat of a younger branch of the Golbornes.

* Webb's Itin. 1622.

† Idem.

NEWTON,

Or *Newton juxta Tattenhall*, is a componant part of the manor of Tattenhall, and the property of Thomas Tarleton, Esq.

PARISH OF WAVERTON,

CONTAINS THE TOWNSHIPS OF

WAVERTON,	AND
HATTON,	HUXLEY.

WAVERTON is situated about four miles S E. E. from Chester, and originally belonged to Ilbert, the supposed father of Richard de Rullos, from whose family it passed by marriage of Margaret, heiress of Robert de Rullos, to Robt. Pichote, (or Pigote), and he granted a moiety of the manor of Tattenhall, as also of Hatton, to Hugh, son of Simon de Hatton, on the render of two marks per ann. The Wavertons, a family which assumed the local name, held lands under the Pichots, which were subsequently alienated by them to the Pulfords, of Pulford. These lands passed to the Grosvenors, in the 40th Edw. III. by marriage of Sir Robt. Grosvenor, of Holme, with Johanna, heiress of John de Pulford, and widow of Thomas de Belgreave. It passed, in 1464, to the Duttons, by marriage of Elizabeth, daughter and co-heiress of Robert Grosvenor, to

CHESHIRE HISTORY.

Peter Dutton. The Dutton estate was eventually vested in the Massies, of Coddington, and is now the property of the Rev. Richaad Massie.

Earl Grosvenor claims share of the manerial right of Waverton, in virtue of the estate which he has here.

There is an extensive quarry of red stone at Waverton, which has been worked a great number of years. The stone used in the repairs of the Cathedral of Chester, in 1819, was obtained from hence.*

The *Church* was probably built about the end of the eleventh century, and is mentioned in the Charter of Hugh Lupus, 1093. It was granted to Chester Abbey by Rich. de Rullos, and continued vested in the Abbots till the Dissolution. By patent 33d Hen. VIII. the patronage of the living was granted to the Bishops of Chester; bnt in consequence of some burdensome mortuaries, claimed by the Archdeacon of Chester, on the death of every incumbent,† an Act of Parliament was obtained in 1755, by which such claims were abandoned, and the Rectory appropriated to the Bishop of Chester, the parochial duty to be performed by a resident stipendiary Curate.

The architectural style of the present Church, is that of the early part of the reign of Henry VIII. and consists of nave, and side aisles, divided from the body by three arches. The roof of the nave, which is of carved wood, bears the date 1635. The Chancel is pulled down. The tower and the whole of the Church is of red stone.

There are no Monuments worthy of notice. The Registers commence in 1582.

The charitable bequests amount to 135*l.* 10*s.* the interest of which is distributed to the poor in money or bread.‡

HATTON

Is about six miles S. E. from Chester. It is not mentioned in the Survey, but it no doubt formed part of the manor of Waverton, descending with it from the Rullos to the Hattons, who probably gave name to the township. The Hattons were originally, of Hatton, in Daresbury, and here they fixed their seat.‖—It appears in an Inq. temp. Edward IV. that Peter Dutton, jun. Esq. and Robert Huxley, yeoman, both of Hatton, suffered outlawry for a felony, Peter Hatton, then holding 12 messuages and 320 acres of land in Waverton, and Norbury, near Marbury. From the Hattons, this township passed by marriage of Petronilla, daughter and heiress, to Hugh Dutton, a younger branch of the Duttons of Dutton; and the son of Hugh Dutton dying without issue, the estate was vested in his daughter Dorothy who married first John Walthall, Esq. and afterwards John Massie, of Coddington, Esq. to whom she conveyed the property on the 28th July, 1699. In the mean time, a claim to the estate had been made by John Dutton, son of the uncle of Dorothy, but it was confirmed to the Massies. In 1699, John Massie, Esq. sold the estate to the Honorable Geo. Cholmondeley, Brigadier-General in the Army, ancestor of the present proprietor, the Most Noble Geo. James Marquis of Cholmondeley; no court is held.

Sir Piers Dutton§ was of the Hatton family. He possessed a great property, and in 1539, rebuilt Dutton Hall, in a handsome manner. It would seem he was in considerable favor with Henry VIII. who engaged him as a fit instrument in bringing about a surrender of the Charters of the Cheshire Monasteries, in particular. It was he who arrested the Abbot of Norton, and Randle Brereton, Baron of the Exchequer of the Palatinate; and the freedom with which he executed numerous illegal acts, at last prompted him to the commission of others of more enormity. Petitions were presented to the King against his proceedings. Sir John Done alleges, that the said Sir Piers, being Sheriff, and Raufe

§ See Vignette, p. 77.

* In the spring of 1819, a gang of gypsies settled on a piece of common land in this township—but quitted early in the summer.

† More particularly noticed in pages 94 and 95.

‡ The Harl. MSS. contain a recommendation from the Rev. Geo. Snell, when Rector, to the Bishop of Chester, to confirm to John Tilston, Esq. of Huxley, a CHAPLETT OR ORATORIE, there built by him on the north-east side of the Church. The Bishop's consent is thus notified:—

"The Pallace, 29 Aug. 1640.

"Let an act be sped for the use of this place to Mr. John Tilston, and the owners of his house at Huxley, to bury, sitt, stand, or kneel in, during divine service in the Church of Warton.

J°. Cestr."

‖ Sir Christopher Hatton, so celebrated in the reign of Elizabeth, was of this family.

CHESHIRE

Mainwaringe his Undersheriff, had incurred numerous penalties by an improper exercise of the office; that they *entendinge undue preventment of inquest* for mayntenance of such persons to whom they have been affectionate, had *returned the servants* of Sir Piers Dutton *as jurors*, thereby incurring, under the statute 23d Henry VIII. penalties amounting to 160*l*. That they had received sums of money for returning Writs.—That Sir Piers, calling himself a Ranger of the Forest of Mara and Mondrem, had killed a brick, a *stagg of a harte*, and three does, in harness, in the day and night time. That he had excited a riot of 50 persons against Sir John Done, the King's Forester, and *lettede them to fetche in a stagge of a harte, which by chance was gone out of the said forest.* That he had sent two of his servants, accompanied by Wm. Glasyer, to Peter Feldage, a prisoner in Chester Castle, offering him pardon if he would impeach Pyers Bruen, one of Sir John Done's servants; but he refused, saying, *he knew nothing of the said Bruen but a trew gentleman;* yet notwithstanding which, he did bring the said Feldage before the King's Council, and suborned him to impeach the said Bruen, *for the malice he bore against Sir John Done*, and caused his imprisonment in the Tower, for the space of eighteen weeks. That to avoid being called upon to account, he had obtained a writ of supersedeas, so that no one could sue the s[d] Sheriff or his servants within the s[d] County, for any matter or cause. It appears this petition was heard, and that a writ of outlawry was issued against Sir Piers, for it is stated,* that "Alianor Dutton, the wif of Piers Dutton, hathe a privy seal to the eschætor of the countie Palatyne of Chester, to remove his hands from the possession of such lands and tenements as was seized to the King's behoof *upon an outla'ry of the s[d] Piers;* and he is therefore not seased at the day of promulgaç'on as evydently it is p'ved." This outlawry was afterwards superseded.

* [...]d MSS [...], 776.

Hatton Hall, now occupied as a farm-house, is a specimen of the domestic architecture of the early part of the 16th century. It was originally quadrangular, composed of brick-work, and wood and plaister; towards the moat which surrounds it, (about 12 yards in width,) are relics of stone-work. The entrance gate is wide and lofty, opening with folding doors to the inner court. Large beams curiously carved support the roof. A figure of St. George and the Dragon is over the gateway; the family arms once over it, no longer remain.—This part terminates in a gable, and the entire front of it has been handsomely ornamented. The windows, which project, rest on two carved brackets; and over a door opening to the interior of the building, are the initials of Rowland Dutton and his wife Eleanor Scriven, with the date 1597.—Some remarkably large oak trees, in a state of great decay, remain on the west side of the outer part of the moat.†

The whole of the township is situated in a low part of the county, intersected by miserable roads.

HUXLEY

Is about seven miles S. E. E. from Chester, and was originally granted to the secular Canons of St. Werburgh; and afterwards confirmed to the Abbot and Convent, who alienated it temp. Henry III. to William de Hockenhull, together with the manor of Hockenhull, reserving a rent charge of four shillings, which was exchanged in 1279 for a rent of 44*s*. Wm. de Hockenhull, afterwards granted half of the manor to his brother Richard, who was the ancestor of the Huxleys of Huxley; the other half he gave to his youngest son Simon, on whose death it passed to the elder brother of the deceased, who transferred it to his next brother Hugh, and this Hugh was the founder of another family, which assumed the local name.

Richard's share continued in his descendants till the time of Elizabeth, when Ralph Huxley‡ sold it to Ralph Tilston, descended in the female line from the Huxleys. On the death of Ralph Tilston it passed to his brother John, who settled it on Tilston Bruen (son of his daughter Mary) on the 2d July, 1652. John son of this Tilston, in 1692, settled the property previous to his marriage with Honour, the daughter of Sir F.

† The largest 20 feet in girth a yard from the earth, and 26 feet at the base.

‡ In the 13th Edw. II. a William de Huxley, was indicted for breaking into the Castle of Halton, and committing a robbery there; he said he was a Clerk and not amenable to the Court. Proclamation was therefore made, but no claim being made by the Bishop, he was adjuded a common robber, and part of a gang of other robbers.—Mr. Ormerod supposes this William to be a native of the township, who had assumed the local name, and not connected with the family of the manerial lords.

CHESHIRE Winnington, Knt. of Stanford Court, co. Worcester.—The male line ending, Huxley was sold in the spring of 1753, to Randle Wilbraham, Esq. of Rode, and has descended with Rode to the present proprietor, Randle Wilbraham, Esq.

Hugh's share after three generations, vested in Robt. de Huxley; and a co-heiress brought it in marriage to Henry de Clive, of Clive, in the hundred of Northwich, and it continued in the family till the marriage of the daughter of Sir George Clive, with Thomas Wilbraham, Esq. of Rode. Sir George Clive, here noticed, was knighted in the field by William Fitz William, Lord Deputy of Ireland, in the month of August, 1588.—He was Chancellor of the Irish Exchequer, a Lord of the Privy Council, and Supervisor of the River Shannon.

The present Manor is within the Tattenhall Leet, but it was originally included, together with Shotwick, in the Abbot's fee of Salghall. HISTORY.

Lower Huxley Hall is an ancient mansion within a moated site, a short distance from the river Gowy. It was garrisoned for the Parliament in Sept. 1644, by Colonel Croxton. Webb* notices it as being a seat of the Clives in 1622. It is now occupied as a farm-house.

The Higher Hall passed to the Cholmondeleys with the other estates of the Savage family, who purchased it from a younger branch of the Hockenhulls in the reign of Queen Elizabeth.† In 1622, this Hall was occupied by the Birkenheads, of Backford; it has since shared the fate of the Lower Hall, and become a farm house.

* Itinerary.

† Orm. 436; Lysons 810.

PARISH OF BACKFORD,

(PART OF.)

COGHALL, OR COGHULL,

Generally pronounced *Caughall*, is about three miles and a half N. E. from Chester, adjoining the Canal from the Dee to the Mersey. It is not noticed in the Survey; but at an early period it was possessed by a family which assumed the local name.—Ralph de Coghull was Lord in the 6th Edw. I. and his great-grandson Roger de Coghull was summoned by the Black Prince, with forty-two other Cheshire Gentlemen, to do homage for lands which they held as tenants in capite.‡ Roger de Coghull died about the beginning of the 15th Century, and left two daughters coheiresses, one of whom married Sir John Massie, of Puddington, Knt.; the other Sir John Osbaldeston, of Chadlington, co. Oxford. The first Share passed with the Puddington property to the present proprietor, Sir T. S. M. Stanley, Bt. of Hooton; the other is vested in the Feoffees of Whitchurch Grammar School.

‡ Orm. 442.

There are only two houses in the township. Some parts of the old timber house, which was the residence of John Massie, Esq. in 1600, still exist; there are some stately trees near it. It has been tenanted by the Ameries, under the Masseys and Stanleys, about two centuries.

A tradition exists, that the *Butter Hill* in this township, was the place where the country people deposited their produce during the continuance of the plague in Chester.

*** A very aukward error occurs in introducing the Parish of Bunbury as forming a portion of the Hundred of Broxton: it was discovered too late to apply a remedy. It should have been under the head of "Eddisbury Hundred."

END OF DESCRIPTION OF BROXTON HUNDRED.

INTERIOR OF THE RUINS OF BIRKENHEAD PRIORY.
(PRESENTED BY M. GREGSON, ESQ.)

The Hundred of Bucklow.

PARISHES.

ASHTON-SUPER-MERSEY	GROPPENHALL	MOBBERLEY	AND
BOWDEN	KNUTSFORD	ROSTHERN	WARBURTON.
BUDWORTH	LYMM	RUNCORN	

Parochial Chapels—(from Leycester.)

DARESBURY — ASTON — NETHER-KNUTSFORD — OVER PEOVER.

Chapels of Ease—(Leycester.)

HALTON	NETHER WHITLEY	HIGH LEGH	AND
THELWALL	STRETTON	OVER TABLEY	RINGEY.
POOSEY	LITTLE LEGH	NETHER-KNUTSFORD	

ASHTON-SUPER-MERSEY PARISH,

CONTAINS THE TOWNSHIPS OF

ASHTON. | SALE.

ASHTON is seven miles south from Manchester, but only part of the township is within the parish. In the reign of Henry IV. a portion of the manor was held by the Carringtons, of Carrington, under the Barons of Dunham-Massey, from whom it passed by a female heir to the Booths, and from them descended to the Earls of Stamford and Warrington, who are the present proprietors. This moiety carries with it the manerial right.

CHESHIRE

The other share was held under the Boydells of Dodleston, by Robert de Ashton, John Daniel, and the Handfords, of Handford. William Handford, Esq. is stated in an Inq. p. m. 7th Hen. VIII. to hold inter alia the manor of Ashton on Mersey, in socage, from the heirs of Sir John Boydell, of Dodleston, Knt.—From the Handfords it passed to the Breretons: an Inq. p. m. 22d. Eliz. states Sir Urian Brereton, Knt. to hold inter alia the manor of *Ashton on Mersey bancke*, in right of his wife Margery Handford, from Thomas Gravenor, and Wm. Marbury, Esqrs. in socage, as of their manor of Dodleston. The Breretons continued in possession till 1674, when they sold it to Sir Joshua Allen, whose descendant the Viscount Allen, again sold it to George Earl of Warrington, in 1749. The Earl of Stamford and Warrington is the proprietor of the entire Manor, for which a Court Baron is held.

The *Old Watling-street*, leading to the ford over the Mersey, adjoins this township.

The *Church* is rather a handsome building, of stone, with a nave and chancel, and at the west end a small belfry.

The advowson of the Rectory was originally attached to the Ashton share of the manor. In 1679, it was the property of Richard Mascie, Esq. of Sale, who settled it in 1684, on his six youngest daughters, in common amongst them. In 1737, these shares became by descent and purchase, the property of Dr. Mainwaring and Thomas Ellison Clerk, and in 1746, were passed by fine to the use of Dr. Mainwaring and Mr. Noble.—Eventually, the entire advowson became by purchase the property of the Rev. Richard Popplewell Johnson, A. B. who is the present Rector and patron.

There are few Monumental Memorials here. In the chancel is an inscription to the memory of the Rev. Massey Malyn, of Sale, L. L. D.

On a marble slab in the Church—

Near this place lieth the body of Thomas White, M. D. who died July 20, 1776, aged 80. Also Rosamond his wife, who died April 23, 1777, aged 70. Beneath this marble lieth also the body of Charles White, Esq. Member of the Corporation of Surgeons, and Fellow of the Royal Society, who after rendering himself eminent in his profession for the space of 60 years, by dexterity and extent of knowledge scarcely exceeded by any of his cotemporaries, retired to the enjoyment of rural and domestic felicity, in the society of his family and friends, at Sale, within this Parish. He died on the 20th of February, 1813, aged 84. Also the body of John Bradshaw White, who died April 27th, 1799, aged 27.

HISTORY.

SALE.

This township is not noticed in the Survey; but it was held under the Barons of Halton, as appears by reference to the Feodary of Halton, temp. Edward II. "*Dominus Petrus de Warburton tenet villam de Sale, pro decima parte Feodi Militas.*" Under the Warburtons, the ancient family of the Massys, of Sale, held lands here. According to Leycester,* "It seems Massy, of Sale, had anciently one moiety of Sale, and Holt of Sale, another moiety, though now scattered." A portion of Holt's possessions were purchased by Sir Geo. Booth, of Dunham Massey, Aug. 4, 1604.

* Page 359.

The Massys continued to hold their possessions, and claim a manerial right here, till 1684, when Richard Massie, settled Sale Hall, and the demesne lands upon his eldest daughter Katherine, whose daughters Katherine and Anne, married Walter Noble, Esq. and Peter Mainwaring, M. D. The Noble and Mainwaring shares were purchased by the Egertons of Tatton, and Mr. John Moore, of Manchester, claims a reputed manerial privilege, in right of purchases made by him from the Egertons. However, no Court is held; and the chief rents are reserved by George John Legh, Esq. whose predecessors, the Leghs, of East Hall, possessed the Mainwaring share under the Doctor's will, and sold it to Mr. Moore.

The Holt moiety of Sale, no longer exists as an entirety: it has become by purchase the property of various individuals.

The *Old Hall* of Sale is the property of Mr. Moore; a modern House has been erected on the site of the former one. Another mansion on the western side of the township, surrounded by flourishing plantations, is the residence of the widow of the late Chas. White, Esq. of Manchester. This is said to have been the seat of the Mascies, of Lymm and Audlem.

A *School*, with a Dwelling adjoining, for the Master, is situated in this township, endowed with land obtained by the inclosure of Sale Moor.

CHESHIRE HISTORY.

THE PARISH OF BOWDON,

CONTAINS THE TOWNSHIPS OF

BOWDON	CARRINGTON
ALTRINCHAM	DUNHAM-MASSEY
ASHLEY	HALE
BAGGILEY	PARTINGTON
BOLLINGTON	TIMPERLEY;

AND HALF OF THE TOWNSHIPS OF

AGDEN	ASHTON.

BOWDEN is beautifully situated on an elevated piece of land adjoining the river Bollin, a short distance east of Dunham Massey Park, commanding delightful prospects on the north and south sides.—At the time of the Survey it was held by Hamon de Massey, first Baron of Dunham Massey; and was subsequently divided. Roger Massy of Hale, possessed of a moiety, sold it to Agatha de Massy for £4. 7s.* in money, and two robes, one for himself and another for his wife, rendering annually one lb of cummin seed at the Feast of St. Martin. Agatha afterwards transferred the share to her younger son Robert, who gave to Adam de Bowden two oxgangs of land here, rendering annually one penny upon the Altar of St. Mary, of Bowden, for the salvation of the souls of the said Robert, his wife, and ancestors, and for his heirs, and for the soul of Matthew de Hale.† The Bowdens continued in full possession till the 7th Elizabeth, when Urian Bowden sold to William Booth, of Dunham Massey, Esq. certain parcels of land in Bowdon. It would appear the Bowdons had alienated other lands to the Vawdreys, for in the 11th Eliz. Thomas Vawdrey of Bowdon, sold to Hugh Crosby of Over Whitley, several parcels of land here; which lands Hugh Crosby subsequently disposed of to Sir Geo. Booth, of Dunham Massey, for £220.

* Temp. Henry III.

† Temp. Henry III.

The other moiety of Bowdon was given by the Barons of Dunham Massey to the Prior of Birkenhead, temp. Edw. I. After the Dissolution, the estate was attached, together with the Church, to the Bishopric of Chester; the lands afterwards were divided, but the advowson of the Church still continues vested in the Bishops, which, with the remaining lands, are held on lease by the Earl of Stamford and Warrington. The manor is within the Leet of Dunham Massey.

There was a Church here long before the Conquest. The Survey thus notices it:—"*Ibi Presbyter et Ecclesia, cui pertinet dimidia hida.*" It is dedicated to St. Mary. Leycester quaintly observes, "The Vicarage of Bowdon, is said to be worth £120. per ann.—Our common proverb is—*Every man is not born to be Vicar of Boden.* The true reason of the proverb I cannot affirm."

The Church consists of a nave, chancel, and side aisles, with a tower, containing a peal of six bells. At the end of the side aisles, are two private chancels, attached to the Earl's Manors of Dunham Massey and Carrington. The ceilings of the side aisles (which are divided from the nave by five pointed Gothic arches, rising from octagonal pillars, with capitals) are neatly carved in oak. Three pointed arches separate the Carrington Chapel in the north aisle, from the chancel; the Dunham Chapel, in the south aisle, is separated by two similar arches. To these Chapels were formerly attached two Chantry Priests:‡

"Penc' Joh'is P'civall nup. cantarist. nup. cant. de Bowden, p. ann. iv*l.* xviii*s.*

"Henrici Tippinge nup. incumben. cant. de Bowdenne, p. ann. xl*s.* iii*d.*"

‡ Pension Roll, 1553.

There are several particularly handsome monuments in the Church.

CHESHIRE

There are two large ones in the *Dunham Chancel;* that on the east side occupying nearly the whole of it: it is handsome but heavy. The inscription is—

This Monument is erected to the ever valuable memory of the Hon. Langham and Henry Booth, younger sons of the Right Hon. Henry late Earl of Warrington: both of them began their early pilgrimage on the Lord's day, and after having fought a good fight, cheerfully resigned their souls into the merciful hands of their God and Saviour Jesus Christ, finishing their course in the 40th year of their respective ages—the former on the 12th of May, 1724; the latter on the 2d of February, 1726-7—do now rest in hope to receive their bodies immortal and glorious in the great day of the Lord. In the sight of the universe they seemed to die, but they are in peace, and their hope full of immortality, for God proved them, and found them worthy of himself, for hon'ble age is not measured by number of years, but they being made perfect in a short time, fulfilled a long time, and pleasing God, were beloved of Him, so that living among sinners, they were translated.—Wisd. chap. 3 & 4.

The other monument, which is divided into two compartments, is somewhat remarkable—

Beneath lieth the body of the Right hon'ble Henry Booth, Earl of Warrington, and Baron Delamer of Dunham Massey, a person of unblemished honor, impartial Justice, strict integrity, an illustrious example of steady and unalterable adherence to the liberties and properties of his country, in the worst of times; rejecting all offers to allure, and despising all dangers to deter him therefrom, for which he was thrice committed close prisoner to the Tower of London, and at length tried for his life upon a false accusation of High Treason, from which he was unanimously acquitted by his Peers, on the 14th of January, 1685-6, which day he afterwards annually commemorated by Acts of Devotion and Charity: In the year 1688, he greatly signalized himself at the Revolution, on behalf of the Protestant Religion, and the Rights of the Nation, without mixture of self-interest, preferring the good of his country to the favor of the Prince who then ascended the Throne; and having served his generation according to the will of God, was gathered to his fathers in peace, on the 2d of January, 1693-4, in the 42d year of his age, whose mortal part was here entombed, on the same memorable day on which eight years before his trial had been.

The other compartment is thus inscribed—

Also rest by him the earthly remains of the R. Hon'ble Mary Countess of Warrington, his wife, sole daughter and heir of Sir James Langham, of Cottesbrooke, in the county of Northampton, Knt. and Bart. A Lady of ingenious parts, singular discretion, consummate judgment, great humility, meek and compassionate temper, extensive charity, exemplary and unaffected piety, perfect resignation to God's will, lowly in prosperity, and patient in adversity, prudent in her affairs, and endowed with all other virtuous qualities, a conscientious discharger of her duty in all relations, being a faithful, affectionate, and observant wife, alleviating the cares and afflictions of her husband, by willingly sharing with him therein; a tender indulgent, and careful mother, a dutiful and respectful daughter, gentle and kind to her servants, courteous and beneficent to her neighbours, a sincere friend, a lover and valuer of all good people, justly beloved and admired by all who knew her, who having perfected holiness in the fear of God, was by him received to an eternal rest from her labours, on the 23d of March, 1690-1, in the 37th year of her age, calmly and composedly meeting and desiring death with joyful hope and steadfastness of faith, a lively draught of real worth and goodness, and a pattern deserving imitation, of whom the world was not worthy.—Heb. xi, 38.

The sides of this monument are supported by two female figures, beneath which is inscribed—

To perpetuate the remembrance of so much virtue, till that great day shall come wherein it shall be openly rewarded, this monument is erected as a mark of dutiful respect and affection, by the care of their son, George, Earl of Warrington, who reveres their memory.

There is a piscina in one of the angles of this Chancel—it contains also a gallery for the use of the family of Dunham Massey.

There are curious whole-length figures of William Brereton, of Ashley, and his wife Jane Warburton, in the Carrington Chancel; their hands are clasped, and they rest on cushions. There are seven kneeling figures beneath, the third holding in its hands a scull. An infant in swaddling clothes, is introduced between the fifth and sixth figures.—Underneath, on a tablet, a long Latin inscription, stating at the conclusion, that Jane died on the 2d March, 1627, aged 63; her husband on the 29th August, 1630, aged 68.

In the Nave is a handsome monument by Westmacott, inscribed—

In a vault near this place were interred, the remains of Thomas Assheton, of Ashley, Esq. on the 9th day July, 1759, aged 64; and in the same vault Harriet Assheton, who died at Manchester, Jan. 1775, aged 74; also the remains of Thos. Assheton Smith, of Ashley, Esq. son of the above Thomas and Harriet, who died April 16th, 1774, aged 49, years, to whose memory William Henry Assheton, Esq. erects this monument.

Under a female figure, elegantly executed, above this inscription—

Quis desiderio sit pudor aut modus tam cari capitis.

A mural Monument to the memory of

Hugh Kirkpatrick Hall, Esq. of Jamaica, and late of Ashley, who died Jan. 27, 1788, aged 38; also his wife Martha, daughter of Marsden Kenyon, Esq. of Manchester, who died Jan. 14, 1780, aged 26.

In the Middle Aisle—

P. Lancaster, A. M. Ecclesiæ quondam Vicaries qui annos 74 natus, obiit Mar. 7, A. D. 1763.

Within the Altar railing—

———o. Gerard nuper de Riddings primus et ultimus ejus nominis et loci hic repetitur die ——— Anno Domini 1672.

The following grateful testimonial, on a brass plate sunk in the flag over the Dunham Vault, must not be omitted—

Hoc sub marmore, communi antiquorum de Dunham Massy Baronem dormitorio, Georgius, nobilissimus dominus Delamer, inhumatur, qui cum insigni pietate, fidelitate, et affectu, nulli secundus, Deum, regem, et patriam, ad sexigesimum secundum ætatis suæ annum coluisset, terrestrem coronulam coronæ cœlesti, decimo die Augusti anno salutis nostræ 1684, commulavit. Gulielmus autem Andreius, honoratissimi domini obitum plorans (cui jam ultra annos triginta continuos fideliter inservierat, cujusq. sortis asperioris quam Dominus pro rege subiit, qua servo licuit, particeps) hoc fœlici et perenni ejus memoriæ amoris juxta et officii sui monumentum posuit, dicavit, consecravit, et solum addidit, ut vità sua cum officio erga nobilem illam familiam finita, hujus ad tumuli introvitum cineres conquiescant, usquidem in novam cum domino æternamque vitam expergiscantur. Obiit 25° die Julii, anno Domini 1685.

There were a variety of other monuments in the Church, chiefly to the Booth family; they are noticed in the Harl. MSS. 2152, 33.

The present Vicar is the Rev. J. T. Law, A. M.

The Registers commence in 1628.

Lysons. There is an ancient *Grammar School* here* to which, about 1600, Edw. Vawdry left £4. per annum. In 1806 the School House was rebuilt, together with a House for the Master. There are Charity Schools at *Seaman's Moss*, and at *Little Heath*, endowed by the interest of £1000. given by Mr. Walton, who died in 1757, and who had long lived in the Dunham Massy family. The Master of the School at Seaman's Moss has a house, and £40. per ann. Little Heath School is superintended by a Mistress, and is merely a preparatory school for boys and girls.

ALTRINCHAM

Is of the ancient fee of the Barony of Dunham Massy.† In the reign of Edward I. Hamon de Massy created Burgesses here, together with a Guild Mercatory, about 1290 ‡—By Charter 13th Edw. I.—"Rex concessit Hamoni de Massy unum mercatum per diem Martis apud manerium suum de Altringham, et unam feriam per tres dies duraturam, videlicèt, in vigilia, die, et crastino festi Assumptionis Beatæ Mariæ." The Tuesday's market still continues; but the fair is on the 25th July, and the last fair day Nov. 11th.

Leycester.

"In a rental of Dunham Massy, 3d Hen. IV. 1402, I find there about forty freeholders or charterers in Altrincham; the rest of the tenants, not exceeding eighteen, were at will. It appears by this rental, as well as by another of my own, temp. Hen. VII. that in those ages, till Hen. VIII. the ancient tenants in our county had generally no leases for lives, as now they have: and the rents which at this day we call old rents, were in those ages the utmost value of such tenements on the rack, so much have these late ages outstripped the former for value, as well for land as other commodities.—At this day, 1669, there are above twenty charterers in this town, whereof Robert Parker's, of Oldfield-hall, in Altrincham, gentleman, is of greatest value; next to it is that belonging to William Leycester, of Hale Lowe, gentleman. Most of all the rest are very small parcels, not worth reckoning up; the chief Lord being Geo. Booth, of Dunham Massy, Lord Delamer. There are so very many small cottages erected here by the permission of the Lords of Dunham Massy, that it is now become a nest of beggars."||

|| Leycester.

The Chief Officer of the town bears the title of Mayor, but it does not appear that he exercises any Magisterial functions. The police government is vested in Constables.

The situation of the town is pleasant and desirable, and since the establishment of the Duke of Bridgewater's canal, and the locality to Manchester, Altrincham, has obtained a small share of notice in a manufacturing point of view. Cotton factories have been erected here, and a manufactory for bobbins, the lathes turned by steam. Vast quantities of potatoes are raised in this township, for which there is always a ready sale at Manchester.

Oldfield Hall was alienated by the Parkers in 1672. It is now the residence of the proprietor Wm. Rigby, Esq. who has rebuilt it in a very handsome style.

The Chapel of Ease to Bowden is dedicated to St. George, and was built by subscription in 1799; the Vicar of Bowden has the appointment of the Minister.

‡ See Charter in the "Antiquities," p. 203,—Signed, "Dominus Reginaldo de Grey, tùnc justiciario Cestriæ," &c.

CHESHIRE

It is of brick; and a Curacy, the estimated value of which is £91. 13*s.* 6*d.* arising from dividends of Stock, seat rents, and surplice fees: the registers coeval with the foundation.

ASHLEY

Formed part of the great Fee of Dunham Massy, and is noticed as such in the Survey. In or shortly before the reign of Henry III. Hamonde de Massy, the then Baron of Dunham Massy, gave a moiety of this township to Robert de Massy, which his son Richard afterwards exchanged with Geffrey Dutton, of Cheadle, for his land in Walton, viz. the half of Nether Walton, and for eight shillings rent from William, son of Kenewret, of Newton, near Chester. Geoffry Dutton, of Cheadle, gave to Hamon de Dutton his youngest son, *totum manerium suum de Ashley*, about 1286, and Hamon assumed the local name, which his descendants bore till towards the conclusion of the reign of Henry VIII. when Thomasina, daughter and heiress of George Ashley, of Ashley, Esq. brought the manor in marriage to Richard Brereton, of Lea Hall, near Middlewich, youngest son of Sir Wm. Brereton, of Brereton, by whom she had issue George Brereton, and two daughters, Agnes and Jane.

George Brereton, Esq. married Sibill, daughter and heir of William Arderne, of Timperley, Esq. Gent. and had issue ten sons,—William, Richard, George, Ottiwell, George, John, Edward, John,* Thomas, Randle; and two daughters, Lucretia, and Jane. The estate continued vested in the Breretons, till the middle of the 17th century, when Thomas Brereton (who died in 1660), left his whole inheritance to be divided amongst his three sisters, who married into the Barlow, Tatton, and Ashton families. The manor afterwards became the property of the Smiths, and is now possessed by William Henry Assheton Smith, Esq. representative of Ralph Assheton, Esq. the husband of the youngest coheiress of Thomas Brereton, before mentioned. This Thomas built the Domestic Chapel at Ashley, in 1653.

HISTORY.

Ashley Hall is now occupied by Thomas Pickford, Esq. and adjoins the river Bollin. It has an ancient appearance, the front of it covered with cement.

BAGGILEY

Was attached to the Great Barony of Dunham Massy, at the time of the Survey. In the reign of King John, Hamon de Massy gave to Matthew de Bromhall, Bromhall, Duckenfield, and two parts of Baggiley, and it is supposed a branch of this family assumed the local name. In 1319, Sir Wm. Baggiley was proprietor of the manor, and his son John Baggiley, made a feoffment of it, together with the manors of Hyde, and Leveshulme, co. Lanc. to Sir John Legh, of Booths, stipulating that Sir John should settle them on the said John Baggiley, and his heirs male; in default of which, the manors of Baggiley and Leveshulme, on William, John, and Jeffery, sons of Sir John Legh, and their heirs male in succession, &c.

The Leighs continued proprietors till their line terminated in Edward Legh, who died in 1688; and he sold it a short time before his death. In 1722, Baggiley was the property of Joshua, Viscount Allen, and in 1749, it was purchased from John Viscount Allen, by Joseph Jackson, of Rostherne, who dying in 1803, he bequeathed it to his cousin the Rev. Millington Massey, who assumed the name of Jackson. It is now the property of his daughter and sole heiress. No Court is held for the Manor.

Baggiley Hall, (at least the remains of it) exhibits specimens of handsome domestic architecture. It is altogether of oak, and wicker work, with bay windows; the interior affording some fine remains of carved work in oak.† On *Baggiley Moor*, which is near the Hall, is a large tumulis; at the west end of the Moor, is a handsome mansion, the property of the Miss Houghton.

* It would appear they were desirous of preserving the name of John in this generation of the family. A MS. note in Sir Peter Leycester's own copy of Antiquities, (in my possession) after noticing "John Brereton, another son, died young, buried at Bowdon, 27th June, 1575;" says,—"Also another John Brereton, son of George Brereton, of Ashley, Esq. baptized at Bowdon, June 20, 1576; he was afterwards Sir John Brereton, Knt. the King's Serjeant at Law, in Ireland, but he dyed without issue; whose widow married the Lord Chiefe Justice Bramston: Sir John left all his personall estate, which was greate, to his widow, and to Sidney Colledge in Cambridge, where he was educated; and to Randle Brereton, his youngest brother; which Randle lived in London, and marryed, and had issue a daughter, marryed to Mr. Bourchir, of Glocestershire; and also a son called Randle Brereton, who had an estate in Lincolnshire, and is the only heire male of all the family of the Breretons, of Ashley, now remayninge, 1672."---H.

† A fine view of Baggiley Hall, is given in Mr. Ormerod's County History.

CHESHIRE HISTORY.

Dr. Gower, in a letter to the late Rev. Mr. Harwood, of Chester, on the authority of Dr. Piercy says, that one of the Leghs, of Baggiley, wrote several historical poems, temp. Hen. VII. The MS. is described to be in folio, entitled "*Scottish Fielde,*" and the style resembles that of Peirce Plowman. "It would seem," says Mr. Ormerod, "that the author had been present—

"Then we tild down our tents
That told were a thousand."

He thus describes himself at the conclusion of the rhymes—

He was a Gentleman by Jesu	Have yearded there longe,
That this jest made:	Before William Conquerour
Which say but as he sayd,	This country did inhabitt;
For sooth and no other.	Jesus bring them to blisse
At BAGILY that bearne	That brought us forthe of bale,
His biding place bad,	That hath bearkened me here,
And his ancestors of olde time	Or heard my tale. &c.

BOLLINGTON

Is about six miles N. W. from Knutsford. It originally formed parcel of the Barony of Dunham Massy, and took its name from the river Bollin, which runs through it. Hamo de Massy, temp. Hen. III. gave a moiety of Bollington in free marriage with his daughter Agnes, to Geoffrey Dutton, rendering yearly a pair of gilt spurs at the Nativity of St. John the Baptist; their descendants subsequently assumed the name of Cheadle; and this portion passed by a female heir to the Radcliffes, Earls of Sussex.—An Old Rental, 3d Hen. IV. says, "Henricus Ratcliffe ut de jure uxoris suæ tenet medietatem Villæ de Bolinton in socagio, reddendo in termino Johannis Baptistæ unum par calcarium deuratorum, vel octo decem denarios."* On the 15th Aug. 1536, Robert Earl of Sussex sold his lands in Bollington and Thelwall, to John Carrington, Esq. of Carrington, and from the Carringtons it passed to the Booths, by marriage of Jane, daughter and heiress of John Carrington, Esq. with Sir George Booth, of Dunham Massy, towards the conclusion of the reign of Elizabeth, and is now the property of the Earl of Stamford and Warrington. The other moiety is held of the Barony of Kinderton, one half of which Robt. de Mara, temp. Henry III. gave to Richard son of Gilbert de Quike (Wike), and to Robert son of Hugh de Ditton, rendering three shillings yearly; *Adam filius Roberti juvenis de Ditton*, released all his right in Bollington, to Richard son of Gilbert de la Quike; and afterwards *Thomas le Eyr de Bolington*, granted the fourth part to William Mere de Mere, *Domino suo*, for £20. William Mere, of Mere, Esq. 42d Eliz. sold it to James Brampton, of Toynton, near to Horncastle, co. Linc. for £350. and James Brampton, of Legborne, co. Linc. disposed of it to Sir Geo. Booth, of Dunham Massy, for £450. 45th Eliz. The other 4th part of Bollington, Robert de Mara the elder gave to Gilbert de Bolinton, to be held by the eighth part of half a Knight's fee; because the said Gilbert had resigned it up *in plenâ curiâ Roberti*, in the reign of King John. This part fell to the Leghs, of Booths, but it is now by purchase the property of the Earl of Stamford and Warrington.

Leycester.

The township is within the jurisdiction of the Court Leet of Dunham Massy. The jurisdiction of the Baron of Kinderton, over the moiety, has long been disused; but a right was exercised by the Meres over it, and a Court is held for it by P. L. Brooke, Esq. to whom it passed from the Meres.

CARRINGTON

Is not noticed in the Survey, but it was held in fee of the Barons of Dunham Massy, and gave name to a family which took the local appellation. The Carringtons flourished here for nearly 400 years; and Carrington eventually passed to the Booths, by marriage of Sir George Booth, of Dunham, to Jane, sole daughter and heiress of John Carrington, of Carrington, Esq. temp. Eliz. He had no issue by her, but enjoyed the property which he recovered by a tedious suit at law.†—The entire township is possessed by the Earl of Stamford and Warrington.

DUNHAM MASSY,

So called from Hamon Massy, the First Baron, was held by him under Hugh Lupus. The original proprietor Elward, was dispossessed at the Conquest.—Hamon de Massy third in descent, gave to his brother John, all the lands in Moreton, which Matthew de

† By this Jane he had no issue, nor did they live long together; yet he inherited all the lands of her father, the same being strictly settled by her father, previous to marriage, to descend to the Booths; the settlement provided, "that if the said Jane, should after marriage be detected of incontinency, the estate should remain with the Booths." SEE COLLINS' PEERAGE.

CHESHIRE

Moreton held, with housebote and haybote, in his demesne wood of Bidston, for Podrington, which his uncle Robert Massy held, "*Faciendo Servitium dimidii Feodi Militis.*" Temp. Hen. II. or Richard I. He also gave to Robert son of Waltheof, all the lands which his father held of him and his ancestors, namely, Etchels, by service of half a Knight's fee: *et ego Hamo retineo ad opus meum Cervum, et Bissam, et Apium de Hulesswood,*" i. e. Hart, Hind, and Boar. Hamon restored to Robt. Bredbury and Brinnington, on finding a sumpter Horse, and a Man, and a Sack, for the carriage of his arms and apparel, when the Earl of Chester shall in person lead an army into Wales; and give aid to Hamon for his ransom, if taken prisoner, and to make his eldest son a Knight, and when his eldest daughter is married.*

Hamon Massy, the 5th in descent, gave the Advowson of Bowdon, to the Priory of Birkenhead, in the 6th Edw. I. 1278. In the 16th of the same King, the Barony was found to be held of the King in capite, by service of five Knights' Fees—"Inveniendo quo quolibet feodo unum Equum coopertum, vel duos discoopertos infrà divisas Cestershiriæ tempore guerræ, cùm omnibus suis peditibus, tenentibus terram forinsecam, infrà feodum prædictum: faciendo servitium suum secundùm purportam Communis Chartæ Cestershiriæ."

Sir Hamon de Massy, sixth in descent, was the last Baron. He married Isabella, daughter of Humphrey de Beauchamp, "who died on the marriage night before Carnal Copulation."† He soon afterwards married her sister Alice, and by her had issue Hamon, who died without issue, and four daughters, Cicily, Isabel, ———, and Alice. On the death of his son, Sir Hamon obtained a divorce from Alice his wife, and married Joan Clinton, sister of the Earl of Huntington; who advised him to sell the reversion of the manor of *Doneham*, with appurtenances, after his and his wife's death, to Oliver de Ingham, Judge of Chester, which he did for 1000 marks, and an annuity of 40 marks. This Hamon was sued at Chester 1st Edw. II. by Peter Dutton, (called sometimes Peter de Warburton, ancestor to the Warburtons of Arley,) relative to a piece of waste ground, conceived by him to lie in Warburton; Hamon pleaded that his father was seized of the same, and that the land in question lay in Dunham and not in Warburton; moreover, that he was one of the King's Barons, and held his lands of the King in capite (as Earl of Chester) in Barony immediately, and ought not to proceed to trial without a Jury of Knights, and discreet men of the county.

† Leyecester.

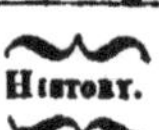

HISTORY.

Sir Hamon de Massy was possessed only of the manors of Dunham, Kelsall, Altrincham, Bidston, Saughall, and Moreton; but in the rental of Dunham Massey, 3d Hen. IV. John Davenport of Bromhall *tenet villas de Bromhall, Duckenfield, Baggiley, et Etchells, per servitium mitilare, et reddendo annuatim £2.*—"Davenport de Henbury tenet terram suam in Werneth, redendo per ann. *5d.* Itèm tenet Bredbury, Romiley, Bruninġton, (nuper Adam de Bredbury, et Matilda Holland) per servitium militare; et idem inveniat Domino de Doneham unum Championem ad pugnandum pro eo, si fuerit appellatus: et si dictus Dominus fecerit aliquam appellationem ad aliquem alium, tàm in brevi de recto quàm aliquo alio modo, dictus Champio pro eo pugnabit: et inveniet unum *Hoblar*, et *Sacket*, Jugg, ad custodiendum Carriagium suum per quindecem dies in Guerris de Wales."—It would seem, therefore, that the services of these and many other towns, formerly belonged to the Barons of Dunham Massy. Hamon, the last Baron, died in the 15th Edw. III. it appears, then, that the family continued in possession of the Barony about 260 years.

Considerable disturbance now arose in the possession of it after it had passed to the Stranges, Lords Knocking, heirs to Oliver de Ingham: John Fitton was the chief claimant; he had married the eldest sister and coheir of the last Baron. The heiress of Fitton having married into the Venables family, and the coheiress of William Venables, of Bollin, having married Robert, afterwards Sir Robert Booth, he renewed a claim in the reign of Henry VI. when it was agreed, that Sir Robert should have half of the manors of Dunham Massy, Altrincham, and Hale.‡

* It was this Hamon that founded the Priory of Birkenhead, in Wirral, sometimes called Birkhedde, and Birket; he dedicated its Church to St. James. "I find, (says Leycester) Oliver, Prior of Birkenhead, subscribed a witness in the reign of King John. I conjecture it might be founded about the reign of Hen. II. and Speed saith they were of the Order of the Black Monks."

‡ Dated 16th July, 11th Hen. VI. 1433.

Leycester thus notices this controversy :—" But now fell great suits concerning the Barony of Dunham Massy, after the death of Hamon, and Joan without issue of their bodies ; for Richard Fitton and the heirs of the other sisters, entred into the mannor of Dunham, as heirs to the said Hamon ; at which time Oliver Ingham was in the King's service beyond sea, to wit, the Steward of Gascony ; and then, by the King's command, Hamon Massy, of Tatton,* and others of the council of the said Oliver, came to the manor of Doneham, and entred in the name of Oliver, and Rd. Fitton and his partners went out of Doneham, and so the said Oliver Ingham died seized of the said manor with its appurtenances : and after the death of Oliver Ingham, Richard Fitton and his partners entred again, and the heirs of Oliver (who were Mary daughter of John Corson, and Joan wife of Roger le Strange, of Knocking, the elder) brought a writ of *Novæ Disseisinæ* against the co-heirs : and after Henry Duke of Lancaster buys out all the right of the co-heirs, as also the rights of the heirs of Oliver ; and so the Duke being possessed of the manor of Doneham, with its members, gave it to Roger le Strange, lord of Knocking."

Thus it was that the Booths obtained a footing in Dunham Massy.—Sir Robert Booth, of Dunham, Knt. was younger son of John Booth, Esq. of Barton, co. Lancaster, and, together with William his son and heir, had conferred on them for their lives, the office *(conjunctim vel divisim)* of Sheriff of Chester.† Sir Geo. Booth, seventh in descent, was created a Baronet on the Institution of the Order, in 1611 ; and his grandson of the same name, was made Baron Delamer of Dunham Massy. The Barony of Dunham Massy descended to Mary, daughter and heiress of George Booth, second Earl of Warrington ; on whose death‡ it passed to her son George Harry, who had by a new creation in 1796, conferred on him the titles of Earl of Stamford and Warrington, and Baron Delamer of Dunham Massy. He died in 1819, and was succeeded by his eldest son, the Lord Grey, now Earl of Stamford and Warrington.

The Booths were a family so intimately connected with Cheshire History, during the greater part of the 17th century, that a few particulars relative to them cannot but be acceptable. Clarendon thus describes Sir George Booth :—" He was a person of one of the best fortunes and interest in Cheshire, and for the memory of his grandfather, of absolute power with the Presbyterians." He was thrice Member for the County in the Long Parliament ; but during the Civil Wars, espoused the cause of the Parliament ; and was included with Sir Wm. Brereton in a Parliamentary order for arming the county, and seizing on the warlike stores of the King's Friends. But, as has been frequently the case, (and was singularly illustrated in the case of Gen. Monk) he abjured the cause in which he had embarked, and became as warm a supporter of the Royalists as he had before been of the Roundheads. Early in 1659, he received a commission from the King, then at Brussels, by which he was appointed Commander of the King's forces in Cheshire, Lancashire, and North Wales. As the Royalist cause gained ground, numerous attempts were made to re-establish Monarchical Authority ; and amongst them Sir George seized the City of Chester for the King, but was prevented obtaining possession of the Castle, by the resolute defence of the Governor, Colonel Croxton.—In the end, Sir George sustained a signal defeat at Winnington, by Lambert, who, with a candor which did not mark the bulletins of a conqueror of the present age, fairly allows that his opponents bravely rallied within a quarter of a mile of the scene of defeat, " disputing the place very gallantly, both parties shewing themselves like Englishmen."—Sir George's party was completely dispersed, and he was seized in his flight at Newport Pagnell, and committed close prisoner to the Tower. On his liberation in Feb. 1659-60, he took his seat in Parliament, and was one of the Committee of twelve who carried to Charles II. the answer of the House to his Majesty's letter. His sufferings in the royal cause had been very great, and the House resolved to reward his services with the sum of £20,000. but with a high spirit, he

* This Hamon Massy was a younger brother of Massy of Tatton, and afterwards the first Massy of Bixton, in Lancashire, in right of his wife.

† This, observes Sir Peter Leycester, " is the first patent for life in this kind that I meet withal in our county ; howbeit after Edw. IV. got the crown, he presently made William Stanley, of Hooton, Sheriff, and so William Booth, Sir Robert's son, was ousted of his Sheriff-ship."

CHESHIRE

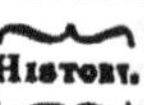

requested that the grant should be only £10,000. which was agreed to by the Commons on the 2d, and by the Lords on the 3d of August.—He had also the Barony of Delamer, in addition to that of Dunham Massy conferred on him; with liberty to propose six gentlemen for Knights, and two for Baronets. The policy of the times, however, not according with his Lordship's opinion, he left the Court in disgust; and enjoyed the otium cum dignitate on his own estates. His son and successor Henry, represented the county in the Parliaments 31st and 32d Car. II. and on the resignation of his father in 1693, received the appointment of Custos Rotulorum. His zeal in defending the liberties of the country against the aggressions of the Crown, and the activity which he manifested in promoting the Exclusion Bill against the Duke of York, soon marked him out as an object of Royal Persecution. His name was erased from the list of Magistrates, he was deprived of the office of Custos Rotulorum; after succeeding to the Baronial titles, he was three several times committed to the Tower, on undefined charges, and was the first and second time liberated without being legally accused.—On his third commitment, he remonstrated with the House of Peers, and then the House formally demanded why he was absent from his seat? This brought the question of his imprisonment to issue, and his trial was ordered to take place before a specified Assembly of Peers, Judge Jefferies, who was his personal and rancorous enemy, being appointed High Steward on the occasion. Notwithstanding this formidable array, and the addition of an abundance of perjured witnesses, Lord Delamer was acquitted, to the extreme joy of the populace. His Lordship lived secluded at Dunham, till the landing of the Prince of Orange, when he raised a large body of men, in this county and Lancashire, and in December 1688, joined the Prince. Lord Delamer was one of the Noblemen selected to carry the Message from the Prince of Orange to the King; and so delicately did he execute the Commission, that James, observed during his residence in France—that the Lord Delamer, whom he had used ill, had treated him with much more regard than the other two Lords to whom he had been kind, and from whom he might better have expected it. On the establishment of William III. his Lordship was appointed Lord Lieutenant of the City and County of Chester, and Custos Rotulorum of the County; he was also in April, 1689, made a Privy Councillor, and Chancellor and under Treasurer of the Exchequer. Becoming in about a year afterwards the object of Parliamentary Jealousy, he resigned the latter office, but was created Earl of Warrington, with a pension of £2000. per ann.* and in the Patent of Creation, his services are particularly enumerated. The estates of Dunham Massy have continued to his descendant, the present Earl of Stamford and Warrington, who succeeded his father George Harry Earl of Stamford and Warrington, in May, 1819.

There is no doubt but what the Barons of Dunham had a Castle here.† Hamo de Masci held it against Hen. II. in 1173. Not a relic now remains of the structure, and its site is even doubtful. Some conjecture, however, may be formed, from the following account of the Old Hall of Dunham, given by Mr. Ormerod.—"It appears to have been a large quadrangular pile, finished with gables within and without. The gables within the Court were indented and scolloped, and large transom windows introduced. The exterior fronts appear to be finished at a later period, with pilasters and other ornaments, in imitation of Italian architecture, and large octagonal turrets were placed at the corners. It stood within gardens laid out in the stiff taste of the time, and surrounded by an ample moat, in one angle of which is drawn *a large circular mound*, with a modern summer-house on the top of it.‡—The tradition of the family refers the original formation of the mound to the purpose for which it here appears used; but as there is not the slightest memorial existing to that effect, it can scarcely be doubted, from its form and situation that it was *the last relic of the Castle* of Hamo de Masci, and like the similar mounds in the other Castles of Cheshire, was the site of the Norman Keep Tower."

* Which was paid only the first half year. The works of this illustrious Patriot, composed of Political Tracts, Parliamentary Speeches, Family Prayers, &c. were collected and published in 1694.

† Noticed by Benedict, Ab. Petrob. ("Hamo de Masci tenuit, contra Regem, castellum de Duneham, castellum de Ulleworda") and, Walter of Coventry—("Haimo de Masci tenuit Castellum de Doneham et de Ullerwell.")

‡ See print of it, in the DELICES DEL' ANGLETERRE.

Dunham Massy was rebuilt in 1730, from the design of Mr. J. Norris.* It is a brick building in the quadrangular form, and is a large and handsome mansion.—The collection of paintings here is familiar to the recollection of the admirers of the Arts: there are a great number of portraits by Hans Holbein, Cornelius Jansen, Vandyke, Sir Peter Lely, Sir Geofrey Kneller, &c.† The collection of family plate is said to be superior in splendor and value, to most in the Kingdom. The parks, which abound with remarkably fine timber, give pasturage to upwards of five hundred head of deer.—There was formerly a fine *Heronry* here.‡

HALE

Is noticed in Domesday-Book. It was held by Hamon de Massy, and was in fee of the Barony of Dunham Massy. The Massies of Hale, a branch of the Dunham family, were settled here for many generations. They are now extinct Within Hale is the Hamlet of RINGEY, where is a Chapel of Ease to the Church of Bowdon; " Of which (says Leycester) I have little to say, save that it was much frequented in the late war by schismaticall Ministers, and, as it were, a receptacle for Non-Conformists; in which dissolute times, every pragmatical illiterate person, as the humour served him, stepped into the pulpit, without any lawful calling therunto, or licence of authority." These observations are equally as applicable to certain itinerent and illiterate preachers of the present day. This Chapel was rebuilt in 1720, by the grandfather of the present Lord Crewe, who gave £200. towards its endowment; it has been since augmented by Queen Anne's Bounty: and the value of it, according to the returns made in 1809, is £58. 16*s*. 6*d*. The patronage is vested in Lord Crewe.

The township is within the jurisdiction of the Dunham Massy Leet, In 1808, the interest claimed by Lord Crewe in the Manor, was sold to the Earl of Stamford and Warrington, the sole manerial Lord.

PARTINGTON.

This township was anciently of the Fee of the Barony of Dunham Massy. It was at an early period divided amongst the Bodons, the Millingtons, Holdenes, Sunderlands, Walleys, and the Carringtons. In 1666, Lord Delamer had a third part, which had belonged to the Carringtons; the remainder was divided among the families of Warburton, Owen, Hadfield, and Partington. The whole, however, is now vested in the Earl of Stamford and Warrington.

Partington is about 19 miles N. W. from Knutsford. The *Hall* is occupied as a farm-house. A house in this township called *Millbank*, was purchased by Mr. Speer, in 1807, from the Trustees of Walter Kerfoot, Esq.—There is a Dissenting Meeting House here.

TIMPERLEY

Is about 8½ miles N. N. W. from Knutsford; it formed part of the Fee of Dunham Massy, and at a very early period a moiety was possessed by a family which assumed the local name, and from them passed to the Masseys, Chattertons, and Radcliffes. From the coheiress of the latter, who married Parre, a fourth

* There is an engraving of it by Kip, in the NOUVEAU THEATRE DE LA GRANDE BRETAGNE.

† Of these may be enumerated Sir Thomas Gresham, and Christiana Duchess of Lorraine, (daughter of Christian II. King of Denmark), by Holbein; Henry, the first Earl of Warrington; Sir John Booth, Knt.; Lady Diana Cecil (daughter of the second Earl of Exeter), wife of Henry Vere Earl of Oxford, and afterwards of Thomas Bruce, Earl of Elgin, and her sister, Lady Elizabeth Cecil, wife of Thomas Earl of Berkshire, by Cornelius Jansen; the Countess of Oxford and Elgin above-mentioned; Lady Killigrew; Philip, Earl of Pembroke and Montgomery; Lady Anne Carr, Countess of Bedford, and Henry Danvers, Earl of Danby, by Vandyke; Anne, Queen of James II.; the Duchess of Portsmouth; the Countess of Ranelagh; the Countess of Meath; Sir George Howard and his Lady; the Hon. Archibald Grey; the first Earl of Shaftesbury; Lady Anne Cecil, the first Countess of Stamford; Henry, the first Earl of Stamford; George, Lord Delamer, and his Lady, (daughter of the first Earl of Stamford) and William Cavendish, Earl of Devonshire, by Sir Peter Lely; the Duchess of Orleans, sister of King Charles II. by Largilliere; Barbara Villiers, Duchess of Cleveland; Henry the first Earl of Warrington, and his second daughter, Lady Mary Robarts; John Churchill, Duke of Marlborough; Lady Elizabeth Delves, daughter of the first Earl of Warrington; and the Hon. Langham Booth, by Sir Godfrey Kneller. There is a curious ancient portrait of Elizabeth, the Queen of King Edward IV.; and there are several portraits of the Warrington family by Dahl, Dobson, and other artists; and one of Frances, the celebrated Duchess of Richmond, in the reign of James I. (the artist's name unknown.)—LYSONS.

‡ The hamlets of SUNDERLAND, and DUNHAM WOODHOUSES, are, incorporated with the township of Dunham Massy.

of the manor passed by purchase to Sir Wm. Booth,* and has descended to the Earl of Stamford and Warrington. The other portion passed by marriage to the Breretons, of Ashley, and was subsequently vested in Sir Amos Meredith,† in right of his wife, daughter of Robert Tatton, of Withenshaw, Esq. husband of Anne, one of the sisters and co-heirs of Thos. Brereton, Esq. who died 1660.—The other moiety of Timperley was held under the Barons of Dunham by the Cheadles, and their representatives, the Buckleys of Cheadle, in 1702, this estate was the property of Lord Bulkeley; but in consequence of purchases made by the Earl of Stamford, it is united to the Dunham Massy estate.

Bank Hill, and *Riddings*, in this township, were anciently seats of the Vawdreys, a family of great antiquity, descendants from Claude Vaudrey, to whom Hugh Cyveilioc gave lands in Knutsford, Marbury, and Atherley. Thomas Gerrard, who purchased Riddings, and who died in 1672, deduced his descent from the Harrow branch of the Gerards, of Ince.

Timperley Hall, is a handsome modern built brick mansion, and was the property of the Rev. Croxton Johnson, Rector of Wilmslow.

AGDEN.

Part of this township only is in the Parish of Bowdon: it is about 5 miles N. N. W. from Knutsford. It was formerly written *Aketon*, and *Acton*. William, son of Simon de Lee, was possessed of Agden in the reign of Hen. III. and he gave one half of it to his son in law, William Rag, who assumed the local name.—Matthew Somervyle, Lord of Alpraham, released unto this William and his heirs, the impleading of him and his tenants in his court of Alpraham, but must appear at his court of Davenham.‡ This moiety passed to John Daniel, of Agden, who married Ellen, daughter of William de Aketon; on his death she married Thomas Warburton, and outlived him. She then settled his lands here on William Venables, brother to Roger Venables,‖ Minister of Rosthern, and on Ellen his wife, daughter of Thomas Daniel, son of John Daniel before mentioned temp. Hen. IV. The Venables family terminated in George Venables, of Agden, Esq. whose daughter and heiress Elizabeth, in 1727, married Sir Philip Touchett Chetwode, of Oakley, Bart. from whom it has descended to Sir John Chetwode, Bart. the present proprietor.

The other moiety was held of the Barony of Dunham Massy by Robert Warburton,§ by military service.

William Venables, who married the heiress of Daniel, and settled at Agden, was grandson of Hugh Venables, Baron of Kinderton, and nephew of Sir Richard Venables Baron of Kinderton, who was killed in the Battle of Shrewsbury.

The manor now owes suit and service at the Court of Dunham; the jurisdiction over the Kinderton moiety is disused.¶

The *Hall* is in a state of extreme dilapidation; but its situation is particularly pleasant.

*** Ashton is before spoken of; see page 361.

* 2d Edward IV.

† "A Baronet of Nova Scotia."—P. L. MS. note.

‡ About 1270. ‖ Of the Kinderton family. § 3 Henry IV.

¶ Ormerod.

PARISH OF GREAT BUDWORTH.

CONTAINS THE TOWNSHIPS OF

BUDWORTH	LITTLE LEGH
ANDERTON	MARBURY
APPLETON-cum-HULL	MARSTON
ASTON-juxta-BUDWORTH	PICMERE
BARNTON	STRETTON
BARTERTON or BARTINGTON	NETHER TABLEY
COGSHALL	OVER WHITLEY
COMBERBACH	NETHER WHITLEY
DUTTON	WINCHAM.

With the exception of Prestbury, this is the most extensive Parish in the County; it is nearly fifteen miles long, and ten miles wide.

BUDWORTH.

This town says Leycester, hath its name from the old Saxon Word *Bode*, which signifies a dwelling, and *Wurth*, a place by a water. It is about two miles N. E. E. from Northwich; situated on a gentle elevation, near two large sheets of water called *Picmere*, and *Budworth Mere*, and is a componant part of the Manor of *Aston juxta Budworth*, included within the Court Baron held by the Warburtons of Arley, for that manor. "It hath two yearly fairs, one on Candlemas Day, February 2, the other on Lady Day, 25th March, the toll of which belong to the King."* At the Conquest Budworth was held by William Fitz Nigell, Baron of Halton, from Hugh Lupus, and from William by Pagan. Temp. Hen. III. it was possessed by Geoffrey, son of Adam de Dutton (ancestor of the Warburtons of Arley) whose posterity in the reign of Edward II. assumed the name of Warburton, on removing their residence to Warburton; about the beginning of the reign of Henry VII. they removed their seat to Arley, in Aston, where Peter Warburton built a handsome house in 1495.

* Leycester.

Geoffry, son of Adam de Dutton, gave a third part of Budworth to the Priory of Norton, temp. Henry III. to pray for his soul for ever. After the Dissolution, Henry VIII. sold all the lands of the Priory in Budworth, and Comberbache, to John Grimsdiche, of London, by Charter dated July 1, 1544, who afterwards sold part of them to John Eaton, of Crowley, and he sold them to Peter Leycester, Esq. of Tabley, in 1548, in whose successor, Sir John Fleming Leicester, Bart. they are now vested. Another part was sold to one Malbon, of Budworth, who re-sold them to Oasley.—Another portion was bought by Hale, of Browneslow, in Budworth, who have the custody of the King's original grant to Grimsdich.† A small part was purchased by Potter. The other two-thirds are held by the Rev. Rowland Egerton Warburton, heir of Sir Peter Warburton, Bart. from the King, in right of his Duchy of Lancaster, and Fee of Halton, to the Barony of which Budworth was attached.

† Leycester.

The *Church*, which stands in a delightful situation, is dedicated to God and All Saints. It consists of nave, chancel, side aisles, and two transepts, with an elegant tower,‡ containing a peal of eight bells. Six pointed arches, resting on clustered columns, divide the nave and side aisles. On the sides of the chancel are ten ancient carved oak stalls, with *subsellia.*—"I suppose (observes Sir Peter Leycester) there was a Church here before the Norman Conquest, for I find in Domesday

‡ Under the great west window of the tower, is the coat of Sir Warburton; it is supposed to have been repaired or built in 1520.

CHESHIRE

Book, '*Ibi Presbyter, et duo Villani, &c.*' and a Priest supposeth a Church; though I confess it is in other places of that Book usually said of such towns as had Churches,*—'*Ibi Presbyter et Ecclesia.* I find on the left hand of the steeple door on the outside, towards the bottom of the fabric, these words engraven in the stone in an ancient character, Argille Egarw Widua, and on the right hand of the same door, opposite to that writing, Wymincham: whereby it may seem that the widow Egard is commemorated as a Special Benefactor in the structure of the steeple." Sir Peter particularizes a number of coats of arms on the steeple, among them Dutton (with a fret in the 2d and 3d quarters not added before the reign of Edward III.) the Priory of Norton, and of Warburton, &c.

The Church of Budworth was originally given to the Priory of Norton, by Wm. the Constable (the younger) temp. Hen. I. which gift Roger Lacy afterwards confirmed. At the Dissolution, Henry VIII. gave the Rectory, together with that of Runcorn, to Christ Church Coll. Oxf. by grant of 11th Dec. 1546.†

In the Chancel are a variety of monuments, chiefly mural.

The north transept is the burial place of the three families of Brooke (of Mere), Barry (of Marbury), and Leycester (of Tabley), and is divided into three cemetries. In the first, on a flag stone—

Thomas, first son of Thos. Lord Viscount Kilmorey, and Frances his wife, was buried March ye 17, 1680.

There are several achievments in the Barry division. In that of the Leycesters is the Monument of Sir Peter Leycester, with the inscription‡—

Hic requiescunt corpora domini Petri Leicester,‖ de Nether Tabley, in comitatu Cestrensi, Baronetti, et dominæ Elizabethæ uxoris ejus, filiæ tertiæ et natu minimæ Gilberti Baronis Gerard, de Gerard Bromley, in comitatu Staffordiensi, quam sibi peperit Elionora sua, filia unica et ex asse hæres Thomæ Dutton de Dutton, in agro Cestrensi, armig. ex qua Elizab. prædictus dominus Petrus Leicester genuit tres filios, Robertu', Byronu', et Thomæ,' totidemque filias, Elianoram, Elizabetham, et Byronam; qui quidem Petrus obiit undecimo die Octobris, anno Domini 1678, et ætatis sexagesimo nono ineunte, et prædictæ domina Elizab. ex hac luce migravit Jan. 26, anno Dom. 1678, ætatis quinquagesimo nono ineunte; quibus beatam speramus resurrectionem.

On a large Mural Monument—

Hic jacet Franciscus Leicester, de Tabley, Baronettus, domi et peregre liberaliter educatus, linguasum sciens, antiquitates præcipue studiosus, in nullo eruditionis genere hospes; hæc habuit otii oblectamenta, capessendæ reipublicæ, si ita libuisset, idoneus. Rempatriam, a majoribus pro salute impeditam, honesta œconomia restituit. Vixit fidei illibatæ amicis servis, et pauperibus charus, quibus nisi vixisset, jampridem esset vitæ pertæsum. Obiit anno salutis 1742, ætatis 68. Juxta sita est Francisca uxor ejus dilectissima, vidua Briani Thornhill armig'i filia et hæres Joshuæ Wilson arm'ri in com. Ebor. pudica, placida, et bene merita. Obiit anno salutis 1716, suæ ætatis 33; reliquerunt unicam filiam Meriella.

On the north side side of the last—

Here lyes Francis Pigote, of Marsham, in Berkshire, Esq. a worthy, sensible, just, and most valuable man, who dyed in the 83d year of his age, 1694. Also Elizabeth, his wife, mother of Meriel, Lady Leicester, by her first husband, Francis Watson, of Aston, in Shropshire, Esq. a Lady very highly esteemed in her life, and much lamented at her death, which was in the 86th year of her age 1692.

On another monument—

Hic jacet Robertus Leicester de Tabley, Bart^{us} raris ingenii animique dotibus instructus; utere lector secundi Caroli testimonio, profitentis palam, civen se perdidisse, quo non superesse meliorem. Obiit anno salutis 1684, ætatis 41. Juxta sita est uxor ejus filia Francisci Watson de Aston, in com. Salop. arm'ri.

Hoc tumulo Meriella, jacet pia filia, mater,
Indulgens, uxor pia, faceta comes
Vicinis urbana, benignaque semper egenis,
Sinceræ cultrix et piettis erat.

Obiit anno salutis 1707, ætatis 69. Habuerunt tres filios, Robertum, Franciscum, Petrum, et unicam filiam Meriellam. Robertus obiit apud Mersham, in com. Berc. anno salutis 1675, ætatis suæ 7, et ibidem repultus est.

The south transept of the Church is appropriated as a Chancel for the Warburtons of Arley. Under the

* To this, is added in a MS. note, supposed by Sir Peter, "Acton had 2 Presbit^y and no church named."—H.

† "In this church is yet the case of a fair organ, having the coats of arms of Warbuton of Arley, Leycester of Tabley, and Merbury of Merbury, carved thereon. These organs, as tradition hath it, came from Norton, bought after the dissolution of that Priory, and were in good order till the pipes thereof were taken out and spoiled by the Parliament soldiers, in the late war 1647, which some Scotchmen among them called WHISTLES IN A BOX."—LEICESTER. In a MS. note,—"Since ye restauration of K. Charles ye 2^d, there is a new paire of Organs set up."—H.

‡ The old monument has been removed, and the inscription copied on thepr esent one.

‖ This is taking a liberty with the old mode of spelling the family name—"LEYCESTER."

CHESHIRE

gallery is an altar tomb of red stone, on which is the figure of a Knight in armour. Near the head is a shield, with the quarterings of Warburton,* Winnington, Grosvenor, and Pulford; the motto, "*Je voll droit avoir.*" Inscribed on a tablet underneath—

HIC JACET JOH'ES DE WARBURTON DE ARLEY, IN COM. CESTR. MILES QUI DUXIT IN UXOREM MARIAM, FIDIAM WILLI' BRERETON DE BRERETON, IN COM P^RD MILITIS PER QUAM HABUIT QUARTUOR FILIOS, QUINQUE FILIOS. OBIIT IN ANNO 1575, ÆTATIS SUÆ 52. QUI FUIT IN RELIGIONE CO'STANS, AMATOR LITERARU' ET AMICU' PAUPERU'.

On a mural monument—

Underneath this tomb doth lye the body of Sir George Warburton, of Arley, in the county of Chester, Baronet, who dyed May 18, anno Domini 1676, being the fifty-first year of his age, and was interred 26 of the same moneth; who had to his first wife Elizabeth, eldest daughter of Sir Thomas Midleton, of Chirck, in ye county of Denbigh, Knt. by whom he had issue two sons and five daughters; and had to his second wife Diana, second daughter of Sir Edward Bishoppe, of Parham, in the county of Sussex, Knt. and Baronet, by whom he had issue five sons and eight daughters, by which Diana this was erected.

To this inscription was subjoined some verses: they are preserved in Cole's MSS.—Near Sir Robert Leycester's monument in the Tabley cemetry, a mural monument—

Here lies Peter Leicester, youngest son of Sir Robert Leicester, Baronet, a youth of very promising parts, who died in the 9th year of his age, 1685. Also Meriell his sister, wife of John D'Anvers, Esq. eldest son of Sir Pope D'Anvers, of Northamptonshire, Bart. a lady justly valued as an ornament to her sex.

On a Mural Monument in the north aisle of the Chancel—

Sacred to the memory of the Rev. Richard Eaton, late Richard Selby, M. A. Vicar of Great Budworth, who at the age of 69 years, died at Pole, on the 7th day of July, 1787, much and deservedly lamented. He was student of Christ Church, Oxford; and presented to the Vicarage by the Dean and Chapter of that College, in the year 1741. In May, 1747, he married Dorothy, sister of George Eaton, of Pole, Esq. and took the surname of Eaton, pursuant to the will of the said George Eaton. He resided constantly within the Parish, and performed the parochial duties in an exemplary manner upwards of 40 years. This memorial, as a testimony of the most sincere and unfeigned affection, was erected by his afflicted sister, Hannah Selby, of Berwick-upon-Tweed.

There is a *School* in the Church-yard, founded by John Dean, Rector of St. Bartholomew's the Great, in 1600; the Vicar has the appointment of the Master.—

* Arg. 2 chevrons gu. on a canton of the second a mullet, or.

HISTORY.

It is endowed with the interest of £200. given by Mr. Pickering, of Thelwall, and a Mrs. Glover.

The great tythes were held on lease by the late Wm. Massey, Esq. of Moston.

The present Vicar is the Rev. Wm. Hamilton Warren, A. M. instituted Nov. 28, 1787.

ANDERTON

Is not noticed in Domesday. In the time of Edw. I. Urian de Sampier (St. Pierre) held Anderton, from whom it descended to the Suttons, of Sutton near Macclesfield; it was purchased from them by Sir Peter Warburton, temp. Eliz. and afterwards became the property of the Stanleys. of Alderley; it is now vested in Sir John Thomas Stanley, Bart. of Alderley and Winnington. The Lysons say, that Urian St. Pierre, died seized of Anderton in 1286, and he had it by gift from Richard de Lostock. It passed by female heirs from the Pierres, to the Cokesays and Grevilles, and from them to the Suttons.

"It is now commonly said of this village, by the neighbourhood that here is neither gentleman nor beggar, charterer, cottager, nor ale house, but a common without end, for that the common is circular, lying round about the township; and the demaine hath been set to Derry Men and tenants, so as no gentleman of long time hath lived there."†

APPLETON-CUM-HULL

Is about 8 miles N. W. from Northwich, and about 4 miles and a half S. S. E. from Warrington. At the time of the Conquest, it was held by Osbern Fitz Tezzon, ancestor of the Boydells of Dodleston. In the reign of Hen. III. Appleton, together with its hamlets of HULL and STOCKTON, was the property of Geoffry Dutton, from whom it descended to the Warburtons of Arley. It is now vested in the Rev. Rowland Egerton Warburton, who holds a Court Baron for the Manor.

The estate of BRADLEY in this township, was the property of the Savages; in the reign of Henry VII. it was held by the Gregs, and passed from them in 1677, by marriage of Katherine an heiress, with William Brock, Esq. of Upton, whose daughter and sole heiress brought it in marriage to John Egerton, Esq. of Oulton. In 1800, it was purchased by Richard Wilson, Esq. of

† Leycester.

CHESHIRE

Lymm, who re-sold it to his brother-in-law Wm. Fox, Esq. of Statham, who is the present possessor.

There is a *School* at Appleton, founded by Sir Geo. Warburton, who died in 1743; it does not, however, possess any endowment.

The wastes here were inclosed under the provisions of an Act of Parliament passed in 1764.

ASTON-JUXTA-BUDWORTH,

Was originally held from the Earl, by William Fitz Nigell, Baron of Halton. John Baron of Halton, gave the manor of HIELD in Aston, to Methroso Punterlinge, temp. Hen. II. he rendering a Welsh lance on the Feast of St. Bartholomew annually. In the reign of Henry III. Geoffry Dutton, before named in Appleton, purchased it from Hugh the Welsh Deacon,* son of Hugh del Hield for twenty-four silver marks; and he gave it to his daughter, Agnes de Dutton.—Towards the conclusion of the reign of Henry III. Robert de Denbigh, and Margaret his wife, purchased it from Geoffry the son of Geoffry de Dutton, for three silver marks, and a Wich-house, in Northwich; Robert dying without issue, Margaret brought it in Marriage to Nicholas de Leycester, in 1276, who was afterwards Knighted. In 1355, John Leycester, of Tabley, sold it to Wm. del Heild, and Goditha his wife, with the reservation of an yearly rent of 40*s*. It was eventually divided between Margaret and Emme their daughters and coheirs; whose descendants possessed the manor, till a moiety was purchased by Thos. Leycester, Esq. of Tabley, in 1500; and in 1601, the other half became vested in the Leycesters, by purchase of Dorothy Leycester, widow.—The manor of WETHALL in this township, was part of the portion of Margaret Dutton, and passed to the Leycesters. The manors of WETHALL and HEILD together, contain about one third of the township of Aston.† There is a Court Baron for the manors of Great Budworth, Aston juxta-Budworth, and Comberbach. The manor of Aston is now the property of the Rev. Rowland Egerton Warburton.

ARLEY HALL, the original residence of the Warburtons, was built by Piers Warburton, Esq. of Arley, who died in 1495: it still exists, and is composed of wood and plaister, cased with brick. The present house, built about 1755, is of a quadrangular form, containing in front 114 feet by 130 in depth, the interior forming a court, 68 feet by 40, laid out as a flower garden.

HISTORY.

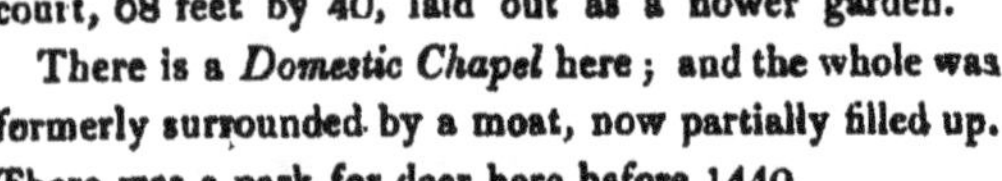

There is a *Domestic Chapel* here; and the whole was formerly surrounded by a moat, now partially filled up. There was a park for deer here before 1449.

BARNTON.

Is about two miles N. W. W. from Northwich.—At the Conquest it was held by Mundret, of the Earl; previous to which it had been held by Dunninge and Ulviet. Temp. John, William son of Henry, the son of Serlo, granted to Hugh Dutton, of Dutton, half of Barnton, which Robert de Meisnilwarin (Mainwaring) held of William, sending yearly a pair of white gloves on the Anniversary of the Nativity of St. John the Baptist, for which grant, Hugh gave three marks of silver in *pleno comitatu Cestriæ*. In the time of Edw. I. the Duttons had possession of the entire manerial right of Barnton. At present Barnton is divided, and the proprietors of lands are all freeholders of inheritance.

The Starkeys, of Barnton, were settled here before the reign of Edward III. and may boast of a regular descent from that period. On the 1st of May, 1758, Piers Starkie settled his lands in Barnton, first on Edmund, eldest son of his late uncle Nicholas Starkie; Edmund died a bachelor; secondly, on Nicholas Starkie, Edmund's brother; thirdly on Legendre Starkie (grandfather of the present heir male of the family), who sold by decree of Chancery, the lands in Barnton to his cousin Nicholas Starkie, of Preston, son of Wm. Starkie, of Manchester, in the representatives of whom they are now vested.‡ There are no manerial privileges exercised.

BARTERTON,

Sometimes called Bartington, is about 4 miles N. W. W. from Northwich; it was formerly written Bertrinton. In the reign of Richard I. Kingsley of Kingsley, was Lord of the Manor of Barterton. A fourth of this township, Margery one of the daughters of Rich. de Kingsley, gave to her son Richard,|| by her husband Hugh de Cholmondeley, which descended to her from

* Leycester.

‡ Ormerod.

|| Temp. Henry III.

† In giving his account of Aston, Sir Peter Leycester observes, "Here should follow the descent of Warburton of Arley; but Sir George Warburton denied me the perusal of his evidences, so as it could not exactly be performed; wherefore I have omitted the same."

CHESHIRE her father's inheritance. Wm. Lancelyn, Lord of another fourth, as descendant of a co-heir of Kingsley of Kingsley, sold the Royalty thereof to Sir Hugh Dutton, in the reign of Edward I. who by purchasing various parcels of land, eventually became possessed of nearly the whole township.

It descended with the other Dutton estates to the Gerards and Fleetwoods, and subsequently passed by various sales to Henry Charles Harvey Aston, Esq. whose grandfather purchased it in 1784.

COGSHULL,

Or Cogshall, is about three miles and a half N. N. W. from Northwich. Richard Baron of Shipbrook, held half of Cogshull in the time of the Conqueror, and Pagan held it from Richard. Previous to the Conquest it was held as two manors by Levenot and Dedon: the other half of Cogshull was held by Randle (the supposed ancestor of the Mainwarings); before the Conquest it was possessed by Ulviet, *et liber homo fuit.* Hugh de Durholme obtained the whole temp. Edw. I. and gave it to Lacy Earl of Lincoln, who granted it to John le Fauconier, "pour le bone service, qu'il nous ad fait, et unquore ferra si Dieu plait, toute cele terre de Coggeshulle ove ses appurtenances, la quele Huward iadys nostre vallet avoit de nostre done en countée de Cestre, rendant dece par an a nous et nous heires un chaperon de Faucon à la Feste Seint Michael," &c.*— It passed afterwards into various hands; and in 1666, was possessed by the Merburys, Ashtons, Piggots, Massys, Richardsons, Pownalls, Greens, and Lows.

* Leycester.

Cogshull is now considered part of the Lordship of Over Whitley. *Burge Hall*, or Burgess Hall, (now called *Cogshull Hall*) was formerly the seat of the ancient family of Burgess, which became extinct in the male line temp. Hen. III. one of the coheiresses of which brought half of this estate to the Starkies, who, in 1689, bought the other moiety, which has descended from the Booths to the Ashtons. Richard Starkie dying in 1722, directed the estate to be sold; and it was eventually purchased by Mr. Peter Jackson, of Frandly, who left it to his natural son Mr. Peter Shackerley.

COMBERBACH,

HISTORY. Is situated about four miles N. W. from Northwich. Roger the Constable, temp. Ric.I. granted, Deo et Beatæ Mariæ, et fratribus servientibus beatis pauperibus Sancti Hospitalis de Jerusalem, totam medietatem de Comberbach; illam scilicèt quam Willielmus de Comberbach, de me tenuit; unà cùm salina in Northwich quæ pertinet ad Astonam juxta Budworth, in puram et perpetuam elemosynam; et si Ricardus Fitton, vel hæredes sui prædictum feodum super me vel super hæredes suos recuperaverit ego et hæredes mei prædictam donationem prædictis hospitaleriis in feodo et hæreditate; reddendo eis annuatim sex denarios pro omnibus quæ ad domum et ad fratres ejusdém domus pertinent. Hiis testibus, Henrico Priore de Norton," &c. John, the son of Hen. de Comberbach, afterwards† gave to Adam, the son of William de Litley, in Aston-juxta-Budworth, all his lands in Comberbach, entailing them on him and his heirs, and in default, on his brother Robert.

† August 1 1335.

The other moiety of Comberbach was granted to the Priory of Norton, by Adam de Dutton, ancestor of the Warburtons; and after the Dissolution, Hen. VIII. sold all the lands composing it, to John Grimsdiche, of London,‡ reserving a chief rent of 7*s.* 7*d.* Grimsdiche sold the greater part of this property to Robert Eaton, whose descendant still possesses a considerable estate in the township.||

‡ 1544.

Comberbach is dependant on the manerial Court of Aston-juxta-Budworth, and the manor is vested in the Rev. Rowland Egerton Warburton.

DUTTON,

Is noticed in the Survey, as having been held by three persons; one part Odard held of the Earl, in capite; another part was held by Fitz Nigel, Baron of Halton; and a third part by Osbern Fitz Tesson. Odard held the largest portion, which before the Conquest had been the property of one Ravene; the shares of Fitz Nigel and Osberne, were held under them by Edward, who was the original Saxon proprietor—such was the mutability of property in those days of military despotism. Eventually the three shares became vested in Odard, and his descendant assumed the local name, and

|| Leycester says, the Grimsdiche property, after being sold to Robert Eaton, was "lastly bought by George Low, of Hartford, from John Eaton, of Over Whitley, about 14 or 16 years ago, 1666:"— He afterwards adds, in a marginal note, in MS. "By vertue of an instayled deed made at ye marriage of John Eaton, his son has recovered the lands from George Low, and is in quiet possession."—H.

was the founder of the Duttons of Dutton. From this time (says Leycester) did the ancient family of Dutton assume their surname; for Odard being seated here in the Conqueror's time, his posterity were sir-named *de Dutton*, from the place of their residence, where they have continued ever since to this present 1666, about 600 years; a family of great worth and antiquity, and as it were almost a constant succession of Knights—but now, alas! ready to change its name, being devolved by a daughter and heir unto the Lord Gerard, of Gerard's Bromley, in Staffordshire.

From this family branched the Warburtons of Arley. About the reign of Edward I. Peter Dutton seated himself at Warburton, and assumed the surname *de Warburton*. Geoffrey de Dutton, temp. Hen. II. was the founder of the Duttons of Chedhill, who afterwards took the local name; and Hamon Dutton, a younger son of the Chedhill family, establishing himself at Ashley, also took the local name, temp. Edw. I. The Duttons of Hatton, and other respectable families, originated in the same source.

It may be interesting to give a short account of the Duttons of Dutton:—

ODARD,* the founder of the family, has been before noticed. HUGH the son of Odard, had confirmed to him the lands of his father. HUGH DE DUTTON, on the confirmation of his lands by the Baron of Halton, gave to William the Baron's son, a palfrey and a sparrow hawk; as his father before him had given to the Baron, his coat of mail and his charging horse.—HUGH DUTTON, the 4th in descent, married the daughter of Hamon Massy, Baron of Dunham Massy, and considerably aggrandized the estates of the family by purchases. Sir Peter Leycester mentions another HUGH, who bought Preston, near Dutton, and Little Legh.—It was this Hugh whom Roger Lacy the Constable acquitted of finding a *judger* to serve at Halton annually for Little Legh; and who had conferred upon him the "Magistracy, rule, and authority over all the letchers, whores, and minstrels of Cheshire," by John the Constable;† and all minstrels licensed by the Duttons, were exempted from the statute of rogues.—HUGH DUTTON, 6th in descent, built the Chapel of Poosey, about 1236, which stands upon land bought by him in Aston-juxta-Dutton.‡ SIR THOMAS DUTTON built the Chapel at the Manor-House of Dutton, towards the end of the reign of Edw. III. he was Sheriff of Cheshire in 1268. SIR HUGH DUTTON: He sued the Prior of Norton before the Commissioners of the Bishop of Lichfield and Coventry, at the Visitation of the Archdeaconry of Chester, in 1315, for not finding a Chaplain, and Lamp at Poosey Chapel, according to the original grant: when John Olton, the Prior, confessing the same, was ordered to find them. He was made Steward of Halton in the 20th Edw. II.—SIR T. DUTTON was made Seneschall, Governor, and Receiver of the Castle and Honor of Halton, by William Clinton, Earl of Huntington, and also of all his lands and manors in Cheshire and Lancashire. Leycester says, "he was indicted for that he and others came with armed power, when King Edw. III. was out of England, within the verge of the lodgings of Lionel, the King's son, Protector of England, and assaulted the manor of Geaumes, near Reading, in Wiltshire, and there slew Michael Poynings, the uncle, and Thomas le Clerke, of Skipton, and others, and committed a rape on Margery, the wife of one Nicholas de la Beche, *for which the King pardoned him*, and he found Sir Bernard Brocas, Sir Hugh Berewyk, Philip Durdanyt, and John Haydoke, his sureties." Previous to this, he had been in several commissions employed for the apprehending of certain malefactors, robbers, and disturbers of the peace in the county; one of which was directed to him as Equitator in Forestâ de Marâ, and to Richard Done, Forester of the same forest.|| In 1379, William Eltonhead, Prior of the Hermit Friars of the Order of St. Augustine, at Warrington, granted to him a perpetual Chantry, to pray for the souls of himself, family, and descendants; to

‡ Leycester.

* "This Odard's, or Hudard's sword, is at this day, 1665, in the custody of the Lady Eleanor, Viscountess Kilmorey, sole daughter and heir of Thomas Dutton, late of Dutton, Esq. deceased; which sword hath for many ages past been preserved as an heir loom, by the name of HUDARD'S SWORD, as so at this day it is by tradition received and called."—LEYCESTER.

† See account of this in page 23, and page 212.

|| "There is a certaine obscure division betwixt the Forest of Mara and the Forest of Mondrum, and under two several Bailiffwicks, at and before this time. In the 31st Edward I. Richard Warre was forester of the Forest of Mondrum, and Rich. Done of the Forest of Mara." MS. note.—H.

CHESHIRE

HISTORY.

which the Prior and Convent were bound under a penalty of 3*s.* 4*d.* to be levied by the Provincial Prior upon omission of such form of service; and if for a week or fortnight it should be omitted, then they were to double the time omitted; if neglected for six months, then on pain of suspension; and if for a year, then to be excommunicated, until the time omitted be made up. This document was witnessed by the Abbots of St. Werburgh, and Vale Royal; and the Priors of Norton and Birkenhedde. This Sir Thomas Dutton was twice Sheriff of Cheshire.—SIR LAWRENCE DUTTON added to the family estates, the manors of Church Minshull, and Aston-Mondrum, by marriage with the heiress of Henry Minshull de Church Minshull. He had license from the Earl to carry away the Chapel of Kingsley, formerly belonging to Sir Peter de Thornton, being within the boundary of the Forest. By his will, he ordered his body to be buried at Norton, and gave his black horse to the Convent there for a heriot. SIR PET. DUTTON, 12th in descent, married Eliz. daughter of Sir Wm. Butler, of Bewsey, Lord of Warrington.* He took part with Hen. Percy, surnamed Hotspur, and obtained a pardon for his rebellion, dated at Cirencester, Nov. 3, 1403. Great contention fell between this Sir Peter Dutton, and Sir William Athurton, of Athurton, in Lancashire; they made inroads on each other; and on one occasion, Sir Peter, Sir Ralph Bostock, Richard Warburton, Thos. Warbuton, John Done, John Manley, Hugh Dutton, of Hatton, William Leycester, Sir Peter Legh, and John Carrington, were all sued by Sir Wm. Athurton, for carrying off forty of his oxen, and forty cows, from his fields at Athurton, and for assaulting his servants. The case was referred to John Duke of Bedford, Regent of England in the absence of Hen. V. who awarded restitution on both sides. In 1423, Sir Peter was made Keeper of Northwood Park, in Over Whitley, from which he gave an oak tree for the repairs of Witton-bridge, and another oak tree for the repair of Farnworth Chapel. He died in 1433.—JOHN DUTTON, his successor, died in 1445.—SIR THOMAS DUTTON was slain, together with his son, at the Battle of Blore Heath, Sept. 1459.—JOHN DUTTON was Steward to the Priory of Norton, and had £3. as an annual fee.—ROGER DUTTON, married Joan, daughter of Sir Richard Aston, of Aston.—LAWRENCE DUTTON, died without lawful issue; but he had an illegitimate son, to whom he gave a Messuage in Preston on the Hill, called the *New Manor.*

* Leycester.

Upon the failure of issue male, great disputes and suits at law arose between Sir Piers Dutton, of Hatton, as next heir male, and the daughters and co-heirs of Sir Thomas Dutton, of Dutton, and their heirs. It was at last arranged, after a seven years' suit, by an award of Henry VIII. 16th May, 1534, by which, the lands allotted to the *co-heirs,* were the Lordships of Church Minshull,† Aston in Mondrum, and Keckwick, and all the lands which the ancestors of Dutton held in Kingsley, Norley, Chorlton, Coddington, Poulton-Lancelyn, Bradley, Budworth-in-le Frith, Milneton, Barnton, Over Whitley, Aston near Mouldsworth, Helsby, Frodsham, and in Chester.—The lands awarded to Sir Piers Dutton, the next male heir, were—the manor of Dutton, with the advowry of the Cheshire Minstrels, the advowson of Poosey Chapel, the Lordships of Weston, Preston, Barterton, Little Legh, Ness in Wirral, Little Mouldsworth, Acton, Hapsford, and all the lands which the ancestors of Dutton held in Weston, Clifton, Preston, Barterton, Legh, Nesse, Little Mouldsworth, Acton, Hapsford, Stony Dunham, Mich Barrow, Stoke, Picton, Arrowe, Northwich, Halton, Thelwall, Onston, Middlewich, Stanthorne, and Higher Runcorne.—A tolerable opinion may be formed from this enumeration of the great possessions of the Family.

SIR PIERS DUTTON,‡ of Hatton and Dutton, was the fifteenth of the family lineally descended from Odard. He built the Hall and Offices at Dutton House, and in 1539, joined it to the Chapel, from which it had previously been separated, He was Sheriff of Cheshire in in 1543, and died in 1546.—JOHN DUTTON, married Eleanor, daughter of Sir Hugh Calveley, Knt. of Lea, near Eaton. He had several illegitimate children.—This John (says Leycester) had also John Dutton, bastard son, who was afterwards gardener at Dutton, and died 1664; and Elizabeth a bastard daughter, married Mr. Marshall, Chaplain to the Lord Gerard, of Gerard's Bromley, *mother to the two famous women-actors now at*

† "By wch ye Chomleyes came Lords of Minshull, and of Aston." M. S. note.—H.

‡ See his portrait, page 77.

CHESHIRE

London, called the two Marshalls. This John sued Raufe Dutton, of Hatton, for all the lands there, as heir at law, but matters were accommodated by an award of the Earl of Leicester, in 1572, by which Raufe was to transfer to John, the lands in Claverton, and Handbridge, in Chester, and in Littleton, in Cheshire; also the property in Hawarden, and Mancot, co. Flint, and 500 marks in money.—THOS. DUTTON, married Thomasin, daughter of Roger Anderton, Esq. of Anderton, co. Lanc. and by her had John, who died without issue, and ELEANOR, who became sole heiress. She married Gilbert Gerard, afterwards Sir Gilbert Gerard, son and heir of Thomas Lord Gerard, in 1609, by whom she had Dutton Lord Gerard, whom she survived; she was succeeded by Charles, fourth Lord Gerard, her Grandson.* Digby, his son, died 1684, leaving a daughter, Elizabeth, who married James Duke of Hamilton, and in 1711, he took the title of Baron Dutton, of Dutton.†

Charles, sixth Lord Gerard, having no issue, settled his estates on the Hon. Frances Fletewood, his sister, and the heirs of her body, by will dated March 14th, 1706; bequeathing to his brother Philip, who succeeded to the title, only £60. per ann. for his life!‡ Chas. Gerard Fleetwood, Esq. who succeeded to the Dutton Estate, in 1745, sold it to R. Lant, Esq. of Putney, co. Surrey, and his sister brought it in marriage to John Bullock, Esq. of Faulkburn Hall, in Essex. About 1776, Thomas Langford Brooke, Esq. of Mere, purchased it from Mr. Bullock, and it is now vested in Philip Langford Brooke, Esq. A Court Baron is held for the manor.

The *Hall* affords some fine specimens of ancient domestic architecture, and is beautifully situated above the River Weaver, partially surrounded by a large moat. A part of the east side of the quadrangle now exists, which is composed of timber, and plaister, the usual materials of the old Cheshire houses. The great hall of the house is a capacious apartment 40 ft, by 20 ft. separated from the entrance passage by a screen supported by pilasters, tastefully ornamented. An inscription runs round the lower part of the ceiling; now nearly destroyed, but it is thus given by Sir Peter Leycester,‖ who transcribed it in 1642:—

HISTORY.

‖ Tab. MSS. Orm. 483.

"Memorandum, that after long suite made by the heires generale of the Duttons against S'r Piers Dutton, then of Hatton, Knight, and now owner of this house and Dutton lordshyp, dependinge continually before all the nobility of the King's Most Hon. Councell, and all the Judges of this realme, by the space of seven years and above, the same Sir Piers was approved heyre male by right inheritance of the house, and all Dutton landes, and so adjudged by the right honourable award of the most famous Prince Henry the Eighth, under his broade seale."

Over the Arch of the Hall Porch are a variety of ornaments, and this inscription:—

Syr Peyrs Dutton Knight, Lorde of Dutton, and my Lady Dame Julian hys wiff made this Hall and buyldyng, in the year of our Lorde God a MCCCCCXLIImo who thanketh God for all.

The door, and the ornaments on and above it, are beautifully executed, and every lover of antiquity must wish for their careful preservation.

NEWBROOKE, or NEWBURGH, an estate in this township, was the residence of a younger branch of the Holfords, held under lease from the Duttons, and their successors.

LEGH, or LEGH-JUXTA-BARTERTON.

This township is sometimes called *Little Legh*, and is about three miles and a half N. W. W. from Northwich. It appears from the Survey, that it was included in the possessions of the Barons of Halton. About the reign of King John, Simon Fitz Osberne, then possessed of the village, granted it to Hugh Dutton, son of Hugh Dutton, of Dutton, and to his heirs, paying an-

* This Eleanor, whom Leycester describes as "a person of such comely carriage and presence, handsomness, sweet disposition, honor, and general repute in the world, that she hath scarce left her equal behind," died at Chester, Jan. 26, 1663, aged 36, and was buried in Trinity Church.

† In 1806, the Marquis of Douglas, was summoned to Parliament by writ, as Baron Dutton, of Dutton, in Cheshire, and took precedence according to the date of the original creation in 1711.

‡ Under a settlement made by Charles, fourth Lord Gerard, in 1660, his estates were limitted to his sons, by his wife Jane Digby, in tail male; with remainder to the heirs male of Thomas first Lord Gerard; and remainder to the right heirs of the said Charles Lord Gerard, and it was under this settlement, that Elizabeth Duchess of Hamilton, succeeded to a portion of the estates of the Gerards.

nually two silver marks at the festival of St. Martin.—Clatterwig, a hamlet of this Township, was purchased by Sir Thomas Dutton, from Hugh de Clatterwig, temp Hen. III.—Leycester says, "In this township is an ancient chappel of ease, called *Little Legh Chapel*, within the Parish of Great Budworth. It was lately repaired by the Inhabitants of Little Legh, 1664, whereunto £5. was given towards the repair thereof, by the parishioners of Great Budworth, *me præsente*.*

Little Legh descended from the Duttons, to the Gerards and Fleetwoods, and was purchased by the Leighs, of Stoneley, Warwickshire; and has subsequently passed to the Leighs of Oldlestrop, Gloucestershire, who are the present proprietors.

MARBURY.

At a very early period Marbury was vested in the Barons of Shipbrook; about the reign of Hen. III. Warin Vernon, then Baron, confirmed the manor to Wm. de Merebirie, probably of the Vernon family.†—In the reign of Edw. I. Simon son of Randle Merbury, married Idonea, daughter and heir of Thomas de Walton, and was the founder of the Marburies of Walton. The Marburies became extinct in the male line in the person of Richard Marbury, Esq. 1684; and in 1708 the estate was sold by his sisters Elizabeth Thackeray, Mary Woods, and Catherine Marbury, to Richard Earl Rivers, of Rock Savage, under a decree of Chancery.—The Earl dying in 1714, Marbury was purchased from his Trustee, by James Earl of Barrymore, his son-in-law; it then passed to his second son, the Hon. Rich. Barry, who dying without issue, it became vested in the eldest son of his next brother, the late James Hugh Smith Barry, Esq. who left it to his natural son, John Smith Barry, Esq. the present proprietor, and High Sheriff for the County in 1819.

The *Hall* of Marbury is an extensive brick building, ornamented with a stone portico; it was considerably enlarged by James Earl of Barymore, by whom wings were added. Its situation is truly picturesque, on the bank of an extensive lake, covering nearly two acres.—It possesses a most valuable collection of ancient pictures and statues, collected chiefly at Rome, by the late owner, J. H. S. Barry, Esq. who removed them hither from his seat at Belmont, in this parish, and who left them as heir looms, directing that a room adjoining the house should be built for their reception; but this part of the will has not yet been fulfilled, probably owing to the general residence of the present proprietor on his Irish estates.‡ The most remarkable antiquities here, say the Lysons, are a statue of Antinous, personifying Abundance; a group of *Paris equestris;* a colossal bust of Lucius Verus; and a *puteal* surrounded by figures in bas relief, now converted into a vase.—The Pictures are chiefly of the Italian School.

MARSTON,

Is not noticed in Doomsday Book; but it formerly belonged to the Barons of Kinderton. Andrew Prior of Norton, granted to Sir Wm. Venables, *charissimo amico nostro*, to find him the celebration of Divine service in his chapel, at Marston, during his life time, when either he or his wife should be there; and also leased to Robert his son, clerk, their tythe of the mill, and of the fishing there,|| temp. Hen. III. It passed from the family of Venables to the Vernons, with the Kinderton barony, and was sold about 1757, by Lord Vernon, to Sir Peter Leycester, Bart. father of the present proprietor, Sir J. F. Leicester, Bart.—A Court Baron is held for the manor, which is included within Sir John's leet of Witton-cum-Twambrookes.

PICKMERE.

Is not mentioned in Doomsday Book, "whereby it seemeth to be waste at that time.§ In the reign of King John, it was divided into two fees; one of which Raufe Mainwaring gave to Hen. de Audley in marriage, with his daughter Bertrey, together with the townships of Smallwood and Snelston, and a mark of rent in Ches-

* This is a Chapel of Ease for Legh, Barnton, Bartington, and Dutton. In 1718, it was completely rebuilt, and has been augmented by Queen Anne's bounty. The Minister is appointed by the Vicar of Budworth. A School has always been held in the Chapel, but the Master's Salary, which arises from interest of money left by a person unknown, is only forty shillings per annum. The Chapel is a mean building of brick, standing defenceless in the highway.

† "There is no great difference between the coat armour of Merbury and Vernon; the fesse in Merbury being Ingraled; the other plaine."—MS. note.—H.

‡ He directed also that a mausoleum should be erected; but it has not yet been built.

|| Marston is situated near the Meres of Marbury and Picmere.

§ Leycester.

ter, on land belonging to one Fagun. This moiety in 1666, was divided among the families of Merbury, Daniell, Leycester (of Nether Tabley) Swinton, Key, Deane, Antcebus, and Warburton, (of Arley). The other moiety together with the manor of Wincham, Wm. Venables gave to Maude, his sister, in marriage, to be held by half a Knight's-fee; it afterwards became the property, by female descent, of the Bruyers, Hulses, and Troutbecks, and from the latter passed to the Talbots, Earls of Shrewsbury; in 1600, the Earl of Shrewsbury sold the moiety to his tenants, "every tenant buying his own, and so are become particular tenants at this day."*

* Leycester.

STRETTON,

Was vested in the family of Starkey, so early as the reign of Henry II. when Roger Fitz Alured granted it to Richard Starkie, and his heir, to be held by the service of the tenth part of a Knight's Fee. It was no doubt originally held under the Halton Barony. In 1714, the Starkies became extinct in the male line, by the death of Philip Starkie, when the property devolved to his two sisters, co-heiresses. One of them dying without issue, the manor passed to the heirs of the other sister, Frances, married to Thomas Coppock, whose only son dying without issue, Stretton became the property of his daughther, who married Michael Renwick, Esq. of Liverpool, father of Thomas Renwick, M. D. the present proprietor.

Stretton *Lower Hall*, was the residence of the elder branch of the Starkies, and was in 1719, sold under a Decree of Chancery, by the heirs of Philip Starkie, to Henry Wright, of Mobberly Esq.; in 1790, the Rev. Henry Offley Wright exchanged the estate with T. L. Brooke, of Mere, Esq. for lands in Mottram; who, in Nov. 1807, sold it to Mr. Long.

Moss Hall was sold at the same time to Hen. Clarke, Esq. of Belmont.†

† Lysons.

The *Upper*, or *Over Hall* is "supposed to have passed in marriage, to the Bradshaws, by whose representatives it was sold to Mr. Peter Dutton, of Warrington, the present proprietor.‡ All the Halls are occupied as Farm-houses.

‡ Ormerod.

In this township was an ancient Chapel of Ease to Great Budworth, called *Stretton Chapel*; it was in a ruinous state in 1666.

NETHER TABLEY,

Is sometimes called in old deeds Little Tabley. At the time of the Survey, it was held by one Gozeline under the Earl; Ostebrand was the possessor previous to the Conquest. In the reign of Hen. II. Adam de Dutton was the proprietor, holding it of the Prior of St. John of Jerusalem in England, by the rent of 6d. payable at the Feast of St. Michael. Adam was the younger son of Hugh Dutton, of Halton, and ancestor of the Warburtons of Arley. Towards the conclusion of the reign of Edw. III. Geoffry Dutton, grandson of Adam, gave the township to his daughter Margaret and her heirs. She married, first, Robert de Denbigh, who died without issue; and about 1276 married Nicholas de Leycester, whose descendants are the possessors at this day.

The following is a brief sketch of the leading heads of this very respectable family:—

Sir Nicholas Leycester, Knt. was Seneschal and Constable of Cheshire. He died in 1295.—Roger Leycester "bought out all the freeholders of Nether Tabley, and made that township entirely his own."||—He died 1359, surviving his father 53 years.—Nicholas Leycester married Mary, daughter of Wm. Mobberly de Mobberley, and by her had John Leycester, Raufe Leycester, (founder of the Leycesters of Toft), and Elizabeth, who married Wm. Mainwaring, of Over Peover, and from whom descended the Mainwarings of Over Peover. Nicholas died in 1349.—John Leycester served in the French wars under the celebrated John of Gaunt, Duke of Lancaster, in 1373. It appears by his accounts, audited by John Tilly, one of the auditors of Sir Thomas Felton, (then Judge of Chester)§ that he accounted for £266. 13*s*. 4*d*. allowed him for payment of Jenkyn Mobberley, Esq. and other soldiers who served under him, and for his own pay for 210 days, at 3*s*. per diem; there was also pardoned to him £38. 10*s*. in the way of gratuity,¶ on which he gave to the Lady Felton "a white ambling palfrey." He built the Manor Hall of Tabley within the lake,** where it now stands, "previous to which, it stood with-

|| Leycester.

§ Dated Southampton, on the eve of St. John, 49th Edward III. 1375.

¶ Leycester.

** See the vignette, page 214.

out the lake, near the Saffron yards," where there is yet a trench to be seen, which environed the old hall about with water; which old hall I conjecture, was the residence of the Hearts of Nether Tabley, whose freehold was bought out by Roger Leycester.* He died in 1398.†—WM. LEYCESTER, 5th in descent: he married Agnes, sister to Sir Piers Dutton, of Dutton; and his second wife was Pillaryne, widow to Robert Massy, of Hale, and sister to Sir John Cradock, Knt. He died in 1428.—JOHN LEYCESTER, who died in 1462.—JOHN LEYCESTER, his son, died in 1496.—THOMAS LEYCESTER died about 1526.—JOHN LEYCESTER died in 1543. PIERS LEYCESTER died in April, 1577, and was buried in our Lady Mary's Chapel at Budworth. "In the Lady Mary's Chapel, was anciently the image of the Virgin Mary, cut in wood, curiously trimmed and decked, her shoes gilded, and hair fastened on her head; set on a frame of wood about two feet high: it was taken down about 1559, hewed in pieces, and burnt in the Vicar's oven.‡—PETER LEYCESTER died in 1581. He had three daughters, Alice, Elizabeth, and Katherine, who became heirs to the land brought by their mother Elizabeth, daughter and heir of Edward Colwich, of Colwich, co. Stafford, but all the ancient lands were entailed on ADAM LEYCESTER, who died in 1591. His widow Dorothy, built the *Gate House* at Nether Tabley. PETER LEYCESTER died 1647.—SIR PET. LEYCESTER, (created a Baronet, Aug. 10, 1660) born in 1613, the celebrated Author of "*The Antiquities*," &c.‖ Sir Peter embarked manfully in the Royal Cause, and was therefore soon fixed upon as an object of Parliamentary vengeance. In 1655, he was incarcerated by them within the walls of a prison, and afterwards compounded for his estates in the sum of £778. 18*s*. 4*d*.—It was about this time that he directed his attention to genealogical studies, commencing, as might be expected, with his own family, and attempting to deduce his descent from the ancient Earls of Leicester. Previous to 1650, he had access to the manuscript hoards of the Grosvenors, Duttons, and several other families of the County; and the two following years were employed by him in the collection of his materials for the History of the Hundred of Bucklow. Thus did Sir Peter occupy his time till the Restoration, two years after which, he was created a Baronet; and in 1673 he published his work, under the title—

"*Historical Antiquities*, in two Books. The First Treating in General of *Great Brettain* and *Ireland*.—The Second Containing Particular Remarks concerning Cheshire. Faithfully Collected out of Authentick Histories, Old Deeds, Records, and Evidences, by Sir Peter Leycester, Baronet. Whereunto is annexed a Transcript of *Doomsday Book*, so far as it concerneth *Cheshire*, taken out of the original Record.

Frustra fit per plura, quod potest fieri per pauciora.

London, printed by W. L. for Robert Clavell, in Cross-Keys Court in Little Britain, M.DC.LXXIII."

The volume is dedicated to "His Most Serene and Most Excellent Majesty Charles II." but it would seem a misunderstanding had occurred, between Sir Peter and his publisher, Clavel; for on the back of the title page of the Copy, in the Author's possession, is written,

"Augustissimo ac Potentissimo Principi, Carolo Secundo, Dei gratiâ Magnæ Bretanniæ Ffranciæ, et Hiberniæ Regi ffidei Defensori, &c.

"Author ipse, non nisi Pace vestrâ Regali prius impetratâ, se suumq. librum ad pedes Maiestatis vestræ omni cum humilitate provolvit; quippe-qui sub vestris dum prodeat alis, tutior vagetur per terras: opus sanctantæ Maiestati impar; utpote cujus summi Imperii amplitudo sublimiorem mandet calamum. Hæc omnia (de quibus versatur) tua sunt: proin tute tibi-ipsi fias patronus; quiâ tibi præter teipsum par nullus est. Cui omni quâ potest, reverentiâ devotissimus vester ligeus hoc laboris sui specimen. PETRUS LEYCESTER, D. D."

"This is the Author's dedication to the Kinge; but Mr. Clavell, (who had the printinge of this booke committed to him) caused the Dedication (as you see in the

* Leycester.

† In a marginal note, relative to the copy of the Seal given in the "Antiquities," is written, "Here is Wm. Leycester's Seale put for John Leycester's." And afterwards, in reference to the seal of Wm. Leycester, in the following page—(358)—"Here is John Leycester's Seale put in the place of Wm. Leycester's."—H.

‡ Leycester.

‖ In a marginal note, p. 361 (error) "Antiquities," in enumerating Sir Peter Leycester's issue, is this MS. note put to the name of Byron Leycester, his third daughter, in a different hand writing to those which precede:—"Byron married —— Venables, of Agden, Councellor at Law, a younger brother: but he compassed the estate from his elder brother, 1675."—H.

page immediately before)* to be put in English, thinkinge thereby the book would sell the better: but that dedication in English is none of myne; and then I caused him to print this Latin Dedication of my owne, which he did, and sent me some of them downe; promisinge me withall to insert this and not the other, into all the rest of my bookes then not sold of,—but I see he failes my expectation.---P. L."

The dispute with his publisher was not the only one in which Sir Peter was engaged: his work occasioned a long controversy with Sir Thomas Mainwaring. Sir Thomas claimed descent from the ancient Earls Palatine of Chester, by marriage of one of the family with Amicia, the asserted daughter of Hugh Cyveilioc, about 1170. Sir Peter denied this statement, and observes, "Now because I found that some are displeased at my placing of Amice, sometime the wife of Raufe Mainwaring, Judge of Chester, among the base issue of Hugh Cyveliok Earl of Chester; and also that I am informed, that three eminent Judges and four Heralds are of opinion that she was legitimate, and not a base daughter, it is very necessary that I put down here my reasons why I have so placed her, protesting withal, that I have not done it out of any prejudicate opinion or calumny intended in the least, but only for the truth's sake, according to the best of my judgment, and that after a long and diligent scrutiny made herein; for I must ever acknowlege myself to be extracted out of the loyns of this Amice by my own mother: but you know the old saying of Aristotle, *Amicus Plato, Amicus Socrates, sed Magis amica veritas.*"

The Learned Antiquary then proceeds to give his reasons "that Amice was a Bastard," and truly they are cogent ones in the set-out. "If Hugh Cyveiliok had no other wife but Bertred, then Amice must certainly be a Bastard; for she was not a daughter by Bertred, as is granted on all sides. But Hugh never had any other wife; ergo, Amice was a Bastard."

Sir Thomas Mainwaring warmly answered this argument, in "A defence of Amicia, daughter of Hugh Ceivilioc Earl of Chester, wherein it is proved that she is not a bastard." Sir Peter replied in "An answer to Sir Thomas Mainwaring's Book, entitled, 'A defence of Amicia,' &c. London, 1673, 8vo." Three of these dry pieces of argument were published on each side, and ballads were sung in various parts of the county, ridiculing the writers and their subject. In the end, a legal inquiry was resorted to; and at the trial at Chester, in 1675, the matter in dispute was adjudged to be in favor of Sir Thomas.—Sir Peter Leycester was an indefatigable searcher into the "Depths of Antiquitie," and left behind him a vast collection of abstracts of evidences, pedigrees, &c.†

To return to the descent of the Leycesters: the direct male line terminated in 1742, in the person of Sir Francis Leycester, Bart. leaving issue one daughter only, married, first, to Fleetwood Legh, Esq of Bank; secondly to Sir John Byrne, of Timogue, a Baronet of Ireland, whose son, Sir Peter Byrne, assumed the name and arms of Leicester, under a special Act of Parliament, and was succeeded by the present proprietor, Sir John Fleming Leicester, Bart.

The *Old Hall* of Tabley, stands on an island, situated in a noble lake, a neat bridge connecting it with the grounds. Its shape was originally quadrangular, but the east side only remains, and the front is covered by luxuriant ivy. In the Hall is a fine bay window ornamented with the Leycester pedigree in stained glass.—There is a domestic Chapel on the south-east side; it is built of brick, with large bay windows; at the west end is a small bellfrey.‡

Tabley House, the present seat of the family, is situated about a quarter of a mile from the Old Hall; and was completed about 1769, under the superintendance of Mr. Carr, of York. A fine portico, of the Doric order, is supported by four columns, each formed of a single block of Runcorn stone, 23 ft. 4 in. high, and 9 feet in circumference, nearly as large as those which support the portico of the County Hall at Chester. The front has a centre, and indented wings, connected by corridors. The grand saloon is 72 feet by 32 feet, exclusive of the window part, and is fitted up as a gallery for the works of painters of the British school. There is here a fine portrait of Lord Byron, the heroic Governor of Chester during the siege, by Vandyke.—The stables are behind the house, forming a quadran-

* The Dedication in English.

† There is a miniature of the Antiquary extant in the possession of Sir J. F. Leicester, Bart.

‡ See Vignette, page 214.

CHESHIRE

rangl: of considerable extent.—The house is about two miles from Knutsford, in an extensive park.

OVER WHITLEY

Includes in its limits the Hamlets of *Norcot, Anterbus, Middle Walke, Seaven Oakes*, and *Crowley*.*—It is generally called the LORDSHIP OF OVER WHITLEY, and is held of the Fee of Halton, in fee-farm.—Antrobus is noticed in Domesday, as being held by Levenot; it afterwards passed to the Barons of Halton. In the 10th Edw. I. Henry de Lacy had grant of free warren here, and a market and fair at Congleton. A family which assumed the local name, was settled here at an early period, but in the reign of Henry VI. Henry Antrobus sold it to Thos. Venables, whose descendants long resided here. In Aug. 25th Eliz. Thos. Venables dying without issue, the property became vested in Frances Venables, who brought Wincham and Antrobus in marriage to Thomas Lee, Esq. of Dernhall, from whom it descended to E. V. Townshend, Esq. of Wincham, who sold the Venables estate in Over Whitley to Sir Edm. Antrobus, Bart.† descendant in the male line from Henry Antrobus.

* Leycester.

THE POLE is the residence of Geo. Eaton, Esq. whose ancestors possessed a considerable estate here for many generations. The estate which belonged to the Prior of Norton, in Comberbach, was purchased by Robert Eaton, soon after the Dissolution.

NETHER WHITLEY,

Is about 4 miles N. W. W. from Northwich, and was held of the Fee of Halton at the Conquest. Randle Blundeville gave it to Alfred de Combre, temp. Richard II. He was the son of Reginald de Combrey, of Leigh Comber, co. Salop, and his son left two daughters, co-heirs: Alice, married Sir Robt. Touchet, of Buglawton and Tattenhall: and Agnes, married Adam de Dutton, youngest son of Hugh Dutton, of Dutton, ancestor to the Warburtons of Arley. Temp. Henry III.‡ Thomas Tuschet was Lord of Nether Whitley, and it continued in the Touchets till the direct male line became extinct in Wm. Touchet, Esq. who died about 1684. His daughter and heiress married Philip Chetwode, of Oakley, Esq. in whose descendant, Sir John Chetwode, Bart. it is now vested.

‡ Leycester, page 387.

HISTORY.

The *Chapel* of Nether Whitley, which is a small brick building, with bay windows, and a nave and chancel, is in the parish of Great Budworth, to which it is a Chapel of Ease.—About 1600 it was completely rebuilt by Thomas Tuschet, Esq.; and Thomas Pierson, Minister of Brampton, co. Hereford, born at Weaverham, and brought up by Mr. Tuschet, in Oct. 1683, left £250 towards maintaining a Minister, and £50. more for maintaining a Minister at Witton Chappel.|| About 1631, lands were purchased in Antrobus, which yielded yearly (1678) £3. 10s.§

|| Leycester.

§ Ibid.

Grimsditch Hall, is now by purchase, the property of Thos. Grimsditch, Esq. a descendant from a younger branch of the Grimsditch family, of Macclesfield. So late as the year 1726, the ancient male line of this respectable family continued in possession here; but on the death of Mr. Daniel Grimsditch, it successively passed to the Chetwodes, and Blackburnes. Part of the land of the Grimsditch demesne is in the township of Newton.

WINCHAM,

At the Conquest, was held by the Baron of Kinderton, under Lupus, previous to which it had been held by Dot,¶ and others. Temp. Ric. I. Wm. Venables, Baron of Kinderton, gave Wincham and half of the township of Picmere, to his sister Maude in marriage; and she gave it to Nicholas de Elets, for the service of half a Knight's Fee.—It continued in the Elets family till about 1233, when Henry de Elets sold the whole manor with its appurtenances to Wm. Venables, and the sale was confirmed by John Scot, Earl of Chester and Huntington. William de Venables bought out certain lands in Wincham, possessed by William son of Guy de Wyncham, which lands were eventually divided between his daughters, Lettice and Beatrix. All the manor of Wincham fell to Beatrix, who married Raufe de Wasteneys, excepting Twambrookes, and Wincham Mill;** afterwards the manor passed in moieties to the Leghs of Easthall, and the Cholmondeleys, by marriage with Alice and Margaret, daughters and co-heiresses of the last of the Wastenyes family. One moiety passed by marriage from the Leghs to the Masseys of Wincham, and the Leghs of Westhall; on the 14th June,

¶ See Edge, page 337.

** Leycester.

† So created in 1814; in February 1815, Sir Edward was granted two horses argent, as supporters to his shield, being used formerly by the Lords of Rutherford, whose title became extinct, and whose barony and estate Sir Edmund purchased.

1566, Anthony Grosvenor, of Ridley, purchased this moiety from Richard Legh, for £220. and sold it again the following year to Roger Pilston, of the Temple, and John Grosvenor of Tushingham; from whom it was purchased by Sir Richard Egerton, of Ridley; and afterwards became the property of the Harcourts.—The other moiety descended from the Cholmondeleys to the Buckleys of Eyton, near Davenham, and from them to the families of Leftwich and Harcourt; in the latter of whom the whole manor then became vested. About 1668, the manor was sold to Robert Venables, Esq. of Antrobus, who had previously possession of two messuages in Wincham;* and his daughter Frances, brought the estate in marriage to Thomas Lee, Esq. of Dernhall, who settled it on his third son Robert; and his son Robert had issue two daughters, Elizabeth and Hester, the former of whom died without issue,; and the latter married Charles Legh, Esq. of Adlington, but having no children, Wincham passed by her will to Edw. Townshend, Esq. of Chester, fourth son of John Townshend, Esq. by Frances, daughter of Nat. Lee, Esq. of Dernhall, eldest son of Frances Venables, daughter of Robert Venables before mentioned,—and Edward Venables Townshend, Esq. son of Edward Townshend, is the present proprietor. No Court is held for the manor; and the township is under the jurisdiction of the Witton leet, where the Constables are sworn.

*Leycester.

The *Hall* is pleasantly situated on a gentle elevation, near the river Weaver.

Moses, sc.

RUINS OF BIRKENHEAD PRIORY, WIRRAL.

PARISH OF GROPPENHALE,

CONTAINS THE TOWNSHIPS OF

GROPPENHALE. | LATCHFORD.

GROPPENHALE,

Is situated about two miles S. from Warrington; and at the time of the Conquest belonged to Osbern Fitz Tezzon. It was afterwards given to William the son of Samson, who, about the reign of Richard I. released it to Hugh Boydell.—In the reign of Edward I. Sir John Boydell gave a place called *Caterich*, in Groppenhale, to Robert, his youngest son, who granted the same to Thomas, son of Sir Hugh Dutton, of Dutton; but he subsequently released it to William, son of Sir William Boydell, of Dodleston, who had right of free Warren granted him in Dodleston, Groppenhale, and Lachford: he died without issue male, and his estates were divided between his sisters and coheirs, Margaret, who married Owen Voel, and Joan, wife of Sir John Danyell, of Groppenhale, but Howel ap Owen Voel, released to Sir John and Joan his wife, all the property of Groppenhale Wood. The estate here was thus vested, when about 1388, it passed by a female heir of the Daniel family, to Peter Legh, of Lyme. A moiety of Groppenhale, descended to Hugh Reddish, in right of Margaret his wife, daughter and co-heir of Thomas Boydell; from whose family it passed in 1556, to Wm. Merbury, of Merbury, Esq. in right of Maud his wife, daughter and heiress of Thomas Reddish of Catterich. Both moieties are now the property of Thomas Legh, Esq. and John Smith Barry, Esq. of Marbury.

In 1712, a *School House* was built here at the expense of Mr. Thomas Johnson, who endowed it with lands in Appleton, which produced in 1812, twelve guineas per ann.

The *Church*, which is dedicated to St. Wilfred, was a rectory so early as the reign of Henry III. when the Boydells were the patrons; the patronage, however, has since been vested in several families, but it is now the property, by purchase, of the present Rector, the Rev. John Burnett Stewart, A. M. presented December 21, 1808. The building is of stone, with nave, chancel, side aisles, and tower; the nave and side aisles divided by pointed Gothic arches, springing from handsome octagonal capped columns.*—In the east window of the south aisle are some rich remains of stained glass.†

The monumental memorials are not numerous, nor remarkable: they are chiefly to the Middlehursts; but there is one to the memory of Wm. Brock, Esq. of Bradley with Appleton, who died May 10, 1674, aged 54. The stone figures of the Boydells, in armour, noticed by Randle Holme, no longer exist, and the probability is, they are buried beneath the flooring.

LACHFORD,

Is about a mile and half S. E. of Warrington. Wm. son of Sampson, released the manor to Hugh de Boydell. During the Earldom of the Black Prince, Sir John Daniell and Joan his wife, obtained the township, with permission to keep two fairs yearly, on the 5th and 6th of May, and the 17th and 18th of October; also to have two weekly markets, on Wednesday and Friday. The manor originally passed with one of the co-heiresses of Wm. Boydell, temp. Edw. III. to Hoel ap Owen Voel, whose son assumed the name of Boydell. Thomas Boydell, his grandson, left two daughters, co-heirs, with whom the manor passed in moieties to the familes of Reddish and Albrugham. The former became vested in the Merburys; but the latter was sub-divided between two co-heiresses, married to Byron and Holt; the share of the Holts passed by sale to the Brookes and Irelands; but Byron's was sold in severalties. The parish of Groppenhale forms one of the principal suburbs of Warrington; and there is in Lachford a handsome *Chapel of Ease* to Groppenhale, consecrated in 1781, of which the Rector of Groppenhale is the Patron.

The old Roman Road into that division of the kingdom now called Lancashire, crossed the Mersey in this township, by means of a Ford, which gave name to the Village. Temp. Ric. I. Randle Blundeville granted to Hugh Boydell, the passage or ferry over the Mersey, from Thelwall to Runcorn. In 1308, John Boydell granted to the Friars Hermits of St. Austin, at Warrington, free passage through Lachford, on the condition of an annual Mass being said for the soul of himself, his parents, &c. In 40 ann. reg. Edward III. the Black Prince appointed certain individuals to arrest all persons passing the ferry by boats, between Runcorn and Cross-ferry, and to commit them to Chester Castle—the order was in this form:—

Edwardus illustrissimus R. Angliæ filius, Princeps Aquitainiæ, et Walliæ, Dux Cornubiæ, et Comes Cestriæ, omnibus, &c. Constituimus Galfridum filium Galfridi de Warburton, militis Will'mum de Mere, Will'mum Wylme, Johannem filium Will'mi Danyel, &c. ad arrestandum, conjunctim vel divisim omnes gentes quæ faciunt passagium per batella ultra aquam de Mersey inter Runcorne, et Crosse Ferry; et per ballivos usque ad Castrum Cestriæ ducendum, moraturos super deliberatione sua duximus ordinandum."

It would appear from an Inq. p. m. of Thomas Boydell, 20th Richard II. that there was a bridge over the Mersey here at that period, for it states, after reciting that he held Lachford, &c. "cu' passagio pont's de Warrington." This Bridge, however, could not have existed long, for we find that the Earl of Derby erected a bridge, on the occasion of a visit from his Royal relative,‡ and to accomplish which, he possessed himself of the road called Bridge-street, on the Warrington side, and afterwards threw up a causeway across the Lachford marshes. On his death, he left the bridge free of toll to the public. His successors kept the bridge in repair, until soon after the Restoration, when owing to the seizure and appropriation of the Stanley estates by the Republican Government, the then Earl was unable to undertake the task on account of the expense. A Meeting of the Gentry of Cheshire and Lancashire was therefore held, at which it was agreed, that the Bridge should be repaired at the joint charge of both counties. In consequence of the approach of the Scotch Rebels in 1745, the Bridge was destroyed on the 24th June, by the Liverpool Blues, commanded by Col. Graham; but in 1747, it was rebuilt of stone at the expense of the Crown, and a watch-house was erected on the centre of it. The present bridge, which is of wood, on massy stone piers, was lately rebuilt, under the direction of Mr. Harrison, the celebrated Architect, and the charge defrayed equally by the counties of Chester and Lancaster.

‡ Temp. Hen. VII.

* One bears the date 1559.

† "In the east window of the south aisle of Groppenhall Church, are some remains of figures of Saints, apparently coëval with the window, which is in the style of the 14th century."—LYSONS.

THE PARISH OF KNUTSFORD,

CONTAINS THE TOWNSHIPS OF

OVER KNUTSFORD	OLLERTON
NETHER KNUTSFORD	AND
BEXTON	TOFT.

Knutsford was formerly a Parochial Chapelry, but was made a Parish by Act of Parliament in 1741.

KNUTSFORD

Is about twenty-four miles from Chester, and fifteen from Manchester. It was originally held under Lupus, by Fitz Nigel, Baron of Halton, under whom it was held by Erchbrand; "but whether (says Leycester) that Knutsford, so held by this William Fitz Nigel. comprehended any more than that which is now a distinct Township of itself, called *Knutsford Booths*, and is at this day in Halton Fee, is some quere."* Temp Edw I.† William de Tabley was Lord of both Knutsfords, and gave a charter empowering the inhabitants to constitute Burgesses. He afterwards obtained a Royal Charter for a weekly market here on Saturday; and a fair yearly, *in vigiliâ, et in die, et in crastino Apostolorum Petri et Paul, id est*, June 28, 29, and 30—This charter was dated at Walsingham, Aug. 3, 20th Edward I. and was subsequently confirmed to William his son, another fair being granted yearly, *in vigiliâ, et in die, et in crastino Apostolorum Simonis et Judæ, id est*, Oct. 27, 28, and 29. This confirmation was dated at Hartford, Feb. 1332, 6th Edw. III.‡ The manor being held by the Tableys, under the Massys of Tatton, was pursuant to agreement divided between Wm. de Tabley, and Sir John Massy, temp Hen. III.; but on the death of the heir of William de Tabley, in 1352, his moiety was divided amongst co-heirs; and eventually, in the early part of the 15th century, the entirety was possessed by Sir Hugh Hulse. Hugh Hulse, Esq. in 1590, sold the whole to Richard Brereton, Esq. of Tatton; and the Royalty being thus invested in the Lords of Tatton, Richard settled his estates on Sir Thomas Egerton, Lord Chancellor of England, ancestor of the Earl of Bridgewater.|| The manor subsequently descended from Lord Brackley, in the same way as Tatton, to Wilbraham Egerton, Esq. M. P. the present proprietor, who holds a Court Leet, and Court Baron, the tolls of market and fairs being attached to it.

Knutsford is a neat town, in a most desirable situation, divided into King-street, Princess-street, Minshull-street, Silk Mill-street, the Market Place, and Swinton Square; and here the Midsummer and Michaelmas Quarter Sessions for the County are held, in a handsome Hall, built under the superintendance of the architect, Mr. Moneypenny.

The Manufactures are trifling: In 1770, a large building was erected in Silk Mill-street, for the purpose of a Mill for twisting silk; the business, however, was not carried on with any spirit; and it was then occupied as a Cotton Mill. This scheme also failed, and the premises are divided amongst labourers.—A considerable manufacture of thread, was formerly carried on here, but at present it is neglected, and almost discontinued. There are races annually at Knutsford, in the month of July, which attract a vast concourse of spectators from the surrounding country. A custom, perhaps peculiar, prevails here, of strewing the streets on public festivals, or on the marriage of an inhabitant, with brown sand: the streets and footways are cleanly swept, and adorned in a fantastic manner with sand and flowers. The gates leading to Tatton Park, at the end

* Knutsford was formerly a Parochial Chapelry of Rosthern, and took its name from the circumstance of King Canute having crossed the BIRCHEN with his army after a victory.

† About 1292.

‡ The present fairs are held on Whit Tuesday, July 10, and Nov. 8th, and are chiefly for Yorkshire goods.

|| Leycester says "Nether Knutsford comprehended the Cross Town, and hath in it an ancient Parochial Chappel, daughter of the Mother Church of Rostherne, situated in the very confines of Nether Knutsford, towards the domain of Booths."

CHESHIRE HISTORY.

of King-street, form a handsome ornament to the town; and near this is the *Spinning School*, founded and supported by the praiseworthy benevolence of Mrs Egerton, of Tatton. Here eighty day scholars have the benefit of gratuitous instruction in reading, writing, and arithmetic: six orphan girls are also educated and maintained in this school, in a way calculated to make them good servants, and situations are obtained for them by the humanity of the amiable patroness.

The *Church* is of brick, with stone facings and battlements; it consists of a nave and side aisles, with galleries over them, and a handsome tower,* containing a ring of six bells.—In 1741, an Act of Parliament was obtained for making Knutsford a distinct Parish and Vicarage, and the old Chapel was taken down. The present Church was built in what was called the Ten-Tree-Croft, and in 1744, it was consecrated. It is dedicated to St. John. The patronage is vested in the Lords of Over Knutsford, Nether Knutsford, and Ollerton, the latter, however, belonging to one proprietor, is only entitled to the alternate presentation. The present Vicar is the Rev. Harry Grey, A. B. presented Sept. 9, 1809. The Register commences 1581.

The Monumental Memorials are few and uninteresting: there is a handsome pyramidal monument to Ralph Leycester, Esq. of Toft, and Katherine his wife: the former died Dec. 20, 1776, aged 77; the latter Feb. 25, 1799, aged 90.

There was a *Free School* here before the Reformation, supported by certain lands, granted on the abolition of Chantries to the Leghs, of Booths, subject to an yearly payment of £5. 6*s*. 8*d*. to a School-master.—Under the Act before mentioned, the Old School-house was taken down and the present one erected, which is kept in repair by the Inhabitants. Some land, then let at £3. 4*s*. per ann. but which brought in annually† £25. was given to the School; in lieu of £80 stock. Willoughby Legh, Esq. of Booths, appointed the Master.

† 1812.

OVER KNUTSFORD,

Sometimes called *Knutsford Booths*, formerly belonged to the Fee of Halton. Temp. Edward I. William de Tabley leased this township and Norbury Booths, to Sir John Orreby during his life. Sir John afterwards sold his title therein to John Legh, Esq. and Ellen his wife; and Wm. de Tabley afterwards released to John Legh and his heirs all his right in Knutsford Booths, and Norbury Booths, dated in March 1300. The male line of this respectable family became extinct towards the conclusion of the 16th century in the person of Peter Legh, Esq. and his daughter and heiress Ruth, brought the estates in marriage to her husband, Thos. Pennington, Esq. of Chester. Willoughby Legh, Esq. is the present proprietor.

BOOTHS, the seat of the family, is about a mile S. E. from Knutsford, and was built by Peter Legh, Esq. in 1745, John de Legh, the founder of the family, was the son of Agnes de Legh, by Sir Wm. Venables, her third husband, representative of the Bradwell branch of the Venables family. Sir John Legh, sixth in descent, was one of the intrepid partizans of Margaret of Anjou; and his successor, John Legh, married Emma, daughter and heiress of Rt. Grosvenor, Esq. of Hulme, and had on the partition of his estates, the property of Hulme, or the demesne land of Allostock.

The site of the Old Chapel of Over Knutsford, before noticed, is marked by a pillar.

BEXTON,

Is about a mile S. S. E. from Knutsford; it appears from the Survey, that Hamo de Massy held one moiety of *Olretune*, and Ranulfus, ancestor of the Mainwarings, the other. Sir Peter Leycester was in error, when he stated that it was waste at the Conquest. Temp. Hen. III. Robert de Bexton had possession of a moiety; of which he gave a fourth part to Thomas de Picmere, in marriage with Margery his daughter. In 1304, Adam de Tabley was Lord of half of Bexton, which he settled on Thomas, son of Thomas Daniell, in 1361.—The other moiety had long been divided in severalties; but they were purchased and united by John Croxton, and in the reign of Elizabeth, sold to the Cholmondeleys, who re-sold the whole to the Daniells, towards the conclusion of the 17th century. In 1726, the manor passed by will of Sir Sam. Daniell, Knt. to his great nephew, Samuel Duckenfield, Esq. of Duckenfield, whose father married Hewitt Parker, Sir Samuel's niece. It subsequently passed to John Astley, Esq. who married the widow of Sir William Duckenfield Daniell, Bart. the younger brother and heir of Samuel Duckenfield, Esq.

* There is a flag-staff on the tower, on which is displayed on proper occasions, the Imperial Flag of England.

About 1775, Bexton was purchased by the Guardians of the present Sir John Fleming Leicester, Bart. whose property it now is, and who holds a Court Baron, for the manor. The ancient hall of Bexton is now occu- as a farm house.

OLLERTON,

Or *Owlerton*, is about three miles S. E. from Nether Knutsford. At the Conquest it was divided between Hamo de Massy, and Ranulfus, ancestor of the Mainwarings. Temp. Edw. I. Sir Richard Massy, of Tatton, had obtained possession of nearly the whole of the manor, which had previously been in severalties, and was Lord of the manor.—In the reign of Hen. VI. it passed from the Massys to the Egertons, and has descended with the Tatton estates to Wilbraham Egerton, Esq. M. P. the present proprietor, who holds a Court Baron for the manor.

The description of a portion of this township, as given in Domesday, is evidently a clerical error, and is intended for Frodsham, which it follows in the order of transcription.—It is thus entered in the Survey :—

" Ipse comes tenet *Alretune*, Godric tenuit; ibi una tenæ geldabilis : Terra est dimidia caruca. Wastæ fuit et est.

" Ibi Presbyter, et Ecclesia habent unam virgatem terræ; et molinum ibi hiemale, et duæ piscariæ et dimidium : et tres acræ prati : et silvâ una leuvâ longitudine, et dimidiâ leuvâ latitudine : et ibi duæ haiæ : et in wich dimidia Salina serviens aulæ.

" Tertius denarius de placitis istius hundredi pertinebat tempore Regis Edwardi huic manerio : tunc valebat octo libras, modò quotuor libras, wasta fuit."

All this is clearly descriptive of Frodsham; and as Mr. Ormerod well observes, " the *molinum hiemale* would be supplied by a mountain torrent descending from Overton hill; the fisheries, in the broad estuaries of the Weaver and the Mersey; the wood, along that part of the line of natural forests, then stretching along this district; the deer toils on the verge of the chace of Mara, recently formed by the Earl; the salt-work, correspondent with the other salt-work reserved for Earl Edwin's other manor, at Acton; and the third penny of the hundred would be appropriately due to a manor held by Earl Edwin, before the Conquest, and constituting one of the free burgs of the Earldom after it.

TOFT,

Is not noticed in the Survey. It is about a mile and a half S. from Knutsford. At a very early period a family resided here, which assumed the local name; and held a moiety of Toft of the Halton Barony in Socage; and the other moiety from the Baron of Dunham Massy, also in Socage. The Tofts continued here till towards the conclusion of the reign of Henry VI. when they became extinct; and Robert Leycester, Esq. grandson of Joan, daughter and heiress of Robt. Toft, of Toft, obtained possession; and it still continues vested in the Leycesters, the present respectable proprietor being Ralph Leycester, Esq.

The Tofts continued here about two hundred and fifty years; and, as relative to Hugh Toft, fifth in descent, Sir Peter Leycester has the following curious passage :—

" Sir John Seyvill, Knt. brother of the Hospital of St. John of Jerusalem, and procurer of the pardon or indulgence of the Castle of St. Peter (by Virtue of this Indulgence of Pope Alex. V. granted to all those who have put their helping hand to the fortification of the said Castle, that they should chuse themselves a Confessor) now granteth to Hugh de Toft, and Alice his wife, because of their charity and aid towards the said Castle, full liberty by the Pope's authority, to chuse themselves a Confessor; whereunto the seal of the Indulgence for the said Castle as affixed : Dated *Apud Templum Bruer' Anno Domini* 1412; and on the Back of the said deed is written in Latin, which I have here put into English as followeth—' The Lord Jesus Christ, who hath given to his Disciples power of binding and loosing, absolve thee; and I by the Apostolical Authority of St. Paul, and the whole Mother Church, by the help of both which and the Pope's Indulgence, do absolve thee from all thy sins, of which by contrition thou hast confessed, or hereafter shall confess. And I grant thee full remission of all thy sins, that thou mayest have eternal life for ever. Amen.—And if it happens that thou recover not this present Infirmity, I reserve it for thee even in the very point of death.' "

Robert de Toft, son of Hugh Toft, was Constable of the Castle of Halton, with a salary of £40. per ann. which he received at Chester by the hand of William de Alcumlow, Bailiff of the Serjeantcy, from Robert

CHESHIRE HISTORY.

Paris, the King's Auditor at Chester, 23d Richard II. for the Ward and Custody of the said Castle for himself and divers Esquires and Archers, then being in the said Castle by appointment of the King's Council.*

RAFE LEYCESTER, who married Joan, daughter and heiress of Robert Toft, Esq. of Toft, died sometime between Michaelmas Day and the 12th Oct. in the 14th year† of Ric. II.—ROBERT LEYCESTER, the third in descent, was the first who was stiled *de Toft*. In the 20th year of Hen. VI. he and John Legh, of Booths, committed an assault on Dennys Holland, a servant in the employ of Geoffrey Massy, of Tatton, in the night time, and chased and destroyed the Deer in Tatton Park, for which they paid £20. each.‡ SIR RAFE LEYCESTER, seventh in descent, was knighted at Leith, on the 11th May, 1544, when the Earl of Hertford commanded the English army, and Knighted other Cheshire gentlemen. In the 5th Eliz. he was entrusted to receive certain sums of money in the way of loan, in Denbighshire; and to deliver such commands under the Privy Seal, as were sent to him.‖ SIR GEO. LEYCESTER, ninth in descent from Rafe, was Knighted in the 44th Eliz. and the following year was made Sheriff of Cheshire by patent. By a Commission dated at Amersford, May 15, 1586, he was appointed by the Earl of Leicester Capt. of 150 foot, and Hugh Starkey then servant to Sir Christopher Hatton, his Lieutenant.—RAFE LEYCESTER, his successor, died at Mobberley, in June, 1640. ANTHONY, his third son, was a warm partizan of the Royal cause; he was taken prisoner by the Parliament troops, and sent to Stafford, where he died in 1646.§—From this period to the present time, Toft has continued uninterrupted in the Leycesters, and is now the property of Ralph Leycester, Esq.

Toft Hall, the seat of the Leycesters, is a venerable building; but has recently been coated with cement. The situation is delightful, and the approach to it is through a fine avenue of flourishing elms.

* Leycester.

† Leycester says the fourth: error.

‡ "This was a great some in those days; more than £100. now. In H. 8, a man might have bought a good cow for a noble."—Marginal MS. note to Leycester.—H.

‖ The Leycesters of Toft, at this period, were possessed of considerable property in Norfolk and Northamptonshire.—See Leycester, p. 380.

§ MS. note to Leicester.—H.

THE PARISH OF LYMM,

Consists of only One Township, including the Hamlets of

BROWN EDGE
HEATLEY
OUGHTRINGTON
REDDISH
AND
STATHAM.

LYMM,

Or as it has been sometimes spelt *Limme*, is about five miles E. from Warrington.—It appears from the Survey, that Gilbert Venables, Baron of Kinderton, held a moiety of the town, formerly held by Ulviet; the other moiety was held by Osbern Fitz Tezzon.—Each of them presented to the Church, and at the present day, the patronage is alternate. In 1316, Gilbert de Lymm, released all his right in the advowson of the Church, to Thomas Legh, of Westhall, in whose descendant, Egerton Legh, it is still vested; the other moiety is in the Warburtons. The moiety of the manor held by Osbern, was in the following century given to John Lacy, the Constable, who gave it to Adam de Dutton, the ancestor of the Warburtons, who held a Court Baron.—The other moiety, held by the Lymms, descendants of the Barons of Halton, passed by settlement to Robert Domville, husband of Agnes Legh, grand-daughter to Thomas Legh. In 1539, this settlement was confirmed.—Afterwards the moiety passed

CHESHIRE

from Robert, in William Domville, and he, in 1697, bequeathed his estates to John Halstead, of Manchester, son and heir of Eleanor Halstead, his eldest sister, and to Wm. Massy, of Sale, son of Ursula, his younger sister; both of them, however, dying without issue, the Halstead share descended to Domville Halstead, who took the name of Poole; and his executors put it up to sale in parcels, when the chief portion was conveyed to James Wylde, Esq. in March, 1796, and he is the present proprietor. The other share, and a fourth of the manor, is now the property of Robt. Taylor, Esq. great grandson of Anne Taylor, sister and coheiress of Wm. Mascie before mentioned, with remainder to his brother, the Rev. Mascie Domville Taylor, now resident in Chester. No Court is held for this portion of the manor.

The scenery in the neighbourhood of Lymm is varied and picturesque; and there are several fine and beautiful falls of water, from an extensive mill dam, into a romantic vale, where they join the stream of the *Dane*.

Lymm Hall is the seat of Robert Taylor, Esq. It was the seat of the Domvilles, and is a building of considerable antiquity, partially moated, and situated on a commanding elevation. The principal entrance room affords in its bay windows some fine specimens of stained glass.—Opposite the gates, is the Ancient Cross, the lower steps of which are cut in the solid rock.

DANE BANK is the seat of James Wylde, Esq. and was formerly the residence of the Halsteads.

OUGHTRINGTON HALL, the residence of Trafford Trafford, Esq. is a handsome building, commanding a fine prospect of the adjoining country. The Lodge is after a design by Mr. Harrison, of Chester. The property was formerly possessed by the Leighs of West Hall, and descended from John Legh, Esq. to the present proprietor. In alluding to the crest of this very respectable family (on a wreath a thresher, per pale arg. and purpure, having on his head a cap quarterly, of the same, and in his hands a flail, striking a garb, or: the inscription, "*Now, thus*") Mr. Ormerod quotes "Hearnes curious discourses," edit. 1771,—"The auncyenttest armorial device I know or have read, is that of Trafords, of Traford, in Lancashire, whose crest is a labouringe man with a flayl in his hande, threshinge, and this written motto '*Now, thus,*' which they say came by this occasion: that he and other gentlemen opposing themselves against some Normans, who came to invade them, this Traford did them much hurte, and kept the passages against them; but that at length the Normans having passed the river, came sodenlye upon him, and he disguising himselfe, went into his barne, and was thresshynge when they entered, yet being known by some of them, and demanded why he so abased himself, answered '*Now, thus.*'"—Whether the legendary story has any foundation in fact, is not now to be ascertained; this crest, however, it is satisfactorily explained, was granted about 1500, by Dalton, then Norroy, King of Arms.

HISTORY.

The *Church* of Lymm, which is dedicated to the Virgin, is of considerable antiquity; and the steeple was rebuilt about 1521. It stands upon elevated ground, and consists of nave, chancel, and side aisles with a strong tower. There are two chancels, one of them belonging to the Domvilles, and the other to the patron of the moiety of the advowson.—The monuments are few. Above the Acton's seat, on a tablet—

Near this spot is interred the Rev. Egerton Leigh, archdeacon of Salop; he was forty years rector of the mediety of this parish, which he enlightened by his example, instructed by his precepts, comforted by his charity, and general benevolence, and died full of faith and hope in Christ, on the 17th Sept. 1798, in the 66th year of his age.

Over a piscina in the south wall, on a white marble tablet—

To the memory of John Legh, of Oughtrington Hall, in this parish; an active and enlightened magistrate, a warm and steady friend, an affectionate and provident parent. This monument was erected by filial love and gratitude. He died April 11, 1806, aged 76 years.

Not on this narrow spot, these mould'ring walls,
For just reward his social virtue calls:
On some bright page the books of life unfold,
His claim to high desert shall there be told.
The constant exercise of virtues giv'n,
To fit us for society in Heaven;
Religious faith, integrity unmov'd,
Calm resignation by affliction prov'd;
An ardent interest in the public weal,
In his friend's cause, a firm efficient zeal;
Each warm affection, and each watchful care,
That children from the fondest parent share;
These fix unshaken, Leigh's eternal claim,
To bliss unbounded, and immortal fame:

These stop our tears, and urge us to ascend,
And join in glory our departed friend.

Susannah, wife of John Leigh, Esq. died January 11, 1804, aged 67 years; her life was a life of piety and faith; her maternal tenderness endeared her to her children, her amiable disposition won the the hearts of her friends, her benevolent charity was the solace of the poor, her death was the death of the righteous.

The tithes of the parish are taken generally, and equally divided by the Rectors, who perform alternately Divine Service.

There is a *Free Grammar School* at Lymm. In 1698, Sir George Warburton, and Wm. Domville, Esq. of Lymm, gave waste lands in Lymm, to maintain a Master and Usher; and the Rev. John Legh, of Ollerton, gave £50. to defray the expense of enclosing the land. This land now brings in about £140. yearly, two-thirds of which are taken by the Master, and the residue by the Usher. Independent of this, the master divides about £60. per ann. being the average income for teaching writing and arithmetic. The School-house, which is of stone, is situated near the Church.

An establishment for clothing the poor, brings in nearly £40. per ann. and this is divided every New Year's Day.

The *Mill* at Lymm was some time ago used for splitting iron.

THE PARISH OF MOBBERLEY,

CONTAINS ONLY ONE TOWNSHIP.

MOBBERLEY,

At the time of the Conquest, was held by Bigot, under the Earl; it had previously formed part of the large possessions of Dot. It afterwards passed to the Aldfords of Aldford; but in the reign of Richard I. Augustine de Brethmete had half of it, which he settled on his brother Patrick during his life, and it was afterwards confirmed to John, the son and heir of Augustine, by Sir Richard Aldford, of Aldford, and Randle Blundeville, temp. King John. It thus continued settled, till Sir Raufe Mobberley, in the 34th Edward III.* having no male issue, left it to his nephew John Leycester, of Tabley, together with the advowson of the Church. Some time afterwards, a composition took place between this John Leycester, and John Dumbell, of Mobberley, and Cicily his wife, by which he released to them all the lands in Mobberley, together with the advowson of the Church, on condition, that they should settle fifteen messuages, &c. the third of a windmill, and the third of all the uninclosed wastes there, belonging to the moiety, on Raufe Leycester his younger brother, to descend to him after their death.—From this Raufe, the lands descended to the Leycesters, of Toft, in whom they are now vested, and form about one third of the moiety. Another part of the moiety, descended to the Hulses, in marriage with Margery, daughter and heiress of John Dumbell, and from them to the Troutbecks, and Talbots, Earls of Shrewsbury. The remaining third part of the moiety was granted to John Legh, of Booths, by Sir John Arderne, of Aldford, by deed dated in 1303.—This share passed by marriage with Maud, heiress of John Legh, to the Ratcliffe's, of Urdeshall, in Lancashire, and afterwards became divided.

* 1359

The *Manor House* of Mobberley, says Leycester, which at last came to the Talbots, of Grafton, in Worcestershire, "stood close by Mobberley Church, where now (1672) the house of Mallory, of Mobberly standeth: but the ancient fabric which was more spacious, and very ruinous, was not long since taken down; which old house, with the demain thereof, together with the advowson of Mobberley Mill, was bought by Andrew Carrington, of Mobberley, gent. from George Talbot, of Grafton, Esq. about the 14th Jac. Part of which demain was soon sold after by Carrington to Robert Robinson, of Mobberley, gent."

The Mobberley Moiety of the Manor has descended to Ralph Leycester, Esq. of Toft. The two-thirds share (that of Dean Mallory, Dean of Chester, temp. James I. and Charles I.) is now possessed by the Rev. J. H. Mallory, together with the advowson.—The remaining moiety formerly the property of the

Ardernes, is vested in Lawrence Wright, Esq. of Mottram Andrew. Mr. Leycester, and Mr. Wright hold Courts for their respective manerial shares.

The *Old Hall*, which has lately been rebuilt, is the residence of the Rev. J. H. Mallory. There are two other Manor-houses, but they are occupied by farmers.

The *Church*, which is dedicated to St. Wilfred, consists of nave, chancel, and side aisles, with a tower containing six bells. The Chancel is worthy of the inspection of the curious in Church architecture; it contains a rood loft, a relic closet, two stalls for the Priests, and a piscina. In the windows are remains of inscriptions nearly obliterated: one of them, "——— te p' a'i'a Hamonis Ley'———ra' ———t anno d'. m^{mo} ccc^{mo} lxxxx^{mo}."

There are memorials also of the Ardernes of Alderley, Troutbecks, Leycesters, Massys of Dunham, Mobberley, Legh of Booths, Venables, &c.—Leycester notices, that "there is engraven in the stone, under the ledge or border on the west end of the steeple, and on the south-west corner, as followeth—'*Orate pro bono statu domini Johannis Talbot, militis, et Dominæ Margaretæ uxoris suæ*,' and then beginning again just over the said border, in the very corner of the steeple, '*Patrone Ecclesie;*' and so passing along to the south side of the steeple, '*Anno Domini milesimo quingentissimo tricesimo tertio. Richard Plat, Master Mason.*' So that Mobberley steeple seems to have been built with free stone, and the Church repaired, anno 1533, 24th Henry VIII."

There are numerous monumental memorials here, to the Manleys of Alderley, Mallorys, Wrights, Orrels of Mobberley, Harrisons of Cranage, &c.

The parish tythes are vested in the Rector, the Rev. John Holdsworth Mallory, presented Sept. 21, 1795.

In 1669, a *Free Grammar School* was founded at Mobberley by the Rev. Wm. Griffiths, who endowed it with the interest of £200.

About 1206, "Patrick de Mobberley founded here a small *Priory of regular Canons of the Order of St. Augustine*, in honor of God, the Virgin Mary, and St. Wilfred, to abide and dwell for ever in the Church of Mobberley; whereunto he gave all that half of the Church of Mobberley with its appurtenances, which belonged to his grant, so as the parsons of the other half of the Church of Mobberley, which was not of his grant, might challenge no right in the said tenements; and he constituted one Walter, a canon, the first prior thereof. I suppose this Priory continued not long, the said Patrick having no further estate in Mobberley, than only for his life."*

* Leycester p. p. 316. 317.—Ormerod, 330.---Mr. Ormerod has a curious collection of Charters, &c. relative to this Priory, the last four of which are those of Sir Gilbert Barton, Knt. lord of Mobberley, at what period is not known;* by the first he confirmed to the Priory the grant of Patric; he added the tythes of the mill by the second; by the third he granted the entire demesne of Mobberley to the canons of St. Mary's priory, at Roucester; and by the fourth, he annexed the advowson of the Priory to the Priory at Roucester.

* Supposed to be between 1228 and 1240.

THE PARISH OF ROSTHERN,

CONTAINS THE TOWNSHIPS OF

ROSTHERN	MILLINGTON
HIGH LEGH	OVER TABLEY-CUM-SUDLOWE
MERE	TATTON.

Exclusive of the Chapelry of OVER PEOVER, and half the townships of AGDEN and BOLLINGTON, noticed under the head Bowdon.

ROSTHERN,

Or Rosthorne, is about three miles and a half N. of Knutsford. At the time of the Survey, it was held under the Kinderton barony, by Ulviet. Temp. Hen. II. it was possessed by a family which assumed the local name; and we find that the daughters and heirs of Homfray de Rosthorne, granted all their lands here to Robert de Manwaring. It then became divided, and a moiety passed to a younger branch of the family of Venables, who had a mansion here. In 1320, this share was conveyed by Wm. Venables to the ancestor of the Leghs of Booths, and Peter Legh, Esq. sold it to the father of Wilbraham Egerton, Esq. M. P. the present proprietor. The other moiety passed with one of the heiresses before-mentioned to the Masseys of Tatton, and has passed with the Tatton Estates to Wilbraham Egerton, Esq. M. P. who is lord of the entire manor, and holds a court for it.

A small distance from the Church is a mansion formerly the seat of a branch of the Massie family, of Coddington, lessees under Christ Church College, Oxford, under which it is new held, with the tithes, by W. Egerton, Esq.

The *Church* stands on the bank of an extensive lake, in a truly picturesque situation.—It is dedicated to St. Mary. Although no notice is taken in Domesday of the existence of a Church here, the probability is, that it was an accidental omission; for it is ascertained by a deed dated so far back as 1188 that there was a Church here before that period.* The advowson passed to the Masseys of Tatton, and from them to Sir Hugh Venables, of Kinderton, in whose family and descendants it continued vested till the close of the last century. Wilbraham Egerton, Esq. is the present lessee of this impropriate rectory. The Rector is the Rev. Shalcross Jacson, A. B. presented (on the last vacancy) the 5th July, 1809. The Registers commence in 1599.

It appears from Gastrel's Notitia, that in 1507, Sir Thomas Lovell and Edmund Dudley, Esq. on the King's behalf and by his command, conveyed to the Priory of Lawnd, Leicestershire, the Parsonage of Rostherne, which was appropriated the same year to the said Monastery, which was obliged to pay to the Bishop of Coventry and Lichfield £1. 6s. 8d. (which are now paid to the Bishop of Chester by Christ Church College) and £23. 6s 8d. to the Vicar, which is paid by the College; and the rest decreed by Chancery paid by their tenants, which decree was obtained 11th Car. I. From the Dissolution, 27th Hen. VIII. to 38th Hen. VIII. it (the impropriate rectory) remained in the King's hands, and was then given to Christ Church.

"The steeple of this Church (says Leycester) was built in stone Anno Domino 1538, 25th Hen. VIII. as appears by the figures cut in stone on the south side of the said steeple; over the figures is written, "*Orate pro anima Domini Willielmi Hardwick Vicarii hujus Ecclesiæ, et pro animabus omnivm parochianorum suorum qui hoc sculpserunt.* The Church consists of nave, side aisles, and chancels, three of them being attach- to the manors of Agden, Tatton, and Mere; another was divided between the possessors of the *East Hall* of *High Legh*, and *Over Tabley.* On a slab against the

* See deed in Leycester, p. 347, in which the name of Hugh Novant, is introduced, who was consecrated Bishop of Coventry in 1188.

north wall of the Chancel, is the recumbent figure of a Knight, in chain armour, a shield on the left side bearing two barrs, and the right hand resting on the hilt of the sword. In the Chancel is also a Tablet inscribed—

M. S. Edvardi Massey, gen. et Elizæ Bowes uxoris ejus, necnon eorum filiorum et filiarum, ut infra Rogeri Whichcote, Rich. Myddelton, M. D. F. R. S. et Mariæ uxoris, Elizabethæ, Wilfridi, Mariæ, et Petri Hall mariti, Henrici et Elizabethæ uxoris, Caroli, Helenæ. Marmor hoc Samuel Massey, M. D. natu minimus de Wisbech in Insula Eliensi, pietatis ergo posuit 1795.

There are several other insciiptions to the Massys in the same chancel.

In the Over Tabley Chancel, a mural monument, with a Latin inscription, to Samuel Daniel, of Over Tabley, who died in 1726.

In the same Chancel—

Near this place are deposited the remains of Anna Maria Legh, late wife of George Legh, of High Legh, Esq. in this parish.--. She was the sole daughter and heir of Francis Cornwall, Baron of Burford, lineally descended from Richard Plantagenet, Earl of Cornwall, King of the Romans, brother to Henry the Third, King of England. The beauties of her mind and person gave lustre to her parentage, her modest and amiable deportment gained her universal esteem. She was an excellent wife, a tender parent, and a good Christian. She died the 7th day of July, 1741, aged 30 years, leaving one son, Henry Cornwall; and two daughters, Lætitia and Anna Maria. To her beloved memory, George Legh, her late husband, has caused this monument to be erected.

In the Over Tabley division of the same Chancel, on a black and white marble monument—

Sacred to the memory of Elizabeth Brooke, wife of the late Peter Brooke, Esq. of Mere Hall, in this county, daughter and heiress of Jonas Langford, Esq. of the Island of Antigua. She died the 15th Decr. Anno Dom. 1809, aged 75 years.

A pyramidal memorial to—

Jonas Langford Brooke, Esq. died at Milan, July 19th, 1784, aged 26.

On a pyramidal monument of white marble, by Bacon, jun.

Sacred to the memory of Thomas Langford Brooke, Esq. of Mere Hall, in this county, who died Decr. 21st, 1815, in the 47th year of his age, most highly respected by all who knew him, for the integrity of his character, and the excellence of his heart. He married Maria, eldest daughter of the Rev. Sir Thomas Broughton, Bart. of Doddington Hall, in this county, by whom he had Maria Elizabeth, married to Meyrick Bankes, of Winstanley Hall, in the county of Lancaster; Jemima, Peter Langford, Thomas Langford, John Langford who died young, William Henry Langford, Charles Spencer Langford who died young, and Jonas Langford.

There are many other memorials of the Brooke family.

There is a very fine Monument in the Tatton Chancel, which occupies nearly the whole of the west end. Beneath a sarcophagus, is a tablet supported by the figures of Hope and Patience; the whole executed by Bacon, of the Royal Academy. It is inscribed—

To the memory of Samuel Egerton, Esq. of Tatton Park, whose remains were deposited in the family burying place under this Chapel, on February 19, 1780, according to his special direction under his last will.—Be it also recorded, that in the same sacred vault rest the several bodies of his father, John Egerton, eldest son of the Hon. Thos. Egerton, by Hester, daughter of Sir John Busby of Addington, Bucks; and which Thomas was third son of John Earl of Bridgewater, by Lady Elizabeth Cavendish, (second daughter of William, Marquis, afterwards Duke of Newcastle.) He was buried the 11th of August, 1724. Also of his mother Elizabeth, daughter of Samuel Barbour, Esq. by Elizabeth, daughter of Rowland Hill, Esq. of Hawkstone, in the County of Salop, who was buried Feb. the 10th, 1743. Also of his grandmother Elizabeth Barbour, wife of Samuel Barbour, Esq. who was buried April the 17th, 1745. And also of his dear wife Beatrix, youngest of the three daughters and co-heirs of the Rev. John Copley, of Battey, in the County of York; who was buried the 1st of May, 1755. And also, that in the parish Church of Shenstone, in the county of Stafford, were deposited the remains of his uncle, Samuel Hill, Esq. of Shenstone Hall, who was buried Feb. the 26th, 1758, from whom as heir at law by his Mother he inherited considerable property in the county of Lancaster. The above-mentioned Samuel Egerton, Esq. was without opposition chosen to serve as one of the Knights of the Shire for the County of Chester, the first Session of the fifth Parliament of George the IId. May the 31st, 1754. He was at every subsequent election returned, till the time of his death. Having served the county near twenty-six years. He was born the 28th Dec. 1711. and died the 10th of Feb. 1780.

On the plinth—

How they demean themselves each in their mortal state of probation, is truly known to Him only from whom no secrets are hidden, but will one day be declared in the presence of the Host of Heaven.

On a tablet—

Sacred to the memory of Elizabeth Egerton, youngest daughter of John Egerton, of Tatton Park; she died the 23d day of October, 1765, aged 48. Her remains rest in the vault beneath. This tablet is gratefully inscribed by her niece Elizabeth, wife to Sir Christopher Sykes, Bart. of Sledmore House, East Riding, Yorkshire.

On a pyramidal monument, against the south wall—

John, y[e] son of John Egerton, of Tatton, Esq. born Oct. 14, 1710, died Oct. 4th, 1738. Esteemed by all who knew him well, for he was cheerful, humane, and open-hearted, steady in principles, sincere in religion; faithful to his friend, and true to his country; the kindest husband, and the fondest father. He married Christain, youngest daughter of John Ward, of Capesthorne, Esq. who erected this monument to her husband's memory. He left two daughters, Elizabeth, and Christian.

Above this is an Infant bearing a profile of the deceased.—On a tablet beneath—

Here lies Christian Egerton, wife of John Egerton, Esq. died Dec. 22d, 1777, aged 68; she was an affectionate wife, a tender mother, sincere in religion, charitable to the poor; in life beloved, in death lamented.

On a mural tablet in the *Agden Chancel*—

In memory of Robert Venables, son of John Venables, of Agden, Esq. by Brizena, his second wife, daughter of Sir Peter Leycester, of Nether Tabley, Bart.—He married Elizabeth, the eldest daughter of John Wedgwood, of Harracles, Esq. in the county of Stafford, by whom he had no issue, and died at Mere in this parish, the eighth day of July, A. D. 1757.

There are a variety of other memorials to the Leghs, Masseys, &c.

The present Rector is the Rev. Shalcross Jacson, A. B. presented July 5, 1809. The Registers commence in 1599.

Near the Church is a *School*, founded originally by W. Hough, who endowed it with £10 The School was formerly held in the lower part of the steeple, and the parishioners appoint the Master.

In this Township is BUCKLOW HILL, which gives name to the Hundred.

HIGH LEGH,

At the Conquest, was held by Gilbert de Venables, under Lupus; it is situated about five miles N. W. N. from Knutsford. So early as the reign of Edw. I. the township was divided between two families which had assumed the local name: Hugh de Legh possessed the *East Hall*, together with a moiety of High Legh; and his successors continued here till the reign of Hen. VII. when a long litigation commenced between the daughters and co-heirs of the then proprietor, and Thomas Legh, of Northwood, who claimed as next heir male, in virtue of an entail, and the moiety was awarded in his favor; and has continued to his lineal descendant George John Legh, Esq.

In the time of Elizabeth, Thomas, grandson of Thomas Legh, of Northwood, erected a large stone mansion here,* with a domestic chapel. The house, which was finished with gables, had projecting bay windows.

Over the entrance, was a large turret four stories high, embattled with two spires rising from the summit. It was taken down towards the conclusion of the last century, when the present house was built on its site. The East hall Chapel still exists, on the west side of the Hall; it is of stone 48 feet long by about 27 in width. It is fitted up with strong oak benches, and the whole exterior has a truly venerable appearance.—In the east window are two figures, male and female, the former bearing the coat of Legh, the latter of Trafford—and underneath is (incorrectly) inscribed:—

" ——— tatu Thome Leigh, armingari, dominus de Leigh, et ——— bella uxor e—— filie et herede Georgi Trafford de la Garet, qui is— Capellam foundaverunt Anno Dom. 1581."

The other moiety of High Legh, was possessed by Thomas de Legh, ancestor to the Leghs, of *West Hall*; but one half of this moiety was afterwards perchased by Sir Richard Massy, of Tatton, in the reign of Edw. I. About 1286, Roger de Montealto, seneschallus Cestriæ, confirmed to Sir Richard Massy all the lands and tenements, *cùm boscis et wastis*, which he had of the grant of Raufe, son of William de Hawarden, in the Township of Legh. This was witnessed by Robt. Grosvenor, then Sheriff of Cheshire. This portion has descended with Tatton, to Wilbraham Egerton, Esq. M. P. The other moiety of the half is vested in Egerton Leigh, Esq. of *West Hall*, which is now occupied as a farmhouse. It was a fine specimen of ancient domestic architecture, and formerly of considerable extent. The building, however, is now mixed with modern work.

The *West Hall Chapel* is a short distance north of the Hall, and was lately re-erected, from designs by Mr. Harrison, the county architect. It is 51 feet long by 42 in width, and with the exception of the front, is of red stone. The front faces the road; and consists of a pediment, supported by four Iönic pillars. On a tablet above the entrance is inscribed:—

Deo. opt. max.
Hoc ipso situ ædiculam
Jam vetustate sublapsam,
Posuit Proavorum Pietas,
A. D. 1408.
Hoc Sacellum, pace reduci,
Restituendum curavit
Egertonus Leigh,
A. D. 1814.

* Engraved in the Views by Watts.

This Chapel was consecrated by the present Bishop of Chester, Oct. 31, 1816. It had a small endowment from Egerton Leigh, Esq. and was subsequently increased by Queen Anne's Bounty, to the amount of £1,800.

*** Mr. Ormerod introduces in a note, the following families, extinct and existing, as descendants of the West Hall family; Leigh (now Trafford) of Oughtrington; Leigh, of Brownsover, co. Warwick, (Bart.) Legh, of Booths; of Adlington, of Baguley, of Annesley, co. Nottingham; of Egginton, co. Derby; Legh, of Lyme; of Birch, co. Lancaster; and Ridge: Leigh, of Rushall, co. Stafford; of Longborow, and of Adlestrop, co. Gloucester; of Stoneley, co. Warwick, (Baron Leigh); of Newnham Regis, co. Warwick (Earl of Chichester); of Stockwell, co. Surrey, of Isall, co. Cumberland; Legh, of Betchton; Legh (now Townley) of Townley, co. Lanc.; and Legh, of Middleton, co. York.

SWINEYARD—a hamlet of High Legh, was the residence of a junior branch of the Leghs, of East Hall; it is now the property of G. J. Legh, Esq. but is occupied as a farm-house.

NORTHWOOD, another hamlet, was the seat of the Leghs, of East Hall, previous to succeeding to the estates of the elder branch. It is the property of Trafford Trafford, Esq. (late Trafford Legh) of Oughtrington, and is occupied as a farm-house.

SWINTON—another hamlet, originally belonged to the West Hall family, the branch settling here, assuming the local name; it is now divided between the East and West Hall estates.

MERE,

After the Conquest, was held by Gilbert de Venables, Baron of Kinderton, It subsequently became the property of a family which assumed the local name;* and they continued here till 1652, when it was sold to Peter Brooke, Esq. ancestor of Peter Langford Brooke, Esq. the present proprietor,† who holds a Court Baron for the Manor.

Mere is about three miles N. W. from Knutsford, and, says Leycester, "undoubtedly took its name from the Mere therein."

The *Hall* was built towards the middle of the 17th century; but it has been much improved by the late proprietor. It is chiefly of brick, and is a large and handsome building, surrounded by fine woods.

The Cocker family resided for several generations at the Strethill farm, in this township; previous to the year 1666, however, it was purchased by Henry Legh, of the East Hall.

The annual sum of £3. was left by one William Grantham, for educating fifteen poor children of the township.

MILLINGTON,

Is nearly four miles W. N. W. from Knutsford.—At the Conquest it was held by William Fitz Nigell.—John the Constable of Cheshire, temp. Hen. II. gave to Wrono of Stretton, half of Millington, namely that which he had in his demesne, rendering yearly a little Irish Nag, called *a hobby*, at Midsummer. It would appear,‡ that one half of Millington was held of the Baron of Halton, by the eighth part of a Knight's fee, and the other half of the same, in socage, paying annually two shillings. "Possibly (observes Leycester) the yearly rent in tract of time, might be continued in lieu of the Irish hobby aforesaid."

From the Millingtons, the manor passed to the Hayfords; on the death of whose representative, Jane Thorold, in 1796, it passed to Sir John Thorold, who died in 1815; and from his children by Dame Jane Thorold, his wife, the estate was purchased by the present proprietor Wilbraham Egerton, Esq. M. P. who holds a Court Baron for it.

OVER TABLEY,

Is about two miles W. N. from Knutsford, and at the Conquest was held under the Halton Barony; but it was soon afterwards divided in three parts. In the reign of Hen. II. Roger de Mainwaring gave a third part to the Monastery of St. Werburgh, at Chester; this part afterwards passed to William de Tabley, and he gave it to Sir John Grey, son of Sir Reginald Grey, who granted it to Roger Leycester, of Nether Tabley, in 1296, and it is now vested in Sir John F. Leicester, his successor. A second part, in the time of Edw. III.

* Leycester says, "whether originally a Venables, I cannot positively affirm."

† "Youngest son of Thomas Brooke, of Norton, Esq."—Peter Brooke, the purchaser, was Knighted in 1660, and was Sheriff of Cheshire in 1669.

‡ Leycester, p. 315.

CHESHIRE HISTORY.

was possessed by Adam Tabley,* under Sir William Boydell, chief lord. It afterwards passed to Thomas Daniell, of Bradley, in Appleton. On the death of Sir Samuel Daniell, last male heir, in 1726, the estate passed to Sir Wm. Duckenfield, Bart. who afterwards added to his name that of Daniell. About 1780, a moiety of this estate was purchased from John Astley, Esq. (who married Lady Daniell) by Peter Brooke, Esq. in trust for his son Thomas Langford Brooke, Esq. of Mere; the other moiety was purchased by the guardians of Sir J. F. Leicester, Bart. the present proprietor.—The other third part of the moiety was possessed by another family of the Tableys, of a place called the Hall of the Wood, in Over Tabley; but Matthew de Tabley being attainted of felony in 1483, his lands were seized by the Crown. Leycester says, "I find John Leycester, of Nether Tabley, Esq. excepting against the lands being held under the Halton Barony, 1, Henry VII. and complaining to the Judges at Chester, that these lands were held of him by homage and fealty, and twelve pence yearly rent;† and praying that he may be restored to these lands, as Chief Lord of the Fee. But he had too potent a person to deal with: and King Henry VII. granted the lands to Sir William Stanley, of Holt Castle, Lord Chamberlain; but he being beheaded for treason in 1495, the lands again escheated to the King; and Henry VIII. leased them to Randle Brereton for his life, whose son Roger Brereton also had them for his life. These lands afterwards continuing in the King's hands, Robt. and Roger Chornock, of London, purchased them, and sold them to Piers Leycester, of Nether Tabley, Esq. for £240. of which a moiety was paid in hand, and a bond given for the residue; but Peter Tabley, of Over Tabley, Esq. purchasing their lands at £9. per ann. in the King's Books, the Chornocks purchased them at the rate of 18*d.* in the King's Books, and cheated the said Piers Leycester, by a fraudulent conveyance, so that he could not enjoy these lands; and it was agreed in the Court of Requests, in 1559, that the Chornocks should restore the money which they had received, and deliver up the bond obligatory to be cancelled; and so Daniell had the lands which his posterity now enjoyeth, 1666."‡

The manor of Over Tabley is now divided in moieties belonging to the Leicesters of Tabley, and the Brookes of Mere, who hold Courts Baron for them. The Leicester share is claimed as a portion of their ancient estate in the township; the Brooke share was purchased by them from John Astley, Esq. in 1780, as before noticed.

There was formerly a Chapel of Ease here, adjoining the highway, built in the reign of Henry VI.

SUDLOWE, a hamlet of the township, formerly belonged to the Leghs, of Booths, but is now possessed by Sir J. F. Leicester, Bart.

A large mansion of brick was built here by Mr. Astley, but a great portion of it has been taken down, and the remainder is occupied as a farm house.

TATTON,

Is about two miles N. from Knutsford. At the Conquest, half of it was held under the Barons of Halton, and the other half was held by Ranulfus, the supposed ancestor of the Mainwarings. In the beginning of the 12th Century, Alanus de Tatton was possessed of the manor, who stiled himself Dominus de Tatton.—About 1286, William grandson of Quenild de Tatton, granted a great part of the township to Sir Richard Massy, and Isabel, his wife, which was confirmed by Peter Hackham, Prior of the Hospital of St. John of Jerusalem in England. It appears, that in the reign of Edw. I. one moiety of Tatton was held of the Barons of Dunham Massy, and the other of the Prior of St. John of Jerusalem; the latter Leycester supposes, was the half which, in the Conqueror's time, belonged to the Halton Barony. In the reign of Henry III. Alan de Tatton, had the royalty of all Tatton, the lands in which called *Bruchel*, he granted to William, the son of William Massy, whether, however, he had any more than a moiety *of the town*, is not to be ascertained, for it is clear that William, grandson of Quenild de Tatton, had no small share. So early as the reign of Edward I. Sir Richard Massy was the proprietor of all the manor,

* "This Adam de Tabley I conceive was a Massy, for he sealed with Massy's coat of arms."—LEYCESTER.

† "This 12d. rent is at this day paid to Leycester by Thomas Warburton, of Tabley Hall; which tenement is parcel of the Hall of Woodlands."—LEYCESTER.

‡ In a MS. note on Leycester is added, "Sir P. Egerton, his pretended estate for the waste in Poole, no better if looked into."—H.

or nearly so; and it continued in his descendants till the death of Sir Geoffrey Massy, who was living in 1475. Joan, the daughter and heiress of Sir Geoffrey Massy, married Wm. Stanley, son and heir of Sir Wm. Stanley, of Holt Castle, and had issue a daughter, (and also heiress) likewise named Joan.*—Sir Wm. Stanley was Lord Chamberlain to Hen VII. and brother to Thomas Stanley, first Earl of Derby of that family;† he was beheaded in 1495, for his adherence to the impostor Perken Warbeck, and his lands and goods were confiscated to the King. He had in ready money and plate, in the Castle of Holt, 40,000 marks, exclusive of jewels, furniture, cattle, &c. His lands let at £3000. per ann. old rent, an immense income in those days; and he aspired to the Earldom of Chester, but his ambition was checked by a refusal, and distaste of the Monarch.‡—Joan, daughter and heir of William Stanley, by Joan Massy, his wife, had two husbands; first, John Ashton, son and heir of Sir Thomas Ashton, of Ashton-super-Mersey;|| he died in 1513, without issue: secondly, Sir Richard Brereton, son of Sir Randle Brereton, of Malpas; by whom she had issue Richard Brereton, (who died without issue) and Geoffrey Brereton, their heir. Anne Brereton, a daughter, married John Booth, of Barton, in Lancashire, in 1540. Sir Richard died at Islington, in 1557. Geoffrey Brereton, married Alice, daughter of Piers Leycester, of Nether Tabley; and Rd. Brereton, their son and heir, who died issueless, in 1598, left all his estate to Sir Thos. Egerton, Lord Chancellor of England; and from the Earls of Bridgewater, the property has descended with the other estates, to the present proprietor, Wilbraham Egerton, Esq. M. P.

The Park of Tatton is upwards of ten miles in circumference, containing about 2000 acres of land, part in tillage, and adjoins Knutsford on the north side.—The house is in a pleasant situation, built of white stone, and the front entrance is under a noble stone portico, supported by four immense Corinthian pillars, from the quarry at Runcorn. The whole is from designs by Messrs. Samuel and Lewis Wyatt. The interior of the house is splendidly fitted up; and the library contains a valuable collection of books, many of rare occurrence. On the whole, it is one of the most superb structures in this or any other county.—In the park is a noble Lake; there was another fine sheet of water near the house, but the locality of its situation rendered it necessary to have it drained.

With respect to the descent of the Egertons, it may not be improper here to say, in addition, that Thomas Egerton, afterwards Vicount Brackley, who became possessed of Tatton, was the natural son of Sir Richard Egerton, of Ridley, brother in law of Richard Brereton, of Tatton, by Alice, the daughter of a respectable yeoman, of Bickerton, named Sparke. Tatton was vested in this branch of the Egertons, till 1780, when Samuel Egerton, Esq. M. P. left Tatton, and his other Estates to his sister, then wife of William Tatton, Esq. of Withenshaw, from whom it has descended, to his grandson, Wilbraham Egerton, Esq. whose father assumed the name of Egerton.

NORSHAGH, a hamlet of Tatton, has passed with the Manor, for which a Court Baron is held.

* Johanna in Latin.—In 32d Elizabeth, Joan, Johanna, and Jane, were agreed, in the Court of Queen's Bench, to be all one name.—See Leycester, p. 371.

† "He had another brother, Sir John Stanley, Lord of Alderley, in right of Elizabeth, daughter of Thomas Wener, sen.r and heir of Sir Edw.d Wener, Knt. in ye first of Hen. 6th, ut paten. chartulis penes Robtu Wener, 1688."—From a MS. note to Leycester.—H.

‡ He had by Joyce his wife, daughter of Edmund Lord Powis, and widow of John Tiptoft, William Stanley above mentioned; and Jane, who married Sir John Warburton, of Arley, one of the Knights of the Body of Hen. VII.

|| She was then only eight years old.

THE PARISH OF RUNCORN,

HISTORY.

CONTAINS THE TOWNSHIPS OF

RUNCORN, SUPERIOR	KECKWICK
RUNCORN, INFERIOR	MOORE
CLIFTON	NEWTON-JUXTA-DARESBURY
WESTON	PRESTON-ON-THE-HILL
ASTON	THELWALL
ASTON GRANGE	OVER WALTON
SUTTON	NETHER WALTON
DARESBURY	HALTON
ACTON GRANGE	NORTON
HATTON	STOCKHAM.

Of these, three are in the Chapelry of Aston, ten in the Chapelry of Daresbury, and three in Halton; two in Runcorn,—and Clifton and Weston.

RUNCORN

SUPERIOR AND INFERIOR.

These townships, formerly called *Romicofan*,* are not noticed in Domesday, but there is no doubt of the lands being attached to the Halton Barony. It was here, observes Leycester, that magnanimous Virago, Elflede, countess of Mercia, widow of Ethelred, the Chief Governor, and sister to Edward the Elder, built a Town and Castle in 916.† Probably it was then in a more flourishing condition than it now is, for it is a very poor village (1668).—These Townships were formerly copyhold land to the Manor of Halton, until the land-holders bought out their lands in fee farm, to hold in free and common socage of the manor of Enfield, in Middlesex, the grant dated 4th Charles I. The Duttons, of Dutton, had for a long period freehold lands here, which were afterwards sold to Savage, of Rocksavage, with which estate they have descended. In 1133, William Fitz Nigel founded here a Monastery of Canons regular, whose son William subsequently removed them to Norton, about the time of King Stephen.

The Marquis of Cholmondeley, as Lessee of Halton Fee, holds a Court Leet and Baron for Runcorn, as an appendage of the Fee.

Runcorn, within the last few years, has increased in size and population, in an extraordinary manner; and the salubrity of its situation for sea-bathing, renders it the resort of numerous invalids. The Duke of Bridgewater's Canal‡ passes through the village; and there is a daily communication with Liverpool, by means of Steam Packets.—Great quantities of stone are cut here, and forwarded by the Canals to all parts of the country, and particularly to Liverpool, the facings of the immense docks there being furnished from the Runcorn quarries. The great connexion which Runcorn forms between the coasting and inland trade,|| gives to it all the bustle of a considerable port, and a Supervisor is now established here, for whom a suitable office, or Custom House, has recently been built on the wharf.§—

* Higden.

† See Florentius, Huntington, Stow, &c.

‡ The Duke built a house at Runcorn for his occasional residence.

|| The Canal at Runcorn is 60 feet above the level of the river; and the fall is by ten locks, contrived by the celebrated Mr. Brindley. See page 86.

§ The privilege of clearing out certain commodities from hence, without touching at the great port of Liverpool, has recently been granted by the Commissioners of Customs.

CHESHIRE

The Mersey, near the Church, is not above a quarter of a mile in width, and this situation, called *The Gap*, has been thought a desirable one for a Bridge; but whether it will ever be erected is very doubtful, although numerous Meetings on the subject have been held, and approaches to it have actually been commenced. At this point the River is fordable, and a ferry has, from time immemorial, been established here.* In 1190, the ferry (then called *navis de Widnesse)* was supported at the voluntary charge of certain individuals resident in Runcorn.†

The *Church* is of great antiquity, certainly existing before the Conquest, "for we read in the ancient roll, that Nigell Baron of Halton, gave the Church of Runcorn, to Wolfaith, a Priest, his brother, in the reign of the Conqueror."‡ It is in a most romantic situation, on a rock overhanging the River, surrounded by trees. It is "called an ancient parish Church, Allhallows of Nether Runcorn, dedicated to All Saints.‖ The patronage is vested in Christ Church College, Oxford, to whom it was given by Henry VIII. The building consists of nave, chancel, and side aisles, The pillars in the south aisle have been removed, to make room for a gallery; but those in the north aisle are clustered, with rich capitals, from which spring four pointed arches.—The nave and chancel are separated by a screen, ornamented with carved work, above which is a rood loft §.

HISTORY

There are an immense number of Monumental Memorials; the church yard is much crowded with them; but very few are worthy of notice. In the Chancel are several monuments of the Brookes, of Norton, the Lessees of the Rectory.

On a pyramidal monument within the rails of the Altar, executed by Bacon, is a fine female figure, placing a wreath on an urn, on which appears a medallion with a profile: the inscription—

In Memory of Sir Richard Brooke, Bart. of Norton Priory, who died March 6th, 1795, in the 42d year of his age; every action of his life displayed such a benevolent disposition and goodness of heart, that his death was universally lamented, but most of all by his relict Mary, daughter of Sir Robt. Cunliffe, Bart. of Saighton, in this county, who erected this monument, as a memorial of his worth, and of her affection.

On a large monument on the north side, ornamented with the arms of Brooke impaling Wilbraham,—

M. M. S. Domini Thomæ Brooke de Norton, baronetti, et dominæ charissimæ uxoris ejus per quadraginta ac novem annos sese mutuo peramantium. Ille vitam probe institutam placide reddidit sexto id. Julii MDCCXXXVII, ætat. LXXIII. Illa partibus suis rite peractis leniter obdormivit quarto hon. Decemb. MDCCXXXIX, ætat LXXXII.—Horum honoratos juxta cineres suos requiescere voluit Thomas Brooke, A. M. Ecclesiæ parochialis de Walton, in agro Lancastriensi vicarius, mortuos parentes indies dum vixit valde desideravit, indies tacite deflevit, filius, et quos huc ad avitum sepulchrum vix ægre comitatus est vivus, propensior dememum secutus est moriens. Decimo sexto Kal. Septemb.

* A Charter relative to this ferry, temp. Hen. I. is given by Mr. Ormerod.

† With respect to the Bridge, &c. the design was proposed by Mr. Telford, at a Meeting held for the purpose at Liverpool, in March, 1817. That gentleman observes in his "Report," that the only eligible way is by means of suspension, over so great a breadth. "It is well known that Chain Bridges have long been employed with success over very considerable openings. Major Rennell mentions one nearly six hundred feet in length over the Sampoo River, in Hindoostan; and in a treatise on Bridges lately published in America, eight Chain Bridges are described, more especially one of two hundred and forty-four feet between the abutments upon the Merimack, over which it is said, horses and carriages pass freely at any speed, without any perceptible motion of the floors." Mr. Telford therefore recommended a bridge on the suspension principle, as the only one applicable to the situation and breadth (2000 feet). He states his full conviction of the practicability of the measure, without interruption or injury to any of the neighboring River or Canal navigations, and estimates the total expense, on a liberal calculation, at £84,990, to be completed in three years, or in less time, viz.:—

Masonry, in Pyramids, (on two of which the centre opening of 1000 feet will rest) Abutments, Retaining Walls, and Parapets, including Iron and Timber, in Curbings and Ties connected therewith	£23,598
Malleable and Cast Iron work, and Painting	37,576
Roadway over the Bridge	15,000
Earth-work in Approaches	1,000
Contingencies...	7,717

Nothing further has yet* been done with respect to this grand scheme; a Bridge, however, on the same principle, projected by the same skilful engineer, is now erecting over the straits of the Menai, upon the success of which (and there is no doubt of it) may probably hinge the eventual commencement of the Bridge over the Mersey at Runcorn.

* Nov. 22, 1819.

‡ Leycester, p. 351.

‖ Ibid.—In a MS. note—" but since the printinge of this booke, I find it called the Church of Saint Bartholomew, at Runcorne. In the booke of the evidences of Sir Willoughby Aston, of Aston, page 15, num. 136."—H.

§ There are a few specimens of painted glass in the Church windows.

Anno { humanæ salutis MDCCLVII
æt. LXIV.
sacerdotii initi XXXVII.

Stop here awhile, and with attention read,
This the short lesson of a teacher dead.
My frailties, for I own I had my share,
Call on thee loudly, reader, to beware.
My virtues (if I haply any shew'd)
Point out to peace and bliss the only road.

Vale et fruere.

On a white marble pyramidal monument by Bacon, arms impaling Brooke and Patten; with a cherub drawing away the drapery and disclosing the inscription—

In memory of Sir Richard Brooke, Bart. of Norton Priory, in this county, who died on the 6th July, 1781, aged 65 years; and of Frances, his wife, daughter of Thos. Patten, Esq. of Bank, in the county of Lancaster, who died April 12th 1778, aged 47 years.

In the north-east angle of the north aisle, a pyramidal monument of grey marble—

In memory of Sir John Chesshyre,* who departed this life, on the XV of May, MDCCXXXVIII.

A wit's a feather, and a chief's a rod—
An honest man's the noblest work of God.

On a similar monument—

Near this place lieth the body of Arthur Rawdon, Esq. late of Hallwood, in this county, who died June the VIth MDCCLXVI, in the XLIIId year of his age. Out of respect to his memory, this monument is erected by his widow, Arabella Rawdon, who died XXIVth Dec. MDCCCVI, aged LXXXIII. Here also lieth the body of Sarah Chesshyre, widow of William Chesshyre, late of Hallwood, Esq. who died Dec. XIX, MDCCLXXVII, aged LXXVII.

On a marble mural monument, adjoining the chancel screen—

Hic situs est N. Alcock, fil. D. A. ex bona uxore sua M. Breek. In Academ. Oxon. et Lugdun. Batav. M. D. Coll. Med. Lond. et R. S. Socius. necnon apud Oxonienses in Chymia et Anatomia per multos annos celeberrimus Prælector; vitam iniit XXVII, finivit VIII Dec. MDCCLXXIX. Fratres superstites M. Alcock et Thos. Alcock. A. M. hujus ecclesiæ vicarius hoc marmor posuerunt in memoriam doctissimum et dignissimi viri.

Thomas Alcock, A. M. pacis justiciarius, hujus ecclesiæ vicarius natus est VIII° Octb. MDCCIX, mortuus XXIV° Aug. MDCCXCVIII.—Spe resurrectionis ad vitam eternam.

In the middle of the Church, on a brass plate—

Here lieth interred the body of John King, clerk, who died the 28th day of February, anno D~ni 1635. He gave towards the mantayninge of a Preacher in the chappel of Halton £5. yearly for ever, out of his land. To the poore and schoole of Halton £VI. yearly for ever. VIIIs. yearly for ever to the mending of the ways in Halton. And Ursula his wife hathe given £30. for a stock to the poore whomen in Halton.

In the Church-yard, on an upright stone—

Mrs. Janet Morrison, daughter of William Morrison, Esquire, of Greenock, in North Britain, died at Runcorn, on the 6th day of Feb. 1801, in the 31st year of her age. This stone is erected by Æneas Morrison, the husband of Mrs. Janet Morrison, to designate the spot where her remains are deposited, that her infant children, when they shall have attained a more mature age, may approach it with reverential awe, and pledge their vows to Heaven to respect her memory, by imitating her virtues.

Near the south wall of the Church-yard—

Underneath this stone, lie the remains of Robt. Chesshyre, of Rock Savage; he departed this life Sept. 9th, 1802, aged 27 years.

'Tis mine to-day to moulder in the tomb,
To-morrow may thy awful summons come.
Wake, thou that sleepest, then—awake, or know,
Thy dream will terminate in endless woe;
Wake, and contend for Heaven's immortal prize,
And give to God each moment as it flies;
Secure then mayst thou recollect the past,
And with a sacred triumph meet thy last.

The Registers commence in 1661. The present Rector is the Rev. Frederick Master, presented June 1, 1816.

Botanists may find on the shore, between Runcorn and Weston Point, a variety of rare plants.†

The *Castle*, as is before noticed, was situated on what is called the *Castle Rock*, but from the extent of it, as collected from the site, it does not appear to have been of great extent,—indeed, merely as a post, commanding the Ferry, and navigation of this part of the Mersey.—It was, however, strongly fortified, and was surrounded on the land side by a ditch, emptying itself, and communicating with the River, on the north side.

CLIFTON,

Is about two miles N. N. E. from Frodsham; but it is now generally called *Rock Savage*, which name it took from the splendid mansion erected here by Sir John Savage, in 1565, and who then abandoned the old seat of Clifton Hall, which then assumed the name of the *Old Hall*. But few remains, however, of Rock Savage now exist; but a reference to the annexed engraving, will afford a correct idea of this once magnificent house.

In the time of Henry II. John Lacy, Constable of

* Prime Serjeant to Queen Anne and George I.

† Greswell's account of Runcorn.

Engraved by J. Fort Manch

ROCK SAVAGE.

Engraved for Hanshall's History of Cheshire

Chester, and Baron of Halton, gave the manor to Galfred, or Geoffry de Dutton, whose posterity afterwards assumed the name of Cheadle, from their residence there. In 1327, the two daughters and coheiresses of Sir Roger de Cheadle, divided the inheritance, when Clemence, the eldest daughter, who married William, the son of Raufe Baggiley, had for her share Clifton and lands in Cheadle and Hulme. Agnes, the other daughter, married Richard the son of Robert de Buckley, and had the capital messuage of *Chedill*, with the advowson of the Church of Chedill, and other rents and services. Isabel, who was daughter and heiress of Clemence, married Thomas Daniell the younger, of Bradley in Appleton, who was afterwards knighted, by whom he had an only daughter and heiress, Margaret, who, temp. Edw. III. brought the estate in marriage to John Savage, who was the founder of the Savages of Rock Savage—a family of great note, and some celebrity. Sir John Savage, fifth in descent, had the charge of the left wing at the decisive battle of Bosworth, in 1485; and was particularly instrumental in promoting the accession of Henry VII. In 1484, Sir John and eight of his brothers, were presented with the freedom of Chester, in which year he was Mayor. He was eventually slain at the battle of Boulogne, in France, in 1492.—Leycester says, "he was a valiant man, and an expert soldier, and made Knight of the Garter by Henry VII. He had a bastard son, called George Savage, parson of Davenham, who had several bastards, to wit, George Savage, Priest, Chancellor of Chester; John Wilmslow, Archdeacon of Middlesex, begot on one Wilmslow's daughter; Elizabeth, married —— Clayton, of Thelwall: she was begot also on Wilmslow's daughter; Randle Savage, of the Lodge, begotten on the daughter of one Dyes, of Barrow; Margaret, married —— Colstensoke, of Over Whitley, who was begot also on Dyes' daughter; Ellen married —— Hayes, of Letley, in Aston juxta Pickmere; she was also begot on Dyes' daughter; Edmund Bonner, first Dean of Leicester, and after twice Bishop of London, begotten on Elizabeth Frodsham, first married to one Edmund Bonner, a sawyer, with Mr. Warmingham, who begot other children on her afterwards, and dwelt at Potter's Handley, county of Worcester. Sir John Savage, 7th in descent, killed one John Pauncefote, Esq. for which he and his father were indicted for murder, and arraigned in the King's Bench; the younger Savage as principal, the elder as accessary, who confessed the facts: on the mediation, of Cardinal Wolsey, and Charles Earl of Worcester, then Chamberlain to the King, * they were pardoned, on paying a fine of 4000 marks, and undertaking not to come into the counties of Worcester and Chester, during their lives, without the King's license, which the younger Sir John Savage afterwards obtained, in 1524. Sir John Savage, eighth in descent, built the magnificent mansion at Rock Savage, in 1565, and first called himself of Rock Savage, in distinction from Clifton, in 1575. He was seven times Sheriff of Cheshire, and three times Mayor of Chseter, dying in his mayoralty in 1597, aged 73. The tenth in descent, Sir Thomas Savage, was created a Viscount by Charles I. in 1626. John, Lord Savage, eleventh in descent, was created Earl Rivers in 1639. He died at his house in Frodsham, "commonly called Frodsham Castle," on the 10th Oct. 1654, and that very night was the same house by accident of fire burned. Richard, the twelfth in descent, dying without issue male, the title reverted to John Savage, his cousin, a Priest of the Church of Rome, but he died without assuming the title."—It appears from a settlement made by Earl Richard, that this John Savage had a life interest in the Rivers estates, which, on his death, descended to Lady Penelope Barry, daughter of Elizabeth Countess of Barrymore, who was daughter of Earl Richard. Lady Penelope Barry married James, second surviving son of George Earl of Cholmondeley, and died without issue in 1786; when the estates descended to her husband's great nephew, the present proprietor, George James, then Earl, but now Marquis of Cholmondeley, and Earl of Rock Savage.†

The remains of Clifton Hall, says Webb, "stand a

* Sir John, the younger, married first, Elizabeth, daughter of the Earl.

† Rock Savage continued in repair till it fell to the Cholmondeleys, when it was much neglected, and went into decay: and Mr. Pennant notices a gentleman, born in the house, who lived to drive a pack of fox hounds through it! In 1640, it was thus described: "We next beheld the magnificent fabric of Rock Savage, overlooking the waters and goodly marshes round about the skirts of it, and

CHESHIRE

little distance from Rock Savage, in the Park, like an aged matron, well contented to go to her grave, having seen in her life time her daughter advanced to such an height of honourable dignity."

WESTON,

Is about two miles N. N. W. from Frodsham. It was originally held under the Earl by the Baron of Halton, and under him by Odard and Brictric.—Odard was the ancestor of the Duttons, and it continued in their family from the conquest, till it passed in marriage with the other estates to the Gerards, of Gerard's Bromley, by whom, and their successors, the Fleetwoods, it was disposed of in severalties. Weston is at present possessed in parcels by the executors of the late Robert Cheshyre, Esq. the Miss Orreds, Mrs. Todd, and Mr. Wm. Banks, but no Court is held.

The situation of Weston is delightful; and from its adjoining the Rivers Mersey and Weaver, the neighbourhood affords a busy scene.

THE CHAPELRY OF ASTON,

CONTAINS THE TOWNSHIPS OF

ASTON, ASTON GRANGE, AND SUTTON.

ASTON JUXTA SUTTON,

AND

ASTON JUXTA FRODSHAM,

Were among the possessions of Odard at the Conquest, who held them under Wm. Fitz Nigel, Baron of Halton, in 1086: at this early period they formed one township.—Temp. Henry II. Gilbert de Aston, probably of a branch of the Duttons, which had assumed the local name, held Aston, whose descendant is the present proprietor, in the person of Henry Charles Aston, Esq. High Sheriff of Cheshire, 1818. The direct male line became extinct on the death of Sir Thomas Aston, Bart. in 1744, when the title was transferred to a collateral branch; but the estates were left by will to Catherine, the wife of the Hon. Henry Hervey, D. D. the fourth son of John Earl of Bristol, who assumed the name of Aston, and was grandfather of H. C. Aston, Esq. A Court is held by him for Aston, and other manors, at Sutton.

HISTORY.

The Hall of Aston is situated on an elevated piece of ground a little beyond Frodsham Bridge, on the Warrington road, commanding an extensive and beautiful prospect: it is a modern building of white stone.

It appears amongst the Aston deeds,* temp. Henry III. that Sir Richard Aston, fifth in descent, together with Hugh and Richard his sons, and Sir Robert Aston, were possessed of a *Corrody* in the Abbey of Norton, " so as each of them should have, and have had by themselves, for finding a yeoman, a page, three horses, a brace of greyhounds, and a goss-hawk, according to their estate, with their chambers, and such easement that belongeth to their degree; whereunto the priors and abbots of the said monastery, in all their time (considering the great possessions given out of the lordship of Aston to the said house) were consenting grantinge and yielding, as for their right of old time, granted and had." Leycester mentions a curious matrimonial deed relative to Sir Robert Aston, sixth in descent, whose father, Sir Richard, " did covenant with John Hawarden, Citizen of Chester, that Robert, son of the said Richard, should take to wife Felice, daughter of the said John; and if Robert die before marriage, then Thomas, another son of the said Richard, should have her to wife; with other covenants, in case Robert should die before he attained unto fourteen years of age, or matrimony had; 7th Edw. III." Sir Rich. Aston, 8th from Gilbert the founder, was treasurer to Queen Philippi, wife of Edward III. of her lands in *Ambrage*,† in Wales, and steward of Hopesdale. In the 12th Ric. II. he served in the Spanish wars; and 10th Hen. IV. was Steward of Halton. Sir Thomas

* Leycester, p. 211.

† Qu. Handbridge?

so contrived in the situation, that from the lower meadows, there is a fine easy ascent up, upon the face of the house, which, as you approach still nearer to it, fills your eye with more delight, as is the nature of true beauty: and to see now the late additions of delectable gardens, orchards, and walks, would make one say, it longs to be the abode of so honourable a master as it doth service to. Yet never since the foundation of it, was it more graced, than when it pleased our gracious Sovereign (Jac. I.) in 1617, to accept the Princely entertainment, which there, for his Majesty and his whole train, was prepared by the Honourable Sir Thomas Savage, his Royal Majesty taking his repast there, and killing a Buck, in Halton Park, after he was that morning come from Bewsey, where his Highness had lain, at the Right Worshipful Sir Thomas Neland's, Vice Chamberlain of Cheshire, whom then, of his free grace, he knighted."

Aston, 17th in descent, was made a Baronet in 1628, and in 1635, was High Sheriff of Cheshire. He was a strong partisan for Charles I. and having the command of some troops, was encountered on the 28th January, 1642, by Sir William Brereton, near Nantwich, who defeated him. Sir Thomas, however, escaped; but he was afterwards taken in Staffordshire, and conveyed to Stafford, where endeavouring to make his escape, he was struck violently on the head by a soldier. The effect of the blow was a violent fever, which terminated his life at Stafford, on the 24th March, 1645.

In this township is a place called *Middleton Grange*. Leycester supposes it to be the same as is called *Mid Eston* in Domesday, which then belonged to the monastery of St. Werburgh, at Chester. In 1236, it was confirmed to the Priory of Norton, by John Lacy, Baron of Halton. "Here was anciently a chappel called *Middleton Chapel*,* where the Prior and Convent of Norton were bound to find a Priest, to say mass on Sundays, Wednesdays, and Fridays, for ever; which chapel, being out of repair, and service said there only on Sundays, for forty years, it was complained of by Richard Aston, son of Sir Robert Aston, at a visitation in 1425, and an order was made by Richard Stanley, then Archdeacon of Chester, "that whereas the Prior and Convent of Norton, long before the same was an Abbey, did covenant with the Abbot of Vale Royal, to find at their own proper cost a fit chaplain to officiate here three days a week, as aforesaid; it was ordered that the said agreement should be kept and observed. But these varicnces concerning Middleton Chapel, between Robert Abbot of the Monastery of St. Mary of Norton, and Richard Aston, of Aston, Esq. were composed by the mediation of Thomas Dutton, Esq. and his wife. But after that Middleton Chapel fell into decay, another Chapel was erected in later days, somewhat nearer to the Hall of Aston, called *Aston Chapel*, situate within the Parish of Runcorn; and in lieu of finding a Priest to officiate there by the Abbot of Norton, the King (after these lands came into his hands) gave £5. yearly rent to the maintenance of a Minister here, and which sum is yearly paid to this day,† by the King's Auditor, at his office, in Chester. And this Aston Chapel was lately made a Parochial Chapel in our days, by the grant of John Bridgeman, Bishop of Chester, dated the 16th of April, 1635, by the procurement of Sir Thomas Aston, of Aston, Bart. and so it is now become a Parochial Chapel for burial, baptism, and other rites, for Sutton, Aston-juxta-Sutton, Middleton Grange in Aston aforesaid, and Aston Grange."

* Leycester, page 209.

† 71.

ASTON GRANGE,

Was given to the Monks of Stanlow, who were subsequently removed to Whalley, by Lacy the Constable; it was therefore NOT given to the Prior of Norton as is stated by Sir Peter Leycester. At this period it was called *Maurice Aston*.‡ After the Dissolution, the manor was purchased from the Crown by Richard Brooke, Esq. in whose descendant, Sir Richard Brooke, Bart. it is now vested.

‡ Lyson p. 757.

SUTTON-JUXTA-FRODSHAM,

Is not noticed in the Survey; but was held of the Fee of Halton. Adam de Dutton, ancestor of the Warburtons, held this township temp. Richard I. and it descended with the other estates to the late Sir Peter Warburton, Bart. who, about 1807, sold the manor to the grandson of the present Henry Charles Aston, Esq. the proprietor, who holds an Annual Court for it.

Adam de Dutton, gave to God, and to the building of the Church of the Blessed Mary, at Norton, and to the Canons serving God there, three shillings yearly rent, issuing from his Mill in Sutton-juxta-Halton; and on his death, the whole of the Mill. Sutton was long the seat of the Warburtons; they had a Park here, and had a mansion in the township, temp. Hen. VII. Geoffry de Dutton obtained a license from the Canons of Norton, for an Oratory here, in the early part of the 12th Century.

Middleton Grange, before mentioned, has passed with the manor of Aston.

Aston Chapel is situated about a quarter of a mile N. of Aston Hall. It is of red stone, and consists of nave, chancel, and belfry.

There are a number of Monumental Memorials to the Astons, the most remarkable of which are the following:

On a large wooden tablet, a genealogy of Aston.

On a marble tablet, the arms of Aston, impaling Pulteney—

The Lady Magdalen Aston, daughter and coheyre of Sr John Pulteney, of Pultney, com. Leicester, Kt. dyed the 2d of June, 1635.—Had issue Jane, Robert, Thomas, and Elizabeth, (three of which

early saynts dyed in her life) Thomas (a chyld of great hope) survived her, but soone left her inheritance for her grace. He dyed the 23d of January, 1637, æ'tis sexto; to whose memories her sad husband, his father Sr Thomas Aston, Baronett, dedicates this sacred amoris ergo.

Heere reader, in this sad, but glorious cell
Of death, lyes shrind a double miracle,
Of woman and of wife, and each soe blest,
Shee may be Fame's fair coppy to the rest;
The virgin heere a blush so chaste might learne,
Till thro the blood she Virtue did discerne;
Heere might the bryde upon her wedding daye
At once both knowe to Love and to obey,
Till she grew wife as perfect and refynd,
To be but body to her husband's mynd;
The tender mother here might learne such love
And care, as shames the pelicane and dove.
But Fame and Truth, noe more, for should you fynde
And bring each grace and beauty of her mynde,
Wonder and envy both would make this grave
Theyre court, and blast that peace her ashes have.

Near this place lie the bodies of—

(1.) Sir Thomas Aston, Bart. who by his second wife (Anne, coheir of her father Sir Henry Wilughby, of Risley, in the county of Derby, Bart. and sole heir of her mother Elizabeth, the first wife of the said Sir Henry, and one of the daughters and co-heirs of Henry Knolls, of Stanford, in the county of Berks, Esq. by Margaret, the only daughter and heir of Sir Ambrose Cave) had issue one son Wilughby; and two daughters, Magdalene, married to Robert, the eldest son of Sir Francis Burdett, of Formark, in the county of Derby, Bart. and Mary married to Michael Biddulph, of Polesworth, in the County of Warwick, Esq. He was born on the 29th of Sept. 1600, and having distinguished himself both by his learning and courage in the defence of Church and State, dy'd in the service of his King, on the 24th March, 1645,—(2.) John his brother, who with great prudence and fidelity preserved the estate and evidences of his family from being ruin'd by sequestration and plunder during his life, which ended on the 1st of April, 1650, for whom this monument is erected by their heir, Sir Wilughby Aston, Bart. 1697.

THE PAROCHIAL CHAPELRY OF DARESBURY,

CONTAINS THE TOWNSHIPS OF

DARESBURY	NEWTON
ACTON GRANGE	PRESTON-ON-THE-HILL
HATTON	THELWALL
KECKWICK	OVER WALTON, AND
MOORE	NETHER WALTON.

* Leycester, page 238.

DARESBURY

Was held under the Barons of Halton. Temp. Hen. III. a family which assumed the local name settled here. " Rogerus de Hiberniâ granted unto Beatrix, daughter of William de Daresbury, and to the heirs which shall be begotten on her body by Robert of Ireland, son of the said Roger, all his land in Leverpool, in Lancashire."* In 1291, Henry le Norreys, was lord of Daresbury, in right of Margery Daresbury, his wife. His successor, Alan le Norreys, had a son also called Alan le Norreys, whose daughter and heiress Clementia, in 1344, married Wm. Danyers, son and heir of Sir John Danyers, of Daresbury, in whose family the township became vested.† On the death of John Daniell, Esq. in 1736, the estate passed to his brother Edward, who mortgaged it to the Astons; and his son John Daniell finally sold it about 1755, to George Heron, Esq. father of the present proprietor, the Rev. Geo. Heron, A. M. The only manerial authority exercised is a Game Deputation.

Daresbury Hall is built on a most commanding site, the view stretching as far as the eye can reach; it is a handsome brick house, and the residence of the respectable possessor, the Rev. G. Heron.

There is a *Grammar School* here, endowed with the interest of £185. the sum total of various subscriptions made for the purpose, in the reign of Elizabeth.

Daresbury Chapel nearly adjoins the road to Warrington, from which town it is about five miles, and three from Runcorn. It is of stone, the south aisle rebuilt in 1773, by the Lord of the manor. It possesses a fine tower, and consists of nave, chancel, and side aisles. Between the nave and chancel are the remains of a rood loft, with some rich carved work.

In the centre aisle, on a stone—

Sacred to the Memory of the Rev. Joseph Blackburn, who departed this life the 20th of June, 1787, aged 83, after being Minister of Daresbury 32 years.

There are memorials of the Starkeys, Winningtons, Rutters, Byroms, Cookes, &c.—The Harl. MSS. notice several stones in the the Church-yard, marked with crosses-florée, with swords beside them, " indicating most probably the sepulchres of crusaders."‡ These are no longer to be seen.

† This family was commonly called Daniell.

‡ Ormerod, page 541.

ITINERARY OF THE COUNTY, &c.

CHESHIRE

HISTORY.

ACTON GRANGE

Is about three miles S. W. S. from Warrington. It is not noticed in Domesday, and Leycester is of opinion it was then waste.—The first notice of its possessors, is that of its being attached to the estates of the Priory of Norton, and it continued the property of that foundation till the Dissolution, when it was purchased with other property, by the Brookes, now of Norton, in whose descendant, Sir Richard Brooke, Bart. it is vested.

HATTON,

Is about seven miles N. E. N. from Frodsham. In the reign of Hen. III. Geoffry, the son of Adam de Dutton, gave the town to William, son of Hothy of Hatton; whose descendants probably assumed the name of Hatton. In 1661 Peter Hatton and his sons sold the manor in severalties, the principal part to Robert Pickering, Esq. In 1760, Henry Pickering, Esq. his descendant, sold the large mansion and farm of *Quisley Birches*, to Mr. Hordern, of Macclesfield, from whose son it was purchased by the father of the present proprietor, Mr. Watt, of Warrington.

The principal estates here which belonged to the Warburtons of Arley, including the manerial right, were bequeathed by Sir Geo. Warburton, of Arley, Bart. to Thomas Sloughter, Esq. High Sheriff of Cheshire in 1755, from whom they passed to Mrs. Sloughter, of Chester, his daughter, and she sold them to Mr. Geo. Litton; and from his Representatives they were purchased by Major General Heron. They were again sold to Mr. Claughton, of Warrington, Attorney-at-Law; and are now the property, by purchase, of the Rev. Geo. Heron; but no Court is held for the Manor.

In 1803, an Act of Parliament passed for the Inclosure of Waste Lands here.

KECKWICK,

Although not mentioned in the Survey, is known to have been held of the Fee of Halton. It was possessed by the Duttons of Dutton, so early as the reign of Hen. I. and the residence of the earlier branches of that ancient family was in this township.* By an award of Hen. VIII. it was allotted with other lands to the daughters and coheirs of Sir Thos. Dutton, of Dutton, in 1534, and became the portion of Margaret, who married Thomas Aston, of Aston, Esq. in whose descendant, Henry Charles Aston, Esq. it is vested.

* Ormerod, 507.

The Constable of Keckwick, is sworn in at the Court Leet of Halton.

MOORE,

Or *More*, is about four miles S. W. from Warrington, and parcel of the Barony of Halton. It was given by Roger Lacy, the Constable, to his brother Richard, who becoming leprous, was buried in the Chapter House, at Norton. The inhabitants were formerly copyholders under the Barons of Halton, but in 1628, by a Royal Grant, they bought their own land, to hold in fee-farm of the manor of Enfield, Middlesex. The Marquis of Cholmondeley holds a Court Leet and Baron for Moore, as an appendage of Halton fee. Previous to 1666, an estate here was purchased from the Brookes by Richard Rutter, Esq. supposed to be a descendant of the ancient family of Le Roter, afterwards called Rutter, of Kingsley; but on the death of his representative, Richard Rutter, Esq. in 1758, this estate passed in marriage with Rebecca, an only daughter, to Peter Kyffin Heron, second son of George Heron, Esq. of Daresbury, and father of General Heron, the present proprietor, who has a seat here.

NEWTON-JUXTA-DARESBURY,

Is about four miles and a half N. E. E. from Frodsham. Leycester says, "this town is not of so great antiquity, for I find it granted by parcels, and enclosures, and closes, some in Henry III.'s time, some in Edw. I. and some in the reign of Edw. II. by the ancestors of Warburton, of Arley, before they had relinquished their proper sirname of Dutton, who were lords thereof, from King John's time, unto this present 1666."

In 1743, Sir George Warburton bequeathed it to his natural son, Thomas Sloughter, Esq. who sold it to the Littons; it is now the property of the Rev. George Heron.†

† See Hatton.

In this township is the manor of HALLUM, given by John Lacy, to Adam de Dutton, whose son Geoffry gave it to two of his attendants, Grimsditch and Hallum. The Hallums became proprietors of the whole, and had possession till 1471, when they sold it to Sir John Needham, ancestor of Lord Kilmorey, who is the present proprietor.

PRESTON-ON-THE-HILL,

Is about four miles N. E. E. from Frodsham; it was

formerly known as Preston-juxta-Dutton, and was purchased by Hugh de Dutton from Henry de Nuers, and Julia his wife, in the reign of King John, rendering eight shillings yearly at the Feast of St. Martin. This was confirmed by Randle Earl of Chester. It passed with the Dutton estates to the Gerards; and in 1705, Charles Lord Gerard conveyed it to trustees for the payment of his debts; but his nephew Charles Fleetwood, sold it to Fulke Greville, who, in 1769, sold it to Thomas Brock, Esq. of Chester; and it is now the property of his nephew, Thomas Brock Yates, Esq.

At Preston (or as it is generally called *Preston Brook)* is a large range of Warehouses, and considerable business is transacted here, it being the place of trans-shipment of goods, &c. between the Mersey navigation, and the Grand Trunk and Duke of Bridgewater's Canal.

THELWALL,

Which is situated about three miles and a half E. S. E. from Warrington, is a very ancient town. It was here that King Edward the Elder, in 920, built a tower and castle, "so called (says Leycester) from the stakes and stumps cut from the trees, wherewith it was environed about as a wall; and King Edward made it a garrison."* No notice is taken of it in the Survey, and it is thought it was then waste.† Roger of Poictou, son of Roger de Montgomery, first Earl of Shrewsbury, was lord of all the lands in Lancashire, between the Ribble and Mersey; and gave half of the fishery in Thelwall to the Abbot of Shrewsbury, temp. Hen. I. The other was granted to the Prior of Norton, by William Fitz Nigel, temp. King Stephen. In the reign of Henry III. Edmund Lacy, the constable, gave to Geoffry de Dutton two thirds of Thelwall, and he transferred it to his youngest son Thomas. Temp. Edw. III. the estate was possessed by the Claytons, and continued in their possession till 1561, when it was sold by John Clayton, to Rich. Brooke, of Norton, Esq.; Thomas Brooke, son of the above, disposed of it to John Moores, M. D. of Lon. in 1621; whose nephew John Moores, of Kirtlington, co. Nottingham, sold the property to Robert Pickering, Barrister-at-Law, in 1662, and his descendant, Henry Pickering, Esq. is the present proprietor.

The *Chapel* here was built by the Brookes', and was originally a domestic Chapel. It was suffered, however, to fall into a state of extreme dilapidation; and continued so till 1782, when it was repaired, and fitted up for Divine Service, with an augmentation from Queen Anne's Bounty. Mr. Pickering appoints the Minister.

This township being parcel of Halton Fee, a Court Leet is held for it, and a Constable sworn, on the eve of Palm Sunday annually.‡

OVER WALTON,

Or *Higher Walton*, is about two miles and a half S. S. W. from Warrington. It was at an early period‖ held under the Lords of Daresbury, although originally under the Barons of Halton; and was given by Margery de Daresbury, daughter and heiress of William de Daresbury, to her son Alan le Norreys, whose successor probably assumed the local name. Temp. Edward III. the township passed by a female heir to Simon de Merbury, and continued in his descendants till towards the middle of the 17th century, when Sir Peter Brooke, of Mere, bought it from Thomas Merbury, of Walton; and it is now the property of Peter Langford Brooke, Esq. who holds a Court Baron for the Manor.—The *Old Hall* is occupied as a farm-house.

NETHER WALTON

Is about two miles S. from Warrington; and was given by John Lacy, the Constable of Cheshire, to Adam de Dutton.—His son Geoffry, gave a moiety to Richard Massey, of Sale, one of his gentlemen, temp. Edw. I. in exchange for the Manor of Ashley; the other was possessed by the ancestor of the Waltons.—The Masseys sold their share about 1660, in severalties, the other, subsequently the property of the Merburies, has passed with the preceding township to Peter Langford Brooke, Esq.

THE CHAPELRY OF HALTON,

CONTAINS THE TOWNSHIPS OF

HALTON, NORTON, AND STOCKHAM.

HALTON.

"This town (says Leycester) in common pronunciation is called *Hauton*, and is as much as a town on a hill; for *hawe*, and *howe*,§ is an old English word for a

* Camden, Polychronicon, Florentius, &c.

† Leycester. ‡ See Halton. ‖ 1314. § From the French HAUT.

CHESHIRE

HISTORY.

hill: howbeit in our Norman way of writing, it is usually written Halton; in Domesday-book it is written *Haletune*."—The Barony of Halton was given by Lupus, the second Earl, to his cousin Nigel,* together with the Constableship of Cheshire,† by military service, that he should lead the vanguard of the Earl's army to the wars in Wales, and conduct the rearguard in returning therefrom.—This office was of great importance; for on it depended the disposal of the Earl's troops, horses, armour, and other provisions of war, throughout the whole county, in some degree similar to the present office of Lord Lieutenant.—This Nigel had two sons, William and Richard; by the first of whom he was succeeded in his Barony. In 1086, the following towns, in Cheshire only, were held by William, viz.:—

In Cestre Hundred.
NEWTON
LEE, one half
BRUGE, one half

Dudestan Hundred.
CLUTTON

Riseton Hundred.
BARROW

Wilaveston Hundred.
NESTON, one half
RABIE, one half
CAPELES, i. e. Capenhurst
BERNESTON.

Mildestvich Hundred.
GOOSTREY, one half
LACHE..

Hameston Hundred.
OVER ALDERLEY, one half

Hameston H.----continued.
MILLINGTON
KNOTSFORD
OVER TABLEY
NETHER PEVER, one half
TATTON, one half.

Tunendon Hundred.
HALTON
WESTON
ASTON
NORTON
ENDLEY
DUTTON, a part of
LITTLE LEGH
ASTON-JUXTA-BUDWORTH
GREAT BUDWORTH
AND
WHITLEY.‡

This William founded the Priory at Runcorn, in 1133; and gave Newton, near Chester, to the Monastery of St. Werburgh, together with the service of Hugh, son of Hudard (Hugh de Dutton) of four oxgangs of land; and the service of Wiceline of two oxgangs. He died towards the conclusion of the reign of Henry I. and was buried at Chester; leaving issue WILLIAM (who succeeded him), Agnes, married to Eustace Fitz John, "a great Baron of the realm,"|| and Maud, who married Aubert de Grelley. WILLIAM the 3d Constable removed the Canons of Runcorn to Norton, temp. Stephen. He gave half of Raby to the Abbey of St. Werburgh. His death took place in Normandy, and leaving no issue, his estates were divided between his two sisters. EUSTACE FITZ JOHN was the 4th Baron, in the right of his wife Agnes; and Randle Gernons restored to him all the honors held by his predecessors. Eustace was the son of John Monoculus, called so because he had but one eye; Hoveden called him "*luscus et proditor nequam*," a wicked traitor with one eye—alluding to his father's infirmity: Eustace defended Malton Castle, in Yorkshire, against King Stephen in 1137; and became heir to Serlo de Bergo, his father's brother, who built Knaresborough Castle, but died without issue. He had two wives, *first* Beatrix, sole daughter and heiress of Ivo de Vescy, by whom he had the Baronies of Malton and Alnwick, and had issue William de Vescy, who took the arms and assumed the name of Vescy: *secondly*, Agnes, sister and coheiress to William the younger, Constable of Chester, by whom he had issue Richard the Constable.§—Eustace was slain in the Welsh wars, together with Robert Curcy, and many others, in 1157.—RICHARD the 5th Constable, married Albreda, or Aubrey, the daughter and heiress of Robert de Lizours, and half sister to Robert Lacy, Baron of Pomfret Castle, who also made her his heiress. It was in right of this Aubrey, that her posterity enjoyed sixty Knights' fees of the Honor of Pomfret. He died previous to 1178, but the precise year is not known.—JOHN, the son of Richard, and the sixth Constable, founded the Abbey of Stanlow, in 1178, which was translated to Whalley, in 1296. He gave Hield, in Aston-juxta-Budworth, to Methrose Punter-

* "This Nigel, if we may believe Pecham, page 189, was the son of Ivo (Vice-comes, or governor of Constantia, in Normandy) by Emme, sister to Adam Earl of Bretagne: Sed quære."—LEYCESTER.

† "They were Constables of Cheshire in fee, that is, to them and their heirs by descent, as it were, after the manner of the Lord High Constable of England."

‡ From Leycester.

|| Leycester.

§ Agnes and Eustace founded a Nunnery at Watton, in Yorkshire; and also a Monastery there. He and his first wife founded the Monasteries of Malton and Alnwick, and the Hospital of Broughton.

linge, for the render of a Welsh lance annually on St. Bartholomew's Day; and married Alice, sister of Wm. Mandevyle, by whom he had Roger, his successor, who assumed the name of Lacy; Eustace de Cester; and Rd. de Cester (to whom Roger gave the township of Moore); Richard died of Leprosy, and was buried at Norton: he had also two other sons, Geoffry and Peter, and a daughter named Alice. Dr. Whittaker, in his History of Whalley, is of opinion that this Peter was the long lived Rector of Whalley; Sir Peter Leycester, however, in his MSS. entitles the Rector, "*Petrus de Lascy, bastardus, dictus etiam Petrus de Cestre, Rector Ecclesiæ de Whalley.*"—In 1181, the Constable, and Richard Peche, then Bishop of Coventry and Lichfield, superseded Hugh de Lacy, Governor of Dublin, whom Henry II. disgraced, for marrying the daughter of the King of Connaught, without the Royal license.—He died at Tyre, in the Crusades, in 1190.*

ROGER, the first who assumed the name of Lacy, and the seventh Constable, was sirnamed *Hell*, "from his fierce and magnanimous spirit."†—He called himself Lacy, on succeeding to the possessions of Robert Lacy, of Pomfret Castle, who died in 1194, and in the following year, a fine was levied at Winchester between Roger, and his grandmother Aubrey, in which she settled on him the great inheritance of Robert. Roger Lacy was one of the most powerful Barons of the Realm, and, next after the Earls, among those whom King John most doubted, and required to swear fealty to him, in 1199, on the death of Richard I. which they did on condition that they should all have their lands restored; the Constable, however, before the restoration, was compelled to deliver his son and heir to the King as a pledge—and here we have another instance of the frightful tyranny of the feudal ages.—He was entrusted among other dignitaries of the Kingdom, with conducting the Scotch King to Lincoln, to do homage to John. In 1201, Roger was sent into Normandy with a strong military force, to suppress the disturbances there; and three years afterwards he kept the Castle *De Rupe Andeliaci* against the French, with so much persevering gallantry, that after all his victuals were spent, having endured a year's siege, and repeated assaults, he mounted his horse, and made a sortie, chusing to die like a soldier, rather than be starved to death. After slaying great numbers of the besiegers, he was with much difficulty taken prisoner, and sent strongly guarded to the King of France, who in admiration of his valour, granted him his parole.‡—It was this illustrious Baron who played off the *ruse de guerre*, in relieving Earl Randle, when besieged by the Welsh at Rhyddlan.‖ He aggrandized the extensive estates of the Barony, by the purchase of the Barony of Penwortham, co. Lancaster, from Robert Bushell, to hold of the King in capite, paying three hundred and ten marks of silver.—The Church of Rochdale he gave to the Abbey of Stanlow, together with the town of Little Wolneton; and presented Osbert de Wethall with a moiety of Nether Peover cùm Little Peover, paying to him annually six shillings and eight pence, and rendering foreign service of the 20th part of a Knight's fee. He married Maude de Clare, by whom he had issue John Lacy, Constable of Chester and Earl of Lincoln.§ This Roger died Oct. 1, 1211.—JOHN LACY, the 8th Constable, was amongst those excommunicated by Pope Innocent III. for conspiring against King John.—Matt. Paris says, "In 1218, there came to the siege of Damiata, a city in Egypt, many strangers out of divers parts of the world. Out of England came the illustrious Randle Earl of Chester, with Saher Earl of

* "This John, Constable of Cheshire, had a clerk called William, AN EXCELLENT ASTROLOGER, who in 1186 writ of the conjunction of the planets that year."—LEYCESTER.

† Leycester.

‡ "Sub libera custodia detentus est."—M. PARIS.

‖ See an account of it page 23, and 212.

§ Pecham notices another son of Roger's, viz. Robert Constable, of Flamborough, co. York, whose posterity took the name of Constable; from which Robert in a direct line are descended Sir Wm. Constable of Flamburgh; Sir Philip Constable of Everingham; Christopher Constable, of Hatfield, Esq.; James Constable, of Cliffe; Esq.; John Constable, of Carthrop, Esq.; Marmaduke Constable, of Kirby, Esq.; Sir John Constable, of Dromanby, with many others then living, 1622.—COMPLEAT GENTLEMAN, page 190.—In noticing the seal of this Hero, Dr. Whitaker observes, there is something evidently allusive to the temper of Roger de Lacy, a serpent inflicting a mortal wound on the throat of a gryphon, or dragon, the ancient cognizance of the Welsh Princes, with whom the Earls of Chester lived in almost continual feuds.

CHESHIRE

Arundel, and the Barons Robert Fitz Walter, John Constable of Cheshire, Wm. de Harecourt, with much Company." In 1232, Henry III. granted to John Lacy the Earldom of Lincoln (which he held in right of his wife).* On the 17th July, 1230, he had been presented by the same King with the manors of Colingham and Berdsey. In 1233, John Scot (then Earl) and Lacy, were bribed with 1000 marks by the Bishop of Winchester, and joined the King's party, having previously taken part with Richard the Earl Marshal, against the King. This John died in 1240, after a long sickness, and was succeeded by EDMUND his son and heir, who was the 9th Baron of Halton; and whom Henry III. married to Alice, daughter of the Marquis de Saluces, in Italy, and cousin to the Queen of England. Edmund died on the 5th June, 1258, and was buried at Stanlow. HENRY, the 10th Baron of Halton, and Earl of Lincoln, was presented by Edward I. in 1284, with the Castle and Lordship of Denbigh;† and was in great favour with that Prince. He was the Chief Commissioner for the rectifying and discovering the abuses and briberies of the corrupt Judges of that time, whose conduct was complained of in Parliament, in 1290: among the offenders were Sir Thomas Weyland, Chief Justice of the Common Pleas, who was banished, and all his goods confiscated; Sir John Lovelot compounded for 3000 marks; Roger Leycester, Clerk, for 1000 marks; Sir William Brompton for 6000 marks: these were all of the Common Pleas; but several other rapacious Judges were also punished. At the Parliament held by the King at Carlisle in 1307, he was placed next to the Prince of Wales, as the Chief Nobleman of the Realm. He was employed in all state affairs of consequence; in 1293 he was sent Ambassador to the King of France, to demand satisfaction for the goods of English merchants seized by the French. On the death of Edmund Earl of Lancaster, he had the command of all the Royal troops in Gascony, and was for a time Vice Roy of Aquitaine. In 1298 he expelled the French from the neighbourhood of Thoulouse. and raised the siege of the Castle of St. Catherine. He led the advanced guard at the battle of Falkirk, in 1299, so fatal to the Scots. During the absence of the King, in the Scotch Wars, he was Protector of England. In 1285, he confirmed to the Prior and Canons of Burstow, a place called Ruddigate, before granted to them by Henry Torbock and Ellen his wife; provided that one leprous person of his fee of Widness, if any should be found, should be admitted into the said house, and be reasonably maintained; and on his death, another to be admitted; and that the names of Henry Lacy, and his wife Margaret, should be inserted in their Martyrology, and their names written in their canon. He married first, at the age of six years, Margaret, daughter and sole heiress of Sir William Longspèe; by whom he had issue Edmund and John, who both died young; and two daughters, Alice and Margaret; Alice only survived, and marrying Thomas Plantagenet, Earl of Lancaster, Leycester, and Derby, the Barony of Halton became united to the Earldom of Lancaster. Henry Lacy had no issue by his second wife Joan, daughter of William Martin Lord Keimis.

HISTORY.

'Brookes and Fern say, that Edmund, eldest son of Henry Lacy, was drowned in the draw-well in Denbigh Castle; but I am told by the Monasticon, that in 1282, Edward I. gave to Henry Lacy, two cantreds in Wales, to wit, *Roos* and *Roweynock;* and that the King, in the same year, gave to Edmund Lacy, his son, a young girl in marriage, but five years old, namely Maud, daughter and heiress of Patrick de Chaworth, by Isabel Beauchamp, his wife, daughter of William de Beauchamp, Earl of Warwick. But this Edmund Lacy died young without issue; and John his brother, running hastily in his youth upon a turret in Pomfret Castle, in Yorkshire, fell down from the walls, and was killed. This great Henry Lacy, Earl of Lincoln, Constable of Cheshire, Baron of Halton, Pomfret, Blackburnshire, Roos, and Roweynock, and Protector of England, died on the 5th of February, 1310, at his house in Chancery-lane, in London, now called Lincoln's-inn, and was buried in St. Paul's Church, London, in the new work which was of his own foundation, under a goodly monument, with his armed pourtraicture cross-legged, as one that had taken a voyage in defence of the Holy Land. He was aged 60 years.‡'

The Plantagenets.—THO. PLANTAGENET, the 11th Baron of Halton, was beheaded at his Manor of Pomfret, in 1321, for rebellion against Edw. II. and leaving no issue,

* Leycester, page 271.

‡ Leycester, page 275.

† The title he took was, "Henricus de Lacy, Comes Lincolniæ, Constabularius Cestriæ, Dominus de Roos et Rowynock."

CHESHIRE

his lands were forfeited to the Crown. The 12th Baron of Halton was HENRY of LANCASTER, who had all the lands and manors of his brother Thomas Plantagenet, restored to him. But we shall pass over the regular succession in the House of Lancaster, merely stating, that on the deposition of Richard II. by Henry of Bolingbroke, the Duchy of Lancaster, and Barony of Halton, were united to the Crown of England,* and so continue at the present day; the Most Noble the Marquis of Cholmondeley, however, holding it on lease from the Crown. Among the privileges of the Barony of Halton, which were very extensive, were the office of Constable and Marshal of Cheshire—the ward of the streets of Chester during the Fair—the right of having a Castle and Prison at Halton—to hold Halton as a free borough, and have free burgesses there—to have a weekly market there on every Saturday; and two fairs, one for seven days, at the Festival of the Nativity of the Virgin; the other for two days, at the Festival of St. Catherine—to hold a Court for the cognizance of offences, and for all pleas and actions within the Barony, except such as belong to the dignity of the Earl's sword—to have a Master Serjeant and eight under Serjeants within the fee; to have the advowries of all such as should put themselves under the Baron's protection—to hold the town of Congleton as a free burgh—exemption from toll at Halton, Congleton, &c.

A Coroner is appointed for Halton Fee, and a Court Leet is held by the Steward. There are also three *Halmote*† Courts held yearly at the Castle, in April, August, and December. There were formerly two annual Courts Leet, and a Court Baron, every fortnight; but at present there is only a Court Leet and a Court Baron, in October. The jurisdiction of the Fee extends over 32 townships, for which Constables are sworn at Halton, viz. Daresbury, Hatton, Keckwick, Lymm, Middleton Grange within Aston juxta Sutton, Newton, Preston, Sutton, Stretton, Sevenoaks, Toft, Tabley, Weston, Higher Walton, Lower Walton, Lower Whitley, Whitley Superior, Aston juxta Budworth, Aston juxta Sutton, Appleton, Antrobus, Barnston, Bexton, Budworth, Cumberbach, Cotton, Church Holme, Cogshill, and Crowley. The view of frank pledge and Court Leet for Thelwall, as parcel of the fee of Halton and Duchy of Lancaster, are held yearly at Thelwall, on the eve of Palm Sunday. The Marquis of Cholmondeley, as Lessee under the Crown, claims Courts Leet at Runcorn and Moore, as dependencies of the Barony. A distinct Court is held at Widness for the Lancashire dependencies; and Congleton is separated from the jurisdiction by Royal Charter.

† Courts Baron.

HISTORY.

The *Castle of Halton* is built upon a hill, from which the township takes its name, but the date of its foundation cannot be ascertained. It is not noticed in the Survey; although it is supposed to have been built soon after the Conquest. Very little historical event is connected with this fortress; notwithstanding its situation rendered it a strong and important military post. Piers Plowman has the following, as a proverb locally allusive—

——— " Thoro the pas of Haultoun,
Poverte might passe whith oute peril of robbynge"—

And it is traditionally stated that the neighbourhood of the Castle was at a very early period much infested with gangs of robbers: indeed, in the reign of Edward II. these freebooters became so bold as actually to steal armour from the Castle itself. This fortress was a favourite place of recreation with the celebrated John of Gaunt; and in the reign of Elizabeth, it was converted into a prison for popish recusants, of whom Sir John Savage had the custody. During the civil wars Halton Castle was occasionally possessed by both parties; in August, 1644, the Parliament forces had possession,—and subsequently it became a Prison for debtors: eventually it fell into the ruinous state it now remains.

During the Protectorate a survey of the Castle was made, and it was even then in a state of ruin: it was described as consisting of a gate-house, with five rooms over; a great hall, with two ranges of buildings over it, containing nine rooms unfinished, and a prison for the honour of Halton. At this time Colonel Henry Brooke was the Steward. Some relics of the building exist on the Mersey side of the hill,‡ but they are chiefly confined to a window, and to the external wall. The area of the great Court is now used as a Bowling-

‡ See Vignette, p. 15.

* The Claims made by Henry Duke of Lancaster, Constable of Cheshire, Baron of Halton, &c. &c. will be found in a long Latin answer to a Quo Warranto, copied by Leycester, p. 280.—The PRODARY in Leycester, p. 288.

Engraved by J. Fitler Manch^r. from a Drawing by Pennington furnish'd by Math^w. Gregson Esqr. of Liverpool

RUINS OF HALTON CASTLE.

Engraved for Hanshalls History of Cheshire.

CHESHIRE

green, and is a place of great resort from the surrounding country, and from Liverpool, and Chester. The view from it is varied and truly delightful. The site of the ancient Gate House is built upon, and occupied as an Inn, adjoining which on the right hand side, are the Court Room and Prison. Over the Chimney-piece of the Court Room, is the following Inscription, on a grey marble tablet :—

" 7th Dec. 1737.—At a Court of Revenue held for the Duchy of Lancaster, before the Right Hon. George Earl of Cholmondeley, Chancellor of the said County,—It was ordered by them, that 500l. be forthwith raised, and paid for the rebuilding this Court House, Gaol, and Court Yard.

Commissioners to survey the same J. S. Cotton, J. Lee, H. Legh, R. Leicester, P. Davenport, and W. Congreve, Esqrs.

The Hon. James Cholmondeley, Lord of this Manor.

J. Pickering, Esq. Steward.

W. Middlehurst, Deputy.

H. Sephton, J. Orme, Undertakers,

10th Nov. 1738.—Finished."

The *Chapel of Halton* was, in 1650, in a state of great decay; although 40 years before it had been used for Divine Service. It was, however, rebuilt before 1705, about which time Sir John Chesshyre increased the endowment of it with £200. eventually augmenting it to £600.; in addition to which there are several smaller benefactions. The patronage was vested in Sir John Chesshyre and his heirs, and is now in the Chesshyres, of Rennington Place, Hertfordshire. The Chapel is situated on the hill, near to the Castle, and is a small mean building of stone.

In 1733, Sir John Chesshyre, of Hallwood, built a *Library* here, which he furnished with about 400 volumes of useful and valuable books—these have since been considerably increased. The Catalogue is on vellum, containing an extract from the donor's will, together with the rules for its government. The rules direct that it shall be open for the use of divines and the neighbouring gentry, particularly his own descendants, at stated hours on Tuesdays and Thursdays, when the Curate, who is also the Librarian, shall attend; and for this purpose a convenient room and fire-place are provided for the Curate, and a landed income of £10. per annum is appropriated for the provision of fuel, &c. the overplus to be expended in the purchase of books. Over the Library door is this inscription :—

HISTORY.

" Hanc Bibliothecam, pro communi literatorum usu, sub cura curati Capellæ de Halton proventibus ter feliciter augmentatæ, Johannes Chesshyre, miles, serviens D^{ni} Regis ad legem, D. D. D. Anno MDCCXXXIII."

There is a *Charity School* here, but when, or by whom founded, is not known. In the time of Bishop Gastrell, the Master's salary was £11. per annum; it is now about £20. This, together with rent charges on lands, of about £3. per annum, arises from the interest of money given by different benefactors. There is an *Alms House* " for six poor, decayed, and honest old servants," which was founded in 1767, by Pusey Brooke, Esq. who endowed it with £54. 12s. per annum, and the Pensioners are appointed by Sir Richard Brooke, Bart. of Norton Priory.

In this township is HALLWOOD, the former seat of the Chesshyres, which was built by Thomas Chesshyre, Esq. the father of Sir John Chesshyre the Serjeant. It passed to Mrs. Arabella Rawdon,* sole surviving child of William Chesshyre, Esq. (widow of the Marquis of Hastings' uncle) who in 1774, sold it to Robert Newton, from whom it passed by purchase in 1799, to Sir Richard Brooke, Bart. the present proprietor. It is now occupied as a Boarding School by Mr. Blake.

NORTON

Was given by William the younger, Constable of Cheshire, to the Canons of Runcorn, in exchange for lands in Runcorn, and he removed the Canons to Norton. At the Dissolution, Norton, with its other appurtenances, Stockham, Acton Grange, Aston Grange, and Cuerdly (co. Lanc.) were purchased by Richard Brooke, Esq.† whose descendant Sir Richard Brooke, Bart. is the present proprietor.

" There is a certain hamlet, a place called *Endley*, now belonging to the township of Norton, and enjoyed as part of the same, which William Fitz Nigell held as a distinct thing by itself, as appears by Doomsday-book. This afterwards came to Aston of Aston; for Richard Aston, son of Gilbert, gave to God and St. Mary, and to Randle, Prior of Norton, all his land of Hendeley, with its appurtenances, about King John's reign.— Here was anciently *a Church* belonging to the Priory, dedicated to St. Mary; but this Church was pulled down after the Dissolution of Abbies. The place of the Priory is now the seat of Brooke, of Norton, who enjoyeth the whole town of Norton entirely.‡ The

* She died at Chester, and was buried at RUNCORN.

† 1545, 37th Hen. VIII.

‡ Leycester.

Brookes are descended from the Brookes of Leighton, in Nantwich hundred, of which family I find one Adam Dominus de Leighton, sub. Henry III. whose son was styled William de la Brooke de Leighton, and his son stiled Ricardus de Doito, 5th Edw. I. that is, *of the Brook*, for *doet* in French, is a brook in English; and under the said manor house in Leighton, a brook runneth, from whence their posterity assumed the sirname del Brook. Thomas Brook, of Leighton, gentleman, the last of the family, in the direct line, died about 1652, very aged. The reversion of his lands came to Francis Cholmondley, third son of Thomas Cholmondley, of Vale Royal, who now enjoyeth the same, 1666.*"

* Leycester.

HENRY BROOKE, the fourth in descent from Richard Brooke, of Norton, youngest son of Thomas Brooke, of Leighton, who purchased Norton in 1545, was created a Baronet in 1662. He was Sheriff of the County four successive years, commencing in 1644, being appointed by the Parliament.

The ABBEY OF NORTON† was dissolved in 1536; but it appears the execution of the Act was strenuously opposed by the Abbot. Sir Piers Dutton, who was then Sheriff, accordingly took into his custody the refractory Ecclesiastics. This he communicated as follows:—‡

‡ Harl. MSS. 601.

"At Dutton the III^{de} day of Auguste. I have taken the bodies of th' Abbot of Norton, Rob. Jamyns, and the straunger, a cony'g smythe, two of the said Abbotts s'vunts, also Rondull Brereton, Baron of the King's Excheker of Chest'r, and John Hall, of Chest'r, m'chunt, and have theym in my custody and kepyng, and the rest I entende to have as spedely, and to be w^{t} you w^{t} theym, God willyng, in all convenyent spede as I possible may."

Mr. Ormerod, with his accustomed research, has given a very interesting account of the proceedings connected with the dissolution of the Priory of Norton. Two months after this event (the imprisonment of the Abbot) the insurrection, which terminated in the "*Pilgrimage of Grace*," broke out in Lincolnshire, at the time when the King's Commissioners were employed in the spoliation of Norton: a simultaneous movement, but on a small scale, took place in Cheshire. The Commissioners were compelled to seek refuge in a tower of the Abbey; nearly 300 men took part with the Abbot, and more were expected to join the malcontents; but this movement was quelled by the promptitude of the Sheriff.*

* Orm. p. 503.

The following curious letters, relative to this local insurrection, are copied from the Tanner MSS. in Bod. Lib.

Sir Pearce Dutton, Knighte, shewinge the insurrection of the Abbot of Norton, made againste the Comissyioners w'h weare sent by Kinge Henry the 8 to suppress his Abbey, and howe he rescued them, and comitted the Abbot to prisson.

Pleaseth it yor good Lordshipe to be aduertesed Mr. Combes and Mr. Bolles the Kynges Comissyoners within the county of Chestere were lately at Norton within the same county for the suppressyng of the Abbey theare, and when they had packed vppe much juelles and other stuffe as they had theare, and thought vpon the morowe after to departe them, thabbot gadered agre (sic) coppany to gedere to the number of towe or thre hondred persones, so that the sayd comyssyoners weare in feare of their lyues and weare fayne to take a tower theare: and therevppon sent a lettore vnto me asserteninge what danger they wearin, and desyred me to com to assyst them, or els they weare never lyke to come thence; wch lettore came to me about 9 of the clock in the same night. I came thether wth muche of my loueres and tenants as I had neare about me, and found diuers fyeres made theare, as well w^{t}hin the gates as without. And the said Abbot had caused an oxe and other vittales to be kylled and prepared for such his company as he had then theare: and it was thought in the morowe after he had come forthe to have had a great number moare, notwthstanding I vsed pollessy and came sudenly vppon them, so that the company that weare theare fledd, and some of them took poole and wateres, and it was so darke that I could not fynd them, and it was thought yf the matter had not byn quickly handled, it wold have growne to further inconvenience, to what danger, God knoweth: howbeit I took the Abbot, and thre of the channones, and brought them to the Kyng's Castell of Halton, and theare comytted them to ward to the Constable, to be kept as the Kyngs rebellious, vpon payne of a thousand pounds: and afterwards sawe the said comyssioners w'th their stuffe conveyed thence, and William Perker, the Kyngs servant, who is appoynted to be the Kyngs fermor there, to be restored to his possession, whearfoare it maye like yo'r good Lordship that the Kyngs grace may have knowledge heareof, and that his pleasure maye be further knowne theirin, w'ch I shal be alwayes redy and glad to accomplishe to the vttermost of my powere, as knowethe our Lord God who euer preserve yo'r good Lordshipe with muche honour. At Dutton the xii of October, an'o 1536, by y'or assured

PE'RUS DUTTON, Kt.

To the Right Honorable and my singuler good Lord Sir Thomas Audley, Knight, Lord Chanseler of England, this be deliuered.

† Norton was made an Abbey long before the reign of Henry VI.—See Ormerod, page 502.

CHESHIRE

The answer to this curious epistle is as follows—

By the Kyng Henry the 8th to direct to S'r Peerce Dutton to hang vp the Abbot and others of Norton in Cheshire.

Trusty and wellbeloved we greete yo' well, and have as well seene the letters wretene from you S'r Peares Dutton to our right trusty and welbeloved Counselore Sir Thomas Audley, Knight, our Chanselore of England, declaring the treaterous demeanore of the late Chanones of the Monastery of Norton, used at the being theaire of our Comyssioners after the suppressyon thereof, and y'or wisdome, polleey, and good endeavore vsed for the apprehensyon of the same, for the whiche we give vnto you our right harty thanks, and shall vndoubtedly consider y'or faythful service therein, to yo'r singular reivyn and comforte hereaftere, as other letteres written from yo' S'r William Brearton to our right truely and right welbeloved Counselere the Lord Cromwelle, Keeper of our Privie Seale towching the same mattere, for y'r good endeavores also therein, and wee geve vnto yo' our right harty thanks: for answer whearvnto ye shall vnderstand that foresasmuche as it apperethe that the sayd late Abbot and Channones have trayterously vsed themselves against vs and our realme, our pleasure and comaundemente is, that yf this shall fully appeare to yo' to be true, then yo' shall emediately vppon the sight herof WITHOUTE ANY MANOR further delaye, cause them to be hanged as most arrante traytores in such sondrey places as y'e shall thinke requisite for the terible example of all otheres hereafter: and bearin fayelle ye not traville with suche dexterety as this matore maye be fyneshed with all possyble dillegence. Gevene vnder our sygnete at our Castell of Wyndesore the xxth of October the xxviijth yeare of our reyne, an'o 1536.

To our truesty and welbeloued
servant S'r Pearse Dutton,
and S'r William Brearton,
Knights, and to every of
them.

This order was not carried into effect; for in consequence of the amnesty granted by the Duke of Norfolk to the Yorkshire Rebels, it was respited by Sir Wm. Brereton.*

The *Old Hall of Norton* was besieged by the Royalists in the early part of the year 1643. This occurrence is thus noticed in a cotemporaneous phamphlet, "Cheshire's Successe:"—They brought cannon with many horse and foot, and fell to batter it on a Sabbath-day. Mr. Henry Brooke had 80 men in the house; we were careful he should lack no powder; with all other Master Brooke furnished them fully. A man upon his tower with a flag in his hand cryed them ayme, while they discharged their cannon, saying, 'Wide my Lord on the right hand; now wide two yards on the left: two yards over my Lord, &c. He made them swell for anger, when they could not endamage the house, for they only wounded one man, having lost 46 of their own, and their canoneer."

HISTORY.

The present Hall is built on the substructure of the Old House, in a low but picturesque situation. Several of the vaults of the old Abbey remain in the cellars. In the garden is a tolerably executed antique figure of collossal dimensions, of St. Christopher.

STOCKHAM

Is about three miles N. E. from Frodsham. It belonged to the Priory of Norton; and on the dissolution of that Abbey, it passed by purchase to Richard Brooke, Esq. in 1545; from whom it has passed to the present proprietor, Sir Richard Brooke, Bart.

In the account of Runcorn Church, is omitted the monument of the late respected Vicar, which is placed in the North aisle.

"Near the South wall are interred the remains of the Rev. W. E. Keyt, M. A. late Vicar of Runcorn, who died March 9th, 1816, aged 48 years: during an uninterrupted residence of sixteen years, he contributed much by a series of kind offices, and pious exertions, to the temporal and spiritual benefit of his parishioners. He was a man adorned by the Author of all excellence with distinguished talents and peculiar worth; the zealous and impressive Minister, the polished Scholar, the disinterested Patriot, the sufferer's Advocate, and the poor man's Friend.

"This marble was erected by his parishioners, to prolong the remembrance of his virtues, and their regret and esteem."

HALTON,

Described by King, in the "Vale Royal," 8vo. edition, vol. 1, page 84.

HAULTON is a proper strong castle, all of stone, standing on a high hill, a mile west from Runcorn, (in which parish it is contained) and two miles north-east from Frodsham, with a chapel, and a pretty town upon, and round about the said hill, founded by one Nigel, Baron of Haulton, and Constable of Chester; of whom the Lacies descended, that were Constables of Chester,

* The arms of the Abbey of Norton were those of its founder, Gules, a pale fusillé Or.

and lastly, Earls of Lincoln, whose issue ended in one daughter, married to Thomas Earl of Lancaster; so that the honour resteth now in the Duchy of Lancaster.

In this castle, every fourteen days, on a Saturday, is a court kept for all matters done within a certain circuit thereof; it hath also a prison for thieves and felons, taken within the said precinct, which are every sessions presented at Chester.

Also, once a year at Michaelmas, do the Queen's Majesty's Officers of the Duchy of Lancaster, as auditors, attornies, and receivers, come and lye certain days in the said Castle, and there keep a law-day.

Speers Dutton was determined to have made this town a market town, if death had not prevented him. It hath a small market every Saturday, and once a year, on the nativity of our Lady, a fair.

SKETCH OF THE CASTLE ROCK, AT RUNCORN, 1819.

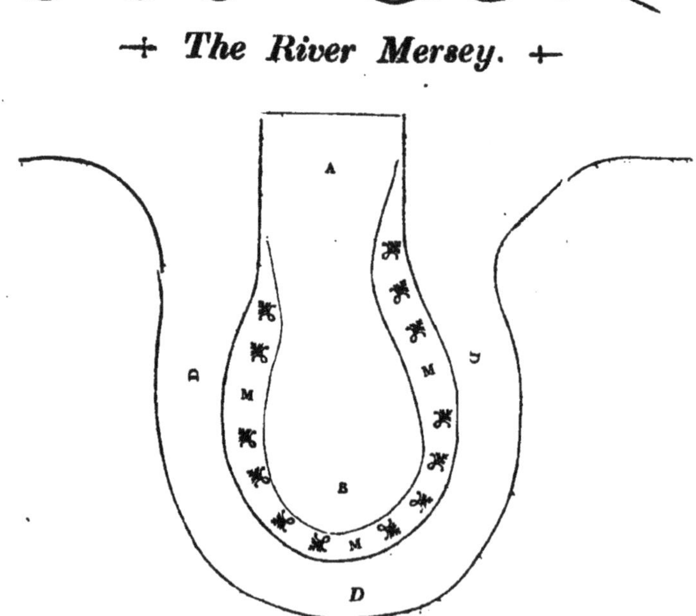

"LITTLE remains to be seen of any thing like the Ruins of a Castle, or Fortification, at present. The rock that bears that name, seems as though it had some time been a place of defence. The Area A. B. is a level place of land, forty yards by thirty, partly surrounded by a Mound, M. M. covered by trees and brambles. This Mound in some places may be seven feet high above the Area A. B. by from ten to eighteen broad; but what may be under this mound is not ascertained, as no one was ever known to examine it; the present appearance would indicate the existence of old ruins, though the surface seems a very luxuriant soil. D. D. D. is a Ditch, about twelve feet wide, and may have been ten or twelve feet deep, but is now filled up to the level at *D.* At A. there is no appearance of a mound, and the rock has been cut straight and perpendicular of late years, by the late Duke of Bridgewater, to improve the River, which at this place is three hundred yards wide at low water, and about four hundred at high water. This contracted part of the river is called Runcorn Gap, but above and below expands to about twice the breadth it is here. At this point, (the Castle Rock,) is the place where the Bridge speculators intend to carry a Chain Bridge over the Mersey, but which is by no means the most eligible situation for such an undertaking, as the road approaching it would be so circuitous; whereas, by placing it about one hundred yards higher up the river, the road would approach it in a straight line, and the shore on each side being rocky, would afford as good a foundation as at the Castle Rock."—INFORMATION OF MR. MOULSDALE, RUNCORN.

VIEW OF LIVERPOOL, OPPOSITE THE CHESHIRE SHORE, IN 1724.

The Hundred of Eddisbury.

CONTAINS THE PARISHES OF

LITTLE BUDWORTH
BUNBURY* (part of)
MIDDLEWICH (part of)
OVER
TARPORLEY
ST. WERBURGH (part of)
WHITEGATE, or NEW CHURCH
BARROW
GREAT BUDWORTH (part of)
FRODSHAM
INCE
PLEMONDSTALL (part of)
TARVIN (part of)
THORNTON
WEAVERHAM
DELAMERE†

Description of the Hundred of Eddisbury,

FROM KING'S VALE ROYAL.

THE Hundred of Eddisbury may well prove the antiquity of itself, and of other hundreds; for that whensoever they had their division, this got its name from the place, which then was of no small account, and was the city, town, fort, or whatsoever other great foundation, which had been built by that noble Elfleda,

* See pages 110, 115, 118, 119, 120, 121, 122: inserted by error, under head "BROXTON HUNDRED."

† See pages 48, 49, and 50.

the Mercian Lady; for various conjectures are made by writers hereof, and that place was called Eddisbury, giving name to this hundred, the form and fashion whereof, by reason that rivers and brooks bound it almost round about, is something irregular though it comes nearest to a pentagon of any other figure, saving that one of the five sides is unequal to all the other four, and that is it which is extended from about Thornton, towards Wirral hundred to Ridley, touching near Cholmondeley, in Broxton hundred, which is a longer side than all the rest.

Our view shall begin where we come over Frodsham bridge, from whence lies a lower way to the parish church; the town a fair continued street, with handsome buildings, and at the west end of it a fair house, which having been a castle, continues still the name of Frodsham Castle, though long since used for a relying seat of pleasure to the honourable owner thereof, Sir Thomas Savage, and stands within view of Rocksavage itself.

The church is fair, and pleasantly situated on the hill over the town, and extends the bounds of the parish to a large precinct: those buildings about the church carry the name of Overtown, in relation to another village beneath called Nethertown, together with the Woodhouses, a member of it. And over them all, a high towering hill, with a beacon upon it; and between all these and Mersey, which here is grown to be a petty sea, lies a fair and fruitful marsh of a large extent; and all this and much more make but that one lordship belonging to that honourable man last named; and next unto it another almost of the same nature and condition, both high and low, called Hellesbey, well known by that craggy high rock called Helsby Tor, at the foot whereof is a high road way to Chester.

Let us here, if you please, take with us a sight of a goodly vale of the fertile and fruitful marshes, towns, and fields, lying toward Mersey side, and wherein this hundred shoots out one of her nooks into the parish of Ince, a goodly lordship of Sir Thomas Cholmondley's, formerly spoken of: and of Thornton, another of Sir George Booth's, with both their churches and their precincts pleasantly situated, and friendly neighbouring one another; whereof Thornton extending her limits to the towns which you see on this side Hapsford, where Edward Greg, a gentleman for special employments in his Highness's Court of Exchequer at Chester, being examiner there, hath a fair seat, and Dunham, for the high situation called *super montem*, where also Robert Whitby, gentleman, and alderman of the city of Chester, hath a very pleasant house seen afar off: and unto this add, that third of Elton, where hath been a long descent of gentlemen who derive unto them from the late rehearsed great lordship, the name of Frodsham.

But let us now go on, and being come to the water, that from the original beginning of it we have formerly called the Beeston Water, and which will now lead us by the bounds of this hundred, till we come to the furthest southern point of that, our course shall be as it directs us. We may see on our left hand a fair lordship called Manley, wherein is an ancient seat and a fair house belonging to the Birkenheads, of Manley, whose owner was in our remembrance Richard Birkenhead, Esq. a learned counsellor at law, and recorder of the city of Chester, his eldest son Adam Birkenhead, Esq.

And now we take with us the view of Mouldsworth, which they distinguish into two, the Great and Little. And herein the goodly ancient house called the Pool, or the Pile, and fair demesnes, the habitation of the Hardwares, a race of worthy gentlemen, the heir whereof, Henry Hardware, Esq. is now in minority, but the inheritance of the house belongeth to Sir Robert Cholmondley, and so we leave Ashton, a fine township, behind us; and turning us a little to look upon Bridge Trafford, so called of the Bridge which giveth passage over that water, and in which a long continued race of gentlemen of that name, have a seemly seat, the owner now being Mr. Trafford, we see Barrow, a fine lordship, belonging also to Rocksavage, and therein the mansion house of John Savage, Esq. one of our city aldermen, and a magistrate in the government, in the country a man in estimation answerable to his worthy name.

We pass on to Kelshall, situated very high in the skirt of the forest, and is a lordship of Sir John Done's, Knight: beneath which, taking with us an ancient house of the Trevors, called Horton, we come to the town and parish church of Tarvin; in which town, besides the fair church and vicarage, which is in the gift of the Lord Bishop of Coventry and Lichfield, we see a very ancient seat now ruined, of a branch of the Bruines, gentlemen of long continuance. But this house and demesne is come to the heir of a late famous lawyer, William Brock, a younger house of the Brocks of Upton; and a little way distant from the town, a large sweet farm belonging to Rocksavage, called Holmstreet, which was a long time a breeding place of the Whalleys, gentlemen of good account. The lordship itself of Tarvin, with many members thereof, all belonging to the same Hon. Sir Thomas Savage, of whom we often make honourable mention.

Not half a mile distant from the same church, we may see a finely seated comely house called Hockenhall, and giving name to gentlemen that have possessed the same in succession for a long continuance, carrying the same name, though for the present the owner of it, John Hockenhall, Esq. hath passed some term in it, and lives not at it: at the one side of which demesne lies Hockenhall Plot, a place well known, being the passage over our said water in our great London roadway to Chester, wanting nothing but a bridge for carts to pass that way when that river riseth, which were a very necessary and charitable work to be done. Which river now leads us by another fair and fruitful demesne, in the midst of a fine lordship, taking name from a passage over the same water, called Stapleford, having been, for an ancient continuance, the seat of gentlemen of great esteem in one well known of the name of Bruines, the owner now, and long hath been, and long I would he might be, John Bruine, Esq. who might, if he affected praise, perhaps receive from me some little remembrance; but all he gets, it shall be this, to pray him to look for his praise amongst those his predecessors, of whom he may take notice in Deuteronomy the 16, 17, 18, and 19.

And now we turn our face a little eastward, to take with us Burton, wherein there is a fair and fine conceitedly built house of brick, which belongeth to Mr. John Werden, a gentleman well descended, and one whose well known deservings are like to add great estimation both to that and to his other possessions. Next to this lies Duddon, wherein one branch of the Hockenhalls have a pretty seat, and Mr. Ralph Done, one of the descendants of the Dones, of Flaxyards, another; and more towards the Forest, a fair house and demesne of Edenshaw, the mansion-house of John Hurlestone, Esq. and near unto this lies Howfield, a member of the same township of Clotton.

Towards this river side, which now hath parted itself into that stream, which we have thus far followed, and that other which we crossed over at Hurley, in Broxton hundred, we come to Tenton, or Tearton, a lordship divided into many parts, but the greatest parts of them belong to the Davenports of Bramhall, before mentioned, and one house and demesne of one descent of the Bressies, which hath been a great name of gentlemen.

And so we cannot here but stay to look upon the next stately house and fine demesne of Beeston, the name both of the house, the township, and that famous and far-seen castle, built there by the last Ranulph, the famous Earl of Chester; and without question it was a place, when such strong holds were in request, of admirable and impregnable strength: it is mounted upon the top of a very steep hill of stone; the chief tower whereof, in the very summit of it, had a draw-well of an incredible depth to serve it with water I have measured it, and notwithstanding that by the great number of stones, which, from the ruinated walls, those that repair thither do cast in, it is supposed, as the well in the outward, to be half stopped up, yet it is of true measure, 91 yards deep, and the other above 80 yard, deep by M. S. and from that tower a circular wall of a large compass, containing a fine plot of ground within the circuit of it, and in the midst of that another well, which by the long descent of a stone, before it falls down to the water when you hear the fall of it, must be of a huge depth; and the foot of that whole wall stands so deep on every side, that, saving one way up to the gates of the Castle towards the east, and those very fair and stately, men can hardly find footing to stand on any part of the said hill. Concerning which, though I have no reason to fit my belief upon any, either idle prophecies, as they call them, or vain predictions of vulgar report; yet neither will I be so scrupulous, as not to make mention of the common word thereabouts used, that Beeston Castle shall save all England on a day; nor so envious, as not to take notice of Old Leland's bold conjecture of the future exalting of the head of it in time to come, whereof I only say this, that I wish every man to look upon what grounds he gives credit to any old dreams: to the place I wish all good, and to the name of Beeston I could also wish a continuance while the Castle stands, being now possessed by an ancient Knight, Sir Hugh Beeston, of much respect; but now, through want of issue male, like to pass into another name, the heir being now married to one of the younger sons of the Hon. and often mentioned Knight and Baronet, Sir Thomas Savage.

Being almost at the head of this water, our guide hitherto, we will take with us the uttermost nook of this hundred, lying southerly upon our right hand, and then return: we come next to Spurstow, a lordship, with the fair house, demesne, and the ancient continued race of gentlemen, in a direct line of the same name, the owner now George Spurstow, of Spurstow, Esq. for the antiquity of whose ancestors I could mention some memorable arguments from the matches of great houses with them, and of them in great places; as also from their being the first that bore the office of High Sheriff in this county palatine, which I have seen testified in a deed of credit among the evidences of that house; but though my duty and my love bind me to do all I can for the estimation of that house, yet my own poor alliance to some that have interest in that blood, makes me more sparing with that precinct: John Aldersey, Gentleman, termed also of Spurstow, hath a fine ancient and fair demesne, and the birthplace of that most worthy to be honoured Aldersey of London, whom the parish stands bound ever to remember, with praises to God, for the preacher's and minister's great stipend there; as also the school master's and usher's, together with the yearly gifts of ten pounds to the poor for ever.—But on the east side of Spurstow lies Haighton, and therein an ancient race and seat of the Haightons, gentlemen of good esteem, and another of the Buckleys; and on the west side, a stately house and great demesne of Ridley, the possession of that honourable descent of the Egertons, sometime a great man of this house, and now the principal seat of that worthy Knight Sir Richard Egerton, formerly mentioned, and of whom for worthy respects I could oft still willingly make mention. Here lay that famous pool, a shallow but a broad water, heretofore a great nurse for fish and fowl; but of late years, and in our remembrance, drained dry, and made more profitable in a goodly meadow for hay: and true it is, that though this pool, though not beginning here as some writers suppose, the head of the water of the Weaver is fetched, which afterwards soon grows to so great a name; and upon the northwest side of Ridley lies the township of Peckforton, sometime belonging to the great name of the Corbetts, in Shropshire, but now Sir Hugh Beeston. And herein is a fine ancient seat of one branch of the Calveleys, and now possessed by my much respected friend Mr. Thomas Calveley, to whom I wish as great good as a friend can to a friend.

Now we see the mother church of all these townships, and many more, the church of Bunbury, the name derived from that Bishop that was sainted by the name of Boniface (but which of them I take not upon me to relate) shews, that the church which was dedicated to that name, and still gives name to the township and whole parish, is of great antiquity; the church a fair one, and unto it not many years ago was added to the south side of the chancel a very fine chapel, by one of the Egertons, Knights of Ridley, which serves for a burial-place to the heir of that house; and hath some monuments, with inscriptions in tables of brass, of some of that family; in which church, in the middle of the chancel, is the vault where the Calveleys are usually buried, under a fair monument, adorned with their arms.

Not far from the church, we see the ruins of a college, which was founded by that famous Calverley, or Calveley, and most finely built and furnished for the maintenance of six priests, who had there their beginning, and such employments as the devotion of those times required, which afterwards was among other such like foundations dissolved, and turned to better uses. And the rectory of the parish being in the hands of Queen Elizabeth, of noble memory, the same was purchased by that worthy citizen of London, Thomas Aldersey, merchant tailor, and a parishioner, born here of those Alderseys, of Spurstow, a little before-mentioned; and the same by him bestowed, part amongst his kinsfolk and friends, but the greatest part founded a preacher's place of one hundred marks per annum, to which he also added a fine house, which he built for that purpose, with a pretty parcel of land unto it, and and twenty *li.* per annum, for an assistant to the preacher, and to be a curate there; and likewise built a new fair free-school, and laid unto it two convenient dwellings, one for a school-master, with twenty pounds per annum stipend, and one for an usher, with ten pounds per annum for ever. Ten pounds per annum to the poor there, besides other charitable gifts to that parish: all which he saw actually effected and performed many years in his life, and fully established by act of parliament before his death: and I may add, that his godly intendments have been by the several persons enjoying those places since he founded them with such incessant pains, laborious diligence, and great learning, endeavoured to be fully effected, as I think the snaky tongue of the fury Envy herself cannot but spit forth the truth of it; and I know there be some that do and shall bless God all the days of their life, that ever they saw and heard the power of the ministry of God's truth in that place; and if any do complain of the small crop of that great harvest, and indefatigable pains there taken, let them impute it to the barrenness of the soil, and want of due care and attention in the hearers, and not to the labours of the workmen, whose comforts I know lie stored up in the conscionable discharge of the duties enjoyned them. The bestowing of the preacher's place there, and the rest, are in the disposing of the master, wardens, and some others of the worshipful company of haberdashers of London; who are much directed therein, when occasion serveth, by that well-disposed and well-deserving gentleman Mr. John Aldersey, of Spurstow, the owner of that ancient house and land, from whence the worthy founder had his descent: by the prudent and godly care of which said worshipful governors, the said places have been, and yet are, most worthily supplied by very learned, godly, and able men. But now fething in one nook of this hundred, and of the parish where we be, lying farthest east, a lordship called Wardhall, where have been a seat and a large demesne of an ancient family of the Prestlands, Esquires, of long continuance; whereof I take it all the heirs male are now failed, the lands being come, in our days, by purchase, to the house of Woodhey.

Along this township lie the well-known pavements or stone causeway, called Watfield Pavement, so termed of the founder, and to the repairing of which were given a pretty house and grounds to it, situate in the middle thereof; the pavement itself being two miles in length, and the disposing and government thereof left to the citizens of Chester.

Near the west-end of it is situated a fair house, called the Cleys, the dwelling of a younger brother of the Davenports of Calveley; and upon the north side of it stands the township of Calveley, whence that great name had first their denomination. Now the principal seat and demesne therein yet remain, and have been long the habitation of one race of the Davenports, the owner thereof, now Arthur Davenport, Esq. and near unto it another fair house, the seat of the Mainwarings, of Calveley, Gent. Beneath this, more north, lies Wettenhall, where are a chapel, and also an ancient seat and demesne of the long continued race of the Breretons, of Wettenhall, now Richard Brereton's, of Wettenhall, Esq. a gentleman of well known experience in the government of the country.

Hence we return westward again, and come by Alpraham, wherein were anciently a house and name of the Pages, now wholly extinct: and here the lofty pile of that sweet and delicate seat of the Hall of Tilston Fearnhall, shews itself, the remembrance of the builder whereof stops again the walk of my pen, and I wish I could neither think upon the happiness of my years there spent, nor upon the unrecoverable loss I there sustained, in the departure of my dear master, the renowned last deceased owner of Woodhey.

Near to this we see the ruins of a house indeed, but no decay of the name or the owners thereof, which was Flaxyards, the ancient seat of the Dones, who were called Dones of Flaxyards; between whom and the Dones of Utkington I have heard was no little emulation, until it pleased God the heirs male of Utkington, failing, were glad to knit with the heir of Flaxyards that so the union of both by marriage might make one greater name; as now we see in the person of the worthy Knight, Sir John Done, of Utkington, a gentleman very complete in many excellencies of nature, wit, and ingenuity; which, together with his diligence and well-pleasing service to his Majesty, who took his pleasure and repast in his forest of Delamere, in the year 1617, where this gentleman being chief forester and keeper, ordered so wisely and contentedly his Highness's sports, that he freely honoured him with knighthood, and graced his house of Utkington near hereunto with his Royal presence, making him Sir John Done of Utkington; of which name the country speaks much of brave Knights, his ancestors, and especially the last of them, his grandfather, by his mother.

But before we go far, let us take with us the view of Tarporley, both town and church and parsonage, all well known by their situation and making; a thoroughfare of great passage upon the great road-way to Chester, a lordship of the said John Done's, and a fit place for keeping the sheriff's, town's, and hundred courts for that hundred.

From whence we go by Eaton and Rushton, two great lordships in one; a great part whereof hath belonged to a race of Hintons, whose heirs-male are thought to be all extinct, but the chief lord there is the same Knight last named.

We go from thence to Darley, a fair seat and demesne of one house of the Starkeys, Esq. of good account, the now owner there, Henry Starkey, of Darey, Esq. ; near unto which are situated another great house, and well known seat of another worthy race, called Egertons of Oulton, whereof have succeeded for some descents Knights of no obscure note; and now the most complete successor of them, Sir Rowland Egerton, Knight and Baronet, whose great alliances and worthy parts have enabled other countries to deprive this his birth-place of such an ornament. In this edge of the forest, near hereunto, stand a little church and town, which in relation of Great Budworth (and no great thing it is, yet a parish by itself) formerly mentioned, is called Little Budworth: in the same is a fair Mere, as there is at Great Budworth, from whence begins a brook, which if we follow but a little way, brings us to Dernhall Grange, once a famous place, as it should seem, by the residence of some of the Earls of Chester, of whom Sir John Scot, the last of the seven famous Earls next after the Conquest, died there; but afterwards made a place for the entertainment of those Monks from whom the Abbey of Vale Royal was founded; or rather, as some think, was the Abbey itself, which afterwards, as it were, was removed thither as a more wholesome seat: and because this place, as amongst woods and waters, was not, forsooth, lightsome and pleasant enough for their fat worships; for some write it, and think, the name came from Dernhole; howsoever it was then, it is now a fine seat with a sweet house of brick lately erected, and now the possession of Henry Lee, Esq. heir to Sir Richard Lee, formerly mentioned, and a gentleman, for his sober and wise carriage, of very worthy esteem. Along the park side of Dernhall lies Swanlow, and therein many good farms that have been of the abbey lands.

And here we approach again upon our old acquaintance, the River Weaver, whom we need follow but a little way, ere it brings us to that famous seat which it gave name unto, how long since were a hard task to search for; where have sitten that great descent of the Stanleys of Weaver, and now is one of the mansion-houses of Thomas Stanley, of Alderley, or Weaver, Esq. of whom we spoke before.

And so we come first to Over-church, situate, somewhat remote from many of her parishioners, and near half a mile from the town itself, which being one of the main goodly possessions which the abbot and convent of Vale Royal enjoyed, obtained by them, or by their means at least, to be made a mayor town, which government they hold till this day, as also a fee and liberty of a good precinct, wherein strangers and all are liable to their arrests; near unto which is a fine gentlemanly seat, called Knights Grange, now the lands of the Lady Mary Cholmondley, formerly mentioned: and not far from this a very pleasant house and demesne of one other branch of the house of Peover, now the possession of Thomas Mainwaring, of Marton, Gentleman. And so a little further we pass by Whitegate, which though it shews you but a chapel, yet challengeth, by a statute in the year —— Henry VIII. to be an entire parish of itself. The vicarage there is in the gift of the said Mr. Mainwaring: and so we come to the famous Vale Royal.

THE ABBEY OF DERNHALL,

IN THE COUNTY OF CHESTER,

Translated afterwards unto Vale Royal.

THE FOUNDATION CHARTER.

EDWARD, eldest son of the illustrious King of England, to the Archbishops, &c. greeting; Know ye, that

CHESHIRE

HISTORY.

we for the health of our soul, and of the souls of all our predecessors and heirs, or other our successors, have given, granted, and by this our charter, confirmed, for us and our heirs, and all our successors, to God and the blessed Mary, and to the monastery of the said glorious Virgin of Dernhall, of the Cistercian order; which we, being sometime in danger at sea, have founded in our county of Chester, in the diocese of Coventry and Lichfield; and to the Abbot and Monks that serve, or shall hereafter serve, Almighty God, and our Lady there, that place wherein the said Abbey is situate, with all the manors of Dernhall and Over, together with the park, in wood, in plain, in men, and other things or liberties whatsoever, and with other things pertaining to the said manor, as fully and freely as ever we have held the same without any reservation.

And furthermore the whole wood of Langwith, in the county of York, with the lands, heath, marsh, and all other their appurtenances, as fully, freely, wholly, and peaceably, as our lord the king our father held the same, and gave the same unto us, with the advowsons of the churches of Esseburn, of the Castle of Peak, of Frodsham and of Weverham, with their chapels and other their appurtenances: granting and desiring, that the aforesaid, with their chapels, may be appropriated to the same monks and to their successors for their maintenance in God's service.

We have granted likewise unto the same monks, and confirmed all reasonable gifts of lands, men and alms, either in present by us conferred upon them, or in time to come to be conferred by the liberality of any other whosoever, or otherwise purchased, or to be purchased, as well in churches as in worldly matters and possessions.

We have likewise granted by this our charter, for us and our heirs, to the aforesaid Abbot and Monks, of our gift, that whensoever it shall fall out, that we, or our heirs, of common course shall take tallage of our demesne lands, the same Abbot and Monks, and their successors for ever, may take tallage in their manors, without the special command of us or our heirs.

Wherefore we will, &c.—Witnesses, the Reverend Fathers Walter, Archbishop of York, N. of Winchester, G. of Worcester, R. of Coventry, Bishops. Edmund, our most dear Brother. Gilbert of Clare, Earl of Gloucester and Hereford. John of Warren, Earl of Surry, Humphrey of Bohun, Earl of Hereford and Essex. Henry of Alemayne, Philip Basset, Roger of Mortimer, Roger of Clifford, Reginald of Grey, then Justice of Chester. James of Audelegh, Robert Wallerand, and Robert Burnell, Master of Fremgham; John of London; and others.

Given by our hand at Winchester, the second of August, in the 54th year of the king our father.

METHINKS it is not altogether improbable, that some such like occasion might long ago, by the presence of a king (and it may be King Edward the First, who founded here the Abbey) give this denomination to the goodly tract of grounds, betwixt the forest and the river Weaver; by his hunting, or other princely sports, to term it *Vallem Regalem*, as the late occasion of our gracious sovereign, his making the house here four days his royal court, while in his fore-mentioned return out of Scotland, he solaced himself, and took pleasing contentment in his disports in the forest, he confirmed it indeed to be a Royal Vale, where it was the joy and gladness of our hearts to behold how graciously his highness spent there the King of Heaven his own day in the service of his God; and where he was pleased to hear our Reverend the Dean of Chester preach unto him God's truth, and could at his dinner recount the heads and chief points of his sermon as punctually as if his highness had been acquainted with the preacher's notes; and where his Majesty, the day following, had such successful pleasure in the hunting of his own hounds of a stag to death, as it pleased him graciously to calculate the hours, and confer with the keepers, and his honourable attendants, of the particular events in that sport, and to question them whether they ever saw or heard of the like expedition, and true performance of hounds well hunting, at which his highness's princely contentment we had much cause to rejoice; and the rather, for that the diligence and service of Sir John Done, had so prosperously prepared his Majesty's sports, which he also as graciously accepted: this Vale Royal was the seat of a noble race of the Holcrofts for two descents, but of late is come by purchase to the Lady Mary Cholmondley, widow, a lady of great possessions, whom we have had several occasions to mention heretofore, and who, for her wisdom, virtue, and careful provision for her child, and great hospitality, deserveth worthy remembrance. We see, beyond this Sandy Way, where hath been the descent of the Eatons, Gentlemen; and Hertford, where Mr. Thomas Row hath built a very delicate little house: and so we look as far as this hundred reacheth to Winnington, which is a fair stone bridge over the river Weaver, which now having met with the Dane, grows very haughty and proud, and hath once or twice of late swelled and foamed too impatiently, because it may not be employed with boats and carriages from the Mersey's mouth, which it thinks itself sufficient enough for, if it were cleared of some wears and stoppages by the way: and going first by Walterscote, a very ancient seat of the Litlers, gentlemen of good worth, and now the possession of Ralph Litler, gentleman: it hastens to Weaverham, which receives name from it, and is a parish, with a church and pretty town, having been also a member of the abbey of Vale Royal, and holding still a great liberty, with a court and prison, of no mean power and jurisdiction of the chief lordship thereof, now in the hands of the worthy Thomas Marbury, Esq. formerly spoken of: and in this liberty I may not omit one ancient seat, having been one of the Abbey Granges, which never were any of the meanest buildings; and this called Helperstone Grange, hath belonged to the Warburtons, so called of the Grange, and now possessed by Peter Warburton, Esq. learned in the law, whom my love will not let me pass in silence, though I say no more, but that which is in every man's expectation, that his worthy parts would soon fit and prepare him, if his own modesty kept him not back, to come and make a supply to the want that death and great preferments bring upon us of the great lawyers of our country, though we have yet good store of them. The vicarage thereof, being a pretty living, after the expiration of a lease for years in being, belongs to the Reverend Bishop of this diocese.

From hence the Weaver shall bring us to Acton Bridge, where we must part with it, and so turn us more westerly, to look upon that township of Acton, wherein there is a house of one James Row, Gent. a freeholder of this precinct, and an ancient seat of the Farrars; and so we take with us Craughton, or Crawghton, where Sir Gilbert Ireland, Knight, the heir and possessor of a great fair house in Lancashire, called Hutt, hath a fair house and demesne.

And next unto this Kingsley, a fair lordship, whereof much of the lands belong to Rocksavage. Mr. Cambden derives Sir John Done's name from one Randal of Kingsley, to whom the Earl of Chester, Randal the First, gave the forestership of this forest, and he to the Dawnes, to hold by right of inheritance, which since fell to be called Dones; and therein also is an ancient seat of the Rutters, of Kingsley, Gentlemen, of long continuance; and not far off, a fair brick house, belonging to one of the Gerards, called Crown Wood.

But we pass thence to Mewton, a lordship on the edge of the forest, belonging to Sir John Done; and so to Alvandley, a pretty township, wherein is a chapel, and a very fine house, that belongs to Henry Arden, Esq. of Harden, formerly mentioned: and so having but only the Deel farm, the ancient inheritance of Sir John Done; and beneath it Cutnall, a very fine seat and demesne, the possession of J. Nuttall, Esq. a man of good sufficiency; we pass by Norley, where one of the Halls, a freeholder, hath a pretty seat; and by Cuddington, wherein are divers pretty farms, we fall into the spacious forest of Delamere itself, having gone round about the same in the view of this hundred; which forest is a delectable place for situation, and maintaineth not only a convenient being and preservation of his Majesty's deer, both red and fallow, whereof there is no small store, but also a great relief to the neighbouring borders and townships round about it; yielding plenty of pasture in the vales, wood upon the hills, fearn and heath, by some called ling, in the plains; great store of fish and fowl in the meres; puits, or seamews, in the flashes; both the kinds of turf for fuel, one they call flea-turf, because it is flead from the upper face of the ground in void places; the other deep-turf, because it is digged out of pits, whereof there is abundance. Upon the highest hill of all, and about the middle of the forest, is seen a very delicate house, sufficient for the dwelling of the chief forester himself when it pleaseth him, and is called the Chamber in the Forest; there being likewise in several parts dispersed on every side of the said forest, pretty and handsome lodgings, with fees and commodities thereunto belonging, for the keepers in each walk.

I might venture to wade into a long discourse of these two towns, or rather cities, which not only add tales, but even the writers, both ancient and modern, do make report of; but because few other circumstances do concur, and not so much as the ruins of any piece of them do remain, the names only of the Hundred of Eddisbury, and a stately old tree, which they call the Finny Oak, which are said to be derived from the town or city of Edelfled, and the fort or castle of Finborow, only excepted: I had rather leave to the credit of those reports and writers, than labour farther for a thing, which if we find, we can never recover.

I also let pass some old prophecies, some conceited names of trees, of moss-pits, pools, long shoots of old archers, as also the horse race one or two, and the late new-found well, which I hope I may take the liberty to leave untouched, because I suppose my long journey in this little hundred hath well nigh tired my reader already.

PARISH OF LITTLE BUDWORTH,

CONTAINS ONLY THE TOWNSHIP OF

LITTLE BUDWORTH-CUM-OULTON.

LITTLE BUDWORTH, or *Budworth in the Frith*, is about four miles N. E. E. from Tarporley; it is described as *Little Budworth with Oulton*, but it formerly was a part of the parish of Over, and is described as such in the charter, for endowing the Bishopric of Chester, 38th Henry VIII. It was originally a portion of the hundred of *Dudestan*, and was retained by the Earl at the time of the Conquest. Hugh Ceivilioc granted the manor, together with a moiety of the forestership of Mara, [between the years 1153 and 1160] to Robert le Grosvenor, father of Robert le Grosvenor, whom he succeeded. Robert le Grosvenor, son of Randle, brother of the before-mentioned Robert, was the father of Richard le Grosvenor, who held Budworth for King Edward I. as Earl of Chester, in capite; and Richard le Grosvenor, his son, recovered a moiety of the forestership of Mara, from Richard Done. Warin Grosvenor, supposed to be the son or brother of Richard, held the office of Bailiff for the Manor of Over; and he had a younger son Thomas, to whom he gave a messuage and forty acres of land, in Budworth, which Thomas again gave to John Grosvenor, his son, and he transferred this property to Mabell, the wife of Thomas Budworth. The manor continued vested in this branch of the Grosvenors, till the death of Richard le Grosvenor, who left Cecilia, his daughter, sole heiress; who married twice, into the families of Bromley and Mere. She had issue by Mere; and subsequently married John Bradburne, whom she survived. Temp. Henry VI. Henry Sartrude, a priest, had the manor from John Bradburne and Cicely, on whom he settled it for the life of the latter, with remainder to Thomas del Mere and his heirs. In the reign of Henry VI. William del Mere was succeeded in the manor by Margaret his sister, the wife of Walter Troyford, and they sold it in the 10th of the same King to William Trowtbeck, Esq. together with a fourth of the manors of Little Neston and Hargreve, for 1000 marks. Certain lands, however, in Budworth, continued for several generations vested in the female line of Robert Grosvenor.*

Budworth remained in the Troutbeck family till the death of Sir William Troutbeck, who left Margaret, his daughter, wife of John Talbot, his sole heiress, temp. Henry VIII. The Talbots thus obtaining possession, Budworth passed with their other estates to the Earls of Shrewsbury; but the share of the Forestership was sold to the Dones of Utkinton, in the reign of Henry VIII. The Earl of Shrewsbury holds a Court Leet and Baron for the manor.

* This branch of the Grosvenors, bore the ancient arms of the Grosvenors; Azure, a bend Or.

CHESHIRE

The CHURCH, which is dedicated to St. Mary and all Saints, previous to the Dissolution, belonged to the Nunnery of St. Mary in Chester, when it was called the Free Chapel of Budworth le Frith, within the parish of Over. The living is an augmented Curacy, of which the Bishop of Chester is patron and impropriator, although the lessee of the great tythes finds the curate. In 1810, the living, including augmentation and other fees, amounted to £45. 18*s.* 6*d.* The Old Church consisted of a tower, nave, chancel, and north chancel, the latter occupied as a pew by the Oulton family; but the tower only remains of this fabric, the body of the church being rebuilt of stone, pursuant to a bequest of £1000. left by a Mr. Ralph Kirkham of Manchester, who was educated at the school within this parish.

In a window in the Egerton's pew, on some fragments of stained glass, is incribed

Egerton—fieri fecit—fecerunt—qui—M.CCCCC.

Adjoining the altar, on the South side, on a grey and white marble monument—

In memory of William Kirkham, Esq. of Little Budworth, Cheshire, who died on Thursday, March 31, 1803, aged 72 years.

Adjoining the latter, on a similar monument—

Near this place are interred the remains of Ralph Kirkham, Esq. merchant, of Manchester, whose unaffected, humane, and amiable conduct through life, endeared him to all his acquaintances. His strict attention to every duty, enjoined by the gospel, justly entitled him to the exalted character of a truly good Christian. Out of his ample property, which he acquired by honest and honourable dealing, he bequeathed one thousand pounds to rebuild this church; and five thousand more to other charitable uses. He died on Tuesday the 5th of June, 1798, aged 65 years.

Over the Vestry door, on a tablet of stone—

This church is augmented with £200. by lot, by proposal of 20£. a year out of the Rectory, by Samuel Lord Bishop of Chester, in conjunction with £200. from the Governors of the Bounty. The £400. in money is laid out in a purchase of lands at Thornton, in this county.

Near to the Park Wall of Oulton, is the *School House*, erected in 1706, at the cost of Catherine Lady Egerton, widow of Sir Philip Egerton, and daughter and heiress of Piers Conway, of Hendre, in Flintshire. The annual salary of the Master is £10. and he is to teach eight poor children, who are nominated by Sir John Grey Egerton, Bart. In addition to the above endowment, 10*l.* per annum, was left by W. Kirkham before mentioned, for the education of twelve children, of the parish of Budworth, who are nominated by his representatives.

HISTORY.

OULTON,

Or, as it was formerly called *Aldington*, or *Aldeton*, is now occupied by the extensive demesne grounds of the ancient family of the Egertons, represented by Sir John Grey Egerton, Bart. The Egertons, of Egerton, have possessed it since the reign of Richard III. when it was held by them under the successors of the Grosvernors of Little Budworth. Temp. Edw. IV. it was sold by Matthew de Bechton to Hugh Done, son of Sir John Done, of Utkington. This Hugh had, by his wife Anne (the daughter of James Lord Audley, slain at Blore Heath) one daughter, and sole heiress Elizabeth, who married John Egerton, Esq. of Egerton, about 1500, to whom by this marriage passed a messuage and 100 acres of land in Oulton. It continues vested in the same family to the present day.

Sir John Grey Egerton, Bart. is descended from one of the most ancient and respectable families that adorn this county, so peculiar for the long line of ancestry which its families boast. Some particulars relative to the Egertons will be found under the head "EGERTON" in Broxton hundred, p. 338. They originated from the marriage of William Belward with Mabilla, daughter and co-heir of Robert Fitz-Hugh, the head of the powerful Barony of Malpas, in the reign of Henry I. The direct line of this William terminated in David de Egerton, temp. Edward II. who left two sisters, coheirs; but the male line was preserved in Urian, David's uncle, and continued in regular descent by the Egertons, of Heaton, (co. Lanc.) Sir Philip, a younger son of Sir Rowland Egerton, of Egerton and Oulton, was created a Baronet in 1617, and the title passed to Sir Thomas Egerton, Earl of Wilton; on whose death it became the right of the present worthy Baronet. Sir John Grey Egerton was one of the representatives of Chester in Parliament, from 1807, to 1818. Few families can boast a more illustrious line of genuine English ancestry than the present head of the House of Oulton—a line which has been elevated to the Peerage in two of its branches. On the Ridley branch, Camden bestowed the epithet of "*Familiæ clara et vetusta;*"

Engrav'd by J. Pigot

VIEW OF  OULTON.

The seat of Sir John Grey Egerton Baronet M.P.

Engraved for Hanshalls History of Cheshire.

and Leland in his Itinerary describing the family says, "The auntientes of the Egertons dwelleth now at Oldeton, and Egerton buildeth ther now."* The first house of the Egertons is at Egerton, in Malpas paroche; he hath also the manor of Oldeton." The house here alluded to has long ceased to exist; and the present *Hall of Oulton* is an elegant and capacious mansion of brick, with stone facings, of which the annexed accurate plate will afford a much better idea than any verbal description. The double flight of steps in front leads to the great hall, a truly elegant room, with a black and white marble flooring, the walls ornamented with pilasters in the Corinthian style, and the whole lighted from capacious windows, partially filled up with stained glass.† The *Park* is an enclosure of about 320 acres, and as it once, no doubt, formed part of the adjoining forest of Delamere, it is marked by the same inequality of surface. In a recess on the South side is the Roman Altar, found at Chester.‡ The grounds are delightful. A great part of Little Budworth is the property of the Earl of Shrewsbury.

THE PARISH OF MIDDLEWICH,

CONTAINS (IN THIS HUNDRED) ONLY

THE TOWNSHIP OF WEEVER,

WHICH lies about three miles W. S. W. from Midwich. At the Conquest it formed a portion of the extensive estates of Bigot, and became attached to the Fee of Aldford, being held under the Ardernes, by a family which assumed the local name. In the 55th Henry III. Henry de Wever was a forester of the chace of Mondrem, and was fined *5l.* by Reginald de Grey, the Justice, "*promala custodiâ ballivæ suæ, et destructione memoris.*" Temp. Edward III. another Henry de Wever held the township of the Fee of Aldford, by finding two men to guard the Castle there forty days, during the war. The township continued vested in the Wevers till the death of Thomas de Wever, whose daughter, Elizabeth, became the heiress, and married Sir John Stanley, son of the first Lord Stanley, temp. Henry VI. and on his death she married Sir John Done, of Utkinton. Elizabeth, the widow of Thomas de Wever, died possessed of a third part of the manor, and of Woodlegh in Bredbury, leaving her daughter Elizabeth, last mentioned, sole heiress, who survived her husband, Sir John Done. Subsequently the estate passed to Thomas Stanley, the eldest son of Sir John Stanley, by Elizabeth Weever, and from him to Thomas his son, who was described as Thomas Stanley, of Weever, Esq. The manor was thus finally vested in the Stanleys, and continued so till the beginning of the 18th century, when it was sold by John Stanley, to the Wilbrahams of Townsend; and it is now the property of George Wilbraham, Esq. of Delamere Lodge and Townsend.

One wing still remains of *Weever Hall*, which continued to be the residence of the Stanleys till about 1660, and was a building of no small dimensions, composed of timber and plaister, much in the style of the older class of Cheshire houses.§

* Philip Egerton, 26 Henry VIII.

† There are some fine paintings in the house; amongst them portraits of Lord Strafford, Archbishop Laud, Sir Thomas Moore, Archbishop Juxon. &c.

‡ See page 292. Mr. Ormerod says, that in the same recess were deposited two large fragments of the ancient Cross of Sandbach. They were brought by Sir John Crewe, from Sandbach, and placed by him in a field fronting Utkinton Hall. When the hall became a farm-house, Mr. Allen removed them to the Rectory at Tarporley, and after his death they were sent to Oulton.

§ Mr. Ormerod has the following, copied from the papers of the Wilbraham family:—"On Sunday the 3d of August, 1715, about eight o'clock in the morning, in the gate place leading to the barns belonging to Weever Hall, the ground suddenly fell in to the breadth

THE PARISH OF OVER,

CONTAINS THE TOWNSHIPS OF

OVER. | OULTON LOWE.

WETENHALL.

NOTE.—*The Hamlets of* SWANLOW *and* WINSFORD *are attached to Over.*—LITTLE BUDWORTH *was formerly a Chapelry of Over.*

OVER

Is a small market town, about five miles from Middlewich; a market and fair were granted here by charter of the 10th Edw. I. to the Abbot and Convent of Vale Royal; the market to be held on Wednesday, and the fair on the Feast of the exaltation of the Cross, including the preceding and following day. Over was numbered amongst the immediate possessions of the Earl till the 54th of Hen. III. when it was granted by Prince Edward to the Abbey of Dernhall, and passing afterwards to the Monks of Vale Abbey Royal,* continued vested in them till the Dissolution, when it was granted to Sir Thomas Holcroft, in exchange for the Manor of Cartmel, for 466*l.* 10*s.* 10*d.* with a reserved rent of 10*l.* 0*s.* 4*d.* The Holcrofts continued the proprietors till Over was sold to Edmund Pershall, merchant, of London, from whom it was purchased about the middle of the 17th century, by Thomas Cholmondeley, whose descendant Thomas Cholmondeley, Esq. of Vale Royal, is the present proprietor.†

Over, which is a borough by prescription, is under the jurisdiction of a Mayor, who is thus annually chosen: Mr. Cholmondeley holds a Court Leet and Baron for the manor, and in October two juries are impannelled, one for the Borough, called the Grand Jury, the other for the lesser townships, called the County Jury. From twelve names returned by the Grand Jury, the Lord of the Manor selects the Mayor. The Mayor is sworn in by the Clerk of the Court, and again at the Winter Session, when Leavelookers are appointed.—Within the borough and lordship the Mayor executes all the functions of a Justice of the Peace; his processes are executed by a Serjeant at Mace. On retiring from office, he bears the title of Alderman, but no longer retains a judicial authority of any description. Licenses for inns and public-houses, are signed by the Mayor, and the County Magistrates: and at the Quarter Sessions the Mayor takes his seat on the bench.

The town consists of a long straggling street, in which at certain intervals are the remains of several crosses. Many marvellous traditionary stories are told here of the former population and great importance of this town, which want only historical facts to corroborate them.

In this township is WOODFORD HALL DEMESNE, granted to Thurstan de Wodeford, by Randle Blundeville; from whom it passed to the Egertons of Bulkeley. In the reign of Philip and Mary, it was held by Hugh Starkie, of Oulton; and was afterwards purchased by the Maistersons, of Nantwich, who sold it to Sir John Booth, Bart. of Dunham Massy. George Booth, Esq. Prothonotory, of Chester, the translator of *Diodorus Siculus,* was heir to Woodford; he died in 1719, and was buried at St. Oswald's in Chester.—

of two yards diameter, with a rumbling noise, and continued until Tuesday. The hole could not be fathomed by a pole of 12 feet, but the earth tumbling in from the sides, the chasm became nine yards in diameter, yet not so many feet deep, and full of salt water.

* Vale Royal was within the limits of Over Parish, till by an Act of Parliament, Whitegate was taken from it.

† Mr. Cholmondeley represented the County in Parliament during several Sessions.

From his grand-daughter, by his daughter Catherine Howard, wife of James Howard, of Boughton. Esq. the estate was bought by Sir George Prescot, Bart. who resold it to the present proprietor, Mr. Richard Dutton, of Waverton. At Bridge-end House, in the township of Over, was born the far-famed Prophet *Robert*, or as he is called in the Vale Royal MSS. *William Nickson*. The story of this ideot is well known, as is the trash called his "*Prophecies*." Little can now be said relative to him, further than what has already appeared in preceding publications. But to omit him altogether in a history of Cheshire, might be deemed an unpardonable crime; we have therefore collected all that is necessary to be known of Nickson in the accompanying note, chiefly copied from the account given by Messrs. Lysons.*

The CHURCH of Over is dedicated to St. Chad; the present incumbent is the Rev. Thomas Crane, instituted Dec. 5, 1810. The impropriation of this church was given by Randle Gernons to the Benedictine Nunnery at Chester; but it does not appear to have existed before the Survey.

On the foundation of the Abbey of Vale Royal, the Nuns of Chester released to it the tithes of a part of this parish, those of Radford, Little Over, Sutton, and Merton, for which they received 105*s.* 2*d.* from the rents of Middlewich; these tithes were, however, subsequently received by the Nuns. In 1475, there was a final award of the portion of tithes by the Abbot, Prioress, and Sir William Stanley, Chamberlain of Chester,

* The earliest printed account of Nixon and his productions, was that published by Curll in 1714. He is described as an illiterate plow-boy, his capacity scarcely exceeding that of an ideot; he seldom spoke, unless when he uttered his prophecies, which were taken down from his mouth by the bye-standers. An anonymous author of the "Life of Robert Nixon, the Cheshire Prophet," places his birth in the reign of Edward IV. but Oldmixon, in his life of him, says that he lived in the reign of James I. A letter annexed to this pamphlet, which has the signature of Mr. Ewers, states, that in 1714, there was an old man, named Woodman, then living at Coppenhall, who well remembered Nixon, described his person, and furnished many particulars relative to him. The tradition at Vale Royal House, where the above-mentioned MSS. have been long preserved with great care and secrecy,* favour the former account; and were it not so much connected with Vale Royal and the Cholmondeley Family, who are known not to have settled at that place before 1615,† the story would have more the air of probability, if placed at a period so remote. If, according to Oldmixon's account, so extraordinary a person had lived at Vale Royal in the reign of James I. we might expect to find some mention of him in the parish register, either at Over, or Whitegate, both of which have been searched in vain; and it is almost incredible that he should not have been noticed by his cotemporaries; yet no mention is made of him either by Webb, who in his History of 1622, speaks much of the Cholmondeley family, and relates a visit of King James I. to Vale Royal for four days; and by the industrious Randle Holme, who has recorded all the remarkable events and circumstances of his time. Indeed, whatever be the age assigned to Nixon, if his stories and his prophecies had been known in the 17th century, it seems very extraordinary that neither of the Holmes should have inserted a single iota concerning him, in their voluminous collection relative to this county; and that Fuller, who published his "Worthies" immediately after the Restoration, when many of Nixon's prophecies are said to have been fulfilled, should also have omitted to notice him.—The story of Nixon's death is, that having been sent for by the King, he was accidentally starved, as he had himself foretold; this is said to have happened at Hampton Court, where two places are pointed out by the person who shews the Palace, each of which has been said to have been the scene of his famishment. This part of the story will not bear the test of inquiry better than the others; there is no entry in the parish register of the burial of such a person in the reign of James I.; one of the closets pointed out as that in which Nixon was by accident locked up, was evidently built in the reign of William III.; and it is needless to observe, that the whole Palace was built subsequently to the reign of Henry VII. which is by some said to have been the time of Nixon's death. When, in addition to these circumstances, it is observed, that the particulars relating to the Cholmondeleys in the printed accounts of Nixon, are at variance with the real and known history of that family, we cannot help recording his story as very suspicious, if not wholly legendary. Mr. Oldmixon says, that when Nixon prophecied the Cholmondeley family was nearly being extinct, the senior Thomas Cholmondeley, Esq. having married Sir Walter St. John's daughter, a lady not esteemed very young; that Nixon prophecied, that "when an eagle should rest on the top of the house, then an heir should be born to the Cholmondeley family;" and that the prophecy was fulfilled by the birth of a son and heir by that lady. In a letter adderssed to Mr. Wm. Ewers, of Nantwich, we are told that this birth of a son and heir, happened about the year 1698, more than threescore years after Nixon is supposed (even by those who place him in the 17th century) to have lived; and Oldmixon says, on the authority of a sister of Mrs. Cholmondeley, that the son then born, was the heir, who in his time possessed the Vale Royal estates. It may be observed that the above mentioned Thomas Cholmondeley, had a son by his first wife, who married and had issue; and it was not till after the death of this son without male issue, that the estates devolved to his son, by Sir Walter St. John's daughter.

Lysons, p. 515.

Ibid.

CHESHIRE HISTORY.

which is noticed in the Leger Book of Vale Royal Abbey. At the Dissolution, Bishop Bird obtained a grant of the Rectory of Over, together with the advowson of the Vicarage, with the reversion to his successors, which they still retain; but the great tithes are held under the Bishop by Charles Cholmondeley, Esq.

The Church of Over was rebuilt by Hugh Starky, Esq. in 1543, and his remains rest under an altar tomb in the North wall; on the tomb is his effigy in brass, and the inscription—

Of your charite pray for the soule of Hugh Starkey, of Olton, Esquier, gentilm˜ Usher to King Henry the VIII. and son to Hugh Starky, of Olton, esquier, which Hugh the son decessyd the yere of our Lord God M.CCCCC.... On his soule Jhu˜ have mc˜y.

There is another altar tomb in the front of the Chancel steps, containing the ashes of Hugh Starky, the rebuilder of the church. The inscription now obliterated, ran thus—

Hic jacent corpora Hugonis Starkey de Olton arm'i, Margaretæ uxoris ejus.

In the South aisle, in stained glass, are the figures of John Starkey, of Oulton, and Agnes his wife. The male figure is in plate armour. In the East window are some fine remains of tabernacle work, also in stained glass. The registers commence in 1558; but the baptisms are imperfect from 1564 to 1590, and the burials from 1567 to 1596.*

THE SCHOOL, which was removed from the township of Dernhall, is situated at the corner of the church road, near the Cross. It was founded in 1689, by Mrs Elizabeth Venables, and her son, Thomas Lee. Esq. for children of the parishes of Over and Whitegate, and of the township of Weever, in Middlewich parish.—The endowment was originally only 20*l.* per annum in lands, which now let for about 55*l.* per annum. The school was removed in 1803.

SWANLOW

Lies within the jurisdiction of the Manor of Over, and is the property of Thomas Cholmondeley, Esq. of Vale Royal.

WINSFORD,

Or as it is sometimes called *Winsford Bridge*, is a hamlet of the township of Over, lying between that place and Davenham, on the opposite side of the Weaver, where there is a fair held on the 8th of May, and a market on the Saturday. There are extensive Brine Pits here, on both sides of the river.

OULTON LOWE,

Was held at the Conquest by the Earls; from whom it is supposed to have passed to the Kingsleys, Randle de Kingsley afterwards giving a moiety of it to Godfrey de la Lowe,† who was the father of John, Randle, and Henry; Randle had issue by ——, Richard, his eldest son and Ralph de Oldeton: Richard succeeded to his father's lands in Oulton, and Randle became possessed of Oulton, being the founder of a family which assumed the local name. Richard was living in the 4th Edw. I. when Nicholas, the son of John de Wettenhall, obtained from him the grant of a messuage and 10 acres of land in *Oldinton*. The Oultons continued here some generations: when it appears that Joan, or Johanna, second of the three coheiresses of John de Olton, became possessed of the manor, with whom it passed in marriage to Peter Starkye, the second son of Thomas Starkye, of Nether Hall, in Stretton, whose descendants continued here till towards the conclusion of the 17th century, when it was purchased by the Egertons of Oulton, and it is now the property of Sir J. Grey Egerton, Bart.

† Vill. Cest.

Darley Hall, the ancient seat of the Starkies,‡ was taken down by the father of the present proprietor. It was moated; and the site of it is now occupied by a farm house.

WETENHALL,

Or Wettenhall, is about seven miles N. N. W. from Nantwich. At the time of the Survey, it formed part of the estates of Gilbert de Venables, Baron of Kinderton. In the reign of Henry I. it gave name to a family, one of whom, Adam de Wetenhall, was appointed Governor of Carnarvon Castle in 1289. John de Wetenhall, temp. Edw. II. had six daughters and coheiress; two of them died without issue; two divided the share which their father possesesd of the Ba-

* In 1755 the Vicarage was augmented, and three years afterwards lands were purchased, value 400l. half of which was given by the Executors of Wm. Stratford, LL. D. the residue from Queen Anne's Bounty.—ORM.

‡ Hugh Starkie, who rebuilt the Church of Over, had a natural son, Oliver Starkie, a Knight of Malta, and subsequently Grand Master of the Order.—Of this family was Ralph Starkie, the Collector of the Cheshire Pedigrees, and author of a Poem, entitled, " Introa-

rony of Wich Malbank; and the other two, Margaret and Elizabeth, brought their moieties of Wettenhall in marriage to Sir Adam Bostock, and Sir Richard de Manley. In the reign of Henry V. Adam de Bostock held as of fee a moiety of the manor, with the appurtenances, in the forest of Mondrem, from the King, as Earl; but this share in the reign of Henry VIII. passed to Sir John Savage, as the son of Anne, grand-daughter of Ralph Bostock. It afterwards passed (44th Eliz.) to the Wilbrahams by fine; and is now the property, by purchase, of Henry Tomkinson, Esq. of Dorfold. The other moiety, that of the Manleys, continued in that family till the 4th of Elizabeth, when Wm. Manley, Esq. and Thomas his son, passed the manor by fine, to John Brereton, Esq. of Eccleston. It continued vested in the Breretons till the reign of Charles I. when Richard Brereton died seized of half of Wetenhall, with messuages in Chester, and the advowson of the Church of St. Mary there; and his son John sold his moiety of Wettenhall, to Roger Wilbraham, Esq. of Dorfold, from whose descendants it was subsequently purchased by Henry Tomkinson, Esq. about the middle of the last century.

The *Hall* of Wettenhall is a curious building, erected in 1630. The front is terminated by three gables, with long windows,* and is in good repair. It is occupied as a farm house.

Near the hall is the *Chapel* of Ease to Over; it is built of brick. In 1719, it was augmented by Queen Anne's bounty, and the Archbishop of York contributed 50*l.* The Vicar of Over appoints the Minister, whose salary in 1810, amounted to 105*l.* 5*s.* 11*d.*

TUNIO;" from which (given in the prospectus of a History of Cheshire,) the following is an extract:—

"With Erdeswicke and Bostock, Ralfe Starkie was cotemporary, of the family of the Starkies of Stretton; a Statesman, a Poet, and an Antiquary. His two first characters do not so immediately concern us; though, what can be a stronger evidence of the powers of the human mind, than to see the abilities of a Burleigh, a Spencer and a Camden, all united in the same person! The Antiquarian Collections of his, still remaining, are the following: Rolls of Cheshire Families, 1595; a book of Alphabetical References to these Rolls; and a book of References to Mr. Erdeswicke's Cheshire Manuscripts. He has besides given us, all the Royal Grants of our Palatinate Immunities; and an exact Account of all the Imports and Exports from the Harbour of Chester, during five years of the reign of Queen Elizabeth,* with the Amount of the Revenue arising from these Port Duties. His Legacy, however, of Cheshire Collections, would certainly have been more extensive, if the jealousy of James the First had not issued a warrant† for the seizure of all Mr. Starkie's State Papers; and, amongst these. many of his antiquarian ones perished. Sir Thomas Wilson, Secretary of State, who executed this warrant, certifies the seizure of so large a number as 45 pacquets of Mr. Starkie's papers.

"You will naturally remark the very particular number that was certified. But these hackneyed figures, had not at that time been elevated above the innocent insignificance of their Peers, by the unhappy lunacy of party, and that distraction of the times which is so greatly to be lamented. Whether you remark it, however, or not, as I have mentioned our antiquary in two of his superior characters, permit me to speak of him in his third; and to give you a single stanza from his historical, political, and moral poem, addressed to his Mistress, Queen Elizabeth. The principal subject is the melancholy reign of Edward the Second, whose Ghost is supposed to recount his several misfortunes, in 581 stanzas—

Why, shou'd a wasted spirit spent in woe,
Disclose the wounds receiv'd within his breast?
Is't not enough, that Fortune proves his foe,
In whose sad frowns is folded his un-rest?
Is'nt not enough, to know himself distrest?—
Oh! no, surcharged hearts must needs complain:
Some ease it is, though small, to tell our pain."

"I have given you this specimen, divested of its antiquated spelling. And I must not conceal from you, for the honour of our antiquary, that this poem has, in one instance, been attributed to the great Spencer. It is mentioned with a perhaps; but it is most untruly conjectural. The poem is in Mr. Starkie's own hand writing; it has never been even surmised as Spencer's, by the several writers of his life; and a copy of it is now existing, with a variety of alterations and additions, to move the compassion of James the First. The author stiles himself Infortunio—as being the unfortunate Ralph Starkie, that in 1619 had unhappily incurred the displeasure of this jealous Monarch; who ascended the throne of England at least four years after the death of Edmund Spencer, which happened about 1598.

"Ralph Starkie, you will find to be more favourable to our antiquities. For I have now in my own possession a very curious Heraldrical Manuscript, formed from all the visitations then in being; with fair draughts of old Seals, Coats, Arms, and Devices. In the first page is the following remark—'This book is augmented in very many places out of Mr. Sampson Erdeswicke, Moth, and other good Gatherings, by me Ralph Starkie, of London, merchant, second son of John Starkie, of Oltone, in the county of Chester, Esqr. 1610.'—A lineal descent of which family has been left us by his namesake, the Antiquary, under the description of the family of Starkie of Darley, or Olton-Lowe."‡

* From the 20th, to the 26th. † August 14th, 1619.

‡ "Starkies is at Dorle, a v miles from Northwich, a scant mile from Oldeton, and a 3 miles from Vale Royal."—Leland's Itin. vol. vii. p. 32.

CHESHIRE

THE PARISH OF TARPORLEY,

HISTORY.

CONTAINS THE TOWNSHIPS OF

TARPORLEY.
EATON,

RUSHTON,
AND
UTKINTON.*

TARPORLEY

Is a market town of little consequence, about ten miles from Chester, on the great road leading from thence to London. It was held under the Barons of Kinderton; but in 1281 it appears to be possessed by Hugh de Thorpley, who had a grant of a market every Wednesday; and an annual fair of three days at the feast of Holyrood; but these privileges were 12 years afterwards transferred by him to Reginald de Grey,† receiving half the perquisites of the fair and markets. From an inquisition p. m. of the 12th Richard II. Reginald de Grey of Ruthin is stated to hold a moiety of Tarporley, with the advowson of the Church, and the *Hermit's Chapel* near the town, from the King as Earl. It continued in the Greys (afterwards Earls of Kent) till the 23d Henry VIII. when Hugh Dennys obtained the manors of Tarporley, Rushton, and Eyton. Wm. Hinton afterwards (1 Edward VI.) purchased the manors, but his descendants alienated them, so that in the first of Mary, only a third of the manors remained vested in the family. A moiety of Eaton and Rushton was sold by them to William Yardley, of Caldecote; of which Sir John Egerton, of Egerton, died possessed in 1614, having purchased it from the Yardleys. This has descended to Sir John Grey Egerton, Bart. the present proprietor. The other parts, forming the entire manor of Tarporley, with the moieties of Eaton and Rushton, passed by purchase to the Dones of Flaxyards; and this share of the property, together with the forestership of Delamere, has descended from the Crewes to the Ardernes, and is now the property of John Arden, Esq. joint Lord with Sir John Grey Egerton, Bart.

The Manor of Tarporley was apportioned to Mrs. Jane Done, eldest sister of John Done, Esq. of Utkinton, who by deed of February 12, 1662, settled her estates to the use of herself for life, with remainder to her sister Mary for life, with other remainders; on the determination of which, the property was to be divided into six parts: two sixths were limited to Sir John Arderne (son and heir apparent to his sister Eleanor) and his heirs; and the other four sixths to Henry, Ralph, James, and Philip, his younger brothers. Before the final adjustment, these estates were involved in a Chancery suit: but in 1725, a decree was issued, dividing them between the children of Eleanor, youngest sister of Mrs. Jane Done, who married Ralph Arderne, Esq. viz. two sixths of the manors, with the Hall of Utkinton, to Sir John Arderne, Knight; one sixth to Henry Arderne; a sixth to Ralph Arderne (whose eldest daughter brought it in marriage to Jonathan Hulley); a sixth part to the Dean and Chapter of Chester, as devisees of Dean Arderne; and the remaining sixth to Philip Arderne, who devised it to the Duckenfield family; from whom, in 1733, it was purchased by Philip Egerton, Esq. of Oulton, the father of Sir John Grey Egerton, Bart. the present proprietor. The two sixths of the manor, including Utkinton, is the property of John Arden, Esq.; and Henry Arden's share is vested in Mrs. Clegg;‡ James Arden's share was sold by the son of his eldest grand-daughter to Mr. J. Shaw, of Idenshaw, who bequeathed it to his fourth son, Henry

* Tarporley township contains 1108a. 16p.; Eaton 1262a. 2r. 35p.; Rushton 1717a. 2r. 25p.; and Utkinton 1779a. 2r. 15p.

† Justiciary of Chester, and one of the most powerful Barons of the Realm—from his grandson Henry de Grey, sprang the Barons Grey de Wilton.

‡ Lysons, p. 790.

Arden Shaw, who died in ——. The manerial rights are held by each possessor in rotation, according to the lots agreed upon by them.*

*Orm. page 22, vol. 1.

It is ascertained that Tarporley had formerly a Mayor; in 1297, Richard Francis occurs as filling that office; William de Hulgrave in 1348; and in the 12th Ric. II. Richard de Chalenor. The office was eventually disused, *why* is not now known, and the government is at present vested in two Constables. The town consists of a long, well paved street, having a general appearance of neatness: at the South end of which is the Manor House, now the property of the Dean and Chapter of Chester. On a long beam in the west front, are the two following lines—

> Ralphe Done, Esquyer, the Lorde of this place,
> Was an ayde to this building in every case.

At the extremity of the beam are the words *John Wytter*, 1586.

Beneath on a large ledge, in one line—

Peneys quoth Jhon Newsome hatthe kept hys promes just, in buldyng of thys howse in Awgust, anno 1585.

On an ornamented shield appears the crest of the Dones, the arms of Davenport, and the crest of the Cholmondeleys, with R. D, W. D, H. C, and T. W, at the four corners. In the meadows, near the church, are a few traces of the entrenchments thrown up by the Parliamentarians in 1642. In a plea to a *quo warranto*, temp. Henry VII. the Earl of Kent, as Lord of the Manor, claims the right of punishing bakers offending against the law by the pillory: maltsters by the tumbrel; scolds by the thew, i. e. being placed on a stool called a *cucking stool:* indeed, with the exception of the power of capital punishment, the rights of the Lord varied very little from those of the Barons of Malpas.

The Church, which is dedicated to St. Helen, is built of red stone, and is of considerable antiquity. It consists of tower, chancel, and side aisles, the east ends of which are enclosed as chancels. The North Chancel belonged to the Dones of Utkinton, the other to the Flaxyards branch of that family.

The living is a Rectory; the present Incumbent the Rev. Philip Egerton, M. A. instituted Feb. 3, 1816, on the death of Dean Cholmondeley. The corn tithes of the entire parish belong to him, as does the tithe on hay for the township of Tarporley. The townships claim a modus of 12*d*. per statute acre for meadow land, and 8*d*. for upland. The small tithes are taken in kind, or by payments in lieu thereof. The advowson descended with the manor through the Greys, Capels, and Dennys, to the Hintons, who sold it to the Starkies. John Starkie of Oulton, sold it to Ralph Done of Utkinton, in whose family it continued; and by the settlement of Mrs. Jane Done, was determined in a similar way to the manor of Tarporley.*

*See p. 434.

There are a great number of monuments in the church; the following only are selected, as being particularly connected with the manerial proprietors, &c. On a flag-stone in the Chancel—

Here lieth the body of Crewe Arden, M. A. of Trinity College, Cambridge, and Rector of this parish. He was inducted on the 28th of February, 1778, and departed this life at his Parsonage House, on the 25th day of August, 1787, aged 37 years. During the possession of this living, he made his parish his constant residence, and the welfare of his parishioners his principal delight and care. He was a generous, charitable, and truly religious man. His death was a most severe affliction to his family and numerous friends, and his funeral was attended with the general lamentations of his parishioners, by whom his memory will be long revered.

On a stone tablet in the South aisle—

Near to this place are deposited the remains of Henry Arderne, of Tarporley, who departed this life the 27th of September, 1775, in the 50th year of his age. Also the remains of Catherine Arderne, relict of the above Henry Arderne, who departed this life the 19th of June, 1777, in the 52d year of her age. Likewise the remains of John Arderne, son of the above mentioned Henry and Catherine Arderne, who departed this life the 30th of July, 1779, in the 19th year of his age.

Within the Chancel rails, on the North wall, a large handsome mural and altar monument; with the full-length figure of Sir John Crewe, Knt. his hands closed, and his eyes turned up to heaven. At his head and feet are two figures of weeping boys, and above an arch supported by fluted pillars, his shield of arms; below is inscribed on a tablet—

Here lyeth (in hopes of a joyful resurrection) the body of Sir John Crewe, of Utkinton, in the county Palatine of Chester, Knt. son of John Crewe, Esq. grandson of Sir Randle Crewe, Knt. Lord Chief Justice of the King's Bench, descended from y[e] ancient family of y[e] Crewes, of Crewe, in y[e] s[d]. county, and from w[ch] (by a younger son) was descended ye 1st Lord Crewe, Baron of Steane, in ye county of Northampton. He was a lover of y[e] Constitution both in Church and State, and consequently an enemy to Popery and arbitrary Government: steadfast to y[e] establisht religion, but charitable to such as dissented from it, who he thought were to be won over rather by mildness than severity, by ye force of reason yn by persecution. He was exemplary in his devotions, and careful to have his family join with him twice a day therein. His loyalty was unshaken and conformable to ye laws of his country. He strenuously maintained ye Revolution principles, and rejoyct in ye happy prospect wch was ye natural effect of them, ye establishmt of ye present Royal Family, and therein ye preservation of ye British liberties and ye security of ye Protestant Religion. He was open, free, and obliging in conversation, a lover of learning and learned men, delighted in a country life, bearing no office but yt of Chief Forester of ye Forest of Delamere, in this county, wch he held by inheritance. He was a dutiful son, an affectionate husband, a kind relation, and a faithful friend; good to his servants, generous to his tenants (whose posterity will enjoy the effects of his bounty) charitable to ye poor, universally belov'd, and as generally regretted at his death. He married 1st Mary, daughter of Thomas Wagstaffe, of Tachbrooke, in the county of Warwick, Esq. a lady of admirable endowments for piety, charity, and steadiness in friendship. His second wife (by whom this monument is erected, in obedience to his will) was Mary, daughter of Sr Wilughby Aston, of Aston, in ye county of Chester, Bt. He died May ye 19th, 1711, in ye 71st year of his age.

Adjoining the above—

Here lieth interr'd the body of Dame Mary Crew, relict of Sr Jno Crew, of Utkinton, Knt. She departed this life the 8th of April, in the 67th year of her age, Anno Dom. 1734.

After the death of her first husband, this Lady married Dr Chamberlain.

Near the altar is an elegant white mural monument, with a well-executed half-length of Sir John Done, of Utkinton, in the costume of the reign of James I. his left hand resting on the hilt of his sword.—As a motto under the shield of arms—*Omnia mei Dona Dei;* the inscription on a black marble tablet—

Hic juxta situs est Johannes Done, de Utkinton, in Com. Palat. Cestriæ eques auratus, Forrestæ de Delamere jure hæreditario Præpositus, a Rege Jacobo 1mo Utkintonæ Equestir dignitate ornatus. Vir omni virtutum genere eximio præditus. Uxorem duxit Dorotheam Thomæ Wilbraham de Woodhey in comitatu dicto armigeri filiam. Obiit die XIVo Aprilis ano Dom. MDCXXIX.—D. Joannes Crewe de Utkinton, eques auratus, Avo optime merito posuit.

The following inscription appears on a black marble tablet, in the North-east corner, near the altar—

Hanc juxta parietem jacet Johannes Crewe de Utkinton, in comitatu Cestriæ, Armiger. Filius Ranulphi Crewe de Crewe in eodem Comitatu Militis, natu minor, qui duxit Mariam Johannis Done de Utkinton pr'dicti Militis, Filiam secundam ——— et obiit Duodecimo die Maii, Anno Christi 1670.*

On a magnificent altar monument, opposite to that of Sir John Crewe, are the representation of two females in white marble, an infant at the feet of the first. The head of the other female reclines on a cushion, and she holds in her left hand a book. The inscription is very long, to the memory of Jane Done, one of the coheirs of John Done, Esq.; also of Mary Crewe, the second daughter of Sir John Done, wife of John Crewe, Esq. The monument was erected by Sir John Crewe, of Utkinton, in 1698.†

It appears that in this parish were formerly two CHANTRIES, *The Chapel of the Rood*, and *The Hermit's Chapel*. The Chapel of the Hermit was presented to in 1385, by Reginald de Grey, and in 1397, when John Achworth was the Priest. In the Register at Lichfield it is described—"*Lib'a capella s'ci Leonardi, sive le Hermitage juxta Torplegh.*" Mr. Ormerod says, "Accident disclosed the site of this chantry, whilst these sheets were transcribing for the press.‡ In ploughing up a field called the Hermitage Field, about half a mile N. W. of the church, the workmen laid bare the foundations of a small cell, built with red ashlars, but which were so slight, that the plan could not be traced. Near this was found a stone coffin, containing the remains of a human skeleton, the thigh bone and skull tolerably perfect. The Hermit had chosen for his retirement a delightful knoll, which commands the Broxtons Hills and the Vale of Chester."

The SCHOOL is in the Church Yard; the arms of Done impaling Wilbraham, with the date 1636, appear over the door. The Master, who is appointed by John Arden, Esq. (who also keeps the building in repair) has £20. per annum paid by the Dean and Chapter of Chester; the scholars, however, pay for their education.

The CHARITIES are chiefly:—£12. per annum, left by John Crewe, Esq. in 1668, charged on lands in Tattenhall, for apprenticing poor children of Tarporley

* This monument was removed from the wall under the second window, in the North side of the North Chancel, in August, 1811.

† Jane Done left 20l. per annum to the School here; and 200l. for the binding apprentice poor children in Tarporley and Utkinton.—Mary Crewe left 200l. for the binding apprentice the eldest sons and daughters of cottagers, her tenants, in such places as were not provided for by her sister's benefaction.

‡ Orm. Part I. published May 1, 1816.

and Utkinton. Two apprentices nominated by John Arden, Esq. on the recommendation of the Rector and Churchwardens, are annually put out by the Charity. A rent charge of £13. left by Mrs. Mary Crewe, in 1685, for apprenticing the sons or daughters of the tenants of herself and heirs, in Clotton, Eaton, Rushton, Alpraham, Kelsall, or elsewhere, except Tarporley, and Utkinton. This charity is under the controul of John Arden, Esq. A rent charge of £6. per annum, left in 1704, by Sir John Crewe, Knight, to be paid in equal portions to four poor women, placed in alms-houses built by him, to be selected from the tenants of Utkinton Hall, the townships of Utkinton, Tarporley, Eaton, and Rushton; Utkinton and Tarporley to have the preference. This charity is also managed by Mr. Arden. The sum of £507. 12*s.* was expended in 1722, in purchasing an estate in Davenham, of about 33 acres, which then let for about £30. per annum. The present rental is 90*l.*; one third of which is shared amongst the poor of Tarporley, another third amongst those of Utkinton, and the remainder to the poor of Eaton and Rushton. This is appropriated by the Minister and Churchwardens. In Nov. 1741, the Rev. Thomas Gardiner left 100*l.* for the instruction of poor children in Utkinton, Eaton, and Rushton.—This is managed by the Rector. The Rev. Crewe Arden's legacy of 100*l.* is also managed by the Rector.

RUSHTON AND EATON.

These manors were granted by John Scott to Hugh Fitton, together with the vills of Great and Little Eaton. This Hugh, who was the ancestor of the Fittons of Gawsworth, committing a felony, the Earl seized on them, and they passed, along with the Earldom to the Crewes; but Henry III. by letters patent, granted them to John de Grey; from whose descendants, Barons of Wilton, they passed through the Greys of Ruthin, the Capell, Dennys, and Hynton families, to the present Lords, Sir J. G. Egerton, Bart. and John Arden, Esq.

Rushton Hall, continued in the Hintons, and their representatives, the Maddocks; and was sold by the Marchioness of Lansdowne, daughter and heiress of the Rev. Hinton Maddock, to her uncle Richard Maddock, Esq. who resold it to Sir John Siddorn.

Flaxyards, the former seat of the Dones, is now occupied as a farm-house. It is moated, and in a truly pleasant situation.

The Welds, a very ancient family, resided in Eaton from the time of Henry III. to the reign of Charles II. when they removed to Newbold Astbury. Of this family was Sir Humphrey Weld, of Lullworth, in the county of Dorset, Lord Mayor of London.

The *Boothurst* Estate, passed in marriage to the Ardens, from whom it descended to the father of Mrs. Clegg, who sold it to Mr. Thomas Hough.

UTKINTON,

Was held under the Kinderton Barony, and was possessed by the Dones, as early as the reign of King John, and continued in the direct line of this family till 1629, when on the death of Sir John Done, the succession of his daughter was contested by Sir Ralph Done, of Duddon, a younger branch of the Flaxyards family, and heir male. He failed, however, in his suit, and the property was divided between Jane, Mary, Eleanor, and Frances. In 1725, pursuant to an award of Chancery, the estates were again divided into six shares, each valued at 4,200*l.* among Richard, eldest brother of Sir John Arderne; John Arderne, of Boothurst; Ralph Arderne, of Clayton Bridge; James Arderne, of the Oak, in Sutton; and the Dean and Chapter of Chester, to whom Dean Arderne had bequeathed his estate; Mrs. Arderne's son, Richard, taking two shares.* This division was the consequence of a litigation, which commenced in 1715, on the death of Mrs. Knightly, relative to the further provisions of Mrs. Done's will.

* See Tarporley, page 431.

The two first shares are the property of John Arden, Esq.; the third, with the share of Utkinton and Tarporley, including the *Shaw Farm* Estate, is vested in Mrs. Clegg; the fourth share of Willington, Utkinton, and Tarporley, with the advowson, was sold to Edward Warren, merchant, in March 1727, for 1000*l.*; resold by him to Sir Nathaniel Duckenfield, of Duckenfield, for 1762*l.* 13*s.* and is now the property (being purchased by his father, Philip Egerton, Esq.) of Sir J. G. Egerton, Bart. The fifth is in the Dean and Chapter of Chester; and the sixth in the Representatives of James Arderne, of the Oak, with the exception of the advowson, which was sold to his cousin, Richard Arderne, of Harden.

CHESHIRE HISTORY.

A great part of *Utkinton Hall* has been taken down; the remainder is now a farm house. It is desirably situated; and what exists of the former building bears the marks of considerable antiquity, composed of timber and plaister, and stone on the ancient Court side. An octagonal pillar of oak pierces the interior of the house, and supports the roof.—The painted glass, which formerly enriched the windows, is preserved at Vale Royal. The *Chapel*, consecrated by Bishop Bridgeman, in 1635, is now a cheese room.*

" To what base uses may we not return!"

All the family pictures, together with the library, which contained a valuable and rare collection of books and tracts, have been removed. They remained here, however, so late as 1755. The Hall was attacked and plundered by the Royalists under Col. Werden, and Colonel Marrow, Governor of Chester, of plate, jewels, writings, &c. in 1644; and although the booty was ordered to be restored by the House of Commons, in Oct. 1648, it seems Mrs. Marrow had carried off the greater part of the valuables.

John Done, of Utkinton, was one of the " seaven valiant and generous esquiers of the county of Chester," who had the command of the 2000 archers raised by Ric. II. " especiallie chosen out for the keepinge of the King's p'son in safetie."

THE PARISH OF ST. OSWALD,†

CONTAINS IN THIS HUNDRED

THE TOWNSHIP OF IDDINSHALL,

WHICH consists of only two houses, is about a mile and a half S. W. from Tarporley, and is completely detached from any other part of the parish. Previous to the Conquest, it belonged to the secular Canons of St. Werburgh, and it appears from the Survey, that it was retained by them. Before 1093, two thirds of the manor was possessed by the Earl Hugh, but he confirmed a third of it to the monastery. The residue was given to a family which took the name of Idineshall; and Robert de Idineshall gave to his brother John all his lands here, which the latter quit-claimed to the Abbot of Chester. At the Dissolution, the manor was given to the Dean and Chapter of Chester, but it was afterwards extorted from them by Sir Richard Cotton, in 1550, and he sold it to Richard Hurleston, Esq. from whom it was purchased by Sir Peter Pinder, temp. Eliz. but this title became extinct by the death of Sir Paul Pinder, about 1700, and the estate passed to Paul Williams, Esq. of Pont-y-Gwyddel, in right of his mother, who was the representative of that family.—From the Williams's it passed by female heirs to the Hydes, and Giffards, of Nerquis, in the county of Flint. It is now the property of Miss Giffard, of Nerquis. The present hall is occupied as a farm-house; the site of the old hall occupies an area of four acres, and is moated.

* The first sermon preached in it by Mr. Harvey, in 1700.

† In Chester.

THE PARISH OF WHITEGATE,

CONTAINS THE TOWNSHIPS OF

DERNHALL,
MARTON,

AND PART OF
OVER.

The Church of Whitegate is situated about four miles S. W. from Northwich, and stood at the gate of Vale Royal Monastery. It was made a Parish Church by Act of Parliament passed in the 33d Henry VIII. but it appears to have been used for all the purposes of a Parish Church long before that period; the Act reciting, that it had time out of mind been made so by authority of the Pope, for the tenants, &c. dwelling on the Monastery Demesne, as well as for the tenants in *Foxwist, Gaville, Salterswall, Over, Merton,* the *Brockhouses,* and all other houses within the precincts of *Over* Parish. It was consecrated as the Parish Church of our *Blessed Lady the Virgin of Whitegate;* all the usual tithe to be paid to the Rector, except that on corn, which was reserved to the King.

The advowson of the Vicarage was granted in the 36th Henry VIII. to John Cokke; but before 1597, it passed to the Holcrofts, of Vale Royal, and from them to the Mainwarings of Merton, who were patrons in 1625. Previous to 1643, the Cholmondeleys obtained it; and it is now vested in Thomas Cholmondeley, Esq. The living is an augmented Vicarage, valued according to the returns of 1810, at 88*l.* 15*s.* 9*d.* The Church is a neat modern building. There are no monumental memorials of interest. The Registers commence 1565. The present incumbent is the Rev. Edmund Lally, instituted as Vicar in 1772.

In this parish is Vale Royal, the seat of Thomas Cholmondeley, Esq. M. P. and formerly the *Monastery of St. Mary,* of which some notice is taken in the introduction to this hundred, but it requires a further notice here.—It appears from the *Chronicle of Vale Royal,* that Prince Edward, the son of Henry III. having been in danger of shipwreck on his return from the Crusades, made a vow to the Virgin, that if she saved him and his companions, he would found in England a Monastery for 100 Monks of the Cistercian order; this vow, according to the above legendary authority, was attended by a miraculous circumstance, for as soon as the vow was made, the vessel was soon out of danger, and being arrived in port, her illustrious burden disembarked; when the ship instantly divided, and was immediately swallowed by the waves! So much for the origin of this far-famed Monastery. On the 5th of the *ides* of January, 1273, some Monks from Dore Abbey, in the county of Hereford, were placed at Dernhall, and in 1281, they were removed to Vale Royal, which had been consecrated in August, 1277, by Anianus, the second of the name, Bishop of St. Asaph, the establishment then receiving a reinforcement in the persons of the White Monks of Conway.* On the second of August, 1277, the King in person laid the first stone at the High Altar, dedicating the place to the honour of Christ, the Virgin Mary, St. Nicholas, and St. Nicbasius; other stones were laid by Queen Eleanor, by Gilbert de Clare Earl of Gloucester, Edmund Earl of Cornwall, John de Warren Earl of Surrey, William Beauchamp Earl of Warwick, Maurice de Croun, Otho de Grandison, John de Grey Baron of Manchester, Robert Tiptoft, and Robert de Vere. Burnet Bishop of Bath and Wells, joined the Bishop of St. Asaph, in the celebration of High Mass, on this auspicious occasion. The *Chronicle* before mentioned tells us, that for ages antecedent to the building of the Monastery, on the Festivals of our Lady, the shepherds had heard music and heavenly voices; and that old people who had lived at the erection of the Monastery, had seen the building glittering in the night with a miraculous brilliancy, visible at an

* They had been removed to Maenan, near Llanrwst, on the destruction of their Monastery, on the site of which Conway Castle was built.

immense distance. Previous to the building being completed, a temporary residence was fitted up for the Abbots. The first Abbot was John Chamneys; a man possessing great influence with the King.—The second Walter de Hereford, a true member of the Church Militant; for it is recorded of him, that a Knight and his armed followers attempting to pass through the territory of the Monastery, he immediately attacked and defeated him. This was at the close of the 12th century.—The third, John de Hoo, an infirm man, and hated by his neighbours; rather, therefore, than live on such terms, he gave in his resignation; and was succeeded by Richard de Evesham. This Abbot was a personage of most exalted piety; and if we may judge from what is recorded, he possessed great influence in the other world: Monks who had died and visited the regions of purgatory, appeared again before him, to obtain his benediction as the only passport to bliss.—The fifth Abbot was Peter;* in his time (about 1330) the Monks took possession of the new and splendid Monastery, built at an expense of 32,000*l.*† an enormous sum in those days. On this occasion, the influx of illustrious visitants was so great, that the Abbey, extensive as it was, could scarcely accommodate them; and at the same time the park was consecrated by Beck, Bishop of Durham. The Leger Book notices the presents made on the occasion in the following manner:—

* 1327.

Hæc sunt exhennia missa domp'no Petro Abb'i de Valle Regali contra festu' Assumc'o'is b'e Marie, a'no d'mi 1330.

	£	s.	d.
D'no Hamone le Massy 1 bukke 6 cunicl. pr	£0	0	9
D'no Olivero de Ingham, Justic. Cestriæ, 1 dol. vini	4	0	0
Dn'o Petro de Thornton, 2 cign. 3 purpays	0	12	0
Dn'o Abb'e de Basingwerke, 12 bidentes			
Dn'o Abb'e de Deulacress, 2 vacc. 12 bidentes, 1 hinnulin	2	8	0
Fr'e Roberto de Shadel, 1 virtul'm, 6 porcell, 6 altil. 20 pull.	0	4	0
Fr'e Ricardo de Ewyas, monacho de Deulacress, 1 bukke	0	4	0
Fr'e Rogero de Waleford, auc. 6, capon 6, porcell. 3, pull. galliner 20, caseos 11	0	2	0
Fr'e Robto Grymbald, 1 porc. 6 auc. 4 capon	0	5	0
D'no Rob'to vicar de Wev'ham, 1 bove. 1 vit'l'm, 1 bident. 5 porcell.	0	13	0
Dn'o Will'o Cortays, capell. de Gosnar, 1 bove,	0	10	0
D'no Jo. de Venables, 2 bident	0	2	0
John de Wetenhall, 40 panes, 1 barell. 12 plenu. servic. ciph. albor, 12 discos. 12 salsar, 6 caseos	£0	6	0
Jo. de Bredkyrch, 1 bove. 13 capon, 1 purpays	0	10	0
Comitate de Kyrkeham, 1 bove	0	13	4
Comitate de Overe, 6 bidentes	0	6	0
Will. de Grosvenour de Budworthe, 2 bidentes	0	2	0
Waltero de Tame, bidentes 1	0	1	0
Will. de Mulleton, 1 bidentes	0	1	0
Henr. fil. Galfridi de Wev'ham, 12 pull. gallinar	0	1	0
Rob'to de Hertford de Swanlowe, 3 auc. 4 pull.	0	1	0
Rog. de Crowton, 5 auc. 1 bident, 7 pull.	0	3	0
Ric'o Freysel, 1 bident	0	1	0
John [illegible], [illegible] bidentes, [illegible] pull.	[illegible]	[illegible]	[illegible]
Ric. Prescot, 1 bovic'l'm	0	1	0
Hen. fil. Ric. Pymme, 1 bident	0	1	0
Joh'ne Alcock, vitl'm, 1	0	1	0
David. Vaccar, vitl'm, 1	0	1	0
Hug. de Sutton et Hug. de Fox, bident. 1	0	1	0
John Christian, 3 auc. 3 pull.	0	0	6
Ric. Russel, Cestriæ, 2 salmones‡	0	6	0
Ric. fil. Nich. de Oaston, 1 bident	0	1	0
Rob't. Janecock, 1 bident	0	1	0
Joh'e de Bradeford, 1 bident	0	1	0
Hondykyn de Holden, 3 auc. 3 pull.	0	0	6
Will'o Snell, 3 pull.	0	0	3
Ric. le Brett de Daneham, 6 capon,	0	1	6
Will'm Judicatore, 1 bident.	0	1	0
David de Bertumley, 1 bident.	0	1	0
Jo. le P'ker, 2 aucus, 2 gallin,	0	0	6
Ran'o le Fox et Steph. de Merton, 1 bident	0	1	0
Jo. le Coks, 3 aucars, 6 pull.	0	1	0
Ralf. del -heth, 3 auc. 6 pull.	0	1	0
Will. fil. Gilbert, 1 bident	0	1	0
Will. del -hethe de Blackedene, 1 bident	0	1	0
Will. Horn, 1 bident	0	1	0
Joh'e Horn, 1 bident	0	1	0
Tho. Horn, 5 auc.	0	1	0
Will. le Tynkere de Blakeden, 3 auc. 3 gallin	0	1	0
Will. fil. Dony, 1 bident	0	1	0
Galf. Dony, 1 bident	0	1	0
Ric de Stockall, 1 bident	0	1	0
Ada. fil. Ric'i cl'ici juxta ecclesia', 1 bident	0	1	0
Hugo. fil. Jo'is Capell. 12 pull.	0	0	6
Warino Horne, 5 aucas, 3 gallin. 3 anat	0	1	0
Hugo. le Twe, 8 capon.	0	1	0
Sum'e Totall	£13	8	4

† According to Shuckburgh's calculation, in Anno—
1250, £.26 was worth £.13
1300, ditto —— 68
1350, ditto —— 77
1800, ditto —— 562

‡ At this period, it will be seen, that Salmon were infinitely more valuable, and of course more scarce, than they are at present, 1819.

CHESHIRE

HISTORY

This document affords a curious contrast to the prices of the present day.

The tenants of the Monastery, it would seem, soon became disgusted with their landlords, the Monks, and this disgust at last broke out into acts of personal violence. In 1321, some of the Monks passing beyond the limits of their domain, were attacked by the Bulkeleys, the Leightons, and Winningtons, and only saved themselves from the sword by their activity; in the same year, John Boddeworth was less fortunate; he was cruelly murdered by the Oldyntons, who played at foot-ball with his head!—In 1329, a quarrel ensued between the Abbot Peter, and the inhabitants of Dernhall, on account of their restriction to the mills there; an appeal to arms was the consequence, but they were subdued, and most of them made their submission to the Abbot with ropes round their necks; ten, however, forfeited all their goods and cattle. Seven years afterwards an insurrection of the Dernhall and Over tenantry, of a more formidable nature, took place: they assembled in a body, and waited at Herebache Cross the coming of Hugh le Fren, then Justice of Chester, to whom they declared their grievances, asserting that they were not vassals of the soil, but free tenants.—The Abbot enraged at their proceedings, threw the ringleaders into prison. Soon afterwards, however, a large party of them, under pretence of making a pilgrimage to the Shrine of St. Thomas at Hereford, went on an expedition to the King himself; but some excesses being committed by them on the road, they were imprisoned at Nottingham. Yet a spirit of determination, worthy of a good cause, animated them; Henry Pymeston, Adam Hychekyn, John Christian, and Agnes his wife, contrived to lay their case before the King in Parliament in London; when a command was issued to Henry de Ferrars, Justice of Chester, to enquire into the facts—but the Abbot producing his charters, he obtained a signal triumph over his tenants, in an order to chastise them in any way he thought proper, to prevent their future importunities. At this time it transpired that the Justice had been bribed by the Abbot with the sum of 100*l.*; and this circumstance they succeeded in laying before the King at Windsor. Another Royal precept was then directed to Prince Edward, Earl of Chester, to remedy the grievances of these poor men; and thirty of the tenants met the Abbot in person at Chester—here again they were unsuccessful. As a last resource, they fled with their families and goods, to the Queen, and as the tenants of her son the Earl, they stated their long list of grievances. The Queen immediately wrote an imperative letter to the Abbot, which compelled him to seek his peace at Court. A circumstance occurred at this period, which shews the turbulent state of the times: the Abbot was on his way home through the county of Rutland; and near Exton, he found the road occupied by his refractory tenantry, who had placed themselves under the order of Sir William Venables, of Bradwall, with whom the Abbot had a quarrel, on account of his brother, the Baron of Kinderton. A battle immediately took place, and William Fynche, who led the Abbot's palfrey, was killed by an arrow. The tenants manfully sustained the contest till the remainder of the Abbot's attendants came up, who rescued him from his danger, after much blood had been spilled. The people of the country, it seems, took part against the Abbot, and he was carried before the King at Stamford. But here the tenantry again became the victims of monastic oppression—a decision contrary to their claims took place; and John Waryng, John Parker, Henry Pym, Jack Blackden, Richard Blackden, Richard Bate, John Christian, jun. William Bate, John Christian of Over, Agnes his wife, Randle de Lutelovre, and William de Lutelovre, were indicted for Fynche's murder; but it does not appear that they were put upon their trial, for they were discharged with the forfeiture of all their goods to the Abbot. The others were imprisoned at Weverham, and placed in the stocks; and Pym, the leader, forfeited all his goods and lands in Dernhall, and was sentenced to offer up a wax taper during the remainder of his life, in the Church of Vale Royal, during High Mass, on Assumption Day.—In 1337, owing to the exactions of the Abbot, Sir William Clifton, of Clifton, opposed the levying of the tithes of the Monastery, attacked the gatherers, flogged the Secretary through the streets of Preston, maimed the hunting palfrey belonging to the Rector of Kirkham, and actually entered the church at the head of his armed followers, during the celebration of the Sacrament of Baptism. For this affair Sir William had to humble himself in a full chapter of the order, before the Abbot of Westminster.* About the beginning of the fourteenth century, an order was issued to Richard Sutton and Urian de St. Pierre, as Serjeants of the Peace, to seize the Abbot and certain of the Monks, who were charged with giving succour to a banditti which then infested the county; indeed, one of the Monks was actually charged as a principal: but so far did the ecclesiastical rights of the time obtain, that the Serjeants reported on this precept, that the Abbot and Monks remained within their own demesne, and could not be seized with infringing the rights of Holy Mother Church. Indeed, an indirect sanction to the fraternity was given by the King himself, for he ordered, that the *privileges* of the Monastery should be respected.—Robert was sixth Abbot of Vale Royal, 1342; and Thomas, the seventh Abbot, in 1366. Stephen, 8th Abbot; in 1379, he was one of the witnesses to the grant of a chantry to Sir Thomas Dutton, in the Church of the Augustine Friars, at Warrington. Henry de Weryngton ninth; William tenth; Thomas de Kirkham eleventh; William Stratford twelfth; John Buckley thirteenth Abbot; the last named distinguished himself by taking the command in person of the tenantry of the Abbey, at the battle of Flodden Field—they amounted to 300 men, and under him commanded Sir George Holford, and John Bostock, Esq. The last Abbot was John Harwood, a man of considerable talent and unbending firmness, and upon him, as the head and representative of the Monastery, fell all the troubles of the Reformation and Dissolution.

The then Reformation commenced with the inspection of the Monasteries, generally, by Commissioners; and amongst those selected to visit the religious houses in Cheshire, was Thomas Legh, Esq. who wrote to this effect as to the *morality* which prevailed in the "monastic seclusions of austere virtue:"—"That there lackythe nothing but good and godly instruction of the rude and poor people, and reformation of the heddies in these p'tyes, for certyn of the Knights and gentilmen, and most com'only all, lyvythe so incontine'tly havynge ther co'cubynes openly in ther houses wt v. or vi. of ther chyldren, *putting from them ther wyfes*, that all the contrey thereat be not a litill offendyd, and taketh evil example." Some time after this, a demand was made to the Abbot to surrender Dernhall, where the chief part of the wheat used in the Abbey was grown; this was answered by a letter from the Abbot to the Royal favourite Cromwell, stating the situation of the Monastery with respect to its lands; in one part of which he says, "I do perceave by youre laste letteres, that your Lordship is enformed, that I have in my hand the Maner of Knighte, the Maner of Bradford, the Maner of Heffreston, the Ferme of Conersley, besyde the demeasnes of my Monastery, and also the personages of Frodsham, Kirkham, and the tenth of Over, and that they be sufficient to furnishe the Monastery of corn and pasture. My Lord, it is truth, the moast part of the grounds belonging (to) Knighte, Bradford and Conersley, be let out to ferme for tearme of yeares unto diveres of my tenants; and the forsayd Maner of Heffreston is let unto one person in ferme; and as touching a great parte of the tenths of Weverham and Frodsham, they are let out to sundry persons, for terme of yeares; and the whole personage of Kirkham is let out to farm for many years; and I have not the tenths of Overe, but in ferme of the Prioress of the Noones of Chestere at her will and pleasure; and moreover I have not in wheate, of the tyeth of the parish of Weaverham and Frodsham yearly above xii. bushel or thereabouts; and the moast part of the demeasne ground of the Abbey is sound *(sand)* ground, and will beare no wheate. So that the substance of the finding of my house in wheate is gotten and had at the Maner of Darnhall," &c.—"wherefore yf it might please your good Lordship, that if thear be *any other ground* that I have in my lande that might please your good Lordship to have, the same *shall be at your pleasure during your lyffe, without any rent for the same*, paying ——— the premeses notwitstand." This letter is stated to be "Scribled at Vale Royal, this xxi day of March,† by your humble, obedient, and dayley oratour, *John* Abbot of Vale Roial."—This liberal offer, notwithstanding, was not accepted: the overthrow of monastic establishments was fixed; and on the 7th Sept. in the 30th Henry VIII. a deed, purporting to be signed by the Abbot, and thirteen of the Monks, was obtained. But this was unequivocally declared to be a gross forgery; and two days after the asserted date of surrender, the Abbot wrote a letter to

† No year named.

* It should be recollected, that the whole of this narrative is founded on an ex-parte statement.

CHESHIRE HISTORY.

Cromwell, of which the following is in part a copy:* the commencement is imperfect, and it runs thus:—

" * * * * * * * * * * me, and my brethren, the Kyng's most graciouse as dred commyssion, wherein his graciouse plesure was, that, for the gratwytye that his grace trusted in me and my brethren, that we wold clerlye of one consente surrendre into his graciouse hands o[r] Monast'ye, beyng of his most graciouse fundacion, and whereof your Lordship is steward. My good lorde, the truth is, I, nor my said brethren, *have never consented to surrendre* our Monast'y, nor yet doo, nor never will doo by our good willes, unless it shall please the King's grace to giff to us commandem't so to doo, which I can not p'ceve in the comicyon or Maister Holcroft so to be. And yf any informacyon be giffon unto his Magestye, or unto your good Lordship, that we shulde consent to surrendre as is above sayd, I assure your good Lordship, upon my fidelitye and truthe, there was never non such consente made by me nor my brethren, nor no person or persons had auctoritye to do so in our names. Wherefore I humbly beseech your good Lordship, in whom is my single trust under God and the Kynge's Maj'tye, to be meane for us unto his grace, so that wee may continewe in our said Monas t'ye to pray for his most Noble Grace and your good Lordship, which we shall dayley doo, according to our bounden duties, during our lyves. I assure your Lordship I am cumynge upwards as fast as my sekeness will suffer me, to beseeche your Lordship of charite to be good to our poor Monastery. I send unto your Lordship the Bill indented, made by me and my brethren, which, in presence of worshipfull men, I offered to Mr. Holcroft, which to take he refused.—And thus o[r] Lord God preserve your Lordship in good helthe. Wrytten at Lychefyld the IX day of September, by your pôu'r bedeman.

JOHN, Abbot of Vale Royal.

The unfortunate Abbot persevered in his journey to London: but it was altogether unsuccessful, and he remained firm in his determination not to sacrifice the Monastery. In this emergency, the only resource was to indict him capitally; and accordingly at a Court held at Vale Royal, on Monday after the Feast of the Annunciation (30. Henry VIII.) before Lord Cromwell and fourteen Jurors, a bill was found against the Abbot, charged with numerous crimes, viz.

†" That John Harwood, late Abbot of the Monastery of our Blessed Ladie of Vale Royal, consented to the slaying of Hugh Chaliner, his Monke; and that the daye before the saide Monkes throat was cut, the saide Monke *saide unto a childe*, being his brother's son, of XII years of age or thereabouts, that he, the saide Monke, would be with his brother at Chestore before the Assumption of our Blessed Lady then next after, or else he said he should suffer death, if he tarried any longer in the said Monasterie.—And furthermore the sayd Jury saith, that the sayde late Abbot sayde unto Richard Nightingale, that if the said Richard Nightingale wolde go in the Kynge's warrs at the tyme of the insorectyon, that he should syt in no howse of his, nor that he wolde not take hym for hys tenant, nor do the Kynge's grace service at his putting. And further the sayd jury saith, that the tenant asked the said Abbot who should be ther Captayn at the sayd insorection, and he answered and sayd unto them, that it made no matter for them, for they shold do no service to the Kyng his grace, for no house of his nor at his bidding; and if that Peter Dutton, Knight, and Hugh Starkey, Esquire, had not byne, the sayde Abbot woulde have caste certayn of them into prison.—Furthermore the sayd jury sayth, that when there came a license to the Vicker of Weram, for towe poor people to marry together, from the officere of our most soverayne Lorde the Kynge, Supreme Head, under God, of the Chorche of England, the said Vicker sayd, at that time, that the sayd license was not lawful, and caste it away in despite, and over sayd that the Kynge's grace was not lawfully married.—Furthermore the sayd jury saith that Roger Harwood, brother of the late Abbot, in the tyme of the insorectyon, asked of one William Robinson, of the Lordship of Werham, and of others, what tydings? and the sayd Robinson and others sayd to him, none; and then the sayd Roger sayd to them, I can shewe to you good tydinge, for the Commons be upp, and sayd that the Kynges good grace did overpresse his poore Commons. And the jury sayd, that Roger Bromfield, and others his father's servants, and partakers, tooke and led away out of the Haywoode, a certein load of

* Harl. MSS.

† The original Inq. in the Bodleian Library.

woode, and ***** where John Cowper, Baylyffe of Overe and Weram did arreste to the Kynge's good graces use; and that Ralphe Bostocke is a common honter within the libertyes."

It is not now to be ascertained whether any proceedings took place on this badly-set-up attempt to destroy the poor Abbot; indeed it is said* that he was allowed to end his days on a small annuity. The Abbey, with the whole of its extensive estates, were now seized by the rapacious Monarch; and in the 3d Henry VIII. the site of the once famous Abbey of Vale Royal, the Granges of Conersley, Bradford, Ernesley, and Merton, Petty Pool Hill, and Dam, and Bradford Mylne, in Whitegate parish, together with Heffreston Grange, and Onston Mylne, in Weverham, Ernesley House in Whitegate and Weverham, and Oakmere Pool, were granted to Thomas Holcroft, the great persecutor of the Monks, for the small sum of 450*l.* 10*s.* 6*d.* subject, however, to a reserved rent of 3*l.* 5*s.* 8*d.* to the King. The same year, Sir Rowland Hill, Knight, merchant of London, had a grant of Dernall, with its appurtenances.—In the 37th of the same reign, Sir Thomas Holcroft, who had been created a Knight, obtained the entire Manors of Over and Weverham, with all their privileges, for 464*l.* 10*s.* 10*d.* subject to the rent of 10*l.* 0*s.* 4*d.* The Bishop of Chester was presented with the impropriation and advowson of Weverham; and the Dean and Chapter of Christ Church, Oxford, got the impropriation and advowson of Frodsham.

* Willis.

The actual revenues of the Abbey were estimated in the 18th Henry VIII. at 548*l.* 4*s.* 11*d.*; and some idea of the splendor of this establishment may be formed from the circumstance that Cromwell himself was the Abbot's Seneschall, who had the power of life and death in the Courts of Over and Weverham, at which presided a Coroner and Bailiff.

Of the Granges and Manors adverted to in the account of the Abbey, it may be necessary to give a few particulars:—

Hefferston Grange is a short distance west from Weverham, which separates it from Whitegate; it is now the property of Nicholas Ashton, Esq. of Woolten Hall, Lancashire. It passed with the general grant to the Holcrofts, and from them to the Warburtons of Arley; and the sister of Peter Warburton, Chief Justice of Chester, brought it in marriage to the Henrys, of Broad Oak, co. Flint; she marrying the celebrated Matthew Henry, the still popular expositor on the Bible. She had several daughters and a son, who died without issue. On his death,† Hefferston Grange passed to his sister Elizabeth, who married John Philpot, Esq. of Chester, and by him had a daughter, who brought it in marriage to the present owner. The house is occupied by Thomas Brooke, Esq. of Minshull, High Sheriff of Cheshire in 1810.

Knights Grange was granted to the Starkies; in the 38th Eliz. John Starkie, and Hugh his son and heir, passed it by fine to Sir Randle Brereton, for £1000. It was afterwards purchased by Lady Mary Cholmondeley, and passed with the other estates to the Cholmondeleys of Cholmondeley. About 1770 it was sold by the late Earl Cholmondeley to the father of the present proprietor, Thomas Cholmondeley, Esq. of Vale Royal.

Hernslow Grange—is partly in the parishes of Whitegate and Weverham, near the road leading from Chester to Northwich, and about three miles from the latter place.

Bradford Grange, or *Manor*, is about half way between Winsford and Northwich. In the reign of Edw. I. it was possessed by a family which had assumed the local name some time before; but it was surrendered by Henricus de Bradford to the King, who gave it to the Abbey of Vale Royal, and he had in return conferred upon him the Serjeantcy of the Eastgate in Chester, with the estate of Brewers Halgh.‡

‡ Brewers Hall, now called.

Conewardsley Grange was granted to the Abbey in the 4th year of Edw. I.

For the following description of the present *House of Vale Royal*, this history is chiefly indebted to Mr. Ormerod's work:—

It consists of a centre with two wings of red stone. The basement appears to be a portion of the Old Abbey. The greater part of the former edifice was rebuilt by the Holcrofts in the time of Elizabeth, at least the architecture bears the style of that date. The old house was lighted by windows, projecting in the centre

† Philip Henry, Esq. afterwards assumed the name of Warburton, and represented the City of Chester in Parliament in 1747.

CHESHIRE

on brackets. Several towers ornamented the front, and a great flight of steps ascended to the great hall, which occupied nearly the whole of the first floor of the centre. The steps and towers, however, are now removed, the wings shortened, and large windows introduced at proper intervals. It now bears no features of monastic gloom; and the approach to it through beautiful grounds, is singularly striking.—The present entrance is by a beautiful porch, in the centre of the front, a long corridor from which leads to the anti-room, which is hung round with ancient implements of war, the horns of deer, &c. The windows of this room and the corridor, are enriched with a profusion of stained glass, chiefly heraldic, and allusive to the Cheshire families; it was this glass which formerly ornamented the Hall of Utkinton. From this room is a communication with the sitting rooms, and domestic apartments. On the other side is the great hall, beyond which are the library and drawing-rooms. The hall is a noble room, 70 feet long, the roof supported by carved ribs of oak. This is hung round with family and other portraits.—Among the pictures at Vale Royal, are the following: Charles I. putting on his cap for execution, by Dunning; an ancient painting of two ladies, with children in their arms; Thomasin, of Tarvin, the celebrated penman; the first Lord and Lady Londonderry, of the Pitt family; the first Viscount Savage, Miss Mainwaring, sister of Arthur Mainwaring, the Poet;* Sir Lionel Tollemache, Bart. father of Jane, the wife of Thomas Cholmondeley, Esq. and Lady Tollemache; Sir Hugh Cholmondeley the younger, in a dress of green silk, with a large ruff; Lady Mary Cholmondeley, his wife, "the bold Ladie of Cheshire;" Queen Elizabeth; Lord Ross, supposed to be poisoned at Naples; his mother, Elizabeth Lady Burleigh; Sir Richard Myddleton, of Chirk Castle; Francis Cholmondeley, Esq. a younger son of the first Cholmondeley of Vale Royal; Ann, sister of Henry Viscount St. John, second wife of Thomas Cholmondeley, Esq.; Thomas Pitt, Esq. Governor of Fort St. George, in the East Indies, the owner of the Pitt Diamond, which is represented in his hat; Catherine Cholmondeley, Countess of Leinster; John Minshull, of Minshull, and his Lady; one of the Cholmondeleys of Holford; Seymour Cholmondeley, Esq.; a Duke of Somerset, by Rubens; James II. by Sir Peter Lely, Charles II. by the same painter, &c. &c.

HISTORY.

The old hall of Vale Royal suffered considerably during the Civil Wars, from the soldiers of Cromwell, by whom it was plundered; and it is said the only piece of plate left by them in the house, was a gold salver, enamelled with the arms of Lady Cholmondeley. At that time they drove away some cattle, when a white cow broke away from them, and found its way home from a considerable distance. The breed is supposed still to exist, and is shown at Vale Royal; the ears tipped with red.

From the year 1542, when Cheshire first sent Representatives to Parliament, the Cholmondeleys have uniformly furnished a County Member.

DERNHALL

Is about six miles W. S. W. from Middlewich. It is not noticed in the Survey; but it is supposed to have been included in the possessions of the Earls, who had a Seat here; and where John Scot, the last of the Palatinates, died by poison in 1237.† On the founding of Dernhall Abbey, the manor was given to the Monks, and continued their property when they removed to Vale Royal. An account of the disturbances that took place between the Abbot of Vale Royal and the Dernhall tenantry, will be found in page 441. In the Leger Book it is stated, that "the natives owe suit to the Court *indefinitely*, at the *will* of the Lord or his bailiff, and if warned over night must attend in the morning; that if lands are transferred by tenants to their sons during their lives, that the sons must perform their suit due to the Abbot, or redeem it at his will; that they must resort to the Abbey Mills, and pay pasturage for their hogs; that they must purchase from the Abbot, *at his own price*, a *power of marrying their daughters out of the manor*; and pay their *leyrwyte*, if they went astray carnally." When any native died, the Abbot became entitled to his pigs and capons, his horses at grass, his domestic horse, his bees, his pork, his linen and woollen cloths, his money in gold and silver, and his brazen vessels; but by a *concession* of Abbot John, the wife might have the metal, the Abbot having the option of purchasing the vessels. In addi-

* Her Mother was a Cholmondeley.

† 1244. Lysons.

tion, the Abbot was to have the best good for an heriot, and the Church the next; all other animals to be equally divided between the Lord, the wife, and the children, and if no children, between the Lord and the wife!—If there be any standing corn, the wife shall choose between that and the corn gathered, and divide with the Abbot the corn he chuses; the other *to be the Abbot's entirely*. No native to make a will without a license from the Abbot. Before a division of the property took place, there should be payment of the expense of the wake and funeral of the deceased, and in the division, heifers should be shared as other animals; that sheep had been divided in the same manner, before Warin Grosvenor, who when bailiff, brought the practice into disuse, *from dislike to the Abbot*. That the Abbot may purchase a hare or a duck for 2*d*. and a duckling in Lent for 1½*d*. from any of the natives.—That the land of the deceased shall remain in the hand of the Lord, until a heir should be found, who must pay fine for it *at the Lord's will*. That the natives in time of war, shall keep watch for a time unlimitted at Dernhall Court, if watch then be kept at Chester Castle, or purchase a release from service from the Abbot.—That the natives shall not sell hay or corn, if the Lord wishes to purchase it; that the fines shall be levied once a fortnight, rent paid quarterly, and no goods of the deceased sold for debts, expenses of funeral wake, or burial, without the license of the Bailiff.—That the tenants shall keep the Lord's pigs and horses, have the care of his park, and feed his hounds."

As has been before noticed under the head of Vale Royal, Dernhall became the property of Sir Rowland Hill, who levied a fine of the manor, and passed it to Sir Reginald Corbet. Temp. James I. it was sold to Richard Lee, Esq. Thomas Lee, Esq. was the father of the American General Lee; and it was purchased from him by the father of the late Thomas Corbet, Esq. who died in 1808.

Dernhall Grange, which is a large and handsome brick mansion, is the property of William Thompson Corbet, Esq.

MARTON,

Or as it is sometimes called *Merton*, is about four miles and a half S. W. S. from Nantwich. It was given by Randle Blundeville to Randle de Merton, son of Randle, "forestario fideli meo," and either he or his son gave it in 1305 to the Abbey of Vale Royal, in exchange for Gayton in Wirral, and Lach on Rudheath, Gayton being inconveniently situated with respect to locality. This exchange took place at the instance of the King, and for his compliance, Randle de Merton was rewarded with a grant by patent of the Earl's Eye, in Chester,* and the Bailiwick of the hundred of Caldey, then valued at 5 marks per annum.—Gilbert Glegg, marrying Johanna, eldest daughter and co-heiress of Stephen de Merton, possessed Gayton, Caldy, the Earl's Eye, &c. in right of his wife, and the whole of his property is still vested in Gilbert's descendant, John Baskervyle Glegg, Esq. of Gayton.—But to proceed with Merton: the manor being ceded to the Monks of Vale Royal, it continued vested in them till the Dissolution, when Sir Thomas Holcroft sold Merton Grange to the Mainwarings of Merton, in which family it continued till about 1690, when Charles Mainwaring, Esq. sold it to Thomas Fleetwood, the ancestor of Sir Thomas Fleetwood, whose widow, the Countess de Front, sold it to T. Cholmondeley, Esq. of Vale Royal, the present proprietor, who is also the Lord of the Manor.

The house, formerly called *Merton* Land, is situated about a mile N. W. from Over. It is composed of wood and plaister, surrounded by a moat, and in excellent repair.

* The Earl's Eye is thus accurately described in the grant:—" ——— et 3 acr. prati de d'nicis terr Castri nostri de Cest. infra insulam quæ vocatur Erls Eye et metas et divisas subscriptas, scilicet, a ponte Cestriæ super aquam de Dee versus Boughton, et in circuitu de Dee usque ad Claverton ford, et de Claverton ford usque ad fossatum de Newbold, et sic per fossatum illud usque Honebrugge, et de Honnebrugge usque ad pontem, Cest." &c.

HISTORY.

THE PARISH OF BARROW,

CONTAINS ONLY ONE TOWNSHIP, IN TWO DIVISIONS.

Great and *Little Barrow* are about five miles E. N. E. from Chester. Little Barrow is situated at the northern extremity of the parish, the greater part of which is elevated ground, commanding truly picturesque views towards the Forest Hills, and a variety of rural and romantic scenery.* It is noticed in the Survey (Bero) as being the property of William Fitz-Nigel, Baron of Halton. Randle de Blundeville, granted to Thomas Despencer, a right of free warren in Barrow; and temp. Edw. I. Hugh le Despencer, Earl of Winchester, possessed the manor of Little Barrow, with twenty acres of land in Great Barrow, which he obtained from Richard Chamberlain. On the attainder of Hugh le Despencer, Edw. III. gave Great Barrow to Sir Roger Swynerton, and shortly afterwards Little Barrow was added to the gift. In the 38th Edw. III. Robert de Swynerton granted two parts of the manor and the advowson of the chapel, with the reversion of the third part, to John Beck, Rector of Checkley, and John Heycok, Chaplain; but in the same year he re-granted them to the said Robert;† and Maud, daughter and sole heiress of Sir Robert Swynerton, brought Barrow in marriage, to her husband Sir John Savage, of Clifton. The manor continued vested in the Savages till the death of Richard Earl Rivers, when in compliance with an act of the 7th Geo. III. it passed to the Lady Penelope Barry, daughter of the Earl of Barrymore, by his wife Lady Elizabeth Savage, sole heiress of Earl Rivers. This Lady marrying James, second son of George, second Earl of Cholmondeley, on her decease, in 1786, Barrow passed to her husband's great nephew, the present Marquis of Cholmondeley.‡

The CHURCH is situated about a mile from Stamford Bridge. It is dedicated to St. Bartholomew, and consists of a body, north aisle, and chancel added in 1671, by Dean Bridgeman, then Rector, Bishop of Sodor and Man, and Dean of Chester. It is a mean building; to which was added, with very bad taste, in 1744, a strong modern tower. In the reign of Henry II. the church was given by Robert de Bachepus, to the Knights Hospitallers, who had a preceptory here. In 1313, on the presentation of Osbert Gyfford, acolyte, it was called "the free chapel of Barwe, within the prebend of Tarvin."—The benefice is a Rectory, of which the Marquis of Cholmondeley is patron. The present incumbent is the Rev. John Clarke, A.M. instituted Feb. 10, 1816. The registers commence in 1572, but they are imperfect between 1668 and 1681. The corn tithes of the whole parish belong to the Rector: 1*d.* the statute acre for meadow land, and 9*d* for upland, is paid in lieu of tithe hay—but the occupier of Barrow Hall farm pays 7*s.* 6*d.* for hay tithe.

There are no particular monumental memorials in the church.

The *Charities* consisted of various sums left by different persons, to the amount of £121. 10*s.* the whole of which were expended in the erection of the tower, in lieu of which six guineas annually was charged to the

* The parish contains about 3000 statute acres.

† The Lysons say, on the authority of Hollinshead and Dugdale, that Barrow was given by Randle Blundeville to his nephew William de Albini, Earl of Arundel, but on a partition of his estates, Barrow passed to Nichola, wife of Roger de Somery, who made it one of his chief seats.

‡ The four halls of the townships, Great Barrow, Little Barrow, Morley, and Park Halls, are now occupied as farm-houses.—In the former, which is a timber and plaister building, is a curious massy bedstead, in elegantly carved oak, the head-board decorated with the arms of Queen Elizabeth, supported by the lion and dragon, the latter the cognizance of the Tudors. The bed-posts are sunk several inches into the floor, which is of plaister; the room is entered by a small arched door way, and was probably the state apartment of the hall. This apartment is well worthy the inspection of the curious.

church rate as interest; this sum is now appropriated to the education of poor children, for whom a school has been built. A legacy of 20s. per annum is paid by the Corporation of Chester, left by Mr. John Brereton, and distributed amongst poor widows.

PARISH OF GREAT BUDWORTH,

CONTAINS, IN THIS HUNDRED, THE TOWNSHIPS OF

CASTLE NORTHWICH, HARTFORD, AND WINNINGTON,

Forming part of the Chapelry of Witton, and separated from the rest of the parish by the Weaver.

Castle Northwich is on the direct line of the road from Chester to Northwich, about eighteen miles from the former. It is not noticed in the Survey, but it is a place of considerable antiquity, and in old records is called *Castleton*, and *Le Castele juxta Northwyche.*—The fortress from which it takes its name was situated at the point of junction of the Dane and Weaver, where the latter river was forded by the Watling-street. Not a vestage of the building exists, but the site of the fortress is to be seen in a small field, on the right hand of the Chester road, immediately above the Hollow-way. It consists of two mounds, the highest nearly circular, and about 90 feet in diameter.* Of the period of its erection we have no account; but from a charter, temp. Ric. I. which runs thus:—"Hionus filius Ricardi de Castello, dedi, &c. Lidulpho de Twamlowe *totam terram Castelli de Norvico habendam,*" &c. it is supposed to have been destroyed at that early date. We may therefore infer, that it was built by the Saxons. From the Twamlows, the estate passed to the Wyningtons, their descendants, and in an Inq. p. m. temp. Edw. III. it is noted "quædem placea terræ vocata le Castell juxta Northwych."—In an Inq. of Sir John Warburton, of Arley, temp. Eliz. it is described as a third part of the manor of Castle Northwich. The earliest account we have of Northwich as a proprietary, is that it belonged to the Kinderton Barony; for in the reign of Henry III. Hugh de Venables granted to Roger his son, the whole of Castle Northwich, for his homage, and rendering annually, on the feast of St. John, a pair of white gloves. Eventually the manor passed in marriage with Letitia, daughter and co-heir of Sir Wm. Venables, to Sir Richard Wilbraham, Knight, ancestor of the Woodhey family. The manor is now the property of Earl Dysert.†

Castle Northwich is a mere suburb to Northwich, being separated from it by a bridge of one arch over the Weaver.

HARTFORD

Is about a mile and half S. W. W. from Northwich; it is noticed in the Survey as parcel of the Barony of Kinderton. Before the reign of Edward III. it was held by a family which assumed the local name; from whom it passed to the Hortons, Masseys of Rixton, Holcrofts, Marburys, and Davies. In July, 1694, Henry Davies, of Dodleston, Esq.; Wm. Jones, of London;

* In Erdeswick's MSS. in the Harl. Coll. it is thus noticed:—"At Northwiche stood sometime a very stronge castell, on the top of a verie high hill, called the Castell of Northwich, and a certaine circuit about that place is still called the Castle Town of Northwich, and is a distinct thinge and several from the town of Northwich, only the name and great trenches give any shew or evidence thereof."

† The late Lord Penrhyn claimed an interest in this manor, and gave a deputation in right of his Lady, who descended from the Winningtons, and who it is said kept a moiety of the Castle at an early period.—Lysons, p. 538.

CHESHIRE gent.; and Anne Joliffe, of Clapham, Surrey, conveyed to John Lowe, of Winnington, and Jeffery Houghton, of Northwich, the manor, reputed manor, or Lordship of Hartford, or Hertford. The Lowes sold the estate in severalties, which terminated in eleven shares; these shares are now in fewer hands, some of the lords holding two and three each. The privileges of this manor, being alternately held, are, the holding a Court Baron, and the appointment of a gamekeeper. The Constables of Hartford are sworn in at Sir John Leicester's Court at Witton, where he holds a Court Leet for Hartford. The manor contains about 1000 acres. In 1795 the waste lands were inclosed. A small portion of Hartford is in the parish of Weverham.

WINNINGTON

Is about a mile N. W. from Northwich. Previous to the Survey, it was held by the ancestors of the Mainwarings and Boydells; and it appears from a deed of very early date, that William de Boidele, granted a moiety of the manor to Lidulph de Twamlow, whose son Robert assumed the local name.—It continued in the Winningtons till the conclusion of the reign of Henry VIII. when it passed in marriage with Elizabeth, daughter and heiress of Richard Wynnington, to Sir Peter Warburton, Knight. Sir George Warburton passed it to his third son, who married Anne, the second daughter of Sir Robert Williams, of Penrhyn, Carnarvonshire. Hugh Warburton, Esq. a General in the army, had by his wife Martha, daughter and coheir of Edward Norreys, of Speyke, co. Lanc. Anne Susannah, who married Richard Pennant, Esq. created Lord Penrhyn, of the kingdom of Ireland; and on his death, she sold it to Sir J. T. Stanley, Bart. the present proprietor.* HISTORY.

The *Hall* of Winnington is a large building, but has nothing particularly striking in its appearance; the situation, however, is delightfully picturesque, close to the most romantic part of the river Weaver. There are some good paintings here.

Winnington Bridge was the scene of a sharp conflict during the Civil Wars, between Lambert and Sir George Booth's forces, in which the latter was defeated. This occurred on the 19th August, 1659, when Captain Morgan, of Golden Grove, was killed in the encounter.

*Lady Penrhyn died without issue, Jan. 1816.

THE PARISH OF FRODSHAM,

CONTAINS THE TOWNSHIPS OF

FRODSHAM (BOROUGH AND FEE)
FRODSHAM (BOROUGH AND LORDSHIP)
HELSBY,
ALVANLEY,
MANLEY,
KINGSLEY,
NEWTON,
NORLEY (PART OF)

FRODSHAM

Is about eleven miles from Chester, on the Warrington road.—It was amongst the possessions of the Earl at the Conquest; and between the years 1209, and 1228, Randle Blundeville, then Earl, granted the Burgesses, 110 in number, an exemption from all tolls, excepting that on salt in the wiches; and that all pleas should be judged within the borough by the Provost, except those belonging to the Earl's sword, reserving to himself the resort of the burgesses to his mills and oven.—This Earl it is supposed, occasionally resided at the Castle of Frodsham, from the circumstance of several of his charters bearing that date. According to the *Villare Cestriense*, Frodsham belonged at a very early period to a family which assumed the local name, but the estate was forfeited, one of the name having in an affray slain the favourite of the Prince. In 1279, the manor was granted by Edw. I. to David, brother of Llewellyn, Prince of Wales, but he also forfeited it for treason, and was executed in 1283. Temp. Henry VI. the King granted to his brother, Edmund of Hadham, father of Henry VII. the manor of Frodsham, and Edmund died possessed of it; but it should be recollected, that during this time, the capital lordship remained altogether vested in the Earldom.—Early in the 17th century, Frodsham was vested in the Savages of Rock Savage; Richard Earl Rivers, gave it to the Duke of Shrewsbury and the Earl of Oxford, as trustees, for the use of Earl Rivers for life; remainder to John Rivers, afterwards Earl Rivers, a Catholic Priest, who never assumed the title; remainder to his issue; remainder to Bessy Savage; remainder to his own right heirs. A litigation, however, ensued on the bequests; and by an act of the 7th of George III. this manor and other estates were vested in the Earl of Barrymore, for the use of John Earl of Rivers for life, remainder to Lady Penelope Barry, daughter of Elizabeth, the sole daughter and heiress of Richard Earl Rivers. These estates were subsequently brought to James, the second son of the second Earl of Cholmondeley, in marriage with Penelope; but on his decease, they passed to his nephew, George James, now Marquis of Cholmondeley, who is entitled to the tolls of the markets and fairs.

In the time of Henry VI. William Torfort was Serjeant of the Peace for the Fee of Frodsham, with the custody of the gaol of Frodsham. Temp. Elizabeth, Sir John Savage was Bailiff of the manor of Frodsham, with the power of making presentments and attachments. He was also Constable of Frodsham Gaol.—The town has the right of market,* but in consequence of its locality to Warrington, it is but thinly attended. There are two small fairs on May 15, and August 21.—Frodsham forms a long open street, extending about a mile; another street leads to the church. Below the elevation on which the town is situated, is an extensive marsh, subject to frequent irruptions from the Mersey. In 1793, and 1802, the tide burst down the embankment, and flowed within 100 yards of the centre of the town.† Not a relic remains of the Castle of Frodsham, which was destroyed by fire in October, 1654, the dead body of John Earl Rivers then laying in it. The building is described to have been of stone, with walls of enormous thickness; the whole in the Norman style of architecture. Some distance east of the town, is a handsome stone bridge over the River Weaver, at its junction with the Mersey. Temp. Edward I. the burgesses of Frodsham found eight soldiers in time of war, when Chester Castle should be besieged.

The CHURCH is situated on very elevated ground, in the township of Overton, and is dedicated to St. Lawrence. The present Incumbent is the Rev. John Fanshawe, M.A. By charter of Hugh Lupus and Ermentrude, 1093, the tithes of Frodsham were given to Chester Abbey; but the advowson was vested in the manor, till the great Monastery of Vale Royal was founded, to which the Rectory and the Advowson of the Vicarage were given; the Monks of St. Werburgh receiving 4*l*. per annum in lieu of tithes. At the Dissolution, the Rectory and Advowson were given to the Dean and Chapter of Christ Church, Oxford; under whom the great tithes are leased by Richard Massey, Esq. of Moston, and re-leased by him to Mr. John Higson, of Frodsham. The whole of the parish pays tithe: the Peel Hall and Kingsley Hall Estates, Cattenall, and part of Crewood,‡ are protected by a modus: the parish generally pays a modus in lieu of tithe hay. The manerial lord has tithe of pigs and geese in Frodsham and Manley. The church is composed of a tower, containing a peal of six bells; with nave, chancels, and side aisles. Three arches, two of them semi-circular, on the side next the tower, separate the nave from the chancels. Of the pillars on which the arches rest, three are cylindrical, and one octagonal; the decorative part, particularly the capitals, in a style apparently coeval with the Conquest. The Chancel at the east end of the South aisle, is kept in repair by the owner of Kingsley Hall; the other by the Lessee of the great tithes. On the right hand of the altar is a handsome stall for the officiating priest.

The monumental memorials are few and uninteresting. On a tablet in the South aisle—

"Near this place, lies the body of Peter Bennet, carpenter, of Frodsham, who died of a dropsy, October 21, 1749, aged 50. In 33 weeks he was tapped 58 times, and had 1032 quarts of water taken from him."

Near the North door, on a mural monument—

* On Saturday.

† Orm. vol. I. page 32.

‡ Crew-wood

CHESHIRE

Near this place lies the body of Francis Gastrell, late Vicar of Frodsham, who departed this life 5th April, 1772, in the 90th year of his age. Also the body of Jane, his wife, who departed this life the 30th October, 1791, in the 81st year of her age.

On a marble monument in the body of the church—

M. S.—Underneath lies interred the body of Robert Hyde, of Cattenhall, Esquire. He married Eleanor, the daughter of John Mather, of Chester, Gent. by whom he had one son and five daughters, who all survived him, except the youngest daughter. He was a loving husband, an indulgent father, a faithful friend, an honest man, a true son of the Church of England He lived much beloved, and died much lamented, Feb. 24, A. D. 1715, of his age 36.

On a stone near the altar—

M. S. of George Villiers, A. M. late Vicar of Frodsham, obt. June 24, A. S. 1774, æt. 50.

The Registers commence in 1558, but they are imperfect from 1642 to 1661. In the list of burials occur the following instances of longevity :—

159$\frac{2}{3}$, Feb. 12. Thomas Hough, cuj. ætas cxli.

———— 13.—Randle Wall, cIII.

1695, April 13.—Margaret Knowles de Hellesby, aged 107.

1791, Nov 21.—Thomas Blain, of Norley, aged 102.

A Chantry was established here by Randolph the son of Roger, who gave two bovates of land and tithes in Aston, to St. Chad and St. Werburgh, for the parson of Frodsham to find a resident Chaplain to perform Divine Service in honor of God and St. Werburgh; but this soon fell into disuse, and its endowments were tranferred to Vale Royal Abbey.

In 1793, a portion of common land in Frodsham and Helsby was inclosed under the provisions of an Act of Parliament.

The *Free School* of Frodsham was established about 1660; and is a neat building of stone, in the Churchyard.—It was built by subscription. The Master is elected by 24 feoffees, including the Vicar and Churchwardens for the time being, There is a good house for the Master, whose salary exceeds £100l. per annum.* A salary of £7. is secured to the Usher, charged on an estate in Overton.

The Organ was given by John Wilkinson, Esq. of Newton, and was erected in 1790. Part of the Organist's fee is the possession of a tenement called the Organ Lot.

HISTORY.

The *Charities* are principally,—An estate close to the town, left by Mrs. Gastrell, to the Vicar and his successors; it is charged with the payment of £10. annually to the Charity at Warrington, for the relief of Clergymen's widows and orphans.—The interest of 100l. distributed to the poor by the Churchwardens, bequeathed by ——— Banner.—Ten shillings per annum charged on a Meadow in Frodsham Marsh.—The rent of a field called Brook Furlong, left by Mr. Chesshyre, of Stockham, in the parish of Runcorn, for the poor housekeepers of Frodsham.—Twenty shillings charged on an estate in Huntington, for the same purpose.—A donation of bread, charged on the school lands.—The interest of a certain sum, for the poor of Newton.

FRODSHAM BOROUGH and LORDSHIP, include the hamlets of *Woodhouses*,† *Overton*, *Bradley*, and *Netherton*, which form a distinct township, and are within the Marquis of Cholmondeley's Manor of Frodsham, from whom the greater part of the land is leased.

† See introduction to Hundred.

Overton, as has been before noticed, is an elevated ridge of land above Frodsham. Here is the hill on which stood a beacon, communicating with other signal posts in North Wales, Lancashire, and Shropshire.

Bradley adjoins Overton, and formerly belonged to the Gerards of Kingsley. The Mill, which is situated on a small stream, is noticed at an early period in the Inquisitions of the Dones of Utkinton.‡

‡ Orm.

Netherton spreads from Overton Hill to the marshes below. The Nangreaves resided at Netherton Hall from the time of Elizabeth till 1815, when, on the death of Lieut.-Col Waring Nangreave, the family became extinct, but it is now possessed by an illegitimate branch.

NEWTON

Is a township included within the Manor of Kingsley. J. S. Barry, Esq. and John Arden, Esq. are the principal landholders. It adjoins Frodsham on the North-west side.

HELSBY

Is about three miles S. W. W. from Frodsham. About

---

* Arising from various bequests. One of these, 3l. per ann. left by Mr. Trafford, subject to the condition of the Master being approved of by the Apothecary's Company at Chester.—Gastrell's Notitia.

1230 it was possessed by a family which assumed the local name. In the 17th Edw. II. William de Hellesby and his wife Hawisia, passed the manor to Peter de Thornton; but subsequently Margery, the sister of William de Hellesby, joined with the nephew of Ralph Starkie, in putting in a claim against the legality of the fine. It does not appear, however, it was attended with any success, for on the death of Peter de Thornton, his estates were divided amongst his eight daughters, and Helsby was divided between Elizabeth, wife of Hamon Fitton, Baron of Dunham Massy, and Maud, the wife of Henry de Beeston. The Fitton share passed by female heirs to Venables and Trafford. In the 33d Elizabeth, Edmund Trafford, Esq. passed the moiety to Thomas Rowe, for £300. and afterwards it was possessed by the Hobarts. About the middle of the 17th century, Sir Henry Hobart, Knight, sold it to John Savage, first Earl Rivers. The Beeston moiety was thus disposed of: Margaret, grand daughter of Sir George Beeston, living in the reign of Elizabeth, brought the estate in marriage to William Whitmore, Esq. of Leighton. Their heiress marrying Thomas Savage, it became his property, and was bought by John Earl Rivers. The whole of the manor thus became vested in the Savages, and has descended with the other estates to the present proprietor, the Marquis of Cholmondeley. The manor is considered parcel of the borough and lordship of Frodsham, and the inhabitants serve as jurors in the Court there, but they have their own Constables.—The situation of the village is strikingly picturesque; Helsby Tor, so prominent in the Cheshire views, towering above it.

ALVANLEY,

It appears from the Survey, was held by Leuric, Saxon Lord of Wimbolds Trafford, which was taken from him by the Conquerors. The Earls soon after had it in possession; and before the reign of John, it was occupied by the Fiz-Alans, Earls of Arundel, as a part of Dunham, and under them by Robert de Alvandelegh, and Richard de Perpunt.—Early in the 13th century,* Philip de Orreby purchased it from the Fiz-Alans; and Agnes his daughter and heiress, temp. Hen. III. brought the manor in marriage to Walkelin de Arderne,† the ancestor of John Arden, the present proprietor.

Of this family was Sir John Arderne, who had a grant from Randle Blundeville, of the Fee of Aldford, with a jurisdiction over about twenty townships.—Also Dean Arderne, whose bequests form so great a portion of the income of the Dean and Chapter of Chester.—Rich. Pepper Arden, was the youngest son of John Arden, of Harden and Alvanley; he was a scholar at the Grammar School of Manchester; from which he removed to Trinity College, Cambridge, and took the degrees of B. A. and M. A. He was subsequently called to the Bar, obtained a silk gown, and in 1784 was appointed Solicitor General, and two years afterwards Attorney General and Chief Justice of Chester. In 1788, he received the appointment of Master of the Rolls, and on the 18th of June, in the same year, he was knighted He was elected M. P. for Newton, in 1782, and two years afterwards represented Aldborough. In 1790 he was M. P. for Hastings, but being elected for Bath in 1794, he vacated his seat for the former place. In 1801, he was elevated to the Chief Justiceship of the Common Pleas, and he was raised to the Peerage, by the title of Baron Alvanley, in the same year. He died in 1804, and was buried in the Rolls Chapel, Chancery-lane. The title descended to his son, the present Lord.

Alvanley Hall is now occupied as a farm-house; the old house was called by Webb, in 1622, a very fine house belonging to Henry Arderne, Esq. but it has long since been disused as a family seat.

Alvanley Chapel is about three miles S. S. W. from Frodsham; the site of it was originally an Oratory, founded by Catherine, the widow of Ralph Arderne, and daughter of Sir William Stanley, of Hooton, Knt. temp. Henry VI.—It had, however, a very small endowment, by no means adequate to the maintenance of a Minister, and in 1787 it was disused; but it has recently been appropriated to Divine Service, although the Curate's salary is scarcely 20*l*. per annum.‡ It is in the patronage of the Arden family.

KINGSLEY

Is about three miles S. E. from Frodsham. It ap-

* Between 1208 and 1226.—Orm.

† The Representatives of this Walkelyn are entitled to quarter the Ducal Coats of Normandy, and those of the Earls of Arundel, Chester, and Mercia.—Orm.

‡ Alvandley, certif. value 5*l*. 10*s*. per annum. viz. 5*l*. interest of 100*l*. left by Thomas Hignett, and 10*s*. interest of 10*l*. left by

CHESHIRE

pears from the Survey, that it was one of the few instances of estates being continued to the Saxon proprietor.—" Dunning tenet de comite Chingeslie:" but it was possessed by him for a very short period, for Randle, third Earl of Chester, granted it, probably on the death of Dunning's direct heirs, to Ranulph, who took the local name, and was also appointed a Master Forester in the Forests of Mara and Mondrem. Richard, the son of Ranulph de Kingsley, married Joan, the daughter of Alexander Sylvester, of Storeton, Forester of Wirral; she died without issue—but by another wife, he had a son, and five daughters, co-heiresses. viz. Emma, the wife of William Gerrard; Agnes, wife of William Lancelyn; Amicia, wife of Randle le Roter, of Thornton; Joan, wife of Henry Done, and Margaret, wife of Richard de Cholmondeley. The share which passed to Randle le Roter passed subsequently to the Roters, or Rutters, of Kingsley; Lancelyn's share being purchased by the Gerrards about 1302, half of the manor continued in that family for more than three centuries; the Dones' share continued in the family till the middle of the 17th century, when it passed by female heirs to the Crewes and Ardernes. Sir John Savage purchased Gerrard's moiety in 1561, and Thomas Earl Rivers buying Rutter's share, the manor is now vested in John Smith Barry, Esq. High Sheriff of Cheshire in 1819—natural son of the late James Hugh Smith Barry, Esq. grandson of Richard Earl of Barrymore, who married the heiress of Richard Savage Earl Rivers.*—Mr. Barry holds a Court Leet and Court Baron for Kingsley.

* Lysons, [pa]ge 661.

Cattenhall Estate is in the township of Kingsley; and about the middle of the twelfth century it was the residence of Randle Venator, or *the Hunter*, who gave it to God, St. Mary, and Sir Inhel the Priest, and his successors. It would appear that the latter established here an hermitage.—The estate soon after became vested in the Monastery of St. Werburgh, at Chester, from which it was conveyed to William Gerrard, of Kingsley, subject to the annual payment of 30*s*. and the finding two Chaplains in Cattenhall Chapel, to pray for the souls of Sir Richard Kingsley and his successors. Cattenhall was subsequently vested in the Gerards and Astons; and eventually became the property of Robert Hyde, Esq. who dying issueless, he left it to his nephew Robert Hyde, Esq.; and on the termination of the family in the male line, it passed in marriage to the Giffords, of Chillington, co. Salop, and is now the property of Miss Gifford, of Nerquis, co. Flint. The Old Hall of Cattenhall no longer exists.†

HISTORY.

PART OF NORLEY

Is in this township. There was formerly an ancient hall here, belonging to the Halls. It was rebuilt in 1782; and passed from William Hall, to his nephew, George Whitley, Esq.‡ who died in 1819. It is now the property of George Whitley, Esq. his son.—A handsome modern built mansion, called *Norley Bank*, is the property of John Nuttall, Esq.

MANLEY

Is about four miles S. S. W. from Frodsham. It is noticed in the Survey, as being the property of the Earl; but in the reign of Henry III. it was vested in a family which had assumed the local name, and held it under the Dones of Utkinton, as of their Fee of Kingsley. It continued vested in the Manleys till 1574, when Richard Birkenhead, Esq. Recorder of Chester, purchased the Manor from William Manley, a minor. It was re-sold by Adam, son of Rich. Birkenhead, to the Rev. Gregory Turner, Rector of Sephton, near Liverpool, by marriage with whose daughter it passed to Henry Legh, of East Hall, about 1630. About 1652, Mr. Legh sold it to Wm. Davies, of Ashton; and on the death of Thomas Davenport Davies, Esq. without issue, the manor passed with his estate, in marriage, to Sir Matthew Deane, of Dromore, co. Cork, Bart. Lord Muskerry, Sir Matthew's brother,

---

Richard Lincock, Surplice Fees belonging to Frodsham. Voluntary Contributions about 8l. per annum, of which 2l. 18s. were given by Mr. Richard Arderne, of Stockport, who nominated the last Curate, and 2l. 18s. to his elder brother's widow. After the death of Ann Churchman, is left to the Curate 60l. by John Dugdale, her husband.—See GASTREL'S NOT.

† Crew-wood, an old seat of the Gerrards, is partly in this township, together with Peele Hall, a moated mansion, and an ancient seat of the Ardernes. A house is built on the site of the latter, the property of George Whitley, Esq.—In Inquisitions, temp. Edw. III. salt-pits are noticed as being in existence in this town; and at the present day there are some brine springs here.

‡ Several years Town Clerk of Chester.

sold it to Thomas Lowton, Esq. in 1789.—In 1814, Mr. Lowton died, and bequeathed the manor, with other estates, to his nephew, Thomas Wainwright, who has assumed the name of Lowton.

The situation of Manley is truly romantic; and here is the extensive quarry of white free stone, from which the materials of the Castle of Chester, Eaton-house, and other buildings, have been obtained.

THE PARISH OF INCE,

CONTAINS ONLY ONE TOWNSHIP.

INCE.

The name of this township is evidently derived from the British word Ynys, an island, or peninsula. It is situated about seven miles W. by S. from Chester. At the period of the Survey, it formed part of the possessions of the secular Canons of St. Werburgh, at Chester, and it was afterwards tranferred to the Abbot and Monks of that foundation.—Towards the conclusion of the twelfth century, the Abbot, in a petition to Hubert, Archbishop of Canterbury, stated, that in Wirral, and in their Manor of Ynys, they had lost by inundations of the sea, 30 carucates of land, and were daily losing more. It recited further losses sustained in the Welsh Wars, and solicited the Archbishop, and the Bishop of Worcester, for leave to appropriate their Church of Campden for the repairs of the Abbey, the choir only being rebuilt, and the rest of the church and belfry being ruinous.*—In the 22d Richard II. the Abbot obtained a license, to fortify the Manor-house of *Inisc*, the same as his other Manors of Sutton and
† Saighton. Salghton.†—At the Dissolution, Ince was obtained by Sir Robert Cotton, who sold it to the Cholmondeleys. In 1722, Charles Cholmondeley, Esq. sold it to Sir George Wynne, Bart. on the death of whose son-in-law, Richard Hill Waring, Esq. it passed to his great nephew John Scott, who assumed the name of Waring— About the year 1805, the whole estate,‡ with the patronage of the Curacy, was purchased by Edward Yates,§ Esq. and Robert Peel, for 80,000*l.* and subsequently Mr. Yates is become possessed of the whole, excepting indeed the *Holm House* property, partly in the Lordship of Thornton, the property of George John Legh, Esq. of High Legh.

The village of Ince stands on an elevated rock, in a situation commanding much variety of scenery. Considerable remains of the *Abbot's Grange* still exist at a short distance from the church, within a moated site, exceeding a statute acre. Two sides of the quadrangle are pretty perfect; the sitting and sleeping rooms of the Monks are occupied as a farm-house; and the hall is converted into a barn, which retains eight large bay windows.¶

Since the property has been vested in Mr. Yates, great improvements have been made in the township by that gentleman. A commodious Inn has been built, conveniences for bathers have been prepared, a a fine quay erected, and many acres of land are already rescued from the river by embanking.—A considerable

* This is a very strong proof of the great antiquity of the foundation of the Church of St. Werburgh, when it is thus stated, that so early as the year 1200, the whole building was in a state of dilapidation.

‡ About 1600 acres, with the impropriation of the great tithes.

§ High Sheriff, 1812.

¶ Mr. Ormerod says, the interior has been used as a burying-place, from the circumstance of many human bones having been discovered in it.

business is carried on here in the conveyance of farm produce from the neighbourhood to Liverpool; and from the attention lately paid to the only two roads to the township, there is a prospect of Ince becoming, at no distant period, a place of some importance.

THE CHURCH is on the highest point of the rock on which stands the village: it is dedicated to St. James, and is an augmented Curacy, valued in 1810, including surplice and other fees, at 105*l.* 5*s.* 11*d.* per annum.—The present incumbent is the Rev. Mr. Church. The building is of considerable antiquity, of red stone, with a strong tower, forming a prominent object in the neighbouring views. On the South side of the steeple is the date 1673.

HISTORY.

There are few monumental memorials in the church.

On a brass plate in the Chancel:—

Infra sacræ sunt conditæ exuviæ Saræ, Ricardi Holt, de Aulà juxta pontem in par. de Bury, in com. Lanc. gen. filiæ, Robertiq; Bellis. A. M. hujus Ecclesiæ Pastoris, uxoris dilectissimæ, quæ dotibus animi præclaris prædita, vitæ integritate adornata, sincera pietate Deo probata, et ad cælum, per Jesu Christum matura, a nobis, pro Dolor! decessit; discessit ad beatos cælicolas, ad patrem cœlestem, ad Xtum mediatorem, sanctorumq; Παννηγυριν, quibuscum perennes agit triumphos, Gloria donata Dei, Jan. 5, anno Domini MDCCVI.

PARISH OF PLEMONDESTALL,

CONTAINS, IN THIS HUNDRED, THE TOWNSHIP OF

BRIDGE TRAFFORD,

WHICH is situated immediately S. W. of the parish of Thornton and is about four miles and a half from Chester. At a very early period it was vested in the Crown, as part of the Earldom of Chester, and under it was held by the *Troghfords*, who continued the proprietors till the death of Thomas Trafford, who was killed in the battle of Naseby, leaving as sole heiress Alice, wife of John Barnston, Esq. of Churton, whose descendant, Roger Barnston, Esq. is the present proprietor.

On the site of the ancient hall of Bridge Trafford, is erected a farm-house.—The manerial rights are exercised by the Dean and Chapter of Chester; and the tenants pay service at St. Thomas's Court.

THE PARISH OF TARVIN,

CONTAINS THE TOWNSHIPS OF

TARVIN-CUM-OSCROFT,	DUDDON,
HOCKENHULL,	ASHTON,
BRUEN STAPLEFORD,	KELSALL,
BURTON,	GREAT MOULDSWORTH,
CLOTTON,	HORTON-CUM-PEELE,

And FULKE STAPLEFORD, *the latter in the Hundred of Broxton. The whole parish contains about* 10,000 *acres.* WILLINGTON, *an extra parochial township, pays corn tithe to Tarvin.*

TARVIN

Is about five miles N. E. E. from Chester; and the roads to Northwich and Nantwich diverge here. At the time of the Survey it belonged to the Bishop; and continued the property of the Bishops of Lichfield and Coventry till 1550, when Richard, then Bishop, granted the Manor to Sir J. Savage, Knt. with a reserved yearly rent of 31*l*. The Savages held Tarvin from the Crown, as of the Earldom of Chester, by military service, at half a Knight's fee;—and from them it passed with the other estates to the Cholmondeleys, who sold it* to Mr. Thomas, and he sold it to the present proprietor, Mr. William Cotgreave, who holds a Court Leet and Baron for the manor.—Sir John Savage procured a charter for a market here, but it is now disused; two fairs, however, are held, on the [illegible]th April, and the [illegible]d December.—In right of this manor, the Bishop of Lichfield and Coventry exercised a jurisdiction over the neighbouring townships of Hockenhull and Kelsall, which, although within its liberties, were nevertheless exempted from the controul of the Foresters of Delamere; but these townships are not now included in Tarvin leet.

* In 1786.

In this township is *Holmes-street-Hall*, formerly called Holme-street Manor-house, which was included in the purchase of the manor made by the Savages; but passed afterwards to the Starkies, Sprostons, Barkers, and Symkins. Mrs. Darell, heiress of the latter, bequeathed it to Mr. Daniel Vawdrey, whose son sold it in 1767 to Thomas Brock, Esq. from whom it has passed to the Cluttons.

Prior's Heys is in the hamlet of Oscroft, attached to Tarvin, a little distance on the East side. It belonged to the Bruens, from whom, with other property, it has passed by purchase, to the Wilbrahams of Rode. The estate is extra-parochial.

A branch of the Bruens of Stapleford, settled in Tarvin, temp. Richard II. but it is supposed became extinct towards the conclusion of the 17th century.

During the Civil Wars, Tarvin was a considerable military post occupied by the Republicans.—On the 12th November, 1643, there was a skirmish between the garrison and the Chester forces; and in the following January, another battle took place. In August, 1644, Tarvin was possessed by the Royalists, and sustained a severe attack from the Parliamentary troops

In September of the same year, it again fell into the hands of the Parliament, when it was strongly garrisoned and fortified; and even the rumour of the approach of the King, in May, 1645, did not induce the surrender of the post. It continued in the hands of the Parliament till the conclusion of the war.†

† See Burghall's Diary.

On the 30th April, 1752, the town was nearly destroyed by fire: it began accidentally, at the west end. The wind was very high, and the flames spread rapidly, and in two hours, the greater portion of the village was a mass of ashes. Collections were generally made, on the behalf of the sufferers, throughout the county; and to the eternal honour of the City of Chester be it recorded, that its inhabitants subscribed near £300. for their relief.

The Church is dedicated to St. Andrew. It consists of body, side aisles, and chancels.—It belonged originally to the Bishops of Lichfield and Coventry; and in 1226, Alexander de Savensby, then Bishop, endowed a Prebendall Stall in his Cathedral, with the advowson of this Vicarage; previous, however, to this, he had given the Church to St. Andrew's Hospital at Denwall,‡ annexing to it, in 1238, the Rectory of Burton, as a compensation for Tarvin. In the reign of Queen Anne, the Stall of Tarvin was united to that of Holford, as one of the Canonries on the new foundation. In 1796, it was annexed to the Dean and Chapter of Lichfield, and by the Act empowering this transfer, the advowson of the Vicarage was separated from the Prebend, and with other advowsons, given to the Bishop. The present Vicar is the Rev. John Oldershaw, presented August 2, 1796. The impropriator has the corn tithes of a portion of the neighbouring extra-parochial township of Willington, which belonged to the Abbey of Whalley. The Parish Registers commence in 1563, but are imperfect from 1682 to 1687. They contain some curious notices; one of them, a true Sternholdian composition by the Parish Clerk:—

‡ Wirral.

"Burials—25 Jan. 1623—John Bruen, of Stapleford, Esquyer. Nulli pietate secundus—

"An Israelite in whom no guyle
Or Fraud was ever found;
A Phœnix rare,
Whose Virtues fair,
Through all our Coasts do sound."

1638. April. Eliz. dau'r of John Harvey, of Tarvin. Slayne, with Mrs. Alice Arderne's darte.

1654.—Notices of five persons named Gaskin, dying of the plague May 10, 16, and 18.

The following are a few of the monumental memorials:—

CHESHIRE

Here sleep the remains of the Rev. Thomas Dickenson, A. M. 50 years resident Vicar, who died June 12, 1796, in the 82d year of his age.

Here lie the remains of Charlotte Dickenson, Relict of the Rev. Thomas Dickenson, A. M. who died the 10th of March, 1815, in the 78th year of her age.

Here lyeth interred John Hardware, of Molesworth, Esq. who dyed 17 Feb. 1661, having been twice married, first to Mary the dau'r of Thomas Gardiner, of Salop, Esq. by whom he has issue one son, that died young; she died 1 Feb. 1652. Afterwards he married Mary, daughter of John Angel, of Crowhurst, Esq. and left issue one son Henry, a quarter of a year old at his father's death.

In the *Bruen Chancel*, at the east end of the south aisle, are painted memorials of

John Bruen, Esq. co. Cest. who dyed Jan. 28, 1625.

Mary, dau'r and coh. John Tilston, of Huxley, Esq. wife to Jonathan Bruen, of Bruen Stapleford, Esq. ob. 15 May, 1651.

On a brass plate—

Henry Hardware here interred is, that Alderman was of late
In the City of Chester, where he was a grave Magistrate,
Within that Citye the sword before him twice had borne.
He ruled with prudente policye, as Citizens grave can well informe,
And so deceased the v. of March 1584.

On a painted tablet—

Mrs. Jane Done (of Duddon) obiit. Ap. 29, 1722, a.° Ætat, 66.

On a brass plate—

Underneath lieth interred the body of Edward Done, Esq. of Duddon, who departed this life July 5, 1718, aged 54 years of his age.

On an adjoining brass plate—

Hic jacet corpus Josephi Gerrard, hujus Ecclesiæ nuper pastoris, obiit Jan. 8, 1708, æt. 58.

On a flag-stone, outside the Chapel—

Near to this place lie the remains of John Thomasen, for thirty-six years Master of the Grammar School, in that capacity approved and eminent, but highly excelling in all the varieties of writing, and wonderfully so in the Greek character. Specimens of his ingenuity are treasured up, not only in the cabinets of the curious, but in the public libraries throughout the kingdom. He had the honour to transcribe for her Majesty Queen Anne, the Icon Basilike of her Royal Grandfather: invaluable copies also of Pindar, Anacreon, Theocritus, Hippocrates's Aphorisms, and that finished piece the Shield of Achilles (as described by Homer) are among the productions of his valuable pen.

As his incomparable performances acquired him the esteem and friendship of the great and learned, so his affability and humanity gained him the good will of all his acquaintance, and the decease of so much private worth was regretted as a public loss.—Obiit Jan. 25, 1740, a°. æt. 54.

HISTORY.

Dum mortale perit, littera scripta manet.

There are very few remains of the richly painted glass which formerly ornamented the windows of the church, the destruction of which was a sacrifice to the fanaticism of the celebrated John Bruen, of Stapleford.

There are several instances of longevity in this parish:—Ralph Nield, buried here in 1760, lived to the age of 107 years, leaving a *sixth* wife behind him.—In 1791, the waste lands in Tarvin were inclosed, when lands were allotted to the Impropriator and Vicar, in lieu of tithes.

The *Grammar School* of Tarvin was founded in 1600, by John Pickering, merchant, and endowed by him with £200. for the purpose of educating twenty children. This sum was laid out in the purchase of lands in Tattenhall, producing £15. per annum, and 3*l*. per annum interest.—The establishment is under the direction of twelve trustees.*

ASHTON-JUXTA-TARVIN,

Is about eight miles E. N. E. from Chester; and was at a very period held by the Mainwarings of Warmincham, under the Barony of Shipbrook, from whom it passed to the Tressels and Veres. About 1580, Sir Christopher Hatton purchased it from the Earl of Oxford, and it passed by subsequent sales to the families of Crewe, Davies, and Whitley. The executors of Roger Whitley, Esq. sold it in 1718, to Mr. Leonard Grantham, who re-sold it ten years afterwards to Mr. Cornelius Hignett, of Darland, whose two daughters and heirs, were married to Thomas Aldersey, M. D. (who died issueless) and to Samuel Aldersey, Esq. of Aldersey, brothers. It is now the property of Samuel Aldersey, Esq. of Aldersey, grandson of the before-named S. Aldersey, Esq.; but no Court is held for the manor.

The *Hall* of Ashton is a stone building, with bay windows, and is the property of Mr. George Speakman, to whom it descended from the Robinsons of Ashton.

Ashton Hayes was formerly† the seat of the Smiths of Hough; but the representatives of the family sold

† Temp. Hen. VIII.

* Six of the children of the school are selected from Tarvin township; the remainder from the other townships of the parish.—There is another school in Tarvin on Dr. Bell's system, for the education of 150 children.

it, towards the conclusion of the 17th century, to Roger Whitley, Esq. In 1722, the then proprietor, sold it to Bruen Worthington, Esq. of Dublin; and in 1809, his grandson, the Rev. Richard Worthington, disposed of it to Booth Grey, Esq. eldest son of the Hon. Booth Grey, third son of Harry, fourth Earl of Stamford.—It is a handsome mansion, and the present proprietor has, by various purchases, made it the head of a considerable estate. The situation is beautifully picturesque, embosomed in woods, midway in the eminences which bound the forest.

BURTON

Is about three miles N. N. W. from Tarporley; previous to the Conquest, with the other estates in Tarvin, it formed part of the possessions of the Bishop of Lichfield and Coventry. At an early period, it was possessed by a family which assumed the name of the township; and before the reign of Edward II. it had passed to Robert le Bruen, who held it from the Bishop. The male line of the Bruens failing, in the middle of the 18th century, it was sold under a decree of Chancery; and is now, with other estates, the property of Randle Wilbraham, Esq. of Rode. No Court is held for the Manor.

Burton Hall was the seat and property of the Werdens, but it is now occupied as a farm-house.—Sir John Werden was created a Baronet in 1672, and his two daughters married on the same day the two sons of the Duke of St. Alban's. On the death of George Duke of St. Alban's, in 1787, the Werden estates here passed to his sister Charlotte Beauclerk, who was married to Andrew Drummond, Esq.; and his grandson, George Harley Drummond, Esq. of Stanmore, co. Middlesex, is the present proprietor. The hall is a fine old house, nearly covered with ivy.

CLOTTON-CUM-HOOFIELD

Is about two miles N. W. W. from Tarporley; and it appears from the Survey, that it was possessed by Ilbert, Lord of Waverton and Eaton, soon after the Conquest. Previous to 1093, Richard de Rublos, the supposed son of Ilbert, gave the tithes of Clotton, and Clotton Mill, to Chester Abbey; Gilbert de Pichot marrying Richard's daughter and heir, succeeded as capital Lord of Clotton, under whom it was held by the Wavertons. The three daughters of Hugh de Waverton married into the families of Clotton, Huxley, and Messington, and brought them in shares the Manor of Clotton.

The *Clotton's share* passed to the Overtons; and the heiress of Roger de Overton brought it in marriage to Thomas de Swetenham, whose daughter Margaret married Thomas Wilbraham, Esq. of Woodhey.—It continued in the Wilbrahams till the marriage of Grace, daughter and co-heiress of Sir Thomas Wilbraham, with Lionel Earl of Dysart; and is now the property of Earl Dysart.

The *Huxley share* passed in marriage with a daughter and heiress to Roger le Praers; and a sister and heiress, Elena, marrying Nicholas Bruen, of Stapleford, brought it to that family. It has subsequently, with the other property of the Bruens, passed to the Wilbrahams of Rode, from whom it was purchased by Mr. James Hassall.

The *Waverton*, or *Messington share*, passed very early to the Dones of Utkinton, probably by purchase; it is now vested in their representative, John Arden, Esq.—No Court is held for the Manor.

Hoofield, or *Hulfield*, is a hamlet of Clotton, and gave name to a family. John de Hulfield was seized of a fourth of the vill of Clotton, temp. Edw. III.

DUDDON

Is about three miles N. W. W. from Tarporley. Temp. Edward I. the widow of Robert de Clotton held a fourth of the manor; but it has subsequently passed, in the same manner as Clotton; and the manor is claimed by the Wilbrahams of Rode. It was formerly vested in the Dones (of Flaxyards) and the Bruens, and from the former the Ardernes claim an interest in the township, and possess a considerable estate, called *Duddon Hall*, now occupied as a farm-house. The township affords some beautiful situations.

HOCKENHULL

Was originally a dependency of the Bishop's manor of Tarvin; but it became vested in a family which took the name of the lordship.*—It continued several centuries in this family; and in 1713, it was sold by their representatives to Mr. Hugh Wishaw, of Chester, whose son sold the estate to John Walsh, Esq. M. P.

* Temp. Henry III. William de Hockenhull gave to Richard his brother, half of the township of Huxley.

for Worcester, in 1761, for 7600*l*. Ten years afterwards it was re-sold to Thomas Brock, Esq. who bequeathed it to his nephew, Richard Yates, Esq. who died in his infancy. The estate was then vested in the Rev. William Brock, Rector of Davenham, and he devised it to the eldest son of his eldest niece, who married Thomas Clutton, Esq. of Kursley, co. Hereford; and his eldest son having succeeded to the property, has taken the name of Brock.

The manerial Court is held with that for the township of Cotton Edmunds and Abbot.

The present *Hall* of Hockenhull is occupied as a farm-house, but it is in a very ruinous state.

HORTON-CUM-PEELE,

Or *Little Mouldsworth*, is composed of two estates, HORTON and PEELE. At an early date it was possessed by the Duttons; subsequently by the Vernons, Cholmendeleys, and Savages. In 1629 the *Horton Hall* estate was vested in a family named Travers, or Travis:* and was subsequently purchased from the Marchioness of Lansdowne, by her uncle, Mr. Richard Maddock. The house is of brick, and is occupied by a farmer.

Peel Hall Estate was vested in the Hardwares, of Bromborow; and passed by subsequent sales to Colonel Roger Whitley, originally a zealous royalist, and the companion of King Charles in his exile. In 1681 he was returned as the Representative of Chester by the Whig party, and in 1692, 1693, 1694, 1695, he held the office of Mayor of Chester. On the passage of William III. to Ireland, he entertained the Sovereign at Peel Hall. Elizabeth, heiress of Thomas Whitley, Esq. brought this estate in marriage to Other, second Earl of Plymouth, about 1706. In 1813, the Earl of Plymouth sold the estate to Booth Grey, Esq. the present proprietor.—The old Hall of Peel, it is conjectured, stood within a circular moat in the garden, and was probably built as a defence against the ravages of the Welsh. The present house was originally erected in 1637, but little can be traced in the remains of the style of its architecture.

KELSALL

Is about three miles N. E. from Tarvin, and nearly eight miles from Chester. At the time of the Conquest, it is supposed to have been held by Baldric, under the Earl;† but it soon passed from him, and was vested in the Bishop of Chester, who held it under the Baron of Dunham Massy.‡ Previous to the reign of Edward IV. it was possessed by the Dones, of Flaxyards; and on the general division of the Dones property, Kelsall fell to the share of Eleanor, wife of Ralph Arderne, Esq. A moiety of the manor is now vested in John Arden, Esq. and Booth Grey, Esq. claims the other, in right of a purchase from the Earl of Plymouth, in whom were vested the Whitley Estates of Mouldsworth, Ashton, and Kelsall.

Formerly Kelsall was an important military post, commanding the principal means of approach to and from Chester, and the Forest of Delamere. The trace of the old pass of Kelsall still exists in a field on the right hand of the road leading to Chester. So late as the year 1745, it was in contemplation to strengthen the position, and on the rumour of the approach of the Pretender, a wide ditch was cut across the road, and other means taken to prevent his approach to Chester on this side.§

There is a quarry of excellent stone in this township, the property of Joseph Gunnery, Esq. of Liverpool.

The general appearance of Kelsall is truly picturesque; embracing some of the most romantic scenery to be found in the county.—Kelsall Hall is occupied as a farm-house.

Some further explanation as to the descent of the Kelsall property may not be deemed superfluous:—The Earl of Plymouth sold the greater bulk of his lands in Kelsall, to Mr. Ralph Norton, and to Mr. Edward Briscoe, of Kelsall. Mr. Norton subsequently sold

* The Travis family sold it to Jacob Jones, about 1719; Thomas Maddock, Esq. Alderman of Chester, bought it of Jones in 1749. The Marchioness of Lansdowne was his grand-daughter, and sold it in 1787.—LYSONS.

† "Baldricus tenet de Hugone comite Cocle;" &c. but Sir Peter Leycester gives this description to Coghall, in the hundred of Broxton.—See ANTIQUITIES.

‡ A family which took the local name, had considerable property here.—Temp. Edw. II.

§ A Regiment called the Liverpool Blues, was particularly active at this period in the royal cause.—So great was the consternation which prevailed, that the inhabitants of the village and neighbourhood actually buried numerous articles of plate and furniture.—Information of Mr. Finchett, sen. of Kelsall, living February, 1820.

CHESHIRE

his share to Samuel Woodhouse, Esq. of Bronte house, near Liverpool; and Mr. Briscoe's share has been purchased by Joseph Gunnery, Esq. solicitor, of Grove House, also near Liverpool; on Mr. Gunnery's estate is an excellent quarry of White Free Stone, worked by Mr. Gunnery, mason, and surveyor of the County Bridges;* and near the border of the forest lands is a fine chalybeate spring, throwing up a considerable quantity of water, which forms a small brook, and ultimately falls into the Gowry. This well has obtained great favour in the opinion of the country people, who attribute to its sanative qualities, cures almost miraculous. Mr. Woodhouse, before-mentioned, holds a great portion of the late Earl Plymouth's lands in Kelsall, and the *Whitewood* property.†

GREAT MOULDSWORTH

Is about nine miles N. E. E. from Chester. It is not noticed in the Survey; but it was held under the Savages, by the Manleys, of Manley, so early as the reign of Hen. VII. The capital manor is here spoken of; for the mediate manor was held by a family which took the name of the township, temp. Edw. III.—Before the reign of Elizabeth, it was sold to the Birkenheads; and in the 36th of the Queen, R. Birkenhead, Esq. of Manley, passed over a considerable estate in Great and Little Mouldsworth. The manerial rights were vested in the Hardwares of Peel, before the 17th century; but a large estate here was vested in John Davies, Esq. of Manley, in 1671; and soon after this, the Tilstons had possession of the manor, from whom it passed to Mrs. Elizabeth Lightbody, and on her death it was bought by Dr. Haygarth, of Bath,‡ who is the present proprietor.

‡ Recently of Chester.

An estate of the Whitleys, in this township, has been purchased from the Earl of Plymouth, by Booth Grey, Esq. of Ashton Hayes, and a curious built house of their's still exists here.

BRUEN STAPLEFORD

Is about seven miles E. by S. from Chester. The Le Brun's, who settled here so early as 1230, gave name to the township. In 1262, Robert Le Brun gave lands in the township to Thomas, the son of his sister Eva. The family continued in uninterrupted possession till early in the 18th century, varying their name from Le Brun to Bruen, Bruyn, and again to Bruen. Richard III. in the first year of his reign, granted a pardon to John Bruen, then Bailiff of Flint, for all murders, rapes, rebellions, &c. practised by him to that date, Feb. 21.—In 1696, on the death of John Bruen, Esq. the estate passed to his uncle Jonathan Bruen, who died in 1715, leaving an only daughter, married to John White, Esq. Having no issue living, the estates were thrown into Chancery; and under a decree of that Court, were sold in 1752 to Randle Wilbraham, Esq. of Rode, who is the present proprietor.

HISTORY.

Of the Bruen Stapleford family, was the celebrated puritan, John Bruen, of bigotted religious principles, but of an excellent general disposition. He married the daughter of Henry Hardware, Esq. of Chester, and in the earlier days of his manhood lived a life of gaiety, if not of dissipation. In 1587 his father died, leaving him as it were guardian to his twelve brothers and sisters, and charged with their bequests. This induced him to adopt a life of economy; and as a commencement, the Park of Bruen Stapleford was cleared of its deer, and converted to a more profitable purpose; and the domestic arrangements of the family were on a rigid system of religious discipline. It is to be lamented, that his blind puritanic zeal, led him to acts, which are by no means amiable in the abstract: the painted glass in his own Chapel, and in the Church of Tarvin, did not suit his religious prejudices, and accordingly it was removed, a greater part being broken; the windows being were glazed at his own expense.|| The hospitality and charity of Mr. Bruen were unbounded: "many that passed betwixt England and Ireland, through Chester, would take up his house for their lodging place, that they might rejoice their hearts in

* The stone used in the building of the Grand Stand, on the Race Course, Chester, was procured from this quarry.

† Information of J. Gunnery, Esq.

|| In the service of Mr. Bruen, was an old and faithful servant, named Robert Pasfield, and the plan he adopted to retain in his memory the numerous Sermons which he heard, strongly reminds one of the modern system of MNEMONICS:—He was a man of no learning, but "invented a girdle of leather, long and large, which went twice about him: this he divided into several parts, allotting every book of the Bible to one of the divisions; for the chapters he had leather thongs also to every division, and he divided the verses by similar means. By this help to memory, he was enabled to repeat to

seeing his face, hearing his voice, and conferring and advising with him."*

Mr. Bruen died in January, 1625, aged 65.†

In HARGREAVE STUBBS, in this township, is a CHAPEL, founded in 1627, by Sir Thomas Moulson, Baronet, Alderman of London. He endowed it with £40. per annum, and also an adjoining SCHOOL with £20. "for the government, education, and instruction of youth in *grammar* and VIRTUE." The surplus of the money from the lands appointed to the endowment, if any, to be appropriated by the trustees for the relief of the poor. These lands now set for upwards £150. per annum. The trustees are the Bishop and Dean of Chester, Earl Grosvenor, Rev. J. Oldershaw, Randle Wilbraham, Esq. of Rode, and the Rev. Rd. Massie, of Chester.

The extra parochial township of

WILLINGTON,

Or *Willaton*, is about three miles N. N. W. from Tarporley, and formed part of the possessions of the Earls. It was subsequently held from the Earls by the Stapleford and Despenser families. Henry Despenser becoming possessed of the entire township, gave it to the Abbot of Stanlow, who afterwards removed to Whalley, subject to a rent of 10*l.* to be paid at Chester, on the feast of St. John. It continued to be vested in the Monks of Whalley till the Dissolution, when it became the property of the Leighs of Booths, and was afterwards possessed by the Dones ‡ Descending to Mrs. Jane Done, it has passed with the Tarporley estates in the same manner as Utkinton.

Corn tithes are paid by the township to the Rector of Tarvin. *Willington Wood* is a well-known object in the County Views.

HISTORY.

‡ Between 1593, and 1629.

his Master, the purport of the sermons in a very accurate manner.— Mr. Bruen called it "the girdle of verity;" and after Pasfield's death, hung it up in his study.

* Copious particulars of the life of this estimable man, will be found in the Rev. Mr. Hinde's "Faithful Remonstrance."—Lond. printed by R. B. 1641.

† His sister Catherine, also eminent for her piety, became the wife of Wm. Brettargh, Esq. of Brettargh Hall, co. Lanc.

THE PARISH OF DELAMERE,

CONTAINS THE TOWNSHIPS OF

DELAMERE, KINGSWOOD, EDISBURY, AND OAKMERE.

A general notice of the Forest of Delamere will be found in page 48.

DELAMERE

Is bounded eastwardly by the parish of Budworth, and road from Frodsham to Tarporley, including the road; westwardly by the townships of Tarvin and Kelsall. Northwardly by the before-mentioned road from Chester to Northwich, from the boundary of the Forest, near Kelsall Toll-bar, to the Edisbury road, and by the inclosures called *Edisbury Lodge*, and by the road leading from Chester towards Middlewich, including the road; northwardly by the townships of *Willington* and *Utkinton*, including the several old inclosures within the respective townships.

KINGSWOOD

Is another township, created by the late Inclosure Act. It is bounded eastwardly by the townships of Kingsley and Norley; westwardly by Ashton, Manley, and Alvanley; northwardly by Frodsham Lordship and Newton; southwardly by the road leading from Ashton to Norley, including the road.

CHESHIRE HISTORY.

EDISBURY

TOWNSHIP, is bounded eastwardly by Norley and the road from Frodsham to Tarporley, and by the Edisbury road, including the roads; westwardly by Kelsall and Ashton; northwardly by the before named road from Ashton to Norley; and southwardly by the Chester and Northwich turnpike-road, including the road.

OAKMERE

TOWNSHIP, is bounded eastwardly by the parish of Budworth, and the townships of Newchurch (Whitegate) and Sandiway; westwardly by the road from Frodsham to Tarporley; northwardly by the townships of Norley, Coddington, and Bryn; southwardly by the road leading from Chester to Middlewich.

Such are the present parochial divisions of this extensive tract of land, of which a further account appears in a foregoing portion of this work.* A few interesting particulars may be added:—At one period, this forest spread over nearly the whole of the hundred of Edisbury, and a great portion of Nantwich hundred. That portion next the Mersey was called the Forest of *Mara*, or *Mere;* the remaining part, stretching in the direction of Nantwich, was the Forest of *Mondrem.* By successive encroachments and inclosures, it was reduced, at the period of the late Act being obtained, to 7755a. 2r. 35p.—Originally the jurisdiction over the forests was vested in the families of Kingsley of Kingsley, Grosvenor of Budworth, Wever of Wever, and Merton of Merton: early in the 12th century, the Master Forestership of the whole was granted to Ralph de Kingsley (ancestor of the Dones) by the tenure of a horn. Half of the vert and venison of Mara, was given by Hugh, the second Earl of the name, to Robert le Grosvenor, together with the vill of Budworth, from whom it descended to the Talbots, and subsequently to the Dones of Utkinton, who assumed the entire and exclusive jurisdiction of the Forest. The privileges vested in the Master Forester were very extensive and curious: amongst them, he claimed† to have all swarms of bees, the right shoulder of all deer taken; he had also the power of beheading any thief taken in the fact.—The forest was well stored with large timber, and many precepts occur, for sending trees, to repair the Castle and Dee Mills, at Chester. There were probably deer here so late as the reign of Charles II. In the reign of Charles I a plan was proposed to destroy the herds of deer which still ranged over the cultivated districts on its borders.—The *Old Pale* was inclosed by Royal precept, in the 11th of Edw. III. The *New Pale* was inclosed in the 17th century.

* See page 48.

† See account of the suit of Richard Grosvenor against Richard Done, 31st Edward I.—ORMEROD, vol. 1, p. 51.

PARISH OF THORNTON,

CONTAINS THE TOWNSHIPS OF

THORNTON,
ELTON,
HAPSFORD,
WIMBOLDS TRAFFORD,
AND
DUNHAM-ON-THE-HILL.

THORNTON,

Or *Thornton-le-Moors*, is about five miles N. E. from Chester, and stretches to the Mersey.—At the time of the Survey, it was held by Bigot; in the reign of John, it became a part of the fee of Aldford, and was given by Richard de Aldford, to Peter, the Clerk to the Earl. This Peter is said* to have been a younger son of David le Clerk, who possessed a Moiety of Malpas Barony.—Randle, the son of Peter, assumed the name of Le Roter, and was founder of the Roters, or Rutters, of Thornton, This family terminated in Sir Peter de Thorneton, Knt. about the reign of Edward III. In the 24th of that

* Collins.

CHESHIRE

King, in a Plea to a Quo Warranto, he produced a grant of Randle Earl of Chester, of a fishery in the Dee, from Chester to Eaton, with exemption from toll at Chester, and free suit of the Mayor's Portmote Court, as also freedom from toll at the Wiches. He married Lucy, daughter and heiress of Sir Wm. Hellesby, by whom he had eight daughters, one of whom, Katharine, was outlawed for felony. The distinct manor of Thornton, on his death, descended to Hamon Fitton, Baron of Dunham Massy, in right of his wife Elizabeth, youngest daughter of Sir Peter. Thornton subsequently passed in marriage with Joan, sister of Peter Fitton, only daughter of Hamon, to Richard Venables, the youngest son of Hugh, Baron of Kinderton. It then passed with female heirs to the families of Booth and Trafford, between whom it was held in moieties.—About 1597, Trafford's moiety was purchased by Sir Peter Warburton, and afterwards passed in marriage to the Stanleys of Alderley, who sold it to the Booths of Dunham Massy. In 1724, Thornton passed by will of the Hon. Langham Booth, a younger brother of George, the last Earl of Warrington, to George Legh, Esq. of East Hall; and it is now the property of George John Legh, Esq, of High Legh.

Earl Grosvenor, in right of his Manor of Aldford, exercises a paramount manerial right, for although a Court Baron is held by Mr. Legh, the tenants are summoned to the Leet at Aldford; and his Lordship appoints a gamekeeper. About two thirds of the entire township, which contains about six hundred Cheshire acres, are the property of Mr. Legh.

The *Holme House Farm*, is in the parishes of Ince, Stoke, and Thornton, but it is nevertheless within the latter manor. There are sixteen Cheshire acres in the Parish Glebe of Thornton Church, six acres of Stockport, seven of Over, ten of Little Budworth, and seven of St. Martin, Chester.*

*Ormerod.

A moated site may still be traced a short distance east of the Church, which was probably the situation of the Old Hall of the Le Roters: the present Hall is occupied as a farm house.

There was a Church, here previous to the Conquest: "*Ibi Ecclesiæ et Presbyter, et una acra prati.*"† The patronage of the living descended regularly with the manor, till the advowson was sold, about 1708, by the Earl of Warrington, for £500. to the Rev. Richard Hill, LL.D. from whose nephew, Thomas Harwar, Esq. it has become vested in Lord Berwick. The present Rector, is the Hon. Richard Hill, instituted 25th March, 1799.

†Domesday

HISTORY.

The *Church* is in a very picturesque situation, built of red stone, and is dedicated to St. Helen. It consists of nave, chancel, south aisle, and a strong tower in which are three bells. In the south wall is a piscina, under a neat arch, trefoiled. Five of the arches which separate the aisle from the Chancel, are pointed. The Church was well repaired about 1715.

The Monumental Memorials are various. There are several inscriptions to the Gerards of Wimbolds Trafford, the Bunburies, the Cottinghams, &c. &c.

On a pyramidal marble monument, on the north wall—

In Memory of the Rev. Rowland Chambre, late Rector of this parish. He was presented to this Church in the year 1760, where, no predecessor having resided withing the memory of man, it devolved upon him to refit the parsonage, erect several additional buildings, and decorate the grounds about it. He resided here during his incumbency, and died the 10th day of December, in the year of our Lord 1796, aged 65.

Hæc domus ultima.
Tendimus huc omnes.

On a blue and white marble mural monument in the south aisle—

Here lyeth interred with his ancestors, Peter Cottingham, Esq. first Secretary to the Lord Chancellor Macclesfield, who dyed the 30th of January, 1743, aged 71. Also, Jane Cottingham, his dearly beloved wife, who dyed the 25th of November, 1751, aged 76.

On a mural monument of white marble adjoining the last—

Underneath lies interred the body of Richard Cottingham, of the city of Chester, gent. eldest son of John Cottingham, of Dunham on the Hill, gent. He married Mary the only daughter and heir of John Gregg, of Elton, gent. by whom he had issue one son, mamed John. He departed this mortal life, the 27th Aug. 1720, in the 49th year of his age.

In the Frodsham Chapel—

Here lyeth interred the body of John Farrar, of the city of Chester, gentleman, late one of the Attornies of his Majesty's Court of Exchequer, who married Eleanor, daughter of John Frodsham, Esq. of Elton, who departed this life the 6th day of July, 1684.

On an elegant mural marble monument, beneath a

sarcophagus, surmounted by the family crest, the arms on the entablature—

Sacred to the memory of the Rev. Edward Harwood, Rector of this parish. deceased September, 1760.

Mary Folliott, his daughter, wife of James Folliott, Esq. merchant, of the city of Chester, March, 1764.

Theodosia Folliott, their daughter, September, 1768.

Elizabeth Harwood, wife of the Rev. Edward Harwood, April, 1772.

Elizabeth Irivisa, daughter of Elizabeth Harwood, May 1789.

James Folliott, Esq. December, 1790, who died at [illegible] Hall, and whose remains were deposited in the Chancel of the Church at Congleton, in the County Palatine of Chester.

The Parish Registers commence in 1574, but there is a deficiency from 1682 to 1688.

There is a *School* here, built by subscription, before 1722, and which has within the few last years, been rebuilt by the Parishioners. The Master's salary arises from the rent of half of the seven acres of land in Elton; the other half, about fifteen pounds per annum, is given indiscriminately to the Poor of the Parish.

ELTON,

Is about four miles and a half W. S. W. from Frodsham, in a low, swampy situation. At the time of the Survey, it was included in the possessions of the Earl, but was subsequently attached to the fee of Aldford.—In the 4th of Edw. II. John de Arderne, then Lord of Aldford, gave Elton in marriage with his sister Cecily, to Wm. de Wastenys, under the tenure of a rose annually. It continued in the same family till after the 12th Henry IV. when William de Wasteneys enfeoffed Sir Hugh de Holes, with the manor. The Holes continued the Lords, till the marriage of John Troutbeck, with Margery, the heiress of Thomas de Holes. Margaret Talbot, heiress of the Troutbecks, died possessed of it in 1531; and 66 years afterwards, a moiety of the manor was conveyed by the Talbots to Sir Edw. Brabazon. A great portion of the estates here was sold by the Brabazons to the Crewes, and was purchased during the Civil War, by the Greggs of Hapsford.—Soon afterwards, the heiress of Edw. Gregg, brought their estates in Elton in marriage to Roger Barnston, Esq.; whose descendant Roger Barnston, Esq. of Churton, and Chester, inherits a great share of them.

There are estates here belonging to Townshend Ince, Esq. and Bell Ince, Esq.; the manerial rights, however, are exercised in right of the fee of Aldford, by Earl Grosvenor.

A family which assumed the local name, settled here at an early period, certainly before 1268, and their interest in the township passed by marriage to William de Frodsham, the male line of whom became extinct in 1765, in Peter Frodsham, Esq. of Elton; his property fell to three sisters, coheiresses, one of whom was the mother of the Rev. Geo. Hodson, Rector of Liverpool, and in right of her, and his two aunts Alicia and Catherine, he became possessed of three fifths of the estate.—About 1789, this property was purchased by Charles Goodwin, Esq. of Farndon, from whom it passed to his niece, the daughter of Mr. Walter Thomas, merchant, of Chester, who married Hugh Maxwell, Esq. a Colonel in the Army, and he is the present proprietor. The other portions of the estate are possessed by a family named Platt; excepting, however, seven Cheshire acres, purchased by the Parish of Thornton.

Elton Hall is a large old mansion, occupied as a farm-house; it is of brick, finished with gables, and appears to have been built about the middle of the 17th century.

HAPSFORD

Is about five miles S. W. W. from Frodsham; and at a very early period was held by the Fitzalans, Earls of Arundel, in right of the manor of Dunham. A moiety afterwards passed to the Eltons, and from them to the Duttons, of Dutton, who in the beginning of the Reign of James I. possessed the whole manor. It passed with an heiress to the Gerards of Gerards Bromley. The lands of the township were soon afterwards sold, but the Royalty remained vested in the Gerards, and afterwards passed to the Fleetwoods. The manor is now the property of Hugh Maxwell, Esq.* who has assumed the name of Goodwin. A Court Baron has occasionally been held for the manor.

*See Elto

Hapsford Hall is an old timber mansion, in a state of extreme decay. The estate attached to it is the property of Roger Barnston, Esq.

WIMBOLDS TRAFFORD,

Is about five miles from N. E. E. from Chester, and was vested in the Fitzalans; from whom it passed to the Bruyns, of Bruen Stapleford, and descended with their estates by purchase, to Randle Wilbraham, Esq. of Rode; who sold it to the late George Edward Ger-

rard, Esq. on whose death, it became the property of his eldest daughter, Dorothy, who married the Rev. Richard Perryn, A. M. of Standish, in Lancashire, and he is the present owner.

The *Hall* is a handsome brick mansion, built by Mr. Gerrard, surrounded by some fine timber.

DUNHAM-ON-THE-HILL,

Or *Stony Dunham*, is about seven miles from Chester, on the direct road to Frodsham. It was amongst the possessions of the Earl, by whom it was granted to the Fitzalans Earls of Arundel. On the attainder and execution of Edmund Fitzalan, 20th Edward II. it was given by Queen Isabella, to John Hotham, Bishop of Ely, but in the reign of Edw. III. the Fitzalans being restored in blood, they regained possession of Dunham. Temp. Henry VI. it was purchased from the co-heirs of Thomas Earl of Arundel, by Wm. Troutbeck, Esq.* and has descended with the other estates of the Troutbecks, to the Earls of Shrewsbury.

It appears from an Inq. post mort. temp. Edw. IV. that Sir William Troutbecke, claimed a moiety of the Office of Keeper of the Bridge Gate, in Chester, with a moiety of the Serjeantcy of Bridge-street; also the Custody of the Garden and Orchard of Chester Castle, on the condition of finding sufficient Kale for the Earl's table. In addition, he claimed nine fishing stalls, and two boats in the Dee, with a right of fishing, reserving the Royal fish to the Earl.

A Court Leet and Baron is held for the Manor.

Dunham Hall is occupied as a Farm House.

* See account of St. Mary's Church, Chester, for further notice of the Troutbecks.---The contract for building the Chapel there, is still in the possession of the Earl of Shrewsbury, dated "the Mononday next before the feste of the Natyvyte of Seynt John the Baptist, in the yere of Kyng Henry the Sixt after the Conquest xi." It is agreed to be "battellet above, like to the littel closet with inne the castell of Chester," &c.

THE PARISH OF WEAVERHAM,

CONTAINS THE TOWNSHIPS OF

WEAVERHAM,	CUDDINGTON,
ACTON,	ONSTON,
CROWTON,	WALLERSCOTE.

With parts of Norley and Hartford.—The Hamlets of Milton, Gorstage, and Sandiway.

WEAVERHAM is about four miles N. W. from Northwich; and previous to the conquest, was possessed by the Saxon Earl Edwin. It was then seized by Hugh Lupus; and continued the property of the Earls, till Edw. I. gave it to Roger Clifford, who on his way from Palestine, married the Countess Lauretania at Beaufort, in France, and endowed her with this manor.—On his death, however, the King seized the manor into his own hands, and transferred it to his newly founded Monastery of Vale Royal, to which it was attached till the Dissolution, and followed its fate in becoming the property of the Holcrofts. It was afterwards sold to the Marburys of Marbury, whose line terminated in three sisters, co-heiresses, and they sold it, in 1708, under a Decree of Chancery, to Earl Rivers.—On his death, the Manor, with other estates, was purchased by James Earl of Barrymore, and has fallen to the present proprietor, J. S. Barry, Esq. of Marbury, but whose general residence is in Ireland.

The Abbots of Vale Royal, had a prison here, and

Cheshire

exercised great authority over the neighbouring townships. His Bailiff was the Judge; and it was also a part of his duty to act in a military capacity, in summoning the tenants of Weaverham fee to Chester Bridge in time of war, &c. At the present time the jurisdiction of the leet extends over the townships of Lostock, Twemlowe, Swettenham, and Lower Withington.—Weaverham. Weaverham is divided into what is termed the town and lordship, the first including Weaverham and Milton, the latter Sandiway, and Gorstage, each having a distinct Overseer; but the rates are equalized at the end of the year.

The houses are built chiefly of timber; in the principal street are two *May Poles.* Salt was made here about 1600.

The Hamlet of Sandiway is partly in Whitegate Parish.

The *Church* is dedicated to St. Mary; and consists of nave, chancel, side aisles, and a handsome tower.—In the north aisle is a chancel belonging to the family of Hefferston Grange; the other chancel belongs to Crowton Hall.

The presentation is vested in the Bishops of Chester; and the present Rector is the Rev. Thos. Armitstead, B. D. instituted Oct. 21, 1806.—The Registers commence in 1694.

On the north side the communion table, on a marble monument—

Near this place are interred the remains of the Rev. Thomas Hunter, M. A. by Diploma from the University of Oxford, late Vicar of this parish, who died Sept. 1, 1777, aged 67. Also, of Mary his wife, who died March 10, 1782, aged 71.

In the Crowton chancel, on a tablet—

This was done at the cost of Mrs. Hannah Halton, to the memory of her kind husband Thomas Halton, gent.—He died at Crowton Hall, October 18, 1675, being 66 years of age, and lyeth buried in this Chapel.

On the south wall, a mural marble monument—

Near this place are deposited the remains of Colonel John Mompesson, of the King's 8th Regiment of Foot, and Lieut.-Governor of the Isle of Wight. Obiit Oct. 3, 1768, aged 46. Erected by Jenny Gaarben, and Frances Oliver, his only surviving daughters.

The *Vicarage*, which is in a delightful situation, has been recently rebuilt by the present Rector. The glebe consists of about fourteen Cheshire acres; two-pence in the pound on servants' wages is claimed here, as at Coddington, as tythe, but it is not enforced. The Lord of Dutton has the tithe on pigs, geese, hemp and flax, in Acton. Composition for all small tithes are paid by the occupiers of the estates in Crewood, Crowton Hall, Dutton, Bottom, and Thave House. A modus in lieu of tithe hay is generally paid in Sandiway, Gorstage, Cuddington, Crowton, and Onston.—The Bishop, as Impropriator, has the corn tithe, which is leased to E. Starkey, Esq. of French Wood, Lancashire.

History.

The Charities consist of £[illegible] a funded legacy by Mr. Clowes, of Liverpool, for six poor decayed housekeepers and their wives, in Weaverham, to be selected by the Vicar—if none are found, then to deserving widows, or to deserving old maids, to be paid on St. John's Day. The interest of various sums, amounting to about £150. is distributed at Christmas by the Vicar and Churchwardens. There are two small estates in Crowton and Gorstage, belonging to the parish, which produce annually about £50. The Gorstage property was left by William Barker of Sandiway in 1700; a twentieth part is paid to the Vicar for a commemoration sermon, on Easter Monday, a portion is given to the poor, and the residue is apportioned in apprenticing six poor girls of the parish.*

*Ormerod.

ACTON

Is sometimes called *Acton in Delamere*, and is about four miles W. N. W. from Northwich As early as the 17th Edw. II. it was held of the Abbot of Vale Royal, by Peter Lord of Thornton. It was afterwards held by the Duttons of Dutton; and passed from them to the Gerards and Fleetwoods. It was sold by the latter to Mr. Scrase, of Brighton, and purchased from him by the present proprietor, N. Ashton, Esq. of Hefferston Grange.

CROWTON,

Is about five miles N. W. from Northwich. It is not noticed in the Survey. At a very early period it formed part of the Fee of Kingsley, and was divided amongst heiresses, wives of Gerard, Kingsley, Done, and Thornton. In the reign of Chas. II. Lord Brereton claimed a moiety of the manor, one fourth by descent from the Egertons, Thorntons, and Kingsleys, the other fourth, by the purchase of his ancestors, in 1302, from the granson of William Lancelyn, who married a coheiress of Kingsley: this portion subsequently passed from the Breretons to the Crewes.—Another fourth passed with a coheiress to the Dones, and from them by female heirs to the Birkenheads and Irelands: from them it was purchased by Thomas Hatton, Esq. and he sold it to the Crewes. In 1802, the estates held here by John Crewe, Esq (since ennobled) were purchased by George Wilbraham, Esq. The last fourth, passed with Emma, a coheiress of Richard de Kingsley, temp. Hen. III. to Wm. Gerard, Esq. whose descendants were seated at Crewood for many generations. It is now the property of Ralph Leycester, Esq. of Toft, in right of his grandmother, one of the two daughters and coheirs of the Gerards. A moiety of the Crewood estate was bought by Mr. Leycester of Gen. Warburton, who married the other heiress.

Crewood and Crowton Halls, are occupied as farmhouses. They possess no particular features of style or antiquity.

Crowton is within the jurisdiction of the Leet of Kingsley.

Ruloe House is the property of J. S. Barry, Esq.—It has recently been put in complete repair, and is beautifully situated. Mr. Ormerod states, and with great chance of accuracy, that Ruloe appears in the parish Registers in 1683, under the spelling of *Roe-loe*, and is most probably the spot which gave name to the ancient *Hundred of Roelau.*

CUDDINGTON,

Called *Cuddington-cum-Bryn*, was included in the Fee of Kingsley, and has regularly descended from the Lords. It is about five miles S. W. from Northwich, and the lands are principally divided between John Arden, Esq. John S. Barry, Esq. and George Wilbraham, Esq—*Cuddington Common*, containing four hundred and sixty acres, was inclosed and allotted in 1766.

The greater part of the township is the property of George Wilbraham, Esq who resides at a beautiful mansion here called *Delamere Lodge*, built after an elegant design by Wyatt, in a singularly romantic situation. Mr. Wilbraham's father removed hither from the ancient seat of the family, Townsend, in Nantwich. A curious M.S. diary, continued by the ancestors of Mr. Wilbraham, from 1542, to 1732, is in his possession; a copy of it is also possessed by Bootle Wilbraham, Esq. M. P. of Latham House, Lancashire, a branch of the ancient family of Woodbey: it relates chiefly to family and county occurrences.

ONSTON

Was granted by Randle Blundeville, to his godson, Randle le Roter, and was probably sold in parcels, soon after the time of Edw. I. It is now considered as part of the Lordship of Kingsley, and is included in the Court Leet of that Fee.

WALLERSCOTE,

Was given by Adam de Wringle to the Nuns of Chester, and continued attached to their establishment till the Dissolution. It was held under them by the family of Littler, or Littleovers, and they had a seat here in 1622. In the 17th Car. I. it was sold by them to Hugh Cholmondeley, ancestor of the present Marquis It afterwards became the property of the Wades; and Anne, daughter and heiress of Peter Wade, Esq. brought it in marriage to the late Peter Legh, Esq. of Booths.—Willoughby Legh, Esq. is the present proprietor.

Wallerscote Hall is the only house in the township, and is occupied as a farm-house.

NORLEY—PART OF.

This township was possessed by a family which took the local name, terminating temp. Edward III. in an heiress, who brought estates here to Robt. Leigh, Esq. of Adlington; and his descendants possessed them in the 16th century.

A large estate in this township is the property of Geo. Whitley, Esq. to whom it has descended from the Halls, who were settled here at a very early period; certainly before the reign of Hen. III. Mr. Whitley, father of the present proprietor, was the sister's son of Wm. Hall, Esq. who erected the present *Hall of Norley*, and died in 1795.

Norley Bank, partly in this parish, was built by the late James Croxton, Esq. and his executors sold it to the late John Nuttall, Esq. of Bury, Lancashire.—In 1811, the estate was sold to the Rev. Rowland Egerton, (7th son of the late Philip Egerton, Esq. of Oulton), husband of Emma, daughter and heiress of James Croxton,* Esq. by his wife Emma, the youngest sister and

* The Croxtons, of Norley, were a branch of the Croxtons, of Croxton Green, in Cholmondeley, temp. Elizabeth. They had estates also at Gonsley in Wybunbury, from whence they removed to Chester. Jas. Croxton, Esq. was buried at St. Mary's, July 25, 1707.

coheiress of Sir Peter Warburton, Bart. of Arley. In 1813, on his eldest son succeeding to to the Arley property, Mr. Egerton assumed the name of Warburton.

*** Omitted in the description of Thornton Church, page 463:

On a Marble Mural Monument—

" In memory of George Edward Gerrard, Esq. one of his Majesty's Justices of the Peace, and one of the Deputy Lieutenants of this county, who was born in Chester, April 23, 1723; and died at Trafford, August 20, 1794.—In public and private life, his conduct was the result of a mind governed by the principles of uniform rectitude and integrity. As a magistrate he was intelligent and active; as a husband tender and affectionate; as a father mild and provident; as a master just and benevolent; as a friend zealous and sincere; as a christian pious, steady, and orthodox, constantly evincing his faith by the works of righteousness. He married Elizabeth, the only daughter of Geo. Johnson, Esq. of Warrington, a women of singular piety and discretion; who having feared the Lord all her days, departed this life, July 21, 1766, in the 37th year of her age. They had issue two daughters and one son: the latter died an infant, and was interred in the Chancel of St. John's Church, Chester. Dorothy, their eldest daughter, married the Rev. Rich. Perryn, A. M. Rector of Standish, in Lancashire · by whom, as a testimony, however small, of his gratitude and respect, this monument is erected."

END OF DESCRIPTION OF EDISBURY HUNDRED.

Mosses, sc.

The Hundred of Nantwich,

CONTAINS THE PARISHES OF

ACTON,	COPPENHALL,	SANDBACH,	
AUDLEM,	MARBURY,	WISTASTON,	AND PART OF
BADDILEY,	MINSHULL,	WRENBURY,	WHITCHURCH.
BARTHOMLEY,	NANTWICH,	WYBUNBURY,	

PARISH OF SANDBACH,

(PART OF)

CONTAINS THE TOWNSHIPS OF

HASSALL. | BETCHTON.

HASSALL is about two miles and a half S. E. from Sandbach; it is described as *Eteshall*, in the Survey, and then belonged to the Barony of Wich Malbank.— Temp. Edw. I. Hassall was the portion of Eleanor, a coheiress, and she granted her lands to the Audley family. Henry de Aldithlegh, granted the township to Henry de Betlelegh. It was in the possession of a family which assumed the local name before the 18th
Cent. Edward III. for we then find,* that Richard de Hassal gave to Adam de Hassal, his chaplain, the manor of Hassall, with remainder to Richard Hassal, jun. and Ellen, daughter of Robert de Betchton, and their heirs. After this, the Hassals having considerable property in Hankelow, settled there; and Ralph Hassal, who was found son and heir by an Inq. p. m. 10th Elizabeth to Wm. Hassal of Hankelow, dying possessed of Hassall and Hankelow, the former, by the mediation of several gentlemen, his friends, was awarded, in order to accommodate a dispute between his two sons, to Ralph, the elder, and he afterwards sold the manor to Wm. Leversage, of Wheelock, Esq.; and Wm. Leversage, Esq. of Betchton, sold it to Thomas Stephens, who was the lord of the manor in 1662, but (says Vill. Cest.) Mr. Wm. Wild, was Lord of the Hall, commonly called Little Hassall.—In 1726, the Hall was conveyed by Richard Lowndes, then Lord of the entirety, on the death of Mr. Wild, to trustees, for five hundred years, for the purpose of raising £2,400, as the portions of the nine children of Richard Lowndes, the son of the before-named Richard.—In 1746, under a decree of

Cheshire

Chancery, the term (500 years) was sold to Mr. Joseph Fluitt, of Chester, and he assigned it to Rd. Lowndes, the son, who left heiresses Joan, the wife of Wm. Penlington, M. D. and Anne, wife of Edw. Salmon, Esq. The Manor, the term in the Hall, and a moiety of the Bostock Hall estate, passed to Mr. Salmon, whose son sold the whole to the Rev. John Armitstead, by whom the same was transferred to Mr. Daniel, who died in 1818, and since his death, the interest has been purchased by Mr. Lowndes. The remaining half of the Bostock Hall property, the possession of John Penlington, Esq of Rode Heath, has been united to the other portion, by purchase from Mr. Salmon.

Bostock Hall is a mansion of some antiquity, and has been surrounded by a moat. It is now occupied by a farmer.

Hassall Hall is a handsome old house, the gardens, which are extensive, laid out in the style of the early part of the 18th century.

BETCHTON,

Or *Bechton*, is about two miles S. E. S. from Sandbach; it is not noticed in Domesday, but was as early as the reign of Edw. I. possessed by the Audleys, under whom it was held by a family which assumed the local name. About the reign of Richard II. it became, by fine and marriage, divided between the families of Fitton and Davenport. The Fitton share passed by purchase, temp. Eliz. to the Egertons of Wrinehill, in trust for the Freeholders, who are the present proprietors of the manor, and elect four lords, who are lords for life. They hold a Court Leet and Baron, and divide the quit rents. The Lords in 1817, were the Rev. Rd. Levett, Mr. John Wilson, Mr. Thomas Summerfield, and Mr. John Podmore. The Davenport share, passed with the other Henbury estates, in marriage with Isabella, an heiress of the Davenports, to Sir Fulk Lacy * This moiety, it is supposed, passed to the Wilbrahams, by purchase from the Beestons, but it is not satisfactorily ascertained whether the manerial rights attached to it were those of the Audleys, or the Davenports. However, George Wilbraham, Esq. of Delamere Lodge, has the estate and manerial interest, and gives a game deputation. No Court is held.

History.

* Ormerod.

Betchton Hall, occupied as a farm-house, is built of timber and plaister, on the site of an ancient mansion, formerly with a demesne attached, the property of the Rev. Prebendary Jackson, of Chester, who died in 1796, and his niece, Miss Day Jackson, is the proprietor.

PARISH OF BARTHOMLEY,

CONTAINS THE TOWNSHIPS OF

BARTHOMLEY,
CREWE,
HASLINGTON,
ALSAGER,
AND
BARTERLEY (co. Stafford.)

A small portion of the Township of HASSALL, is in this Parish.

BARTHOMLEY

Is about seven miles and a half E. from Nantwich. It appears from the Survey, that it was attached to the great Barony of Wich Malbank, but was soon afterwards held under the Barons, by the family of Praers, in whom it continued till about the 20th Edward III. when Elizabeth, heiress of Thomas Praers, brought it in marriage to Sir Robert Fulleshurst. In the 21st Elizabeth, Sir Christopher Hatton obtained the manor from Robert, Thomas, and George Fulleshurst; but it was subsequently sold to Randle Crewe, from whom it has descended to the present proprietor, Lord Crewe.

The *Church* is dedicated to St. Bertoline, and the advowson is attached to the manor. It consists of a nave, chancels, side aisles, and tower. The side aisles are cut off from the nave by a line of pointed Gothic arches,

CHESHIRE

springing from the capitals of clustered pillars. The roofing of the nave, is of wood, richly carved, put up in 1589, and enriched with the arms of Acton, Delves, Egerton, Venables, &c. At the end of the north aisle is the Crewe chancel; under an arch in which is the recumbent figure of an ecclesiastic, on an alabaster slab, conjectured* to represent Robt. Fulleshurst, the Rector, who died 1475.

Ormerod.

In the Crewe chancel in the south aisle, built by Sir Randle Crewe, on a large white mural monument,—

Underneath lieth the body of Mrs. Anne Crewe, daughter of the late John Crewe, of Crewe, relict of John Offley, of Madeley, Esq. and mother of the present John Crewe, of Crewe, Esq. who died May 15, 1711, aged 62 years.

Beneath—

Elizabeth, the younger daughter of John Crewe, of Crewe, Esq. who had children only by his first wife Carew, the daughter of Sir Arthur Gorge, of Chelsey, in ye county of Middlesex, Knt. and left no issue male; relict of Charles the youngest son of Sir Christopher Turnor, of Milton Erneys, in the county of Bedford, Knt. and sometime one of the Barons of the Exchequer,—prepared this monument to be erected for a memorial of her husband, theyr only child Elizabeth, and herself.

He dyed 13th August, 1693, } aged { 42
Theyr daughter 25th Oct. 1694, } aged { 4
She on 20th June, 1696, } aged { 45

And their bodies are enclosed in the vault beneath.

On a mural monument—

Beneath lieth the body of John Crewe, Esq. of Crewe, son of John Offley, Esq of Madeley, in the county of Stafford, who died August 26, 1749, aged 68, to whose memory this monument was erected by Sarah his wife, who departed this life May 8th, 1751, aged 69, and is likewise here interred.

Against the north wall is the monument of Sir Robt. Fulleshurst, one of the four Squires of the renowned Lord Audley, at the Battle of Poictiers; he died in the 13th year of Richard II. It is an embattled altar tomb, around which, in bas relief, are the mutilated figures of Knights and females, under Gothic arches, beautifully ornamented with crockets. The figure of Sir Robert is on the top, represented in armour; a collar of S. S. is on the neck, and on the forehead is a fillet, inscribed Ich Nazarenus. The feet rest on a lion.

HISTORY.

Within the Communion rails is a tablet, inscribed—

M. S. Mariæ uxoris dilectissimæ, Brianus Shaw, A. M. hujus ecclesiæ Rector brevem hanc tabellam demortuæ virtutibus imparem mœrens posuit—Obiit Aug. 28, 1697.

On a brass plate on the south wall—

Zacharius Cawdrey servus Domini nostra Jesu Christi, evangelista et Rector ecclesiæ Parochialis de Barthomley, in Comitatu Cestriæ, filius Zachariæ Cawdrey evangelistæ et vicarii ecclesiæ parochialis de Melton Mowbray in comitatu Lecestriæ, nepos Roberti Cawdrey, evangelistæ et rectoris ecclesiæ parochialis de North Luffenham in Comitatu Rutlandiæ, hic juxta dilectissimæ conjugis Helenæ Cawdrey et charissimi alumni Johannis Crew, (filii Johannis Crew de Crew, armigeri) exuvias depositarus est suas si Deus voluerit, lætam expectans earundem resurrectionem et restitutionem. In mundo labor, in terra quies, in cœlo gloria. Et deposuit xxi° die Decemb. anno Domini 1684.

There are various other memorials, amongst them to the Malbons, of Bradley; Rt. Hodson, Esq. of Doddlespool Hall, in Barterley, died Sept. 2, 1816, aged 77.

The present Rector, is the Rev. Edward Hinchcliffe, A. M. presented Dec. 30, 1796.†

In 1722, the sum of £610, in which was included a gift of £300, by John Crewe, Esq. was appropriated to the purchase of the *Ravenshawe Estate*, in Audley, for the benefit of the School and Poor. In 1817, the rental was £30. of which £10. 4s. is given to the Schoolmaster, and the remainder is distributed amongst the different townships of the Parish. About twelve children are educated here, and the school is free to two children nominated by Lord Crewe, two by the Rector, and the descendants of the Rev. Mr. Steele, of Claycroft, the founder. The interest of £110. is given weekly in bread to the Poor of Crewe and Barthomley. The rectorial tithes are those of Barthomley, Alsager, and Barterley, but the Rector has frequently disputed those of Haslington, which are possessed by Sir J. D. Broughton, Bart. and Mr. Sparrow, of Wolseley, co. Stafford, Lord Crewe has the tithes of Crewe.

† Burghall, in his Diary, says, "the enemy now drawing nearer to the town, [of Nantwich] spread themselves into Stoke, Hurleston, Brindley, Wrenbury, and all the country about, robbing and plundering every where; till Dec. 22, they passed over the river to Audlem, Hankelow, Buerton, Hatherton and on Saturday they came to Barthomley (giving an alarm to the garrison of Crewe Hall); as they marched they set upon the Church, which had in it about twenty neighbours, that had gone in for safety; but the Lord Byron's troop, and Connought, a Major to Colonel Sneyd, set upon them, and won the Church; the men fled into the steeple, but the enemy burning the forms, rushes, mats, &c. made such a smoke, that being almost stifled, they called for quarter, which was granted by Connought;

CREWE

Is about four miles S. W. S. from Sandbach. It appears from the Survey, that it was attached to the Shipbrook Barony, but it wes afterwards transferred to the Barony of Wich Malbank. The Crewes were settled here at a very early period, certainly before 1150.— Amicia, the widow of Thomas de Crue, temp. Edward I. released to her daughter Jane, all that she had in Crue, in right of her dower. Thomas de Crue died in the 21st Edw. I. and he held his lands here by military tenure, sending an armed man twice a year to *keep the peace during the Chester Fair*.*—Jane, or Joan, married Richard de Praers, of Barthomley, and had issue Randle, who died without issue; and Thomas, whose heiress Elizabeth brought Crewe in marriage to the celebrated Sir Robt. Fulleshurst, had also a portion of the Barony of Wich Malbank, which had been granted to Sir Randle de Praers, 6th Edw. I. by Randle de Merton. Crewe continued vested in the decendants of Sir Robert till the reign of Henry VIII. when Thomas Fulleshurst, who was Sheriff of Cheshire in the 20th of that King, sold his share of Wich Malbank Barony to Sir Hugh Cholmondeley; and in 1578, Sir Christopher Hatton purchased from him the Manor of Crewe. About 1610, Sir Randle Crewe, descended from the original possessors, and afterwards Lord Chief Justice of the King's Bench, bought the manor from the Representatives of Sir Christopher Hatton, and thus restored the former patrimony of the family to the direct line.

Sir Randle Crewe, descended from Patrick, a younger brother of Thomas de Crue, whose daughter Joan, brought the estate to the Praers family. Sir Thomas Crewe, brother of Sir Randle, was the founder of the family of Crewe of Stene, in Northamptonshire, ennobled by Chas. II. His elder son, Sir Clippesby Crewe, continued the direct male line, and his youngest son John, was the founder of the Crewes of Utkinton.—John Crewe, grandson of Sir Randle, was the last of the newly-settled family in the direct line, and his daughter and sole heiress Anne, married John Offley, Esq. of Madeley, co. Staff. whose son assumed the name and bearings of Crewe. The property continues vested in the grandson of the last named, John Lord Crewe, elevated to the Peerage in 1806, after being one of the Representatives of the County in six successive Parliaments. Sir Randle Crewe, the restorer of the original family, was born in 1558, at Nantwich, being the second son of John Crewe, of Nantwich, by Alice, the daughter of Humphrey Mainwaring. He was appointed Chief Justice of England in the 22d Jac. I. and in that office, says Fuller, "served two Kings though scarce two years in his office, with great integrity. * * * * King Charles's occasions calling for speedy supplies of money, some great ones adjudged it unsafe to venture on a Parliament, for fear, in those disinterested times, the physic would side with the disease, and put the King to furnish his necessities by way of loan. Sir Randle being demanded his judgement of the design, and the consequence thereof (the imprisoning of recusants to pay it) openly manifested his dislike of such preter-legal courses, and thereupon, Nov. 9, 1626, was commanded to forbear his sitting in the Court, and the next day was discharged from his office, whereat he discovered no more discontentment than the weary traveller is offended when told that he is at his journey's end."—Two years after his discharge, he wrote a letter to the Duke of Buckingham, dated June 28, in which he nobly says, alluding to the judgment he had given, "God doth knowe, it was a great affliction to me to deny any thing commanded me by the King that my heart soe loved, and to whom I had been soe bound, Prince and King: but had I done it, I had done contrary to that all his Judges resolved to doe (and I only suffer), and if I had done it and they had deserted me therein, I had become a scorne to men, and had been fitt to have lived like a scritch owl in the dark." An unsuccessful attempt was again made to have him

but when they had them in their power, they stripped them all naked and most cruelly murdered twelve of them, contrary to the laws of arms, nature, and nations. Connought cut the throat of Mr. John Fowler, a hopeful young man, and a minor, and only three of them escaped miraculously, the rest being cruelly wounded. Christmas-day, and the day after, they plundered Barthomley, Crewe, Hasling-ton, and Sandbach, of goods and clothes, and stripped naked both men and women."—This atrocious act formed one of the articles against Charles I.

* Military assistance was no doubt rendered necessary, from the turbulence of the Welsh.

CHESHIRE

HISTORY.

restored to the office of Chief Justice, in 1641, and the subject was brought before Parliament by Mr. Hollist. Sir Randle was then eighty-two years of age; he died at his house, at Westminster, Jan. 13, 1645-6, and was buried at Barthomley.

Crewe Hall is one of the finest specimens of the Grecian style of domestic architecture in the kingdom It was begun in 1615, and completed in 1636. A great part of the interior retains the original decorations, particularly the stair-case. The gallery, nearly one hundred feet in length, contains the Library, and family pictures, which are very numerous. On the north side of the house, is the Chapel; the windows over the communion table, containing the Annunciation, and the Offering of Isaac, in stained glass.—During the Civil Wars, Crewe Hall was garrisoned by the Parliament forces, but on the 28th December, 1643, it was taken by Lord Byron. A determined resistance was made by the besieged, who slew sixty of the assailants, and wounded many more; "but wanting victuals and ammunition, they were forced to yield it up, and themselves, one hundred and thirty-six, became prisoners, stout and valient soldiers, having quarter for life granted them."* The King's troops retained possession till the relief of Nantwich. "Feb. 4, (1643) The Nantwich forces assaulted Crewe Hall, then kept by Capt. Fisher, which was presently surrendered, on condition that he and his men, about one hundred and twenty, with the wounded, might depart safe, leaving their arms; many of them came that same day to Nantwich, where they were entertained."† The House sustained very little injury during the siege.

* Burghall.

† Burghall.

In 1727, a *Free School* was founded at Crewe, by Mr. Thomas Leadbeater, who endowed it with the interest of £120. The School-house and that of the Master, were built by subscription; the Master is appointed by Lord Crewe.

HASLINGTON

Is about four miles S. S. W. from Sandbach, and was formerly parcel of the Barony of Wich Malbank, passing to the Vernons by one of the coheiresses of the last Baron. The last heir male of the Haslington Branch of the Vernons, was Sir George Vernon, Baron of the Exchequer in 1631. His heiress married a Derbyshire branch of the Vernon family, from whom Haslington was purchased by the Aislabies, of Studley Park, co. York. It was afterwards alienated to Messrs. Sparrow, and Henshall, who sold it to the late Rev. Sir Thomas Broughton, Bart.

WINTELEY is a large lake, on the Sandbach side of the township, near which is an ancient Chapel for Dissenters, said to have been built so early as the reign of Elizabeth.

OAKHANGER HALL was formerly the seat of the Actons, from whom it passed to the Manleys, of Lache, and subseqeently to John Ready, Esq. who married the heiress of the Manleys.

CLAYHANGER HALL was purchased by John Bridge Aspinall, Esq. the present owner, from the late Rev. Weston Bayley: it has been much enlarged, and is the head of a considerable estate.

HALL O' HEATH, is occupied as a farm-house, but was formerly the seat of the *Heaths*, from whom it passed with a female heir to the Mores, and from them, temp. Eliz. by marriage with Cecilia More, to Alexander Walthall, ancestor of the present proprietor, Peter Walthall, Esq. of Wistaston.

BRADLEY HALL is occupied as a farm-house, and was for several centuries the property of the ancient family of the *Malbons*, now extinct. It is now the property, by purchase, of J. Ford, Esq. of Abbeyfield.—In the centre of the Village, is a large moated area, supposed to have been the site of the old Hall of the Vernons. Their later residence is at the east end of the village, the form quadrangular, and moated, but of the original building only one side remains, and that chiefly occupied by a large apartment, probably the great hall, but which tradition says was a domestic Chapel.

HASLINGTON CHAPEL was built by the Vernons for their own accommodation, and that of their tenants, but it was never consecrated. It was formerly called *libera Capella*, and had Chaplains regularly instituted to it.—The great tithes attached were appropriated by the Vernons, but the Rectors of Barthomley have laid claim to them. The patronage of the Curacy, and the impropriation, is exercised by the Lord of the Manor. The Registers commence in 1648.

ALSAGER,

Or *Alsacher*, is about six miles S. E. S. from Sandbach. It formed a portion of the great Barony of Wich Malbank, and was vested in the Vernons, and subsequently in the Minshulls. Temp. Hen. III. it was

CHESHIRE

HISTORY.

held by a family which assumed the local name, but which became extinct in the direct male line in 1768. The Manor and Hall, observes Mr. Lysons, which were inherited by the three sisters of John Alsager, Esq. (who then died) are now under the wills of Mrs. Mary and Mrs. Judith Alsagar,* the property of Catherine, relict of Richard Sheridan, Esq. and her three maiden sisters, the elder of whom, Anne, has assumed the name of Alsager.

In 1790, the three Mrs. Alsager obtained an Act of Parliament to enable them to build a CHAPEL here, dedicated to our Saviour. It is situated on a piece of waste ground, and is built of stone, with a handsome tower steeple. It is a Curacy, the glebe and impropriation fees valued at £110. 10s. per annum.—The appointment of the Minister is vested in the manerial Lords; it is endowed with about sixty acres of land, and has the privilege of burial and baptism

A *School* was also built here by the same Ladies, for the education of boys and girls, endowed with thirty acres of land, but only eighteen have as yet been inclosed. The appointment of the Master is now vested in Trustees, but the Minister has the preference for the situation.

*Bearing date, 1792.

PARISH OF COPPENHALL.

CONTAINS THE TOWNSHIPS OF

CHURCH COPPENHALL, | MONK'S COPPENHALL.

CHURCH COPPENHALL is about five miles N. E. from Nantwich, and was originally attached to the Barony of Wich Malbank, at which period, it is supposed, both townships were united. It was afterwards alienated from the Barony, and possessed by the Waschetts, from whom it passed to the Orrebies, about the end of the 13th century, and was vested in them for some time.—It then passed by female heirs to the Cubets, of Leghton, and the Hulses, from the latter of whom it was inherited by the Vernons, and in 1616, Sir Thos. Vernon died seized of it. The Ravenscrofts were afterwards the proprietors, and it passed from them by marriage with the daughter and heiress of Hall Ravenscroft, Esq. to the Delves family. Sir John Delves Broughton, Bt. General in the Army, is the present proprietor. There was an estate formerly here belonging to the Knights of St. John of Jerusalem.

SHAWE HALL in this township, of which the moated site only remains, was the ancient seat of the Fulshursts of Crewe. The lands appurtenant to it were given temp. King John, by Randle Mainwaring to Robert de Leycester; it passed subsequently to Henry Hiccockson, and he gave it to Thomas Shawe, of Church Coppenhall. It is the property of Miss Jackson, of Nantwich.

The CHURCH is dedicated to St. Michael; the present Rector the Rev. John S. Catlow, A. M presented Feb. 6, 1805: it is in the gift of the Bishop of Lichfield and Coventry. It was formerly called the CHAPEL of Coppenhall, and within the parish of Wybunbury; but in August, 1373, it was endowed as a distinct Benefice. It is a mean but curious building, with nave, chancel, and side aisles; the belfrey of wood. The pews are ornamented with grotesque figures of animals, &c. The floor is of clay, with blocks of wood to kneel upon, chained to the seats. In the windows are some neat specimens of stained glass.

There are no monumental memorials worthy of particular notice.

MONK'S COPPENHALL

Was at a very early period held by the Waschetts.—Idonea, widow of Wm. Waschett, gave permission to the Abbot of Combermere to erect a Mill in Coppenhall, on a piece of water called Worithern, and to make a Pool for it. In the reign of Edw. I. John de Mere, and Maud his wife, gave all their lands here to the

Abbey of Combermere. Soon afterwards Adam, Abbot of Combermere, conveyed the Estates to Robert Burnell, Bishop of Bath, who gave to the Abbey £213. 6s. 8d. and part of Grenfordley, to relieve the necessities of the Convent. Monk's Coppenhall passed from the Bishop's descendant in marriage to the Lovels, but on the attainder of Lord Lovel, temp. Hen. VII. it was forfeited to the Crown. In 1616, Sir Thomas Vernon died possessed of it, and it subsequently became the property of the Cholmondeleys, who sold it to Mrs Anne Elcock, of Poole, whose nephew and heir, Wm. Massey, Esq. is the present proprietor.

PARISH OF WISTASTON,

CONTAINS ONLY ONE TOWNSHIP.

WISTASTON,

Or *Winstanton*, is about three miles N. E. E. from Nantwich. It was attached to the Barony of Wich Malbank, and held under it by a family which assumed the local name. It was afterwards divided between the families of Egerton and Alexander, and passed from the latter by a female heir to Richard Walthall, Esq.—The other moiety passed in marriage with Ellen, co-heiress of Hamon de Wistanston, to Adam de Praers, and from his family by a daughter to Hugh Malpas, of Checkley. It afterwards passed in marriage with two daughters, to two brothers of the Peshall family, whose representatives sold it to the Delves', of Doddington.—The Rev. Sir Thomas Broughton, Bart. in exchange for an estate in Hunsterson, conveyed it to Peter Walthall, Esq. who is the proprietor of the entirety. It appears from Woodnoth's Collections, that the manor was held by the service of finding horses when required, for the use of the Earl, and providing a man and horse to keep Chester Fair twice a year, according to the custom of the fairs.

At a very early period, the ancient family of Bressey *(Brescy)* had an estate in this parish. Little is known of their precise origin; but in an old deed, without date, of William Malbank, Baron of Nantwich, he states, that "he has received of Robert de Bracy, his *black nephew*, ye homage and service of three K^ts^ fees, viz. for Wistaston," &c. The seat of this family is described to be at Wilcots, Wilcocks, or Wilde-cats-heath; no such places, however, are now known: but in the adjoining township of Willaston, is an old mansion called Bressey Hall, the property of W. Sneyd, Esq. It was from the Bresseys above-mentioned, that the Braseys of Chester descended.—There is another ancient house here, called the Red Hall, the property of John Bayley, Esq. but occupied as a farm-house.

The Church, which is an ancient structure, pleasantly situated, is dedicated to St. Mary; the present Rector, the Rev. Wm. Morgan, A. B. presented May 14, 1789. In old deeds, it has been described as the *Free Chapel of Wistanston*, and it is probable it originally was within the boundary of Wybunbury parish.—It is built chiefly of wood, with nave, chancel, and side-aisles; at the west end is a small belfrey. The Registers commence as early as 1572. The advowson was, till the beginning of the 17th century, vested in the two lords of the divided manor, but the presentation is now solely in P. Walthall, Esq.

The whole of the parish tithes belong to the Rector.

History.

CHURCH MINSHULL

PARISH, CONTAINS ONLY ONE TOWNSHIP.

CHURCH MINSHULL,

So called to distinguish it from Minshull Vernon, is about six miles S. from Middlewich. It was formerly in the parish of Acton, and attached to the Barony of Wich Malbank, but on its division, it fell to the portion of Philippi Basset, and afterwards was vested in the Lovels. The mesne manor was possessed by a family which assumed the local name soon after the Conquest, and from whom it passed with an heiress, temp. Edw. III. to the Duttons. On the death of Sir Thomas Dutton, temp. Henry VII. without male issue, a division of the Dutton estates took place in 1534, and Church Minshull passed to the representatives of Elinor Cholmondeley, the eldest of the co-heirs and was possessed by the Cholmondeleys. A younger branch of the Minshulls continued the male line, and resided at Minshull till the death of John Minshull in 1654, when his estate passed in marriage with Elizabeth, his sole heiress to Thomas Cholmondeley, Esq. of Vale Royal, who thus became possessed of the whole property.—Eventually the estate was sold, together with the impropriate Rectory and advowson of the donative, to the late Sir Richard Brooke, Bart. of Norton Priory, whose younger brother, Thomas Brooke, Esq. possesses the whole parish, excepting only the *Lea Green Hall Estate*, which is the property of Mr. John Done, of Tarporley, by purchase from Sir George Prescot. It is occupied as a farm-house. A general air of neatness pervades the village, which is in a very picturesque situation.

The CHURCH is dedicated to St. Bartholomew. In the confirmation charter of Randle Gernons to the Abbey of Combermere, it is described as the Church of Munschulf, and the Rectory was leased of the Abbey by the Minshulls before the reign of Henry VIII. It was afterwards vested in the Daniels of Daresbury, and was sold by them to John Minshull. It subsequently passed with the Minshull Hall estates. The building is of brick, with nave and side aisles. The tower contains five inharmonious bells. The vault of the Cholmondeleys is at the east end of the Church.

The monuments are few, and of little interest: on a painted tablet over the north east door,

In the middle of this chancel lyeth interred ye body of Jane, daughter of Sir Lionel Tolmache, of Helmingham, in the county of Suffolk, Bart. and late the wife of Thomas Cholmondeley, of Vale Royal, in ye County Palatyne of Chester, esquire, who had yssue several sonns and daughters, of whome Robert, Elizabeth, Jane, Mary, Anne, and Diana, dyed ye 14th of April, anno D'ni 1666.

On the outside of the east end, on a blue slab—

Near this place lye interred the bodys of Thomas Minshull, late of Erdswick, in the county of Chester, and Alice his wife, who was daughter of James Trollope, of Thirlby, in the county of Lincoln, Esq.—They left two sons and five daughters. This monument is erected by the three surviving daughters, in dutiful remembrance of parents upright and just in all their ways. Both they and their children suffered great wrongs by unjust people. He was loyal to his King and true to his Country. His mother was sister to Sir Edward Fytton, of Gawsworth, in Cheshire, who suffered for King Charles the First, of blessed memory.

The Parish Registers commence in 1561, and contain the following remarkable instance of Longevity:—"1649, Thomas Damme, of Leighton,* buried the 20th of Feb. being of the age of seven score and fourteen."

In 1614, the Rev Christopher Minshull, left the interest of £200. for the support of a *School*, to which was added the interest of £50. by Mr. Wilbraham, of Dorfold, and £50. by other benefactors, for the like purpose.

In 1785, a *School House* was built, the school previously being held in the Church.

The present incumbent is the Rev. E. Clementson.

* Leighton is in Nantwich Parish, and there are crofts there, still called DAMME'S CROFTS.

CHESHIRE

The following are Extracts from the Church Wardens' Book for the Parish, commencing in 1670 :*—

	£	s.	d.
1670.—Spent and payd at ye great Visitation	00	12	04
1672.—For ffive quartes of wine and bread for the Sacrament	00	05	04
1673.—Ffor 3 hundreds of Latts and fetching them ...	00	10	00
1676.—July 4th Receved the sume of one pound ffour shillings, being the ffree gift of William Woodstocke towards the maintaiuing of a free schoole at Church Minshull...	01	04	00
1679.—To~rds redeeminge a Turkish slave...	00	01	00
1684.—Charges at the Archbishop's visitation ye first time	00	18	00
To Arthur Warburton, for a diall	00	02	00
1686.—Paid Will. Holdford for 4 urchins	00	00	08
1687.—Paid to three poor men who had theyr corne destroyed by the great haile storme in Alvanley	00	02	00
1688.—Paid for binding ye Church Bible	00	13	00
Paid to 4 men that were wounded by ye Turke	00	01	06
1691.—To Wm. Walls for 8 hedghogs†	00	01	04
1694—Paid to Thomas Robinson, and Thomas Parkinson for 24 hedghogs	00	04	00
1695.—Paid to a man wth his hand cut off	00	00	02

1704.—April 3.—We whose names are underwritten, &c. request and desire the Church Wardens to prosecute ye cause now in the Bps. Court, agst Daniel Harrison, upon suspicion of incest with Mary his daughter.—and likewise to endeavour to procure letters patent for a Brief for building a Church at Minshull aforesaid.

HISTORY.

	£	s.	d.
1703.—For drawing a load of stone from Manley... ...	0	5	0
For three quarts of wine, bread, and bottles ...	0	6	8
1704.—Charges about Thomas Deakin, and the woman that the Quaker had with child	0	2	0
1708.—Spent on Gunpowder Treason day	0	2	0
1712-13.—Spent when the peace was concluded... ...	0	2	0
1715.—For meat at the Visitation	0	10	0
For tobacco and ale	0	7	0

1717.—Oct. 10.—An agreement of the Parishioners to indemnify the Church Wardens for Mr. Ruddall's charge for buying the 5 bells :— A long list of subscribers follow ; the principal of whom were—

	£	s.	d.
"Charles Cholmondeley, Esq.	10	10	0
Madame Anne Cholmondeley...	10	0	0
Mr. Rich. Vernon	5	5	0
Mr. Hugh Wade	4	4	0
Roger Wilbraham, Esq.	4	4	0
The total sum collected	128	18	6

Mr. Ruddale's bill was—

	cwt. qr. lb.	£	s.	d.
Minshull 5 bells weighed at Shrewsbury	34 0 0			
which at £1. 10s. 0d. per cwt. amounts to ...		255	8	0
Clappers, baldriggs, fitting		1	18	6
For hanging the bells		15	5	0

The Timber for the bell frames being the gift of the Worshipful Chas. Cholmondeley, of Vale Royall, Esq.

	£	s.	d.
To Mr. Morphitt, for making the font	1	15	0

* In the possession of Mr. Davies, surgeon, Chester.

† It would seem from the numerous entries in the books, as to destroying vermin, that hedghogs must have been very numerous in the township.

THE PARISH OF ACTON,

CONTAINS THE TOWNSHIPS OF

ACTON,	BRINDLEY-CUM-BURLAND,
POOLE,	FADDILEY,
WORLESTON,	ALSTANTON,
STOKE,	EDLASTON,
ASTON IN MONDREM,	HENHULL,
CHOLMONDESTON,	COOLE PILOT
HURLESTON,	NEWHALL.
BADINGTON,	

The Parochial Chapelry of Wrenbury is in this Parish.

ACTON,

Or *Aghton*, is about a mile N. E. from Nantwich, on the Chester Road. Morcar, a Mercian Earl, is described as having his seat here previous to the Conquest. It formed parcel of the Barony of Wich Malbank, and passed by a coheiress from Wm. de Mabedeng, to the Vernons, and from them by another coheiress to the Littleburys, who sold their share of the Barony (an 18th) including Acton and Hurlestone, and Dorfold Hall, to John de Wetenhall. Ellen, sister and coheiress of John de Wetenhall's grandson, married Sir Henry Ardern, whose son Ralph was seized of these manors, and died about 1420. In the 28th Henry VI. Robert Ardern, Esq. paid a fine on his estates here to Henry Wetenhall; and in the 4th of Henry IV. the King granted letters of alienation to Thomas, son of Henry de Wettenhall, for the manor of Dorfold, and messuages and lands in Acton, Hurleston, Nantwich, and he enfeoffed Thomas Ferrars with the estates, to the use of Sir John Bromley, who passed them to the Lord Stanley. In 1522, Thomas, Earl of Derby, died possessed of this property, which, it is conjectured, he held merely in trust, for the Bromleys then had possession of Dorfold, and had resided there several generations. Dorfold was purchased from the Bromleys, by Sir Roger Wilbraham, and in the 44th Elizabeth, he passed over to Ralph Wilbraham, his youngest brother, the manors of Acton, Hurleston, and Dorfold. The descendants of this Ralph continued at Dorfold till April, 1754, when Roger Wilbraham sold Dorfold, and other estates, to J. Tomkinson, Esq. father of H. Tomkinson, Esq. the present proprietor, who holds a Court Baron for the Manor.

The present *Hall* of Dorfold was built in 1616, by Mr. Ralph Wilbraham, on the site of the old mansion of the Bromleys. It is of brick, with large bay windows, and immense chimnies, and still retains much of its original form. The drawing room is a very handsome apartment.

The *Church* is dedicated to St. Mary, and the present Vicar is the Rev. Edw. Hinchcliffe, A. M. presented March 7, 1798. The foundation is of considerable antiquity, the Survey noticing that two priests resided at Acton. The Church was an appendage to the Barony of Wich Malbank, and a grant of it to Combermere Abbey was confirmed by Randle Gernons, together with its three Chapels of Nantwich, Wrenbury, and Minshull, in 1130. After the Dissolution, the Rectory and Advowson were granted to the Wilbrahams, of Woodhey, whose representative, the Earl of Dysart, is the patron.

The building is handsomely finished with red stone, with nave, chancel, side aisles, and a fine tower containing six bells. The side aisles are divided from the nave by five pointed arches on the sides, above which is a row of windows. The top of the tower was much

CHESHIRE. injured in 1757, by a storm, and the reparations of it,* and of the interior, have been done in a very aukward though costly manner.

There were four *Chantries* here at the Dissolution; at the south-west angle of the nave, is the *Dorfold Chancel;* that of *Woodhey* is at the south-east: in the north-west angle is St. Mary's Chantry, in which is the monument of Sir Wm. Mainwaring: it is in the shrine form,' handsomely ornamented, and surrounded by the family crest: at the edge of the tomb was formerly the inscription:—

Hic jacet Willielmus Manwaring, quondam Dominus de Badelye, qui obiit die Veneris xx°, ante festum Pentecostae, anno Domini m°. ccc°. nonagesimo nono.

In the *Dorfold* Chancel, on a mural monument—

M. S Spe resurgendi hic jacet Francisca, filia natu minima Thomæ Ravenscrofte, de Bretton, in agro Flint. armig. uxor 1ª. Radulphi Wilbraham de Dorfold, in com. Cestriæ armig. cui peperit 17 liberos, reliquit 13, viz. filios 9, filias 4, quæ gravi et diuturno morbo confecta firma in Christo fide, et invicta animi patientiâ, in cœlum rediit cum vixisset annos 49.

Obiit { die Septembris 5°, anna salutis 1706.

On a mural tablet—

To the deare memory of Mary Wilbraham, wife of Roger Wilbraham, of Derfould, Esq. daughter to Thomas Ravenscroft, of Bretton, in Flintshire, Esq. who, through the panges of childbed passed to eternal rest, ult.° April, anno D~ni 1632, ætat. suæ 37.°

Here lyes the earthy part of her whose name
Gives honour to this stone; who knew no flame
But that of zeale, and conjugale pure love;
Ambitious of no place but Heav'n above.
More paynes to put on Christ, than clothes she tooke,
The law her glass, where she loved most to look.
Meeke she was, yet her vertues caused a strife,
Whether she was Christian more rare, or wife:
A better daughter or a mother; more
Bounteous to friends, or kinder to the poor;
During this strife, ere it was thoroughly tried,
Whilst grace grew, nature weaken'd, and she died.

On another tablet nearly opposite—

To the memory of Elizabeth, daughter of Rog. Wilbraham, of Derford, Esq. by Mary his wife, daughter of Thomas Ravenscroft, of Bretton, Esq. She dyed Decemb. ye 6th, anno D~ni 1645, ætat. suæ 24.

Here lyes her body—hould! some one replies,
'Tis not her body, 'tis the marble lies;
For her fayre clay, ere death could reach her bed,
Sly sickness (to cheat them) thence ravished,
And in its roome conveyed a skelleton,
Which scarce her looking glasse or frends could owne:
A skelleton so bare, that as she lay,
She seemed a soule abstracted from its claye.
Thus lightened, she could act, and never faint,
But moved more like an Angell than a Seynt;
Whilst, through these weather-beat thin walls of skin,
Each looker on might see what dwelt within:
Sound judgment, joyn'd to active piety,
Wit, sweetness, patience, and humility.
A virgin, too! save that, just such another
In all perfections as her neighbour mother.

In the *Chancel,* is a memorial, with a long inscription, of Samuel Edgeley, vicar of Acton, who died 18th Dec. 1721, aged 89. He was vicar 47 years.

HISTORY. In the *Woodhey Chancel,* an altar monument in white marble, with the figures of Sir Richard Wilbraham, of Woodhey, Bart. in plate armour, and his wife Elizabeth; on the south side, the inscription—

Lectissimorum conjugum par. Ricardus Wilbraham eques et baronettus, Thomæ Wilbraham de Woodhey, armigeri, et Franciscæ filia Hugonis Cholmondeley, de Cholmondeley, equitis filius; unica et pientissima uxor, nomine et re Gratia, Johannis Savage de Rocksavage, equitis et baronetti, filia. Utrosq' cœlo, dignos, terris majores, reddiderant pietas, virtus, fides, hic fortis, justus, sapiens; illa benefica, affabilis, pia, numerosa sobole, filiis sex, filiabus septem, donati. Mortuus est 3° Apri~s, an° Dom^i MDCXLIII, ætat. LXIV.—Mœrens uxor marito et filiis omnibus supervixit: Infœlix! conjugis pariter et prolis vidua mortua est 8° Marti^i MDCLXI, ætat LXXVI. Ne posteros capiat oblivio hoc sacrum nurus fideli commisit marmori.

On the north side,—

Siste advena, qui vir hic situs sit te moræ pretium erit. Thomas Wilbraham, baronettus, Richardi Wilbraham, militis ac baronetti, ac

* On the 16th of Oct. 1643, Lord Capel advanced with the King's forces towards Nantwich, and took possession of Dorfold Hall, and Acton Church, but evacuated both during the following night. Both places were made garrisons by the Parliament; but Dorfold Hall was taken by Lord Byron, Jan. 2, 1644; and Acton Church, after making a stout defence under the orders of Captain Sadler, during which it was several times assaulted, and the Royalists lost six men, fell into the same hands about a fortnight afterwards. On the 25th Jan. the siege of Nantwich was raised, and the garrisons of Dorfold and the Church, nearly 1,500 men, were obliged to surrender to Sir Thomas Fairfax. Upwards of sixty officers were amongst the prisoners, and in the number Colonel (afterwards General) Monk, who was sent Prisoner to the Tower.

CHESHIRE

Gratiæ conjugis, filius hæresq. Uxorem duxit Elizabetham, Rogeri Wilbraham, equitis aurati (Regi Jacobo libellorum supplicum magistri) filiam cohæredem. Physicis, theologicis, perlegendo, scribendo, plurimum versatus; summa humanitate, sapientia, amœnitate, et probitate æternum celebrandus; paucis tamen (humilitate propria, sæculoq. iniquo) celebris. Septem habuit filios, filiam unicam, amicos plurimos, inimicum neminem. Tempora optimus supervixit pessima, cœlumq'. rediit Oct. XXXI anno salutis MDCLX.—Amantissimo et optimè merenti conjugi uxor mœrens P. usque dum dilectos cineres complecti datum sit, luctûs monumentum spirans, et majus ipsa seperfutura.

At the end of the *Woodhey Chantry*, are the remains of an altar, and in the north wall is a piscina.

There is a *School* at Acton, originally founded by subscription, for the maintenance of that furious fanatic, Burghall, the non-conformist Minister. At present the salary of the Minister is about £20.

An *Alms House* here, for two old men, was founded and endowed by one of the family of Wilbraham; it has not been particularly ascertained by whom, but Sir Thos. Wilbraham, or a Lady Wilbraham, are mentioned as being the founder. It is endowed with 18 statute acres of land adjoining the house, and the aged inmates receive each £4. annually, with certain articles of cloathing. The Earl of Dysart, as Representative of the Wilbrahams, is the Trustee.

POOLE

Is about two miles N. N. W. from Nantwich, and is in three divisions, called *Barratt's Poole*, *War Poole*, and *White Poole*, each forming a distinct manor. Barratt's Poole is the property of Sir J. G. Egerton, Bart. War Poole, of the Earl of Dysart, and White Poole of William Massey, Esq. Earl Dysart holds a Court Baron for his Manor, which owes service to the Barony of Nantwich. Barratt's Poole was possessed by the Egertons at a very early period, certainly before the reign of Henry VIII. and was held by them from the Abbot of Combermere The Elcocks, of Stockport, held lands in White Poole, and War Poole, before the reign of Edw. VI. which continued vested in their descendants till the death of Mrs. Anne Elcocke, in 1812, when the manor of Whitewall with other estates, passed under her will to Wm. Massey, Esq.

Poole Hall is now occupied as a farm-house, and formerly belonged to the Leycesters, and passed from them to the Taggs, of Acton.*

WORLESTON,

Or *Wordleston*, is about three miles and a half N. from Nantwich. It formed part of the Estates of the Barony of Nantwich, and on their division, passed to Eleanor Malbank, and subsequently to the Audleys.—It was then possessed by a family which adopted the name of the township, and about 1290, Walter de Worleston sold a moiety of it to Robert de Harcourt, which moiety passed with daughters to the Cholmondeleys and Bromleys.† The other share continued vested in the Worlestons, till near the conclusion of the following century, when it passed by coheiresses to the Crewes and Knolles. The coheiresses of Crewe brought estates here to the Boydells, Leycesters, and Chetwodes,‡ ancestors of the Chetwodes of Oakley, and they had a seat in the township. Another coheiress brought an estate here to a younger branch of the Leycesters of Tabley, who also settled here. This portion is the property of George Harley Drummond, Esq. by inheritance from the Werdens; the other part was purchased from a Mrs. Craven, by Mrs. Anne Elcocke, and has descended with her other estates.

Worleston Rookery, is an ancient mansion, the property of Daniel Vawdrey, Esq.

Rease Heath Hall, was the seat of a collateral branch of the Wilbrahams; but in 1772, it was purchased from the Windsors, who succeeded to it, by Henry Tomkinson, Esq. of Dorfold,

STOKE

Formed portion of the Barony of Wich Malbank, and eventually fell to the share of Philippi Basset, from whom it fell to the family of Praers. Randle de Praers gave the manor to his son Randle, whose descendants assumed the name of the township. It passed from the Stokes, by female heirs, to the Beestons and Astons. Previous to 1622, Edw. Minshull, Esq. purchased from the Astons, and his family lived at Stoke Hall for upwards of a century. It appears from the Villare Cest.

* Webb, in his Itinerary 1622, speaks of an old house here, which belonged to the Boydells, "a respectable family then worn out."

† Mr. Ormerod supposes it to be this moiety which was possessed by the Drummonds, from the Werdens of Burton, and which was purchased by William Massey, Esq. of Poole Hall, from H. Drummond, Esq.

‡ Lysons, p. 467.

that Isabel, daughter and heir of Randal de Stoke, about 1380, married Wm. Beeston, whose grand-daughter Isabel, married Sir Robert Aston, of Aston. In 1719, the manor and Hall of Stoke were sold by Edw. Minshull, Esq. to Mr. Thomas Williams, whose son sold them in 1753 to Roger Wilbraham, Esq. In 1781, Richard Craven, Esq purchased the property, and his daughters now possess it.

The wife of the great Poet Milton, who survived him, and died at Nantwich in 1726, was of the Minshull family.—Indeed, it has been noticed,* that the Poet himself had a connexion with the county, being a branch of the Miltons, or Milnetons, who descended from a natural son of Hugh Ceivilioc: but this is merely traditionary. It is certain that there were some respectable families of the name in and near to Nantwich during the Civil Wars.

ASTON,

Or *Aston in Mondrem*, so called from its being within the limits of the ancient forest of Mondrem, is about four miles N. from Nantwich. It formed parcel of the Barony of Wich Malbank; and subsequently was possessed by the families of Crue, Praers, and Minshull.—Temp. Ric. II. Johanna, daughter and sole heiress of Henry Minshull, brought an estate here in marriage to Edmund Dutton, of Dutton. In the 30th year of Hen. VIII. Richard Cholmondeley, Esq. held the manor of Sir Thomas Fulleshurst, by military service, and it continued vested in his descendants till May 1748, when Aston Hall was purchased from the Earl of Cholmondeley by Mr. John Darlington, and his daughter married Henry Tomkinson, Esq. of Dorfold, who is the present proprietor. The royalty, it is stated,† passed in the same manner as the Crewe Hall estate, and was purchased in 1802, by Henry Tomkinson, Esq.

The family of *Brayne* settled here certainly so early as the reign of King John, and continued till the beginning of the present century, when Mr. John Brayne sold *Brayne Hall* to the late Mrs. Elcocke. William Massey, Esq. her nephew, is the present proprietor.—The House is occupied by a farmer.‡

CHOLMONDESTON,

Is about five miles N. W. from Nantwich. It is noticed in the Survey as being attached to the Barony of Wich Malbank from which it passed with other portions to Philippi Basset. It was afterwards vested in the Crues; and it is noticed|| as being held by Thomas de Crue, temp. Edw. I. by the custom of finding a judger (juryman) in the County Court, and an armed man to attend Chester Fairs, and guard the gates.—Under the Crues it was held by the Wetenhalls, who became extinct about 1600, by the death of William Wetenhall, whose daughter Susan, married Lawrence Wright, Esq. and in right of her he possessed a fourth of the manor, subsequently purchasing the other shares, from his wife's relatives. Soon afterwards, he sold the entire manor to Sir Thomas Egerton, afterwards Earl of Bridgewater; and temp. Jac. II. the Earl re-sold it to Sir John Werden, of Chester, from whom it has dedescended to George H. Drummond, Esq. the present proprietor.

HURLESTON

Is about three miles N. W. from Nantwich: it is not noticed in the Survey, but it formed a portion of the Barony of Nantwich, and on the division of the estates thereof, the manor fell to the share of Auda, the wife of Warin Vernon. It subsequently passed with Acton, as before noticed, to Hen. Tomkinson, Esq. who is the present lord. A Court Baron belongs to the Manor.

BADINGTON

Is about two miles and a half S. S. W. from Nantwich; and, with the last-mentioned manor, is not noticed in Domesday Book. It was an integral part of the Nantwich barony, being a dependency of that division which passed from Eleanor de Malbank, to the Audleys. The Chettreltons§ were afterwards the mesne lords; but William Chettleton dying without issue temp. Richard II. it passed in marriage with his sister Arabella, to William Bromley, of Bromley, co. Staff. in whom it continued vested a great number of years; when Isabel, daughter of Sir John Bromley, brought the manor in marriage to Wm. Needham, from whom it

* Orm. Vol. 3, p. 191. † Lysons, p. 471.

‡ Webb notices the Actons and Weavers, as having seats in the township.

|| Vill. Cest.

§ Or Chettletons, Lysons, p. 472.

descended to the representative of his family, the Lord Kilmorey. In this township was the ancient Hall of the Bromleys, but there are now no remains of it.—Sir John Bromley, above noticed, was one of the distinguished warriors who composed the army of Hen. V. in France. At the battle of Corbie, in Picardy, 1415, when Sir H. Stafford Lord Bourchier, who commanded the right wing, was defeated, and the standard of Guienne, which he bore, taken by the French, Holinshead records, that "Whereat one John Bromley, of Bromley in Staffordshire, esquier, a neere kinsman unto the Lorde Bourgchier, was even streit so pearsed at hart, as he could not containe him, but by and by run eagerlie upon the French, and with his souldiers, in whom wroth and teene had alreadie inflamed furie and desire of revenge, did so fiercelie set upon them, that they were not only beaten backe, but also forced to abandon the place. At this pushe, the Capteine cutting through the thickest, strake down the Champion that bare the standard, and so giorouslie recovered it againe, and after duringe the fight (where as manie of the French lost their lives) courageouslie over his shoulders advanced it himselfe. The rest that fled awai our people pursued in chasing and slaughter unto Corbie very gates. So in victorie, honour, and great joy, with our small loss (in comparison) thanks unto God's Majestie, the chieftaine brought his hoste into his campe and order againe." For this and other acts of valour, Lord Bourchier gave to John Bromley an annuity of £40. In July 1418, the King returned to France, and John Bromley had the charge of the advanced guard. In April, 1819, he was knighted by the King in the field, and made Governor of the Castle of Damfront, and Seneschal and Constable of Bosseville le Rosse, and March. In the 6th of Hen. V. Sir John distinguished himself in a fight between three hundred English and eight hundred French: it appears* the former had been dispatched by the Earl of Warwick as a garrison from a small fortress near Cawdebeck, and were under the orders of Sir John and George Umfreville. The French were defeated by them, with the extraordinary loss of their Commander and two hundred *slain* and two hundred wounded. In this contest Umfreville was killed, and Sir John, and Walter Audeley, then only eighteen years old, were wounded. John Bromley died in the month of September of the following year; and the next year died Walter Audeley, at Warwick, on the 17th day of July; he was buried at Acton, near the body of his gallant companion in arms.

* Hollinshead.

BRINDLEY AND BURLAND.

The former of these townships, lies about five miles W. N. W. from Nantwich; the latter about three and a half W. N. W. It appears, that temp. Edward I. Burland was a dependency on that portion of the Barony of Wich Malbank, which fell to the share of Auda Vernon.---They are considered to be dependencies on the manor of Faddiley, and in 1671, Sir Thos. Mainwaring and Sir Thomas Brereton were the joint Lords; Courts Baron are held for them; but the inhabitants attend the Court Leet of Earl Dysart for Faddiley.—After the death of Sir M. Mainwaring, of Peover, his family moiety was sold in 1798, by Lord Grey, and Ralph Leycester, Esq. devisees in trust, to Hen. Tomkinson, Esq. of Dorfold, who is the present proprietor. The Brereton moiety, which descended to them by marriage with the Honfords of Honford, is now the property of Earl Dysart,—Branches of the Wilbraham family, formerly resided at Brindley and Burland; and the Allens, a very ancient family, had also a seat at Brindley for more than two centuries.

Brindley Hall is now occupied as a farm-house; it passed by marriage from the Allens to the families of Hewitt and Holford, and the Executors of Allen Holford, Esq. the last heir male, who died 1788, sold it to Mr. Richard Darlington.

Burland Hall was formerly the residence of a branch of the Griffins, of Barterton, and subsequently of the Hewitts.† Edward Griffin, Esq. who was the last heir male of the Burland family, died in 1771, and was buried at Nantwich.

† Lysons.

Swanley, or *Swanlow Hall*, in Burland, was the occasional residence of the Mainwarings of Kerminchan; it is now occupied by a farmer, and is the property of H. Tomkinson, Esq. of Dorfold Hall.

In 1717, Mr. George Harley, left thirty-three acres of land for the maintenance of four poor widows, or elderly women, of Burland, Brindley, or Faddiley, and for those divisions of the Parish, called Hurleston-quarter, and Cholmondeston-quarter.

CHESHIRE

FADDILEY,

Is about five miles W. N. from Nantwich.—This township belonged to that share of the Barony which was the portion of Auda Vernon. It was held as a dependency on the Lordship of Woodhey, then possessed by the Golbornes, in whom it continued vested till the reign of Edward IV. when it passed in marriage with Margaret, the heiress of John Golborne, to Thomas Wilbraham, of Radnor.*—Richard Wilbraham, the tenth in descent from the last named Thomas, was Master of the Jewel House, and Revels, to Queen Mary, representing in the first three years of her reign, the county of Chester in Parliament.—It is said he was a great patron of the Lord Chancellor Egerton, in his early life, then settling upon him £20. annually, which the Chancellor received to his dying day.—Rd. Wilbraham, twelfth in descent, was a great sufferer in the civil wars; he compounded for his estate with £2,500. and died about Oct. 31, 1660.—Richard Wilbraham, his son, thirteenth in descent, had an income then exceeding £3000. per annum, and was named as a knight, in the intended Order of the Royal Oak. In him the direct male line terminated, in 1692—he was the third Baronet of the Family. The family estates passed in marriage with Grace Wilbraham, to Lionel Tollemache, Earl of Dysart; and they are now the property of the present Earl of Dysart.

The village is composed of cottages, and a few farm houses; and about a mile S. W. are the remains of *Woodhey*, the ancient seat of the Wilbrahams, which is now converted into a farm-house. In 1700, Lady Wilbraham, widow of the last Baronet, built here a Domestic Chapel, endowing it in 1703, with £20. per ann. for the Minister, £2. for the Clerk, and £3. for repairs. For this purpose, a rent charge of £25. per ann. was settled on the manor of Newton, co. Stafford, by her will, dated 1707.—The manor of Woodhey has sunk in that of Faddiley, for which a Court Leet is held, which extends over Baddiley, Brindley, and Burland.

HISTORY.

ALSTANTON,

Or *Austerson*, formed part of Nantwich Barony, and became the property of Eleanor, subsequently passing to the Lords Audley. It was possessed by a family which adopted the local name, and was afterwards inherited by the Bulkeleys, Wetenhalls, Praers, and Bromleys, from the latter of whom it passed with the other estates, in marriage, to Sir William Needham, whose descendant Lord Kilmorey is the present proprietor.

EDLASTON

Was part of that portion of the Barony of Wich Malbank, which fell to Auda Vernon. It was afterwards in the possession of the Edlastons; when temp. Edward I. Richard Edlaston gave it to Rich. de Foulhurst, in whose descendants it was vested till about the latter end of the reign of Hen. VIII. when, with other portions of the Barony, it was purchased by the Cholmondeleys.

It is now the property of the Marquis of Cholmondeley. The ancient Hall is occupied as a Farm House.

HENHULL,

With the last-mentioned township, was included in the share of Auda Vernon. As early as the reign of Edward II. the family of the Henhulls possessed it, and in the reign of Edward IV.† it was divided amongst the coheirs of Richard Henhull. It was afterwards in the Claytons, and in 1573, was purchased from them by the Cholmondeleys, and is now the property of the Marquis Cholmondeley. Webb notices a "fair seat" of the Claytons here, "a family almost worn out."

† Vill, Cest.

COOLE PILATE,

Or *Pilot*, is about five miles S. S. W. from Nantwich, and the manor has descended in the same manner with Austerson, to Lord Kilmorey. There were two fami-

* This Thomas is *supposed* to be the 5th in descent from Sir Richard Wilburham, who took his name from the manor of Wilbraham, in Cambridgeshire.—William Wilburham, Esq. who died Aug. 1537, bequeathed his body to be buried before the Image of the Virgin, in Acton chancel, and left *xs.* towards purchasing a tower bell, if the Parish would find the remaining sum necessary for the purpose; if not, then the money to be expended in a *pix*, and two cruetts of silver, for the service of the High Altar on good days. He further willed, that twelve white gowns should be given to twelve poor men—that twelve torches be held about his body on the day of burial—that eight tapers be held over it, in the midst thereof should spring out a larger one—and that one penny be given to every person attending his funeral who would accept of it. He required his executors to buy a marble stone to put upon him in the chancel, with pictures of himself and his wife, with their arms; that £11. be put out *in sure keeping*, to pay 11*s.* yearly to a well disposed Priest to sing during twenty years, for him, his Children, &c. the service to be performed in Woodhey Chapel, &c.

lies who possessed estates here; the Whitneys and St. Pierres. The property of the former, which continued in their family from the 12th Richard II. to 1744, is now possessed by Henry Tomkinson, Esq. of Dorfold, being purchased from Mr. Hugh Whitney, by Mr. Henry Darlington. The St. Pierres property passed by a female heir to the Hortons, about the reign of Henry IV. the last male heir of which family died about 1740, when the estate descended to Dr. Davenport, of Ley-[illegible], co. Wilts, and in 17[illegible], it was purchased from his representatives by Joseph Skerrett, Esq. who is the present proprietor. A farm-house is built on the site of the Old Hall.

NEWHALL

Is about five miles S. W. S. from Nantwich. It formed part of the Estates of the Nantwich Barony, which were apportioned to Eleanor de Malbank, and she granted the Manor to Henry de Audley, which was confirmed by Earl Randle. It continued for many generations, in the Audleys, from whom it descended to the Touchetts. In the reign of Henry VIII. it was vested in Sir Anthony Browne, who surrendered it to the Crown; and afterwards was possessed by George Cotton, Esq. who sold it, with the Court Leet, &c. to Thos. Egerton, Esq. Solicitor-General, 33 Elizabeth.* Not long after this purchase, the township was passed to the Cottons of Combermere, from whom it has descended to the present proprietor, Lord Combermere.

The ancient *Castle of Newhall* is noticed as being in existence when the first grant was made to Henry de Audley, and its situation is described by Leyland, as a "place of the Lorde Audeleys, in Cestreshyre, betwixt Cumbermere and Nantwiche, caullid *Newhaull Tower.* It is now downe. There be motes and fair water."—There were some remains of it existing in the time of Dugdale. It is conjectured† to have been erected by one of the Barons of Kinderton, as a protection against the predatory incursions of the Welsh. From an Inq. relative to the Griffins, of Barterton‡ it appears they held certain lands, by the service of watching and warding at the Castle of Newhall, in war time, with three men.

A Court Leet and Baron is held for the Manor by Lord Combermere, to which the inhabitants of Wirswell and Wrenbury owe suit; and Constables are appointed by the Court.

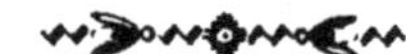

WRENBURY PAROCHIAL CHAPELRY,

Comprizes WRENBURY cum FRITH, BROMHALL, CHORLEY, WOODCOTE, part of DODCOTT cum WILKESLEY, SOOND, and NEWHALL—the latter has just been described.

WRENBURY-cum-FRITH,

Is about five miles S. W. by W. from Nantwich. As a portion of the Barony of Wich Malbank, it fell to the Audleys, in the manner noticed in the accounts of the townships in Acton.—The *Manor* of Wrenbury is vested in Lord Combermere,‖ and John Cross Starkey, Esq. but the Marquis of Cholmondeley holds a Court Leet; and the district of *Wrenbury Frith* is divided in equal shares between those Noblemen.

Mr. Starkey's estate here was held by his ancestors at a very early period; it fell to them by marriage of Thomas Starkey, of the Stretton family, with Eleanor, eldest daughter and coheiress of John de Olton, temp. Richard II. It continued in the direct male line, till the death of Thomas Starkey, in Oct. 1802; and under his will, his widow Eleanor, passed the Wrenbury Hall estates to her nephew, John Cross, Esq. son of William Cross, Esq. of Bloomsbury, by Mary, sister of Eleanor, and he assumed the name of Starkey.

It would appear, from the Records in the Exchequer at Chester Castle, a Manor of Wrenbury was held by the family of Le Strange, temp. Edward II.

Wrenbury Hall, the property of John Cross Starkey, is a handsome house, surrounded with extensive plantations. The general situation of the township is very flat.

The *Chapel of Wrenbury* is built in the Gothic style, with nave, side aisles, chancel, and a handsome tower.

* Before this period, this branch of the Egertons were settled at Christleton.—LYSONS, p. 478.

† Orm. p. 203.

‡ Harl. MSS. 2038.

‖ His Lordship has two-thirds of the Manor, as parcel of the Estates of the Abbey of Combermere.

The roof, excepting that of the Chancel, is of carved oak. It has frequently been called a *Parish Church*, but this is a vulgar error Webb says, "it was so deemed in 1622; but it differs in no respect from the other Parochial Chapels in Cheshire, and has never been instituted to as a Parish."*—The Rev. Gilbert Vawdrey, is the Minister of the Chapel, which is an augmented Curacy, in the gift of the Vicar of Acton. The tithes, which were appropriated by Combermere Abbey, together with those of Acton, were granted at the Dissolution to Robert Needham, Esq.

* It is noticed as a Parish in the Population Returns.

The Vicar of Acton, is charged with the payment of £10. per ann. to the Curate. The Registers commence in 1593.

Amongst the Monuments are the following:—

A mural pyramidal monument to the memory of Elinor Starkey, relict of Thomas Starkey, Esq. of Wrenbury Hall; born July 10th, 1739, died April 7th, 1811.

On a similar monument to the last,—

Sacred to the memory of Thomas Starkey, of Wrenbury Hall, in this township, Esq. who departed this life on the 31st day of October, 1802, in the 69th year of his age; and lies here interred with his ancestors. He was descended from a very ancient and honourable family, who in the page of early history are found to have possessed the township of Stretton, and other large demesnes in Cheshire. His immediate lineal descent was from Richard Starkey, of the Lower Hall, Lord of Stretton; from which root emanated the family of Starkey, of Over Hall, in the 16th year of King Edward the First, 1287.---The deceased was Lord of the manors and demesne of Wrenbury cum Frith, in this county, which were possessed by his ancestors for many centuries, who there signalized themselves by their eminent virtues, from the time of King Richard II. He was blessed with a most amiable disposition, and a fine and independent mind. Gentle in his manners, humble in his deportment, sincere in his friendships, kind to his dependents, universal in his hospitality, he was beloved by all, but chiefly by his afflicted widow, who mourns a most tender husband and faithful monitor. Such was the man; the Christian rises higher: for to a pious course of life, and firm reliance on the Saviour's merits, he added a fervent devotion and charity to his fellow creatures. To perpetuate his memory, and to give a lasting memorial of her just regard, Elinor, his widow (by whom he has left no issue) hath erected this monument.

A beautiful figure of a sick man, in a recumbent position, pointing to the Bible, is above the inscription; behind which is a female figure, supporting the head, and pointing with the Cross to Heaven.—On another mural monument by Bacon, jun.

Sacred to the memory of John Jennings, of London, Esq. who departed this life February 1, 1808, in the 69th year of his age. He was a kind and affectionate relative, a true and constant friend, courteous, humane, benevolent; unremitting in his endeavors to console the afflicted, assist the indigent, and alleviate distress; but as a Christian, he placed no confidence in these moral virtues, the merits of his Saviour being the only ground of his hope for acceptance and salvation. He lived universally esteemed, and died sincerely lamented. As the last tribute of affection, his sister, Elinor Starkey, hath erected this monument.

On a wooden tablet, ornamented with the arms and crests of the family, memorials of the Starkeys, from Lawrence Starkey, Esq. buried Dec. 8th, 1611, to Thomas Starkey, Esq. buried March, 14, 1714. The whole of these are on the south side of the Chancel.

On the south side of the Chancel, on a tablet of white marble—

Beneath lies interred the body of Stephen Cotton, Esq. who died Dec. y[e] 7th 1727, aged 27 years; to whose memory this small monument was erected by his brother Sir Robert Salusbury Cotton, Bart.

Vere, youngest daughter of Sir Thomas Cotton, Bart. was beneath interred, Sept. 23, 1730, aged 17.

On a wooden tablet—

Under this stone, in this south side, half part of Wrenbury Chancell, belonging to Combermere, lyes the body of Geo. Cotton, Esq. fifth and youngest son of Sir Robt. Cotton, of Combermere, in the county of Chester, Knt. and Bart. and of Dame Hester his wife, sister and heir to S[r] John Salusbury, of Lewenny, in the county of Denbigh, Bart. who died the 8th day of July, 1702. There also lyes inter'd, Hugh Calveley Cotton, gent: an infant, eighth son of Thos. Cotton, Esq. and Philadelphia his wife, daughter and heir of his Excellency Sir Thomas Lynch, Knt. late Governor of Jamaica. He died June the 24th, 1707.

On a white marble monument—

Underneath lieth the body of Lady Elizabeth Cotton, obiit Aug. 16, 1745, aged 63. Also the body of Sir Robert Salusbury Cotton, Bart. her husband, obiit Aug. 27, 1748, aged 53.

The Charitable Bequests are—50*s*. annually to the poor of Wrenbury, arising from 50*l* the amount of several donations, payable from Lord Combermere's estate in Newhall.—15*l*. per ann. the amount of several donations, payable by Lord Combermere —33*l*. per ann. to the Poor of Wrenbury.—50*s*. an annuity to the Minister; 4*l*. 5*s*. for the Minister, payable by Lord Combermere; 1*l*. for the Minister, arising from Land in tenure of J. Holland, Esq.—1*l*. to the Poor of Newhall, arising from Land in tenure of J. Holland.—1*l*. to the Minister of Burleydam.—4*s*. to ditto, payable from Lord Combermere's estate.—10*l*. to the Schoolmaster of Wrenbury.—30s. to ditto, payable from Lord Combermere's estate.—3l. for placing out one apprentice, payable from ditto.—5s. to the Poor of Wrenbury, arising from land in the tenure of Richard Purcell.—2s. 6d. to the Poor of Chorley, arising from land in the tenure of Rd. Purcell.—The whole of the above annuities are paid, applied, and distributed, by the Minister, Churchwardens, and Overseers of the Poor, on St. Thomas's Day. 2l. to the Minister of Wrenbury, for a Sermon on St. Mark's Day.—2l. to the Poor of Newhall.—6l. for placing out two Apprentices.—The above sums are also paid, applied, and distributed on St. Mark's Day, by the persons above mentioned.—10s. to the Minister of Wrenbury, for a Sermon on the 8th of Sept.—1l. to the poor of Wrenbury and Chorley, on the same day. To be paid and distributed by the persons above mentioned.

BROMHALL

Is about three miles and a half S. W. S. from Nantwich. It is noticed in Domesday, as being part of the possessions of William Malbedeng; and it passed from his descendants with the other divisions of the Barony, to Eleanor de Malbank, and from her to the Audleys. The Cheteltons were at a very early period settled here as mesne Lords, and the manor subsequently passed, by the marriage of Annabella, temp. Edw. III. to William de Bromley. Eventually it became the property of the Needhams, and is now possessed by Lord Kilmorey.

The *Hall* is occupied as a farm house.

CHORLEY,

Is about six miles S. W. from Nantwich. It was included in the possessions of William Malbedeng; and on the division of the Barony, passed to Eleanor Malbank, and from her to the Audleys and Harcourts.—Robert Harcourt possessed it temp. Edw. II. and his daughters, coheiresses, brought it in marriage to Hugh Cholmondeley, and Robert Cholmondeley. In 1561, both shares were vested in Hugh Cholmondeley of Cholmondeley, ancestor of Geo. James Marquis Cholmondeley, the present proprietor.

The Cholmondeleys had a seat here so late as the reign of Hen. VII. Sir Richard Cholmondeley distinguished himself in the military events of that period, and had an important command at the Battle of Flodden Field. He was afterwards appointed to the Lieutenancy of the Tower, and was the last of the family who resided at Chorley. By his will, dated in 1521,* he left his estates to his brother Roger, who was settled in Yorkshire, and in default of heirs male, to the Cholmondeleys, of Cholmondeley. Roger was the ancestor of the gallant Sir Hugh Cholmondeley, who so stoutly defended the Castle of Scarborough, and was created a Baronet in 1641. Sir Roger Cholmley, who was Chief Justice of England, and founded Highgate Grammar School, was a natural son of Sir Richard Cholmondeley.

DODCOT-CUM-WILKESLEY†

Is about five miles S. W. S. from Nantwich, and is situated partly in this parish and in that of Audlem.—It was held under the Nantwich Barony by Dot, and Godric, and no doubt took its name from the former, the direct ancestor of the Dods of Edge. Hugh Malbank, in his foundation Charter of the Abbey of Combermere, includes the manor of Wilkesley, and it was confirmed by his successors. At the Dissolution, Sir Geo. Cotton possessing himself of the adjoining abbey demesnes, the manor has passed with the other estates to Lord Combermere.

BURLEYDAM CHAPEL, is in the Audlem division of the township, close to the side of the road. It is a neat building, surrounded with iron rails, brought from Leweny. The plan is that of a Cross. There are no monumental memorials worthy of notice. Near the altar, on a large tablet, are the arms of Sir Lynch Cotton, the founder, and his wife. The site of

THE MONASTERY OF COMBERMERE,

Is in the Acton portion of the township. It was founded by Hugh de Malbanc, who placed in it Monks of the *Cistercian* Order; and dedicated it to the Virgin Mary and St. Michael. The endowment was liberal; it consisted of lands adjoining, the manor of Wilkesley, a fourth part of Nantwich, the Churches of Acton and Sandon, free pasture in the woods and moors near Nantwich, the Chapelries dependent on Acton and Sandon, &c.—Randle Gernons, in a Charter of Confirmation, after reciting the gifts, &c. of the founder, grants to the Monks the Church of Acton, "Cum Capellis suis, videlicet, Wiko Malbano, de Wrennebury, et Munschulf." It then proceeds: "Concedo etiam dictis monachis et eorum successoribus, quod habeant liberam curiam et

* Lysons.

† Spelt in old deeds Wivelesde, Winclestle, and Winkesley.

CHESHIRE

tholneum, et assisam panis et cervisie, et uthesium et blodwit, et catalla felonum, forisfacturas et felonias, et omnes mensuras, et omnimodo amerciamenta et emendas de omnimodis transgressionibus hominum et tenentium ipsorum vel aliorum quorum: cunq' existentium infra terras vel limites seu bundas ipsorum monachorum nostrorum infra dominium meum Cestresire, et habeant in predicto manerio furcas, et infangtheof et utfangtheof in manerio predicto in perpetuum."

He acquitted the Monks and their successors from all tolls in the City and County of Chester; and excepted them or their tenants from pleading before any one but the Earl or his Chief Justice. This Charter was dated at Chester in 1130. Besides these grants, there were a great number of private benefactions of much value, mentioned in Tanner's *Notitia*. It is supposed* the Abbey of Poulton was furnished with Monks from Combermere; and on their removal to Dieulacres, they were considered as dependent on Combermere.

Ormerod.

The following is a list of the Abbots:— A. D.

William the first Abbot; living in	1153
Robert, temp. John Scott, the Earl.	
G——, ...	1240-41
Adam	1296
William de Lee, present at the dedication of the Abbey of Whalley, in May, ...	1306
Richard de Rodiherd, 1296; he died 1316, and was buried at Whalley.	
Gregory; supposed about	1335
Robert, about	1382
Thomas Lymmor, 2d Henry IV.	
Roger, ...	1453
Robert, ...	1468
John, ...	1468
John, ...	1498
Roger, ...	1504
John, ...	1515
Christopher, ...	1519

John Massy—July 27th, 30 Henry VIII. surrendered the Monastery to the King, and retired on a pension of £50. per ann. which was paid to him in 1556.†

HISTORY.

In a valuation 32d Hen. VIII. the lands of the Monastery were estimated at £275. 17*s*. 11½*d*. Soon after the Dissolution, the site of the Monastery and adjacent land, including the cemetry, and the lake, were granted to George Cotton, Esq. and the same grant included lands in Dodcote, co. Salop: Cliffe, in Drayton-in-Hales, in the same county; Eardley Grange, co. Stafford. Wincell Grange, Cheshire; Newton Grange, in Ashburne; and Cotes Grange, or Cote Field, in Haslyuton, co. Derby, of the total value of £64. 18*s*. 7*d*.—This George Cotton, who was subsequently Knighted, was the son of John Cotton, of Cotton, in Shropshire, Esquire of the body to Henry VIII. His younger brother, Sir Rich. Cotton, had a still greater share of the lands of dissolved Abbeys.

The Cottons are a family of the highest respectability, several of whom have represented the County in Parliament. The present proprietor of the beautiful estate of Combermere, was, as has been before noticed, ennobled for his brilliant services in the Peninsular Wars.‡

The late Sir Robert Salisbury Cotton, father of Lord Combermere, represented the County in Parliament from 1780 to 1796. The present seat of the family, which still retains the name of *Combermere Abbey*, stands on the site of the Monastery, and the walls, chiefly, are those of the Old Abbey,|| recently coated, and ornamented in the pointed Gothic style.—The situation is delightful, on the margin of the beautiful lake of Combermere, which is considerably above half a mile in length. Leland, in his *Itinerary*, says, "A mile from Combermere Abbay, in time of mind, sank a pease of a hill having trees on hit, and after in that pitte sprang salt water, and the Abbate there began

† The Arms of the Abbey: Quarterly, or and gules, a bendlet sable, debruised by a Crosier in pale or, the head sinisterways.

‡ The services of Lord Combermere, have been marked by extraordinary heraldic distinctions; ARMS: Azure, a chevron, between three cotton hanks* Argent, in the chief point suspended by a ribbon Gules, fimbricated Azure, a representation of the Gold Cross conferred upon his Lordship, for his services at Talavera, Fuentes d' Honore, Salamanca, Orthes, Toulouse, &c. &c. SUPPORTERS: two falcons rising proper, gorged murally Gules. CREST: on a wreath a falcon close proper, dexter leg elevated, holding a belt proper, buckled Or. *Addtional Crest*: a mount Vert, thereon a Dragoon of the 20th regiment, mounted on a horse sable, accoutred proper, in the act of charging; above, on an escrol, the word "*Salamanca*."

|| The present library is supposed to have been the ancient refectory.—A drawing of the remains of the Abbey was made by Buck.

* Supposed to allude to the strings which were fastened to the legs of the Falcon.

CHESHIRE

to make salt; but the menne of the wichis componid with the Abbay, that ther should be no salt made. The pitte yet hath water, but much filth is faullen into hit."

SOUND,

Or *Soond*, was formerly possessed by a family which assumed the name of the Township; and passed by marriage with their heiress to the Chetwodes, temp. Edw. IV. whose descendants, the Chetwodes of Oakley, still have an estate here.

In 1662, the manor was vested in the Crown.

The Marquis of Cholmondeley is the present proprietor.

HISTORY.

Soond Hall is now a farm-house, which originally belonged to the Sneyds of Bechton, Staffordshire; about 1770, the father of the present possessor, Mr. Beckett, purchased it from them.*

* Lysons

WOODCOT,

Is a very small township, and was originally a portion of the Barony of Wich Malbank. Temp. Richard II. the St. Pierres held lands here; as did also the Fulleshursts, in the reign of Henry VI. The Starkeys of Wrenbury, held lands here from the Touchetts, about the time of Henry VII.

THE PARISH OF NANTWICH,

CONTAINS THE TOWNSHIPS OF

NANTWICH,	LEIGHTON,	AND PART OF
ALVASTON,	WOOLSTANWOOD,	WILLASTON.

NANTWICH.

This manor was given by Hugh Lupus, with a variety of other estates, to his kinsman William de Malbedeng, or Malbanc, and erected into the *Barony of Wich Malbank.* The best idea may be formed of the extent of the possessions of the Baron, by a recapitulation of their names :—

In *Dudestan Hundred:* Tattenhall, and Golborne Bellow.

In *Riseton:* Ulvre.

In *Willaveston:* Wervin, Poole, Landican, Upton, Thingwall, and Knoctorum.

In *Mildesvic: Eteshall*, Church Minshull, Minshull Vernon, and Sproston.

In *Warmundestrou:* Nantwich, Acton, Willaston, Wrenbury, Chorlton, Marbury, Norbury, Wirswall, Walgherton, Buerton, Hatherton, Wistaston, Barksford, Barterton, Worleston, Barthomley, *Essetune, Wivelesde*, Titley, Stapeley, Wisterston, Bromhall, Poole juxta Worleston, *Tereth, Cerlere*, Baddiley, Coppenhall, Poole, Aston juxta Poole, and Cholmston.

In *Atiscross:* Claitone and Wepre.†

It appears that William Malbedeng had a grant of the entire Hundred of Nantwich, and three-fourths of the lands of the Hundred; the remainder were divided between the Bishop, Richard Vernon, of Shipbrooke, and Gislebert Venables, of Kinderton.—William was a great patron to the Church, and previous to the year 1093, gave to the Abbey of Chester, all Whitley, a third of Wepre, two bovates of land in Salghall, the tithes of Salghall, Clayton, and *Yroduc*, the Church and tythes of Tattenhall, and a Saltwork in Nantwich. Immediately on his elevation to the new dignity, he made Nantwich the seat of his Baronial authority, and built a Castle there.* The precise time of his death is not known, but it is certain he was living in 1093, having witnessed the Earl's Charter to Chester Abbey.

* Lysons 704.

Hugh de Malbank, second Baron, gave a fourth

† The two last in Flintshire. The townships in *Italics*, so described in the grant.

part of the *vill* of Nantwich, to his newly-founded Abbey of Combermere.

WILLIAM DE MALBANK, the third and last baron of Nantwich, in the direct Norman line, died in the reign of Edward I. leaving three daughters, coheiresses, Philippa, Auda, and Eleanor, between whom the estates of the Barony were divided.

The first named, married Thomas Lord Basset, of Hedrington, by whom she had three daughters, Phillipa, Joan, and Alice. Her share consisted of a third of the manor of Wich Malbank, with the Castle, a third of Newhall, Aston juxta Hurlestone, Acton, Haslington, Coole, and Woolstanwood; rents and services in Barthomley, Crewe, Leighton, Aston-juxta-Mondrem, Cholmondeston, Stoke, Landican; two parts of Tranmere, Buerton, Alvaston, Church Minshull, Wistaston, Rope, Willaston, White Poole, Norbury, Wirswall, Rowe Shotwick, and Thingwall. This was afterwards subdivided amongst the daughters of Philippa, the eldest of whom marrying Henry Earl of Warwick, had the Castle.* She died without issue; and her portion, which is to the present time called the Countess of Warwick's Fee, fell to the Crown, and was granted by Edward I. 1277, to Randal de Merton; who conveyed it to the Praers family in the same year, and from whom it passed by female heirs to the Fulleshursts. Joan the second daughter of Lord Basset, married Reginald Valletort, and on his death William de Courteney; but dying without issue, she left her portion to the family of Sanford. Alice, the third daughter, married Lord Biset; and her portion subsequently, by gift and purchase from her representatives, was inherited by Robt. Burnell, Bishop of Bath and Wells, from whom it was possessed by the Lovells; and they purchased the other portion of the Barony, which had passed in marriage from the Sandfords to the Brownings. Francis Lord Lovell being attainted, Sir Thomas Stanley got a grant of his shares; Sir Thomas also being afterwards attainted, the shares were granted to Sir A. Browne, and afterwards to William Lord Paget.

Auda, the second daughter of William de Malbank, married Warin de Vernon, Baron of Shipbrooke. Her portion consisted of a third of Nantwich, Coole, Woolstanwood, Hurleston, and Acton; two parts of Haslington; rents and services in Audlem, Hankelow, Tittenley, Marbury, Baddeley, Faddiley, Brindley, Burland, Edlaston, Barret's Poole, Stapeley, Weston, Wybunbury, Hough, Shavington, Walgherton, Church Coppenhall, Henhull, Alsagar, Wigsterson, Pensby, and a third of Chorlton. Warin, their son, died without issue, and this share, like the preceding, fell to three daughters, coheiresses. Margaret, the eldest, had two coheiresses, one of whom brought a small portion to the Leftwich family, in whom it was a long time vested. The share of the other daughter, passed to the Vernons, and from them, in marriage, to the Savages. Auda, second daughter of Warin Vernon, married William Stafford, and his son sold her share to the St. Pierres. It was afterwards possessed by the Mainwarings of Kermincham. Rose, youngest daughter of Warin, maried John Littlebury, whose son sold their portion of the Barony to John de Wetenhall. It was subsequently subdivided between two coheiresses of the Wetenhalls, one of whom brought a share to the Ardernes; the other to the Bromhalls and Davenports.

The share of *Eleanor*, who died unmarried, consisted of a third of Coole and Woolstanwood; two parts of Newhall, Aston-juxta-Hurleston; rents and services in Bechton, Hassall, Worleston, Wrenbury, Chorley, Barksford, Monk's Coppenhall, Over Bebington, two parts of Barnston, Baddington, Bromhall, Sound, Alstanton, Barterton, Chorlton, Tiverton, and half of Wardhull. These estates she conveyed to Henry de Audley, Hugh de Pascy, &c. in trust for Audley and his heirs. They were eventually divided between the co-heirs of the Audleys, and passed to the Touchetts and Fitz Warrens; the share of the latter became by marriage the property of the Bourchiers Lords Fitz Warren. In tracing these descents, the authority of the Lysons has been chiefly relied on: the minor ramifications of the property will be found under the heads of the various townships composing the Barony.

Early in the reign of Elizabeth, the greater portion of the estates, originally forming the Baronial possessions of Wich Malbank, were possessed, by purchase and otherwise, by Sir Hugh Cholmondeley; an Inq. p. m. as to Sir Hugh, states him to have been the Lord of $\frac{14}{16}$ths of the Manor or Barony of Nantwich, with all

* The Castle, say the Lysons, was subsequently purchased by the Lovells, and attached to their share of the Barony.

the lands and messuages therein; and the Booth Hall, or Court House, and the Escheator's Hall; the Lovel and Audley shares being held in capite, and the remainder as the 20th part of a Knight's Fee, of the Earldom of Chester. Robert, eldest son of Sir Hugh, was created Baron of Wich Malbank, Sept. 1st, 1645; and his nephew Robert, subsequently became possessed of the title and family estates.—The present Marquis of Cholmondeley, has a portion of the feudal rights of the Barony, for which he holds a Court, in addition to the Hundred Court; but persons living within certain limits of the town, owe suit and service to Lord Crewe's Court for the Audley and Warwick Fees. The Abbot's Fee, being the 4th of the vill of Wich Malbank, is now the property of Lord Dysart, who holds a Court Leet for it.

There are no remains in existence of the CASTLE of Nantwich, which was situated near the Welsh Bridge. It was in ruins even before the reign of Henry VII. about which time, most of the materials, particularly the stones, were removed, and employed in the enlargement of the south transept of the Church, called the Kingsley's aisle. The site of the Castle is the property of the Marquis of Cholmondeley.

The estate, attached to the Fee of St. John of Jerusalem, formerly possessed by the Wilbrahams, and Leghs of Booths, is the property of Sir John Chetwode, Bart.—It appears from the Harl. MSS. that the Barony of Nantwich included the following townships, viz. :—

Acton	Buerton	Henbull
Alsagar	Bunbury	Hough
Alstanton	Burland	Hurleston
Alvaston	Chettleton, 2-3ds	Leighton
Aston	Cholmondeston	Wich Malbank
Aston in Mondrem	Chorley	Marbury
Audlem	Church Coppenhall	Church Minshull
Baddiley	Monk's Coppenhall	Newhall
Badington	Coole	Norbury
Bartherton	Crewe	Barret's Poole
Batthomley	Edlaston	White Pool
Basford	Faddiley	Row Shotwick
Over Bebington	Hankelow	Shavington
Beeston	Haslington	Soond
Brindley	Hassall	Stapeley
Bromhall	Hatherton	Stoke
Tiverton, 2-3ds	Weston	Worleston
Thingwall	Wirswall	Wrenbury
Tittenley	Wistaston	Wardle, (a half.)
Tranmere, 2-3ds	Woolstanwood	

In the same MSS. the shares of the Barony are thus explained, previous to Lord Lovell's attainder, when they were thirty-six in number, viz. Lord Lovell twelve shares, or one third; Lord Audley eight, or two parts a third; Lord Fitzwarine four, the remainder of the second third; Sir John Savage had a half, or six shares of the last third; Sir William Davenport two shares, Henry Mainwaring two; and Robert Fulleshurst, and Ralph Leftwich, held the other two shares.

Ancient state of Nantwich.—Of the primitive state of this place, little is known, but there is great probability that it was a Roman Station. Its Welsh name, *Hellath Wen*, (the town of white salt), affords a strong inference that it was founded by the Ancient Britons, and its present name is derived from the British; *Nant*, a vale. and *wich*, a salt spring.—With respect to its ancient jurisdiction, it appears there was established here soon after the Conquest, a Mercatorial Guild or Brotherhood, being a politic institution, and the groundwork of Bodies Corporate. It is stated,* that the present School House, in the Church Yard, was the Hall of this Society, and that persons not incorporated were not allowed at their death the particular solemnities of the Church, and to have only the third bell tolled. In judicial matters this Guild had the assistance of the Court Leet, and it provided six perpetual Chaplains to say mass for the brethren belonging to it. It is supposed this Institution is the same noticed on an inscription in the Church, as being the Brethren and Sisters of the Holy Cross. They were suppressed, and the revenues forfeited, under the statute of Edward VI.; notwithstanding which a bailiff, one of its chief officers, continued to be chosen annually at the Leet, and was considered the first officer in the town, although he possessed not a tittle of legal authority. This election, however, which took place at the first Court after Michaelmas, ultimately fell into neglect, and the present jurisdiction of the town is vested in the Constables.—The other ancient officers of the Guild, were *the Rulers of Walling*—the *Heath Keepers*—the *Leave Lookers*—

* Ormerod.

the *Ale Tasters*—the *Fire Lookers*—and the *Kennel Lookers*.

The duties of the Kennel Lookers, were, in some degree, similar to those of the public scavengers. They inspected the channels and water courses in the town, and directed the cleansing of the streets and the public wells. This office, as a formal appointment, no longer exist. The Fire Lookers were inspectors of ruinous or dangerous chimnies, and had authority to remove timber improperly introduced near the fire-places of houses. The Ale Tasters regulated the assize of bread, and inspected the publicans. The Leave Lookers' was an office of some authority: they inspected the markets, regulated the weights and measures, and destroyed all unwholesome meat. It was the business of the Heath Keepers to superintend the town's right to Croach, or Croach Common, now called *Beam Heath*,* and prevent trespassers encroaching upon it. The Rulers of Walling, attended to the regulation of the Prices of the Brine, and the manufacture of Salt. The office was held by the most respectable of the Proprietors, who were sworn to execute the office uprightly. They appropriated the quantity of brine to each wich-house, and inspected the pits. The Institution of these particular civic offices, like those within the township of a military origin, are alike involved in great obscurity— That Nantwich must have been a place of considerable importance, is pretty evident, from the establishment of a fortress here at a very early period—certainly before the Conquest; and we find that the Earls of Mercia had a mansion in the adjoining village of Acton. On the creation of the Barony, this "Sov'reign of a limitted domain," made a chace on the Weaver, to which was given the name of the *Forest of Chouhyl*. There exist no remains whatever, of the Chantry at Nantwich, dependent on Combermere.

On the advance of the Norman army to the northern parts of England, a considerable force was assembled here; against which it is highly probable that Gherbod, or Hugh Lupus was sent; for it is ascertained from a curious source,† that Lupus, on its overthrow, presented Gilbert le Grosvenor, ancestor of the Grosvenors of Eaton, with considerable lands wrested from the Saxon proprietors. During the Earldom of Randle II. Nantwich suffered severely by an inroad of the Welsh. It appears from Partridge's History of Nantwich, that in 1438, the town was nearly destroyed by a fire; and in 1583, it had a similar visitation, which ori-

* The following is the grant of the Heath to the Inhabitants, temp. 14 Edward I.—

"**This Covenant**, between Richard Alvaaston, clerk; William, son of William Alvaaston; Thomas, the son of Cradock, of Weston; William Cottigreen, and Agnes his wife, of the one part; and all the men of the town of Wich Malbank, on the other part; on the 10th of April, in the year of redemption, 1285, and to continue between the parties for ever. The said Richard, William, Thomas, William and Agnes, do hereby covenant, and by this document confirmed by themselves, and for their heirs, administrators, or assigns, to the said men of Wich Malbank, and their heirs, that they shall have for ever, free common of pasture, for all manner of cattle, in any part whatsoever, to the wood and waste of the township of Alvandeston, at all times of the year, except only the forty days, between the feasts of St. Michael and St. Martin; so that neither the said Richard, William, Thomas, William and Agnes, their heirs, administrators, or assigns, shall never inclose any of the said wood or warte, nor claim any part for themselves, their heirs, administrators, or assigns; but that the same shall for ever lie in common. Nevertheless, by virtue of the grant and agreement aforesaid, all the men aforesaid, of the town of Wich Malbank, do grant and agree, for themselves, their heirs, and assigns, to the said Richard, William, Thomas, William and Agnes, and their heirs, administrators, or assigns, that it shall be lawful for them to improve in such manner as shall seem to them most meet, without the interruption or contradiction of the said men of Wich Malbank, a certain portion of the said waste, lying within the division hereafter mentioned, namely, from the Ford, under Schallarn, in the field which is called Brock-field, near the Sonst-rest, following the Knowl on the other side of the Crooked-brook, to the Seich, which is opposite Marlar. From thence ascending by the said Seich to the Great-oak, and from thence directly to the Redclough, so divided by the bounds and meet there drawn. Thence following the Redclough, from the same side, to Robut's-hey. So that the men of Wich Malbank, nor their heirs, or assigns, shall have any common within the said place, while it shall be inclosed, nor ever shall or may claim the same. And because the parties aforsaid will that this instrument do stand ratified, firm, and inviolable, they have entered the same on the roll at Chester, called the Domesday-Book. And for greater security, each party have affixed their seals: These witnesses being present, namely, Sir Reginald Grey, Justice of Chester; Sir Rd. de Massie; Sir Ralph de Vernon; Sir Richard de Sandbach; Thomas de Crewe; Thomas de Perns;* William de Woodnot; Thomas de Allsterton; William de Clerk."—The annual races are run here. *Qy. Paers?

† The depositions in the chivalric suit of Scroop and Grosvenor.

CHESHIRE

HISTORY

ginated through carelessness at the Waterlode, near the Weaver, on the 10th December. It commenced in a house with a thatched roof, which was quickly destroyed, and spreading rapidly on the east and south sides, reduced those quarters of the town into a heap of cinders. It commenced at six o'clock, and burnt with great fury till six o'clock on the morning of Dec. 11th. Nearly six hundred buildings were reduced to ashes, including two hundred dwelling-houses. The damage was estimated at £30,000, an immense sum; but the sympathy excited by this calamity was so great, that a general collection was made throughout the kingdom, and Queen Elizabeth contributed £2000. and the use of timber in the Forest of Delamere, to a great amount. Nantwich was for a long series of years sorely afflicted with the plague; four years after the fire, the ague carried off more than one hundred and forty of the inhabitants: in 1596, George Fallowes, who had received his discharge from the Cadiz expedition under the Earl of Essex, introduced the flux, which proved fatal to a great number of people; and eight years afterwards, on the 12th of June, nearly five hundred of the inhabitants were swept away by the plague, which continued its ravages till the 2d of March, 1605. This melancholy visitation was brought from Chester.*—James I. honored the town with a visit, which is noticed by Webb in his *Itinerary*.†

The following particulars of the siege,‡ extracted

* It was at this time, that the Assizes were held in Nantwich, and the Court of Exchequer at Tarvin, in consequence of the progress of the plague at Chester.

† "One happiness I will not forget to report, which it pleased our most gracious King, his most excellent majesty, to add unto them in the year 1617, the 25th August, who vouchsafed to make that town the lodging-place for his royal person; and after he had for some hours accommodated himself in the house, then his royal court, of Thomas Wilbraham, Esq. it pleased him to walk so far as to the brine seth, and with his eye to behold the manner of the well, and to observe the labours of the briners (so they call the drawers of the brine), whose work it is to fetch it up in leather buckets fastened to ropes, and empty it into the troughs, which troughs convey it into the wich-houses; at which work those briners spend the coldest day in frost and snow, without any cloathing more than a shirt, with great cheerfulness. And after his majesty's gracious enquiry among the poor drawers, of many things touching the nature of the same brine, and how they proceeded to convert it into salt, most princely rewarding them with his own hand, his majesty returned to the court. The next day his majesty was likewise pleased to appoint a sermon to be preached before him in the church, and of his princely graciousness to stay while an oration was pronounced by one of the scholars of the school; which sermon was then performed by a divine of our own country, both by birth and dwelling, Mr. Thomas Dodd, Archdeacon of Richmond, and to which his majesty gave so great attention, and with the same was so affected, as it pleased his highness to grace the preacher with his princely and free election of him into the number of one of his chaplains in ordinary; which, for the honour of our country, and for an addition to the worth of this our eloquent and sweet preacher, I thought fit here to record."

* 1642. ‡ September 23.*—Col. Hastings was called into Cheshire to assist the army against the Deputy-Lieutenants of the militia, which were at Nantwich with a competent number, but a kind of peace was agreed upon between them, Dec. 23, which was afterwads disliked by the Parliament. Colonel Hasting's soldiers did much hurt by plundering. January 28,† was a hot skirmish at the further end of Nantwich, between Sir William Brereton's forces, and Sir Thomas Aston's: † 1643.
Sir Thomas, intending to take the town, came in the morning with two hundred men, but was repulsed by about eighty led by Captain Bramball, and in his retreat was set on by Sir William's company, who took prisoners one hundred or near it, and killed divers; he took also eighty horse with arms, cloak-bags, and pillage, to the value of a thousand pounds. Immediately upon this victory, came to the aid of Sir William, Colonel Mainwaring, Captain Duckenfield, Capt. Hyde, Captain Marbury, with other gentlemen, and their companies of horse and foot well appointed, to the number of two thousand, who many times issued out, and brought in much provision and many prisoners. Sir William, in the name of the Parliament, sent out his warrants, and summoned all from sixteen to sixty to come to a general muster at Tarporley and Frodsham, Feb. 21; which the Commissioners of Array hearing of, issued out of Chester with all their forces, and two great pieces of ordnance, and entrenched themselves on the side of Ruddyheath, near to a place called The Swan's Nest, where Sir William met them with his forces.

February 22d.—The army had the advantage of the wind and ground; shots were made on both sides, but little or no hurt done.—The night before, three hundred of the Parliament side had taken Beeston Castle, who coming down to assist the military, were met by the horse of the Array on Te~erton Town-field, where one of Colonel Mainwaring's Officers was slain on the Parliament side, and a few others of the King's, who were buried at Tarporley.

About Easter, Whitchurch was filled with many soldiers for the King, of which the Lord Capel was commander, who did much hurt by plundering the country, especially about Nantwich.

April 11.—The Nantwich forces hearing the Whitchurch-men, now grown strong, intended, with many carts, to fetch away all that was left at Mr. Massey's, raised almost all their strength, both horse and foot, about one thousand, and marching towards Burleydam Chapel, met the enemy, who after a little skirmish fled to Whitchurch. They slew five, and took two or three prisoners, without the loss of one

CHESHIRE HISTORY.

from Burghall's Diary, given in the *Vale Royal*, clearly shows the share of misery Nantwich endured arising

man, except three taken and carried off. Sir Richard Wilbraham died a prisoner in Shrewsbury, about this time.

The next week, the Nantwich forces went and faced Chester, and when they came to Boughton they killed one of the guards, which greatly frightened the city, but they returned speedily.

On Tuesday morning, at break of day, the Nantwich forces went to Cholmondeley Hall, where they were informed four hundred of the army were billeted, whom they found ready to receive them. A fierce battle was fought; at last the Nantwich forces, having slain and wounded many of them, drove them into the house, and so returned, many of their own being hurt and slain, with a booty of six hundred horses; the report was, that fifty or more of the enemy were slain in and about the house.

April 24.—The Cavalries from Whitchurch and Cholmondeley came near to Nantwich (their horse being then out of town), and took a great prey from Dorfold, Acton, Ranmore Sound, and all that neighbourhood; namely, all the cows and young beasts they could find, with horses and household stuff from many, to a great value, and carried all away with them; the Nantwich forces not daring to pursue them, lest the town should be endangered, for they were in number fifty horse, besides divers foot companies, and had given two alarms to the town two days together; but when Sir W. Brereton, with his horse was returned, which was May 30, a considerable number of horse and foot went towards Whitchurch, and near the town took Captain Morrice, a Lieutenant, a Quarter-master, and three or four common men, and brought them prisoners to Nantwich, with about sixty cows and young beasts.

May 17.—Lord Capel with his forces, to the number of fifteen hundred, came near to Nantwich, almost to the end of Haspinal street, and discharged against the town; which returning the like, slew some of his men, and wounded others. They endeavoured to have planted four pieces of ordnance about Malpas field, but finding the town inconvenient, and the town gunners flinging wild balls among them, between one and two on Thursday morning they returned to Whitchurch with shame, hurting no man; but they killed a calf of Mr. T. Mainwaring's, and broke barns for hay, on which the soldiers rhymed:

> The Lord Capel with a thousand and a half,
> Came to Barton-Cross, and there they kill'd a calf;
> And staying there until the break of day,
> They took their heels and fast they ran away.

June 12th.—Four or five companies of dragoons went towards Holt, and being then the time of the fair, and coming into Farn unexpectedly, gave them a great alarm, and frightened them not a little; from thence they went to Shockledge, whence they took ninety-eight beasts, oxen, and other cattle, with many horses, and returned safe at night to Nantwich; they plundered Mr. Leche's house at Carden, who was one of the arrays, and in shooting against the house, which opposed them, they killed a woman servant, and brought Mr. Leche and others prisoners to Nantwich.

June 17th.—J. Bostock of Tattenhall, counsellor at law, and clerk of the council of war at Nantwich, being found guilty of adultery with one Alice Chetwood, in the minister's house, on the Sabbath-day, at the time of divine service, was adjudged to stand in the market-place, at the highest of the market, with a paper on his breast, signifying his offence, which was executed accordingly; the whore, with another paper, standing by him.

August 3d.—Lord Capel with about three thousand men came to Ranmore, not at once, but in different parties; at the first, two or three troops appeared, so Nantwich went confidently against them with the forces that were ready, Sir William Brereton being then at Stafford: the enemy seeing this, brought up more of the horse that staid behind at Baddington lane, and advanced towards them; but when the Nantwich men saw the enemy increase so, they retreated in time, without loss of any save one Richard Massey, and Lieutenant Ashbry, who was slain by one of his own men by chance.

That night the enemy with all their ordnance, carriages, &c. lay quietly on Ranmore, and on Friday morning, about six o'clock (there being a very thick and dark night) they set upon the town, on the side between March-lane, and the Weaver; and being very near the walls before they could be seen by the townsmen, they fired very fiercely, and played mightily with their cannon, but did little hurt; the townsmen, out of their works, returned the like, both with ordnance and muskets. This hot work lasted till nine or ten o'clock, when the sun dispelled the mist; the enemy then perceived themselves to be too near their works, and so fled away space, and they of the town followed them with shouting, and killed about forty of them, and wounded sixteen, and from that time Nantwich was quiet from the Lord Capel and his forces; only their frequent coming near it occasioned burning many houses, cots, and barns, that afforded them shelter; and that very night and the next day the garrison were employed in that business.

A report that Nantwich was besieged brought many of the allies out of Lancashire and Staffordshire, both horse and foot, to have aided the town, but the enemy being departed they returned back; among the rest, there came the Moorland dragoons as far as Haslington, Saturday August 5th, where they quartered that night; in their return they gave a strong alarm to Mr. Biddulph's house in Staffordshire, where was a garrison. This Biddulph was a great papist.

August 10th.—Sir William Brereton being at Stafford, went with his forces against Mr. Giffard's house of Chillington, a garrison furnished with three great pieces of ordnance, and one set of drakes; they besieged it, and playing hard upon it two days, on Friday the besieged yielded, being sore battered and not able to hold out any longer. The house was surrendered upon fair quarter given; they took Mr. Giffard, his two sons, a seminary priest, and above sixty others, and carried them prisoners to Stafford, and arms for two hundred men, and store of ammunition, and all this with the loss of one man and a boy; Sir William Brereton returned to Nantwich, and that night Sir T Middleton with all his forces, seven great pieces of ordnance, four cases of drakes, and about forty carriages of ammunition came to him.

August 28th.—Captain Croxton and Captain Venables, with their companies and others, went to Durtwich, and cut in pieces all their pans, pumps, salt-pits, and works, and carried some of their pans off, so their salt making was spoiled, which served Shrewsbury, Wales, and many other places of the kingdom. The provocation to this was, that Lord Capel had issued a proclamation, that none under his command should fetch any salt from Nantwich.

October 14th.—Report came to Nantwich, that Lord Capel, with three thousand six hundred men, and one hundred and forty carriages, great ordnance, and a mortar piece, was coming against them. On which sad news, the townsmen and many others, and a double guard, sat up all night, but heard no more of the enemy, than that they were at Whitchurch, Combermere, Marbury, &c.

October 16th.—About one in the afternoon the enemy got to Acton with all the carriages, before any intelligence came to town; when two companies of foot and some dragoons issuing out towards Acton, set upon the enemy, and drove them into the Church, which they fortified for safety; some of them also took Dorfold House, where being sheltered, the Nantwich forces were fain to retreat, firing at them, as occasion served, over the wall. The enemy dispersed themselves into the fields, and down Henshall-lane, to Beam-bridge, continually shooting at the town, but came not near the walls; which the townsmen observing, some few active men, of their own head, leaped over the walls with their muskets, and ran disorderly towards the enemy, firing one at another all that afternoon till night, when the enemy fled, both horse and foot, some slain and eight or nine taken, and then all was quiet on both sides. At night, all the townsmen and countrymen that came in to the aid of the town, and a great number of horse and foot, watched carefully at the walls, expecting hourly when the enemy would assault the town, being so near as Acton and Dorfold; and on Tuesday morning, when a great assault was feared, tidings came that the enemy were marched away; at first it was not credited, but it proved true, they marched off about midnight. That morning Sir William Brereton, Sir Thomas Middleton, and Colonel Greaves, with almost all the army, save what they left for the security of Wem, came to aid Nantwich, not hearing of the enemy's departure. They presently sent forces after them, and brought in about forty prisoners of the meaner sort; the best escaped. So they preserved the town without the loss of one man.

October 23d.—Some of Sir Thomas Middleton's troops went into Wales and fetched in Sir Edmund Broughton from his own house at Broughton, and two of his sons, and brought them prisoners to Nantwich.

Every day after Dec. 13th, till Sabbath-day, they had alarms at Nantwich from the enemy; on the Sabbath at sermon time, they heard the enemy were advancing towards them, whereupon the Captain, with the soldiers, and Serjeant-Major Lothian, who led them, went out, and hearing the enemy were at Burford, a mile from Nantwich, they drew towards them, and before the foot could come up, they charged some of the enemy's horse, slew some and wounded others, and took some prisoners; yet not without a great loss to the town, for Major Lothian, a discreet and valiant man, was taken prisoner, and when the foot was coming up they fled; yet that night gave an alarm to the town, which from the time of taking Beeston Castle had no rest, day or night, but were upon guard continually.

The enemy now drawing nearer to the town, spread themselves into Stoke, Hurleston, Brindley, Wrenbury, and all the country about, robbing and plundering every where till Dec. 22; they then passed over the river to Audlem, Hankelow, Buerton, Hatherton, &c. and on Saturday they came to Bartomley (giving an alarm to the garrison of Crewe Hall), as they marched they set upon the Church, which had in it about twenty neighbours, that had gone in for safety; but the Lord Byron's troop, and Connought, a Major to Colonel Sneyd, set upon them, and won the Church; the men fled into the steeple, but the enemy burning the forms, rushes, mats, &c. made such a smoke, that they being almost stifled, they called for quarter, which was granted by Connought; but when they had them in their power, they stripped them all naked, and most cruelly murdered twelve of them, contrary to the laws of arms, nature, and nations. Connought cut the throat of Mr. John Fowler, a hopeful young man, and a minor, and only three of them escaped miraculously, the rest being cruelly wounded. Christmas-day, and the day after, they plundered Bartomley, Crewe, Haslington, and Sandbach, of goods and cloaths, and stripped naked both men and women. [N. B. This was one of the articles entered against King Charles; had he pleaded when brought to judgment, at Whitehall.]

On St. Stephen's day the Parliament's army (leaving some to keep Nantwich) marched to Middlewich, Holmes Chapel, and Sandbach, and in Booth-lane met the enemy, where there was a great fight, but in the end the Parliament forces were worsted, and retired to Middlewich, the enemy following them and driving them quite away; there the Parliament left their Magazines and two hundred men that were slain and wounded on the other side.

January 4.*—The enemy besieged Doddington Hall, kept by Capt. Harwar, with a hundred and sixty men; they took it without resistance, though they had all necessaries for a fortnight, which the enemy got, Harwar and his men being sent off to Wem with their cloathes, not being allowed to go to Nantwich, which night and day they assaulted and harrassed by their continual alarms.

* 1643.

Saturday January 12.—The besieged sallied out, and fetched in seven carriages, drawn with great oxen, and provisions in them, which so enraged them, that they fired Thomas Evenson's barn, Sabbath Church's lodge, and some others, and many stacks of hay.

January 16th.—Some of each company issued out at the sconce in Mr. Mainwaring's back-yard, where the enemy were entrenched; they quickly entered their works, killed some of them, drove the rest away, and brought in cloaths, arms, and ammunition, with the loss of one Blackshaw. The day after the enemy shot against the town very

latter, but the town was taken from them by Lord Grandison, on the 21st Sept. 1642.—Throughout the

much, and discharged their cannon ninety-six times, but did no execution at all.

ridge's ry of wich.

About this time, Lord Byron sent the following summons:*—

To the Commanders, Soldiers, and Inhabitants of the Town of Nantwich.

"That it may appear to all the world, that neither I, nor the army under my conduct, desire the blood or ruin of any (as we have been most falsely and maliciously scandalized in that behalf,) but that our chief aims and endeavours are to reduce the people to their obedience to his majesty, and settle the country in peace without shedding of blood. I have thought good, before I engage myself upon the town, to let you know,—1st That I do in his Majesty's name charge and command you to deliver up the said town of Nantwich, with all the arms, artillery, ammunition, and other things therein, into my hands, for his majesty's use; and that all commanders, soldiers, and others, immediately lay down their arms and submit to his majesty's mercy.—2d. I promise pardon to such as shall readily lay down their arms and submit, and shall give safe conduct to such as shall desire to go to their own houses in the country, and will protect both them and the inhabitants of the town in their persons and estates, except such as his Majesty hath excepted.—3d. If you refuse these conditions, I shall, by God's help, use other means for the recovery of his majesty's rights, and vindicating of his and the country's wrongs; whereby, if you and those many good people who are forced to be among you shall perish, both your own blood and theirs shall rest upon your heads. I am content to allow two hours for the return of an answer, and admit a cessation of arms till that time be expired.—If you send two men of quality, the one a soldier, and the other a town's-man, to treat with me (or such as I shall appoint), of the time and manner of the render of the town, I will give safe conduct and caution for their safe return. John Byron."

To this a verbal answer was returned, importing, that the town was kept for the use of the King (what hypocrisy!) and the Parliament, and by their special directions; and that they were resolved to keep it against him and his forces so long as God should enable them. As soon as this answer was received, the cannonading the town began, and about eleven o'clock at night the enemy planted a short piece of ordnance near Dorfold House, and shot into the town many red hot balls, one of which lighted into a rick of kyds in Mr. Wilbraham's back yard, which made a terrible fire, but through God's mercy, and the industry of many women, who were employed to quench it, not much hurt was done, only the enemy shooting continually with their cannon, killed a daughter of John Davenport's, the first that was slain since the siege began. The besieged seeing many of the enemy sheltered in and about Mr Minshull's house and barn, sallied out again, fired the barn, and a cote or two of Dutton's, which they burned to the ground, took two prisoners, and killed nine or ten; they brought in a woman too, who had ten half crowns in her pockets, without the loss of a man.

These vigorous measures not producing the desired effect, Lord Byron was determined to storm the town; but before he put his resolutions into practice, sent the following summons:

To the Inhabitants and Commanders of the Town of Nantwich.

"Whereas I am most certainly informed, as well by divers of the soldiers who are now my prisoners, as by several other creditable persons, that you are not only in a desperate condition, but that the late summons I sent to the town hath been suppressed and concealed from the inhabitants thereof, and they must grossly abused, by being told that no mercy was intended to be shewed by this army to the town, but that both man, women, and child should be put to the sword: I have therefore thought fit once more to send unto you, that the minds of the people with you may be dispossessed of that false and wicked slander which hath been cast upon this army; and I do charge you (as you will answer Almighty God for the lives of those persons who shall perish by your perfidious dealings with them) that you impart and publish the sad summons I sent to the people with you, and that you yield up the town of Nantwich into my hands for his Majesty's use, and submit yourselves to his Majesty's mercy which I am willing to offer unto you. Though I am confident that neither of yourselves, nor by any aid that can come unto you, there is any possibility for you to escape the hands of this army; if you please to send two gentlemen of quality to me, the one a commander, the other a towns's-man, whereby you may receive better satisfaction, I shall give safe conduct and hostage for their return. I do expect a present answer from you. John Byron."

To which the following answer was returned.

"We have received your last summons and do return this answer; that we never reported or caused to be reported that your lordship or the army intended any such cruelty, we thinking it impossible for gentlemen and soldiers so much to forget humanity: and if any have informed you otherwise, it is their own conceit, and no reality. Concerning the publishing of your former summons, it was publicly read among the soldiers and town's-men as your trumpeter can inform you, and since that time multitudes of copies have been dispersed amongst the town's men and others, and from none hath it been concealed or detained. For the delivery of this town; we may not with our consciences, credits, or reputations, betray that trust reposed in us for the maintaining and defending this town as long as any enemy shall appear to offend it. Though we be termed traitors and hypocrites, yet we hope and are confident, God will evidence and make known to the world in his due time (though for the present we should suffer) our zeal for his glory, our unfeigned and unspotted loyalty towards his Majesty, and sincerity in all our professions. George Booth."

Three days after, at break of day they strongly attacked the town on every side; and the soldiers and townsmen as stoutly defended themselves for an hour or more: very great valour was shewn on both sides, but at last the enemy fled away as fast as they could, leaving their scaling-ladders and wood-kids they had brought with them, some arms, and a hundred dead bodies behind them, whereof Captain Sandford was one, who was killed upon the spot, where one

whole of the Civil wars, Nantwich was firm in its devotion to the Parliament; indeed it might be considered

of his firelocks was sore wounded and brought into the town, but died quickly. The town soldiers had the pillage of them all, and their arms, and lost but six common men. There was found in Captain Sandford's pockets, when he was stripped, a paper containing the order of the assault for taking the town. The field word was, God and a good cause. A letter also was found upon him, dated January 13, in these words:—

"To the Officers, Soldiers, and Gentlemen in Nantwich:

"GENTLEMEN,

"Let these resolve your jealousies about religion: I vow by the faith of a Christian, I know not one Papist in our army, and as I am a Gentleman, we are not Irish, but true born English, and real Protestants born and bred. Pray mistake us not, but receive us into your fair esteem, and know we intend loyalty to his Majesty, and will be no other than faithful in his service. Thus believe, from your's,

"T. SANDFORD."

Another was found, dated the 15th, viz.

"GENTLEMEN,

Mr. Drum can inform you, that Acton Church is no more a prison, but now free for honest men to do their devotion therein: wherefore be persuaded from your incredulity, and resolve: God will not forsake his anointed. Let not your zeal in a bad cause dazzle your eyes any longer, but wipe away your vain conceits, that have too long led you into error: loth I am to take the trouble of persuading you into obedience, because your erroneous opinions do most violently oppose reason among you; but, if you love your town, accept of quarter; and if you regard your lives, work your safety by yielding your town to Lord Byron, for his Majesty's use. You now see my battery is fixed, from which fire shall eternally visit you day and night, to the terror of your old and females, and consumption of your thatched houses. Believe me, Gentlemen, I have laid by my former delay, and am now resolved to batter, burn, and storm you. Don't wonder that I write to you, having Officers in chief over me; it is only to advise, because I have some friends among you, for whose safety I wish that you accept Lord Byron's conditions, for he is gracious, and will charitably consider you. Accept of this as a summons, that you forthwith surrender your town, and by that testimony of your fealty to his Majesty, you may obtain favour. My Firelocks, you know, have done strange feats, by night and by day, and hourly we will not fail in our visits of you; you have not yet received my alarm, wherefore expect suddenly to hear from

"T. SANDFORD,
"Captain of Firelocks.

"From my battery and approaches before the
Welsh Row."

The siege continued; things began to be very scarce, both for man and horse; many cattle being within the walls, for fear of plundering, wanted forage; a special Providence now appeared, for it pleased God, upon the thawing of the snow, the Weaver began to rise, and the enemy fearing the water would take down the platt, which they had laid over it a little below Beam-bridge, for their free passage to relieve one another: they therefore, on the 24th of January, conveyed all their ordnance over the river, together with their carriages, and most of their horse and foot, towards Acton Church, and on the the 25th, the river was risen so high, that their plat was carried down, so that they could not pass the river; which the townsmen and soldiers perceiving, took advantage thereof, and issued out to the enemy's works, driving such as were left in them away, throwing down their works, bringing in much hay and fuel, burning Mr. Jeffrey Minshull's new house, barn, and stable, and many other dwellings, where the enemy had been harboured. The same day, Sir William Brereton, General Fairfax, and many other Commanders, and the Lancashire forces, to the number of 3,550 horse, and 5,000 foot, marched towards Nantwich, to raise the siege; coming over Delamere Forest, they met with some of the royalists, and in the skirmish took forty prisoners, and killed some; at Bar-bridge they met more of them, killed some, and took thirty prisoners, and still drawing to Hurlston, they saw the whole body of the enemy at Acton: the battle began very fiercely about half an hour after three in the afternoon, and before five, many of the train-bands issued out of the town, and fell upon their rear, whereupon they fled, and were utterly routed. Sir Mic. Earnley, Sir F. Butler, Colonel Gibson, Colonel Warren, Colonel Fleetwood, and many Captains, Lieutenants, and soldiers, about 1,600, were taken prisoners. One brass cannon, four smaller, all their carriages, magazines, and provisions, which were all immediately brought into the town; and if day-light had not failed, but few of them would have escaped; but the night being very dark, they did not pursue them, and many remained on the field all night; few were slain on either side; about forty of the King's, and three or four of the others, and but few wounded. The Cavaliers in Acton Church, and Dorfold, quickly called forquarter, which was granted them; and the Saturday after the market began again, and plenty of all provisions at reasonable rates.

Monday, Steel, late Governor of Beeston Castle, was shot to death in Tinker's Croft, by two soldiers, according to judgment against him; he was put into a coffin, and buried in the Church-yard. He confessed all his sins, among the rest, that of uncleanness: he prayed a great while, and to the judgment of charity died penitently.

Some Parliament forces being billetted in and about Tarvin, were set upon by the Chester forces, and some wounded, and others taken prisoners; but a company of Parliament dragoons making haste, overtook and rescued them, killed a Captain, and some others, wounded many, and took eight prisoners, whom they sent to Nantwich.

Wednesday, January 30.—A solemn thanksgiving was kept for removing the siege, but not in the Church, for the prisoners had been kept there, and it was not cleansed, but in some houses of the town, fitted for that purpose.

February 4.—The Nantwich forces assaulted Crewe Hall, then kept by Capt. Fisher, which was presently surrendered, on condition, that he and his men, about one hundred and twenty, with the wounded,

Cheshire

as the rendezvous for the disaffected of the Counties of Chester and Lancaster at that distressing period, and is in fact noticed as such by Lord Clarendon. It was the head quarters of Sir William Brereton till Chester surrendered; and in Jan. 1646, it was ordered to be dismantled, and the garrison was discharged.

Description of the Town.—The situation of Nantwich, although generally little above the level of the Weaver, is nevertheless pleasant and healthful, and is about twenty miles S. E. from Chester; it occupies a considerable portion of land. It has a market every Saturday; the toll of cattle and vegetables is the right of the Marquis of Cholmondeley, but that on corn and fish is Lord Crewe's. Burnell, Bishop of Bath, in 1282, obtained the grant of a Fair here, for three days, on the Feast of St. Bartholomew. It still continues to be held: there are two other Fairs on the 26th March, and 15th Dec.

The general appearance of the town is very ancient: the houses are mostly composed of timber and plaister, of which stile of building the Crown Inn affords a very excellent specimen. The principal streets are Hospital-street, the Welsh-row, and Beam-street, from which other passages diverge. At the end of the streets, are *Alms Houses.* The alms houses at the end of Hospital-street, have a stone gateway in front, and the inscription—" Sir Edmund Wright, borne in this towne, sole founder of this alms-house, a'no Dom. 1638."—Those in the Welsh-row, are dated 1613; and the inscription on those at the end of Beam-street is, " These Alms-houses, were erected in the year of our Lord 1767, by John Crewe, of Crewe, Esq. in trust of the wills of Sir Thomas Crewe, Knt. and Sir John Crewe, Knt."—The Alms-houses in Love-street, are endowed by benefactions from a Mrs. Ermine Delves.

The other streets,* &c. are High-street, Pepper-street, Pillory-street, Barker-street, Mill-street, Middlestych, Sparbacon-lane, Love-lane, the Swine Market, Wall-lane, Church-lane, Castle-lane, Dog-lane, Mason's-yard, Wood-street, Bakehouse-lane, Marsh-lane, and Fulhurst-lane.—Some dispute has arisen, on the origin of the name of the *Welsh Row,* which, at a very early period was called *Frog-row;* but it may be easily traced to its peculiar situation, as being the principal suburb of the town that first fell a sacrifice to the frequent incursions of the Welsh. Indeed, to particularize an instance, it is recorded in a M.S. supposed to be written by a Curate of Nantwich,† that Mr. T. Maisterson,‡ who served in France under the the Black Prince, and subsequently under Henry IV. and V. de-

might depart safe, leaving their arms; many of them came that same day to Nantwich, where they were entertained.

February 13.—A solemn day of thanksgiving in Nantwich and Acton Churches, and on Thursday after a day of humiliation.

* A handsome Stone Bridge over the Weaver, separates Hospital-street from the body of the town.

† History of Nantwich, 8vo.

‡ The Maistersons, observes Mr. Ormerod, in an extract from the Harl. MSS. although they never appear to have possessed manerial property in Cheshire, or to have resided at any other place than Nantwich, were a family of high antiquity and importance, distinguished by military prowess, and connected by marriage with the best families of the county. The first of the family known to have settled here was *Robert Filius Magistri,* or Masterson, temp. Edw. I. His grandson Thomas, was with Edward III in the French wars, and with the Black Prince in Spain, in aid of Pedro the Cruel. He was in the advanced guard with John of Gaunt against the French, " where Sir Bertram de Cleaquim, Constable of France, and the Marshall Dandrehen were, which part of the army were in the cruelest fight, notwithstandinge that Henry the Bastard that usurped, restored and staid his men thrise that day when they were on the point to fly. For the great valour of the sd Thomas, shewed that day, upon ther return to Burdeux, the Duke of Lancaster did win the sd Thomas to his service, and by indenture interchangeably did bind him to serve him in the warrs, upon honourable termes and honourable conditions, and to pay him yearly the sum of xl. per annum, out of his receipts of his Manor of Halton." Returning from Spain he found " that the Prince was behind with him for his pay for himselph, his men at arms and archers, the sum of 2738 fortz of Gwyan gold, wch sd money he could never be payd, although the Prince appointed his recevors in Cheshire, John Sonde, and Jo. Allen, to make payment thereof."—Temp. Ric. II. he was made Escheator of Cheshire, and again served under the Duke of Lancaster in his endeavor to obtain the Crown of Castile. On the Duke's rebellion against the King, this Thomas fought for him at the Battle of Shrewsbury, in consequence of which, his house was spoiled, and all his goods carried away by Lord Percy's servants, and for a restitution of which he afterwards petitioned Hen. IV. " Lastly, he recd. his pension of xl. per ann. of King Hen. V. of whom he was greatly esteemed for the service done to his father and grandfather. He lived in the last year of Henry V. so as I conceave he was livinge in the beginninge of Hen. VI. his reign. I gather by this his great age, for he served Edw. III. the Black Prince his sonne, John of Gaunt Duke of Lancaster his brother, Richd. II. Henry IV. Henry V. and saw the entrance of King Henry VI." Richard the

CHESHIRE fended his house in Pillory-street, which was moated, against such of the inhabitants who had joined the Welsh on the *other side* of the River.

The inhabitants of Nantwich* are privileged not to serve on Juries that are not within the jurisdiction of the town. So early as the reign of Edw. III. it was stated to have been a prescriptive right, and was then confirmed, as it was subsequently in the reign of Elizabeth.

There are no remains of the *Chapel of St. Anne*, which was situated near the Bridge in the Welsh Row, nor of the *Chantry of Cistercians*, dependent on the Abbey of Combermere. The present handsome *Bridge* was erected in 1803, when the old stone bridge, which was built in 1663 at the County expense, was taken down. A wooden bridge existed here at a very early period; and a stone bridge which succeeded it, was washed down by a flood in 1637. Mr. Partridge notices a *Hospital for Lepers*, dedicated to St. Lawrence, which was situated in the Welsh Row, opposite to the Chantry or Priory, before noticed.

The manufacture of SALT here, formerly so extensive, is now reduced to a single establishment.—The brine pits of Nantwich may be traced to a very remote antiquity. In the Charter of Hugh Malbanc to Combermere Abbey, he grants them the tythe of salt of his own salt pits, and of others, and the salt of the Blessed Virgin, and the salt of Friday, and the salt for the Abbot's table, as freely as at his own board.† The brine pits were closed by order of Hen. III. to annoy the Welsh. In the reign of Hen. VIII. Leland says there were three hundred salt works here; and in the reign of Elizabeth there were two hundred and nineteen; but the dreadful fire that then occurred, injured or destroyed nearly the whole of them. In 1624, there were not more than one hundred remaining; and since that period, owing to the discovery of the springs at Northwich, and other parts of the county, of a very superior strength, the manufacture continued rapidly to decline. The *Old Biat*, supposed to be the first discovered in the town, is still in existence; and notwithstanding its vicinity to the River, from which it is distant only six feet, it still retains its original strength of brine. It is noticed by Mr. Partridge, in his History of Nantwich,‡ that "enriched by the profits and gratefully sensible of the benefits accruing from the saline springs, which so copiously flowed around Nantwich, every Ascension Day our pious ancestors sung a hymn of thanksgiving for the blessing of the brine. That ancient salt-pit, called the *Old Biat*, (ever held in great veneration by the town's people) was on that day bedecked and adorned with green boughs, flowers, and ribbons, and the young people had music, and danced round it; which custom of adorning and dancing continued till a very few years ago."—The origin of the term *Biat*, as applied to this pit, remains undiscovered; but the word *Biot* has a local meaning tantamount to a support, or a stay: the curious in etymology may endeavour to trace the allusion.

HISTORY.

‡ An. 1774.

In the Welsh Row is situated *Towns End*, the remains of the ancient seat of the Wilbrahams, a family which branched from the Woodhey stock.‖ The Wilbraham *Alms Houses*, are in the immediate neighbour-

son of Thomas, was Seneschall to the Earl of Essex for the Manors of Adderley and Sponley; another of the family fell at Flodden, and in the disputes between Charles I and his Parliament, their descendants took an active part.—In an Inq. p. m. 1 Jac. I. Thomas Maysterton, gent. is stated to have held two hundred and six acres of land, &c. in Nantwich from the King in socage, by fealty, as parcel of the estates of the dissolved priory of Trentham.

* In Derrick's letters to Lord Southwell, 12mo 1760, the town is thus noticed: "In our way we stopped to dine at Nantwich, a well-built market town, famous for white salt, and excellent cheese. Whilst dinner was providing we took a view of the Church, which is built in the form of a Cross, old, large, and handsome. Many of the stalls of the Monks are standing to this day, encumbered with a great deal of carved work: the pulpit is remarkably beautiful. Here we were shown the monument of *the founder!* SIR ROGER DE CORRADOC, an ancient British Knight, who was said to be immediately descended from the renowned Caractacus. It is of white marble but much defaced by Cromwell's soldiers, from whose violence nothing neat, elegant, or venerable, was sacred. They were possessed of this town for a year or upwards, during which time they turned the Church into a stable for their horses. There is a charge of five shillings put down in the Church-book, for pitch, to purify the place on their departure."

† As has been before noticed, there is little doubt but what the Romans procured salt here.

‖ A curious journal was commenced by Richard Wilbraham, Esq. in 1612, and was continued by his successors till 1732. It notices, in addition to family affairs, all the leading local incidents of that period. After describing the visits of Jac. I. to Townsend, it mentions the entertainment there in 1640, of the Earl of Strafford and suite, then Lord Lieutenant of Ireland. In 1659, August 11, Sir George Booth, in his fruitless attempt to raise a party for Charles II. made this

hood, and were founded in 1613, by Sir Roger Wilbraham, Knt. for four poor men of Nantwich, and two of Acton. Each pensioner has a distinct apartment, a small plot of garden ground, and an annuity of forty shillings per annum. They have also a coat of grey cloth with blue facings.

The *Porch House*, was an ancient building adjoining Fullesburst-lane, and in the reign of Edward IV. was in the possession of H. Wettenhall, Esq. of Dorfold.*

The *Grammar School* is situated on the north side of the Church-yard, and was founded by John and Thomas Thrash, wool-packers, of London, temp. Eliz. On the south side is the inscription, "Rich[d] Dale, Friee Mason, was the Maister Carpenter in making this buyldinge, Anno Domino 1611." It has an endowment of £9. 14*s*. appropriated to the gratuitous instruction of six boys.

The Charity School here for forty boys, is called— *The Blue-cap School*, and was endowed principally by the Wilbraham Family,

In Pillory-street, is the Meeting-house of the unostentatious *Society of Friends*.

The *Methodist Chapel*, is in Hospital-street, and is rather a handsome building; the *Unitarian Chapel* is also in the same street.

The *Independents' Chapel* is in Church-lane, and was built by the late Captain Scott;† formerly in the army, and a zealous Calvinistic Preacher.

The last sectarian place of worship is the *Baptists' Chapel*, in Barker-street.

The *Town Hall* was built in 1720; in which is a Sessions Room, towards the erection of which the Prince of Wales, afterwards George II. contributed £600. and his effigy adorned the front of it. In 1737, owing to the wretchedness of its construction, a great portion of this building fell down; several persons lost their lives, and numbers were bruized. It would seem that this catastrophe did not operate as a caution; for a few years afterwards, during the sitting of the Session, a tremendous shaking of the Hall took place, which so alarmed the court and spectators, that in the hurry to escape the threatened danger, many people were dreadfully injured.‡

A *Market House* is erected on the site of the Old Hall.

Mainwaring's Hall, which was situated in Beam-street, no longer exists. It was moated.—There were two branches of this family settled here, viz. Peter, bastard son of William Mainwaring, of Peover, by Jane Praers; the other descended from Wm. Mainwaring of the Kerminchaм family.

Wright's Hall, which was situated in Barker-street, was occupied by the Wrights of Mottram St. Andrew.

Church's Mansion is in the Hospital-street, and was originally moated. Of this family was Saboth Church, Vicar of Tarvin; and Mr. Saboth Church, a non-conformist of some note.‖

The *House of Industry* is in a pleasant situation, near Beam Heath. It was built in 1780, and a grant of land for the purpose was made by the Earl of Cholmondeley.

seat his head-quarters. The house is supposed to have been built in 1571, and was a spacious brick edifice, with bay windows, and extensive gardens. It is the property of George Wilbraham, Esq. of Delamere Lodge, the representative of the family.

* A brewery is now erected on the site of it.

† On the west wall, in Queen-street Chapel, Chester, is a neat white marble tablet, inscribed to the memory of the Captain and his two wives; below which they were interred.

‡ The removal of the Sessions from Nantwich to Knutsford, is said to have been the effect of these accidents.

‖ The following curious warrant, authorising a search for arms, is copied from the original, in the possession of Mr. Dicas, solicitor, Chester: it is singularly coincident with the bills passed in Parliament, in 1819:—

To Lieutenant Roger Mainwaring and Cornett John Johnson, and to either of them.

By and from the Lord Lievtenant of this Covnty, and by vertve of the Statvtes of this Kingdom concerning the Militia, you are hereby in his Maiestes name desired, required, and commanded forthwith, taking to yovr assistance the Constables, or one of them of the respectiue townships (who also are hereby reqvired to be aiding and assisting therein) to make diligent Search for, and to seize and take into yo. Cvstody the sev:[e]all pesons here und[e] named, being Papist, or such who haue refvsed or not taken the oaths appointed by an Act of Parliam[t]. made in the first year of his Maiesties Reign, intitvled an Act for Abrogating the Oaths of Allegiance and Svpremacy, and appointing other Oaths, and all the Armes, excepting their Walking Swords, w[ch] you shall find in their own possession, or in the possession of any other, for their, or any of their vse or vses And also the persons and arms of all svch Strangers as you shall haue jvst cavse to svspect to be disaffected to the Go-

Nantwich was the birth place of several prominent characters: *John Gerrarde*, the botanist, was born here in 1545, and died in 1607. *Harrison* the Regicide, and Parliamentary General, was a native of this town; and here resided for many years, the widow of our immortal poet Milton, daughter of Mr. Minshull, of Stoke; she died here in 1726.

The CHURCH* is an elegant structure, the architec-

---

uernment. And that yov bring the said persons and armes to vs at Nether Knvttesford with all convenient speed. And also that in the day time yov diligently search the seueral hovses and places of abode of all the said persons, and other hovses, places, and grovnds to them belonging, for all the horses of the persons herevnder named; and that you bring vnto vs a Note in writing of all svch horses and their Colovrs and Markes as yov' shall any where find, and in whose cvstody they were found. And for so doing this shall be yovr warrant; Hereof fail nott. Giuen vnder our hands and seals at Nether Knuttesford the Nynth day of March, Anno Regni Dom. William Tertii Dei grat. Regis Angl. &c. Octavo; Annoq. Dm. 169$\frac{5}{6}$.

Sir William Meredith, Baronet
Thomas Cholmondeley, of Vale Royal, Esq. and
Mr. Francis Cholmondeley, his brother
Sir Philip Egerton, his house to be searched, but his person not to be seized.
John Egerton, Esq.
Mr. Thickness
Mr. Dod, of Broxton
John Massey, of Coddington, Esq.
Mr. Peter Weston, of Christleton
Mr. Monke Davenport
Mr. Saboth Church, of Namptwich
Sir Rowland Stanley
Sir James Poole
Wm. Massey, of Puddington, Esq.

And yov are hereby fvrther reqvired and avthorized to Seize all the serviceable Horses of the Persons herein named, and to bring the same vnto vs at Knvttesford; Given vnder our hands and seales att Knvttesford aforesaid, the Tenth day of March Ann. Dm. 169$\frac{5}{6}$.

(Signed)
THOMAS LEE.
ROGER MAINWARING.

* "Before I proceed to other matters, it may be proper now to discuss the question,---Whether the Church of Nantwich was ever a Chapel of Ease to the Church of Acton? I hold the negative opinion. First, then, let us see what constitutes a Parish Church, and if ours is found to have always possessed the necessary requisites, we may confidently conclude Nantwich Church was never a Chapel to that of Acton; this I shall endeavour to prove. In the primitive Church of the English Saxons, parishes were limited only in regard to the ministering Presbytery, who had their limits assigned them by the Bishop, and not in regard to parochial profits; for in those times the whole profit of each diocess made a common treasure to be disposed of by the Bishop and his Clergy; but afterwards, when devotion grew to a higher pitch, divers laymen of the best quality built churches, and endowed them with peculiar maintenance for the incumbent, who should there reside; which maintenance, with other ecclesiastical profits which came to the hands of every such several incumbent, was by this means restrained from the common treasury of the diocess, and annexed to the particular church so founded; and out of these lay-foundations chiefly came those kind of parishes which at this day are in every diocess. The first express limitation of profits to be given to this or that Church, as in the laws of King Edgar, Anno 970, where there is a threefold division of Churches. The first is called *Senior Ecclesia*, or the Mother Church; the second, a Church that had a place for burial; the third, a Church without a place for burial.—Where it is ordained, that a man not having entered a Church of his own, should pay his tithes to the next Mother Church where he heard God's service. And that the other Churches might not be over impoverished by those of later foundation, the founders of churches whereto the right of sepulture was annexed, were to settle above a third part of their tithes upon their new built churches. But these new erections in old parishes bred new divisions, and by connivance of the times became whole parishes. For the right of sepulture was, and regularly is, a character of a parish church, or *ecclesia*, as it is commonly distinguished from *capella* a chapel. And a *quore impedit* brought for a church, where the defendant pretended it to be but a chapel, the issue was not so much, whether it was a church or chapel, as whether or no it had *baptisterium et sepultura*. For if it had the right of administration of sacraments in it, and sepulture also, then it differed not from a parish church. Those other churches, which in Edgar's laws are spoken of, which had no places of burial, are those which at this day are called chapels of ease, built for oratories, but not diminishing any thing of the mother church's profit. Thus speaks the learned Seldon. From which I conceive it clear, that Nantwich church, which always possessed the distinguishing requisites, was *à principio* a parish church, and never a chapel of ease to that of Acton; I mean not however to say that Acton was not the older church; it might be so, and till such time as this was built, no doubt, according to the laws then established, the inhabitants of Nantwich, and the neighbouring villages, paid their tithes to it, as being the next mother church; but after Nantwich church was built (which was before Hugh Malbank built the Abbey of Combermere, though in his grant he passeth it by the name of *capella*) it is more more than probable, the founder, according to the custom of those times, endowed the new built church with some portion of the tithes that were formerly paid to the church of Acton, namely, besides the tythes of the town, those of Alvrasdeston, Willaston, Woolston-Wood, and Leighton, which lay near and convenient to this new-built church, and furthest off from Acton; and so made it a parish. 'Tis not probable that a church almost as large as a cathedral, that had a dean and six priests belonging to it, that had a right of sepulture and the sacraments, should be a chapel of ease to another, in whose jurisdiction or deanery that other lay. The deed made by Robert, son of Robt. de Hextal (long

CHESHIRE

ture in the Gothic style, of the early part of the 14th century, and dedicated to St. Mary. It was originally dependent on the Church of Acton, and is noticed as such by Sir Peter Leycester, and various other writers.*—It is a Rectory, in the gift of Lord Crewe, valued at £106. 3s. 9d.† The building has a nave, chancel, side aisles, and two transepts, and is in length, from east to west 155 feet 2 inches, the chancel occupying 51 feet 9 inches, the nave 75 feet broad, and the chancel 24 feet; breadth of the transepts 98 feet 2 inches; height of the tower, which contains six bells, about 110 feet. The whole is of stone, considerably dilapidated externally, and in the Cathedral form; the fine octagonal tower rising from the centre, ornamented with battlements and pinnacles. The tower springs from four arches, the piers finished with pillars, with the capitals highly ornamented. The Chancel is an elegant building, the eastern window of which is singularly beautiful. Representations of the Annunciation, the Crucifixion, and other scriptural subjects, are sculptured on the orbs which terminate the intersection of the groins.‡

* Ormerod, p. 234.

HISTORY.

The wooden stalls in the Chancel are richly carved, and in excellent preservation.||—There is a beautiful stone pulpit projecting from the piers of the central tower.—The whole of the Choir is vaulted with stone; the sides ornamented with curious tabernacle work.—Notwithstanding the elegance with which the entire fabric has been finished, the interior is sadly disfigured with galleries,§ and other modern absurdities, termed improvements.

The *Monumental Memorials* are numerous and varied; a few of the principal inscriptions follow:—

In the Chancel, on the north side, on a painted tablet,

Here beneath lyeth ye body of Thomas Mastersone, of Wich Malbane, Esq. who first married Frances, coheyre to Sir John Done, of Utkinton, Knt by whom he had yssue 2 sons & 2 daughters, which all dyed yonge; after he married Mary, daughter to Tho. Maunwaringe, of Martyn, Esq. and had yssue Mary, Rich. & Katherine, y^t^ all dyed yonge, Thomas. Robt John, Elizabeth, Mary, Katherine, Frances, Bridget, Margrett, and Hellena, all now livinge, ye said Tho. dyed on the 16th. Feb. an^o^ D'ni 1651.

On another tablet—

Here beneath lyethe the body of Thomas Maisterson, of Wich

---

before Richard II. in whose time the Abbot of Combermere pretended a title thereto, as being a chapel annexed to Acton) proves its exercising the administration of the sacraments by the grant of certain lands for the health of his soul, and the soul of his friends *Deo et beatæ Mariæ, et ecclesiæ beatæ Mariæ de Vico Malbano* for the maintenance of a perpetual priest to be elected by him and his heirs, *cum concilio et consensu totius parochiæ* And warrants the said lands, *Deo et altari beatæ Mariæ ecclesiæ predictæ*. Thus its right of administering the sacraments appears from the warranting these lands to the altar, and the word *ecclesia* shews it to be a church and not a chapel. And that it had an undoubted right of sepulture before the Abbot's claim, the 22d of Richard II is proved as well by the monument of Sir David Craddock, knight, who lies buried in the cross aisle; and that it was possessed of this right before the foundation of Combermere, appears by the houses and possessions of the dissolved abbey, which are upon the church-yard, a spacious spot of ground within the very heart of the Abbot's fee, but no part of it. I say my point is proved by these evidences; as likewise by numerous other deeds still extant, but too many to be here cited; one will be sufficient for the purpose.

A TRANSLATION OF A DEED

PROVING NANTWICH CHURCH TO BE A PARISH CHURCH AND NOT A CHAPEL.

"To our well beloved children in Christ as well known. William Howe, and Sybyll his wife, with all others whatsoever. We William Rudduck, and William Lynch, Stewards of the guilds or fraternities of Wich Malbank, lawfully deputed, send greeting, that by the prayers and suffrages of the saints ye may obtain celestial joys. Forasmuch as out of the goods bestowed upon you, ye have munificently contributed to the maintenance of the guilds aforesaid, and six priests, daily to officiate in the church of the Blessed Mary, in Wich Malbank aforesaid, for their brethren and sisters, alive and dead; we admit you to the participation of all the masses which in the said church shall be celebrated, and to all other works and suffrages, which by our brethren are performed, by the tenour of these presents in life as well as death. Farther granting, that after death, your souls shall be commended and offered by the prayers of the saints, priests, and brethren of the guild aforesaid; masses, exequies, and prayers being performed for them as for other your brethren deceased, is accustomed to be done. In witness whereof, the seal of our said office is hereunto appended. Dated the 8th day of January, 1461."—*King's Vale Royal.*

† Parl. Ret. 1809.—The *Notitia* states the value at £27. 3. 4d. In 1719, Mr Bromhall, Mr. Crewe, and Mr. Wilbraham, subscribed £50. each, to augment the living; which, with other donations, amounted to £200. and with this sum were purchased the tithes of Alvaston, and the Nantwich division of Willaston.

‡ The north transept, according to a MS. in the Harl. Collection, was dedicated to St. Mary, and was a distinct Chapel.

|| They are twenty in number, and tradition says, were brought from Vale Royal Abbey, at the Dissolution.—*See Pennant.*

§ The arms of the Earls and Barons of the Palatinate are painted on the front.

Malbanke, Esq. who married Mary, daughter to Thomas Palmer, of Marston, in ye county of Stafford, Gent. by whom he had issue two sonnes and one daughter, Thomas, Richard, and Mary, all now livinge: the said Thomas died on the 7th day of Aprill, a° D'ni 1669.

In the Chancel—

"AN EPITAPH UPPŌ Y^E DEATH OF JOHN MAISTERSON, GEN. 1586.

Nowe Malbanke mourne, lament your losse, lay mirth asyde be sade.
Lett fall your straeninge siluer tears, for him that made you glade;
Your Joy and Jewell wears to duste, his bones are clad in clay;
Your Piller and your Proppe is gone, gone is your gemme and stay.
The turrett trees and stedfast towre, is batterd to the grounde.
The captane cheefe of all the charge, dead in the campe is founde.
Traile downe youre Ensignes & retire, the steede hath loste his breathe,
Lett trumptr sound, strike on the drum, the dumpe of dreadfull deathe.
Fowle of youre scattringe shott at one's, dragg on your pearring picke,
Close up youre gates, shutt up youre doores, you neuer saw the like.
Pull downe youre hangings and begene to attire your walls with blake,
Send forthe youre greefed sighes, youre happe is gone to wreack.
This dismall day canicular, one this tenthe of December
Youre towne was burnde, youre friend did die, that was youre cheefest member.
Youre extreame losse he did repaire, he wypte youre tears away,
But now youre glorie and youre gain, shall be no more youre staye,
John Maisterson hathe changed his life, to Malbanke heauie greefe;
Good chaunge to him, hard chaunge to them that felt his sweet releife.
Unto the poore he franckly gaue, the needie shall him wante,
To those that lacke, his happie hand was neuer proued scante.
When this poore Towne to ashes fell, deuourde with firie flame,
By pittie moued, he founde the way, howe to repare the same.
Whoe by the grace of our good Queene and nobles of this lande,
This poore towne was builte up againe, in state as it dothe stande.
The timber had eis been growing in woods, which nowe sweete dwelings are,
Soe had the seats and plotts of ground, remained to this day bare.
Had he not bin, this Towne had bin noe Towne as nowe it is;
That which he had, he did procure, the trauaille all was his.
His deeds well doon noe faute can foyle, nor deathe the same expell,
Noe ruste nor tonge can tuch his life, nor furies slaight can quell.
Nor thoghe that deathe doth put downe life, & nature yealds her dewe,
Yete this town shall from age to age, his pearles fame renew.
The livinge and the unborne tow, and all that shall succeede,
The roofes and walls shall blase his fame, for this his worthy deede.
His endless labour in this case deserues an endless crowne,
With goulden garlands of great thankes, & wraythes of high renoune.
The Sonn shall witness of his woorks, surusyde with his bemes so brighte,
Soe shall the moone and statly stars, that vewe the same by nighte.
And all good hearts shall yeald him prayse and moniment his name,
And so long as the worlde endures shall spreade abroad his fame."

In the Nave—

To the memory of Richard Minshall, Gent. son and heire of Mr. Thomas Minshall, of this town of Nantwich. He married Elizabeth, daughter of Richard Wilbraham, of Lincoln's Inn, Esqr son and heyre of Mr. Richard Wilbraham, of this town. He lived wonderfully beloved, being of a most sweet, pleasant, affable, and generous nature; upright in his dealing, charitable to the poor, and a great lover and maker of peace He died very piously upon the 17th day of February, 1637, being the 56 year of his age, leaving behind him no child: but his good name, which is most dear, and sorrowful wife, here registers in his deserving character.

I wish so long a peace unto thy vrne
As till in harbour svch another greet,
If so vntil the world to ashes tvrn,
The ashes will vnreck'd belike to rest.

At the foot of an adjoining monument, erected by Geoffrey Minshull—are the four following lines, being all of the inscription now legible—

Within this glasse a pattern you may see
Of humane change and time's mortality:
In vaine it were t' expresse: this place hath tride
Their birth, their breeding, how they lived and died.

Against the south-east pier of the tower in the south transept, on a mural monument—

Marmori huic vicini una obdormiscunt senex proavus, puerq' pronepos, uterque Richardus Wilbraham.

Ille ex patre fuit Radulpho, filio filii Ranulphi, filii secundi Thomæ Wilbraham de Woodhey, ar. prognate. Vir præter pietatem, qua claruit, Sapientiæ mensura, judicii pondere, et annorum numero olim insignis; qui ex uxore sua Elizabetha filia Thomæ Maisterson generosi quatuor habuit liberos, videlicet Richardum Wilbraham armigerum, Rogerum Wilbraham equitem auratu', Thomam Wilbraham generosum et Radulphum Wilbraham de Derfold, ar'. Obiit 2° die Feb. a° sui Jesu 1612. Ætatis sui 88°.

Iste primo genitus fuit filius Thomæ Wilbraham ar' (filii et hæredis Richardi Wilbraham ar', filii Richardi senioris prius memorati) ex Rachaele conjuge ejusdem Thomæ, filia et hærede Josuæ Clive de Huxley ar' susceptus; puer optimæ spei, candidissimæ indolis, ingeniiq' præcocissimi, qui dum procul prægressi vestigia, virtutem anhelans, sequeretur, animam in cursu hoc efflans, idem cœlum, idem et sepulchrum invenit. Obiit 23° die Julii a° salutis 1633. Ætatis 12°.

Near the above—

H. S. E.

ROGERUS WILBRAHAM de Vico Malbano Arm. Vir (ex indole) minime famæ appentens: Morem vero gravitate Scientiæ copia, vitæ integritate, non incelebris qui religionis, et Literarum Studiis pene totus incubuit: Nec amicis interim nec Patriæ defuit, Uxorem habuit Aliciam Dorfoldensem Cognatem sibi, et Cognominem, amore, et virtute multo intimius conjunctam; undecim liberorum pater, quatuor tantum

CHESHIRE

reliquit superstites, Duos filios, totidemque filias; Ranulphus natu maximus hoc posuit Monumentum Optimo parenti, filius pientissimus.

Obiit Anno { Æræ Christianæ MDCCVII. / Ætatis suæ LXXXV.

On a brass plate near the last monument, a long inscription relative to Ralph Wilbraham, who died 1637. The following lines are at the foot of it:—

Quas tulit acceptas Christi Wilbrahamus aurore,
In Christi moriens membra refudit opes;
Scilicet hæredem cum se sentiret Olympi,
Hæredem contra scripsit E ipse Deum.

On the opposite side—

M. S.

Thomæ Wetenhall de Vico Malbano in Com. Cest. Arm. et Catherinæ uxoris ejus ex qua unicum filium Thomam et quatuor filias Catharinam, Amiciam, Margareta, et Susannam seperstites suscepit qui quidum Thomas Obiit XVIIII° Octob-Anno MDCLXXVII° Cathaina vero XIV° Maij Anno MDCLXXXIII°.

On an altar tomb of red stone, is the figure of a Knight in armour, lying on an alabaster slab, the head reclining on the head of a lamb. The sides of the tomb are ornamented with shields bearing quatrefoils. The monument is much mutilated. It is said to be the memorial of a Sir John Cradock.

Under an achievement—

Anna uxor Johannis Brock, generosi, filia atq. hæres Gulielmi Mainwaring de Wico Malbano generosi, hic jacet sepulta: obiit quarto die Decembris a°. Domini 1666.

Under a painting of an aged man and woman, in the north transept—

Hereunder lyes the body of Thomas Church, gent. aged 71, who married Anne, daughter of Thomas Mainwaring, gent. and dye' the 6 of July, anno 1634.

A memorial of—

Thos. Wickstead, Esq. who died Jan. 11, 1769, aged 60, and of his wife Grissel, only daughter of Charles Fletcher, of Wigland, Esq. who died Aug. 18, 1784, aged 82.

In the Chancel, are two recumbent figures on an alabaster tomb, the male figure in a furred robe. It originally bore this inscription, now defaced:*—

Johannes Crewe, ex antiqua familiâ de Crewe, oriundus, vir pius, susceptum ex Alicia Manwaring uxore reliquit sobolem Ranulphum, Thomam, Lucretiam, Prudentiam. Vixit ann. 74, obiit anno domini 1598.

* Harl. M.SS.

The living is a Rectory; the present incumbent, the Rev. Anthony Clarkson, A. M. presented Jan. 2, 1793.

HISTORY.

ALVANDESTON,

Formed portion of the Nantwich Barony, and passed subsequently with the share of Phillippi Basset. It then gave name to a family which had possessions in it; and it is ascertained, that after the reign of Edw. I. the Mainwarings had an estate here. About the reign of Henry V. the manor was vested in the Bromleys, and continued in their descendants for many generations. Ultimately the lands became alienated, and the greater part of the village is now possessed by Messrs. Forster, of Nantwich. *Beam Heath*, noticed in the account of Nantwich, is in this township. It was granted to the Monks of Combermere, and the Inhabitants of Nantwich; and the confirmation of the latter's rights is given in a preceding page, together with the agreement witnessed by Reginald de Grey, Justice of Cheshire.— It was stipulated that it should for ever remain uninclosed; but in 1803, an Act of Parliament for its inclosure was generally agreed to. The heath contained about four hundred statute acres; and it was enacted that not more than two hundred acres should be turned into tillage; thirty acres to be appropriated to the cultivation of potatoes for the poor, and for the gravel pits and clay; a portion of it to be annually set apart for *an outlet or boozy pasture;* and a certain number of leys to be reserved for the resident householders of Nantwich. The Rector is entitled to the tithes of the portion in tillage; but the whole is exempt from the poor rates of the township.

In 1788, an old mansion, formerly the property of Richard Vernon, Esq. was purchased by Messrs. William and Thomas Forster.

LEIGHTON,

Is about five miles N. E. N. from Nantwich, and falling to the lot of Philippi Basset, subsequently passed to the Countess of Warwick, and from her to the Praers of Barthomley, and the Fulleshursts: it is now included in Lord Crewe's court leet for Crewe and Barthomley. At a very early period William (de Lecton) who assumed the local name, conveyed the manor to Randle de Oldeton; and about 1328, it was acquired by exchange with the Oldetons, by the Erdeswicks, and their posterity remained here till the 17th century. In 1625, it was bought by Lawrence Eyton; and the manerial right was vested in Henry Styche, Esq. of a Shropshire family. Passing to the Werdens, it is now by inheritance from them, the property of G. Harley Drummond, Esq. whose father purchased the great tithes from the Wilbrahams.

The *Hall* of Leighton has been converted into a Farm House.

The Brookes of Leighton, were descended from the Leightons; and their estate here, was purchased, temp. Elizabeth, in failure of issue male, by Lady Cholmondeley, and passed from her to the Cholmondeleys of Vale Royal.

WOOLSTANWOOD,

On the division of the Barony was shared by Phillippi, and Eleanor Basset: two-thirds of the homage and service to the former, and the remainder to the latter. The Bulkeley family had estates here; as had also the Griffins of Barterton, who possessed the Mill, and the chief house, the Egertons of Broxton, the Sparkes of Nantwich, and the Brookes of Leighton, who held from the Earl in capite.—Certain manerial rights were vested in the Cholmondeleys, certainly as early as the reign of Elizabeth; but they were purchased from them about the commencement of the present century, by the late Mrs. Anne Elcocke, of Poole, from whom they have passed to William Massey, Esq. her nephew.

NANTWICH-WILLASTON

Is principally the property of Wm. Sneyd, Esq.—The corn tithes are vested in the Rector of Nantwich; but the tithe on hay belongs to Miss Windsor, of Shrewsbury.

THE PARISH OF BADDILEY,

CONSISTS OF ONLY ONE TOWNSHIP.

BADDILEY.

It is situated about three miles S E. from Nantwich, and was parcel of the Barony of Wich Malbanc. Falling on its division to the share of Auda Malbanc, it eventually passed to the Vernons, and the Praers family; and from them to the families of Bromley, Mainwaring, and Hondford. The Bromleys released their interest in the estate to the Mainwarings, and it was for a long time divided between them, the Hondfords, and their representatives the Breretons. Subsequently, however, the Mainwarings were possessed of the whole of it; and it was sold by the executors of the late Sir Harry Mainwaring, Bart. to Wm. Rigby, Esq. of Oldfield Hall, who re-sold it to the guardians of Charles Wicksted, Esq. the present proprietor * The court baron, held for the Manor, is under the jurisdiction of Lord Dysart's leet for Faddiley.

* Lysons.

The *Hall*, the ancient seat of the Praers family, was composed of timber and plaister, and moated. There was a Park attached to it. Philip Mainwaring, Esq. who died in 1642,† left a valuable library here as an heir-loom, expressing also a desire that it should be increased by his successors; but it is not stated that this desire was attended to.

† Lysons.

Near the site of the Hall, which is occupied as a Farm-house, is

The CHURCH, dedicated to St. Michael, a mean building, originally of timber and plaister, like the barns in its vicinage. The nave has within the last few years been rebuilt with brick. It consists of a nave and chancel; and in the latter are some seats, with ancient carving, and the monument of Sir Thomas Mainwaring, Bart.

Underneath lyes interred Sir Thomas Mainwaring, Bart. son and heir of Sir John Mainwaring, Bart. the twenty-ninth heir-male of the Mainwarings of Peover, since King William the Conqueror's time. He married Martha, eldest daughter of William Lloyd, of Halghton, in the county of Flint, Esq. He departed this life ye 20th and was intered the 24th of September, in theyear of our Lord, 1726. The sd Dame Martha Mainwaring, his widow, whom he lovingly made his heir, survives: and in her dear memory of him erected this monument.

There are a few memorials to the Davenports, of Blackhurst.

The advowson of the living was originally attached to

CHESHIRE

the Manor; but was given by William de Praers, to the Abbey of Combermere, in 1354. It was reunited to the manor at the Dissolution; and the patronage is still retained by the Mainwarings of Peover.

The present Rector is the Rev. Peter Wright, presented February 14th, 1796; the Registers commence in 1579.

HISTORY.

WHITCHURCH PARISH,

EXTENDS INTO CHESHIRE, AND INCLUDES THE TOWNSHIPS OF

WIRSWALL, | MARBURY, | NORBURY.

WIRSWALL.—The whole of this manor, previous to the Conquest, was part of the possessions of King Harold. Afterwards it was included in the Barony of Wich Malbanc, and fell to the lot of Philippi Basset.—James Lord Audley, temp. Richard II. held two thirds of the Manor, which descended to the Touchetts. The Earls of Shrewsbury had lands here from the time of Henry VI. to Philip and Mary: and the manerial rights are now divided between Earl Shrewsbury and Lord Combermere.

On a commanding elevation, is situated the ancient *Hall* of the Wicksteds, who remained here many generations: towards the conclusion of the last century, Mary, daughter and heiress of Rich. Wicksted, Esq. married Simon Ethelston, of Marbury, whose grandson, the Rev. Charles Wicksted Ethelston, A. M. is the present owner.

THE PAROCHIAL CHAPELRY OF MARBURY.

MARBURY-CUM-QUOISLEY is about eight miles from Nantwich, and three from Whitchurch, in the neighbouring county of Salop. Although considered a distinct Parish, it is dependent on Whitchurch. The early descent of this manor is similar to that of the last-mentioned township. It was held from the Praers family by the Lords Strange. Temp. Richard II. Ankarett, daughter and heiress of John le Strange, married Richard Talbot, father of the great Earl of Shrewsbury. In the 40th Elizabeth, Edw. Talbot, Esq. and Jane his wife, for the sum of £2000. passed over the manor to Sir Thomas Egerton, Lord Keeper—and it is now the property of his descendant the present Earl of Bridgewater: it is somewhat remarkable that "notwithstanding the numerous and extensive purchases and acquisitions make by Lord Brackley in Cheshire, that this is the only manor vested in his lineal representative.*

QUOISLEY, or *Coisley*, is a hamlet of Marbury, formerly the property of the Order of St. John of Jerusalem. A considerable estate here is the property of John Knight, Esq. of Whitchurch, purchased in 1789.

Marley Hall—is in this hamlet, and for two centuries was the ancient seat of the Pooles; it is now a farmhouse. The Pooles, in a direct line, became extinct by the death of Charles Poole, Esq. whose daughter and heiress marrying Thomas Tatton, of Marley Green, died in 1731. The Tattons sold the estate to Robert Heath, Esq. of Hanley, in Norbury, and he bequeathed it to his cousin the Rev. Cudworth Poole, nephew of Charles Poole before-named. On his death it fell to his godson Domville Halsted, Esq. who assumed the name of Poole, and was father to Domville Halsted Cudworth Poole, the present proprietor. The present family of the Pooles, have erected a handsome mansion on the border of *Marbury Mere*, which is an extensive and picturesque lake.

Hadley Hall, in Marbury, formerly the seat of the Hulses, and a branch of the Breretons, is the property of the Rev. Mr. Ethelston, but is occupied by a farmer.

The CHURCH, which is of red stone, composed of nave, side aisles, chancel, and tower, is situated on a most romantic spot on the edge of the lake. It is of some antiquity; a range of pointed arches, divide the nave from the aisles. The chancel is altogether an

* Ormerod.

CHESHIRE

addition to the original structure. The Minister is appointed by the Rector of Whitchurch; but it is not ascertained when the Church was annexed to Whitchurch. The Registers commence in 1538.

In 1688, a *School House* was built by subscription; but the endowment by Mrs. Bickerton extended only to four Children.

NORBURY.

The descent of this township is similar to the two last, as it respects the inheritance from the Nantwich Barony. Early in the 16th century, the manor was vested in the Crown; and in 1543, was granted to Sir Thomas Gresham, who soon afterwards conveyed it to Sir Hugh Cholmondeley, who was Knighted in 1544, and from him has descended to the present Marquis.

Althurst, or *Altridge Hall*, was for many years the residence of the Cholmondeleys, but it was taken down many years ago. The *Manors* of Norbury and Althurst (say the Lysons), have descended to the present Marquis of Cholmondeley. A younger branch of the Bromley family, now extinct, were settled for a considerable time at the *Lower House*, in Norbury, and are said* to have possessed, in 1662, a third part of the manor.—Roger, a younger son of William Bulkeley, settled at Norbury, upon an estate given to him by his father, and assumed the local name. Of this family was Sir John Norbury, Lord Treasurer of England, whose descendants settled in Surrey. He was the son of David Norbury, whose daughter and heiress brought the estate here in marriage to Sir Wm. Hulse, and his posterity resided in the township many generations, but in the end they removed to Astley, in Quoisley. Sir Hugh Hulse, Chief Justice of the King's Bench, who was made one of the five Judges by Richard II. on his assumption of the Government in 1389, was son of a younger brother of Sir William: Sir Hugh's granddaughter and heiress married Sir Wm. Troutbeck.

* Harl. MSS.

HISTORY.

Hanley Park, was for many years the residence of the Heaths; but on the death of Robt. Heath, Esq. in 1766, it passed with Marley Hall.

Swanwick was the seat of a family of that name, who long resided there, and were originally from Wirswall: it is supposed they became extinct about 1600.

AUDLEM PARISH,

CONTAINS THE TOWNSHIPS OF

AUDLEM, BUERTON, HANKELOW, TITTENLEY,

AND PART OF

DODCOTT-CUM-WILKESLEY, AND SOUND.*

* See Wrenbury.

AUDLEM, or *Aldelime*, is about seven miles S. E. from Nantwich, and formed portion of the Shipbrook Barony. Very soon after the Conquest, the Traylebewes were the mesne lords, and eventually assumed the local name, continuing in possession till the time of Edward III. when a division of the manor took place between the aunts (coheirs) of Sir Thomas de Aldelym, married in the families of *Hoghe* and *Wrenbury*. The Hough division, after a long succession, was purchased by Wm. Mascie, Esq. The Wrenbury division descended from the Wrenburys, to the Wettenhalls, and the subdivision of this moiety, passed with their other estates, to the Tomkinsons, from whom it was purchased by Mascie Taylor, Esq. of Chester. The Massey subdivision of Audlem descended to the Masseys of Tatton; but the whole of the property is now enjoyed by M. Taylor, Esq.

Moss Hall, belongs to Mr. Taylor, and is of some antiquity, composed of timber and plaister, and lighted by bay windows. So late as the year 1760 it was the seat of the Mascies and the Taylors.

In the 24th Edw. I. a Charter for a fair and weekly market, was granted to Sir Thomas de Aldelym, but it subsequently fell into disuse; in 1817, however, it was revived by the present lord of the manor, M. Taylor, Esq. to take place annually on the day after the Feast of St. James the Apostle.

CHESHIRE

THE CHURCH, which is dedicated to St. James, was given, temp. Edward I. by Thomas de Aldelym to St. Thomas's Priory, at Stafford, and it was afterwards appropriated by the Friars.

At the Dissolution, the appropriation and advowson, were granted by Patent to Rowland Lee, then Bishop of Lichfield and Coventry. Eventually, they passed by sale to the Cottons, of Combermere, and are now possessed by the Right Honorable Lord Combermere.

The present Rector is the Rev. Wm. Cotton, LL. B. presented Oct. 18, 1802. The Registers commence in 1642:

The Church consists of nave, chancel, side aisles, and tower. Six pointed Gothic arches on the south, and five on the south side, divide the nave from the aisles. It is an ancient building, in a truly picturesque situation. The Hankelow chancel is at the end of the north aisle.

The following inscriptions are on tablets in the Chancel—

Sacred to the memory of Nathaniel Wetenhall, Esq. son of Gabriel Wetenhall, Esq. and Catherine Cope. He married Arabella, daughter of Brigadier-General Edward Montague, only brother of George Earl of Halifax. He died in the 77th year of his age, 1778, Feb. 6. His remains, and those of his father and mother, are deposited in this chancel. This monument is erected by his affectionate widow Arabella Wetenhall.

On an adjoining monument—

Near this place are deposited the remains of Arabella, daughter of Brigadier-General Montague, and widow of Nathaniel Wetenhall, Esq. who died July 20, 1798, aged 85 years. In memory of her many virtues, and as a tribute of grateful affection, this tablet was erected by the Honorable Martha Vernon.

BUERTON

Is about seven miles and a half S. S. E. from Nantwich. It was included in the possessions of William de Malbanc, and passed to the share of Philippi Basset, but the mesne royalty became vested in a family which assumed the name of the township, and passed from them to the Houghs and the Pooles, in whom it continued till 1725, when F. Poole, Esq. sold the manor to the Broughtons, and it is now the property of Gen. Sir John Delves Broughton, Bart.

HISTORY.

The Gamuls, originally of a Staffordshire family, were settled here certainly as early as the reign of Edw IV. and of this family was the eminently faithful Sir Francis Gamul, whom Charles I. created a Baronet. He was dispossessed of his seat here by the tyrants of the day, and his life estate in it was sold to Wm. Plymley, of Norton, Salop, Gent. in 1653.* On the death of Sir Francis, however, in the following year, the property reverted to his daughters, his son dying without issue: and Mr. Brerewood who married Sidney, sold the estate to Sir Geo. Warburton.

The site of the *Old Hall*, is occupied as a farm-house, the property of Sir J. D. Broughton, Bart.

TITLEY,

Or *Tittenley*, was also a portion of the Nantwich Barony, and passed afterwards to the Vernons and the Savages. Temp. Edward I. Thomas de Titesle, was the mesne lord and his successors, who continued the local name, were settled here as late as the reign of Henry VIII. about which time Humphrey Titley sold his property to Robt. Needham, for £500.

There was a *Park* attached to the *Hall* of Titley.—Lord Kilmorey is the present proprietor.

HANKELOW

Is about five miles S. E. from Nantwich, and it is highly probable was included in the possessions of the Baron of Wich Malbanc. Its descent to the Vernons is similar to that of Titley. Under the latter it was held by the Hassals for ten generations; but on the division of the estates of Ralph Hassal, in 1622, the manor became the property of Wm. his youngest son, and afterwards of the two daughters of William, married to John and Rowland Wibbenbury. Rowland purchased his brother's interest; and the whole was afterwards purchased by James Bayley, Esq. of Wistaston, grandfather of the present proprietor, and lord of the manor.

The *Hall* of Hankelow is a handsome mansion of brick, and was sold by Mr. J. Richardson of Beeston, (whose father bought it from the Wetenhalls) in 1817, to Thos. Cooper, Esq.—The Wetenhalls of Hankelow were a family of great respectability, and it is supposed became extinct in the direct line in 1663.

The portion of the townships of *Newhall* and *Dodcott-cum-Wilkesley*, are spoken of elsewhere.

* The only original picture of Sir Francis, is in the possession of the Rev. T. Edwards, of Aldford.

PARISH OF WYBUNBURY,

CONTAINS THE TOWNSHIPS OF

WYBUNBURY,	HATHERTON,	BLAKENHALL,
WILLASTON,	BASFORD,	CHECKLEY,
STAPELEY,	SHAVINGTON,	BRIDGEMERE,
ROPE,	WESTON,	HUNSTERTON,
BARTERTON,	CHORLTON,	LEA,
HOUGH,	WALGHERTON,	DODDINGTON.

WYBUNBURY

Is situated close to the borders of Staffordshire, and about three miles E. from Nantwich. Previous to the Conquest it was included in the possessions of the Bishop of Lichfield, and continued so vested till the removal of the see to Chester, temp. William I. Under the Bishop it is supposed to have been held by the Barons of Nantwich. It afterwards passed to the Vernons, and under them was held by the Praers family.
* 1277. Temp. Edw. I.* Robert de Prayers, gave up the manor and Church to the Bishop of Lichfield and Coventry, and they are now vested in his successors, under whom the Rev. Robt. Hill, of the Hough, is the lessee of the manor. The Rectory is divided: John Mellor, Esq. has lease of the tithe of corn and hay, for Backenhall, Bridgemere, Checkley, Chorlton, Doddington, Hatherton, Hunsterton, and Walgherton; Richard Congreve, Esq. of Burton, Wirral, and his sister, are lessees of the tithes of the other townships, excepting, however, two-thirds of Willaston, which belong to the Dean and Chapter of Chester.

The CHURCH is dedicated to St. Chad, and consists of nave, chancel, side aisles, and tower, which has six bells. The sides of the great western door are carved in several episcopal figures; over one of the windows, is a statue of the Virgin and Child. Six fine pointed arches separate the nave and side aisles. The roof, which is of oak, is richly carved in a variety of armorial devices, &c. The tower is lofty, supported by buttresses, and terminated with pinnacles. It is apprehended, however, that it is in a dangerous state: it leans considerably in a direction nearly N. E. drawing with it in the same direction, the body of the Church itself.

In the south aisle is an altar tomb, canopied by a large arch of white marble. Reclining on it are the figures of a Knight and his Lady; the former clad in mail. The inscription—

Here lieth Sr Thomas Smith, of Hough, Kt. and Dame Anne his wife, doughter to Sr Wm. Brereton, of Brereton, Knt. who had issue one sonn and one daughtr. whch Sr Thomas died the 21st of December, 1614, whose ladie in remembrance gave him this monument.

In the nave, a monument, the inscription nearly illegible, but blanks are left for the dates. The following is stated to have been the inscription*— * See Orm. p. 253. Harl. MSS. 2151,111.

Virtuti et dignitati Joannis Woodnet armigeri, Shaventoniæ Woodnetensis domini, viri prosapi et antiquo stemmate, legum Angliæ piissimi et consulti Professoris, Cestrescirensis nobilitatis antiquatæ assertoris egregii, rerum heroicarum jurisq. honorarii, scientissimi, qui adversis aliquamdiu jactatus, tandem (Christo vindice) hic in sepulchris majorum pacificum quietis portum appulit, et resurrectionem beatificam expectat.

Quid gloriaris carnem? Heu, Vermem!
Quid antiqua predia? imo tædia.
Quid generis splendorem? ah rorem!
Quid longa serie clavos repetivos atavos
Et affines? ecce finis?
Solum Jesum Christum tibi crucifixum
Et te mundo gloriare.
Obdormivit placentissime in Christo —— die ——
anno salutis —— ætatisq.

At the end of the north aisle, two figures in brass of a warrior and his lady;—the inscription is—

CHESHIRE

Here lyeth Rafe Delves, esquyer, of Dodenton, and Katerine his wyfe, the whiche Rafe died the seconde day of Marche in the yeare of owr Lord God A MCCCCC and XIII, on whose sowllys Allmyghty Jhu have mercy.

At the east end of the same aisle, on tablets—

P. M. Henrici Delves de Dodington, Baronetti, (Thomæ filii) qui Catherinam, Rogeri Wilbraham, equ. aur. uniusq. magistrorum libellorum supplicum, filiam et cohæredem, primo in uxorem duxit: e qua filios Henricum et Thomam in cunis defunctos, ac Thomam Delves, Bar: filias vero, Mariam Tho. Mainwaring de Pever, Bar: Katherinam Edw° Glegg de Gayton, ar: et Graciam Josuæ Edisbury, (filio et hæredi Johannis Edisbury) de Pentry yr Claud in agro Denbigh, ar. enuptas genuit; deinde Mariam, Ranulphi Leicester, civis Lond. filiam, copulavit. Qui quidem Henricus obiit XXIII° Maii a° ab incarnat. D'ni MDCLXIII° ætat. LXIII°.

P. M. Thomæ Delves de Dodington, eq. aur. et Baronetti, (Henrici filii) qui Mariam Thomæ Wilbraham de Woodhey natam primo in uxorem duxit, e qua Henricum Delves, Baronettum, Laurentium vero, Ricardum ac Thomam sine prole defunct filios suscitavit. Deinde Mariam, Edwardi Baber, de Chew, in com. Somersetensi, servientis ad legem, unam filiarum, (Roger. Wilbraham, mil. unius magistrorum libell: supplicum relictam) copulavit qui quidem Thomas patriæ charus, præcipua cujus munera maximo cum honore subivit, obiit XXIII° Apr. a° ab incarn. D'ni MDCXLVIII°, ætatis LXXIIII°. Posito hoc marmore a° D'ni MDCLXIX.

Beneath the tablets—

Prædict. Tho. Delves, Bar: qui hæc monum. posuit, duxit in uxore. Eliz. filiam unicam Halli Ravenscroft de Horsham, in Sussexia, ar: sub tumulo marm. in ecclesia. Horsham prædict. conditamq. e qua suscepit Mariam in cunis defunctam, et Thom' ac Henricu' superstites.

* There was a *School House* at Wybunbury, built by subscription about two centuries ago; in 1707, Thos. Heath bequeathed a Cottage as a residence for a Schoolmaster, and a portion of his personal estate to instruct poor children. The money amounted to £100. and it was appropriated in 1735, and 1748, to the purchase of lands, which† produced £30. per ann. of which sum £14. 13*s*. 4*d*. is devoted to the purposes of the School. This, with some trifling donations, and the rent of a few houses, is the whole endowment. The scholars are taught reading, writing, and accounts.

*Lysons.

† 1810.

The present Rector is the Rev. J. F. Muccleston, A. M. presented Feb. 5, 1802.

WILLASTON,

Formerly called *Wigstanton*, and vulgarly *Wisterson*, is partly situated in Wybunbury parish, and partly in Nantwich parish. It was included in the Barony of the latter place, and passed to the share of Phillipi Basset, under whose descendants it was held by the family of Cheney, or Chanu, as early as the reign of Edw. I. It was vested in their posterity till 1533, when John Cheney, Esq. conveyed it to Richard Sneyd, Esq. Recorder of Chester. From him descended the Sneyds of Keele and Bradwell, Staffordshire, and in their representative the manor is now vested.

HISTORY.

Bressey, or *Brassey Hall*, in this township, is a venerable mansion, formerly a seat of the respectable family of the Brasseys.

A handsome mansion, built by Mr. John Bayley, of Nantwich, is now the property, by marriage with his daughter, of Charles Salmon, Esq.

STAPELEY

Is about two miles and a half from Nantwich, and originally formed part of the Nantwich Barony. It was subsequently held by the Vernons and Audleys; and Richard de Audley made a grant of the whole to Peter de Stapeley, who held it by the tenth part of a Knight's service. Peter was the grandson of Reginald Fitz Herchenbald, who was Seneschall of Nantwich in the 12th century.‡

‡ Ormerod.

In the 24th Edward III. the manor was purchased by Richard Rope; whose descendants continued here many centuries. It would seem, however, that a division of the property had taken place, for we find from an Inquisition p. m. 4th Elizabeth, that Laurence de Rope, died possessed of *a moiety* of the manor only; but his grand-daughter Cicily, is described‖ as bringing the manor in marriage to her husband Richard Greene, of Congleton.

‖ Vill. Cest.

In 1662, the Earl of Ardglass, *Mr. Milton*, and Richard Green, were joint Lords, but it is unknown how they obtained possession. The share of Green was purchased by Milton, and afterwards was held by the family of Stubbs.

In 1765, the late Mr. William Salmon, of Nantwich, purchased the property; and it is now held by Charles Salmon, Esq. and William Salmon (minor) nephew of Charles Salmon.

The *Hall* of Stapeley is the property of James Bayley, Esq.—There is an elegant mansion here belonging to William Harwood Folliott, Esq. of Chester, inherited by him in right of his wife Catherine, the daughter and heiress of John Burscoe, Esq.§

§ See Thornton.

ROPE

Is about two miles and a half E. N. E. from Nantwich, and together with the last township, formed part of the Fee of the Nantwich Barony. It was apportioned on the division of the estates, to Philippi Basset; and became eventually, (the descent not known) the property of the Ropes. Lawrence Rope, Esq. dying without issue in 1580, the manor was purchased by Henry Delves, Esq. It afterwards passed with Doddington to the Broughtons, and is now the property of Sir John Delves Broughton, Baronet, a General in the Army.

BARTERTON,

Is two miles S. S. E. from Nantwich, and being a part of the Barony, passed to the Audleys. About the reign of King John, Wm. Ruffus, who resided here, was the mesne Lord, and sold it to Bertram de Griffin, for 100 marks, to be held by payment of 13*s.* 4*d.* homage and service, and the annual presentation of a pair of gilt spurs. James de Audley, the Chief Lord, also granted to Griffin an acquittance from pasture for his perambulatory Serjeants of the Peace. The Griffins continued in possession for many generations; and about the middle of the 17th century, Richard Griffin, Esq. sold the manor to Thomas Delves, from whom it passed to his descendant, Sir J. D. Broughton, Bart.

The *Hall* of Barterton, formerly the seat of the Griffins, is occupied by a farmer.

HOUGH

Is about three miles E. S. from Nantwich. It is not noticed in Domesday, but it is supposed it formed part of the Barony of Wich Malbanc, and passed to the Praers family, under whom it was held by a family which assumed the local name. Temp. Richard II. on the death of Richard Hough, Ellen and Margaret his daughters, were left coheiresses. Ellen married Richard del Massye, a younger branch of the Sale family, and eventually obtained possession of the entire manor, which descended to his heirs.

About 1517, Thomas Smith, Alderman of Chester, purchased the property from Ralph Mascy, Gent. with other estates in Aldelym, Nantwich, &c. He was subsequently several times Mayor of Chester, and was Knighted. On the termination of the male line of the Smiths, towards the close of the 17th century, the manor was purchased by the Walthalls, of Wistaston.

In 1763, in exchange for a moiety of Wistaston, Peter Walthall passed the manor to Sir Bryan Broughton Delves, Bart. and the manor is now the property of Sir J. D. Broughton.

A mansion in Hough, now the residence and property of the Rev. Robt. Hill, was formerly the seat of the Bromhalls. In 1806, the Cliffe estate, the residence of the late Robt. Clarke, Esq. was purchased by Sir Thos. Broughton, Bart.

HATHERTON

Is about four miles S. E. S. from Nantwich; and although originally parcel of the Barony, was severed from it, and possessed by the Orrebys, from whom it passed to the Rod's and the Corbets. About 1576, Thomas Hulse, heir of Robert Corbet, sold the manor to the Smiths, of Chester.*

The Manor of Hatherton, was sold by the representatives of Sir Thomas Smith, about 1700, to Mr. Salmon, and in 1784, it was purchased from his grandson by Charles Bate, Esq of Nantwich. Mr Bate, dying in 1814, left the manor to his wife, on her death to her nephew Mr. Matthew Mare, of Basford, co. Staff. and to his issue male; the remainder to his brother Matthew Mare, &c.

The site of *Hatherton Hall*, the ancient seat of the Smiths, is occupied by a farm house, the property of Mrs. Sparrow.

BASFORD,

Or *Barkersford*, (spelt *Berchesford* in Domesday) is about five miles E. from Nantwich, and after forming a part of the Barony, passed to the Audleys. The mesne manor, was divided between the Harcourts and Woodnoths, but the division and descent of the latter is unknown. Temp. Edw. II. Robert, the son of Robert de Harcourt gave a fourth of the waste to Robert the son of William de Praers; and in 1298, a similar grant was made to Robert Vicar of Wybunbury, by Robert Woodnoth. The manerial rights of the Harcourts passed with an heiress to Hugh Cholmondeley, whose daughter and heiress Lettice married R. Bromley. The Bromleys continued here many years; and about 1563, the reversion of the manor was sold by John Bromley,

* It is remarkable that in 1625, Sir T. Smith served at the same time the offices of Mayor of Chester, and High Sheriff of the county.

to Thomas Clutton. It appears Sir Hugh Cholmondeley died seized of the Clutton share (by purchase) 39th Elizabeth. Sir Hugh Cholmondeley the younger, afterwards gave the manor to his son Thomas Cholmondeley, of Vale Royal; but it was subsequently sold by the devisees of Seymour Cholmondeley, Esq. to Dr. Joseph Crewe, Rector of Barthomley, whose son John Crewe, Esq. re-sold it to the late Rev. Sir Thomas Broughton, Bart. It is now the property of his son, Sir J. D. Broughton, Bart.

About 1700, *Basford Hall*, the ancient seat of the Bromleys and Cholmondeleys, was destroyed by fire; its site is occupied by a farm-house.

SHAVINGTON,

Shavington cum Gresty, or *Shavington Woodnoth*, is about four miles and a half E. from Nantwich. It formed originally two manors, and passed from the Nantwich Baronial possessors to the Vernons, in marriage with Auda Malbanc. The Woodnoths were the mesne Lords for a long succession of generations, certainly as early as the reign of Henry III. They became extinct in the male line in 1637,* and in 1666 the Smyths of Hough were in possession, and the descent subsequently appears the same as that of Hatherton to the family of Mares.

The Manor of GRESTY was possessed by Sir John Griffyn, temp. Hen. IV. and became divided in territory after the reign of Henry. V. for in the 15th Henry VI † it appears that Robert Davenport held a moiety of *two barbed arrows* in *Grayston*, &c. as an appendage of the Nantwich Barony. Towards the conclusion of the reign of Elizabeth the share of the Davenports in the Barony of Nantwich was purchased by Sir Hugh Cholmondeley; this sale of course included Gresty. This portion is now the property of Sir J. D. Brongton, Bt. the other portion passed to the Bates, of Nantwich.

In 1661, *Shavington Hall demesne*, the ancient seat of the Woodnoths, was purchased by the ancestor of the present proprietor, John Turner, Esq. who has erected a handsome mansion on the site of it.

WESTON

Is about six miles N. E. from Nantwich. It is not noticed in the Survey, but it is supposed to have been antecedently included in the possessions of Earl (King) Harold. The Griffyns of Barterton exercised manerial rights here as early as the reign of Edw. II. but on the death of John Griffin, temp. Henry IV. the manerial rights became vested in the Smiths of Hough. Eventually the manor became the property of the Delves family, and it is now that of their descendant, Sir J. D. Broughton, Bart.

Weston Hall is occupied as a farm-house.

CHORLTON,

Is about five miles and a half S. E. from Nantwich, and formed part of the Nantwich Barony. Two parts of it, subsequently to the division, was possessed by the Griffyns; the other part was vested in Thomas, son of Roger de Chorleton. Temp. Edward II. the entire manor was the property of Robert de Praers. Temp. Edw. III. a sixth of the manor was obtained by John Delves, from John Bresey, who had married an heiress of the Praers family. In the reign of Richard II. Isabel, widow of Sir John Delves, had the whole of the manor, which has descended to Sir John Delves Broughton, Bart.

WALGHERTON,

Is about four miles S. E. E. from Nantwich, and formed part of the Barony; but on the partition, it fell to the share of the Vernons. About 1270, the manor was conveyed by Henry de Waschet to Fulke de Orreby, from whom it passed to the Corbets and Smiths, with Hatherton. In 1666, the manor was the joint property of Sir Thomas Smith, and Sir Geo. Vernon.—In 1668, it was conveyed by George Vernon and others to Hall Ravenscroft, Esq. whose daughter and heiress marrying Thomas Delves, Esq of Doddington, the manor has passed to his descendant Sir J. D. Broughton, Bart.

It appears, that so early as 1539, the Hall demesne was purchased by Sir Henry Delves, from Richard Kardiff.‡

‡ Lysons, page 83[illegible].

BLAKENHALL,

Is about five miles and a half S. E. E from Nantwich. Unlike the last-mentioned township, it was included in the possessions of the Baron of Kinderton.—In the time of Henry I. it was possessed by a family which bore the local name, and they continued to hold the manor for several generations. About the middle of the reign of Richard II. John Delves bought it from Thomas de Blackenhale, but it was held from the fee of

CHESHIRE

HISTORY.

Kinderton. Sir John Delves Broughton, Bart. is the present proprietor.

CHECKLEY

Formerly called *Chacklegh*, or *Chackley*, is about seven miles S. E. E. from Nantwich; and with Bridgemere, Hunsterton, Lea, and Doddington, is supposed to have been included in the vill of Blakenhall.* It is partly in the county of Stafford.—The Lysons thus state the descent: the manor was at a very early period vested in the Praers family, and passed from them with a female heir to the Blakenhalls. Temp. Edward III. a third of it was the property of John Bressey, and he sold it to Sir John Delves. The residue passed with other female heirs to the families of Malpas and Perhall, or Persall. About 1662, Thomas Delves, Esq. afterwards Sir Thomas Delves, Bart. purchased it from Sir John Persall, and it has descended to the present proprietor Sir J. D. Broughton, Bart.

* Ormerod p. 264.

Checkley Hall, the ancient seat of the Persalls, is occupied as a farm-house.

Heywood Barnes, an estate possessing manerial rights, was bequeathed by the late Rev. Sir Thos. Broughton, Bart. to his youngest son, the Rev. H. D. Broughton, of Broughton, Staffordshire, into which county the property runs.

Wrinehill, is a hamlet of Checkley, which is often termed *Checkley cum Wrinehill*: it is in Staffordshire, and therefore beyond the boundary of this work. It passed from the Hawkstones to the Egertons, of Egerton, and is now the property of the Earl of Wilton.

BRIDGEMERE,

Or *Bridesmere*, it is supposed was included with Blakenhall in the Barony of Kinderton. Long before the 8th Richard II. it was possessed by a family who took the local name. Richard de Bridesmere dying temp. Henry IV. left Thomas Maylor and Richard de Madeley, his heirs, but Richard de Madeley, having killed John de Birches,† the whole was vested in Richard de Maylor. It afterwards passed to the Hulses; but before the reign of James I. it reverted to the Vernons as paramount lords. Sir Bryan Broughton Delves, Bart. having purchased the manor from Lord Vernon, it is now the property of Sir J. D. Broughton, Bart.

† Ormerod.

HUNSTERTON,

Or *Hunsterson*, is about five and a half miles S. E. from Nantwich, and was also included in the Vill of Blackenhall. It was continued in the estates of the Kinderton Barony till 1762, when it was purchased by Sir Bryan Broughton Delves, Bart. The mesne manor was vested in a family which took the name of the township, certainly before the reign of Edward III. The manerial rights have long since been disused. The Delves family had a very early proprietary share of lands here, as had also the Mores, of Hall o' Heath.

LEA,

Or *Lee*, it is conjectured, was parcel of the vill of Blackenhall, and is five miles S. E. from Nantwich, pleasantly situated on the margin of a small stream. A family which settled here at an early date, assumed the local name, and from a younger branch, which afterwards settled at Quarendon, Buckinghamshire, sprang the Lees, Earls of Lichfield. The township was for many generations held by the parent stock under the Kinderton Barony, by military service. Temp. Car. I. Hen. Lee, Esq. sold the whole to Hen. Delves, Esq. of Doddington, in whose descendant Sir J. D. Broughton, Bart. it is now vested. The site of the old *Hall* is occupied as a farm-house.

DODDINGTON

Was included in Blakenhall vill, attached to the Kinderton Barony. It lies about five miles and a half S. E. E. from Nantwich. Previous to the reign of Edw. II. a family which took the name of the township had possessions here. The mesne manor, which had been vested in the family of Praers, was, with Blackenhall, and one sixth of Chorleton, passed, temp. Edward III. to John Delves, by John Bresey, who it is supposed, married the heiress of Wm. Praers.

The Delves's, were originally of Delves Hall, in the county of Stafford.

Richard de Delves his son, was, temp. Edward II. constable of *Heleigh* Castle.' John de Delves, third in descent, was one of Lord Audley's esquires at the Battle of Poictiers, where he distinguished himself by his valor, and had a grant of part of Lord Audley's armorial bearings. He was appointed Esquire of the body to Edward III. and was Knighted by that monarch in the 33d year of his reign. In the 38th of the same King, he was appointed one of the Judges of the King's Bench, and deputy to the Justice of Chester, and in the same year, had license to fortify his house at Doddington. He founded a Chantry in Handbridge, in Chester, which he handsomely endowed, and died in 1369 without issue. He was buried in Audley Church, in Staffordshire, where a handsome monument with his effigy is erected.

John Delves, nephew of the last, and fourth in descent, represented the county of Stafford, in Parliament, and died 18th Richard II.

John Delves (5th) his son and heir, served in the wars in France in the reign of Henry IV. He died 7th Henry VI.

Richard Delves (6th) died in the 24th Henry VI. and was succeeded by his brother and heir.

John Delves (7th) was appointed Warden of all the Mints in England; was a strong partizan of Hen. VI. against the House of York. He was proclaimed a rebel, traitor, and enemy at Westminster, 11th Edward IV. In 1460, Queen Margaret gave him the charge of Sir John and Sir Thomas Neville, sons of the Earl of Shrewsbury, then Prisoners in Chester Castle. In 1471, he was killed at the Battle of Shrewsbury, and attainted the year following.

John (8th) his son was taken prisoner at Tewksbury, and afterwards beheaded.

Ralph (9th) and Henry (10th) succeeded.

Sir Henry Delves (11th) cousin of the last, was Sheriff of Cheshire in the 29th and 37th Henry VIII. and subsequently represented the county in Parliament.—He died Aug. 6, 1559, and was buried at Wybunbury.

John Delves (12th) died in June, 12th Elizabeth; and Henry Delves (13th) took part with the unfortunate Charles I. against his Parliament.—The Castle of Doddington was taken possession of by the Parliament troops, early in the contest, and surrendered, with the garrison of one hundred and fifty men, to Lord Byron, on the 4th Jan. 1644. In February following it was again possessed by the Parliament.

The last Baronet in the direct male line was Sir Thomas Delves (17th) who died in 1752, and his daughter and heiress Elizabeth marrying Sir Bryan Broughton, Baronet; Doddington, with the other estates, has descended to his representative, the present proprietor, Sir John Delves Broughton, Bart.

Doddington Hall is a handsome and spacious edifice of stone, the building of which was commenced about the year 1777, after designs by Mr. Samuel Wyatt.—It is situated in a fine, extensive Park, in which is a beautiful avenue of venerable oaks. On the south side is a fine lake.

Near the north front, are the remains of the ancient castellated mansion, built about 1364. The Doddington Hall, mentioned in the Diary of the siege of Nantwich, no longer exists; in the portico of it, were the figures of the Lord Audley and his Esquires, which were removed to the staircase of the ancient family mansion, on the Hall being taken down; and there they still remain.

END OF ITINERARY OF NANTWICH HUNDRED.

PLAN OF BICTON CASTLE.

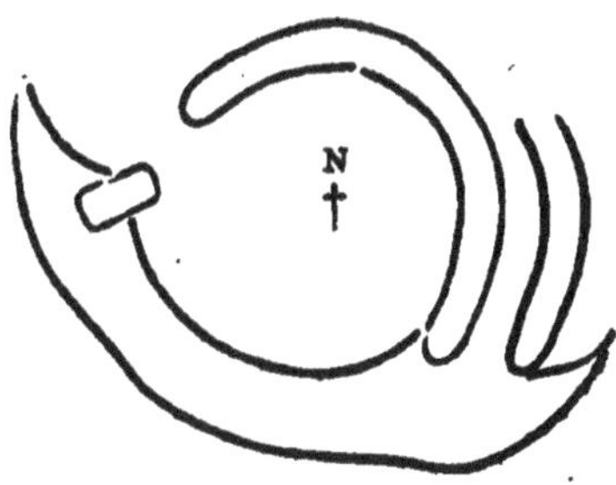

The Hundred of Macclesfield,

CONTAINS THE PARISHES OF

ALDERLEY,	MOTTRAM-IN-LONGDENDALE,	STOCKPORT,
ASTBURY, (PART OF)	PRESTBURY,	TAXALL,
CHEADLE,	ROSTHERN, (PART OF)	AND
GAWSWORTH,		WILMSLOW.

THE PARISH OF GAWSWORTH,

CONTAINS ONLY ONE TOWNSHIP,

GAWSWORTH,

CHESHIRE

WHICH lies about three miles S. W. from Macclesfield, and has five nominal divisions, *Tidnor-end*, *Shallow-end*, *Stubbs-end*, *Mill-end*, and *Woodhouse-end*.—It appears from the Survey, that it was included in the possessions of the Earl, and held by him. Earl Randle, however, granted to Hugh the son of Bigod, the manor of Gawsworth, together with the right of holding his own Courts, without pleading at Macclesfield, rendering, annually, to the Earl, a caparisoned horse. The Aldfords succeeded to Bigod's estates, and Richard de Aldford subsequently granted to Herbert de Orreby, the manor in fee, with acquittance of all service, except finding one man in time of war to assist in the defence of Aldford Castle. The Orrebys continued in possession till the reign of Edward I. when Thomas de Orreby dying, the manor passed in marriage with his heiress Isabella, to Thomas Fitton. The succession of the Fittons continued till the death of Sir Edw. Fitton, Bart. in 1643, who left the manor to his nephew Chas. Gerard, first Earl of Macclesfield. Immediately on the death of Sir Edward Fitton,* his four sisters—Penelope, who married Sir Charles Gerard, Knt. Mary, the wife of Sir John Brereton, Knt. Jane, the wife of Thomas Minshull, Esq. and Frances, wife of Henry Mainwaring, Esq. took possession of his estates; but they were ejected by Wm. Fitton, grandson of Sir Edw. Fitton, then Treasurer of Ireland, who claimed under a deed of Sir Edward's in favor of his next male heir. At the Restoration, however, Sir Edward's will in favor of his nephew, Charles Gerard, was fully established. The litigation between the families was long and rancorous; and it is stated in a rare pamphlet printed at the Hague in 1663, that the deed under which William Gerard held, had been forged, to accomplish which several had joined in a Conspiracy.† Mr Ormerod says, "whether the conduct of Fitton was met by similar guilt on the part of Lord Gerard, God only can judge; but his hand fell heavily on the representatives of that noble house: in less than half a century the husbands of its two coheiresses, James Duke of Hamilton, and Chas. Lord Mohen, were slain by each others hands, in a murderous duel, arising out of a dispute relative to the partition of the Fitton estates; and Gawsworth itself passed to an unlineal hand, by a series of alienations complicated beyond example in the annals of the county." But to proceed with the descent of the manor:

HISTORY.

From the second Earl of Macclesfield it passed to Lady Mohun, the daughter and heiress of his sister and coheiress Charlotte Mainwaring. Under the will of

* Lysons.

† See this more at length, in Mr. Ormerod's History of Cheshire, under the head—Gawsworth, page 291.

CHESHIRE

Lord Mohun, it became afterwards the property of his second wife Elizabeth Lawrence, from whom it passed to her daughter Ann Griffith, (by a first marriage,) and was purchased, together with Bosley, in 1727, by her husband the Right Hon. Wm. Stanhope, Vice Chamberlain of the Household. It is now vested in his descendant, the Earl of Harrington—who holds a Court Leet and Baron for this manor and Bosley.

The township is built in a very straggling manner, but the situation is rather picturesque, on the side of the road to Congleton.

The *Old Hall* of Gawsworth is a short distance west of the *Church*, situated on a pleasant bank; and from what remains may be traced its original quadrangular form. It is composed of timber and plaister. Over the door-way, are carved the arms of Fitton, and as a motto on the garter which ornaments them, are the words "FIT ONVS LEVE." Beneath—

Hæc sculptura facta fuit apud Calviæ in Hibernia per Richardum Rany, Edwardo Fyton, milite primo d'no presidente totius provinciæ Conatiæ et Thomoniæ, anno D'ni 1570.

The grounds are diversified, and have been laid out with considerable taste, according to the times in which they flourished. In the midst of them, is a memorial to the singular Author of the play of *Hurlothrumbo*, performed at the Haymarket Theatre in 1722; he was a dancing master, and contrived to be introduced as a table companion to the principal families of the neighbourhood:—

Uuder this stone rest the remains of Mr. Samuel Johnson, afterwards ennobled with the grander title of Lord Flame; who after having been in his life distinct from other men, by the eccentricities of his genius, chose to retain the same character after his death, and was at his own desire buried here, May 5, A. D. MDCCLXXIII, aged 82.*

The last built Hall of Gawsworth, erected by Lord Mohun, is of brick, very plain in its design, and has occasionally been used as a residence by Lord Harrington.

HISTORY.

There is a large painting of F. Fitton, Esq. in one of the rooms, around the frame of which is inscribed—

"Francis Fyton, married wt Katherine Countes of Northu'br. dowger, a° 1588, eldest of the daughters and coheires of Joh' Nevill, Kt. Lord Latymer, being thyrd sone of Edward Fyton, of Gawsworth, Kt. (who married Mary ye younger doughter and coheir of Sir Vigitt Harbutell, in Northu'br. Kn. and Elenor, her elder sister married wt Sr Thomas Percy, Kn. afterward ataynted, being father by her to Thos. and Henry Percy, Knts. and both in their tymes Earles of Northu'br. and restored by Q. Mary) brother to Edward Fyton, Kn. Lord of Conaghte and Thresorer of Ireland, and sone and heyre to th' aforesayd Edward, which Threasorer and his wife deceased in Irlande, and lye boathe buried in St Patric's church, in Dublin."

The parish of Gawsworth is supposed to have been originally incorporated with that of Prestbury. Towards the middle of the 13th century, the Church is noticed merely as a *Chapel*, in an agreement between the Abbot of Chester and "John de Birchill, presbr *capellæ* de Gawsworth."

THE CHURCH, which is a Rectory, is dedicated to St. James, and consists of nave, chancel, and tower, in which is a ring of five bells. The whole is of considerable antiquity. The tower is ornamented with finely sculptured pinnacles. On the south side of the Church is a porch; and the roofing is finished with battlements. There are some very fine remains of stained glass in the windows. The situation is delightful.

There are numerous monuments here to the Fitton family, some of them finished in the richest style of the 17th century, with effigies.†

A monument to

Sir Edward Fitton, son of the Lord President of Connaught.

Another—

To Sir Edward Fytton, who died May 10, 1619: erected by his Lady. To Sir Edward Fytton, Bart. of Gawsworth. To Francis Fytton, Esq. husband of the Countess Dowager of Northumberland.

Near the Altar, memorials of—

Anne, wife of Edw. Thornicroft, Esq. only daughter of Sir Raphe Assheton, of Middleton, Bart. Born Aug. 7, 1655, died Dec. 30,

† Ormerod, page 295.

* The following lines are at the foot of the preceding:—

Stay thou whom chance directs or ease persuades,
To seek the quiet of these sylvan shades,
Here undisturbed, and hid from vulgar eyes,
A wit, musician, poet, player, lies,
A dancing master, too, in grace he shone,
And all the arts of op'ra were his own.
In comedy well skill'd he drew Lord Flame,
Acted the part, and gained himself the name.
Averse to strife how oft he'd gravely say,
These peaceful groves should shade his breathless clay,
That when he rose again, laid here alone,
No friend and he should quarrel for a bone;
Thinking that were some old lame gossip nigh,
She possibly might take his leg or thigh!

1712.—Edw. Thornycroft, her husband, died May 11, 1726, aged 71. Mary their daughter, and wife of Peter Davenport, Esq. died Oct. 8, 1721.—Henshaw Thornycroft, of Thornicroft, Esq. died May 10, 1780. Mary, his wife, died Feb. 26, 1774.—Frances, the wife of Edward Thornicroft, of Thornicroft, Esq died Dec. 29, 1809.—Ann, Viscountess Barrington, his second wife, died April 13, 1816. Edward Thornicroft, Esq. died Jan. 20; the last heir male of the ancient family of the Thornicrofts, of Thornicroft; a truly pious and benevolent Christian.

In the Chancel, on a marble monument—

In memory of the Rev. John Hammond, A. M. forty-one years Rector of this Parish; also, Alice his wife, who was the second daughter of Sir Foulke Lucy, of Henbury, in the county of Cheshire, Knt. She was interred the 14th Oct. 1697, aged 37; and he on the 15th April, 1724, in the 73d year of his age, leaving three sons and three daughters.

An inscription underneath notices the monument to have been erected by the Rev. John Lucy, of Charlecote, in the county of Warwick, in memory of his ancestors.

Near the Altar, is a tablet—

To the memory of the Rev. Miles Lonsdall, who died Dec. 5, 1785, aged 50.

The present incumbent is the Rev. H. F. Mills, presented in 1803.

The Rectory is an ancient mansion; the entrance hall of which is truly singular.

There are several Parochial benefactions; amongst them £200, left by the widow of the late Rector, the Rev. John Tickell, A. M.

THE PARISH OF ASTBURY,

CONTAINS, IN THIS HUNDRED, THE TOWNSHIPS OF

SOMERFORD BOOTHS. | EATON.

SOMERFORD BOOTHS

Is about three miles N. W. from Congleton, and is noticed in some old deeds, as *Somerford-juxta-Marton*. At a very early period, the township was possessed by the Baggileghs of Baguley; and about the reign of Henry VI. the Wetenhalls obtained lands here, in marriage with a daughter of the Bagguleghs.

Temp. Edw. I. the family of Swettenham, connected by family ties with the Somerfords, who had property here as early as the reign of Richard I. were settled in this township, and it is highly probable they were here at a much earlier period. They continued here so late as the year 1768, when on the death of Edmund Swettenham, Esq. the family became extinct in the direct line; but his great nephew Roger Comberbach, Esq. of Chester, assumed the name of Swettenham, on his accession to the estate. His son Clement Swettenham, is the present proprietor,

The *Hall*, called *Somerford Booths*, is erected on a pleasant site on the bank of the River Dane. The *Old Hall* is also near the River, and bears the æra of its foundation, in its gables and bay windows. It has lately, however, been much altered after the Gothic style.*

EATON,

Sometimes spelt *Yeaton*, is not noticed in Domesday, but is supposed to have been described under the head of Congleton, in conjunction with HULMWALFIELD.

At a very early period the manor of Eaton, was held by the Praers' of Baddiley, under Aldford Fee. About the middle of the reign of Richard II. John de Honford held the manor of Eyton, with part of the Vill, in right

* The Lysons notice a farm in this township, called SHANEWICK (stated in some old records to be a manor) now the property of Sir T. S. M. Stanley, Bart. to whose grandfather it was bequeathed by Wm. Massey, Esq. of Puddington, in whose family it was vested so early as 1450.

of his wife Margery de Praers, from John Arderne.—It was afterwards possessed by William Maynewaringe, nephew to the before-named Margery, who bequeathed the whole to his cousin John Honford. The manor was successively in the Starkeys, and Breretons; and Sir Thomas Brereton, last male heir, by deed of July 19, 1667, conveyed it to Wm. Rode, of Rushton Janes, co. Staff. In 1752, Thomas Rode, his descendant, sold the estate to George Lee, Esq. and on his death, April 4, 1773, it fell to George Ayton, Esq. who married Mr. Lee's niece, and he took the name of Lee. It is now the property of Sir Edmund Antrobus, Bart. having been purchased by his brother Philip, from Mr. G. A. Lee, and his son.

The Constables of Eaton are sworn at the Hundred Court, the Leets of Aldford and Gawsworth having long since been neglected.

The *Hall* is pleasantly situated about one mile N. of Congleton. Sir Edmund Antrobus gives a game deputation for the manor.

ROSTHERN.

(PART OF)

SNELSON,

Or *Snelleston,* is about five miles S. E. from Knutsford, and was allotted at the Conquest to Ranulphus, the founder of the Mainwarings. On the marriage of Henry de Aldithley to Bertra, daughter of Ralph Mainwaring, she had the township given to her as a dowry. The township subsequently became divided, and a family settled here which assumed the local name, and possessed a great portion of the property. They continued here several generations, and about 1640, the heiress married ——— Parker Esq. of Astle, in whose descendant, Colonel Thomas Parker, the principal estate of the township is vested. There are no manerial rights exercised.

NETHER ALDERLEY,

CONTAINS THE TOWNSHIPS OF

NETHER ALDERLEY, OVER ALDERLEY, AND GREAT WARFORD.

NETHER ALDERLEY,

Is about six miles N. W. from Macclesfield. At the Conquest it was vested in Bigot, and passed to the Aldfords, his successors. About 1202, Sir J. Arderne married the heiress of Aldford, and the township continued in the Ardernes till the death of Sir John Arderne, about 1423, without male issue; whose daughter and heiress married Thomas Stanley, Esq. of Elford, in Staffordshire, second son of Sir John Stanley, Knight of the Garter, and great uncle of John Stanley, to whom Over Alderley fell in marriage with the heiress of the Wevers. The reversion of the manor was sold by a grandson of Thomas Stanley, to Sir Wm. Stanley, of Holt, who was beheaded by Hen. VII. when the estate was vested in the Crown. Henry VIII. afterwards granted it to Urian Brereton, Esq. Groom of the Chamber to Anne Boleyn, and he was decapitated for a supposed adulterous connexion with his Royal Mistress. The manor was again seized by the Crown, and with Aldford and Etchells, granted for a term of years to Sir

CHESHIRE

Edward Peckham, Cofferer of the King's Household, with reversion to Margaret Moreton, for her life. In the 3d and 4th of Philip and Mary, they were purchased by Robert Tatton, and Sir Edward Fitton; and Sir Edward Fitton sold his purchase to Sir Thomas Stanley, the ancestor of Sir J. T. Stanley, Bart. the present proprietor of Nether and Over Alderley.

The ancient seat of this branch of the noble and illustrious family, was in this township. It was of considerable antiquity; and was nearly rebuilt by Sir Edw. Stanley about 1754, twenty five years after which it was destroyed by fire. The out-offices, however, were saved, and were subsequently converted into a farmhouse. The present residence of this respectable family, is at the Park-house, on the south side of the Park.

The Park of Alderley is of considerable extent, and boasts of some of the finest beech trees in the county,* planted by Sir Thomas Stanley, the first Baronet, about 1640. The park abounds with beautiful scenery, considerably heightened by a fine piece of water, called *Radnor Mere*. Rising above the grounds, is that singular ridge of land, called *Alderley Edge*, the summit of which, like the insulated hill of Beeston, commands one of the finest prospects in the county, but it differs from it in one respect, having the advantage of a good drive to the top of it, near which has been found, in small quantities, copper, lead, and ore. There was a beacon here in 1622;† and on the threatened invasion in 1803-4, it was fixed upon for a similar purpose.

† Webb.

In this township, were formerly four halls, viz. *Heywood Hall*, *Sossmoss Hall*, *Fallows Hall*, and *Monk's Heath Hall*. Heywood Hall was the property of a family of the same name, from whom it passed to the Hollinsheads,‡ and the Fallows; William Fallows, Esq. of Derby, sold it in 1801, to Sir J. T. Stanley, Bart. Sossmoss Hall, was formerly possessed by the Wyches, of Davenham, from whom, in 1753, it was purchased by Sir Edward Stanley, and is now the property of Sir J. T. Stanley. These are now occupied as farmhouses. Fallows Hall and Estate, called La Falwitz in old deeds, was, temp. King John, granted by Robt. de Aldford, to his youngest brother Henry de Falwitz, who gave it to his son Thomas. It was held by his successors for a long period of years, and about 1685, Wm. Fallowes, Esq. sold it to the ancestor of Thomas Parker, Esq. of Astle, who is the present owner.—Monk's Heath Hall, was, as early as the 15th century, the property of the Wards, of Capesthorne; it was afterwards vested in the Antrobus family; and, about 1671, was purchased again by the Wards. In 1748, this family became extinct; and the estate is now, by the marriage of his grandfather with the daughter and heiress of John Ward, Esq. the property of Davies Davenport, Esq. M. P. for the county.

Alderley CHURCH is dedicated to St. Mary, and the present incumbent is the Rev. Edw. Stanley, A. M. presented by his brother Nov. 15, 1805. It is built of grey stone, in various styles, but the greater part is of considerable antiquity. It consists of tower, (with six bells) nave, chancel, and side aisles; from which the nave is separated by gothic arches, rising from octagonal columns. At the west end of the nave is an organ gallery, the front decorated with the armorial bearings of several of the neighbouring families. The Stanley gallery is at the east end of the south aisle, also ornamented with the armorial quarterings of the family.—There are memorials here of the Stanley, Ward, Hollinshead, and other families.

Under the Stanley gallery, on a flag-stone, is this inscription—

Here lieth the body of Thomas Stanley, Esq. eldest son of Thos. Stanley, Esq. and Joan, daughter of Thomas Davenport, of Henbury, Esq. He married Ursula, daughter of Richard, and sister of Sir Hugh Cholmondeley, Knt. and had issue Thomas, who died young, and Randle, his heir and successor; also Dorothy, who died unmarried; Elizabeth married to Roger Downes, Esq. of Shrigley; and Frances married to Henry Delves, of Doddington, Esq. He rebuilt the houses of Alderley and Wever, and died August 1st, 1591.—Also, the body of Sir James Stanley, Bart. who died without issue, A. D. 1746, and was succeeded by his brother Sir Edward Stanley, Bart. who died at Alderley, in 1755.---Also, the body of his sister Mary Stanley, who died unmarried at ye Park House, in Alderley, in 1766.

On a brass plate, in the chancel, a memorial of Tho-

* According the statement of the Lysons, "they vary in girth from 12 to 14 feet, and continue of nearly the same girth to the height of 20 feet: the largest contains 192 feet of timber in the boll, and 128 in the branches."

‡ Of which family was the Historian.

mas Hollinshead, Esq. of Heawood, buried August 16, 1703, aged 63, with the inscription—

ΕΛΠΙΖ ΕΙΜΩΝ ΤΟΥΣ ΓΟΝΕΙΣ ΠΡΑΞΕΙΝ ΚΑΛΩΣ.

The memory of Edward Skipton, Master of Arts, and Rector of this Church, who dyed eight day of September, in the year of our Lord Christ one thousand six hundred and thertye.

Here lyes below an aged sheepheard clad in heavy clay,
Those stubborne weedes which come not off unto the judgement-day,
Whilom he led and fed with welcome paine his careful sheepe,
He did not feare the mountaines highest tops, nor vallies deepe,
That he might save from hurte his faithful flocke, which was his care,
To make them stronge he lost his strength, and fasted for their fare,
How they might feed and grow, and prosper, he did daily tel,
Then having shewe'd them how to feede, hee bade them all farewell.

At the Altar rails, on a slab—

Hic jacet Philippus Ward de Capesthorne, armiger, Joannis et Margaretæ filius junior, supervivens autem et hæres. Uxorem habuit Penelopen, Caroli Edmonds ar. filium hæredemq. ex ea suscitabat et reliquit Joannem.

Natus 12 } Apr. { 1635.
Obiit 26 } Apr. { 1687.

The *School House* was built by the Rev. Hugh Shaw, Curate of the Parish in 1628—it has since been endowed with £100. by Mr Thomas Deane, when tenant of Park House, who died 1695; £100. from John Parker, Esq; £50. from Mr. George Baguley; 50s. from Mr. Robert Marbury. The Rector is one of the Feoffees, and they have the nomination of the Master. The School House is repaired by the Parish.

OVER ALDERLEY,

At the period of the Survey, was held in moieties between Wm. Fitz Nigel, and Bigot, brother of Bigot, then Earl Marshal of England.—The mesne manor was subsequently held under the Barons of Halton, by Robert de Montalt, the last Baron of that name. The daughter of his aunt Leuca, (who married Philip de Orreby, the younger) became the sole heiress, and she married Walkelyn de Arderne, and brought to him the manor of Over Alderley in marriage. His possession of the other moiety of it (say the Lysons) may be accounted for by descent from the Aldfords, whose ancestor Sir Robert de Aldford, married Sarah daughter of Richard Fitz Eustace, Baron of Halton, and it is probable he had in marriage with her the moiety which Richard possessed by inheritance from William Fitz Nigel. Walkelyn de Arderne, who was for some years Chief Justice of Chester, had possession of both the Alderleys; but they were separated on the death of his grandson; and not re-united till the reign of Elizabeth. Peter Arderne, who died in 1346 had two daughters, Christiana, married to John Fitton, of Bollin, who died without issue; and Margaret, who married Richard Weever, of Weever, whose great grandson of the same name had an only daughter, and she married John, third son of Thomas Lord Stanley,* younger brother of the first Earl of Derby. Thomas Stanley, the 7th in descent from John, was the first Cheshire Gentleman created a Baronet after the Restoration. The fine beech trees on the border of the mere, were planted by him. The large estates of this respectable family are now vested in their lineal descendant, Sir John Thomas Stanley, Bart. The manor is held of the Fee of Halton.

* Lysons.

HISTORY.

A third part of the manor was bought by the present proprietor of Sir J. F. Leicester, Bart. This portion was separated from the other parts at a very early period; and in 1337, Richard Mottershed conveyed it to the Grosvenors, from whom it passed with a coheiress to the Leycesters, of Tabley.

The HULME HOUSE property in this township, consisted of lands granted to Robt. le Grosvenor, of Allostock, temp. Edw. III. by the Hargreaves, Bradfords, and Hulmes. It afterwards passed in marriage to the Leycesters; and in the 18th Henry VII. John Leycester, Esq. sold it to Francis Hobson. Subsequently it passed to the family of Downes, of Pott Shrigley; and in 1784, Peter Downes, Esq. sold it to Joseph Fowden, who re-sold it in 1796, to Robert Hibbert, Esq. of Birtles, and he is the present proprietor. On this estate several ancient relics have been discovered; particularly a Roman urn, about 6 inches high, and 18 inches in circumference.

In the higher part of the township is the HARESHILLS ESTATE, the property of Wm. Hibbert, Esq. purchased from Sir J. F. Leicester, 1797.

GREAT AND LITTLE WARFORD,

Originally formed one township, and was held at the Conquest by Ranulfus, from whom it passed to the Mainwarings, his descendants, and was held by them in the reign of Hen. III. The Lysons say, that it was held under the Mainwarings by the Poutrells; and that Roger Mainwaring gave it to his brother Ralph. It would appear, that the Poutrells made claim to the manor, for in 1286, Lawrence Mainwaring fully established his right to it against Richard Poutrell. About 1337, the manor was conveyed by Geoffrey of Stockport, and his wife Eleanor, to John de Motlow; but before the reign of Henry VI. the Masseys of Puddington were in possession, by what means is not now known, and continued the proprietors till they became extinct, when the manor, with the other estates, passed to their representative, Sir T. S. M. Stanley, Bart. who holds a Court Baron.

THE PARISH OF WILMSLOW,

CONTAINS THE TOWNSHIPS AND HAMLETS OF

CHORLEY,	FULSHAW,	MORLEY,
DEAN ROW,	HOUGH,	STYALL.

WILMSLOW,

Anciently called *Le Bolyn*, is about seven miles from Macclesfield, on the Manchester road, and what is very singular, the township is confined to the Church and the Church Yard. The great divisions of the parish, are included in *Bollin Fee*, *Pownall Fee*, *Chorley*, and *Fulshaw*.—At a very early period, the whole was held by the Fittons. The name "*Bolyn*" arose from its situation on the banks of the Bollen. Rd. Fyton, temp. Hen. III. granted Fulshaw to the Order of St. John of Jerusalem. By an Inq. of the 30th of the same King, the manor of Bolyn is described as being held by the service of attending the King's army at Chester, with all the family of Fitton, armed with bows, &c—This family continued here in the direct male till the death of Peter Fitton,* without issue, whose sister and heiress Johanna, married Richard Venables of the Kinderton family. It is ascertained from an Inq. post mortem, 4th Hen. VI. that Wm. de Venables held the manor of Bolyn, and the advowson of Wilmslow Church, by military service, viz. by finding thirty-three men for a guard in the combes in the Forest of Macclesfield, during the hunting season, &c.—Temp. Henry V. Richard Venables died without issue, and his estates fell to his sisters Douce and Alice,—the first married to Sir Robt. Booth, (of the Barton family) the other to Sir Edmund Trafford, of Trafford, near Manchester. The Venables' estates then became divided.

* 42 Edward III.

POWNALL FEE,

Fell to the Trafford share, with the advowson of Wilmslow Church. This family continued in uninterrupted succession, till the death of Humphrey Trafford, Esq. who died issueless in 1779. The property then passed to the Traffords of Croston, and it is now possessed by them. The Court Baron held for the manor, extends over Chorley, Hough, and Morley.

BOLLIN FEE,

Became the property of the Booths, as before noticed; from the heiress of whom,† the manor passed with the estates to her son, the father of the present Earl of Stamford and Warrington. The Court Baron, &c. includes within its authority, Bollin-cum-Norcliffe, Dean Row, and Styall.

The *Hall* belongs to the Earl of Stamford; but is now used as a farm-house. It is supposed it occupies the site of the mansion of the Fittons.‡

HOUGH was the residence of a branch of the Davenport family during the Civil Wars.

A family of the name of Ryle, settled in Styall before the 16th century.

† See Durham Massy.

‡ Ormerod.

Hawthorn Hall is in the Hamlet of Morley.—It passed from the Lathams to the Leighs and Pages; Thomas Leigh Page sold the property to Mr. Ralph Bower, Wilmslow, in whose children it is now vested.

Pownall Hall, also in Morley, recently rebuilt, was the property of a respectable family of the same name, which terminated in the direct male line so early as 1328; it then passed to a branch of the Fittons, and from them them to the Newtons of Newton, near Butley. Peter Mainwaring, of Smallwood, obtained the estate in marriage with Catherine Newton; and from those who subsequently became possessed of the Hall, it was purchased by John Worrall, Esq. the present proprietor.

The Church of Wilmslow is dedicated to St. Bartholomew; the present Rector, the Rev. Joseph Bradshaw, A. M. instituted March 28, 1814. The building is situated on the bank of the Bollin, and consists of nave, chancel, side aisles, and tower, containing six bells. Five pillars supporting pointed arches, divide the nave and side aisles. The Church has a number of monumental memorials. Near the Altar, are the figures of Sir Robert Booth, and his wife Douce Venables; the original inscription was—

Hic jacent corpus Roberti del Bothe militis quondam D'ni de Bolyn, Thorneton, et Dunh'm, qui obiit in festo s'ce Tecle virginis Domini mill'mo ccccLx° et corpus Dulcie ux'is d'ci Rob'ti del Bothe que obiit in crastino s'cte be'e Virginis anno Domini mill'mo cccc° quinquagesimo tercio, quorum animabus p'p'tietur Deus. Amen.

On an altar tomb in the chancel, the figure of the Rev. Henry Trafford, who died in August 1537.—Memorial of the Rev. Croxon Johnson, who died Jan. 30, 1814, aged 53—of Peter Ledsham, who died July 22, 1678—John Usherwood, died Oct. 3, 1705, aged 39—Samuel Finney, Esq. died Feb. 22, 1795, aged 32—Peter Davenport, Esq. died Sept. 22, 1800, aged 66.—In the Pownall Fee Chancel, under two canopied recesses in the wall, is the tomb of an ecclesiastic, and also of a female, her head reclining on a wheat sheaf.

A Chancel, built by the Leghs of Hawthorn Hall, is on the south side of the Church.

There is a *School* at Wilmslow, for ten children, founded by the Rev. Henry Hough, Rector of Thornton-le-Moors; the endowment, however, is but £5. per ann. About 1780, a *House of Industry* was built on *Lindow Common*, which was supported by lands, given by the Freeholders, producing an annual rental of more than £200.*

CHORLEY,

Is within the Court held for Pownall Fee. The Hall was the seat of the Davenports as early as 1400, when Thomas youngest son of Sir Ralph Davenport, married the heiress of Honford, of Chorley. Another branch of the Davenports, possessed lands here, at a much earlier period, under a grant from Edmund Fitton to Richard Davenport, grandson of Sir Roger Davenport, of Davenport, living in 1291, by the tenure of two shillings yearly, and a flitch of bacon during pannage in Fulshaw Wood.

In 1612, the Chorley Hall estate was sold by Wm. Davenport, to Francis Downes, Esq. In 1640, it was purchased by Sir Thomas Stanley, of Alderley, ancestor of Sir J. T. Stanley, Bart. the present proprietor.—The House is of considerable antiquity, built partly of stone and timber, with bay windows, and gables. It occupies a moated site; and is let as a Farm House.

FULSHAW

Was given by Richard Fytun to the Order of St. John of Jerusalem, and the Duke of Leeds, as lessee under the Crown of the property belonging to the ancient Preceptory of the Order at Iveley, in Derbyshire, holds a Court Leet and Baron for the manor.

The lands of the township, were granted by the Order to Richard del Short, and Robert Crosse de Fulshagh, by deed dated at Malcheburne, Michaelmas, 1277. In the 5th Elizabeth, Humphrey Newton obtained the manor by fine, of Thomas de Verdon; and in the 39th of Elizabeth, William Newton disposed of the manor for £200. to Thomas Leigh, Esq. It was subsequently (1666) divided between the Newtons, and the Lathoms, of Hawthorn Hall. The Newton moiety was

* Mr Wright, Rector of Wilmslow, who was ejected from his living during the Civil Wars, sustained a regular siege in the Rectory House, from Col. Duckenfield, the Parliamentary commander. One or two of his maid servants were killed He was then eighty years old; but lived nevertheless to see the restoration of Charles II. when he was himself reinstated. His death is thus noticed in the Parish Register:—"Oct. 1661. The 20 daye aboute nyne of the clocke in the nighte, Mr. Thomas Wright, gentleman, parson of Wilmeslow, ended his lyfe, and was buried in the tombe on the northe syde of the Chancell, the 23d daye of the same month of October, 1661."

 soon after sold to Roger Wilbraham; and in 1682, he sold it to Mr. Samuel Finney, ancestor of the present proprietor P. D. Finney, Esq. The other moiety passed to John Leigh, Esq. and was afterwards in several hands. In 1787, Mr. Page, of Hawthorn Hall, had possession; but in 1800 it was sold in portions to various purchasers.

Fulshaw Hall is a venerable brick house, with bay windows, and gables.

PARISH OF NORTHENDEN,

CONTAINS THE TOWNSHIPS OF

NORTHERN, OR NORTHENDEN | ETCHELLS (PART OF.)

NORTHENDEN,

Is about four miles W. from Stockport, and was held by Ranulphus and Bigot at the Conquest. It was afterwards possessed by the Baron of Dunham Massy, who gave it, with the advowson of the Church, to Chester Abbey, and the Abbot claimed view of frank pledge, temp. Edw. III. On the Dissolution, the property of the Abbey here, was involved in the troubles created by Sir R. Cotton; and notwithstanding the new Bishop had lands settled upon him in the township, he was compelled afterwards to surrender them to the Crown. Before the 22d Eliz. the manor was vested in the Tattons of Withenshaw, and still continues the property of their descendant Thomas Wm. Tatton, Esq. who holds, half yearly, a Court Leet and Baron.

WITHENSHAW, in this township, was described as a distinct manor, temp. Elizabeth. It is the property and seat of Mr. Tatton. The Hall is a handsome building, recently improved and modernized, but some parts of the old house still remain. During the Civil Wars, it was garrisoned for the King; but after a long siege was captured by the Parliament troops, Feb. 25, 1644, "there being then in the house (says Burghall) only Mr. Tatton, some few gentlemen, and a few soldiers, who had quarter for life." During the siege Captain Adams was killed, and buried at Stockport, and it is probable, many fell during the contention, as, a few years ago, six human skeletons were found in the garden lying by the side of each other.*

KENWORTHY is a hamlet in this township, and was in the reign of Edw. I. the property of Robert, youngest son of Sir Alan de Tatton, then Lord of Tatton.—Mr. Tatton has an estate here; two other estates pay chief rents to him; and another estate is the property of the Shelmerdines.

The CHURCH is dedicated to St. Wilfred. The present Rector, is the Rev. Thomas Maddock, A. M. Prebendary of Chester, presented May 25, 1809. The building consists of nave, chancel, side aisles, and tower. Five pointed arches, springing from octagonal columns, separate the nave from the side aisles. There are two Chapels at the end of the aisles, belonging to the Tatton family.

The monumental memorials of this family, are very numerous; but none of them of material interest.†

ETCHELLS,

Is partly in the parish of Stockport; it was anciently vested in the Ardernes, and Stanleys; before the 22d Elizabeth, Robert Tatton, Esq. held the manor from the Queen in capite; and it has regularly descended with the Withenshaw estates. The tenants of this manor are exempt from attending the Hundred Courts, by grant from Henry VII.—Separate Overseers are appointed for the Northenden and Stockport divisions of the parish; and the poor rates are distinct.—A Court Leet and Court Baron is held for the Manor.

* Lysons.

† They are given in Mr. Ormerod's work.

[...]SHIRE

THE PARISH OF CHEADLE,

CONTAINS THE TOWNSHIPS OF

CHEADLE BULKELEY, CHEADLE MOSELEY, HANDFORTH-cum-BOSDEN.

CHEADLE BULKELEY

Is about six miles S. of Manchester, and it is probable the original *vill* of Cheadle, included the whole parish. It is not noticed in the Survey; but there is little doubt it was held by the Earl. A family which assumed the local name, was settled here before 1180, for Hugh Cyveilioc quit-claimed to Robert de Chedle four porkers, which he used to pay the Earl, " by an agreement made for love before his Barons."* The son of Hugh de Dutton, was the ancestor of a family settled here, which also took the name of the township; and which terminated in two heiresses, married to the families of Baggiley and Bulkeley; the former thus acquiring the divisions called Cheadle Hulme or Moseley, and the latter Cheadle Bulkeley, with the advowson of the Church. The Leghs, of Lyme, acquired the Baggiley share, by marriage with the heiress of that family. Sir Piers Legh married the widow of Sir John Savage, and the estate passed to her son by Sir John, and descended to Sir John Savage, who was killed at Boulogne, temp. Henry VII.—The Bulkeleys held their portion for many generations, and got possession of the entire manor, by the marriage of Sir Richard Bulkeley, Knight, with Margaret, daughter of Sir John Savage, about 1558.

*Vill. Cest.

On the death of James Viscount Bulkeley, the manor was sold in 1756, under the provisions of an Act of Parliament, to the Rev. Thomas Egerton, of Cheadle, who devised it to the Beresfords; and in 1806, they conveyed it to John Worthington, Esq. of Ringway, who is the present proprietor. In 1810, an Act of Parliament was obtained, for the inclosure of the waste lands in this parish.

The CHURCH is dedicated to St. Mary; the present Rector is the Rev. Henry Delves Broughton, A. M. presented Aug. 1, 1807. The building consists of nave, chancel, side aisles, and tower with six bells.—The nave is divided from the side aisles by four pointed arches.—In the north aisle is the Cheadle Moseley Chancel; and in the south aisle, the Hondford Chancel.

The monumental inscriptions are few in number.—The following are selected :—

Within this Chancel rest the remains of Bertie Markland, Esq. many years in the Commission of the Peace, and a Deputy Lieutenant of the County of Lancaster: who died at the Rectory House in this parish, on the 20th day of May, 1817, aged 66 years. In the discharge of his duty as a Magistrate, he was upright and impartial, as a friend and neighbour conciliatory and sincere; a loyal subject to his king, and a Christian in faith and practice. In the same grave is interred the body of Anne Markland, his affectionate wife, by whose death, on the 29th of October, 1816, in her 65th year, a happy union of 40 years was dissolved. This tablet is consecrated to their memory by their surviving relations.

At the top of the monument is an open book, inscribed—

" Watch and pray, for ye know not when the time is."

There is a large altar tomb in the Hondford Chancel, representing two Knights in plate armour. On another altar tomb is also the figure of a Knight in armour.—On a tablet, in the centre, is the inscription—

Here lyeth the body of Sir Thomas Brererton, of Handforthe, Baronett, who married Theodosia, daughter to the right Hon. Hon'ble, Lord Ward, and the Lady Frances, Barronesse Dudley. Hee departed this life the 7th of January, ann. Dom. 1673, ætatis suæ 43.

In the Mosley Chancel, engraved on a brass plate—

Hic jacet Humphridus Bulkeley, armiger, filius et hæres Richardi Bulkeley, armigeri, et Katherinæ uxoris filiæ Georgii Nedham de Thornset, in comitatu Derbiæ, armigeri. Richardus filius fuit primogenitus Richardi Bulkeley militis (de Beawmaris et Cheadle) per uxorem priorem. Humphridus Bulkeley, prædict. obiit octavo die Septembris, anno Domini 1678.

CHESHIRE

CHEADLE MOSELEY,

Or Cheadle Hulme, is about four miles S. S. W. from Stockport, and passed through the Chedles and Leighs to the Savages, and from them in marriage to the Marquis of Winchester,. It was purchased from him by Sir Nicholas Mosley, Knt. Lord Mayor of London, in 1559. About 1695, the heiress of Sir Edw. Mosley, Bart. brought it in marriage to Sir John Bland, Bart. of Kippex Park, co. York; and his grandson, under the authority of an Act of Parliament, sold it in 1754, to John Davenport, Esq. of Stockport, from whom it passed to the Bamfords, of Bamford, co Lancaster.—William Bamford, Esq. dying without issue male in 1807, it is now possessed by his representative in the female line, Lloyd Bamford Hesketh, Esq.

Bradshaw Hall is occupied as a farm-house.—In 1550, it was purchased from Sir John Savage by James Kelsall, Esq. and it is now the property of his descendant, Jane, niece of Oldfield Kelsall, Esq. who died in 1817, and wife of the late Rev. Chas. Prescott, B. D. Rector of Stockport.

HONFORD-cum-BOSDEN,

Handforth, Handford, or *Hondford,* is about five miles S. W. S. from Stockport, and BOSDEN is a hamlet of this township. As early as the reign of Henry III. the manor was vested in a family which took the local name, and which was settled here till about 1566, when it passed with an heiress, Margery, to Sir John Stanley, Knt. Before the 22d Elizabeth, the manor was held of the Stanleys, by Sir Urian Brereton, Knt. Sir Thomas Brereton, 8th and 9th May, 1666, conveyed his estates to trustees, with remainder to his wife, Dame Theodosia Brereton, remainder to Sir Thomas's issue, remainder in tail mail to Nathaniel Booth, of Mottram Andrew, and his heirs, &c. This Nathaniel Booth, Esq. was certainly in possession as early as 1678; and his successor Mr. Booth, June 14, 1764, agreed with Mr. E. Wrench, for the sale of the manor, together with lands, &c. in Chester; two years afterwards the estates were conveyed to Mr. Wrench. In April, 1804, E. O. Wrench, Esq. of Chester, conveyed the same to Joseph Cooper, of Hondford, yeoman, in fee; and on the 9th Nov. 1805, Mr. Cooper devised the estate to trustees, to be sold; in Feb. 1808, it was purchased by Mr Wm. Pass, of Altrincham, who is the present proprietor.

HISTORY.

The *Hall* and demesne are the property of Lawrence Wright, Esq. of Mottram St. Andrew, by purchase from the Leghs, of Chorley, on whom they devolved from the Booths. Sir J. Stanley, who held the manor temp Hen. VIII. was natural son of James Stanley, Bishop of Ely. He founded a Chantry in the Collegiate Church of Manchester; where an altar tomb covers the remains of his father. This Sir John Stanley was in no small degree connected with the political events of the day; we find in the 38th charge brought against Cardinal Wolsey—"That the said Cardinal did call before him Sir John Stanley, Knt. which had taken a farm by covent seal of the Abbot and Convent of Chester, and afterwards by his power and might, contrary to right, committed the said Sir John Stanley to the prison of Fleet by the space of one year, until such time as he compelled the said Sir John to release his covent seal to one Leghe, of Adlington, which marr'd one Lack's dau'r, *which woman the said Lord Cardinal kept and had with her two children!* whereupon the said Sir John Stanley, upon displeasure taken in his heart, made himself monk in Westmr and there died."*—Of Sir Wm. Brereton, another proprietor of the manor, some particulars will be found in the account of the siege of Chester, and Nantwich. At an early period in life, his aversion to the Established Church was notorious; which was no doubt increased from the circumstance of being the friend and neighbour of Judge Bradshaw, and Colonel Duckenfield, and the son-in-law of Sir Geo. Booth, who was the chief corner-stone of the Puritan cause in Chester.†—He was made a Baronet in 1626 7, and represented the County in the Parliaments of the 3d, 15th, and 16th years of the reign of the unfortunate Charles I. He was particularly honoured by the Parliament on the termination of the war, being appointed Chief Forester of Macclesfield, and Seneschal of the Hundred; he had also a large share of the property confiscated from the Papists; and on the death of Laud, Archbishop of Canterbury, he obtained a grant of the Palace at Croyden. He died April 7, 1661, and was described as a notable man at a thanksgiving dinner, having terrible long teeth, and a prodigious stomach, to

* Lord Herbert's History of Hen. VIII. p. 300, edit. 1672.

† Clarendon.

turn the Archbishop's Chapel into a kitchen, and swallow up the palace and lands at a morsel.*

Hondford, is supposed, by Mr. Whittaker, to have been the site of one of the smaller Roman fortresses; but Mr. Watson was of a different opinion, fixing the situation near Hale.

PARISH OF PRESTBURY,

CONTAINS THE TOWNSHIPS OF

PRESTBURY,
ADLINGTON,
BUTLEY-CUM-NEWTON,
NEWTON-JUXTA-BUTLEY,
LYME HANLEY
POYNTON,
WORTH,
WOODFORD,
MOTTRAM ST. ANDREW,
TITHERINGTON,
BOLLINGTON,
FALLIBROOME,
UPTON,
HENBURY-CUM-PEXHALL
BIRTLES,
CHELFORD,
OLD WITHINGTON,
LOWER WITHINGTON,
CAPESTHORNE,
MARTON,
SIDDINGTON,
NORTH RODE,
BOSLEY,
MACCLESFIELD,
SUTTON DOWNES,
WINCLE,
KETTLESHULME,
HURDSFIELD,
RAINOW,
WILDBOARCLOUGH,
MACCLESFIELD FOREST,
AND
POTT SHRIGLEY.

PRESTBURY

Is about three miles N. N. W. from Macclesfield; and at a very early period, was no doubt a place of some importance and considerable population. The existence of the Church is not noticed in the Survey, and it is conjectured, that it was destroyed by the Norman invaders.—The manor of Prestbury subsequently was possessed by the Earls of Chester; and Earl Hugh Cyveilioc granted it, together with the advowson of the Church, to the Abbot of Chester, and it continued vested in the Monastery of Saint Werburgh till the Dissolution; when the whole was transferred to the Dean and Chapter, but eventually shared the fate of the other possessions of the Church, and fell into the hands of Sir Richard Cotton. Temp. Elizabeth,† the Leghs of Adlington, were the proprietors, and the manor, and rectory, have descended to their representative Richard Legh, Esq. who holds a Court Leet and Baron. The north end of the street which forms the town, is terminated by a neat bridge over the Bollin, nearly adjoining which is

The CHURCH.—It is dedicated to St. Peter, and the present Vicar is the Rev. John Rowlls Brown, present. July 10, 1800. The building consists of nave, chancel, and side aisles, separated from the former, by five pointed arches. In the tower are six bells. Some parts of the Church are of considerably antiquity. At the end of the North aisle is the Legh Chancel; that formerly in the south aisle, was appropriated to the Worths, of Titherington.—Under a shield in stained glass in the east window of the Adlington chancel, is the inscription—

Orate pro bono statu Thomæ Legh de Adlington armigeri, et Sibelliæ uxoris suæ uni' filiarum Uriani Brereton de Hondford, militis defuncti qui hanc fenestram fieri fecerunt in anno Domini 1601.

On the right of this, a pyramidal monument, with the Legh arms, inscribed—

To the memory of Charles Legh, Esq. of Adlington, in the county of Chester, who died the xxvi of July, MDCCLXXVII, aged LXXXIV years. He married Hester Lee, eldest daughter and coheiress of Robert Lee, Esq. of Wincham, in the said County, by whom he had an only child Thomas Legh, Esq. who died at Wincham the xv day of June, MDCCLXXV, aged XL years.

On a brass, in the north wall of the chancel—

* Mysteries of Good Old Cause, 1665.

† Ann. reg. 22, Aug. 6.

CHESHIRE

Hic sepult. jacet cadaver Theodosiæ filiæ septimæ Nathanielis Boothe, armigeri, nuper de Mottram Andrew, quæ mortem obiit die 4 Martii 170½. Hic sepultum jacet cadaver Mariæ octavæ et natu minimæ filiæ Nathanielis Boothe armigeri, nuper de Mottram Andrew, quæ mortem obiit die 16° Octobris 1696.

Over the recumbent figures of a Knight and Lady, in the south aisle, is a mural monument to the memory of Mary, the wife of John Marsden, D. D. daughter and heiress of John Acton, Esq. of Bache, in this county, who died Jan. 4, 1771, aged 41.—In the same aisle, on a brass

Here lyeth the body of Bithia, wife of William Swettenham, of Swettenham, Esq. who departed this life April 30th 1742. Here also lyeth the body of Thomas Swettenham, of Swettenham, Esq. son of William and Bithia Swettenham, who departed this life March 20th, 1748, aged 54.

On the north side of the altar, on a slab, in the wall, the recumbent figure of a Knight in armour, the head resting on a helmet—

Here lyeth the bodye of Edwarde Warren, of Poynton, Knight, wyche dep'ted from thys transitory lyffe the XII day of October in the yere of our Lord God M°CCCCC°LVIII, whose soule God pardon.—Amen.

On a similar stone, close to the latter, bearing a large ornamented cross—

Hic jacet Reginaldus Legh, armig. filius Roberti Legh mil. quondam d'ni d' Adlyngton qui Reginal's fuit p'cipuus adjutor in edifacac'o'e campanilis, et porticon eccl'ie edificavit de p'priis obiit XVI die Julii an. d. M.CCCC°LXXXII°.

In a wide arch, opposite to the last, the figure of a man in armour, and his lady, recumbent :—the inscription is destroyed; but it was to this effect—

Hic jacent Rob'tus Dounes armig', et Matild' ux' ej', et Rob'tus Dounes fil' dicti Rob'ti et Emmota uxor ej' filia Rog'i Bouthe armig'. et dict' Rob'tus Dounes obiit in vigilia s'c'i Laurenc' martyris an'o D'ni 1495.

On a brass in the Chancel—

Joseph Ward, A. M. formerly of Wadham College, Oxford, and Vicar of Prestbury 33 years, who died Feb. 7, 1772, in the 61st year of his age.

To the memory of Lætitia Catherine Hibbert, wife of Robert Hibbert, jun. Esq. of Birtles, and daughter of Henry Augustus Leicester, Esq. of Tabley, in this county, who died 11th July, 1817, in the XXXth year of her age.—"Blessed are they that keep his testimonies, and that seek him with their whole heart."—PSALM CXIX, v. 2.

HISTORY.

The townships of Upton, Titherington, Siddington, and Fallybroome, are considered as excepted from the impropriation, and pay tithe of corn to the Vicar; the tithes of Capesthorne, belong to Capesthorne Chapel, to which they were given by John Ward, Esq. of Capesthorne.

There is a very ancient small building on the south side of the Church, supposed to have been the remains of an old place of worship, built by the Normans, instead of the Saxon church then destroyed. On the front of it, the following inscription is introduced:—

SACELLUM HOC ANTIQUISSIMUM PERHIBETUR HUJUS PAROCHIÆ ORATORIUM. VETUSTATE RUINOSUM, UNA JAM PRIDEM PARTE COLLAPSA, OMNI FERE ALTERA COLLABASCENTE, NE PRISCÆ PIETATIS VENERABILE MONUMENTUM FUNDITUS CORRUERET SUMPTIBUS SUIS RESTITUIT, GULIELMUS MEREDITH, BARONETTUS, A. D. M.DCC.XLVII.*

ADLINGTON,

Is about five miles N. W. from Macclesfield; and at the Conquest, with Macclesfield, formed two great townships, held subsequently by the Norman Earls. Early in the 12th century the manor of Adlington was possessed by a family which bore the name of Corona. About the reign of Edw. II. John Legh, of Booths, married Ellen, heiress of the Corona family, and had with her the manor.—From the above period to 1781, the Leghs continued here in uninterrupted succession, when on the death of Charles Legh, Esq. without issue male, the direct line of the family terminated: after the death of his widow, in 1806, the manor devolved, pursuant to Mr. Legh's will, to his cousin, Richard Cross, Esq. of Shaw Hill, near Preston, co. Lancaster, who has assumed the name of Legh.

The Park of Adlington is of considerable extent.—The *Hall* is an extensive quadrangular building, in the ancient style of the Cheshire timber and plaister mansions. The principal front is of brick, ornamented with a handsome portico, and projecting wings. The *Domestic Chapel* of Adlington is in the south-east angle.

* Dugdale notices the following inscription as having formerly illustrated a grave-stone in the Church-yard:—

Those goods I had whilst I did live,
Unto four monkes I freely give
To eate, and drinke, and make good cheere,
And keep my *obite* once a yeare.

CHESHIRE HISTORY.

of the front; in the north front is the great hall of the house. During the Civil Wars, Adlington Hall shared the fate of many other mansions. It was in the first instance garrisoned by the Royalists, but was compelled to surrender after a fortnight's siege on the 14th Feb. 1645. Burghall observes, that "a younger son of Mr. Legh, and 150 soldiers had all fair quarter and leave to depart, leaving 700 arms, and 15 barrels of gunpowder." A court leet and baron are held for the manor twice a year.

BUTLEY,

Butleigh, or *Butley-cum-Newton*, is about three miles N. W. from Macclesfield. It appears, that Uluric, a Saxon, who possessed estates in this township, was, no doubt for certain good services not explained, permitted by the Normans to retain his lands here. As early as the reign of Hen. III. the Pigots had possession of the manor, held of the Prince in capite by military service; and they continued the Lords till the death of Robert Pigot, temp. Edw. VI. when it was divided between his daughters. Temp. Elizabeth, a moiety was purchased by the Leghs, from Gilbert Gerard, who bought the share of Elizabeth, the eldest daughter; the share of Mary was also purchased by the Leghs; and eventually they became the proprietors of the village and manor, which are the property of R. C. Legh, Esq. who holds a Court Leet and Baron for them.

Butley Hall is the residence of the Rev. John Rowlls Brown, Vicar of Prestbury.

Foxwist Hall was formerly possessed by the Duncalfs, which family is now represented by two maiden ladies, residing in Adlington.

Willett Hall was originally the seat of the Butleys, and after passing from them to the Mottersheads, and the Brookes of Mere, is the property of the Wrights, of Mottram, and Offerton.—Thomas Newton, the celebrated Latin poet, was born in Butley.

NEWTON-JUXTA-BUTLEY,

Or *Butlegh*, was originally a part of the township of Butley. It was held by the Newtons, of Pownall, for a long period; and on the death of William Newton, about 1620, it passed into several hands, but is now the property of R. C. Legh, Esq.

The *Chapel of Newton*, although long since ruinated, is still continued in the list of Chapels of the Diocese.

LYME HANLEY,

Or *Lyme Handley*,* is about seven miles N. E. N. from Macclesfield. It was granted by Richard II. to Margaret the daughter of Sir Thomas Danyers, as a reward for his bravery at the battle of Creçy, when he rescued the standard of the Black Prince Earl of Chester, and took prisoner Tankerville, Chamberlain of France. She was Sir Thomas's third daughter, and married Piers Legh, who was her third husband. He was Knighted soon after, but in 1399, on the advance of the Duke of Lancaster into the Palatinate, he seized Sir Piers, who was warmly attached to the King, and caused him to be beheaded at Chester on the 1st of Aug.

Dr. Cowper says, his head was fixed on the Eastgate, and his body afterwards interred in the Church of the White Friars, previous to being removed to Macclesfield. Holinshead, in noticing the military murders observes, "the Duke (of Lancaster) caused one of King Richard's faithfull and trusty friends, Sir Piers a Leigh, commonly called Perkin a Lee, to lose his head, and commanded the same to be set upon one of the highest turrets about the citie; and so that true and faithfull gentleman for his stedfast faith and assured loialtie to his loving Sovereign, thus lost his life."

The township continued in uninterrupted descent from Sir Piers Legh to Thomas Peter Legh, Esq. of the Lyme family; and he settled all his Cheshire Freehold Estates, including Lyme, and the Lancashire property, on his natural son Thomas Legh, Esq. M. P. for Newton, in the county of Lancaster, and his heirs: remainder to his second natural son William; further remainder to his niece Charlotte Anne Ormerod, and the issue of the marriage between his sister Martha Anne, wife of Lawrence Ormerod, of Ormerod, Lancashire, who is the representative of the regular branch of the Lyme family.

Lyme Hall, the seat of Mr. Legh, is a large quadrangular mansion of dark coloured grit stone, the south and west fronts are in the Palladian style, from Leoni's designs. The east and west fronts are in plain stone, the former opening to an extensive conservatory nearly one hundred and twenty feet long. There is a handsome portico to the south front, which is supported by beautiful columns of the Iŏnic order. The apart-

* The prefixture of *Lyme* to its name, has its origin in the situation being on the *lime* or border of the Forest of Macclesfield.

ments of the house are capacious. In the room adjoining the dining-room, the arms of James I. decorate the chimney-piece; and a representation of deer hunting, finished in stucco and painted The domestic Chapel ornamented in the Iönic style, is under the magnificent drawing room, which remains in its original state, excepting, however, the narrow windows, which have given place to modern ones. This apartment is wainscoated, with pannels and niches, and the ceiling is much enriched. In the upper part of the house, is a gallery one hundred and twenty-four feet long, in which are numerous portraits, including those of Sir Peter Legh, Knt. and Dr. John Hewitt, beheaded in 1658. In other apartments are portraits of the gallant James Earl of Derby, (beheaded at Bolton) with his illustrious Lady; Admiral Piers Legh, by Kneller, &c. &c.—Over the hall fire-place, is the portrait of an old man, who was seventy years park keeper; in his hundred
* 1705. and second year,* he is stated to have hunted a buck in a chase of six hours' duration. Considerable alterations and improvements were made in the house in 1817-18, under the direction of Mr. L. Wyatt.

In Lyme park, which contains about one thousand
† Ormerod. Cheshire acres,† is a herd of upwards of twenty wild cattle, similar to those in Lord Tankerville's park, at Chillington, chiefly white, with red ears. They have been in the park from time immemorial, and tradition says they are indigenous. In the summer season they assemble on the high lands, and in winter seek shelter in the park woods. They were formerly fed with holly branches, with which trees the park abounded; but those being destroyed, hay is now substituted. Two of the cows are shot annually for beef. There is a breed very much like them in a domesticated state, in Vale Royal park, the seat of T. Cholmondeley, Esq. A singular custom prevailed here, which was established upwards of a century ago, by the old Park-keeper before noticed, of driving the red deer: he was accustomed in the months of May and June, to mount his horse, and riding round the park hills with a rod in his hand, collect the deer together, and then drive them like a herd of cattle with the greatest ease. At the Deer Clod apposite the Hall, they would stand for any length of time, the young ones keeping close to their dams, and the old stags rearing up at each other in harmless combat, for at that season of the year, they dare not make use of their horns which are extremely tender. Obeying the order of the keeper, they would then rush into the Horse-pool, and swim the entire length of it; after this they were permitted to separate. The custom is now seldom practised.

POYNTON,

Is about four miles and a half S. S. E. from Stockport. Originally included in the possessions which the Earl had in the Hundred, it was subsequently granted to the Poutrells, and from them passed to the Stockports about the time‡ when the town from which they ‡ Rand.
took their name, was made the head of a Barony — Blundeville.
Temp. Edw. III. Poynton passed with the Barony of Stockport to Sir John de Warren, in right of his mother Cicely, daughter of Sir Nicholas de Eton, of Stockport, and wife of Sir Edw. Warren, whose father Edw. Warren, was supposed to be descended from the Earls of Warren. Considerable obscurity exists in tracing the descent of this connexion, and it gave rise to the History of the Warrens, by Mr. Watson. From Sir Edw. Warren, the descent is clearly traced. It appears by an Inq. p. m. temp. Elizabeth, that Sir John Warren held the manor from the King, by the annual render of two shillings, or a sparrow hawk. On the 11th May, 1544, Sir Edw. Warren was Knighted by the Earl of Hertford, at Leith; and about 1584, built a hall at Poynton. Sir Edward Warren, the 11th in succession, served in the Irish Wars, and was Sheriff of Cheshire in the 40th Elizabeth. Sir George Warren, K. B. was the last male proprietor of Poynton, and he died Aug. 31, 1801, leaving a daughter, Elizabeth Harriet, married to Viscount Bulkeley, in whom the manor is now vested, and who holds a Court Leet and Baron twice a year.

The *Hall* of Poynton, built by Sir Edward Warren, as stated above, was entirely pulled down by Sir G. Warren, who erected a handsome and extensive edifice on its site, in the Iönic stile. The park is extensive, and beautifully diversified; but it is now used as a ley.

On the right hand of the road from Stockport to Macclesfield, is POYNTON CHAPEL, also re-built by Sir George Warren, in a very neat manner. It is supposed
it was first founded in 1312,§ at which period the Abbot § Ormerod.
of Chester granted to Nicholas de Eton, and Joan his

wife, that he should find a Chaplain in the Chapel of Poynton for ever, for the benefit of them and the rest of the inhabitants.

In 1500, John Veysey, Vicar-General of the Diocese of Lichfield and Coventry, sequestrated the tythes belonging to Chester Abbey, because the Abbot had not found a Chaplain.

The patronage is vested in Lord Bulkeley; and the Registers commence in 1723.*

WORTH,

Is about five miles S. E. S. from Stockport, and was originally included in the *vill* of Poynton. It was at an early period possessed by a family which took the name of the township.† Temp. Hen. V. Worth passed to Roger Downes, of Shrigley, in marriage with Agnes, daughter and heiress of William de Hulme, who it is supposed was the representative of the Worths, in the female line. It continued vested in the Downes family, till it was sold by the present Edward Downes, Esq. to the late Sir George Warren, and has passed to Viscount Bulkeley. Worth is included in the Leet Court of the Hundred of Macclesfield.

WOODFORD

Is about five miles N. W. from Stockport; it is not noticed in the Survey, but it was included in the list of Sir John Arderne's estates, temp. John, and he settled it on his brother Eustace. It passed from the Ardernes, through the Stokeports and Etons, to the Warrens. About 1370, it was purchased from the Warrens, by John Davenport, of Weltrough;‡ and from him it has descended to the present proprietor, Davies Davenport, Esq. M. P. who holds a Court Leet and Baron for it.

Woodford Hall, the ancient seat of the Davenports, is occupied by a farmer.

MOTTRAM ANDREW,

Or *St. Andrew*, is about five miles N. W. W. from Macclesfield. A family, which took the name of the township, possessed it at a very early period, from whom it passed in marriage with Agnes, daughter and heiress of Adam de Mottram, to David Calveley; and it continued vested in the Calveleys till about the middle of the 17th century, when it became (supposed by sale) the property of a younger branch of the Booths, of Dunham Massy. The manor was afterwards alienated by Nathaniel Booth, Esq. to Richard Cooke, Esq. of Macclesfield, in 1716; and after some litigation, it was purchased from the Trustees in 1738, by Wm. Wright, of Offerton, from whom it has descended to his grandson, the present proprietor, Lawrence Wright, Esq.

Mottram Hall is occupied by Mr. Wright. The *Higher House*, and the *Lower House*, belonged about 1650, to two branches of the Mottershead family; but have subsequently become the property of Mr. Wright.

Lea Hall is the property of Mr. Mather; it formerly belonged to a branch of the Masseys.

TITHERINGTON,

Or *Tyderington*, is about a mile and a half N. of Macclesfield; it is not noticed in the Survey, but it is conjectured it formed a dependency on the Earl's manor of Macclesfield, being separated from that town by the Bollin.

A family which adopted the name of the township, were in possession long before the reign of Henry III. holding it by the service of a Knight's fee in the Welsh marches.—Subsequently to the 21st Edward I. Titherington passed with an heiress to the Worths, who were the proprietors till the end of the 17th century, when Samuel Heath, Esq. of Dublin, heir of Jasper Worth, sold it to Wm. Abney, for £1280. in November, 1695. It afterwards became the property, by sale, of the Perys, and the Robins, of Stafford; the latter devised it to John Hicken, Esq. and his trustees, in 1768, sold it to John Acton, Esq. for £8,600. In 1769, Mr. Acton conveyed it to his son in law, Wm. Brooksbank, Esq. whose sons dying issueless, the town-

* The Park of Poynton boasts some thriving plantations, and very fine timber; but its subterraneous riches, in coal, are immense, and probably exhaustless. It is said they were thus discovered:—An old tenant of one of the farms, was obliged to procure his water from a considerable distance, and frequently petitioned Sir George Warren to sink a well for him: but his request not being attended to, he gave notice to quit the premises. This induced Sir George to pay more deference to the man's desire, and the well was begun. The spring lay at a great depth; but before the workmen found the water, they discovered a large vein of very superior coal. A colliery was immediately commenced; and continues to be worked with great success.

† Supposed to be descended from the Worths, of Titherington.—Ormerod.

‡ Lysons, page 734.

CHESHIRE HISTORY.

ship is now vested in his daughter Anne, wife of Edw. Hardinge Stracey, Esq.

BOLLINGTON

Is about two miles N. of Macclesfield, and is included in the manor of Macclesfield Forest.

The land-owners are copyholders from the Crown. There are considerable Cotton Works and Collieries here.

FALLIBROOME,

Anciently called *Falingbrome*, and *Falygreve*, altho' not noticed in Domesday, is nevertheless supposed to have been included in the Earl's manor of Macclesfield. It was granted by Hugh Cyveilioc to Sir Richard de Fytun, and passed from his successors to the families of Venables and Booth; and the latter selling their estates in severalties, the manor has fallen into disuse.

UPTON,

Is about a mile and half N. N. W. from Macclesfield; and, with several of the preceding townships, is unnoticed in Domesday. Like them, however, the probability is, it was part of the great Lordship of Macclesfield. The Stapletons (a Yorkshire family) were settled here at an early period; and Edwyn Stapleton was succeeded by —— Darcy, Esq. after whom, the Booths became the proprietors. About 1740, it was sold by them to John Ward, Esq. whose eldest daughter and heiress married the grandfather of Davies Davenport, Esq. M. P. and he alienated it to John Ryle, Esq. of Park House, near Macclesfield, who is the present proprietor.—The situation of the township generally is very picturesque.

HENBURY-CUM-PEXHALL,

Is nearly two miles W. S. W. from Macclesfield.—It appears from the Survey that this township was originally included in the list of the Earl's Estates. The Mainwarings of Warmincham held this manor of the Fee of Halton; and it passed from them to the Tressels. Temp. Edw. III. Oliver *de Burdeaux* obtained it in marriage with the heiress of Sir Warin Mainwaring; and in the same reign, a large portion of it was purchased by Sir John Davenport, of Woodford, and his descendants continued the possessors, till the death of
* 1664. Isabella,* the wife of Sir Fulk Lucy, one of the Representatives of the County in Parliament, when he sold it to Sir Wm. Meredith, Bart. About 1779, his grandson, Sir William, alienated it to John Bower Jodrell, and his son, F. Jodrell, Esq is the present proprietor.

Henbury Hall, the residence of Mr. Jodrell, is a handsome mansion, considerably improved and beautified by its present owner.

BIRTLES,

Lies about two miles and a half W. N. from Macclesfield; and was as early as the 14th century vested in a family of the same name; and at the commencement of the 17th century it was possessed by their representatives, the Swettenhams, in right of Mary, the wife of Thomas Swettenham, married in 1602. In 1783, Thomas Swettenham Willis, Esq. sold the manor to Joseph Fowden, and he resold it in 1791, to the present proprietor, Robert Hibbert, Esq.

CHELFORD

Is about seven miles due W. from Macclesfield, and is supposed to have included in its boundary, the township of Old Withington. About 1264, the manor was given to the Abbot of Chester, by Robert Pigot, on the condition of furnishing a Chaplain to say Mass for the repose of his soul in Chelford Chapel, three days in the week, and the remaining four days before the altar of St. Nicholas, in Prestbury Church. At the Dissolution it was severed from the Dean and Chapter of Chester, in the suits with Sir Richard Cotton. In the 22d Elizabeth it was held by Henry Mainwaring, of Carincham, and has subsequently passed to the Mainwarings of Peover. The Constables of Chelford are sworn at the Court of Barnshaw.

A *School House* was built here by the Rev. John Parker, and endowed with £20. per annum; for the poor children of the township.

In this township is the Hamlet of ASTLE, or *Asthulle*, which passed with Chelford, to Chester Abbey. At a very early date, it was held of the Order of St. John of Jerusalem by Adam de Asthulle. It is now the property and seat of Thomas Parker, Esq. Colonel of the Royal Cheshire Militia, by marriage of an ancestor in 1650, with the heiress of the Snelsons, of Snelson.

The *Hall* is a very handsome building, and the picturesque scenery of the grounds is much improved by an artificial lake.

The present CHAPEL of Chelford, is a modern brick building, on the bank of the lake. It was consecrated

CHESHIRE in 1776. There was a Chapel here as early as 1267. At the Dissolution, the Chaplain was Edward Acton, who had a salary of £4. 6s. 8d. from Chester Abbey. It is now an augmented Curacy, the patronage vested in Thomas Parker, Esq. The registers commence in 1679. The Parkers have a vault here, with an Altar Tomb, on which is the name of the Rev. John Parker, of Astle, who died Nov. 1, 1795. There is also a memorial of R. S. C. Brooke, Esq.

OLD WITHINGTON,

Is nearly seven miles and a half N. N. W. from Congleton, and, as before noticed, is conjectured to have been included in the *vill* of Chelford. Indeed the county rate is at present assessed on the townships jointly, under the description of Chelford-cum-Old Withington. It is not noticed in the Survey. The Pigots, and the Worths, had estates here; but the manor was among the earliest possessions of the Ardernes of Aldford, and was held under them by the Camvilles, of Clifton Camville, Staffordshire.

In the reign of Henry the Third, Walkelyn de Arderne granted to Robert de Camville release of all homages or rents due to him in Old Withington, in reward of the services rendered by him in the wars in Gascony. This Robert afterwards granted to Oliver Titton, and John de Baskervyle, about 1266, the manor, in moieties. The whole eventually became vested in the Baskervyles, and continued in their family by direct descent, till, pursuant to the will of Wm. Glegg, Esq. of Gayton, in 1758, whose daughter Maria he married, John Baskerville, Esq. assumed the name of Glegg, and is the present proprietor of Withington and Gayton. The Constable of the township is sworn at the Hundred Leet. No Court is held for the Manor.

The *Hall* of Withington is an extensive building, considerably amplified and improved by Mr. Glegg, and is seated in a pleasant part of the Hundred.

LOWER WITHINGTON,

(A part of which is within Marton Chapelry) is seven miles N. N. W. from Congleton. Although not noticed in the Survey, there is little doubt but what it was included in the possessions of the Earl; for it is stated,* that Randle Blundeville gave this township, with twenty shillings rent from the Mill at Macclesfield, to Robert the son of Salmon, on the render of a pair of gilt spurs; in return for which, Robert quit-claimed to the Earl, all the lands which his father held in Normandy. Robert de Salmon, afterwards gave to his daughter Mary, in marriage with Vivian de Davenport, a moiety of the township; Ellen, wife of Matthew del Mere, grand-daughter of Gilbert Salmon, brought to her husband the other half of the township. Temp. Richard II. the Del Mere share, was settled by Matthew del Mere on Randle Mainwaring of Peover. The Davenports were afterwards possessed of the whole manor,† and continued in possession till towards the close of the 17th century; subsequently it became the property of the Parkers, and is now vested in Thos. Parker, Esq. The township is subject to the Leet of Weverham.

* [Vill. Cest.]

† Lysons, 733.

HISTORY.

The singular elevation called *Tunsted Hill*, is in this township; and is supposed to have been the site of a village, anterior to the Saxon æra.‡

‡ Ormerod.

Wheltrough Hall, an ancient timber mansion, was formerly the seat of a branch of the Davenport family, from whom descended the Davenports of Bramhall, Henbury, and Woodford. Towards the close of the 17th century, the family either became extinct, or had quitted Cheshire, for the estate became vested in the Hollinsheads, of Sutton, from whom it passed in marriage with an heiress, Frances, to her husband Peter Brooke, Esq. of Mere. In 1792, her grandson, Thomas Langford Brooke, sold it to the Rev. John Parker, of Astle, and from him it has passed to the present proprietor, Thomas Parker, Esq.

CAPESTHORNE,

Which is about five miles W. S. from Macclesfield, was included in the possessions of the Earl; and subsequently passed with Gawsworth to the Ardernes.—Very early in the 13th century, it was vested in a family which adopted the name of the towship, for in 1238, Thomas de Capesthorne, contracted with Lucia de Orreby Lady of Gawsworth, to do service ward at Aldford Castle, she finding him an haubergeon.—Temp. Edward III. Sarah, the daughter and heiress of Randle Capesthorne, brought the township in marriage to her husband John de Ward. The Wards continued in uninterrupted possession, till the death of John Ward, Esq. in March, 1748, when in right of his wife, Mary, eldest daughter of John Ward, the manor became the property of Davies Davenport, Esq. of Woodford, grandfather of Davies Davenport, Esq. M. P. the present proprietor.

The *Hall* is a large building, erected in the early part of the 18th century, pleasantly situated on the margin of a fine sheet of water, supplied from a lake called Reed's Mere.

Capesthorne *Chapel*, was built by John Ward, Esq. last of that name and family, who endowed it with the tythes of the township. It was twice augmented in 1722, and 1723, with £200 by Mr. Ward. The Minister, is appointed by Mr. Davenport. The Registers commence in 1722.

MARTON

Lies nearly four miles N. W. from Congleton; and it appears from the Survey it was held by the Earl — A moiety of it was subsequently obtained by marriage of Richard de Davenport, with Amabel, daughter of Gilbert Venables, Baron of Kinderton, and great grandfather of Gilbert, the first head of the Barony. They continued possessed of this moiety in regular succession; and it is now, together with the other moiety (purchased by Richard Davenport, Esq. in 1760) the property of D. Davenport, Esq. M. P.*

Marton *Hall*, is a timber mansion of considerable antiquity, with centre and wings. In the hall are hung up a few old lances.

The *Chapel* is a short distance N. E. of the hall, and consists of nave, chancel, porch, and tower, finished with a low spire. It is chiefly of timber; and some of the windows contain a few specimens of ancient stained glass. In the Chapel Yard, are two figures in armour, much decayed, supposed to be the effigies of Sir John Davenport, who built the Chapel, about 1343, and his son Sir Urian or Vivian Davenport.—On the Dissolution, this Chapel, or Chantry, was granted to the Davenports, and the patronage of the Curacy is vested in Davies Davenport, Esq. The Registers commence in 1584.

SIDDINGTON

Is about five miles N. W. from Congleton.—It was included in the estates of Bigod; and the paramount royalty descended to the Ardernes of Aldford. A branch of the Davenports, it is supposed, settled here before the 16th Edw. III. and assumed the local name.†—About the end of the 15th century, Emmote, daughter of Robert de Sydington, brought the manor in marriage to Edward Fitton, of Gawsworth, and on the termination of the Fittons in the direct line, this estate went to their heirs in general, from whom it was purchased by the Wards, of Capesthorne, and has descended with other property to the present possessor, D. Davenport, Esq. M. P.

The *Chapel* of Siddington, is a short distance from the Hall, built chiefly of timber and plaister. The chancel is divided from the nave by an elegantly enriched carved oak screen. A license to baptise and bury here, was obtained in 1721, from which date the Registers commence.

The *School* was endowed with £8. per ann. about 1710, by John Fowden; the appointment of the master is vested in the Bishop.‡

A family named *Loges*, were settled here at a very early period, and the estates which they held in the township, passed to the Davenports, and the Parkers, of Coppenhall.

In this township are the Hamlets of HENSHAW,§ and THORNYCROFT, which gave name to distinct families. The Henshaws, or Henchals, continued here in regular succession, till the marriage of John Thornycroft, Esq. with Eleanor, heiress of John Henshaw, Esq. in 1712.

Henshaw Hall is occupied by a farmer. The male line of the Thornycrofts, terminated in Edw. Thornycroft, Esq. who died Jan. 20, 1817, and was buried at Gawsworth, leaving the manor, with its dependencies, vested in two sisters for life, with remainder to the Rev. Charles Mytton, Rector of Eccleston, and his issue.

Thornycroft Hall is now used as a farm-house.

NORTH RODE

Is about three miles and a half N. E. from Congleton, and was included in the numerous estates of Bigod, and fell to the Ardernes, under whom it was held by the Mainwarings of Warmincham, and their followers

* Mr. Ormerod observes, that the manor has been in this respectable family, ever since the marriage of Richard de Dauneport, with Amabilia Venables, about 1176—645 years!

† Ormerod, 560.

‡ Lysons, 732.

§ Hofinchel, in the Survey.

the Tressels; and from them it passed to their successors, the Veres, Earls of Oxford. Sir Christopher Hatton then became the Proprietor, and after him his representatives, the Crewes, of Crewe. Lord Crewe sold it a few years since to John Smith Daintry, Esq. of Macclesfield, who is the present possessor.

BOSLEY,

Anciently called *Bosley and Lea*, or *Lea Bosley*, is about five miles E. N. E. from Congleton, and was held under the Earl by Hugo de Mara, whose estates were formed into the Barony of Montalt. On the death of the last Baron, it was granted by the Crown to the Stanleys.* Soon after the death of Thomas Stanley, first Earl of Derby, temp. Hen. VII. it was vested in a branch of the Leghs, and they assumed the surname of Macclesfield, exchanging it with the Duke of Buckingham, for Mere, and lands in Chesterton. After the Battle of Flodden, the manor was given to Sir Edward Stanley, created Lord Monteagle. Subsequently reverting to the elder branch of the Stanleys, James Earl of Derby sold it to Sir Edward Fitton, of Gawsworth; and from his descendants it has passed with Gawsworth, to the Earl of Harrington.

The *Chapel* of Bosley, is built of brick, with an ancient tower. The Vicar of Prestbury is the patron. The Registers commence 1728.

THE CHAPELRY OF MACCLESFIELD,

CONTAINS THE TOWNSHIPS OF

MACCLESFIELD, KETTLESHULME, SUTTON DOWNES, HURDSFIELD, WINCLE, RAINOW, WILDBOARCLOUGH, AND MACCLESFIELD FOREST, POTT SHRIGLEY.

MACCLESFIELD

Is about one hundred and sixty-six miles from London, and eighteen from Manchester. It is thus noticed in the Survey:

Ipse Comes tenet Eduinas Macclesfeld, Comes tenuit; ibi II hidæ geldabiles. Terra est X carucarum. In dominio est una caruca, et IV servi; ibi molina serviens curiæ. Silva VI leuvis longitudine et quatuor latitudine; et ibi VII haiæ erant; pratum bobus. Tertius denarius de hundret pertenet huic manerio. Tempore R. Edwardi valebat VIII libras, modo XX solidos. Wasta fuit.

It appears from this, that Macclesfield had previously been considerably depopulated,—the woods attached to Earl Edwin's demesne were six miles long and four in breadth, with six inclosures, or decoys, for deer and wild goats. No notice whatever is taken of the Church, which had no doubt been antecedently in existence, but was then in ruins.

Soon after the Baronial establishments of the Earl, it became in some degree a place of importance and of military strength, a fortification being erected, which was kept in repair by the Lords of Aldford, and other tenants of the Earl. Some Courts were then established here, and the Earl's Justice fixed on the town for the seat of his tribunal. Executions of his sentences, were here carried into effect, on the site of a piece of land, called the *Gallows-tree-hey*. On the lapse of the Earldom to the Crown, the abolition of these distinctions followed as a consequence, and the manor of Macclesfield became vested in the Crown.

Temp. Randle III. the town was made a free burgh for one hundred and twenty burgesses, each of whom paid to the Earl 12*d*. and in the 45th Hen. III. Prince Edward his son, then Earl, granted a Charter, a translation of which is subjoined.†—The privileges thus granted to Macclesfield, were subsequently confirmed by Edward III. at York, Feb. 26, 1334; on the 14th Nov. 1390, by Richard II. at Westminster; by Edw. IV. 30th Jan. 1465; by Elizabeth, at Westminster, May 13, 1564, and Sept. 1, 1595; and by Charles II. under whose charter the present civic government of the town is administered.

The Corporation of Macclesfield consists of a Mayor, and 24 Aldermen; of whom, including the Mayor,

* It had been previously vested in the Earl of Salisbury by Royal grant, dated 1337.

† Copy of the Charter granted by Edward Earl of Chester, to the Corporation of Macclesfield. Translated from the Latin:—

Edward the illustrious first-born of the King of England, to the Archbishops, Bishops, Abbots, Priors, Counts. Barons, Justices, Sheriffs, Officers, Servants, Bailiffs, and all his faithful Subjects, health! Know ye, that we have granted, and by this our present Charter have

four are Justices, and are annually elected. They claim toll of fairs and markets; and hold half yearly sessions, before the Mayor, Justices, and Recorder, for the trial of assaults, and misdemeanors, not having cognizance of felonies. What are called *Privy Sessions*, are also held weekly, for the settlement of local disputes, and adjustment of pauper cases, &c.

In 1796, an Act was obtained for the inclosure of the waste lands; and the shares of them, together with the mines, and minerals, which were apportioned to the King as Lord of the Manor, became the property by purchase of the late Mr. C. Cooke.

The Records of Macclesfield are not of very remote antiquity, and those in existence enable the reader to form but a vague opinion of the progressive increase of the town, either in wealth or population.

Sir John Savage, when Mayor of Macclesfield, fell in the Battle of Flodden, and with him a great number of the burgesses; tradition asserts, that a similar fate attended many of the men of Macclesfield at the Battle of Bosworth, but this tale is no doubt built on a perversion of facts by no means uncommon in history—Indeed, it is added, that the Mayor and Burgesses petitioned Henry VII. on the subject of the calamity which the town had sustained in the loss of so many of its inhabitants, and Dr. Aikin, in his Description of the Country round Manchester, states that a copy of this identical petition was in existence in the Town Chest, praying, that although they were unable to fill up the vacancies in the Corporation as demanded by the Charter, it might not, therefore, be abrogated, inasmuch as the townsmen had fallen in the King's service. No such document, however, is now to be found.

The principal market was formerly held by prescription, on Mondays, but by the Police Act, obtained in 1814, it was altered to Tuesdays. Considerable business is transacted here in the Corn Trade; the fairs, of which there are five in the year, take place May 6, June 22, July 11, Oct. 4, and Nov. 11.

The situation of Macclesfield is at the foot of the hills which divide Cheshire from the neighbouring Counties, and on the borders of the former Forest of the same name; a branch of the Bollin runs through the lower part of the town. The principal manufacture of the town, is silk, cotton, &c.; it formerly consisted of wrought buttons of silk and mohair. This species of trade may be traced back nearly two hundred years; and the buttons, which were curiously worked with the needle, were employed in the ornamenting the full suite so much worn in the reigns of William III. Anne, and George I. and II.*

Silk Mills were erected here, nearly a century ago,

confirmed for ourselves and our heirs, to our Burgesses of Macclesfield, that our Town of Macclesfield may and shall be a free Borough; and that our Burgesses of the said Borough, may have a Merchant's Guild in the same Borough, with Liberties and free Customs belonging to the said Guild; and that they shall be free throughout all our County of Chester, as well by water as by land, of Tolls, Passage Money, Pontage, Stallage, Lastage, and all other customs, excepting Salt at the Wyches. And that they may have Common of Pasture, and Housebote, and Heybote, in our Forest, as they used to have; saving to ourselves our Mast, and Mast-money; and that they shall not be impleaded nor judged, in any Plea out of their Borough. And if any of them shall happen to be at our mercy for any forfeiture, he shall pay no more than TWELVE PENCE before judgment; and after judgment, a reasonable amercement, according to the nature of the fault, unless the forfeiture belong to our sword. The Burgesses aforesaid, shall grind their corn at our mill to the twentieth grain, as they were used to do; and they may nominate their officers, by our assent and appointment, or by that of our Bailiffs. They may have and hold their Burgages and the lands belonging to them, freely and quietly for TWELVE PENCE a year; and may give, sell, or mortgage the same to whomsoever they will, excepting Religious Houses, as they used to do; saving to ourselves the liberty of our Oven in the said Town. Wherefore we will and firmly command, for ourselves and our heirs, that our Burgesses aforesaid shall have all the aforesaid privilleges, and enjoy all the Liberties appointed, as is more fully set forth. As witness, Lord Erardo de Valory, Fulcone de Orreby, our Justice of Chester; Ralphe de Basset, Thomas de Orreby, our Escheator of Chester; Hugh de Clifford, John le Breton, Keepers of our Wardrobe; Thomas de Moulton, and others. Given under our hands, at Guildford, the 29th day of May, in the 45th year of the reign of our Lord and Father the King. A. D. 1261.

EDWARD.

* The following account of this curious trade, is copied from Aikin's Manchester, page 437.—" In the wild country between Buxton, Leek, and Macclesfield, called the FLASH, from a Chapel of that name, lived a set of pedestrian chapmen, who hawked about these buttons, together with ribbons, and ferreting, made at Leek, and handkerchiefs, with small wares, from Manchester. These pedlars were known on the roads they travelled by the appellation of FLASH-MEN, and frequented farm-houses and fairs, using a sort of slang, or canting dialect. At first they paid ready money for their goods, till they acquired credit, which they were sure to extend till there was no more to be had, when

and a great trade in that article, and in cotton, is now carried on, so much so, that within the last forty or forty-five years, the population is nearly doubled.

At the commencement of the silk trade, an Act of Parliament was obtained, imposing a penalty on the wearing of moulds, covered with the same stuff as the coat; this, after having fallen into disuse, was again attempted to be enforced in 1778, by the extraordinary project of hiring informers. But the result, as might be expected, was unfavorable, inasmuch as it tended to promote the more general use of metal buttons.*

In addition to the cotton factories, there is a great manufactory here of fustians, linen cloth, &c. Upwards of thirty mills for silk throwsting, preparatory to being used by the weavers, are established. There were formerly large smelting and brass works, a short distance east of the town, called the smelting houses, consisting of a specious building, a large windmill for grinding the ore; a range of low buildings called calamy-house, where the calamine was washed, brass-houses, smelting-houses, &c; but these have been discontinued some years.

The manor of Macclefield, is vested in the Crown, as a portion of the Earldom of Chester. About 1270, say the Lysons, it was settled on Eleanor, the wife of Prince Edward; and after going through many hands, subsequently to the death of Charles I. the manor and borough were sold to Peter Brereton and John Winstanley; and the Manor and Hundred, held under lease by the Mainwarings, to Samuel Rowe.

In 1762, the Earl of Harrington obtained a lease from the Crown of all Cottages erected on the waste, and other encroachments within the manor; also, all Coal-pits, with all profits of Court for the Manor; all mines, excepting royal mines, and all stone-quarries.

In 1765, the same Earl had a lease of the manor and borough of Macclesfield; the royalties of coal, peat, and turf; the profits of the two fairs yearly, with all Manerial Courts, commons, wastes, and encroachments thereon.

In 1776, the Crown granted a lease of all fines and alienations upon surrenders within the manor and forest, and all heriots, reliefs, perquisites of Court, and other profits, to the Duke of Leeds. The springs and water courses which supply the town, together with the toll at fairs and markets, bring in a considerable income, and are vested in the corporation.

On the passing of the Inclosure Act in 1791, it was ascertained that no Courts had been held by the Earl of Harrington, under authority of the leases; and that the only Court which sat, was a three weeks Court by the Mayor, for the trial of actions—that no copyhold estates were held of the manor, nor any profits of Courts received—that the Corporation received the profits of the fairs—and that no advantage had accrued to the Lessee from any mines, excepting coal mines.

By this enactment, all encroachments within the manor, except such as had occurred within sixty years, and had no buildings erected on them, were reserved to their respective possessors: the manerial right of the Crown to the soil, mines, and minerals of the waste grounds, were abolished, reserving only coal mines,—and as a compensation for such concession, an allottment of 118a. 2r. 34p. was made to the King, which, with the right of digging coal,† were sold in 1803, under the Land-tax Redemption Act, to C. Cooke, Esq.

A Court of Record, is held once a month, at Macclesfield, for the liberty of the Hundred, which includes Over Alderley, Nether Alderley, Birtles, Bollin Fee, Bosley, Bramhall, Bredbury, Brinnington, Capesthorne,

they dropped their connexions without paying, and formed new ones. They long went on thus, inclosing the common where they dwelt for a trifling payment, and building cottages, till they began to have farms, which they improved from the gains of their credit, without troubling themselves about payment, since no bailiff for a long time attempted to serve a writ there. At length a resolute officer, a native of the district, ventured to arrest several of them; whence their credit was destroyed, they changed the wandering life of pedlars for the settled care of their farms; but as they were held by no leases, they were left at the mercy of the lords of the soil, the Harper family, who made them pay for their impositions on others. Another set of pedestrians were called the BROKEN-CROSS GANG, from a place of that name between Macclesfield and Congleton. These associated with the Flash-men at fairs, playing with thimbles and buttons, like jugglers with cups and balls, and enticing people to lose their money by gambling. They at length took to the kindred trades of robbing and picking pockets, till at last the gang was broken up by the hands of Justice. The character of Autolycus, in Shakespeare's Winter's Tale, seems to have been a correct model of this worthy brotherhood."

* Beauties of England, page 258.

† Of which there were four seams differing in depth, extent, and value.

CHESHIRE

Cheadle, Chelford, Mottram-in-Longdendale, Newton-in-Prestbury, Northenden, Pownall-fee, Romilly, Siddington, Snelson, Somerford Booths, Stockport, Great Warford, Werneth, Lower Withington, Old Withington, Woodford, and Worth.

Bosley was formerly considered in the forest boundary. Adlington, Butley, Gawsworth, Macclesfield, Norbury, Poynton, Prestbury, North Rode, and Torkington, lie in the jurisdiction of the Forest and Hundred.

There is a distinct Court for the Manor and Forest; and a Court Leet for both jurisdictions. The office of Keeper of the Gaol at Macclesfield, which was hereditary, passed at an early date with the daughter of John the Gaoler, to the family of Mottram, in whom it continued some generations; from them it fell to the Savages, and to their representatives the Cholmondeleys. The Gaol is now the property of the Corporation. The Savages had formerly a Park here, which extended to Park-lane, about a mile S. S. W. On being broken up, which took place many years ago, the land was sold in lots by Lord Cholmondeley.

The *Castle Field*, adjoining the road to Congleton, is supposed to have been the site of a castellated mansion belonging to the Savages.

Having before shortly adverted to the silk manufacture of this town, it may not be deemed superfluous, to go a little further into detail: Although the silk business had been previously established here, the great stimulus to its present extent was given by Mr. Charles Roe, the son of a Clergyman, of Derbyshire, who settled in Macclesfield about the middle of the last century.

The first model of a silk mill, had been brought from Italy to Derby, where a manufactory was established; and Mr. Roe, having obtained a knowledge of the mechanism, erected a large and improved machine here, in 1756, in a building at the end of Park Green. Mr. Roe's success, soon introduced competitors, for in a few years, twelve mills were in work, viz. Roe, Robinson, and Stafford; Greaves and Huxley; Jonas Hall; Braddock and Hall; Wm. Hall; Thomas Hall; John and John Rowbotham; Philip Clewes; Greaves and Johnson; James Rowson; Joseph Simpson; and James Mayson.

HISTORY.

About 1785, Cotton Spinning was first commenced here, by some Lancashire speculators, who built a large factory on Bollin Bank, at the Waters; the town began to rise rapidly in its population; and in 1790, a further increase to trade took place by a new establishment for the manufacture of silk.

In 1787, the first Bank was opened in Jordan Gate, by Hawkins, Mills & Co. and on their declining business, they were succeeded by the present respectable firm of Daintry & Ryle; they were followed by Critchley & Turner, in 1816; since then Messrs. William, John, and Thomas Brocklehurst & Co. have opened a Bank.

There are no particular features of beauty or antiquity in the *Public Buildings* of Macclesfield.

In Roch-wall-gate, a very short distance S. of the Church, are some small remains of the ancient mansion of the Dukes of Buckingham, which Smith* notices as "a huge place all of stone, in manner of a Castle, which belonged to the Duke of Buckingham, but now gone to decay."

Webb, in his Itinerary, 1622, observes "In this towne are yet seene some ruines of the ancient Manor House of the renowned Duke of Buckingham, who (as yet report goethe) kept there his Princely residence, about the time of King Edward IV. of whose great hospitality there, much by tradition is reported." It is somewhat extraordinary, notwthstanding these positive descriptions of the Duke of Buckingham, the records of the town are entirely silent as to the family.

The *Court House*, and *Gaol-tenement*, are of grey stone, situated near the Church, in the market place.—During the Disturbances of 1819, the former was converted into a guard room for troops. The King's Bake-house, the *furnus villæ* of the Earl's Charter, continued vested in the Crown till 1818, when it was sold to Mr. T. Jones, the Postmaster, and is used now as the Post Office.

Bate Hall, in Chester Gate, has for a long period been let as a Public House; it was formerly the residence of the Stopfords, ancestors of the Earls of Courtown.

The *Grammar School*† of Macclesfield was founded

* See Description of Cheshire, 1585.

† The following is a portion of the "Will of Sir John Percyvale,

CHESHIRE

HISTORY.

at the beginning of the 16th century. Like many other excellent charities, in this instance the letter of the endowment has not been strictly attended to. The original site of the School, was near the Parochial Chapel, on the east side; the place is now called *School Bank*. The present building is in King Edward-street, and including the Master's residence, forms three sides of a quadrangle; it was purchased from the trustees of Sir R. Davenport, Knight.

In 1552, King Edward VI. further endowed the school with sixteen acres of land near Chester, several crofts, closes, meadows, and houses, in and near the City; part of the Prebend's lands of St. John's College, which belonged to the Petit Canoury—late in the possession of Richard Brereton, Esq.*—In the Charter granted by this King, no notice whatever is taken of the original foundation, nor of the estates purchased under it in Tytherington, Rainow, Hurdsfield, and Sutton; it is therefore supposed that, owing to some legal informality, they were seized by the Crown. The charter directs that the school shall be called *The Free Grammar School of King Edw. VI.*—that it shall be taught by one Master and Under Master, and governed by XIV Trustees,† to be chosen by the Inhabitants of Macclesfield, and the Parish of Prestbury, who are made a Body Corporate, with a Common Seal, and have the power of filling up vacancies.

The lands, &c. thus granted are to be held under the

KNT. the first founder of Macclesfield Free Grammar School.

xxth. January, M.CCCCCII.

To all People to whom this present writyng indented shall come, John Percyvale, Knyght, and late Maire of the citie of London, sendith gretyng, in our Lord God evrelastyng. Wherefore this tyme, I consideryng that in the countrie of Chestre, and specially about the towne of Maxfild, fast by the which towne I was borne, God of his aboundant Grace hath sent and daily sendeth to the Inhabitants there copyous plentie of children; to whose learnyng, bryngyng forth in conynge and virtue, right few teachers and scolemaisters been in that countre, whereby many children for lak of such techying and draught in conynge, fall to idleness, and consequently live dissolutely all their dais, which with the gracious mocion of the most Revrende Fader in God, and my singular good Lord, Thomas Archbishop of York, hath moche stered me of such little good as God of his Grace hath me sent, to purved a preest to sing and pray for me and my friends at Maxfild aforesaid, and there to kepe a free Gramar Scole for evermore." [The will then goes on to describe the lands, &c. and proceeds]—"And I have intreated and besought my said singular good Lord to ordeyne and purvay, at my costs and charges, after the rate of xvj years purchase, Vm'rc. more above the said Xm'rc to the encrease and augmentation of the salary of the forsaid preest and scolemaistre, and he may alway be a man graduate, to the better relievying with spirituall comforte of all the contre there as by prechyng and techyng, and good example givyng. The which londs and ten'ts of the yerely value of Vmrc. to the said londs and ten'ts, of the yerely value of Xmrc. my said singular good Lord, of his speciall goodness, hath granted me to purvey and ordeyne in the best wise he can, and so to make the same londs and ten'ts to amounte to the sume of the yerely value of Xli. Wherefore and whereupon I, the said John Percyvale, by this present writyng endented, make and declare my will as to the disposicion of all the said londs and ten'ts, as well of the said Xmrc. by yere, ready purveyed, as of the said other yerely mrc. to be purveyed, that is, to wete, of the said hole Xli. by yere, in the manner and form hereafter ensuying, that is to say, first and formost I will, that myn executors, with the advice of good lerned counsell, shall see that the title, right, and interest of all the said londs and ten'ts, of the yerely value of Xli. as is aforesaid, shall stond clere, good, and sufficient to the performance of my purpose and entent aforesaid, to be executed after the maner and fourme hereunder declared, the which title, right, and enterest so found good and sufficient, I woll that myn executors without delay shall make trew payment and contentation unto my said singular good Lord, as well of the said Xvjli. vjs. yot. being behynde unpaied of the purchase of the said yerely Xmrc. as for the hole purchace of the said yerely Vmrc. yf my said good Lord do purvay therefore and purchace it; and that done, I woll that then all the same londs and ten'ts by good and ordynate conveyaunce shall be put in feoffement to these persones folowyng, that is to say [naming them.] To hold to them and to theyr heires for ever, to the intent that they and their heires of thissues and p'fets of all the said lands and ten'ts shall fynde and susteone a virtues preest conynge in gramer and graduate. The same preest to sing and say his devyne s'vice daily as his disposicione shall be, in the parishe chirch of Maxfild aforsaid, praiyng for my soule, and the soule of Dame Thomasyne my wyfe, the soules also of our faders, moders, benefactors, and the soule of Richard Sutton, gentilman, for the good and holsome counsell which he hath given me to the p'fourmance of this my will, and for all X'an soules. An I woll that the same preest shall alway keep and contynew in the said town of Maxfild a free gramer Scole, techyng their gentilmen's sonnes, and other good men's children of the towne and countre thereabouts, whereby they shall now grow in conyng and virtue to the laude and praise of Almighty God, and to their own comfort and p'fite." &c.

* Valued temp. Edward VI. at £8. 17*s.* 4*d.* per annum.—HARL. M.SS.

† The present Trustees are D. Davenport, Esq. M. P. J. Glegg, Esq. Edw. Downes, Esq. Thomas Parker, Esq. Francis Jodrell, Esq. Laurence Wright, Esq. Lord Bulkeley, the Vicar of Prestbury, Rich. Legh, Esq. John Ryle, Esq. J. S. Daintry, Esq. Thos. Legh, Esq. Edward Stracey, Esq. and the Rev. Walter Davenport.

manor of East Greenwich, by the annual payment of twenty-five shillings to the Court of Augmentation of the King's revenue. The original school-house was sold in 1750, and the Governors then purchased the present one.

In 1774, they obtained an Act of Parliament, empowering them to make further exchanges and purchases—to appoint such a number of sub-masters as might be necessary in the various branches of literature, &c. and to increase the salaries of the head master and ushers at discretion.* The Act further gave them authority to make statutes for the school, with the advice of the Bishop of Chester; to dismiss the masters for improper conduct, with the approbation of the Bishop. When the Act passed, the revenues of the school were £170. per ann.; they are now £700.

The present Agent for the School is David Browne, Esq. a gentleman to whom all the recent historians of Cheshire have been under great obligations for the very valuable matter communicated by him relative to the Hundred; the head master is the Rev. David Davies, D. D.

In the reign of Elizabeth, Brounswerd, the celebrated Latin poet, was master of the school; he was buried in the chancel of the Parochial Chapel.

Mr. Ormerod notices within the town four Halls, viz. *Stapleton Hall*, formerly the property of the Stapletons, of Upton, near Macclesfield, now converted into shops; *Ogden Hall*, now occupied as a private house, formerly Ogden's, afterwards Swettenham's, of Somerford Booths, and now the property of J Green, Esq. of London, whose mother purchased it from the Swettenhams; *Worth Hall*, occupied as a private house, formerly Archbishop Savage's, and his occasional residence on coming into the town from Mottram Andrew; *Pickford Hall*, formerly the property of the Pickfords, of Macclesfield, has been taken down, rebuilt, and is the residence of William Ayton, Esq.

Adjoining the School-house field, is the *Walley Heys*, in the vicinity of which are several *tumuli*, not far south of the supposed line of a Roman road from Condate to Rainow.

* The Seal of the Trustees is of oval form, the ends pointed; in the centre, the figure of an old man with a book in his left hand, and a rod in his right.—Around, is the inscription, "SIGILLUM LIBERE SCOLE DE MACCLEFFELD."—Over the central figure the letters E. R. at the feet a rose.

The PAROCHIAL CHAPEL of Macclesfield† was founded about 1277, by Queen Eleanor, and is dedicated to St. Michael. It is dependent on the Church of Prestbury. The curate is appointed by the Mayor, with the sanction of the Bishop of Chester; he is a King's Preacher, and has a Salary from the Crown of £50.—The Registers commence in 1572.

The building is composed of nave, chancel, side aisles, and tower, the latter originally crowned with a spire.—There are Chapels belonging to the Leghs, of Lyme, and the Savages, on the south side of the south aisle.—The entire fabric has lately undergone a thorough repair. Early in the last century, the nave was entirely rebuilt, and the chancel was singularly placed at the end of the south side aisle.

The *Savage Chapel*, was built by Thomas Savage Arch-Bishop of York, in 1501; his body was buried at York, but his "heart at Maxfield, where he built a Chapel at the side of Maxfield Church, and intended to have made a College there." It originally communicated with the Church. The door-way is under a turret on the west side. In a window projecting over the entrance, are carved the arms of England, and those of the founder, impaling the secs of Rochester, London, aud York. The entire front is much enriched.

Under Gothic arches, in the interior, on the north side, are two altar tombs; one of them supporting the recumbent figure of a man in armour, his head lying on a helmet, with a dog at his feet. The other tomb also bears the effigy of a warrior, in armour, with a collar of SS.—These are memorials of the Savage family.—On the opposite side, and near the entrance, are altar tombs, but the figures have been removed from them. There is another arch in the east end, with an enriched canopy, below which is a magnificent altar tomb, on which are a male and female figure in alabaster. The sides of the tombs are ornamented with three male and three female figures in niches. The following inscription was legible on the edge of the arch in 1584:—

"——— *Sir John Savage, which was made Knight in the wars of* ——— *which died the 26th day of July, in the year* MCCCCCXXVII, *and Lady Elizabeth*

† See annexed engraving.

Engd. by J. Pigot from a Drawing by I. Mills.

MACCLESFIELD PAROCHIAL CHAPEL.

Engraved for Hanshalls History of Cheshire.

his wife, dau ——— to ——— which Lady Elizabeth died the — day of ——— anno domini"

In the Chancel, on the east side, is a large mural monument, on which is a figure recumbent, in a robe and wig; above it a canopy, supported by four Corinthian pillars. The inscription is—

Here lyeth the body of the Right Hon'ble Thomas Earle Rivers, Viscount Colchester and Savage of Rock Savage, Baron of Darcy of Chich, who died the 14th day of September, 1694, at his house in Great Queen-street, within ye parish of St. Giles-in-the-Fields, in the County of Middlesex, and was here interred the 14th day of October following, in the 67th year of his age.

Below, on the front of the tomb, in continuation of the inscription—

He married two wives, ye first was ye Lady Elizabeth Scrope, one of ye three coheirs of the Right Hon'ble Emanuel Earle of Sunderland, Baron Scrope, of Bollon, and Lord President of the King's Councell in ye North, by whom he had yssue the Hon'ble Thomas Viscount Colchester, dec'd, who married ye Lady Charlotte Stanley, eldest daughter of ye Right Hon'ble Charles Earle of Derby, Baron Stanley (Strange of Knokyn) and Mohun, Lord of Man and ye Isles, but left noe issue male; and ye now Right Hon. Richard Earle Savage, Baron Darcy of Chich, and Lieutenant of the County Palatine of Chester, as alsoe Custos Rotulorum for ye said County Palatine, Lieut.-Gen. of Horse under his most excellent Ma'tie King Wm. ye 3d, and Capt. of the troop of Guards, and the Ladys Elizth and Annabella Savage, yet living, with several other Children who died young. His second wife was the Lady Arabella Bertie, daughter of ye now Right Hon'ble Robert Earle of Lindsey, Baron Wiloughby of Eresby, Great Chamberlain of England, Lord Lieutenant of the County of Lincoln, and Custos Rotulorum for the parts of Holland, Kestevan, and Lindsey, in the same County, and one of his Majesty's Most Hon'ble Privy Councell. She survived him, and is now living, but never had any issue.—This tomb was erected in the month of September, 1696.

Near the last monument, a stone, ornamented with a cross. The edge of it, in 1584, bore the inscription—

Hic jacet Corpus D'ni Georgi Savage, qui obiit die ——— mensis——— *1552.**

Nearly opposite the two last monuments, is an altar tomb, on which are the figures of an armed man, and a female—there are inscriptions on three tablets within the nich. The first is—

Memoriæ Sacrum viri clarissimi prudentissimi, piissimq. D. Joannis Savage, equites aurati, antiqua Savagorum gente oriundi, de tota republica Cestriensi et Hamptoniensi optimè meriti, 5to Decemb. anno 1597o, ætat 74, in dolorem consanguineoru' et bonorum omnium vita functi. Thomas Savagus miles et baronettus, majore filio nepos, in uxorem duxit Elizabetham filia' Thomæ Baronis Ducie de Chich prima', et per eam favore Principis indulgentiori existens sorte thalami et affinitate cineri, in successione proximus isti honori, pietatis, ergo singularis, hoc posuit monumentum.

On the other tablet, are some long Latin verses.—In the north-east angle, are several brass plates, affixed to a board. One of them has the effigies of Roger Legh, and his wife, with their six sons, and six daughters behind them, kneeling. Underneath is inscribed,

Orate p' a'i'abus Rogeri Legh, et Elizabeth ux'is sue qui quid'm; Rogerus obiit' IIIo die Novembris ao Dom'ni Mo CCCCVIo. Elizabeth vero obiit vo die Octobris ao D'ni MoCCCCLXXXIXo quor' a'iab' p'picietur d'.

On a label issuing from the man's mouth, now defaced, was—

In die judicii libera nos Domine.

From the woman's mouth—

A dampnac'o'e p'petua lib'a nos D'ne.

Between the figures, above, a representation of the Pope, kneeling at an altar; behind which is the figure of our Saviour; beneath—

The p'don for saying of v pater nost', v aves, and a cred, is xxvi thousand yeres and xxvi dayes of pardon.

In the Chancel was an alabaster monument for one of the Leversage family, with the effigies of the deceased.

In the Legh chancel, is the memorial of Sir Piers Legh, before noticed, inscribed—

Here lyethe the bodie of PERKIN A LEGH,
That for King Richard the death did dye,
Betray'd for Righteousness:
And the bones of Sir Peers his sonne,
That with King Henry the Vth did wonne,
In Paris.

This Perkin served King Edward III. and the Black Prince, his son, in all their wars in France, and was at the battle of Cressie, and had Lyme given to him for that service; and after their death, served King Richard the Second and left him not in his troubles, but was taken with him and beheaded at Chester by King Henry IV. And the said Sir Peers his son, served King Henry V. and was slain at the battle of Agincourt:—In their memory, Sir Peter Legh, of Lyme,

* Mr. Ormerod has a query, whether this George Savage was not the Rector of Davenham, and father of the infamous Bonner?

Knt: descended from them, finding the said old verses written upon a stone in this Chapel, did re-edify this place, A. D. 1626.

In the same chancel, on a mural monument—

P. M. S. D'næ Letticiæ Legh, de Lyme, D'ni Georgii Calveley de Lea Baronetti filiæ, et uxoris charissimæ sev'di Thomæ Legh, S. S. T. P. Ecclesiæ Parochial' de Walton et Sephton, in agro Lancast'l, Rectoris vigilantiss'i, et D'ni Petri Legh de Lyme, equites aurati, filii natu tertii. Obiit Oct. xivto anno salutis MDCXLVIII. Et Letticiæ, Thomæ et Letticiæ Legh, filiæ pientissimæ. Obiit Febr'ii xximo anno D'ni MDCLI°, anno ætat xvi. Atque Thomæ Legh de Lyme, armigeri, Rev'di Thomæ et Letticiæ p'dict' filii natu secundi, qui spe beatæ resurrectionis animam Deo piè reddidit Sept'bris xxii° anno salutis MDCXCVII anno ætatis sue ferè LXI.—H. M. liberaliter constituit Petrus Legh de Lyme armiger anno MDCCXII.

A brass plate, with a memorial of William Legh, schoolmaster of Macclesfield, obiit 1630.

Another brass plate to the memory of Caleb Pott, M. A. schoolmaster of Knutsford, Sandbach, Newcastle, Audlem, and Macclesfield, obiit 1690.

Engraved on a brass plate—

Joanni Brownswerdo, Macclesfeldensi Ludimagistro, viro pio pariter ac docto, hic sepulto et repulverescenti, Thomas Newton, Butlensis, pietatis, gratitudinis, et officii ergo, P.

Alpha poetarum, Coryphæus grammaticorum,
Flos pædagogῶn, hac sepelitur humo.
Obiit 15 Apr. 1689.

CHRIST CHURCH, was built in 1775, by Charles Roe, Esq. The fabric is of brick, in length about one hundred feet, and about sixty-six feet in breadth. It is generally well finished, but in a very tasteless manner. It has a lofty square tower, containing a peal of ten bells, which forms a conspicuous object in the views of the town.

Over the altar, is a bust of the founder, by Bacon, with Genius weeping over it, holding a cog-wheel in her hand.

The inscription—

" Whoever thou art, whom a curiosity to search into the monuments of the dead, or an ambition to emulate their living virtues, has brought hither, receive the gratification of either object, in the example of Chas. Roe, Esq. A gentleman who, with a slender portion on his entrance into business, carried on the button and twist manufacture in this town, with the most active industry, ingenuity, and integrity; and by a happy versatility of genius, at different periods of life, first established here, and made instrumental to the acquisition of an ample fortune, the silk and copper manufactures, by which many thousands of families have been since supported. The obstacles which envy and malevolence threw in his way, retarded not his progress: enterprising, emulous, and indefatigable, difficulties to others were incitements to action in him. His mind was vast and comprehensive, formed for great undertakings, and equal to their accomplishment.—By an intuitive kind of knowledge, he acquired an intimate acquaintance with the mineral state of the earth; and was esteemed, by competent judges, greatly to excel in the art of mining. In that line his concerns were extensive; and the land-owners, as well as proprietors, of the valuable mine in the Isle of Anglesea, are indebted to him for the discovery.

It pleased the Almighty to bless his various labours and benevolent designs. His grateful heart delighted to acknowledge the mercies he received. God was in all his thoughts. And actuated by the purest sentiments of genuine devotion, which burnt steadily through his life, and the brighter as he approached the Fountain of Light, he dedicated to the service of his Maker, a part of that increase his bounty had bestowed, erecting and endowing at his sole expense, the elegant structure which incloses this monument; and which, it is remarkable, was built from the surface of the ground, and completely finished, both inside and out, in so short a space as seven months.—READER, when thou hast performed the duties which brought thee hither, think on the founder of this beautiful edifice, and aspire after the virtues which enabled him to raise it. He died the 3d of May, 1784, aged 67 years, leaving a widow and ten children (who have erected this monument as a tribute to conjugal and filial affection) poignantly to lament a most indulgent husband, a tender father, and a general loss."

A monument to the memory of the Rev. D. Simpson, A. M. who died March 29, 1799, aged 54; he was the first Minister.

The patronage of this Church is, under an Act of Parliament, passed in 1779, vested in the heirs of Mr. Roe.

The living is a perpetual cure and benefice, subject to the Bishop of Chester. There have been several donations to Charities connected with the foundation; among them, Miss Roe left £600. in 1787, for the education of poor children, and £100. interest to be appropriated to the purchase of bibles.

In 1813, Thos. Allen, and Martha his wife, left £10. per annum, to be given in clothes on St. Thomas's Day, to spinsters and widows not receiving relief from the parish.

In 1703, an *Alms House* for three poor widows, was founded in Macclesfield, by Mr. Stanley, who endowed it with £6. annually.

The *Dissenters* from the Established Church are very numerous in Macclesfield.* They have several places of worship.

* A Dissenting-school of quite a new description, was established here in 1819, by a notorious seditious character, called PARSON HAR-

MACCLESFIELD

Remarkable occurrences connected with Macclesfield.

1270—Manor conferred on the Princess Eleanor, by Prince Edward.

1279—Chapel of St. Michael founded.

1513—Sir E. Savage, and a great number of Burgesses fell at Flodden.

1649-59—General Fairfax at Macclesfield, and entertained at the *expense* of the Corporation: cost 1*s.* 6*d.**

1662—Dreadful tornado in Macclesfield Forest, accompanied with a fall of hail; some of the stones were four inches in circumference.—"There arose a great pillar of smoke, in height like a steeple, and judged twenty yards broad, which making a most hideous noise, went along the ground six or seven miles, levelling all in the way; it threw down fences and stone walls, and carried the stones a great distance from their places, but happening upon moorish ground *not inhabited*, it did the less hurt. The terrible noise it made so frighted the cattle, that they ran away, and were thereby preserved; it passed over a corn field, and laid it as even with the ground as if it had been trodden down by feet: it went through a wood and turned up above an hundred trees by the root; coming into a field full of cocks of hay ready to be carried in, it swept all away, so that scarce a handful of it could afterward be found, only it left a great tree in the middle of the field, which it had brought from some other place. From the Forest of *Maxfield* it went up by a town called *Taxal*, and thence to *Waily Bridge*, where, and no where else, it overthrew an house or two, yet the people that were in them received not much hurt, but the timber was carried away nobody knew whither. From thence it went up the hills into Derbyshire, and so vanished. This account was given by Mr. Hurst, Minister of Taxal, who had it from an eye witness.

1745—The inhabitants of Macclesfield were alarmed by a visit from the army of Prince Charles Edward Stuart, the Pretender to the Crown of England, who marched into this town at the head of his troops, on Sunday the 1st December, O. S. and set up his standard at his head quarters, a house in Jordan-gate. The Scotch remained but two days in Macclesfield, and though undisciplined and boisterous, they did not injure the persons or destroy the property of the inhabitants, except in the article of food, of which they took a supply. They amounted to some thousands of men, chiefly of the Highland Clans, led by their Chieftains. They were mostly armed with the broad sword and target.—On the 3d of December, at six o'clock in the morning, they quitted Macclesfield on their destined route to London, arrived in Leek about 10 o'clock in the forenoon, and rapidly advanced towards Derby.

1770—Public Library established.

1804—Contested Election for a Recorder. For Mr. Abercrombie 112; for Mr. Roe, 128—31 Burgesses did not vote.

1809—Grand celebration of the Jubilee.

1811—Macclesfield Courier first published.

———Macclesfield Theatre opened, April 15.

1812—Dreadful riots in the town.

1813—First stone of Macclesfield Sunday School laid, April 21—grand Masonic procession.

1814—Police Act passed.

———A Dispensary established.

HISTORY.

It appears from a variety of valuable information relative to this hundred, furnished by David Browne, Esq. that Macclesfield had formerly three principal gates in its walled fences or "*haia*;" viz. the *Chester-gate*, in the direction of that city; the *Jordan-gate*, described in some old Law proceedings as "portam Jordani de Macclesfield ducentum de Cockshute," which Jordan, it is probable, had the custody, of the gate as a military service: it leads to *Cockshute-lane*. *Wall-gate* is now called *Church Wall-gate*, and leads to the lower part of the town. It is conjectured this gate had a postern near the extremity of *Back Wall-gate*.

The present Curate of Macclesfield, is the Rev. Lawrence Heapy, A. M. appointed in 1800.

* This must be an error. It is copied from an 8vo. History of Macclesfield, published in 1817.

CHESHIRE HISTORY.

SUTTON DOWNES,

Or *Sutton*, is about two miles S. S. E. from Macclesfield. It is included in the Forest of Macclesfield.—It was formerly two mesne manors, Sutton and Downes, which respectively gave names to families. The Suttons had a grant of the manor from Hugh Ceivilioc, some time between 1153, and 1181.

The first possessor from the Earl was Adam the son of Onyt, and his successor assumed the local name.—The Suttons for a long time held the office of Bailiffs of Macclesfield Forest. The *original* line terminated in the reign of Henry VII. and the first of the *second* line of the Suttons, was John Sutton, nephew of the founder of Brasenose College, Oxford, and Master of Burton Lazers. Richard Sutton, 4th in descent from him, was killed at Chester, in 1601. On his death the estate passed to his two sisters and coheirs, one of whom was the wife of Sir H. Davenport, a branch of the Bramhall family; the other of Sir Philip Monkton, ancestor of Lord Galway. The share which fell to the latter was purchased by Sir Humphrey Davenport, who was made Baron of the Exchequer in 1630; and his great grand-daughter, brought the manor in marriage to Sir Rowland Belasyse, from whom the Earls of Fauconberg descended.

In 1819, the property was vested in the Countess of Lucan, who died in that year; it is now the property of her heirs.

The *Hall* of Sutton, is about a mile S. of Macclesfield, and is occupied as a farm-house. Its situation is romantic, at the juncture of two streams which empty themselves into the Bollin, and surrounded by some fine old timber. The only wing of the ancient building now remaining, is of wood and plaister, finished with gables. The hall of this curious fabric is well worthy of inspection. In the front of this wing, are several antique figures carved in wood, one of which represents a warrior in scale armour, holding a mace in his hand.

The Manor being within the liberties of the Forest of Macclesfield, was held by the service of free forestry, its owner being bound to follow the standard of the the King with the arms with which he guarded his Bailiwick.*

Three estates in the township were held by the same service:—

Heghlegh, Healie, or Hoghlegh, was possessed by Richard de Heghlegh, temp. Edward I. In the reign of the Third Edward, Robert Foxwiste forfeited the estate for felony. Some time in the reign of Eliz. it was possessed by the Leghs, of Lyme, and still continues in their descendants.

The vill of Downes gave name to a very respectable family.

The other estate was held by the Dicons, then by the Stanleghs. of Stanleghs, in Disley; and before the 23d Elizabeth, the Savages were vested with it.

Langley Hall, a short distance N. E. of Sutton Hall, was formerly the residence of the Clowes' family. Charles Clowes, Esq. their descendant, about 1808, sold it to the present proprietor, David Yates, Esq.

Ridge Hall was for many generations vested in a younger branch of the Leghs, of Lyme. Thos. Legh, Esq. Mayor of Macclesfield in 1761, sold it to Wm. Norton, M D. whose sister bequeathed it to the present proprietor, her great nephew, William Smyth, Esq. Professor of Modern History at Cambridge.

Hollins, or Hollinshed, gave name to a family settled here as early as the reign of Hen. III. They afterwards removed to *Cophurst*, and subsequently to Heywood in Alderley. Hollinshead the Chronicler was of this family, and possessed Cophurst. The male branch of the family, it is supposed, has long since been extinct; but the name is still very familiar in the county, being borne by many respectable families.—The estate is now the property of the heirs of John Stonehewer, Esq. of Foden Bank. Cophurst is the property of Mr. Bullock, whose father purchased it from the late Col. Legh, of Lyme.

The Oaks, possessed many generations ago by the Ardernes (of the Alvanley family) is now the property of David Davies, D. D. in right of his wife, Frances Mere, youngest daughter of the late Rev. P. Mere, Vicar of Prestbury, who married Martha, youngest coheiress of John Arderne, Esq.

WINCLE,

Is about six miles S. E S from Macclesfield. The

* These foresters were entitled to timber, firewood, and other perquisites; they had also the liberty of fishing within the forest, and of taking foxes, hares, squirrels, badgers, otters, musketts, and eagles.

Monks of Combermere had formerly a Grange here. At the Dissolution, the Cottons obtained possession of it, from whom it was purchased by the father of the present proprietor, J. S Daintry, Esq.

Bishop Gastrell describes the CHAPEL of Wincle, in his Notitia, dated May 16, 1717, as being very handsome,* without communion table, pulpit or font; the sacrament, however, had been administered, although no children were christened. Since that period, the whole fabric has been substantially rebuilt with stone. The windows contain some specimens of ancient stained glass. Is is a Curacy, in the gift of the Vicar of Prestbury.

WILDBOARCLOUGH

Is about four miles from Macclesfield; and includes a dreary, inhospitable district, thinly inhabited, spreading to the Derbyshire border.

MACCLESFIELD FOREST

Lies four miles S. S. E. from Macclesfield, high among the hills, and, with the last township, is the property of the Earl of Derby, Forester and Hereditary Steward.—It is also very thinly inhabited.

The CHAPEL is a low mean building of grey stone, the interior fitted up with oaken benches. It is stated by Bishop Gastrell as not being consecrated.

HURDSFIELD

Is not more than two miles E. N. E. from Macclesfield, and, like Wincle, and Kettleshulme, is almost exclusively copyhold. In this township is *Swanscoe Park*, which formerly belonged to the Derby family, as an appendage of the Stewardship of the Forest; during the Rebellion, however, they were dispossessed by Sir Wm. Brereton, and it was held by the Breretons till 1667. In course of time it was sold to Mr. Thomas Ward, of Manchester, whose grandson, Mr. T. Ward is the proprietor. There are still some remains of the old park wall.

RAINOW

Is nearly three miles N. E. E. from Macclesfield — The township consists of a considerable number of houses, chiefly cottages, a few manufactories, nearly the whole of them built of stone.

The CHAPEL of Rainow was rebuilt some years ago; the patronage is in the Vicar of Prestbury.—*Jenkin*, or *Saltersford Chapel*, also in this township, is built in the most dreary part of this inhospitable district. It takes its name from its situation near *Jenkin's Cross*, and was built about 1739, by the subscriptions of the neighbourhood. The Registers commence in 1770.

In a secluded situation below the Chapel, is *Saltersford Hall*, a curious old mansion of stone, built towards the conclusion of the 16th century. This was formerly the seat of the Stopfords; one of whom, James Stopford, was a Lieutenant in the forces in Ireland under the orders of the Parliament, and eventually acquiring a large property in that kingdom, settled at Tarah Hall, co. Meath. The Earl of Courtown, descendant of this James Stopford, is the present proprietor of the estate, from which he derives the title of Baron of Saltersford.

The *One House*, another old stone mansion, has long been the residence of the Hulleys, supposed† to represent a younger branch of the Hoghleghs, of Taxall.

The *Kerridge Hill* is a prominent feature of the scenery of this region, which abounds with inequalities of surface, deep vallies, and small streams. On the Bollington side of the Hill, is a large quarry, from whence stone, flags, and slate, are procured. The Roman road from Manchester to Buxton crossed this township, and it is probable one of their smaller stations was in its immediate vicinity.

In *Hedgerow*, in this township, lived Margaret Broadhurst, who attained the extraordinary age of 140 years.‡ She was a native of Over, and became a servant in the family of Downes, of Shrigley. She then married Humphrey Broadhurst, a farmer's laborer, and had nine children. Her food was of the most simple description. A few years before her death, Sir George Booth sent for her to Dunham Massy, and offered to maintain her during the remainder part of her life; but her improved fare did not suit her previously acquired habits, and she told Sir George, that if she did not return to her former food, she should die. It is stated that she was buried at Prestbury about 1650, but there is no notice of the circumstance in the Registers. The letter states that she went by the name of the *cricket of the hedge*; and adds, alluding to her age, that " the computation

* Built temp. Car. I.

† Ormerod.

‡ See letter from the Rev. F. Brokesby to Mr. Thomas Hearne, at the end of the 6th vol. of Leland's Itin. dated 1711.

is very moderate," for one Mrs. Brideoak asking the old woman how old she was, she replied, "I was fourscore years old when I bore that *snicket*," meaning her daughter, who was then sixty years old! This dubious anecdote is introduced to gratify the lovers of the marvellous.

POTT SHRIGLEY,

Lies nearly four miles and a half N. N. E. from Macclesfield, and at a very early period received the name of *Shrigley*, from a family which inherited considerable estates here. The family of Downes was settled here certainly before the reign of Edward III. and continued in uninterrupted possession till the recent sale of the Shrigley property to William Turner, Esq. of Mill Hill, near Blackburn.

The *Hall* is built in a pleasant situation; and, altho' reparations and additions have, at various periods, been made to it, still bears many of the features of the old Cheshire mansions, being finished with gables, &c. The ancient hall of this edifice is still perfect.

Pott-Shrigley CHAPEL nearly adjoins the Hall; it was founded by Geoffrey Downes, about the reign of Henry VII. and endowed with lands of considerable value, which were subsequently seized by the Crown, in the confiscation of Church property. The building consists of nave, chancel, and side aisles, the division of the latter being formed by two pointed arches. The tower is embattled, and contains three bells. There are a few remains of stained glass in the windows, and the roofs of the chancel and nave, are of oak, painted. It is on the whole a very neat edifice, and was considerably beautified by the late Mr. Downes. In the chancel, on the south side, is a memorial of Peter Downes.*

In this township are *Pott Hall*, and *Berristow Hall*, which were purchased from James Beech, Esq. of Shaw, near Cheadle, Staffordshire, by Mr. Downes. It is supposed that Berristow Hall, was the residence of the Shrigleys, who preceded the Downes family in the possession of property here. Pott Hall gave name to a family settled here for many generations. It appears from the Herald's visitation in 1663-4, that Edmund Pott, of Pott, then aged 23, was 5th in descent from Roger Pott. The family, in the direct male line, terminated in heiresses, and, says Mr. Ormerod, "another of similar name, now represented by Henry Potts, Esq. of Chester, is *traditionally* said to be descended from it, and alienated an estate in this township in the last century." Why the *doubt* of the descent, as inferred from the term "traditionally," is here introduced, it would be difficult to discover, when we have the positive fact, that when the ancestor of Mr. Potts sold his estate here, called the Cockshutt Hey, he reserved a piece of land (parcel of it) which now lies waste, and is Mr. Potts's property.

* This gallant officer was a Midshipman in the Leander, and was mortally wounded on the 17th August, 1798, in the action between that ship and the Genereux, near Candia, in which he so eminently distinguished himself, as to receive the thanks of Sir T. B. Thompson, his commander. He was born at Butley, the 9th day of September, 1778.

THE PARISH OF TAXALL,

CONTAINS THE TOWNSHIPS OF

TAXALL | YEARDSLEY-cum-WHALEY.

TAXALL lies on the borders of Derbyshire, about eight miles S. W. from Macclesfield, and eleven S. E. from Stockport. The River Goyt separates it from Derbyshire. Its situation gives it an extensive command of prospect.

During many generations this manor was vested in the Downes, of Sutton Downes and Overton, a branch of the Shrigley Family.

In the 16th Edward I. it was possessed by Robert de Downes, and his descendants in the male line had possession till the death of John Downes, temp. Jac. I This John left four daughters, Margaret, Mary, Anne, and Sarah, "from whom the estate was wrested by their uncle Edmund, as heir male, which Edmund was the son of Reginald, who joined with his son Edmund in conveying the manor and advowson to J. Shallcross, Esq. of Shallcross, in Derbyshire, to whom John Downes, second son of Reginald Downes, of Downes, confirmed the same by a release, in 1715"—Some curious notices relative to the manerial rights of the Downes, are given in a note by Mr. Ormerod;* amongst them, is mentioned a boast of Reginald Downes, that "hee could bring all Taxall to his Court to be kept in his compass window, commonly called by the name of the bay window, adjoining to the house-place, (the kitchen) at Overton, where the Courts had been formerly kept." Also, "That hee when y[e] King came a hunting, allways rowsed the stagg, and when y[e] King came to y[e] Forest, Mr. D. held y[e] King's stirrup, and y[e] Lord Derby held his stirrup; and that y[e] Lord Derby, instead of actually holding y[e] stirrup, put his strop or whip, and held it towards y[e] stirrup whilst Mr. Downes mounted." That "hee held his land by a blast of a horn on a Midsummer Day, and paying a pepper-corn yearly." There was a tradition once prevalent in the family, that they had liberty to hang and draw amongst themselves, and that "a spot of land near Overton Hall, which goes by the name of the gallows yard, was the place where offenders were executed."

Furnished by Mr. Browne.

The manor, including the Overton Hall Estate, was sold by the Shallcross's early in the last century, to the Dickensons of Manchester, by whom it was resold to the late Foster Bower, Esq. uncle of the present proprietor, Francis Joddrell, Esq.

The *Old Hall* of Overton has been taken down, and on its site is erected a farm-house. Taxall-lodge was built by Mr. Bower, for his own residence. There are some very thriving plantations in the township.

The CHURCH, which is dedicated to St. James, is in a pleasant situation on the stream of the Goyt. It consists of nave, chancel, side aisles, and a tower containing three bells.---Within the chancel rails, are several memorials of the Shallcross's. On a brass plate, in the chancel, an inscription to the memory of Edward Potts, A. B. Rector of Taxall, ob. July 5, 1753—On the north wall, a monument to Michael Heathcote, gentleman of the pantry, and yeoman of the mouth to Geo II. who died in 1768.

There are the remains of an ancient Cross in the Church-yard.

The Rev. John Swain is patron and incumbent of the Rectory.

WHALEY,

Or *Yeardsley-cum-Whaley*, is about nine miles S. E. from Stockport, on the road from Manchester to London through Buxton. The estates here are copyhold of the Court of Macclesfield Forest.

Yeardsley Hall, was for more than a century, the seat of the Joddrells. About 1776, a greater part of the Old House was taken down, with the intention of rebuilding it in an improved form; but this design was subsequently abandoned, and it is now occupied by a farmer. The Leghs, of Lyme, are the proprietors of *Bottoms Hall*, in this township.

PARISH OF STOCKPORT,

CONTAINS THE TOWNSHIPS OF

STOCKPORT,	BREDBURY,	OFFERTON,
ETCHELLS,	BRAMHALL,	MARPLE,
BRINNINGTON,	DISLEY STANLEY,	ROMILEY,
HYDE,	NORBURY,	WERNITH.
DUCKENFIELD,	TORKINGTON,	

STOCKPORT

Is about seven miles from Manchester, and 175 miles from London, irregularly built on the banks of the Mersey. In the ancient History of this Town, a vast deal of speculation must almost necessarily be embraced. Although not noticed in the great Survey, there is little doubt but what it was then a military position, and had been so from the period when the Roman Legions settled in Chester and Manchester. It is probable that, on the Danish and Norman invasions, a great part of this district was depopulated by them, and that Stockport severely suffered in the general devastation. The late Rev. J. Watson, in his "History of the House of Warren," has gone into the History of the Town at some length, and in a way that manifests deep research. In allusion to its antiquity and form of Government, he observes, "After William the Conqueror thought himself firmly established on his throne, he bestowed many provinces and counties of this realm on the great barons who assisted him. These strengthened the counties respectively allotted to them, in the mode that seemed adapted to secure their possessions from the incursions of their neighbours. The Counties Palatine (as they have since been called) were judged to be in greater danger than the others, and greater attention was therefore paid to their defence. Thus, in the adjoining county palatine of Lancaster,* Roger Pictavensis. the Earl, caused his whole jurisdiction to be surrounded with a chain of forts; some of which I shall mention, as their situations are immediately connected with the illustration of my subject. One of these forts was at *Widness*, where a Baron was stationed to protect that part of Lancashire from the incursions of the Cheshire people; and as the jealousy was mutual, opposite to this, on the Cheshire side, was *Halton Castle:* and Nigel, or rather William, son of Nigel, was fixed there with the same title, and stationed in such a manner, as to guard the country from any surprise, either from Warrington, another Lancashire barony, or Runcorn Ferry. The next barony on the Lancashire side, above Warrington, was *Newton*, erected as well to strengthen the former, as to oppose any passage out of Cheshire over the river Mersey at Hallingreen Ferry; and lest from this station, and over this ferry, damage should be done to the inhabitants of Cheshire, the Earl of Chester made Hamo de Masci another of his Barons, and placed him opposite to the above, at *Dunham*. Another barony of the Lancashire palatinate was *Manchester*, erected as a guard on one side against any incursion from Stretford, and on the other, against the military station which appears to have been in very early times at Stockport. Now as all the above Lancashire Barons were made in the reign of the Conqueror by Roger Pictavensis, it seems to follow, that the barony of Stockport is as old as the rest within the county of Chester; for why should every other Lancashire barony be guarded against, which lay opposite to Chester, and not that at Manchester? If such an opening into the county was permitted to remain unguarded, the other establishments must have been useless. When the Castle at Stockport was first erected is uncertain; but the site on which it stood has the name of Castle Yard to this

* Lancashire was not erected into a Palatinate till long after the grant of Cheshire to Gherbod, the predecessor of Lupus.—H.

CHESHIRE

day. That there are no records to determine its origin, is a proof of its antiquity. If the hints given by Mr. Whittaker are well founded, it is antique indeed.—"The town of Stockport," says this gentleman, "appears evidently the one common centre to three or four very variously directed roads of the Romans. The High-Street advances to it from Manchester; and the Pepper-Street hastens to it from Hanford; and in the parish of Ashton, and near the foot of Staley Bridge, is a third road, commonly denominated Staley-Street, for a mile together, the main line of which lies pointing clearly from *Castle-Shaw* to Stockport. These are sure signatures of a Roman station. This must have been fixed upon as the site of the castle, and was the area of the Castle Hill at Stockport. That is exactly such a site as the Romans must have instantly selected for such a station; that is, a small area, detached from the level ground of the Market-place, and connected with it only by an isthmus. The area must have been the actual site of the castle in the earliest period of the Saxon residence among us; as the castle must have originally communicated its name to the town, and as both were denominated Stockport, because the former was a port or castle in a wood. The area is about half a statute acre in extent; the site is still incomparably strong in itself, and the position is happily fitted for the ford.—The station must have had a steep of one hundred or one hundred and twenty yards upon three sides of it; and must have been guarded by a foss across the isthmus. The Roman road from East Cheshire must have been effectually commanded by it; being obliged, by the circling current of the Mersey, to approach very near to the castle; and being evinced, by the remaining steepness of the neighbouring banks, to have actually ascended the brow in a hollow immediately below the eastern side of it." More might be urged in proof of their being a *castrium* in Stockport in the time of the Romans, if the point was not already sufficiently established: and that a fortress was maintained here in the Saxon times, the very name of the place demonstrates: and, besides its signification, as given by Mr. Whittaker, *Stoc*, or *Stoke-port*, may likewise signify a wooden castle; Stoke Castle, in Norfolk, being interpreted, in Spelman's Icenia, by *Capella Lignea*: or Stoke may also mean a place or settlement in general; as, *Stoke-Curey*, where the Curries lived; *Wood-stock*, the Woody-place; so also *Stoke-port*, the Place of the Castle But which ever of these derivations is correct, it plainly has a reference to the Saxon times, and is confirmed by the very current tradition, that the Danes were repulsed here, and great numbers of them slain.—Nichols has thus expressed himself in his book "*De litteris inventis.*"

> Fama refert, Danos ubi nunc Stopporta locatur,
> Affectos olim clade fuisse gravi:
> Inde urbi nomen, prædonum incursibus obex
> Quod datus, hic Anglis sit quoque parta salus.*

"This etymology is wrong, because the name was *not* very anciently written *Stopport;* but the tradition is probably right; for a field below the castle, called the Park, is fuller of human bones, to a larger extent, than would be necessary for the burial ground of the garrison. Stopport was probably a corruption from *Stoke-port*, as some centuries ago it was almost uniformly written. In the year 1173, the castle was possessed by Geoffrey de Constantine; but whether he held it in his own right, or of the Baron of Stockport, or even against him, by order of the Earl of Chester, is unknown."

HISTORY.

With respect to the Barons of Stockport, much difficulty has prevailed in ascertaining the family and origin of the "N—, Baron of Stockport," mentioned in the Vale Royal. Dugdale was of opinion, that this "N." certainly was one of the Barons of the Palatinate, but, adds he "N. doth not stand for the first letter of his name, but is commonly used where the Christian name is unknown."† Mr. Watson says, that the Castle of Stockport was in the reign of Hen. II. defended against that monarch by Geoffrey de Constentin.‡ When this Castle was built is quite uncertain; but it is highly probable that it stood on the site of a Roman Fortress.

Although entirely unnoticed in Domesday by its present name, Stockport no doubt was a place of considerable importance at a very early period. Mr. Ormerod conjectures, that the name, inverted, may be found in that of the adjoining township of *Portwood*, and this

† Harl. MSS. 1967.

‡ History of House of Warren.

* In ages past, the place where STOPPORT stands
Marked the repulse of hostile Danish bands;
And thence, according to the voice of Fame,
The Angles, safely gain'd; the town, its name.

CHESHIRE HISTORY.

is very rational: for that Stockport was the head of a large parish antecedent, to the Norman invasion, can admit of little doubt—the whole district, indeed, in those days of difficulty and danger, may have been wasted, and in a measure destroyed, by the rapacity of the invaders. During the previous inroads of the Danes, Stockport, or its immediate neighbourhood, as has been before noticed, was the scene of a signal overthrow of those marauders,—and its situation in a military point of view, was certainly one of the first importance.

It has been before stated, that Geoffrey de Constantine held the Castle of Stockport, temp. Hen. II. but it does not appear, whether he was the possessor, or merely the Commander of it as a fortress. It is ascertained, however, that subsequent to that reign, the Despensers were the proprietors, and under them it was held by the Stokeports. On the seizure of the estates of Hugh le Despencer, the partizan of Simon de Montfort, the Barony of Stockport was taken by the Earl, under whom it was held by the Lords of Stockport in capite "per forisfacturam Hugonis Dispenser."* It appears the first Robert de Stockport, held his lands immediately from the Baron of Dunham Massy, and this Robert is supposed to be the grandson of Robert Fitz Waltheof, who had Etchells settled upon him also from the Baron of Dunham Massy. Sir Peter Leycester much doubted whether this family (the Stockports) had any collateral connexion with the ancient Barons.

The History of the Barons of Stockport have their only certain detail from Robert de Stockport. The SECOND Baron was Sir Robert de Stockport, Knt. Sir Richard de Stockport was the THIRD Baron. He left two coheiresses, Joan and Maud; the former was married first to Sir Nicholas de Eton, and afterwards to Sir John Ardern. This Sir John had Stockport, Poynton, and Wideford, for his life, and part of the lands in Etchells, by agreement, in consequence of which, Nicholas, son of Sir Nicholas de Eton, released to Sir John Ardern, all his right to those manors, with the advowson of the Churches, &c. and his son Robert confirmed the same eight years afterwards (1340). Sir John Ardern, then granted to Robert de Hampton, parson of Alderley, and Richard de Mancester (his Chaplain,) the manor of Stockport, the manors of Poynton, Wydesford, and Etchells, but they re-granted them, together with the Church advowson, to him for his life, and at the same time granted to Robert, the son of Nicholas de Eton, and his heirs, the reversion of the manor and advowsons, on Sir John's death —Sir Nicholas de Eton, FOURTH Baron of Stockport; Nicholas, FIFTH Baron; Robert de Eton, SIXTH Baron; Sir Richard de Eton, or de Stockport, SEVENTH Baron. This Richard died without issue male, and the estates descended to John, son of Edward de Warren, Knt.; he was the son of Cecily, sister of Robert de Stokeport (or Eton) father of Richard de Stokeport, Knt. father of Isabel de Stokeport.—It is from this period that the Warrens commenced their descent in the Barony, and they are now represented by Lord Warren Bulkeley, in right of his wife, only daughter and heiress of Sir G. Warren, K. B.

The Local History of Stockport embraces a considerable share of that of the manufactures of the country; but is not marked by any peculiar feature of general interest: About 1260, Robert de Stokeport, granted to the Burgesses a Charter, entitling them each to a homestead, and an acre of land, on their rendering a shilling annually: they had also at the same time the grant of a Weekly Market (on Friday), and a Fair yearly, on the Feast of St Winefred, to continue seven days.

This town had its share of the troubles during the Civil Wars:—On Saturday, May 10, 1645, Lord Fairfax's regiment of horse, commanded by Col. Spencer, removed from Macclesfield to the neighbourhood of Stockport, where they remained a week, and then marched into Yorkshire; stating as a reason for this movement, that Sir Wm. Brereton had withheld their pay from them. On the 17th August following, a great number of Scots, six thousand horse, and one thousand heavy dragoons, made Stockport their head-quarters, on their way from Congleton; they were commanded by Major-General Leslie. They stated they had come from the siege of Hereford, on that day week, and their object was to intercept the King in his expected march into Scotland. On the Thursday before, the King was in the neighbourhood of Bakewell, and had spread great alarm in that district. On the 25th of the same month,

* The Lords of Stockport had estates in Barrow, Winnington, Etchells, Bredbury, Brinnington, Poynton, Woodford, Romiley, Hattersley, Wodeley, Offerton.—Bredbury, Brinnington, and Etchells, were subinfeudations from the Dunham Massy Barony.

Major Jackson, commanding eight troops of Lancashire horse, who had marched from Lancashire in the rear of the Scots, came from Yorkshire to Stockport. The Major, with Capt. Markland, and others, were quartered at Bramhall; the day but one afterwards, they marched on their way to Latham House.—In the preceding year the town had been occupied by a division of three thousand cavalry and infantry of the Parliament army, commanded by Col. Duckenfield. On the 25th May, they were attacked by Prince Rupert, and put to the rout; leaving many dead and wounded behind them. The Prince then entered the town, placing in it a few Dragoons, and proceeded on his way to Manchester.

During the Scotch Rebellion, the Pretender's army twice passed through Stockport, in their advance and retreat.

Dr. Aikin states, that in Stockport were erected some of the first mills for winding and throwing silk, on a plan procured from Italy. The persons concerned in the silk factories were reckoned the principal people in the place; but, on the decline of this trade, the machinery was applied to cotton spinning, and the different branches of the cotton manufacture are now the chief staple of the town. The people of Stockport first engaged in the spinning of reeled weft, then in weaving checks, and lastly in fustians; and they were so ingenious as to attempt muslins, which were introduced at the time of the invention of the machines called mules, whereby the thread was drawn finer, and spun softer, than that of the weft. The manufacturers here, with this advantage, produced a species of flowered muslin with borders, for aprons and handkerchiefs, by casting a coarse shoot for the figures, and neatly trimming off the float, before bleaching, with scissars, so that the figure was a good imitation of needle work. The cotton trade of Stockport is now so considerable, that, besides a large number of cotton spinning-shops, here are twenty-three spacious cotton factories, most of them worked by steam-engines. The making of hats is likewise a considerable branch of employment. Weaving fustians has extended from hence over Cheadle, Gatley, and Northenden, where a few checks or furnitures had been woven before.

About the year 1775, the cotton manufacture was introduced here from Lancashire;* and about 1780, the manufacture of checks and fustians was first commenced.—From this period the increase in the manufactures and population of Stockport is astonishing. In 1750 the burials in Stockport were 206; in 1800 they exceeded 650. In 1818 there were forty-five cotton spinning factories here, and upwards of sixty in the manufacture of muslins, fustians, &c. There can be no doubt, that a great proportion of the prosperity of Stockport, is to be attributed to the convenience afforded by the Duke of Bridgewater's canal, which runs through the immediate vicinity of the town, communicating with all the principal rivers in England, and spreading the industry of its inhabitants to the most remote parts of the globe.

The Police of the town is superintended by two Constables; there are also two resident Magistrates, the Rev. Chas. Prescot, and Holland Watson, Esq. There are four Church-wardens who enjoy considerable privileges.†

The PUBLIC BUILDINGS are few in number: In 1792, a *Dispensary*, on a large scale, was established here, of which Lord Warren Bulkeley was appointed the first President. *Sunday Schools* were instituted in 1784, in which year no less than six were opened; but they soon declined. The Methodists, however, supported their's with their characteristic determination, and in 1794, they had nearly seven hundred scholars in it. —At the present period upwards of seven thousand children are educated by the Establishment and the different Sects. In 1805, an extensive School House was erected, 132 feet in length, 75 in width, and four stories high: it arose from a general subscription of the Inhabitants, and has accommodations for more than three thousand five hundred children. Since its establish-

* The JENNY, a machine in its infancy for spinning ten threads of cotton at once, was invented in 1776, by James Hargreaves, a weaver, near Blackburn. This was subsequently improved by that great mechanical genius, Rd. Arkwright, then a barber, at Bolton. The History of this great man is so well known as to require no further notice here.

† The Church-wardens are hereditary; they were called PRÆPOSITI, or Posts, and are the owners of the manors of Brinnington, Bredbury, Norbury, and Bramhall; they execute the office by Deputy.

CHESHIRE

ment about twenty-five thousand children have received here the most important rudiments of education.

It would seem that there was formerly a manor attached to the Rectory, called *Church-gate*, for which a Court was held; the lands were held by the service of being foreman of the Jury, when the Rector held his Court.*

* Terrier 1700.

The *Free School* was founded by Sir Edmund Shaa, or Shaw, goldsmith, and Alderman of London, in 1487;† he endowed it with £10. per ann. The present income of the School is about £50. per ann. and the Master is appointed by the Goldsmith's Company.

In 1683, Edward Warren, Esq. founded an Alms House here for six old men, endowing it with 20s. per ann. for each of its inmates. Another benefactor allows them 5s. yearly, and coals.

The Parish Church of Stockport is dedicated to St. Mary.—The Old Church, which is supposed to have been erected early in the fourteenth century, was taken down in 1813; it consisted of nave, side aisles, chancel, and tower; and a private chancel on the south side of the great chancel, belonging to the Vernons of Hurleston, Lords of Marple.

In 1809, an Act was obtained for rebuilding this structure, and a further Act for enlarging the powers, was granted in 1815. The first stone of the present Church, was laid on Monday, July 5, 1813, by Wilbraham Egerton, Esq. one of the County Representatives, and the building was completed early in 1817, at the estimated expense of £30,000. It is a noble pile, occupying a commanding site at the east side of the Market Place. The style of architecture is the florid Gothic. It is built of the Runcorn stone, and consists of a nave, chancel, side aisles, and lofty square tower, finished with battlements and pinnacles, with a fine ring of eight bells. It is highly creditable to the spirit and piety of the town.

The present Rector is the Rev. C. Prescott, instituted in 1820: the living is estimated at £1,200. per ann. The Registers commence in 1584.

On the east side of the Chancel, is a mural monument to the memory of the late Sir George Warren.—It is a tasteful piece of sculpture by Westmacott. The inscription is—

HISTORY

To the memory of Sir George Warren, late of Poynton, in this county, Knight of the Most Honorable Order of the Bath, descended lineally from the noble and ancient race of the Earls of Warren and Surrey, many years Representative in Parliament for the town of Lancaster, Lord of the Barony and Manor of Stockport, &c. &c. whose remains lie intered in a family vault near this place; in whom the tender affections of the parent, the polished manners of the gentleman, the amiable qualities of the friend, and the social endearing attractions of the neighbour, were conspicuously united. Elizabeth Harriet Warren Bulkeley (Viscountess Bulkeley), wife of Thomas James Warren Bulkeley, Viscount Bulkeley of Cashel, in the Kingdom of Ireland, and Baron Bulkeley of Beaumaris, in the Kingdom of England, his dutiful only daughter and heiress, by his first wife Jane Revell, the only daughter and heiress of Thomas Revell, of Fetcham, in the county of Surrey, Esq. deceased, has dedicated this monument, as a grateful tribute of her affection and filial piety, and as a lasting record to posterity of her sincere love and regard for the best and tenderest of parents. Obiit Aug. 31, 1801, ætat. 67.

On the north side of the Chancel, a mural monument:

Radulphus Wilhelmi Wright, de Mottram Andreæ armigeri, et Franciscæ Aliciæ conjugis, filius. Natus est secundo die Maii MDCCXXXI; obiit vicesimo quarto die Aprilis MDCCLIII et intra hanc ecclesiam ad australe latus sepultus est.

O rarest pattern of untainted youth,
Of purest manners, probity, and truth,
Humane, benevolent, of social mind,
The friend of virtue, and of human kind.
From your own Heav'n could you no longer stay?
Unkind to leave us till we'd learnt the way;
To leave us thus forlorn without relief,
The only time you ever gave us grief.
If Heaven, in pity to the growing race
Had lent your virtues for a longer space,
What youth must not have felt the influence
Of your just conduct, and your manly sense.
But, ah! too soon remov'd, in you we've lost
A bright example when we want it most.
Tho' in these rites your absence we deplore,
Soon must we meet again and part no more,
In happier climes and on a safer shore.
Till then, accept this stone, this verse receive,
All that a Father's fondness now can give.

Una reponuntur cineres
Henrici
Wilhelmi Wright de Mottram Andrew armig:
et Franciscæ Aliciæ conjugis,
filii natu maximi.
Nati 1 die Septembris MDCCXXVII. denati
30 die Mart. MDCCXXVIII.

† Brother of Dr. Shaa, who preached the celebrated Sermon at St. Paul's Cross, in favor of the Duke of Glocester—Richard III.

[Here follow the names and deaths of their five children, Elizabeth, Maria, Frances, Laurence, and Purefoy.]

Talium est requum Dei. Hoc marmor charissimis liberis pater mœrens P. MDCCLVI.

Near Sir George Warren's monument, on a small tablet—

In memory of Jane Frances, daughter of Robert Langley Appleyard, of London, Esq. and Jane Mary his wife, and grand-daughter of the Rev. Charles Prescot, Rector of this Parish. Died 13th April, 1812, aged 4 years and 9 months.

On another monument an inscription—

Near this place (by permission of Peter Legh, of Lyme, Esq) were interred the remains of George Clarke, of Hyde, Esq. who died the 11th Nov. 1777, aged 62 years; and also, Edward Clarke, Esq. his younger brother, who died the 6th September, 1776, aged 60 years, being of the elder branch of the family of the Hydes, of Hyde, and Norbury.

Above the Communion steps is an ancient arch, indented in the wall, under which, it is supposed, was a recumbent figure. On the opposite side of the Chancel, under cinquefoil arches, neatly ornamented, are three stalls for the Priests. Near to them is a piscina. Within the stalls, is the figure of Richard de Vernon, Rector of Stockport twenty-eight years, who died July 16, 1334. The head reclines on a cushion, and the feet are supported by a dog. The inscription round the slab (much mutilated) is—

Ici gist Richard Vernouna personne ceat Eglise.

Near to this is a monument, with a long Latin inscription, to the Rev. Legh Richmond, who died in July, 1769—also, a memorial of his son, Henry Richmond, M. D. who died Oct. 4, 1806, aged 64 years.

At the end of the south aisle, a mural monument—

At the foot of this pillar lie the remains of John Ardern, of Harden, Esq. who died in London, May y[e] 27th A. D. 1703, an. ætat. 40.—He left issue behind him 2 d[rs.] Margaret and Catherine, by Anne y[e] 2[d] d[r] of S[r] W[m] Ingleby, of Ripley, Bart. who in just esteem to her husband's virtues, erected this monum[t] to his memory, and to admonish thee (Reader) that hee was worthy thy imitation; for as he was singularly happy in all y[e] virtues of a private conditio' so y[t] the great concern he shewed in procuring y[e] authority of y[e] legislature to enable him to do honourable right to his family, tho' to y[e] diminution of his own revenue, shows y[t] his goodness was not confin'd to himselfe; and his knowne abilities might have rendered him a public blessing, had not the circumstances of y[e] times he lived in, and those strickt rules by which he govern'd himselfe, hindred him from entering upon public action.—Reader, farewell; imitate his virtues if thou can'st, or honor at least the memory of him who possesst 'em.

St. Peter's Church, or rather *Chapel*, is a small neat brick building, erected in 1768, by Wm. Wright, Esq. and endowed with about £200. per ann. arising from a rent charge on lands in Mottram St. Andrew, pew rents, and a trifling augmentation from Queen Anne's Bounty.—On the north side of the Chapel, is an elegant white marble tablet, inscribed—

In memory of the Rev. George Edward Leigh, A. B. late Minister of this Church, son of John and Susannah Leigh, of Oughtrington Hall. He died May 5, 1808, in the 36th year of his age, and was interred in the family vault at Lymm. He was endeared in every relation of life by a most benevolent disposition, and by cheerful piety in the discharge of his sacred duties; his early death was lamented by who knew him.

On a large mural monument, in the middle of the north side of the building—

To the memory of Wm. Wright, of Mottram St. Andrew, in the county of Chester, Esq. As a Magistrate he was upright, vigilant, and intrepid, but always tempered the severity of justice with the sweetness of a benevolent heart. Of virtue and learning he was the patron and example. In his private conduct he was temperate and regular; severe in examining himself, but candid to others; tender and affectionate to his wife and family, and to sum up all, the friend of human kind.—To his pious munificence we owe this Chapel of St. Peter, erected and amply endowed by him in his life-time, and also a provision for poor and deserted children of this town, where he resided many years. Nor was his bounty confined to the place of his abode, but largely extended through the course of his life to every useful institution, and proper object of compassion. Supported by a lively faith in Christ, and an entire resignation to the will of God, after a life of 73 years, embittered with pain and trouble, he was rewarded with an easy death, on the third day of December, 1770. To show to after-times the bright example of every Christian virtue, and as a small testimony of his gratitude to the memory of his kind relation, this monument is erected by the Rev. Henry Offley Wright.

On a tablet, on the north side of the Altar—

To the memory of the Rev. Thomas Bentham, A. M. son of the Rev. Samuel Bentham, of Ely. He was born within the precincts of that Cathedral, and educated at St. John's College, Cambridge. In the year 1737, he succeeded to the Vicarage of Aberford, in the county of York, where his laborious discharge of all parochial duties for thirty years, recommended him to the pious founder of this Chapel, to which he was presented upon its consecration. Anxious to promote the glory of God, and the good of mankind, he devoted his time and talents to the duties of his sacred office. In the public discharge of his ministry, he was watchful, zealous, prudent; in the intercourse of private life benevolent, humble, pious; recommending what he taught by the uniform tenor of his own example. He died May 2d, 1790, in the 76th year of his age.

CHESHIRE HISTORY.

In addition to the Churches, the Calvinists have two Chapels, the Methodists three; the Unitarians one; the Roman Catholics one (at Edgeley); and a Meeting-house for the Quakers.

During the late disturbances, a strange medley of religious blasphemy, and sedition, was preached to the lazy, the ill-disposed, and the illiterate, in what were called the Union Rooms—a place set apart for the purpose. It was here Harrison the seditionist expounded his dangerous doctrines—and it was here that M'Ghinnis, who shot Mr. Birch, the constable, became his proselyte, and was afterwards convicted and executed for the offence at Chester; Bruce, his accomplice, was transported for life, in 1820.

BRINNINGTON,*

* Or Burnt Town.

Adjoins Stockport. It is not noticed in the Survey, but it is ascertained that at a very early period it was possessed by the Barons of Dunham Massy.—It was afterwards granted, and confirmed by Hamon, the third Baron, to Robert Fitz Waltheof, together with Bredbury, and Etchells. It is conjectured this Robert was the ancestor of the Barons of Stockport. In the 1st of Edw. III. Robert Dukenfield obtained the manor from William the son of Walter de Stockport; and it descended with Duckenfield, to the late John Astley, Esq. In 1812, William Fox, Esq. agreed with the trustees under the will of James Harrison, Esq. (purchaser from Mr. Astley) for the purchase of the manor of Brinnington, with several estates therein, which were paid for into the Court of Chancery in 1813, when possession was given, but the conveyance was not made complete till 1815.† The lands included in the conveyance, were 458 acres, which, with fourteen afterwards purchased by Mr. Fox, and two farms of sixty-one acres belonging to Mr. Thomas Marriot, constitute the whole of Brinnington, as distinguished from Portwood ‡

† Ormerod.

‡ Same.

The populous Hamlet of Portwood, in this township, contains 554 acres, and is principally the property of Messrs. Borrons. The *Hall* is occupied by a farmer. This hamlet may be said to form a component part of the town of Stockport, so greatly has the population lately extended itself.

A Court Baron is held for the manor and township of Brinnington. The Constables are sworn at the Hundred Court. The proprietor of the manor is one of the four *præpositi* of the parish of Stockport. Brinnington moor was inclosed a few years ago, and great improvements have lately taken place here, under the regulation of an Act of Parliament.||

HYDE

Is nearly four miles N. E. E. from Stockport. So early as the reign of John, one half of the township was possessed by a family which bore the local name; the Bagguleys were in possession of the other moiety, but it was obtained from them by the Hydes, temp. Hen. III. Sir John Hyde, THIRD in descent from Matthew de Hyde, served in France under the Black Prince.—Robert Hyde, NINTH in descent, was ancestor of the Hydes of Wisthatch, of which family was Edw. Hyde, Earl of Clarendon, Chancellor of England, and grandfather through his daughter Anne Hyde, Duchess of York, of Anne and Mary, successively Queens of England. Early in the last century, the male line direct terminated in Edward Hyde. It is now the property of George Hyde Clarke, Esq. whose grandfather George Clarke, Esq. Lieut.-Governor of New York, married Anne, one of the daughters and sole heiress of Edward Hyde, Esq.

Hyde Mill, or *Hyde Hall*, the seat of Mr. Clarke, is a building of considerable antiquity, but it underwent some modern improvements in the time of the late proprietor. A great part of the interior is in its original state. It is rather pleasantly situated on the River Tame; but the rapid introduction of manufactories into the neighbourhood, has materially deteriorated from the romantic beauties of the adjacent scenery.

There is a Court held for the Manor, subject to the Hundred Court.

Hyde Chapel is a Meeting House for Dissenters.

DUCKENFIELD,

Or Dukenfield, is about six miles and a half N. E. N.

|| Hamon de Massy gave the manor to Robert Fitz Waltheof, for which Robert was to serve him in his chamber, and to carry his arms and clothes when the Earl in person went into Wales; Hamon was to find him a sumptre man and a sack, whilst with the army; and Robert was to swear that if Hamon was in captivity, he should help to set him free, and also help to make his son's Knight, and to marry his eldest daughter; in token of which, Robert gave Hamon a gold ring.—Lysons.

from Stockport. It was originally included in the fee of Dunham Massy, and was given by Hamon to Matthew de Bromhall, or Bretberie. About 1327, it was purchased from William de Stockport, by Robert de Dokenfield, whose family had resided here from the Conquest, and whose descendants continued in possession till the death of Sir Robert Dukenfield, created a Baronet in 1665. His widow Penelope (who assumed the name of Daniell on being possessed of the estates of the Daniels of Tabley,) brought the manor and other estates in marriage to John Astley, Esq. a Portrait Painter of considerable celebrity. On her death, Mr. Astley re-married, and had issue, the present proprietor Francis Duckenfield Astley, Esq. High Sheriff of Cheshire in 1807, and who was almost the last of those gentlemen who maintained the dignity of the office by a large retinue, and a spirited munificence.*

Duckenfield Lodge is the residence of Mr. Astley, and is in a truly delightful situation on the bank of the Thame, opposite to Ashton-under-Lyne. Near the Lodge is an ancient place of worship for Dissenters.

Duckenfield Hall is divided into two tenements; one of the wings contains a domestic Chapel, founded in 1398, in the Chancel of which is a memorial of Sir Robt. Duckenfield, Bart. who died in 1729. This building is described by Sir Peter Leycester, as a Chapel of Ease to Stockport, and is included as such in the Diocesan catalogue.

This township is yearly increasing its population; it contains several extensive collieries, and cotton factories.—The Moravians had an establishment here; but disagreeing with the late Mr. Astley, most of them removed to Fairfield in 1785, where they still remain. Many of them, however, continued in Duckenfield, where they have a Chapel, a house for the Minister, and a boarding school fo rgirls.

The township of Duckenfield abounds with mines and quarries, which yield a considerable revenue. Iron ore is found in great quantities; and the smelting of iron seems to have been carried on here at a remote period, the scoriæ of iron being met with in abundance in a field called *Brun Yorth*, a provincial pronunciation for burnt earth.

The coal pits are from 60 to 105 yards in depth, according to the bearing of the strata. The borders of several of the old pits are planted with fir trees, which thrive well, form small woods, and give a pleasing appearance to the adjacent country.

Of the family which took the local name, was the celebrated Colonel Robt. Duckenfield, the Parliament Commander. He was born on the 28th August, 1619. In 1643, he was appointed a Commissioner for sequestrating estates, and raising money for the Commonwealth. In 1644, in conjuction with Col. Mainwaring, he had command of the troops sent to guard the Bridge at Stockport against Prince Rupert. He afterwards served at the siege of Withenshaw. In 1650, he was made Governor of Chester; and in the month of August in that year, he was appointed to the command of the Broxton and Wirral divisions of the seven hundred men to be raised in Cheshire. He was a member of the infamous Court Martial which sentenced to death the illustrious Earl of Derby; and it is stated, that Henry Bradshaw having obtained for the gallant Earl a pardon, it was placed in the hands of Col. Duckenfield, *who suppressed it!*—His next appointment was to the command of the troops sent against the Isle of Man, where he arrived on the 25th Oct. 1651.

Subsequently, Duckenfield, and Henry Birk(en)head represented the County in Parliament, which assembled July 5, 1653, and sat till the 12th Dec. of the same year. In 1659, he had £200. voted to him by Parliament, for his services in suppressing the insurrection of Sir George Booth. It will be seen from this hasty sketch, that he took a very active part in the oppressive measures of that period. Soon after the Restoration, he was brought to trial for the share he had in the trial of the Earl of Derby, and was afterwards imprisoned in the county for being concerned with many others in carrying on a plot to seize the King and Tower, to kill the Queen, and as many of the French nation as should be found there, and restore the Parliament.† From this time to his decease, we perceive nothing further about him. It is conjectured he died previous to 1665, in which year his son was made a Baronet by Charles II.

* Sir N. Duckenfield, Bart. the descendant of the ancient stock of the Duckenfields, resides at Warfield, in Berkshire, but inherits no part of the estate.

† Ormerod.

CHESHIRE

BREDBURY.

After the Conquest this manor was held by Ricardus de Vernon, and subsequently passed from the Shipbrook family to the Dunham Massy family. Temp. Hen. II. Waltheof held Bredbury under the Masci family. It was afterwards possessed by the Stockport family. In the time of Edw. III. Bredbury was held by the tenure of doing service to the King in time of war, with an uncaparisoned horse. It was about this reign, that in consequence of two subinfeudations, the Ardernes of Alvanley, and the Davenports of Henbury, had manerial rights here.

The ARDERNES had their lands in the township by the marriage of Peter de Arderne with Cecilia, the daughter of Adam de Bredbury; and their portion of the township has descended to the present representative of the family, John Arderne, Esq.

The DAVENPORT share was held by them from the Warrens, Lords of Stockport, and was originally in the Woodford branch of the family, but it was eventually obtained by the Henbury line of the Davenports.

John Arden, Esq. holds a Court Baron for the "Manor of Bredbury-cum-Goyt;" the manerial rights formerly exercised by the Davenports, have fallen into disuse.*

Harden Hall is a fine old house, built about the middle of the 16th century. From its resemblance to *Poole Hall*, in Wirral, Mr. Ormerod supposes it to have been erected by the same Architect. It was originally built of grey stone, in a pleasant situation on the bank of the Tame. The front is lighted by very large bay windows, and the building is rendered conspicuous by a turret which rises considerably above the general level of the roof. The great hall is a fine room, about 33 feet long by 24 feet in width. The walls are decorated with a great number of old family pictures, which, it is to be lamented, are not taken more care of by the present proprietor. Some of them are completely spoiled, and the others are in a state of rapid decay:† most of these pictures it is said‡ belonged to the Crewes, and were brought from Utkinton Hall; amongst them is the portrait of Mrs. Jane Lane, who assisted the escape of Charles II.; she is represented as concealing the Crown under her cloak.

HISTORY

BRAMHALL,

Bromhall, or *Bromhale*, is about three miles S. W. from Stockport. Previous to the Conquest, the township was divided into two manors. At a very early period, it was possessed by a family which adopted the local name, and, temp. Hen. II. Hamo de Masci, confirmed to Matthew de Bromhall, the Manor of Bromhall, Duckenfield, and two portions of Bagguley.

About the reign of Hen. V. the property passed with an heiress to John Davenport, Esq. ancestor of William Davenport, Esq. who holds a Court Baron, and who receives quit-rents from every estate in the township.

The *Hall* of Bramhall, is a venerable mansion, composed chiefly of timber and plaister, in a picturesque situation on the side of a small rivulet. The original form of the building was a quadrangle. The great hall is a noble room, with large bay windows. The drawing-room, which is approached by a spiral staircase of solid oak, forms a wainscoted square of nearly thirty-six feet. On the door posts appear the date 1592.—In this apartment are portraits of Sir Wm Davenport, and Dorothy his Lady, 1627; Sir Wm. Davenport and his wife Margaret, aged 44, in 1628; Wm. Davenport and his wife Elizabeth Gregory, with their five children; J. Warren, Esq. aged 40, 1580; Sir Edw. his son, aged 32, 1594; Sir Urian Legh, of Adlington, in a Spanish costume, holding in his right hand the truncheon of a Commander.§ Beyond the drawing-room is an apartment called the *Plaster Room*, the walls of which are hung round with ancient military weapons, buff suits, &c. The bed-chamber, called the *Paradise Room*, adjoining this, has a bed, on which is worked in worsted by Dame Dorothy Davenport, the History of the Fall; this piece of work was commenc-

* The Davenport portion passed by a female heir to Sir Fulke Lucy. John Arden, Esq. and Sir Fulke Lucy, were joint proprietors in 1662 The Lucy moiety being purchased by the Ardens, the whole is now their property.—LYSONS.

† In one of the sleeping rooms is a curious old carved oak bedstead, not much dissimilar to the one in the Hall at Barrow.

‡ Lysons.

§ Sir Urian had a command in the expedition to Cadiz, in 1596, where he was Knighted. It is believed by the Adlington family, that Sir Urian is alluded to in the old ballad printed in PERCY'S RELIQUES OF ANCIENT POETRY, beginning—

> Will you hear a Spanish Lady,
> How she woo'd an Englishman?
> Garments gay as rich as may be,
> Deck'd with jewels had she on.

ed in 1610, and was completed in 1614 The *Banquetting Room* is a noble apartment, 42 feet in length by 21 feet in breadth; the roof is of wood, enriched with quatrefoils, the wainscoat painted with flowers, and grotesque figures. There are remains of stained glass in the windows.

In the south east angle of the building is the *Domestic Chapel*, an ancient structure with a flat roof, supported by brackets; the windows contain specimens of stained glass. Its erection is attributed to the reign of Richard III.

Over the Davenport Vault here, is an inscription to—

Martha, wife of William Davenport, Esq. who died December 25th, 1810, aged 63.

DISLEY STANLEY,

Is about six miles S. E. of Stockport. Jordan de Dystelegh, held lands here, temp. Edw. I. by the service of being one of the foresters of Macclesfield; these lands passed to the Suttons and Sherds, or Sherts.—John de Sherde was settled here as early as the reign of Edward III.

STANLEY was a hamlet on the north side of Disley, but is now annexed to it; Grym de Stanlegh held it, temp. Edward I. by the same service as the Sherdes held Disley. The Manor is vested in the Leghs, of Lyme.

The situation of the township is very pleasant, on the borders of Derbyshire.

The CHAPEL of Disley, consists of a nave, and chancel, with a stone tower, containing a ring of six bells. The chancel and vestry are of brick. The whole of it was rebuilt, consecrated, dedicated to the Virgin Mary, and made parochial, in 1558; and the Leghs, of Lyme, have vested in them the appointment of the Curate.—There are some beautiful specimens of heraldic stained glass in the chancel window. The Registers commence in 1591.

On a flag-stone is a memorial of Joseph Watson, buried June 3, 1753, aged 104; he was Park-keeper at Lyme upwards of 64 years, and was the "first that perfected the art of driving the stags."

It appears from the Ecclesiastical Survey, 26 Henry VIII. there was formerly a Chantry here: "Cantaria in Dystley Deyn Thomas Davenport, capellanus, ib'm. Valet in terris et tenementis eidem cantarie spectan. per a'm IIII*l*. Xma inde VIIJs."

There is a *School* here, endowed with £10. 5*s*. per ann. by the Leghs, who have the appointment of the Master, but his salary is unsettled.

NORBURY

Is nearly four miles S. E. S. from Stockport, and was held by Bigot at the Survey. A mesne manor was subsequently possessed by a family which took the local name, and the heiress of which brought it in marriage, temp Hen. III. to Robert de Hyde.

About the end of the 17th century, the Hydes sold the manor to the Leghs of Lyme, in whom it is now vested, and who hold a Court Baron for it.

Norbury *Hall*, a building of timber and plaister, is in a state of ruin.

Norbury CHAPEL is a low building of brick; the Curate, the same with Poynton, is appointed by the Leghs. The Registers commence in 1723.

In 1760, Peter Legh, Esq. built a *School House* here, but it is not endowed.

TORKINGTON

Is scarcely three miles S. E. from Stockport. It formed, with Norbury, and other townships, part of the extensive fee of Aldford. The mesne manor was subsequently held by the Ardernes of Aldford, and under them by the Leghs of Booths, and the Manor is now possessed by John Legh, Esq. but no Court is held.—The *Hall* is occupied by a farmer

On the sides of the Macclesfield Road, is erected the populous village of BULLOCK SMITHY, taking its name from an ancient house of that name.

A neat *Lodge* was built in Torkington, by the late Mr. Legh, where he occasionally resided.

OFFERTON

Is little more than two miles and a half S. E. S. from Stockport. There is no doubt but what it formed part of the Fee of Aldford, and was included in the Survey with Norbury. From a family which subsequently took the local name, it fell by marriage of an heiress to the Wyningtons. On the death of Ralph Winnington, near the close of the 16th century, this property was divided between the Wrights of Nantwich, and the Bradshaws of Marple. The manor and hall of Offerton, are now vested in Lawrence Wright, Esq. of Mottram Andrew; but he does not hold a Court Baron.

The *Hall* is occupied by a farmer; it is of brick, finished with gables, and of considerable antiquity.

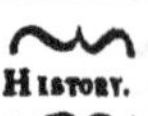

MARPLE

Is about five miles E. S. E. from Stockport. Mr. Ormerod is of opinion the ancient manor of Merpull, alludes "obviously to the ancient expansion of the waters of the Goyt, in the vale below." It is not noticed in the Survey; but in the time of Earl Randle a grant of lands called Merpul and Wibreslegam was made to Robert, son of Robert de Stockport.—Subsequently Robert re-granted this property to his sister Margery and her husband Wm. Vernon, who was Chief Justice of Chester in 1230-2; he was ancestor of the Vernons of Harleston. In the 30th Edward. I. Richard de Vernon granted the manor of Marple to John de Mottram; and in the 3d of Edward II. Robt. Mottershead remitted the manor to Richard de Vernon.

On the death of Sir George Vernon, temp. Elizabeth, Marple fell to the portion of his daughter Margaret, wife of Sir Thomas Stanley. Subsequently the manor was sold by Sir Edward Stanley, to Thomas Hibbert, Esq. The manerial rights are now disused.

Marple Hall was conveyed by Sir Edward Stanley, July 7, 1606, to Henry Bradshaw, yeoman, for £270.

In Sept. 1631, *Wyberslegh Hall* was settled on Hen. Bradshaw, grandson of the above, by Barnard Wells, of Hope, in Derbyshire; and both of these Halls, the latter occupied by a farmer, are the property of John Isherwood, Esq. High Sheriff of the county in 1815.

Marple Hall, is a noble old house, finely situated on the rise of a hill above the Goyt, and is the residence of Mr. Isherwood, who is descended in the female line from the notorious John Bradshaw, President of "the High Court of Justice," which condemned King Charles I.*

He was born at Wyberslegh Hall; and in the register of Stockport Church, his birth is thus entered:—

"1602.—John the Sonne of Henry Bradshaw, of Marple, was baptized the 10th of December."

In the margin is the word traitor, with a line under it.

Henry Bradshaw, elder brother of the "President,"

* The Judge relates in his will, that he had his school education at Bunbury, in Cheshire, and Middleton, in Lancashire; and tradition adds, that he was also for some time at Macclesfield; with the strange circumstance annexed to the tale, that he wrote the following sentence on a stone in the Church-yard there:

My brother Henry must heir the land,
My brother Frank must be at his command:
While I, poor Jack, will do that
That all the world shall wonder at.

Bradshaw served his clerkship with an attorney at Congleton, to which place he returned after residing some time in Gray's Inn, and acted as counsellor at law. The first time of his being employed in the affairs of Government, seems to have been in the year 1644. In 1646 he was more eminently distinguished, being appointed one of the three Commissioners of the Great Seal for six month. In the February following, both Houses voted him the office of Chief Justice of Chester; and he was also made one of the Judges for Wales. On the third of January, 1648-9, when the Lords had adjourned their house, and it was found on their journal, that they had rejected the ordinance for the trial of the King, the Commons voted the business to be performed by themselves alone, and chose Bradshaw, then serjeant, and others, for assistants. On the 10th, the commissioners appointed for the trial met, and elected Bradshaw, who was absent, as their president; but allowed him to appoint a deputy to supply his place at Guildhall, where he sat as Judge. His conduct in the High Court, which condemned the dethroned Monarch to a violent death, has been so frequently related by historians, that we shall avoid entering into the detail, and only observe, that the strong attachment to republican principles which appears to have actuated him on that occasion, animated him to the latest period of his existence; for when on his death-bed, he was advised to examine himself about the matter of the King's death, he affirmed, that if it was to do again, "he would be the first man that should do it." On February the 14th, 1648, he was one of the thirty-eight persons whom the House had voted to compose a Council of State, and invested with extraordinary powers. In the March following, he was appointed Chief Justice of Wales; and in June, 1649, had £1000. voted to him by the Parliament.—On the escape of Duke Hamilton, and some other state prisoners, an act was passed, constituting a new court of justice, and Bradshaw was made president. This caused a very unexpected change in his affairs; for on the same day that Cromwell dissolved the Long Parliament, and by that means destroyed the Commonwealth, it occasioned him to lose the Protector's confidence; for, equally the opposer of unlimited power, whether exercised by a king or an usurper, the Judge disdained to submit in silence to illegal authority. After expelling the Members of the House, Cromwell went to break up the Council of State, and prefaced his design with these words: "If you, gentlemen, are met here as private persons, you shall not be disturbed; but if as a Council of State, this is no place for you, since you cannot but know what was done in the House in the morning: so take notice that the Parliament is dissolved." To this Bradshaw boldly replied, "Sir, we have heard what you did at the House in the morning, and before many hours all England will hear it. But, Sir, you are mistaken, to think that Parliament is dissolved; for no power under hea-

Engraved by J Pigot. Manch.[r]

A VIEW OF THE AQUEDUCT AT MARPLE IN CHESHIRE.

Engraved for Henshalls History of Cheshire.

CHESHIRE HISTORY.

was a very prominent character during the Rebellion. He signed the Petition* from the County for making the Presbyterian the Established Religion of the Land.—He was a Magistrate; and was Serjeant-Major in Col. Duckenfield's Regiment, under Lord Fairfax, and Lieut.-Colonel in Colonel Ashton's regiment of foot—He had subsequently the command of the Macclesfield Hundred Militia, which was at the battle of Worcester, where he was wounded. He sat on the trial of the Earl of Derby at Chester, in 1652

* July 6, 1646.

At Marple were several forms for an apology or answer of Col Bradshaw,† to the Charge against him, of having sat on Lord Derby's trial, when the matter came before the Committee in 1660: he there states, that being an officer under Cromwell he was ordered by him to be present at the Court Martial at Chester; that not knowing what danger he might incur if he absented himself, he occasionally attended at the management of it, but did not sign the warrant for his execution; that he interposed as much as he could for the Earl's pardon, and actually presented a petition to Col. Mackworth (President of the Court) in behalf of the Earl, and earnestly pressed it; that being sent for by the Earl, he immediately attended, and wrote to his brother, President Bradshaw, to use his utmost endeavours to spare the life of the Earl; that he never had any thing which belonged to the Earl, his Countess, or any of theirs; that he was a poor man, in debt, with a small estate, and had a wife and eleven children to maintain, who were unprovided for. That he intended in future to demean himself as became an obedient subject, craved the benefit of his Majesty's most gracious pardon, and prayed their Lordships that his errors might be imputed to his much-lamented ignorance and mistake. On the 14th Aug. 1660, he had his discharge from Alexander Thane, Usher of the Black Rod. On the 15th March, 1661, he died, and was buried at Stockport.

† Ormerod.

There is a CHAPEL of Ease here, recently rebuilt with stone; the tower containing the old bells of Stockport Church. The living is in the gift of the Rector of Stockport; and the Registers commence in 1655.

Henry Bradshaw, who survived his brother, the President, founded a School here, on a small scale, endowed with the interest of £100.; it has since been augmented by other benefactions, and the income is now £8. 17s. per ann. In the neighbourhood of this township is a fine Aqueduct over the river, a sketch of which accompanies this.

ROMILEY

Is about four miles east of Stockport, situated on the hills bordering on the neighbouring county of Derby.

In the Survey it *(Rumelie)* is described as being

ven can dissolve them but themselves; therefore take you notice of that." This speech completely alienated the Protector's affections from him, though at the same time it appears to have impressed him with respect: for, in a conference with Desborough, he observed, that his work, after dissolving the Parliament, was not completed, till he had also dissolved the Council of State, which "I did in spite of the objection of honest Bradshaw, the President." Before this, the sum of £2000 per annum had been settled on him by the Parliament. In the year 1654, Bradshaw was returned as representative for this county; and his behaviour was so inimical to Cromwell's designs, that the latter exerted his authority to prevent his being a second time returned. He also required him to resign his commission as Chief Justice of Chester; but this he steadily refused, alledging, that he held that place by a grant from the Parliament of England, to continue quam diu se bene gesserit: and whether he had carried himself with that integrity which his commission exacted from him, he was ready to submit to a trial by twelve Englishmen, to be chosen even by Cromwell himself. The firm adherence of Bradshaw to what he supposed were the principles of liberty, and which Cromwell was unquestionably violating, prevented his being any more employed in state affairs during the Protectorship; yet, after the death of Oliver, he was again returned for Cheshire to the Parliament that met in January, 1658-9; and soon after appointed one of the Commissioners to hold the broad seal for five months, but was dispossessed of his high office by the army, who dissolved this parliament, or assembly, as it was called, by force. After the Restoration, twenty-three persons, who had sat as Judges on the King, were attainted, though in their graves. Bradshaw, who died in the year 1659, being among the number, his body was taken up, and on the 30th of Jan. 1660-1, the day appointed for this act of retributive justice, as it was termed, was drawn on a sledge to Tyburn, where he, Cromwell, and Ireton, were hanged on the several angles of the gallows, under which their mutilated trunks were afterwards buried; their heads having been first cut off, and fixed on Westminster Hall. By the Judge's will, dated the 22d of March, 1653, it appears that he was possessed of various manors, &c. in Kent, Middlesex, Berks, Southampton, Wilts, and Somerset; and that he made many charitable bequests; among which was the sum of £700 to purchase an annuity for maintaining a free-school at Marple. The probate copy of his will is yet at Marple Hall; but the observance of its provisions was completely interrupted by the changes made in the destination of his property at the Restoration. The general opinion, that he possessed lands in Cheshire, is probably erroneous, as they are not mentioned in the above record.—BEAUTIES OF ENGLAND.

waste, and included in the possessions of the Earl, from whom it passed to the Barons of Dunham Massy.—Temp. Edw. III. it was held by Isabel, daughter of Richard de Stockport, and from her it descended to the Ardernes, Etons, and Warrens. About 1620, the Davenports held it under the Warrens. In 1703, it was the property of Reginald Bretland, Esq. and at the present time the manerial rights are claimed by John Arden, Esq. and Thomas William Tatton, Esq.; the former claims in right of the Ardernes, his ancestors,—the latter by the purchase in 1768, of the *manors of Wernith and Romiley.*

There is no Court held; the Constables are sworn at the Macclesfield Leet.

CHADKIRK CHAPEL is in this township, nearly opposite to Marple Hall. There was a manor here at the Survey, held by the Earl's tenant, Gamel. The Chapel was in ruins about sixty years before 1746, when it was rebuilt by subscription; the patronage is vested in the Rector of Stockport. Serjeant Bretland left £5. for an orthodox preacher here, requesting the Rector of Stockport would add as much more; but it had not been paid in 1718. The annuity of 5*l* ℘. *an.* is now paid by T. W. Tatton, Esq. who holds the Bretland estates on which it was charged.

There was formerly a *Chantry* here, which is noticed in the Ecclesiastical Survey.

WERNITH

Is on the north side of Romiley. In the reign of Edward III. it was held by Isabel. It passed for several centuries with the last township. In 1662 it was possessed by Sir Fulk Lucy; the manor is now vested in Thomas William Tatton, Esq. but no Court Baron is held.—The Constables are sworn at the Macclesfield Leet.

Wernith Hall was purchased in 1812, by J. B. Isherwood, Esq. from the Rev. Mr. Coke; and Mr. Isherwood resold it in 1815, to Mr. Andrew, of Comstall Bridge. The highest part of the Cheshire Hills, *Wernith Low*, is in this township.

THE PARISH OF

MOTTRAM IN LONGDENDALE,

CONTAINS THE TOWNSHIPS OF

MOTTRAM,	GODLEY,	MATLEY,	HOLLINGWORTH,
NEWTON,	HATTERSLEY,	STAYLEY,	TINTWISTLE.

MOTTRAM* forms that bleak and dreary promontory extending to the borders of Yorkshire—or, rather the parish of Mottram includes that inhospitable district.—The township of Mottram is about seven miles N. E. from Stockport. Formerly the entire of the parish was called Tintwistle, or "Tengestvisie," and it is so noticed in the Survey.

Before the year 1300, the De Burghs had property here; and in the 11th Edw. II. Thomas Earl of Lancaster, who was subsequently beheaded, had a grant of the estates from Thos. de Burgh. Sir Robert de Holland, a dependent of the Earl's then got possession of the property, from whom it passed to his representatives, the Lovells, who retained it till the attainder of

* The population, as appears from the parish register, has more than doubled since the last century, and is still augmenting. Formerly there was hardly sufficient business for one butcher, excepting at the Wake; but now several are maintained from the additional employ afforded by the increased consumption. The inhabitants are supplied with water from springs: on the very top of the hill is a fine well, and two others are on its different sides. Most of the hills in this vicinity have springs, either issuing from their sides, or summits, all which are of soft water. The scenery in the neighbourhood of Mottram is very grand. The rugged and steep rocks, occasionally ra-

SSHIRE

486. Francis Lord Lovell, temp. Hen. VII.* In the 4th Hen. VII. LONGDENDALE was granted in fee to Sir Wm Stanley, of Holt, together with the interest which the Lovels had in the Barony of Nantwich. In 1495, it again reverted to the Crown. Subsequently the Wilbrahams of Woodhey had a grant, and the manor is now vested in their representative, Wilbraham Tollemache, Earl of Dysart, who holds courts for Mottram and Longdendale, the jurisdiction of which extend over the whole parish.†

There are extensive moor grounds in this neighbourhood, which abound with grouse.

The CHURCH is dedicated to St. Michael, and the present Vicar is the Rev. James Turner, instituted about 1794. The Church consists of nave, chancel, and side aisles, with a tower containing eight bells. There are private chancels at the end of the side aisles, belonging to Hollingsworth and Stayley Halls. In the south chancel is a full length figure of Ralph Stanley, in complete armour, with his wife on his left side. In the Chancel, on an altar tomb, on which is a recumbent figure of Serjeant Bretland, is this inscription :—

HISTORY.

H. S. E. quicquid mortale fuit Reginaldi Bretland, A. L. S. familia non ignobili orti, virtute, doctrina, ingenio praeclari, qui consultando prudens, eloquendo facundus, agendo fortis, pacis studiosus, escarum fugax, clientibus in maximis fidus.—Rex aliorum sibi commissas tam diligenter quam suas administrabat; neque constituere litium rationes quam controversias tollere maluit Nullus illi per otium dies exiit. Vitae tandem satur, animam virtutibus onustam beneque de

lieved by bold and swelling eminences, and those declining into vallies cloathed with verdure, constitute some very picturesque and romantic prospects. The CAR TOR is a very singular precipice; its perpendicular height is eighty feet. The summit and sides have oak trees growing on them; and from the former vast rocks are pendant, which seem to frown destruction on every thing beneath. The face of the precipice exhibits various strata of rock, coal, or slaty matter, and free-stone; all as regularly disposed as if they had been placed by the art of a mason. Between the Car Tor and the opposite and well-wooded hills of Derbyshire, the Mersey hurries along its craggy bed, and greatly contributes to the grandeur of the contiguous scenery. The most distinguished natives of this town were Mr. LEE, formerly an eminent stock-broker' under the Royal Exchange, who raised himself to affluence by his persevering industry; and LAWRENCE EARNSHAW, more favored by the endowments of mind than the gifts of fortune, which were but very moderately dispensed to him. The cottage wherein this extraordinary man was born, soon after the commencement of the last century, stands in the high road to Wednescough Green, and is contemplated by the neighbouring inhabitants with nearly as much veneration as the admirers of Sir Isaac Newton express for the place of his nativity. He was early apprenticed to a taylor, and afterwards to a clothier; but neither of these employments being congenial with his disposition, after serving both for eleven years, he placed himself for a short time with a clock-maker of Stockport. With the very little instruction he obtained from his desultory education, he became one of the most universal mechanists and artists that was ever known. He could have taken wool from the sheep's backs, manufactured it into cloth, and made every instrument necessary for the clipping, carding, spinning, reeling, weaving, fulling, dressing, and making it up for wear, with his own hands. He was an engraver, painter, and gilder; he could stain glass, and foil mirrors; was a blacksmith, whitesmith, copper-smith, gun-smith, bell-founder, and coffin-maker; made and erected sun-dials; mended fiddles; repaired, tuned, made, played upon, and taught, the harpsichord and virginals; made and mended organs, and optical instruments; read, and understood Euclid; and in short, had a taste for all sorts of mechanics, and most of the fine arts. Clock-making, and repairing, was a very favourite employ to him; and he carried so far his theory and practice of clock-work, as to be the inventor of a very curious astronomical and geographical machine, containing a terrestrial and celestial globe, to which different movements were given, representing the diurnal and annual motions of the earth, the positions of the moon and stars, the sun's place in the ecliptic, and various other phoenomena, with the greatest correctness. All the complicated calculations, as well as the execution, of this ingenious work, were performed by himself; and one of the machines, curiously ornamented, was sold to the Earl of Bute for £150. About the year 1753, he likewise invented a machine to spin and reel cotton at one operation, which he shewed to his neighbours, and then destroyed, through the generous apprehension that it might take bread from the mouths of the poor — This was previous to the late inventions by which the cotton manufacture has been so much promoted. He also contrived a simple but ingenious peice of mechanism for raising water from a coal mine.— He was acquainted with that equally self-taught genius, the celebrated BRINDLEY, and when they occasionally met, they would continue to occupy many hours in discoursing on the principles of science, and their own respective modes of operation. Earnshaw possessed a singular degree of sobriety, not even drinking a glass of ale for many years after he was grown to manhood. His mien and countenance were not peculiarly stamped with intelligence, but, on the contrary, might, at first view, be considered as indicative of stupidity, yet when animated by conversation, his features beamed with the irradiations of intellect. He conversed with fluency, and clearly explained the subjects of his discourse in the dialect and peculiar phrase of his country. But all his trades, and all his ingenuity, were employed to a certain degree in vain; for the expense incurred through the maintenance of a sick wife and family, prevented his attaining affluence. He died about the year 1764.

† The manors of Micklehurst and Arnfield are appendages of the estate.—LYSONS.

CHESHIRE

repub. meritam, placidè Deo reddidit die tertio Aprilis, anno Dom. 1703, ætat. suæ 62.—Semper laboremus; omnia sunt hominum tenui pendentia filo; dum loquimur fugerit invida ætas, cape quam minimum credula postero.

The Church was built about 1487, and towards its erection, Sir Edmund Shaa bequeathed a sum of money.* The Registers commence in 1562.

* Lysons.

The advowson of the living fell to the crown on the attainder of Lord Lovell, and Henry VIII. annexed it to the property of the Bishop of Chester, who still leases it, and enjoys its revenues. The Bishop is the patron.

There is a *Free School* here, well endowed.†

NEWTON,

This township was, as early as 1302, in the possession of a family which bore the local name;‡ and they continued here till 1692, when Alexander Newton sold the mesne manor to Sir Charles Duckenfield, Bart. It has subsequently passed with the manor of Duckenfield.

GODLEY,

Or *Godelegh*, gave name to a family settled here before the reign of Henry III. In the 12th Edw. II. Wm. de Baggulegh, and William his son, obtained the manor from from Robt. de Godelegh.|| It subsequently passed to the Mascies of Sale, and the Newtons. No manerial rights are now claimed; and the estates here are in the hands of several proprietors.

|| 1319.

HATTERSLEGH

Is nearly six miles N. E. E. from Stockport. It was held of the Manor of Longden, under the Earls, by the Stockports, and after them by the Hattersleghs; it subsequently passed to the Carringtons,§ and descended with other estates to the Booths of Dunham Massy.—The Earl of Stamford and Warrington is the present proprietor, and holds a Court Baron for the Manor.

STAYLEY,

Or *Staveley*, was held at a very early period by the Macclesfields, and under them by a family which assumed the local name, who continued here in the direct male line till the reign of Elizabeth, when Elizabeth, daughter and heiress of Ralph Stavelegh, married Thomas the son of Thomas de Ashton, and brought to him this township.—It was subsequently conveyed by a co-heiress to the Booths, and has passed with their other estates to the present Earl of Stamford and Warrington, who holds a Court Baron for it.

HISTORY

On the Hills behind the Old Hall, noticed by Webb, as "a fine old manor belonging to Sir George Booth," is the ancient British fortress of Bickton Castle.¶—The inner slope or rampart is 27 feet, perpendicular height 6 feet, outer slope from the top of the rampart to the bottom of the ditch 35 feet, inner slope of the ditch 16 feet, depth of the ditch 8 feet, width at the bottom 6 feet; height of the rampart above the level of the ground 8 feet; breadth of the gateway 16 feet.**

¶ See page 513.

** Ormerod.

MATLEY.

Temp. Edward II. lands here were obtained by Wm. de Baggelegh from Richard de Mattlegh. Subsequently, by sale or otherwise, the Mascies of Sale had a portion of the manor, and afterwards the Booths, from whom it has passed to the present respected and noble head of the Dunham Massy family, who holds a Court Baron for it.

HOLLINGWORTH

Is supposed to have been included, as *Holisurde*, in the Earl's waste lands, at the period of the Survey.—It was afterwards a dependency on the Earl's Lordship of Longdendale, under which it was held, temp. Edw. III by John de Holynworth, whose descendants continued in possession till 1734, when Jacob Hollingworth sold the manor to Mr. Daniel Whitle.

In Nov. 1792, John Whitle left the manor to his brother Daniel, which Daniel died, leaving issue a son and daughter, living in 1811.††

†† Ormerod.

In 1800, the *Old Hall* was purchased by Mr. Geo. Hadfield, who made it his residence.

Thorncliffe Hall was also purchased, in 1810, by Mr. Hadfield, from the Tattons, of Withenshaw.

† The endowment consists of lands in Haughton, in Bunbury Parish, houses in Manchester, and a rent charge in Chadkirk of £5. per ann. given by Robert Hyde, of Cattenhall, Esq. The Haughton estate was purchased with £200. given in equal portions by Robert Gartside, of Nantwich, and Sir Richard Wilbraham, of Woodhey; and the Manchester Houses were purchased with the timber on this estate, which was valued in Bishop Gastrell's time at £165. The nomination of the Master is now in the Minister and Churchwardens; it was formerly in the Bishop and Parishioners.

‡ The Lysons say it was acquired by Thomas de Newton, in marriage with the daughter and heiress of Thomas de Davenport.

§ The Carringtons, temp. Elizabeth, held their lands here, by the annual render of a barbed arrow to the heir of the Stockports.

CHESHIRE. — HISTORY.

The Earl of Dysart, the representative of the Wilbrahams, deputes a gamekeeper for the manor.

TINTWISTLE.

It appears that no mesne manor ever existed in this township. On its eastern side is the CHAPEL OF WOODHEAD about six miles from Mottram, on the Yorkshire borders, founded by Sir Edmund Shaa, under his will bearing date in 1487, in which he says, "I woll have two honest preestes oon of them to syng his mass and say his other divine service in a Chapel that I have made in Longden Dale, in the countie of Chester, and pray especially for my soule, and for the souls, &c. and I woll that he have for his salarie yearley for evermore, the some of £4. 6s. 8d." In 1662, the Chapel was in a state of extreme decay; but it has been repaired, and the patronage is vested in the Bishop. The building is of grey stone; the situation singularly commanding and romantic, above the stream of the Etherow.

END OF ITINERARY OF MACCLESFIELD HUNDRED.

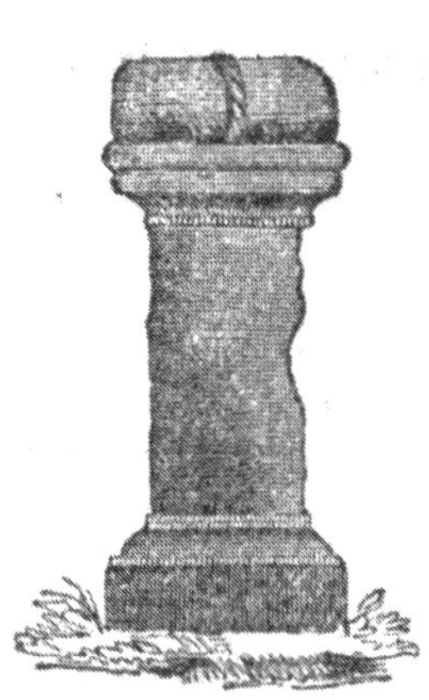

A ROMAN ALTAR, of which the above are accurate front and side views, was found on Thursday the 29th of March, 1821. As the dedication of it is singular, and as excited a good deal of discussion among the curious, a minute description will not be unacceptable. The field, in which it was discovered, is called the DANIELS, Great Boughton, near Chester, and is the property of Mr. Simon Faulkner, gardener.—It is situated near the junction of the Roman Roads to MANCUNIUM (Manchester) and MEDIOLANUM (Chesterton, in Staffordshire) about 350 yards from the Black Lion Mr. Faulkner having made a contract to furnish a quantity of sand, or the new building at Eaton, some workmen were employed to cut it away, and in levelling a tumulus about half way up the field, on the west side, they struck against hard substance, which upon inspection proved to be the Altar in question. The ornamental parts have been neatly executed, particularly the mouldings and the finishg of the scrolls. The inscription, which is quite perfect, may be thus Anglicised—"THE TWENTIETH LEGION—THE MIGHTY, THE VICTORIOUS,—TO THE NYMPHS ND FOUNTAINS."* The Altar, is of red sand stone, and was found embedded in a sandy soil, surrounded by a heap of stones, no doubt originally forming the temple in hich it was kept. Its height is four feet; the middle of the column two feet; the base and capital about two feet three inches. The THURIBULUM is an inch in depth. is conjectured that the fountain or well to which, with its guardian "NYMPHS," it was dedicated, has been filled up, as there is none in its immediate vicinity, but the eld abounds with springs of water, which spontaneously burst forth their chrystal streams. The altar was detached from the pedestal, a rough piece of similar stone, early twenty inches wide, and six inches thick, and was in a half inclined position, supported by the soil. The inscription is the same behind as in front, with e exception of the word FONTIBUS, which is cut FONTBUS. It has been suggested, the letters V. V. allude to a vow made previous to its erection by the edicators, and should be rendered VOTUM VOVIT; but when the uniformity of the application of these initials is adverted to, there can be no doubt but what they are scriptive of the Legion, VALENS VICTRIX—the Valiant, the Victorious. Supposing the Altar thus discovered to have been erected when the Twentieth Legion FIRST RIVED here, it is 1778 years old; if when they quitted England, 1491 years--taking a medium, it may be stated that this Altar is ONE THOUSAND EIGHT HUNDRED D SEVENTY ONE YEARS OLD!—CHESTER CHRONICLE.

* Dr. Whittaker says, this Legion was composed of Citizens of Rome, not mercenary troops, and Agricola fixed their head quarters at Manchester—HISTORY OF ANCHESTER.

The Hundred of Northwich,

CONTAINS THE PARISHES OF

ASTBURY, BRERETON, GREAT BUDWORTH, CHURCH LAWTON, DAVENHAM, MIDDLEWICH, SANDBACH, SWETTENHAM, AND WARMINGHAM.

THE PARISH OF MIDDLEWICH,

CONTAINS THE TOWNSHIPS OF

MIDDLEWICH, KINDERTON, MORESBARROW-CUM PARME, SPROSTON, BYLEY-CUM-YATEHOUSE, STUBLACH, RAVENSCROFT, CROXTON, NEWTON, SUTTON, CLIVE, WEEVER, WIMBOLDSLEY-CUM-LEA, OCCLESTON, AND MINSHULL VERNON.

MIDDLEWICH* is about eighteen miles E. of Chester, and nearly one half of the built town, is within the adjoining township of Kinderton. It appears from the Survey, that it was held by the King and Earl so early as the reign of the Confessor, and was subsequently included in the territorial possessions of Hugh the Second Earl. On the extinction of the authority of the original Earls, the royalty passed to the Crown, in which it has since been vested, and is held by lease by Thomas Wright, Esq.†

From a plea to a Quo Warranto, temp. Hen. VII. the burgesses of Middlewich claimed peculiar privileges, viz. that yearly at at the Court after the Feast of St. Michael, they might elect a Chamberlain, who was to be assisted by two Bailiffs. The latter to have at each Court, to be held from fifteen to fifteen days, *unam*

* The following account is from the "BEAUTIES OF ENGLAND." —"Its name was derived from its centrical situation between the WICHES, or Salt Towns; and its origin has been supposed at least as remote as the time of the Romans; the road to it from Northwich being mentioned by Camden, as raised with gravel to such a height, as to be readily known for a work of that people. Its government is vested in a certain number of burgesses; and its privileges are similar to those of the other Salt Towns. The salt manufactured here, is made from brine springs, well saturated; but the quantity is at present inconsiderable, though it might readily be increased on demand.—Some additional employ to that furnished by the salt works arises from a cotton manufactory established a few years ago."

† The lease which was granted Aug. 10, 1792, for fifty years, commencing Oct. 10, 1791.

WRENBURY CHURCH.

Eng[d] by J. Piper

MIDDLEWICH CHURCH.

Eng[d] for Hanshalls History of Cheshire.

sextam cervisiæ, to be there drunk, and not carried away, paying for each *lagena* of the beer, a farthing below the usual price; the beer to be supplied by two brewers at each Court, going through the brewers in rotation.—They also claimed to boil and sell salt, giving the thirtieth boiling to the Prince (Earl) and to be free from toll, murage, and homage, throughout the whole county

The present government of the town is vested in two Constables, who are sworn at the Court held by the Crown Lessee.

A considerable manufacture of Salt is still carried on here.—The Fairs are held on Holy Thursday, and the 25th July.

The town is pleasantly situated at the junction of the rivers Croco and Dane.

There are two markets weekly, on Tuesdays and Fridays, the former is chiefly for butcher's meat.

During the Civil Wars, Middlewich and its neighbourhood partook largely of their consequent miseries. There was a sharp contest here between the Royal troops, commanded by Sir Thomas Aston, and a division of the Parliamentary Army, under Sir Wm. Brereton. Sir Thomas Aston has detailed the whole of it in a letter addressed to Earl Rivers, Lords Cholmondeley, and Kilmorey, the Hon. T. Savage, &c. It is dated "Pulforde,* March 17, 1642." He observes, that at the approach of the enemy, under Brereton, before Wheelock Bridge, from Northwich, "The Welsh forces advanced so unwillingly, though it were but to line hedges, that two troops of horse were sent down to face the enemy in a narrow passage, within half-musket shott, where several of them were shott, otherwaies the foote would not have advanced or stayed by it. * * * Another part of the enemie approaching another passage, called the Wallwich Bridge, Captaine Prestwiche's troop was commanded thither to stay by the foote, which was of Capt. Massie's company, which he alsoe did, till all those foote likewaies were commanded off, and made good there retraite. Upon the approach of the third partie from Nantwich, I appointed the two trained bands of two hundred men, to make good that avenew, beinge the streete end toward Booth-lane, which was well advantaged by ditches and bankes on bothe sides, which, with the addition of some small trenches that they presentlie made, were convenientlie defensible, but (for ?) those that would have stayed in them. And to check their approach, I drew out a partie of sixty commanded horse, the other troopes beinge to back them into the lane, there beinge no other ground for horse; and to make way for them to charge, I drew off some commanded musketeers, six score before, to line the hedges that the enemie might not take advantage of the ditches on both sides to gall the horse in the flank, upon their charge. But the enemie advauncinge with a great body of musketiers, on either side the lane at a great distance before their horse, our musketiers and the lieutenant who commanded them, after the first fire given on them, *fell down and crept awaie*, leaving their armes; so that the enemies foote receyvinge no check, our horse could not charge, but to be flanked and cutt off by the musketiers on both sides the lane. And Colonell Ellis having drawne a piece of ordnance in the rear of our horse they were forced to wheel off to let his ordnance play, findeing the greatest of their force and strength to be then comeing upon them. I then called a party of Captaine Spotwood's dragoniers to make good the Church Yarde, and placed a guard in the breaste works at the other ende of the towne, drew the other piece of cannon to the Churche-yarde, and planted it there with advantage to scour the streete. They attempted to approach in: I then brought up a companie of musketiers of Col. Ellis, commaunded by a Captaine, whom I knew not, to assist the two trayned bande companies, whoe were to make good that passage; but these as soon as they came up neere to where the cannon was pointed, *laide themselves all downe* in a sorte of hollow way, and theire arms by them, soe that I was forced to ride amongst them, and *with my sworde beate them up*, and myselfe on horseback brought them up to the hedge where the other musketrey lay, but neither these nor those *durste put up their heads, but shott theyre pieces up into the ayre*, no one foote officer beinge bye them to save or order theme. During all whiche time my owne troope, it appears, Captain Ratclyffes, and Lord Cholmondelyes troopes, stood directly in the reare of them, and not a man moved, although divers of theire horse were shott under them, till our cannon made but one shott, which grased a great way shorte, and mounted over their heads, and a second shott went into a banke, not fourtie yardes from the cannoniere, at which the enemie made greate shoutings, and advanced faste upon our foote, *who all instantlie forsook theire stande and came awaye*, leavinge the horse within pistol shott of the enemie, though there was somewhat of a trench between them; at which the horse wheeled back. But all men there must witness that I staid them per force, standinge fully exposed to shott till the cannon was brought off, and noe one ffootman was left with it but Col. Ellis himselfe, who drew it off with his own hands, some of the horsemen helpinge to bringe it off to the Church. Before this, upon the falling of those of Broxton hundred and the Welsh, from the first hedge, all the whole stand of pikes in the reere of the horse *cleerly run awaye*, and all the musketeers placed for the defence of the ende of the streete leadinge to Booth-lane; did quitt their trenches, haveing *never discharged their shott, nor even scene theire enemie*, or any cause of feare but theire fellows flyinge. The horse then made a hastie yet an orderlie retreate into the Lewon streete, and soe passed to the Church yarde, expectinge to have founde it made goode by the parties left there for the purpose. I found all the foote wedged up *in the Church*, like billets in a wood pile, noe one man at his arms, trusting then only to the cannon to scowre the two chiefe streetes, which lay with as much advantage as was possible for pieces to be placed: and that the enemie came down Dog-lane, as well as approaching by the principall streetes, and advanced briskly upon our horse, who were in the condition of sheepe in a penn, and quite exposed to slaughter, and frustrated of the use and effect of our ordnance upon the enemie. I then commanded them to draw up in a field at the ende of the towne; but that entrance being barricadoed by Captaine Spotswoode, occasioned a separation of them, that they dispersed several waies, and by reason of distress could not meet of three fields breadthe, and till they came beyond Kinderton House. I nexte repayred to the cannon I had placed to scoure the streetes, and founde no cannoniere with them, the other drawinge the cannon off, at whiche, beinge offended, he saide he could not get one ffootman to assiste him; nor could I draw out ten musketiers foorthe from the Church, would it have saveed the worlde. Amongst them was even Coll. Ellis himselfe, the cannon being deserted entirelie, but, as I understand not howe the matter was, I shall not now proceed to censures.—The enemie falling directly in three streetes upon me, and likewise attacking me in the Churche-yarde, and the horse being marched out of sighte, I *quite alone*, all I could possibly hope to do, was to reallie the horse againe if possible, to wheele aboute, and fall on the reere of them; but, by reason of severall crosselanes, I had lost the whole body of the horse, save some few stragglers, with which I had smal hope to repell the enemie that had repulsed us. Perceivinge that the enemie had possessed the towne, and hearinge that our horse had turned towards Warrington, I sent a messenger after them, to order them to reallie at Rudheath, intendinge to go by Brereton, and with that convoye, to redeeme and receave the addition of the Lord Brereton's forces; but they were advanced (by whose conduct I know not) past recall; yet I went to him myself, bothe to give him an accompte of the action, and to know his resolution." The letter detailing this valorous action, of which some of the recent brilliant exploits in the Italian peninsula, would form a suitable counterpart, then goes on to lament the occurrence in very strong terms. Sir Thomas himself made good his retreat by way of Kinderton; those who took refuge in the Church, among whom were Sir Edward Mosley, Capt. Hurleston, Captain Massie, of Coddington, Capt. Starkie, of Stretton, &c. were made prisoners.*

The CHURCH is dedicated to St Michael; it is a fine building, consisting of nave, chancel, side aisles, and a handsome tower, with a ring of six bells. Five pointed arches separate the nave from the side aisles. The capitals of the columns on which the arches rest, are ornamented.† On the roof of the chancel, at present obscured by the plaister, is the inscription, " This

* It appears from Burghall's Diary, that Sir Thomas Aston entered the town on the 10th March, when his soldiers committed great plunder; Sir William Brereton, appeared before the town on Sunday the 12th, and discharged several shots against it; the battle was fought on the Monday. On the day after Christmas-day, 1643, there was on action at Booth-lane, between Lord Byron's troops and those of the Parliament, when the latter were routed, with the loss of 200 men.

† Gastrell, in his Notitia, says, " There was, as 'tis said, an old Chapel on the north side of this Church, belonging to the family of Wever, Lords of Wever, but pulled down at the Dissolution of Abbies;—no remains."

roofe was builded at the coste of Sir Wm. Brereton, Knt. patron of this Church, an. D'ni 1621. Vivit post funera virtus. Raphe Walley, of Stanthorne, and Rd. Hatton, of Detton, surveors of this worke, 1621, Robt. Hallyby, being Preacher and Vicar." One of the chancels belonging to the Kinderton Barony, has over the door "Peeter Venables, 1632." It was purchased from the Bulkeleys, and the parish, by the Kinderton family, and in 1689, the Bishop confirmed the sale, on condition that it should be repaired by the Barons. The other Kinderton chancel is in the north-east angle of the Church, inclosed by a neat oak screen; over a shield of arms of the Venables' alliances, is "Peter Venables, Baron of Kinderton, A. D. 1633."

In this chancel, on a large blue slab, is the inscription—

The Hon. Peter Venables, Baron of Kinderton, dyed the 19th day of January, 1679, leaving by Katherine his wife, sister of the Right Honorable Lord Ferrers, two daughters, Catherine and Anne. Catherine dyeing in a short time after him in her infancy, his ancient house and estate, which had continued in his name and family by an uninterrupted succession from the Conquest, descended to the said Anne, as his sole daughter and heire, who married the Right Honourable Montague Lord Norreys, afterwards Earle of Abingdon.

On a similar slab adjoining the last—

The Honourable Catherine Venables, wife of the Honourable Peter Venables, last Baron of Kinderton, eldest daughter of Sir Robt. Shirley, of Astwell, in ye county of Northampton, and of Staunton Harold, in the county of Leicester, Baronet, and grandchild of the Right Honourable and Most Noble Robert Devereux, Earle of Essex and Ewe, Viscount Hereford, Lord Bourchier and Lovaine, Baron Ferrers, of Chartley, in Staffordshire, and Viscount Tamworth, Baron Bourchier and Louvaine. Dyed July ye 6th, 1717, in the 65th year of her age.

Engraved on a small brass plate, in the north angle, is a representation of a female figure kneeling, with a son and two daughters behind. Over the head of the son, is "*A'no etatis u'decimo;*" above the daughters' heads, *Elizabetha (Maria) superstites.*—Beneath in old English letters—

Here lyeth buried under this gravestone, Elizabeth Venables, the wife of Thomas Venables, Esq. Baron of Kinderton, the eldest daughter of Sir William Brereton, of Brereton, Knt. who dyed the —— day of June, 1591.

Adjoining this, a mural monument of marble—

Discite mortales, quam sunt mortalia vana,
Discite mortales, nulla secura dies:
Nulla secura dies; tenui pendentia filo
Omnia sunt hominum: mors inopina venit:
Attamen est nobis Christo morientibus ipsa
Mors, lucrum, requies, gaudia, vita nova.
Munde furas igitur, caro sævi, frende Satanu,
Vivimus, haud morimur: mors gemebunda malis.
Hæc vos spectando moveant spectacula nostra,
Quo mens majori flagret amore Dei;
Mundus in hoc mundo fac vivas, condito messes,
Condito, non semper tempora messis erunt,
Denique venturi vos mutet gloria mundi,
Commoveat Christus, comoveatq' salus.
Non obiit, requiescere
obiit anº D'ni 1591.

On a marble mural monument—

H. S. E.

Franciscus Leveson, Richardi Leveson, de Lilshull, mil. barn. ex sororis filia nepos, ex testamento adoptivus hæres, nomen ejus et insignia concessione regia assecutus. Patrem habuit Richardum Fowler de Harnedge Grange, in co. Salop. ar.; matrem Margaretam filiam Richardi Baronis Newport et Rachaelis filiæ Johannis Leveson, sororis dicti Richardi; uxorem habuit annam filiam Petri Venables, Baronis de Kinderton, e quâ filios suscepit Richardum et Petrum in cunis defunctos, Franciscum superstitem, et Franciscam filiam. Vixit annos XXV, mens. IX. dies XXV. diem obiit Kindertone XVII Aug. A. D. MDCLXVII.

Near the last, on a blue slab—

Hic jacet Franciscus Leveson, filius tertio-genitus ac adhuc unicus Francisci Leveson armigeri, nuperrime defuncti, qui obiit VIIº die mensis Septembris, aº D'ni MDCLXVIIIº, ætatis unius anni trium mensium et XXIIII dierum.

In other parts of the Church, are memorials of—

The Rev. John Hulse, of Elworth Hall, in Sandbach, founder of the Hulsean Prize, and the office of Christian Advocate in the University of Cambridge, who died Dec. 13, 1790, aged 82 years

Mary and Anne, daughters of Smith Kelsall, of Bradshaw, gent. by Jane his wife daughter of Thomas Yate, of Middlewich, gent. who died Feb. 5, 1735, the former aged 4, the latter 2 years. Matthew and Penelope, son and daughter of the same; the former died Feb. 20, 1735, aged 4 months: the latter July 6, 1737, aged 5 months. Mary, daughter of the said Thomas Yate, by Mary his wife, daughter of Leftwich Oldfield, of Leftwich, Esq. died March 30, 1723, aged 9 years. Said Thos. Yate, died July 25, 1743, aged 80 years; said Mary Yate, Aug. 10, 1754, aged 78. Lucy Kelsall, died May 13, 1755, aged 16.—Thomas Yate, M. D. eldest son of the above Thomas and Mary, died March 24, 1785, aged 73.

Daniel Vawdrey, died March 29, 1801, aged 68, and Mary his wife, died Feb. 1, 1774, aged 30.

&c. &c. &c.

There were formerly numerous shields of arms in this Church, of the Fitton, Massie, Swettenham, Cotton,

Rope, Doddington, Grosvenor, Brereton, Moston, Venables, Bulkeley, &c. families.

The present Vicar of Middlewich, is the Rev. James Stringer, presented Jan. 31, 1811.

Till about the middle of the 15th century the patronage of the living was vested in the Touchetts, as an appendage of their manor of Tattenhall.*—In that century, under the sanction of the Abbot of St. Werburgh's at Chester, Sir Thomas Stanley presented; and in 1494, the Priory of Stone. In 1504, the Church was appropriated to the Monastery of Leuton, co. Notts.; and at the Dissolution, the impropriation of the Rectory was possessed by the Crown; and subsequently by the Breretons. The latter afterwards sold the tithes to various persons, and in 1817, they were thus appropriated.† The Patron of the Vicarage had the tithes of Midlewich, Newton, Occleston, Sproston, and Wimboldsley, except the estate of Lea Hall, belonging to Sir J. F. Leicester, Bart. Mr. William Court, is the impropriator in Sutton. Geo. Wilbraham, Esq. in Clive, and Weever; in Croxton, H. Tomkinson, Esq; Daniel Vawdry, Esq. in Ravenscroft, and Moorsbarrow-cum-Yatehouses; in Stublach, J. P. Brandreth, M. D. Lord Vernon, in Kinderton; and W. Rigby, Esq. in Minshull Vernon. All the tythes, including Easter Dues, &c. belong to the impropriators, excepting the tithe of two farms in Minshull Vernon, belonging to Hervey Aston, Esq. which were left to the Vicar of Middlewich.

* Ormerod.

† Ormerod.

On the 16th Dec. 1663, William Lord Brereton, conveyed the Advowson of the Vicarage to Robert Lowe, and John his son, and they re-conveyed it on the 15th March, 1677, to Samuel, second son of the before named Robert. It afterwards passed in marriage with Martha, daughter of Samuel Lowe, of Newton, to Edward Moreton of Church Hill, in Over; and subsequently, in marriage with Jane, daughter of James Moreton, son of the above, to Isaac Wood, of Winsford. It is now the property of Isaac Wood, Esq. of Newton.‡

KINDERTON

Is about a mile and a half from Middlewich, of which a considerable portion is within this township. Shortly after the Conquest, the dignity of BARON OF KINDERTON was conferred by the Earl on Gilbert de Venables, a younger brother of Stephen Earl of Blois,‖ and annexed to the dignity was a large territorial possession, viz.

Eccleston,	Wincham,	Brereton,
Alpraham,	Mere,	Kinderton,
Tarporley,	Over (part of)	Davenport,
Wettenhall,	Peover	Witton,
Hartford,	Rosthern	AND
Lymme (one half)	Hope (co. Flint)	Blakenhall.
High Legh	Newbold Astbury,	

He had also a joint share with Hamo and Ranulphus, of Baggiley and Sunderland.§

The name of Gilbert's son, Second Baron of Kinderton, is not recorded. Gilbert, IIId Baron; Sir Wm. Venables IV; he obtained a license from Andrew, Prior of Norton, for a Domestic Chapel, at *Merston*. V. Hugh de Venables; VI. Sir Roger de Venables: in 1261, he recovered possession of the Church of Astbury, against the Abbot of Chester, but he retained it a very short time. The Monks, with whom, as may well be supposed, he was not in much favor, recorded his death as a judgment from Heaven, "*miserabilitet obiit!*" The trial took place, according to the Chronicle of the Abbey, in 1259, and it states that he obtained the verdict by a *false assize*. VII. Sir Wm. Venables: he restored to the Monks of Chester the Advowson of Astbury, during the time of Abbot Byrchehylles.¶—VIII. Sir Hugh Venables.—IX. Sir Hugh

‡ "Thomas Wood, of Middlewich parish, had a child born on St. Martin's Day, in the morning and Christened about noone, called Anne, whiche had on either hande one thumbe and five fingers, and upon the right foote five toes, and on the lefte foote six toes; and it had a grate eye and a small, and lived eight hours after it was christened, and buried at Middlewich the same day, 7° Edward VI. 1553."—Extract from an ancient register taken by Sir P. Leycester, and copied in Wharton's Calendarium Ecclesiasticum, 1657.

‖ Previous to the year 1093, he gave Astbury Church, and a moiety of Newbold, to the Abbey of St. Werburgh, at Chester.

§ In addition to the foregoing, Arclid, a moiety of Bollington, Bradwell, Castle Northwich, Checkley, Doddington, Hartford-cum-Horton, Hunsterston, Lea, Marston, Moresbarrow-cum-Parme, Moreton, Alcumlowe, Piemere, Radnor, Somerford, Sproston, Stanthorne, and Utkinton, are noticed in the Harl. MSS. as being attached to the Barony.

¶ This Sir William was the ancestor of the Leghs of Booths, the Venables of Bradwell, &c.

Venables.—In a plea of Hugh to a Quo Warranto, he claimed in right of his Barony (temp. Edward III.) amongst other rights, the gallows, pillory, tumbrell, and thew. If any robber be taken within the fee of Kinderton, he shall be brought up within three days, when he shall be arraigned if the accuser demands, and trial take place, and according to the inquest judgment shall be given in Court: but if the thief is unwilling to put himself on the inquest, then he shall be immediately taken to Chester Castle; and tried according to law, and if convicted capitally, he shall be brought back by the Baron's officers to Kinderton, and be there executed on the Baron's own gallows. He also claimed *pelfe*, by which he explains, that if any resident on his demesne shall have committed felony, or wounded any one dangerously, and fled, he shall seize all his goods and chattels by his beadle, and after presenting to the Earl at Chester what belongs to him, have for himself the best of his beasts of burden, and the best of all his horned kine, &c. his malt, and grain of every description, within one quarter; all his carts, ploughs, &c.—These claims were resisted by the Earl, but a Jury decided in favor of the Baron. X. Hugh Venables; he was Sheriff of Cheshire, 2d Rich. II. XI. Sir Rich. Venables, Knt. He was Sheriff in 1386, as Deputy to Hugh Earl of Stafford. In the 4th of Henry IV. he espoused the cause of the Percies, and fought with them at the Battle of Shrewsbury, where he was taken prisoner, and beheaded. XII. Hugh Venables. XIII. Hugh Venables, died without issue; his title and estates descended to XIV. Sir Hugh Venables, his nephew. He fell at the fight of Bloreheath, where he distinguished himself under the command of the Ld. Audley. Dying also without issue, Rt. Grosvenor, of Holme, delivered the estates to XV. his great uncle Hen. Venables, notwithstanding an Inq. in favor of Rd. Coton and Ralph Bostock, the sons of his Aunt. He was the last heir male of the direct line, and settled the estates on Wm. Venables (XVI.) son and heir of Thomas Venables, of Golborne, and his heirs male: this William was the great grandson of Hugh Venables, tenth Baron of Kinderton. Thomas Venables XVII. Baron; he was slain at Flodden. The XVIII. Baron was Sir Wm. Venables; he was grandson of William the sixteenth Baron; he was Sheriff of the County in 1526. Sir Thos. Venables, XIX Baron; he was one of the Gentlemen of Cheshire Knighted by the Earl of Hertford, at Leith, in 1544. XX. Sir Thomas Venables. XXI. Peter Venables, only two years old on the death of his father, the late Baron. He caused to be executed at his sole expense, the first collection of County Heraldry, including 520 shields of arms. His grandson Peter Venables, was the XXII. and last Baron of Kinderton in the male line; he died in 1679, leaving two daughters, Catherine, the wife of Robert Earl Ferrers, who died soon after her father without issue; and Anne wife of Lord Norreys, afterwards Earl of Abingdon to whom the Barony and estates descended, who also died issueless. The Barony then passed to the Vernons of Sudbury, co. Derby, in right of Mary, sister of the last Baron, the wife of Thomas Pigot, Esq.; she had issue Anne, sole heiress, wife of Henry Vernon, Esq.; and their son George Venables Vernon, Esq. succeeded to the Barony under the will of Peter Venables, his great uncle. Mr. Vernon was raised to the peerage, as Baron Vernon, of Kinderton, on the 12th May, 1762.*

An enumeration of the towns included in the ancient Barony of Kinderton is given in the preceding page; but the jurisdiction of the Courts over several of them has long since been disused: Marston, Wincham, Hart-

* The crest of the family of Venables, is thus accounted for—it is ROMANTIC enough to be sure, and is recorded in a PATENT OF AUGMENTATION of the Arms and Crest of Thos. Venables, of Goulborne, in the county of Chester, Gent. who was lineally descended from Sir Gilbert Venables, Knight, cousin-german to King William the Conqueror His crest was a Demie Dragon, gules, issuing out of a Welson, or Wyer to take fish, argent. " A terrible Dragon made his abode in the Lordship of Merston, in the county of Chester, where he devoured all such persons as he laid hould on, which the said Thomas Venables hearing tell of, considering the pitiful and dayly destruction of the people, without recovery, who, in following the example of the valiant Romans, and other worthy men, not regarding his own life, in comparison of the commodity and safeguard of his countrymen, did in his own person valiantly and courageously set on the said dragon; when first he shot him through with an arrow, and afterwards with other weapons manfully slew him, at which instant the said dragon was devouring of a child; for the which his worthy and valiant act, was given unto him the Lordship of Merston, by the ancestors of the Earls of Oxford, the lords of the fee there. And also ever since the said Thomas and his heirs, in remembrance thereof, have used to bear, as well in the arms as in the crest, a Dragon." The Patent of Augmentation is dated the 30th of October, in the year 1560.

ford, and Castle Northwich, are included in the Leet of Witton, purchased from Lord Vernon, by Sir Peter Leicester, Bart.

The Court Leet and view of Frank-pledge, for the Barony of Kinderton, extends over Kinderton, Bradwell, Sproston, Moresbarrow, Moston, Alcumlow, Somerford Radnor, Newbold Astbury, Davenport, and Arclid. The Halmote Court has jurisdiction over Kinderton, Bradwell, and Sproston. The usages and practice of these Courts, vary nothing from those of others.

The last time the power of capital punishment was exercised by the Barons of Kinderton, was in 1597, when Hugh Stringer was tried for murder in the Court Baron, convicted and executed. The Proprietor of the *Hangman's Butts* in Ravenscroft, was compelled by his tenure, to find an executioner, and the place of execution is now called the *Gallows Field.*

The old *Hall* of Kinderton was taken down before 1760; it was situated on the River Bank, two fields distant from the site of the ancient *Condate.** The moat is still, in part, to be traced, and it appears to have inclosed several acres of land. No remains whatever of the ancient Hall is in existence, nor is its stile of architecture known.

Kinderton Lodge is in another part of the township.

MORESBARROW,

Or *Moresbarrow-cum-Parme*, is not noticed in the Survey. The township is at present divided in two estates. Edw. I. gave the manor to the Abbey of Vale Royal; and after the Dissolution, Edw. VI. granted it to Thomas Brown; from whom it subsequently passed to the Brookes, of Norton, and the family of Venables. About 1792, Lord Vernon, sold the Manor of Moresbarrow, and the Hamlet of Parme, to Josiah Perrin, of Warrington, who left them, by will, to his daughter Sarah, under the stipulation that she should not marry a Scotchman; but disobeying the injunction by marrying Wm. Geddes, of Warrington, a Scotchman, the manor descended to Maria and Josiah Perrin, the children of Joshua Perrin, nephew of Josiah. The whole is now vested in Maria Perrin, widow of Mr. Joseph Cheetham, of Stockport.

The Berringtons, originally from Berthinton, or Barton, in Bucklow, were the proprietors of *Moresbarrow Hall* estate, temp. Edw. I. Two bastard sons of their descendant Adam Berington, burnt down the Hall, in consequence of some family dispute. After several

* Camden, and Salmon, were of opinion Congleton was the site of Condate; Horsley, Baxter, and Stukeley, conceive it was near Northwich; whilst Reynolds says he expects Middlewich WILL BE FOUND TO BE THE VERY PLACE. With respect to Kinderton being the locus in quo, Mr. Whittaker says he discovered the road from Mancunium (Manchester) towards Condate, by its elevated and well-gravelled surface in many places. Its whole length from New Bridge to Bucklow Hill is denominated STREET; which Horsley and Percival have written Kind-street; but it is invariably spoken King-street by the people, and leads directly to Kinderton, leaving Northwich about half a mile to the right. Here, therefore, the termination of the road, and the length of the distance, invite us strongly to search for a station. The name of Cundate is loudly echoed in that of Kinderton. And what is much more weighty, this is the first place convenient for a camp about the requisite distance from Manchester. The Kind-street, pointing down the bank of the river to the bridge of Ravenscroft, forded the channel two or three yards to the right of the bridge, and entered the field beyond it; and HERE IT HAS BEEN ACTUALLY DISCOVERED. This is denominated the Harbours Field; and was plainly the site of the Roman station. The particular position of the ground betwixt the rivers Croco and Dane is a strong argument of itself.—The appellation of the close is an additional evidence; the Har-bourb's Field signifying the area of the military station: the site and name, the remains about it, and the tradition concerning it, are decisive proofs. The ground is nearly a parallelogram, about ten statute acres in extent, bounded by a natural bank, lofty and steep on one side, with the little Croco curling at the foot of it; and by another bank less lofty, but more steep, on a second side; with the Dane running directly under it; the former river falls into the latter at the angle of the field. On the third side, but several yards within the bridge, are considerable remains of a ditch rising up the ascent, and exhibiting marks of having been once continued along the hollow of the adjoining lane.—On the fourth the ancient ditch retains its original appearance, being a steep foss, about ten yards in depth, and eight in breadth at the top: this was formerly converted, like part of the other, into the course of a road, but has lately been made the channel of a current. Such was the station of Condate. A road has been discovered issuing from it, commonly called the Roman road, which appears, from its direction, to have led to Mediolanum, in Shropshire. Another went by Holme-street Hall, to Chester; and a third extended by Street-forge, and Red-street to Chesterton, near Newcastle. The most accurate account of the distance between Manchester and Kinderton, states it to to be about twenty-two English miles, which are very nearly equal to twenty-three and three quarters of Roman; a distance that corresponds with the number in the tenth Iter of Richard.

times changing ownership, the estate is now the property of Daniel Vawdrey, Esq. of Tushingham-cum-Grindley. The remains of a moat describe the site of the *Old Hall*.

There was another estate in the township, considered as nearly one third of it, which, subsequent to the reign of Henry III. was vested in the Wincham branch of the Venables family.*

Vill. Cest.

SPROSTON

Is about two miles E. from Middlewich, and belonged, to the Nantwich Barony, but was subsequently, it is supposed, exchanged with the Baron of Kinderton for more immediate property.

This manor has descended with the other estates of the Kinderton family to Lord Vernon. It is included within the jurisdiction of the Baronial Courts. It would seem that at one period the township was divided, as the Breretons granted a moiety of the vill of Sproston to the Sandbaches, to be held by render annually of two steel spurs, or three pence.† The other moiety was possessed by the Croxtons, of Croxton.—The *Hall* is occupied as a farm-house.

† Harl. MSS.

BYLEY,

Or *Byley-cum-Yatehouse*, is about a mile N. E. N. from Middlewich. It was originally held under the Earl by Hugh de Mara, founder of the Montalt Barony, from whose descendants it passed to the Lords of Aldford. During the Justiceship of Phillip de Orreby, Richard de Aldford gave the manor to the Abbey of Pulton, the Abbot of which had a grange here. The Monks of Birkenhead had also an estate here, by which, temp. Edw. III. they claimed manerial rights. Waren de *Biveley* had a third estate here, which he exchanged with the Abbot of Dieulacres for Ravenscroft. On the Dissolution, the manor was purchased from the Crown by Geoffrey Shakerley, of Shakerley Hall, co. Lanç. and it is now the property of Charles Watkin John Shakerley, Esq. A Court Leet and Baron is held for the Manor. The *Hall* is occupied by a farmer.

RAVENSCROFT

Is about a mile N. from Middlewich. It is supposed to have been included in the Vill of Croxton, as it was at one time held from the proprietors of that manor.—Waren de Byley, as is before noticed, got possession of this manor by exchange with the Abbot of Dieulacres, and removed his residence here, and assumed the local name;‡ but his direct line became extinct in the fourth generation, Roger de Ravenscroft dying without male issue, and his daughter Margery, married Roger Croxton, of Croxton.

Ravenscroft was alienated by Cicily Ravenscroft, in 1704, she conveying it to Peter Yates, whose descendant Thomas Yates, sold the estate to his relation John Seaman, from whose son it was bought in 1808, by the present proprietor Daniel Vawdrey, Esq. The *Hall* is of considerable antiquity.

Colonel Croxton was a prominent character in the disturbances in Cheshire during the great Rebellion. He was twice Governor of Chester Castle, in 1650, and 1659, when its surrender was demanded by Sir George Booth, to whose summons he is said to have replied—"That as perfidiousness in him was detestable, so the Castle which he kept for the Parliament of England was disputable; and if he would have it, he must fight for it; for the best blood that run in his veins, in defence thereof, should be as a sluice to fill up the Castle trenches."

STUBLACH

Is three miles N. of Middlewich; like several of the preceding townships, it is not noticed in the Survey.—According to the *mise* book, it would seem it was formerly considered as two hamlets, STUBS and LACHE.—A family, which assumed the local name of Stubs, or De Stolbis, gave lands in Leyes, or Leche, to the Abbey of St. Werburgh. The descent of the township, it is supposed, has been in the families of Page, Delves, and Prescot; from Sir Geo. Prescot, Bart. it was purchased by the late Wm. Harper, Esq. of Everton, Liverpool, one of whose daughters married Pilkington Brandreth, M. D. the present proprietor.

A portion of the estate of EARDSHAW lies in this township, including the *Hall*, which is of brick, in a very ruinous state, although a building of considerable extent, and venerable appearance.

NEWTON

Adjoins Middlewich on the West side, a considerable portion of the houses of which, is built on land within this township. Temp. John, Simon de Newton, held

‡ A descendant of his, marrying Isabella, heiress of Ralph Holland, of Bretton, co. Flint, was the founder of the Ravenscrofts, of Bretton.

Cheshire

this Manor, and that of Sutton and Wimboldsley. His son, who took the name Del Holt, had possession of the same townships, and their descendants had also possession till about the reign of Henry VI. subsequent to which they were alienated. The manor of Newton eventually became vested in the Crewes, of Crewe, and from the present Lord Crewe it was purchased by the late James Roylance, Esq. under whose will, with the estate called the *Manor House*, a handsome modern
* 1812. building, it has passed* to the present proprietor, Wm Court, Esq.

There are handsome houses in the township the property of John Braband, Esq. and Isaac Wood, Esq.

SUTTON

Is about a mile and a half South of Middlewich.—The manerial descent is similar to that of the last mentioned township.

The late Mr. Roylance purchased the manor from the late Daniel Carbonel, Esq. of London, who bought it from Thomas Yates, M. D. to whom it was devised by the Vernons of Middlewich. It was originally parcel of the Kinderton Barony.

Mr. Court is the present proprietor. The *Hall* is occupied by a farmer.

CROXTON

Lies about a mile N. W. from Middlewich. Soon after the Conquest, it was granted, together with Newton, and Nether Tabley, to Gozelin, a Norman; afterwards it passed to Orme the Harper, ancestor of the Touchetts, under whom it was held by Wulfric.—Liulph de Croxton, his son, then became the Lord, and was succeeded by three of the same name. Richard de Croxton, son of the last Liulph, became heir on the provision, that he will not alienate any of his lands in the Township from his son by sale, waste, incumbrance, or mortgage; that he will *not endow any future wife* with the same, bestow any part of it on any Religious House, or give it with his body when he dies.

In the 8th of Hen. V. the male line became extinct by the death of Ralph Croxton. Margaret Croxton, his heiress marrying Hugh Mainwaring, bastard son of Randle Mainwaring, of Over Peover, by Emma Farington, he became Lord of Croxton. From the Mainwarings it passed by marriage to the Oldfields of Bradwell; and temp. Car. I. Mainwaring Oldfield sold the manor to Roger Wilbraham, of Dorfold.

In 1754, Roger Wilbraham re-sold to the late James Tomkinson, Esq. whose son, Henry Tomkinson, Esq. is the present proprietor, and holds a Court Baron for the Manor.

This township, which takes its name from its vicinity to the rivulet of the Croco, is celebrated for its fine dairy land.

The *Hall* is occupied as a farm house; it has been a respectable house.

CLIVE

Is nearly two miles S. W. from Northwich. So early as the reign of John, Warin de Clive was the Lord, of whose descent some further notice will be found under the head "*Huxley*." Richard Clyve, of Huxley, (temp. Elizabeth) was the last heir male of this family, when the property descended to Rachael Clive, daughter of Joshua Clive, Esq of Huxley; she married Thomas Wilbraham, Esq. of Townsend, and the manor is now the property of his lineal descendant George Wilbraham, Esq. of Delamere Lodge.

An estate in this township passed in marriage, previous to Richard II. from the Clives to the Congletons, who conveyed it to the Wevers; their representative Sir Thomas Stanley, had estates here in 1607. The Wilbrahams subsequently became the proprietors. Another estate passed similarly to the Hulses, who resided at Clive Hall, but removed to Elworth, in Sandbach.—The Rev. John Hulse left Clive Hall to the University of Cambridge.†

WIMBOLDSLEY,

Or *Wimbersley*, it appears from the Survey, was held in equal shares by the Earl and Bigot: the moiety of the latter descended with his other estates, componant parts of the great fee of Aldford. The Earl's share passed to the Barons of Shipbrook; and Warin, Baron of Shipbrook, granted it to Richard, son of Matthew

† Webb speaks of a "fair old house, called the Nuns' House, near Clive, with a demesne which belonged to Sir Thomas Holcroft, and subsequently to Thomas Marbury. This house stands near Winsford Bridge, and probably belonged to the Nuns of Chester. It is a farm-house, the property of Messrs. Salmon.—Lysons.

CHESHIRE

de Vernon. It is supposed he or his descendants assumed the local name; and it passed from the Wimboldesleys, to Richard del Holt, son of Simon de Newton.

After being several generations in the Holts, it passed to the Coltons, about 1495, and fifty years afterwards they sold it to the Breretons of Ashley, who subsequently alienated it to the Lowndes family.

In 1758, the Trustees of Sir P. Leicester, Bart. purchased it from the devisees of Robt. Lowndes; and Sir J. F. Leicester is the present proprietor.

Lea Hall, now occupied as a farm house, was about 1766, the residence of the celebrated Dr. Fothergill.—Chalmers* says, although he rented it only by the year, yet, "he spared no expense to improve." During the recess from Midsummer to Michaelmas, "he took no fees but attended to prescribe gratis at an Inn, at Middlewich, once a week."

* Biograph. Dictionary.

Courts are occasionally held for the Manor.

OCCLESTON

Is about three miles and a half S. S. W. from Middlewich, and before the reign of John, gave name to a family which continued Lords till after the reign of Henry V. In the 37th of the following Henry, Rich. Bunbury held the township in socage from Lord Audley. The Bunburys were the proprietors till the 12th James, when Sir H. Bunbury sold it to Wm. Moreton, Esq. of Moreton, for £600. and ten years afterwards he sold it to Sir John Davenport, of Davenport, for £1049.

The Manor subsequently became vested in the Whitmores of Apsley, and is now the property of Edw. Vernon, Esq. The manor is within the jurisdiction of the Courts of Shipbrook.

MINSHULL VERNON

Is about four miles S. S. W. from Middlewich. At the time of the Survey, it was included in the possessions of William Malbedeng. It was from the transfer of this township to the Vernons, at the time of the division of the Baronial estates, that it received its present name.

Oulton. From the Vernons the manor passed to the Oldintons,† and in 1322. John de Oldinton enfeoffed John le Feme, Chaplain, with Minshull Vernon, Erdeswicke, and Oldinton.

HISTORY.

The Oldintons, says Mr. Ormerod, terminated in three coheirs, Johanna, wife of Peter Starkey, of Nether Hall, in Sutton; Ellen, wife of Thomas Starkey, of Wrenbury; and Margaret, wife of Rich. Fitton, of Pownall. The manor became divided between the two latter. Eventually the whole became vested in Thomas Aston, Esq. of Aston; and remained so till 1701, subsequent to which the township became the property of Henry Newport, Earl of Bradford, who by will in 1736, in the event of the death of John Harrison, an infant, without issue, left his estate to Mrs. Anne Smith, of Berkeley Square, London. She left them to William Pulteney Earl of Bath, whose heir and brother Lieut.-Gen. Pulteney, died in 1767, leaving the Bradford estates to Wm. Pulteney, Esq. afterwards Sir Wm. Pulteney, Bart. On his death, in 1806, Minshull Vernon, passed to the Earl of Darlington. About 1812, his Lordship sold the manor, and a large estate, to Wm. Rigby, Esq. the present proprietor.

The hamlet of HULGREVE was at a very early period vested in the Vernons, and Richard, son of Warin Vernon, assumed the local name. Temp. Hen. V. the *Manor*, as it is called, became the property of John de Beeston, by marriage with Margaret, daughter and heir of William de Hulgrave. The estate was subsequently vested in the Astons; and is now the property of H. C. Aston, Esq.

The *Hall* is of considerable antiquity, situated on the bank of the Weever.

The hamlet of ERDSWICK was included in the estate of the Hulgraves, temp. Edw. II. In 1328, Thomas de Erdswick, exchanged Erdswick for Leighton, with the Oultons, and it afterwards was divided between the Starkies and Minshulls; from the latter, Erdswick Hall was purchased by Mr. Richard Vernon, of Middlewich, and he left it to a person of the same name, but no relation, temp. Anne. From "a political attachment,"‡ Mr. Vernon devised Erdswick to Wm. Murray, Esq. subsequently Earl of Mansfield. It is now the property of the Earl of Mansfield.

‡ Lysons.

The *Hall* is occupied by a farmer, but it is in a very ruinous state. It has been of considerable size, built in a quadrangular form, of stone and timber; it has bay windows, and is moated.

HISTORY.

THE PARISH OF WARMINCHAM,

CONTAINS THE TOWNSHIPS OF

WARMINCHAM,
TETTON,
ELTON, AND
MOSTON.

WARMINCHAM,

Or *Warmingham*, is about three miles S. from Middlewich, and with ELTON, and TETTON, was at one period the property of Ranulphus, ancestor of the Mainwarings, whose estates included lands in Warmincham, Tatton, Blacon, Nether Peover, Over Peover, Warford, *Cepmondwich*, *Owlarton*, Snelson, Cogshull, Wheelock, Tetton, Northenden, Sunderland, and Baggiley, in this County; together with Warburne, in Norfolk.

In the 1st Edward II. Warmincham and its dependencies passed to Sir Wm. Tressel, of Cubblestone, in right of his wife Maud, daughter of Sir Warin Mainwaring. The property successively passed to the Tressels and Veres, one of whose descendants, temp. Eliz. sold the property here to Sir Christopher Hatton, and his representatives re-sold to Sir Randolph Crewe.—The estates are now the property of Lord Crewe, who holds a Court Leet and Baron for the three manors; to which also residents in Moston and Wheelock owe suit and service.

Near the Church is the moated site of the ancient seat of the Tressels, which Sir John Tressel obtained a license to fortify, temp. Edw. III.

OLD HAUGH, on the western side of Warmincham, was the residence of the Smiths, of which family was Wm. Smith, Rouge Dragon Pursuivant at Arms,* who made extensive collections of County Heraldry.

The CHURCH is dedicated to St. Leonard; the present Rector is the Rev. Willoughby Crewe, presented Oct. 15, 1816. The building is situated near to the Wheelock; it consists of body and chancel, which were rebuilt in 1797; the tower was erected in 1715.

On the south wall of the chancel, is a small monument, with the following inscription, followed by some silly lines—

Here rest the remains of Randulph Crewe, LL. D. late Rector of this parish, born Feb. 6, 1717, died May 29, 1777. Also, the remains of Anne Crewe, relict of the said Randulph Crewe, born Nov. 2, 1722, died Dec. 29, 1795.

In the Chancel on a brass plate—

Here William Lingard's body lies,
Late parson of this place,
Whose soul in Abraham's bosom rests,
Through Christ's merits and grace.
Amongst his good deeds manifold,
Inscribe this on his stone,
What coste and charges, he was att
Upon a neighbour's sonn,
First at the schoole, then at Cambridge,
Then with his people here,
Where he hath kept God's will to preache
The space of 16 yeare.
Then full of days, and of the age
Of seventie yeare and foure,
Was here interrd when cruell Death
Would let him live no more.
Viz. August XVIII°, 1620.

In the nave, a marble monument—

Juxta jacent reliquiæ Gulielmi et Francescæ Vernon, ille obiit, sexto die Junii, anno Domini 1732°, ætatis 52°; illa obiit quinto die Martii, anno Domini 1727,° ætatis 42.

On a marble monument—

Beneath are interred the remains of Ralph Vernon, who died 19th

* A notice of this gentleman is given in Chalmers' Biographical Dictionary.

July, 1728, aged 84 years. Also the remains of Mary, his former wife, who died 25th Nov. 1760, aged 41 years. Also the remains of Anne, his second wife, who died 6th May, 1803, aged 83 years.

At the south end of the Church, is the monument of Maud, or Matilda, heiress of the Mainwarings, who married Sir Wm. Trussel, and subsequently Oliver de Bourdeaux, a servant of Edw. II. It bore the following inscription, now obliterated—

Yey git Dame Maud Manwaryn. jadis campagne Oliver de Burdax, de qui Dieu ——— sa alme ——— urage marci, et qui pour l'alme de elle priera, trois cents jours de pardon* avera.

Mr. Thomas Minshull founded a Free School here, which he endowed with two pieces of land, let for about £15. per ann. Other endowments have been entirely lost, excepting one of the interest of £20. per ann.

* Copied by Sir William Dugdale.

HISTORY.

MOSTON†

Is about two miles and a half W. N. W. from Sandbach. It is supposed to have been included with Warmincham in the Survey. It gave name to a family settled here at a very early period, certainly coeval with Edward I. It subsequently descended with the Venables' estates to the Vernons; and the late Lord Vernon sold the manor to the late Rev. John Armitstead, father of the present proprietor, Lawrence Armitstead, Esq. of Grange.

† In the singular augmentation of the Venables' arms, in page 567, this township is erroneously printed Merston.

THE PARISH OF DAVENHAM,

CONTAINS THE TOWNSHIPS OF

DAVENHAM,	STANTHORNE,	MOULTON,
SHIPBROOK,	NEWALL,	EATON,
WHATCROFT,	SHURLACH-CUM-BRADFORD,	AND
BOSTOCK,	WHARTON,	LEFTWICH.

DAVENHAM

Is situated on the river Dane, and is about two miles S. from Northwich, and nearly four miles N. E. from Middlewich.

Formerly this township was annexed to the estates of the Shipbrook Barony, but on the division of the property, eventually passed to William Harpur, Esq. and is now the property of Edward Hoskins Harpur, Esq. At an early period, the estates here, were divided into two manors, *Over* and *Nether Davenham*, and for many generations were vested in the Bretts, holding under the Vernons and Savages as Chief Lords; from the Bretts they passed in marriage to the Holfords and the family of De la Wyche, which had long been settled in Davenham. Allen, the last male heir of the Holfords, alienated his estates to his brother in law Thomas Highlord Ravenscroft, Esq. on whose death, in 1795, Wm. Harpur, Esq. of Liverpool, purchased them from his Trustees; and they are now the property of J. H. Harpur, Esq.

The ancient Hall of Ravenscroft, was long occupied by the widow of Mr. Ravenscroft, who had a life-interest in it.

The Wyches went from hence to Alderley, and as there is no certain record of the disposal of their Davenham estates, it is supposed they were sold in parcels, a greater part of which are now, probably, the property of Mr. Harpur.

The CHURCH of Davenham is rather a neat building, with a spire, which was erected in 1680, and the Chancel about twenty-seven years since, by Dr. Cotton, Dean of Chester, then Rector.—On the north side of the

Chancel, is the Leftwich Chapel, belonging to the Hall of that name, and within which township, the whole building stands. It is dedicated to St. Wilfred, and the present Rector is the Rev. James Tomkinson, A. B.

The Priory of Birkenhead, had formerly vested in it the advowson of the living; but about 1285, it was sold by the Prior to the Baron of Shipbrooke, and, according to Vill. Cest. for seventy marks. Continuing for some centuries united with the Manor of Shipbrook, it was eventually separated, and after being possessed by several families, was purchased by the father of the present proprietor, Henry Tomkinson, Esq. of Dorfold.

It appears from Smith's Collection, that George Savage, (the illegitimate son of Sir John Savage, killed at Boulogne) when Rector of Davenham, has seven bastard children by three different women, one of whom, was afterwards the celebrated Bishop Bonner, by Elizabeth Frodsham.

There is a *Free School* here, endowed with £20. per annum, for the Master, which has been increased by the Parish. This endowment is a rent-charge on Shipbrooke Hill Farm, and the produce of some trifling benefactions.

SHIPBROOKE,

(Probably from *Sheep*-brook) is nearly two miles S. E. from Northwich, and was the seat of Richard de Vernon, created by Hugh Lupus one of his Barons.

Warin Vernon, the fifth Baron in succession, son of Warin, who had married one of the co-heiresses of the Baron of Wich Malbank, left three daughters co-heiresses, married in the families of Wilbraham, Stafford, and Littlebury.* Ralph Vernon, Rector of Hanwell, the younger brother of Warin, had some long law-suits with his nieces relative to the Barony; but it was in the end determined that a moiety of the Baronial estate including this township (the seat of the Barony) and the Manor of Minshull Vernon, should be awarded to Ralph. This portion of the estate,† was settled on his illegitimate son Sir Ralph, who attained the extraordinary age of 150 years.‡ This Ralph married Mary, daughter of Lord Dacre, and Maud Grosvenor (widow of John Hatton, who on one side is described as his second wife, and on the other as his concubine)|| and had issue male.

In 1325, he made a settlement upon the marriage of Sir Ralph (his grandson, or as some pedigrees represent him, his great grandson) with Agnes, daughter of Richard D'Amory, Chief Justice of Chester: by this Deed, in the event of male issue failing from Sir Ralph and Agnes, the Vernon estates were settled on Richard, eldest son of the before-named Sir Ralph *the Old*, by Maud Grosvenor, passing by a younger son, Thomas, by his wife Mary, whose descendant James Vernon, some years afterwards, contested the validity of the deed, and after considerable litigation, it would appear a compromise took place, for James Vernon recovered Haslington,§ but Shipbrook, and a moiety of the Barony, passed to the descendants of Richard. On the death of Sir Ralph Vernon the younger (of Mottram), who by Agnes D'Amory, his wife, left an only daughter, married to Hamo le Strange, Shipbrooke became the inheritance of Sir Ralph Vernon, son of Richard, on whom the estates were entailed. This Sir Ralph leaving no male issue, Shipbrooke passed to his younger brother Sir Richard Vernon, afterwards slain at the Battle of Shrewsbury, leaving two sons, Sir Richard, who died in France, and left an only daughter married to Sir Robert Foulshurst, and Sir Ralph, on whom Shipbrooke devolved, Ralph Vernon, son of the last-named Sir Ralph, left an only daughter and heir Dorothy, married to Sir John Savage, K. G. slain at the siege of Boulogne, 1492. In consequence of this marriage, the Savages became possessed of half the Barony, with the manor of Shipbrooke, and the Royalties of Davenham, Leftwich, Moulton, Shocklach, and Wharton, sold in the beginning of the 18th century, by the Savages, to Richard Vernon, Esq. of Middlewich and by him devised to Henry Vernon, Esq of Hilton, in the county of Stafford, one of the lineal descendants of Sir William Vernon, grandson of Warin, third Baron of Shipbrooke.

In 1765, the representatives of Mr. Vernon, procured an Act of Parliament for the sale of his estate, when

* Lysons.

† Woodnoth's Coll.

‡ In the Pedigrees of the family, he is called "Sir Ralph the Olde" and "The Old Liver".

|| Ibid.

§ Woodnoth's Coll.

it was purchased by Wm. Tomkinson, Esq. of Manchester, and he devised it to Edward Tomkinson, Esq. who assumed the name of Wettenhall, by whom it was sold to the predecessor of Edward Hoskins Harpur, Esq. the present proprietor. There are no remains of the ancient *Hall* of the Vernons.

WHATCROFT

Is about three miles S. E. from Northwich. At an early period the Manor was vested in the Bulkeleys, ancestors of the present Lord Bulkeley, who removed into North Wales more than two centuries ago, still, however, retaining their manor.

In 1756, an Act of Parliament was obtained for the sale of this and other estates, late the property of James Lord Bulkeley, when the Manor was purchased by the Robinsons; and it is now the property of James Topping, Esq. Barrister at Law, who married the heiress of the Robinsons.

BOSTOCK

Is rather pleasantly situated, about three miles N. W. W. from Middlewich. It formerly gave name to the descendants of Osmerus, Lord of Bostock, temp. William I. and they possessed it some centuries. Towards the latter part of the 15th century, an heiress of the Bostocks brought it in marriage to the Savages.* It was afterwards vested in the Whitmores, of Apley, in the county of Salop, who sold it to Wm. Tomkinson, Esq. whose nephew Edward Tomkinson, Esq. sold it to Thomas France, Esq. father of James France France, Esq. High Sheriff of the County in 1819.

The *Hall* was built by T. France, Esq. in 1775, and is the residence of the present proprietor. The ancient Hall, an old building of timber and plaister, and moated, was taken down in 1803.

An ancient Oak, on Bostock Green, is said to have marked the centre of the county.

STANTHORNE

Is about two miles W. N. W. from Middlewich. It appears from Woodnoth's Collections, that in the 13th and 14th centuries, the manor was vested in a family named Rabers, *Little Stanthorne*, as it is called, being at the same time held by the Duttons. Subsequently the Whalleys were seized of the manor; and it was afterwards, by purchase, the property of Sir John Byrne, Bart. from whom it descended to his grandson, Sir John Fleming Leicester, Bart. and from him it was purchased by Richard Jones, Esq. of Manchester.

The site of the ancient *Hall* is occupied as a farm house, and described by a moat.

NEWHALL,

After many descents was, temp. Elizabeth, vested in the Savages, from whom it passed to the Stockleys.—Subsequently the Hall and other estates were purchased by the Whittakers; and at this time the proprietor is E. Vernon, Esq. by marriage of an ancestor with the heiress of the Whittakers. The *Hall* is used as a farm house.

SHURLACH

Is a mile and a half E. S. E. from Northwich, situated in rather a pleasant part of the county. The royalty is vested in the Shipbrooke Barony; but the lands are divided amongst several proprietors.

WHARTON

Lies about two miles and a half N. N. W. from Middlewich, and the same remarks which occur under the head "*Shurlach*," are applicable to this township.

MOULTON

Is exclusively the property of Thos. Cholmondeley, Baron Delamere. This estate was formerly vested in the Bostocks.

EATON,

Or *Ayton*, is about three miles S. W. from Northwich. At one period it was divided between the families of Praers and Bulkeley; but, temp. Henry VIII. Thomas Bulkeley sold his share to the Breretons,† and subsequently they became the proprietors of the entirety of the manor. Previous to 1672, however, the estates became by purchase, the property of the Cholmondeleys and Lindseys, and the manor is now vested in Thomas Cholmondeley, created Baron Delamere, in 1821.‡

* The Lysons observe in a note, that a younger branch of the Bostocks continued here some time, and is supposed to have become extinct about a century ago. The last of this name in the Parish Registers, is Thomas Bostock, interred Dec. 26, 1704.

† Vill. Cest.

‡ The Bulkeleys had a seat here. Bishop Gastrell notices a monument in Davenham Church, to William Bulkeley, Esq. of Ayton, who died in the reign of Edward IV. Leland says the two Bulkeleys, i. e. of Whatcroft and Eaton, contended either to be the senior House, and he adds "Bulkle of Eaton's Stok cam to a daughter, and Leftwich had her, but Sir Gul. (William) of Brereton brought Eyton."—Lysons.

CHESHIRE — HISTORY.

LEFTWICH

Is about a mile from Northwich. Temp. William I. the manor was given to the Vernons, Barons of Shipbrooke, as parcel of the Barony, and they possessed it till the beginning of the 13th century, when Margaret, sister and heiress of Warin Vernon, brought it to Sir Richard Wilbraham, in marriage, and their daughter and co-heir, Maud, brought it also in marriage to Robt. de Winnington, whose son Richard assumed the local name. He was the founder of the family of Leftwich, who resided here many generations; but in the beginning of the 17th century, Elizabeth, the daughter and heiress of Ralph Leftwich (last male Representative of the family) married William Oldfield, Esq. and brought with her the estates; and his descendant, Jane, sister and coheiress of Bowyer Oldfield, Esq. last heir male of the family, in 1736, sold the manor to Thomas Highlord Ravenscroft, Esq. from whom the Honorable Booth Grey purchased it in 1790, and his heir sold it to the father of J. H. Harpur, Esq. the present proprietor. A farm-house occupies the site of the ancient *Hall* of Leftwich, of which a cut is given in page 469.

THE PARISH OF ASTBURY,

CONTAINS THE TOWNSHIPS OF

NEWBOLD ASTBURY,	EATON,*	RADNOR,
BUGLAWTON,	HULMEWALFIELD,*	SMALLWOOD.
CONGLETON,	GREAT MORETON,	SOMERFORD BOOTHS.*
DAVENPORT,	ODD RODE,	

ASTBURY,

Or *Newbold Astbury*, is about a mile from Congleton, on the Manchester Road. At one period the township consisted of two Manors, vested in the families of Venables and Astbury, from the last of which it passed with a female heir to the Somerfords, and subsequently to the Oldfields, from whom it was purchased by Archdale Palmer, Esq. but how his rights have ceased does not now appear.

Richard de Venables had possession of the advowson temp. John; and the manor, or a portion of it, was claimed by the Venables family, certainly so late as the 44th Edward III.† after which the Hawkstones had possession, and Ellen daughter and heir of Sir John Hawkstone, brought his estates in marriage to Wm. Egerton, of Caldecote, ancestor of the Egertons of Wrinehill, in whose descendant, Sir John Grey Egerton, Bart. the manor is now vested, and he holds a Court for it.

WALL HILL HALL, in this township, now a farm-house, was formerly the seat of a branch of the Rode family.

The CHURCH is dedicated to St. Mary; the present Rector the Rev. O. Crewe, presented Oct. 30, 1782.—Previous to 1093, this Church was given by Gilbert Venables, Baron of Kinderton, to the Abbey of Chester; subsequently, however, his descendants obtained possession of the Church; and retained it till the 13th year of Richard II. when the matter was tried at Chester, before Humphrey Duke of Gloucester, Chief Justice, and the right of the Abbey fully confirmed. At the Dissolution, the Advowson was involved in all the series of litigation which resulted from the proceedings of Sir Richard Cotton.

In 1607, Ralph Egerton presented to the Rectory; and subsequently the Hackets, Egertons, and Hampsons. In 1782, Peter Brooke, Esq. was the Patron.

The tithes of the whole parish are vested in the Rector. The *præpositi* of the parish (the Mayor of Con-

* The townships marked (*) are in Macclesfield Hundred.

† Comson's Coll.

gleton, the proprietors of the Halls of Brereton*, Davenport, Eaton, Great Moreton, Little Moreton, Somerford, Radnor, and Oddrode) elect the Churchwardens.†

The building consists of nave, chancel, and side aisles, with porches on the west and south sides. The tower is crowned with an elegant spire. Five pointed arches, springing from clustered pillars, divide the nave from the side aisles: two similar arches separate the private chancels from the chancel. The east window is finely finished. The roofing of the church is of oak, beautifully carved, that of the north aisle has the date 1701: the name of *Richard Lownes, carpenter*, and 1616, and 1617, occur in the body of the Church.—Beautifully finished oak screens, divide the chancel from the nave; there is a rood loft on the west side, with oak stalls, &c.

The whole building is elegantly finished, and the windows contain some fine specimens of ancient stained glass.‡

In the north west angle of the Chancel, is an altar tomb; the inscription—

T(homas) B(ellot) was buried November the 10th, anno D'ni, 1654. Mors mihi lucrum.

* At one period included in the parish.

† See Stockport.

‡ The Editor is indebted for the following particulars, to an intelligent friend in Congleton:—"Astbury Church, is one of the handsomest Country Churches in the County of Chester. It is of a Gothic construction, very elegant, lofty and light; was greatly adorned with painted glass, in the windows, and carving and images, tho' now mostly destroyed, either at the Reformation, or in the Civil Wars, particularly an Organ was then destroyed by the Religious Fanatics: the beautiful stained glass in the windows, and other ornaments were then broken. The windows were stopped up with broom branches, the Church was closed, Divine Service suspended, burials took place without any ceremony, marriages were celebrated at the Public Cross, before a Civil Magistrate, and so continued until the Restoration, 1660. At that period, the Church was repaired and made clean, the service resumed, but no monuments were placed therein, neither was an Organ erected, and such it remains, through the supineness and lukewarmness of the principal persons in the parish. It was pewed all over, instead of the forms before used. The walls on the inside adorned with scripture paintings, but all were defaced by the Church being, by some Vandal churchwarden, white washed. There were a few images of Angels below the roof in the north and south isles, but they are mostly defaced and pulled down. The font is a very plain stone basin, lined with lead, but the cover and other ornaments very elegant, done in beautiful carving in wood. The east ends of the north and south aisles are claimed as the burial places of the Moreton, Wilbraham, the Bellot, and Shakerley familes, of which there are some decent memorials erected. The civil government of the church is vested in eight of the principal families in the parish, and two of them act by rotation as Church-wardnes, which is done by deputy:—1. Congleton, and Eaton Hall. 2. Rode Hall, and Moreton. 3. Bellot, near Moreton, and Davenport. 4. Somerford, and Brereton Hall, though now Brereton is not in the parish, yet it was so formerly. They are called the posts of the parish. The repairs of the Church are supported by a Constable Lay through the parish, or more, if not sufficient.

	£.	s.	d.
1. Astbury pays one Mize	2	15	6
2. Congleton	£4	0	0
3. Buglawton	2	6	4
4. Davenport	0	19	0
5. Hulmwalfield	0	16	0
6. Eaton	1	5	0
7. Moreton	1	6	8
8. Odd Rode	2	16	0
9 Radnor	0	6	4
10 Somerford Booth	1	10	2
11 Somerford	1	1	0
12 Smallwood	3	2	3
	£22	4	1

The usual common yearly expenses of the Church, did amount to Thirty Pounds; they are now considerably more. The east end of the north isle contains the monuments of the Moreton and Wilbraham families; in the south aisle, monuments of the Bellots, Shakerleys, &c. and an altar tomb, with an effigy of a man in armour unknown, the only ancient one in the Church. Near to the communion rails, on the south side of the middle aisle, is an altar-tomb with an effigy of a Lady, inclosed with rails. The chancel is seated in the cathedral form, and service was performed here in that manner; there is an eagle also, upon which the Gospel used to be read. All the ceiling over the middle aisle is elegantly adorned with carved oak, and over the altar a beautiful ornament of wood, on which, at the end, are representations of our Saviour's hands and feet, of a flesh colour; there is also, another such ornament, but has no figures thereon; they are each covered very much with carved work and tracery, and have a pleasing appearance. The Church is covered with lead, and the ceiling of the middle and south aisles, is beautifully covered with square pannels, and flowered ornaments, not so the north aisle, which is quite plain, having been done by inferior workmen, and at a different period. The Chancel is separated from the choir and isles by wood screens and carved work, and there was also a rood loft and there stood the organ, which was destroyed in the time of the usurpation. The north, west, and south aisles, which as before noticed, are seated in the cathedral form, have desks, from which the psalms were chaunted,

On a marble mural monument, in the north-east aisle—

Here lie the remains of Peter Shackerley, of Somerford Hall, Esq. and likewise of Ann, his first wife, the daughter of John Amson, of Lees, in the county of Chester, Esq. This tribute of filial affection was erected by Eliza Buckworth, their only surviving child, to the memory of the best of parents, Anno Domin' 1796.

Memorials of Dorothy Maria, the infant daughter of C. W. J. Shackerley, Esq. and of G Shakerley, his son.

In the south-east angle a monument, round the edges of which is inscribed—

Hic jacet D. Maria Egerton, ex antique Grosvenorum familia oriunda, nup' Ric, Egerto' de Ridley, equitis aurati uxor, plena annoru' xxv° * * * *

At the end—

Rodolphus Egerton de Ridley, maritus charissimus in memoriam officiosæ pietatis uxori bene merenti hoc monumentum posuit a° D'ni 1609°.

On the north side of the nave, on a monument—

Near this place lies interred, the body of George Lee, of Eaton Hall, in this Parish, Esq. who departed this life the 4th April, 1773, aged 71 years.

There is a private Chancel at the east end of the north aisle, belonging to the proprietors of Odd Rode, the windows of which formerly contained some splendid stained glass. There still remain a piscina, a relic closet, and some of the altar steps, adjoining the latter is a tomb, on which are slabs, inscribed—

Dame Mary Jones, died the 19th of April, 1743, aged 85.

Sir William Moreton, Knt. Recorder of the City of London, died the 14th March, 1763, aged 67.

Dame Jane Moreton, died the 10th of February, 1758, aged 61.

The memorials of the Wilbrahams of Rode, are at the opposite end of this Chancel. On a marble monument affixed to the pillar:—

Ricardus Ranulphi Wilbraham, armr. et Mariæ uxoris ejus filius primogenitus, antiqui stemmatis germen speciosum, flos juvenum patriæ spes, sui nominis decus, sub ævi flore præreptus, hic jacet, et terreni patrimonii factus exhæres, cœlestem creavit hæreditatem sexto die Feb. MDCCVI. Sparge rosas, plecte corollas, abi et fuge viator.

---

and the lessons occasionally read. The communion table and rails are quite plain, and raised by three steps above the floor, and flagged.— It was once adorned with garlands and flowers, and the seats and floor covered with rushes, but this custom has now fell into disuse. There are five doors to the church: two on the north, two on the south, and a large one on the west side; there are also a south and north porch from the side of the latter a road once existed which led to the steeple— it is now walled up, and a passage cut on the west side. The steeple is square, with a spire about forty yards high, and contains four large old bells, the tenor defective and out of tune, with a clock; the steeple stands at the north-west side of the church yard. In the Churchyard, is an ancient tomb, covered with a Gothic arch, and two altar tombs, on the sides of which are some tracery, but to whom unknown, although supposed to be some of the Venables family, the owners at the conquest. The Brereton family pretend a claim thereto, and have put an epitaph in modern letters in Latin, to that purport.—At the time of the Doomsday record, it is written thus:—" Gilbert Venable holds of the Earl Newbold Astbury, Ulvit a Barkman, did hold " it; there is one hide and half of land, liable to taxes. There is " one Redman or Barkman, that holds 100 acres, and the Presbyter " or Priest has 100 acres. The whole is 5 Carucates, and plow " lands of 500 acres. There are three villains or slaves, and two " borderers or house holders, and one acre is pasture. There is a " wood, one mile long and the same broad, and there are two inclosed " pastures of old land. In the time of Edward the Third, it was valued at twenty shilling: the modus is eight shillings. Gilbert Venables gave to God, and St. Werburgh (at Chester), the Church of " Astbury, with half the wood, and open land, and every thing thereunto belonging."—When the Church was erected cannot now be ascertained, as there are no dates to be found; probably about the year 1300, or later, though not much, as a part at the north-east end is of different stone and building, and seems much older. The stone, it is supposed, was procured from Congleton Edge, as there are yet remains of considerable quarries, the stone of which appears similar, with the exception of the older part of the edifice. This Church is a valuable Rectory, belonging to the Crewe family, is in value about £3000, per ann. and to the Curate the Crewes give a salary of about £200.

Dimensions of the Church.

Length inside	100 feet.
Width	78
Width, middle aisle	34
Side aisles	22
Width of middle aisle passage	8
Side aisles' passage	6
Height of middle aisle	51
Ditto side aisles	20
Steeple width (it is square)	22
Height thereof to the square	60
Height to the top	120

On the screen which separates the body of the Church from the Chancel, over which the rood loft, and the organ stood, are the arms of England, temp. Charles II. also the Lord's Prayer, Belief, and the Ten Commandments, written in old text hand, under which is the reading desk, on the south side of the middle isle. The pulpit is plain, covered with crimson velvet, and is placed in the middle aisle, adjoining to a pillar on the north side thereof, so that the Minister stands facing the middle and south aisles, and his back and the pillar towards the north aisle, which is very inconvenient."

On the north wall, on a pyramidal monument, on a tablet surmounted by a sarcophagus—

Near this place is buried Randle Wilbraham, of Rode, in the County Palatine of Chester, Esq. of which he was Vice Chamberlain; also Deputy Steward of the University of Oxford, and Barrister at Law. He was second son of Randle Wilbraham, of Townsend, in Namptwich, in the same county, Esq. by his wife Mary, daughter of Sir Richard Brooke, of Norton, in the said county, Bart. He died Dec. 3d, 1770, aged 76. His great industry and abilities carried him to the highest reputation and practice in his profession, which he adorned with sound knowledge, clear judgment, and steady integrity. He sate many years in Parliament, where his public conduct superior to interest, or faction, shewed him a lover of his King and Country, the Laws and Constitution of which he well understood, and well maintained, loyal, upright, and independent. His private virtues shone in the husband, father, and friend; tender, careful, affectionate, candid, and easy. The natural goodness of his heart he improved by sincere religion; he was a true Christian, and a firm Member of the Church of England. He married Dorothea, daughter of Andrew Kenrick, Esq. of Chester, Barrister at Law.—She died Nov. 18th, 1754, aged 50, and was also interred here.

Below the tablet—

Ann Wilbraham, daughter of Randle and Dorothy, died Dec. 5, 1769, aged 39, and lies buried here.

On a tablet—

Here lieth interred the body of Richard Wilbraham Bootle, Esq. only son and heir of Randle Wilbraham, Esq. of Rode Hall, in this county, born Sept. 20, 1725. He married May 31st, 1755, Mary, daughter and sole heiress of Robert Bootle, Esq. of Lathom, in the county of Lancaster, by whom he had six sons and eight daughters, of whom eight survived, namely—Edward, born March the 7th, 1771, and Randle, born Jan. 10th 1773; the daughters, Ann, married to Sir Richard Pepper Arden, Master of the Rolls; Mary, to William Egerton, Esq. of Tatton Park, in this County; Francisca Alicia, to Anthony Eyre, Esq. of Grove, in Nottinghamshire; Sybilla Georgina to William Farington, Esq. of Shawe Hill, in Lancashire; Emma, to Charles Edmonstone, Esq. Barrister at Law, London; Elizabeth unmarried.—He was elected one of the Representives in Parliament for the city of Chester, at the Accession of his present Majesty, October, 1760, and served in five successive Parliaments, where his conduct was uniform in support of his King and Country, in the respectable character of an independent country gentleman. He died March 13th, 1796, aged 71 years.

On the west side of the monument of Randle Wilbraham, on a tablet,—

This monument is erected to the memory of Mary, wife of Richard Wilbraham Bootle, Esq. of Lathom House, in Lancashire, and Rode Hall, in this Parish; she was born on the 17th of March, 1734 and closed a life of exemplary usefulness, benevolence, and charity, on the 10th of April, 1813, in the 80th year of her age.

Beneath this, on another tablet—

Sacred to the memory of Lalitia, wife of Randle Wilbraham, Esq. of Rode Hall, who died on the 30th of March, 1805, aged 27.

Sleep on, fair form! and wait th' Almighty's will,
Then rise unchang'd, and be an Angel still!

On the south wall of the south aisle, on a tablet—

Near this place lies interred the body of Edmund Swetenham, Esq. late of Somerford Booths, in the county of Chester, who departed this life, May the 7th, 1768, in the 77th year of his age. Also, of Susannah, relict of the said Edmund Swettenham, and daughter of Richard Wilmot, late of Derby, in the county of Derby, M. D. She died the 18th of May, 1790, aged 77.

On another tablet—

Near this place rest the mortal remains of Roger Swetenham, Esq. of Somerford Boothe, in this county, whose life was distinguished by every thing worthy of the man and the Christian; he was a most tender and affectionate husband, a most kind and indulgent father, and a very sincere and faithful friend. He died 27th of January, MDCCCXIV, aged 55.

There is a piscina, and a stall for the Priest, in the Chancel, at the end of the south aisle; also at the east end, an ancient figure in plate armour and gorget, his surcoat bearing the Davenport arms. Inscribed on a slab is—

Hic jacet Amia Bellot de Groevenour' familia oriunda nuper Bellot de Moreton uxor, quæ obiit primo die Septembris a'no D'ni, 1612.

On the adjoining slab—

Hic jacet Edwardus Bellot, super de Moreton, ar. qui obiit VII die Augusti an. Dom'i 1622.

A monument, with a Latin inscription, to John Bellot, of Moreton, Esq. died Nov. 9, 1659.

On another monument, a Latin inscription to the memory of Sir John Bellot, Bart. who died July, 1674.

In the south-east angle of the Church-yard are four recumbent figures, on altar tombs, ascribed to the Breretons; within the arch of that on which recline the figures of a Knight and his lady, is this inscription, cut at a much later period than the workmanship of the monument—

Hic jacent Radulphus Brereton miles et domina Ada, uxor sua, una filiarum Davidis comit. Huntingdonis.*

* Among the records in the Tower, is a license from Edw. I. during his Welsh wars, in 1282, to John de Stanley, Rector of Astbury, for bringing provisions for the support of his household at St. Botolph's fair.—The following instance of longevity occurs in the Registers of the parish: "Alice Walker, widow, aged almost 105, buried Nov. 28, 1747."

Cheshire

History.

CONGLETON

Is about 161 miles from the Metropolis, in a highly interesting part of the county, and situated on the banks of the Dane, over which is a handsome bridge of stone, built in 1782.*

* The following particulars have been handed to the Editor by the same Gentleman who favored him with the notes on Astbury, in the preceding pages, for which he will be pleased to accept his best thanks :—

" Congleton, is a Market Town, on the east-side of the county of Chester, pleasantly situated on a gentle declivity, on the south side of the River Dane, in a sandy situation; and intersected by two small branches which arise on the moss near to the town, on the south.--- This town is exceedingly well watered, as springs arise in most parts of it, of excellent water. Congleton is about one mile in length, but of different breadths, as the streets are in general single, and not closely built, as most other populous towns are. It was anciently built of wood and plaister, being seated in the midst of woods, but latterly has become modernized, and is mostly built of brick and slate. The Church stands on the south side of the town, in a high situation, and was newly built of brick in 1741-2, to an old steeple of stone, which was the same height, but in 1785, it was raised much higher; there are six bells in the tower. The outward appearance of the Church is rather mean, but yet it is particularly well finished and neat in the interior. There are several large and genteel houses in the town; and on the site of the old Guildhall, a new one has been erected, with a colonade. But the most elegant building is the Silk Mill, which was erected on the side of the river, by Messrs. Pattisons, & Co. in 1751 and 1754, of brick, five stories high, and about sixty yards in length. This building presents a beautiful appearance if viewed from off the Bridge, which is of stone, supported by three arches, erected in 1782, at the expense of seven hundred pounds. The principal houses in the town, and vicinity, belong to Messrs. Pattison, T. Johnson, F. Johnson, W. Lowndes, in the West-lane; Miss Antrobus, Mr. Watson, W. Read, G. Read, Moody Hall, Mrs. Swettenham, in the town; Lady Warburton, Daisy Bank; and Mr. Malbon, of Dane-bank.— There is a delightful and interesting prospect from either Daisy-bank, or the Hill-field, on the north of the town, commanding at one view the grounds beneath, the church on an eminence, the high grounds behind, and the hills of Biddulph, near Congleton Edge Mole in the perspective. The Church is merely a Chapel of Ease under Astbury, the Mother Church, about one mile distant, in the gift of the Mayor and Corporation. The Salary, with part of the Surplice fees (a part with the tithes go to Astbury) is about £200. per ann. The present Minister is the Rev. S. Williamson. There is a Methodist Chapel newly erected, nearly the size of the Church, on the old situation. There is also a Calvinistic Chapel; and an Unitarian Chapel, but its frequenters are by no means numerous. There are three Sunday Schools in Congleton, belonging to the Church, the Methodists, and the Calvinists; and upwards of three hundred Children are taught gratis, mostly supported by Charity Sermons. The town is governed by a Mayor, Eight Aldermen (two whereof are Justices) Sixteen Common Councilmen, Recorder, Town Clerk, Two Serjeants at Mace, &c. The Mayor is chosen annually on the Monday before Michaelmas Day, as are also the Justices, &c. There is a weekly market on Saturday, well frequented, and four Fairs, held on the Thursday before Shrove Sunday, May the 12th, July the 13th, and Nov. 22d, for cattle, horses, and Yorkshire goods. As the town lies near to the Collieries, and to the Coal Wharf, on Congleton Moss, it is well supplied with Coals at about 14s. per ton. This town was much noted formerly for the manufacture of a kind of shoe-tie, and other wares, called Congleton prints, the which, since Buttons and Buckles came in use, are now entirely neglected and unknown. About fifty years ago there was a great Silk Ribbon Manufactory here, for Coventry, but latterly it is gone to nothing, as at one time nearly half of the women and children were employed therein. But since Messrs. Pattisons established the throwsting Silk Mills here, many others have been erected, and now it has become the principal business of the town. About twenty large and small mills, mostly propelled by water, are now in work for the London and other markets.

It was formerly customary on Shrove Tuesday to have a great holy-day, and spend the afternoon in logging at cocks, &c.; but happily this cruel practice has long been abolished. The 29th of May, 4th of June, and 5th of Nov. were also days devoted to mirth and jollity, by ringing of bells, bonfires, adorning the streets and houses with branches of oak, and the windows with flowers, &c. but circumstances have rendered the greater part of them useless. The inhabitants are now better employed, and the masters do not allow such holidays. By the account of Congleton taken in Doomsday book, it seems then to have been a small village, the same as the neighboring townships. In Leycester's Antiquities, it is said thus to be: " The same Bigot holds Congletone (Congleton). Godwin held it. There is one hide of land liable to pay taxes. The whole land is four carucates, two with two villains (or slaves), and four cottages. There is a wood one league long, and one broad, and there are two inclosed pastures. It was waste and so it is found: it is now, (1068) worth four shillings" It is now worth £20,000. It seems according to a traditional account, that it was very small, and that " Ralph the Third Earl of Chester journeyed twenty miles eastward, and founded a town, and called it Condate, and then seven miles more eastward, and founded an Abbey, and called it Dieu la Crea." Which, as the situation is by a river, and there being plenty of spring water, seems probable, for it was a place of some consequence about 1290: Henry Lacy, Constable of Chester, granted to Congleton, a Charter, to the effect—that there shall be a Brotherhood, or Company of Merchants; also, household, and bayhold; free liberty of all their cattle in the commons of Congleton, to go and pasture; to have liberty to get and dry turf and peats, and keep any number of hogs.— To be free throughout all Cheshire, from all tolls, &c.; not to be

CHESHIRE HISTORY.

From the earliest period recorded, to the 13th century, Congleton was a depency on Bigot's fee of Aldford. In the 53d Henry III. the manor was settled by Sir Peter Arderne on his son John, married to Margaret the daughter of Griffin, Lord of Bromfield. Previous to the death of John Arderne, which took place

compelled to go out of their town on any affairs done therein but the same to be tryed there. Not to pay above twelve-pence on a reasonable amerciment if any offence was there committed. To grind their corn at his mill to the twentieth grain; to chuse a Mayor; to have all their lands and houses for ever, paying yearly for each house 6d. and for each acre of land 12d. and to sell the same when agreeable; to behead any felon if caught in the fact, or to keep him three days in the stocks, and then to send him to Halton Castle, to be there tried. Henry VI granted a charter in 1454, to remove the mills to the place where they now stand, and to cut the river a new course, the same direction in which it runs at present. The stream formerly ran under the town, and washed away a part of Mill-street. He also granted to them an injunction, to prohibit any other corn mill in the town, paying to him yearly £1. 6s. 8d. In 1524, Henry VIII. granted to the inhabitants an exemption to appear in any other court than their own, and also to be free through Chester. Queen Elizabeth, in 1583, granted them the privilege of chusing a Mayor out of the Burgesses of the town yearly, and a mandamus to be free from toll throughout all England. James I. granted, in 1615, a new charter, confirming therein all former grants, and allows them a Mayor, eight Aldermen, Sixteen Capital Burgesses, two Serjeants at Mace, one to be Catch-pole or Sheriff, the other the Gaoler; to have a New Fair, for two days, to commence on Thursday before Shrove Sunday, and to have the tolls thereof; to chuse the Mayor and Justices yearly, on the Monday before Michaelmas-day. In 1666, Charles II. granted them a new charter, and confirmed most of the former privileges.—This is the last charter, the obtaining which cost £89. 11s. 6d.

Singular Customs extracted out of the Accounts of Congleton.

		£.	s.	d.
1584	(Richard Green Mayor), Joseph Smith, tending the Townwood	0	6	7
1588	William Tilman, his quarter's wage 2l. 0s. 0d. Davenport the reader 1l. 0s. 0d.	3	0	0
1589	(John Hobson, Mayor) paid Mr. Trafford's man the Bearward	0	4	4
	Gave to Sir John Hollingsworth's Bearward	0	2	0
	Jane Smith, towards the Exhibition of Besse Riddleworth	0	9	6
	Lord Darcy's players	0	5	0
	Furniture Money to Sir William Brereton, and other Justices	1	18	0
	Jane Smith, for her exhibition of Besse Riddleworth, her Burial Sheet, as there were no Coffins then in use	0	11	2
1590	To Widow Broadhurst, for making the Surplice, and Thread 3d.	0	1	8
	Bestowed on Mr. Caudwell when he Preached in the Chapel	0	7	4
1591	To the Constables, for taking Highfield and Rathbone to Halton Castle	0	8	0
	Straw for the Cock-pit	0	8	0
1592	Gave to the Players	0	5	0
	Alderman Smith, and William Drakefoot's journey to London, on Town's business	3	12	7
	Gave to my Lord Admiral's Players	0	7	0
	Mending the Cockpit 5s. 8d.	0	1	8
	To Arthur Checkley, for saying the Service on the Sabbath Day	0	1	0
	Mare for two days	0	2	0
1594	William Broster, the Minister and Schoolmaster, Quarterage	3	6	8
	(Only one Bell in the Steeple,) 27th Elizabeth.			
	Mr. Oldfield, son-in-law to Richard Spencer, cast two more Bells, the first and second, and bound himself in a bond of £40. to uphold the said bells during his life to continue sound and tuneable, and accord with the Great Bell.			
	Gave to Mr. Damas for Preaching 10s.; To Mr. Palmerford, 5s.; Gave to Mr. Gerard, of Stockport for Preaching 2s.	0	17	0
1595	Gave for Wine to the Rushbearers	0	3	8
	Job Creswell, and T. Savage, their expenes to borrow Money at Nantwich, but could not	0	2	8
	Gave to the Poor this quarter 27s. 3d. do. more 32s. 9d.	3	0	0
	Gave to Darmer for preaching 10s.; do. James Hulme 5s.	0	15	0
	Gave to Verdon for taking Horton to Halton Castle, a felon	0	6	8
1597	Spent in a Banquet gave to Sir John Savage	1	4	0
	Disburst to Mr. Hangton's man, of Hangton, who had been with him	1	5	0
	To the Queen's Players	1	0	0
	For Candles used at the Six o'Clock Service Prayers	0	2	10
	Mr. Broster, for saying Prayers, Winter Quarter	0	10	0
	Mr. Smith of Manchester, preaching on NewYear's Day	0	10	0
	Mr. Lawton, for making four Sermons (he should have been Schoolmaster)	1	0	0
1599	Gave to Mr. Carr, of Middlewich, for preaching four Sermons	0	5	0

in the 1st of Edw, II. it passed to Henry de Lacy, Earl of Lincoln, Baron of Halton, and Constable of Chester, who granted the inhabitants the following Charter:

"Know all men present and to come, that we, Henry de Lacy, Earl of Lincoln, and Constable of Chester, have granted, and by this our present Charter,

		£.	s.	d.
	Gave to a Preacher who preached on a Saturday, and on St. Martin's Day	0	5	0
	Gave for Wine to those who brought Rushes from Buglawton to our Chapel	0	3	0
	Wine and a gallon of Sack, bestowed on Sir Edw. Fitton, Gawsworth	0	4	8
1600	Gave to Shelmardine the Bearward	0	6	8
	One year's Wage to the Clockmender	0	2	0
	Second quarter to Shenton the Schoolmaster	3	4	0
	Paid James Barker to fetch Shenton's Books, and Clothes, from Oxford	1	6	8
1601	Gave to the Bearward at the Great Cock Fight on May 5, 6, and 7	0	6	8
	Wine, Sugar, and Cakes, to Sir John Savage, Knt.	0	5	0
	Clods, 19 loads, to make Butts at the Wakes, at the Bearward's Green	0	4	0
	To the Bearward	0	5	0
	Spent on Sir Wm. Brereton, and on Mr. Brereton, and Sister	0	10	0
	Spent on Sir J Savage, and on the Lord Keeper	0	8	7
	Ten quarts of Wine for the Gentlemen at the Great Cockfight	0	6	0
	And upon a Preacher 6s. 8d. more on Sugar 1s. 8d	0	8	4
	Dressing the School at the Cockfight 4d. Clods for the Cockpit 5s. 10d.	0	6	2
	Cash gave to Counsellor Molesworth, for his opinion about keeping the Water on the Common, by reason of Somerford Mills, and the Intack.	0	10	0
	For horse hire, to go to London in the cause of the Lord of Somerford	2	6	8
	Mr. Mayor, and Mr. Smith, when they went to Croxon to Mrs. Oldfield, at the same	0	1	1
	Mr. Mayor, and Richard Green's expenses, four days and nights in London, 31s. 6d. Horses and Ostler 23s. 7d.	2	15	1
	Mr. Bragreve, Her Majesty's Attorney, 20s. to his man, Mr. Wardle, for his pains in procuring the Privy Seal against Mr. Oldfield and wife, 3s. 4d. Privy Seal 11s. To Mr. Ockerson, our Attorney, 3s. 4d. Box to put the Privy Seal in, 3d	1	17	11
	Richard Green's expenses coming home again 15s. 4d. Shoeing a Gelding 6d	0	15	10
	Mr. Davenport, our Counsel in the cause, his Fee and Writing the Information, and a pottle of Burned Wine (2 quarts) 2s.	1	2	0
	Two quarts of Wine, and one of Burned Sack, and Cakes, bestowed on the Worshipful Mr. Warburton of Arley	0	3	0
	Spent in Wine, Cakes, and Sugar, on Sir John Savage	0	6	8
	The same on Mr. Brereton, Liversage, Davenport, and others	0	3	0
	Expenses at repairing the Cockpit, in Clods, Straw, and Windings	0	7	0
	Wine to Mr. John Brereton, at the Great Cockfight	0	3	0
	Wine to Sir John Savage, and a Gentleman, on the first day of the Cocking	0	2	4
	More to him and Mr. Wilbraham 6s. 8d.; More on Wensday, two pottles of Wine, ½lb. Sugar, Prunes, Apples, and Beer 5s. 10d.	0	12	6
	More to him and Brian's daughter, two pottles of white wine	0	2	0
1602	Bestowed on Sir Wm. Brereton, Knt. and Mr. Warburton, and Egerton, at the Great Bear Bait, in Wine, Sack, Spice, Figs, Almonds, and Beer	0	11	10
	To Mr. Ireland, the Preacher, one quarter's wage,	0	6	8
1603	To Sir Wm. Brereton, and Mr. Mainwaring, when they proclaimed the King (James), March 24,	0	4	4
	To the Queen's players 13s. 4d.; Repairing the Cockpit, 1s. 10d.; the great Cock Match was fought on April 6,	0	15	2
	The Profits of the Mill, one year, £65. 8s. 1d.; the Miller's share is one-sixth heap of the Corn and Malt	65	8	1
	Rent paid to the Crown for the Land Mills	0	19	7
1607	To the Rush-bearers, Wine, Ale, and Cakes	0	6	0
	To Mr. Wardle, the Preacher of Bosley, for his Sermon on the 6th September, by the consent of the Overseer	0	5	0
	Paid one year's Interest for £20. to Mr. Hawarth 40s.	2	0	0
	Clear profits of the Mill £101. 8s. 5½d. They relieved the Poor at a great expense, and treated the Preacher in Wine and Sugar, and gave to one of them 2s.	0	2	0
1609	Gave to four Ringers on the King's Holyday, (suppose Nov. 5.)	0	2	0
	For the Ox Money for the King's Provision, the same paid each year	0	7	10
	Paid to the Curate and Schoolmaster his quarterage	4	0	0
	Bought a Service Book, cost 5s,	0	5	0

have confirmed, for us and our heirs, to our free Burgesses of Congleton, that the said Town may be a free Borough, and that the Burgesses of the same Borough may have at their pleasure for ever, a Guild-Merchant, with all liberties and free customs to such a Guild appertaining. They also may have Household and Haybold, and Common of Pasture, for all the Beasts and Cattle every where within our Territory of Congleton, with unlimited fuel, without the deliverance of any one on our part when they shall need; as of Turves and Peats, to be digged, dried, and taken any where in the Turbury of Congleton. And that they shall be quit of Pannage, how many Hogs soever they shall have within the bounds of Congleton. And that by virtue

		£.	s.	d.
1610	Gave to the Players and Bearward, at the Wake, August 20	0	15	0
	Paid Henry Kent the Expenses of a New Charter	26	13	4
	Paid Mr. Halliday £20. and Interest 30s. for a debt due when when Mr. Edw. Drakefoot pawned the Town's Lands	21	10	0
1611	To Thomas Green, the Bearward	0	6	8
	Mr. Carter, his wage for Church and School, at 5 marks a quarter	2	9	0
	Bearward and Bullward, gave to them at the Wakes	0	15	0
1613	Gave to Mr. Hardern to fetch Shelmadine and his Bears 1s. 3d. when the Great Cockfighting was at Whitsuntide, and he refused to come, and Brack the Bearward and his Bears came, gave to him 6s. 8d.	0	7	11
	Spent on Mr. Orian, Marden, Liversage, Oldfield, and their Wives, Wine	0	8	4
	Fetching the Bears at the Wakes, 3s. 6d. ditto two more Bears 1s. Bearward 15s.	0	19	6
	Paid John Wardle, for saying Service in the Chapel three weeks	0	13	4
	Paid 1lb. Candles used in the Chapel on Christmas Day in the Morning, as it was customary to have 6 o'clock Prayers then	0	0	4
	A gratuity to His Majesty 50s.	2	10	0
	Thorley, the Curate, his quarter's Wage 3l. to the Town Clerk 6s. 8d. his quarter's wage	3	6	8
1616	Three gallons of Claret Wine, at the Grand Cock Fight	0	9	0
	To the Warden Master 3s. 4d.; to the Bearward 8s; King's Players 10s.	1	1	4
	The Bells were hung in Leather Thongs (Quere: how were they rung?)			
	Wine to Lord V. Brian 8s. and Beer, Bread, and Fruit, to Lady Brian 6s.	0	14	0
	Claret Wine bestowed on Sir John Savage	0	17	10
	Ordered, that a Bushel of Malt be Brewed against his next coming.			
	Wine, six quarts, for the Communion Service, 3s.; Bread 6d.	0	3	6
	This was the first for that purpose.			
	Mr. Caps, the Curate, his quarter's wage (he was the first that had orders)	7	10	0
	A Prayer Book, and Statute Book, to be read in the Chapel	0	4	0
	The Clerk three quires of Paper to make a Book of Orders	0	1	0
	Ox Money is still paid 13s. 4d.; King's Provision 2l. 0s. 0d	2	13	4
1617	Gave to Lady Savage a Purse 10s. and Money in the same 4l. 19s.	5	9	0
1618	There was in this Mayoralty only 78 Inhabitants in the Town, and Lordship, called over in the Hall, Sept. 28.			
1621	Gave, with the Overseers' consent, to the Prince's Players 20s.; the King's Players 28s. 4d.; Lady Elizabeth's Players 10s.	2	18	4

So is continued until 1700 in this manner.

ADDENDA TO A FORMER ACCOUNT.

1622 About this time arose the saying of Congleton selling the Word of God to buy a Bear.

Thus: there being a new Bible wanted, for the use of the Chapel, and as they were not able at that time to purchase one, they had laid some money by, for the purpose. In the mean time the Town Bear died, and the said money was given to the Bearward to buy another; and the Minister was obliged to make a further shift, and use the old one a little longer, until they could purchase one. Some say they gave to him the money thence arising at the sale of the Old Bible laid by, having bought a new one.

ACCOUNT OF THE PLAGUE IN 1648.

"Watch and Ward against the infection or sickness said to be at Newcastle and Namptwich.

"The Infection in Congleton appeared at one Laplove's House, which was warded night and day at 1s. each.

"Dec. 18, 1641.—The dead Corps was covered with a cover and tied with incle, and was carried on a ladder to be buried. His wife and others dye. Burial fees paid to Henry Thursley and F. Stubbs 8s.

Dec 20. It is in Moody-street, bought a pott and piggin, cost 5d. to carry drink to the infected. Morrison procured Berrison to watch and ward night and day, at the houses and cabins shut up.

Dec. 28. It is at Croslidge; Little Bess attends the infected.—

	£.	s.	d.
Paid in part for coffins to bury the dead of the plague	£0	10	0
Mody-street all them per day	0	3	5
Croslidge	0	2	1
Paid Francis Stubbs, the Burier, one Week	0	7	0

of a Charter of grant and confirmation of the liberties of our Boroughs, which we have from our Sovereign Lord the King, they are acquitted for ever throughout all places in Cheshire, as well by land as by water, under the defence and protection of us and our heirs, with all their Merchandises from Toll, Stallage, Passage, Pavage, Pontage, Lastage, and Murage; and from all other impeachments which touch Merchandises, except reasonable amends, if they commit trespass. And that they may not be impleaded nor adjudged out of their own proper Borough, of any Plea which sounds as a transgression committed within the limits of the said Town. And if any of them in our mercy shall fall by default, it may not exceed twelvepence; and after judgment a reasonable amercement according to the quantity of the offence. And that they shall grind their grist at our Mill of Congleton, at the twentieth grain, while the Mill shall be sufficient. And that our Burgesses aforesaid may choose for themselves by themselves, a Mayor and Catchpole, and Aletaster; and shall present them at the appearance of our great Court there, upon Tuesday next after the feast of St. Michael; and our Bailiffs shall take their Oath for their faithful service to the Lord and Commonalty — Also we grant for us, our heirs, and assigns, that the aforesaid Burgesses, their heirs, and assigns, may have their Burgages, and Lands pertaining to their Burgages, and also the Lands which within the aforesaid Lordship may reasonably be approved or rented, by Oath of the aforesaid Burgesses, without hurt of their liberty, or their Common aforesaid; and hold them peaceably and quietly for ever; to wit, every Burgage, sixpence yearly, and for every acre of Land, twelvepence, at the accustomed rent days. And that they make to our Court three appearances yearly at certain days. Yet a Writ of Right issuing in the said Court, they shall do suit, from fortnight to fortnight, for all other manner of services and demands. And that their Burgages and Lands aforesaid, they may lawfully sell, give, mortgage, or alienate as they please, except to religious persons. And that if the Bailiffs of the Town shall take any Felon, the Felony being known, they may lawfully behead him, and the Felony being unknown, they shall hold him (if they will) in the Stocks for three days, and afterwards send him to our Castle of Halton, with the Chattels found with him, saving to them the Pelf which belongs to the Serjeants. And we Henry, and our heirs, all the aforesaid Liberties, Burgages, Lands, and Tenements, with all their Appurtenances and Free Usages of the said Town, to the aforesaid Burgesses, their heirs and assigns, against all people, will warrant, acquit, and for ever defend. In witness whereof, to this present Charter our Seal we have put, these being witnesses; John Deyville, William le Vavasour, Robert of Stockport, Geoffrey of Chedle, Knts. Richard of Rode, Graham of Tideby, Bertram of Saxeby, Vincent of Wombivelle, Gervase a Clergyman, and others."

	£.	s.	d.
To Henry Bransward and Son, for 3 days in burying	0	1	6
Thurdley the burier dead: John Stubbs hired at 7s per week, to bury, and continue.			
The town send to the Justices of the County, and a Letter into Staffordshire, to them for relief of the poor in the Plague.			
Paid to Mr. Brook, the Physician, for his advice at the Plague	0	1	0
Paid to Mr. Langley for a Sermon on the Day of Humiliation	0	10	0
Paid to Thursley's widow his dues for burying the dead	1	17	8
For seventeen quarts of wine for the Sacrament	0	11	4
Bread	0	0	6
Collected	0	6	2
Paid to Little Bess for Wormwood, Soap, Candles, and Pitch, for Moody-street	0	6	9
Paid to Newcomb, for Reading Prayers			

	£.	s.	d.
Paid for a Cart, Saddle and Thrill	0	10	0
Wheels, and Axletree to carry the Dead to their Graves	0	9	0
Money collected for the Sick, and paid by the Constables in the neighbouring Townships, and given to private persons, and borrowed by the Town up to the 19th of July, 1642, amounts to	83	0	0
Paid to a Man for killing Newton's Cat, when his son died, for fear of infection	0	0	4

All the clothes of the infected were boiled in water, and pitch, and frankinscence burned in the cabins, for fear of infection. The plague was first brought to North Rode Hall, in a box of clothes sent from London, from an infected person there. Those who opened the box, at Rode Hall died, and the whole county became infected. Few persons came to the Town, grass grew in the streets, and all intercourse ceased. Money when taken was put into water; and letters were held to the fire before opened, and taken at arms' length from the person who delivered them.

Like the Charter, granted by Hen VII. to the City of Chester, this appears to be rather one of confirmation than creation, inasmuch as the grantees are therein described as "free burgesses." Further confirmations and additions to the privileges of the town took place in the reigns of Henry VIII. and Elizabeth, by which the inhabitants were exempted from attendance on the County Courts. The Corporation consists of a Mayor, eight Aldermen, and sixteen Capital Burgesses; two of the Aldermen being Justices, have the same jurisdiction as the County Magistrates in the Borough, holding general Sessions of the Peace, the Mayor presiding. These authorities are claimed under a Charter granted by James I. in 1624-5. The present High Steward of the Borough, elected by the Corporation, is Randle Wilbraham, Esq. of Rode, who holds a Court Leet; his Deputy is Mr. John Lockett, solicitor.

In 1637, the celebrated President Bradshaw served the office of Mayor of Congleton, and he was subsequently made High Steward, as appears from a Resolution of the Body, of Jan. 21, 1655-6: "That John Bradshaw, Esq. of this Borough, learned in the law, be continued High Steward of, and Council for, this Borough, as formerly, and be paid the same salary, quarterly for counsel, as heretofore hath been paid, and that he be acquainted herewith."

The *Guild Hall* of Congleton was built in 1805, and contains a place of confinement for debtors, and two arched cells for felons: the market people assemble under the Piazza. There was an ancient Chapel near the Bridge, subsequently used as a Work-house; it is now taken down, and a House of Industry on a large scale, erected on Congleton Moss.

In the 15th century, in consequence of the injury which the town had sustained from inundations, a petition was presented to Henry VI. and in 1451, the Corporation had the Royal permission to turn the course of the River Dane, and remove the King's Mills, which were at the same time granted to the Corporation in fee farm.

In 1603, and 1641, the town suffered dreadfully from the plague; of which, and some local occurrences, several particulars are given in the preceding notes.

The manor was formerly parcel of the Barony of Halton, and passed with that Barony to the Plantagenets, by marriage of the Earl of Lancaster with the wealthy heiress of Henry Lacy Earl of Lincoln, Constable of Chester; it thus became vested in the Crown, and was annexed to the Duchy of Lancaster. Charles I. granted it in fee-farm to Ditchfield and others,* and subsequently it was vested in a family named Toxteth, from whom it passed with successive female heirs to the Grahams, and Rawdons.

In 1745, Peter Shackerley, Esq. purchased it from Sir John Rawdon, and it has descended with Somerford Radnor, to the present Lord, Charles Watkin John Shackerley, Esq. whose rights were recognised by an Act of Parliament, in 1795, on the inclosing of the wastes.†

There were formerly two Chapels in Congleton, dependent on the Mother Church; the lower one we have before mentioned. They were both in existence in 1450, but the latter was disused above a century ago, and is described by Bishop Gastrel, as having then (1724) been put into repair. There is an entry in the Corporation books for the expenditure of "Sack and Claret for the Lord Brereton, when Brereton bells were cast in the Old Chapel in 1633."

The New CHAPEL OR CHURCH, was rebuilt, and enlarged in 1740, but the tower was not removed till 1786, previous to which the Church was higher than it. It is a neat building of brick, with a square tower, containing a clock, and a ring of six fine-toned bells. The pews are of oak, and the Chancel is decorated with neat paintings of St. Peter and St. Paul. Bishop Gastrel says, "The right of electing or nominating a Curate to this Chapel was, with the advice of the Chancellors of London, York, and Chester, upon a case stated, adjudged by the Bishop to be in the Corporation, anno 1698; after which Mr. Malbon, elected by the Corporation, was nominated by Mr Hutchinson, rector of Astbury, who was presented to that living by Sir Andrew Hacket. In 1722, on Malbon's death, the dispute revived between the Rector and the Corporation; but the Bishop nominated by lapse."—The Corporation at this time claim the right.

* Lysons.

† The Corporation possess one of those ancient instruments of punishment for a scolding woman, called A BRIDLE; a similar instrument is called *the branks* at Newcastle-on-Tyne.

CHESHIRE

The monuments are very few. There are memorials of the Smiths, Sydebothams, Starkeys, Alsagers, &c.— The latter family became extinct in the male line in 1768, on the death of John Alsager, Esq. and his sisters who survived him, all died unmarried, previously founding the Chapel of Alsager, in the adjoining parish of Barthomley. In the south aisle, on a marble tablet is inscribed—

Here lieth interred the body of Samuel Pattison,* late of London, merchant; a person of unspotted integrity, of exemplary virtue, and endowed with every amiable quality that can adorn human nature, therefore universally regretted by his family and his friends. He resided during a year before his death, in this town, as Director of the Silk Mills, where by his great abilities, and unwearied application, he rendered the most important services; and enjoyed the satisfaction of living to see all the works completed, and the manufacture brought to perfection. Obiit 27 May, 1756, æt. 30.

There is a *School*, erected in the year 1814, free to the Children of all Burgesses and Freemen, who are inhabitants. The Master is nominated by the Corporation, and has a house, garden, and a small close of land, an old stipend of £16. and the interest of other benefactions,† amounting in the whole to upwards of £20 per ann.

As there are few persons in the County but what have heard of the story of the good people of Congleton selling their Church Bible to *buy a Bear*, the following version of it is given by the author of an 8vo. History of Macclesfield, &c. 1817:—

"The predilection of the inhabitants of Congleton in the seventeenth century for the elegant divertisement of Bear-baiting, is proved from their own records. In this respect, however, they were more censurable than the rest of their countrymen, to whom the savage exhibition of dogs tearing a bull to pieces, or one well lacerating another, afforded the highest gratification. Peculiar circumstances, indeed, seem to prove that the Burgesses of Congleton preferred Bruin to their Priest, for it is recorded that in 1621, they sold their Bible to buy a Bear; which has since been used as a stigma of contempt by the malignant, but at which the present inhabitants of Congleton have the good sense to laugh, and even they themselves facetiously call their Borough, 'Bear Town' There are two accounts given of this curious transaction, the first of which, and indeed the most probable is, that there being a New Bible wanted for the use of the Chapel, and the Corporation was not able to purchase one, though they had laid up part of the price. Meanwhile, the town-bear died, and the *Bearward* not having money sufficient to purchase another, he applied to the Corporation for assistance, who after mature deliberation thought it expedient to take the money laid by for the purchase of a Bible, and give it to the Bearward to buy a Bear. The other tradition, which bears very hard indeed upon the morality of the good Burgesses of Congleton, roundly asserts, that they actually sold their Bible, and gave the price of it to the Bearward to purchase another *Ursa Major!*"

HISTORY

BUGLAWTON

Is not mentioned in Domesday; but it certainly became the seat of the Touchetts, soon after the Conquest, at which period their founder Orme *the Harper*, had considerable estates in this part of the county,‡ and his descendants continued here many generations. Sir Robert Touchet, Knt was one of the *barons* who, temp. Edward II. met at Sherborne, and swore to "stand by each other," until they had amended the state of the realm; but he afterwards submitted to the King. Sir John Touchet, was slain in an engagement with the Spanish fleet off Rochelle, in the 44th Edw. III.— Another Sir John Touchet assumed the title of Lord Audley, in the 4th of Henry IV. in consequence of his marriage with the sister and coheiress of Nicholas Lord Audley. James Lord Audley commanded the Lancastrian troops at the fight on Blore-heath, 38th Hen. VI. where he was killed: his son John Lord Audley, was Lord High Treasurer of Ireland. James, the next Lord, was beheaded on Tower Hill, having been found amongst those engaged in the battle of Blackheath, in 1497. His son James, was restored to his rank and property, and probably as a boon to the rapacity of the King, surrendered Buglawton to Henry VIII. in 1535.

* He was partner with Mr. John Clayton, who erected the first Silk Mill in Macclesfield, abou 1752.

† The interest of £20. per ann. was left by Mr. Hulme, in 1736.

‡ The derivation of the name of Touchet, says Sir P. Leycester, in his MSS. is from *Citharista*, or *Touch-it*.

Thirty years afterwards, the manor was vested in the Bagnalls; and in 1596, Sir Henry Bagnall sold it to Sir Randle Mainwaring, from whom it was purchased by John Stafford, Esq. of Macclesfield, and again from him by Samuel Egerton, Esq. of Tatton. It is now the property of Wilbraham Egerton, Esq. M. P. who claims an heriot of the best beast, on the death of the owner.

Beglawton Hall, is severed from the manor, and was purchased from the Bullocks in the year 1807, by R. Keymer, Esq.

In this township is a spring containing sulphur, a small quantity of Epsom salts, and calcareous earth, which has been found serviceable in scorbutic cases.

A ruinous farm house called *Cronley*, formerly gave name to a family which became extinct temp. John.

MORETON-CUM-ALCUMLOW,

Or *Great Moreton*, at the time of the Survey, is supposed to have been waste, as it is not noticed there — Mr. Ormerod has very little doubt but what it formed parcel of the Kinderton Barony; and from an Inq. p. m. temp. Jac. I. it was found to be held from the Barony, by the render of two shillings. It was possessed by a family which took the local name, and from whom it passed in marriage with a female heir to the Bellots, about the middle of the 14th century. Sir Thomas Bellot, the last Baronet of the family, sold Great Moreton, to Edw. Powis, Esq. of Staffordshire, whose son Thomas Jelph Powis, Esq. sold it to the late Holland Ackers, Esq. of Manchester. It is now vested in James Ackers, Esq. his brother, and Geo. Ackers, Esq. his son, for their lives, with remainder to the said George Ackers, Esq. and his issue

The Barons of Kinderton claim the right of having the Constables sworn in their Court; no Court is now held for the manor.

Great Moreton *Hall* is a large ancient building of timber and plaister. In front of the house were the steps of an old Cross, removed about 1806.

The hamlet of ALCUMLOW is attached to this township, and is held by the same title as Astbury, by the proprietor, Sir J. G Egerton, Bart.

ODD RODE,

Or *Little Moreton-cum-Rode*, are noticed as two manors in the Survey, and were subsequently granted to Hugh de Mara, and Wm. Fitz Nigel.. They are described in Domesday, as having inclosures for taking wild deer, and an aery for hawks. The present divisions of the township are distinguished by the names of *Little Moreton* and *Rode*. A branch of the Grahams of Lostock, settled in LITTLE MORETON certainly early in the 13th century, the third of whom assumed the name of Moreton, and his descendants in the male line, continued till the death of Sir W. Moreton, in 1763, when his nephew, the Rev. Richard Taylor, took the local name, and was father to the present proprietor, the Rev. Wm. Moreton, of Westenham, in Kent.

In the 12th Hen. VIII. Sir Wm. Brereton, made an award between Mr. Wm Moreton, and Mr. Thomas Rode, of Rode, in a dispute *which should sit highest in the churche, and foremost goo in procession:* when he very judiciously awarded between these two sticklers for *pre-eminence*, "That whyther of the said gentylmen may dispende in landes by title of enheritaunce 10 marks or above more than the other, that he shall have the pre-eminence in sitting in the Churche, and in gooing in procession, with all other lyke causes in that beha'f."

The *Hall* is a large old building, with a moated site, the entrance to which is from the north side, over a bridge. The Hall was built in 1559, and is a very fine specimen of the timber mansions of the time. There is a fine gallery here, 68 feet long by 12 feet, lighted by a range of bay windows. There is a figure of Fortune over the window at the west end, with the motto *qui modo scandit, corruet statim.* On the east side is a small Chapel, the east window containing some scriptural texts in old English. The House is occupied by a farmer, but considerable attention is paid to its preservation.

RODE.—A family which bore the local name, were settled here before the reign of John, and from their descendant Randle Rode, Esq. Roger Wilbraham, of Townsend, purchased, in 1669, his moiety of Rode; it is now the property of Randle Wilbraham, Esq. whose grandfather built the present *Hall*, which has been greatly improved by the present proprietor.

SMALLWOOD

Is about three miles S. E. from Sandbach, and is not noticed in the Survey. Sir Ralph Mainwaring gave

CHESHIRE

* Smelewde.

it* in marriage with his daughter Bertrea, to Henry de Aldithley, and it continued vested in the Audleys, till shortly after the 10th of the reign of Edward III. soon after which it passed to the Hawkstones; and about the year 1400, it came by marriage to a branch of the Egertons, and subsequently was possessed by the Wilbrahams and the Willoughbys.

In the 22d James I. Sir F. Willoughby† passed the manor and twenty-four messuages to Thos. Hood, for £1000—The further descent of the manor is similar to that of Moreton; and it is now vested in George and James Ackers, Esqs. for their lives, with the same remainder as noticed in Moreton. Some years have elapsed since a Court has been held.

In this township is *Overton Hall*, belonging to the Masters and Fellows of Caius College, Cambridge, and now occupied as a farm-house.

SOMERFORD-CUM-RADNOR.

A family assuming the local name, settled here at a very early period, continuing till the reign of Elizabeth, when it terminated in a female, who brought it in marriage to a branch of the Oldfields, of Bradwell. In the first year of the 18th century, the manor was purchased from them by the Shackerleys, of Holme, whose representative on the female side, Charles Watkin John Shackerley, Esq is the present proprietor.

The *Hall* is a fine building, principally built in the first year of the present century, commanding some delightful scenery, with the Dane running through the grounds.

Of the original boundary of the hamlet of RADNOR, little can be now said with certainty: Dr. Williamson states, that temp. Henry III Henry de Blakenhall remitted to William de Van,‡ for six marks of silver in hand, all the right in the Vill for eight barbed arrows yearly rent. It subsequently passed from the family of Venables, to the Wilbrahams, who held it till about 1620, when Sir Richard Wilbraham sold the manor (?) for £900 to Philip Oldfield, Esq. The landed interests of Somerford and Radnor, are now united, and Mr. Shackerley holds a Court Baron for them, although Mr. Starkie, of Wrenbury, claims a manerial right, and has a game deputation.

HISTORY.

DAVENPORT

Is about five miles N. W. W. from Congleton, and is noticed in Domesday as being amongst the estates of the Venables' family. It was soon after granted to Orme, the ancestor of the Davenports, and he assumed the local name. Richard Davenport the *second* from Orme, had a grant of the Master Foresterships of the Forests of Leeke and Macclesfield; Thomas the *third*, and Richard the *fourth*, was exempted from suit, &c. to the County Court of Chester, by Randle Blundeville; Vivian the *fifth* had a grant of the Magisterial Serjeancy of Macclesfield Hundred, thus placing in his power and at his disposal, the lives of the Earl's subjects without any appeal whatever. The allusive crest of the Davenports (on a wreath, a felon's head couped proper, haltered, or) began to be worn about his time on the helmets of the Master Serjeants, terrifying the numerous hordes of banditti which then infested those dreary tracts.|| Roger Davenport, *sixth*; Sir Thomas, Knt. the *seventh*, whose second son was founder of the Davenports of Weltrough; Sir John *eighth*, who founded a chantry in Marton Chapel: he was distinguished "by his great statture and military achievements;" Sir Ralph, the *ninth*, who bound himself to Richard II. to serve the King with three archers well mounted and armed, to make war for a year in parts beyond the seas "where God pleased;" Ralph the *tenth*; he joined the Percies against Henry IV. but obtained indemnity; John *eleventh*; John *twelfth*; Ralph *thirteenth*; John *fourteenth*; John *fifteenth*; John *sixteenth*; John *seventeenth*.

In 1671, John Davenport, the *twentieth* in male descent from Orme, died, and the manor passed in marriage with the eldest daughter, and co-heiress, to Robt. Davies, Esq. of Manley. Sir Matthew Deane, Bart. who married the heiress of Davies, sold Davenport about 1740, to Richard Davenport, Esq. of Calveley, representative of the eldest existing male line of the ancient proprietors, who dying without issue male in 1771, it

† The first proprietor of this family was Sir Hugh Willoughby, who with his crew was frozen to death in 1553.

‡ Mr. Ormerod conjectures this to to be an abbreviation of Venables.

|| There are several curious documents in the possession of the present head of the family, specifying the names of the robbers taken and executed, with the rewards, viz. for a Master Robber 2s. *and a salmon*; for the others twelvepence each.

passed under his will to his grand-daughter Phœbe,* wife of Eusebius Horton, of Catton, in the county of Derby, and it is now vested in their eldest daughter Anne.

HULME WALFIELD

Is about two miles N. W. from Congleton, and is the only township of Astbury parish north of the Dane, belonging to the hundred of Northwich. As it is not noticed in the Survey, it is supposed to have been at that period, either waste, or included in what occurs under the head of Congleton. It takes its name from *Hulme* and *Walfield*, divided into many shares before the 35th Edward III. and so late as Charles I. was possessed in unequal portions by the Traffords, the Honfords, the Massies, and the Leversages.

The acreage of the township is about one thousand statute, nearly one half of which is the property of John Ford, Esq. of Abbeyfield, in whom the *Hall* is vested, and who claims manerial rights. Sir T. S. M. Stanley has about 160 acres here; Mrs. Heywood about 300 acres; Mr. Starkey, of Wrenbury, 120 acres, and a claim of maneriel rights, giving a game deputation; the residue is the property of Lady Warburton, who resides in a handsome mansion upon it.

PARISH OF SWETTENHAM,

CONTAINS ONLY TWO TOWNSHIPS,

SWETTENHAM AND KERMINCHAM.

SWETTENHAM is nearly four miles N. W. from Congleton, and about seven E. from Middlewich. It is not noticed in Domesday, and is conjectured, from being subsequently a dependency of Weverham, to have been retained by the Earl.

Peter de Swettenham, the first lord who assumed the local name, held the manor, temp. Henry III. and he and his immediate successors did homage to the Abbot of Vale Royal, to whom the paramount royalty was granted; part of the services attached to the homage, was to find forty soldiers for the Welsh wars.—Joan the daughter and heiress of Thomas de Swettenham, brought it to the Davenports of Davenport, in the 16th century.

In 1671, John Davenport, Esq. of Davenport, sold the manor and advowson to Thomas Swettenham, the representative of the original proprietors, and his successors continued here till 1780, when the manor and advowson passed to the widow of Thomas, the last male descendant, with remainder to a Mrs. Heys, and on their death to John Eaton, Esq. a distant relation, who assumed the name, and was father of the present proprietor, Millington Eaton Swettenham, Esq.

The dedication of the CHURCH is unknown: it is of brick, with side aisles, and a tower, forming a prominent object in the adjacent views. There are memorials here of the Sneyds, Mainwarings, &c. The Registers commence in 1570; and the present Rector is the Rev. Thomas Swettenham Eaton Swettenham, presented Sept. 6, 1814.

KERMINCHAM,

Or *Carincham*, is about five miles and a half N. W. from Congleton. It appears from the Survey, it was included in the territorial possessions of the Barons of Montalt, from whom it was afterwards held by the Swettenhams, and subsequently by the Mainwarings, a younger branch of the Peover family, whose personal property in it became extinct in 1797, on the death of Sir H. Mainwaring, of Peover, when the manor devolved to John Uniacke, son of Frances, eldest daughter of Roger Mainwaring, who made a settlement, and to the sisters of Frances, viz. Mary wife of Richard Jones, and Catherine wife of Thomas Lowfield. The latter still retains her share, and has since purchased that of Mr. Uniacke. Mrs. Jones devised her share to Catherine, her niece, wife of J. R. Parker, Esq. of

CHESHIRE

Youghall, in Ireland, whose son Roger Parker, has taken the name of Mainwaring.

The *Hall* is in a very neglected state, situated in a small park.

Kermincham Lodge is a handsome modern building, the occasional residence of the Proprietor.

Rowley, an estate in this township, was, temp. Henry VIII. possessed by a family of that name, who sold their property here to Randle Mainwaring.

The Rowleys, Viscounts Longford, are descendants of the above.

HISTORY

THE PARISH OF BRERETON,

CONTAINS ONLY THE TOWNSHIP OF

BRERETON-cum-SMETHWICK.

BRERETON-cum-SMETHWICK

Is about six miles E. of Middlewich, and three miles N. of Sandbach. It is noticed in the Survey as being among the territorial possessions of Gilbert de Venables, Baron of Kinderton. A family which assumed the local name, had a grant of it, as early as the reign of Wm. Rufus. It is noticed in Hollinshead's Chronicle, that Sir Wm. Brereton, 13th in descent from the founder of the family, was busily employed in the Irish Wars; and in 1534, he with his son John Brereton, was inshored at Howth, with 250 soldiers well appointed. He was sent the same year to summon Maynooth Castle, a strong fortification, which he subsequently took by storm, running up to the "highest turret of the Castle, and advancing his standard on the top thereof, notifienge to the Deputie, that the fort was woone." The same author further observes, that some time after this, travelling to Limerick, to bring in the Earl of Desmond, he died on his journey, and was buried in the College there.

In 1624, Sir Wm. Brereton was created Lord Brereton, of Leighlin, in Ireland, on the death of Francis Lord Brereton. In 1722, the male line of the family became extinct, and the manor passed by Lord Brereton's will to his sisters Jane and Elizabeth; the whole subsequently becoming vested in Elizabeth, was left by her to Sir Charles Holte, Bart. of Aston, in the county of Warwick, her sister's son. Heneage Legge, Esq. of Aston, whose aunt was the first wife of Sir Lister Holte, Bart. then became the proprietor.

In 1817, an Act of Parliament was passed for dismembering the estates, in order to satisfy the claims of certain mortgagees; and although the estate has several times been advertised for Sale, it has not yet obtained a purchaser.

Brereton Hall was the residence of A. Bracebridge, Esq. by marriage with the daughter of Sir C. Holte, Bt.

The *Hall* of Brereton was erected by Sir William Brereton, temp. Elizabeth. It is a noble mansion of brick, and has the date 1577 in several of the windows.

The vignette in the preceding page, affords a pretty accurate sketch of its style.*

The first stone of this house, was, it is said, laid by Queen Elizabeth, who subsequently visited its hospitable owner. The front is to the west, the wings terminating in gables; the centre is ornamented with two turrets, with bay windows. The door way has the date 1586. The dining room is a noble apartment.—In the windows and round the top of the staircase, are the arms of the principal gentry of the county, together with other devices in stained glass. Some windows of painted glass, representing the Saxon and Norman Earls of Chester, were removed by Sir Lister Holte to Aston Hall, in Warwickshire: but in 1817, they were taken to Liverpool for the convenience of sale, and there disposed of.†

Webb describes the Hall, as "The stately House of Brereton;" and Camden says, that Sir Wm. Brereton had of late "added very much credit and honor to the place, by a magnificent and sumptuous house that he had there built."

There were several fine paintings in the Hall, one of them a beautiful portrait of Elizabeth. The situation of the building is on a gentle eminence, with a small lake in front, which from neglect is become stagnant. The timber which formerly graced the Park, has been cut down, and the whole presents a melancholy scene of comparative desolation. Near it is *Bag Mere*, in which according to the tradition of the neighbourhood, trunks of trees were observed to rise, and float for several days, previously to the death of an heir of the Breretons.—This circumstance was attested to Camden by several creditable persons; and is apparently believed by him, and ascribed to unknown but preternatural causes; tho' there appears no occasion to resort to supernatural agency to account for the rising of the trees; and if any coincidence of time, as the report suggests, was observed between their swimming on the surface, and the decease of an heir of the Breretons, such a coincidence could only have been accidental.

The hamlet of SMETHWICK was given by Ralph Brereton, temp. John, to his nephew, Orme de Smethwick, and his heirs, paying yearly *twelve pence* to Brereton Chapel. Early in the eighteenth century, the hall and land were purchased from the representatives of the Smethwicks, by the ancestor of the late Edward Thornycroft, Esq. of Thornycroft, on whose decease they passed by will to his sisters for life, then passing to the Rev. Charles Mytton, Rector of Eccleston, and his issue.

The *Hall*, which is of considerable antiquity, and in a ruinated state, is occupied by a farmer.

A Court Leet and Court Baron is held at Brereton, including Smethwick.

The CHURCH is dedicated to St. Oswald; the present Rector, the Rev. Wm. Fell, LL.D. was presented July 10, 1807. Formerly dependent on Astbury, it was made parochial temp. Richard I. The advowson was sold in 1807, by order of Mr. Bracebridge's Assignees. The building is of stone, containing a nave, chancel, side aisles, and tower, with five bells. The whole in the pointed gothic style, with oaken roof, elegantly carved, and finished. The Registers commence in 1538.

In the south aisle is an elegant monument, with busts, inscribed, on tablets—

Here lieth interred the body of Wm. Smethwicke, of Smethwicke, Esq. who, mindful of his death, erected this monument for himself and his wife, pious to God, pious in good works; which William was born Oct. 1, anno D'ni 1551, and died June 16, anno D'ni 1643.

Here alsoe lieth the body of Frances Smethwicke, daughter of Sir Anthony Coleclough, Knt. married to Wm. Smethwicke, aforesaide, and lived in wedlock with him 58 years, a devout and hospitable

* Sir Wm. Brereton married Margaret daughter of Sir John Savage, of Rock Savage; and it is conjectured from the similarity of the style of building to that of the ancient Hall of Rock Savage (see plate), that they are the work of the same architect.

† The statement so prevalent at that time, that these windows formerly belonged to the Chapter House of Chester Cathedral, is too absurd to demand a formal contradiction.

matron, borne Anno Dom. 1557, in the County of Kildare, in Ireland, Novemb. 6, and died 1° of May, 1632.

Mors absorpta est in victoria.

On another tablet, below—

Mortis in hac camerâ speculare hic nobile compar,
Par ætate sua, par pietate sua;
Una fides vivis, mens una, unita jugumq;
Traxit honoratum copula lustra decem.
Vita una juncti, tumulo hic junguntur in uno,
Uni quis strueret bina sepulchra pari
Ille inopum, memor ille Dei, memor ille sepulchri,
Condidit hic, sub quo conditor ipse rogo.

Within the communion rails, on an elegant monument, a Latin inscription, to the purport—that

In ancient times the Church of Brereton was a donative Chapel in the parish of Astbury; that the ancestors of Sir William Brereton, Baron of Malpas, who erected this monument in 1618, were buried in the Church Yard, at Astbury, where their tombs still existed; but that after the Chapel of Brereton had been made parochial, the ancestors of the said Sir William Brereton, patron of the Church of Brereton, had been buried in the chancel of that Church.

PARISH OF SANDBACH,

CONTAINS THE TOWNSHIPS OF

SANDBACH, BRADWELL-cum-HOLLINS, ARCLID, WHEELOCK, HASSAL, BETCHTON.*

SANDBACH

Is about twenty-five miles from Chester, and one hundred and sixty-two from London. It is noticed in the Survey, among the estates of Bigot. Before the reign of John, a family had possession here, which assumed the local name. Richard de Sandbach was Sheriff of Cheshire, in 1230. The manor passed from the Sandbaches to the Leghs of Booths, and from them to the Radclyffes, the latter afterwards selling it to Sir Randolph Crewe, from whom it passed in marriage to the Offleys. It is now, with Crewe, and the other estates, the property of Lord Crewe, who holds a Court Leet and Baron for the manor. The Leet was granted to Sir John Radclyffe, by Elizabeth, an. reg. 21, with a market on Thursday, and two fairs,—one to be held on the Thursday and Friday before the Nativity of the Virgin, the other on the Tuesday and Wednesday in Easter week. The situation of the town is low, but it is on a dry, sandy soil, and by no means unpleasant.†

The *Hall* is built on the branch of a small stream,

* Hassal and Betchton are in Nantwich Hundred.

† SANDBACH (commonly called *Sandbitch*) standeth on a high bank upon the small river of Wheelock, and is but a little town, with a fair church built of stone; lately make a market town by Sir John Radcliff, who is Lord thereof. It hath a small market every Thursday, and yearly two fairs; that is to say, on Tuesday and Wednesday in Easter-week, and Thursday and Friday before the Nativity of our Lady. In the market-place do stand, close together, two square crosses of stone, on steps, with certain images and writings thereon engraven; which, as they say, a man cannot read, except he be holden with his head downwards; and this verse (as they hold opinion) is engraven thereon:—

In Sandbach, in the Sandy Ford,
Lieth the ninth part of Dublin's hord.
Nine to, or Nine fro,
Take me down, or else I fall.

They also affirm, that the said crosses were set up there before the birth of Christ; but that is not so, for the story of the passion is engraven thereon; but whether the said verses are written thereon, or no, I know not. Certain I am, that on Sunday morning, the 1st of November, 1561, there were three chests made of tin, or such like metal, found near the said river, but nothing in them. On the covers were certain letters, or characters, engraven, which chests were carried to the Sheriffs.—KING'S VALE ROYAL.

SANDBACH (*Sandbeach*) is very pleasantly situated on an eminence near the little river Wheelock, about four miles from Middlewich. It was made a market town in the 17th century, by its lord, Sir John Radcliffe, of Ordsall, Lancashire, whose ancestors had long possessed the manor. In the market-place are two square crosses, ornamented with various images, and a carved representation of the Crucifixion. The town was formerly famous for the goodness of its malt liquor; and worsted-yarn, and stuffs for country wear, were ma-

HISTORY.

which empties itself into the Wheelock. It is of considerable size, chiefly composed of timber and plaister, with gables and bay windows.

In the Market Place are the *Ancient Crosses*, for the restoration of which the lovers of antiquity are indebted to the indefatigable exertions of Mr. Ormerod.—The substructure, says that gentleman, consists of a platform of two steps, on which are placed two sockets, in which the crosses are fixed. At the angle of each stage of the platform, are stone posts, on which rude figures have been carved. The platform and sockets are five feet six inches in height. The present height of the greater cross is 16 feet 8 inches, and that of the smaller one 11 feet 11 inches, making the greatest present height from the ground 22 feet 2 inches.—At this period, it would be a task almost impossible to accomplish, to ascertain the cause of these magnificent relics of the skill of other days being erected; a writer, however, in a periodical work,* says, the Cross was "put up in the year 608, when Penda returned a Christian convert from Northumbria to Mercia, attended, according to Bede, by four Priests deputed to preach the Gospel through his dominions, Cedda, Adda, Betti, and Diuma.†

Abbey Field, the seat of John Ford, Esq. is within the township of Sandbach. The Fords were settled here soon after 1686, when Ellen, the widow of Wm. Ford, Esq. of Ford Green, Staffordshire, purchased an estate here, called *Hind Heath*, which has descended to the present respected proprietor. The demesne takes its name from an adjoining field, which belonged to the dissolved Abbey of Dieulacres. The house is a very neat and elegant structure, nearly the whole of which has been built by Mr. Ford, whose ancestors were at Ford Green, so early as the 12th century.

The Elworth estate, was given by Richard de Bradwall, to his son Thomas de Helleworth, temp. Edw. I. and it continued in the Ellworths till near the close of the 17th century, when it passed in marriage to the Hulses. The direct male line of the Hulses became extinct on the 13th Dec. 1790, by the death of the Rev. John Hulse, who left, by will dated in July, 1777, the whole of his estates to the University of Cambridge, for the purpose of "founding three Scholarships in St. John's College, and a prize for the best dissertation on the evidences of Christianity, and for establishing the offices of Christian Advocate, and an Annual Lecturer."‡

The *Hall* of Ellworth he devised to Thos. and Elizabeth Plant, his servants; Thomas still lives, and his son is the present occupier.

The Hill estate is the property of Thos. Twemlow, Esq. of Peatswood, Staffordshire.

Sandbach, and its immediate neighbourhood, was the scene of several skirmishes in the great rebellion.

The Church is dedicated to St. Mary; the present Rector the Rev. Richard Lowndes Salmon, A. M. presented Jan. 15, 1787. The building consists of nave, chancel, side aisles, and tower, in very good repair.—The whole is of red sand stone, and of pointed Gothic architecture. Six pointed arches on each side, divide the nave and side aisles.—It appears from the Survey, there was a Church here before the Conquest. Afer the Dissolution the impropriate Rectory of Sandbach, late belonging to John Broughton, was granted to William Tipper and Richard Cartwright; and it is now in the following shares: Lord Crewe impropriator in Sandbach; John Latham, M. D. and Wm. Chesworth, in Bradwall; George Wilbraham, Esq. in Bechton; in Hassal and Wheelock, the Rev. R. L. Salmon; and the Rev. W. W. Moreton, in Arclid. The advowson of the Vicarage is now vested in the Representatives of the late Rev. John Armistead, who bought it.—The Vicar has, with few exceptions, the Vicarial tithes of Sandbach, exclusive of the Chapelries. The curate of Holmes Chapel has a portion of both Rectorial and Vicarial

nufactured in large quantities by its inhabitants; but latterly its trade has considerably decreased.—Beauties of England.

* Catholic Magazine, vol. 1, page 308.

† Those who wish to see a detail of the circumstances connected with the restoration of the Crosses, are referred to Ormerod's Cheshire, vol. 3, p. p. 57, 58.

‡ The annual Salary of the Christian Advocate to be £70; to the Lecturer £60; to each Scholar £30; and £.50 for the Prize. Preference to be given for the Scholarships, to natives of Cheshire, and particularly to the son of the Curate of Sandbach, the Vicar or Curate of Middlewich, the Curate of Witton, or to the sons of Clergymen born in Sandbach, Middlewich, or Witton. The Bishop of Ely to be visitor of this trust.

CHESHIRE tithes in his Chapelry: those of Goostry are much divided; and, generally speaking, the impropriations in the two Chapelries belong to the family of Mainwaring of Peover, Booth of Twemlow, and Hall of Hermitage. From two estates in Sandbach township, the Rector of Brereton has corn tithes. The Registers commence in 1562.—The Church font, is of an octagonal form, ornamented with the leaves of the acanthus, and dated 1669. It bears an inscription somewhat singular, inasmuch as it may be read in the common way, or like the Hebrew, &c. from the right to the left:—

NIΨON . ANOMHMA . MH . MONAN . OΨIN.

In the nave is a marble monument, inscribed—

Sacred to the memory of Richard Jackson, Esq. of Betchton House, in this parish, who died in Sept. 1718, and Elizabeth his wife, the only daughter of Wm, Oldfield, Esq. and Letitia his wife, who died Dec. 24, 1769. Also of the Rev. Richard Jackson, D. D. Canon of York, Lichfield, and Chester, and only son of the above Richard Jackson, Esq. who died Nov. 12, 1796; and of Ann, his his wife, daughter of Dr. Richard Smallbroke, Lord Bishop of Lichfield and Coventry; who died April 6, 1785. Also of the Rev. Rd. Jackson, L. L. B. Vicar of Colwich and Longdon, in the county of Stafford, and only son of the above Richard and Ann Jackson, who died Jan 24, 1792. This monument was erected 1799.

On an adjoining monument—

Sacred to the memory of John Welles, Esq. who departed this life the 15th of May, 1803, aged 63 years. This monument is erected by his faithful and affectionate wife, who lost in him the tenderest husband. Also, to the memory of Ann and Elizabeth Welles, sisters, of exemplary piety. Ann departed this life Jan. 4, 1787, aged 90 years; Elizabeth departed this life June 21, 1787, aged 86 years.— Also, of Ann, widow of the said John Welles, who departed this life the 15th of May, 1815, aged 61 years.

On a marble monument in the chancel—

Proh dolor! lugubre hoc mortalitatis speculum, mœsta gratanter posuit parochia in memoriam viri nuper admodum reverendi Thomæ Welles, A. M. qui bonis omnibus triste sui desiderium reliquit, 2do die Januarii,

Anno { Dom. 1728
Ætat. 66
Vicariat 33.

There are other memorials of—

John Furnivall, Esq. of Betchton, one of his Majesty's Justices of the Peace for the county of Stafford; died at Maple Hayes, Aug. 29, 1806, aged 64: buried at St. Michael's, Lichfield,—of John Amson, of Leighs, Esq. died Jan. 9, 1735, aged 50,—of Wm. Hurst, of Sandbach, gent. died Jan. 14, 1724, aged 66,—of Hugh Mee, A. M. Vicar of Sandbach, died July 19, 1732, aged 29,—of Elizabeth, relict of Wm. Hurst, died April 8, 1741, aged 68,—of E. Mee, relict of Hugh Mee, died Dec. 2, 1785, aged 80,—of Anne, wife of Thos. Hulse, buried Aug. 9, 1750, aged 63,—of Thos. Hulse, buried April 19, 1753, aged 72, &c. &c. HISTORY

In the Wheelock chancel,* on a mural monument—

In memory of Edward Powys, of Wheelock, Esq. who departed this life Sept. 29, 1768, aged 59, much lamented by his acquaintance. This monument is erected by his relict Catherine Powys, and his son Thomas Jelf Powys, Esq.

On an adjoining monument—

In memoriam Thomæ Moulson de Whelocke, armigeri, qui obiit tertio die Septem', annoq' Domini 1648.

Most of the Charitable funds have been expended in the purchase of lands; one purchase has been remarkably fortunate: the discovery of a coal mine on an estate at Cobridge, Staffordshire, purchased with the parish money, amounting to about £850. per ann. which is partially laid out in the purchase of Stock. The whole is thus divided:

Sandbach	one-half,	Wheelock	1-12th,
Betchton	1-6th,	Hassal	1-12th,
Bradwall	1-9th,	Arclid	1-18th.

There is a *Free School* in Sandbach, founded in 1718, by Mr. Francis Wells. The endowment is about £25. per ann. By the directions of the founder, twenty boys were to be taught reading, writing, and arithmetic, and three of them to be educated for the University.

BRADWALL,

Or *Bradwell*, is about two miles and a half N. W. from Sandbach, and is supposed to have been waste at the time of the great Survey. It was, however, attached to the Barony of Kinderton, and was recognized as a manor dependent on the Baronial Court. A family which assumed the local name was settled here at an early period, certainly before 1287, and the site of their mansion may yet be traced in the *Hall Field*.— The manor continued vested in the Barons of Kinderton till 1807, when Lord Vernon sold it to John Latham, M. D. who five years before, had possession of Bradwall Hall Demesne. This estate had been attached to the property of the Venables', as manerial lords, and it passed from a younger branch, by co-heiresses, to the Beringtons (of Moresbarrow) the Oldfields (of Heswall); and in 1719, Wm. Oldfield, Esq. conveyed the estate (including the south aisle of Sandbach Church)†

* Screens formerly divided the chancels from the nave, &c.

† In the south aisle of the Church is a chancel or oratory attached

CHESHIRE

to Charles Ward, Esq. of Dublin; the trustees of whose son in law, John Jerris, Esq. conveyed it to the present proprietor.*

The *Hall* is a handsome building of brick, with extensive pleasure grounds.

In 1811, an Act of Parliament was obtained for inclosing the waste lands. A Court Leet and Baron is held for the Manor; but the township, as before noticed, owes service to the Courts of Kinderton.

HOLLINS is a hamlet of Bradwall.

HASSAL.†

This manor, previous to the Conquest, was in moieties, and temp. Edw. II. was divided between the families of Hassal and Wood. Subsequently it was vested solely in the Hassals, and Ralph Hassal, Esq. sold it to Wm. Leversage, Esq. of Wheelock, from whom it passed by sales to the families of Stephens, Powis, Lowndes, and Daniels, the last proprietor of this name, Walter Daniel, Esq. died in 1818, when Wm. Lowndes, Esq. purchased the remainder of a term of 500 years, granted by Richard Lowndes, Esq. in 1726.‡

There is an estate in this township which belonged successively to the families of Bostock, and Lowndes, but it has been divided between the coheiresses of the latter.

The *Hall* is the property of Mr. John Penlington, of Rode Heath, but is occupied by a farmer.§

§ Lysons.

BETCHTON

Is above two miles S. E. S. from Sandbach. It is not noticed in Domesday, but it is ascertained by an Inq. of the 16th Edw. I. to have passed with Hassal to the Audleys. A family which adopted the local name had possession of the township, and continued here several generations till the reign of Edw. III. when it was divided between the Davenports and Fittons, by marriage with the daughters of Peter Legh, of Booths, to whom the estate was passed by Matthew de Betchton. The moiety which belonged to the Davenports (say the Lysons) was acquired in marriage with the heiress of Peter Legh, to whom it was conveyed by the Betchtons, to Sir John Davenport, of Davenport, and was afterwards settled in the Henbury branch, in which it continued till the marriage of the heiress of that branch with Sir Fulke Lucy, in the 17th century. It is probable this moiety passed to the Wilbrahams, to whom the Betchtons sold the permanent royalty which had belonged to the Lords Audley. A moiety of the manerial rights of the township is vested in George Wilbraham, Esq of Delamere Lodge; the other moiety was sold by the Fittons, temp. Elizabeth, to the Egertons of Wrinehill, in trust for the freeholders. The freeholders are the present proprietors, and elect four lords, who are joint lords for life, holding a Court Leet and Baron, and dividing the quit rents: the Rev. Richard Levett, Mr. J. Wilson, Mr. Thomas Summerfield, and Mr. J. Podmore, were the lords in 1817.‖

HISTORY.

‖ Ormerod.

Betchton Hall, is occupied by a farmer,; it is built of timber and plaister, in a very pleasant situation.—In the 17th century it belonged to a branch of the Leversages, of Wheelock, from whom it subsequently passed to the Jacksons: on the death of Dr. Richard Jackson, Prebendary of Chester Cathedral, in 1796, it passed to his three nieces, daughters of Mr. William

to Bradwall Hall. There was also anciently a domestic Chapel, nearly adjoining the Hall on the north side, some walls of which were remaining 15 years ago (1819).—ORMEROD.

* George Ormerod, Esq. author of the splendid folio County History, married, in 1808, Sarah, daughter of John Latham, Esq.

† In the Hundred of Nantwich.

‡ September, 1820, the estate was offered for Sale by Auction, at the Crown Inn, in Nantwich, under an Order of Chancery, made on an appeal between Henry Watkinson Whatton (who married the daughter of W. Daniel) and others, Plaintiffs, and Geo. Daniel Spencer Daniel, and others, Defendants, when it was thus described in the printed particulars:—

"A Capital Messuage divided into Two Tenements, with all requisite and convenient Offices, Lawn, Pleasure Ground, Orchard, and a most excellent Garden walled round, and planted with choice Fruit Trees, Fish Ponds well stored with Fish, a Cottage and Gardens, and one hundred and thirteen acres two roods and one perch, more or less, of Arable, Meadow, and Pasture Land, statute measure, lying within a ring fence, the whole being Tythe Free, and the Poor Rates remarkably low, with *The Manor of Hassall*, and all Rights, Royalties, Privileges, and Immunities, incident and appertaining thereto.—The Manor is Freehold, and the remainder of the Estate is Leasehold, and held for the remainder of a term of 500 years, of which 424 years are unexpired. There are a great number of valuable Timber Trees on the Leasehold part of the estate; and although the Purchaser will not be entitled to cut down the same for sale, and therefore will not be required to pay for the same by valuation or otherwise, it is obvious that his power of preventing or enabling the Reversioner to sell the said Timber, may possibly by agreement between them be a source of considerable Emolument to a Purchaser."

Day, of Sandbach, who assumed the name of Jackson, the last of whom died in 1820, bequeathing the great bulk of her property to Mr. Richard Baxter, of Chester.

ARCLID,

Or *Arcliffe*, is about two miles E. N. E. from Sandbach, and was held from the King by the Barons of Kinderton, under whom it was held, temp. Edward I. by the Bernards; it was afterwards possessed by a family which took the local name, and subsequently by the Hassals, the Withenshaws, the Clottons, and the Mainwarings; the last of whom sold it in 1670. It is now the property of the Rev. W. M. Moreton, whose ancestor purchased it the beginning of the last century.

The *Hall*, the property of the Rev. W. M. Moreton, is occupied as a farm-house, and is in a romantic situation, not far from a small lake called *Taxmere*.

A mesne manor, noticed in the Vill. Cest. is not now used; but the paramount royalty passed with Kinderton to the Vernons, from whom it was purchased by the late Mr. Ralph Leeke, of Middlewich.

An estate in this township, formerly the property of the Lingards, is now in the possession of Thos. Twemlow, Esq. of Liverpool.

WHEELOCK

Is two miles S. S. W. from Sandbach, and is noticed in Domesday, under the name *Hoiloch*. A family bearing the local name had possession of it as early as the reign of Henry II. if not before.

In 1439, on the death of Richard de Wheelock, without heir, it passed to Thomas Worth, who married the heiress of the Wheelocks, and his daughter and heiress brought it in marriage to the Leversages. During the Great Rebellion, Wm. Leversage, of Betchton, sold the manor, to the wrongful disinheritance (as is said by Dr. Williamson) of his nephew, then a minor, to Thomas Stephens, Esq. of Lypiat, Gloucestershire, who held it till 1662; it was subsequently sold to Richard Vernon, Esq. of Middlewich, from whose trustees it was purchased by Edward Powis, Esq. of Moreton. It was purchased from the Powis's by the late Holland Ackers, Esq. of Manchester, together with the manors of Great Moreton and Smallwood, and is now the property of James Ackers, with remainder to Geo. Ackers, Esq. son of Holland Ackers, Esq. and his issue. There is no Court held for the mesne manor, and the inhabitants attend the Leet of Warmincham.

The *Hall*, an ancient mansion, is now occupied as a farm-house.

Whitehall in this township, a modern mansion, was the residence of the Rev. R. L. Salmon.

In consequence of the Grand Trunk Canal passing through the township, the population has greatly increased within the last twenty years; a great part of the village, however, on the north side of the River Wheelock, is in the township of Sandbach, and here the late Wm. Whitehead, Esq. established Salt Works, erected an Inn, and a mansion for himself, and made other great improvements: there are salt works, a brewery, a factory, and warehouses on the south side of the stream.

The brine springs in this township are plentiful, and are about sixty yards from the surface.

THE PAROCHIAL CHAPELRY OF

HOLMES CHAPEL, OR CHURCH HOLME,

CONTAINS THE TOWNSHIPS OF

HOLMES CHAPEL, COTTON, AND CRANAGE.

HOLMES CHAPEL,

Or *Hulme*, is about four miles N. E. from Middlewich, and before the reign of Edward II. was possessed by a family which took the local name, and held it under the Barony of Halton. It continued a long time the property of the Hulmes, when it passed to the Needhams of Cranage; and in 1760, the late Lord Kilmorey sold it to Thomas Bayley Hall, of Hermitage, the present proprietor.

The CHAPEL consists of nave, chancel, and side aisles, with a square tower, of red stone, terminating in battlements, and pinnacles. The nave is supported by wooden pillars; the side aisles are of brick. Two wooden tablets in the Chancel contain an account of such of the family of the Halls, and their relations by marriage, as have been buried at Holmes Chapel.

In the chancel, a memorial of Ann and Cotton Hall, infant children of Thomas Hall, of Cranage.

At the Chancel end of the south aisle, on a marble monument—

Requiescat in Pace. Thomas Hall, nescio an immortali Deo ab pietatem, an mortalibus ob humanitatem charior. Obt. 25°. M'tii 1715. Joanna prædicti conjux mœstissima, hicce etiam placide requiescat. Obt. 27° Jani. 1721-22.

In the south aisle a tablet

To the memory of Strethill Harrison, Esq. of Cranage Hall, who died April 27, 1801, ætat. 52; and of two of his daughters, who died young.

Another tablet in the same aisle

To the memory of Anna, wife of the Rev. James Eyton Mainwaring, of Ellaston, in Staffordshire, daughter of Mr. Vawdrey, of Millgate, died April 8, 1789, a°. æt. 26.

In the south aisle at the west end, on a tablet—

William Arthur Hodges, Esq. Captain in the 47th Regiment, having been twice wounded in the battle of Vittoria, fell at the storming of St. Sebastian, in Spain,

Aug. 31, anno { Domini 1813, Ætatis 26,

A tablet, in memory of—

Wm. Archer, Esq. second son of Rd. Archer, Esq. of Shrewley, co. Warwick, obiit 24 July 1787, a°. æt. 37.

The Curacy is in the gift of Vicar of Sandbach. The Registers commence in 1680.*

The Lysons say that a considerable estate in Church Holme belonging formerly to the Hulmes, passed afterwords to the Bulkeleys and Cottons.

Eardshaw, or as it is frequently pronounced *Yearnshaw*, in this township, a reputed manor, was in 1457, the property of Hugh the Page, whose ancestor temp. Edward III. was Bailiff of Drakelow. John Page, a descendant, sold Eardshaw to Sir Henry Delves, Bart. of Doddington; passing by subsequent sales to the Townsends and the Prescots, it became the property, with Drakelow, of Wm. Harper, Esq.

The *Hall* is occupied as a farm-house.

COTTON

Is about three miles N. E. from Middlewich. It is not noticed in the Survey; but Dr. Williamson says, this place had for immediate Lords the Frasers, till Adam Fraser, in 1204, pawned the whole village to Roger Lacy, Constable of Chester, for eighty marks of silver, to pay his debts with: whose son John Lacy, granted it to Gilbert de Cotton, son of Judas Kelly; ever since which the Cottons have been the lords of the place.

In the 6th year of Richard II. Robert Cotton, of Cotton, who bound himself to serve under Sir Thomas de Carington, with a horseman and three archers, in the Crusade made by the Bishop of Norwich, settled on Robert Grosvenor, and Thos. Davenport, of Betchton, all his lands, &c. in Cotton and Hulme.

In the 5th of Henry VI. Sir Thos. Grosvenor remitted the same to Thomas Cotton, of Cotton, who in the same year passed his lands here to Thos. Hassall, Vicar of Sandbach. This Vicar again settled the manor on the Cottons; and about 1653, Thomas Cotton sold it to Sir Thomas Cotton, Bart. of Connington, in Huntingdonshire.† William, 5th in descent from Sir Thomas, dying without issue male, the manor descended to his only daughter Frances, wife of Dingley Ascham, Esq. and in 1738, he sold the manor and township to Thomas Bayley, Esq. of the Inner Temple, who bequeathed the whole of his fortune to his mother Jane Bayley, and she in 1745, left the township to her son-in-law, Thomas Hall, of Hermitage, who married her daughter Elizabeth, whose son Thomas Bayley Hall, Esq. is the present proprietor, of the estate and impropriate tythes. There is no Court held for the manor.

The *Hall* is an ancient mansion of timber, occupied as a farm-house.

CRANAGE,

Or *Crannach*, is about four miles E. N. E. from Middlewich. At an early period it was vested in the Croxtons, and subsequently in a collateral line which assumed the local name. In the 49th Edw. III. Alice, daughter of William de Crannech, brought a moiety of the vill in marriage to Wm. Nedham, son of Thomas Nedham, of Nedham, co. Derb. Sir Robt. Nedham, 5th in descent, purchased the other moiety, and thus vested

* In 1723, Richard Vernon, of Middlewich, gave the interest of £200. to the Chapel, and the Halls, of Hermitage, have frequently been its benefactors. The endowment exceeds £80. per ann. In 1707, Thomas Hall, Esq. founded *Schools* for ten boys and ten girl, endowing each with £4. out of the Hermitage estate, the nomination of the Master and Mistress being vested in his heirs. Since then there have been some trifling additions to the endowment.

† Son of the founder of the Cottonian Library, who was a descendant of the Cottons, of Cotton Edmunds, in Broxton Hundred.

CHESHIRE

in himself the entire manor. In 1756, it was purchased from Lord Kilmorey by the trustees of the present proprietor Thomas Bayley Hall, Esq.

The Abbots of St. Werburgh, in Chester, had a paramount jurisdiction over the manor, by virtue of various grants from the Croxons, and claimed to hold a Court Leet for it with their other townships, at their Manor House, at Barnshaw. Sir H. M. Mainwaring, Bart. the present proprietor of the Lordship, claims the same privileges.*

* Ormerod.

About 1650, several parcels of the township were sold by the feoffees of Lord Kilmorey; one of these estates is the property of Lawrence Armistead, by purchase from his father the Rev. J. Armistead.

The ancient stone bridge over the River, on the site of one built by Sir John Nedham, temp. Hen. VI. has been taken down, and a wooden one erected in its stead, after plans by Mr. Harrison, the county Architect.

The estate of HERMITAGE, in this township, is the residence of T. B. Hall, Esq. It was given by Roger Runchamp to the Priory of St. John of Jerusalem, under which it was held by a branch of the Cranages, till 1334, when it passed with an heiress to Rich. Darlington, and with an heiress of that family, temp. Hen. VI to Hugh Winnington; on the death of the last heir male Thomas Winnington, about 1590, it was eventually sold, about 1657, to John Leadbeater, and is now the property of Mr. Hall. The waste lands here were inclosed in 1779.

THE CHAPELRY OF

GOOSETRY-CUM-BARNSHAW,

CONTAINS THE TOWNSHIPS OF

BARNSHAW-CUM-GOOSETRY, TWEMLOWE, BLACKDEN, AND LEES.

BARNSHAW-CUM-GOOSETRY,

Is about six miles N. E. E. from Middlewich; altho' mentioned as two distinct townships, they are now united in one. They were originally attached to the Baronies of Montalt and Halton.—The Lysons state that Goosetry and Barnshaw were given by Hugh Fitz Norman to the Abbey of St. Werburgh, in Chester; the Monks had a Chapel and Manor-house in Barnshaw, built soon after they obtained possession of the manor, and Abbot Thomas,† had licence, from W——, Abbot of Dieulacres, to have divine service celebrated for ever, "saving the indemnity of the Mother Church of Sandbach, and of the Chapels of the same, according to the form of the bond which he held from the Abbot."‡

HISTORY

The remains of the Old Mansion in Goosetry are still to be traced near the site of the present Chapel.

After the Dissolution, Barnshaw was granted to Hen. Mainwaring, of Carincham; and it continued vested in his descendants till about 1754, when it was sold to the Mainwarings of Peover, and it is now the property of Sir H. M. Mainwaring, Bt. who holds a Court Leet for this manor which includes Lees, Chelford, Hulse, Cranage, Plumley, Over, Blackden, and Tabley, the Constables for which are sworn in at Barnshaw. "A Court Baron is held for the four townships only first named, the manerial rights of the remaining townships being vested in other proprietors."§—The clear account given by Mr. Ormerod, of the Chapel of Goosetry, is a sufficient reason for copying it verbatim:—

The Chapel of Ease to Sandbach, in this township, is in the patronage of the Vicar. From the mention of the Chapels of Sandbach in the license for Thomas (de Capenhurst ?) to found a Chantry in his Manor House of Barnshaw, this Chapel, as well as that of Hulme, may be deemed antecedent to the date of that license, (1249-65 ?) The domestic Chantry of Barnshaw was certainly distinct from this, and the license for it precisely resembles those for the Chantries at Weston, and other manors, where public places of worship were in existence previously. A license to bury at Goosetry the bodies of those who died in the township, was granted in 1350, on account of the distance from the mother Church, and the danger from inundations, alluding probably to the floods, which might affect the fords of the Dane: In this license, all oblations for funerals, or otherwise, are reserved to the Church at Sandbach.‖

The CHAPEL, which was made parochial in 1350, is

† Mr. Ormerod suggests Abbot Thomas de Capenhurst.

‡ Chart. St. Werburgh.

§ Ormerod.—Information of Sir H. Mainwaring.

‖ "Extracts from the Lichfield Episcopal Registers, 2070, 180."

CHESHIRE

a neat brick building, the tower erected in 1792. The burial ground is skirted by a small stream.

The present Curate is the Rev. Mr. Littler, to whom the author has to express his acknowledgements for several interesting communications.

On the south aisle of the Church on an altar-tomb, an inscription—

Underneath lie the remains of the Rev. Thos. Burroughs, A. M. Rector of Pulford, and Curate of this Chapelry, who departed this life the 4th day of April, 1809, aged 73 years.

In the north-east angle of the Chapel, on a mural monument—

Sacred to the memory of John Glegg, late John Baskervyle, Esq. of Old Withington, who departed this life the 19th Jan. 1784, aged 78 years; also of Mary his wife, the daughter and heiress of Robert Glegg, Esq. of Gayton; she departed this life the 21st Feb. 1784, aged 72 years.

On an elegantly finished mural monument on the south wall, ornamented with naval devices—

In a vault underneath this tablet are deposited the remains of Walter Booth, Esq. a senior Post Captain, in the Royal Navy; he died the 21st of March, 1810, aged 60 years. He was the eldest son of Ralph Griffiths, of Caer Rhyn (Hûn) in the county of Carnarvon, Esq. by Mary, daughter of the Rev. Charles Everard, and niece of the late Thomas Booth, of Twemlow Hall, Esq. having in compliance with the will of his maternal great uncle, the last heir male of that ancient family, assumed the name of Booth. Also the remains of Ann Parry, eldest sister of the above Walter Booth, and Relict of the Rev. Owen Parry, of Perfeddgoed, in the county of Carnarvon; she died the 5th of May, 1797, aged 41 years.

On a variegated tablet near the last—

In the family vault near to this tablet are deposited the remains of Thomas Booth, Esq. of Twemlowe Hall, in this Chapelry, who died Aug. the 23d, 1786, aged 92 years. There are also deposited in the same vault, the remains of his nephew and heir, the Rev. Chas. Everard, of Twemlowe Hall, who departed this life March the 7th, 1792, aged 67 years.

On an ancient wooden tablet, in the Vestry—

John Baskervyle, of Old Withington, in the County Palatyne of Chester, who took to wife Magdaline, daughter to George Hope, Esq. of Queen's Hope, in the County of Flint, &c. He had issue six sons, viz. George, who died in his minority; Thomas, Laurence, Randle, John, and Henry; and six daughters viz. Rebecca, Elizabeth, Magdalene, deceased; Katharine, Mary, and Elizabeth, surviving. He died ye 16th of Feb. anno Domini MDCLXII. and about the 63d yeare of his age.

On flag stones are memorials of the Baskervyles, Jodrells, Amsons, Mainwarings (of Kermincham) Booths, &c. &c.

HISTORY.

In 1684, Mrs. Elizabeth Staplehurst left the interest of £200. to the Minister for teaching the poor Children of the Chapelry.—The Registers commence in 1561.

TWEMLOWE

Is about six miles and a half E. N. E. from Middlewich. At a very early period the Croxons were possessed of the Manor; their successors, the Lidulphs, were then the proprietors; and they granted the greater part of it between the Abbey of Vale Royal, and the Abbey of St. Werburgh.

The Lysons say, the portion given to Vale Royal Abbey was held under it by the Hardings, descendants of the Lidulphs, from whom it passed by female heirs to the Knutsfords, and from them to the Booths and Jodrells. The estate which was given to the Abbey of St. Werburgh, passed at the Reformation to the Brookes, of Norton.

The greater part of the township is the property of the Booths and Jodrells; the manerial rights are vested in the former, and the estate of the latter was left to the late wife of Egerton Leigh, Esq.* No Court is held for the Manor; the township is subject to the Leet Court of Weverham.

The MANOR HOUSE of Twemlowe, is an ancient House, formerly moated, of which there are still some remains, and standing on the brow of a hill, commanding some romantic views. Another mansion, the seat of the Leghs, was built by Egerton Leigh, Esq. who married one of the daughters of Francis Joddrell, Esq.

BLACKDEN

Is a small township, and is supposed to have been included in Goosetry, and to have belonged to the Goosetries, whose coheiresses married into the families of Kinsey, and Eaton. Of the former, there were formerly three branches settled in Blackden†; and "the immediate male representatives of Robert Kinsey, who married the heiress of Goosetry, ended in Thomas Kinsey, father of Margery, wife of Thomas Baskerville, of Old Withington, and Alicia, wife of Hugh Holinshead, of Heywood. From the first mentioned of these coheirs, are descended the Gleggs, of Old Withington; John Glegg, Esq. the present proprietor, purchased, in 1814, the share of the other coheir from Mr. William

* Ormerod.

† Ibid.

Fallows, of Derby, descended from the daughter of Hugh Hollinshead, before mentioned. This share is reported to be two-thirds of the manor."*

The Eaton share is now the property of Mr. Kinsey, of Knutsford, whose ancestor, John Kinsey, married Elizabeth Eaton, in whom the property of the family became vested.

Blackden *Old Hall* is the property of Mr. Glegg, and is occupied by a farmer.

The other *Hall*, the property of Mr. Kinsey, is a timber mansion and formerly occupied by the family; it still contains a number of family portraits.

The Constables of the township are sworn at the Leet of Barnshaw, although the inhabitants do not attend the Courts there.

LEES,

About three miles N. N. E. from Middlewich, is noticed in Domesday, and was divided between the Earl and the Baron of Halton. It was subsequently possessed by the Lidulphs, and Robert of that name, gave his property here to Chester Abbey, for the repose of the souls of his ancestors, much to the satisfaction of the holy brotherhood.

After the dissolution it passed to the Shackerleys, and is now the property of Charles Watkin John Shakerley, Esq. of Somerford Hall.

An estate here was possessed by the Amsons, which ultimately fell to the Shackerleys, by marriage with an heiress.

* Ormerod's History of the County of Chester, from information of John Glegg, Esq.

GREAT BUDWORTH PARISH,

(PART OF.)

PAROCHIAL CHAPELRY OF NETHER PEOVER,

CONTAINS THE TOWNSHIPS OF

PLUMLEY,*	GREAT PEOVER,
NETHER PEOVER†,	ALLOSTOCK.

PLUMLEY,

Is about three miles and a half S. W. from Knutsford. About 1119, the manor was given by Roger de Mainwaring to the Abbey of Chester, under which it was held by mesne lords till the Dissolution. About 1227, half of the manor passed in marriage with Joan, daughter of Richard de Lostok, heir to her two brothers, who died without issue, to William de Toft, a younger brother of Roger de Toft, whose posterity settling at HOLFORD,‡ (a hamlet of this township) assumed the local name. The Holfords possessed the moiety of the manor of Plumley, till the death of Christopher Holland, Esq. in 1581, when it passed in marriage with his heiress to the Cholmondeleys. Robert Cholmondeley, Earl of Leinster, left this estate to his illegitimate son Thomas Cholmondeley, and his grandson Robert, dying without issue, bequeathed it to his wife Jane, who afterwards married Seymour Cholmondeley, Esq.

* In Bucklow Hundred, but introduced there in the account of Great Budworth.

† In Bucklow and Northwich Hundreds.

‡ Lysons.

ITINERARY

OF THE

HUNDREDS OF CHESHIRE;

INCLUDING

EVERY PARISH AND TOWNSHIP,

COMPILED, ARRANGED, AND WRITTEN,

FROM ANCIENT DEEDS,

FROM

Domesday Book, Leycester's Antiquities, Lyson's and Ormerod's Histories of the County, and other authentic sources of information,

WITH

Notices of Principal Land Owners,—Noble and Knightly Families, &c. their Seats;

Families extinct and existing—Ancient Fortifications,—Roads, &c. &c.

Brown, del.

THE ORATORY IN THE REFECTORY OF ST. WERBURGH'S MONASTERY, CHESTER.

HUNDRED OF BROXTON.

PARISHES.

ALDFORD,	ECCLESTON,	MARY ST.	SHOCKLACH,
BUNBURY,	FARNDON,	MALPAS,	TARVIN, PART OF
CHRISTLETON,	GUILDEN SUTTON,	OSWALD ST.	TILSTON,
CODDINGTON,	HANDLEY,	PLEMONSTALL,	TATTENHALL,
DODLESTON,	HARTHILL,	PULFORD,*	WAVERTON,

HINDMARSH (Malpas) Extra-parochial.

THE PARISH OF ALDFORD,

CONTAINS FOUR TOWNSHIPS

ALDFORD,	CHURTON, PART OF,
BUERTON,	EDGERLEY.

Cheshire

Aldford is 5 miles S. E. of Chester, pleasantly situated on the banks of the Dee, over which it has a good bridge. In former times, it had a Market on Tuesday, granted to Walkelin de Arderne, about 1253, and a fair for three days, at the Festival of the Holy Cross. It is somewhat remarkable, that Aldford is altogether unnoticed in the Survey. It no doubt, however, formed part of the extensive estates of Bigot, at the Conquest; and took its present name about the time of Randle Blundeville. In the reign of Henry II. Robert de Aldford took to wife Mary, daughter of Richard Fitz Eustace, baron of Halton;* and it is probable about this time the Castle, which it once possessed, was erected. Aldford afterwards became the head of a great fee, held in capite by military service from the Earls.—Richard de Aldford was the Lord in the time of King John.—Between the 10th of King John, and the 13th Hen. III. Sir John Arderne† succeeded to the fee of Aldford, and occupied the Castle. By the Charter of Confirmation granted to him, he is entitled to the privilege of free duel in his Court, and ordeal by fire and water, "*Et libertate duelli habendi in curiâ suâ, et cum juisio ignis et aquæ*, et cum omnibus libertatibus et aisiamentis intra villam et extra villam, et cum advocatione ecclesiarum et capellarum, et cum omnibus prædicto feodo de Aldeford pertinentibus." The witnesses to the charter,

History.

* Ormerod.

† This Sir John Arderne is supposed to be the son-in-law of Richard de Aldford.

CHESHIRE — HISTORY.

Lymm.

The manors of Plumley and Holford, with Holford Hall, were purchased in 1791, by Thomas Langford Brooke, Esq. of Mere, from Thomas Asheton Smith, Esq. to whose grandfather Thomas Asheton, Esq. they were given by Mrs. Cholmondeley, before named.*

Holford Hall was rebuilt by Dame Mary Cholmondeley (heiress of the Holfords) who resided in it during her widowhood; it is of this widow James I. spoke, when he called her "*The bold Lady of Cheshire*," in allusion to her long law suits with the Holfords. The hall is occupied as a farm house.

The other part of Plumley appears to have been subdivided; the greater portion belonged to the Mobberleys, and passed from them to the Leycesters. Sir J F. Leicester, Bart. is the present proprietor.

The Tenants owe service to the Court of Barnshaw.

GREAT AND LITTLE PEOVER

Lie about three miles S. W. from Knutsford. The manor of both these townships has been from a very early period held in moieties, which have passed thro' the same hands: a moiety of Great and Little Peover passed by sales from the Peovers to the families of Harding, Bonetable, Mobberley, and Grosvenor, and by marriage about the reign of Edw. IV. from Grosvenor to the Ancestors of the present proprietor, Sir J. F. Leicester, Bart.—The other moiety was formerly possessed by the family of Poole, or De la Poole, and temp. Henry VII. it passed from them to the Holfords. Mary, daughter and heiress of George Holford, having married Sir Hugh Cholmondeley, of Cholmondeley, a law suit arose between this lady and the heirs male of Holford, which, after forty years litigation, terminated in a friendly award, by which this moiety of Great and Little Peover, with other estates, were divided between them. Sir John Leicester's ancestors purchased the moiety and he is now the proprietor.

The CHURCH was first built about the reign of Hen. III.; it consists of nave, chancel, side aisles terminating in chancels, and a handsome stone tower, with four bells. The smaller chancels belong to the families of Brooke, of Mere, and Shackerley, of Hulme. Four rude wooden arches, divide the nave from the side aisles.

The Shakerley chancel was added to the Church in 1610; in it is a handsome mural marble monument, inscribed—

M. S. Galfridi Shakerley,† de Shakerley, in agro Lancastriensi, qui a castris reportavit gloriam adhuc adolescens. Ob fidem utrique Carolo et Ecclesiæ periclitanti præstitam iterum, iterumque carcere conclusus, rei familiaris dispendium, et quicquid iniquum excogitavit parricidalis democraticorum furor, eadem animi constantià quâ prius discrimina belli sustinuit, adversis major nec secundis impar. A rege tandem retaurato ad equestrem dignitatem promotus arcis Cestrensis præfectus fuit; hoc munus, ab eo sponte depositum, Petrus, primogenitus ex Catherina filia Gul. Pennington de Muncaster, in Com. Cumbriæ, armig. pari vigilantia ac fide administravit; ex eadem lectissima conjuge (cujus ossa sunt hic recondita) tres insuper suscepit liberos Galfridum, Catherinam, et Annam. Jana, uxor altera quam postea duxit, charissima filia Joh. Doulben de Segroit, in com. Denbigh, arm. quæ geminos peperit filios, Georgiam et Johannem, amoris ergo hoc monumentum mœrens posuit.

Obiit anno { Domini MDCXCVI, ætatis suæ LXXVIII.

† This gallant soldier signalized himself during the battle between Poyntz and Sir Marmaduke Langdale, at the siege of Chester:—"The heath upon which Sir Marmaduke Langdale was drawn up, carries the name of Rowton Heath; a mile beyond which, in the London road from Chester, is another heath, called Hatton Heath. The order which Sir Marmaduke had received from the King, was only to beat Pointz back. Sir Marmaduke performed the same effectually; for having marched his men over Holt Bridge undiscovered by the enemy, who had taken the out-works and suburbs of the city on the east side thereof, and Pointz coming in a marching posture along the narrow lane between Hatton Heath and Rowton Heath, Sir Marmaduke having lined the hedges, fell upon him, and killed a great many of his men; and having so done, ordered Colonel Shackerley, who was best acquainted with that country, to get the next way he could to the King (who lodged then at Sir Francis Gamull's house, in Chester) and acquaint him, that he had obeyed his orders in beating Poyntz back, and to know his Majesty's further pleasure. The Colonel executed his orders with better speed than could have been expected; for he gallopped directly to the river Dee, under Huntington House, got a wooden tub (used for slaughtering of swine) and a batting-staff (used for batting of course linen) for an oar, put a servant into the tub with him, and in this desperate manner swam over the river, his horse swimming by him (for the banks were there very steep, and the river very deep) ordered his servant to stay there with the tub for his return, and was with the King in little more than a quarter of an hour after he had left Sir Marmaduke, and acquainted the King, that if his Majesty pleased to command further orders to Sir Marmaduke, he would engage to deliver them in a quarter of an hour; and told the King of the expeditious method he had taken, which saved him the going nine or ten miles about, by Holt Bridge (for the boats of Eaton were then made useless); but such delays were used by some about the King, that no orders were sent, nor any sally made out of the City by the King's party, till past three o'clock in the afternoon, which was full six hours after Pointz had been beat-

Beneath, on the same monument—

H. S. E. supradicta Domina Jana Shakerley, dignissimo marito conjux optima, filiis mater indulgentissima, pia, pudica, prudens, post undecim pene actos in laudabili luctu annos quem defleverat secuta est XVI^to die Maii anno Domini MDCCVII, et ætatis suæ LIX.

On a mural marble monument—

To the perpetuall memory of ye pious, prudent, and virtuous lady Katherine, daughter of William Pennington, of Muncaster in the county of Cumberland, Esq. the first wife of Sir Geffery Shakerley, of Hulm, in the County of Chester, Knight, by whom she had two sons and two daughters viz. Peter ye eldest, Geffery ye younger son, Katherine ye eldest daughter, and Ann the younger daughter, who married Charles Hurleston, of Newton, near Chester, Esq. This monument is erected by ye said Peter Shakerley, eldest son of the said Sr Geffery Shackerley, Knight, by the sd Katherine his first wife, anno Domini 1725.

A mural marble monument to the memory of Mrs. Shakerley, who died July 25, 1767, aged 89 years.

On the south side of the east window, a marble mural monument inscribed—

Here lies interred, George Shakerley, of Gwerselt (syllt) in the county of Denbigh, Esq. He married Anne, youngest daughter of Sir Walter Bagot, of Blythefield, in the county of Stafford, Bart. and by her had four sons, and six daughters, four of whom only survived him. He was a gentleman of quick apprehension, a pregnant fancy, and a strong memory, all which natural advantages he improved by an assiduous application to his studies at Westminster and Oxford.—The acquaintance of men of learning and virtue was his ambition and delight, and where he made a friendship he was sure of keeping it, being constant and unaffected in his devotions, honest and just in his actions, sincere and steady in his friendship, easy and polite in his manners, open and unsuspecting in his temper, spirited and inoffensive in his conversation. Thus possessed of every quality wch could make him agreeable and useful in private life, after a long and painful struggle, on the 2nd of February, 1756, in the 73d year of his age, he died, as he lived, with a pious and patient resignation to the Divine will.

Within the communion rails, on a brass plate, in a flag stone—

Here lyeth the body of Jane Cholmondeley, relict of Thomas Cholmondeley, of Holford, Esq. and daughter of Edward Holland, of Denton, in Lancashire, Esq who departed this life December the 16th, 1696, ætat. suæ 78.

On the stone—

Also here lyeth interred the body of Rich. Cholmondeley, fourth son of Thos. Cholmondeley, of Holford, Esq. who deceased August ye 16th an'o Domini 1665.

There are several other memorials of the Cholmondeleys, amongst them, on a brass plate let into a stone,

Here lyeth the body of T. Cholmondeley, late of Holford, Esquyer, the onely sonne of Robert Lord Cholmondeley, Baron of Wich Malbank, Viscounts Kells, Earle of Leinster, sonne and heyre of Mary, daughter and heyre of Christopher Holford, of Holford, Esquyer, which sayd Thomas dyed the sixth of January, MDCLXVII.—

Mortalitatis exuvias hic deposuit Thomas Cholmondeley, nuper de Holford, armig. cujus superstes virtus adulantis statuæ dedignatur pompam; satis es quod publico dolore pollinctus erat: in Deum pius, in Regem fidelis, in bello magnanimus, in pace beneficus, in omnibus gratus: usque ad invidiam honestus simul et amatus Denatus VIII. Id. Jan. MDCLXVII.

On a small stone near the altar rails, a memorial of Hugh Cholmondeley, gent. son of Thomas Cholmondeley, Esq. died 28th March, 1625.

The Curate is nominated by Sir J. F. Leicester. The Registers begin in 1570.

There is a *School* in the Chapel Yard, built in 1710, by the Rev. R. Comberbach, when Curate, on land given by Sir Francis Leicester. It was originally endowed with £645. and in 1799, and 1810, it was further augmented by bequests from a Mr. T. Barton, and Mrs. Mary Antrobus; the latter of which is distributed in bread.

ALLOSTOCK

Is about five miles S. W. from Knutsford; and soon after the Conquest was possessed by the Grosvenors, an account of whom occurs under the head of "Eaton," in Broxton Hundred. Some circumstances, connected

en back; and so Pointz having all that time for his men to recover the fright they had been put into in the morning, Poyntz rallied his forces, and with the help of the Parliament forces who came out of the suburbs of the city to his assistance (upon whom the King's party in the city might then successfully have fallen) put all those of the King's to the rout, which was the loss of the King's horse, and of his design to join Montrose in Scotland, who was then understood to be in good condition.

"This is what my father, the said Colonel Shakerley (afterwards Sir Geffrey Shakerley) hath often declared in my hearing; and since no mention is made of him in all this History,* (though he faithfully served the King in all the wars, was personally engaged in almost all the field battles for the King, sold part of his estate to support that service, and was for many years sequestered of all the rest) I thought it my duty, as his eldest son and heir, to do that justice to his memory, to insert this here, under my hand, that it may be remembered to posterity. "PETER SHACKERLEY."

"From Pennant's Wales, 4to edit. 1784, p. p. 482. 483. 484."

* Meaning Clarendon's History of the Rebellion; this account being written by Peter Shackerley, Esq. in one of the blank leaves.

with the celebrated suit of arms between Sir Robert le Grosvenor, and Sir Richard le Scroope, are highly curious, not only in a family, but an historical point of view:—In the examination of John de Holford at Nantwich, on the 1st of Oct. 1386, he deposes, "Qu'un des progenitors du dit Jurré vient en le temps de Conquest, ouesq. Hugh de Louf, Cout de Cestre, et apres le Conquest mesme celuy Hugh departs le Seignorie de *Lostock* de un *Hame* (Hulme) qui fuist occis *en le batail a Nampwich*, et dona une parte du dit seignorie a Monsieur Hugh Ronchamp. progenitour du dit Jurré q'uest appellé Nether Lostock, et l'autre parte il dona a Robert Fitz Monsieur Gilbert de Grosvenour appellé Over Lostock."

Three years afterwards, Stephen, the Abbot of Vale Royal, in reference to the connexion between the Grosvenors and Hugh Lupus, and the dispute as to the Bend, *or*,—said, after quoting the authorities of ancient monuments, and writings,—"que Hugh Loufe, conte du Cestre, le primir après la Conquest, *nevieu de William le Conquerour* d' Engleterre, vient en Engleterre one William le Conquerour susdit: et ouesq' le dit Hugh, armé en les armes susditz (c'est assvoir, Azure, oue un bend d'or) et mesmes les armes tanque a sa mort il usoit," &c.—Raufe Grosvenor, 4th in descent from Gilbert, fought under Earl Randle II. at the battle of Lincoln.—Robert, 6th in descent, occurs in several deeds as the Lord of Little Meoles and Hilbree, in right of the hundred of Caldey. It was not till the reign of Edward III. and his expeditions into France, that the dispute about the Coat of Arms first arose, at which time Sir Robert Grosvenor, Knt. was then a minor; but his guardian, Sir John Daniell, valiantly maintained his ward's armorial rights, as appears from his Challenge mentioned in the deposition of John Leycester, of Toft:—Monsieur Johan Danyell chalangea les dits armes en noum du dit Monsieur Robert, q'i avoit espousè la fille du dit Monsieur Johan Danyell, encontre un esquier de Cornewall appelle Carminow." It was this Robert who married Joan, daughter of Sir Robert Pulford, and sister and heiress of John Pulford, being widow of Thomas, son of John de Belgreave.—In the trial of arms, which began in the 10th year of Richard II. and ended in the 13th of the same reign, Sir Richard Grosvenor proved, that the Bend, *or*, was used by his ancestors at the Conquest, by Raufe le Grosvenor, at the Battle of Lincoln, by Robert le Grosvenor in the Crusade under Richard I. by Robert le Grosvenor in the Scotch Wars under Edward II. at the Battle of Cressy, and by Sir Robt. himself as harbinger to Sir James d' Audley, Lieutenant to the Black Prince, and in Berri, at the Tower of Brose, in Guienne, in Normandy, at the Battle of Poictiers, at the Battle of Najara, in Spain, 1367, and at the battle of Limoges, in 1370, under the Black Prince. Sir Richard Scrope, per contra, proved that the same coat had been borne by his ancestors as early as 1052. The decision is well known, and is unnecessary to detail here; but the Tabley M.SS. insinuate; that "Sir Richard Scrope overweighing the other with powerful friends, had the coat awarded to him."*

With respect to the descent of the Pulford estates, some curious particulars are given in the Tabley M.SS. It appears that the right of Sir Thomas Grosvenor to them was contested by Sir Robert Legh, who pretended a right to them under the settlement made by Thomas de Belgreave and Joan his wife; in order to settle family differences, it was agreed that Sir Thos. Grosvenor should take a solemn oath on the body of Christ, in the presence of twenty-four gentlemen. Accordingly (and it admirably illustrates the superstition of the times) Robert del Birches, Robert de Legh's Chaplain, celebrated a Mass of the Holy Trinity, and consecrated the Host, and after the Mass (albo cum amiclo stotâ, et manipulo indutus) held forth the Host before the Altar, whereupon Sir Thomas Grosvenor knelt before him, whilst the settlements were read, by James Holt, Robt. de Legh's Counsel, and then swore upon the Lord's body, that he believed in the truth of these Charters.—After this, Sir Laurence Merbury, Knt. Sheriff, and fifty-seven principal Knights and Gentlemen of Cheshire, affirmed themselves singly to be witnesses of the oath, all elevating their hands at the same time towards the Host. Sir Thomas Grosvenor then received the Sacrament, and Sir Robert de Legh and Sir Thomas, kissed each other, *in affirmationem concordiæ prædictæ*. Sir Robert then acknowledged the right of the lands to be in Sir Thomas Grosvenor, and an instrument to that

* Amongst the witnesses examined on the part of Scrope, was the celebrated Geoffrey Chaucer, then forty years old.

effect was signed by all those present. Ralph son of this Sir Thomas, was the Ancestor of the Grosvenors of Eaton.

The Grosvenors had their chief seat at HULME in this township (which was purchased temp. Henry III. of Gralam de Runchamp) till the death of Robert Grosvenor, Esq. in 1465, when the male line of the elder branch became extinct, and his estates were divided between his daughters and coheirs. The manor of Allostock is divided between Sir John Leicester, Bart. who possesses two-fifths, and C. W. J. Shakerley, Esq. who has three-fifths. Sir John inherits one-fifth from his ancestor, who married one of Robert Grosvenor's coheiresses; the other was purchased of the Stanleys of Hooton, whose ancestor married another of the coheiresses. Mr. Shakerley inherits one-fifth from his ancestor, who married the heiress of John Legh, of Booths, by one of the coheiresses of Grosvenor; the other shares, in the absence of documentary proof, are supposed to have been acquired by purchase.*

Sir John's share and Mr. Shakerley's, are considered moieties of the manor, and each proprietor holds a Court Baron. *Hulme* is not now considered a distinct manor.

The *Hall* of Hulme is built on a moated site of about an acre, surrounded by a moat nearly twenty yards in width. The approach to the house is over an ancient stone bridge; very little of the original mansion is now to be seen: the only relic possessing claims to curiosity, is an immense arch of oak carved, which supports the basement story. The House is occupied by a farmer.

* Lysons.

THE PAROCHIAL

CHAPELRY OF WITTON,

CONTAINS IN THIS HUNDRED, †

THE TOWNSHIPS OF

WITTON-CUM-TWAMBROOK,

NORTHWICH,

LOSTOCK GRALAM, OR NETHER LOSTOCK,

BIRCHES, HULSE, AND LACHE DENNIS.

WITTON-CUM-TWAMBROOK

Adjoins, and in fact forms part of, the township of Northwich. This manor, and that of *Le Crosse*, were vested in the Barons of Kinderton, and continued in their descendants, the Lords Vernon, for many generations. In 1757, however, Lord Vernon sold them to Sir Peter Leicester, and they are now the property of Sir J. F. Leicester, Bart. who holds a Court here for Witton-cum-Twambrook, Marston, and Wincham.

In 1558, Sir John Deane, then a Prebendary of the Cathedral of Lincoln, and Minister of the Church of St. Bartholomew the Great, in London, founded a Free Grammar School, in Witton, endowing it with lands in Wirral, and several houses in Chester,‡ which, altho' then of comparatively small value, now produce an income considerably exceeding £100. per ann. The venerable founder, in the statutes made by him, appears to have had due attention to the bodily health and recreation, as well as the mental improvement, of the pupils; he orders, that "a week before Easter, and Christmas, according to the olde custome, the scholars shall barre and keep forth of the schoole the schoolemaster, in such sort as other scholars doe in great schooles; and that as well in the vacations, as the other days aforesaide, they use their bowes and arrowes onely, and eschewe all bowleing, cardinge, dyecing, quiteinge, and all other unlawful games." He also ordered that if the rents of the estates exceeded the annual income of £12. then an Usher should be appointed. At the present period the management of the School is vested in twelve feoffees, who appoint the Master, and select the Scholars.

The Parochial CHAPEL of Witton, is a neat Gothic structure, situated on a rising piece of ground. It was nearly re-built in 1560 or 1570, and again considerably beautified in 1722, to which many of the neighbouring gentry contributed; Mr. Vernon, of Middlewich, gave £200. on condition that he and his heirs should have the appointment of the Curate. It is endowed with Queen Anne's bounty.||

The building consists of nave, chancels, side aisles, and a neat embattled tower, containing six bells. The roofs are of oak, enriched with carved work: five pointed arches divide the nave from the side aisles.

† Castle Northwich, Hartford, and Winnington, are noticed in Edisbury Hundred.

‡ Described in the Harl. MSS. as being parcel of the possessions of the Monastery of St Anne, in that City.

|| The patronage is now vested in Sir J. F. Leicester, as Manerial Lord.

There are now existing very few monumental memorials of interest.

The Chapelry is in four divisons, viz. Witton, Northwich, Lostock, and Hartford, each of which choose their own Churchwardens. The Registers commence in 1561.

NORTHWICH.

The extensive Salt Works in this Township are noticed in the Survey, and the manor was then vested in the Earl. On the termination of the line of Earls, the whole was seized by the Crown; and in the 12th Ric. II. the township was granted to John Holland Earl of Huntington, subsequently created Duke of Exeter. On his attainder, in the first year of Henry IV. the estates were conceded to his son John, who was the 2d Duke; but on the attainder of Henry Holland, the 3d Duke, the Crown again obtained possession.

Richard III. amongst other valuable gifts, granted this manor to his then favorites Sir Thomas Stanley, Knt. Lord Stanley, and Geo. Stanley, Lord l'Estrange, his son; and it continued for many generations in their descendants Earls of Derby. In 1784, however, the present Earl sold it, under the authority of an Act of Parliament, to James Mort, Esq. of Witton House, who died in 1793. His son Jonadab also dying in 1799, bequeathed the estate to Anne his only sister, wife of Mr. Thomas Wakefield, and he sold the manor in 1808, to Arthur Heywood, Esq. who re-sold it soon after to the present proprietor, John Pemberton Heywood, of Wakefield, Barrister-at-Law.

The Lord of the Manor holds a Court Leet and Baron, at the former of which the Constables, Market-lookers, &c. are sworn in. He has also the right of market and fairs, and *pickage* and *stallage*. The Fairs are held on the 10th April, (for cattle only) the 2d Aug. and 6th of Dec.: the Market is held weekly on the Friday.

The whole manor and township are in the Hundred of Northwich, altho' the River Weaver divides it, the stream ceasing to form the boundary between the Hundreds of Northwich and Edisbury, immediately within the manerial limits. The part of the township on the western side of the River, is about a third of the whole, and is bounded by the townships of Castle Northwich and Winnington. On the south side, the township is divided from Castle Northwich by a brook, called *Lamprey Ditch*, formerly abounding with those fish, but which the increase of navigation on the Weaver, has entirely destroyed. The whole of the manor and township scarcely exceeds ten statute acres.†

The following particulars are compiled, chiefly from Mr. Ormerod's work: Near the entrance of the town from Chester, is an ancient house, the property of Mr. J. Barker; above which rises a singularly curious garden, consisting of five terraces, one rising progressively above the other. In 1642, this house was conveyed by Sir Humphrey Davenport, Knt. to Wm. Bentley, M. D. a gentleman of rather eccentric disposition, as he caused his body to be interred at the very summit of the garden, in a summer house, with this inscription:

> Depositum Gulielmi Bentley, M. D. de re Medica optime meriti, de amicis non minus; qui per quinquaginta saltem annos artem, quam suam fecit, pie, perite, benigne, exercuit, eoq; feliciter ornavit. Tres habuit uxores, quibus conjux simul et amicus fuit, primæ desiderio novissimæ curâ, hic facet, spe beatæ resurrectionis. Obiit Sept. 13, An Dom. 1680, ætat. 79.

It is supposed that this Garden was the principal fortification thrown up during the Great Rebellion, by Sir Wm. Brereton; and in the soil, numbers of cannon balls have been found.

On the Edisbury side of the River, immediately adjoining the Bridge, is the *Old Sessions House*, built at the expense of George II. when Earl of Chester.

Northwich is the scene of all the great County Meetings, two memorable instances of the *liberty of speech* which prevails on such occasions, occurred in the years 1821 and 1822. There is great business done here in the Manufactory of Salt, and its population consists chiefly of those immediately employed in the works.—It is one of the great thoroughfares between Liverpool and London, and between Manchester and Wales, *via* Chester.

This town partook pretty largely of the troubles consequent on the Civil Wars. Sir Wm. Brereton threw up a strong military post here, which, Dr. Cowper says, "soon greatly harrassed the county round, and not only took many prisoners, but plundered several mansions and places in the neighbourhood, and brought in great numbers of horses and cattle, as also large quantities of goods and provisions of every kind." On the 10th of March (1642-3) the Doctor records, that Sir Thomas Aston marched from Chester to Middlewich,

† Ormerod.

and endeavoured to make that place defensible, and from hence Sir Wm. Brereton was ineffectually attacked by a party of Royalist Dragoons, under Captain Spotswood. He made an attack from Northwich upon the Royalists on the Sunday following, and the next day advanced again from Northwich, and being backed by the Nantwich forces, stormed the town of Middlewich, and gave Sir Thomas Aston a complete defeat.—In December of the same year, Sir William experienced a complete defeat from the King's forces, recently reinforced from Ireland; and the Parish Register notices that a garrison of Royalists was then placed here. In August, 1643-4, the Parliamentary troops regained possession, and in an expedition against it, Col. Marrow was shot, in a skirmish, at Sandiway.

Sir John Birkenhead, the celebrated Author of the first Court Newspaper *(Mercurius Aulicus)* was born here, in 1615.

LOSTOCK GRALAM

Is about two miles E. N. E. from Northwich. It belonged to Hame, who was slain at the battle of Nantwich, on the advance of Hugh Lupus to take possession of his new Earldom.—Hugh de Runchamp had a grant of it from the Earl, and Gralam, his son, assumed the local name. It descended from the Lostocks to the Holfords, and from them, with the Holford Hall estate, in Plumley, to Peter Langford Brooke, Esq. of Mere, who holds a Court Leet for the Manor.

BIRCHES

Is two miles and a half E. S. E. from Northwich.—Temp. Edw. I. Emme, daughter of Stephen de Moreton, gave the village to Nicholas her son, he paying to Geoffrey de Lostock, a pair of white gloves for their lands. This Nicholas, it is supposed, took the local name, and it continued in his family till the reign of Edw. II. when Nicholas Winnington purchased lands here, and the estate ultimately became vested in him and his descendants for many generations.

In the reign of Charles I. a coheiress of the Winningtons brought it in marriage to Ralph Starkey, of Morthwaite, and be continued to hold it till 1662.—Previous to 1695, a Mrs. Elizabeth Dobson had possession of the Manor, and she settled it on Thomas Cholmondeley, and Peter Shackerley, as trustees; and in the event of Peter Shakerley dying without issue, on the heirs of Thomas Cholmondeley, in trust, to educate two boys from the profits of the estate, one of whom is to be the son of a Counsellor, bred up in an Inn of Court, and the other the son of an orthodox Divine of the Church of England. The trust is still fulfilled, and the estate is now vested in Thomas Cholmondeley* Lord Delamere.

* Elevated to the Peerage, 1891.

The *Hall* is an ancient brick mansion, and is used as a farm house.

The township owes suit and service to Mr. Brooke's Court for Lostock Gralam.

HULSE

Is nearly four miles S. E. from Northwich, and is considered to be within the Lordship of Goosetry-cum-Barnshaw. It formerly gave name to a family from which sprang the Hulses of Little Neston, Norbury and Clive. It was vested in the Monks of Chester Abbey, and it is conjectured Hulse formed part of the estates of Runchamp. The manor is vested in Sir H. M. Mainwaring, Bart. Mr. Edward Antrobus has estates here.

LACHE DENNIS

Is four miles E. S. E. from Northwich, and is included in the grants made to Vale Royal Abbey, by Edw. I. Abbot Walter exchanged the estates with Randle de Merton, for Merton. So early as the reign of Edw. VI. the Shakerleys had property here, as had also Venables of Antrobus. The whole of the estate is now vested in Charles Watkin John Shakerley, Esq. There are no manerial rights.

RUDHEATH,

(Lordship of) part of which is in the Chapelry of Witton. This district is extra-parochial, but includes portions of the surrounding townships. The Lysons describe it as being principally in the parish of Davenham. With Hoole, and Over Marsh, this was appointed a Sanctuary for Criminals. A great portion of the Heath has been inclosed, and extensive plantations have been made. "It is observable (says Mr. Ormerod) that the numerous cottages which are scattered in the solitary lanes round this district, contain inhabitants, whose objects are not very dissimilar from those of the lawless race to which Rudheath anciently afforded protection." The Harl. MSS. contain an account of the boundaries being ridden by Randle Earl of Chester.

...SHIRE The *Lordship* extends over many estates in the adjoining townships, and passed with the Earldom to the Crown; it was afterwards granted to the Portland family; and was purchased from the late Duke, by John Marshall, Esq. On the 22d Feb. 1643, an action was fought here between the Royal and Parliamentary forces, but neither party could claim the victory. HISTORY.

PARISH OF CHURCH LAWTON,

CONTAINS ONLY ONE TOWNSHIP.

CHURCH LAWTON.

It is situated on the borders of Shropshire, about six miles equi-distant between Congleton and Sandbach.—The township, which had been divided in two unequal portions, was vested in Hugo de Mara, or Fitz-Norman, founder of the Barony of Montalt, and he gave it to the Monks of Chester Abbey. Temp. Hen. III. one moiety of the township was held under the Abbey by a family which bore the local name; and according to the Harl. MSS. Robert, son of Vivian de Davenport, settled on lands here in the 56th Henry III. and he also assumed the local name. The pedigree states him to be *ancestor* of the Lawtons, of Lawton, and the assertion is borne out strongly by the armorial bearings of the Lawtons, which differ only from those of Davenport, in the substitution of a fesse charged with a cinquefoil for the Davenport's chevron.

After the Dissolution, the manor and patronage of the Church, were purchased from the Crown by Wm. Lawton, Esq. of Lawton.* ...d Hen. VIII.

It appears from an Inquisition p. m. 6th Edward VI. that William Lawton held the manor, &c. from the King in capite by military service, as the 20th part of a Knight's Fee.

The manor and advowson are now the property of William Lawton, Esq.

The *Hall*, the seat of Mr. Lawton, is in a beautiful situation; it is a capacious brick mansion, with wings, commanding extensive views into the neighbouring counties.

The CHURCH is dedicated to All Saints, and the Registers commence in 1559. The present Rector is the Rev. Lancaster Wettenhall, presented the 27th Dec. 1782. The building is of brick, plain, with an embattled stone tower; on the south side of which is an ancient door way, highly ornamented with mouldings in the early Norman style.

The monumental memorials are very few: amongst them are some of the Lawton family: A monument of J. Cartwright, Esq. of *Lee Hall*,† in the parish, who died in 1718.

Whitelock, in his *Memorials*, noticed a fatal accident, which occurred in the Church, in June, 1652, when eleven persons were struck dead by lightning.

† Now occupied as a farm-house, the porperty of Mr. Cartwright, of Sandbach.

END OF ITINERARY OF NANTWICH HUNDRED.

The Hundred of Wirral,

CONTAINS THE PARISHES OF

BACKFORD,	EASTHAM,	STOKE,
BEBINGTON,	HESWALL,	THURSTASTON,
BIDSTON,	NESTON,	WALLASEY,
BROMBOROW,	OVERCHURCH,	WEST KIRKBY,
BURTON,	SHOTWICK,	WOODCHURCH,

AND THE *Chapelry of BIRKENHEAD.*

THE HUNDRED OF WIRRAL, DESCRIBED BY JOHN LELAND.

WIRRAL requireth a larger description than any of the other hundreds; because it is, in a manner, a country of itself; as a Peninsula, enclosed between the two great rivers of Dee and Mersey, and having the main sea at one side, is by this means nearly environed round about with salt water. It is twenty miles long, and six miles broad; and beginning within half a mile of the city of Chester, and within two bow shots of the suburbs, without the Northgate, at a bridge called Stone Bridge, and there is a dock for ships to ride at a spring tide, called Port Pool.

Half a mile lower is Blacon Head, as an armlet of the ground pointing out, where is an old manor belonging to the Earl of Oxford. A mile by water lower, hard on the shore, is a little village called Saughall.—A little less than a mile lower is Crabhall village. A mile lower is Shotwick Castle, on the shore, belonging to the King. Shotwick Townlet is three quarters of a mile lower; and two miles lower is a road in Dee, called Salt House; and on the shore a Salt House Cottage.—Then is Burton Head, whereby is a village, almost a mile lower than Salt House.—Two miles lower is Denhall Road; and against it a firm place belonging to Mr. Smith: and within this land is Denhall village. More than two miles lower, Neston road, and inland a mile in the country is Neston village.—About three miles lower is a place called the Red Bank: And half a mile inland, is a village called Thurstington.—A mile, and more lower, is West Kirby, a village near the shore.—And half a mile lower is Helbree, at the very point of Wirral.

HELBREE ISLAND.

This island of Helbree, as a full sea, is all environed with water; and then the Trajectus is a quarter of a mile over. But at low water, a man may go over the sand. It is about a mile in compass, and hath sandy ground, which abounds with conies. There was a cell of Monks of Chester, and a pilgrimage of our Lady of Helbree, which idolatry is now suppressed.

Hitherto Leland, and other places I pass over to be brief. Hereafter followeth the particular names of all the villages and townships.*—*From King's "Vale Royal,"* 8v. *edit. vol.* 1. *p.* 40.

* The names of the villages and townships in this hundred, as particularly described in the Vale Royal, are—Blacon, Crabhall, Mollington Tarend, Saughall Magna, Saughall Parva, Wood Bank, P. Row SHOTWICK, Shotwick, Puddington, Treves, P. BURTON, Denhall, Ness, Neston Parva, cum Hargreen, M. P.; NESTON Magna, cum Ashfield, Leighton, Gayton, P. HESWALL, cum Ouldfeld, P. THURSTASTON, Caldey, Caldey Magna, cum Tend Albinis in Newbold et Larton, P. WEST KIRBY, Newton cum Larton, Meoles Parva, Meoles Magna, Kirby in Whaley, Liscard, Poulton cum Seacomb, P. BIDSTON, P. CLAUGHTON, cum les Granges, Oxton, Upton, Moreton, Brimstage, Saughall Massie, Prenton, Landican, Pennesby, Thingwall, Barnston, Thornton, Tranmore, P. BEBBINGTON Inferior, Bebbington Superior, Poulton Lancelot, cum Lespitell, Hooton, Poole Inferior, Stanney Parva, P. STOKE, P. BACKFORD, Capenhurst, Ledsham, Franckby, Raby, Willaston, Stanney Magna, Stourton, C. BRUMBRO, P. EASTHAM, cum Plimyard, Poole Sup. Whitby, Arrow, P. WOOD CHURCH, Childer Thornton, Sutton Magna, Sutton Parva, Croughton, Chorlton, Lea, Irby, Greasby, Knocktorum.

THE PARISH OF BACKFORD,

CONTAINS THE TOWNSHIPS OF

BACKFORD, MOLLINGTON, AND
CHORLTON, LEA, CAUGHALL.*

* In Broxton Hundred.

BACKFORD

Is about three miles and a half N. E. from Chester. It is conjectured that the township was, soon after the conquest, vested in the Barons of Dunham Massy, and that the Church was subsequently given by them to the Priory of Birkenhead, temp. Henry II.

In the 10th Henry V. the direct male line of the Massies of Tymplegh, became extinct, when the township descended to Cecilia, daughter and heiress of Edw. Massie. This Cecilia was married to Richard de Chadderton. In the reign of Edw. IV. the manor was possessed by John Parre, in right of his wife Ellena, a coheiress of Richard de Radclyffe, who married Margaret, the daughter of Richard de Chadderton. The Parres continued in regular succession here, till the reign of Elizabeth, when Robert Parre sold the property to Thomas Aldersey, from whom Henry Birkenhead, Esq. became the purchaser, in 1571. The Birkenheads became extinct, in the male line, in the beginning of the 19th century, on the death of Thomas Birkenhead, when the manor was divided between his nieces Frances, wife of John Glegg, Esq. of Irby, and Deborah, wife of Wm. Glegg, Esq. of Grange. Major-General Birkenhead Glegg, is the present proprietor of the township, excepting only two thirds of a small estate near to the Church, which belong to Mr. Meacock, of Stanney; and Mr. Fallows, of Fallows Hall, Alderley.

The *Hall* is a handsome brick mansion, put into a state of thorough repair in 1821-2, for the residence of Major General Glegg.

The CHURCH is dedicated to St. Oswald; the Registers commence in 1562. The present Vicar is the Rev,

Thomas Armitstead, B. D. instituted April 29, 1803. On the Dissolution, the impropriate Rectory, and the advowson of the Vicarage, formed part of the endowment of the See of Chester: the late Rev. Sir Henry Poole, Bart. leased the great tithes from the Bishop of Chester. All the other tithes belong to the Vicar, excepting half the tithes of Chorlton, which (together with the Rectorial tithes of that township) are claimed by the Rector of Mary's Church.—Lea pays a modus, in lieu of tithe hay. The Church consists of a tower, nave, and chancel, the former supposed to have been built in the reign of Henry VI. The interior of the Church is composed of three aisles, separated by pillars.

There are some remains of stained glass in the east window, in which the letter R. is introduced. The whole was nearly rebuilt in 1728.

The Charitable Bequests are but few: £100. vested in the funds in the name of the Vicar, John Feilden, Esq. and B. Glegg, Esq. A small field rented by Mr. Feilden, at £6. per ann. From these receipts a weekly distribution of bread is made to the Poor on Sundays; and on Easter Sunday, there is a general distribution of the residue.

A monumental inscription, on the south wall of the Chancel—

Here lyeth the body of Ralph Morgell, of Moston, in the county of Chester, Esq. Registrar of the Consistory Court of Chester.—He married Margaret daughter of Edw. Glegg, of Gayton, Esq. and had issue John, Henry, Rafe, Edward, Thomas, William, Isabella, and Margaret, wife of William Glazlour, of Lay, Esq. He died the 4th of January 1678. He left the poor of Backford £10. the use of it to be given in bread yearely for ever.—Blessed are the charitable.

Adjoining this, on a board—

Margareta, nup. Ranulph Morgell, gen. uxor, et Edwar. Glegge, de Geton, filia, obiit 12° die Octobris, 1627.

Near to the latter—

Here lyeth the bodys of Rafe Morgell, gen. and Elizabeth his wife, who had issue Rafe, William, and Elizabeth Morgall. He died Nov. 27, 1683, and she died May 9, 1685. They gave £5. to the Parish of Backford, the use of it to be given to the Poore, on Good Friday, in money, for ever.

On a marble tablet over the chancel door,—

Underneath lieth the remains of Sarah, relict of Gwin Lloyd, Esq. of Hendwr, in the county of Merioneth, and sister to Sir Rowland Hill, Bart. of Hawkstone. She died at Backford Hall, April XIV, MDCCLXXXII, aged LXXIV.

On a pyramidal mural monument—

To the memory of the Rev. Samuel Griffith, D. D. Rector of Avington in the county of Berks, who died 29th April, 1796, aged 64.

Near to the south porch, on an altar tomb—

Here lie interred, Anne, Mary, and Sarah Griffiths, daughters of Thomas Griffiths, of the City of Chester, Esq. and Alice his wife, daughter of Harry Vigars, of Eaton, in this county, gent. Anne died April 8, 1758, aged 10 weeks; Mary died April 30, 1758, aged 3 months; Sarah died Feb. 17, 1776, aed 16 years. Thomas Griffiths was interred here the 9th of August, 1784, aged 59.—Also Alice, his relict, mother of Anne, Mary, and Sarah, 6th Sept. 1796, aged 61.

CHORLTON*

Is nearly four miles N. from Chester, and is divided from the Hundred of Broxton, by the line of the Canal from Chester to Whitby. So early as the year 1186, lands in this township were granted to Chester Abbey; and at the Dissolution the Estate possessed by the Monks, fell into the hands of Sir Rich. Cotton. Subsequently the property of the township became alienated, and the principle owners now† are Richard Wickstead, Esq. † 1820.
James Swan, Esq. and George Ormerod, Esq. Author of the magnificent History of the County. The minor proprietors, are Major Gen. Glegg, Jonathan Lowe, and John Grace.

In this township is an estate, formerly the property of the Hootons, of Hooton, from whom it descended to the Stanleys; in 1791, Wm. Pownall, Esq. of Chester, purchased from Sir Wm. Stanley, Bart. and alienated some small portions thereof. Mr. Pownall, in 1799, re-sold it to the late Wm. Nicholls, Esq. F. S. A, Deputy Registrar of the Archdeaconry of Chester; and on his death, by will, dated in 1809, it devolved to his wife Dorothea, daughter of the Rev. Wm. Russell. In 1811, Mrs. Nicholls sold this estate to the before-named Geo. Ormerod, Esq. representative of the second branch of the Ormerods, of Ormerod, in Lancashire.

MOLLINGTON TORRANT,

Or *Great Mollington*, is about two miles and a half N. W. N. from Chester. It appears from the Survey, it was held by Robert de Rodelent, who was killed in 1088, in a skirmish with the Welsh. How the manor then descended is not now known; but temp. Edw. II. William *Torrand*, de Mollington, was proprietor. In

* There isa field it this township, the rent of which is apropriated to the reduction of the Poor Rates.

the reign of Hen. V. Edmund de Eulowe died seized of lands here, leaving his property to Katherine the daughter of Rd. de Hatton, who married Roger Booth, Esq. the fifth son of John Booth, Esq. of Barton.

The Booths continued the Lords till the male line terminated in John Booth, or Bothe; and he by his will, dated Oct. 8, 1542, directed his body to be buried at Chester, and left his property to his niece Agnes Booth; she died Feb. 20, in the 44th Elizabeth. Soon after this the manor became vested in the Gleggs of Gayton; and Mary, sole daughter and heiress of Robert Glegg, Esq. brought the manor in marriage to John Baskervyle, Esq. of Old Withington, who sold it on the 26th, Jan. 1756, to Thomas Hunt, Esq. whose family had for a considerable time been settled in Mollington, and resided on an estate which was sold by — Gamull, Esq. to Francis Leche, Esq. a younger branch of the Leches, of Carden.

Mary Hunt, widow of Thomas Hunt, Esq. and their daughter Anna Maria Hunt, conveyed their estates here, and the manor, in 1797, to John Feilden, Esq. of Blackburn, in Lancashire, who is the present proprietor.

Mollington Hall, the seat of Mr. Feilden, is a handsome brick mansion, delightfully situated, and surrounded by fine plantations. It was built in 1756.

Courts Leet and Baron are held for the manor.

LEA

Is about three miles N. N. W. from Chester.—Formerly this manor was the property of the Monks of Chester, and was subject to their Court for Upton.—After the Dissolution, this manor, with Whitley and Overpool, were granted to Wm. Glasier, Esq. and John Glasier, Gent.

In 1709, owing to the foreclosure of a mortgage, a Decree of Chancery vested the manor in Geo. Naylor, Esq. and his descendant, in 1718, sold it to Thomas Bootle, Esq. of the Inner Temple. In 1802, this property was purchased by the present proprietor, John Feilden, Esq.

The *Hall* is a respectable building, occupied as a farm-house.—No Court is held for the manor.

In the 13th century, a considerable estate here was the hereditary property of the Master Cook of the Abbey of St. Werburgh.

ST. OSWALD'S PARISH, CHESTER.

(PART OF)

CROGHTON,

Or *Croughton*, is about four miles N. E. from Chester, and is situated beteeen the townships of Stoke and Backford.

In 1093, Hugh Lupus gave the Manor to the Monks of Chester, and they retained it till the Dissolution, when, with other property granted to the Dean and Chapter, owing to the informality which has been before adverted to,* it fell into the hands of Sir Richard Cotton, whose son Geo. Cotton, Esq. sold it to Rich. Hurleston, Esq. Anne and Mary Hurleston, daughters of John, and nieces and coheiresses of Charles Hurleston, Esq. of Newton and Picton, brought the manor in marriage, about the middle of the 18th century, to Henry John Needham Viscount Kilmorey, and John Leche, Esq. of Carden; the former holds his share; and Hurleston Leche, Esq. son of John Leche, Esq. is the present proprietor of the remainder.

*ee the account of ester Cathedral.

In this township is a singularly romantic Valley, called *The Dungeons*, through which it is, with great probability, conjectured, a branch of the Mersey flowed, till it united with the stream of the Dee, near Chester.

STOKE, OR STOAK PARISH,

INCLUDES THE TOWNSHIPS OF

STOKE AND LITTLE STANNEY.

STOKE is about five miles N. E. of Chester. It is not noticed in the Survey, and the earliest Baronial possessor was Roger de Soterlegh, early in the 12th century. It is conjectured that Edmund de Soterlegh, who presented to the Church in 1316, transferred the township to the Roters, of Thornton, about 1326, whose successors the Thorntons had possession till the division of their estates among the co-heirs, when Stoke fell to Ellenor wife of Sir Thomas Dutton, of Dutton. The estate subsequently, it is said,* passed in marriage with the other possessions of the Duttons, to the Gerards, of Gerards Bromley, which family afterwards sold Stoke to the Bunburies of Stanney, about the middle of the last century,† and the whole is now the property of Sir Henry Bunbury, nephew of the late Sir F. C. Bunbury, Bart. well known for his attachment to field sports, and particularly racing. A Court Leet and Baron are claimed for the Manor, but they have not been held for many years.

* Ormerod.

Two small houses here belong to the poor of Eastham.

The roads in this parish are in a wretched state of neglect, and the whole township has a miserable appearance.

The *Hall*, an ancient timber house, was situated within a moated site, and occupied by a farmer.

The *Canal*, from Chester to Whitby, passes through this township.

There is a *Free School* in this parish, built on Little Stanney Green, under the provisions of Sir Thos Bunbury's will, dated Aug. 22, 1682, who left for the endowment of it Two Hundred Pounds, and more than Three Hundred Pounds, to the Parochial Poor: his liberal example has not been followed by his successors. It should, however, be remarked, that, like many other excellent Institutions, this has sunk into insignificance, from the circumstance of the money being long lost to the parish, *owing to its being vested in private hands*. The present Salary of the Master is only Six Pounds a year, One Pound of which was left by Mr. Henry Marsh, and the remainder is paid by Sir Henry Bunbury.

The CHURCH is dedicated to St. ———, and is of considerable antiquity, built of red stone, nearly surrounded by trees, and crowned with a mean wooden belfry, in a state of great decay, and extreme danger.‡ The body of the Church is in length about 60 feet, in breadth about 27 feet, divided by a heavy arch, on the east side of which is a transept of wood, projecting into the Church-yard, considerably increasing its width. This transept was the burial place of the Bunburies, and contains a number of their monumental memorials. A screen of oak, above which has been a rood loft, separates the body from the Chancel, which is in the style of the early part of the 16th century. Under a clumsy gallery of oak, at the west end of the body, is a very ancient font, ornamented in the Saxon style. It is about 2 feet in diameter, and nearly 3 feet high.

The general style of the building is nearly as early as the time of William I. In 1349, Sir Peter de Thornton, gave the Church to the Dean and Chapter, of St. John's, Chester; and in October, of the same year, they presented Adam de Wygan, one of their Chaplains, to the cure. The living is a Curacy, in the gift of the Bunburies, who possess the impropriation and the advowson. The great tythes belong to the impropriator, and the tythes of hay and potatoes to the Curate. Mrs.

---

† The Bunburies had previously possessed an estate in Stoke, valued, in an inquisition, p. m. 37 Hen. VI. at 63s. 6d. rent.

‡ As the present proprietor of the township is an absentee, he might show that he has not forgotten the respect due to the burial place of his ancestors, by putting the Church in good repair, and building a tower for the bells.

CHESHIRE

Brown of Whitby, holds the tithes of the portion of that township, in this parish.*

In the south wall of the Church, near the porch, is this inscription in Longobardic letters, supposed to relate to one of the early Rectors :—

Magister Andre' cus' a'i'e p'p'itiet' d's.

A short distance from this, on a shield, carved on a stone,—

Hic jacet corpus Henrici Trafford, Clerici, qui obiit vicesimo quarto die Augusti, anno ætatis suæ quinquagesimo quarto, annoque recuperatæ salutsis M.DC.LIV.°—Servavi resurgam.

Amongst a great number of other memorials, on a large white alabaster monument, against the north wall of the Chancel, in capital letters,—

Neere this place lyeth interred the body of Henry Bunbury, Esq. eldest son of Henry Bunbury, of Stannie, in the Countie of Chester, Knt. together with Ursula Bunbury, the daughter of John Bailey, of Hodsden, in the countie of Hartford, Esq. his most loveing wife.

He } dyed { Feb. 1, Anno D'ni. 1664, } aged { 66 years,
She } dyed { Mar. 20, Anno D'ni. 1652, } aged { 53 years.

The most deare parents of Thomas, John, Henry, William, Joseph, Richard, sons, and Susan, Mary, Anne, Elizabeth, and Ursula, daughters; John dyed in the service of his King and Countrie in Ireland, A. D. 1642. Mary and Anne dyed in theire minoritie. In memorie whereof the fower youngest sons and two daughters have erected this monument, Anno Salutis 1688.

On the north side of the altar, on a painted board, ornamented with armorial bearings,

Here lyeth the body of William Bunbury, third son of Henry Bunbury, of Bunbury, and Stanney, in the county Palatine of Chester, Esq. He married Mary, the second daughter of Sir Richard Skeffington, of Fisherwick, in the county of Stafford, Knt. and had issue five sons and two daughters, John, Skeffington, Francis, and Ursula, died in their minoritie; Charles, William, and Mary, * * * * * * * He died y[e] 23[d] of October, 1676, being his birth day, aged 47 years. She died the 22[d] of April, 1711, aged 82 years.

On a painted tablet—

Here under lyeth the bodye of Edw. Morgan, of Goulden Grove, Flintshire, Esq. He married Ursula, daughter to Henry Bunbury, of Stanney, and had issue Edward, Elizabeth, and * * * * * * He died 22d November, 1682, aged 58 yeas. The said Ursula died 27th Nov. 1709, aged 72. He was son and heir of the noble captaine Edw. Morgan, who was slain at Winnington Bridge, Aug. 1659, by Elizabeth, dau. of Thomas Whitley, of Aston, Esq. who was son and heir of Robt. Morgan, Esq. by Katherine, dau. of William Jones, of Castle March, Knt. son and heir of Edward Morgan, Esq. originally descended from S[r] Tudor ap Eidnefydd Vychan, one of the xv families or houses of genteel account in North Wales.

HISTORY.

On a flag stone—

Here lyeth Ursula, daughter of John Bailey, of Hodsden, Esq. late wife of Henry Bunbury, of Stanney, Esq. she died A. D. 1652, March 20, and was aged 53.

On a monument, near a tattered banner, and two achievements, for Sir Henry Bunbury, and his Lady Susanna Hanmer—

Neare this place lyeth the body of Sir Thomas Bunbury, Bart. who first married Sarah, daughter of John Chetwood, of Oakeley, in the county of Stafford, Esq. by whom he had issue sons and daughters, whereof Sir Henry his heire, and Mary, survived him. Afterwards he married Mary, the daughter of Humphrey Kelsal, of Heath syde, in the county of Chester, Gent. by whom he has had issue 2 daughters, Priscilla and Lucie, both living. He dyed 22d of Aug. 1682.

On a marble monument—

Here lye the remains of Sir Henry Bunbury, Bart. who dyed the 12th of February, 1732, and was buried the 16th following.

Near him lies also, Sir Charles Bunbury, his son, who dyed April y[e] 10, 1742. And between y[e] two is interred, Susanna Lady Bunbury, daughter of Wm. Hanmer, of Bettisfield, Esq. in com. Flint, mother of Sir Charles, and wife of Sir Henry Bunbury, to whose memory she erected this monument. She died Sept. the 23d, 1744.

On a wooden tablet, emblazoned—

Here lyeth the body of Thomas Bunbury, Gent. fourth son of Sir Henry Bunbury, of Stanney, Knt. He first married Margaret, sole dau. of Wm. Wilcocks, of the Oakes, in the county of Salop, Gent; and had issue Martha, Henry, Elizabeth, and Anne. She died 1632, aged 37. He afterwards married Elinor, fifth daughter to Henry Birkenhead, of Backford, Esq. and had by her eleven children, whereof six died in their minority. Thomas, Dulcibella, Joseph, Benjamin, and Diana, only survived him. He died the 9th day Dec. anno 1668, aged 63 years; and she died the 20 of Dec. a°. 1675, aged 70 years.

On another tablet—

Here lyeth the body of Lydia Bunbury, daughter to Thomas Bunbury, of Stanney, in the countie Palatyne of Chester, Esq. by Sarah, daughter to John Chetwood, of Oakley, Esq. his first wife.—She died the VI day of June, in the year 1675, and in the 11th year of her age.—Firmum in vita nihil.

LITTLE STANNEY,

It is supposed, is included with Great Stanney, under the head *Stanei*, in the Survey, and was held by the Earls.—The Bunburies of Bunbury, had possessions here certainly as early as the reign of Richard I. at which time a family was settled here, bearing the local

* It appears from the Harl M.SS 1965, 40, that the Abbot of St. Werburgh claimed the right of burial at Wervin Chapel, from all the townships in the parish, for which they allowed the Rector of Stoke two marks of silver yearly.

CHESHIRE

name. About the reign of Edw. III. the daughter and heiress of David de Stannich, brought the township in marriage to David de Bunbury, from which period, down to the present, the Bunburies have held possession. Sir Henry Bunbury claims Courts Leet and Baron for the Manor, but they are not held.

The *Hall*, at present occupied by Mr. Meacock, was the ancient seat of the Bunburies when it was the good old fashion for landlords to reside on their own estates; it is built chiefly of timber, and encompassed with a moat. The *Old Hall* still remains, and is a singularly curious room, with a heavily ornamented roof of wood. On the wainscoat, at the upper end, are inscribed a series of verses now nearly defaced. The building is surrounded by extensive barns and grainaries.—When this building began to decay, the Bunburies fixed their seat at a more modern building, which, alluding to the *bon vivants* who frequented it, was jocosely called "*Rake Hall,*" and still retains its nomenclature. On a pane of glass in the kitchen window, dated Dec. 15, 1724, is recorded the names of the following visitants then present, viz. Sir Charles Bunbury, Sir R. Grosvenor, Sir William Stanley, Sir Francis Poole, Amos Meredith, Colonel Francis Columbine, Edward Mainwaring, Thomas Glazeour, Scherington Grosvenor, Seimour Cholmondeley, William Poole, and Charles Bunbury, jun.

As has been before noticed, the Bunburies no longer reside on their paternal estates—and to this circumstance may be mainly attributed the miserable state of the roads and buildings in the townships.

With respect to the family, it has been observed,* that either from seclusion, from a wish for privacy, or from intermarriages with other counties, the Bunburies have been little connected with the county of Chester, and much cannot be told of earlier generations beyond their estates and alliances. One warrior graces the pedigree, Sir Roger de Bunbury, a commander in the French wars of Edward III. who is said to have added the *Chess Rooks* to his paternal armorial coat, in compliment to his skill in military tactics †

In the Harl M.SS. 2046. 35, is a document admirably illustrating the feuds of the great families of the County during the reign of Edward IV. It is a petition without date, running thus :—

HISTORY.

"Sheweth mekely unto yore gode Grace yowre. Orator William Stanley of Hoton, squier, how that one Richard Bunbury, of Stanney, squier, with 20ty. harnessht men with him in forme of warre, and contry to youre lawes and proclamac'ns, upon Palme Sunday last passed, came to the town of Wervyn and Pickton, and there soght the servants of yo'r s'd supplyant, in theire howses and chambers, and all theire places, theym to have beaten, maymed, murthered, and slayne, if the said Richard Bunbury had found the s[d] servants in either of the s[d] townes, and their soght them; and hath kept them from their tenures sith the s[d] Sunday, unto the makeyng hereof, unto their great hurte, to the said poore tenants, should in that behalfe, &c. Wherefore your s[d] suppliant mekely besecheth youre Highness, the p'mises tenderly considered, and in way of charity, to call before you the s[d] Richard Bunbury, and to p'vide to the s[d] poore tenants remedy in such wise as your peace may be kept, and the s[d] poor s'vantes be at their habita'cons."

Henry Bunbury, Esq. father of the first Baronet, was an active loyalist, and had his estates sequestrated by the Republicans for five years, during which period he was closely imprisoned at Nantwich. He was allowed as sustenance only a fifth of the produce of his lands, and when he was set at liberty, a fine of 2,200*l.* was levied upon them. His entire loss was about 10,000*l.* exclusive of his Hall at Hoole, near Chester, which was destroyed during the siege of that city.

Chester has several times been represented by Members of this family.—The grandfather of the late Baronet was on very intimate terms with Farquhar, the Dramatist, who drew from him, the gay and good humoured character of Sir Harry Wildain. The graphic talents of the late Henry Bunbury, Esq. paticularly in satire, are well known; and his son, Major-Gen. Sir H. C. Bunbury, K. C. B. it may not be deemed improper to state, had the office of communicating to the late Emperor of France, his sentence of perpetual exile to St, Helena.

* See Ormerod, Vol. 2, p. 215.

† The Arms of the Bunburies, are,—Argent, on a bend sable, three chess rooks argent.—Crest, on a wreath two swords in saltier, croped through the mouth of a Leopard's face, or, blades proper, hilted or,

Engraved by [illegible] from a Drawing by [illegible].

WEST VIEW OF HOOTON IN CHESHIRE,

The Seat of Sir Thos. S. M. Stanley Bart.

Engraved for Hanshalls History of Cheshire.

CHESHIRE

GREAT STANNEY,

An extra-parochial township, adjoining Stoke, and one of the most miserable districts in the Hundred.—It appears from the Survey, that it was, with Little Stanney, included in the possessions of the Earl, and from him it was transferred to the Barony of Halton.

In 1178, it was given by John the Baron, to the Monastery of Stanlow. After the Dissolution, the township fell to the possession of the Warburtons; and in the 36th Hen. VIII. it was obtained from John Warburton, of Bromfield, and Sibilla his wife, by Henry Bunbury, Esq. for five hundred marks, the acreage then stated to be 670. From him it has descended to the present proprietor, Sir H. Bunbury, Bart.

In the most desirable part of the township, on an artificial terrace still existing, near two hundred yards in length, the Monks of the neighbouring Monastery built a Grange. This situation, now called *Grange Cow-worth*, includes an area of about six statute acres, the whole surrounded by a moat; and the site of the buidings has frequently been discovered in turning up the soil. It would appear, that at one period, the township formed part of the parish of Eastham. The Chartulary of St. Werburgh, temp. Hen. III. says, that the Church of Stanlow pays annually one stone of wax to the Church of St. Werburgh, between the octaves of St. Peter and St. Paul, the apostles, and another on the feast of St. Nicholas; in lieu of which it receives all the profits and offerings of Stanney and its appurtenances, which the Monks of Stanlow cultivate with their own hands; provided that as long as any seculars remain in Stanney, they pay to the *Mother Church of Eastham* all its Ecclesiastical rights, as before the arrival of the Monks at Stanlow.

Stanlow Monastery.

The site of this religious establishment is still to be traced on a rock, jutting out into the Mersey, from the marshes between Whitby and Ince.

Previous to the departure of John, the 6th Baron of Halton, for the Holy Land, in 1178, he founded here a Monastry of Cistercians, endowing it with "the land of Stanlaw, and the vills of Mauricaceston and Staneye."

The succession of the Abbots, was as follows:—

HISTORY.

1 Radolphus, died in 1209
2 Osbern ....
3 Charles ....
4 Peter ....
5 Simon ....
6 Richard de Thornton, died in 1269
7 Richard Northbury died in 1272
8 Robert Hauworthe ....

Osbern, the second Abbot, had granted to him by Randle Earl of Chester, at the instance of Roger de Lacy, a deafforestation of the domains of the Abbey, and a permission to destroy beasts of chase; and large grants were made to the Abbey, of lands in Lancashire. The 4th Abbot, it is presumed, presided when the large grants were made to the Monastery by John de Lacy, of the Churches of Eccles, and the moieties of Blackburn, Stanynges, Hordern, Newton, &c. The 6th Abbot is supposed to have been one of the family of le Roter, which settled at Thornton. It was in the time of the 8th Abbot, that the Establishment removed to Whalley, and certainly not without sufficient reason, when we contemplate their melancholy situation: In 1279, there was a dreadful inundation from the sea, as appears from the Chronicle of St. Werburgh:—"*Mare erupit* III *non. Februar. die S'tæ Werburgæ, et incredibilia mala fecit apud Stanlaw et alibi; insuper pontem Cestriæ confregit et asportavit, cursum solitum supra modum excedens.*" Seven years afterwards, the great tower of the Church was thrown down by a violent storm; and in 1289, a large portion of the Abbey was burnt down. The same year,* the Abbey Lands suffered so much from an inundation, that an indulgence of forty days was granted to all who assisted the Abbey by contributions; and Roger, Archbishop of Mount Royal, and Aimo, Bishop of Versailles, gave indulgencies to all who undertook a pilgrimage to Stanlow, to pray for the souls of the Lacies there buried.

* Ormerod.

Representations of these calamities were made to Pope Nicholas IV.; and Henry de Lacy, having offered the site of the Church of Whalley, permission was granted the Monks to remove, on condition that they should have twenty added to their numbers, and that four of them should be left at Stanlow to perform Divine Service. In Jan. 1294, this removal took place; but the taking possession of this new situation was not accomplished without considerable opposition from the Monks of St. John at Pontefract, who pleaded a prior right to Whalley; from the Hospitallers near St. Botolph; and even from their Patron, the Earl, who took forcible possession of the Church, on the death of Peter de Cestria, the last secular Rector of Whalley, and would not surrender it till he forced them to release to him the Chapel of St. Mary, at Clitheroe, and other privileges. The Monks having obtained possession, read the revocation at the Church, "the people in crowds invoking judgments on the Simoniacks."* From this period to the Dissolution, Stanlow continued attached to the Monastery of Whalley, the Monks of which, it is said, maintained here thrice the number (four) stipulated for in the representation made to Pope Nicholas: "*Per servicium inveniendi* XII *capellanus idoneos apud Stanlowe, ad divina continuè celebranda.*" After the Dissolution, the Monastery fell into the hands of the rapacious Sir Richard Cotton; and his son Geo. Cotton, Esq. temp. Elizabeth, sold the property to Sir John Poole, of Poole, Knt. The Rev. Sir Henry Poole, Bart. his successor, died in 1820; and in him the direct male line terminated—having issue two daughters only.

The site is well described in the folio history of the county;† and is occupied by a farm-house and barns, in which some of the ancient door-ways are preserved. From the middle of the yard, a subterraneous excavation in the solid rock, passes under the adjoining buildings, nearly due east, and emerges at a distance of nearly sixty yards, towards the confluence of the Gowy with the Mersey; from whence another similar passage, branching off at right angles to the north, led to a small circular apartment, also in the solid rock, which was discovered within the last few years, when the sea burst violently upon it, and laid bare several leaden coffins, containing, probably, the ashes of some of the *Chaplains* sent here for the celebration of Divine Service.‡

There was a causeway leading to Stanlow, between the sea, and the townships of Great Stanney and Poole, including nearly 120 acres of land; about seventy or seventy-five years ago, it was completely swept away, so that there is now no regular communication between Great Stanney and Ince.

The Stanlow estate, consists of nearly two hundred and thirty acres of grass land, now deemed extra-parochial.

* Ormerod—History of Whalley, &c.

† Ormerod, vol. 2, p. 220-221.

‡ The bones of the Lacies, several of whom were interred at Stanlow, were removed from thence soon after the establishment of the Monastery at Whalley.

PARISH OF EASTHAM,

CONTAINS THE TOWNSHIPS OF

EASTHAM,	CHILDER THORNTON,
HOOTON,	GREAT SUTTON,
OVER POOLE,	LITTLE SUTTON, AND
NETHER POOLE,	WHITBY (PART OF).

EASTHAM,

Is situated about nine miles N. of Chester, in one of the most desirable parts of the Hundred. It was included in the possessions of the Earl, and in the Survey, this parish, with the adjoining one of Bromborow, are united in the same description, although the latter contained the Church and Manor House of the original vill of Eastham.§

About 1152, Randle Gernons, then Earl, gave Bromborow and Eastham, with their Churches, to the Monks of St. Werburgh's, at Chester; a short time previous to which, the Church of Eastham had been built, the

§ Ormerod.

Engraved by J. Tisot of Manch.r from a Drawing by Pennington furnish'd by Math.w Gregson Esq.r of Liverpool

THE VILLAGE OF EASTHAM.

Engraved for Hanshalls History of Cheshire.

Engraved by J. Pigot. Manch^r. From a Drawing by T. Chubbard furnish'd by Math^w. Gregson Esqr. of Liverpool

EASTHAM BOAT HOUSE.

Engraved for Hanshalls. History. of Cheshire.

HISTORY.

parish Church being Bromborow.* As a distinct manor, therefore, Eastham may trace its origin to this period.

The Manor and Church continued vested in the Abbey of St. Werburgh, till the Dissolution, when it fell into the hands of Sir Richard Cotton, from whom it was obtained by Sir Rowland Stanley, of Hooton, he paying a fee-farm rent of £30. a year. It is now the property of his descendant Sir Thomas Stanley Massey Stanley, Bart.

Carlet,—an estate in this township, lies close to the Mersey, about a mile from the Church,—here is one of the principal Ferries to Liverpool.† The Hill above the Ferry-house commands a truly delightful prospect.

PLIMYARD is a hamlet of this township, the property of Sir Thomas Stanley Massey Stanley, Bart.

The *Hall* is an ancient stone building, supposed to be on the site of the Grange belonging to the Monks of Chester Abbey.

The CHURCH is dedicated to St. Mary; the present Rector is the Rev. Thomas Trevor Trevor, LL.D. instituted May 4, 1797—on the presentation of the Dean and Chapter of Chester, who generally appoint one of the Prebendaries.—The Rectorial Tithes of Eastham, Hooton, and Childer Thornton, belong to Sir T. S. M. Stanley, Bart.; those of Over Poole, and Nether Poole, to Sir Hen. Poole, Bart.; of Great Sutton, to Thomas White, Esq.; of Little Sutton, to the Rev. Thomas Edwards, of Aldford; and those of the portion of Whitby, to Mr. Hignet, of Foulke Stapleford ‡

The *Vicarage House* is a capacious mansion, most delightfully situated.

The Church is an extensive building of red stone, crowned with a handsome spire steeple, rebuilt about sixty or seventy years ago.—The interior consists of nave, chancel, and side aisles, the latter divided from the body of the church by four pointed arches, resting on octagonal pillars. At the end of the North aisle is the Stanley chancel. A great portion of the church was, it is said, rebuilt from designs by the celebrated architect Inigo Jones; but Mr. Ormerod argues the improbability of this, from the circumstance that, among some mutilated letters under the chancel window, is the date "17 E. R." viz. 1574, in which year Inigo Jones would only be two years old."

There are a number of monumental memorials here, but few of any particular interest: in a window on the south side of the Church—

Orate pro bono statu Ranulphi Pull, Cl'ici—Qui hanc fenestram vitream fecit. A. D. 1423.

Hic jacet Margeria, nuper uxor Willielmi Stanley, armigeri, ac filia Joh'nis Bromley. militis, quæ obiit die dominica, 13° die mensis Augusti, anno D'ni 1469.

There are two altar tombs of the Stanleys, of Hooton; on one of them, which is surmounted by a cross, there is inscribed round the edges—

William Standley, of Houton, was buried heare the fourth of Janunuary, the yeare of our Lord God, 1612. Death rest in the ende. His wife was Ann Herbert, and left by her livinge one son and six daughters.—Death * * * * * * miseries.

On the surface marble of the other tomb, in capitals—

Here lyeth the bodye of the Honourable Charlotte Lady Stanley, wife to Sir William Stanley, of Hooton, Bart. and daughter to the Right Honourable Richard Lord Viscount Molyneux, who deceased the 31st day of July, 1662.—*Requiescat in Pace.*

Inscribed on a brass plate on the tomb—

Here lyeth the body of Sir Rowland Stanley, of Hooton, Knt. who deceased the 5th day of April a° 1613, and was here buried the 23d day of the same moneth, in the yeare of his age 36.

On the east side of the chancel door, an achievement for James Poole, Esq. of Poole, who died Dec. 13, 1613.

On flag stones within the Altar rails,

Here lyeth the body of Richard Banner, clarke, and Vicker of Eastham, who died the vi day of December, 1655.

Here lyeth, waiting the comeing of the Lord, the body of George Becket, who was Vicar of this Church 29 years, and died in the year 1694, aged 63.

On a marble tablet, against a pillar in the middle aisle—

Sepulturæ consecratum Gulielmi Currey, hujus parœciæ, et Helena, uxoris ejus. Qui spe in Christo stabilita, id sibi unicè negotium fecerunt, ut vitam Christi servo dignam agerent, Deo ut placerent.—Obiit ille 15° Oct. 1779, æt. 72, illa 16 Martii 1785, æt. 82.—Juxta sepultus est Gulielmus Currey, arm^r pærfatorum Gulielmi et Helenæ filius, qui moribus virtuti aptissimis, avilem et militarem vitam feliciter explevit. Obiit 17 Ap. 1798, æt. 58. Elizabetha uxor Gu-

* In the confirmation of the grant by Pope Honorius, it is described, "*Eccl'ia de Brombro', cum Capella de Estham.*"

† See the accompanying plate.

‡ The Rector, says the author of the "*Beauties of England*," is entitled to ALL fish caught in the Mersey on Sundays and Fridays. This statement is inaccurate.

CHESHIRE HISTORY.

lielmi Carrey, hujus parœciæ, armigeri, Femina pia, benevola, moribus universim suavissimis prædita, corpore infirmo, animo æquo, per omnem fere vitæ cursum cum adversa valetudine conflictata, ad æternam requiem migravit 23 Oct. 1785, æt. 63.

The following, with the first memorial noticed in this account, existed in 1593—

Pray for the soule of Peter Stanley, of Byckersteth, Esq. one of the younger sones of Will'm Stanley, of Hoton, Kt. and Elizabeth his wife, being daughter and heire of James Scaresbreck and Margaret his wife, which Margaret was daughter and heire of Thomas Atherton, of Byckersteth, Esq. which made this window, Anno 1543.

There is a parochial *School*, in Childer Thornton, erected about the year 1630, by the Parishioners. The Minister and Trustees appoint the Master, whose stipend arises from gifts and legacies. Mr. H. Marsh left a house and land in Stoke, from which Twenty Shillings are given to the Master of Thornton School, Twenty Shillings to Stanney School, and the remainder to the poor of Eastham. These lands produced about £20. per annum.

The Church Registers commence in 1611.

HOOTON

Is about nine miles N. W. from Chester, beautifully situated above the Mersey. It appears from the Survey, that it was included in the possessions of the Barons of Shipbrook. About the reign of John, the township became by marriage the property of Randle Walensis, whose successors assumed the local name. Temp. Richard II. on the death of William de Hoton, his estate passed to William de Stanley, in right of his wife Margery, sole heiress of William de Hoton. Since which time, to the present, a period of nearly five centuries, the Stanleys have lived here in uninterrupted succession. The present proprietor is Sir Thos. Stanley Massey Stanley, Bart.

The Stanleys were a younger branch of the Audleys, of Staffordshire.

William de Stanley was the first who settled in Cheshire, temp. Edw. II. when he married Jane, daughter and one of the coheirs of Sir Philip Bamville, of Storeton, Knt. Chief Forester of Wirral—to which office he succeeded.

Several of this family have been highly distinguished in the Annals of the Country. Sir John de Stanley, was made Knight of the Garter, and Lord Deputy of Ireland; he was the brother of William Stanley, of Hooton, and marrying Isabella de Latham, was the founder of the noble family of the Stanleys, Earls of Derby.

William Stanley, fourth in descent, married Agnes, one of the daughters and heirs of Robert Grosvenor, of Holme, and obtained with her the manor of Buerton, which still belongs to the Stanleys. He was made Sheriff of Cheshire, temp. Edw. IV. and Carver to the King. The old tower of the former House at Hooton, was built by him. Sir Rowland Stanley, temp. Henry VIII. is noticed as being the oldest Knight in the land.*

In June, 1661, Wm. Stanley was created a Baronet by patent. In 1792, on the death of Sir Wm. Stanley, Bart. the direct male line failing, the estates of the family fell to John Stanley Massey, Esq. of Puddington, (who assumed the name of Stanley) under a settlement made by Sir Rowland Stanley, in April, 1743, previous to his marriage with Elizabeth, daughter of Thomas Parry, Esq. of Perthymael, Flintshire †

The *Hall* of Hooton, a print of which accompanies this notice, was built after the year 1778, (when the ancient house was taken down) from the designs of Mr. S. Wyatt.‡ The stone was obtained from the Storeton quarry.—The Hall is a very handsome edifice, and the circular stone stair-case is generally admired. The situation is truly delightful; commanding a noble view of the fine expanse of the Mersey, from beyond Liverpool, to Ince and Weston point.

The *Old Hall*, of which a view is given in the folio County History, is thus described by Mr. Ormerod: it was a "very large quadrangular building, one of the rooms of which was decorated with rude paintings of the Earls of Chester, executed on the wainscoat. One side was occupied by a strong stone tower, embattled and machicolated, from which rose a slender turret of extraordinary height. It was erected by Sir William Stanley, who had for this purpose a license, enrolled in the Exchequer at Chester, dated Aug. 10, 2 Hen. VII.

Sir Wm. Stanley, who rendered his name detestable in every English ear, by his treacherous surrender of Deventer to Philip II. of Spain, was of this family.

* King.

† Ormerod.

‡ The entrance lodges, in the township of Childer Thornton, are singularly neat and beautiful buildings, also after Mr. Wyatt's designs.

He was a man of great personal bravery, and distinguished himself in the Irish Wars, in 1578; it is recorded that he sustained a charge of 400 foot and 30 horse, belonging to the Earl of Desmond, "in close fight for eight hours, not having himself in his company above six score persons to the uttermost."—In the latter part of his life he stood high in favor with Philip, by whom he was appointed Governor of Mechlin, where he died. A Court Baron is held for the Township.*

OVER POOLE

Is about seven miles N. of Chester, and was included in the possessions of the Barons of Nantwich; and Nether Poole is supposed to have been included in the same description in the Survey.

The earliest subsequent account we have of the township, is its being given by Catherine, the wife of Hameline de Bardulph to the Monastery of St. Werburgh, at Chester, and the Abbot claimed here the customary manerial rights. After the Dissolution, it was granted by Elizabeth, to William and John Glazier, Esqs. subject to a fee-farm rent payable to the Dean and Chapter of Chester. It afterwards passed to the Pooles, and is now the property of the representatives of the late Rev. Sir Henry Poole, Bart. A Court Leet and Baron is annually held for the Manor.

NETHER POOLE

Adjoins the last mentioned township. So early as the reign of Henry III. a family was settled here which assumed the local name, and it terminated in three heiresses Gillian, Basilia, and Alice de Pulle, who quit-
An. 1220. claimed their lands here to William le Hare, of Pulle.† This William is supposed to have been the founder of the regular line of the Pooles of Poole, lately become extinct in the male line by the death of the Rev. Sir Henry Poole, Bart.

About the reign of Edward I. a branch of the family settled in Devonshire, and there founded the Pooles of Shute.

Thomas Poole was made Sheriff of Cheshire, *durante bene placito*, temp. Hen. VIII. He was Seneschal of Birkenhead Priory at its Dissolution; and built the present Hall of Poole.

This family possessed considerable property in the County; an Inq. p. m. Edw. VI. describing them as having lands in Nether Bebbington, Great Neston, Liskard, Bradwall, Salghall, Capenhurst, Kirby, Moreton, Woodchurch, Neston, Leighton, Oscroft, Hurleston, Occleston, Buerton, Oldfield, Handbridge, Backford, Thingwall, and lands attached to the office of Seneshal of Birkenhead. James Poole, died of the wounds he received during the siege of Chester, when the estates of the family passed to his younger brother Thos. Poole, in whose descendants they afterwards continued.

Poole Hall is a very fine old building, chiefly of stone, and from its being nearly covered with lichen, has a truly venerable appearance. Each end of the east front terminates in an octagon turret, of a height corresponding with the centre gable of the north front. The house is approached by an embattled porch leading to a spacious Hall, beyond which is another extensive apartment, both of them decorated with numerous family and other portraits. Solid blocks of oak compose the stairs; one of the upper rooms is wainscotted; and over the chimney piece of the hall is the date 1574.

The House and its immediate vicinity, command some fine marine views—it is occupied by a farmer.

WHITBY,

Which is partly in the parish of Stoke, is a little more than six miles N. E. of Chester. It is not noticed in the Survey, but was included in the possessions of the Barons of Nantwich; and William Malbedeng granted it to the Abbey of Chester in 1093, the Abbot claiming the same rights here as in Poole.

After the Dissolution, the Glaziours obtained a grant of the township, from whom it passed by sale to the Morgells of Moston; and passed with their heiress, to Henry Bennett, Esq. Mr. Hewitt, of Hoole, subsequently purchased the estate from Sir John Williams, Bart. of Bodlewyddan, and John Townshend, Esq. who married the daughters of Hen. Bennett, Esq. of Moston; and in two or three years afterwards, sold it to the Right Hon. Earl Grosvenor, who holds a Court for the Manor. Mr. Grace is the owner and occupier of an estate in the township.

The Canal from Chester terminates in this township, and from the rapid intercourse between that City and

* Some of the ancient portraits still exist; among them, one of Edric Sylvester, Ancestor of the Storetons. Attached to Hooton, is the ancient Hamlet of ROVEACRE, also the property of Sir T. S. M. Stanley, Bart.

and Liverpool, Whitby is raised to the importance of a small port. A steam packet plies between this and Liverpool daily; a comfortable Inn is established here; and Lodging Houses, with Hot and Cold Baths, have been erected for the accommodation of the Valetudinarian.—A powerful Steam Engine was built at the north end of the basin, to supply the Canal with water from the Mersey, but since the union with the Nantwich branch, it became unnecessary, and was taken down.

LITTLE SUTTON

Is about seven miles and a half N. N. W. from Chester, and forms an inconsiderable village on the road between Chester and the Ferries to Liverpool.

So early as the reign of Edward the Confessor, the secular Monks of Chester held Sutton—here was one of the Abbot's four principal Manor Houses, and Richard II. granted to the Abbot letters patent, empowering him to fortify his Manor Houses of Sutton, Inise, and Salghton.

After the Dissolution, the Manor was granted to the Dean and Chapter of Chester, but was subsequently seized by Sir Rich. Cotton, on whose death Sir Hugh Cholmondeley, of Cholmondeley, obtained possession, and it passed from him to the Cholmondeleys of Vale Royal, who continued to hold it, subject to a fee farm rent to the Dean and Chapter.

It was purchased in 1798, by Mr. White, of London, and is now the property of his son, John White, Esq. who holds a Court Leet and Baron for Great and Little Sutton.

The ancient *Hall* of Sutton has been taken down, and a farm-house built on its site. There are now no remains of the *Abbot's Manor House;* but Mr. Ormerod conjectures that it stood about 400 yards S. W. of the present Hall, where, in 1611, a curious discovery was made in digging for the foundation of a farm house. In this place, a little below the surface, an ancient cemetry was found by the workmen, about 42 feet square, containing many bones and skulls. This inclosed space was in twenty-five compartments, supported by thirty-six pillars; each compartment about seven feet square; and in these compartments the bodies were laid in rows It was conjectured that the pillars supported a floor above, probably that of the domestic Chapel. These pillars were about 2 feet 6 inches high, rounded inwards towards the middle, where their diameter did not exceed seven inches; the diameter at the tops and bottom was 12 inches. Two steps remained on the North side leading to the room above, near which was the stone frame work of a door, with an inscription, which was destroyed by the workmen before its purport was ascertained.

GREAT SUTTON

Adjoins the preceding township, and was included in the possessions of the Abbot. It is also the property of Mr. White. It did not originally belong to the Abbots, for it was divided, according to the Survey, between the Bishop of Chester, and the Barons of Malpas.

CHILDER THORNTON

Is about eight miles N. N. W. from Chester. It belonged to the Abbey of Chester; and continued so vested till the Dissolution, when Sir Richard Cotton seized upon it, and subsequently granted it in fee-farm to Wm. Mayo, (or Baxter) and Richard Bavand. In the 38th of Elizabeth, the former passed lands here to Robert Cotgreave, for the sum of £500—The property here is chiefly divided, but Sir T. S. M. Stanley, W. W. Currey, Esq. the Representatives of the Spurstows, and Joseph Wilmot, Esq. claim manerial rights, and the privileges of a Court Leet and Baron. The principal land-owners are Sir T. S. M. Stanley, Bart. the Minor Canons of Chester Cathedral, under the will of Mrs. Barbara Dod;* W. W. Currey, Esq. Major in the army; Joseph Wilmot, Esq. in right of his wife, daughter of Mr. Litherland; Robert Vyner, Esq.; and the Representatives of the Spurstows.

* May 29, 1703.

There is a *School* here for the education of fourteen children, established about 1660, which is kept in repair by the parish, and has a few trifling legacies, as an endowment.

THE PARISH OF BROMBOROW,

CONTAINS THE TOWNSHIPS OF

BROMBOROW, AND BRIMSTAGE.

Bromborow, or *Brombrorough*, is about eleven miles north from Chester. Early in the 10th century, a monastery was founded here by Elflida, which was then called *Brimesburg*;* but it had ceased to exist before the Survey was made, and the township itself was included in the description of Eastham. The Charter granted by Edward I. when Earl, for a Market every Monday, and an annual Fair of three days, at the feast of St. Barnabas, is no longer enforced. The Dean and Chapter of Chester, had a grant of the Manor, at the Dissolution, but with many other of their estates, it was seized by Sir Richard Cotton, and was granted to the same parties who held Childer Thornton, with the exception of the Old Manor House and demesne, the Water Mills, and a Wood called William Drife, which were obtained by Henry Hardware, gent.—Subsequently the Manor was sold to Bishop Bridgeman and from him to his son Sir Orlando Bridgeman, Knight and Baronet, and Keeper of the Great Seal. He conveyed it to — Greene, who resold the estate in parcels, excepting the Manor and Court, and Hall, which were purchased by Edward Bradshaw, one of the Aldermen of the City of Chester.† From his son Sir James Bradshaw, of Risby, Knt. the manor and hall were purchased by James Mainwaring, Esq. his brother-in-law, the present proprietor, about 1681.—Mr. Mainwaring is a descendant of the Mainwarings of Whitmore, in Shropshire, and is representative and heir male of this ancient stock; lineally descended from Ranulphus, who possessed Warmincham, Peover, &c. at the time of the Survey.

The *Hall*, the seat of Mr. Mainwaring, is a handsome old house, most delightfully situated, commanding many fine views on the Mersey, the opposite shore, Liverpool, &c.

The *Court House*, the old seat of the Hardwares, is a stone building, with bay windows and gables. The moated site of the Manor House of the Abbots, adjoins the Court House, and the line of fortification is still visible.

The Church is dedicated to St. Barnabas, and is of high antiquity. On the separation of Eastham from the Manor, as has been before noticed, a New Church was built there, which, together with Bromborow Church, were given to the Abbey of Chester; and Pope Honorius, in his charter of confirmation, describes the Mother Church, distinctly: "*Eccl' de Brombro'* cum capellâ de Eastham" At the Dissolution, the impropriation, which is now vested in Mr. Mainwaring, fell into lay hands. The nomination of the Curacy, is in the Dean and Chapter of Chester.

The Church consists of a body and chancel, and an aisle on the north side separated from the body by four pointed arches. The door way is very ancient, and it has been doubted whether some parts of the building are not remains of the Saxon Monastery of Brimesberg.

BRIMSTAGE,

Brunstath, *Brinstall*, *Brumstagh*, or *Burnstache*, is about four miles N. E. of Great Neston, adjoining the last described township At a very early period the Domvilles were settled here, the elder line of which family is now represented by the Earls of Shrewsbury:

---

* Gibson, in the Saxon Chronicle, conjectures from the similarity of names, that here was fought the decisive battle between the forces of Athelsten, and those of Aalaf and Constantine, in which the former was victorious. This battle is said to have taken place in 937.—The invading fleet of the Danes was composed of 615 vessels of various sizes.—The supposition, however, is rather too far fetched; for instead of this fleet entering the Mersey, all our ancient writers place it in the Humber.

† He was the Lord of Bromborow in 1666.

CHESHIRE HISTORY.

another branch subsequently settled at Lymm, and continued till early in the last century. It is conjectured,* that the Domvilles were a younger branch of the Barons of Montalt. The manor passed from John Domville, temp. Richard II. to Sir Hugh Holes, who married Margery, heiress of the Domvilles; and the Holes's possessed the estate till the latter part of the reign of Henry V. when Margaret, sole heiress of Thos. Holes, brought the whole in marriage to Sir John Frontbeck, of Dunham, who was killed at Blore Heath. The manor of Brimstage is now possessed by his descendant, the Earl of Shrewsbury, and the tenants owe service to the Leet at Raby.

* Ormerod.

The *Hall* is situated at the extremity of the village; it is built of stone, and occupied by a farmer. Adjoining it is a very ancient square tower, of considerable height; the lower apartment was the Chapel, the roof of which is vaulted.

In February, 1398, Hugh Hulse, and Margery his wife, obtained a license to build an oratory here; it is therefore supposed that this tower formed part of an extensive house, of great strength, and that it was built in the reign of Hen. V.

It was tenanted in 1592, by J. Poole, Esq. of Poole, who superintended the estates of the Talbots, in the neighbourhood.

THE PARISH OF BEBINGTON,

CONTAINS THE TOWNSHIPS OF

NETHER BEBINGTON, POULTON LANCELYN, HIGHER BEBINGTON, TRANMERE, AND STORETON.

NETHER BEBINGTON

Is about thirteen miles N. of Chester, and nearly five N. E. N. from Great Neston. In the reign of Richard Cœur de Lion, Hugh de Boidele of Dodleston, granted the manor to Robert de Lancelyn. The Lancelyns continued here in uninterrupted descent, till the reign of Henry VIII. when, after the death of Wm. Lancelyn, the last heir male, his daughter and heiress Elizabeth brought it in marriage to Randle Greene, Esq.† In 1756, Edward Greene, Esq. last heir male, died, and the estates passed to his sister Priscilla, who married John Parnell, Esq. On her death they were vested by her bequest, in the present proprietor Joseph Greene, Esq. formerly Kent, having assumed the present name in compliance with Mrs. Parnell's will. Mr. Greene holds a Court Leet and Baron for this Manor, and Poulton Lancelyn.

This township affords some delightful views of the Mersey, with the port of Liverpool, and the high grounds of Lancashire.

The CHURCH, which tradition says was formerly called *White-church*, is situated a considerable distance from the Village. It is dedicated to St. Andrew, and the present Rector, is the Rev. Roger Jacson, A. M.‡ instituted Nov. 15, 1777.

About 1093, Seward, gave the "Chapel of Bebington," and part of the Manor, to the Monastery of St. Werburgh, at Chester, which gift was subsequently confirmed by his descendant William de Lancelyn. It continued vested in the Abbots till the dissolution, when it fell, with other of the Church estates, into the hands of Sir Richard Cotton. Eventually it was vested in the Stanleys, of Hooton, from whom it passed to a branch of the Pooles, of Poole. The Rev. Hugh Poole, son of Hugh Poole, Rector of Bebington, dying without issue, his sister brought the advowson in marriage

† Of the family of Greene, of Greene Norton, co. Northampton.

‡ This Gentleman executed the important duty of Chairman of the Quarter Sessions, for a considerable period, with great credit to himself and advantage to the County.

to —— Jacson, Esq. a younger son of the Jacsons of Hallwood, co. York.

The CHURCH consists of a nave and south aisle, the latter divided by a range of massive Saxon arches — The eastern part of the Church is in the style of the conclusion of the 15th century. The windows are large and uniform. The pillars between the body and aisle at the eastern end, are clustered. At the end of the south aisle is a strong and handsome tower, crowned with a beautiful spire. The external appearance of the building is very imposing, and it is a prominent object in the view from the opposite shore.

There are but few monumental memorials:—On a small brass plate in the Chancel—

Radulphus Poole, Hugoni Patri, tam suggesto quam sepulchro eodem, successor, collectus fuit ad patres. Aprilis v° 1662.

Nearly adjoining this, on a marble tablet, an inscription—

To the memory of John Jacson, son of the present Rector, who died March 11, 1799, aged 20, after a painful illness of seven years' duration.

On the south side of the Altar, on a large pyramidal monument of black and white marble,

In memory of Edward Green, Esq. only son of John Green, Esq. by Priscilla, his wife, dyed without issue, May 19, 1756, aged 50.

On a monument of black marble, opposite the last,

Priscilla, eldest daughter and heiress of Edw. Green, Esq. widow of John Parnell, Esq. of Chester, died December 18, 1792, aged 86.—Ursula Green, spinster, died Dec. 1791, aged 84. Edward Parnell, Esq. son of John and Priscilla, died unmarried, Aug. 1776, aged 39. Elizabeth Green, spinster, died May, 1751, aged 41. Within these rails their remains are deposited, with those of numerous ancestors, resident at Poulton Lancelyn, in this parish, for more than seven centuries, and Lords also of the Manor.

"The righteous shall be had in everlasting remembrance."

On a mural monument, at the east end of the north aisle—

Near this are interred, in hopes of a blessed resurrection through Jesus Christ our Lord, the bodys of the Greens of Pooton Lancelyn, Esqrs. viz. Edward 1631, Randle 1639, Henry 1653, Richard Jan. 1677, his wife, daughter to Sir Thomas Bunbury, Bart. May, 1678, Edward 1694, John 1711, his wife Priscilla, Dec. 15, 1742, the Rev. Thomas Green, Jan. 17, 1746.—Thomas Green, A. M. R[r] of Woodchurch, erected this 1742.

In 1655, a *Charity School* was founded here for the Children of Great Bebington, and the demesne of Poulton; it was endowed by the Landowners with twenty acres of land, from a common then inclosed. The Master is elected by Trustees; the Rector of Bebington, and the Proprietor of Poulton, being of the number. Among other benefactions to the parish poor, are several sums of money for providing parish cows. There are now ten, which are let out by the Rector and Churchwardens, at five shillings a year for each cow, for the purpose of forming a fund to keep up the stock. The cows are inspected annually. In 1692, there were twenty-nine cows kept; the price of a cow then was less than £3. at the present day about £9.

POULTON LANCELYN

Or *Poulton-cum-Spital*, is about fourteen miles from Chester.—Soon after the conquest, it was held by the Lancelyns under the Boydells, of Dodleston, by a charter, by which the former were to pay twenty marks, and send four men every third year to repair the works at Dodleston Castle.

The descent of the Lancelyns to the Greens, is the same as noticed in the last described township. The whole of the township is the property of Joseph Greene, Esq. with the exception only of a small tenement belonging to Robt. Vyner, Esq. of Gautby, co. Lincoln.

There is some beautiful rural scenery in the township. The *Hall* is in a pleasant situation, commanding bold and extensive views. In the grounds adjoining are to be traced the remains of the Castle or fortified house of the Lancelyns. It was situated near the meadows called the *Marfords*, so termed from a ford anciently here, over a large pool, which was formed by the tides, before the receding of the waters from this coast.

There was a CHAPEL, temp. Henry III. in the *Hamlet of Spital*,* in this township. It was dedicated to Thomas à Becket. There are now no remains of it. It is mentioned in Tanner's *Noticia*, as being in existence in the reign of Edward I. and was for the reception of Lepers. Divine Service was performed here by the Almoner of the Abbey of Chester, and Mass said for the souls of the Bishops, the Earls, Abbots, and Monks of Chester; for this service, the Almoner had the revenues of the Church of Ince, with the exception of 20s. paid to the Monastery of St. Werburgh.

* An abbreviation of *Hospital*, from which the township has its name.

Cheshire

STORETON

Is about five miles N. E. from Great Neston, and the Manors of *Great* and *Little Storeton* are included in this township. The situation is one of the most barren and dreary in the hundred. The earliest account we have of it, is its presentation, together with Puddington, to Alan Sylvester,* by Randal Meschines, Earl of Chester.

On the death of Ralph, son of Alan, the township was especially granted to Alexander, son-in-law of Alan Sylvester,† who assumed the local name. The Master Forestership of Wirral thus became vested in him. He left two daughters, Johanna and Agnes; the former of whom dying, the entire estate became vested in the latter, wife of Sir Thomas Bamville; and their daughter Jane, marrying Sir William Stanley, Knight, brought with her part of the estates of the family, and thus the Stanleys became settled in Cheshire. Ellen and Agnes, also daughters of Sir Thomas Bamville, had the residue of the property divided between them. Ellen married William Lakene, and Agnes, John de Becheton. Ultimately the whole of the estates became vested in the Stanleys, and are now the property of Sir T. S. M. Stanley, Bart. who holds Courts Leet and Baron for the Manor.

The *Hall* is occupied by a farmer; and the remains of the old mansion of the Storetons are still to be traced in some buildings of white stone, now used as barns, &c.

In this township is a Quarry of remarkably fine white stone.

BEBINGTON SUPERIOR

Was held by Robert de Bebington, from John de Worleston, by the render of a rose on St. John's Day annually. From the Bebingtons it passed in marriage to the Minshulls, of Minshull, and continued vested in them till the reign of Elizabeth, when Elizabeth daughter and sole heiress of John Minshull, brought it in marriage to Thos. Cholmondeley, Esq. of Vale Royal. About the middle of last century, the township was sold in parcels by Charles Cholmondeley, Esq. M. P.

The principal proprietors at present are Daniel Orred, Esq. of Chester, and Thomas White, Esq. of the same City. Mr. Orred's purchase was made directly from the Cholmondeleys; and Mr. White, father of the present proprietor, made purchases at different periods.—Gamekeepers are appointed for the reputed Manor by both of these gentlemen, each laying claim to the manerial rights.

Randle de Bebington, and William, Randal, James, John, and Charles, sons of his eldest brother, lost their lives in the conflict of Flodden Field. The Bebingtons of Chorley and Nantwich are descended from this stock.

In this township is the *Rock Ferry*, formerly a considerable medium of thoroughfare between Chester and Liverpool, but now completely eclipsed by the adjacent ferries of Whitby, Eastham, Tranmere, and Birkenhead.

An occasional seat of the Minshulls, Derby House, is the property of Dr. Watson, of Preston, Lancashire.

TRANMERE

Is about seven miles N. E. of Neston, and sixteen miles from Chester. It was formerly called Tranmull, and gave name to a family as early as the reign of Henry III. A daughter of Richard de Tranmere, temp. Edw. III. married John de Bebington, and brought with her a moiety of the manor, which subsequently descended to the Minshulls, and Cholmondeleys, by the latter of whom it was sold. The other moiety became, by marriage, the property of Robert Holme, of Tranmere, and William Holme, the 8th in descent from him, temp. Jac. I. sold it in parcels.

The manerial rights are now claimed by Francis Richard Price, Esq. of Bryn y Pys, Flintshire, proprietor of the Priory of Birkenhead, and Daniel Orred, Esq. of Chester, who purchased estates here from the Cholmondeleys, and both of these gentlemen appoint gamekeepers.

The Kents, formerly considerable landowners in the township, became extinct temp. Charles II. when Elizabeth, their heiress, married Edward Glegg, Esq. of Grange.

* Steward to the Earl.

† The Charter runs thus:—"Hugo Comes Cestriæ, Constabulario suo, Dapifero suo, et universis Baronibus suis, et omnibus Hominibus suis. Salutem. Noveritis me dedisse Alexandro Magistro filii mei, Aunabellam filiam filii Alani Salvagii, cum totâ sua hereditate, videlicet, Storeton et Pudington, et omnibus eorum pertinentiis, tenendà in feoda et hereditate, liberè et quietè de me et heredibus meis, sicut Carta patris mei testatur. Testibus, Bertramo de Verdon, Johanne Constabulario."

 From this township sprang the family of Holme, of which were the four Randle Holme, celebrated in the History of Chester, and well known to all in any degree versed in its antiquities.*

* THE RANDLE HOLME, FATHER, SON, AND GRANDSON, HERALDS.

After having searched the different Biographical records, it is with a degree of surprise and regret that we find no mention made of these indefatigable Heralds; whose manuscripts have contributed so largely, to furnish our great seminary of literary curiosities, the British Museum; and afforded accurate information both to the antiquarian, and historian. These three characters being born before the commencement of the register, in the parish in which they resided, we have not been able to ascertain the exact period of their birth.

The first RANDLE HOLME was the son of Wm. Holme, stationer, who lived in the Bridge-street, Chester; which William, I find, entered on the books, of the united Company of Stationers, Painters, Glaziers, and Embroiderers; the 12th of June, 1592, and his son Randle, June 3d, 1598. He was leave-looker, of the city, anno 1618. Sheriff, anno 1616, and Mayor anno 1633. He died early in the year 1654, and was buried January the 30th in the body of St. Mary's Church; where a handsome monument was erected to his memory, with a Latin inscription, which still remains in good preservation.—He it was who laid the foundation of his son's heraldrical knowledge, who succeeded him on his demise.

RANDLE HOLME, son of the aforementioned, was brought into the Stationer's Company, according to his own entry, October the 16th, 1622: thirty-two years before his father's death, to whom he was Sheriff, anno, 1613—He was Mayor, 1643.

In searching the Catalogue of Harleian Manuscripts, No. 2002, Section 13th, we found the following item:—

Copie of a commission of Charles I. empowering Randolph Holme Mayor of Chester, Sir Robert Brerewood, Kt. Recorder, Sir Orlando Bridgeman, Kt. Attorney of his Courts of Wards and Liveries, and Vice Chamberlaine of Chester, Nicholas Ince, Richard Dutton, Charles Walley, Randolph Holme, sen. Col. Francis Gamull, and Thos. Throp, Aldermen of the said City, to sieze upon the effects of absent rebels, and of such of their adherents, as were, or had been in actual rebellion against him; the said effects (of what kind soever) being within the city, or county of the city of Chester; or within five miles of the said city, within the county palatine of Chester; giving likewise commands how they should dispose of the same. This bears Teste at Oxford, the first of January, anno Regni 19. fol. 299.

Copie of *Daniel King's certificate, importing that he had received from Mr. Randle Holme, an original Grant, under the Broad Seal and Hand of King Charles I. which he hoped to show to King Charles II. for the benefit of the loyal sufferers of the city of Chester. Dated 26th July, 1662. fol. 301. b.

This Grant I take to be the Commission mentioned in the last section or article; and it may be easily imagined that the rebels, when gotten into power and into possession of Chesster, would be revenged to the utmost on all those who acted by its color and authority; so that it is no wonder if the Holmes' were suddenly oppressed, and (at long run) brought to ruin. I remember a son of the third Randle Holme, (son to the second who was Mayor when this commission was issued; who was son to the old Alderman, named in the same commission) and, I think, his name was also Randle. He was Tapster or Chamberlaine in the Golden Talbot Inn, in Liverpool, A. D. 1694; his poor father the third Randle then living.

The second Randle Holme, was undoubtedly the greatest character of the three; in the year 1688, he published a Work, entitled, "The Accademie of Armoury, or a store-house of Armoury and "Blazonry, &c. &c."—'*Every man shall camp by his Standard, "and under the Ensign of his Father's house. Numb.* ii. 2. *&c.*' "By Randle Holme of the city of Chester, Gentleman Sewer in extraordinary to his late Majesty King Charles II. and sometimes "Deputy for the King at Arms." Chester, printed for the Author, MDCLXXXVIII. There is also a curious engraved title, with this inscription; "Domum Tho. Simpson de civit. Cestr. Ald. et just. pacis."

By an address to the public, printed at the end of the contents of this large work,† (consisting of upwards of eleven hundred pages) we find it was his intention to publish another volume, but must lament, that a work so full of curious information, should never be published,‡ for want of that pecuniary support, which the compiler was incapable of affording.

There are several pieces of poetry, in praise of his work, by his son, his Doctor, his Apothecary, and his Printer!

To each chapter of this work, are prefixed plates, and dedications to those Gentlemen who contributed towards its publication; and with great fatigue, trouble, and expense, did Randle Holme wade through this elaborate work, which for want of pecuniary support, never was completed. He died March 15th, 1699, and was buried in the north aisle of St. Mary's Church.

He was succeeded by his son, the THIRD RANDLE HOLME. This man amassed a considerable property during his life-time. That part of Glover's-stone, called Holme-street, entirely belonged to him. He was Sheriff, anno 1705, but did not live to be Mayor. He married Margaret, daughter of Griffith Lloyd, Esq. of Llanarmon, in the county of Denbigh; by whom he had issue, five children, who all died young.—CHESHIRE BIOGRAPHY.

* Author of the Vale Royal of Cheshire.

† "Thus far have I with much cost and pains, caused to be printed for the public benefit; what remains (and is ready for the press) is as followeth in the succeeding contents; which if encouraged by liberal and free contributers, may appear in the world, else will sleep in the bed of its conception, and never see the glorious light of the Sun."

‡ The M S. materials for this work, are now in the British Museum.

In this township is one of the great ferries to Liverpool, to which two Steam Vessels ply throughout the day; besides numerous daily boats. Many of the Liverpool Merchants and Tradesmen have retiring houses in this township, which has already become considerably increased in its population.

Holt Hill commands a truly delightful view of the Mersey, and the opposite coast of Lancashire, &c.

BIRKENHEAD

Is about nine miles N. N. E. from Neston, and nearly sixteen miles and half from Chester. About A. D. [illegible], Hamon de Mascie founded here a Priory, dedicated to St. James, for sixteen Benedictine Monks. The estate at a very early period was attached to the Great Barony of Dunham Massy.

In 1279, Hamon de Masci, gave to the Priory the Rectory of Bowdon, and it was also further endowed with the Rectory of Davenham, and the vills of Over Bebington, Salghall Massey, Bidston, Moreton, Claughton, and Tranmere, and the Rectories of Backford, and Bidston—besides numerous other estates of less importance, but in the whole producing a very considerable revenue.*

The list of Priors is rather imperfect: the earliest on record is

Oliver, temp. John .. ..
Robert de Bechinton .. .. 1338-9.
———, a Monk of Birkenhead, .. 1339.
Roger,.. .. .. 1379.
Robert, ... 1428.
Thomas Bovere, ... 1455.
Thomas Reynforth,.. .. .. .. 1460.
Nicholas, ... 1495.

* * * * * *

Altho' Leland states, that this Priory was "a Celle to Chester," it is much doubted, and particularly by Tanner, from the fact of the right of election being vested in the Monks, and the distinct valuation of the establishments, temp. Henry VIII.

Those who are desirous of a long written description of the remains of the Priory, can refer to Mr. Ormerod's work; the accompanying engraving affords a pretty accurate delineation of part of the present exterior:

* Amongst other rights claimed by the Prior, temp. Edward III. was that of ferrying passengers from Birkenhead to Liverpool, and of building houses (Inns?) for their accommodation,—so that, in fact, Birkenhead is returned in 1822, to what it was in the reign of the Third Henry.—The charges then were for a horseman 2d, a foot passenger ¼d.—and they were thought very exorbitant.—Another privilege possessed almost exclusively by the fraternity, was that of electing a Prior from amongst themselves, which, however, it appears, they subsequently lost, as the right of the advowson of Birkenhead occurs in the 19th Edw. III. as being vested in the Barons of Dunham Massy.

CHESHIRE

The ruins of the Priory form a square of about 25 yards The most perfect part of the building, an oblong room, about 46 feet by 23 feet, was used as the Parochial Chapel till the year 1820, when the present Church was built.

In this Chapel is a plain monument, with this inscription—

Near this place lie the remains of Richard Parry Price, Esq. F. R S. who after bearing with uncommon fortitude a very long and lingering illness, died May 14, 1782, aged 45. He was a tender husband, an affectionate father, a sincere friend, and a good Christian. This monument was erected to perpetuate his virtues, by his much afflicted widow.

The silent dead nor praise nor trophies seek,
Yet what truth dictates gratitude may speak.

The remaining buildings are in a state of great decay, and unless some effective means be taken for the preservation of such venerable relics, the whole will speedily be a mass of ruins.

On the Dissolution,* the site of the Priory and the Manor of Birkenhead, were granted to Ralph Worseley, Esq. of Worseley, in the county of Lancaster, whose eldest daughter, and co-heir Alice, brought the estate in marriage to Thomas Powell Esq. of Horseley, about the year 1572. In 1629, Thomas Powell, Esq. of Birkenhead, was created a Baronet.

About 1715, John Clieveland,† Esq. Mayor of Liverpool in 1708, and Member of Parliament for the Borough in 1710, purchased the estate from the representatives of the last Baronet;‡ and in 1716, Mr. Clieveland devised the estate to his son William, who, with his brother John, dying without issue, the property devolved on their sister Alice, wife of Francis Price, Esq. but subsequently married to Thomas Lloyd, Esq. of Gwernhayled.

Francis Richard Price, Esq. of Bryn y Pys, in the county of Flint, great-grandson of Alice Clieveland, is the present proprietor of the Manor of Birkenhead, comprising all the land from high water mark, to Bidston Light-house, including the Woodside Ferry.

HISTORY.

The situation of Birkenhead is truly delightful, opposite to the great town of Liverpool, from which, on Sundays, there have frequently been importations of from 15,000 to 20,000 persons in one day. An excellent and capacious Inn has been built Messrs. Hetherington, Grindrod, & Addison, of Liverpool, called the Birkenhead Hotel—and a magnificent Quay, affording ample protection for the numerous steam and other boats which are continually plying from hence to Liverpool. A few years ago, the township was composed of a few straggling houses,—it has now assumed the appearance of a respectable town, formed into regular streets of elegant houses. The increase of the population has of course corresponded.

In 1811, there were only *sixteen* inhabited houses here, *seventeen* families, and *one hundred and ten* inhabitants; in 1822, there were *twenty-nine* houses, *thirty-six* families, and *two hundred* inhabitants.

The CHURCH is an elegant and substantial building of red stone, composed of nave, aisles, and tower, crowned with a neat spire, forming altogether an interesting feature from Liverpool, and the River views. There is a ring of six tuneable bells in the steeple.—Mr. Price has the appointment of the Minister of the Church, whose income has been increased by Queen Anne's Bounty.

The *Hall*, or as it has generally been termed, *Birkit House*, is a short distance from the Priory; it possesses no particular excellencies as a building, but has a most desirable site. During the Civil Wars, it was garrisoned by the King's troops, who thus commanded the passage of the River. On the 22d Sept. 1644, it was taken by the troops of the Parliament.

* Its revenues were then estimated at £90. 13s. a clear annual income.

† Of this family was Clieveland the Poet.

‡ Lysons.

CHESHIRE | HISTORY.

THE PARISH OF BIDSTON,

CONTAINS FOUR TOWNSHIPS,

BIDSTON,	SALGHALL MASSIE,
MORETON,	CLAUGHTON,

OF ALL OF WHICH NO NOTICE IS TAKEN IN THE SURVEY.

BIDSTON,

Is about eighteen miles from Chester, and was formerly attached to the Barony of Dunham Massy.—Henry Earl of Lancaster, purchased from the Massys the manor of Bidston; and eventually, the manor of Dunham with Bidston, and its other dependencies, were given in Exchange by Henry Duke of Lancaster, to Roger le Strange, Lord Knockin. After the death of Roger le Strange. temp. Henry VI. Bidston was alienated to the Stanleys Earls of Derby, who continued the proprietors till 1653, when Charlotte de Tremouille, Countess of Derby, and her son the Earl, sold it to Wm. Steele, Esq. and temp. Charles II. he re-sold it to Lord Kingston. Subsequently Bidston was sold to Sir Robert Viner, Bart. a while Lord Mayor of London; and is now the property of his descendant, Robt. Vyner, Esq. of Gaultby, in the county of Lincoln, who holds Courts Leet and Baron for it.

It was during the embarrassments of his family, occasioned by the part they had taken against the Parliament, that Charles 8th Earl of Derby retired to his estate here, where he lived in economical retirement.

The *Hall*, the ancient seat of the Stanleys, and a favorite residence of Wm. Earl of Derby, Lord Lieutenant and Chamberlain of Cheshire, temp. James I. is built of yellow-coloured stone. The front is finished with gables, and lighted by bay windows, and the whole has a very venerable appearance. The village is small, but cleanly.

The CHURCH is situated in the lower part of the town; over the western door of which are the armorial bearings of the Stanleys. It consists of nave, chancel, side aisles, and tower, and is kept in tolerable repair.

B. Keene, Esq. Registrar of the Diocese, leases the Rectory, with the tithes, &c. under the Bishop of Chester, and appoints the Curate.

It formed part of the endowment of the neighbouring Priory of Birkenhead, and was appropriated by it. In the 33d Hen. VIII. the Impropriation and Patronage were given to the Bishop of Chester. The Registers commence in 1679.

The *Charity School* is supposed to have been founded in 1636, when the sum of £200. was raised for its endowment. The *School House* was built upon a piece of land given by Lord Strange. The income of the land attached to the school is about £10 per ann.

FORD, sometimes called *Bidston-cum-Ford*,* is a Hamlet of the Township.

In conformity with an Act of Parliament passed in 1762, a *Light House* was erected here by the Corporation of Liverpool, the expenses attending which are defrayed by a trifling duty on all ships sailing to and from Liverpool. It is a strong building, well adapted for the purpose, and adjoining it are a range of *Signal Poles* and *Flags*, belonging to the Merchants of that town.

In 1814, about 1530 acres of inferior land here were let at an annual rent of 44s. per acre.

SALGHALL MASSIE—MORETON.

Salghall is about nine miles N. N E. from Neston. The Manor is the property of Robert Vyner, Esq.† and his tenants attend the Court at Bidston.

Moreton is nearly nine miles and a half from Neston; the entire face of the township has a miserable aspect. The tenants attend Mr. Vyner's Court at Bidston.

A small CHAPEL OF EASE, formerly in this township was destroyed about 1690.‡

CLAUGHTON

Is partly in this parish, and in the adjoining one of Woodchurch. It formerly belonged to the Prior of

* Lysons.

† See Bidston.

‡ Gastrel Notit.

 Birkenhead, and after the Dissolution became the property of the Worsleys; from Alice, their coheiress, it passed in marriage to Thomas Powell, Esq. of Horsley, and is now the property of Francis Richard Price, Esq. Although a Gamekeeper is appointed, there is no Court held.

THE PARISH OF WALLASEY,*

CONTAINS THE TOWNSHIPS OF

WALLASEY, LISCARD, POULTON-cum-SEACOME.

Wallasey is about twenty miles N. E. from Chester. It appears from the Survey, that it was included in the possessions of Robert de Rodelent, on whose death it became attached to the Fee of Halton.

In the reign of Henry VI. the Manor was held by Sir Thomas Stanley, and Henry Litherland, and subsequently the whole was vested in the Stanleys. After 1668, part of the estate was alienated by the Earls of Derby, and passing to the families of Steele and Kingston, became the property of the Vyners, R. Vyner, Esq. being the present proprietor.

A portion of the Manor was obtained by Sir John Egerton, Knt. as early as the commencement of the reign of James I. and is now the property of his descendant, Sir John Grey Egerton, Bart. Mr. Vyner, and Sir John, are the joint Lords of the Manor. An estate here, which was the property of F. R. Price, Esq. has been purchased by John Tobin, Esq. of Liverpool, and with it the old Hall of Wallasey.

The *Mock Beggar Hall* estate, now called Leasowe Castle, has been purchased from the Egertons, by the widow of Lewis Boodeè, Esq. The house is turretted, and handsomely built, and realizes almost the stories we have heard of palaces in a wilderness,—for a more wild and desolate tract of land than the Leasowe† now about to be inclosed, is rarely to be met with.

Notwithstanding the barren appearance of this district, there is a tradition, that at one period "a man might have gone from tree top to tree top, from the Meoles stocks to Birkenhead"‡

At the north-west point of this parish is the *Black Rock*, projecting far into the sea, so well known to those navigating the Mersey to Liverpool; and near to which, at high water mark, is a mass of sandstone, indented by the operation of the sea, into natural caverns, of the *secrets* of which, the neighbourhood abounds in many marvellous stories. These caverns are called the *Red Noses*.

There were Horse Races on the Leasowe so late as the year 1750, when they were discontinued. These Races were of very early origin; the celebrated Duke of Monmouth run his horse here, won the plate, and presented it to the daughter of the Mayor of Chester.

The Church|| is dedicated to Saint Hilary.—It is a divided Rectory, a moiety of which belonged to the Priory of Birkenhead; but on the Dissolution, it was attached as part of the endowment, to the Bishopric of Chester, and still remains so. The Rev. T. Armitstead, of Backford, holds it in lease from the Bishop of Chester.

Gastrell's *Notitia* says, "There were formerly *two* Churches here, one called Walley's Kirk, situated in the present Church-yard, the foundation of which is yet visible, and Lee's Kirk, near a narrow land still called the Kirk-way, but which one became ruinous, and the,

* Formerly called *Kirkby in Walley*.

† About 220 acres. The Sand Hills, by the Inclosure Act, are to remain, as a protection from the fury of the Irish Sea.

‡ See Ormerod, Vol. II. p. 262.

|| See Vignette, page 263.

other wanted a Priest: they were both taken down, and the present one was built in their stead."

Lees Kirk, observes Mr. Ormerod, must have been the Chapel belonging to the Priory of Birkenhead; *Walleys Kirk*, is obviously a corruption of the name of the Parish Church, uniformly called "*medietas Rectoriæ de Kirkebye in Walleia*," in the Registers at Lichfield.

The other moiety of the Rectory, originally given by William de Waleya to the Convent at Chester, was, on the Dissolution, attached to the Bishopric of Chester also.

The steeple, erected in 1530, has been preserved in the repairs of the Church, the body of which is rebuilt. There are very few monumental inscriptions; amongst them the following:—

Sacred to the memory of George Briggs, who died 8th of February, 1814, aged 85. He resided nearly 60 years as Curate and Rector of this Church, endeared to all who knew him as a Minister and a Friend, by pureness of knowledge, by love unfeigned.

Led by Religion's bright and cheering ray,
He taught the way to Heav'n, and went that way;
And while he held the Christian life to view,
He was himself the Christian that he drew.

Another memorial—

Within these sacred walls are deposited the remains of Elizabeth Penketh, who departed this life on the 2d Dec. 1778, æt. 33. Also, of Ellen Johnson, eldest daughter of the late Thomas Johnson, Esq. of Newton, in this county, who departed this life on the 9th of April, 1783, æt. 34. Erected by an affectionate sister, M. A Johnson.

The *Rectory House* stands near to the Church; the present Rector is the Rev. Augustus Campbell, A. M. instituted February 18, 1814.

In 1656-7, Major Henry Meols built a *School House* here, and endowed it; his brother William also gave £125. as a further endowment, which was appropriated in the purchase of a house and lands: a close of land was subsequently given to the school by Hen. Young.

In 1799, the old school was pulled down and the present one erected by subscription. The Master is appointed by the Minister and Church-wardens. The existing endowment is a House, Garden, four Fields, in all about 22 statute acres, and the interest of £100. left by the late Rector, the Rev. George Briggs.

The *Charities* are £7. yearly, left by Hen. Robinson, to be given in bread to the poor every Whit Tuesday; the repairing of an Inscription in the Church to be defrayed out of it. The interest of £64. to be distributed on St. Thomas's day; and the interest of £20. to be given on Whit Tuesday.

A Rent-charge of £2. 16s. charged on fields belonging to Mr. Tobin, left by Mr. Thomas Cleave, of London.

Several handsome houses have, within the last few years, been erected in this township, and the adjoining one of Poulton-cum-Seacome.

LISCARD

Is about eleven miles N. E. from Neston. At a very early period, certainly in the reign of Edward II. the township was held by Richard de Aston, under the Barony of Halton. After the reign of Henry VIII. the family of Meoles were settled here, and on their termination in the male line, the reputed manor, with that of Great Meolès, passed in marriage to the Houghs. In 1804, the executors of John Hough, Esq. sold the estate to Mr. John Penketh, of Sea Bank.

The Abbot of Basingwerk had an estate here.

POULTON.

Poulton in Wallasey, with Seacome, is about ten miles N. E. from Neston. It is not noticed in the Survey. Temp. Henry VI. a moiety of the manor belonged to the family of Bold.

In the reign of Elizabeth, the Houghs held estates here under the Pooles, of Poole. Subsequently the manerial rights were divided between Thomas Meoles, Esq. of Chester, and Wm. Whitmore, Esq. of Thurstanton. In March, 1693, both these shares were purchased by Mr. James Gordon, and they were the property of his son in 1718. In 1774, James Gordon devised the estates to Richard Smith, Esq. Captain in the Navy, and afterwards appointed a Rear Admiral.—The present proprietor is Richard Smith, Esq. of Urswick, in Lancashire. At the Spring Assize, for Cheshire, 1816, the Jury, in an action *Smith v. Smith*, contrary to the direction of the Chief Justice, Sir William Garrow, decided that the manerial rights and privileges were exclusively vested in Richard Smith, although no manerial rights had been exercised in the Township.

Seacome Ferry is a place of great resort from the opposite town of Liverpool.

PARISH OF OVERCHURCH,

Is about seventeen miles N. W. from Chester. This Parish contains only one Township.

UPTON,

Was formerly included in the possessions of the Barons of Nantwich, from whom it passed, with other property, to the family of Praers, and from them to the Orrebies. Agnes, daughter and heiress of Philip de Orreby, marrying Walkelyn de Arderne, brought this manor as her dower. About 1310, Sir John Arderne gave Upton in marriage with his daughter, to John de Warwick, whose daughter Margaret, brought it in marriage to the Bolds, of Bold, in Lancashire. In April, 1614, Robt. Davies, of Manley, purchased the manor from Henry Bold, and he subsequently sold it to the Earls of Derby, who alienated it, and eventually it fell into the hands of the Cunliffes. The present Sir Foster Cunliffe, Bart. having disposed of the estates here to Thomas Clarke, Esq. of Liverpool, he conveyed them to John Webster, Esq. of Poulton in Wallasey, the present proprietor.

The *Hall* is a heavy low building, with bay windows, built on the best situation in the village.

The CHURCH stood nearly a mile from the Village, and at the commencement of the last century, was in a state of extreme decay. In 1709, the Parishioners sold two of the bells to defray the expenses of repairs, the steeple having been beat down by a storm, and only fourteen families being liable to the costs.

In 1813, the entire fabric was taken down, and a small Church erected on a piece of waste land near to the town.

The Rectory formerly belonged to the Abbey of St. Werburgh, at Chester, and on the Dissolution was given to the Dean and Chapter, but they lost this with their other estates.

It is now the property of Sir T. S. M. Stanley, Bart. who appoints the Curate.

PARISH OF WEST KIRKBY,

CONTAINS EIGHT TOWNSHIPS.

WEST KIRKBY,	LITTLE CALDEY,	GREASEBY,	LITTLE MEOLES,
GREAT CALDEY,	FRANKBY,	GREAT MEOLES,	NEWTON-CUM-LARTON.

WEST KIRKBY

Is nearly eighteen miles from Chester. The earliest account of it is being included in the possessions of Robert de Rodelent, who gave the Church to the Abbey of Utica, in Normandy; but after this it appears, the Abbot, for the consideration of Thirty Pounds to be paid yearly by the Monks of Chester, gave up to them all his rights here, and in Hilbury, together with St. Peter's Church, in that City.

The Manor, was formerly held under the Abbey of Basingwerk by a family who adopted the name of the township.

In 1668, the manor was the property of the Earl of Bridgewater, but being afterwards sold in parcels, the freeholders in succession enjoy the manerial rights, and hold a Court Baron.

The CHURCH is dedicated to St. Bridget. The present Rector, is the Rev. T. T. Trevor, instituted March 29, 1803. As as been before noticed, it was obtained from the Abbey of St. Ebrulf (Utica) by the Monks of

Chester; but being subsequently seized by the Earls of Chester, in the reign of King Stephen, it was given to the Abbey of Basingwerk. This occasioned a long litigation between the Abbey and the Monks, which terminated in the advowson being vested in the Monks, with whom it continued till the Dissolution, when it was given by Charter to the Dean and Chapter, in whom it is now vested.

The tithes of the whole parish belong to the Rector exclusively.

The Church adjoins the Village, and is situated a small distance from the Irish sea. It consists of tower, nave, and chancel; in the latter is a piscina, and two stalls for the Priests, under niches.

There are few monumental memorials of interest.—Among them are these inscriptions:—

On a tablet of red stone,

H. S. E. Johannes Vanzoelen, nuper de civitate Bristoliensi Generosus: qui obiit tert. die Septembris, a° D'ni 1689.*

In a small Chapel, at the end of the north aisle, a monument—

To the memory of Edward Glegg, of Grange, Esq. who married Elizabeth, daughter and heiress of John Kent, of Tranmore, Gent. and died the 4th of August, 1714, leaving issue William, Edward, John, Abigail, and Silence.

A memorial of—

John Glegg, of Caldey Grange, Esq. who died the 23d day of April, 1749, aged 37; also, Catherine and Mary, his issue by Mary his wife, who died Feb. 28, 1758, aged 39.

The Registers commence in 1692.

A *School* was founded in Grange, by William Glegg, Esq. in 1636, who endowed it with fifteen Cheshire acres of land in Greaseby, producing in 1819, £45. per ann. In 1676, the salary of the Master was augmented by a rent charge of £30. from Mr. Thomas Bennett, of Newton, on an estate in Newton. The appointment of the Master is vested in the Bishop of Chester, and the Churchwardens of West Kirkby.

It is stated † on the authority of the Rev. Mr. Newton, that the remainder of Mr. Bennett's estate was subsequently left to the poor of the parish, to be distributed at the will of his executors, with a limitation of a rent charge of £56. per ann. for the purchase of bread for twelve poor people every Sunday, and £24. to clothe twenty-four of the parish poor, which is still done. In 1814, the entire proceeds of the estate, were £327. per annum.

† Ormerod.

LITTLE CALDEY

Is about nine miles and a half N. W. N. from Neston, and the village generally is composed of miserable huts.—It was included in the possessions of Robert de Rodelent, and passed from his descendants, to the Thurstanstons, an illegitimate branch. Agnes, heiress of this branch, brought the township in marriage to Patrick de Haselwall, from whose representatives it subsequently passed to the Calveleys, Davenports, and Egertons, of Caldecote. The Browns had afterwards possession, and subsequently the Whitmores, between whose representatives and Elizabeth Smart, the manerial rights are now divided. There was formerly a Hundred of Little Caldey, the profits of which were given by Edward I. as Earl of Chester, to Randal de Sutton; the daughter and heiress of this Randal married the ancestor of John Glegg, Esq. proprietor of certain lands in Chester, called the Earl's Eye, granted with the hundred of Caldey to Randal de Sutton.‡

‡ Lysons.

The tithes of Great and Little Caldey were given to the Abbey of St. Werburgh, by Hugh Lupus, the second Earl.

The Village of DAWPOOL, or as it was anciently written Dalpoole—*(de la Pool?)*—obtained probably from its local situation, adjoins the sea, below Caldey; being a reputed manor, the representatives of the Whitmores appoint a gamekeeper.

In 1820-1, a Steam Packet establishment was projected here by some sanguine inhabitants of Chester. Public Meetings were had, Subscriptions were entered into, Surveys were made by inexperienced persons, and a good deal of expense was incurred. The opinion of the celebrated engineer, Mr. Telford, was then obtained, and his Report put the proposal to rest. Many experienced people, however, conceive that Dawpool offers peculiar advantages for such a situation.‖

GREAT CALDEY,

Formerly called *Grange*, is seven miles N. W. N. from Neston. At the time of the Survey it was held

* He died whilst the army of the Duke Schomberg on the way to Ireland was encamped in the townships of Great and Little Meoles.

‖ For further information, reference may be had to the *Chester Chronicle* for that year.

CHESHIRE

See West Kirkby.

by Hugh de Mara. It was afterwards given to the Abbey of Basingwerk,* and subsequently united to the Earldom. In 1552, Hen. VI. gave the manor of Hull Grange (Great Caldey) with a Swannery on Newton Carr, to John Glegg, Esq. of Gayton, and it continued vested in his descendants till the death of Wm. Glegg, Esq. in 1785, when the estate, under a decree in Chancery, was purchased by John Leigh, Esq. of Liverpool, excepting some land belonging to the Parish Poor, and the Trustees of Northwich School.

The site of *Grange Hall*, is occupied by a farm-house. Newton Carr, a waste of about 220 statute acres, is included in the Wallasey Inclosure Act.

FRANKBY

Is nearly seven miles N. N. W. from Neston, and formed part of the manor of Upton, till the beginning of the 17th century. At an early period it was vested in the Praers family, and passed from them to the Orrebies, Ardernes, and Bolds.

About 1614, a descendant of the latter sold it to Robert Davies, who 21st James I. resold it to Peter Day, or Daa, in whose representatives it continued for above a century.

In 1780, it was alienated by them; it was afterwards the property of Mr. Bond, of Daisy Bank, Congleton, and is now that of Peter Phillips, Esq. who purchased it in 1805, and who holds a Court, subordinate to that of Upton.

GREASEBY

Is nearly eight miles N. N. W. from Neston. The tithes of this township, with those of Storeton, were given by Lupus to Chester Abbey.

In 1086, Nigell de Burceio was Lord of Greaseby.—R. de Rullos, in whom the town was afterwards vested, gave the whole of it to the Abbey of St. Werburgh, he and his brother Robert retaining "nothing in the same but prayer and alms." The Monks had full possession till the Dissolution, when the manor was granted to the Dean and Chapter, who speedily lost it owing to the omission in their Charter; and James I. confirmed it to George Cotton, Esq. son of Sir Richard Cotton.—He conveyed it to Thomas Bennett; and afterwards it was included in the estates of the Gleggs, of Irby;—they sold it to Mr. Robt. Peacock, of Upton, the present proprietor, who holds a Court in the township, altho' "the freeholders contend there is no Manor, and it is so stated by Dr. Williamson.*"

HISTORY.

GREAT MEOLES

Is about eleven miles N. N. W. from Neston, and is the extreme township of the hundred, next to the Irish Channel. It was amongst the possessions of Robert de Rodelent. Previous to the reign of Hen. III. the township was possessed by a family which assumed the local name, and continued the Lords in uninterrupted descent till 1695, when Thos. Meoles, then residing in Chester, died, and left his property to his sister, Ann Meoles, who also dying without issue, she bequeathed the estates to her cousin Charles Hough, a descendant in the direct line of the family of Meoles.

Mr. William Ramsbottom, of Liverpool, surgeon, in right of his wife Jane Hough, grand-daughter of Charles, is the present proprietor.

LITTLE MEOLES

Is nearly ten miles N. W. N. from Neston, and was given to Robert de Rodelent. On his death in the Welsh wars, the Grosvenors, and Meoles, were the Lords, the Lancelyns, of Poulton, retaining the mesne manor. From the latter it passed to the Bromboroughs, temp. Edw. II. but in the reign of Hen. VIII. it had reverted to the Lancelyns as Capital Lords. It subsequently passed by sale to the Stanleys, of Alderley, in whom it now continues, the present Sir J. T. Stanley Bart. by settlement previous to marriage, having vested it in his brother the Rev. Edward Stanley, for life, remainder to Sir John and his heirs. There is no Court held for the Manor.

The waters of *Hoyle Lake*, wash this township which shoots out into a promontary, on which the father of the present Sir John Stanley built an excellent Hotel, much frequented in the Bathing Season, notwithstanding the totally barren aspect of the country.

Hoyle Lake was formerly called *Lacus de Hilburgheye* and *Heye Pol*, and was vested in the Monks of St. Werburgh. A safe anchorage is afforded here to vessels going to and from Liverpool in stormy weather.

It was in this neighbourhood that, in 1690, the celebrated Duke of Schomberg encamped his army, on his way to Ireland.

NEWTON-cum-LARTON

Is about eight miles N. N. W. from Great Neston.

* Lysons.

It appears from the Harl. MSS. that this township was at a very early period vested in the Banastres, of Lancashire. After this the manor was divided between them and the Barons of Kinderton. After the death of Lady Venables in 1557, it is supposed this moiety passed by sale to the Masseys of Puddington. The descent of the other moiety is obscure.

The *New House Estate* here, was the property of a branch of the Coventry family, from whom it passed to Thomas Bennet, of Newton, who, in 1668, was joint Lord with Edward Massey, Esq. of Puddington, and Henry Newport, of Larton.

The manerial rights are now claimed by the Rev. Roger Jacson, in right of his wife, a descendant of the before-named Thomas Bennett, who bequeathed a great portion of his estate for the endowment of the Free School at West Kirkby. An estate here, belonging to the School at Woodchurch, produced about £80. per ann. in 1820.

HOOSE,

An extra-parochial township, adjoins West Kirkby. In 1579, it was the property of Randle Probye, but in 1668, it was possessed by John Field and Robert Ormeston.

About 1755, the Gleggs, of Backford, had possession, and in 1803, John Glegg, Esq. sold it to Samuel Baxter. In 1812, Mr. Charles Monk, purchased it, together with the manor, and afterwards re-sold to J. T. Swainton, Esq. of Larkhill, near Liverpool, who has erected here a neat Cottage, for his occasional residence.

ISLAND OF HILBREE,

(PART OF ST. OSWALD'S PARISH, CHESTER.)

This island, which is about twenty miles from Chester, forms part of the parish of St. Oswald, having been given to the Abbey of St. Ebrulf, of Utica, by William the First, and by the Abbot subsequently released to the Abbey of St. Werburgh, at Chester.— From that preriod it has been considered as belonging to the above parish; originally, however, it was attached to the parish of West Kirkby.

A Cell of Monks was established here by the Abbot, and this religious establishment was dedicated, to the Virgin Mary. Hollinshead says "thither went a set of superstitious fools in Pilgrimage to our Lady of Hilbery, by whose offerings the Monks there were cherished and maintained."

Leland observes, that "at the floode it is al environed with water as an isle, and then the trajectus is a quarter of a mile over and four fadome deep of water, and at ebbe a man may go over the sande. It is about a mile in compace, and the ground is sandy and hath conies," as it has at this day. But old Henry Bradshaw, in his marvellous life of St. Werburgh, gives an account of the miraculous interference of that Saint, on behalf of Richard Earl of Chester. He was on a pilgrimage to the well of St. Winefred opposite, when he was attacked by a strong party of the Welsh, and forced to take shelter in Basingwerk Abbey. The insecurity, however, of his place of refuge, induced him to make an appeal to St. Werburgh, and it was heard promptly: the Virgin saint, like Moses of old, instantly threw up sandbanks, which separated the waters, and the Baron of Halton, his Constable, came to his succour with a body of troops, and rescued him from his peril. The legend thus ends :—

> And where the host passed over betwixt bondes,
> To this day ben called the *Constable* Sondes.

This wonderful intervention of the Saint, gave still greater celebrity to the island; devout pilgrims crowded to it from all parts, and the pious Monks profited no little by the credulity of the visitors.

The cell had a grant of £3. issuing from Little Meoles, by Robert de Lancelyn, temp. Richard I. William Lancelyn, his son, quit-claimed for ever to the Monks the fishery of the Lake: *lacus de Hildburgheye, qui vocatur Heye-pol*. The last named William gave likewise a house in little Meoles to the Monks, and the grant was confirmed by Robert Grosvenor and his wife Margery, *dominos capitales*.

The cell and the pilgrimages no longer exist, nor is there the slightest relic of the building, either in walls or site.

So early as the Earldom of John Scot, there were lights placed on the island, and he contributed towards them 10s. per ann. There are now no lights, but there are two large land-marks for the purposes of assisting the navigation into Hoyle Lake.

THE PARISH OF THURSTASTON,

INCLUDES TWO TOWNSHIPS:

THURSTASTON, AND IRBY (PART OF).

THURSTASTON, or *Thurstanston*, is about fifteen miles from Chester. At the Survey it was included in the possessions of Robert de Rodelent. On his death,* his estates were divided amongst many proprietors, and this township fell to one who assumed the local name.

In the beginning of the reign of Edward I. it passed from the Thurstastons, in marriage with Agnes, the heiress to Patrick de Haselwal, who was the father of David, founder of the Haselwalls of Haselwall. It passed from the Haselwalls to the Whitmores, about the reign of Richard II.† John de Whitmore was Mayor of Chester in 1369, and his descendant William Whitmore in 1473. The Whitmores continued the proprietors till the death of John Whitmore, Esq. last male heir, in 1751, when the estates became divided, and at the commencement of 1816, they were in twenty-four equal shares,‡ the rents being received, and the Courts held jointly. Six of these were vested in Mrs. Brown, sole representative of the Whitmores, being daughter and heiress of Catherine, fourth daughter and co-heiress of John Whitmore, Esq. and the only one that had issue. Eight in Whitmore and Elizabeth Smart, the issue of Baptist Smart, M. D. by a second marriage, which Baptist Smart had married for his first wife Lucy 6th daughter and co-heiress. Five in Col. Hugh Maxwell Goodwin, and Anne his wife, daughter of Walter Thomas, merchant, of Chester, and niece and heiress of Charles Goodwin, Esq. of Farndon,‖ who purchased from Dorothy, the second daughter and co-heiress. The other five, were the property of the late James Okell, Esq.§ of Fron, in the county of Flint, in right of his wife, sister and heiress of Wm. Dix, to whom the same were devised by Mary the fifth co-heiress.¶

‡ Ormerod.

¶ Ormerod.

Under a late decree of the Court of Chancery, the Manor and Hall of Thurstaston, are vested in Mrs. Browne.**

The CHURCH, which was given by Matthew de Rodelent to Chester Abbey, is dedicated to St. Bartholomew: the present Rector is the Rev. J. Fish, A. M. At the Dissolution, the patronage was given to the Dean and Chapter of Chester, and they are now the patrons. The door-way of the Church is Saxon, with zig-zag mouldings, and the Chancel is in a circular form.

The *Hall*, anciently the seat of the Whitmores, is now a farm-house.

There is a monument in the Church to the memory of Lucy, the daughter of John Whitmore, Esq. who married Baptist Smart, M. D. of Cheltenham, and died 1744.

IRBY

Lies partly in this parish, and partly in Woodchurch, and is about five miles N. N. W. from Great Neston. In 1093, it was given by Hugh Lupus to the newly founded Abbey of St. Werburgh, and was vested in it till the Dissolution, when it fell into the hands of Sir R. Cotton, who sold it to John Harpur, Esq. In the 44th of Elizabeth, it was obtained from the Harpurs, by Thomas Leigh, Esq. for £400. From his daughter it

* He was murdered by a party of Welsh marauders, on the 3d July, 1088.

† See monumental Inscriptions, Trinity Church, Chester.

‖ Mr. Goodwin was for many years a grocer in Chester, and afterwards retired to Farndon.

§ Mr. Okell practised many years as a Surgeon, in Chester.

** By the same decree the manor and nearly all the estate of Little Caldey, have devolved to Whitmore and Elizabeth Smart; the remainder of Caldey, and a greater portion of the lands in Thurstaston to Mr. Goodwin, and his wife; and a moiety of Haselwall manor and advowson, with all the lands in Haselwall and Oldfield, and a part of Thurstaston, to Mr. Okell.

CHESHIRE

was purchased by Edward Glegg, Esq. of the Grange, about 1655. It is now the property of Major-General Glegg, of Backford.

The *Old Hall*, stands within a moated area, of which three sides still remain; and it was here that the Abbot attended to hold his manerial Courts.

HISTORY

THE PARISH OF HESWALL,

CONTAINS TWO TOWNSHIPS,

HESWALL-CUM-OLDFIELD, CAYTON.

HESWALL, or *Haselwall*, is about three miles N. W. N. from Great Neston, and was included in the estates of Robert de Rodelent. On his death, it fell into the hands of Patrick de Haselwall, whose descendants continued here till early in the 14th century, when, on the death of David de Haselwall, it fell to his two daughters, Eliza, wife of Robert de Calveley, and Eustasia, wife of William de Egerton, who afterwards married John de Barnston. Eliza had issue one son, and on the death of his widow, Catherine, her husband's sister, brought the half of Heswall to her husband Arthur Davenport, from whom the moiety has descended to Davies Davenport, Esq, M. P.

The Egerton share continued vested in that family till the 4th of Elizabeth, when Sir Ralph Egerton passed the moiety of the manor, the advowson, and the fishery, to Thomas Browne, for £500.

In 1699, it was purchased by William Whitmore, Esq. and on the distribution of the Whitmore estates, it became the property of James Okell, Esq.* The *Hall* is a short distance from the Church.

* See Thurstaston.

A Moiety of the HAMLET OF OLDFIELD, in this township, is the property of Mr. Hough; the other moiety descended to James Okell, Esq. with the half of Heswall. Patrick de Heselwall, temp. Henry III. gave Oldfield in marriage with his sister Alice, to Guy de Provence, and his grandson Richard assuming the local name, was the ancestor of the Oldfields, of Northwich hundred.

The CHURCH consists of nave, chancel, side aisles, and tower. It is in various styles, having been rebuilt and repaired at different periods.†

The Registers commence in 1539, and the present Rector is the Rev. B. Penny, A. M. instituted July 23, 1807.

Amongst the monumental memorials are the following: On a marble tablet on the right hand of the Altar,

Sacred to the memories of Sir William Glegg, Knt. and dame Elizabeth his wife, who both lie interred at Esher, in Surrey.—He was the eldest son of Edward Glegg, of Gayton, Esq. by Catherine daughter of Sir Henry Delves, of Doddington, Bart. Lady Glegg was daughter of Sir Robert Cotton, of Combermere, by Esther, sister and sole heir of Sir John Salisbury, of Lleweni, Bart. Sir William died Jan. 9, 1706; Lady Glegg, March 5, 1711. Their youngest son, William Glegg, of Gayton, Esq. the last male heir of that ancient family, rests within these rails. He married Lucy, daughter of Richard Diot, of the city of Westminster, Esq. and died Nov. 9, 1758, in the year of his age 70.

A painted memorial of—

Elizabeth, daughter of Edward Pickford, citizen of Lincoln, late wife of Edward, son and heir of William Glegg, of Gayton, Esq. she died without issue May 27, 1649.

On a tomb-stone in the Chancel—

Here lieth the remains of J. Radenhurst, clerk, B. A. late Rector of this Parish, who departed this life, 21 June, 1807, in the seventy-seventh year of his age.

† On the north side of the Church, is the arms of Whitmore, "Vert cheequy, Or," carved in white marble, with three quarterings. 2d. "Argent a Chief Azure," for Haselwall.—3d. "Or, a Lion rampant, between three Martlets, gules," a female branch of the last.—4th. "Party per fesse, Vert and Gules, an Eagle displayed, Or."—Under these is an oval Medallion, in white marble, representing a winged figure thrusting a lance into the mouth of a dragon—with *Sigillum Willielmi de Hesel Well.*—Whitmore's motto "EITHER FOR EVER," supposed taken from using the two first coats at pleasure.—The colours are added from the Visitations.—ORMEROD.

On a brass plate,—

Here lies William Ramsbottom, late Rector of Heswall. He died the 15th day of November, 1702, in the 70th year of his age; and having been Rector there thirty-six years, obtained his place of rest, and by the power of Almighty God, will be raised again to Glory.

On a tombstone,

Hic jacet reverendus Joannnes Norris, A. M. quondam hujus Parochiæ Rector. Obiit Nov. 10, A. D. 1762.

The advowson of the living belongs to the Lords of the manor. It is divided between Mr. Davenport and Mr. Okell.

The Manerial Lords have the Friday's Fishery; and the Rector that of Sunday.

GAYTON

Adjoins Heswall, and was included in the possessions of Robert de Rodelent. On his death it was seized by the Earl, who granted it temp. Henry III. to Reginald Tibermont, and he afterwards resigned it in order that the King might give it to the Abbey of Vale Royal.—The Monks afterwards exchanged it with Randle de Merton, for Merton, and the King gave Randle, in addition, the bailywick of Caldy Hundred, Lache-on-Rudheath, and the Earl's Eye, in Chester. Gilbert Glegg, of Gayton, marrying Johanna, daughter and heiress of Stephen de Merton, became possessed of her estates, temp. Hen.VI. John Baskervile Glegg, Esq. (whose father John Baskervile,* Esq. assumed the name of Glegg, in consequence of his marriage with Mary, only daughter and heiress of Robt.Glegg, Esq) is the present proprietor, and Bailiff of the Hundred of Caldy, holding his Court Baron and view of Frank-pledge, to which the Lords of the township within its jurisdiction, (Poulton-cum-Seacome, Thornton Hough, Leighton, Gayton, Heswall, Thurstaston, West Kirkby, Great and Little Meoles, Hoose, and Newton-cum-Larton) owe suit and service.

Thomas Glegg was a warm friend to the House of York, during the Wars of the Roses. He seized stores and money worth 20,000 marks, at Gayton, coming to King Henry, for which he was imprisoned in Chester Castle, but subsequently (12th Feb. 8th Edw. IV.) obtained a pardon.

Gayton Hall, where William III. slept,† on his way to Ireland, when William Glegg was knighted, is the occasional residence of the proprietor, and is a handsome brick mansion, fronting the estuary of the Dee, surrounded by well grown trees. The situation, although commanding fine views of the Welsh coast, &c. is particularly bleak.

* Of the family of the Baskervilles, of Old Withington.

† In June, 1689.

THE PARISH OF WOODCURCH,

CONTAINS NINE TOWNSHIPS.

WOODCHURCH,	ARROW,	BARNSTON,	IRBY, (PART OF)
LANDICAN,	OXTON,	PENSBY,	UPTON, (DO.)
KNOCKTORUM,	THINGWALL,	PRENTON,	CLAUGHTON, (DO.)

Woodchurch is about seventeen miles N. N. W. from Chester, and six miles from Neston. The first notice we have of the township is in the Charter of Chester Abbey, where it is called *Wude Church*, A. D. 1093. It continued vested in the Abbey till the Dissolution, when it was granted to Peter Grey, Esq. He sold it to the families of Bostock, and Hiccock, and they conveyed it to Robt. Hiccock, Esq. of London.—He re-sold it to the Crosses, of Lancashire, but it was again bought by Mr. Hiccock. His sons conveyed it to Robert Leenes, towards the seventeenth century.

Some alienations took place before the manor was bought by Dr. Wilson, Bishop of Sodor and Man, and under his will it has passed, with Landican, and Knoc-

CHESHIRE torum, to the present proprietor, Thos. Patten Wilson, Esq. M.P.

The CHURCH is dedicated to the Holy Cross; the present Rector is the Rev. Joshua King, A. M. instituted 1822.

It is supposed* that the Church formerly stood in the adjacent township of Landican, and this is deduced from the first syllable *Llan*, which, in the Welsh language, points out the seat of the Church, as Llanferras, Llanrhaidr, &c. and from the circumstance of the Survey noticing a Priest being there. Of the *fact*, however, we have no certain data; all that we now know is, that the Church is in the township which bears its name.

* Ormerod.

It appears the advowson descended with the manor till the latter part part of the Reign of Richard II. and how it subsequently became alienated cannot now be ascertained. In the beginning of the 17th century, it was vested in the Adams's; in 1673, Hugh Burches, of Dublin, was instituted to the Rectory in right of his wife Margaret, heiress of the Adams's; and from him the advowson descended by female heirs to Ellen, daughter of Mr. Peacock, wife of the Rev. Brian King, the late impropriator and patron, and who has exclusively all the parochial tithes. The Registers commence in 1572.

The Church is a neat building of stone; it consists of nave, chancel, side aisle to the north, and a tower, in the style of the latter part of the 15th century.

The Parsonage House is a handsome dwelling, near the Church gate, built about 1719.

There are a variety of monumental memorials here, amongst them, on a tablet, in the chancel,

Underneath lyeth interred the body of William Hockenhull, gent. eldest son of George Hockenhull, of Prenton, Esq. by Mary his wife eldest daughter to George Leicester, of Toft, in the county of Chester, Esq. The said William had to wife Barbara, daughter and coheir of Richard Massey, of Sale, in the said county of Chester, Esq. (who lineally was descended from the ancient family of Massey, Baron of Dunham Massy, in the said county) by whom he had two daughters, Mary and Anne, and John, born after his father's death. He died 28th Dec. 1698, in the — year of his age.

On a marble tablet,—

Sacred to the memory of George Ball, of Irby, gentleman, who departed this life on the 1st of February, 1777, aged 54. And of Catherine Weller Ball, who died on the 18th of July, 1787, aged 89.

On a tablet in the chancel,—

HISTORY. Here lyeth the body of Mary, eldest daughter of George Leicester, of Toft, Esq. and wife to George Hockenhull, of Prenton, Esq by whom he had issue ten children, whereof three sons, William, George, and Ralph, and three daughters, Anne, Mary, and Dorothy, survived her. She died 27th Dec. 1681, in the 37th year of her age.

On another tablet—

Here lyeth the body of Robert Hicock, late of Woodchurch, in the county of Chester, who, by Elizabeth his second wife, daughter to Elias Foster, of Newchurch, in com. Cest. gent. and relict of William Gamull, of Crabhall, in the said county, gent. had issue a son and daughter, viz. George and Mary. He died 14th Dec. 1690, aged 65.

On a large tablet in the Church, entitled *Catalogus Mecœnatum*, is a list of the Parish Benefactors.

William Gleaves, Esq. Alderman of London, left by will, in 1665, the sum of £500. towards building and endowing a Free School; £100 were expended in building, and the residue in the purchase of lands, from which the Master had a salary of £80. per annum.* When Bishop Gastrell made his visitation, there was a Library attached to the School, containing upwards of 390 volumes. Twelve Trustees, including the Rector, appointed the Master. The School is now newly built in the Township of Arrow.

* 1820.

In 1525, James Goodier, of Barnston, left 20 marks to buy 20 yoke of Oxen for the Parish Poor; it was afterwards laid out in the purchase of Cows, which were hired to the Poor at the rate of 2s. 8d. yearly. In 1679, the Bishop of Chester awarded that this Charity should be under the direction of 14 Trustees, ten of whom to be chosen annually, the remaining four to be the Minister, Church Wardens, and the owner of Prenton Hall. At one period 92 Cows were provided by this Charity, which is now fast falling into decay.†

† See Bebington.

The *Parsonage House* is near to the Church; it is a commodious building, for which a license was granted in 1709.—The Parish Registers commence in 1572.

Dr. Sherlock, Rector of Winwick, who died in the year 1689, gave nineteen years before £50. for the purchase of fifteen Cows for the poor of Oxton, where he was born.

LANDICAN

Is about six miles N. of Neston. It was included

CHESHIRE HISTORY.

in the possessions of the Nantwich Barony, and it is supposed* to to have contained the Vill and Church of Woodchurch in its original limits. On the division of the Baronial property, temp. Henry VI. this Township fell to the lot of Phillippa, wife of Lord Basset. It passed subsequently to the family of Praers, Fulleshurst, and Wilbraham; and the Manor is now claimed by Thomes Patten Wilson, Esq. who appoints a game-keeper.

* Ormerod, p. 289, ii.

KNOCTORUM,

Or *Noctorum*, is about seven miles N. of Neston, in a miserable situation, and with the preceding Township was attached to the Nantwich Barony, and afterwards was vested in the Praers family, who gave it to the Abbey of Chester, to which it continued attached till the Dissolution. It was then transferred to the Dean and Chapter, and lost by them owing to the *error* discovered by Sir Richard Cotton, and seized by the Crown. It was subsequently held under the Crown, with a reserved rent to the Dean and Chapter, and was sold with the same title as Woodchurch. By the last purchase, it became the property of Dr. Wilson, son of the Bishop of Man, and under his will it is vested in T. P. Wilson, Esq. who appoints a game-keeper.

ARROW,

Or *Arrowe*, is about seven miles N. W. from Neston, and was attached to the fee of the Montalt Barony, under which it was held by the Soterleys, and the Roters, of Thornton. From the last it eventually passed to the Duttons, and from them, with their other extensive estates, to the Gerrards. Their successors, the Fleetwoods, alienated the estate early in the 18th century; and the Manor, with a large portion of the Township, is now the property of Mr. John Shaw, merchant, of Liverpool, by purchase from Mr. Macknight, also a merchant of the same place. Mr. Shaw appoints a game-keeper.

OXTON,

Is about seven miles N. E. of Neston, and was at a very early period vested in the family of Domville, from which it passed thro' the Hulses, and Troutbecks, to the Earls of Shrewsbury, in whom it is now vested, and is included in the Leet of Raby.

Although situated on a bold eminence, commanding extensive views of the Mersey, the town of Liverpool, and the high lands of Lancashire, the immediate locality is dreary and barren, presenting a scene of extreme misery and desolation.—Here was born Richard Sherlock, the political writer, temp. Car. I. and II.

THINGWALL,

Is nearly five miles N. W. from Neston, and about a mile S. of Woodchurch, and the local description of Oxton is equally applicable to this Township. It was included in the possessions of the Barons of Nantwich; and temp. Richard II it was vested in the Domvilles, and from them passed to the Earls of Shrewsbury, in whose Leet of Raby the Township is included, and where an agent of R. Vyner, Esq. of Gautby, who possesses the Manerial rights formerly vested in the Lords Kingston, attends, although his immediate tenants in Thingwall, owe service to his Court at Bidston.

In 1668, the Earl of Shrewsbury, Sir Wm. Stanley, and Lord Kingston, claimed the Manerial right.

BARNSTON,

Is about four miles N. W. of Neston. It is written in old evidences *Barnstone*, *Bernston*, *Berinston*, and *Bereleston*, and formed part of the territorial possessions of the Barons of Halton. It was originally divided in moieties, one of which was held by the Troutbecks, under the Earl, the other by a family which took the local name under the Barons of Halton. The Barnstons alienated part of their share as early as the reign of Edward I. and towards the latter end of the reign of Edward III. their connexion with the Township ceased altogether.† The Barnstons were succeeded by the Tyldesleys, and it is supposed that, about the reign of Henry VII. they alienated the moiety, which has long since been unknown. The other moiety, which was possessed by the Troutbecks, descended to the Earls of Shrewsbury, who are the present proprietors, and to whose Leet at Raby, all the tenants owe suit and service.‡

† Roger Barnston, Esq. of Chester, and Churton, is a descendant of this ancient family.

‡ The Lysons say, that the Barnston's moiety eventually became the property of a younger branch of the Bennetts, of Willaston, who sold it to the Macklins, whose property it was in 1810.

The *Hall*, which was in a ruinous state in 1724,* no longer exists.

PENSBY,

Is four miles N. N. W. of Neston, and fourteen miles N. W. of Chester, and was certainly as early as the reign of Henry VI. divided in parcels. A third part of the Manor belonged to the Hospital of St. John, at Chester, although it is with good reason supposed, that at one time the whole Township was in the possession of a family which bore the local name.

Long before 1668,† the Manor was vested in the Gleggs of Gayton, from whom it has descended to the present proprietor, John Baskervyle Glegg, Esq. of Gayton.

* Gast. Nott.

PRENTON,

Is six miles N. E. of Neston, and lies at the extremity of the parish of Woodchurch. At the Conquest it was given by the Earl to the Barons of Shipbrook; but in the reign of Edward III. it was possessed by a family which assumed the name of the Township, It passed from them to the Gleyves and Hocknells; and the latter family terminating in 1782, the Manor and Estate were purchased by Mr. John Lyon, in whose representatives the property is now vested.

The site of the Hall is occupied by a Farm House. There are no Freeholders in the Township.

† The Lysons say, they have possessed it for nearly two centuries.

THE PARISH OF NESTON,

CONTAINS EIGHT TOWNSHIPS,

NESTON,
LITTLE NESTON-cum-HARGRAVE,
NESSE-cum-DENWALL,
WILLASTON,
LEDSHAM,
RABY,
LEIGHTON, and
THORNTON HOUGH.

NESTON,

Is nearly eleven miles N. W. of Chester. Previous to the Conquest it was divided into three shares, one of which remained to the Abbey of St. Werburgh, at Chester;* the other was held under the Baron of Halton, and the third by "Robertus Cocus tenet de Comite Nestone." In the reign of Henry I. or Stephen, the Monks exchanged their share with the Baron of Halton, for his moiety of Raby, thus becoming proprietors of the whole.

In the 6th Edward I. Robert de Montalt held the manner of Neston from the King, in capite, by the service of finding a juror for the County Court, and Court of Willaveston Hundred.

The Montalts terminated in Robert, who, by fine, 1st Edward III. gave all his lands to Queen Isabella, with remainder to the King's Brother, John of Eltham, remainder to the King. In the 12th of the same reign the Queen exchanged, for 1000 marks, the Manors of Lee, Boslee, and Neston, the Castle and Vill of Mold, the Castle and Manor of Hawarden, and the Seneschalship of Chester, to William de Montacute, Earl of Salisbury, in whose descendants they continued till the 1st of Henry IV. when John Earl of Shrewsbury was beheaded for Treason, and six years afterwards, his Estates were confiscated to the Crown. In 1451, these Estates were granted to Edward Prince of Wales, but John Hertcombe claimed them in right of a Trustee,

* The Parish is divided into four quarters: one of which comprehends Great Neston only; another, Leighton, Thornton, and Raby; a third, Ledsham, and Willaston; the fourth, Little Neston, and Nesse.

named by the Earl before his offence was committed, and at last obtained them. A fine was levied on the Manor of Neston, in 1454, to the use of Richard Neville, Earl of Salisbury, and Alice his wife, granddaughter of the Earl who was beheaded, with remainder to their son-in-law Sir Thomas Stanley, afterwards created Lord Stanley.—In the descendants of Lord Stanley, the Manor continued for some centuries; but eventually Neston was alienated to the Whitmores, in discharge of a gaming debt. Bridget, daughter and heiress of Wm. Whitmore, brought it in marriage to Thomas Savage, second son of Lord Savage, whose daughter and heiress married Sir Thomas Mostyn, of Mostyn, Flintshire, Bart. in whose descendant, Sir Thos. Mostyn, Bart. M. P. the Estate is now vested.

A *Market* is held in Neston, every Friday; but how it originated is not known, as there are no records of the existence of any charter.—Fairs are also held Feb. 2, May 1, Sept. 29. A Court Leet and Baron is held annually by Sir Thomas.

A little more than half a mile below Neston, on the shore of the Dee, nearly opposite to Flint, is PARKGATE, well known throughout the Country, as a place of considerable resort for sea-bathing, although from the receding of the tides from this shore, it is not likely long to continue so. About fifteen years ago, Parkgate presented every appearance of the bustle of a Sea Port, there being at that time, five or six stout-built Packets, besides other vessels, constantly employed in the trade with Ireland. At the present period, however, this, as a Packet Station, is completely neglected, and no vessels of burthen can come within a considerable distance of the Quay, although but a few years ago, they rode along-side it. A large sandbank occupies the former channel, and the vast accumulation of sands in the bed of the river, renders it highly probable it will soon be choaked up.

Parkgate consists of a long range of irregular built houses, facing the estuary, and owes its origin to the formation of a quay in the vicinity, by the Citizens of Chester, when the navigation of the Dee to that City was impeded in the 16th century. There is a regular Ferry here to Flint, which affords a great accommodation to those living on the Welsh shore desirous of visiting Liverpool.

A Custom House is still supported at Parkgate, but nearly the whole of its *trade*,—if the word may be used—is confined to the vessels frequenting the adjoining Collieries at Ness.

THE CHURCH of Neston is dedicated to St. Mary and St. Helen; the present Vicar is the Rev. Thomas Ward, A. M. Prebendary of Chester, instituted Jan. 23, 1784. The Registers commence in 1700.

There is little doubt but what there was a Church here previous to the Conquest; and it afterwards became vested in Leucha de Montalt, before named. Her son, Ralph de Montalt, gave the Church to the Monastery of Chester. Richard de Neston, the incumbent, quit-claimed the Church; but on his death, Roger de Montalt, refusing to recognize the grant, seized the possession of the Church by force of arms, and presented to it Ralph de Montalt. The Abbot, however, subsequently obtained the advowson from the Montalts, at the price of the Manor of Bretton, (Brocton) the Chapel and House of Sponne, a mark of silver yearly issuing from the tenement of Bechene, the resignation of the Tythes of Hawarden to the Rector, and the payment of five marks yearly to the incumbent, Ralph de Montalt.—The living thus restored to the Abbey, remained vested in it till the Dissolution, when it was transferred to the Dean and Chapter, with whom it now remains. The Rectorial Tythes, of Thornton, Raby, and Leighton, are attached to the Vicarage; those of Great and Little Neston belong to Sir Thos. Mostyn, Bart.; those of Ledsham to the Dean and Chapter; and Sir T. S. M. Stanley, Bart. has those of Willaston and Ness.

The building consists of Nave, Chancel, Side Aisles, and Tower. The Nave and Chancel are now in one. There are the remains of a rood loft about 40 feet east of the steeple. The Chancel was formerly separated from the side-aisles by pointed arches springing from octagonal pillars, several of which have been removed. It is conjectured the Tower was repaired in 1697, that date appearing on a stone in the north side. The fabric is of considerable antiquity. In 1809, an Organ was erected on the north side of the Church, built by J. Schultz, of Liverpool.

The Monumental remains are not very remarkable.

Near the Communion Table, on a tablet, a memorial of—

The Children of William Ramsbottom, Rector of Haselwall, the first of whom died 1679.

Edward Briggs, obiit. Sept. 14, 1793, ætat 12 years.

Joseph Lyon, Esq. obitt 16th June, 1809, ætat. 58.

Elizabeth Mascle, widow of Thos. Mascle, late of Coddington, Esq. died 30th of December, 1784, aged 76.

An inscription in the Vestry,—

Here lyeth the Ladye of Thomasyn, daughter and heyre to —— Newcomen, Gent. late wife to George Pott, of Stancliffe. She died on the 27th day of November, 1650. By her he had John, George, Arthur, Ambrose, Thomas, Peter, and Samuel: also three daughters, Elizabeth, and Thomasine, and Mary, and a sonne still borne.

On the south side of the Altar, on a tablet,—

Sacred to the revered memory of Edmund Lyon, late of Liverpool, Merchant, who departed this life, at Neston, the 16th of January, 1789, aged 76; and of Anne his wife, formerly Anne Hayes, spinter, who died the 12th January, 1773, aged 52. Also to the respected memory of her Brothers, Thomas Hayes, of Chester, M. D. who died the 2d of August, 1767, aged 53; and Joseph Hayes, of Neston, Esq. who died the 7th of July, 1784, aged 67, sons of Samuel Hayes, formerly of Willaston, in this Parish, Gent. by Martha, his wife, who was daughter of John Ball, Esq. of Irby.—This tablet is inscribed, as a tribute of affectionate gratitude, by their personal Representative Joseph Lyon.

Opposite to this, on a marble tablet,—

Spe vitæ beatioris hic jacet quod mortale fuit Joannis Briggs, A. M. hujus Dioeceseos Cancellarii, et Parochiæ de Mitbley, in comitatu Eboracensi Rectoris. Obiit 7° Octobris, A D. 1804, ætat. 76. Necnon haud longe ab hoc loco requiescunt cineres Edwardi Briggs, ejusdem filii natu minimi, quem diutino morbo absumptum, intra duodecimum ætatis annum mors abripit Septembris 14°, A. D. 1793.

There is now no Free School in the parish of Neston, although Bishop Gastrell notices a School built on Windle Hill, the Master of which was nominated by the Vicar. It had, however, no endowment, and has long since ceased to exist.—Lands in Willaston were left by Thos. Wilcock, of Chester, for the use of the poor of St Bridget's and St. John's parish, Chester, and Neston parish. These lands now produce a considerable revenue. Some smaller charities were laid out in the erection of the North Gallery of the Church, the interest of which is still distributed among the Poor.—The interest of £500. left by Dr. Hayes, is given annually to the poor of Great Neston, as is also the interest of £10. left by Elizabeth, relict of S. R. Stepney, Esq. of King's County, Ireland. The Vicarage House is nearly opposite to the Church.*

LITTLE NESTON cum HARGREAVE,

Is about a mile S. E. of Great Neston. In the reign of Edward III. the Houghs held a fifth of the moiety of the Manor of Little Neston, from whom it passed to Cecilia, widow of Richard le Grosvenor, as next of kin. In the 10th Hen. VI. Walter Twyford, son of Cecilia del Mere, last of the Grosvenors of Little Budworth, passed the Manor of Budworth, and the fifth of Neston, to William Troutbeck, Esq. for 100 marks. The other four-fifths of the Manor were vested in the family of Corona previous to the reign of Edw. II. and before the 3d of Richard II. John le White purchased the rights of the Coronas. This share successively passed through the Hulses, Ewloes, Booths, (of Mollington) and Mordaunts, (of Oakley); and in 1618, Sir Charles Mordaunt, Knt. sold the same to John Cottingham, Esq. in whose descendant John Cottingham, Esq. the Manor, in conjunction with the Earl of Shrewsbury, (in right of the Troutbecks) is now vested; and they hold Courts Leet and Baron for the Manors of Little Neston and Hargreave.†

In Little Neston are extensive Coal Works, held under the Cottinghams by a Company which worked the same. In 1820, 1, & 2, were continued litigations between Mr. Cottingham and Sir T. S. M. Stanley, Bart. grounded on an alledged trespass of the latter, in working under the Manor of the former. In the Autumn Assizes of 1822, the question of trespass and damage came on for trial, when a verdict was given against Sir Thos. Stanley, with £2000. damages. These were thought exorbitant, and an application

* In the Church-yard is a memorial of John Hancock, farmer, who died Dec. 4, 1775, aged 112. At the age of 104, he was in the habit of walking half a mile to a public house; his wife survived him 24 years, being at the time of her death (1799) only 75 years of age,—so that there must have been 63 years difference betwixt them.—The Manor of Ashfield in Neston, which belongs to the Pooles, was purchased by the ancestors of the late Rev. Sir H. Poole, Bart. of the Duttons, in 1717.

† The Manor of Hargreave is situated between Willaston and Raby. It was formerly considered a distinct Manor.

was made to the Court of King's Bench, in Hilary Term, 1823, to set aside the Verdict; the Court, however, on a full hearing of the case, confirmed the finding of the Jury.*

NESS,

Descended from the Duttons of Dutton, to the Gerards of Gerard's Bromley, from whom in 1668, it was purchased by the Masseys of Puddington, in whose representative, Sir T. S. M. Stanley, Bart. it is now vested. A Court Leet and Baron is held for the Manor.

In the Hamlet of DENWALL, now generally called *Dennah*, was the "Poor Hospital of Denwell," endowed with the Church of Burton, by Alexander de Savensby, Bishop of Lichfield, in January, 1238. This hospital no longer exists, but its revenues are still appropriated to the use of the Hospital of St. John, at Lichfield. In Denwall, also, are extensive Coal Works.

WILLASTON,

Is about three miles E. of Great Neston, and originally gave name to the *Hundred of Willaveston*, now Wirral. It was vested at an early period in the Orrebies, from whom it passed to the Mainwarings, Trussels, and Veres, Earls of Oxford, by whom it was sold subsequent to 1502, to the Freeholders, and they exercise the manerial rights.†

The *Hall* is an ancient brick building, with bay windows, finished with gables. It was built by one of the ancestors of the Bennetts, in 1558. The village has a much more respectable appearance than the generality of those in this district of the Hundred.

LEDSHAM,

Is about six miles N. W. N. from Chester. It appears from the Survey, it was the property of Walter de Vernon, brother of the Baron of Shipbrook. In the reign of Richard II. it was possessed by the Gerards of Kingsley; eventually, however, it became the property of the Masseys of Puddington, by purchase from Sir Thos Gerard, Knight, for 1000 marks; and descended to their representative Sir T. S. M. Stanley, Bart. the present proprietor.

The *Hall* is occupied by a Farmer. There are no Freeholders in the Township.

RABY,

Is nearly two miles and a half N. E. of Neston; and presents to the eye a most barren and desolate appearance. At an early period it was divided between the Monastery of St. Werburgh, and the Baron of Halton, but in the reign of Stephen the whole was possessed by the Monks in exchange for a third of the Manor of Neston, and they held lands here as late as the reign of Edward III. Some particulars as to the tenure, &c. of the Rabys will be found in page 284.—In the third of Henry V. Hugh de Holis died seized of half the serjeancy of the Bridge Gate and Bridge-street, Chester, a Messuage and Gardens, and a road under the City walls to the same, the custody of the Castle Garden,‡ &c.—From the Hulses, Raby passed to the Troutbecks, and from them to John Talbot, Esq. of Albrighton, in the county of Salop. In right of the latter, the Earl of Shrewsbury is the present proprietor, and his Lordship holds a Court Leet and Baron at Raby, for this manor, Brumstath, Oxton, Thingwall, Barnston, and Thornton Grange.

LEIGHTON,

Is near to Parkgate on the N. N. E. side, and was included in the possessions of Robert de Rodelent. On his death the paramount Lordship was given to the Barons of Montalt, under whom it was held, temp. Edw. II. by William de Leighton and John Riseings. About the same reign the daughter of William de Leighton brought the Manor in marriage to Roger de Thornton, and his daughter Ellen becoming heiress of Thornton Mayewe and Leighton, brought them in marriage to Richard del Hough. The Houghs continued here in uninterrupted succession till the 27th of Eliz. when the estates became the property of Wm. Whitmore, by marriage with Alice, daughter of Wm. Hough, who died the 10th Feb. 27th Elizabeth. They

* The works alluded to extend nearly two miles under the bed of the river, beneath which is a canal for the purpose of conveying coals from the extremity to the pit mouth.

† The greatest number of shares is vested in Samuel Bennett, Esq. Mayor of Chester, 1818, and his three brothers; and the family have enjoyed property here since the property was sold by the Veres.

‡ Where were these Gardens situated?

CHESHIRE HISTORY.

subsequently passed by female heirs to the Savages and Mostyns, and the present proprietor is Sir Thos. Mostyn, Bart. and M. P. of Mostyn.

Bridget Savage, who brought the Estate to the Mostyns, was a Roman Catholic; and she and her husband after a long and happy life, died within a day of each other at Gloddaeth, in the county of Carnarvon, and were interred at Eglwys Rhôs Church. *

* Pennant.

Part of Parkgate is in this Township; there are Courts Leet and Baron held for the Manor.

THORNTON HOUGH,

Is about two miles and a half N. N. E. of Neston.

The descent of this Township is similar to that of Leighton.

Thornton Grange is the property of the Earls of Shrewsbury by descent from the Troutbecks.

THE PARISH OF BURTON,

INCLUDES THE TOWNSHIPS OF

BURTON AND PUDDINGTON.

BURTON,

Is about eight miles N. W. of Chester, beautifully situated on a rock, which juts out into the Estuary, called Burton Point.

From a very early period the Manor was attached to the Estates of the Bishops of Lichfield and Coventry; but in 1806 it was purchased from the Bishop by Richard Congreve, Esq. (a branch of the Congreves of Congreve, in Staffordshire) who is the present proprietor and holds a Court Baron for it.

Mr. Congrvee resides at Burton Hall, a handsome house, commanding fine views of the opposite shore.

The Church is dedicated to St. Nicholas, and was given in 1238, by Alexander Bishop of Lichfield, to the Hospital of *Denwall*, or Dennah, the Master of which was uniformly appointed to the Rectory till 1495-6, when it was appropriated by Bishop Smith to the Hospital of St. John, in Lichfield, from which the Rectory is now held by lease by Mr. Congreve, but the Hospital nominates the Curate, who possesses the Easter dues; the other tythes are vested in Mr. Congreve.—The Registers commence in 1538.

The Church was rebuilt in 1721, and consists of Nave, Chancel, North Aisle, and Tower; it is a plain building of stone. The Massey Chancel, at the East end of the North aisle, is part of the original Church.

On a white marble monument in this Chancel,—

To the Memory of Sir John Stanley Massey Stanley, Bart. of Hooton, who departed this life on the 24th day of Nov. 1794, in the 84th year of his age; and of Mary his wife, daughter of Thos. Clifton, Esq. of Lytham, who departed this life the 21st day of May, 1770, in the 40th year of her age; also of their two sons, viz. of Sir Thomas Stanley Massey Stanley, Bart. who departed this life on the 19th day of February, at York, in the 41st year of his age, and was buried at Eastham,—and John Stanley, Esq. who departed this life on the 30th day of December, 1790, in the 36th year of his age;—this monument of gratitude was erected by Lady Stanley, relict of Sir T. S. M. Stanley, and daughter of Wm. Salvin, Esq. of Croxdale, Durham, 1797.—Requiescant in Pace!

Near the South door, on a blue flag stone,—

Nathaniel Wilson, May 29, 1702. Alice Wilson had issue, Samuel, James, Joseph, Sarah, Benjamin, Thomas, Bishop of Man, and Mary.

The celebrated Dr. Thomas Wilson, Bishop of Sodor and Man, was born in this Township in 1663. He received his education at Trinity College, Dublin, which he left in 1686, and obtained the curacy of New Church, in the parish of Winwick, of which his uncle, Dr. Sherlock, was Rector. It was by him he was introduced to the Stanleys Earls of Derby, by whom he was appointed Bishop of Man, in 1697.—The then revenues of the Bishopric did not exceed £300. per annum, but by husbanding his resources, he contrived to do great good to the Island generally, and was of especial service in the relief of distressed Mariners,

CHESHIRE

Although he had been offered an English See, the Pious Bishop refused it, from attachment to the inhabitants of Man. His virtues obtained for him the friendship of Cardinal Fleury, by whose interest the coasts of the Island were protected from the ravages of the French ships of war.—In 1707, the Bishop was made D. D. by the University of Oxford, and received the same honor also from Cambridge. He died on the 7th of March, 1755, aged 93 years, having had four children by his wife Mary, daughter of Thos. Patten, Esq. of Warrington. Dr. Wilson, Prebendary of Westminster, was the only son who survived, and he made some large purchases in Wirrel, now inherited by Thomas Patten Wilson, Esq.

In 1807, an Act of Parliament was obtained for inclosing the wastes of the Township.

There is a School here open to all the poor children of Burton, and to four of Puddington. The School-house is of red stone, on the Ness road, towards the erection and endowment of which Bishop Wilson gave £400. Hough, Bishop of Worcester, gave £50. to the same good object. Dr. Wilson, the Bishop's son, gave £200.,* and the lands produce upwards of £30. per annum.

* Lysons.

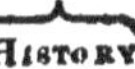

PUDDINGTON,

Or Podington, (formerly written Pudican) is about seven and a half miles N. W. from Chester. It was originally included in the possessions of Hamo de Masci, whose descendants held it under the Stanleys of Hooton, in right of the grant made by Earl Randle to Alan Sylvester. The male line of the Masseys terminated in 1715-16, by the death of Wm. Massey, Esq.—a firm adherent to the tenets of the Roman Church, and a warm supporter of the Pretender. It is stated* that he was engaged in the Battle of Preston, and made his escape to Wirral, *by swimming his horse over the Mersey* below Hooton. He was subsequently apprehended at Puddington, and thrown into Chester Castle. He died soon after, bequeathing his estates to his God-son and adopted heir, Thos. Stanley, Esq. a younger son of Sir Wm. Stanley, Bart. who died in 1740. Mr. Stanley assumed the name of Massey, and assigned the same to his elder brother John Stanley, Esq. On the death of Sir Wm. Stanley, Bart. of Hooton, in 1792, the title and estates devolved to his uncle John Stanley Massey, Esq. of Puddington, whose grandson, Sir T. S. M. Stanley, Bart. is the present proprietor.

* Ormerod.

THE PARISH OF SHOTWICK,

CONTAINS THE TOWNSHIPS OF

SHOTWICK,	GREAT SALGHALL,
ROUGH SHOTWICK, OR	LITTLE SALGHALL,
WOODBANK,	CAPENHURST.

SHOTWICK,

Is situated close to the mouth of the Dee, about six miles N. W. of Chester; there were formerly, (as the termination *wick* or *wich* imports) Salt-works here, used in Leland's time. *Previous to the Conquest*, it belonged to the secular Canons of St. Werburgh, and was confirmed to the Benedictine Monks in 1093. The Manor was held under the Abbots by a family which took the local name, and their heiress Alice, brought the Manor in marriage to Robert de Hockenhull, of Hockenhull, temp. Edward I. On the estate of Hockenhull being sold in 1715, the family resided here; and in 1734, occurs in the Register, a notice of the baptism of the children of Joseph and Martha Hockenhull. But soon after this, the family declined, the estate was mortgaged, and eventually sold to Mr. S.

Bennett, whose great nephew John Nevitt, Esq. (who has assumed the name of Bennett,) is the present proprietor.

The *Hall*, formerly the seat of the Hockenhulls,* is of brick, with large gables. The site of the ancient Hall, near the Church, is still visible.

The CHURCH consists of a Nave, North Aisle, Chancel, and a small Chapel in the Eastern Aisle, with a handsome embattled tower.—Four pointed arches separate the North Aisle from the body of the Church. The Chancel and Chapel windows contain a few remains of painted glass; and in one window are the letters T. A. continually repeated—it is conjectured they are the initials of Thomas Yeardley, when Abbot.

Part of the South door-way is of very great antiquity, probably coeval with the Conquest.

There are few monumental remains. On a flag stone within the railing of the Altar,—

Here lyeth the body of Joseph Hockenhull, Esq. who was interred 17th July, Anno Domine, 1679, aged 64.

The Registers commence in ———

The learned Dr. Samuel Clarke, was for a few years Curate of Shotwick.

The Dean and Chapter of Chester present to the Curacy, and have the impropriation of the tythes of the whole parish, which were leased by them to the late Mascie Taylor, Esq.† and the widow of the late Rev. J. Briggs, A. M. Prebendary of Chester, and Chancellor of the Diocese.

Obit. 1821.

GREAT SALGHALL,

Is about four miles N. N. W. of Chester, and belonged to the Canons of St. Werburgh, previous to the Conquest. Hugh Lupus gave afterwards only a third of the Vill (the *fee* of Salghall) to the Abbey, attaching the remaining two thirds to the Earl's Park Keeper of Shotwick.—The paramount jurisdiction of Great and Little Salghall, are now vested in Charles Trelawney Brereton, Esq. who holds Courts Leet and Baron for Great Salghall, the Leet of which embraces Little Salghall.—The Village includes a miserable collection of wretched Cottages, with roads as bad as any need be in the Hundred.

This township was the residence of Mrs. Mary Davies, "the strange and wonderful old woman that hath a pair of horns growing upon her head," of whom there is an account and portrait in Leigh's History of the County; and in a pamphlet preserved in the British Museum. She was remarkable for having an excrescence on her head, which, when she was sixty years of age, grew into horns; these, after four years growth, were cast and renewed, which happened two or three times before her death. There is a portrait of her in the Ashmolean Museum at Oxford, where, and in the British Museum, one of the horns is preserved.†—A few similar instances have occurred:—in the University Library at Edinburgh, is preserved a horn cut from the head of Elizabeth Love, in the 50th year of her age. In 1790, Mrs. Allen, a woman who had a horn growing on her head, was exhibited in London. ‡

LITTLE SALGHALL,

Was included in the Estates of the Baron of Nantwich; it was subsequently attached to the office of the Park-keeper of Shotwick. In other respects the description of the preceding Township will apply to this.—C. T. Brereton, Esq. is the proprietor.

A reputed Manor exists in this Township, vested in Mr. Brereton, a portion of which was received by him from C. Potts, Esq. in exchange for lands near Chester. This portion, together with lands sold to Mr. Robert Ellison, was bought by Mr. Potts, from Mrs. Elizabeth Sloughter, of Chester, and formed a part of the Estate of the Does of Shotwick, of whom there is a memorial in the Church.

The Tattons and Chamberlains, had also Estates in the Township.

ROUGH SHOTWICK,

Is a Township nearly opposite to Church Shotwick, divided from it by a small stream. It is called *Woodbank* and *Rowe Shotwick*, and is about six miles N. W. from Chester. It was the property of Hugh de Wodebank in 1300, but in 1313 he sold it to William de

* This family terminated in a female, who was indebted to Parish relief for a sustenance.—ORM.

† Lysons.—There is a portrait of her at Doddington Hall.

‡ These appendages to the heads of *females* are very singular the *male* class, it is believed, wear them occasionally.

CHESHIRE Hooton, from whom it passed to the Stanleys of Hooton. In 1637, William Stanley, Esq. sold the Manor to Thomas Hiccock; and on the death of John Hiccock without issue, about 1740, the Estate passed by female heirs to the family of Stubbs, and Boulton.—From the latter it was purchased by Mr. Edward Platt, Attorney, of Chester, by whose will it was left to his daughter Dorothy, wife of George French, Esq. of Chester, and her issue, with a life interest of one-third reserved to Mr. Charles Price, of Chester.

CAPENHURST,

Is nearly six miles N. N. E. from Chester, and it appears from the Survey, that the Barons of Halton were superior Lords of the Township. From their successors, it was held by the Bernstons, by whom it was transferred to James de Pulle, or Poole, under whose descendants the Capenhursts, Cheneys, and Cholmondeleys, were successively Lords of the mediate Manor.—In 1790, the Manor was purchased from the Earl (now Marquis) of Cholmondeley, by the late Richard Richardson, Esq. whose son is the present proprietor, and resides in the Township, in a substantial and modern built house, erected by his father.

The *Old Hall*, chiefly of timber, was taken down by Mr. Richardson, and a farm-house erected on the site. Courts Leet and Baron are incident to the Manor; and all the land of the Township is Mr. Richardson's property. HISTORY.

SHOTWICK PARK,

Formed the domain belonging to the ancient *Castle* of Shotwick, a plan of which, as delineated in its ruinous state, is annexed. This was one of the line of fortresses erected by the Earl for the protection of the frontiers of the Palatinate from the incursions of the Welsh. Shotwick Park, from the advantages of its local situation, and neighbourhood to Chester, has frequently been the scene of embarkation to Ireland and other places, and has, probably more than once, been honored with the presence of the King. Leland thus notices the Castle: "*A myle lower* is Shottewik Castle, on the very shores longing to the King, and thereby ys a Parke." The building was of a pentagon form, strengthened with six towers, one of them stated to be five stories high. The only remains now, are a large mound, of a crescent form, with intrenchments on the Park side.

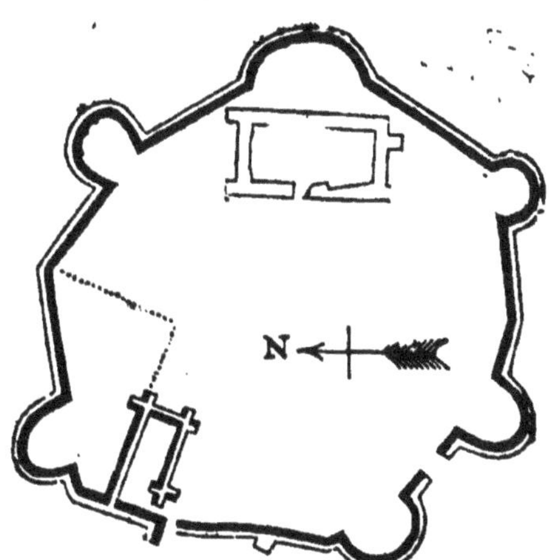

It is stated, that within the memory of man part of the walls, &c. have been carried away to repair the roads.* Lysons.

In 1256, Fulco de Orreby had charge of the Castle from Prince Edward; and in the reign of Edward III. Sir Hugh Calveley had the custody of it.—The Park eventually became vested in the Wilbrahams, to whom it was granted soon after the Restoration; and having passed to the Salisburies of Ledbrooke, in Flintshire, Salisbury Lloyd, Esq. of Ledbrooke, in 1734, bequeathed the property to Thomas Brereton, the husband of his daughter Catherine, who assumed the name of Salisbury. In 1756, Wm. Brereton left these Estates to Owen Salisbury Brereton, Esq. his son by a former wife of the Trelawney family, who dying without issue, bequeathed his Estates to his cousin, the present proprietor, Charles Trelawney, Esq. who has taken in addition the name of Brereton.

LITTLE MOLLINGTON, or MOLLINGTON BANASTRE,

(Part of St. Mary's Parish, Chester,)

Is about one mile and a half from Chester. It was formerly included in the large possessions of Robert de Rodelent, on whose death it reverted to the Earl, and was subsequently given by Edward III. to Robert Banastre, from the County of Lancaster.—It eventually passed from his descendants by an heiress to the Langtons and Hoghtons, and from the latter by marriage with Alicia, heiress of Henry Hoghton, to William Stanley, of Hooton, temp. Henry VI.—Sir T. S. M. Stanley, Bart. is the present proprietor.

The Dobs, of Mollington, now extinct, had an Estate in this township.

BLACON-CUM-CRABWALL,

Or CRABHALL, lies in the parishes of St. Oswald and the Holy Trinity, in the City of Chester. Blacon was granted at the Conquest to Ranulfus, ancestor of the Mainwarings, from a branch of whom, by marriage, it became vested in the Trussels, of Cubbleston, temp. Edward I. and they remained here till the reign of Henry VII. when Elizabeth Trussell brought their Estates in marriage to Edward Vere, Earl of Oxford. His Grandson, Edward, sold the Manor of Blacon, 20th Elizabeth, to John Crewe, and his son Sir Randle Crewe, Knt. Lord Chief Justice of England, "whose great grandson, John Crewe, Esq. dying without issue male, the family estates passed to John Offley, Esq. of Madeley, who married Anne, his eldest daughter. Mr. Offley took the name of Crewe in 1708, and was father of the present proprietor John Lord Crewe."*

CRABWALL, a hamlet of Blacon, was given by Thos. de Mainwaring to John, son of Robert de Erneway, paying one penny for all secular service, *salva custodiâ vadi de Dee, sicut custodiri solet tempore guerre.*—The Erneways afterwards vested the Estate in the Abbey of St. Werburgh, the Abbot, Simon, binding himself to maintain for ever two secular Chaplains, to celebrate Mass for the souls of John Erneway and Margery his wife; one Chaplain at the Altar of St. Leonard, in Chester Abbey, and the other at the Altar of the Virgin, in St. Bridget's Church: the Abbot to be responsible for the same to his Diocesan on complaint of the Mayor of Chester.

After the Dissolution a branch of the Gamuls settled here, and continued till the male line became extinct in 1750, by the death of William Gamul, Esq. who left Crabwall to his three sisters, all of whom died without issue. Under the will of one of them, (Margaret) a moiety passed to William Gamul Farmer, Esq. second son of her niece, in whom also the other share was vested by deed of gift of another sister, Anne Gamul.

Samuel Farmer, Esq. elder brother of the late Wm. Gamul Farmer, is the present proprietor of Crabwall—for which, and Blacon, no manerial rights are exercised.

* Ormer

END OF ITINERARY OF WIRRAL HUNDRED.

THE PARISH OF WARBURTON,

[OMITTED IN PAGE 418.]

...SHIRE

WARBURTON is about nine and a half miles N. N. W. from Knutsford, and six and a half from Warrington. It appears from the Survey, that the Township was in moieties, held by the Baron of Halton, and Osberne Fitz Tezzon, ancestor of the Boydells In the reign of Richard I. Adam de Dutton, a younger son of Dutton of Dutton, became possessed of both moieties, one in right of his wife, with which he endow[illegible] Canons of St. Werburgh, who had a religious house here.

Sir Geoffrey Dutton, of Dutton, second in descent from Adam, followed the Crusaders to Palestine. Peter Dutton, Knt. fourth in descent, assumed the name of Warburton; and Peter Warburton, ninth in descent, fought on the side of Percy, at the Battle of Shrewsbury.—The Warburtons continued in uninterrupted succession till the death of Sir Peter Warburton, of Warburton and Arley, in 1813, when the family in the male line became extinct. Under his will, all his extensive estates were vested in Trustees for the use of Rowland Eyles Egerton Warburton, a minor, his great nephew.

Courts Leet and Baron are held for the Manor. On the east side of the Church is the moated site of the ancient Hall of Warburton.

The gift of a moiety of the township, by Adam de Dutton, to the Premonstratensian Canons then established here, is before noticed.—Very little of the history of the PRIORY of WARBURTON is now known. It appears, however, that the Abbot of Cockersand, in Lancashire, in whom the moiety had become vested, by a series of Charters, quitclaimed to Sir Geoffry Dutton the whole of the grant, excepting only 8 bovates of land, and also gave up the advowson of the Church, which is now vested in the Warburton family. It is customary to present this living with that of Lymm, although distinct presentations have several times occurred.

HISTORY.

Near the bank of the river stands the Church; it consists of a brick tower at the west end, a nave, chancel, and side aisles, wooden pillars separating them from each other. Some part of the building is of considerable antiquity; the portico is of stone, and the date 1645. About six years ago, three stone coffins lying on the north side of the Church were examined, and in one of these was found a remarkably large human skeleton. The coffins bore undoubted marks of great antiquity, and they probably contained the ashes of some of the Canons of the former Monastic establishment. A field on the west side of the Church, still bears the name of the Abbey Croft.

A brass plate in the Chancel has this inscription—

Subtus inhumatur corpus docti, piique viri Richardi Grimsbey, mediet de Lym cum Warburton Rectoris, qui 1mo die Februarii ano 1669, ætatis suæ 67° placide in Xto obdormivit.

ADDITIONS, CORRECTIONS, &c.

MAYORS AND SHERIFFS OF CHESTER, SINCE 1817:

Mayors.	Sheriffs.	Mayors.	Sheriffs.
1818, T. Bradford, *Draper*,..	Chas. Dutton, *Currier*, John Dodd, *Skinner*.	1821, J. S. Rogers, *Skinner* ..	John Johnson, *Draper*, John Gardner, *Upholder*.
1819, J. Williamson, *Builder* .	Geo. Wildig, *Tobacconist*, William Sefton, *Draper*.	1822 Mm. Massey, *Druggist*..	Wm. Davenport, Esq. Edward Ducker, *Roper*.
1820, Wm. Seller, *Brewer*....	Francis Massey, *Brazier*, William Cross, *Distiller*.	1823, Robt. Morris, *Painter*	Jonathan Colley, *Tanner*, G. Walker, *Wine-merchant*.

EXECUTIONS AT CHESTER, IN

1554.—George Marsh, burnt at Spital Boughton, for his attachment to the Protestant faith.

1588.—September 8.—A woman burnt at Boughton, for poisoning her husband.

1589.—Execution of John Taylor, Gaoler of the Castle, for the Murder of Mr. Hockenhull, a prisoner in his custody, for recusancy.

1592.—Execution of William Geaton, servant to the Bishop of Chester, for the Murder of James Findlove, a Scotch pedlar; his body was hung in chains on Groppenhall heath.

1601.—A woman named Candey, executed for conspiring to murder her husband; her paramour, Boon, refusing to plead, was pressed to death in the Castle.

1602.—One Arnet, servant to a Mr. Manley, of Saltney side, hung for murdering his fellow servant.

1654.—Sir Timothy Featherstonhaugh shot by order of the Parliament, before the Abbey Gate, Northgate-street.

1750.—Two Irishmen executed, and gibbetted on the Parkgate road, near the Two Mills, for a Murder.

1768.—Three men hung for burglary; the rope of one of them broke, when lifting up his cap, he exclaimed in horrible agitation, "My God! what am I to suffer?"

1776.—May 4.—Execution of James Knight, for a burglary, at Odd Rode.

1776.—Sept. 21.—Christopher Lawless, Isaac Hutchinson, Alexander Solomon, and Isaac Josephs, executed for robbing the shop of Mr. Pemberton, jeweller. Solomon was accessary before the fact.—They were buried behind the Roodeye Cop, opposite Overlegh.

1777.—April 10.—S. Thorley executed for the horrible murder of Anne Smith, a ballad-singer, near Congleton. After cutting off her head, he severed her legs and arms from her body, which he threw into a brook; part, however, he actually broiled and eat! There was little doubt of his insanity. He was hung in chains on the heath, near Congleton.

1779.—April 16.—William Ellis, for burglary, and William Loom, for discharging a loaded pistol at Charles Warren, of Congleton, executed at Boughton.

——.—Oct. 2.—Sarah Jones executed, for stealing 28 yards of chintz, from the shop of Mr. Meacock, Chester.

1783.—Resolution Heap, and Martha Brown, hung; the former for a burglary at Whaley; the latter for the same offence at Over.

1784.—April 26.—Elizabeth Wood hung, for poisoning James Sinister, at Bredbury.

CHESHIRE

1784.—May 13.—John Oakes hung, for coining.

1786.—April 24.—Execution of Peter Steers, for the murder of his wife, by Poison.

——May 6.—Edward Holt hung, for a burglary at Knutsford.

——.—Oct. 1.—Thomas Buckley, aged 20, hung for a burglary, in Chester.

——.—Oct. 7.—Thomas Hyde, aged 35, hung for Horse stealing.

——.—Oct. 10.—James Buckley, aged 22, executed for a burglary in Miss Lloyd's house, Newgate-street, Chester.

1789.—Feb. 4.—Thomas Mate hung, for the Murder of John Parry, a Constable, in Handbridge. He was 64 years old, and when at the gallows, he charged his wife, 70 years old, with infidelity!

1790.—John Dean, from Stockport, hung for the murder of his wife, who was seven months advanced in her pregnancy. He was hung in chains on Stockport Moor.

1791.—April 21.—Execution of Lowndes, for robbing the Warrington Mail. His prosecution, it is said, cost £2000. He was hung in chains on Helsby Hill, but the gibbet pole was in a short time after cut down by some people in the neighbourhood, and was not again erected.

——.—Oct. 8.—Allen, Aston, and Knox, hung for a burglary at Northern. For the first time the gallows was erected on the north side of the road in Boughton.

1796.—April 30.—Thomas Brown and James Price, executed for robbing the Warrington Mail; they were hung in chains on Trafford Green, and remained there till 1820, when the pole was taken down, the place having previously been inclosed.—In the scull of Price, a robin's nest was found.

1798.—April 20.—John Thornhill hung for the murder of his sweetheart Sarah Malone, at Lymm.

——.—Oct. 4.—Peter Martin, alias Joseph Lowther, hung, for firing at a boat's crew of the Actæon, in the Mersey, when employed on the Impress service.

1800.—May 24.—Thomas Bosworth hung, for forgery, and Alexander Morton, for felony.

1800.—Oct. 18.—Execution of Mary Lloyd, for forgery at Stockport.

HISTORY.

1801.—May 9.—Thompson, Morgan, and Clare, for burglaries, hung at Boughton.—Near the gallows Clare made a spring from the Cart, rushed through the crowd which made way for him, rolled down a gutter-way towards the river—a rapid descent,—and plunged into the Dee. He was drowned; but his body was found, and afterwards hung up with the others. These were the last men hung at Boughton, which had been the scene of execution of criminals for at least two centuries.*

——.—Oct. 3.—Aaron Gee, and Thomas Gibson, hung from what got the name of the *drag*, out of a temporary window way, in the attics, on the south side of the Northgate. The unfortunate men were propelled from the window about five feet, and dropped nearly forty inches, their bodies beating against the windows beneath, so as to break the glass in them.

1809.—May 6.—Execution of George Glover, and William Proudlove, in front of the House of Correction, for shooting at an Officer of Excise, at Odd Rode. When the Drop (used for the first time) sunk, the ropes broke, and the poor men fell to the platform, half-strangled; new ropes were procured, and the sentence was carried into effect about an hour after the accident.

1810.—May 2.—Execution of John Done, for the murder of Betty Eckersley, a woman of bad cha-character, at Lymm. He denied the crime to the last moment.

——.—Oct. 10.—Execution of Smith and Clarke, for a burglary and felony in the shop of Mr. Fletcher, Watch-maker, Eastgate. The conduct of Smith on the drop was exceedingly unbending and audacious, and the night before his execution he played at cards with some of his companions. They were buried in St. Martin's Church-yard.

1812.—June 15.—Temple and Thompson, hung for rioting. They were connected with the Luddites.

——.—August 24.—Execution of John Lomas, for the murder of his master, Mr. Morrey, at Hankelow.

* We have seen it somewhere stated, that Criminals were at one period executed on Hough Green.

1813.—April 23.—Edith Morrey executed, for the murder of her husband. An improper intercourse had for some time existed between her and John Lomas, which terminated in her exciting him to destroy her husband, and the crime was perpetrated with circumstances of peculiarly savage atrocity. She pleaded pregnancy at the time of her trial with Lomas.

1813.—June 26.—Execution of William Wilkinson, James Yarwood, and William Burgess, for a rape on Mary Porter, near Weston Point. They were what are locally termed flatmen, and when Wilkinson, (a fine stout man about six feet high) mounted the scaffold, he exclaimed to his fellow sufferers, "Keep up your spirits; never mind, my lads—we are all murdered men. I'm just as happy as if I was going to a play!" and when the halter was placed round his neck, he added, "My new handkerchief fits me nice and tight."

1814.—May 28.—William Wilson, an old sailor, in his 70th year, executed for arson, at Tiverton, near Tarporley. His exit was most extraordinary: on the morning of his death he entertained a number of persons in the parlour of the Constable's house, with an account of his naval exploits; and in his way along the streets to the City Gaol, he chewed bread in his mouth, and threw it at the Beadle, observing he was like Peeping Tom of Coventry. At the City Gaol he said, "What a many people are here to see an old man hung. Here's as much fuss as if there were a hundred to be hung."

1815.—April 22.—Execution of Griffith and Wood, for a Burglary in the house of John Holme, near Stockport.

1817.—May 10.—Execution of Joseph Allen for uttering forged Bank of England Notes to a great amount.—In a declaration made on the morning of his execution, he said he had been "wrongfully accused," and that he "did not know good notes from bad ones."—After his condemnation, he took, for *six days*, no other refreshment than water.

1818.—May 9.—*Abraham* Rostern, and *Isaac* Moors executed, the former for a Burglary at Edgeley, the latter for a similar offence at Cheadle Bulkeley. Both of them acknowledged their guilt.

1818.—Sept. 26.—John Moores executed, for a Burglary.

1819.—May 8.—Joseph Walker executed, for robbing his former master on the Highway, between Northwich and Manchester. He denied his guilt to the last.

——.—Sept. 25.—Execution of Samuel Hooley, and John Johnson, (a man of colour) for a Burglary at Bowden.

1820.—April 15.—Jacob M'Ghinnes executed, for shooting Wm. Birch, at Stockport. He was one of the Radical Reformers, and his intention was to have shot Mr. Lloyd, Solicitor, of that town. He had been a Member of the Established Church, a Methodist, and an Atheist; but on the drop he professed to have a firm belief in the mercies of God.

——.—April 22.—Execution of Thomas Miller, for a Burglary at Bowden.

——.—Sept. 16—Execution of Ralph Ellis, for a Burglary at Elton, and William Ricklington, for setting fire to the Rectory House at Coddington. Ellis confessed his offence. Ricklington was at one time an Atheist, but believed in the doctrine of the *metempsychosis*; he once observed that it was likely he might be a hack horse in the next world!

1821.—May 5.—Execution of Samuel Mealey, for a Highway Robbery at Stockport.

1822.—May 4.—Execution of Wm. Tongue, for a Rape on an infant; and George Groom for a Highway Robbery on a man named Joseph Kennerly.

——.—Sept. 14—Thos. Brierly executed for a Highway Robbery, near Congleton.

1823.—April 14.—Execution of Samuel Fallows, for the murder of his sweetheart, at Disley. Several Galvanic experiments were made on his body previous to dissection.

1823.—May 20.—Execution of John Kragon, for a Rape on an infant, at Stockport.

——.—Sept. 13.—Execution of Edward Clarke, for a Highway Robbery, at Stockport.

ESHIRE

THE KING'S SCHOOL.

Extract from the Foundation Grant by Henry VIII. of which the following is a pretty accurate translation from the original Latin:

"We appoint and ordain, that at the election of the Dean, or in his absence, the Vice Dean and Chapter, there ever be in our Church of Chester, 24 Boys, poor and friendless, to be maintained out of the income of our Church, of good capacities and given to learning, if possible; which, however, we would not have admitted *before they can read and write, and somewhat understand the rudiments of grammar;* and this is at the discretion of the Dean and Head Master. And these Boys we will have maintained at the expense of our Church, until they have made some tolerable proficiency in the Latin Grammar, and have been taught to speak and write Latin, for which end they are allowed the term of four years; or if the Dean or Head Master see cause, of *five*, and no more. But we order, that no one (unless he be a Chorister of our Church) be elected a poor Scholar, that is under the age of *nine* years.

"Moreover we appoint, that one be elected by the Dean and Chapter, well learned in Latin and Greek, of good character and religious life, and endowed with the art of inculcation, who shall infuse religion and cultivate sound learning, as well in the 24 Boys of our Church, as in all others whatsoever, that shall come to our school for Grammatical Instruction. He shall be deemed the Chief in our School, and shall be the Head or Chief Master.

"Again, we will have *another*, elected by the Dean and Chapter, of good character and holy life, well versed in Latin, and qualified to teach; who, under the Head Master, shall ground the Scholars in the first rudiments of Grammar, and from thence shall be stiled the Under Master."

ON CANALS.—We are led to believe, that making the Rivers Mersey and Irwell navigable (the boundary between the two Counties of Cheshire and Lancashire) was the first grand effort at Canal-making, in this Kingdom. This was planned in the year 1712, by Mr. Thos. Stears, Engineer of the Liverpool Docks, then making. This was then considered a bold and an arduous undertaking, and Parliament granted extraordinary powers to the proprietors, insomuch that they are not bound within any limits, but have a ROVING Commission by the said Act, to pass through any lands, in either County, which were thought convenient so to do.—The Act for making the Weaver navigable, was obtained shortly after 1720, and the surplus of the Weaver has nearly defrayed all the County Rates. This plan of expending Public Stock, like the one of the *Liverpool Docks*, has contributed greatly to the enlargement of Liverpool, and nourishment of Cheshire. Both concerns have been greatly extended; the Mersey and Irwell from above Warrington through Cheshire down to Runcorn, and the other from Pickering's lock down to Weston Point, thereby securing a regular passage at all times without delay, in neap tides, to the great advantage of the Public. It is considered that upwards of 1000 tons of goods are carried up to Manchester and neighbourhood by the Old Quay Company annually, and by the Weaver upwards of 360,000 tons of Salt, besides Cheese, &c. &c. are sent annually down to Liverpool; in addition to all the carriage down from Manchester, and up to Northwich from the River Mersey. This has been a source of great trade and mutual wealth to the two Counties. The Duke of Bridgwater's Canal was began at Worsley, in the year 1758. The Ellesmere Canal Act was obtained in 1794, all which have been found useful, although it has been the least productive.—*M. G.*

HISTORY.

MARBURY HALL.—*Anecdote.*—The late Mrs. Holbrooke, the last of the name, and resident at Budworth, whose maiden name was Ashley, happened to be at Marbury Hall, then the residence of Lord Barrymore, when the Officers of the Crown arrived to arrest him for his correspondence with the Pretender. Aware of their object, she had the adroitness to proceed directly to his library, and though occasionally interrupted in the collection, she finally succeeded in carrying away all his Lordship's correspondence, which she did on horseback, wrapped up in a large white *Joseph.* On reaching home, she burnt them, and thus rendered fruitless the search which was making for documents likely to establish his Lordship's guilt. On being brought before the Privy Council, a wrong day was given for that on which it was said he had received a visit from the Pretender, and this was stated by his steward, Mr. A. who produced his memorandum-book, satisfactorily proving, in the presence of George II. and the Council, that he had been with Lord Barrymore "from an early hour in the morning till eventide," and that no other person had visited his Lordship.—It was pretty certain, however, that the Pretender had been on a visit to Marbury; for on the death of his Lordship's second son, the Hon. Richard Barry, the cup out of which "the Stuart" had drank, altho' intrinsically not worth threepence, was engraved and ornamented, and sold for £26.—There was a very fine collection of paintings at Marbury; at one period there were no less than fifteen *Holy Families* by different masters.—*M. G.*

Broxton Hall,—is near the Turnpike-road betwixt Barnhill and Whitchurch, and is distant from the former about three miles; it is well worth the Tourist's attention to visit the *terrace*, from which a most beautiful and extensive view may be obtained. Carden Cliff and Overton Scar, form a picturesque foreground to a view of the champaign country from Chester to Wrexham, the source of the River Dee, a rich tract of country finely terminated by the distant Welsh Mountains, rising in gradual succession. Carden Cliff and Broxton Terrace partake alike, in form and make, of those sudden and abrupt freaks of nature which she so frequently displays throughout her works. From Overton Scar there is a pleasing view of Chester, at the distance of fifteen miles, St. George's Channel, Farndon, Bangor, Holt, and Wrexham, the River Alyn, and the debatable lands in the Marches of Wales. The Scar at Overton, which the wandering Tribe of Gypsies formerly inhabited, rises to a considerable height, and is a huge mass of rock projecting far beyond its base, and forming a sort of cavern beneath, where the Gypsies sometimes slept. As many as sixty have been here in one season; and in a recent hard winter they were relieved by the parish. Owing, however, to some nefarious practices in the neighbouring town of Malpas, some of the fraternity were prosecuted, and they have happily deserted this part of the country; the scene of their festivals, the turf, is now planted with timber trees.

The Allports of Overton.—Dean Cholmondeley observed "I wish to clear up exactly who this Richard was, and when he lived?" He was living in 1644, and was Grandfather of Robert, who married Miss Mainwaring, 1680. He had Messuages, Lands, and Tenements, near Fleet-street, London; in Dorset Court, otherwise Salisbury Court; Hanging Sword Court; and Hanging Sword Alley.—See Nichol's Literary Anecdotes, vol. 1, folio 4.—1719, Richard Allport made his will, and left a legacy to his Sister Lacon for her life, and all his lands to his Neices, Hester, Anne, and Elizabeth Lacon. William Dod, of Edge, Edward Wright, of Stretton, and John Puleston, of Pickhill, Denbighshire, Esq. Executors. He left legacies also to his Cousins, three sons of Thos. Leach, then deceased; a rent of charge of £40. a year for the Curate of Malpas, for daily service in the said Church next preceding Sacrament Sunday; £500. for the Boys' and Girls' Charity School, at Malpas; and £50. to the Blue Coat School, at Chester, in which City he was born. He died about 1723.—*M. G.*

Chester Choir.—In the Gallery there is a fine specimen of the mouldings of the trefoiled heads, running round the the trefoil even to the dripstone.—The Piers of the Choir have the appearance of decorated Piers.—The distinction between the early English small multiplied mouldings, and the bold decorated ones, may be well observed in the arch between the Choir and the Lady Chapel, which is very good early English, and the arches of the nave are good decorated work—they are admirable specimens of the difference of character of the two piers.—The west front presents a fine specimen of perpendicular English fronts; it was usual to have a great window and two side ones, with a large door and sometimes side ones. But Chester has only one side window. The door (see plate) is very rich, with niches on each side.—This edifice, though its exterior seldom attracts the attention it deserves, from the decay of the stone and the destruction of its battlements and pinnacles, yet to those who will take the pains to examine its composition, it presents a fine series of very good work. The Norman (Saxon) portions are small, but the Chapter House, its vestibule, and a passage beside it, the Lady Chapel, and some portions adjoining the north aisle of the Choir, present varied and excellent specimens of early English. The transition to decorated work may be traced, and the completion of that style in the south transept, and part of the nave, with the organ screen, is very well marked. The Bishop's Throne was once the pedestal of the shrine of St. Werburgh, and deserves particular attention. It is of pure decorated character, and though disfigured by paint, is in excellent preservation. The West end, the South porch of the Cloisters, the upper part of the nave and transepts, and the central tower, are *perpendicular* work, mostly of good character, and the stalls and tabernacle work are particularly fine.

Early English Roofs.—In the East passage of the Cloisters there is a fine specimen of the rare occurrence of an additional rib between the Cross-springer and the wall, and between the Cross-springer and the pier rib: having a longitudinal and cross-rib at the point of the arches, not running to the wall, but stopt by the intermediate rib.

Chester Free School.—Early English Stair-case, with a series of arches rising each higher than the former, with shafts and mouldings,—same at Beverley.—*See Vignette, p.* 108.

St. John's Church.—Presents a very fine specimen of Norman and early English, and the tower has been a very rich perpendicular one; but the perishable nature of the stone is such, that nearly all traces of the once excellent pannelling are lost.—The tablets under the windows are like the dripstone, and sometimes fine bands are carried round as tablets. There are fine specimens of these here.—Vignette, 215.

Bebbington Church—is a curious mixture of plain Norman, with a fine Eastern portico of good perpendicular work.

Nantwich Church—contains some excellent work: the stalls are fine, and there are several good windows; the tower, a small octagon over the intersection of the cross, is simple and elegant; and the East end presents a fine composition of buttresses, canopy, and battlements.

Birkenhead Priory—in ruins; has in the chapels, in the vaults, and in the door ways, some very good work. The mouldings of the door ways are of very excellent composition.

CHESHIRE

RUNCORN CHURCH—contains good plain early English work, and good wood carvings.

MALPAS AND MACCLESFIELD CHURCHES, and WITTON CHAPEL—possess some very curious specimens of good architecture.—*From a cotemporaneous work on Architecture.*

IRON BRIDGE.—This House, which forms the extreme boundary of the City of Chester on the South, is so called in the Latin Charter of Edward Prince of Wales and Earl of Chester, son of Edward I.; *why* remains still to be explained. —In 1820, and many years before, the house was licensed as an Inn and Tea Gardens.

WRENBURY CHAPEL—(484)—The Chancel is the property of Lord Combermere and J. C. Starkey, Esq. of Wrenbury Hall, both of whom have vaults beneath it.—There are five heavy bells in the tower.

DELAMERE CHAPEL—(461)—is built of white stone; it is a small neat structure, but sufficiently large for the present population. The present Rector is the Rev. Rowland Hill.

TRINITY CHURCH, CHESTER.—Edmundson mentions a window in this Church where the supporters of the arms of Edward IV. are, on the dexter side, a Bull sable, crowned and hoofed or; sinister a lion quadrant, arg.—Henry Prince of Wales, Earl of Chester, son of Hen. IV. confirmed that part of a former charter, ordering, that the "Parson of Trinity Church should not have tithe of the Roodeye."

LOCAL MILITIA.—Chester, commanded by Col. Barnston, 1102 strong; Congleton, Lieut. Col. Trafford, 934; Macclesfield, Gen. Sir J. D. Broughton, 852; Stockport, Col. Ince, 988.—Total 3876.

The Barons of Malpas had 22 'Squires in their train.—*Harl. MSS.*

PAGE 405.—See note †.—John Smith Barry was born at Rock Savage; he was a keen sportsman, and chased a fox into the very room in which he was born.

PORTS OF CHESTER AND LIVERPOOL.—"Here lyeth the body of Ellen Hicks, wife of Clement Hicks, gent. Her Majesty's Chief Searcher for the Port of Chester and Liverpool, being of the age of 35 years, who deceased 11th April, A. D. 1598."—*Inscription in Trinity Church, Chester.*

Bishop Chadderton, who was enthroned in 1579, "loved the Citizens well, and in token thereof he sent them from Lincolne, a very ffaire basen and ewer of silver, and guillt, with all the Maiors' names engraven in it, whiche had been Maiors in his time; whiche basen and ewer remains at every Maior's house for his time of Mairolty, and is worth 40s."

HISTORY.

34th Hen. VIII. There was an order from the Star Chamber addressed to the Citizens of Chester, as to the mode of the election of Mayor; is it now to be found?

PAGE 293.—Note *.—Such mottos or devices were formerly very common.—There was some years ago, on a low stone house at the verge of the Castle Ditch, Liverpool, a similar inscription.—On a door near the Kitchen, at the Earl of Derby's seat, was the motto "Bring good news and knock boldly."—This part of the house was erected temp. Hen. VII.

NORTHWICH, OCT. 9, 1789.—Early on the morning of the 7th, the Aqueduct of the Staffordshire Canal across Wincham Valley, in this county, gave way, and the water rushed down into the river with great violence. Two corn mills below were in great danger of being forced down—in consequence of this and heavy rains on the night before, there was the greatest flood ever remembered in the Weaver. The water rose from 16 to 18 feet—most of the streets were under water, 6 to 8 feet deep, and almost all the avenues impassable except to boats.—Seven thousand bushels of salt were destroyed, and much injury done to the salt-houses. The town and salt-works surrounded, and in many places immersed in water; the scene was awful beyond description—fortunately, however, no lives were lost, though many were in imminent danger.

1816.—May 31.—An act passed for vesting part of the settled estates of S. Aldersey, Esq. of Aldersey, in Trustees, to be sold, &c. in order to purchase other estates, to be settled to the same uses, &c.

1818.—A King and Constitution Club was established in Chester, of which Colonel Barnston was elected perpetual Chairman.

1820.—A "Whig Club of Cheshire and the adjoining Counties" formed; the Annual Meetings held at the Royal Hotel.

1821.—The Lamb Row, Chester, of which a view is given p. 255, fell down, and all the materials were removed.

1821-2.—The North and South wings of Eaton House were built, and an addition of upwards of 40 acres made to the pleasure grounds.—A Gothic Temple was built at the south end of the terrace, for the reception of the Roman Altar, noticed in page 561, in which it is now placed.

1821.—This year Dr. Law, Bishop of Chester, took a general Survey of his extensive Diocese, submitting to the different Churchwardens, &c. a series of questions as to the state of their respective Churches, Burial-ground, Glebe, &c. This will in after times be of as much, or rather more, importance, as the *Notitia* of Bishop Gastrell.

CHESHIRE

1823.—The tower of St. Bridget's Church, Chester, being in a dilapidated state, the bells were removed, and a great portion of it was taken down.

1823.—April 24 and 25.—Great rejoicings in Chester, in celebration of the Birth of Gilbert Grosvenor, son of Visct. Belgrave, and grandson of Robert Earl Grosvenor. Grand dinners were given, an Ox was roasted on the Roodeye, fire-works were exhibited and there was a grand procession of the Corporation, and Mail and Stage Coaches, to congratulate the Noble Earl at Eaton. The horns of the Ox, splendidly worked in silver gilt, bearing the arms of Chester and of the Grosvenors, were subsequently presented to Earl Grosvenor, by the Committee who superintended the festivities.

1823.—There was this year a contest against Alderman Morris, for Mayor, and Mr. Geo. Walker, for Sheriff. Both of them were, however, elected; there being for Mr. Ald. Morris—504; Ald. Moss—378; Ald. Rogers—293; Ald. Massey—293 For Mr. Geo. Walker—617; Mr. Thos. Whittakers—574.

ERRATA.

P.453.—Line 13, second column, for "part of Norley is in this *township*," read *parish*.

63.—In the population returns, Great Boughton and Churton Heath are noticed as belonging to Aldford Parish; they are in St. Oswald's parish.

64.—Part of Ashton is in Bowden parish.

68.—The Cathedral precincts and Little St. John's, altho' united under one head for the convenience of giving the population returns, have, however, no connexion together.

84.—The River Weaver for about one third of its course, takes nearly a southerly direction, then an eastwardly one, and afterwards, with the Wheelock, a southerly one, receiving, amongst other streams, that of the Dane, before its confluence with the Mersey at Weston Point.—The course of the Rivers in Cheshire are much underrated; the Weaver has been estimated at only 33 miles, whereas the distance between Frodsham and Winsford Bridge only, is nearly 20 miles.—The Mersey (82) also, instead of being, as has been pretty generally stated, 44 miles, is little short of 55 miles, taking into account its various meanderings.*

HISTORY.

* Rev. Peter Maddock.

102.—St. Martin's Church is omitted in the list of Churches, in Chester.

103.—For *Waverton V.* read *Weverham V.*—Tollington Chapel is omitted in Bury parish; as are also St. George's and All Saints, Manchester; the new Chapel in Rochdale; St. Stephen's and St. Phillip's, Liverpool.—In Leyland Deanery, Chorley, and Rufford, should be entered as Rectories, instead of Chapelries. In Amounderness, for *Bisham* read *Bispham*.

104.—There is a Chapel new built at Preston. In Furness Deanery, for *Adlington* read *Aldingham*.

118.—All Bunbury parish is in Edisbury hundred, Burwardsley excepted, which is in Broxton.

125.—Second column, for *per contra*, read *e contra*.

94.—York and Lincoln are each larger than the Diocese of Chester in square miles, and London in population.

95.—Line 13, for "Diocese," read County.

99.—Dr. Majendie was installed Bishop of Chester in the month of   of 1800.—*Edmund* Bowyer Sparke should read *Edward* Bowyer Sparke.

101.—The Rev. T. T. Trevor should be L. L. D. not D. D. —1st. col. line 28, for *Prebends*, read *Prebendaries*.

POPULATION OF THE COUNTY, 1821.—GENERAL SUMMARY.

HUNDREDS, &c.	Houses.				Occupations.			Persons.		
	Inhabited.	How many Families.	Building.	Uninhabited.	Agricultural Families.	Manufacturing Families.	Other Families.	Males.	Females.	Totals.
Hundred of Broxton	2,715	2,963	11	54	1,951	532	480	7,955	7,768	15,723
Bucklow	6,637	7,013	24	129	3,407	2,842	1,122	18,671	18,521	37,192
Edisbury	4,264	4,632	37	71	2,766	1,095	771	12,368	12,225	24,593
Macclesfield	14,551	16,205	192	385	2,898	12,190	1,117	43,267	44,212	87,479
Nantwich	3,832	4,261	17	81	2,507	1,254	500	11,118	11,213	22,331
Northwich	5,799	6,157	40	186	2,038	3,239	880	15,292	15,912	31,204
Wirral	2,427	2,602	27	56	1,624	519	459	6,885	6,996	13,881
City of Chester	3,861	4,529	29	186	830	2,552	1,147	8,975	10,974	19,949
Town of Macclesfield	3,008	3,662	37	64	99	3,240	323	8,421	9,325	17,746
Totals	47,094	52,024	414	1,212	18,120	27,105	6,799	132952	137146	270098
Totals, 1811	41,187	44,502	250	1,239	16,396	23,043	5,063	110841	116190	227031
Increase, 1821	5,907	7,522	164		1,724	4,062	4,062	22,111	20,956	43,067

THE INDEX.

It is considered that the following irregular Index will be amply sufficient for the purpose of *particular* reference, as under each Parish and Township is described the descent of possession, together with any circumstance of note attending its History.—A general Index to a work of this bulk would swell out the pages to a considerable extent, and increase the matter without adding to its generally utility. Owing to a careless blunder by the Engraver, St. Olave's Ward is printed *St. Daves* in the list of References in the Map of Chester.

Chester, Dec. 20, 1823. J. H. H.

ESHIRE HISTORY.

ITINERARY OF THE COUNTY, &c.

HISTORY

ITINERARY OF THE COUNTY, &c.

CHESHIRE — HISTORY.

ITINERARY OF THE COUNTY, &c.

Cheshire

History.

ITINERARY OF THE COUNTY, &c.

NOTE.—The School at Aldford was built, and is maintained, by the munificence of Earl Grosvenor; it is, however, erroneously stated to the contrary in the account given of the Township.

Directions to the Binder; List of Plates, Vignettes, & Plans.

ITINERARY OF THE COUNTY, &c.

Cancel pages 107 and 108; and substitute those given in the last parts.

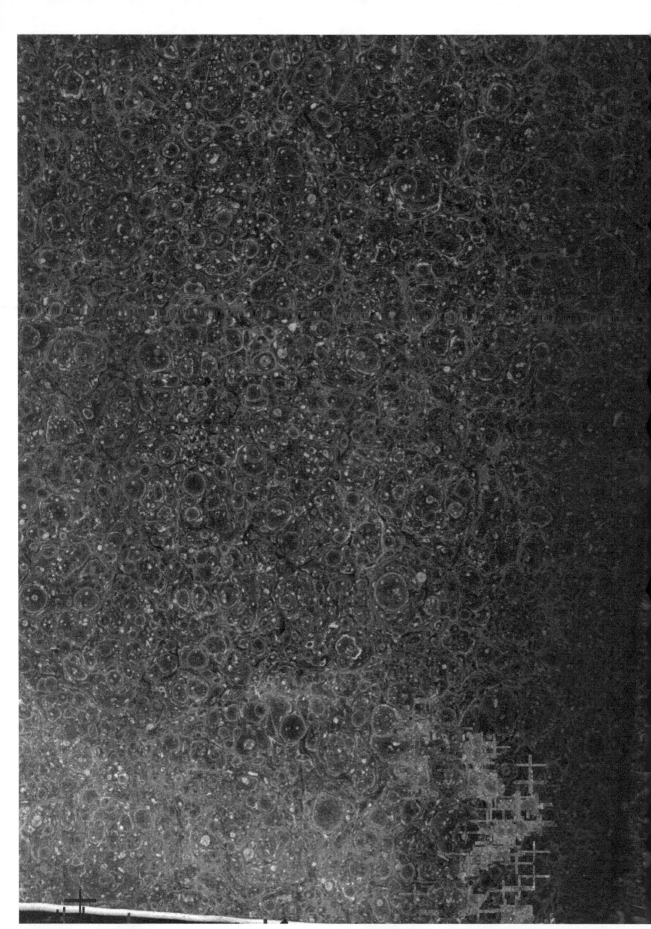

Lightning Source UK Ltd.
Milton Keynes UK
UKHW03f2005270818
327875UK00006B/494/P